THE NEW OXFORD HISTORY OF ENGLAND

General Editor · J. M. ROBERTS

A New England?

PEACE AND WAR
1886–1918

G. R. SEARLE

CLARENDON PRESS · OXFORD

OXFORD
UNIVERSITY PRESS

Great Clarendon Street, Oxford OX2 6DP

Oxford University Press is a department of the University of Oxford.
It furthers the University's objective of excellence in research, scholarship,
and education by publishing worldwide in

Oxford New York

Auckland Cape Town Dar es Salaam Hong Kong Karachi Kuala Lumpur
Madrid Melbourne Mexico City Nairobi New Delhi Shanghai Taipei Toronto

With offices in

Argentina Austria Brazil Chile Czech Republic France Greece
Guatemala Hungary Italy Japan South Korea Poland Portugal
Singapore Switzerland Thailand Turkey Ukraine Vietnam

Oxford is a registered trade mark of Oxford University Press
in the UK and in certain other countries

Published in the United States
by Oxford University Press Inc., New York

British Library Cataloguing in Publication Data

Data available

Library of Congress Cataloging in Publication Data

Data available

Typeset by SPI Publisher Services, Pondicherry, India
Printed in Great Britain
on acid-free paper by
Biddles Ltd., King's Lynn, Norfolk

ISBN 978-0-19-820714-6
ISBN 978-0-19-928440-5 (Pbk.)

3 5 7 9 10 8 6 4 2

TO
BARBARA

General Editor's Preface

The first volume of Sir George Clark's *Oxford History of England* was published in 1934. Undertaking the General Editorship of a *New Oxford History of England* forty-five years later it was hard not to feel overshadowed by its powerful influence and well-deserved status. Some of Clark's volumes (his own among them) were brilliant individual achievements, hard to rival and impossible to match. Of course, he and his readers shared a broad sense of the purpose and direction of such books. His successor can no longer be sure of doing that. The building-blocks of the story, its reasonable and meaningful demarcations and divisions, the continuities and discontinuities, the priorities of different varieties of history, the place of narrative—all these things are now much harder to agree upon. We now know much more about many things, and think about what we know in different ways. It is not surprising that historians now sometimes seem unsure about the audience to which their scholarship and writing are addressed.

In the end, authors should be left to write their own books. None the less, the *New Oxford History of England* is intended to be more than a collection of discrete or idiosyncratic histories in chronological order. Its aim is to give an account of the development of our country in time. It is hard to treat that development as just the history which unfolds within the precise boundaries of England, and a mistake to suggest that this implies a neglect of the histories of the Scots, Irish, and Welsh. Yet the institutional core of the story which runs from Anglo-Saxon times to our own is the story of a state-structure built round the English monarchy and its effective successor, the Crown in Parliament, and that provides the only continuous articulation of the history of peoples we today call British. It follows that there must be uneven and sometimes discontinuous treatment of much of the history of those peoples. The state story remains, nevertheless, an intelligible thread and to me appears still to justify the title both of this series and that of its predecessor.

If the attention given to the other kingdoms and the principality of Wales must reflect in this series their changing relationship to that central theme, this is not only way in which the emphasis of individual volumes will be different. Each author has been asked to bring forward what he or she sees as the most important topics explaining the history under study, taking account of the present state of historical knowledge, drawing attention to areas of dispute and to matters on which final judgement is at present difficult (or, perhaps, impossible) and not merely recapitulating what has recently been the fashionable centre of professional debate. But each volume, allowing for its special approach and proportions, must also provide a comprehensive account, in which politics is always likely to be prominent. Volumes have to be demarcated chronologically but continuities must not be obscured; vestigially or not, copyhold survived into the 1920s and the Anglo-Saxon shires until the 1970s (some of which were to be resurrected in the 1990s, too). Any single volume should be an entry-point to the understanding of processes only slowly unfolding, sometimes across centuries. My hope is that in the end we shall have, as the outcome, a set of standard and authoritative histories, embodying the scholarship of a generation, and not mere compendia in which the determinants are lost to sight among the detail.

J. M. ROBERTS

Preface

Few periods of English history have attracted so rich and voluminous a literature as that spanning the years 1886–1918. Writing this work of synthesis has therefore offered a daunting challenge. How indebted I am to earlier labourers in the vineyard will be apparent from the footnotes to the text and from the Bibliography. The book would also have been much the poorer but for the stimulation and advice of friends and colleagues. I particularly appreciate the input of those who read draft chapters and saved me from many a foolish slip: namely, John Charmley, Roy Church, Stephen Church, Jon Cook, Colin Davis, Eric Homberger, Mark Knights, Adrian Martin, Carole Rawcliffe, Michael Sanderson, and Richard Wilson. Any remaining faults are of course my own.

Throughout the period that I have been preparing this volume I have enjoyed indispensable support from the University of East Anglia in the form of facilities, secretarial assistance, and study leave. I also benefited greatly from the 'time-off' award that I received from the British Academy / Humanities Research Board. Library staff at Cambridge University Library as well as at my own university have given me unfailing help in my book searches.

Thanks are also due to Anne Gelling, Ruth Parr, and Kay Rogers of the Oxford University Press, who put their professional skills at my disposal and steadied the ship when it entered choppy waters. Sadly John Roberts did not live to see the publication of this volume but, despite his declining health, read the entire text in draft and was generous in his encouragement and suggestions. The index was completed by Dr Michael Tombs, to whom I am also grateful.

Finally words cannot express the extent of my debt to my wife Barbara, without whose great patience and support the book would never have reached completion.

November 2003   G. R. SEARLE

Contents

PART II   LATE VICTORIAN ENGLAND
1886–1899

Plates

Tables

Map

Abbreviations

AAA	Amateur Athletics Association
AMC	Association of Municipal Corporations
APS	Aborigines Protection Society
ASE	Amalgamated Society of Engineers
ASRS	Amalgamated Society of Railway Servants
BCU	British Commonwealth Union
BEF	British Expeditionary Force
BMA	British Medical Association
BSP	British Socialist Party
CCO	Conservative Central Office
CID	Committee of Imperial Defence
CIGS	Chief of the Imperial General Staff
CIV	City Imperial Volunteers
COS	Charity Organisation Society
CPA	Corrupt and Illegal Practices Act of 1883
CTC	Cycling Tourist Club
CWC	Clyde Workers Committee
DMI	Director of Military Intelligence
DMO	Director of Military Operations
DNI	Director of Naval Intelligence
DORA	Defence of the Realm Act
EES	Eugenics Education Society
EFF	Election Fighting Fund
EPD	Excess Profits Duty
ETU	Electrical Trades Union
FA	Football Association
FBI	Federation of British Industries
FTL	Fair Trade League
FTU	Free Trade Union
GFTU	General Federation of Trade Unions
GHQ	General Headquarters, British armies, France
GPDST	Girls' Public Day School Trust
GS	General Staff
ICS	Indian Civil Service
ILC	Imperial (Liberal) Council

ILP	Independent Labour Party
IML	Imperial Maritime League
IRB	Irish Republican Brotherhood
JP	Justice of the Peace
LCC	London County Council
LDOS	Lord's Day Observance Society
LGB	Local Government Board
LL	Liberal League
LRC	Labour Representation Committee
MFGB	Miners' Federation of Great Britain
MOH	Medical Officer of Health
NAGL	National Anti-Gambling League
NALGO	National Association of Local Government Officers
NEC	National Executive Committee
NL	Navy League
NLF	National Liberal Federation
NSL	National Service League
NSPCC	National Society for the Prevention of Cruelty to Children
NUM	National Union of Mineworkers
NUR	National Union of Railwaymen
NUWSS	National Union of Women's Suffrage Societies
NUWW	National Union of Women Workers
NVA	National Vigilance Association
OTC	Officers Training Corps
PFA	Professional Footballers' Association
PLP	Parliamentary Labour Party
PRC	Parliamentary Recruiting Committee
RDC	Rural District Council
RPE	Radical Plutocrats Enquiry
SDF	Social Democratic Federation
SF	Sinn Fein
SL	Socialist League
SWMF	South Wales Miners' Federation
TRL	Tariff Reform League
TRTL	Trade Union Tariff Reform League
TUC	Trades Union Congress
UDC	Urban District Council
UDC	Union of Democratic Control
UIL	United Irish League
UUC	Ulster Unionist Council
UVF	Ulster Volunteer Force

VAD	Voluntary Aid Detachment
WEA	Workers' Education Association
WEWNC	War Emergency Workers National Committee
WFL	Women's Freedom League
WLF	Women's Liberal Federation
WLL	Women's Labour League
WSPU	Women's Social and Political Union
YMCA	Young Men's Christian Association

Introduction

In 1900, in the midst of the Second Boer War, the Poet Laureate, Alfred Austin, brought out a new edition of his book of patriotic verse, *Songs of England*. The volume is a paean of praise to the British Empire and to those who had contributed towards its development. The title, however, elicited an unfavourable response from those inhabitants of the United Kingdom who did not see themselves as 'English' at all. Austin was unsympathetic and uncomprehending: 'I meant by "England" to include not just the English themselves,' he explained, 'but all those—Scots, Irish, Australians, even Indians—who "thrill to the sound of England" '.[1]

As A. J. P. Taylor later noted, the word 'England' continued to be similarly used (though not always so tactlessly), well into the twentieth century, to cover, variously, England and Wales, Great Britain, the United Kingdom, even the British Empire: indeed, the original *Oxford History of England* series, to which he was contributing, rested on precisely such a verbal slippage. The difficulty, as Taylor points out, is that Scotland and Ireland (since 1922 Northern Ireland) possess their own separate administrative and legal systems, while Wales, though administratively integrated into England, is culturally quite distinct—especially in its Welsh-speaking areas. As such, these countries deserve, and have received, their own separate histories. Yet, Taylor adds, 'it would be impossible to discover a specifically English foreign policy, and foolish, though not impossible, to discover the specifically English contribution to British budgets or to British overseas trade'. Taylor's solution to the difficulty is also mine: 'Where the Welsh, the Scotch [*sic*], the Irish, or the British overseas have the same history as the English, my book includes them also; where they have a different history, it does not.'[2]

This approach seems particularly well suited to the years from 1886 to 1918. There were many respects in which this period saw a process of convergence within the United Kingdom. For example, the recent Reform Act of 1884 for

---

[1] A. Austin, *Songs of England* (London, 1900 edn.), 'Explanatory'.
[2] A. J. P. Taylor, *English History 1914–1945* (Oxford, 1965), pp. v–vi.

the first time laid down uniform electoral qualifications throughout the national territory (Chapter 4). Many social, economic, and cultural processes were also leaping effortlessly across 'national' boundaries, which amounted to little more than lines on a map. When discussing such trends as urban growth or the emergence of a consumer society, I have therefore felt free to draw my examples from Cardiff and Edinburgh as well as from Leeds and Birmingham (Chapter 3). It would be simply perverse to do otherwise.

There is, in any case, another way in which the fate of the various inhabitants of the United Kingdom were intertwined. When Gladstone raised the prospect of Irish Home Rule in 1886, he unwittingly stimulated a desire for greater national self-determination among the other 'Celtic' nations, and these sentiments remained strong at least until the outbreak of the Great War. Why, then, some contemporaries argued, not give the Scots and the Welsh, as well as the Irish, their own parliaments ('Home-Rule-All-Round') and then leave the Westminster Parliament to concentrate on what were called 'imperial issues'—foreign policy, defence, and the like? Or one might be bolder still and formalize these arrangements in a written constitution, which would specify what was a local and what an imperial matter—in other words, turn Britain into a federal state, in which a place could also be found at Westminster for representatives of the self-governing colonies (or 'Dominions') (Chapters 1, 4, 12).

Such proposals had a superficial attraction but were seldom adequately thought through. In particular, most of their proponents were unclear as to precisely what role there would be in their scheme of things for England, which was more populous and wealthy than Scotland, Wales, and Ireland put together. But simply to raise these proposals made English people more reflective than they might otherwise have been about what made 'England' and its inhabitants distinctive, and goaded some of them into raising their voices 'in praise of St George' (Chapters 1, 15). This is one of the prominent themes of the present volume.

Two other aspects of the book deserve comment. First, 1886–1918 was an age of extremes. Some historians have presented it as a period of imperial pomp and circumstance, which found outlet in a preoccupation with display, ceremony, and dressing-up ('Ornamentalism'), with Lord Curzon, the Indian Viceroy, as a kind of representative figure (Chapter 4). But these years also saw the cult of the simple life, epitomized by that fertile questioner of all established procedures and structures, Edward Carpenter (especially Chapter 15). It must always be remembered that the apogee of Imperialism, with its idealization of war, occurred alongside the belated advent of democracy, the start of the Labour Party, a socialist renaissance (Chapter 7), welfare politics (Chapter 11), and a challenging of traditional gender stereotypes in the face of the prevailing cult of 'masculinity' (Chapters 2, 12, 19). This book attempts to do justice to all these complex—and contradictory—developments.

This leads on to my other theme: the remarkable speed with which the Victorian synthesis unravelled. Contemporaries were themselves conscious of this happening. 'During the last twenty or thirty years', wrote Sidney Webb in 1901, 'we have become a new people. "Early Victorian" England now lies, in effect, centuries behind us . . .'[3] The advent of a new century and the death of the long-lived Queen Victoria in 1901 further stimulated this sense of living through an age of accelerating change. As one journalist put it in May 1901, 'we stand upon the threshold, not so much of a new century—for that merely signifies a mechanical calculation of time—as of a new era in political and social life'.[4]

When Webb invoked a 'New England', he specifically had in mind the recognition that people were 'not merely individuals, but members of a community, nay, citizens of the world'. The dwindling prestige of the old creed of individualism had many consequences: class-based politics, welfare reforms, and a host of collectivist projects, all of them anathema to statesmen of William Gladstone's generation. But change was equally pervasive in other fields of existence. Novel methods of transportation (not least those made possible by the invention of the internal combustion engine) altered the face of cities and reconfigured social relationships. The harnessing of electrical power was another innovation that had major repercussions. The conquest of the air and the development of the submarine enlarged the circumference of mankind's domain. An understanding of the material world was transformed by the development of atomic physics, while the exploration of the unconscious challenged older conceptions of mental life (Chapter 16). The arts, too, experienced a radical break with the past in the form of 'modernism', which brought with it the 'shock of the new' (Chapter 15). All of these developments predated the outbreak of the Great War, though the pace of change undoubtedly quickened between 1914 and 1918, and many of the innovations listed above only reached their full flowering during the post-Armistice years.

But it would be misleading and naive to treat the years 1886 to 1918 as effecting a straightforward progression from tradition to modernity, since the period was marked by continuity as well as by change. As Disraeli had earlier warned Britain's first Marxist leader, England was 'a very difficult country to move, Mr Hyndman, a very difficult country indeed'.[5] Even the Great War, conventionally seen as a revolutionary force, impinged on British society in

---

[3] *Twentieth Century Politics: A Policy of National Efficiency*, Fabian Tract No. 108 (London, 1901), 3.
[4] Cited in G. R. Searle, *The Quest for National Efficiency: A Study in British Politics and British Political Thought, 1899–1914* (Oxford, 1971), 51–2.
[5] H. M. Hyndman, *The Record of an Adventurous Life* (London, 1911), 248.

ambiguous ways, strengthening some older structures and habits of thought as
well as encouraging modernization. For example, the adoption of a war economy meant that new roles were created for women, enlarging their sense of
what was practical and desirable; but, by valorizing combat, war reinforced
older notions of what it meant to be a man or a woman (Chapter 19). The
horrors of war also tempted many Englishmen to look back nostalgically on the
pre-war world and to seek refuge in older religious and cultural values. Many
war-induced changes were only temporary adjustments and 'normalcy' soon
returned (Chapter 20).

All historical epochs can be categorized as 'ages of transition', but this is
especially true of the restless energy, creativity, and often destructive turmoil
of the years 1886–1918—a period which spanned the nineteenth and the
twentieth centuries in more than a narrowly chronological sense. Whether all
of this amounted to the emergence of a 'New England' is for the reader to
decide.

PART I

England in 1886

CHAPTER I

Nationalism and Nationality

> Who dies for England, dies for God . . .
> Who dies for England, sleeps with God.[1]

So wrote the Poet Laureate, Alfred Austin, in 1900. These lines capture the tone of an era in which British people, from all classes and social backgrounds, threw themselves enthusiastically behind a succession of small and medium-sized wars in the belief that they were carrying out God's Will—before finally plunging into the tragedy of the Great War of 1914–18. It is no coincidence that so many of the most enduring of our patriotic poems and songs were composed in these years: 'What Have I Done For You, England, My England?', 'Land of Hope and Glory', 'I Vow To Thee My Country', 'The Yeomen of England', and 'Land of My Birth I Pledge to Thee'. Even the ritual of playing the National Anthem at the start of public events, whether or not the monarch was physically present, only became standard practice during the Great War—which was also the time when Parry wrote his musical setting of 'Jerusalem'.

Yet for a people so enthusiastically singing the praises of national identity, there was an undercurrent of uncertainty, despite the bombastic self-assertion. 'Britishness', writes one historian, was 'a puzzle to itself and the world',[2] and the same applies with even greater force to 'Englishness'. Who, indeed, *were* the English?

I. ENGLISH AND 'CELTS'

England's population, by 1886, had probably reached about 26 million.[3] Yet not all these people would have described themselves, or been described by others, as 'English', while many who more snugly fitted the description were not living in England at all. This is partly because England did not constitute a

---

[1] A. Austin, 'Spartan Mothers', in *Songs of England*, 83–4.
[2] J. H. Grainger, *Patriotisms: Britain: 1900–1939* (London, 1986), 49.
[3] At the 1881 census it had been 24,613,926.

nation-state, but formed a unit within a larger polity, officially known as the 'United Kingdom of Great Britain and Ireland', which linked it to the neighbouring 'nations' of Wales, Scotland, and Ireland.

As recently as 1841 England's share of the population of the United Kingdom had been a modest 56.2 per cent. But Ireland had experienced huge population losses during the mid-century Famine years, followed by a steady decline caused by an unusual demographic combination of late marriage and high emigration. By 1913 Ireland was supporting a mere 4,346,000 inhabitants, approximately one-half of the pre-Famine total: a depopulation without equal in western Europe since the Black Death. Meanwhile the population of the rest of the United Kingdom had continuously grown, though in Scotland at a slower rate than in England and Wales. The result was that by 1881 England already comprised 70.6 per cent of the UK's total population, a proportion that was to rise to over 75 per cent by 1911.[4]

England in the late Victorian period thus dominated the British State to an even greater extent than Prussia, with 61.2 per cent of Germany's total population in 1900, dominated the newly formed Reich. In March 1894 the Prime Minister Lord Rosebery made what was widely considered a gaffe when he proclaimed that England was the 'predominant member of the partnership of the Three Kingdoms', without whose consent Irish Home Rule (and by implication other major constitutional changes) could not take place; as a Scot, Rosebery might have been better advised not to say this, but in a sense he was voicing a truism.[5]

By the 1880s the word 'British' was generally used to describe the totality of peoples within the United Kingdom—the term 'United Kingdomers' never caught on.[6] The 'British' label proved unacceptable to most of Ireland's Catholics, but it caused less offence among the Welsh and was positively embraced by Scotsmen, who superimposed it upon their own 'more restricted' patriotism. Thus were multiple identities fashioned.[7] Yet in 1887 James Bryce, an Ulsterman of Scottish descent, while noting that the 'distinct national feeling' of the Scots and the Welsh was 'happily not incompatible with attachment to the greater nationality of the United Kingdom', argued that the Englishman had 'but one patriotism, because England and the United

---

[4] The 1881 Census recorded the population distribution as follows:

England	24,613,000	(70.6%)
Ireland	5,175,000	(14.8%)
Scotland	3,736,000	(10.7%)
Wales	1,361,000	(3.9%)

[5] However, Wales was a principality, not a kingdom.

[6] H. C. G. Matthew, *Gladstone: Vol. 2 1875–98* (Oxford, 1995), 213, n.

[7] See L. Colley, 'Britons and Otherness: An Argument', *Journal of British Studies*, 31 (1992), 312–15.

Kingdom [were] to him practically the same thing'. Rosebery thought similarly: 'with an Englishman, the love of Great Britain means the love of England—the larger and lesser patriotisms are one.'[8]

This habit of casually eliding Britain with England was not confined to arrogant Englishmen. The author of 'What Can I Do For Thee, England, my England?', W. E. Henley, was himself Scottish, though based in London. Nor, it seems, did the Welsh composer Edward German (né Edward German Jones), otherwise best known for his 'Welsh Rhapsody', find it incongruous to sing the praises of the 'Yeomen of England' in his hit musical *Merrie England* (1902).

All the same, the 'Celtic' nations, as they were often called, were busily forging distinctive identities of their own in the late Victorian period. Wales started off with the advantage of possessing a separate language that was still widely spoken: in the 1880s about 70 per cent of her inhabitants could converse in Welsh, and even as late as 1901 Welsh was the principal language of 13.9 per cent of them, another 32.2 per cent being bilingual.[9] Around the defence of this language and the culture which it supported (a culture all but impenetrable to outsiders), a vibrant sense of national identity was being constructed. The national Eisteddfod, reorganized in 1858, had assumed more or less its present form by 1880. The Principality was also acquiring other potent national symbols: for example, in 1893 a royal charter was conferred on the National University of Wales, to which the National Library at Aberystwyth was attached in 1905.

Scotland's situation differed markedly from that of Wales. In 1881 the number of Gaelic speakers had already fallen to 231,594 (6.2 per cent of the population), nearly all of them located in two Highland counties (Inverness, and Ross and Cromarty). And though Edinburgh boasted a vibrant cultural life, this was an Anglophone culture: Scottish thinkers and artists such as Adam Smith and Walter Scott were as widely read and admired south of the border as in their native land. On the other hand, as we shall see, the 1707 Act of Union had left untouched many features of the old Scottish Kingdom, so that the country still 'retained her Church, her Law, and her Teaching'.[10] Moreover, the establishment during the Edwardian period of chairs in Scottish History at both Edinburgh and Glasgow Universities[11] suggested that the Scots

---

[8] Lord Rosebery, 'The Patriotism of a Scot', 4 Nov. 1882, *Miscellanies* (London, 1921), ii. 111.

[9] *The Statesman's Yearbook for 1910*, 12. However, a decline of the language was beginning to set in during the 1890s (B. Thomas, 'A Cauldron of Rebirth: Population and the Welsh Language in the 19th Century', *Welsh Historical Review*, 13 (1986–7), 433).

[10] Rosebery, 'Patriotism of a Scot', ii. 127.

[11] The Fraser Chair in Scottish History at Edinburgh in 1901—followed a decade later by one in Glasgow, funded from the profits of a successful exhibition of Scottish history, art, and industry (K. Robbins, *History, Religion and Identity in Modern Britain* (London, 1993), 11).

might not for ever be content with an ideology of nationalism that relegated their country to the status of a 'lesser gem' in the imperial diadem. However, for the time being most Englishmen still viewed 'North Britain' ('NB', as it was often called) through a Highland mist of tartans, kilts, bagpipes, and craggy castles.

In nearly all respects Ireland was the least integrated part of the 'British State' and, for those concerned to maintain that state's integrity, quite the most troublesome. Political life in 1886 was dominated by the Irish Home Rule crisis, arising from the demand of the Irish Nationalist Party for a recognition of Ireland's separate individuality through the establishment of a parliament in Dublin. This demand, which Gladstone had belatedly accepted and imposed upon his Liberal followers, excited violent controversy, since in Ireland even moderate national feeling assumed an anti-English hue and separatist ambitions were far more widely entertained there than in Scotland—or even Wales, where Church disestablishment aroused much stronger passions than the prospect of self-government.

The earlier plantation of much of the province of Ulster by English and by Scottish Presbyterian settlers had created an enclave in the north-east of Ireland whose Protestant inhabitants, except in the aftermath of the French Revolution, generally acquiesced in rule from London. But the predominantly Roman Catholic south and west had something of the character of a conquered colony, separate from England in religion, culture, social composition, and historical memory.

At the root of Ireland's sense of separate nationhood was religion, some 90 per cent of her population being Roman Catholic. This set Ireland apart from England and created a barrier between the vast majority of her people and the British state, whose monarchs had to swear at their coronation to maintain the Protestant Succession. Religion also divided Ireland from Scotland and Wales, which, like England, were predominantly Protestant.[12]

On the other hand, 'Nationalist' Ireland did share with the other two 'Celtic' countries certain cultural features. True, by 1881 its ancient Gaelic language, 'Irish', was spoken by only 18.2 per cent of the population, most of them concentrated in isolated communities along the Atlantic seaboard, and the attempts to revive it made by the Gaelic League, founded in 1893, were not entirely successful.[13] However, the desire of Ireland's cultural enthusiasts to get in touch with a distant Celtic past paralleled similar projects that were afoot

---

[12] Though Robbins stresses that Protestantism was hardly a unifying element in Britishness since it took different forms in England and Scotland, whose splits and divisions were scarcely comprehensible south of the border (Robbins, *History, Religion and Identity*, 252). The 'Union of Welsh Independents' was uneasily linked to the Congregational Union of England and Wales.

[13] By 1901 the proportion of Irish speakers had fallen to 14.36%.

in Wales and—less convincingly—in Scotland. Out of this shared endeavour arose a Pan-Celtic movement, which also had links with Manx, Cornish, and Breton enthusiasts.

Although often unobservant of what was happening on what they disparagingly called the 'Celtic Fringe', English patriots felt sufficiently threatened by these developments to redouble their efforts, already under way in mid-century, to discover the essence of true 'Englishness'—through myth, folklore, and history. One expression of this was an insistence on the centrality of the country's Anglo-Saxon heritage. In 1896 there were widespread celebrations of the millenial anniversary of the death of King Alfred the Great, in whose memory a statue was erected five years later in Winchester, the former seat of the Anglo-Saxon kingdom. Scholars were also working to retrieve Anglo-Saxon (*aka* 'Old English') texts.[14] And schoolchildren were encouraged by their reading primers to think of themselves as belonging to a blue-eyed, fair-haired people, and told that the Queen was 'the descendant of the Saxon chiefs who settled in Wessex more than 14 centuries ago'.[15]

Though it was possible to depict the Normans as 'Norsemen' (Northerners, like the Saxons and the Danes), the Conquest proved a little difficult to fit into this narrative. The 'feudal' Middle Ages did, it is true, help shape the national identity through the concept of chivalry, embodied in the Arthurian legends and in the cult of St George, and through the legend of Robin Hood.[16] But most English patriots were relieved to move on to the Elizabethan era, supposedly the heyday of 'Merrie England', where they could sing the praises of 'Good Queen Bess'.

What made the late sixteenth century, in this idealized vision, so attractive to patriots was that it seemed to represent the historical moment when the genius of the English people first revealed itself, partly through the works of Shakespeare, and partly through the activities of those swashbuckling sea-dogs, Hawkins, Raleigh, and Drake.[17] (In 1912 a 'Shakespeare's England' Exhibition was staged at Earls Court, with street scenes designed by Lutyens.) To Englishmen there was the added bonus that this was also a time when Ireland and Wales were still peripheral and Scotland a separate kingdom.[18]

[14] See Ch. 15.

[15] S. Heathorn, ' "Let us remember that we, too, are English": Constructions of Citizenship and National Identity in English Elementary School Reading Books, 1880–1914', *Victorian Studies*, 38 (1994–5), 420.

[16] See Ch. 15 and below.

[17] One of most anthologized poems of the period was Henry Newbolt's 'Drake's Drum', published in *The Island Race* (1898).

[18] A. Howkins, 'The Discovery of Rural England', in R. Colls and P. Dodd (eds.), *Englishness: Politics and Culture 1880–1920* (1986), 70–1, 73. On primers, see 'Constructions of Citizenship', 396–423. See also Ch. 15.

In practice, the myth of 'Merrie England' served a variety of ideological purposes. For example, it inspired the *volkisch* movement to revive the maypole and Morris dancing. The socialist Robert Blatchford, in his famous book *Merrie England* (1894), was more concerned to point up a contrast between the horrors of industrial capitalism and the world that it had replaced. 'Merrie England' was, in any case, more a frame of mind than a distinct epoch.[19] It can easily be mocked, but it was perhaps no more silly or unhistorical than the stories which the Welsh and the Irish were weaving around their collective pasts.

The invocation of Anglo-Saxondom, however, has now incurred the serious charge of racism. In fact, racial definitions of nationhood by no means dominated the field in the nineteenth century. Most English nationalists knew full well that they belonged to a mongrel people. That is why they often insisted on a linguistic test of nationhood: 'Everyone who speaks English as his mother tongue has the right to be called English', declared the journalist St Loe Strachey.[20] A still more common ploy involved the evocation of the magic of 'English earth'. Thus Rudyard Kipling, in *Puck of Pook's Hill* (1906), depicts the (supposedly) unchanging English landscape as a holy place, which had subjected successive waves of conquerors to its spell, creating out of these disparate elements one people.

Others saw 'Englishness' as a set of values that derived their authenticity from the institutional link between the Church of England and the British State. This was the message propagated by the Bishop of Durham, Brooke Foss Westcott, in *The National Church as the Spiritual Organ of the Nation* (1893).[21] Many Anglicans, joined on this issue by some Dissenters, also stressed the contribution made by Protestantism to England's triumphant global mission. 'Once let Popery put her foot again on the neck of England, and there will be an end of all our national greatness', warned the Anglican Bishop of Liverpool in 1900: 'God will forsake us, and we shall sink to the level of Portugal and Spain.'[22]

But, outside Liverpool, sectarian prejudices of this kind, though a potent shaper of *social* identities, no longer intruded as often as they had once done into discussions of what it meant to be English. Significantly, missionaries operating on imperial soil in Africa and Asia were increasingly co-operating

---

[19] Basil Hood, the librettist of the musical *Merrie England*, incorporates within it a play about the medieval characters of Robin Hood and Maid Marion.

[20] Heathorn, 'Constructions of Citizenship', 399. Strachey, editor of the *Spectator*, was a cousin of the writer Lytton Strachey and father of the left-wing publicist John Strachey.

[21] R. T. Shannon, 'John Robert Seeley and the Idea of a National Church', in R. Robson (ed.), *Ideas and Institutions of Victorian Britain* (London, 1967), Ch. 9.

[22] P. J. Waller, *Democracy and Sectarianism: A Political and Social History of Liverpool, 1868–1939* (Liverpool, 1981), 173.

with one another across both denominational and national frontiers: the first World Missionary Conference assembled at New York in 1900. In fact, 'Englishness' now drew less on specifically Christian tenets than it did on the vaguer notion of 'character'.

To define 'character' too narrowly would itself be 'un-English',[23] but it usually denoted a marked capacity for compromise and a belief in combining freedom with order and for displaying such 'manly' qualities as duty, self-restraint, and self-sacrifice.[24] These characteristics were in turn presented as the property of a nation of tough and independent-minded seafarers, an 'Island Race'.

Whatever criterion of Englishness was adopted, the effect (deliberate or otherwise) was to marginalize the other peoples who inhabited the British Isles—as it was still permissible to call the 'North-East Atlantic Archipelago'. Yet it would be misleading to convey the impression that an impassioned debate between competing conceptions of civilization was tearing apart the peoples of the United Kingdom. Cultural enthusiasts and antiquaries, largely drawn from the professional middle classes, numbered at most a few tens of thousands across the four 'nations'. If one wants to see a manifestation of national feeling that commanded mass support, it would be well to turn to the emerging world of organized spectator sports.

For the 1880s was the decade in which football, both in its association and rugby union codes, was sweeping through the entire British Isles—though in Ireland the establishment of the Gaelic Athletic Association in 1884 represented an attempt to revive native games and protect them from the contaminating touch of the Sassenach. The annual clash between England and Scotland in soccer had been established on a regular basis as early as 1872, and rugby contests between England and Wales were also attracting huge crowds, even before the institution in the 1883–4 season of the annual 'Home International' soccer tournament and the 'Four Nations' rugby championship. These competitions, followed from afar by newspaper readers unable to see the matches live, in some ways heightened antagonisms within the United Kingdom. Indeed, in Scotland and Wales football may have acted as 'a vitally important channel for [a] sense of national resentment, which was the nearest either people came to a popular national consciousness' before 1914. Football was also a source of pride for small nations that in other respects seemed doomed to play the role of perpetual underdogs.[25] But these sporting encounters also had

[23] Robbins, *History, Religion and Identity*, 90.
[24] Counterbalancing this equation of English 'character' with 'manliness' was the view of English women as 'mothers of the race'. See the discussion in Ch. 2 and 8.
[25] R. Holt, *Sport and the British: A Modern History* (Oxford, 1989), 237. The Welsh rugby team won the Triple Crown in six out of twelve seasons before 1900 (p. 250).

an integrative value within each of the 'Home' tournaments, united in the annual hope of victory: competition and rivalry can unite as well as divide.[26]

Integration, meanwhile, was operating at many other levels. For a start, the four 'nations' were far from homogeneous. For example, the social structure of the crofter counties in the Scottish Highlands in many ways resembled that of rural Ireland, while the Presbyterians in the Scottish Lowlands readily identified with their co-religionists in Northern Ireland—in 1912 one Scottish MP even suggested during a debate on Irish Home Rule that the predominantly Protestant areas of Ulster should be given the option of joining a Scottish parliament rather than the one in Dublin![27] The Protestant 'Ascendancy' families of Ireland, by contrast, were closely intertwined with English county society.

Moreover, offsetting the fissiparous influence of culture were various economic developments making for a more uniform United Kingdom, among which the most important was internal migration. For the English people, and still more the Scots, Welsh, and Irish, were not neatly confined within their own national territory, but were intermixed in complex ways.

This was particularly apparent in the case of wealthy landed aristocrats, who formed an exclusive class that can best be labelled 'British cosmopolitan'. The Marquess of Lansdowne, for example, owned extensive estates not only in Wiltshire, but also in Ireland, which he seldom visited, and in Scotland. In fact, south of the border, the lure of Scotland's 'romantic' scenery and facilities for field sports proved a powerful magnet for the wealthy and privileged, amongst them the Queen and her court. Conversely, many Scottish noblemen, who thought of themselves primarily as Scotsmen, sent their children to be educated in England (spurning the much better education to be had at home), or married into an English family. A self-confessed Scottish patriot such as Lord Rosebery would figuratively don tartan when it suited the occasion, but blend in with the English aristocracy at other times. Such assimilation was particularly easy for wealthy Conservatives, since their party provided an arena where landed elites from all corners of the United Kingdom could effortlessly join forces.[28]

At a slightly lower social level, the relationship between the English, Scottish, Welsh, and Irish peoples also had its complexities. William Gladstone, Prime Minister in 1886, was the Liverpool-born son of a Scottish corn factor,

---

[26] In any case, at club level professional football was drawing together players from all corners of the United Kingdom: the Tottenham side which won the FA Cup in 1901 contained five Scots, two Welshmen, one Irishman, and three northerners (Holt, *Sport*, 171).

[27] P. Jalland, 'United Kingdom Devolution 1910–1914: Political Panacea or Tactical Diversion?', *English Historical Review*, 94 (1979), 775.

[28] J. Turner, 'Letting Go: The Conservative Party and the End of the Union with Ireland', in A. Grant and K. J. Stringer (eds.), *Uniting the Kingdom?* (London, 1995), 272.

educated at Eton and Christ Church, Oxford, who married into a Welsh gentry family. He thus had family links, as well as political connections, in all parts of Great Britain.[29] So interdependent were the populations of the various nations that it came as no great surprise in 1902 when the Conservative Prime Minister, A. J. Balfour, appointed a fellow Scot, Randall Davidson, Archbishop of Canterbury—to be joined on the episcopal bench seven years later by another Scot, Cosmo Lang, as Archbishop of York.

Service to the Empire—as administrators and as members of the armed services—bound together the peoples of the United Kingdom even more closely, thereby strengthening a consciousness of 'Britishness'. In 1899 Wales supplied 5 per cent of all colonels in the British army, Scotland 12 per cent, and Ireland 21 per cent—in all cases a higher percentage than their share of the total population, which was 3.9, 10.7, and 14.8 per cent respectively.[30] The smaller nations made a proportionately smaller contribution to the rank-and-file. In particular, the British army no longer relied so heavily on Irish privates and NCOs as it had done in 1851, when Irishmen had constituted an astonishing 37 per cent of all non-commissioned personnel; the Irish element was 14 per cent in 1891 and only 9.1 per cent by 1913, by which time 78.6 per cent came from England.[31] All the same, it was appropriate that Kipling should have made one of his 'Soldiers Three' an Irishman, Private Patrick Mulvaney—the other two being a Cockney and a Scotsman.

Most population movement, however, took the form of a direct quest for employment and economic advancement, a quest which often meant moving from one 'nation' to another—easily enough done, since the frontiers to be crossed amounted to little more than lines on a map. Though England received a net inflow of population, not all movement was in this direction. Belfast, a late Victorian boom town, sucked in Irish country folk from its impoverished rural hinterland but also attracted skilled labour from England (and Scotland) into its busy shipyards, engineering works, and textile mills. Indeed, the great shipbuilding firm of Harland & Wolff well illustrates the point: the Harlands originally came from Glasgow, while Wolff was a Liverpudlian of German origins.[32]

---

[29] Though, significantly, not in Ireland, which he only visited once.

[30] I. F. W. Beckett (ed.), *The Army and the Curragh Incident 1914* (1986), 3, suggests fewer: 12 of 89 major-generals were Irish, two of these being Catholics. Kitchener may have been an 'accidental' Irishman, but General Roberts and Admiral Beresford both chose Irish designations on their ennoblement (D. Fitzpatrick, 'Ireland and the Empire', in A. Porter (ed.), *The Oxford History of the British Empire: Volume III: The Nineteenth Century* (Oxford, 1999), 511).

[31] W. J. Reader, *At Duty's Call: A Study in Obsolete Patriotism* (Manchester, 1988), 8. In 1913 Wales accounted for 1.4%, Scotland for 7.6% (I. Beckett, 'The Nation in Arms', in I. F. W. Beckett and K. Simpson (eds.), *A Nation in Arms: A Social Study of the British Army in the First World War* (Manchester, 1985), 11).

[32] Moreover, Pirrie, its managing director, was an Ulsterman born in Quebec.

The fastest-growing area in the United Kingdom during the late nineteenth century was South Wales, thanks to the development of its coalmines and its iron and steel industry. Between 1860 and 1913 Glamorgan's population more than doubled, as it drew in thousands of immigrants from impoverished south-west counties of England such as Somerset and from Ireland, as well as from rural Wales. Many of these 'foreign' immigrants quite quickly assumed a kind of Welsh identity, even if after 1900 few bothered to acquire the language.

However, most of the population movement within the British Isles involved movement into England, where most of the UK's dynamic economic sectors were located. The presence on English soil of Scottish and Welsh people cannot easily be traced, since they came from many different social backgrounds and dispersed relatively quickly. But accent and family loyalties kept alive, over many generations, a sense of separateness from the host society and a sentimental attachment to the ancestral 'home'. Lloyd George did not feel his Welsh identity to be compromised in any way as a result of having been born in Manchester.[33] The nature of Britain's multinational state facilitated such an outcome since, as British citizens, the Scots and the Welsh could hold aloof from total assimilation to English customs and manners without any serious imputation of disloyalty.

Irish Catholics, however, were both more visible and more vulnerable. In fact, most Irish emigrants preferred to escape to the United States, where they would be entirely free from British rule: nearly 81 per cent of them were taking this route in 1886.[34] But a steady stream, between 1,000 and 6,000 a year, continued to move into Great Britain, a total supplemented by seasonal workers seeking employment at harvest time.[35] These Irish people mostly gravitated to the communities that had already been established by their fellow countrymen during earlier decades: that is to say, Glasgow and Greenock in Scotland, and London, Birmingham, Manchester, and Liverpool in England.

By the 1880s the most dramatic phase of Irish immigration had ended. The proportion of Irish-born peaked in 1861 at 601,634, when they constituted about 4 per cent of the population of England and Wales, but thereafter numbers steadily declined: by 1901 they were down to 426,565 (1.3 per cent of the population) and by 1911 to 375,325 (1 per cent).[36] In 1911 Liverpool, with 45,000 Irish-born inhabitants, was still the English city with proportion-

---

[33] Welshmen living in the metropolis also had the option of attending one of several Welsh chapels.

[34] About 300,000 in Canada in 1861, nearly a quarter-of-a-million in the Australian colonies by 1891 (Fitzpatrick, 'Ireland and Empire', 512).

[35] Though such seasonal migration was in decline by the end of the century, about 30,000 travelling Irish harvesters were working in the northern districts of England and the Midlands in 1900 (A. Howkins, *Reshaping Rural England: A Social History 1850–1925* (1991; 1992 edn.), 202–3).

[36] Higher on mainland Britain as a whole, because of the greater Irish concentrations in Scotland, where they comprised 3.7% of the population in 1911.

ately the largest Irish minority, followed by Manchester, which had 28,194. The largest *numbers* of Irish men and women were to be found in London (60,022 in 1901); though this represented under 1.6 per cent of the metropolitan population,[37] there were dense Irish settlements in certain poor East End boroughs, notably Whitechapel and St George's-in-the-East, where the Irish-born comprised 36 per cent and 40 per cent respectively of all residents.[38]

If one extends the definition of Irishmen living in England and Wales to include second- and third-generation residents, the size of the Irish community must at least be doubled. But this would raise issues of national identity which perplexed the Irish as much as it did their neighbours. Could protracted residence in England, or loss of one's brogue, or marriage to a non-Irish spouse, be said to compromise or to dilute one's Irish credentials? What did Irishness really mean?

Such questions were easily answered by those aggrieved over the circumstances in which their families had left the ancestral land. Feeling more like transportees than emigrants, such Irishmen passionately identified with the struggle for national liberation being conducted 'back home'. However, probably only a minority adopted this extreme position. All Irish people could wear the shamrock and sing 'God Save Ireland!' when celebrating St Patrick's Day; Irish folk music and dancing, too, proved popular. But, significantly, attempts to found branches of the Gaelic League in England and Scotland met with little response except from metropolitan intellectuals.

The Roman Catholic Church, to which most Irish immigrants paid varying levels of allegiance, played an equivocal role in the process whereby Irish people assimilated to their new surroundings. On the one hand, the Catholic hierarchy (almost exclusively composed of Englishmen) emphasized their Church's 'English credentials': its favourite anthem, 'Faith of Our Fathers', evoked an era pre-dating the Reformation, suggesting that Catholicism had deep roots in England's past. On the other hand, through its social activities as much as its teaching, the Catholic Church tried as far as possible to fashion a self-contained Catholic community, insulated against the working-class culture of the native majority.[39] In short, torn between the competing demands of ethnicity, religion, and class, the Irish community occupied an ambiguous position, seeking neither absorption into English society nor a defiant independence from it. Instead Irishmen developed 'an intermediate way of

---

[37] D. Fitzpatrick, 'A Curious Middle Place: The Irish in Britain 1871–1921', in R. Swift and S. Gilley, *The Irish in Britain 1815–1939* (London, 1989), 13.

[38] S. Fielding, *Class and Ethnicity: Irish Catholics in England, 1880–1939* (Buckingham, 1993), 27, 30.

[39] M. A. G. O Tuathaigh, 'The Irish in Nineteenth-Century Britain: Problems of Integration', *Transactions of the Royal Historical Society*, 5th ser., 31 (1981), 168.

life'—half in and half outside of England's labour movement, half in and half outside of the civic life of the localities which they inhabited.

Total assimilation would, in any case, have been difficult, given the attitude towards the Irish taken by most English people. The stereotype of 'Paddy' or 'Pat' was by no means an unmitigatedly hostile one. Yet, because they were disproportionately employed at the unskilled end of the labour market, the Irish were often dismissed by other workers as 'no class', and blamed, often unfairly, for a multitude of social evils: unemployment, wage undercutting, overcrowding, urban squalor, and crime and disorder.[40] The notice 'No Irish Need Apply' was often to be seen. Even the well-known Irish trade union activist Patrick Curran thought it prudent to change his first name to 'Pete'.[41]

Moreover, an association had grown up in the English consciousness between Irish Nationalism and the ugly scenes that had been enacted during the Irish Land War: shootings, rick-burning, animal mutilations, as well as lesser criminal activities, such as rent boycotts and intimidation. True, Gladstone's espousal of Home Rule in some respects legitimized Ireland's national aspirations, promoting social as well as political integration between the English and Irish peoples. Yet militant Irish Nationalists continued to be viewed as dangerous as well as disloyal: the 1880s had seen the 'Triangle' gangs launching a bombing campaign in London and other major cities, to combat which the Special Branch of the Metropolitan Police had been established in 1883. As a result of this troubled history, the Irish were still seen by most English people more as strangers than brothers.

2. FOREIGN IMMIGRATION

The most rabid of anti-Irish xenophobes could hardly challenge right of entry to the Irish, who, after all, were full British citizens. The same did not apply to those of foreign nationality. Yet before 1905 Britain had no immigration laws and its inhabitants traditionally prided themselves on an 'open doors' policy which made their country a haven for political dissidents fleeing from oppressive regimes abroad. In this way a stream of foreign radicals, socialists and nationalists, politicians, intellectuals, and rebels (from Mazzini and Herzen to Marx and Engels), had found themselves living in Britain, mostly settling in London.

Many commercial men, whose trade had taken them to England, also chose to settle there: a case in point is the German quarter in Bradford, where the composer Frederick Delius, son of a German wool-merchant, was born.

---

[40] It was demonstrable that the Irish were disproportionately likely to end up in a prison or a workhouse.

[41] Fielding, *Class and Ethnicity*, 36.

England, indeed Great Britain as a whole, thus absorbed into its population many men and women of talent, who greatly enriched its economy, culture, and political life—men such as the German-born conductor Charles (Karl) Hallé, who received a knighthood in 1888 in recognition of his contribution to the musical life of Manchester. However, as the case of the Irish shows, *economic migrants* were less likely to be welcomed.

In the middle years of the century the largest of such groups were the Italians, who colonized in London the Saffron Hill area in Holborn and then spread out to Finsbury, Kings's Cross, and Soho, where they earned their living in the manufacture of plaster statuettes and, more prominently, as street performers and itinerant musicians, much to the exasperation of local residents—during the 1890s one Radical MP, Alfred Jacoby, made repeated attempts to put down the 'organ grinding nuisance'.[42] By the Edwardian period the Italians, who now numbered about 25,000, were diversifying into the catering trades, where they specialized in the selling of ice cream—a product much enjoyed by the English, who continued, nevertheless, to despise its vendors.

'England opened its doors to all comers, but extended a warm embrace to no-one': this verdict also applies to German immigration.[43] In 1911 the census recorded the presence in England and Wales of 53,234 Germans, plying a wide variety of trades. They could be found, for example, working as correspondence clerks, bakers, pork butchers, hairdressers, waiters, and musicians in brass bands.[44] England also attracted a number of prominent German businessmen and financiers, including Ernest Cassel, Ludwig Mond, and Felix Schuster, as well as representatives of German-based firms[45]; such men, some of them Jewish, received a guarded welcome, tinged with dislike. German office workers, too, were unpopular, the National Union of Clerks complaining that these interlopers were taking bread out of their own members' mouths. But, in general, the German community (which comprised only 0.1 per cent of the total population) was broadly tolerated.[46]

Far less easily assimilated were the Chinese and Lascar (East Indian) seamen, some of whom settled in the ports and dockland areas of London,

---

[42] L. Sponza, *Italian Immigrants in Nineteenth-Century Britain: Realities and Images* (Leicester, 1988), 188–93.

[43] R. Ashton, *Little Germany: Exile and Asylum in Victorian England* (Oxford, 1986), 245.

[44] There were also about 4,000 Lithuanians in England and Wales, and approximately double that number in Scotland.

[45] P. Panayi, 'German Business Interests in Britain During the First World War', *Business History*, 32 (1990), 244–5.

[46] The arrival on English shores of a few hundred German gypsies in the early years of the century met with total hostility (G. K. Behlmer, 'The Gypsy Problem in Victorian England', *Victorian Studies*, 28 (1985), 231–53).

Liverpool, Cardiff, and Glasgow. The Chinese community numbered about 1,000 inhabitants.[47] Of those not employed as seamen, most were employed in the laundry trade, the first Chinese laundry having opened on Merseyside in 1887.[48] The Chinese predilection for opium-smoking and gambling attracted some censure,[49] and there were also allegations that young English girls were doped into becoming 'the body slaves of the laundry lords'. However, the police largely ignored such complaints,[50] and while some anti-Chinese disturbances did occur in Liverpool and in South Wales during the labour unrest of 1911, these immigrants were usually left in peace. The same was true of the small community of West Indian sailors which had sprung up in Canning Town.[51]

In fact, outside a few port areas and university towns, most late-Victorian Englishmen would never have set eyes on a 'coloured' person—except in such exotic settings as London theatres, fairs, and show grounds, or during the Queen's two Jubilees of 1887 and 1897, which were attended by 'native princes' from every corner of the Empire. 'Coloured immigration' was on so small a scale that it hardly featured as a serious social or political problem.

Far different was the complex reaction elicited by Jews from Eastern Europe, who, fleeing from Tsarist pogroms, began arriving in large numbers from 1881 onwards. In one sense these were the sort of classic refugees from oppression whom the English had traditionally prided themselves on succouring. But the mass nature of Jewish immigration aroused concern. Admittedly, many simply used England as a transit camp before continuing their journey to their ultimate destination, the United States, where some $2\frac{1}{2}$ million eventually settled. But by 1914 between 120,000 and 150,000 Eastern European Jews had made their home in Britain, over one-half of them in London, the rest in such cities as Manchester, Birmingham, and Leeds. Although Jewish 'aliens' constituted only 0.3 per cent of the total population (far fewer than the Irish), they tended, like the Irish, to bunch in particular areas: the London borough of Stepney alone contained some 42,000 Jews,[52] and in Leeds they also made a dramatic impact.

Unlike the 'old' Jewish community (some 50,000 strong) that pre-dated them, most of the new immigrants were poor and lacking in the skills needed

[47] In 1911 there were 403 Chinese in Liverpool, 247 in London, and 1,319 in the whole of Britain, 480 of them seamen (J. P. May, 'The Chinese in Britain, 1860–1914', in C. Holmes (ed.), *Immigrants and Minorities in British Society* (1978), 122).

[48] The opening of the first 'Chinese restaurant' in Liverpool in 1907 was another significant development.

[49] Havelock Wilson, the seamen's leader, was a vociferous critic.

[50] May, 'Chinese', 80.

[51] The latter, who held British nationality, in any case occupied a somewhat different situation.

[52] J. Schneer, *London 1900: The Imperial Metropolis* (New Haven and London, 1999), 8.

for speedy adaptation to their new surroundings. When trade was bad, as in the mid-1890s, they became scapegoats for economic and social distress, as had previously happened to the Irish. Moreover, many still had no language but Yiddish and so clung to their 'ghettos'. Unsympathetic observers dubbed the Jewish quarters of London 'The New Jerusalem'.

The Chief Rabbi and the Board of Deputies, who provided social and religious leadership for 'Old Jewry', could summon up no enthusiasm for the mass arrival of their co-religionists. They feared that this development might provoke an outbreak of the anti-Semitism from which, in recent decades, England had been largely exempt—certainly by comparison with most Continental European countries.[53] Indeed, the Jewish Board of Guardians effectively repatriated over 50,000 Jews on the ground that, even with help, they stood little chance of becoming self-supporting citizens.[54]

Although overwhelmingly working class, poor Jewish immigrants were slow to blend in with their English comrades, and this stand-offishness was widely attributed to the fact that Jews had been culturally programmed to become profit-maximizers. 'Sweating' was likewise thought to be a pathological form of economic activity for which Jews were primarily responsible. However, a House of Lords Select Committee, set up in 1888 to examine this issue, eventually reached the conclusion that sweating was really a structural problem which owed little to race or cultural conditioning. Before long, Jewish immigrants were belying the stereotypes pinned on them by outsiders by forming their own trade unions and even joining pre-existing ones.

Jews who had been born anywhere in His Majesty's Dominions, along with anyone else in that situation, automatically acquired British citizenship—however temporary or casual the circumstances determining the locality of their birth, and whatever the nationality of either or both of their parents.[55] Those born in a foreign country were differently placed. However, under an Act of 1870 aliens could become naturalized after five years' residence, on payment of a £7 fee, provided that they could prove that they had paid their taxes and obeyed the law. It was later stipulated that applicants should be of good character, and a Home Office circular of 1905 also allowed naturalization to be withheld from those who could not 'speak, read, or write English

---

[53] This is a controversial subject. W. D. Rubinstein, *A History of the Jews in the English-Speaking World: Great Britain* (Basingstoke, 1996), notes that many Britains were 'philo-semites', predisposed, as a result of biblical study, to view the Jews as a favoured race.

[54] D. Feldman, *Englishmen and Jews: Social Relations and Political Culture 1840–1914* (New Haven and London, 1994), 156. Significantly, some immigrants referred contemptuously to the Chief Rabbi as 'the West End *goy*' (D. Englander, 'Booth's Jews: The Presentation of Jews and Judaism in "Life and Labour of the People of London" ', *Victorian Studies*, 32 (1989), 570).

[55] A position reaffirmed by the 1901 Interdepartmental Committee on Naturalisation: Feldman, *Englishmen and Jews*, 381.

reasonably well'.[56] However, few Jewish immigrants availed themselves of this facility, so, at a legal as well as at a social level, 'aliens' they remained.[57]

After 1880 the right of foreign-born Jews even to take up residence in the United Kingdom met with a fierce challenge. In April 1886 the first of many meetings was held in the East End, attended by local MPs, to advocate the placing of barriers in the way of the further immigration of 'destitute aliens'. The restrictionist movement was soon joined by vicious anti-Semites, for example, Joseph Banister and his 'British Brothers' organization. Eventually, in 1905, Parliament jettisoned its traditional concern for the right of asylum, and passed the restrictive Aliens Act.

Immigration was thus throwing up new problems of how 'Englishness' was to be defined. Whatever the legal niceties, did Irish Catholic labourers, or Italian ice-cream sellers, or first-generation Yiddish-speaking Jews think of themselves as 'Englishmen', and could they really be accepted as such? Most contemporaries thought not, though the more liberal-minded contended that assimilation at a later date remained a distinct possibility. The crucial test was neither ethnicity nor religion, but 'loyalty'—as became apparent during the Great War, when the Jews most under threat from public hostility were not the poor denizens of East London, but the rich 'cosmopolitans', who had seemed to be better assimilated.

3. THE ENGLISH EXODUS

Emigration posed a similar problem, but of a reverse kind: did English people cease to be English simply because they had crossed the seas to begin life afresh in some new land? The muckraking journalist Arnold White linked these two anxieties, complaining about England's misfortune in having to take the scourings of Eastern Europe while much of her best blood was leaving for the colonies.[58] But this was to take a wholly negative view of the situation. A more common response was to attempt to exploit the English (and Scottish) Diaspora by creating some new kind of polity which would bring together the 'English people', scattered though they were across the globe.

In fact, over one-third of all emigrants from England and Wales later returned, some because they found the life of the prairie farmer much harsher than they had foreseen, but most because they had always intended to do so.[59]

---

[56] Ibid. 371–2.

[57] On the further problems caused by who was entitled to welfare benefits, see Ch. 11.

[58] John Burnett opined that immigration was 'rendering useless the sacrifice of thousands of our own emigrants who go or are sent abroad' (Feldman, *Englishmen and Jews*, 269).

[59] Famous individuals who did this include the Scotsman Andrew Carnegie and Robert Tressell, the novelist, a middle-class Irishman who settled in Hastings after a spell in South Africa.

The same applies to those who left the country as adventurers, prospectors, miners, and planters. A list of 'temporary exiles' must also include merchant seamen, numbering over 100,000, many of whom would have spent a sizeable part of their working lives overseas.

Then there were the missionaries, a group whose recruitment peaked in 1896. The largest society, the Church Missionary Society, sent out as many missionaries into the field in the 1890s as it had done during the previous forty years—in part because it had recently agreed to recruit single women, who now slightly outnumbered men, but also perhaps in response to the acquisition of new imperial territories. The China Inland Mission was also buoyant, expanding dramatically in the 1880s. By 1899 just over 8,500 British and Irish Protestant missionaries, in total, were working in non-European countries, alongside many Irish Catholics.[60]

Finally there were those serving abroad in an official capacity within the Empire. During the 1890s the Indian Civil Service and the Colonial Service alone employed some 20,000 white men and 146,000 soldiers, as well as many other ancillary workers. These 'Anglo-Indians' were developing a social life which in time impinged upon the home country: polo and snooker were effectively 'invented' by officers of the British army in India, while badminton had been codified in Poona in 1870. So many British citizens were stationed abroad that special schools sprang into existence at home for the education of their children, among the most famous being the United Services College, 'Westward Ho!', where the young Rudyard Kipling, who had been born in Bombay (his father was a museum curator in India), passed part of his boyhood in the company of similar 'orphans'.

The significance of all this restless wandering is that it stimulated the Englishman's belief that he belonged to a people that were virile and progressive because they were outward-looking, actors on a world stage. This belief also found expression in a romanticization of the life of the seafarer, the pioneer, and the explorer.

What, however, of those who settled abroad *permanently*? Between 1861 and 1900 about 4,250,000 people emigrated from England and Wales, numbers rising sharply in the 1880s, declining in the following decade, and then gathering momentum up to the Great War. More than 5 per cent of the population of the United Kingdom left permanently between 1900 and 1914.[61]

As we have seen, most Irishmen chose to emigrate to the United States, but so, interestingly, did over 40 per cent of Scottish emigrants and over 25 per cent of those from England and Wales. Yet by the Edwardian period all the

---

[60] H. Macleod gives the lower number of over 3,000 (*Religion and Society in England, 1850–1914* (Basingstoke, 1996), 147).
[61] A. Offer, *The First World War: An Agrarian Interpretation* (Oxford, 1989), 121.

favourite destinations for the English and Welsh were Empire countries: about 60 per cent (averaging about 100,000 p.a.) made for Canada, Australia, New Zealand, and British South Africa. These first-generation emigrants retained close ties with the 'mother country', the new cheap postal service linking them to the homeland, just as it linked the Irish-Americans to their native soil. This helped keep alive the sense that Britain was not an island state, but rather the centre of a 'Greater Britain' which reached out to all corners of the globe.

Most emigrants were labourers or white-collar workers interested in their own short-term economic advantage. But a substantial minority comprised 'gentlemen' and 'gentlewomen', seeking their fortune or attracted by the prospect of leading an adventurous new life in Australia and Canada. (Some were fleeing from their creditors, and a few were paid by their families to go away!)[62] Whereas some emigrants left England to escape its suffocating class system, these aristocratic and gentlemanly types often saw the colonies of settlement as a congenial alternative to the rapidly democratizing homeland, and tried to re-create a hierarchical social order there: significantly, a two-volume edition of Burke's *Colonial Gentry* appeared between 1891 and 1895.[63]

Others left Britain's shores as part of an organized scheme. Starting in 1882, the Barnardo homes sent deserted and orphaned children to begin a new life as farmers in Manitoba. By the end of the century over 2,000 'children of the Empire' a year were leaving for Canada (others went to Australia), many of them girls destined for a life of domestic service. This later caused resentment among Canadians, who objected to having dumped on them so many waifs and strays, some of whom became criminals.

Organized emigration of this kind took place because of the lingering belief that unemployment was the result of a congested labour market and that 'surplus' labour could be syphoned off from the unhealthy big cities and sent to the sparsely populated colonies, a process whereby decadent townees would, in Arnold White's words, be 'moralised by sunshine and sweat'.[64] The government's Emigrants' Information Office (established in 1886) was studiously neutral: to the annoyance of imperialists, it did not particularly push Empire countries. However, many emigrants received some financial assistance to go there through the recruiting efforts of the Agent-Generals of Canada, Australia, and New Zealand.[65] Moreover, in the mid-1880s the Local Government Board was still sending pauper children to the colonies, particularly Canada,

[62] P. A. Dunae, *Gentlemen Emigrants From the British Public Schools to the Canadian Frontier* (Vancouver, 1981).

[63] D. Cannadine, *Ornamentalism: How the British Saw Their Empire* (Harmondsworth, 2001), 36.

[64] This was his 'solution' to the plight of the Russian Jews: A. White, *The Modern Jew* (London, 1899), 57.

[65] One-half of those making a new life in Australia did so—which was just as well since the passage to Australia cost four times the passage to the USA.

while the Home Office similarly 'exported' children from reformatories and industrial schools. The Unemployed Workmen's Act of 1905 later authorized the funding of assisted emigration for adults.[66]

Working men who had been cajoled in this way or driven into emigration by unemployment and distress often reacted bitterly to their experiences. For example, George Lansbury spent an unhappy year in Australia in 1884–5, where he suffered exploitation, and came back fiercely critical of the emigration 'swindle'. Indeed, trade unionists remained generally sceptical about any kind of organized emigration. On the other hand, to thousands of working-class emigrants the colonies—free, egalitarian, and prosperous—offered the chance of an excitingly fresh start.[67]

Meanwhile nothing could dampen the fervour of Arnold White himself, who wanted to increase British influence in the world by colonizing sensitive areas: he had twice led a party of emigrants to South Africa in the mid-1880s, and thought that if he had been given greater support the Second Boer War need never have been fought. Along with the journalist W. T. Stead, White also managed to persuade the Salvation Army's General Booth to advocate a 'salvation ship' for the transfer of the entire 'surplus population' of urban Britain to an 'Oversea Colony' (perhaps in South Africa, perhaps in British Columbia)—though in the event nothing of that kind materialized.[68]

Thus, from the viewpoint of emigration the Empire was becoming increasingly important. Booth was speaking for all imperialists when he argued that 'to change from Devon to Australia [was] not such a change in many respects as merely to cross over from Devon to Normandy', since in Australia 'the Emigrant [found] himself among men and women of the same habits, the same language, and in fact the same people, excepting that they live[d] under the southern cross instead of in the northern latitudes'. 'The constant travelling of the Colonists backwards and forwards to England', he argued, 'makes it absurd to speak of the Colonies as if they were a foreign land. They are simply pieces of Britain distributed about the world, enabling the Britisher to have access to the richest parts of the earth.'[69]

So emigration had two consequences. It superimposed upon English and British national identities the concept of Empire citizenship, and it also

---

[66] The Poor Law between 1900 and 1913 assisted the emigration of 9,742, the Reformatory and Industrial Schools Act (1891) and Children's Act (1908) helped 3,097 (1900–14), and the Unemployed Workmen's Act another 27,465 by 1914 (S. Constantine, 'Migrants and Settlers', in J. M. Brown and W. R. Louis (eds.), *The Oxford History of the British Empire: Vol. 4: The Twentieth Century* (Oxford, 1999), 172–3).

[67] A. Offer, 'Costs and Benefits, Prosperity and Security', in Porter (ed.), *British Empire: Nineteenth Century*, 709–10.

[68] Nevertheless, the Salvation Army became a very important emigration agency.

[69] W. Booth, *In Darkest England and the Way Out* (London, 1890?), 143–4.

weakened the dynastic or geographical conception of the state by emphasizing the significance of ethnicity.

4. 'OUR KITH AND KIN'

By comparison with the Empire, or even the United States, the Continent of Europe seemed somewhat peripheral to the lives of the late Victorian generation. For example, sporting links with the white colonies went back to the 1880s and were becoming highly formalized during the Edwardian decade: the first official cricket Test Match with Australia took place in 1904, and in rugby union there were visits from the All Blacks (New Zealand) in 1905, the Springboks (South Africa) in 1906–7 and 1912–13, and an Australian team in 1908. By contrast, the only time before 1914 in which the English soccer team met European opposition was during its two tours of Austro-Hungary in 1908 and 1909.[70]

It is also noticeable how the Grand Tour of old tended to give way in this period to a more ambitious kind of expedition, made possible by faster and cheaper steamboats. Its pioneer was Charles Dilke, who in 1866–7, in his own words, 'followed England round the world', first visiting the United States and Canada, and then proceeding via the South Sea islands to Australasia and the Indian Subcontinent, an adventure which he described at length in his influential book *Greater Britain* (1868). Lord Rosebery was, admittedly, a lover of Italy (he owned a villa near Naples), but he paid three lengthy visits to the United States as a young man, while George Curzon, the future Viceroy of India, set off shortly after graduation, in 1887, on a round-the-world trip that took him to Central Asia, Persia, the Far East, and the North-West Frontier, an experience which helped equip him for his future role as a self-appointed 'imperial statesman'. Sidney and Beatrice Webb, who were far more interested in municipal government and social policy than in foreign affairs, twice embarked on a world tour: primarily to Canada and the United States in 1898, and in 1911–12 to India, China, and Japan.

The prominent place occupied in these itineraries by the United States is highly significant. For many contemporaries argued that if 'Englishness' was to be defined by language and by cultural and political habits (such as commitment to the rule of law and to representative government), then the English people were to be found wherever English people settled. And in this case the United States was not really a 'foreign' country, since its inhabitants were fellow members of the 'English speaking race'—or of 'Saxondom', as Dilke put it.

---

[70] England played Austria twice, Bohemia and Hungary once in June 1908, and the following year played Austria once and Hungary twice. Needless to say, England had crushing wins on all seven occasions, the goal aggregate being 48 goals for, 7 against!

There were even those who hoped that the peoples of the United States might, in the not-too-distant future, be reunited with their 'kith and kin' back home. The short-lived *Anglo-Saxon Review*, founded in 1899 by the New Yorker Jennie Jerome, vigorously propagated this unrealistic view. A more influential advocate was Stead, who helped convert Cecil Rhodes to the cause—hence the Rhodes Bequest of 1902 which provided scholarships at Oxford University for young Americans as well as for white colonials. Similar ideas underlay Joseph Chamberlain's notorious speeches at Birmingham in May 1898 and at Leicester in November 1899, which described the Americans as 'bred of our race' and looked forward to the eventual establishment of an alliance between Germany and 'the two great members of the Anglo-Saxon race'.[71] Winston Churchill, already predisposed to favour closer ties with the United States through having an American mother, was strongly influenced by this cult—which had lasting consequences for the so-called 'special relationship' between Britain and America.

America, in fact, was very much in the consciousness of Englishmen in the 1890s. To some businessmen it was feared as the source of an unwelcome trade competition, but the 'Americanization' of life, like it or not, was an indisputable fact—seen particularly in the development of new marketing, retailing, and advertising techniques,[72] and in newspaper layouts (the 'interview', banner headlines, etc.). British life was also profoundly influenced by American inventions, such as the telephone and the typewriter, just as management practice later owed much to 'Taylorism' (time-and-motion studies).

There were also links of other kinds. Following the upheavals of the Franco-Prussian War of 1870–1, a number of wealthy Americans, on their European tour, fled the dangers of Paris for London, which they found equally, if not more, congenial, and where they settled on a long-term basis. One of those families was the Jeromes, whose daughter Jennie (of the *Anglo-Saxon Review*) later married Lord Randolph Churchill. In fact, a surprising number of late Victorian and Edwardian politicians had American wives, among them Joseph Chamberlain (his third wife), Curzon, who married Mary Leiter, and, on the Liberal side of politics, Lewis ('Loulou') Harcourt. By the end of the century London, by now the acknowledged social capital of the world, was attracting many very wealthy Americans, such as William Waldorf Astor, who settled there in 1890. The novelist Henry James was well placed to explore the social

---

[71] J. A. S. Grenville, *Lord Salisbury and Foreign Policy: The Close of the Nineteenth Century* (London, 1964), 170. According to the *Daily Mail* in 1898, both England and the USA were 'civilising Powers', which 'in no distant future' might 'have to stand shoulder to shoulder with Germany against the half-barbarous Power [i.e. Russia] that now threaten[ed] Europe'.

[72] Selfridge opened his famous store in Oxford Street in 1909.

and emotional world of these American expatriates, because he himself belonged to their number.

Such a constant interaction between the two most powerful English-speaking countries fostered the notion that it was inconceivable that Britain should ever go to war again with the United States: a viewpoint officially affirmed by the Committee of Imperial Defence in 1904. Hence the consternation in London in 1895 when the two countries found themselves in serious disagreement over the boundary between Venezuela and British Guiana; fortunately the dispute was amicably settled two years later. Significantly, too, British public opinion heavily backed the Americans during the Spanish–American–Cuban War of 1898.

But even more important than the United States was the Empire. India and many of the 'dependencies' had, for the British home public, the attraction of the exotic—an attraction commercially exploited by department stores such as Liberty's, with its 'Eastern Bazaar'. Not for nothing was the most popular author of the 1890s Rudyard Kipling, who wrote so vividly of 'the great game' involved in the defence of the North-West Frontier. It has controversially been claimed that extra-European territory may also have constituted an arena of sexual opportunity, liberating the travelling Englishman from many of the taboos which prevailed in his native land—contributing, in some cases, to a greater tolerance of other races and cultures.[73] (One of the many downsides to such encounters was the very high rate of venereal disease in troops stationed abroad.)[74]

However, there was always probably more interest in the 'colonies' than in the dependencies, whose peoples, different in race and creed, raised worrying problems of sexual relationships and cultural incongruities. John Seeley, in his best-selling *The Expansion of England* (1883), called India's inhabitants peoples 'of alien race and religion . . . bound to us only by the tie of conquest'.[75] Chamberlain was therefore not being a total eccentric when, in launching tariff reform, he concentrated almost exclusively on what later became known as the 'Dominions'—the self-governing colonies heavily peopled by white settlers. As we shall see, these 'Dominions' played an important role in the British economy, but interest in their affairs was mainly due to the sympathy felt with peoples who came from British stock—the French-speaking citizens of Quebec, the Boer farmers of Cape Colony, and the distinctly unfriendly Irish communities in Australia and Canada were often

---

[73] See R. Hyam, *Empire and Sexuality* (London, 1991).
[74] J. A. Mangan and J. Walvin (eds.), *Manliness and Morality: Middle-Class Masculinity in Britain and America, 1800–1940* (Manchester [c.1987]), 89.
[75] Seeley, *Expansion of England*, 14.

conveniently forgotten, as were the sizeable indigenous populations, who of course formed the majority in South Africa.

In the 1880s interest in the English-speaking colonies was a progressive cause, dear to the hearts of many Liberals, who felt uneasy about India and the tropical dependencies, which they associated with reactionary Tories (it had been Disraeli who had presided over the Queen's acquisition of the title 'Empress of India' in 1876, and who had also been responsible for a border skirmish in Afghanistan which had proved intensely unpopular). Indeed, 'imperialism' was initially a word which conjured up an image of military despotism or, more specifically, the sort of populist autocracy associated with the regime of Napoleon III ('Bonapartism'). It was because he believed the word 'Empire' to be 'too military and despotic to suit the relation of a mother-country to colonies', that Seeley preferred to use the title 'Greater Britain',[76] the term earlier popularized by Charles Dilke. J. A. Froude in 1885 opted for 'Oceana'.

5. FOREIGNERS

A sense of national identity is partly self-generated. But it can also be defined in opposition to 'the other': external national and ethnic groupings that are perceived as potentially threatening. Foreign European nations helped play that integrative role in this period.

Britain's 'divergence' and sense of detachment from Continental Europe was not total. There were close ties of economic interdependence between Britain and countries such as Germany. Europe also had an important *cultural* attraction for many Victorians, since it constituted the heart of a common 'Christian civilization'. Germany was seen as the home of rigorous scholarship and scientific research, and France as the originator of the *haute cuisine* which the wealthier classes slavishly followed. French remained the language of diplomacy, and it was fashionable to read French novels (so much more daring in their subject-matter than English works of fiction). The Prince of Wales popularized the French resort of Biarritz and the spa towns of Baden-Baden (Germany) and Marienbad (in Bohemia, part of the Austro-Hungarian Empire). Indeed, there was a tendency for the wealthy to flee from the traditional resorts in England, now that they were being colonized by the masses, making instead for locations such as the Alps.[77] In 1913 about 600,000 Britons visited the Mediterranean, which for many was becoming

---

[76] R. Koebner and H. D. Schmidt, *Imperialism: The Story and Significance of a Political Word 1840–1960* (Cambridge, 1965), 173.

[77] Big-game safaris in India and Africa also had a following among the very wealthy.

a passion.[78] Finally, the Queen had relatives scattered throughout Europe, while, at the opposite end of the political spectrum, socialists and peace campaigners cherished their links with their European counterparts. All the same, it was probably only a minority of Englishmen in the 1890s who thought of themselves as 'Europeans' in any but a narrowly geographical sense.

The language barrier cannot be underestimated. But the peoples of the Continent were not just seen as unintelligible or strange: they were often insolently dismissed. The excitement of the Risorgimento now forgotten, even the Italians, for all their past cultural achievements, were widely dismissed as decadent and contemptible, both by working-class Londoners with Italian immigrants as neighbours and by upper-class Englishmen who encountered them on their foreign travels, though here class prejudice and patriotic bigotry often combined. 'Foreigners are in fact deceitful, effeminate, irreligious, immoral, unclean and unwholesome', declared the satirical magazine Truth in 1893: 'Any one Englishman is a match for any seven of them.'[79]

In forming a view about the 'Europeans', the English usually differentiated. Not too much notice need be taken of the anthropologists' attempts to distinguish between three European 'races': in ascending order of merit, the 'Mediterranean', the 'Alpine', and the 'Nordic'—a schema at the expense of which Hilaire Belloc later had much fun. More widely held were the views of Lord Salisbury, who, in a famous speech to a Primrose League gathering in May 1898, declared that the world could roughly be divided between 'living' and 'dying' nations, with the 'weak nations becoming weaker and the strong states . . . stronger'. Though he tactfully refrained from specifying, the 'living' group, headed obviously by Britain and the United States (the immediate point of reference in Salisbury's speech), would also have included Germany: the 'dying' would have included Spain and Portugal, with France and Belgium positioned somewhere in the middle. Some Radical idealists formed a deep attachment, strengthened by visits, to various Slavic peoples struggling against Turkish misrule, but Russia, a semi-European power, seemed sunk in barbaric backwardness.

However, attitudes to foreign nations were opportunistic, heavily influenced by the contemporary international situation. The French, widely mistrusted in the 1890s, were later replaced as hate figures by the Germans, once seen as 'cousins' (interestingly, Rhodes had included them in his scholarship scheme), but increasingly feared, not because they were 'backward' or 'decadent' but, on the contrary, precisely because their modernity and efficiency made them serious rivals and, potentially, dangerous foes.[80] And as antagonism mounted

---

[78] J. Premble, *The Mediterranean Passion: Victorians and Edwardians in the South* (Oxford, 1987).

[79] To be fair, the article was rude about Americans and Australians, as well as about the European nations (cited in Sponza, *Italian Immigrants*, 120–1).

[80] See Ch. 8.

between British and Afrikaners in South Africa, hostile stereotypes circulated of the latter, despite the fact that, as hard-working Protestant farmers, they possessed many of the attributes that the English normally deemed praiseworthy.

6. THE EMPIRE AND 'RACE'

To indicate his sense of the inferiority of the Boers, Lord Milner,[81] the architect of British policy in South Africa, was proud to declare himself a 'race patriot'. Like other imperialists, he also strove to foster a wider sense of national identity. Consciousness of Empire must certainly have helped to weaken local patriotisms by involving all the peoples of the United Kingdom in a shared project. Admittedly, the Scots, who had played so important a role in Empire-building—as explorers, missionaries, teachers, and businessmen— would have been riled to hear Salisbury refer to 'the Empire of the English', just as the Irish rightly complained of the way their own exertions in the imperial cause were overlooked.[82] Nor would they then have been appeased when told that, though not of the Anglo-Saxon race, they had earned the right to be called 'English' through the contribution they had made to the winning of the Empire![83] All the same, in Balfour's words, Britons, whatever their differences, 'could feel united in dominion over, and in abstraction from, the millions of colonial subjects beyond their own boundaries'.[84]

How, then, did the British justify their dominion over so many coloured peoples in Africa, Asia, and Polynesia? Charles Darwin's *The Descent of Man* (1871) had left unresolved the question of whether the different human races were sub-species of *homo sapiens* ('polygenism'), or whether the similarity of their constitutions indicated a common origin ('monogenism'). By the 1880s the intellectual ascendancy in anthropological circles had been seized by those who emphasized racial *difference*. In particular, Augustus Keane gave scientific 'backing' to age-old stereotypes in a series of popular books, such as *Man Past and Present* (1899) and *The World's Peoples* (1908), in which the 'Caucasian' peoples ('brave, imaginative, musical and richly endowed intellectually') were confidently placed at the top of the evolutionary tree.[85]

---

[81] German by parentage and education.

[82] Schneer, *London 1900*, 181. Among the Irish Catholics employed in the Imperial Service were Antony MacDonnell and Michael O'Dwyer, the Lieutenant-Governor of the Punjab in 1913 (Fitzpatrick, 'Ireland and Empire', 497–8, 510).

[83] H. E. Madden, in Heathorn, 'Constructions of Citizenship', 396–423.

[84] Colley, 'Britons and Otherness', 325.

[85] D. Lorimer, 'Theoretical Racism in Late-Victorian Anthropology, 1870–1900', *Victorian Studies*, 31 (1988), 426.

However, well into the Edwardian period the scientific discussion of race continued to be vague and inconclusive, with disagreements still raging around how 'race' was to be defined: by language group, culture, skin colour, cranial measurements, and so on. No wonder that the government refused to accede to the demands of the Anthropological Society in the 1890s to establish a 'Bureau of Ethnology' for the guidance of the colonial administrator.

In popular discourse there was even greater confusion, the word 'race' often meaning nothing more than 'nation' or 'people'. (Irish Nationalists commonly described Parnell as the 'great leader of the Irish race'). Edwardian eugenists later adopted the language of race in an attempt to explain and justify the existence of social classes;[86] but they did not have very much to say about the relationship between European and non-European peoples. This is not really surprising: since the superiority of 'whites' over 'blacks' was widely treated as self-evident, it did not constitute a 'problem' requiring rigorous analysis. Had there been a sizeable number of coloured residents in the United Kingdom, such as existed in the United States, things might have been different.

To Rhodes, who had encountered Darwin at second hand through the writings of Winwood Reade, the issues were, in any case, perfectly simple: 'I contend that we are the first race in the world,' he wrote when a young man, 'and that the more of the world we inhabit, the better it is for the human race.' In fact, the most common justifications of Empire rested less upon race than upon the concept of 'mission'. When in 1898 Kipling spoke of the 'White Man's Burden', he was (revealingly) addressing the Americans who had just assumed responsibility for the Philippino peoples following the Spanish–American War, but the phrase was one that well captures the mood of late Victorian imperialism, with its commitment to an ethic of 'service'—an ideology which owed much to the Englishman's sense of having played a pioneering role in the abolition of slavery earlier in the century, as well as to his part in stamping out 'cruel' customs such as 'suttee' in India.

European (and specifically British) technological superiority underpinned this cultural self-confidence—indeed, there was a tendency to rank the different 'races' according to this criterion.[87] 'We give them education, peace, prosperity, and better conditions of life than obtained under their own rule... In return we expect loyalty and co-operation': that, to many unreflecting Englishmen, seemed adequate justification for British dominion over the 'lower races'.[88]

---

[86] See Ch. 11.

[87] It usually resulted in Western civilizations coming top, followed by those of the East, with Africa and the Pacific at the bottom of the pyramid (C. Bolt, *Victorian Attitudes to Race* (London, 1971), 27).

[88] W. Beach Thomas, *The Citizen Books* (1908–10), cited in Heathorn, 'Constructions of Citizenship', 419.

However, by the 1890s there was mounting scepticism among the informed public about how rapidly such 'progress' could be achieved. A succession of unhappy experiences—the 'Indian Mutiny' of 1857, the Jamaica Rising of 1866, the conflict with Islamic fundamentalists in Egypt and the Sudan in the 1880s—had led to a growing dislike of non-European peoples and cultures. This can be seen in official attempts to limit, even prevent, sexual contacts between 'whites' and 'blacks' ('concubinage'). These efforts took a variety of forms, for example, encouraging Anglo-Indian officials to bring their wives with them to India following the improvement of steamships and after the opening of the Suez Canal in 1869 (these 'memsahibs' were then often accused, somewhat unfairly, of creating more rigid distinctions between the races).

Even where there was no dislike, successive British governments were only too conscious of the dangers of tampering with 'native customs', however irrational or objectionable they might appear to English susceptibilities: for example, the polygyny which was commonplace in many Moslem and Asian countries. Even the practice of female circumcision, widespread in north-east Africa, was grudgingly tolerated.

Limits, of course, had to be drawn. The slave-raiding and human sacrifices practised by the Ashanti chief Prempeh led to his being crushed and deposed in 1896. Indeed, having expunged their own sense of guilt in the matter of slave-trading, the British authorities were not only inclined to crack down hard on this practice, but were prone to depict slave-trading as a moral wickedness for which Africans (and Arabs) bore prime responsibility, a stance which led to the categorization of Africa as the 'Dark Continent'—an area of the world where the human race might even be *regressing*.

Queen Victoria, being of an older generation, was in some ways untouched by such attitudes. In a moment of rare common sense, she warned that colour prejudice threatened to break up her Empire: having a curry prepared each day in her palace of residence, on the off-chance that a hungry Indian prince might pay a courtesy call, was her own particular contribution to good race relations. The Queen also defied convention by establishing a close relationship with her devoted Indian servant 'Munshi'. Few of her subjects were so open-minded.

The Aborigines Protection Society (APS) was the butt of satirical comment from those who believed that they had outgrown sentimental 'negrophilia'. Yet neither did scientific racism triumph. This outcome owed something to the influence of missionaries, who often combined with local merchants (whom they saw as allies in the struggle to replace slave-trading with legitimate commerce), but who tended to mistrust European settlers, preferring to see the British government step in as trustees for the native peoples, whom they wanted to protect.

Only a minority of missionaries actually adopted 'native' customs and dress in order to get on equal terms with their spiritual charges.[89] On the contrary, the reports which they sent home usually put in a lurid light the savagery and backwardness of the peoples whom it was their 'calling' to rescue. Yet, taught by their faith that all races were the children of God (even though the 'heathen' had temporarily fallen under the sway of the Prince of Darkness), missionaries, along with the APS, were ever ready to protest against the blatant colonial exploitation of native peoples.

Moreover, although that intrepid explorer and anthropologist Mary Kingsley could write in *Travels in West Africa* (1897) that a black man was 'no more an undeveloped white man than a rabbit is an undeveloped hare', and should consequently be encouraged to develop, under European supervision, along his own lines, there was a general acceptance in official circles of the common humanity of 'whites' and 'blacks', tempered by the belief that the European races would, for the foreseeable future, have to provide tutelage for native peoples. This was also the view of many 'advanced' liberal-minded women, proponents of what has been called 'maternal imperialism'.[90]

But just as the British had erected a hierarchy of Europeans, so they informally ranked the various colonial peoples. Thus, Sir Frederick Lugard respected the qualities of the Hausa tribes in Nigeria, and the 'noble' Bedouin had many admirers, as did the fiery Pathan (Pashtun) tribes, the Sikhs of India (the 'Ironsides' of the Subcontinent), and the Masai in East Africa. Racial stereotyping was often constructed around gender, the above races being deemed 'manly', unlike the Bengalis and the Shona, who were thought 'effeminate'.[91] In 1898 the *Spectator* suggested that the Zulus, the Masai, and the Matabele might be drafted into the British army.[92] The Queen and Lord Salisbury even viewed with equanimity the prospect of Indians fighting in a white man's war, though the socialist Keir Hardie was horrified by it.

However, it is an interesting reflection on the value system of the Indian Civil Service and of colonial administrators in general that the tribes and peoples who most elicited this esteem were either warriors or else the toiling peasantry, for example, the Egyptian fellaheen and those Indians belonging to what Curzon called 'the great mute pathetic cultivating class'. By contrast, 'native' traders and professional men were mistrusted. Indeed, the more highly westernized 'natives', such as the Bengalis ('Babus'), tended to attract con-

---

[89] For example, some CMS missionaries on the Niger in the late 1880s adopted Hausa dress and tried to live alongside Africans on equal terms.

[90] See Ch. 2.

[91] R. O'Hanlon, 'Gender in the British Empire', in *Oxford History of British Empire: Twentieth Century*, 390.

[92] Bolt, *Victorian Attitudes to Race*, 145.

tempt—perhaps because they seemed a threat, albeit a still distant one, to British imperial rule: educated Bengalis had formed the Indian National Congress in 1885. Salisbury thought babus 'misfits', while the head of the African Department at the Colonial Office called 'educated natives' 'the curse of the West Coast'.[93]

Within each native people or tribe, the colonial rulers frequently co-opted local elites—kings, princes, and emirs—and affected to see them as their social equals. Thus Curzon, when Indian Viceroy, called native Indian princes 'colleagues and partners' who, 'amid the levelling tendencies of the age', kept 'alive the traditions and customs, sustain[ed] the virility, and save[d] from extinction, the picturesqueness of ancient and noble races'. Race prejudice was thus, to some extent, tempered and undercut by class prejudice.[94]

Similarly, at home high-class Indians who observed the conventional social niceties, far from being rejected because of their race, were frequently fêted—and not just by the royal family. The Indian prince Ranjitsinhji, after completing his education at Trinity College, Cambridge, played cricket stylishly for England as well as for Sussex, where he was affectionately known as 'Ranji'. The Punjabi (Sikh) Duleep Singh (the 'Black Prince') acted the country squire and entertained the aristocracy on a lavish scale from his residence, Elveden Hall, in Suffolk.[95] At universities and the Inns of Court Indians were less welcome, but in 1885 there were 160 Indian students, mostly at Oxford, Cambridge, and London, and by 1910 their numbers had risen to over 700 across the United Kingdom as a whole.[96] Gandhi read for the Bar at London between 1887 and 1890, followed by Jinnah and, later, Nehru.

Among those studying the law in London there were also a few West Indians, most notably the Trinidadian Henry Sylvester Williams, who hosted the Pan-African Conference in London in July 1900—an early assertion of the claim that 'no other but a Negro can represent the Negro'. Encouraged by his Radical-Liberal friends, Williams later stood as a Progressive candidate for Marylebone Borough Council.[97]

Educated Indians were even more ready to assert their right to take their place as British citizens alongside the white majority. Remarkably, a Parsee priest, merchant, and lecturer, Dadabhai Naoroji, who on three occasions served as President of the Indian Congress Party, managed to defy Salisbury's gibe that the British were not yet ready to elect a black man by getting himself

[93] P. Burroughs, 'Imperial Institutions and the Government of Empire', in Porter (ed.), *History of British Empire: Nineteenth Century*, 182.

[94] Cannadine, *Ornamentalism*, 48, 125.

[95] On his death in 1893 the estate was acquired by the first Earl of Iveagh.

[96] R. Visram, *Ayahs, Lascars and Princes: Indians in Britain 1700–1947* (London, 1986), 178.

[97] Schneer, *London 1900*, 213–25.

returned as a Radical MP for Finsbury Central in 1892. Another Parsee merchant (and barrister), Sir M. M. Bhownaggree, actually represented Bethnal-Green North-East for the *Conservatives* between 1895 and 1905.

Without doubt these were untypical cases. Racial prejudice in late Victorian and Edwardian Britain was rampant, encouraged by spectacular exhibitions in which 'natives' were put on display almost as if they were animals in a zoo. Derogatory stereotypes of Afro-Americans were further reinforced by the entertainer G. H. Elliot, the 'chocolate coloured coon', who first made his appearance in the 1880s, along with the equally popular 'nigger minstrels'. It is also revealing that the clubland phrase used to acknowledge that a person was endowed with high moral qualities, such as truthfulness, loyalty, and courage, was: 'You're a white man!'

On the other hand, there was no *formal* colour bar, and all those born in HM's Dominions (including 'natives' born in a British colony) automatically received British citizenship, with unimpeded right of entry into the United Kingdom.[98] Indians were also free to enter the Indian Civil Service—even if this involved the prior acquisition of an expensive English education and travelling to London to sit the entrance examinations. Naoroji was presented by his white sponsor to the Liberal Association of Holborn as a long-time resident who could justly be called 'an Englishman as well as an English subject'.[99] Considerations of culture and class were thus sometimes enough to override distinctions based on skin pigmentation.

7. SCHOOLING AND PATRIOTISM

A sense of national identity does not automatically generate the political phenomenon called 'nationalism'. Similarly, the habit of imperial command did not arise naturally, but necessitated a particular kind of educational conditioning. For the upper middle class and the aristocracy, induction into the values which supposedly conferred an advantage on an imperial race—service, self-control, team-spirit—began early, notably in the exclusive 'public' schools, many of which self-consciously prepared their pupils for a future career as colonial administrator or army officer.

It was mainly during the Edwardian decade that the public schools, through their cadet forces, began to develop distinctively militaristic features—Edmond Warre, headmaster of Eton from 1884 to 1905, being the trendsetter. But during the previous two decades they had prepared their boys for a life of

---

[98] This position was reaffirmed by the British Nationality and Status of Aliens Act of 1914.

[99] C. Holmes, *John Bull's Other Island: Immigration and British Society 1871–1971* (Basingstoke, 1988), 83–4.

imperial service *indirectly*, through their emphasis on developing 'character' rather than mere intellect. This invariably entailed putting boys of impressionable age through a 'hardening process' (separation from the parental home, bullying, physical chastisement), an experience which allegedly prepared them for the rigours of frontier life. The prefectorial system was also meant to produce leaders, the theory being that boys who, as fags, had learnt obedience, would later acquire the aptitude for command—a command initially exercised over younger boys, but later extendable to 'inferior' classes and races.

The late Victorian school ruthlessly subordinated individuality to the good of a larger group (the house, the school). This value system bred a contempt for acquisitiveness (not that this stopped many ex-public school boys going on to enjoy success in finance and commerce), and strengthened the 'chivalric' values, which were already deeply embedded in Victorian culture and which became an important element in the Imperial ethos.[100] 'Boy tribalism' was in turn fostered by the cult of organized games, which was probably at its height in the late 1880s and 1890s—particularly cricket, which, carrying associations of the traditional village, had become a potent symbol of Englishness. Henry Newbolt's oft-quoted *Vitaï Lampada* (1897), with its refrain, 'Play up, play up, and play the game!', is about the transference of courage and self-sacrifice from cricket team to army regiment. Reports of football matches in school magazines were similarly replete with military imagery and language. War, in short, was often treated as the ultimate sporting experience, though in the late 1890s a new generation of war correspondents, such as George Steevens of the *Daily Mail*, also took a grim pleasure in stressing its violence and brutality.[101]

Many of the top public schools specialized in preparing boys to pass the army examinations (in Wellington in 1868 ninety-six of 312 pupils were preparing for the army), while in 1880 20 per cent of pupils from Rugby and Harrow entered the army. In crack regiments, such as the cavalry and the guards, many officers came from aristocratic families, products of Eton, Harrow, or Winchester—indeed, the tendency was for these army units to become *more* aristocratic in the closing decades of the century and for the ties between the officer corps and the public schools to tighten. But the big public schools expected nearly all their alumni, if of an appropriate age, to come to the aid of the Empire in an emergency.

It is a matter of contention how far the value system of the prestigious public schools percolated downwards, and the extent to which imperialism ever became a cause capable of generating intense enthusiasm among the lower-middle class and manual workers. The ever-expanding public school system

[100] M. Girouard, *The Return to Camelot: Chivalry and the English Gentleman* (New Haven and London, 1981).
[101] Reader, *At Duty's Call*, 32–4.

undoubtedly enabled some of the cardinal features of the prestigious public schools to be imitated by the lesser ones, and even by grammar schools: indeed, the headmasters of these 'lesser' establishments had often been at one of the big public schools, particularly Rugby, which went in for 'exporting' its former staff in this way. Public school values could also be vicariously encountered even by working people through that most popular of genres, the 'public school story', examples of which were probably being read by hundreds of thousands of Board School pupils and young adolescents. Frank Richards's *Gem* and *Magnet* stories of Greyfriars, fabulously popular among working-class youths, began in 1907.

Direct attempts to instil imperial patriotism into the masses, however, were not an unequivocal success. The Education Codes of 1871 and 1876 required elementary schools to put their pupils through military drill, but by the end of the century 'Swedish drill' (a non-militaristic activity) and organized games had largely taken its place—the former encouraged by female members of the School Boards. An LCC report of 1911 specifically warned against the deliberate inculcation of patriotism on the European model, and history was not made a compulsory subject before 1900.[102]

On the other hand, *Deeds That Won the Empire* (1897), written by the Australian lecturer Dr W. H. Fitchett, had gone into its twelfth edition by 1900, and Kipling and Fletcher's *A School History of England* (1911) also achieved high sales. Patriotic school 'readers' were probably even more influential, along with geography books, both of which reinforced the notion of European superiority over non-European peoples.[103] And although, to the fury of imperialists such as Lord Meath, Empire Day, initiated on 24 May 1905, did not secure government support until 1916, many individual schools participated in the flag-waving rituals surrounding its celebration. Elementary schools were even more prone to observe 'Trafalgar Day', which the Navy League had promoted in order to raise consciousness of Britain's position as a great naval power, a campaign which also took the form of disseminating pamphlets, setting prize essays, and so on.[104]

Far more popular among young boys of all classes were the adventure stories which the ex-war correspondent G. A. Henty churned out at six-monthly intervals, 103 between 1868 and 1902—some historical (*With Wolfe in Canada*,

---

[102] V. E. Chancellor, *History For Their Masters: Opinion in the English History Textbook, 1800–1914* (Bath, 1970), 113. As late as 1895 there were still twice as many schools offering needlework as history (D. Vincent, *Literacy and Popular Culture: England 1750–1914* (Cambridge, 1989), 187).

[103] The popular late-Victorian genre which mixed geography and travel narratives was particularly important because it made the strange and the forbidding familiar through naming places after royalty, imperial statesmen, and so on, so facilitating their imaginative appropriation (R. A. Stafford, 'Scientific Exploration and Empire', in Porter (ed.), *History of British Empire: Nineteenth Century*, 294–319).

[104] A. J. Marder, *The Anatomy of British Sea Power* (Hamden, Conn., 1964), 53.

1886), some placed in a contemporary setting (*With Roberts to Pretoria*, 1902), but nearly all of them allowing the young reader to identify with some stirring episode redounding to Britain's fame and fortune. Such accounts (regularly given away as Sunday School prizes) were undoubtedly far more entertaining than actual history books.[105] The 'Jack Harkaway' penny-dreadfuls, and the more respectable *Boy's Own Paper*, started in 1879, to which the once-famous Dr Gordon Stables often contributed, similarly trumpeted the obligations and rewards of imperial citizenship. Finally, youth was the target aimed at by committed imperialists anxious to propagandize among the masses: for example, Lord Meath's Lads' Drill Association, established in 1899.

Meanwhile adults were being familiarized with the imperial message through the medium of the mass-circulation newspapers, many of which, not least the newly founded *Daily Mail*, adopted a stridently imperialistic tone. Propaganda by spectacle could reach an even wider audience. Particularly important in propagating the imperialist message was the 1897 Jubilee, stage-managed by Reggie Brett, the future Lord Esher—a great pageant attended by representatives from all round the Empire, from elected premiers to native princes. To provide an appropriate backcloth to these displays, conscious attempts were made to turn London into a true 'imperial metropolis', replete with symbolic statuary and grand thoroughfares testifying to Britain's global power: the development of Kingsway during the first decade of the new century was meant to serve precisely such a purpose. The refronting of Buckingham Palace, the widening of the Mall, the construction of Admiralty Arch, and the building of the Victoria Memorial outside Buckingham Palace were similarly intended to create a theatrical setting suitable for monarchical pageantry and imperial celebrations.

Museums, such as the Horniman Museum in South London and the Pitt-Rivers in Oxford, proudly displayed the trophies of Empire. So, in a more overtly propagandist way, did a succession of great exhibitions, starting with the 1886 Colonies and India Exhibition in London. The 1899 Greater Britain Exhibition, which was mounted at Earl's Court, had twenty-six acres of ground on which to present its attractions—which included native dancers, monkey performers, and Bedouins.[106] Similar spectaculars were staged at London's Empress Theatre, while in the music halls the irreverently Radical tone commonly found in the 1870s and early 1880s had been largely replaced by the end of the century by open displays of patriotism. In the 1890s there was a vogue for 'Imperial tableaux', in which colonies were depicted as willingly

[105] J. Bristow, *Empire Boys: Adventures in a Man's World* (London, 1991).
[106] In August 1900 one exhibition featured, among its 'natives', Lobengula, the defeated Matabele chief.

subservient and loyal, along with 'the dusky sons of Hindostan'.[107] Travelling panoramas, dioramas, and cosmoramas, featuring imperialistic spectacles such as the battle of Omdurman, criss-crossed the country.

But one must be careful not to paint a scenario in which scheming 'imperialists' brainwashed and manipulated a gullible populace. True, consumers were bombarded with imperialist imagery, which shrieked out at them from all sides—from newspaper advertisements, hoardings, the decoration on biscuit tins, and from other kinds of commercial packaging—'jingo kitsch', it has been called.[108] But businessmen would not have marketed their wares in this way, had the iconography of Empire not been broadly popular. No one coerced working-class families into attending the music-halls—they would certainly have taken their custom elsewhere had they disliked what was on offer. This is apparent from the fate of Lord Meath's organization, which, with its crude propaganda, militaristic values, and obsession with drill, never recruited more than a few thousand volunteers—in startling contrast to the later success of the Boy Scouts.[109]

In short, as the churches had discovered decades earlier, it was not possible to 'indoctrinate' the working classes with an unpalatable message, and the recipients of 'edifying' entertainments were perfectly capable of selecting the entertaining elements and filtering out whatever was uncongenial or could not be fitted into the mind-set through which they viewed the world.[110] It seems reasonable to deduce that the willingness of people of all classes to devote money and time on commodities and activities which had an 'imperialist' bias meant that they were generally popular.

Not that 'imperialism' lacked its critics. There existed a strong strand in popular Radicalism and in socialism which attacked the Empire for its exploitation of the 'native races' and called for the conferral of self-government on them, a cause in which they were joined by some humanitarian Liberals. Other Radicals took a less sympathetic attitude to 'natives', insisting rather that the British government should not involve itself in the horrors of the 'Dark Continent', which simply served to distract attention from social problems at home.

The very grandiosity of imperialistic projects also produced, by way of reaction, a celebration, in Radical circles, of the small-scale and the local. As

---

[107] P. Summerfield, 'Patriotism and Empire: Music-Hall Entertainment 1870–1914', in J. M. Mackenzie (ed.), *Imperialism and Popular Culture* (Manchester, 1986), 27–8.

[108] J. M. MacKenzie, *Propaganda and Empire: The Manipulation of British Public Opinion 1880–1960* (Manchester, 1984); T. Richards, *The Commodity Culture of Victorian England: Advertising and Spectacle, 1851–1914* (London, 1990), Ch. 3.

[109] See Ch. 13.

[110] J. Rose, *The Intellectual Life of the British Working Classes* (New Haven and London, 2001), Ch. 10.

early as 1881 Seeley had noted that some of his countrymen regarded the Empire as 'a kind of excrescence upon England', which deprived them 'of the advantages of our insularity' and exposed them 'to wars and quarrels in every part of the globe'.[111] The so-called 'Little Englander' Radicals concurred. 'Better a "little England" than an England swollen and bloated out of recognition', declared J. L. Hammond.[112] Empires, in G. K. Chesterton's view, were both transient and unreal, and those who extolled them vulgar power-worshippers, lacking in any spark of true patriotism.[113] 'Back to England!' was the cry of these 'oppositional patriots', who wanted love of country to develop from pride in one's native village and the love of one's local landscapes and customs[114]—a vision that perhaps had somewhat more in common with Kipling than either party could comfortably acknowledge. Meanwhile socialists had their own rather different vision of England: interestingly, in his famous anthem Edward Carpenter prophetically called upon 'England' to 'arise', not the working class.[115]

These, however, were minority voices. Most late-Victorian Englishmen, from whatever class, could derive satisfaction from the thought that they constituted a successful imperial 'race'—consolation indeed for the poor and the underprivileged. Imperialism may also have appealed because it gave off a warm sense of camaraderie that was greatly needed at a time when urbanization and industrialization had destroyed many older forms of face-to-face relationship.

8. CONCLUSION

Every Englishman is a citizen in several different ways. He is a citizen of the town of the country district to which he belongs; he is a citizen of England . . . he is a citizen of the United Kingdom, and he is also a citizen of the great British Empire.[116]

For the late-Victorian English, nationality was a problematic concept. Were they primarily 'English' or 'British'? The iconography of patriotism gave off mixed messages as to their identity. For example, the pugnacious John Bull sometimes symbolized England, and sometimes a Greater Britain menaced by impudent foreigners—without ever quite losing his older roles of bemused

---

[111] J. R. Seeley, *The Expansion of England* (London, 1883; 1895 edn.), 341.

[112] Cited Grainger, *Patriotisms*, 144: from Hammond's *Liberalism and the Empire* (1900).

[113] In Lucian Oldershaw, *England: A Nation: Being the Papers of the Patriots' Club* (London, 1904), 11–25.

[114] Ibid. 221, 262.

[115] On 'England Arise', see Ch. 7.

[116] Oscar Browning, 1893, cited in Heathorn, 'Constructions of Citizenship', 418.

shopkeeper or stolid taxpayer being taken for a ride by his political masters. St George was an even more protean figure. As well as embodying the chivalric values,[117] he was, of course, the patron saint of England: in 1894 the Royal Society of St George was founded, under royal patronage, 'to encourage and strengthen the spirit of patriotism among all classes of the English people'. Little wonder if, on the eve of the Great War, some English conservatives sought to raise the banner of St George to express defiance of the rapacious and insubordinate Celts. Yet in the childrens' play *Where the Rainbow Ends*, St George, depicted as an armour-clad knight, 'golden-haired, blue-eyed, English of the English', brings the drama to a close by calling on the youth of England to 'rise' and let their voices ring 'for God, for Britain [*sic*], and for Britain's King'.[118]

Immigration and emigration were also important in raising puzzling questions as to whether nationality was conferred by ethnicity, geographical location, or 'culture'. Most Englishmen assumed the superiority of whites over blacks, and placed the British in the vanguard of the white races. But the 'English race' was not usually thought of in purely biological terms, but was envisaged as the carrier of a distinct set of values and institutions which had been successfully transplanted to the colonies of settlement. Indeed, to an imperialist such as George Wyndham race served the purpose of reconciling allegiance to Empire with various local patriotisms.[119] Yet there was also a tension between those who recognized themselves to be citizens of the Empire and those who believed that 'home' existed wherever people of English stock had settled—in the latter case, we had more in common with our American 'cousins' than with, say, the French Canadians or the Cape Dutch, to say nothing of the coloured races, all of whom lived under the Union Jack.

The English thus switched between apparently contradictory definitions of their national identity, usually without betraying any embarrassment. Indeed, for some, this ambivalence could be a source of cultural energy, especially if they had had lengthy sojourns outside England. To take a famous example, Rudyard Kipling left 'Westward Ho!' for India, where he spent seven years, later moved to Vermont (where he married an American wife), and then took up residence for many months in South Africa, before and during the excitement of the Boer War. After this extraordinarily peripatetic existence he finally settled down, at the age of 36, in his new home, 'Bateman's'

---

[117] Baden-Powell adopted the saint as the special protector of the Boy Scouts, who were encouraged to behave like knights of yore.

[118] S. Riches, *St George: Hero, Martyr and Myth* (Stroud, 2000), 200–6.

[119] E. H. H. Green, 'The Political Economy of Empire, 1880–1914', in Porter (ed.), *History of British Empire: Nineteenth Century*, 356–7.

in Burwash in the Sussex Weald, where he rediscovered England, 'my favourite foreign country'.

In short, though national feeling and patriotism took many different forms,
none was 'natural': each had to be 'discovered' or 'invented'. But these
identities were also inextricably intertwined with issues of gender, age, and
class.

CHAPTER 2

Generation and Gender

Women played a significant part in the running of the Empire—as publicists, missionaries, social workers, or simply as supportive wives. In the iconography of imperialism, female figures, too, were prominent: Britannia (sometimes bearing the crosses of St George and St Andrew on her shield) adorned many monuments, and in 1893 the Prince of Wales, for the first time, named the royal yacht after this mythic personage.[1] Significantly, the relationship between the homeland and its overseas colonies was often depicted in patriotic literature as that of an all-caring mother, surrounded by her dutiful daughters.

All the same, Empire had traditionally been the stage on which masculine dramas were played out,[2] and this presented its (male) apologists with something of a dilemma. Some argued that racial superiority could overpower feminine frailties—a necessary concession if they were to sing the praises of Good Queen Bess or pay respectful obeisance to Good Queen Victoria. But others countered women's demand for the vote with the objection that 'native peoples' would chafe at being ruled by females.[3]

Imperialists also struggled to fit children into their world-picture. Children were often likened to non-European subjects of the Crown, in that both lacked an adult's freedom, though, in exchange for this loss, they were supposedly receiving kindly protection and wise governance. But obviously such a state of tutelage was only *temporary* for British children. Kipling allows the 'boy' in *Kim* to transgress racial boundaries because his youth places him 'beyond caste'—but only until, with maturity, he assumes the responsibility of serving the Empire.[4] And during this transitional period most imperialists thought that children—boys in particular—needed to be prepared, ideologically, for their future role.

---

[1] M. Warner, *Monuments and Maidens: The Allegory of the Female Form* (London, 1985), 45–8.

[2] K. Boyd, 'Exemplars and Ingrates: Imperialism and the Boys' Story Paper', *Historical Research*, 67 (1994), 143.

[3] B. Harrison, *Separate Spheres: The Opposition to Women's Suffrage in Britain* (London, 1978), 34, 75.

[4] John McBratney, 'Imperial Subjects, Imperial Space in Kipling's "Jungle Book" ', *Victorian Studies*, 35 (1992), 277.

If governing an Empire thus fell within an adult, male sphere of duty, then, quite as deep as race or nation, was the bedrock of gender and age. Imperialism might be 'manifest destiny', but human beings were also subject to *biological* destiny. The narrator in Rider Haggard's best-selling *King Solomon's Mines* (1885) voiced a common (male) viewpoint when, from the heart of 'darkest Africa', he observed: 'Women are women all the world over, whatever their colour.'[5]

What, then, were the demographic realities of late-Victorian and Edwardian England? Of England's 26 million inhabitants in 1886, females formed a majority. In 1881 there were 105.5 females to every 100 males, a sex imbalance which rose to 106.3 in 1891 and then to 106.8 in 1901 and 1911.[6] More boys than girls were born, but this was quickly offset by higher male mortality during infancy. Emigration then tilted the balance still further towards females, who also benefited disproportionately from a falling death-rate. In each age cohort (apart from the 10–14 grouping) females enjoyed a better survival-rate than males.[7] By the start of the century life-expectancy at birth, which was steadily rising, stood at 46 years for men but 50 for women; widows significantly outnumbered widowers; and amongst the very elderly (75+) there were approximately three females to every two males. This situation is not radically different from that of more recent times—indeed, though we all now live longer, the gender imbalance has actually widened and the gap in life-expectancy between men and women increased.[8]

Where the late Victorian and Edwardian population really did differ from that of later decades was in age-distribution. Although the birth-rate had been steadily falling since 1876, children and youths outnumbered the elderly by nearly five to one (see Table 2.1).

Thus, despite the new interest in the plight of the aged poor (which was to culminate in the 1908 Old Age Pensions Act), only one in 13.5 people was aged 60 or over.[9] No wonder that early photographs show the streets so full of children and youths. In West Ham, a recently developed urban area, 41 per cent of the residents in 1901 were under 15 years of age.[10] In this respect, late Victorian England more resembled a contemporary 'third world' country such as Egypt than it does a modern European state (see Table 2.2).

[5] (Oxford, 1989), 246.

[6] These figures may be distorted by the greater number of men away from home as seamen, etc., on census day.

[7] Even amongst those aged 20–40—which shows that the undoubted perils of childbearing were outweighed by the industrial accidents and deaths which wreaked havoc among their male counterparts.

[8] By 1951 the overall ratio was 108.2. However, among those aged 15–44, the ratio of women to men, which had been 106.6 in 1881, had narrowed to 103.2.

[9] The female–male ratio in this age group was 122.7 in 1891, 125.3 in 1911.

[10] J. Springhall, *Coming of Age: Adolescence in Britain, 1860–1960* (Dublin [c.1986]), 48.

TABLE 2.1. *Distribution of ages in England and Wales, 1881–1911* (%)

	1881	1891	1901	1911
Under 15 years	36.5	35.1	32.4	30.6
Over 60 years	7.4	7.4	7.4	7.6

TABLE 2.2. *Comparison of age-distribution, 1881 and 1990* (%)

	UK, 1990	England, 1881	Egypt, 1990s
Under 15	19	36.5	40
Over 60	21	7.4	6

So much for the raw biological data. But the *meaning* of age and gender is culturally determined, and in the late Victorian and Edwardian period both children and women were acquiring important new identities.

1. THE YOUNG

Looking back on his own childhood from an Edwardian perspective, Edmund Gosse (born 1849) was struck by the absence in his parents of any sense of childhood as a distinctive stage in human life: 'I had not, until my tenth year was far advanced, made acquaintance' with any other child, and even then 'had not the faintest idea how to "play" ', not having learnt or heard of any 'games'.[11] Though Gosse's austere upbringing, in a Plymouth Brethren household, was unusual even by the standards of the day, this account registers an important historical change: the recognition that children were not miniature adults (or 'Little Women', in Louisa May Alcott's popular novel of 1868), but had their own personalities and needs.

Increasingly, childhood status was being redefined to signify dependence on parents, economic and sexual inactivity, and an absence of legal and political rights.[12] In middle-class milieux this led to an idealization, or 'sacralization', of the child which found expression in the view that childhood was a magic realm, a time of heightened emotional sensitivity. No wonder that, in his *Studies of Childhood* (1895), the psychologist James Sully should have dealt at such length with imagination, play, and art.

Fictional writers sought to evoke this magical thought-world—often in ways that also stimulated the imagination of adults. James Barrie's *Peter Pan* (1904)

[11] E. Gosse, *Father and Son* (London, 1907), 159–60.
[12] R. Cooter, Introduction to R. Cooter (ed.), *In the Name of the Child: Health and Welfare 1880–1940* (London, 1992), 2–4.

and the play which soon rivalled it in popularity, Mrs Clifford Mills's *Where the Rainbow Ends* (1911), were quintessentially Edwardian works. The cult of childhood received a further boost from such diverse classics as Beatrix Potter's stories (like *Squirrel Nutkin*, 1903), Edith Nesbit's *The Railway Children* (1906), Kenneth Grahame's *Wind in the Willows* (1908), and Walter de la Mare's *Peacock Pie* (1912). Edward Elgar provided a musical equivalent to these books in his *Wand of Youth* suites (1907) and in his accompaniments to the children's fairy-play *The Starlight Express* (1915). As well as having access to a huge quantity of books specifically aimed at this constituency, the children of the well-to-do could also play with a wide range of commercially manufactured toys: for example, Meccano sets were first produced in 1908.[13]

Moreover, the falling birth-rate meant that, especially at the upper end of the social scale, average family size was declining: marriages of the late 1860s which lasted twenty years or more produced an average of 6.16 children, those of the 1870s 5.8, those of the 1880s 5.3, those of the 1890s 4.13, and those of 1915 2.43.[14] This may have resulted in children being more valued as individuals. Thus, where space permitted, it was now thought desirable to give each child a separate bedroom—one of many manifestations of the new 'ethic of privacy'.[15]

Admittedly, the aristocracy and gentry still saw little of their offspring, who were handed over to nursemaids and governesses before (in the case of boys) being packed off to boarding school. An extreme case was furnished by two little girls, growing up at Kingston Lacy, who supposed that their father was absent on a long stay in India and only learnt of his death five years after the event![16] But such heartless conduct ran counter to middle-class mores, which encouraged emotional intimacy between parents and children. This more affectionate, informal relationship was quickly exploited by late Victorian advertisers, who tended to depict older children as loveable little rascals—a far cry from the stern attitudes of earlier decades.[17]

This re-evaluation of childhood impacted upon public policy. Prison was now thought to be an inappropriate punishment for young offenders.[18] Similarly, hospitals sprang up to deal specifically with children, who had previously been lumped in with women.[19] In 1907 the Child Study Society was founded to

---

[13] H. Hendrick, *Children, Childhood and English Society, 1880–1990* (Cambridge, 1997), 88–9.

[14] A. McLaren, *Birth-Control in Nineteenth-Century England* (London, 1978), 11, based on Matras, *Population Studies*, 1965.

[15] J. Harris, *Private Lives, Public Spirit: A Social History of Britain 1870–1914* (Oxford, 1993), 93.

[16] P. Horn, *Ladies of the Manor: Wives and Daughters in Country-House Society 1830–1918* (Stroud, 1991), 28.

[17] L. A. Loeb, *Consuming Angels: Advertising and Victorian Women* (Oxford and New York, 1994), 13.

[18] See Ch. 6.

[19] Cooter, 'Introduction', 9.

provide a forum for a new professional grouping, that of child psychologist—one of many indications that childhood was being reconstructed in 'psycho-medical terms'.[20]

Meanwhile a new emphasis was being placed upon children's need for care and protection. In 1885 the age of consent for girls was raised from 14 to 16—a highly significant step in protecting children from the pressures of adult life. Worried about the prevalence of father–daughter incest (a hitherto unmentionable subject), child protection agencies started to give mothers firm advice about the importance of ensuring 'modest' domestic arrangements for their children, and Parliament passed legislation in 1903 and 1908 prohibiting and punishing incest for the first time.[21] (Significantly, neither Havelock Ellis nor Edward Carpenter, Britain's foremost sexologists, would give any credence to the Freudian concept of infant sexuality.)

In fact, in place of the older view that society needed protection from criminal children, the new orthodoxy insisted that it was children who needed protection from cruel or negligent parents.[22] The National Society for the Prevention of Cruelty to Children (NSPCC), founded in 1883 by a Congregational minister, Benjamin Waugh, soon developed many local branches, typically dominated by clergymen and JPs.[23] The organization started entering working-class homes in the 1890s and was soon investigating 10,000 cases a year, instigating numerous prosecutions of parents—only a minority of whom, incidentally, were really poor.[24]

The NSPCC's hand was strengthened by a succession of Acts of Parliament, such as the 1889 Prevention of Cruelty to Children Act, which made it an offence carrying a fine or imprisonment to neglect, ill-treat, or abandon children in ways that would cause suffering; it also placed additional restrictions on child employment. A further Prevention of Cruelty Act of 1894 obliged Poor Law guardians to accept children brought to them for protection,[25] and Poor Law Acts of 1889 and 1899 gave them the authority to terminate parents' rights over abused and deserted children. The pre-war

---

[20] H. Hendrick, 'Child Labour, Medical Capital, and the School Medical Service', in Cooter (ed.), *Name of the Child*, 47.

[21] A. S. Wohl, 'Sex and the Single Room: Incest Among the Victorian Working Class', in A. S. Wohl, *The Victorian Family: Structure and Stresses* (London, 1978), 201.

[22] H. Ferguson, 'Cleveland in History: The Abused Child and Child Protection, 1880–1914', in Cooter (ed.), *Name of the Child*, 152.

[23] Ibid. 150.

[24] Ibid. 148–50; Harris, *Private Lives*, 84; G. Behlmer, *Child Abuse and Moral Reform in England, 1870–1908* (Stanford, 1982).

[25] M. J. Wiener, *Reconstructing the Criminal: Culture, Law, and Policy in England 1830–1914* (Cambridge, 1990), 163.

Liberal governments later extended the state protection of 'minors' deemed to be 'at risk'.[26]

Headmasters in the big public schools, sensitive to the new climate of opinion, now reined in those sadistic floggings beloved of many of their mid-Victorian predecessors. The end of corporal punishment in schools still lay far off. Nevertheless, one historian discerns a trend towards 'a less frequent and less harsh use of beatings, strappings, and beltings over the course of the [nineteenth] century, and the partial substitution of verbal correction and non-corporal punishment'.[27]

On the other hand, in working-class communities, where children were punished less frequently but probably more severely when the occasion seemed to require it, caning and slapping were considered a salutary discipline, provided the correction was administered by the parents and not by 'outsiders'. Indeed, there is some evidence that working-class children were being treated more strictly just when middle-class children tended to be pampered.[28] Such a regime could be half-rationalized as a necessary preparation for adult life, where survival required the poor to develop habits of subordination and obedience.

There was a similar emphasis in the elementary schools on orderliness and conformity, which was imposed by drill and corporal punishment, along with much rote-learning—though the mechanical teaching of the '3 Rs' was not so dominant after the abandonment of the Revised Code in 1897.[29] Working-class girls seem to have enjoyed their schooldays more than boys. But many of the latter fiercely resented the loss of status involved in exclusion from the adult world of work.[30] There were even occasional school strikes, notably in 1911 when protests, originating in South Wales, spread to sixty-two towns, with children picketing schools and marching through the streets, demanding an end to homework and caning, better school meals, and improved heating in school buildings.[31]

---

[26] See Ch. 11. Other protective measures included the 1889 Children's Charter, which restricted long hours of work, co-ordinated local initiatives against cruelty, and provided greater punishments for offenders.

[27] F. M. L. Thompson, *The Rise of Respectable Society: A Social History of Victorian Britain, 1830–1900* (London, 1988), 134.

[28] E. Ross, *Love and Toil: Motherhood in Outcast London, 1870–1918* (Oxford, 1993), 150, 158; Harris, *Private Lives*, 88.

[29] In any case, many teachers had previously gone beyond the prescribed code (J. Rose, 'Willingly to School: The Working-Class Response to Elementary Education in Britain, 1875–1918', *Journal of British Studies*, 32 (1993), 130).

[30] J. Rose thinks the unpopularity of schooling has been exaggerated. For a contrary view, L. Rose, *The Erosion of Childhood: Child Oppression in Britain 1860–1918* (London, 1991), Ch. 17.

[31] S. Humphries, *Hooligans or Rebels? An Oral History of Working-Class Childhood and Youth, 1889–1939* (Oxford, 1981), 92.

Yet, whether children themselves liked it or not, the community was now insisting that they needed to undergo a longer period of tutelage before going out into the adult world—hence the centrality of education. In 1880 schooling had been made compulsory until the age of 10 (parishes could extend this through local by-laws): in 1893 the threshold was raised to 11 and in 1899 to 12. In 1900 local authorities were empowered to raise the leaving age yet higher, to 14, though few did so before 1918.

Compulsory schooling had initially been bitterly resisted by many working-class parents who, even after education had become free in 1891, found themselves deprived of a much-needed supplementary income.[32] Skilled workers, it is true, had always taken a pride in education, both for themselves and for their offspring, this being one of the status distinctions which marked them off from the 'rough' and the unskilled. Gradually, over the next two decades, almost all working-class parents came to view schooling as normal and natural: by the 1900s few of them were treating the attendance officer (who in some rural areas doubled up as the Poor Law relieving officer) as a class enemy—perhaps influenced by the more sensitive way in which lady councillors were handling cases of truancy.[33] In London summonses for non-attendance fell sharply after 1900, and by the turn of the century schoolteachers were often being accorded an exaggerated respect.[34]

Most middle- and upper-class children probably stayed at school until the age of 18, and the children of the commercial classes did so until at least 16. However, a secondary education still lay beyond the reach of most children of manual workers—certainly before the 1902 Education Act (only 5,500 schol-arships were available in 1900).[35] Nor was there a uniform leaving age: children who had attained a particular 'Standard' could be exempted from further schooling. Even after the 1899 Education Act had extended the age of compulsory schooling to 12, many children, taking advantage of various loopholes, continued to leave school earlier.

Moreover, although the trend was to postpone the age at which young boys and girls entered the labour market full-time, the half-time system still operated in the industrial north. Children who had met the Fifth Standard or who had attended school for 300 sessions during the previous five years could combine schooling with factory employment: 175,437 were doing so in 1890, though the numbers had more than halved by 1910. Moreover, one-half of all Lancastrian girls were working as half-timers in local mills, a

---

[32] School fees had ranged from 1d. to 4d. a week.

[33] D. Rubinstein, *School Attendance in London, 1870–1914: A Social History* (Hull, 1969), 114–16; P. Hollis, *Ladies Elect: Women in English Local Government 1865–1914* (Oxford, 1987), Ch. 3.

[34] Rubinstein, *School Attendance*, 49.

[35] Hendrick, *Children, Childhood and English Society*, 66.

practice that became legal at the age of 10 in the 1890s, at the age of 12 in the 1900s.[36]

Finally, at least 145,000 children, three-quarters of them boys, were working for wages while still at school, mainly as street vendors and messenger boys.[37] One expert estimated in 1914 that there were, in all, over 600,000 members of the child labour force, working in shops, agriculture and domestic service, or employed as half-timers in factories and workshops, or doing casual errands as street traders or helping out their mothers in home industries.[38] Nor do these figures include poor working-class children who, usually for no payment, were working very hard on tasks set for them by their parents: young girls sharing domestic chores with their mothers, boys running errands, and both sexes involved in 'outwork' such as matchbox making.

By the end of the century there was a growing anxiety about the excessive use of child labour, particularly among doctors who feared that it was impairing normal physical and mental development.[39] This led to the passing of the 1903 Employment of Children Act, which allowed local authorities to make by-laws that prohibited the employment of children in specified occupations, curtailed street trading, and prescribed maximum working hours and an age threshold. But nearly one-third of authorities did not adopt the Act, while others were not enforcing their own by-laws seriously.[40] Robert Sherrard's *The Child-Slaves of Britain* (1905) uncovered continuing scandals.

The trade unions, anxious about the employment of young children, felt even more threatened by employers' growing resort to the labour of teenagers, who were being substituted for adults in a range of industries, including boot and shoes, printing, and textiles (30 per cent of textile workers and 28 per cent of woollen workers were lads under 20), as well as at the menial end of office work. In Birmingham, 94.5 per cent of all boys aged 15 to 20 had jobs— amongst the working class the proportion would presumably have been higher. Since such boys were generally cast adrift at the end of adolescence, social investigators feared that these 'blind alley occupations' were contributing to high levels of adult able-bodied unemployment. Meanwhile, however, given

[36] J. Lewis, *Women in England, 1870–1950: Sexual Divisions and Social Change* (New York and London, 1984), 57.

[37] J. Walvin, *A Child's World: A Social History of English Childhood 1800–1914* (Harmondsworth, 1982), 77, says about 200,000 in 1908; Hollis estimates the number at 300,000, one-third of them working for more than 20 hours a week (*Ladies Elect*, 443).

[38] Hendrick, 'Child Labour', 51.

[39] Ferguson, 'Cleveland in History', 52.

[40] Ibid. 51, 60. Successive pieces of legislation between 1889 and 1908 also restricted the employment of children in theatres—though perhaps almost as much to remove sexual temptation from adults as to protect children (M. Sanderson, *From Irvine to Olivier: A Social History of the Acting Profession in England, 1888–1983* (London, 1984), 70–1).

their lack of skill and training, young lads could earn good wages (over 15s. a week in engineering and textiles, much more than that in shipbuilding), and the high demand for their labour meant that they could quickly be re-employed should they be sacked, which made them difficult to discipline—another concern for many adults.[41] In the 1880s and 1890s there was also a growing use of young females in the potteries, shoemaking, and hosiery, creating yet more unease among skilled male workers.[42]

These anxieties fed into the wider adult preoccupation with what was coming to be known as 'youth'. From the 1880s until the outbreak of the Great War, the recognition dawned that there was a gap between childhood and adulthood, distinct from either. For example, during the Edwardian years people indulgently discussed the 'flapper'—a boisterous girl 'whose hair is not yet up, and whose skirts have just been let down'.[43] More particularly, the concept of 'adolescence' was gaining acceptance, popularized by the writings of the American psychologist G. Stanley Hall, who stressed the emotional strains and stresses brought on by puberty and advanced the fanciful notion of a stage in life during which youths recapitulated the development of the human species, from savagery to barbarism to civilization.[44] Social 'experts' vied with one another in painting psychological profiles of adolescent youths: E. J. Urwick, for example, could write of 'a species of man-child, in whom the natural instincts of boyhood are almost overwhelmed by a feverish anxiety to become a man'.[45]

Such perceptions were beginning to affect social policy, particularly in the area of prosecuting and sentencing for juvenile crime: children were not the only ones for whom prison was now thought inappropriate—in 1901 only 1,073 youths between the ages of 12 and 16 were gaoled. But, though treated more humanely in some respects, 'youth' was also the butt of much moralistic censure: 'a somewhat unlovely characteristic of the present day', one social worker bemoaned, 'is that there is among the children a prevailing and increasing want of respect towards their elders, more especially, perhaps, towards their parents.'[46] The proliferation of youth 'gangs', each with its

[41] M. J. Childs, 'Boy Labour in Late Victorian and Edwardian England and the Remaking of the Working Class', *Journal of Social History*, 23 (1987), 783–802, esp. 790–2. See also M. Childs, *Labour's Apprentices: Working-Class Lads in Late Victorian and Edwardian England* (London, 1992).

[42] M. Savage and A. Miles, *The Remaking of the British Working Class 1840–1940* (London, 1994), 50, quoting H. Bradley, *Men's Work, Women's Work* (Oxford, 1989).

[43] S. Mitchell, *The New Girl: Girls' Culture in England 1880–1915* (New York, 1995), 183. In the 1890s the term 'flapper' had denoted a very young prostitute.

[44] One of the popularizers was the American who acted as the first Chairman of the Eugenics Society, Dr J. W. Slaughter, author of *The Adolescent* (1911).

[45] J. Gillis, *Youth and History* (New York, 1975; 1981 edn.), 130–1.

[46] Helen Bosanquet, quoted in G. Pearson, *Hooligan: A History of Respectable Fears* (Houndmills, 1983), 55.

distinctive dress code, provoked much disquiet, culminating in the extraordinary panic about 'Hooliganism', following some minor disturbances in the midst of a heatwave during the 1898 August Bank Holiday.

The fear of miscreant youth was but one manifestation of a wider anxiety about the indiscipline of urban life, which homed in upon male activities such as cigarette-smoking, 'loafing' on street corners, and betting—all portrayed as symptoms of modern degeneracy. Though much less was heard about females of the same age, Lily Montagu thought it ominous that the streets should have been swarming with working-class girls with 'a dangerous craving for excitement', their minds formed by the reading of 'mawkish novelettes'.[47] Factory girls, in particular, were often presented as 'flirts',[48] sexually precocious creatures with money and freedom, but no adult sense of responsibility.

To enterprising businessmen, these young people constituted an important market, to supply which a whole range of new periodicals was founded. Some, such as the *Boy's Own Paper* (1879) and the *Girl's Own Paper* (1880), sponsored by the Religious Tract Society, were mildly edifying. Others had fewer pretensions: replacing the old 'penny-dreadfuls', comics came into circulation such as *Comic Cuts* ('100 Laughs for a ½ d') and *Illustrated Chips*, both launched by Alfred Harmsworth in 1890, followed by *Picture Fun* in 1902, and by the first coloured comic, *Puck*, in 1904. By the turn of the century a new generation of magazines, including *Chums* and *Young England*, had broken free from the piety and stuffiness of the evangelical '*BOP*' to preach a 'manly' patriotism, spiced with military values: the *Boy's Journal*, a Harmsworth publication, declared in its editorial address (September 1913) that it was 'essentially a man-making paper for the manly lad'.[49] But most middle-class opinion-formers saw youth, especially working-class youth, less as an opportunity to be exploited than as a danger—no doubt because they had escaped the trammels of childhood before experiencing the disciplines of adult life, the most central of which was family-building.[50]

Children of all classes attended Sunday Schools: by the early twentieth century some 80 per cent of the 5–14 age-group were doing so, though there is some evidence of decline just before the Great War.[51] But otherwise, before the 1880s, few attempts had been made to organize young people's leisure time—the main exception being the Anglican 'Girls' Friendly Society'

[47] C. Dyhouse, *Girls Growing Up in Late Victorian and Edwardian England* (London, 1981), 130.
[48] Lewis, *Women in England*, 184–5.
[49] R. H. MacDonald, 'Reproducing the Middle-Class Boy: From Purity to Patriotism in the Boys' Magazines, 1892–1914', *Journal of Contemporary History*, 24 (1989), 519–39; Boyd, 'Imperialism and the Boys' Story Paper', 148.
[50] H. Hendrick, *Images of Youth: Age, Class and the Male Youth Problem, 1880–1920* (Oxford, 1990).
[51] In the West Riding Wesleyan schools increasingly turned to hosting entertainments like football, rambling, and choirs.

movement, which was very strong in many rural areas.[52] Thereafter 'youth movements' were founded thick and fast. Churches, and groups such as the teetotal 'Band of Hope', proselytized among the young, purveying their distinctive brands of wholesome Christianity. More far-sighted clergymen saw the desirability of luring lads off the streets by organizing football clubs. These were the years which also saw the emergence of militaristic or semi-militaristic organizations such as William Smith's 'Boys' Brigade' in Glasgow in 1883 (35,000 members by 1894), the 'Church Lads' Brigade' in 1891 (which peaked at 70,000 in 1908), the 'Jewish Lads' Brigade' in 1895,[53] and the 'Boy Scouts' in 1908. This development possibly indicates a changed attitude among middle-class volunteers towards the parents of working-class and lower-middle-class teenagers. In the most successful of them, the Boy Scouts, members were enjoined to show obedience to King and Country, even to their employers, but not explicitly to their parents—perhaps because parents were seen as part of the problem, not as part of its solution.

Just as the notion of a 'retirement age' was slowly beginning to reconfigure the lives of the elderly,[54] so the late Victorian and Edwardian period was characterized by a deepening sense of a series of stages through which young children were supposed to pass—though, as we have seen, this varied considerably according to social class. Thus, when compulsory education was first introduced, the schools had been widely utilized by working-class mothers as nurseries in which their tiny tots could be placed. But between 1901 and 1911 the under-3s were eliminated from the school system, and places for 3- to 5-year-olds drastically cut.[55] Similarly, literature was being deliberately targeted at specific age-groups: earlier in the century *Peg's Paper* had been read by a promiscuous audience of young girls and female teenage factory hands, but such mixing seemed inappropriate in a society which had a clear sense of the way in which population was structured by age.

Adult behaviour towards the young was thus becoming more sensitive and humane, but at the same time more censorious and meddlesome. In complex ways this development may have contributed to the stabilization of society by conferring real power on adults, including poor parents who were powerless for

[52] B. Harrison, 'For Church, Queen and Family: The Girl's Friendly Society 1874–1920', *Past & Present*, 61 (1973), 107–38.

[53] R. A. Voeltz, ' "A Good Jew and a Good Englishman": The Jewish Lads' Brigade, 1894–1922', *Journal of Contemporary History*, 23 (1988), 119–27. By 1909 it had a membership of 4,000–5,000, mostly in London—partly aiming to Anglicize Jews by making them more martial.

[54] There was no retirement age for professors—with disastrous consequences for Oxford science (see Ch. 16)! In 1890 the compulsory retirement age for civil servants was set at 65. However, the 1891 Census recorded about 65% of men over 65 as being in employment, that of 1901 61%, that of 1911 56% (P. Thane, *Old Age in English History: Past Experiences, Present Issues* (Oxford, 2000), 281). The fall was largely accounted for by a shrinkage in the size of the agricultural workforce.

[55] Lewis, *Women in England*, 36.

most of their lives.[56] In many households 'father's chair', sacrosanct to the father, was a symbol of the head of the household's authority over his children. But, of course, it often denoted, too, the *paterfamilias*'s superiority over his wife, for late Victorian and Edwardian society was as obviously structured by gender as it was by age.

2. THE POSITION OF WOMEN

In the ideology of 'separate spheres', females were presented as morally superior to males—whether because the division of labour between the sexes had protected them from the dangers confronting many male breadwinners, or because their maternal functions had conditioned them to display tenderness and compassion and to listen attentively to the voice of conscience. In either case, female altruism was constantly being contrasted with male egotism. Biologists reinforced these assumptions by providing (largely spurious) explanations of supposedly innate gender differences: for example, Patrick Geddes and J. A. Thomson's influential *The Evolution of Sex*, first published in 1899, described men as 'katabolic' (or energetic), women as 'anabolic' (or passive). From such beliefs the deduction was drawn that a woman's natural place was in the home, where she could exercise her main influence as wife and mother, presiding, as the 'angel of the house', over her domestic sanctuary and defending family values from the corrosive invasion of market forces. This ideology was underwritten by many women as well as by most men.[57]

Practice, however, diverged considerably from precept: in the United Kingdom as a whole, 29–30 per cent of the total labour force were female. True, the percentage of women in full-time employment fell by about 10 per cent between 1871 and 1911; but it rose slowly thereafter.[58] Most waged women were single or widowed.[59] Indeed, in many sectors of the economy a formal marriage bar operated, as it did in Huntley and Palmer's biscuit factory and in the civil service.[60] Even in the Lancashire textile industry only a minority of the female workforce were married, and a smaller proportion still had

---

[56] On the other hand, one consequence of compulsory education was that it sometimes inverted power relationships within the family, as illiterate working-class parents fell dependent on their literate children in discharging a series of mundane tasks (D. Vincent, *Literacy and Popular Culture* (Cambridge, 1989), 24–6, 50, 72, 103).

[57] No 'right to work' for women was recognized by policy-makers—except for widows with dependent children (C. Briar, *Working for Women?* (London, 1997), Ch. 2).

[58] Harris, *Private Lives*, 129.

[59] The 1911 Census showed that only 103 out of 1,000 married women worked, compared with 301 widows and divorcees, and 677 single women aged 15 and over (Lewis, *Women in England*, 149–50).

[60] Lewis, *Women in England*, 186, 102.

dependent children.[61] This, in turn, meant that the female workforce was preponderantly young: barmaids were thought to be unemployable once they had reached 35, and even shop assistants struggled to get jobs once they were 30.[62]

Yet statistics of full-time employment give a misleading impression. Farmers' wives worked in the interstices of the arduous task of running their home, while working-class mothers often took on part-time casual employment, as 'chars' or in laundries, to supplement their husband's low income or to compensate for his unemployment. Such women were most likely to go out to work *immediately after* the births of their children because it was then that their financial needs were greatest—only to stop when their children were old enough to bring money of their own into the parental home. Many thousands of poor women were also 'outworkers', employed in sweated occupations such as tailoring and box-making, often helped by their small children.[63]

The 1881 census showed that over four-fifths of female employees were bunched into only three occupational categories: domestic service, where they numbered 1,756,000, textiles (745,000) and clothing (667,000). By 1911 the situation had changed, but not dramatically: 70.6 per cent of working females were still confined to these three economic sectors.[64] However, there had been a significant build-up of women working in various branches of engineering; on the eve of the Great War they numbered 128,000, more than were engaged in agriculture and horticulture. But the most momentous change in the female labour market was the growth of middle-class posts—in teaching, retailing, office work, and nursing.[65]

In fact, a majority of the teachers in the Board Schools created by the 1870 Education Act were women—to the annoyance of their male colleagues.[66] Though less well qualified, they constituted 75 per cent of the 230,000 teachers listed in the 1901 Census. Another catalyst for change was the typewriter, the

---

[61] Thompson, *Respectable Society*, 75–6. The Leicester hosiery industry was exceptional rather than normal (P. Thane, 'Late Victorian Women', in T. R. Gourvish and A. O'Day (eds.), *Later Victorian Britain 1867–1900* (Basingstoke, 1988), 194).

[62] Lewis, *Women in England*, 154.

[63] An investigation of boxmakers in 1915 showed that 78% were married and 16% widowed. One-third were totally dependent on these earnings, one-third worked for pin money (Ibid. 57).

[64] According to the censuses, domestic servants fell from 45.2% of the female workforce in 1881 to 39% in 1911; textiles from 19.2% to 17.4%; clothing from 17.2% to 15.2%. These statistics, however, may seriously inflate the numbers employed in domestic service, an unstable category. See E. Higgs, 'Women, Occupation and Work in the Nineteenth Century Censuses', *History Workshop Journal*, 23 (1987), 59–80.

[65] Lewis, *Women in England*, 158.

[66] T. R. Gourvish, 'The Rise of the Professions', in Gourvish and O'Day (eds.), *Later Victorian Britain*, 22.

use of which really took off during the late 1880s.[67] Because of its vague similarity to a sewing machine, this invention drew an increasing number of female employees into what had once been the male-dominated clerical occupation. (The new position of telephonists was dominated by women from the very start.) By 1900 females formed about 20 per cent of all white-collar workers, earning on average 25–30s. a week. The financial rewards might seem small, but such jobs often conferred on women a freedom denied to domestic servants—or to many housebound wives. Hence the popular myth (among men) of the 'fast' female office employee, embodied in books such as Clara Del Rio's salacious *Confessions of a Type-Writer* (1893).[68]

On average women earned much less than men, even when, as in school-teaching, they were doing exactly the same work. Women compositors received $5\frac{1}{2}d.$ for tasks for which men were paid $8\frac{1}{2}d.$, shop assistants earned about 65 per cent of men's income, and female clerks drew less than one-third of the average male salary.[69] Cotton-weavers and actresses were among the few occupational groups being paid roughly the same as their male counterparts[70]—which may explain why both were later so active in the suffrage agitation. Even in textiles, women earned, throughout the industry as a whole, little more than half the wage of their male colleagues—only slightly better than the national industrial average of 43.7 per cent.[71] Outside textiles, young women drew on average a paltry 12s. 11d. per week.[72]

Often women were systematically excluded from well-paid jobs, not only by employers, but also by the tactics of male-dominated unions: for example, they were prevented in this way from operating the linotype machines introduced into printing in the 1890s.[73] Even more blatant were actions such as that of the Bolton Amalgamation, Bleachers' Dyers' and Finishers' Association, which ruled that women could only qualify as one-third members.[74] But women often did worst in all-female jobs.[75] The real problem lay in the notion of a 'woman's rate' (amounting to little more than 10–12s. a week, or else a fixed percentage of male earnings). As a result, women on piece rates (as many were) often had their terms of remuneration changed if it seemed that they were earning 'too

---

[67] The earliest machines go back to the 1850s, but the prototype of the modern machine was the American-made Remington Improved Model I of 1878; 304 Remington Model IIs were sold in 1880, 27,000 in 1887, and 65,000 in 1890 (A. Briggs, *Victorian Things* (London, 1988), 414).

[68] C. Keep, 'The Cultural World of the Type-Writer Girl', *Victorian Studies*, 40 (1996–7), 416–18.

[69] Lewis, *Women in England*, 163, 165–6. Before 1914 over 90% of female clerks were to be found in commercial and business firms, the less well-paid end of the system (p. 158).

[70] Thompson, *Respectable Society*, 215.

[71] Lewis, *Women in England*, 163–4.

[72] Ibid. 8.

[73] Ibid. 175, 180.

[74] Boys were counted as half-members (Ibid. 176).

[75] Ibid. 166.

much'. Women also had to endure fines, which were sometimes deducted from their wages for quite trivial offences—for example, shop assistants calling a customer 'Miss' instead of 'Madam'.[76] Many women accepted these restrictions as natural, and were slow—or too cowed—to challenge them.

For teenage girls from humble backgrounds, the best route to social advancement lay not through work but through making a 'good' marriage: it has been estimated that 10 per cent of working-class females married into middle-class families, compared with 7 per cent of males of the same class.[77] Women did make major gains in status, power, and influence; but these gains mainly benefited those higher up the social scale.

For women who had plentiful cash at their disposal, the expansion of the consumer market certainly brought benefits. In 1913 one trade journal noted that 'a full 90% of advertisers have found it or are finding it, advisable to leave the man practically out of account altogether when designing their announcements'. Instead, advertisers aimed their message at women, now flatteringly portrayed as goddesses of consumption. The launching of no fewer than forty-eight ladies' magazines between 1880 and 1900 was another indication of women's growing power as consumers.[78]

New shopping patterns further contributed to women's increasing self-confidence outside the home, especially in the larger cities, where those with money and leisure experienced greater freedom. For example, department stores now offered enhanced possibilities of enjoying a pleasant day out, in safe but luxurious surroundings, enabling 'respectable' women to meet their friends and share a drink or a light meal without exciting adverse comment or unwanted attentions. Moreover, the provision of ladies' toilets—including public toilets in which women could literally 'spend a penny'—may even have allowed female visitors to stay longer in town and to attend public meetings—with important political consequences. The proliferation of women's clubs during the 1890s was part of the same trend—one that was widening women's 'public space'.[79]

Not only as consumers but also as participants in a widening range of leisure activities, better-off women could enjoy a life far more varied and interesting than had been available to their mothers. For example, the growing popularity of female sport[80] encouraged the design of women's clothing that would leave the limbs free for physical exercise. A kind of knickerbockers found favour with

[76] Lewis, *Women in England*, 164–5.
[77] Savage and Miles, *Working Class*, 39.
[78] Loeb, *Consuming Angels*, 9, 78.
[79] E. D. Rappaport, *Shopping for Pleasure: Women in the Making of London's West End* (New Jersey, 2000), Ch. 3.
[80] See Ch. 14.

cyclists, while the 'rational dress movement' of the 1890s saw restricted dress
being discarded for tailored garments with divided skirts.[81] True, the founder
of the modern Olympic Movement, Baron Pierre de Coubertin, thought
athletics for women to be 'against the laws of nature', echoing male doctors
who warned of serious gynaecological damage.[82] Women often had to fight for
their right to enjoy sport, in the face of the disapproval of elderly ladies of more
conventional dispositions, as well as of the mockery of men ('surtout mes
dames, point de zêle', urged a male observer of a ladies' cricket match[83]). But
they won more of these fights than they lost.

Finally, the fertility revolution was helping women by weakening the assumption that their lives must largely be given over to the bearing and rearing
of children. By the end of Victoria's reign few educated men would have found
acceptable behaviour such as that of Gladstone's friend George Lyttelton, who,
between 1840 and 1857, had fathered no fewer than twelve children, though at
the expense of his wife, who became more and more exhausted with each
successive pregnancy until she eventually died during the birth of her twelfth
child. Forty years later such large families were rare among the aristocracy—by
1911 their average family size had dropped to 2.5 children. Even among the
working-class families investigated by the Women's Co-operative Guild in
1913, many husbands were restraining their sexual appetites out of respect
for the comfort and well-being of their wives, while doctors often warned
their better-educated patients that non-stop pregnancies were injurious to
health.

The late Victorian period also saw the start of a slow secular trend towards a
more family-centred life, in which social pleasures could be shared between
men and women—for example, the seaside holiday which cut across the
boundary of gender and generation. Blatantly 'mercenary' marriages, such as
were still common in landed society, were viewed by outsiders with contempt.
It was an ideal of the companionate marriage that was gaining ground. The
Married Women's Property Act of 1882 had given wives full control over all
their personal property, and, although the divorce law remained substantially
unchanged,[84] a series of measures conferred on magistrates powers to grant
separation orders to women who had been battered by their husbands (after
1897 about 8,000 of these were being granted each year).[85] Courts, in fact, were
increasingly open to the notion that husbands and wives had reciprocal rights

---

[81] Holt, *Sport*, 123.
[82] Figure-skating was the only activity for women in the pre-war Olympic Games.
[83] J. Lowerson, *Sport and the English Middle Classes, 1870–1914* (Manchester, 1993; 1995 edn.), 212.
[84] Harris, *Private Lives*, 75.
[85] More women sought separation from their husband on grounds of his unwillingness or inability to
maintain them (Lewis, *Women in England*, 47).

and obligations,[86] and often ran ahead of public opinion in their verdicts—as when, in *R. v. Jackson*, 1891, the Court of Appeal took the unpopular decision of upholding the right of a wife to move about freely and not be abducted by her husband.[87]

However, not all women's gains were brought about by market forces or by male initiatives: there were many obstacles to female advancement which women themselves had to fight hard to overcome. Contemporaries spoke about the 'revolt of the daughters', a phrase which drew attention to the self-assertion of younger females whose expectations and self-confidence had been raised by middle-class schooling. By 1895 there were between 10,000 and 15,000 private girls' schools in England: of the more prestigious establishments, eighty-six had been created under the terms of Endowed Schools Act of 1869, and another thirty-six owed their existence to the flourishing Girls Public Day School Company, set up in 1872.[88]

By the late 1880s many pupils from such establishments were going on to further study. Girton and Newnham Colleges at Cambridge had been founded for female students in the early 1870s; Lady Margaret Hall and Somerville College at Oxford followed suit in 1879. But although young women could study at Oxford and Cambridge Universities, they could not take degrees. At Cambridge, where the Senate in 1896–7 upheld the status quo by 1,713 votes to 662, the conferral of degrees on females did not take place until as late as 1948! (Oxford was quicker off the mark, making this concession in 1920.)[89]

However, the well-documented saga of the humiliations meted out to females at 'Oxbridge' gives a slightly misleading impression of women's position at the end of the nineteenth century. London University had granted them the right to take degrees as early as 1878, and none of the newly chartered late Victorian and Edwardian universities drew sexual distinctions. By 1900 there were 1,476 full-time female students in England, and another 1,194 in Scotland and Wales (and numbers were rising), to say nothing of the hundreds enrolled in teachers' training colleges. The triumph of Philippa Fawcett, daughter of the woman's suffrage leader, who was ranked above the senior wrangler in Cambridge's Mathematics Tripos in 1890, was only one of many indications that women could compete academically on even terms with the

---

[86] Thane, 'Late Victorian Women', 181. However, some working-class women expected to be knocked about from time to time by their husbands.

[87] Four years later another legal milestone was reached when the Commissioners in Lunacy released a socialist freethinker, Edith Lanchester, who had been incarcerated as insane for choosing to live, out of wedlock, with her working-class lover.

[88] The Company became a Trust in 1906. After 1902 there was a proliferation of girls' grammar schools.

[89] C. Dyhouse, *No Distinction of Sex? Women in British Universities 1870–1939* (London, 1995).

brightest of men, perhaps even outperform them.[90] Three years later Alice Cooke became the first woman to be appointed to a university teaching post—at Owen's College, Manchester.

Other young women fought to earn their living in an overwhelmingly male-dominated world, or even to break into one of the ancient professions. An important symbolic victory was the admission of women into the British Medical Association in 1892–3—even if in 1900 there were still only 434 women licensed to practise as doctors, one-third of whom were working abroad.[91] Christabel Pankhurst took a law degree from Victoria University[92] in 1906, graduating with First Class Honours, having been refused a hearing when she applied for admission to Lincoln's Inn. In 1911 females comprised only 6 per cent of the membership of all the higher professions,[93] but they were an assertive and independent group: at suffrage rallies professional women often paraded under their own banners.[94] Also prominent at such events were actresses and musicians—the latter numbering 22,600, ranging from the formidable composer Ethel Smyth to humble music teachers.[95] Hundreds of women were also earning a living with their pens: in July 1893 Flora Shaw was made Colonial Editor of *The Times*, on a salary of £800, making her London's highest-paid woman journalist.[96] However, it is something of a mystery that no great creative female novelist or poet, writing for an adult readership, should have emerged between George Eliot and Virginia Woolf.[97]

More fundamentally, the ideology of 'separate spheres' was beginning to weaken from the 1880s onwards. True, women had long been welcomed as co-workers in a wide range of reforming crusades, from the anti-slavery movement onwards—especially those which set out to remove abuses which directly victimized women: slavery, the Contagious Diseases Acts,[98] drunkenness, or reckless gambling. In all such reforming pressure groups, women continued to take a very active part.[99]

---

[90] Alfred Marshall, the economist, explained this by women's greater capacity for sitting examinations, and did not think it denoted their intellectual superiority!

[91] Total numbers had doubled by 1909: B. Harrison, 'Women's Health and the Women's Movement in Britain: 1840–1940', in C. Webster (ed.), *Biology, Medicine and Society 1840–1948* (Cambridge, 1981), 52.

[92] A degree-conferring body, based on Manchester, with affiliated colleges in Manchester, Liverpool and Leeds. See Ch. 16.

[93] Lewis, *Women in England*, 194.

[94] But some women, prominent in higher education and professional advancement, opposed the parliamentary vote (Harrison, *Separate Spheres*, 55–6).

[95] Thane, 'Late Victorian Women', 192.

[96] D. O. Helly and H. Callaway, 'Journalism as Active Politics, Flora Shaw, *The Times* and South Africa', in D. Lowry (ed.), *The South African War Reappraised* (Manchester, 2000), 53.

[97] Olive Schreiner was South African, Somerville and Ross were Irish.

[98] See below.

[99] See F. Prochaska, *Women and Philanthropy in 19th Century England* (Oxford, 1980).

Women also seemed naturally suited to philanthropy, which involved the extension of 'home influences' (i.e. middle-class domestic values) into the lives of the urban poor: in 1893 perhaps half-a-million women were working 'continuously and semi-professionally in voluntary activities'.[100] But the sick and the destitute, most philanthropists agreed, should not be given mere handouts. They also needed love, kindliness, sympathy, and understanding, which meant that well-wishers had an obligation to visit the objects of their charitable work in their homes. Women were thought to be exceptionally well fitted for this role—this was the kind of activity in which they might well 'feel themselves at home' in more than one sense. Also, house-visiting might give rise to scandal if a man visited the woman of the house in the middle of the day when her husband was out at work; the arrival of a woman on the doorstep avoided these embarrassments!

But by the 1880s many middle-class women, especially those who had received a good secondary or university education, recognized the need for proper training before they embarked upon their philanthropic projects. The end-result was a cross between the older concept of a woman's proper sphere and a new emphasis upon education and training. In other words, late Victorian philanthropists did not entirely abandon the traditional notion of women's charitable mission, but they began to acknowledge that philanthropy needed to be subsumed into the profession of social work, preparation for which required an appropriate vocational training, so that the necessary techniques, such as the practice of case-work, could be mastered and, equally important, so that the emotions of pity and horror were subjected to the salutary discipline of science.

The various humanitarian associations towards which women were attracted undoubtedly played a part in broadening their minds and giving them a more extended sense of public usefulness. Even philanthropy, originally thought of as an extension of home influences, eventually drew many ladies away from their homes, providing them with experiences which were at variance with the ideology of domesticity. Many middle-class women thereby discovered that they had skills in running large-scale organizations and were quite the equal of men as polemical writers and as public speakers. Others launched out into social investigation: for example, Margaret Loane, the district nurse who was also the author of a series of books on how the poor lived. Through their involvement in a range of voluntary activities, in philanthropy, associational campaigns, in social administration, and in politics, women were also beginning to force traditionally 'feminine' issues (childcare, public health, etc.) on to the public agenda, even indirectly into the arena of national politics.

---

[100] Thane, 'Late Victorian Women', 190.

The movement for women's rights and for the parliamentary vote, which had begun in the middle of the century, went into the doldrums in the 1890s; but a portent of change was the drawing together of a number of provincial suffrage societies into the organization known from 1897 onwards as the National Union of Women's Suffrage Societies (NUWSS), under the leadership of Mrs Millicent Fawcett (sister of Elizabeth Garrett Anderson, the pioneering doctor).

The parliamentary vote was not to be attained until 1918, but long before then women had achieved a significant breakthrough in local politics. Ever since 1869 women ratepayers were eligible to be placed on all local government electoral registers, and in the 1880s they formed some 17 per cent of this electorate overall.[101] Women could also *serve* on some local authorities: by 1885 seventy-eight were members of a School Board, another thirty-seven of a Board of Guardians. This privilege was extended to parish, rural district, and urban district councils when these were established by the Local Government Act of 1894, though females did not gain the right to sit on county and borough councils until 1907.[102]

All of these events achieved wider publicity as a result of the discussion during the 1890s of the so-called 'New Woman', whose 'advanced' aspirations were being voiced by writers such as 'George Egerton' (Charlotte Dunne) in her collection of short stories, *Keynotes* (1893). Another energetic fomenter of the spirit of feminine 'rebellion' was the homosexual Edward Carpenter, who advocated a looser marriage bond and predicted that 'Woman' would no longer be content with serfdom, but aspired to be 'the equal, the mate, and the comrade of Man'.[103] The word 'feminism' did not appear in the 1901 *Oxford English Dictionary*, but the *Supplement* cited it, in inverted commas, from a French usage of 1895, to mean 'advocacy of the rights of women'. By the eve of the Great War the word, in its different forms, had achieved a wider currency, though not all campaigners for the parliamentary vote yet wished to be known as 'feminists'.[104]

3. GENDER ROLES

So far the impression may have been given that women were making progress towards the achievement of gender equality—albeit only after surmounting

---

[101] Hollis, *Ladies Elect*, 31–2.

[102] See Ibid. 43, for the 'bemusing tangle of electoral law'.

[103] E. Carpenter, *Love's Coming of Age* (1896; 1915 edn.), 56.

[104] The current *OED* dates the first use of 'feminism' to 1895 and that of 'feminist' in its adjectival form to 1894, though it did not escape inverted commas until 1898. 'Feminist', as a noun, dates from 1904.

many difficulties and suffering a few setbacks. However, not all the social changes of late Victorian times had the effect of undermining the doctrine of 'separate spheres'. For example, whereas several of the new leisure activities, such as tennis and cycling, brought men and women together on an informal footing, other sports tended to segregate the sexes: professional football, except in the very early years, attracted an almost exclusively male crowd.

Moreover, the cramped, uncomfortable homes of the poor often drove the 'head of the household' out into a world of male conviviality. Throughout this period and well into the next century the culture of the pub remained over-whelmingly masculine, especially in the north; similarly with working men's clubs, where only one out of 512 admitted women in 1897.[105]

Nor is it clear that greater educational opportunities for girls were blurring traditional gender roles. Admittedly, in elementary schools children of both sexes studied certain core subjects. But this led many contemporary moralists to grumble that young girls' frail frames were being overtaxed by an inappro-priate education, to the neglect of the acquisition of domestic skills. The pioneers of women's secondary education were sensitive to this criticism: Girls Public Day School (GPDS) pupils only studied in the mornings, to avoid strain and so that they could be at home with their mothers in the afternoons.[106]

Even in elementary schools, girls continued to be shepherded into tradition-ally 'feminine' areas of study: indeed, by the mid-1890s they were *obliged* by central regulations to learn needlework, while many took the domestic econ-omy option, which covered cookery and, later, laundry work. Education for all, regardless of gender, had certainly not destroyed the notion that, for poor girls, education, if provided at all, should be directed mainly towards turning out conscientious mothers and competent servants.

In the secondary-school and university spheres, the drive for an improved education for females was also ambiguous. At Cambridge University, Newnham College belonged more to the 'separatist' camp: Girton, under Emily Davies, set much higher store by the eventual integration of male and female education. Nor did the headmistresses themselves speak with a united voice. The GPDS schools stoutly resisted Board of Education pressure to introduce a substantial training in housewifery into the syllabus. However, Sara Burstall, headmistress of Manchester High School, disagreed, arguing that most girls were destined for marriage (and should be encouraged to see this as a goal), something too easily forgotten by unmarried female teachers—mathematics, she thought, had 'a hardening influence' on femininity. Were such views a craven

---

[105] Harris, *Private Lives*, 27.
[106] Dyhouse, *Girls Growing Up*, 71.

surrender to male prejudice? Or were London's women teachers, when protesting at the tendency to model girls' education on that of boys, perhaps making a kind of feminist point?[107]

Except in the Quaker schools and in a handful of experimental progressive establishments, fee-paying schools were nearly all single-sex, especially at secondary level. In particular, most of the boys' public schools depended on boarders who were deliberately removed from the 'effeminate' influence of sisters and mothers, as well as from contact with other girls—part of the 'hardening process' designed to prepare them for the all-male realms of imperial service, military life, and national politics. Much of the literature produced for boys was geared to the same end. Henty, according to a study of his work published in 1907, 'wanted his boys to be bold, straightforward and ready to play a young man's part, not to be milksops', and had 'a horror of a lad who displayed any weak emotion and shrank from shedding blood, or winced at any encounter'.[108]

Imperial service and military life, in their turn, contributed to the construction of masculinity. The mid-Victorian years had seen indications of what has been called 'masculine domesticity', that is, the 'domestication' of *men*, many of whom found in the home and family not only a welcome release from work, but also an arena for the display of tenderness and playfulness. But such behaviour led to anxieties that sons might grow up effeminate—hence the growing popularity later in the century of a public-school education. Upper-middle-class males now tended to crave an escape from the stifling environment of home into a life of adventure and male sociability.[109]

This was Britain's version of the 'frontier experience', with its idealization of the life of pioneer, hunter, and trapper. It could be experienced vicariously in books which portrayed the rough life of the bush as an environment where masculinity could develop. But many young men from public-school backgrounds played it out for real, in a colonial setting. A notable exponent of this mode of existence was Robert Baden-Powell, who, among many accomplishments, was the author of a book on pig-sticking, which he wrote during his years as a subaltern in India.

A further consequence was the formation of a peculiar kind of 'male bonding', 'comradely' relationships between men of a similar class (sometimes

---

[107] D. M. Copelman, *London's Women Teachers: Gender, Class and Feminism, 1870–1930* (London, 1996), 223.

[108] W. J. Reader, *At Duty's Call: A Study in Obsolete Patriotism* (Manchester, 1988), 28.

[109] J. Tosh, 'Authority and Nurture in Middle-Class Fatherhood: The Case of Early and Mid-Victorian England', *Gender and History*, 8 (1996), 48–64, 'New Men? The Bourgeois Cult of Home', *History Today*, 46 (1996), 9–15, *A Man's Place: Masculinity and the Middle-Class Home in Victorian England* (New Haven, 1999).

contemporaries, sometimes an older man and a younger acolyte)—relationships far more intense than any later formed with women. This kind of 'homosociality' came about as a result of a life's journey which began in an all-boys' boarding school, and continued in an all-male Oxford or Cambridge college, which replicated many of its rituals as well as attracting virtually the same personnel. So did the world of the army mess, the Bar, and the London club; and what was the House of Commons if not the most prestigious of all male clubs? Life as a colonial administrator or as an officer garrisoned overseas, often separated from wife and female company, created yet another milieu in which intense male friendships could flourish.

Some great imperial figures, for example, Lord Kitchener and Cecil Rhodes, never married. Lord Milner, who once declared that he had married the Empire, did not get round to acquiring a wife until he had reached the age of 67—though he secretly consoled himself during the interim with a mistress in Brixton in South London. Milner's disciple John Buchan depicted such bachelors well through his fictional character Richard Hannay, who confesses: 'Women had never come much my way, and I knew about as much of their ways as I knew about the Chinese language. All my life I had lived with men only, and rather a rough crowd at that...'[110]

More often than not the resulting void was filled by male coteries, some of which came to exercise considerable political influence.[111] These male friendships were rarely homosexual. Baden-Powell may well have been a repressed homosexual, but most imperialist leaders had conventional heterosexual tastes: they simply pursued lives which excluded their wives and mistresses from public life, except in the minor role of 'Society' hostess.[112] Baden-Powell is an extreme manifestation of a particular psychological type, the 'boy-man' permanently stuck in adolescence; the cricketer W. G. Grace had many of the same characteristics. Revealingly, Rider Haggard dedicated his 'adventure yarn', *King Solomon's Mines* (1885), to 'All the Big and Little Boys'.

Meanwhile the imperial experience, coupled with anxieties about the declining birth-rate, was leading to a cult which paralleled that of 'masculinity': that of 'motherhood', widely seen as women's contribution to the imperial race. Mary Scharlieb, a doctor who wrote copiously on health matters, urged that 'every girl should be looked upon as a potential wife and mother'.[113] But

---

[110] J. Buchan, *Greenmantle*, Ch. 14.

[111] For example, Milner's 'Kindergarten': the able young intellectuals and administrators who grouped around Lord Milner.

[112] Upper-class women were not as severely cut off as were their equivalents in the USA. Austen Chamberlain once observed that he could immediately measure his stock by the number of fingers that Lady Londonderry extended to him at receptions. Such influence may, in some cases, have supplied compensation for being denied direct access to power.

[113] M. Scharlieb, *Womanhood and Race Regeneration* (London, 1912), 19.

because working-class females could not be trusted to perform their wifely and maternal tasks responsibly and efficiently, a host of organizations sprang up to teach them, alongside the schools. The ideology of 'Social Maternalism' also underlay the foundation of infant-welfare centres, post-natal clinics, and so on, which were an important aspect of Edwardian life.[114] Rather earlier in the field was the National Association for the Promotion of Housewifery, active in the 1870s and 1880s, a body founded, appropriately enough, by the wife of Lord Meath, the apostle of training for young men.

These initiatives gave rise to a debate about whether, once married, women should be allowed to take paid employment at all, at least on a regular basis. A chorus of male voices discouraged the practice. Doctors, increasingly obsessed with women's bodies, worried over the damage that might be done to their reproductive organs and to the health of their infants. Patriots depicted the falling birth-rate as detrimental to the nation's strength.

Such fears were also articulated by the labour leader John Burns, who firmly declared that a woman's place was in the home. But, in saying this, Burns was also expressing the working man's resentment over female competition in the labour market. A trade unionist told the 1889 Select Committee that, 'when the married women turn into the domestic workshops they become competitors against their own husbands and it requires a man and his wife to earn what the man alone would earn if she were not in the shop'. Most socialists pursued the same line: an ILP pamphlet of 1900 declared that true freedom for women lay in not having to earn 'any wages under *any* conditions',[115] and Ramsay Mac-Donald constantly claimed that only capitalism prevented the male breadwinner from securing a 'living wage'. Respectable artisans, having lost some of their former authority in the workplace, were all the keener to assert their masculinity by establishing themselves as the family provider—whether their wives or daughters liked this or not.

In any event, there was a case for saying that the well-being of the working-class family depended less on the wife bringing in a second income than in the skill and devotion with which she managed the household budget and performed her complicated and arduous domestic tasks.[116] For the poor, marriage thus functioned as a form of social insurance in a harsh environment where two people in a stable relationship, with complementary skills, could more easily survive than could an isolated individual. In many urban areas, 'separate spheres' made good economic sense.

It would seem, moreover, that many working- and lower-middle-class women welcomed the enhanced importance being accorded to housework

---

[114] Ch. 11.
[115] Lewis, *Women in England*, 49–50.
[116] Thane, 'Late Victorian Women', 195.

(now more pleasant, thanks to such new domestic appliances as the gas stove), and took pride in their achievements and pleasure in the creation of a space where they enjoyed respect and a certain autonomy—husbands being generally discouraged from 'getting under their wives' feet' in the kitchen. 'Home Rule' to them had connotations quite separate from happenings in Ireland![117] How widespread these views were can be seen from the great success of the Mothers' Union, founded in 1886, which, with quite the largest membership of all women's societies, modestly campaigned for a better deal for women within the framework of the existing family.[118]

Nor did late Victorian and Edwardian advocates of women's rights present a united front in the face of patriarchal prejudice. All welcomed the enlargement of opportunities made possible by improvements in girls' education and defended a woman's right to choose what sort of life to lead. But Olive Schreiner was unusual in arguing that all adult women should have regular paid employment.[119] The trade unionist Mary MacArthur declared that she, for one, was 'sufficiently old-fashioned' to believe that a woman's place was in the home, while even MacDonald's wife Margaret, a leading figure in the Women's Labour League, once argued that the married woman who abjured paid work would have more opportunity to 'give thought and companionship to her husband'.[120] Forms of state assistance that would guarantee economic independence for wives also had few defenders, Mrs Fawcett claiming that this would destroy the fabric of family life by absolving parents from responsibility for maintaining their children. As for the Women's Co-operative Guild, founded in 1884, its original purpose was to help women become better housewives and consumers.[121]

Working-class women meanwhile, were, facing a dilemma. Should they seek wage equalization at the risk of pricing themselves out of the market? Similarly, should they welcome protective legislation for the practical benefits it conferred, or should they deprecate it, either on grounds of discrimination or, again, because it might deter employers from employing women at all?[122]

Educated middle-class girls eager to pursue a commercial or professional career faced a somewhat different dilemma: how to reconcile their ambitions with marriage and motherhood. This issue had been brought into sharp relief by Alice Gordon's article in the 1895 number of *Nineteenth Century*, which

---

[117] J. Bourke, 'Housewifery in Working-Class England, 1860–1914', *Past & Present*, 143 (1994), 167–97.

[118] Harris, *Private Lives*, 27–8; Harrison, 'Girls' Friendly Society', 111.

[119] Lewis, *Women in England*, 95.

[120] Ibid. 51.

[121] Ibid. 50.

[122] R. Feurer, 'The Meaning of "Sisterhood": The British Women's Movement and Protective Labor Legislation, 1870–1900', *Victorian Studies*, 31 (1988), 233–60.

revealed that, of the 1,486 women who had had a university education, only 208 had subsequently married;[123] many of the rest had presumably settled for the life of 'the glorified spinster'. Anecdotal evidence certainly suggests that university education, by providing many girls for the first time with a room of their own and considerable social independence, was seen by its recipients as liberation from an intolerable restraint, and that many of them had no wish to return to the prison of domesticity. Indeed, during the late 1880s and 1890s a few of these 'liberated' young women came out in open hostility to marriage, with an endorsement of celibacy—a startlingly novel development.[124] Given the existence of about half-a-million 'surplus' women of child-bearing age, many of these young females would never have found a mate in any case.[125] Quite regardless of this demographic reality, some young women clearly chafed at the restrictions imposed by marriage on their hard-won autonomy. On the other hand, it should be emphasized that most articulate and educated women still remained hostile to the notion that a career was an *alternative* to marriage.

In August and September 1888 the *Daily Telegraph* posed the question: 'Is Marriage a Failure?' It would seem, from its readers' responses, that the marital relationship was in many instances being renegotiated, as wives sought a measure of independence from their husbands.[126] Yet marriage, as an institution, remained broadly popular. True, in 'rough' communities cohabitation was common, as the Great War was to reveal, but those participating in these irregular liaisons often married once the woman became pregnant. In fact, illegitimacy rates declined steadily throughout this period.[127] The marriage-rate also fell slightly: whereas in 1881 87.7 per cent of females aged 45–9 had been married at some point in their lives, this proportion fell over the next three decades to 87.1 per cent, 85.7 per cent, and 83.5 per cent by 1911. The main change in marriage patterns, however, was a rise in the average age of first marriage—up by a full year from its low-point in 1871 to over 26 in 1901[128]— another factor contributing to the population slowdown and also, perhaps, to male demands for prostitutes. At the turn of the century, men on average were

---

[123] D. Rubinstein, *Before the Suffragettes: Women's Emancipation in the 1890s* (Brighton, 1986), 188.

[124] P. Levine, ' "So Few Prizes and So Many Blanks": Marriage and Feminism in Late 19th Century England', *Journal of British Studies*, 28 (1989), 170–1.

[125] They numbered 479,000 in 1891, 613,000 in 1901, and 664,000 in 1911.

[126] The controversy, which elicited 27,000 letters, was prompted by two articles written by the actress Mona Caird in the *Westminster Review*. There was a precedent in the 'Marriage or Celibacy?' controversy of 1868 (J. M. Robson, *Marriage or Celibacy? The* Daily Telegraph *on a Victorian Dilemma* (Toronto, 1995)).

[127] Illegitimacy rates per 1,000 unmarried, widowed, and divorced women aged 15–45 fell from 10.1 in 1891–5 to 7.9 in 1911–15 (J. Bourke, *Working-Class Cultures in Britain 1890–1960: Gender, Class, and Ethnicity* (1994), 31). The Registrar-General attributed 7% of the population slow-down to this development (Harris, *Private Lives*, 48).

[128] Thompson, *Respectable Society*, 53.

getting married at just over 27, women at just over 25, much as they do today.[129]

Whatever the views of the 'New Woman', marriage also retained its prestige. Carpenter's unconventional attacks on the institution made even many of his comrades squirm with embarrassment. Socialists tended to rationalize their conventional views by urging the unwisdom of making needless enemies to the cause; others argued that greater sexual freedom was indeed desirable but would automatically follow the abolition of private property, which must therefore be tackled first.[130] Most female advocates of 'the Vote' were equally cautious.

4. SEXUAL MORES

The late Victorian period was Mrs Grundy's finest hour. Two events conspired to make it so. An ill-judged venture in regulating prostitution in certain garrison towns, through the Contagious Diseases Acts, had sparked off nationwide protests: moralists who objected to the state condoning 'vice' joined up with working men critical of police harassment and with Josephine Butler and her 'Ladies' National Association', who denounced a system which subjected prostitutes to humiliating medical examination while letting their male clients go scot-free. In 1885 the Contagious Diseases Acts were finally repealed; but this coincided with W. T. Stead's sensational exposure in the *Pall Mall Gazette* of child prostitution and the 'white slave traffic' in his 'Maiden Tribute of Modern Babylon' articles.

Against a background of intense moralistic excitement, Parliament passed the 1885 Criminal Law Amendment Act, which not only raised the age of consent for girls, but also, for the first time, through Henry Labouchere's Amendment, criminalized all kinds of male homosexual activity.[131] In addition the Act gave the police new powers to close down brothels. The Act had some unintended consequences, not least the driving of hundreds of prostitutes out onto the dangerous streets, which increased their dependence on pimps. Three years later came the sadistic killings of London prostitutes by 'Jack the Ripper'.

'Social purity' organizations had meanwhile sprung up to defend 'civilization' against the many sexual evils that seemed to threaten it. Spearheading the movement was the National Vigilance Association (NVA), a pressure group founded in March 1886. It was headed by a 'born again' Methodist, William

[129] Bourke, *Working-class Cultures*, 50.
[130] See Robert Blatchford's response to Carpenter, in C. Tsuzuki, *Edward Carpenter 1844–1929: Prophet of Human Fellowship* (Cambridge, 1980), 121–3.
[131] The 1898 Vagrancy Act was mainly used against homosexual men. The Criminal Law Amendment Act of 1912 severely increased the penalty for opportuning for 'immoral purposes'.

Coote, who took upon himself the task of censoring the pleasures of both rich and poor. All the Christian denominations joined in the 'purity crusade', the Anglicans through the 'White Cross League', the Nonconformists through the Free Church Council, under the guidance of its President, the Baptist F. B. Meyer.[132]

Books, tracts, lectures, and films were produced in staggering volume from the 1880s onwards, mostly aimed at saving youth from 'corruption'. The campaigners particularly targeted pornography and prostitution,[133] but they also aspired to remove all impurity in word and deed. Thus, working girls were urged by groups such as the 'Snowdrop Bands' to pledge themselves to 'discourage all wrong conversation, light and immodest conduct and the reading of foolish and bad books'—the prevalent (false) assumption being that young girls who became prostitutes had invariably been coerced or led into their way of life through ignorance. The 'Alliance of Honour', a body formed by two Sunday School teachers in 1901, performed a similar mission among young men (clerks, shop assistants, and the like), giving them graphic reminders of the painful consequences of contracting venereal disease.[134]

Boys and girls alike were also warned of the dangers of masturbation ('secret bad habits'), which many doctors (at least during the 1880s) believed could lead to insanity.[135] Headmasters of the big public schools, notably Edward Lyttelton of Eton, expended so much time and energy on this project that one is tempted to question their own mental health. However, it is perhaps understandable that those who presided over institutions characterized by rigid sexual segregation should have been highly sensitive to the charge that an 'unnatural' environment was a breeding ground for unnatural sexual practices.[136] Yet how could young people be warned against 'beastliness' of all kinds without destroying their innocence and stimulating their sexual feelings prematurely? Headmasters, together with the leaders of the various youth movements who shared their intense horror of self-abuse,[137] could never quite resolve this particular conundrum.

The purity crusaders believed that, at the very least, political leaders should be setting a good example to the younger generation, and when this did not happen, they exploded in indignation. The Prince of Wales, for all his womanizing, was too prestigious a figure to be safely attacked, but divorce scandals ruined the careers of the up-and-coming Radical politician Charles Dilke in

---

[132] E. J. Bristow, *Vice and Vigilance: Purity Movements in Britain since 1700* (London, 1977), 131–2.
[133] See Ch. 14.
[134] Bristow, *Vice and Vigilance*, 130–1, 143.
[135] Ibid. 140, 128.
[136] Havelock Ellis made this point forcefully in his controversial book, *Sexual Inversion*.
[137] See the advice given to the Rovers: Bristow, *Vice and Vigilance*, 140.

1886, and later the Irish leader Charles Stewart Parnell in 1890. Mrs Ormiston Chant, better known as the scourge of the music halls,[138] was one of the activists of the Women's Liberal Federation who later tried to block Dilke's political comeback. In taking this line, the 'moral repressionists' believed themselves to be discharging a solemn patriotic duty: after all, had not Rome fallen because of its failure to uphold the sanctity of family life?

Most advocates of women's rights aligned themselves with 'social purity'. Understandably, they wanted females to enjoy the freedom to walk the streets unthreatened by male violence, exploitation, and lewdness, and they had good reason for feeling angry about the 'double standard'. Such women also gave a feminist twist to the issue of venereal disease by publicizing the terrible plight of innocent wives who had been infected by their husbands.[139] But Josephine Butler was unusual in combining her loathing of prostitution with a sympathy for prostitutes, whose rights as citizens she was determined to uphold in the teeth of the often brutal harassment they were receiving at the hands of male policemen and magistrates.[140] More often, moral indignation overbore feelings of humanity.

In the 1890s, in the midst of the fashionable discussion of the so-called 'New Woman', Grant Allen published his novel *The Woman Who Did* (1895). But his emancipated heroine, who refused on principle to marry the father of her child, came to a sticky end, and few contemporary advocates of women's freedom approved of her rejection of marriage: Millicent Fawcett branded Allen as 'not a friend but an enemy'.[141] In June 1889 a small audience attended, wonderingly, the first unbowdlerized performance of Ibsen's *A Doll's House*, a private production at the Novelty Theatre, but only a small minority of women wanted to throw their respectability into doubt by attacking the institution of marriage as such. Even within the privacy of a discussion circle such as the 'Men and Women's Club', set up in 1885, 'liberated' women had little to say about a woman's right to sexual self-expression.[142]

For although women were beginning to challenge many conventional wisdoms, the idea that 'respectable' women did not feel sexual desire and were the custodians of more spiritual values than fleshly men continued to be upheld by most campaigners for sexual equality. Was it a coincidence that the

---

[138] See Ch. 14.

[139] See Ch. 12.

[140] Hence her work on behalf of the 'Personal Rights Association'.

[141] E. Showalter, *Sexual Anarchy: Gender and Culture at the Fin-de-Siecle* (London, 1990), 52. Victoria Crosse responded with *The Woman Who Didn't* (1895).

[142] L. Bland, *Banishing the Beast: English Feminism and Sexual Morality 1885–1914* (Harmondsworth, 1995), Ch. 1. Interestingly, the case histories collected by the Women's Co-operative Guild in *Maternity* do not suggest that working-class wives derived much pleasure from the sexual act, a 'good' husband being invariably defined as someone who refrained from making 'demands'.

'mediums' in spiritualist sessions were always females, or that churchgoing was so much more widespread among working-class women than among their menfolk?[143] Many (not all) advanced women thought not. They therefore reacted with horror to contraception, which they feared would have the effect of still further reducing women to objects upon which men could unleash their passions—even Olive Schreiner, though an advocate of 'voluntary motherhood', took this view.

The wider topic of birth control, however, concerned not merely women. In 1908 the Registrar-General calculated that 79 per cent of the population decline was due to 'deliberate restriction of child-bearing'.[144] Yet what did this involve? In 1879 the Drysdale brothers had founded the Malthusian League to preach the desirability of the poor having smaller families. During the following decade they went further, offering to instruct the poor, and anyone else who cared to listen, in how this could be achieved.[145] Chemists and other entrepreneurs were meanwhile taking advantage of the situation: one hears of public toilets fly-leafed with advertisements promoting their wares, and some couples found that publication of the banns brought them unsolicited advice about how they might conduct their marital life.[146]

However, probably no more than 15 per cent of the women who married before 1910 had resort to such methods,[147] and birth-control clinics did not appear in working-class neighbourhoods until after the Great War. It is therefore probable that the restriction of births was mainly achieved by coitus interruptus, or even by sexual abstinence.[148]

The fact is that 'respectable' opinion still frowned upon all 'artificial' interference with the processes of sexual reproduction—Gladstone thought it the 'saddest & most sickening of subjects'.[149] Such methods of family limitation were still associated with the grubby world of prostitution and with 'Bohemians', and so fell under a stigma only slightly less severe than abortion (still important in some working-class localities, judging from the widely advertised abortifacient pills). Doctors were especially prone to giving lurid warnings about contraceptives, the use of which, some claimed, led to cancer, and also, in the case of women, to hysteria and galloping nymphomania.[150] In 1886, at the

---

[143] J. Cox, *The English Churches in a Secular Society: Lambeth, 1870–930* (Oxford, 1982), 34.

[144] Harris, *Private Lives*, 48.

[145] Alice Vickery Drysdale, the wife of C. R. Drysdale and the first woman to be admitted to the Pharmaceutical Society, argued that a women's Malthusian League would end prostitution by encouraging earlier marriages (J. Lewis, *The Politics of Motherhood: Child and Maternal Welfare in England, 1900–1939* (London [c.1980]), 200).

[146] M. Mason, *The Making of Victorian Sexuality* (Oxford, 1994; 1995 edn.), 63.

[147] McLaren, *Birth-Control*, 11.

[148] R. Woods, *The Demography of Victorian England and Wales* (Cambridge, 2000), Ch. 4.

[149] R. Shannon, *Gladstone: Heroic Minister 1865–1898* (Harmondsworth, 1999), 474.

[150] J. Peel, 'Contraception and the Medical Profession', *Population Studies*, 18 (1964), 136.

NVA's instigation, Dr H. A. Allbutt was struck off the medical register for publishing his birth-control manual, the *Wife's Handbook*, in a cheap edition. The churches joined in the hue and cry, the Anglicans, at their 1908 Lambeth Conference, condemning 'the practice of resorting to artificial means for the avoidance or prevention of child-bearing', though Nonconformists tended to take a more liberal line.[151] The socialist/labour movement was divided on the issue.

The population question in turn gave rise to anxieties about the physical health of the 'race'. 'Social hygiene', as it was known, in fact covered a range of concerns, not just the falling birth-rate, but also the problem of so-called 'racial poisons' (alcohol and syphilis), and eugenics, the 'science' of race improvement. A prominent advocate of all these causes was the Presbyterian minister Dr James Marchant, who in 1904 founded the 'National Council of Public Morals', which aimed at 'the regeneration of the race—spiritual, moral and physical', and who later edited the influential 'New Tracts for the Times' series. One consequence was the increasing 'biologization' of social policy, which now centred on the health of the body, rather than on the fate of the soul—or even the integrity of public life. Nonetheless, the earlier obsessions of the social-purity crusaders long remained on the public agenda.

In no area of sexual conduct was the prevailing puritanism more marked than in attitudes towards homosexuality. The word 'homosexuality' had only recently been coined (by the Swede Hans Benkert in 1869), and it was not used in an English publication until the early 1890s. The turning point came with the Criminal Law Amendment Act, which by criminalizing 'gross indecency' between males even when conducted in private, went a long way towards creating (or 'constructing') homosexuality as a clearly defined condition.[152] The lurid Cleveland Street Case of 1889–90, following a police raid on a homosexual brothel, brought the issue into bolder relief; so did the spectacular fall of Oscar Wilde, who received two years' imprisonment with hard labour when his unsuccessful libel case against the Marquis of Queensberry led to his being put on trial in 1895.

Previously sexual relationships between men had generally been explained as the consequence of a superfluity of male sexual energy, not as a distinctive pathological condition. Indeed, it so happened that, for all his later notoriety as an iconic 'pervert', Wilde himself was bisexual. The intrusion of the law, however, led to sharp distinctions being drawn between 'natural' and 'unnatural' forms of masculinity.[153] Homosexuality, it now appeared, defined a particular character type, not a specific form of sexual activity. Its foremost

---

[151] McLaren, *Birth-Control*, 208, 210.
[152] Sodomy was already a felony, whether involving man, woman, or animal. This continued to be so.
[153] J. Weeks, *Sex, Politics and Society* (London, 1981), 90.

champion, Edward Carpenter, reinforced this view of homosexuals as a race apart by naming them 'Uranians' and 'Urnings' and crediting them with distinctive personality traits.[154] Other homosexuals started to play up to society's preconceptions of them by affecting the dress and manners of the flamboyant dandy—a role which, paradoxically, had previously been associated with the male 'womanizer'.[155]

To a generation so concerned with the social importance of procreation, homosexuality (like masturbation) must have seemed particularly reprehensible. The pursuit of pleasure for pleasure's sake also ran counter to the prevailing work ethic. Deeper than either consideration, perhaps, was the anxiety to maintain firm gender boundaries, 'effeminacy' in any form threatening those masculine values which seemed so important to social cohesion. However, it is significant that, despite some talk about 'Odd Women',[156] lesbianism hardly featured as an ethical/social issue—doubtless because all reference to female homosexuality had been omitted from the Criminal Law Amendment Act. Female homosexuality, when recognized at all, tended to be treated as an aspect of prostitution.[157] Homosexual conduct among men, though more openly discussed, was equally misunderstood, not least by the leaders of the medical profession, most of whom continued to view it as a kind of mental illness.[158]

In the long run, however, both the medical profession and bodies such as the NVA were fighting a losing battle. Indeed, many of their activities might even have been counter-productive. Thus, the heavy insistence on the importance of maintaining firm gender boundaries gave a thrill to breaking this taboo—hence perhaps the contemporary popularity of cross-dressing acts, from the theatrical depiction of Maid Marion to the music-hall routines of Vesta Tilley. In a similar way, the criminalization of homosexuality risked glamourizing this form of 'deviancy'. Finally, the more energetically the NVA tried to subordinate art and entertainment to moral codes of conduct, the fiercer the reaction it provoked—a reaction which led not only to the 'culture wars' of the Edwardian decade but also to the elaboration, amongst the intelligentsia, of startlingly radical views about human sexuality.[159]

Repression thus had the paradoxical consequence of stimulating a new kind of experimental libertarianism. Its leaders were two prolific controversialists,

[154] These terms were drawn from the Austrian sexologist Ulrichs.
[155] A. McLaren, *Twentieth-Century Sexuality: A History* (Oxford, 1999), 98.
[156] The title of Gissing's novel of 1893.
[157] M. Cale, 'Girls and the Perception of Sexual Danger in the Victorian Reformatory System', *History*, 78 (1993), 213; Bland, *Banishing the Beast*, 288–96.
[158] S. Hynes, *The Edwardian Turn of Mind* (1968), 163.
[159] Weeks, *Sex*, 91. On the 'culture wars', see Chs. 14 and 15.

Edward Carpenter and Havelock Ellis, who challenged, head-on, the NVA's belief that the law had a part to play in the regulation of private sexual conduct: 'An act does not become criminal because it is disgusting', Ellis insisted.[160]

A doctor by training and a socialist by conviction, Ellis set out to combat prejudice and ignorance of many kinds. Thus he denied that any medical evidence existed to support the view that masturbation caused insanity, and he was one of the first English writers to deal sympathetically, and in some detail, with female homosexuality—helped perhaps by the fact that his wife, Edith Lees, happened to be lesbian. More fundamentally, Ellis did much to undermine the distinction between what was 'normal' and 'abnormal' by undertaking a calm, dispassionate examination of a wide range of sexual practices, some of them seemingly bizarre or shocking (such as auto-eroticism, a word of his own coinage). The results of these researches were made public in the six volumes of his great work *Studies in the Psychology of Sex*, published between 1897 and 1910.[161]

Ellis himself, however, became the victim of the very prejudices he sought to overthrow when the first volume of the series, *Sexual Inversion* (1897) was condemned in the courts as obscene,[162] forcing him to switch to an American publisher. Ellis's main offence, in the eyes of his many critics, was that he wrote lucidly for the general reader about subjects which had previously been treated, if at all, by Continental psychologists addressing a medical readership in highly technical language—in works such as Richard von Krafft-Ebing's *Psychopathia Sexualis* (1886), which provided both Ellis and Carpenter with much of their material.

Yet, however provocatively unsensational his treatment of sexual abnormalities might have seemed to contemporaries, Ellis was not always entirely non-judgemental. For example, while deprecating the hysteria surrounding homosexuality which followed the Wilde trial and calling for law reform in this field, Ellis conceded that society could not be 'expected to tolerate the invert who flouts his perversion in its face'.[163] Despite his constant invocation of the 'New Spirit', Ellis held other highly traditional views: in *Man and Woman* (1893) he asserted that nature had 'made women more like children in order that they may better understand and care for children',[164] and in his later

---

[160] H. Ellis, *Studies in the Psychology of Sex: Vol 1: Sexual Inversion* (London, 1897), 156.

[161] A seventh volume came out in 1928.

[162] A prominent anarchist bookseller, George Bedborough, was prosecuted for distributing Ellis's book; he pleaded guilty and later committed suicide.

[163] Ellis, *Sexual Inversion*, 157. Ellis had been uncomfortable with the fact that his original collaborator on *Sexual Inversion*, John Addington Symons, was a homosexual. Ellis himself was a heterosexual, though he led an unusual life within an extraordinary *ménage a trois* (involving Olive Schreiner, his long-term mistress, and Edith Lees, his wife).

[164] p. 522.

writing the essence of sexuality is often depicted as the 'courtship' by which the male conquered the female.

Edward Carpenter mounted a much more radical challenge to gender stereotyping by emphasizing the many, often baffling, ways in which which Nature had *intermingled* the male and female elements out of which each individual was composed. Moreover, living openly with his working–class lover, Carpenter celebrated (as well as attempting to explain) what he called 'homogenic love'. Members of the 'Intermediate Sex', he argued, were ideally placed to interpret men and women to each other—and thus to heal gender divisions.[165] Carpenter further contended that 'normal' Uranians were not sensualists—on the contrary, they were 'not so sensual as the average normal man'. Instead, they should be seen as the 'advance guard' of a great movement that would 'one day transform the common life by substituting the bond of personal affection and compassion for the monetary, legal and other external ties which now control and confine society'.[166] Writing as a socialist, Carpenter thus hailed homosexuals as harbingers of a new age of affectional possibilities, in which freedom and love would be one.

Ellis and Carpenter were heroes to those who, on the eve of the Great War, founded the British Society for the Study of Sexual Psychology—a body which initially concentrated on homosexual law reform, but also had papers read to its members on a wide range of other topics.[167] Yet the two men may have made their greatest impact on the artistic avant-garde through their insistence on 'love' as the element binding together the human race, and their 'sacralization' of sex—influencing many later writers, not least E. M. Forster and D. H. Lawrence.

5. VOTES FOR WOMEN

None of these revolutionary musings made an immediate impact on the way in which the advocates of 'Votes for Women' chose to present their case. But the suffragists, too, found themselves forced to confront the vexed issue of gender differences. To what conclusions were they drawn?

Mrs Fawcett, a political economist like her late husband, had initially followed the lead given by John Stuart Mill, emphasizing what men and women had in common as responsible citizens (this was one reason why she

---

[165] The phrase derived from the German sexologist Magnus Hirschfeld.

[166] E. Carpenter, *The Intermediate Sex: A Study of Some Transitional Types of Men and Women* (London, 4th edn., 1916), 13, 116.

[167] 'We are a note of interrogation', said one of its leading figures, Lawrence Houseman (L. A. Hall, ' "Disinterested Enthusiasm for Sexual Misconduct": The British Society for the Study of Sex Psychology, 1913–47', *Journal of Contemporary History*, 30 (1995), 667).

opposed special legislative protection for female workers). By the 1880s, however, she was more inclined to take the view that women needed to be enfranchised precisely because they were *different* from men, and could thus complement the knowledge and wisdom which men brought to public life— not least out of their experience of motherhood. This was a powerful argument now that social reform, and issues of child and maternal welfare in particular, were beginning to bulk large in national, as well as in local, politics. 'Do not give up one jot or tittle of your womanliness, your love of children, your care for the sick, your gentleness, your self-control, your obedience to conscience and duty,' Mrs Fawcett declared, 'for all these things are terribly wanted in politics.'[168] In short, many suffragists now called for 'the feminization of democracy' and spoke of the need for a cultural transformation of society in line with feminine values.[169]

Such a rhetoric was particularly used by women active in local government, who often presented municipal work as a kind of 'compulsory philanthropy', for which traditional female aptitudes and accomplishments were highly suitable. However, this argument tended to be a double-edged sword, since it encouraged belief in the existence of 'separate spheres' and so legitimated the exclusion of women from national—though not from local—politics.

The message transmitted by women's reforming work was also ambivalent, since female middle-class reformers often unwittingly reinforced, in the minds of unsympathetic men, the very stereotypes which perpetuated their own subordination. For women's emphasis upon their own superior morality, rooted in feelings of sympathy and compassion, laid them open to the well-worn accusation that their hearts too often ran away with their heads, and that they were too emotional, even hysterical, to be entrusted with the awesome responsibilities of citizenship.

Women often proclaimed that their mission was to elevate the whole tone of public life. For example, in the anti-drink crusade the female activists were probably more inclined than men to spurn calls for compromise and 'realism'—perhaps because they associated compromise with the shabby powergames from which, as women, they were excluded. However, a common male reaction to this was that they did not want busybody women interfering with the pleasures to which they felt themselves entitled; a standard male antisuffragist argument was that women would probably vote for Prohibition or Local Option (by which local authorities could choose to adopt prohibition),

---

[168] 'Home and Politics', in J. Lewis (ed.), *Before the Vote Was Won: Arguments For and Against Women's Suffrage* (New York and London, 1987), 419.
[169] L. P. Hume, *The National Union of Women's Suffrage Societies, 1897–1914* (Brighton, 1982), 15, 18.

thereby closing down their beloved pubs and depriving the hard-working breadwinner of his well-deserved pint of beer.

In general, male objections to votes for women exhibited a strange mixture of chivalry and misogyny: on the one hand women were idealized, and on the other hand ribald fun was poked at their expense. In one breath the anti-suffragists argued that women, if enfranchised, would vote en bloc to enforce utopian reforms (such as the abolition of war, or the closing of all public houses), and then, apparently unaware of the contradiction, they would declare that women had no need of the vote because men were effectively representing them. The latter argument had some plausibility, in that most of the reforms for which women campaigned in the late Victorian period were eventually carried by a male parliament. But it entirely neglected women's aspirations— their desire for an explicit recognition of their intelligence and public spirit.

Resistance to the suffrage movement, however, relied less upon reasoning than upon sentiments prevalent in those social circles monopolized by men. Not surprisingly, 'clubland' provided a fertile breeding ground for anti-suffragism, no doubt because women's demand for the vote was construed as an attempt by outsiders to invade 'their club'. Most leading 'imperialists', too, were horrified by the prospect of women achieving equal political rights: the great proconsul Lord Cromer, for example, thought that it would disadvantage Britain in her struggle against Germany.

Women's presumed inability to fight in defence of their country was another oft-used explanation of why women could participate in local politics, but not decide great issues of state at Westminster. When suffragists replied that 'progress' meant that in the modern world reason was replacing force as the supreme arbiter in international disputes, they simply reinforced their opponents' belief that the Empire could not be entrusted to 'pacifists', whose minds were clouded by sentimental illusions. Indeed, to suffragist claims that in advanced industrial societies gender differentiation was becoming less pronounced, the anti-suffragists argued that, in fact, the opposite was the case: greater specialization of function was making men and women more *unlike*. 'An adult white woman', declared F. E. Smith, quoting H. G. Wells, 'differs far more from a white man than a negress or pygmy woman from her equivalent male.'[170]

What (limited) successes women had had in carving out new social roles for themselves was also provoking a backlash. As early as 1887 Walter Besant's *The*

---

[170] C. Rover, *Women's Suffrage and Party Politics in Britain, 1866–1914* (London, 1967), 43. 'Natives did not deserve the vote because they were not adequately sexually differentiated; while working men were sufficiently "masculine" and dominant over women to deserve it' (A. Clark, 'Gender, Class and the Nation: Franchise Reform in England, 1832–1928', in J. Vernon [ed.], *Re-Reading the Constitution: New Narratives in the Political History of England's Long Nineteenth Century* (Cambridge, 1996), 250).

Revolt of Man (1887) had prophesied the results of female revolution—a disaster that would only be halted, he argued, when men recaptured the reins of power and legitimate order was restored.

But for most educated men and women alike, the main issue was whether, and in what ways, women could reconcile their new social and economic freedoms (and the possibility of political emancipation) with the responsibilities of motherhood. Charles Darwin had dramatized the emergence and the triumph of *Homo sapiens* in terms which gave the processes of human reproduction a central importance. By dignifying 'motherhood', this development possibly enhanced women's self-esteem, but it also lent itself to arguments designed to imprison women within their maternal functions. Could women's progress as rational beings, asked the traditionalists, only be achieved by imperilling the future of the human race?

When the scientist George Romanes observed in 1887 that it would 'take many centuries for heredity to produce the missing five ounces of the female brain',[171] he was using a 'biological' objection to women's emancipation that was much less frequently employed on this side of the Channel than in France. Jokes about pregnant legislators got much closer to the heart of the anti-suffrage case, which focused upon the womb rather than upon brain-size. The 'medicalization' of women played an important part in the anti-suffrage case: no wonder that so many male doctors came out as virulent opponents.[172]

But equal political rights for women also seemed 'unnatural' to many women. Lord Salisbury saw no reason why women of means should not vote, but his wife disagreed. Revealingly, the famous manifesto published in the *Nineteenth Century* in 1889 by a group of distinguished ladies opposed to the suffrage cause (including Beatrice Potter, later Beatrice Webb) spoke of the impossibility of enfranchising those who were disqualified, 'either by the disabilities of sex, or by strong formations of custom and habit resting ultimately upon physical difference against which it is useless to contend'.[173]

6. CONCLUSION

Gender, like age, was a category which cut across those other divisions (of nationality and of social grouping) which fractured late Victorian and Edwardian England. The labour/socialist movement, in particular, struggled long and hard to hammer out a common line on all the issues which it raised. To the eccentric Carpenter, this was not in itself a bad thing. On the contrary,

---

[171] Lewis, *Women in England*, 84.
[172] Harrison, *Separate Spheres*, 67; 'Women's Health', 27–30.
[173] Cited in Harrison, *Separate Spheres*, 116.

'homogenic love', he thought, was a way of building bridges *between* the social classes, as well as resolving gender antagonisms: 'Eros is a great leveller. Perhaps the true Democracy rests, more firmly than anywhere else, on a sentiment which easily passes the bourns of class and caste, and unites in the closest affection the most estranged ranks of society.'[174] Perhaps Carpenter was right, in a very limited sense: the Cleveland Street scandal, for example, had revealed that many well-bred gentlemen delighted in crossing class lines by engaging in 'rough trade' with Post Office messengers, stable-boys, and the like.[175] Similarly, though no equivalent claims were made by lesbians, some suffragists, from the 1880s onwards, stressed the (chaste) solidarity of sister-hood, a solidarity transcending barriers of caste, creed and education.

Gender allegiances, of course, seldom shaped ideological convictions in so simple a way. After all, many men (not least Carpenter) strongly advocated female enfranchisement, while, conversely, many women clung to the security offered by the doctrine of 'separate spheres'. All the same, sexual tensions did something to stabilize a class-divided society by drawing together people of the same gender but from different social (and political) backgrounds.[176]

This particularly happened on the 'anti' side of the suffrage debate. For patriarchy meant that, at least in his own home, the working man, with his chair on which no one else could sit, the newspaper reserved for his first readership, and his special treats and relishes, was indeed the ruler of his little world, just as much as men from more privileged social circles. And when suffragists tried, rather snobbishly, to establish their case by pointing to the alleged absurdity of denying a lady of property the vote while conferring it on her gardener, they may have given insufficient weight to the feelings of the gardener. Rather in the way that a poor white man could preen himself on his superiority over 'blacks', the errand boy who shouted abuse at the suffragettes was doubtless getting his own back on social superiors to whom he usually had to grovel.[177]

[174] Carpenter, *Intermediate Sex*, 115.
[175] Others noted the power of 'scarlet fever', a fascination with guardsmen.
[176] See Ch. 12.
[177] Harrison, *Separate Spheres*, 22.

CHAPTER 3

Social Identities: Class, Community, and the Masses

The population question raised profound issues of gender, but it had even wider implications because demographic patterns varied so significantly from one social grouping to another. In 1881 only 15 per cent of men in the prosperous London borough of Hampstead had married between the ages of 20 and 24, but 32 per cent had done so in impoverished Bethnal Green, and, though these differences had narrowed slightly by 1911, they had not disappeared.[1] The relatively affluent were also less inclined than the working class to get married at all.

This, in turn, had an impact upon the birth-rate, which was not falling uniformly. The number of children born to the families of male manual workers was 25 per cent higher than to those of non-manual families, a gap which widened to 42 per cent during the period 1910–24.[2] In the 1880s unskilled labourers and agricultural workers still produced a large number of offspring: coalminers, with an average of more than six children, were the most fertile group of all. The gap in family size was partly neutralized by the existence of death-rates much higher in poor districts than in the comfortable suburbs—in York they were almost double. But, even allowing for this, the 'lower' social orders were reproducing themselves at a higher rate than their 'betters'—indeed, some professional groups such as doctors and clergymen were scarcely replacing themselves at all.

It was these figures of 'differential fertility' which later provided ammunition for the Edwardian eugenics movement. Social class, eugenists believed, was fundamentally a biological category, with those who were mentally and physically 'fitter' being pulled upwards into the highest social positions, the 'dregs' falling to the bottom. If this were so, then racial suicide threatened.[3]

---

[1] E. Ross, *Love and Toil: Motherhood in Outcast London, 1870–1918* (Oxford, 1993), 59. The national average was 22%. By 1911 the figures were 10% for Hampstead, 19% for Bethnal Green (p. 61).

[2] J. Lewis, *Women in England, 1870–1950: Sexual Divisions and Social Change* (New York and London, 1984), 6.

[3] See Ch. 11.

Eugenics never captured the allegiance of more than a vocal minority. But even its stout opponents often conceded that it was a misfortune that poorer couples who could least afford to bring up their children in comfort were having such large families, while the well-to-do, by whatever means, were controlling their fertility so rigorously. Such a development could only widen the already alarmingly enormous gaps in wealth and income.

These inequalities were becoming ever more starkly revealed. According to the 'New Domesday' survey of the late 1870s, one-quarter of the land of England and Wales belonged to a mere 710 individuals,[4] a concentration of ownership perhaps more extreme than in any other European country—bar Scotland and Ireland. If these wealthy landlords formed the apex of the social pyramid, its base consisted of a working class, the lower strata of which were living on the margins of existence: 768,938 persons were in receipt of poor relief in 1885, 2.9 per cent of the population of England and Wales.[5]

Inequalities may actually have been at their zenith in this period. Between 1895 and 1914 thirty estates were valued for probate at £2 million or more (an unprecedented number), while a mere 10 per cent of the adult population owned 92 per cent of the nation's wealth.[6] Moreover, as the Fabian Chiozza Money demonstrated in his influential study *Riches and Poverty*, one-half of the national income was being received by only 12 per cent of the population, and one-third by less than one-thirtieth.[7] Nearly 88 per cent of the population fell below the income-tax threshold of £160 a year. Much of the story of England between 1886 and 1914 centres on the attempts that were made at justifying, defending, assailing, and alleviating these inequalities.

What were the main building-blocks of the social system? The family itself still sometimes functioned as an economic unit. The hill farmers of Wales, Scottish crofters, and the peasant proprietors of rural Ireland all relied heavily on the labour of their immediate kin, and even in the agricultural districts of southern and eastern England children were expected, at certain points in the season, to help out their parents. Moreover, in parts of Northumberland the practice survived whereby whole families were hired by the year and paid as a group, being lodged in, or near to, the farmhouse which employed them—this

[4] D. Cannadine, *The Decline and Fall of the British Aristocracy* (New Haven and London, 1990), 55.

[5] M. Rose, *The Relief of Poverty 1834–1914* (London and Basingstoke, 1972), 53.

[6] W. D. Rubinstein, *Men of Property: The Very Wealthy in Britain Since the Industrial Revolution* (London, 1981), 41; J. Harris, *Private Lives, Public Spirit: A Social History of Britain 1870–1914* (Oxford, 1993), 99–100.

[7] C. Money, *Riches and Poverty* (London, 1905; 1911 edn.), 48. The rich were drawing £453 per person, the comfortable £67, the poor £24.

being the most cost-efficient method of labour organization in these remote areas.[8]

On the other hand, in the urban and industrial districts the family seldom played such a role. True, in cotton-weaving the father sometimes had a supervisory function which enabled him to recruit members of his own family, including wife and children over school-age. However, by the end of the century more impersonal and bureaucratic recruitment procedures were largely eliminating such systems. As a result, the family became increasingly separated from the world of work.[9]

This left five important foci of social identity: locality, occupation, class, voluntary communities (especially the Church), and consumption. As with nationality, these categories overlapped in complex ways, sometimes reinforcing, sometimes weakening one another.

1. LOCALITY

Counties had once been 'countries', and they retained a proud sense of individuality. The larger towns, too, still formed a world of their own, a tendency which was in some ways enhanced by the development of local government.[10] Each of the major provincial cities also flaunted a distinctive 'high bourgeois culture', which may have been at its most vibrant in the closing decades of the nineteenth century.[11]

There were other important regional differences. The tenement blocks of the Scottish cities sustained a social life different from England's, and even within England house-types and standards varied: in the North-East two to three rooms were the norm, but, generalizing broadly, the number of rooms increased as one moved south, where five or six were common.[12] Regionalism was at its sharpest in those areas where a single industry predominated, such as the coalfields or the medium-sized textile towns of the North.

Some of the rivalry between nearby regions and towns had a long history—witness the jealous competition between Leeds and Bradford or that between Manchester and Liverpool (the latter having a peculiar ethnic mix which gave it a personality all its own). By the late Victorian period such rivalries were

---

[8] A. Howkins, *Reshaping Rural England: A Social History 1850–1925* (London, 1991; 1992 edn.), 19–20, 51.

[9] But in 1899–1914 31% of men marrying still worked in the same occupation as their father (M. Savage and A. Miles, *The Remaking of the British Working Class 1840–1940* (London, 1994), 45, 54).

[10] See Ch. 4.

[11] S. Gunn, *The Public Culture of the Victorian Middle Class: Ritual and Authority in the English Industrial City 1840–1914* (Manchester, 2000).

[12] F. M. L. Thompson, *The Rise of Respectable Society: A Social History of Victorian Britain, 1830–1900* (London, 1988), 187–8.

being reinforced by more recent social developments: civic pride often centred on the local football side, with the fortunes of which citizens of otherwise quite different backgrounds could identify. 'When Preston won the FA Cup in 1889, the town took to the streets in an intense and spontaneous celebration of welcome with a crowd of 30,000 surrounding the station and a band playing "See the Conquering Hero Comes".'[13]

But between 1886 and 1914 these local identities were being broken down and redefined by changes in methods of transportation. In 1886 horse-drawn traffic still dominated the urban scene in the form of carts, carriages, and omnibuses: in many ways the horse remained, right up until 1914, the most cost-effective mechanism for transporting freight and passengers across short distances. However, in the course of the 1880s horse-drawn omnibuses rapidly gave way to trams, most of which, especially within the larger towns, were electrified during the following decade, often amidst great popular excitement.

But the tram was already facing a formidable new rival. In November 1885 Gottlieb Daimler invented the first effective internal combustion engine. Initially this contraption was fitted to a bicycle, but in 1886 a way was found of applying it to a four-wheeled vehicle. Motor buses made their appearance in 1898: there were already over 5,000 vehicles in operation by 1904 and over 50,000 by 1914, though many cities did not acquire a motor-bus service until after the Great War. Motorized cabs, or taxis as they soon became known, date from 1904. But most motorized vehicles were in private ownership: only 8,465 in 1904, their numbers dramatically expanded, until on the eve of the Great War they totalled 132,000, adding fresh chaos to the roads, where they mingled with the still very large number of horse-drawn vehicles and with the ubiquitous bicycle—in its modern form, essentially an invention of the 1890s.[14]

Trams and buses played an important part in urban expansion. Daringly, the LCC built new estates, devised to alleviate congestion in the city centre, along the routes of new tram lines.[15] Though such planning was very rare before 1914, in the greater London area in particular the age of the commuter had arrived. Londoners had the use of another transport facility in the 'underground', which, in the form of covered cuttings, dated from 1863, but was transformed into the 'tube' and underwent electrification during the 1890s.

In addition, between 1870 and 1912 the already dense rail network increased by a further 50 per cent, largely through the construction of rural and suburban

---

[13] R. Holt, *Sport and the British: A Modern History* (Oxford, 1989), 170.
[14] A. R. Ubbelohde, 'Science', in S. Nowell-Smith (ed.), *Edwardian England, 1901–1914* (Oxford, 1964), 240. The public-service vehicles include taxis. London acquired a service in 1905, Liverpool in 1911 (P. J. Waller, *Town, City and Nation: England 1850–1914* (Oxford, 1983), 163–4).
[15] Waller, *Town, City and Nation*, 30–1.

lines.[16] Here was another development which allowed towns to expand far beyond their earlier limits. By 1900 4,252 suburban trains were pouring daily into London's twenty-two termini.[17]

As a result of all these changes, once-distinct towns sometimes merged into one another to produce what would soon be called 'conurbations' (the word coined by Patrick Geddes in his *Cities in Evolution* of 1915). By 1891 11,670,000 people (over 47 per cent of England's population) were concentrated within six such areas: Greater London, South-East Lancashire, the West Midlands, West Yorkshire, Merseyside, and Tyneside. Both the numbers of the inhabitants of the conurbations and their ratio to the population as a whole steadily rose.[18] London enjoyed an exceptional prominence, but rivalling the national capital were provincial metropolises such as Manchester, Birmingham, and Leeds, each serving the social and cultural, as well as the economic, needs of many satellite towns.[19] Where would this process stop? Writing in 1901, H. G. Wells could envisage the total breakdown of the traditional distinction between town and country; by the start of the following century, he predicted, the Londoner might 'have a choice of nearly all England and Wales south of Nottingham and east of Exeter as his suburb'.[20]

Improved transportation, however, did not simply blur or obliterate civic identities. On the contrary, it often re-created and reinforced these identities by drawing people into the larger towns for shopping and for a host of recreational purposes. Something similar was also happening to many market towns; while some stagnated or declined into little more than overgrown villages, others, prospering from railway links, formed a closer relationship with their agricultural hinterlands and developed into important regional centres. For example, Carlisle, with a population of nearly 50,000 in 1911, not only functioned as agricultural market and commercial hub for a large area stretching into South-West Scotland, but also attracted factories as various as Carr's, the biscuit manufacturers, and the Cowans Sheldon's Engineering works.[21]

Meanwhile, within the larger towns distinct neighbourhoods retained considerable social importance, particularly for working-class women, who often built up rich supportive networks within them. Males from similar backgrounds also had strong ties with their neighbourhoods, as can be seen from

---

[16] Waller, *Town, City and Nation*, 159.

[17] Ibid. 160.

[18] This was paralleled in Scotland by the growth of the Central Clydeside region and in Wales by the expanding industrial area in Glamorganshire.

[19] Gunn, *Culture of the Victorian Middle Class*, 11–14.

[20] H. G. Wells, *Anticipations* (London, 1901), 45–6, 63.

[21] J. Brown, *The English Market Town: A Social and Economic History, 1750–1914* (Ramsbury, 1986), 93.

sports teams: of 148 cricket clubs in Liverpool during the 1890s, sixty-one had street- or place-names.[22] But such loyalties did not preclude a strong sense of belonging to the larger city, nor indeed a sense of membership of even wider constituencies. Moreover, close-knit urban neighbourhoods of this kind were overwhelmingly a working-class phenomenon, and should perhaps be seen as a particular form of class loyalty, rather than as an expression of 'territoriality'.[23]

How stable were attachments to a particular locality? In 1886 the country was still in the throes of a demographic upheaval, movement between the constituent parts of the United Kingdom and emigration to the colonies[24] being accompanied by considerable internal migration. In 1901 28 per cent of men in England and Wales were living outside their 'native' county, a proportion that was to rise ten years later to 36 per cent.[25] No county had fewer than 10 per cent of immigrants in its population, and the home counties had nearly 50 per cent.[26]

Contemporary commentators emphasized the impermanence of urban communities, whose inhabitants, wrote C. F. G. Masterman, were 'still only, as it were, commencing to settle down in their new quarters, with the paint scarcely dry on them, and the little garden still untilled'.[27] In fact, by the end of the century the areas most heavily dominated by newcomers tended to be growing suburbs such as Croydon, or else fashionable resorts such as Brighton—not industrial towns, in most of which over 70 per cent of residents had been locally born and where many families came from the second, third, or fourth generation. Even in London, some two-thirds of the population had been born within the LCC area, while in the East End the proportion was higher still. Though short-distance house-moves, often from street to street, were common among manual workers (Charles Booth found 40 per cent of families had done so within a year in one district of Bethnal Green), urban working-class settlements were perhaps more stable than they had been during the preceding decades of hectic growth.[28]

The well-to-do, on the other hand, were becoming more detached from specific localities, as, from the middle of the century, they began abandoning the inner cities, into which they had formerly poured so many resources and so much energy, for the privatized world of suburban family life. Indeed, by the

---

[22] Another thirty were attached to a church, twenty to a works, eighteen to a school (Holt, *Sport*, 151).

[23] See below.

[24] See Ch. 1.

[25] E. H. Phelps Brown, *The Growth of British Industrial Relations* (London, 1959), 12.

[26] Harris, *Private Lives*, 43.

[27] C. F. G. Masterman, *The Condition of England* (London, 1909), 96.

[28] J. Lawrence, *Speaking for the People: Party, Language and Popular Politics in England, 1867–1914* (Cambridge, 1998), 241–3, 30.

end of the century local industrialists, with strong roots in their native town, were gradually being superseded by a 'business class' with interests that were geographically disparate. This signified the emergence of a 'national' middle class: 'by the early 1900s it was common for businessmen and employers in Birmingham, Leeds and Manchester to have several addresses: a family "home" in Bowdon, Edgbaston or Headingley, a town house in London, a small estate in Scotland, perhaps, or a villa by the sea.'[29]

2. VERTICAL STRATIFICATION: OCCUPATION

At least Masterman was correct in his belief that rural society was in crisis. Between 1870 and 1911 some 2,500,000 acres in Great Britain went out of cereal production, and in some counties, such as Suffolk, large tracts of what had once been farmland were converted to field sports. During these years of agricultural depression many labourers moved into the cities or else emigrated.[30] As a result, the total agricultural workforce in England and Wales (including farmers) dropped from 1,409,117 in 1881 to 1,253,322 twenty years later.[31]

Since it was young people, especially young women, who were most likely to move residence in this way, the age structure of urban and rural districts differed quite dramatically. The 1909 Poor Law Commission learned that old people (those aged 60 and over) constituted 66.9 per 1,000 of London's population and 67.3 in other mainly urban areas, but no fewer than 102 in mainly rural districts. And because the cities contained more people of child-bearing age, they had a higher birth-rate than the countryside, a factor which contributed even more than internal migration to the growing disparity between the populations of urban and rural districts: in London between 1851 and 1891 84.03 per cent of urban population increase resulted from a surplus of births, only 15.97 per cent from net immigration.[32]

Predominantly rural counties, such as Somerset, Norfolk, and Westmorland, grew very slowly: their combined population, 978,000 in 1881, had reached only 1,017,000 thirty years later, a statistic which masks the drift within each county into its larger towns (for example, the population of Norwich grew from 88,000 to 121,000 during the same period). Meanwhile the populations of urbanized and industrialized counties expanded dramatically: Durham from 867,000 to 1,370,000, the West Riding of Yorkshire from

---

[29] Gunn, *Culture of the Victorian Middle Class*, 192–5.

[30] Though emigration was no higher from the agricultural districts than from the big cities.

[31] See W. H. Armstrong, *Farmworkers* (London, 1987).

[32] Waller, *Town, City and Nation*, 26–8. Net immigration represents the difference between those who left London (about one-fifth) and those who entered it (over one-third).

2,237,000 to 3,131,000, and Warwickshire from 737,000 to 1,250,000. Already by 1886 mainland Britain (Ireland being once again an exception) could definitely be categorized as a predominantly urban country—indeed, the most heavily urbanized society in Europe apart from Belgium.

Urbanization in turn involved a redistribution of the male workforce. The 1881 census showed that over Great Britain as a whole agriculture (embracing horticulture and forestry as well as farming) was still the largest single occupation for men, comprising about 1,500,000 out of a male labour force of 8,852,000 (17 per cent).

But, taken together, industrial occupations now dominated. Textiles, the pacemakers of the early Industrial Revolution, still employed 554,000 men and 745,000 women, some 10 per cent of the total workforce. The various branches of engineering accounted for another 8 per cent (11.25 per cent of all employed men). Mining and quarrying, even more overwhelmingly a male domain, absorbed 6.82 per cent of employed males. Building and construction, little affected by the processes of industrialization, also continued to expand: in 1881 they employed 875,000 men, just under 10 per cent of the male workforce. Food, drink, and tobacco, which employed 592,000 people in 1881, had almost doubled the number of their employees by 1914.

The year 1901 saw manufacturing reach the apex of its dominance—which is why the northern industrial towns tended to reach their maximum size in Edwardian times.[33] Yet, as the British economy diversified in the latter decades of the nineteenth century, the tertiary (service) sector grew, relative to the secondary (manufacturing) and the primary (extractive) sectors. Not all of these tertiary occupations were 'advanced'—witness the survival of the very large domestic and personal services sector. In addition, in 1881 as many as 870,000 males (just under 10 per cent of employed men) were working in various parts of the transport industry as railwaymen, hauliers, seamen, and dockers.

But the economic future of the country very much rested with the commercial and financial sectors which, led by the burgeoning City of London, were developing at a very rapid rate: in 1881 they already employed 363,000 people (a 67 per-cent increase over the previous decade), only 11,000 of them females. About 118,000 people, nearly all males, were located in 'public administration': this was to be another important growth area (it registered about a 150 per cent increase by the outbreak of the Great War). Government employment increased fourfold between 1870 and 1914.[34]

---

[33] Harris, *Private Lives*, 126; Waller, *Town, City and Nation*, 125. Even so, only about one-third of workers were employed in manufacturing (Savage and Miles, *Remaking of British Working Class*, 22).

[34] Harris, *Private Lives*, 11–12.

How did the occupational distribution of the workforce affect social identity? It did so by engendering ties of sentiment and mutual obligation between managers and men which were often strong enough to override class divisions. For example, in the West Midlands, where units of production tended to be small and the distinction between employer and employee relatively weak, industrial conciliation and partnership flourished, producing a 'community of interests' which W. J. Davis, the founder of the National Society of Amalgamated Brassworkers, described as follows:

The employers find the capital, business capacity and enterprise, and should have the lion's share of the profits. We find the technical skill and muscle which the product requires ... Therefore you must apportion fairly the profits as between Capital and Labour.[35]

It was usually from the employers that the initiative came in attempts at fashioning occupational solidarity. The kind of face-to-face paternalism long established in some of the Lancashire cotton factories, which encouraged the 'hands' to vote enthusiastically for their employer, had not entirely died out by the 1880s, but it was being replaced by more formal mechanisms of influence and control. 'Enlightened' employers increasingly set up elaborate welfare schemes for their staff, many, for example, providing medical services, running works canteens and crèches, and establishing subsidized savings and pensions schemes. The 1890s also saw the proliferation of works sports grounds and brass bands.

To those with strong religious convictions such activities seemed nothing less than a Christian duty, but even Quaker philanthropists such as the Cadburys and the Rowntrees were not unaware of the material advantages of stabilizing the labour force and encouraging workers to identify their personal interests with the well-being of their firm. This sort of welfare capitalism particularly flourished in the food-processing and chemical industries, which had many female employees; but it was also to be found in the heavy industry sector, where it was practised by the likes of Mather & Platt, the Oldham engineering works.[36]

Pan-class collaboration at the national level was more difficult to organize, though it sometimes happened spontaneously—as in 1901 when the government's export coal duty provoked protests from both coal-owners and the mining unions, drawn together by a common threat to their livelihoods. A more contrived project of this kind came in the 1890s when Lord Winchelsea

---

[35] In 1899: D. Smith, *Conflict and Compromise: Class Formation in English Society 1830–1914: A Comparative Study of Birmingham and Sheffield* (London, 1982), 239.

[36] J. Melling, ' "Non-Commissioned Officers": British Employers and Their Supervisory Workers, 1880–1920', *Social History*, 5 (1980), 197–8.

founded the National Agricultural Union, a body which claimed to represent all agrarian groups, be they landowners, farmers, or labourers—to the annoyance of urban groups already suspicious of the 'doles' being paid out to the rural population.[37] This was neither the first nor the last time that town–country antagonisms flared up publicly. But, in the absence of a tariff such as existed in most other industrialized countries, pan-class collaboration on an occupational basis proved difficult to achieve. On the contrary, vertical stratification tended to weaken in the late Victorian period, under the pressure of antagonisms which were dividing society horizontally.

3. HORIZONTAL STRATIFICATION: CLASS

If class identities were becoming sharper in the closing years of the nineteenth century, this owed much to changes in methods of production. Industrialization, in its earlier phases, had by no means destroyed craft skills; but during the 1890s the emerging machine-tools industry made possible, for the first time, the production of standard interchangeable parts, a development which offered a sharp threat to the engineer's traditional role.[38] As the use of machinery spread, other manufacturing enterprises were reorganized along factory lines: among them, the boot-and-shoe industry, food processing, cigarette manufacturing, and newspaper production. Mechanization similarly transformed life at sea, the fishing smacks of Hull and Grimsby being all but replaced during the 1890s by fleets of steam-propelled trawlers.[39]

By American standards British industry remained small-scale. In 1898–9 the average workshop employed fewer than thirty male workers. Even in 1907, according to the industrial census of that year, there were still only 100 firms which had 3,000 people on their payrolls, and these employees represented a mere 5 per cent of the total labour force.[40] Indeed, until the very end of the century the family partnership remained the most common business form. However, private companies—a kind of halfway house to the publicly floated company—were becoming more important: between a third and a fifth of all companies registered in 1890 were private, a proportion which had risen by 1914 to four-fifths.[41] Limited liability companies proper took surprisingly long

---

[37] See Ch. 7.

[38] By 1907 only 2.7% of engineering workers were employed in workshops (W. Knox, 'Apprenticeship and De-Skilling in Britain, 1850–1914', *International Review of Social History*, 31 (1986), 174–5).

[39] R. Robinson, *Trawling: The Rise and Fall of the British Trawl Fishery* (Exeter, 1986), Chs. 7–8.

[40] Cited in D. Cannadine, *Class in Britain* (New Haven and London, 1998), 114.

[41] P. L. Cottrell, *Industrial Finance 1830–1914* (London, 1979; 1980 edn.), 163. These companies were formed with a view to protecting the family's private wealth should their business fail. The 1907 Companies Act exempted them from having to be filed under public registration, though from 1900 onwards they had to undergo an annual audit.

to take root. Although enabling legislation went back to the 1850s, culminating in the Joint Stock Companies Act of 1862, by 1885 public companies still accounted for only 5–10 per cent of important business organizations, being largely confined to shipping, iron and steel, breweries, and cotton.[42]

The turning point came with the spectacular flotation of Guinness in 1886, followed by that of J. & P. Coats, the sewing cotton combine in 1890.[43] Between 1893 and 1897 the annual registration of new limited liability companies more than doubled—5,148 new companies being created in the latter year. Then came a spate of huge amalgamations in branches of textiles, brewing, iron and steel, wallpaper, and tobacco—the most heavily capitalized public company of all being the Imperial Tobacco Company, registered in 1901.[44] Indeed, the role of the 'promoter' in organizing these flotations was a notable feature of the 1890s, attracting the satirical attention of Gilbert and Sullivan (*Utopia Limited*, 1893) and giving rise to some dramatic scandals, in particular those centred on the remarkable Ernest Terah Hooley, whose bankruptcy in 1898 exposed the many titled people he had employed as 'fronts'. 'Companification' also provided rich pickings for a new kind of unscrupulous financial journalist, of whom the most influential was Harry Marks of the *Financial News*.[45]

Most mergers took the form of a defensive reaction among the older staple industries to new challenges from America and Continental Europe. Intensified competition similarly led to the formation of several international cartels—including the notorious Dynamite Trust and the International Maritime Marine, sponsored in 1900 by J. P. Morgan in New York, which combined five of the biggest passenger-carrying transatlantic shipping companies.

None of these developments necessarily resulted in an immediate loss of control on the part of the original owners or partners, since most ordinary shares with voting rights were often retained within the circle of family and friends.[46] But, over time, there was a growing separation between ownership and management as enterprises became more highly capitalized, making it harder, some contemporaries believed, for able working men to rise out of their class.[47] Larger economic units also tended to bring about more

---

[42] P. L. Payne, 'The Emergence of the Large-Scale Company in Great Britain, 1870–1914', *Economic History Review*, 20 (1967), 520.

[43] L. Hannah, *The Rise of the Corporate Economy* (London, 1976), 21.

[44] Payne, 'Large-Scale Company', 527.

[45] D. Porter, ' "A Trusted Guide of the Investing Public": Harry Marks and the *Financial News* 1884–1916', *Business History*, 28 (1986), 1–17.

[46] Waller, *Town, City and Nation*, 71.

[47] However, over the course of the late nineteenth century there may have been a very small *increase* in upward mobility from the working class, though never more than one in ten; however, those who ascended the social scale mainly entered the ranks of small businessmen and white-collared employees, not the established middle class (Savage and Miles, *Remaking of British Working Class*, 32–3).

impersonal work relationships and the erosion of older practices of employer paternalism.

Marx had predicted that industrialization would inexorably *simplify* the social system, sharpening antagonisms between bourgeoisie and proletariat. Lord Salisbury, of all people, believed that a class war was already in progress. There was *some* evidence to offer hope to the revolutionary and to confirm the apprehensions of the conservative. Trade unionism, for example, expanded significantly from the late 1880s onwards, partly in response to the de-skilling of many artisanal trades: only 750,000 in 1888, membership climbed to 2,000,000 in 1900, 2,250,000 in 1910 and over 4,000,000 in 1913.

Trade-union density was highest among metalworkers (especially in ship-building), coalminers, and cotton operatives. It was weaker, but still significant, among printers, railwaymen, and sections of the building industry. Yet whole areas of industrial life had scarcely been touched by trade unionism—unsurprisingly, since in towns such as Hastings ('Mugsborough'), scene of Robert Tressell's novel *The Ragged Trousered Philanthropists*, there were no large employers whom a demoralized workforce could identify as the class enemy. Neither had industrial organization yet made significant inroads into the white-collar occupations (with the notable exception of schoolteaching). Indeed, the trade-union movement remained an overwhelmingly adult male affair: in 1896 there were only 142,000 female trade unionists, 60 per cent of them in cotton. Youths, too, were largely unorganized.[48]

In any case, membership of a union did not necessarily denote a commitment to advancing the interests of the working class as a whole. The TUC brought affiliated unions together for debates at its annual conference; in the interval the Parliamentary Committee kept a watching brief over legislation that might affect its members. But the fraternal spirit of the TUC was often skin-deep and sectionalism remained very strong. Most coalminers, for example, were geographically isolated from the rest of the trade-union movement and reluctant to make common cause with other manual workers.

A sense of working-class identity was more likely to thrive amongst groups such as the railwaymen, whose membership was scattered in penny packets throughout the land. For them, combination with other unions was the *sine qua non* to securing any kind of parliamentary presence.[49] However, such alliances of convenience did not amount to a deep sense of class brotherhood, as postulated by the socialists. Even the Amalgamated Society of Railway

[48] Females constituted 7.9% of all trade unionists in 1896, 6.5% in 1891, and 10.6% in 1911 (Lewis, *Women in England*, 169).

[49] Though there were, of course, a few 'railway towns', notably Derby, which returned the Secretary of the Amalgamated Society of Railway Servants, Richard Bell, as one of its two members in the 1900 General Election.

Servants was slow to adopt an 'all-grades' movement—the engine drivers had already split away to form their own union in 1881.

Working-class leaders found overcoming such sectionalism to be no easy matter. For the manual working class, which comprised over three-fifths of the labour force (as compared with about two-fifths today),[50] was living in very disparate circumstances. Despite mounting threats to their traditional privileges, engineers who had served an apprenticeship still earned almost double the wages of the labourers who worked alongside them, and were highly conscious of their superiority in terms of status and respectability. The daughter of a skilled tinworker, growing up in Port Talbot, remembers her family as being 'middle class', as against the 'ordinary people', who were lower class.[51]

Another privileged group of manual workers consisted of those who participated in the subcontracting which played so important a part in coalmining, with its 'butty' system. Foremen and supervisors, the 'NCOs' of Britain's industrial army, had an even more complex social identity, since, though manual workers by origins, they often aspired to the lifestyle of the lower middle class.[52]

At the opposite end of the spectrum, constituting perhaps one-tenth of the total population, lived what would today be called an 'underclass' of the very poor: many of them casual workers, suffering from chronic underemployment. These were 'the people of the abyss', on whose fringes were to be found the criminal and semi-criminal classes, including pickpockets and prostitutes, as well as vagrants, mendicants, and paupers. To what extent 'the poor' could be lumped in with the working class proper was a question which puzzled contemporaries.

The marginalization of the 'people of the abyss' was often the result of residential segregation. Many better-paid workers in regular employment could take advantage of cheap workmen's trains and the expanding network of trams, which offered an escape from the overcrowding, squalor, and expense of inner-city life. Unskilled workers, trapped in casual employment, could seldom take this option. Dockers, for example, had to live close to the docks, so that they could hear by word of mouth when a ship awaited unloading. This usually meant living in sub-letted larger houses, the rents of which were actually higher on average than those charged for the modern terraced houses that were springing up in the inner suburbs. This was because slum clearance (under the terms of the various Public Health Acts), plus the demolition of former residential property to make way for the building

[50] G. Routh, *Occupation and Pay in Great Britain 1906–79* (London and Basingstoke, 1980), 5.

[51] In her eyes, the employers and professional men of the locality presumably constituted the 'upper class': P. Thompson, *The Edwardians: The Remaking of British Society* (London, 1975), 141.

[52] Melling, 'Non-Commissioned Officers', 183–221.

of railway termini and new commercial premises, had created a housing shortage which led to rack-renting and overcrowding. London, where this process was particularly marked, had 56,000 one-roomed and 55,000 two-roomed flats in 1901.

But outside London, where social zoning was less marked, different social groups still often intermingled, albeit residing in different types of accommodation. Even in London out-migration did not result in simple class polarization. For a start, publicans and shopkeepers had to stay behind in the residential parts of the old city centres. Nor were manual workers in these areas an undifferentiated mass: even in dockland, stevedores and lightermen, the most skilled workers in their trade, enjoyed higher incomes and esteem than ordinary labourers. Conversely, there were cities with acute housing problems in which slum dwelling was by no means confined to the casual poor. In 1891 52 per cent of Glasgow's total population were living in over-crowded conditions, as were 40 per cent of Gateshead's and 35 per cent of Newcastle's.[53]

Talk of a 'labour aristocracy' cut off from the wider working class by skill, higher wages, and commitment to 'respectability' thus misleads on a number of counts. Skilled craftsmen comprised only 10 per cent or so of the labour force, but the 'respectable' working class—many of them members of the Co-operative Movement or of a friendly society—far exceeded this number.

Moreover, even where labour hierarchies did exist, these could take several forms. In coalmining and ironmaking stratification was based on age and strength rather than skill: this individualized the work relationship by offering almost every male a chance to earn high wages at *some* point in his career. 'Skill', in any case, was a highly problematic concept, often denoting little more than success in controlling entry into a particular occupation.[54] In coalmining even the most highly paid men, the hewers, were unskilled in the sense that they had neither served an apprenticeship nor studied at trade school, but they were not doing the sort of work which blacklegs could easily take over in the event of a strike.

In the years around the turn of the century wage differentials may have contracted slightly. The growth of semi-skilled occupations was meanwhile providing more work in the middle range of working-class incomes—particularly for women. A further indication of slightly greater working-class homogeneity was that intermarriage between families of the skilled, the semi-skilled,

[53] A. S. Wohl, 'Sex and the Single Room: Incest Among the Victorian Working Class', in A. S. Wohl, *The Victorian Family: Structure and Stresses* (London, 1978), 204.

[54] N. Whiteside, 'Welfare Legislation and the Unions During the First World War: Reply', *Historical Journal*, 25 (1982), 444. As for mechanization, far from always entailing a process of de-skilling, it often created demand for *new* skills.

and the unskilled was increasing in the years before 1914—up from about 20 per cent in the 1840s to almost 40 per cent.[55]

In short, there was no simple polarity between labourer and artisan, still less one between the 'rough' and the 'respectable': it makes more sense to see the late Victorian working class as 'multi-layered'. Thus the wealthy Liverpool shipowner Charles Booth, in his pioneering survey of London, broke the manual workers into no fewer than six separate 'classes' or categories, and though he may have had his own ulterior motives in denying the existence of a unified working class, his writings accurately convey the bewildering variety of working-class life.[56]

If working-class society was complex, so was that of the middle class. Indeed, the 'middle class' was in many ways a residual category—a convenient label to pin on people who were neither manual workers nor landed aristocrats. Farmers, often treated as though they constituted the rural middle class, were a particularly disparate occupational grouping. At one extreme stood 'gentlemen farmers' on the fringes of county society, who attended county balls and participated in field sports and whose daughters played the piano in handsomely appointed parlours; at the other extreme stood many small farmers of under 100 acres who were largely reliant upon the labour of family members to scratch a meagre living from the soil.

Even within an urban milieu, middle-class people had few common economic characteristics: some lived off dividends (among them rentiers, many of them female), some off profits (most businessmen), and some off fees (lawyers and doctors), while, as the century wore on, an increasing number (including schoolteachers and a range of officials employed in the public sector) drew salaries.

Moreover, within the Victorian middle class the spread of incomes was colossal. At one extreme there were millionaire dynasties such as the Rothschilds (merchant bankers), the Willses (tobacco manufacturers), and the Grettons (brewers). For a lucky handful of successful professional men, too, incomes could be very high: R. B. Haldane, a successful barrister, was drawing fees worth between £15,000 and £20,000 p.a. before he entered government office, and a permanent secretary (a civil service position) earned between £2,000 and £2,500 p.a.

But most professional men could count on less than £500 p.a.: barristers' earnings averaged £478, GPs' £395, and dentists' £368, while many clergyman, on £206 p.a., had an income lower than that of skilled industrial workers in full employment (boilermakers, for example).[57] Still lower down the income

---

[55] Savage and Miles, *Remaking of British Working Class*, 37.

[56] In some areas it was further complicated by ethnic divisions arising from Irish and Jewish settlement.

[57] Routh, *Occupation and Pay*, 63. Admittedly, these are averages which conceal wide variations: for example, vicars were earning much more than curates and most also had the benefit of a free house.

scale was the elementary school teacher, on £154 p.a. Like other members of the much-mocked lower middle class, the teacher often lived in genteel poverty, aspiring to a middle-class lifestyle without the wherewithal to achieve it—a social phenomenon mocked in the portrayal of Mr Pooter, the City clerk, in *Diary of a Nobody*.[58] Small shopkeepers and clerks suffered the added disadvantage of job insecurity. In the large provincial cities the middle class was headed by a wealthy and influential elite consisting of between 3 per cent and 5 per cent of the urban population, the major industrial, commercial, and professional families, but there was also a 'long social tail of small entrepreneurs, shopkeepers, tradespeople and, increasingly, clerical workers'.[59]

Moreover, the middle class was not divided by income alone. Another important distinction was the one which separated the professional from the 'entrepreneurial' middle class: all businessmen were, to a greater or lesser extent, profit-orientated, while most professional men (and women) were by definition insulated from the direct play of market forces, subscribing, as many of them did, to an 'ethic of service'. Some spokesmen for the professional middle class proudly asserted their separate identity: those who owed their position to 'learning', boasted Karl Pearson, the scientist, were superior, not only to social classes based upon 'birth' and 'manual labour', but also to the possessors of capital.[60]

Significantly, between 1881 and 1901 the growth in membership of the professions outstripped that of the population as a whole. This was especially true of doctors, whose ratio to total population fell from 1,723 to 1,439. This led in the 1890s to a renewed overcrowding of the profession, which, in general, depressed medical incomes.[61] However, the status of doctors had risen—partly as a long-term consequence of the 1858 Medical Practitioners Act, which had discouraged 'quacks', and partly because the profession had succeeded, however disingenuously, in creating an image of itself as performing a disinterested service for the wider community.

---

[58] G. and W. Grossmith, *Diary of a Nobody* (1892).
[59] Gunn, *Culture of Victorian Middle Class*, 18–19.
[60] D. A. MacKenzie, *Statistics in Britain 1865–1930* (Edinburgh, 1981), 76–8, citing Pearson's article, 'Anarchy' of 1881–2. According to Pearson, it was 'labour of the head, which produces all we term *progress*, and enables any individual society to maintain its place in the battle of life'. However, it has been doubted whether many professional men shared this 'professional consciousness' (J. Garrard and V. Parrott, 'Solicitors and Gas Engineers, *c*.1850–1914', in A. Kidd and D. Nicholls (eds.), *The Making of the British Middle Class?* (Stroud, 1998), 148–68).
[61] A. Digby, *Making a Medical Living: Doctors and Patients in the English Market for Medicine, 1720–1911* (Cambridge, 1994), 15, 142–5. The figures for professional growth were: clergy 16%; lawyers 21%; physicians and surgeons 50%, compared with 25% for the population of England and Wales as a whole.

Lawyers never achieved this sort of popularity. But the standing of the late Victorian solicitor compared favourably with the despised attorney of earlier decades, thanks to improved professional training and higher educational standards, coupled with a campaign run by the Law Society to stamp out 'unethical' practices. More to the point, both professions had successfully resisted or deflected earlier attempts by entrepreneurial radicals to open them up to competition. Such an ethic of service perhaps aligned them more closely with landed society than it did with that sector of the commercial middle class that lived on profit.

In general, no one could really afford a lifestyle that qualified for membership of the middle class unless his income carried him over the income-tax threshold of £160 a year. Members of this class were also expected to employ at least one domestic servant. Yet the poorer groups in what would normally be called the middle class could not afford such help (certainly not a live-in servant) and paid little or no income tax, while some privileged manual workers did both. What mainly separated the lower middle class from manual workers was a status distinction: they had received a more protracted education and did not work with their hands. There is indeed an important contrast to be drawn here between mental and manual labour.

All the same, the frontier between middle and working class was poorly defined, with a large and variegated population living in the border-area. The inhabitants of this ambiguous social world, neither typically working-class nor typically middle-class, are sometimes called 'plebeians'. In London, a largely pre-industrial city, a significant percentage of the population still inhabited this frontier zone. How, in class terms, are we to describe groups such as lodging-house keepers, landladies, publicans, street vendors, and superior domestic servants such as governesses and ladies' companions? These could be manual workers who had risen in the world or, equally, they could be middle-class men and women down on their luck.

Thus the middle class shaded off at one end into the working class. But at the other end middle class and aristocracy were beginning to intermingle. Sharing the same public-school education and the values which it imparted, the two groups were also interlinked by marriage: by the end of the century no fewer than 24 per cent of leading City of London bankers had aristocratic fathers-in-law.[62] The prejudice within landed society against trade and industry was still strong, but 'gentlemen' could enter banking or one of the established professions without loss of caste, particularly the law (Lord Robert Cecil and Alfred Lyttleton both took this path). Admittedly, the links between landed society

---

[62] Y. Cassis, 'Bankers in English Society in the Late Nineteenth Century', *Economic History Review*, 28 (1985), 213–14, 218.

and the Bar had weakened in the course of the nineteenth century; all the same, by 1885 21 per cent of all practising barristers were the sons of landowners or rural gentry.[63]

Many businessmen were attracted by the aristocratic way of life: weekending at country houses, participating in field sports, and even buying landed estates. 'Blackburn's large employers consumed increasingly conspicuously, displaying the paraphernalia of matching horses, carriages and liveried servants, and later turning their stables over to Royces and Daimlers.'[64] Some historians have argued that this process of 'gentrification' led to a 'haemorrhaging of talent' from business life, so contributing to Britain's economic 'decline'.[65]

However, it is noticeable that most businessmen who aspired to gentility chose to rent a country house, not to buy one, and that those who did purchase invariably opted for the residence and its surrounding park, rather than acquiring a full-blown estate. As Thompson puts it, this was 'a hatchet job on the traditional aristocratic lifestyle, slicing out the agreeable and pleasurable elements and ignoring the responsibilities for tenants and labourers, and for local administration, that had gone with them'.[66] In any case, with a comprehensive and efficient transport system at their disposal, businessmen who chose to devote their weekends to field sports and country-house entertaining had no need to neglect their work—indeed, a leisure activity such as hunting could facilitate business contacts between, say, bankers and their aristocratic clients.[67]

On the other hand, such social intermingling was bound to have political consequences, indicating, as it did, the emergence of a new 'ruling class', with big landowners coexisting harmoniously with at least a sizeable section of wealthy capitalists, as the former became more entrepreneurial[68] and the latter embraced the delights of an upper-class lifestyle. Contemporaries were acknowledging this development when they talked (often disapprovingly) about the rise of a 'plutocracy'.

To deny the reality of class because there were these difficulties of definition and demarcation would be perverse. But what they do show is that 'class' was not something 'given', a situation into which people were born and irrevocably tied by their economic occupation and circumstances. On the contrary, social position in Victorian England could be as much determined by how people behaved as by the scale and source of their income. Thus working-class

---

[63] D. Duman, *The English and Colonial Bars in the Nineteenth Century* (Beckenham, 1983), 17.

[64] J. K. Walton, *Lancashire: A Social History 1558–1939* (Manchester, 1987), 234–5.

[65] For a critical review of this literature, see F. M. L. Thompson, *Gentrification and the Enterprise Culture: Britain 1780–1980* (Oxford, 2001).

[66] Thompson, *Respectable Society*, 164.

[67] J. Harris and P. Thane, 'British and European Bankers, 1880–1914: An "Aristocratic Bourgeoisie"?', in P. Thane, G. Crossick, and R. Floud (eds.), *The Power of the Past* (London, 1984), 227.

[68] See Ch. 7.

'respectability', that hallmark of social identity (indicating moderation in drinking, providence, self-control, and commitment to domesticity), was not solely found among 'labour aristocrats': it could be achieved, with varying degrees of effort, by all working men and women.[69] Was the front door-step regularly scrubbed or the home left in a state of scruffiness? Would the husband observe strict monogamy, or be tempted by the delights of a less self-restrained existence? More fundamentally still, was the church or the pub the main centre of his associational life?

4. RELIGION AND CULTURE

For all but the very poor, religion probably formed the main cultural determinant of social identity, in complex ways cutting through both middle class and working class. To attach oneself to a place of worship of any kind denoted a wider social commitment. It also mattered what were one's denominational affiliations.[70]

Looking back on his boyhood in Norwich in the 1870s, the journalist H. W. Massingham recalled that 'society was divided into two compartments— Church and Chapel', each section living apart and regarding the other 'with no favourable eyes'. In the main, wrote Massingham, 'the Established Church founded itself on the old-established industries of banking, brewing, wine-selling, and the still more ancient pursuit, which largely prevailed in the Cathedral Close, of doing nothing at all'. On the other hand there was Dissent, which, in Massingham's view, 'had a hold on the shop-keeping class, and in return for being slightly looked down on in this world, cherished rather confident opinions of its prospects in the next, coupled with serious doubts as to the Anglican position there'.[71] There was little social intercourse between the two communities.

In cities with large Irish settlements, such as Liverpool or the East End of London, Roman Catholicism disturbed this delicate equilibrium, because the Dissenters sometimes found themselves in alliance with the Catholics and sometimes in fierce opposition to them. Norwich, however, was more typical of English cities in having a simple polarity between Church and Chapel, Anglicanism and Dissent: a polarity which divided the respectable citizenry

[69] Thompson argues that respectability was a set of values 'derived from past customs and present responses to living and working conditions, rather than ... being either imitative or imposed from outside or above' (*Respectable Society*, 355).

[70] The following discussion applies only to England, and to a lesser extent to Wales: the ecclesiastical structure in Scotland, where the established church was Presbyterian, was quite different—as, of course, was Ireland.

[71] 'Norwich As I Remember It', in H. J. Massingham (ed.), *A Selection from the Writings of H. W. Massingham* (London, 1925), 326–7.

along social, cultural, and political, as well as denominational, lines—although the very poor were largely detached from both camps.

How far did these sectarian divisions mirror those of social class? In general, chapel made a greater appeal to the middling ranks of society, while the Church of England drew more heavily upon both ends of the spectrum. Earlier in the century most Nonconformists had been concentrated in low-status occupations, and to a lesser extent this remained the case. Very few Nonconformists were landowners, and they were scantily represented in the prestigious professions; but many were 'in trade'—as bankers, merchants, and industrialists. Being frugal, hard-working, and single-minded, many had gone on to amass large fortunes. The Quakers in particular were famous for their entrepreneurial acumen and their wealth: one thinks of the Gurneys, who were bankers, the Frys and the Rowntrees, cocoa and chocolate manufacturers, and the Pease dynasty in the North-East, with interests both in banking and the iron trades (the professional football team, Darlington, a town dominated in the late nineteenth century by the Pease dynasty, is known to this day as the Quakers). The Congregationalists, too, contained some very wealthy laymen: for example, the Colmans in Norwich, the Bainses in Leeds, or William Lever in Cheshire.

But wealth was not the same as status, and here Nonconformists were still at a disadvantage. In higher education, it is true, the worst kinds of discrimination had recently ended. In Oxford and Cambridge universities, richly endowed and enjoying considerable political influence and social prestige, undergraduates no longer had to swear allegiance to the Thirty-Nine Articles after 1856; religious tests for teaching fellowships were similarly abolished by legislation in 1871; and celibacy for fellows generally ended in the 1870s and 1880s. Even so, the whole atmosphere of the ancient universities remained permeated by Anglican values.

There was a similar problem at the level of secondary education, revolving around the public schools, dominated by the nine Clarendon schools:[72] Eton, Harrow, Rugby, Winchester, Westminster, Shrewsbury, Charterhouse, St Paul's, and Merchant Taylors. The last two were day schools, the others boarding establishments, but all rested on ancient foundations, which in some cases went back to the fifteenth century. Rivalling them in prestige were a number of more recent schools of a similar social and educational type, founded in two waves, some in the 1840s (e.g. Wellington and Cheltenham), some in the 1860s (e.g. Clifton). Aping the ethos and largely following the curriculum of these prestigious schools were many humbler institutions,

---

[72] So called because they had been investigated by the Royal Commission chaired by Lord Clarendon in 1864.

bringing the total number up to at least 100 by the end of the century.[73] All but a handful of public schools had close ties with the Church of England: their headmasters were eminent Anglican clergymen—often en route to a deanery or a bishopric. Each had a different social catchment area: Eton, for example, was the most aristocratic, while Winchester had strong links with the prestigious professions.

Public-school costs in the late nineteenth century were high, especially in the more famous boarding schools: in Harrow the basic annual fees ranged between £143 and £188, depending on which house a pupil joined. Even the smaller public schools were too expensive for any working-class, or even lower-middle-class, child. Indeed, steps were deliberately taken in the course of the century to end the arrangements whereby clever boys from the locality could be helped into the older endowed schools. By contrast, most members of the middle class could have afforded some kind of public-school education for their sons, if they were prepared to make sacrifices and economize. It was possible in many schools for pupils to take up lodgings in the nearby town—these were the so-called oppidans. In other schools, such as Cheltenham and Bedford, parents sometimes moved to the neighbourhood so that their children could attend as day pupils. Moreover, genteel but impoverished parents were often helped by kindly relatives over the burden of school fees.

Thus not all public-school pupils, even in the great Clarendon schools, came from rich backgrounds. Many were the sons of country parsons and of retired military officers whose pecuniary circumstances were decidedly modest.[74] It is glib to suppose that because those who gravitated to important positions (Anglican bishops, senior civil servants, and the like) had attended a public school, they must have come from wealthy and privileged backgrounds. Some parents of these elite personages died without their estate being recorded in probate—in other words, they left almost no money at all. Moreover, several had come from rather ordinary backgrounds; for example, the fathers of Victorian and early twentieth-century archbishops of Canterbury included an impoverished landowner, a n'er-do-well Birmingham chemical manufacturer, and a small Edinburgh merchant.[75]

But not all Dissenters *wanted* their sons to attend a public school, preferring to send them to one of the educational establishments which their communities had created. In fact, many of the Dissenting schools offered a very good education, with a broader curriculum than was to be found in the public schools, which still had a heavy bias towards the classics and put the idea of

---

[73] In that year 100 schools attended the Headmasters' Conference.

[74] W. D. Rubinstein, 'Education and the Social Origins of British Elites', *Past & Present*, 112 (1986), 163–207.

[75] Namely, Tait, Benson, and Randall Davidson (Rubinstein, 'Education and Social Elites', 177).

a 'liberal education' a long way ahead of vocational training.[76] There was thus a rich profusion of proprietary schools purveying an alternative secondary education, centred on English, mathematics, modern languages, and science, and even, in some schools, including subjects such as bookkeeping. But these institutions had difficulty in matching the ancient Anglican foundations in terms of inherited wealth and prestige. Here was a grievance which rankled.

But a choice existed. Just as the affluent could choose whether to continue worshipping at chapel or else switch over to the Established Church, they could also choose whether or not to send their sons to a public school of the traditional type or to go for a quite different kind of secondary education. Some wealthy businessmen, such as the textile manufacturer Hugh Mason, could easily have afforded a public-school education for their children, but would not countenance the idea of sending them to institutions which held values they regarded as alien: either because, as loyal Dissenters, they disapproved of the Anglican ethos, or because they had a considered preference for a more 'practical' kind of education; or indeed, for both these reasons. This obduracy, however, was crumbling: amongst prominent Dissenting manufacturers, Jeremiah Colman, George Cadbury, G. A. Wills, Joseph Chamberlain, and William Lever all consented to their sons attending either Oxford or Cambridge University, the last two also sending them to a big public school (Rugby and Eton, respectively).

Denominational rivalries counted for less in working-class education or in working-class life. Yet, despite widespread religious indifference among the urban poor, Christianity was far from being primarily a 'middle-class' concern: indeed, it may well be that working men and women, predominantly from the skilled and semi-skilled strata, still formed the majority of every Christian denomination.[77] In particular, most Irish immigrants remained remarkably loyal to the Roman Catholic Church (an exception to the general rule that the unskilled were those least connected with organized religion) and patronized their own Catholic schools.[78] And in Lancashire the Church of England had earlier undergone a revival which had resulted in the foundation of many Anglican schools, which continued to enjoy high levels of working-class support.

[76] In Rugby in the 1860s, 17 out of 22 hours were devoted to classics, three to maths, two to modern languages or science (W. J. Reader, *At Duty's Call: A Study in Obsolete Patriotism* (Manchester, 1988), 94).

[77] C. G. Brown, *The Death of Christian Britain* (London, 2001), 154–5.

[78] About 60% of Catholics in England regularly attended mass, but perhaps the percentage fell as low as 20% in some working-class districts, and with more women than men (S. Fielding, *Class and Ethnicity: Irish Catholics in England, 1880–1939* (Buckingham, 1993), 48–9). Worries about 'leakage' in 'god-less' England led in October 1884 to the establishment in October 1884 of the Catholic Truth Society, which by 1890 enjoyed the blessing of the hierarchy and of the Vatican.

But the greatest density of working-class worshippers was to be found in Nonconformity. The Primitive Methodists, for example, recruited strongly among the coalminers of the North-East and the farm labourers of Norfolk. Most of the other Dissenting communities, some more successfully than others, similarly attracted working men and women. Thus the Baptists performed well in that frontier zone where the skilled working class met the lower middle class: from an analysis of the marriage registers in Bethnal Green, it appears that 55.3 per cent of Baptist husbands were manual workers, as against 24 per cent from clerical occupations. Congregationalism generally appealed to those of greater education and higher social status: even so, in Bethnal Green 38.9 per cent of Congregationalist husbands were manual workers.[79] In the various Dissenting chapels of Lambeth, as elsewhere, shopkeepers and clerks tended to predominate, but membership 'usually sprawled uncomfortably across significant class barriers'.[80]

This had wider social consequences, in that for working men a commitment to chapel signified far more than an acceptance of a particular creed. It also involved an adoption of a way of life which could cut them off from many of their friends, workmates, and neighbours. For example, because of the close ties between Nonconformity and temperance, late Victorian working-class chapelgoers were detached from many of the rituals of everyday life which centred on alcohol (middle-class men could face comparable embarrassments). There was a similar taboo surrounding all kinds of gambling. Perhaps it was for this reason that many working-class converts adopted a militant Evangelicalism which loudly proclaimed 'the blood of the Lamb'.[81] In this way religion bound together middling social groups across the frontiers of class, uniting them in a culture of 'respectability' equally hostile to the cultural pretensions of 'polite society' and the roughnesses of speech and behaviour commonly found amongst sections of the poor.

Late Victorian England was an overwhelmingly Christian country, in that it faced few coherent ideological challenges. Yet the Christian religion was also a source of social and ideological discord. There were two fundamental divisions. The first was that between Protestantism and Roman Catholicism. A deep hatred of Catholic 'superstition' and 'bigotry' (in many areas difficult to disentangle from dislike of the Irish) could easily boil over into disorder. As late as 1897 the Manchester Watch Committee tried to stop Joseph Slattery, author of *Secrets of Romish Priests Exposed*, from addressing a meeting because it feared a riot;[82] and in 1909 serious sectarian disturbances rocked Liverpool,

---

[79] H. McLeod, *Class and Religion in the Late Victorian City* (London, 1974), 33.

[80] J. Cox, *The English Churches in a Secular Society: Lambeth, 1870–1930* (Oxford, 1982), 131.

[81] McLeod, *Class and Religion*, 68–72.

[82] Fielding, *Class and Ethnicity*, 35.

where passions had been aroused by a recent papal encyclical, 'Ne Temere', which banned mixed marriages.

The High Church party within the Church of England also angered Evangelical Protestants, especially after 1894, when its leaders proposed a corporate reunion with the Roman Church. Indeed, 'ritualism' was a bone of contention within the Anglican Church itself. In the 1890s the Liberal leader William Vernon Harcourt took up a campaign against what he called 'lawlessness in the national church', and John Kensit, head of the Protestant Truth Society, achieved notoriety by starting brawls in Anglican churches where 'popish' rituals were conducted—before (or so legend has it) he was eventually killed, in 1901, by a fanatic wielding an iron bar.[83]

The second (and more fundamental) divide was that between Church and Chapel, a division that, in Augustine Birrell's words, ran through the country like 'Offa's Dyke'. The Nonconformists were admittedly a diverse group. The Wesleyan Methodists (with over 600,000 adherents) formed the largest sect, but, having only broken with the Church of England reluctantly in the 1780s, they had never whole-heartedly identified themselves with other Nonconformists, except at times of short-lived excitement. The backbone of Nonconformity comprised 'Old Dissent' (Presbyterians, Baptists, and Congregationalists), who traced their origins back to the seventeenth century. So did the Quakers and the Unitarians, though the latter were too 'peculiar' in their beliefs and practices to be accepted without reservation into the main body of Nonconformity. Indeed, in many respects the Nonconformists were too disunited for their own good, exhibiting what one historian has called the 'riotous pluralism of Victorian religion'.[84]

However, holding the sects loosely together was a sentiment of grievance against the privileges still enjoyed by the Established Church, which found expression in what one historian has called a search for 'dignity', another a display of 'effortless inferiority'.[85] Admittedly, as the various disabilities from which Dissenters had once suffered were gradually removed and as wealthy Nonconformists rose in the world, Nonconformity lost some of its former crusading fervour. The evolution of 'Dissenters' into the more mild-sounding 'Free Churchmen' is undoubtedly connected with these social changes. An improved education, causing many Dissenters to become 'bored' with Chapel, may also have eroded their sense of being a people apart.[86] In particular, the

[83] He probably died of pneumonia and meningitis (P. J. Waller, *Democracy and Sectarianism: A Political and Social History of Liverpool, 1868–1939* (Liverpool, 1981), 192–3).

[84] Harris, *Private Lives*, 167.

[85] See Ch. 4. See C. Binfield, *So Down to Prayers: Studies in English Nonconformity 1780–1920* (London, 1977), and J. Munson, *The Nonconformists: In Search of a Lost Culture* (1991).

[86] Cox, *English Churches in Secular Society*, 139–40.

President of the United Free Churches complained that, since the removal of the University Tests, 'an incessant stream of the sons of our wealthy laymen feeds the ranks of the Anglican Church, through having been educated at Oxford and Cambridge'.[87]

By the 1890s there were even signs of an incipient ecumenicalism in the tendency of different Christian denominations to draw together in the promotion of civic good works, a development which in Bristol embraced Anglicans, Quakers, Congregationalists, Baptists, Wesleyans, and even Roman Catholics. Indeed, the restoration and extension of Bristol Cathedral attracted hefty subscriptions, not just from Anglicans, but also from wealthy Dissenters such as Sir Edward Wills, the tobacco manufacturer (a Congregationalist), and Lewis Fry, from the famous Quaker family.[88] Socially and culturally, a gulf was opening up between 'mainstream Christianity' and those uncompromisingly evangelical sects which cared little for 'progress': the Bible Christians, the Methodist New Connexion, the Christian Brethren, and, in particular, the recently founded Salvation Army, all of whose supporters tended to come from the ranks of the socially marginalized.[89] Conversely, the wealthy increasingly participated in 'a common social round, reinforced by ties of friendship and marriage', while a distinctive urban culture, centred on gentlemen's clubs, debating societies, and concert halls, was drawing together the well-to-do from different sects and parties: significantly, many clubs deliberately set out to discourage the airing of controversial religious and political issues.[90]

Yet even when wealthy Nonconformist laymen had secured full social acceptance within their own localities, they might nevertheless feel themselves disadvantaged on a national stage.[91] For historic sectarian animosities still existed just beneath the surface, and the uproar sparked off by the 1902 Education Act[92] did a great deal to revive a militant spirit among Dissenters just when there were signs that it was in abeyance. Here is a good example of a society being united by its internal divisions: religious discord helping to push into the background the latent resentment between manual and white-collar workers and between rich and poor which might otherwise have torn society asunder.

---

[87] J. Munson, *The Nonconformists: In Search of a Lost Culture* (London, 1991), 84. Mansfield College was opened in Oxford in 1889 to train graduates for the Congregationalist ministry.
[88] H. E. Meller, *Leisure and the Changing City, 1870–1914* (London, 1976), 78–80.
[89] Ibid. 84.
[90] Walton, *Lancashire*, 234; Gunn, *Culture and the Victorian Middle Class*, 24, 98.
[91] H. Macleod, *Religion and Society in England, 1850–1914* (Basingstoke, 1996), 110.
[92] See Ch. 10.

5. THE RISE OF MASS SOCIETY

However, religion was under threat from the spread of commercialized leisure and its secular values, which in turn reflected something more fundamental still: the emergence of a 'mass' society, in which social identities were being reconfigured by new patterns of consumption.

This came about because, for the first time since the dawn of industrialization, rising real wages[93] gave large swathes of the working-class community a surplus which could be spent on other than bare necessities—very small sums individually but, in aggregate, forming a mass market that was eminently worth cultivating by a new class of entrepreneurial retailer.

The so-called 'retail revolution' was both cause and consequence of this relative improvement in living standards. Cheap imported foodstuffs brought about changes in the way less affluent consumers shopped. Whereas prior to 1870 fixed-premise shops dealt mainly in luxury goods and in the relatively high-priced commodities in which grocers specialised (teas, sugars, spices, etc.), with most basic items being bought in markets, the late 1870s saw the emergence of a new kind of retail outlet, the 'multiples', such as Liptons and Home and Colonial, which, through bulk purchases and the resultant economies of scale, were able to undersell their more traditional rivals.

This was not a total innovation, since the Co-operative Movement, with its own wholesale stores, had pioneered this organizational structure at least ten years earlier. The Co-operative Movement was based upon the principle of mutuality, and appealed to the idealism, as well as the self-interest, of the stable working class, particularly in the factory towns of the North. The 'multiples' carried none of this ideological baggage: they were profit-making bodies, from first to last. But they fruitfully copied some of the retailing principles earlier associated with the Co-operative: for example, they sold goods at fixed price for cash only (eschewing the credit offered by little corner shops), which simplified the process of selling (staff did not have to make delicate decisions about who was, and who was not, creditworthy), enabling the organization to expand through the employment of cheap, largely unskilled sales assistants. Vertical integration (the amalgamation under one organization of production, wholesaling, and retailing) was another innovation of the Co-operatives which the 'multiples' later copied: Lipton's, for example, owned the tea estates in Ceylon from which, after processing and packing, the tea could be sold in identically branded parcels in any of their retail stores. The benefits which this development brought to the consumer were immediate and dramatic: when Lipton

---

[93] See Ch. 6.

entered the tea market in 1889, tea was selling in grocers' shops at between 3*s.*
and 4*s.* per pound: Lipton slashed the price to between 1*s.* 2*d.* and 1*s.* 9*d.*[94]

The 1880s was the decade which saw the most rapid expansion in multiple
retailing, with some signs of a slowdown by the late 1890s. The reasons for the
expansion are complex. A growth of demand obviously forms part of the
explanation. The need to achieve a quick 'put-through' of highly perishable
commodities (Lipton's had originally confined themselves to dairy produce)
also put a premium on this kind of business organization. Significant, too, was
the fact that in the 1880s more traditional retailers started off with a prejudice
against stocking some of the new products coming to market (imported frozen
meat, margarine, a wide range of ready-made condiments, etc.), a prejudice
which created a niche which the newcomers were quick to fill.

The retailing revolution began in the food trade, but soon spread to other
areas, such as boots and shoes (Freeman, Hardy, and Willis), pharmaceuticals
(Boots), and bespoke tailoring (Montague Burton). Singer's Sewing Machine
shops were established to sell a new product which its manufacturers could not
readily place except through their own retail outlets. All these organizations
relied upon a few basic principles: concentration on a relatively small range of
goods, which were mainly pre-packaged and priced (allowing for rapid sales),
the prohibition of credit, and heavy advertising. High quality was not what was
on offer—for this, discerning and affluent customers could go to more expensive shops; instead, the multiples strove for cheapness and reliability, to be
achieved through standardization.

Lipton's, for example, started off modestly, with a single shop in Glasgow:
by 1898 there were some 250 more-or-less identical shops the length and
breadth of the United Kingdom. This 'massification' led in time (not all at
once) to the ironing-out of regional variations: the food-and-drinks industry,
for example, would suffer in its profits if a product needed to be varied to meet
the differing tastes of different regions.[95] Similarly with the footwear worn by
working-class males: in 1886 some regions favoured shoes, others boots, and
others clogs, just as in some areas pipe tobacco was more popular than
cigarettes or snuff. By 1914 these regional variations were much less pronounced.

The department stores, the origins of which can be traced further back into
the nineteenth century, also expanded rapidly—mostly out of grocery shops
(Harrods) or drapery establishments (Derry and Toms). Selfridges in London
was the first purpose-built store of this kind: it was opened, with a great
fanfare, by the American entrepreneur of that name in 1909. Here the principle

---

[94] P. Mathias, *Retailing Revolution* (London, 1967), 101.

[95] However, some of the early 'multiples' were confined to one region: see W. Hamish Fraser, *The
Coming of the Mass Market 1850–1914* (London, 1981), 111–12.

was in some respects the opposite of that underlying the multiples: its supply of an array of very different goods under one roof formed the main attraction, allied with the eye-catching displays which encouraged impulse buying. But, again, the department stores had a strict policy of no credit and fixed-price labelling—the latter serving the purpose of allowing upwardly mobile but unsophisticated customers to look at household goods of which they had had no previous experience to find out whether they could afford them—without having to ask and risk making fools of themselves. As Lady Jeune noted in 1896: 'We go to purchase something we want; but when we get to our shop there are so many more things that we never thought of till they presented their obtrusive fascination.'[96] Indeed, shopping in these comfortable and luxurious stores was becoming for many people 'a pastime and a pleasure', a social event which was looked upon as a 'treat' and 'a holiday occasion'.[97]

The burgeoning of the department stores, not just in London but in all large cities (Lewis's in Liverpool, Manchester, and Birmingham, for example), was only possible thanks to improved urban transport systems which drew in customers from over a wide area—though mail-order purchasing was now becoming possible for those beyond their physical reach. It also gives some evidence of the spread of affluence to new social groups (including the emergence of an expanded 'lower middle class' of clerks, commercial travellers, and shop assistants), as well as the opening out of 'space' for women. The new goods on offer included pianos, often sold on a kind of hire-purchase system ('the Three Year System'), which established itself long before its legality was confirmed by the outcome of the Helby–Matthews case of 1895. By 1910 payments of less than 10s. a month without deposit, spread over a far longer period, sufficed to acquire one of these prestigious objects.[98]

Co-operative stores, 'multiples', and department stores did not, of course, displace the traditional corner shop: between them the former accounted for over one-tenth of total retail trade in 1900, 16.5 per cent in 1910.[99] But even small shops usually carried a wide range of branded goods that were available from one end of the country to the other, leading to a greater homogeneity of taste.

Accompanying all these changes, and the precondition for several of them, was an expanding press, which followed broadly the same path as the other mass consumer-goods industries. Technical improvements (the rotary press,

---

[96] J. Walkowitz, *City of Dreadful Delight: Narratives of Sexual Danger in Late-Victorian London* (1992), 49.

[97] F. W. Burgess, *The Practical Retail Draper* (1912), ii. 169, cited in C. Breward, *The Hidden Consumer: Masculinities, Fashion and City Life 1860–1914* (Manchester, 1999), 128.

[98] C. Ehrlich, *The Piano: A History* (Oxford, 1990, new edn.), 98–104.

[99] J. B. Jefferys, *Retail Trading in Britain, 1850–1950* (Cambridge, 1954), 30.

and then the Linotype typesetter, widely used in the 1890s) raised hourly printing rate to ten times that of a hand compositor, and the use of cheaper newsprint, made from 1880s onwards from wood pulp rather than rag or esparto, meant that newspapers were becoming more capital-intensive—no newspaper before 1885 had called upon capital of more than £62,000.[100] This fuelled the quest for high circulations: the heavy costs of installing the new machinery would be more than repaid once circulation passed a high break-even point, but otherwise disaster loomed.

Along with the decline of illiteracy,[101] more consumers now had the time and inclination to buy daily newspapers (though before 1914 most working-class families confined themselves to a 'Sunday'). A new breed of entrepreneur stepped in to exploit these market opportunities. George Newnes, inventor of the weekly magazine *Tit-Bits* (launched in 1880), was followed by Alfred Harmsworth, who copied the format with *Answers to Correspondents*. Out of the profits generated by this, and a wide range of light-hearted magazines (some designed for women), children's comics, and so on, Harmsworth launched his own national newspaper, the *Daily Mail*, in 1896. This newspaper was quite conservative in its format: the front page was initially covered in small ads, a practice not changed until 1902. However, the *Mail* broke new ground by selling for a halfpenny, whereas most established daily papers cost a penny, with *The Times* priced at threepence. Other established papers were obliged to drop their own prices to stay competitive, while other new titles appeared in imitation, among them Pearson's *Daily Express*, founded in 1900, which daringly printed news on its front page. Following Harmsworth's lead, papers dropped the column rule, allowing advertisements and illustrations to dominate the layout.[102]

In fact, this price-cutting was only possible because most popular newspapers now sold at below cost price, the gap being bridged by advertising revenue, which became essential to their commercial viability as never before. Harmsworth realized the importance of this, publishing his circulation figures over the *Mail*'s masthead, and inviting his competitors to follow suit. In fact, the *Mail* had quickly built up a circulation by the end of the century of nearly 1 million copies daily (a figure inflated by the war-induced boom), falling back by 1913 to just over three-quarters of a million—still far ahead of staider titles such as the *Daily News*, which was selling about 375,000 copies, and *The Times*, with a mere 45,227.

As in other aspects of the 'Retail Revolution', newspapers did much to create a national market, within which regional subcultures assumed less importance.

[100] A. J. Lee, *The Origins of the Popular Press in England 1855–1914* (London, 1976), 81.

[101] D. Vincent, *Literacy and Popular Culture: England 1750–1914* (Cambridge, 1989).

[102] R. Williams, *The Long Revolution* (Harmondsworth, 1965), 200.

The technological capacity of the new printing presses, allied to good communications, made it possible for the London dailies to reach nearly all parts of Great Britain by midday at the latest. Some provincial titles, it is true, had an influence which extended beyond their locality, such as C. P. Scott's *Manchester Guardian*, whose circulation figure never exceeded 50,000 before 1914. But the local press, an important focus of identity, was in process of decline: peaking at 171 in 1900, the number of provincial newspapers had dropped to 121 by 1910.[103]

The 'Retail Revolution', with which the development of the popular press was so closely entwined, also meant that people became, at least to some extent, defined by their role as consumers, not as producers. And this, in turn, encouraged new modes of social perception, not least through the agency of advertising, a major business in its own right, employing about 100,000 people and perhaps accounting for 0.55 per cent of GDP by the Edwardian years.[104] Once thought vulgar and fraudulent, 'ads' now proliferated in the high-class journals as well as in the popular press, promoting a bewildering array of foodstuffs and consumer goods, including new inventions which ranged from waterproofing and disinfectants to desiccated soups. Even luxury goods often carried the message that luxury was affordable and accessible. Advertisers thus peddled fantasies quite as much as they addressed material needs, seeking to evoke an imaginary 'community of spenders'—shoppers of the realm unite![105] In this way they helped to link different parts of the country and to forge new kinds of allegiance which often cut across the boundaries of both class and locality.

But was this a healthy phenomenon? Where once the educated had expressed anxieties about 'crowds' and 'mobs', they now talked, with only slightly less apprehension, about the 'masses' and the 'multitude'. 'When the historian of the future speaks of the past century as a Democratic century,' wrote Wells, 'he will have in mind, more than anything else, the unprecedented fact that we seemed to do everything in heaps.'[106]

6. STATUS HIERARCHIES

In some ways such fears of the 'massification' of society were built upon misunderstanding and delusion. In reality, far from coagulating into undifferentiated lumps, the English people retained a highly developed sense of status.

---

[103] Lee, *Popular Press*, 286–7.

[104] T. R. Nevett, *Advertising in Britain: A History* (London, 1982), 70–1.

[105] L. A. Loeb, *Consuming Angels: Advertising and Victorian Women* (Oxford and New York, 1994), 5, 7, 166, 179.

[106] Wells, *Anticipations*, 16.

Shopping, for example, could divide as well as unite the consuming public. Thus some department stores went to considerable lengths to keep working-class customers in their place by opening up bargain basements that could be reached without entering the main store, which was patrolled by intimidating shopwalkers. Working-class housewives, for their part, preferred to stick to shops where they felt at home: 'co-ops', corner shops, and chain stores. Subtle distinctions of status also divided each class internally. Middle-class shoppers, for example, understood that there was a hierarchy of department stores, with Harrods, Whiteley, and Debenham & Freebody at the top, Selfridge's at the bottom.[107]

Working-class life similarly involved minute gradations between different social groups, defined by dress, accent, and manners. Robert Roberts, from the vantage-point of his Salford corner shop, observed that a 'class war' was taking place in his working-class neighbourhood, one in which residents ranked one another according to a highly elaborate social code.[108] Differing patterns of consumption made a major contribution to this kind of working-class stratification, with such items of conspicuous expenditure as fob watches, 'Sunday best' clothes, and artificial flowers under the ubiquitous glass shade in the front parlour all testifying to their owner's high place in the social pecking-order.[109]

Employers sometimes deliberately fostered such elaborate stratification: for example, the railway companies and the Post Office constructed a long promotion ladder for their staff, with innumerable gradations of ranks, rigidly defined, each with its own uniform, status, and salary. But working men and women readily internalized these distinctions—most notably in domestic service, where privileged employees such as butlers and chefs would hardly treat a humble kitchen-maid as an equal. This 'hierarchical vision of British society' may also have been encouraged by the contemporary vogue for antiquarian trappings, such as 'town halls ornamented with statues of historic figures and local worthies, maces, regalia and armorial bearings'.[110]

In no field of late Victorian and Edwardian social life was this obsession with status distinctions so apparent as in sport. We have seen how professional football could recapture, within an urban setting, something of the old intimacy of village life—'a sense of belonging and a sense of pride'.[111] In the English countryside field sports had traditionally performed a similar role. Boxing, too, often united the social classes, though in more complex ways—drawing much

---

[107] J. Benson, *The Rise of Consumer Society in Britain, 1880–1980* (Harlow, 1994), 192, 210–11, 218.
[108] R. Roberts, *The Classic Slum: Salford Life in the First Quarter of the Century* (Manchester, 1971).
[109] P. Johnson, 'Conspicuous Consumption and Working-Class Culture in Late Victorian and Edwardian Britain', *Transactions of the Royal Historical Society*, 5th ser., 38 (1988), 27–42.
[110] Cannadine, *Class in Britain*, 122, 125.
[111] Holt, *Sport*, 154.

of its support from 'toffs' and 'roughs', while being viewed with suspicion by respectable folk from the middling strata.[112]

In general, however, the main effect of sport was to solidify status distinctions. Thus tennis and golf, both rapidly expanding after 1886, enjoyed the devoted support of the aristocratic young, though the rapid development of golf-clubs and of tennis courts shows that their popularity was spreading throughout suburbia; but, unsurprisingly, only one-eighth of golf-club directors before 1914 came from white-collar or skilled artisan backgrounds, and membership criteria were invariably set so as to exclude 'undesirable' types—in which category Jews often figured.[113] Some sports bifurcated socially—the 'crown green' bowling of northern England, with its democratic ethos, developed along quite distinct lines from the southern game of bowls, which was more 'genteel', just as there was a social divide between the two rugby football codes.[114] Other pastimes, such as yachting and motoring, were, by their very nature, socially exclusive because expensive.

The most status-ridden sport of all was cricket. Though Eton versus Harrow matches attracted crowds of about 15,000, tickets were priced specifically to exclude those who merely enjoyed watching the game.[115] Participants in first-class cricket were categorized as either 'gentlemen' (amateurs) or 'players' (professionals), a distinction which was maintained until as late as the 1960s by means of devices such as having the cricketers' names designated differently on the scorecard. Moreover, in the late Victorian period 'gentlemen' mainly batted, while the socially inferior 'players' specialized in the sweatier business of bowling. The servility of professional cricketers also involved their use of separate entrances and an obligation to carry out a range of menial tasks. 'When Kent played Surrey in 1890 a fine spread was laid on for the gentlemen but the professionals "were left to shift for themselves, and thought themselves lucky to get a bit of bread and cheese".'[116]

The term 'amateur' came into general currency in the 1880s, when it acquired a complex set of social meanings. Those who could afford to play the game for love were deemed superior to those who relied on it for their living, a judgement which was legitimized, not just by snobbery, but also by the assumption that prowess at games suffered if a player tried too hard to succeed. When the Amateur Rowing Association was founded in 1882, its rules excluded those who worked with their hands—the aim probably being that of

---

[112] See Ch. 14.
[113] Holt, *Sport*, 131–4. In some clubs the 'artisans', who helped maintain the links, had their own subordinate position. In Scotland, by contrast, sport was less class-ridden.
[114] See Ch. 14.
[115] Holt, *Sport*, 115. The same was also true of the Varsity rugby match.
[116] Ibid. 290.

preventing full-time boatmen from seizing an 'unfair' advantage. C. B. Fry was
the archetypal late Victorian hero, captaining Oxford University at cricket,
soccer, and athletics and representing England in all three sports with apparently effortless ease, combining these achievements with being an accomplished classical scholar and writer.[117] A studied nonchalance also
characterized the conduct of members of the Leander Club (rowing) and of
the Corinthian Casuals, an amateur football club which eschewed the penalty
kick on the ground that this was a violation of the 'gentlemanly' code.

Some of these status distinctions might seem nothing more than a manifestation of class feeling. In England (though much less so in the rest of Britain)
leadership in nearly all sports rested with aristocrats or, at least, with the
alumni of the big public schools. The Jockey Club remained largely an
aristocratic preserve, as did the higher levels of the MCC, cricket's governing
authority, while the proliferation of old boys' dinners and associations from the
1870 onwards denoted the importance of the 'old school tie'. On the other
hand, mere wealth seldom prevailed.[118] Prosperous provincial businessmen, for
example, had mainly to be content with seats on the boards of soccer and rugby
league clubs—a world shunned by true gentlemen.

7. CONCLUSION

Locality, occupation, class, religious affiliation, and 'mass' society coexisted in
complex ways. The forces of localism were clearly in decline,[119] and this had
implications for religious community, since most churches (especially the
Nonconformist chapels) thrived on face-to-face relationships. Admittedly,
religion necessarily fostered an allegiance to ideals which transcended locality—and indeed nationality. Yet the Congregationalists, otherwise known as
Independents, were, as their title suggests, particularly introspective and place-
bound, while, in Jose Harris's view, all the larger sects tended to remain
geographically 'restricted and localized in their marriages until the late nineteenth century, by which time their sectarian exclusiveness was . . . beginning
to give way to a more class-and-culture view of marriage and more tolerance of
marrying-out'.[120]

Class, as preached by the socialists, was indeed a powerful shaper of wider
social identities. But the creation in 1889 of the Miners Federation of Great

---

[117] Ibid. 99. The same was also true of the varsity rugby match.
[118] Ibid. 114.
[119] See Ch. 4 for the way in which the reorganization of parliamentary constituencies in 1885
weakened municipal identities.
[120] Harris, *Private Lives*, 102–3. Very small sects, like the Quakers and Unitarians, had always been
obliged to look further afield.

Britain, linking together largely autonomous county unions, shows how class consciousness, tinged with sectionalism, could develop alongside deep regional attachments.

In any case, how widespread was adversarial class feeling? Direct contact between people from dramatically contrasting backgrounds sometimes sparked off a 'them and us' attitude, not only among manual workers but also among the professional people who sought to understand them: the philanthropist Helen Bosanquet, in her manual *Rich and Poor* (1896), dramatized the ignorance and misunderstanding bedevilling social relationships, while Mrs Loane, a district nurse, declared her doubt as to whether an equal conversation was *ever* possible across the class barrier.[121]

But it was more common for society to be visualized, in traditional terms, as an elaborate pyramid, a seamless hierarchy of social ranks. Class was also held in check by the older force of religious sectarianism, while simultaneously coming under challenge from commercial developments which opposed to its 'producer' ideology a new 'consumerist' perspective on life. What did all this mean for politics?

---

[121] R. McKibbin, *The Ideologies of Class: Social Relations in Britain 1880–1950* (Oxford, 1990: 1991 edn.), 167–96.

CHAPTER 4

Governance and Politics

1. UNITING THE UNITED KINGDOM

It could not easily be predicted, merely from a knowledge of their background, how late Victorian electors would cast their vote. Would the determining factor be class, occupation, ethnicity, religious denomination, or even (in the case of School Board elections) gender?[1] The outcome invariably depended upon circumstance, context, and the interplay of party rivalries. For parties, with their proud histories and distinctive traditions, could reshape, as well as bolster, their adherents' views of the world: social experiences did not automatically translate into political behaviour.[2]

Political parties were, in turn, circumscribed in how they operated by Britain's unwritten constitution, an amalgam of statutory provisions and precedents which had developed, higgledy-piggledy, over many centuries. To a foreign observer, the 'United Kingdom of Great Britain and Ireland' was indeed a peculiar polity. For, though not a federation, neither was it a unitary state of a recognizably modern kind. True, the British government and the Westminster Parliament had untrammelled sovereignty over the entire national territory. But, for administrative purposes, this territory was split into three distinct 'divisions'—'England and Wales', Scotland, and Ireland—for each of which special legislative, as well as administrative, provisions were commonly made.

Wales, which featured in official statistics as little more than a westward extension of England, owed its subordination to earlier conquests at the hands of the English Crown. As a result, most laws which applied to England also applied to Wales, and vice versa; the Welsh Intermediate Act of 1889 was exceptional in recognizing the distinctiveness of the Principality. It is another

---

[1] Female voters could maximize the chances of female candidates by taking advantage of the 'cumulative vote' system, under which voters had the option in multi-member constituencies of casting all their votes for a single candidate. On women and the local-government franchises, see Ch. 2.

[2] J. Lawrence, 'Class and Gender in the Making of Urban Toryism, 1880–1914', *English Historical Review*, 108 (1993), 629–31.

sign of how administratively intertwined were the affairs of the two nations that the march county of Monmouthshire, which had been annexed by Henry VIII, formed part of England, though ecclesiastically it fell within the diocese of Llandaff.

By contrast, the 1707 Act of Union, which linked the kingdoms of England and Scotland, had left most aspects of Scottish life untouched. North of the Tweed there was a separate state church and educational system, and Scottish law, supervised by the Lord Advocate, operated with little interference from English, Irish, or Welsh MPs. From 1885 onwards there was also a Scottish Office, under a separate Secretary of State, to co-ordinate the various administrative offices housed in Edinburgh.[3] This did not satisfy Scottish Radicals such as Dr G. B. Clark, MP for Caithness-shire, who wanted much greater powers of self-government.[4]

In Ireland national dissatisfaction with 'alien' rule touched much higher levels than in Scotland. The 1800 Act of Union gave the Irish a guaranteed 103 MPs at Westminster, but day-to-day administration was exercised from Dublin Castle by officials working to the orders of the Lord-Lieutenant (or Irish Viceroy), normally a senior Cabinet minister, assisted by a Chief Secretary for Ireland, who sometimes rivalled the Lord-Lieutenant in importance.[5] Ireland had lost its fiscal autonomy in 1825 but in most internal matters it required, even more than Scotland, to be regulated by special legislation. Ireland possessed an armed police force (the Royal Irish Constabulary) and justice was dispensed by stipendiary magistrates—both being deviations from the arrangements that prevailed in the rest of the United Kingdom, but thought necessary to cope with the prevailing social and political turbulence. An imperial metropolis delivering policies to a colonial dependency was how British rule in Ireland was widely seen.[6]

Faced by the bitter protests that this system provoked, Joseph Chamberlain and his Radical allies came up in 1885 with an ingenious plan for appeasing Irish Nationalism, while at the same time reforming local government throughout the United Kingdom in ways likely to facilitate the implementation of their favoured land, fiscal, and educational reforms. Its central idea was the establishment of directly elected 'County Boards', to be supervised and controlled in

---

[3] Initially promoted by Lord Rosebery, though later implemented by a Conservative government.

[4] J. Kendle, *Ireland and the Federal Solution, 1870–1921* (Kingston, Ont., 1989), 67.

[5] Some Irish administrative departments were controlled by the Treasury or by Whitehall, others were separate agencies under the formal direction of the Chief Secretary. On the resulting 'mess', see D. Fitzpatrick, 'Ireland and the Empire', in A. Porter (ed.), *The Oxford History of the British Empire: Volume III: The Nineteenth Century* (Oxford, 1999), 496.

[6] J. Turner, 'Letting Go: The Conservative Party and the End of the Union with Ireland', in A. Grant and K. J. Stringer (eds.), *Uniting the Kingdom?* (London, 1995), 260. The notion of Ireland as a colony was, of course, intensely contentious.

Ireland and Scotland (and perhaps Wales) by an elected 'National Council'. This bold devolutionary scheme would hopefully reconcile national diversity with the supremacy of the Westminster Parliament within a modernized system of local government that was coherent, logical, and based upon the consent of the governed.

However, scarcely had the ink dried on this plan than Gladstone dealt it a *coup de grace* by offering the Irish their own parliament. As a political device for meeting the aspirations of the Irish people, Gladstonian Home Rule may arguably have been well judged. But the 1886 'Government of Ireland Bill' suffered from two serious defects. First, it proposed to exclude the Irish from Westminster but to keep control of customs and excise there—raising the inevitable cry of 'no taxation without representation'. Second, the concessions made to Ireland took almost no account of their implications for other parts of the United Kingdom. With some justification, Gladstone's opponents dismissed his scheme as an unworkable muddle. However, the defeat of Home Rule meant the survival of a status quo that was only slightly less confused— particularly if account is also taken of the multiplicity of institutional arrangements that regulated Britain's relationship with its many overseas territories.[7]

Constitution-mongers saw a tidy way of ending all these complications. Why, they asked, not opt for an out-and-out federalization of the Constitution, which would give each 'nation' of the United Kingdom its own parliament? Westminster would then become an 'Imperial Parliament', with the House of Lords turned into an 'Imperial Senate', to which the self-governing colonies could send representatives. This would, at a stroke, unblock 'congestion' at Westminster, satisfy the aspirations of the constituent nations of the United Kingdom, and unify the Empire. Such was the case fervently argued by the recently founded Imperial Federation League, and, over the next thirty-five years, it made many converts.

Unfortunately, several difficulties stood in the way of the federal project. First, colonies such as Canada and New Zealand disliked the prospect of power returning to an imperial capital situated the other side of the globe. Most English Conservatives, too, felt unenthusiastic about the rhetoric of imperial unity, which threatened to subvert a constitutional settlement with which they were broadly satisfied.[8] By undermining the sovereignty of Parliament, alleged the Unionist lawyer A. V. Dicey, federalism would deprive 'English institutions of their elasticity, their strength and their life', weaken the Executive, and lessen the power of the country to resist foreign attack.[9]

---

[7] On the Empire, see Ch. 8.
[8] Turner, 'Letting Go', 266.
[9] A. V. Dicey, *England's Case Against Home Rule* (London, 1886; 1887 edn.), 196.

Nor was there much backing among the 'lesser nations' of the United Kingdom for federalism, as distinct from devolution (or 'Home-Rule-All-Round'), with which it was often confused. Even Scottish Home Rulers, such as Dr Clark, really wanted no more than a greater say in the running of their country—a reform, they affirmed, which would have the effect of strengthening the Empire of which Scotland constituted an integral part;[10] these modest aspirations were partly satisfied by the establishment in 1894 of the Grand Committee system. While patriotic Scotsmen were lukewarm towards federalism, most Irish Nationalists dismissed it with contempt, because they feared any form that downgraded their own national claims, which they presented as unique.

Moreover, it remained unclear from federalist propaganda whether England would receive its own separate parliament.[11] This was part of a wider problem: 'the English would not alter the Imperial parliament, because it was their domestic parliament also: the Acts of Union of 1707 and 1800 had simply brought Scottish and Irish MPs to Westminster.'[12] Finally, the fact that Britain did not have a written constitution or a codified set of laws would have made the distribution of powers between the various parliaments very difficult to achieve.

The absence of a formal constitution conferred considerable importance on the Crown, the institution which had initially united the English and Scottish kingdoms. The monarchy was also at the centre of the Empire, which it helped bind together through an elaborate system of ceremonies and rituals, including the bestowal of 'honours' on colonial officials, native potentates, and 'dominion' politicians.[13] Indeed, as the self-governing colonies developed into what amounted to independent, allied nations, it was arguably the personal position of the monarch which linked each to the 'mother country' and to other British territories.[14]

As far as the United Kingdom itself was concerned, the Commons played an essential role in maintaining political integrity, though in complicated ways. The 1884 Reform Act had, for the first time, created uniform franchise qualifications across its entire territory.[15] But, in so doing, it set up new tensions between the component nations. For, whereas Scotland's electorate

---

[10] J. E. Kendle, *Federal Britain: A History* (London, 1997), 62.

[11] The same problem bedevilled devolution. The *Radical Programme*, for example, was silent on whether England would be given its own National Council.

[12] H. C. G. Matthew, *Gladstone Vol. 2 1875–98* (Oxford, 1995), 253.

[13] See D. Cannadine, *Ornamentalism: How the British Saw Their Empire* (Harmondsworth, 2001), chs. 7–8.

[14] S. Low, *The Governance of England* (London, 1904), 283. The conferral on Queen Victoria in 1876 of the title of 'Empress of India' also shows the importance to Empire of the institution of monarchy.

[15] The two earlier Reform Bills had put Scotland and Ireland on a quite different basis.

was increased by over 160 per cent and that of England and Wales by over 150 per cent, the number of Irish voters approximately trebled—greatly to Parnell's advantage. Far from leading to a convergence between the different kingdoms, the harmonizing of the franchise accentuated the cultural and national differences between Ireland and mainland Britain, exposing the 'Union' to further strains.

Another bone of contention was the failure to accord the constituent nations equal treatment in the accompanying Redistribution Act. Ireland's loss of population since 1801 meant that it was now over-represented: it contained constituencies as small as Kilkenny Borough, which had a total population of little more than 13,000 and an electorate of only 1,500. Even in 1885, Scottish, Welsh, and English constituencies were, on average, much larger than Ireland's. Over the next three decades this imbalance significantly worsened, as England's population increased while Ireland's continued to decline (see Table 4.1). To put it another way, during the Edwardian period England had one MP for every 66,975 persons, Scotland one for every 63,805, Wales one for every 57,301, and Ireland one for every 44,147. Conservatives argued that, in fairness, England should be allocated another thirty-one MPs, mainly at Ireland's expense.

Despite these tensions, electoral politics helped bind the constituent parts of Great Britain together, particularly through the agency of party. For example, the strength of the Liberal Party in Wales (in the 1885 election the Liberals had won all but four of its thirty seats) helped attach the Principality to England; in Scotland, another area of Liberal strength, the Liberals ran a separate organization but one that was closely linked to its southern neighbour. The Conservative Party's writ ran the length and breadth of Great Britain, even though it was essentially an *English* party that viewed the non-English parts of the United Kingdom instrumentally.[16] It was, however, a revealing indication of Ireland's separateness that Britain's mainland party system had not survived there: during the 1880s the Liberal Party had been almost entirely displaced by the

TABLE 4.1. *Number of electors per constituency, 1885–1918*

	1885–6	1900	1914
England	8,983	10,876	13,561
Wales	8,140	9,811	12,744
Scotland	8,008	9,730	12,328
Ireland	7,304	7,566	6,912
UK	8,635	10,185	12,377

[16] Turner, 'Letting Go', 274.

Irish Nationalists in the Catholic South, while the predominant group in Ulster, the Unionists, enjoyed a semi-autonomous status, though linked to the English Conservative Party.

2. GOVERNANCE

The 'rehabilitation of monarchy' was one of the most startling developments of the late Victorian period. By 1886 the Queen, now 67 years of age, had acquired a respect and popularity which made the widespread republicanism of the 1870s little more than an embarrassing memory. School primers stressed Victoria's role as the embodiment of her people's past and present life, which suggests that her longevity may have made her a symbol of stability in a bewilderingly fluid world.

How much actual power, however, did the Queen still have? The British monarch was the head of the army—no titular position, this, as we will see, since it enabled Victoria, and later her son, to exercise something of a veto over changes in military and naval personnel. In foreign policy, too, the Queen, with her numerous contacts abroad, many of them familial, wielded considerable influence.[17]

In theory the monarch's role remained, as Bagehot had earlier put it, 'to be consulted, to encourage and to warn'. In practice, particularly at times of deadlock and crisis, the institution played a more important part than that. Indeed, Victoria notoriously allowed her dislike of Gladstone's personality and policies to lure her on several occasions into blatant partisanship, particularly during the Home Rule controversies of 1886 and 1892–4.[18] Only with the accession of George V in 1910 did Britain acquire a politically neutral monarchy.

Despite royal 'interferences', executive power was principally exercised through the Queen's ministers, more particularly by the Prime Minister, customarily the leader of the party with a Commons majority. The most important agency of government was the Cabinet, numbering between sixteen and twenty-two members, which always included the principal officers of state. The most highly paid minister (with a salary double that of the Prime Minister) was the Lord Chancellor who, from the Woolsack, acted as leader of the House of Lords, as well as heading the judiciary. The Foreign Secretary, Home Secretary, and Chancellor of the Exchequer, the other key ministers, were invariably drawn from the leadership of the majority party.

---

[17] See Ch. 8.
[18] Thus, in 1892 she publicly announced that she accepted Salisbury's resignation 'with regret' (Matthew, *Gladstone Vol. 2*, 334). Gladstone nobly overlooked this slight and gave loyal support to the Queen over the Royal Grants question.

All ministers were responsible to Parliament, but the relationship between the two Houses was mired in controversy. Radicals argued that the hereditary principle must give way before the onward march of popular accountability. But Lord Salisbury, the Conservative Leader, insisted that the duty of the Upper House was 'to represent the permament as opposed to the passing feelings of the English nation'. From this he deduced that the Lords could legitimately reject any measure sent up to it from the Commons which lacked a popular mandate—a claim which, if vindicated, seemed likely to *increase* its powers.[19]

Before 1906 few of the 550 or so peers[20] regularly took part in the House of Lords' deliberations, which were all but monopolized by about twenty ministers and Opposition frontbenchers. Debates were often perfunctory: the 1890 session contained only eighty-nine business meetings, each lasting on average sixty-two minutes, of which no more than eight continued beyond 7 p.m.[21] Only when the Liberals held office did the Lords even pretend to take their responsibilities as a revising chamber seriously.

The House of Commons, though a much livelier assembly than the Lords (Salisbury privately called the latter 'a paradise of bores'), still had very much the air of a gentleman's club. Indeed, newly elected Members often likened their early experiences to memories of their first days at public school. But the systematic obstructionism of the Irish MPs had forced the Chamber to alter its traditional procedures by introducing the closure in 1882 and the 'guillotine' (or gagging clause) five years later. Indeed, the tendency was for governments to take increasing control of the parliamentary timetable, relying on party to supply them with the disciplined majorities which they needed to carry out the promises and programmes around which general elections increasingly depended—a development which became more pronounced during the 1890s.

If ministers relied upon efficient 'whipping' to carry their legislative measures onto the statute book, they also needed an efficient, disinterested, and honest body of officials to oversee their implementation. By 1886 so much could more or less be taken for granted. An order-in-council of 1870 had seen the belated adoption of the principles of the Northcote–Trevelyan Report, first drafted sixteen years earlier. As a result, civil service posts were supposed to be filled by open competitive examinations (in order to guard against the evils of

---

[19] Speech at Hackney in November 1880: A. Roberts, *Salisbury: Victorian Titan* (London, 1999), 494.

[20] As well as UK peers, 26 bishops and archbishops, and 28 'representative' Irish and 16 'representative' Scottish peers sat in the Lords. The Scottish peers elected their 'representatives' at the start of each new Parliament and at subsequent vacancies: the Irish peers for life, as vacancies occurred.

[21] A. Adonis, *Making Aristocracy Work: The Peerage and the Political System in Britain 1884–1918* (Oxford, 1993), ch. 3, esp. p. 60.

the 'patronage' system), with promotion strictly by merit. There was also to be a two-tier entry system, with the senior officials recruited into an 'Upper Division' institutionally fenced off from a 'Lower Division' which performed routine clerical tasks.

In practice, things never worked out in quite this way. For a start, the strict division between 'mental' and 'manual' labour, upon which the Northcote–Trevelyan Report had been predicated, proved irrelevant to the work of many departments. Moreover, the Foreign Office had successfully pressed for exemption from recruitment by open competitive examinations; the practice of diplomacy, it claimed, required before all else discretion and probity—qualities supposedly found within a select caste whose members all knew one another.[22] Other departments, notably the Board of Education, paid lip service to the principle of competitive exams, but in practice used more traditional methods of filling vacancies as they arose.

Nevertheless, Northcote–Trevelyan, vigorously promoted by Gladstone, gave the British civil service a distinctive flavour. The examinations set by the Civil Service Commissioners were, consciously or unconsciously, devised in ways that encouraged a university-educated elite which had received a liberal education. On the eve of the Great War under 20 per cent of all recruits had not attended a major public school (indeed, about 20 per cent came from only four schools: Winchester, Eton, Rugby, and St Paul's), and 78.5 per cent of them had graduated from Oxford or Cambridge University, where nearly 60 per cent had read classics.[23]

Recruited at a relatively young age (23 years on average), these civil servants were encouraged to think that they had committed themselves to a lifetime career, which, given satisfactory performance, would bring them a comfortable, pensioned retirement—set after 1890 at the age of 65. Movement between the public service and the outside world, whether commerce or the professions, was generally discouraged—though lawyers had to be taken in at a later age, after they had demonstrated their professional competence. The British civil service also had a bias against expertise, highly educated gentlemen being systemically preferred. 'I do not know who is to check the assertion of experts when the government has once undertaken a class of duties which none but such persons understand', a senior Treasury official once remarked.[24] The quality most valued in the civil service was sound, all-round judgement.

[22] For the consequences of this, see Ch. 8.
[23] Of the 113 entrants in 1914, Oxford supplied 47% and Cambridge 31.5%. Nine entrants had been educated at a Scottish University, seven at Trinity College Dublin, seven at London University, and one at the University of Wales. After classics, the next most popular university subjects were maths and history. Science, economics, modern languages, and the applied sciences found few takers.
[24] R. Lingen, cited in R. Lambert, *Sir John Simon* (London, 1963), 452.

Almost equally valued was a commitment to 'economy', reinforced by the Treasury's position as the most powerful domestic department.[25] Similar qualities came to the top in the Indian Civil Service and among the District Commissioners who in practice ran many of the Crown Colonies—though for administrators serving abroad, some field training and acquisition of relevant skills had obviously to be provided. But 'programme-driven' administrators such as Edwin Chadwick earlier in the century now had little place in Whitehall.

The late Victorian civil service was very small. According to official statistics, in 1900 its staff, excluding industrial workers, numbered just over 100,000, most of them employed in a subordinate capacity. Even on the eve of the Great War there were only about 450 First Division clerks in total, and a major department such as the Home Office could get by in 1899 with only seventeen First Division clerks (senior administrators).[26]

What of the legal system? The peculiarity of the British state was that it lacked a Ministry of Justice. The head of the judiciary was the Lord Chancellor, who always sat in the Cabinet, assisted by the Attorney-General and the Solicitor-General, who seldom had Cabinet rank. But the separation of powers, whereby the judiciary maintained its independence from both legislature and executive, was more than a fiction.

The Judicature Acts of 1873–5 had recently overhauled the administration of justice, merging the courts of common law with the courts of equity, probate, admiralty, and divorce, to form a new Supreme Court of Judicature. The Acts also formalized the separation between the two branches of the profession: solicitors (who now swallowed up the attorneys and proctors) and barristers. The state loosely supervised the profession, but the legislation by which this was achieved left lawyers largely free to conduct and regulate their own affairs: for example, the Inns of Courts, which provided training for barristers, were ancient corporations, remarkably resistant to the spirit of reform. Lawyers were thus independent professionals, accountable to their clients (who paid them an 'honorarium'), but not public officials. In 1879 a Crown Prosecution Service was set up, but only on a small scale and with very limited powers.

Minor offences were tried before the magistrates' bench by Justices of the Peace (JPs), appointed by the Lord Chancellor's Office from the ranks of local worthies: amateurs, who could nevertheless turn for help on technical points to the town clerk, a trained lawyer. The police, who enforced the law, were controlled in the boroughs by the watch committees and in the counties,

---

[25] However, it was only in 1918 that the Permanent Secretary of the Treasury formally became the Head of the Civil Service.

[26] Numbers had risen to 24 by 1909 (J. Pellew, *The Home Office 1848–1914* (London, 1982), 75).

prior to 1888, by quarter sessions. (The Metropolitan Force came under the direct authority of the Home Secretary.)

This difference between borough and county arose out of the complexities of local government. The 1835 Municipal Reform Act (substantially amended by the Municipal Corporations Act of 1882) had created machinery through which local ratepayers in urban areas could petition for incorporation, after which they would be allowed to elect their own council. By 1886 few large towns, with the significant exception of London,[27] lacked such powers: there were 280 municipalities in 1888, 313 by 1901.[28]

In the rural areas no equivalent bodies existed before 1888. Magistrates meeting in quarter sessions had to deal with administrative matters such as the building of roads and the repair of bridges. Other services were supplied by a variety of ad hoc bodies, nearly all of them nineteenth-century creations, notably the School Boards and the Boards of Guardians, which administered the Poor Law (and did much else besides—for example, enforcing the vaccination laws). Guardians and School Boards also operated in urban areas, though their boundaries seldom coincided with those of the municipal council—which led to much overlapping, confusion, and waste.

In 1888 local government was partly modernized and made accountable to a wider electorate with the Local Government Act, which created fifty county councils for England and another twelve for Wales.[29] Among the former was the London County Council (LCC), whose establishment gave the capital, for the first time, adequate powers of self-government. The county councils inherited all the administrative powers of quarter sessions, except responsibility for the police, which was jointly shared. The 1888 Act also elevated certain boroughs to the status of 'county boroughs', freeing them from dependence on the counties in which they were situated. This administrative category was originally intended to cover only the ten most populous boroughs (each with a minimum population of 150,000). However, as the Bill passed through Parliament, a cross-party coalition of MPs from the affected urban areas succeeded in lowering the population threshold to 50,000. This resulted in the creation of sixty-one county boroughs, a figure which had crept up by the eve of the Great War to eighty-one.

Whereas the county boroughs were entirely autonomous, the county councils shared responsibility with the various municipal councils situated within their boundaries. But this initially left the rural districts and the unincorporated towns in limbo. Then, in 1894, the Liberals passed another far-reaching Local

---

[27] Overall responsibility for London lay with the Metropolitan Board of Works.

[28] P. J. Waller, *Town, City and Nation: England 1850–1914* (Oxford, 1983), 243.

[29] Scotland was given broadly similar powers by a separate Act of Parliament a year later; Ireland had to wait until 1898.

Government Act.[30] Henceforward, all rural parishes with a population of 300 had a directly elected parish council, a secular unit of administration with limited powers of regulation over footpaths, local commons, allotments, and so on.[31] These bodies, in turn, were subordinated to the newly created rural district councils (RDCs), some 600 in all, which inherited the functions of the old Poor Law unions and sanitary districts.

For urban areas which did not aspire to borough status, about 700 urban district councils (UDCs) were also provided.[32] No local government authority existed in London below the level of the LCC other than the ancient vestries, until the legislation of 1899 which created twenty-eight directly elected metropolitan borough councils.

Meanwhile the 640 Boards of Guardians[33] continued to operate much as before (except those that had been brought under the auspices of the RDCs), while the School Boards, some 2,500 in number, survived until the passing of the 1902 Education Act.[34] Several Whitehall departments vied with one another in exercising a loose supervision over these various bodies: for example, the Local Government Board (LGB) dealt with sanitary and health issues and with poor relief, and the Home Office with policing.

If all this sounds complicated, it reflects a reality that was indeed very complicated. Its main justification was that, in British political culture, rationality and efficiency took second place to a determination to check centralizing tendencies by stimulating civic pride and local self-reliance. The various late Victorian reforms partially achieved this objective.

Following the 1894 Act, all local bodies did at least derive their authority from the electorate—which had not previously been the case.[35] In other ways, however, the new authorities seemed to be specifically designed to check democratic ardour. For example, the 1888 Act (initiated, significantly, by a Conservative ministry) followed the model of the Municipal Corporations Act in having one-third of all councillors retire annually and in having a class of aldermen (elected by the councillors themselves), who made up one-quarter of the entire council.[36] This ensured that it would usually take several years before a tide of popular opinion decisively altered the council's political balance.

---

[30] This measure also extended the local government franchise. See Ch. 7.

[31] Those with populations less than 300 could petition the county council to have their own council. Otherwise they had to make do with 'parish meetings'. The parish thus became a living unit.

[32] P. Hollis, *Ladies Elect: Women in English Local Government 1865–1914* (Oxford, 1987), 357. In 1900 there were 694 in England and 53 in Wales.

[33] In 1900 there were 600 in England, 47 in Wales.

[34] London's School Board survived until 1903—see Ch. 10. In 1900 School Boards numbered 2,185 in England, 338 in Wales. The Boards of Guardians survived until 1929.

[35] The secret ballot was introduced for the first time to the election of Guardians.

[36] In the LCC they constituted one-seventh of the Council.

The local government reforms of 1888–94 survived, with very few changes, for over eighty years. But from the outset the administrative arrangements they established were fundamentally flawed. England still had far too many local authorities, with jurisdictions that often conflicted. For example, there were over 1,900 different bodies with responsibility for the building and upkeep of roads (a pressing issue as motor traffic grew), and this situation was not remedied until the creation of a Ministry of Transport in 1919. Likewise, at the end of the Great War there were 186 different police forces, 128 of them in the boroughs: attempts were made by the 1890 Police Act to encourage them to exchange men during an emergency, but, characteristically, the authorities could seldom agree on how to allocate costs.[37]

Moreover, the smaller authorities (and some of the larger ones, too) tended to be run in an amateurish way. The housing reformer Thomas Horsfall tirelessly advocated the institution of paid mayors, on the German model, but he found few backers. On the contrary, many councils continued, right up to the end of the century and beyond, to hire their medical officers of health and even their town clerk on a part-time basis—a system of 'extravagant parsimony' against which Chamberlain constantly railed.

But perhaps the gravest weakness in the 1888 statute was that it allowed so many urban areas to opt out from their counties, depriving the latter of much-needed revenue and still further complicating the already vexed subject of local taxation.[38] (Thus Cheshire County Council lost Birkenhead and Stockport, costing it £457,000 and £161,000 respectively in rateable value.)[39] The original idea, which had been to confer county borough status on the likes of Liverpool and Manchester, may well have been defensible. But why were smaller towns and cities (albeit with important histories), such as Canterbury, Chester, Exeter, Lincoln, and Worcester—none of which met the 50,000 population threshold—allowed to join their ranks?[40]

Even odder is the elevation of the historic counties as cornerstones of local 'democracy' at the very time when they were losing their importance in the definition of parliamentary constituencies. In any case, the counties (whose boundaries were only marginally adjusted) varied widely in their acreage, population, and gross rental. To take two extremes, Lancashire had a popula-tion of 4,437,518 and a total acreage of 1,299,816: Rutland a population of

---

[37] Waller, *Town, City and Nation*, 268.

[38] See Chs. 7 and 11.

[39] J. M. Lee, *Social Leaders and Public Persons: A Study of County Government in Cheshire* (Oxford, 1963), 69. The loss of county boroughs and the Agricultural Derating Act decreased the county's rateable value from £3,139,304 in 1889 to £2,800,000.

[40] Pressure from local MPs, activated by a mixture of local pride and a desire to keep down the rates, supplies the answer.

20,743 and an acreage of 108,700.[41] Nor did county boundaries take much account of recent occupational and residential developments: many inhabitants of the Home Counties, for example, earned their living within the LCC area.[42]

As administrative units, the boroughs and county boroughs made greater sense. But as towns expanded in the wake of improved transportation systems, they, too, ceased to encompass many of those who were dependent on them. 'Areas of administration', H. G. Wells noted in *Anticipations*, were 'still areas marked out by conditions of locomotion as obsolete as the quadrupedal method of the pre-arboreal ancestor.'[43] Thus the emergence of 'conurbations' did not lead to an administrative merger of the historic towns which, in social and economic terms, were running into one another: Manchester and Salford, for example, retained their separate civic identities. In 1901 the boundaries of many county boroughs, including Bristol, Derby, Liverpool, Manchester, and Portsmouth, were enlarged so as to take in the outlying suburbs. More dramatically, historic Birmingham transmuted in 1911 into 'Greater Birmingham', becoming, with its 840,000 inhabitants, the second city in England—though not, as proud 'Brummies' were wont to claim, the 'second city of the Empire', since Glasgow, itself recently enlarged, had a bigger population still, approximately 1 million.[44] But the population of many of these large cities continued to spill over their administrative borders. As for the LCC, it was outmoded almost from the moment of its establishment.

Urban growth, by breeding thousands of 'non-local people', also had implications for the quality of local government. Many wealthy and influential citizens, with a limited stake in any one administrative area, took little active interest in civic life. Simultaneously, new social and economic needs were arising that small-scale local authorities struggled to meet. To achieve economies of scale, the supply of water and electricity would have been better organized on a regional basis. This was the burden of Wells's 1903 paper, 'The Question of Scientific Administrative Areas in Relation to Municipal Undertakings'.

A concern with reshaping local government so as to make areas coincide with functions scarcely exercised the minds of many ministers, MPs, or local

---

[41] Constituency boundaries were left for quarter sessions to define: in Leicestershire the largest division contained 1,673 voters, the smallest 388 (J. P. D. Dunbabin, 'Expectations of the New County Councils and Their Realisation', *Historical Journal*, 8 (1965), 357). Wards of wildly different size also characterized other local authorities: in Liverpool, the Pitt Street ward had 741 voters, Everton 24,270, though each returned three councillors (P. J. Waller, *Democracy and Sectarianism: A Political and Social History of Liverpool, 1868–1939* (Liverpool, 1981), 119).

[42] Moreover, Middlesex, a separate county, was in many ways an adjunct of the LCC.

[43] H. G. Wells, *Anticipations* (London, 1900?), 99, 403.

[44] The boast presumably rested on geographic extent: Birmingham now stretched over 13 miles at one place, making it three times the size of Glasgow and twice the size of Manchester, Liverpool, or Belfast (A. Briggs, *History of Birmingham, Vol 2: Borough and City, 1865–1938* (Oxford, 1952), 155).

councillors, though it fascinated the Fabians who, from 1905 onwards, brought out their 'New Heptarchy' series of pamphlets on the subject.[45] But increasingly Parliament was asked to pass special legislation to resolve difficulties that would otherwise have been insoluble. For example, with Liverpool and Bootle clinging to their separate civic identities, the Mersey Docks and Harbour Board had to be created.[46] The Port of London Authority followed in 1908. As we shall see, the administration of social welfare was soon to necessitate the creation of a multitude of new ad hoc authorities, at local as well as at national level.

3. A RULING CLASS?

But the *machinery* of politics and administration does not tell us much about the *spirit* in which it is operated, a point shrewdly made by Gladstone in May 1890:

The ultimate power resides in the hands of those who constitute our democracy. And yet, our institutions are not democratic. Their basis is popular; but upon that basis is built a hierarchy of classes and of establishments savouring in part of feudal times and principles; and this, not in despite of the democratic majority, but on the whole with their assent.[47]

The House of Lords was, obviously, an institutional expression of the landed aristocracy; law lords were the only life peers. True, 115 new peerages had been created between 1868 and July 1886[48]—an invaluable source of prime-ministerial patronage. Several of these were bestowed on businessmen. But even in 1911 only about one-sixth of the Chamber were first-generation peers from non-landed backgrounds.[49]

As for the House of Commons elected in 1886, its membership was drawn from a scarcely less narrow social constituency. Only 2 per cent of MPs were working-class, while nearly one-half came from aristocratic and landed backgrounds, a proportion that would be still higher if the Irish Nationalists were excluded. Over 30 per cent held active and substantial business interests, while some 52 per cent came from the professions, the law being the most popular.[50]

---

[45] Starting with *Municipalization By Provinces* (no. 125: Oct. 1905). See A. M. McBriar, *Fabian Socialism and English Politics 1884–1918* (Cambridge, 1962), 233.

[46] Waller, *Town, City and Nation*, 244.

[47] Matthew, *Gladstone, Vol. 2*, 322.

[48] That is to say, in addition to peers who had received a further promotion ('step').

[49] F. M. L. Thompson, *English Landed Society in the Nineteenth Century* (London, 1963), 297.

[50] The figures, which amount to more than 100% because of overlapping membership, are based on W. C. Lubenow, *Parliamentary Politics and the Home Rule Crisis: The British Commons in 1886* (Oxford, 1988), App. 3.

At ministerial level the catchment area for those thought suitable for the highest offices was even more severely restricted—regardless of which party was in power. Between them, Salisbury's Conservative Cabinet of 1885–6 and Gladstone's Cabinet of 1886 contained nine landed peers, and there were at least seventeen landowners and gentlemen out of a combined total of thirty Cabinet ministers—a state of affairs not very different from Earl Grey's ministry sixty years earlier. Moreover, of these thirty ministers, fourteen had attended one of the Clarendon public schools (nine were Old Etonians, four Old Harrovians, and one an old Rugbean), and eighteen had studied at Oxford or Cambridge—indeed, of the total number of Cabinet ministers, almost one-half (fourteen) had attended either Christ Church, Oxford, or Trinity College, Cambridge, the two most aristocratic and socially prestigious colleges. By comparison, only four of these ministers can by any stretch of the imagination be called businessmen: W. H. Smith from the Conservatives, and Campbell-Bannerman, A. J. Mundella, and Joseph Chamberlain from the Liberals. Nor was this exceptional: indeed, the aristocratic flavour of the Cabinet actually grew more pronounced during the 1890s, tempered only by the presence of a disproportionate number of lawyers.

That so few working-class men were able to establish themselves in national politics is hardly surprising. The 1883 Corrupt and Illegal Practices Act of 1883 (CPA), by setting limits on election expenditure at constituency level, should, in theory, have lowered the financial barrier and let in more men of modest means. However, nothing in the Act prevented the 'nursing' of constituencies between elections, and this put poor candidates at a continuing disadvantage. Moreover, had there been any serious intention of widening access to the Commons, steps would have been taken to institute payment of MPs (which did not happen until 1912) and to transfer the cost of the returning officers' expenses on to public funds, a reform demanded by many Radical Liberals (at the Newcastle Conference, for example) but not conceded until 1918. As a consequence, few men from humble backgrounds could afford to entertain parliamentary ambitions—except for members of the Irish Nationalist Party, many of whom effectively depended upon financial subventions from their Irish-American sympathizers.

Before the founding of the Labour Party in 1900 and the establishment in 1903 of a central fund out of which its impecunious MPs could be paid, the only working-class politicians on mainland Britain who stood a chance of reaching Westminster were those sponsored by their trade union. The 1885 General Election, the first held on the basis of the new franchise, saw the return of thirteen 'labour' MPs, all loosely attached to the Liberal Party, a number which fell after the election of the following year to only ten—six of them miners, including Thomas Burt, who had first become an MP way back in

1874. Another of these so-called 'Lib-Labs', Henry Broadhurst, a stonemason by trade, was appointed a junior Home Office minister in Gladstone's third ministry (1885–6)—the first working man to hold such a post. But ministerial office still remained well out of the reach of nearly all manual workers, however able.

The failure of more than a handful of businessmen to force their way into the Cabinet is more difficult to explain: contemporaries puzzled over a state of affairs in which government seemed to be so out of kilter with the country's economic base. One important reason for the aristocratic domination of the Cabinet was that landowners (and also barristers) found it easier to combine their way of life with the demands of Parliament than did businessmen, few of whom, in the era of the small family-run enterprise, could risk delegating their authority. This affected the age at which MPs entered Parliament: in the 1890s 46 per cent of peers' sons did so in their twenties or early thirties, the gentry a little later. Professional men usually delayed their parliamentary debut until they had established their careers, usually in their forties. But provincial businessmen, especially those who had personally built up their own firms, had to wait much longer, self-made men of this type first entering the Commons at an average age of 50. Even Chamberlain, the most successful businessman in politics of his generation, did not get elected until he was 40, having first retired from the family business entirely so that he could concentrate on politics. Compare this with his one-time rival and later colleague Lord Hartington, heir to the Duke of Devonshire, who first became an MP at the age of 23—after a safe seat had been found for him, dominated by the family influence.[51]

Because they set off with this initial advantage, aristocratic MPs tended to serve in the Commons for much longer periods.[52] And though only a minority of such Members aspired to ministerial office or thought of politics as a 'career', those who did so often became the true 'professionals', the men whose experience, knowledge, and devotion to public service made them the obvious occupants of the great offices of state.

Social snobbery also came into the equation. From the time of Gladstone's first ministry, formed in 1868, until the Liberals' accession to power in December 1905, the Foreign Secretary was always a peer.[53] By this time the

---

[51] See J. P. Cornford, 'The Parliamentary Foundations of the Hotel Cecil', in R. Robson (ed.), *Ideas and Institutions of Victorian Britain* (London, 1967), 268–311.

[52] The eldest sons of peers, of course, would eventually follow their father into the Lords, as Hartington himself did in 1891.

[53] Before and after that date the few commoners who did hold that office were, without exception, either Irish peers (Palmerston), heirs to a peerage (Lord Stanley), or traditional landowners (Sir Edward Grey).

King had erroneously convinced himself that this was a *formal* requirement!
The principal advisers in the Foreign Office and in the Diplomatic Corps
themselves invariably came from landed families and had received an aristocratic education. All this was still thought necessary for the country's prestige.

Britain was thus being governed at the end of the nineteenth century by a
'ruling class' narrowly based upon landed wealth and the ancient professions,
with values inculcated by the public schools and Oxford and Cambridge
universities. These were precisely the social types who also dominated the
Court, the higher ranks of the Armed Services, and the Diplomatic Corps, and
who, as holders of the office of Lord-Lieutenant, also provided social and
political leadership in the counties.[54] It remained an open question in 1885–6
whether this narrow elite would successfully adapt to the recent extension of
the parliamentary franchise.

4. THE ELECTORAL SYSTEM

In 1885 Parliament had passed a measure of redistribution, hammered out over
many months between Salisbury, then Conservative Leader in the Lords, and
the Liberal President of the Local Government Board, Charles Dilke. It
was in many ways quite radical—too much so for Gladstone's liking.
True, Salisbury succeeded in protecting the agricultural seats from contamination by immigrants from the big towns—an important Conservative objective.
But the Act also had other far-reaching implications for British political culture.

For a start, it represented a move towards the old Radical goal of equal
electoral districts: there was a massacre of the smaller boroughs and a redistribution of their seats to the industrialized counties and the populous urban
districts. Eighty-nine single-member and seven two-member boroughs were
disfranchised and another thirty-nine two-member boroughs lost one of their
seats. Conversely, the London area alone acquired forty-two new single-
member constituencies.

Redistribution changed the nature of electoral politics in other ways.
The multi-member constituency had previously been the norm: in 1880
only 190 MPs across the entire United Kingdom had been returned for
single-member constituencies, compared with 414 for double-membered
and thirty-three for triple-membered constituencies.[55] But after the Redistribution Act only twenty-four territorial double-member constituencies
survived (twenty-one in England, and one each in Wales, Scotland, and
Ireland).

---

[54] For the workings of local government, see Ch. 7.
[55] London was a four-member constituency. Another nine members sat for the six university seats.

This broke up the big cities in ways likely to encourage class-based voting. Birmingham and Manchester had previously each returned three MPs, but both towns were now divided into seven and six single-member constituencies respectively, constituencies based upon the socio-economic characteristics of their districts. This meant that, whereas formerly an MP might see it as his duty to represent his borough in its entirety, after 1885 it was more likely that an MP returned by a comfortable suburban constituency would identify with his counterparts elsewhere rather than with an MP from his own town representing a deprived urban area.

Of more immediate significance was the earlier 1884 Reform Act, which extended the household franchise from boroughs to the counties across the entire United Kingdom. Overall, it enfranchised more than one-and-three-quarter million new electors—in percentage terms, the biggest increase of all the nineteenth-century Reform Acts. Standing in 1885–6 at 5,707,531, the electorate then steadily expanded until by the start of the Great War it exceeded 8 million.[56]

Admittedly these changes fell short of the universal manhood suffrage which Chamberlain and his Radical friends had once called for (the issue of votes for women still enjoyed little support in Parliament, and a backbencher's amendment proposing it had been contemptuously rejected, on Gladstone's advice, by a margin of 136 votes). Not only was plural voting retained, but paupers continued to be disqualified, though the 1885 Medical Relief (Qualifications Removal) Act exempted those who had received treatment in a Poor Law infirmary. The requirement that to exercise the household franchise one had to prove twelve months' continuous residence also penalized the geographically mobile, as did the even tougher conditions surrounding the new (and highly unsatisfactory) lodger franchise.[57] These complications meant that young males, whatever their social background, were under-represented on the electoral registers.

Nevertheless, probably 60 per cent of adult males had the vote after 1884 (two out of three in England and Wales, a smaller proportion in Scotland and Ireland.) In particular, most agricultural labourers and coalminers could now vote. In the boroughs the drawing-up of the electoral rolls was heavily influenced by the whims of registration officials and the interventions of party agents, leading to variations from one constituency to another; but, capricious though the system was, it excluded no category of adult males entirely from the parliamentary franchise.[58] The 1884 Reform Act was thus a

---

[56] Of these, however, up to half-a-million were probably plural voters.

[57] On the complexities of the lodger franchise, D. Tanner, *Political Change and the Labour Party 1900–1918* (Cambridge, 1990), 112–18.

[58] J. Davis and D. Tanner, 'The Borough Franchise after 1867', *Historical Research*, 69 (1996), 306–27.

massive stride towards the 'democracy' that contemporaries, depending on class and political conviction, either demanded, feared, or despised.

In responding to the new democratic challenge, politicians had also to take note of the 1883 Corrupt and Illegal Practices Act, a measure initiated by MPs who had been shocked by the widespread corruption surrounding the 1880 election—and perhaps equally shocked by the escalating cost of securing a parliamentary seat. Under the terms of this essentially cross-party act, a tough maximum schedule was imposed on what candidates and those acting in their name could spend during an election campaign.

The authors of the CPA hoped thereby to encourage the development of an intelligent electorate that would rationally examine the issues, free from grosser preoccupations. If the ideal of citizenship required the people to participate directly in the political process, this ideal was, to some extent, realized. Turnout in contested constituencies achieved what, in retrospect, seem extra-ordinary levels: usually above 80 per cent and reaching a peak of 87 per cent on mainland Britain in January 1910.[59] Moreover, these figures underestimate the electorate's true involvement, since the lengthy process of compiling the electoral register meant that, by the time the polling booths opened, thousands of those entitled to vote were dead or had moved to another part of the country. Deliberate abstention was probably quite unusual.

Interest in politics was maintained by the widespread coverage of parlia-mentary proceedings: traditional journals still carried verbatim reports of leading politicians' speeches. Sunday papers such as the *News of the World* and *Reynolds' Weekly* did, it is true, also regale their readers with sensational items drawn from the police and divorce courts, but, of the daily papers, even the organs of the so-called 'Yellow Press', such as the *Daily Mail*, assumed an interest in politics that would today cause a drastic collapse in sales. With fewer recreational alternatives, political meetings regularly attracted phenomenal audiences. For example, in June 1887 Gladstone, a spectacular crowd-puller, drew a vast audience to his meeting at Singleton Park, Swansea, where 50,000 supporters paraded past his leek-bedecked platform.

Successful public speakers often modelled their oratory on preaching—Lloyd George, for one, regularly attended religious services, not solely or even mainly for the good of his soul, but to see how the great evangelists wove their spells. More controversial, because the theatre was only just beginning to establish its respectability, was the link between politics and the stage—Gladstone himself, significantly, was an enthusiastic theatregoer. In short, the political platform, like the pulpit and the stage, was the site of a kind

---

[59] However, turn-out figures are difficult to calculate because of uncontested elections, plural voting and double-member constituencies.

of performance art, whose successful practitioners were the pop stars of their generation.

An interest in political oratory and debate usually went hand in hand with strong partisan convictions. For politics also had something of the character of a spectator sport, an adversarial contest which was exciting because one could never quite be sure which side would win. Talking informally in 1920, Lloyd George acknowledged that this was still the case: 'The Briton is a fighting man. He likes a fighting speech. Politics is his football match.'[60] In fact, from the early 1880s onwards political parties and football teams imitated one another in many respects: each sported its 'colours' and had its own tribal songs—and each tended to trigger off fighting and mayhem.

Reformers cherished the hope that, in time, violence and misconduct would disappear from public life. In 1872 the introduction of the secret ballot did away with the rowdiness of the open hustings. However, until the 1920s and perhaps beyond, contested elections were frequently accompanied by fighting, as bands of zealots struggled to break up their rivals' meetings and to seize control of symbolically important spaces (for example, market squares). In addition, parties often hired brass bands, which played patriotic airs to raise the spirits of their own supporters—and to disrupt the activities of their opponents. The holding of ticketed meetings, though not unknown, was widely condemned as 'un-English'—because 'un-manly'.[61] Nor did the custom, prevalent in the Conservative Party, of using public houses as committee rooms do much to promote calm, rational debate. All this gave a great deal of amusement and satisfaction, even to those who still did not possess the vote— at least, it did so to the male members of the community. (Most women probably saw things differently.)

The other great pleasure which men and women alike derived from elections centred on the money which contests brought into the community. True, the CPA, as intended, did curb electoral expenditure at constituency level (it dropped from 42s. 5d. per elector in 1880 to 18s. 9d. in 1885), and the maximum schedule did help to protect candidates from unscrupulous agents and grasping voters for whom, traditionally, a contested election was a bonanza. On the other hand, MPs and would-be MPs were still under almost nonstop pressure to subsidize a variety of local 'good causes', charities, sports and social clubs, and so on. Particularly vulnerable to being fleeced in this way were candidates whose political views made them unpopular in their locality. Parliament resolutely refused to tackle this 'abuse', if such it was. Moreover, no

---

[60] Cited in G. R. Searle, *Country Before Party: Coalition and the Idea of 'National Government' in Modern Britain 1885–1987* (Harlow, 1995), 4.

[61] J. Lawrence, *Speaking for the People: Party, Language and Popular Politics in England, 1867–1914* (Cambridge, 1998), 167, 181.

way could be found of stopping the activities of pressure-groups which, though nominally 'independent', regularly intervened at election time in support of one particular party.[62]

In any case, for many years to come, cultural tradition was against electoral purification, since many poor people saw election-day perks and handouts as one of their immemorial rights, and were quite indignant at the prospect of losing them. The number of successful bribery petitions being filed may have declined after 1880,[63] but 'progress' in this field was slow and halting. As Lloyd George, a Welsh Baptist, mischievously reminded his pious Anglican colleague, Charles Masterman, the most corrupt constituencies in the land nearly all happened to be cathedral cities! (Worcester was investigated by a Royal Commission after the 1906 General Election, the last time that this procedure was applied.)

Electoral 'abuses', however, did not always originate from below. For example, labourers who crossed the parson or farmer in parish and rural district council elections still risked victimization. The 'feudal screw' was also applied, on occasions, to tenants and shopkeepers rash enough to defy the authority of the 'big house'.[64] 'Spiritual intimidation' from clergy of all denominations was another infringement of individual freedom about which little could be done.

In one respect, however, the CPA did make a big difference to political life. Through its restrictions on 'paid agency', it forced the parties to rely more upon volunteers at election time, so giving a boost to mass party organization. It was no coincidence that two of the Act's keenest promoters were John Gorst, famous for his part in establishing the National Union of Conservative Associations in 1869, and Chamberlain, the driving force behind the Birmingham Caucus and the National Liberal Federation, founded about a decade later. Local organizations certainly proliferated in the late Victorian period: by February 1888 the newly founded Liberal Unionist Association had 155 affiliated branches covering 257 constituencies, while the National Liberal Federation, which moved to London after Chamberlain's defection, received the affiliation of another fifty Liberal associations.[65] Unofficial bodies, notably

---

[62] e.g. the Union Defence League or, later, the Free Trade Union, or, in a more self-interested way, the brewers (much to the indignation of Liberal activists).

[63] In 1880, 16; 1885, 3; 1886, 0; 1892, 5; 1895, 1 (C. O'Leary, *The Elimination of Corrupt Practices in British Elections, 1858–1911* (Oxford, 1962), 186). This, however, is an unreliable index of corruption, since petitioning was expensive and the parties often preferred to settle their disputes outside the courts.

[64] Hollis, *Ladies Elect*, 364–5. On the operation of the 'feudal screw', see N. Blewett, *The Peers, the Parties and the People: The General Elections of 1910* (London, 1973), 374–6.

[65] T. A. Jenkins, 'Hartington, Chamberlain and the Unionist Alliance, 1886–1895', *Parliamentary History*, 11 (1992), 134–5.

the Primrose League, a valuable adjunct to Conservatism, also blossomed in the new electoral soil.[66]

But the main beneficiaries of these changes were agents and full-time party workers. Significantly, the central organs of both parties, appointed by and responsible to the Leader, rapidly extended their control over the institutions of the mass party after 1885—though the Conservatives were quicker than the Liberals to do this. Earlier fears that British public life was falling under the domination of the wirepullers of the local 'caucus' soon proved to be wide of the mark.

During the 1890s the Conservative Party, under its Chief Agent, Captain Middleton, built up a formidable machine, not only centrally but also in the localities through the establishment of constituency agents (the successors to the solicitors who had earlier helped the parties organize the electoral register). Middleton also encouraged his agents to develop a greater sense of professional identity. As a result, the National Society of Conservative Agents, founded in November 1891, set its own professional exams and qualifying system, published its own periodical, and ran a special Benevolent Fund. By the end of the decade about one-half of all constituencies employed a Conservative agent.[67] The Liberals, who followed suit, had already founded the Liberal Publication Department in 1887.

However, these new services made heavy financial demands on the parties nationally. In 1880 the Liberals' general election fund had been a modest £50,000, but by the time of the two 1910 elections both major parties were spending around double that sum. Thus, in many ways all that the CPA had achieved was to transfer the cost of politics from constituency level to the centre. This, in turn, meant that corruption, outlawed in its cruder, more populist forms, returned through the back door in more subtle guises, as both parties began to exploit their powers of patronage to entice wealthy sympathizers to give big donations to their central funds, which were unaudited and so shrouded in secrecy. By 1895 the Liberals were embarrassed by the revelation that their Chief Whip and Party Organizer had apparently driven a disreputable bargain with two rich business backers, Sydney Stern, a Jewish banker, and James Williamson, the linoleum manufacturer.[68] But the Conservatives and, in particular, the Liberal Unionists had pioneered these misdeeds: the 'Special Fund' raised by the Liberal Unionist Chief Whip between 1890 and 1892 involved blatant honours trafficking, out of which the Conservatives

---

[66] See Ch. 7.
[67] R. Shannon, *The Age of Salisbury, 1881–1902: Unionism and Empire* (Harlow, 1996), 314–17.
[68] P. Marsh, *The Discipline of Popular Government: Lord Salisbury's Domestic Statecraft, 1881–1902* (Hassocks, 1978), 246.

received a 'cut' of £7,500.[69] These problems were to deepen in the years just preceding the outbreak of the Great War and afterwards.

One reason for heavy party expenditure was that general elections were beginning, for the first time, to take on the appearance of a struggle for power between two dominant party groupings, fought out over the length and breadth of the land. This had not always been so. Even in 1880 there were still fifty-two constituencies on mainland Britain, returning eighty-three MPs, which did not go the polls. This figure excludes the university seats[70] and Ireland, where contests continued to be rare occurrences, except in the 'border' areas and on those occasions when a party was internally divided, as the Irish Nationalists were in 1892.

The 1885 Redistribution Act, by reducing the number of double-member constituencies and thus diminishing the scope for cross-party compromise, made contested elections more common, and in the 1885 General Election all but thirteen constituencies polled.[71] In 1886 the number of uncontested elections rose to 148, which was hardly surprising considering the unusual circumstances in which the election was held,[72] but in 1892 there were only thirty-six constituencies without a contest. The Liberal Party's chronic financial embarrassment during the late 1890s[73] then produced a large crop of uncontested elections: 122 in 1895 and 161 in 1900. However, by the early twentieth century it was quite rare for electors to be denied an opportunity of voting.[74]

The development of mass politics was thus uneven, but the overall trend was clear: political parties were starting to recognize the need to put up candidates even in hopeless constituencies—partly to give their supporters an opportunity of 'affirming' their allegiance, and partly so as to maintain a local organization ready to participate in local elections, an important consideration since (albeit very slowly) parliamentary politics were becoming entangled with municipal and county council contests.

---

[69] T. A. Jenkins, 'The Funding of the Liberal Unionist Party and the Honours System', *English Historical Review* (1990), 921–6.

[70] Graduates had an additional vote in their university seat, a sort of non-territorial college. Oxford University and Cambridge University each returned two members, London University returned one. The other university seats were Edinburgh and St Andrews' Universities (1 member), Glasgow and Aberdeen Universities (1), and Dublin University (i.e. Trinity College, Dublin) (2 members).

[71] In all the following statistics, the figure applies to constituencies, not MPs, i.e. it includes the double-member boroughs. By no means all the contests involved a candidate from each of the main parties, of course.

[72] Under a year had elapsed since the last election. Moreover, many Liberal constituency parties, whose member had defected to Liberal Unionism, did not have time to find a replacement.

[73] See Ch. 7.

[74] Except in December 1910, another general election which came hard on the heels of its predecessor.

More fundamentally, parliamentary politics were slowly becoming 'nationalized', as first Irish Home Rule, and later the fiscal question aroused strong feelings that transcended purely local issues and personalities. However, this development took a long time to work itself out. Large landowners still had an advantage if they stood in a constituency where they owned property. Their urban counterparts, leading manufacturers and employers of labour, enjoyed a comparable influence in the boroughs in which their works were situated. Take, for example, the case of Blackburn, fiefdom of the Hornbys, who owned the town's main cotton factory: Sir Harry, Conservative MP for the borough from 1886 onwards, seldom troubled the Commons with his opinions, but he retained an enormous popularity among his constituents, who knew him as the 'owd game cock', because of his generosity to local charities and his innocent habit of wandering the streets with his pockets filled with sweets, that he disbursed to passing children; his parliamentary position therefore remained impregnable—until, during the Edwardian period, national issues rudely thrust themselves on his attention.[75] Sir Harry Hornby was not an isolated figure. Many Liberal MPs enjoyed a similar rapport with their local towns: for example, Jeremiah Colman in Norwich and Sir Charles Palmer in Jarrow.

'Localism' was carried furthest by the nascent Labour movement. The Lib-Lab miners represented 'the politics of locality' in their most extreme form. By comparison, the twenty-nine Labour-sponsored MPs elected in 1906 came from more variegated backgrounds; even so, over one-half of them lived in or near their constituency, and eight had actually been born in its vicinity.[76]

All this notwithstanding, many of the parliamentary candidates running for the main parties in 1885 were 'carpetbaggers'. What mattered increasingly was the platform upon which a candidate stood rather than his personal credentials. By 1910 MPs such as Hornby were recognized to be members of a dying breed.

5. THE SHAPING OF PARTY ALLEGIANCE

The growing 'nationalization' of politics, however, did not immediately remove the considerable regional variations in party fortunes. One striking feature of electoral geography (dating back to 1868) was the weakness of the Conservative Party in Wales and, to a lesser extent, in Scotland. In the 1892 and 1895 elections the Liberals returned 83.3 per cent of Welsh and 61.8 per cent of Scottish MPs—as against 39.3 per cent of MPs representing English

---

[75] P. F. Clarke, 'British Politics and Blackburn Politics, 1900–1910', *Historical Journal*, 12 (1969), 302–27.
[76] Lawrence, *Speaking for the People*, 231–4.

seats. In Ireland, on the other hand, the Liberals had been all but wiped out by 1885; thereafter, parliamentary representation was shared, roughly in the proportion of four to one, between Nationalists and Unionists.

Moreover, even within England there were prominent regional variations. For example, whereas the Conservative Party was dominant in the South-East, in Merseyside, and in Western Lancastria (Greater Manchester and its hinterland), the Liberals flourished in the East Midlands, most industrial areas of Yorkshire, and the North-East.[77]

Such regional allegiances cannot, however, simply be taken at face value. In Wales, and perhaps in Scotland, a sense of national distinctiveness may have found expression in support for the Liberal Party and, even more obviously, in the rejection of a Conservatism which spoke in a pronounced English accent. But, even in the 'Celtic Fringe', this national feeling was not 'pure', since it was also, in part, a manifestation of the strength of Dissent, which, throughout mainland Britain, tended to be closely associated with Liberalism.[78]

In fact, prior to 1886 religion was overwhelmingly the main determinant of voting behaviour, with the Liberal Party closely aligned with Nonconformity, Conservatism with the Established Church. The great rallying cry of Nonconformity, spearheaded by the Liberation Society, was 'religious freedom': Dissenters wanted the various Christian bodies to compete with one another on equal terms, with the state staying neutral, as was the case in the United States of America, which served them as a model of how religious life should be conducted in the modern world.[79] Despite being led by a high Anglican (Gladstone), the Liberal Party showed some sympathy towards these views, in contrast to the Conservatives, who presented themselves as the protector of a national church that symbolized the centrality of Christian values in the nation's life.

By 1886 many of the Nonconformists' disabilities had been removed. The repeal of the Test and Corporation Acts had taken place as long ago as the 1820s. But church rates had only been abolished in 1868, and not until 1881 could

---

[77] Conservative and Unionist vote as a percentage of the total vote in general elections, 1885–1918: Great Britain, 49.5; England, 50.8; Scotland, 43.0; Wales, 38.6; South-East England, 56.2; West Midlands, 55.2; LCC area, 52.7; Wessex, 51.4; Lancastria, 50.7; Bristol Region, 49.6; Central, 49.2; Devon & Cornwall, 49.0; East Anglia, 48.6; East Midlands, 47.6; Yorkshire Region, 45.2; North England, 45.2; Peak–Don, 44.2 (H. Pelling, *Social Geography of British Elections, 1885–1910* (London, 1967), 415). Because these figures omit uncontested elections, they underestimate the regional differences.

[78] Thus, whereas most of England farmers voted Conservative, in Nonconformist areas such as rural Wales dislike of an 'alien' Anglican landlord class naturally drew them towards Liberalism, often of an abrasively radical kind.

[79] The Archbishops of Canterbury and of York, the Bishops of London, Durham, and Winchester, and 21 diocesan bishops (in order of seniority) sat, *ex officio*, in the House of Lords, and this at a time when the Upper House still retained a great deal of legislative importance.

Nonconformists be buried in their own consecrated grounds. In many ways it was still assumed that the Church of England was the national church; only a minority of Anglican clergymen favoured disestablishment and disendowment, though Gladstone had already done this to the Church of Ireland in 1868.

Meanwhile Nonconformists struggled to end the advantages enjoyed by the Anglican Church, particularly at the level of elementary schooling. The 1870 Education Act had merely permitted the setting up of publicly funded 'board schools' in parts of the country where the existing facilities were inadequate; this left Anglican schools in a monopoly position over much of rural England, causing intense anger amongst chapelgoers. Moreover, where School Boards existed, elections to them often pitted Radical Dissenters against Conservative Anglicans in contests marked by bitter sectarian feeling.

Then, in the winter of 1885–6, Gladstone unexpectedly dropped his Home Rule bombshell by committing his party to establishing a subordinate Irish parliament (or 'Assembly', as he preferred to call it), as demanded by Charles Stewart Parnell's Irish Nationalist MPs. In taking this controversial initiative, Gladstone split the Liberal Party. The government which he formed in February 1886 proved incapable of carrying its Home Rule Bill through the Commons (it would, in any case, have foundered in the Lords), with ninety-three Liberal MPs, approximately a third of the parliamentary party, joining the Conservatives in the Opposition lobbies. These dissident Liberals (the 'Liberal Unionists', as they were called) were a diverse group, since they contained not only the acknowledged leader of the Whig faction, Lord Hartington, but also a number of erstwhile Radicals, notably John Bright and Joseph Chamberlain, both of them Dissenters. The Liberal Unionist Party promptly entered into an electoral alliance with the Conservatives. Henceforward, the main line of political division on mainland Britain—as well as in Ireland—was that separating 'Unionists' from 'Home Rulers'.

Yet, strongly held though many people's views were about the future governance of Ireland,[80] most politicians and electors did not base their stand on the Home Rule issue solely on their assessment of its merits. For example, because Nonconformists had invested so much emotional capital in the Liberal Party, most were prepared to give Gladstone the benefit of the doubt over his Irish policy. Particularly in the northern industrial towns, prominent laymen who might otherwise have drifted into Conservatism continued to serve as Liberal MPs and constituency chairmen. As late as 1900 approximately one-third of all Liberal MPs belonged to a Dissenting community: very few Unionists came from such a background. For the same reason, regions as diverse in their occupational and industrial structures as Norfolk, the West

[80] See Ch. 5.

Riding of Yorkshire, and the North-East coalfields stayed broadly loyal to the Liberal cause—thanks largely to chapel influences.

On the other hand, there was, from the start, something unstable about a partnership between English Nonconformists and the Roman Catholics who dominated the Irish Nationalist Movement. The difficulty was memorably captured by the Quaker, John Bright, Chamberlain's fellow MP for Birmingham, when he coined the slogan, 'Home Rule Means Rome Rule'. Chapelgoers continued to feel a lively aversion to 'papist' practices and beliefs, and this was sometimes sufficient to draw them into the Unionist camp, as happened on a large scale, not only in the West Midlands, but also in Cornwall, where Methodism was the dominant creed. In other words, the old church–chapel rivalries were overriden, in certain parts of the country, by a more basic religious division: that between Protestants and Catholics.

Views on Home Rule were also coloured by attitudes to Irish immigration. After 1886 Catholic Irishmen who had the vote on mainland Britain usually backed the Liberals in order to promote Home Rule—except at times when, the Irish Question being temporarily in abeyance, some were tempted to vote Conservative in defence of their church schools. But in Lancashire, where a strident brand of Anglican Protestantism flourished, this provoked a nativist backlash from which the Conservative Party hugely benefited.

Thus ethnicity, religion, and convictions were all important determinants of voting behaviour. But so, too, was class. The accepted wisdom in Victorian Britain was that working-class electors divided their votes between Liberals and Conservatives roughly in the ratio of two to one. Conversely, there was evidence that middle-class voters were turning to the Conservatives in increasing numbers. Interestingly, in the 1885 General Election, held *before* the onset of the Home Rule crisis, the Conservatives had already secured thirty-eight of the forty-eight most middle-class English borough seats.

This process accelerated after the Liberal schism: in the 1886 General Election the Conservatives won forty-three of these forty-eight seats (another four fell to their Liberal Unionist allies), and even in 1892, when the Liberals nationally put up a much stronger performance, the Conservatives still retained forty-two of them. To look at the matter from the opposite end, in 1885 the Liberals won over a fifth of the more affluent urban seats (20.8 per cent), but only 3.1 per cent during the next four elections. In stark contrast, the Liberals, victors in 69 per cent of the poorer urban and mining seats in 1885, still managed to hold on to nearly one-half of them in the next four elections.[81] In some respects, then,

---

[81] This classification of constituencies, heavily reliant on Pelling's *Social Geography of British Elections*, is somewhat rough and ready, its main statistical basis being the number of domestic servants per 1,000 households. There is a small danger that the class definition of a constituency will have been influenced by knowledge of which party it generally supported.

Gladstone, by frightening middle-class voters with his startling solution to the Irish question, unwittingly contributed to a more class-based political system.

At the level of landed society, this development was starkly evident. Some prominent landowners stayed loyal to Gladstone after 1886 (particularly those who had held office in a Liberal ministry), but in general the Whig aristocracy defected, leaving the Liberal Party very weak in the House of Lords, on the county bench, and at the royal court.

Even amongst Dissenters, the higher a man's social status and income, the greater the likelihood that he would abandon the political faith of his fathers for Conservatism or Liberal Unionism. Thus, prosperous Wesleyans deserted Gladstone in droves in 1886, while the predominantly working-class adherents of the Primitive Methodists did not do so—though in the course of the 1890s some of the latter were to be lured away into support of socialism and the cause of independent working-class representation.

However, on balance, the drift to a class-based political system in the 1880s was complicated by Gladstone's insistence that the fate of Ireland was the defining issue of the day. Many working men became enthusiastic Home Rulers after 1886 because they accepted Gladstone's view that securing justice for Ireland was democracy's most pressing task. But other manual workers, including those who had previously supported the Liberal Party, violently disagreed. In areas where Irish immigrants had settled in large numbers, especially Merseyside and in the textile towns of Lancashire, Home Rule was very unpopular indeed; even trade-union officials openly rallied to the Conservative Party, as the best way of frustrating Gladstone's programme. Most dramatic of all was the case of Chamberlain's fiefdom, Birmingham, where all seven seats returned Liberals in the 1885 General Election, prior to the eruption of the Home Rule issue, but which then became a Liberal desert—working-class constituencies such as Bordeseley showing as strong a commitment to Unionism as more affluent residential areas such as Edgbaston.[82] The middle and upper classes showed similar divisions. Symbolic was the situation of Chamberlain and Hartington, who now found themselves, incongruously, joint leaders of the new Liberal Unionist Party.

So British political life after 1886 was truly betwixt and between. The party realignment of that year had gone some way towards creating a class-stratified political system, a process further facilitated by the new electoral arrangements created in 1884–5; but at the same time the passions unleashed by Home Rule cut across these class divisions, preventing that process from fully working itself out. The salience of Home Rule also meant that, for at least the next

---

[82] In 1886 all but one Birmingham constituency returned a Liberal Unionist, the other a Conservative. The Liberals never again won so much as a single seat there until the Ladywood by-election of June 1969.

decade, social issues never dominated the agenda of high politics. Sectarian loyalties, where they survived, were also important in creating cross-class constituencies that were crucial to the fortunes of the Liberal Party nationwide, as well as helping the Conservative Party in certain areas.

It all made for political fluidity. For example, a working man of Irish ancestry living in Manchester (if he qualified for the franchise) might choose to advance the 'national' cause by backing the Liberals, or, as a Catholic, throw his support behind the Conservatives to defend church schools and the principle of a religious education, or (if opportunity arose) express his class allegiances by voting Labour. The political parties had much to play for.

6. PARTY AND ITS CRITICS

At Westminster party friction was generated by small, but not unimportant, differences in the social and economic profiles of the two main parliamentary parties. Conservative MPs included proportionally more landowners and army officers than their rivals, while the Liberals had more active businessmen. Of businessmen in the House, those from the manufacturing sector were more likely to be Liberals, those from banking and finance Conservatives. Moreover, the Liberal Party was somewhat less 'genteel', in the sense of being more associated with newer forms of wealth and status than the more aristocratic Conservatives. This partly reflected the reality that the Liberals, with their sizeable Nonconformist minority, contained MPs who were less likely to have been educated at a major public school or at Oxford and Cambridge. Finally, corresponding with its electoral base, Conservative MPs were predominantly English, the Liberals more representative of mainland Britain as a whole, though many Liberal Scottish MPs were English career politicians seeking a safe seat north of the border.[83]

But these differences, though real, should not be exaggerated. Before the foundation of the Labour Party it was the Irish Nationalists who were the odd men out since, though led by a Protestant landowner, many of their members were tenant farmers or came from the humbler strata of the business and professional worlds (i.e. retailers, journalists, and solicitors), not from higher-status groups.[84] This, plus the fact that they were an overwhelmingly Catholic

---

[83] In 1912 Asquith could privately write from his Lowland Scottish home, 'so far as the eye can see, these rolling hills are represented at Westminster by London barristers' (Turner, 'Letting Go', 258). On the other hand, only a minority of Welsh Liberal MPs were not Welsh.

[84] F. S. L. Lyons, *The Irish Parliamentary Party, 1890–1910* (London, 1951), 169–73, suggests that in the 1892 Parliament 65.5% of MPs represented the 'upper middle-class section', but to reach this conclusion he has had to include large businessmen and even the sizeable contingent of journalists; also, as he admits, Nationalist 'landowners' were often little more than gentlemen-farmers. Moreover, only

group in a self-consciously Protestant Parliament, meant that socially the Irish Nationalist MPs never really fitted into Westminster. Liberal, Liberal Unionist, and Conservative MPs, on the other hand, especially at leadership level, came from not widely dissimilar backgrounds: thus the brother of the Liberal Leader Henry Campbell-Bannerman sat as a Conservative MP; while Edward Grey's Under-Secretary at the Foreign Office, Edmond Fitzmaurice, was the brother of Grey's predecessor, the Liberal Unionist Lord Lansdowne. This did something to soften the asperities of party conflict—but not much, since ideology and policy in this period mattered much more than class.

The fact is that the crisis of 1885–6, which had initially disrupted the unity of both parties, was also responsible for the emergence of a new party system of greater rigidity than anything seen before. Rivalry between different Liberal candidates, common in London between 1868 and 1885, when it ran at nearly 29 per cent, affected only 2.4 per cent of contests between 1885 and 1914.[85] On the other side of politics there were initially greater divisions. The Liberal Unionist Party in the Commons maintained a modicum of independence in the late 1880s (even sitting with the Liberals on the Opposition benches). But, with the Irish generally supporting the Liberals and the two wings of the Unionist Alliance growing closer together, an 'adversarial' system of politics soon developed.[86] By 1903 the Unionist and Liberal MPs were obeying their respective whips in as many as 90 per cent of all divisions. The 1902 reforms of the parliamentary timetable reinforced this trend by giving the executive greater control over the House, so reducing still further the scope for backbench independence.

In the House of Lords cross-bench co-operation continued for rather longer, especially over foreign policy, where the two sets of Leaders genuinely shrank from damaging what they saw as essential national interests. However, as we will see, on controversial domestic issues the Unionist peers maintained a more or less united front,[87] and when the Liberals briefly held office between 1892 and 1895 the Opposition used its crushing majority in the Upper House to vote down or mutilate a range of Liberal measures, not just the Home Rule Bill—such was the intensity of the partisan passions conjured up from the deeps by the Irish quarrel.

---

one-third of these MPs had attended a university, and of these only three had been to 'Oxbridge', most being graduates of the Queen's Colleges and the Catholic University, though, admittedly, six had been to TCD (pp. 165–6).

[85] Lawrence, *Speaking for the People*, 169.

[86] See Ch. 5.

[87] The Liberal Unionist peers, still an independent grouping between 1886 and 1890, soon merged their identity with the Conservatives.

All the same, the dominance of party did not go unchallenged. In particular, at the plebeian end of the social spectrum, suspicion of the 'caucus' continued to generate contempt for party itself. Only later did the Labour Party, with its solidaristic values, grasp that it could turn caucus methods to its own advantage.

Less easily reconciled to the new dispensation were certain intellectuals in politics, old-fashioned Liberals such as Henry Sumner Maine, and A. V. and Edward Dicey. These men deplored what they saw as the artificial polarization of opinion, and, fearing that intelligence and originality were being ground down under the heels of the party machines, attempted to circumvent party politics altogether or, failing that, to mitigate some of their undesirable features. Hence the Proportional Representation Society, founded in 1883, gained many adherents during the 1890s. Others extolled such well-tried methods as the 'conference system' (which had been used to engineer an all-party agreement over the recent Redistribution measure). There were even advocates for such newfangled devices as the referendum (A. V. Dicey pressed it on Salisbury, presenting it as 'at once distinctly and undeniably democratic and in practice Conservative'),[88] while there was much discussion concerning the desirability of establishing a new kind of national politics, perhaps leading to the formation of a 'national government'.

Much of this cavilling against the alleged abuses of the party system originated in a more fundamental disapproval of mass politics. Yet, with the passing of the Reform Acts of 1884–5, the deed had irrevocably been done: a limited kind of 'democracy' was clearly here to stay. But whether the issues that Gladstone had raised when he launched his crusade for Home Rule would succeed, in more than the short term, in distracting the new electors from using their vote in order to change their material circumstances, only time and events would tell.

[88] Roberts, *Salisbury*, 586.

PART II

Late Victorian England 1886–1899

CHAPTER 5

Home Rule and the Politics of Unionism

I. THE AFTERMATH OF THE HOME RULE CRISIS

The party realignment of 1885–6 dealt the Liberal Party a heavy blow, from which it may never fully have recovered. Gladstone's dissolution of Parliament in July 1886, following the defeat of the Home Rule Bill, produced a Commons in which his followers numbered only 191. Even with the support of the eighty-five Irish Nationalists, this did not give him anything approaching a Commons majority. With Liberal Unionist support, the Conservative Leader, Lord Salisbury, returned to 10 Downing Street. Thus began twenty years of almost unbroken Unionist domination.

Gladstone, however, could personally derive some consolation from the Home Rule realignment. By launching his crusade, he had defined for at least another generation what Liberalism meant, sidestepping the social questions which the Radical wing of his own party had been trying to promote. Gladstone had also emerged from the crisis with a better-disciplined, if smaller, party—though, ironically, as a close colleague complained, the 'Grand Old Man' seemed not to 'care a rush' for his followers and colleagues.[1]

The Conservatives, however, had much more to celebrate. During his minority government of 1885–6 Salisbury had found it expedient to work in a loose alliance with the Irish Nationalists—an escapade which was later to cause him considerable embarrassment.[2] But when in 1886 Gladstone raised the stakes so high that he could not be trumped, Salisbury found himself once more acting as defender of the Union. This delighted the Conservative Leader, who had never had any real intention of conciliating the forces of Irish Nationalism, for which he felt a cold contempt. His new role also furnished him with a series of effective populist cries: loyalism versus treason, order

---

[1] 'The moment the question of his personal convenience turns up, or he finds himself out of touch with the party, he is ready to discard it regardless of consequences', grumbled W. V. Harcourt: R. Shannon, *Gladstone: Heroic Minister, 1865–1898* (Harmondsworth, 1999), 553.

[2] With Salisbury's approval, the Irish Viceroy had held a private meeting with Parnell, raising the latter's hopes of an imminent Irish settlement.

versus sedition, and England versus Ireland. From this his party was likely to draw rich electoral dividends; for, as *The Times* noted, with only a little exaggeration, the maintenance of the Empire was 'as dear to the working man of West Ham as it [was] to the masses who work[ed] in other ways in Kensington or Marylebone'.[3]

Home Rule served Salisbury well for yet other reasons. There were obvious advantages flowing from the schism within the Liberal ranks which Gladstone's impetuosity had provoked. Moreover, defending the status quo from Union Jack-bedecked platforms released Salisbury from the irksome and dangerous necessity of saying anything much about contemporary social issues, as his troublesome colleague Randolph Churchill had intermittently been pressing him to do. In this sense Salisbury's position mirrored that of Gladstone.

The Irish Question immediately became entangled with considerations of party advantage and personal ambition, amongst Gladstonians as well as Conservatives. For example, there were Radicals such as Henry Labouchere who embraced Home Rule primarily because they saw this as a way of purging the party of its Whiggish elements. Others stayed loyal to Gladstone in 1886 less because they were persuaded of the merits of reconciliation with the Irish people, than because they had been antagonized by Parnellite obstruction in the Commons and welcomed a settlement which would have ejected the Irish from Westminster. Meanwhile some senior frontbenchers, notably William Vernon Harcourt, were impatient with Gladstone's Irish obsession and only grumpily went along with it because they saw no alternative to doing so.

But cynicism can be carried too far. Tactical cunning was an integral aspect of Gladstone's complex personality. But the Liberal Leader, for all his ignorance of modern Irish society,[4] did fervently believe that the Union would be strengthened, not weakened, by a devolution of power to the Irish people, a conviction that he was able to impart even to a Whig aristocrat such as Lord Spencer, the recent Irish Viceroy. Many Radicals and working-class activists, too, genuinely welcomed Irish Home Rule, because they saw it as a first instalment of 'democracy'. As for the Nonconformists, many of them, already dazzled by Gladstone's aura of moral authority, accepted his view that Home Rule was a 'holy' cause, the attainment of which would entail the consummation of the 'Christian scheme'.[5]

---

[3] 8 July 1886, cited in W. C. Lubenow, *Parliamentary Politics and the Home Rule Crisis: The British House of Commons in 1886* (Oxford, 1988), 319.

[4] e.g. his delusion about the patriotic potential of the Irish landlord class: see J. Loughlin, *Gladstone, Home Rule and the Ulster Question 1882–93* (Dublin, c.1986).

[5] Shannon, *Gladstone: Heroic Minister*, 443–4.

The Unionist case was more straightforward. Most of its advocates simply denied that the Irish constituted a separate people. They also contended that Irish Nationalists had already abundantly demonstrated their unfitness or unreadiness for extensive powers of self-government. It seemed that, given the opportunity, they would ill-treat the minority of Protestant 'loyalists', though comparatively little was said at this stage about the Ulster difficulty. Moreover, A. V. Dicey was not alone in claiming that Home Rule was 'the half-way house to Separation',[6] since Unionists generally assumed that Parnell, whatever he might find it expedient to say, was working for the establishment of an independent state. Such an outcome would be fatal to the greatness and security of Great Britain, not least because it would give England a foreign, and possibly a hostile, neighbour along its western seaboard. Restless colonial subjects and foreign powers alike, Unionists warned, would draw the deduction that London had lost the will to protect its territory and stand by its friends.

The dispute between Home Rulers and Unionists thus aroused intense passions that were capable of dividing families and destroying old friendships. In the process the scenery of British politics was also transformed.

2. SALISBURY AND THE UNIONIST ALLIANCE, 1886–1892

In the long run the Irish quarrel proved to be the making of the Conservative Party. But this was not entirely apparent in the late summer of 1886. Indeed, Salisbury re-entered 10 Downing Street unsure whether his ministry would last more than a few months. The Conservatives had failed to win the 1886 election contest outright: to form a government they needed the support of the seventy-eight Liberal Unionist MPs, of whom between twelve and twenty-one were followers of Chamberlain. Before accepting the premiership, Salisbury had actually offered to serve under the Liberal Unionist Leader, Lord Hartington, though the latter promptly declined the offer, merely promising to give the Conservative government 'independent but friendly support'.

The Liberal Unionists, in fact, were still disunited over what they hoped to achieve. Fearing a drift into 'demagoguery', many of their socially conservative elements—voters, MPs, and peers alike—saw the vindication of the Union as essential to the restoration of good order and the defence of property rights. Joseph Chamberlain, on the other hand, suspected—with some justification—that Gladstone, in launching his Irish crusade, was seeking to divert politics from the constructive social programme into which he had recently invested much time and energy. Moreover, Chamberlain broke with Gladstone in the

---

[6] A. V. Dicey, *England's Case Against Home Rule* (London, 1886; 1887 edn.), 287.

summer of 1886 in the belief that this betokened a *temporary* separation, and that he would soon be welcomed back as the dominant figure in a post-Gladstonian Radical Party once Home Rule had become discredited through its lack of electoral appeal.

Chamberlain and Hartington also disagreed on how Ireland could best be governed. The Birmingham Radical strongly objected to Gladstone's Home Rule Bill, but neither did he favour the status quo: on the contrary, having already expressed his support for a devolutionary settlement, he now began flirting with the federal project.[7] Moreover, though determined to thwart Gladstone, Chamberlain had made it clear from the start that he intended 'never to vote with the Tories unless they [were] in danger, and to vote against them whenever we [could] safely do so'.[8] Such a detached stance played well in areas such as Scotland and the West Midlands, where the Liberal Unionist Party had a strong local following.

Hartington, on the other hand, objected to any tampering with the Union, and saw co-operation with Salisbury as the best guarantee that this would not happen. The Liberal Unionist Leader knew that, had he accepted the premiership, Chamberlain might have been tempted to return to the Gladstonian fold; at the very least, the fragile integrity of the Liberal Unionist Party would have been jeopardized. Hartington also realized the difficulty of heading a coalition in which his Commons followers would have been outnumbered five to one by the Conservatives. This is why he rejected the supreme prize.

Meanwhile Salisbury was experiencing problems with some of his own senior colleagues, the most troublesome of whom was Lord Randolph Churchill, the Chancellor of the Exchequer. Churchill had forced his way to the top of the Conservative Party by a display of wayward brilliance and a reputation for troublemaking which made it expedient to silence him with high office. Once the prophet of 'Tory Democracy' and darling of the activists of the National Union of Conservative Associations, Churchill had more recently reinvented himself as a liberal economist. In a series of public speeches, notably at Dartford in October 1887, Churchill put forward a programme of advanced social legislation of a kind likely to appeal to the Radical Unionists, combining this with savage attacks on the alleged extravagance of the Service Departments.

Churchill's resulting vendetta against the inoffensive War Secretary, W. H. Smith, is hard to explain except as a bid to demonstrate his indispensability and to bend the rest of the Cabinet to his will. Fortunately for Salisbury, Churchill overplayed his hand: in December 1886 he threatened resignation

---

[7] See Ch. 4.

[8] T. A. Jenkins, 'Hartington, Chamberlain and the Unionist Alliance, 1886–1895', *Parliamentary History*, 11 (1992), 113.

for tactical reasons and the Prime Minister chose to interpret this request literally. Asked at a later date to reconsider this decision, Salisbury demurred: 'Did you ever hear of a man who having got rid of a boil on the back of his neck ever wants it back again?'[9]

Churchill left office in high dudgeon, fulminating against 'the "principles" of a stupid Toryism'. Party managers were nervous since, for all his personal faults, the flamboyant Churchill enjoyed a popularity in the Commons and in the country at large which no other senior Conservative could match. Churchill also had the potential to destabilize an already insecure minority government by exploiting his contacts with Opposition politicians. In January 1887 he approached Chamberlain, in many ways a kindred spirit, suggesting that between them they might create a new 'National Party'. However, Chamberlain, who had not been forewarned of Churchill's resignation, reacted coolly.

In the event, Salisbury weathered the storm with the loss of only one junior minister. After Hartington had again rejected Salisbury's offer of the premiership—much to the relief of Conservative Central Office and of most Conservative backbenchers—the vacancy at the Treasury was filled by an experienced former Liberal minister, George Joachim Goschen, quite the most conservative in outlook of all the senior Liberal Unionist MPs. However, Goschen made his joining of the ministry conditional upon the removal from the Foreign Office of the fading Lord Iddesleigh, the former Stafford Northcote. As a result of an unfortunate press leak, Salisbury's attempt at moving Iddesleigh to the Privy Council provoked the latter's indignant resignation. Indeed, on 12 January he visited 10 Downing Street to protest about his discourteous treatment, only to drop dead at Salisbury's feet. Salisbury was distressed by this experience, but it did at least leave him free to combine the roles of Prime Minister and Foreign Secretary, as he had done during his first ministry of 1885–6—a source of satisfaction to a politician whose main interest always lay in diplomacy. W. H. Smith ('Old Morality') replaced his former tormentor Churchill as Leader of the House.

However, the Salisbury ministry was still not out of the woods. On 13 January 1887 a Round Table Conference met in an attempt to reunite the fractured Liberal Party. Hartington did not participate in these talks, which ran on until mid-March, but Chamberlain and his fellow Radical Unionist, G. O. Trevelyan, were prepared to explore the possibilities of an Irish compromise. Equally eager for reconciliation was Harcourt, once a close associate of the Birmingham Radical. However, John Morley, who had effectively

<hr>

[9] R. R. James, *Lord Randolph Churchill* (1969), 311. Salisbury particularly disliked Churchill's commendation of graduated death duties, which he thought would mean a country gentleman paying an extra 9*d.* in the pound.

usurped Chamberlain's former place, showed no wish to compromise; nor, from behind the scenes, did Gladstone.[10]

With the collapse of the Round Table talks, Trevelyan rejoined the Liberal Party, followed over the next few months by other Radical Unionist MPs: by 1892 as many as ten of the Liberals who had voted against the Home Rule Bill were standing once more as Gladstonian candidates.[11] Chamberlain, still unclear about his future, returned to the idea of establishing a 'National' or 'Centre Party', which, he hoped, would exclude 'only the extreme sections of the party of reaction on the one hand, and the party of anarchy on the other'.[12] Churchill responded favourably, and the two men continued their informal exchanges throughout the early summer of 1887. But the venture ran into the ground with the later involvement of Hartington, whose overriding priority remained that of propping up Salisbury's government as the only realistic way of saving the Union—he saw no point in co-operating with a vengeful Churchill out to destabilize that government.

Meanwhile the government's future crucially depended upon its handling of Ireland, where the Irish Chief Secretary, Michael Hicks Beach, confronted an inflammatory situation. Another downturn in the fortunes of agriculture had reawakened the Irish land war, this time in the form of the so-called 'Plan of Campaign', a cunning stratagem invented by Parnell's lieutenant, the Nationalist MP William O'Brien, which involved aggrieved tenants withholding rent from an unreasonable landlord and paying the money into a central fund which could then be used to fight evictions.

Hicks Beach and senior Dublin Castle officials obviously wanted to defeat the 'Plan'—but not in such a way as to encourage the obduracy of the Irish landlords, for whom they felt little sympathy. Indeed, General Sir Redvers Buller, the Permanent Secretary, encouraged his chief to take a friendly view of the tenants' case. The two men also cracked down hard on rioting 'loyalists' in Belfast: in early August 1886 1,200 soldiers were sent into that city to reinforce the police.

Beach's espousal of a moderate Unionism aimed at the resolution of 'reasonable' Irish grievances was well-meaning. However, the polarization of attitudes towards Ireland which Gladstone's offer of Home Rule had provoked meant that Hicks Beach's policies simply looked defeatist in the eyes of his supporters. In March 1887, largely isolated within the Cabinet and suffering

[10] Though he did meet Trevelyan at dinner and helped persuade him to rejoin the party (H. C. G. Matthew, *Gladstone Vol. 2 1875–98* (Oxford, 1995), 307).

[11] Lubenow, *Home Rule Crisis*, 287.

[12] G. R. Searle, *Country Before Party: Coalition and the Idea of 'National Government' in Modern Britain 1885–1987* (Harlow, 1995), 36.

from poor health, Beach resigned. Salisbury gambled by replacing him as Chief Secretary with his nephew, Arthur Balfour.

Though initially this appointment was greeted with a mixture of mockery and incredulity, Balfour had already shown steely ruthlessness during his brief spell as Scottish Secretary in 1885–6, when he had put down a crofters' revolt. Correctly diagnosing that the main problem for the Irish government was a loss of confidence among senior officers of the Crown (a factor in Gladstone's conversion to Home Rule the previous year), Balfour replaced Buller and assembled a cadre of senior officials who shared his determination to reassert the rule of law in Ireland—among them the new Crown Prosecutor, Edward Carson. Salisbury heartily approved of these moves: the Irish 'must "take a good licking" before conciliation would do them any good', he had earlier observed.[13]

Balfour threw all available resources into the fight against the Plan of Campaign. Hicks Beach had already drafted a new Crimes Bill, giving the Irish authorities sweeping powers to suppress disorder and resistance to evictions, but Balfour stiffened its provisions so that 'disaffected' areas could be 'proclaimed': in other words, subjected to a kind of martial law. All who infringed its provisions risked imprisonment, a fate which befell Roman Catholic priests and even Irish Nationalist MPs (notably William O'Brien), as well as liberal-minded English observers, such as the poet Wilfrid Scawen Blunt.

Serious trouble soon followed. In Mitchelstown in September 1887 an illegal demonstration took place. The police, brought in to control and disperse the crowd, panicked and fired into the unarmed assembly; three civilians were killed and others wounded. Balfour, while discreetly tightening up procedures to prevent another such occurrence, publicly backed the agents of the Crown, in defiance of the Opposition as well as in the teeth of Nationalist protests.

These policies carried considerable risks. As Balfour irritably noted, there seemed to be some curious connection between Irish Nationalism and weak lungs. In 1888 a prominent Irish Nationalist, John Mandeville, died of a throat infection seven months after his release from imprisonment, probably because of the dampness of the gaol and the hardships of its regime. The Unionists were nervous about the same thing recurring. When O'Brien protested at being treated as a common criminal by embarking upon an act of voluntary constipation, Dublin Castle was sufficiently alarmed to ask for regular reports on O'Brien's bowel movements, a 'crisis' only ended when the prison doctor smuggled a laxative into the prisoner's food.[14]

---

[13] A. Roberts, *Salisbury: Victorian Titan* (London, 1999), 443.

[14] L. P. Curtis, jnr., *Coercion and Conciliation in Ireland 1880–1892: A Study in Conservative Unionism* (Princeton and Oxford, 1963), 227–8. The glad tidings were passed on to Balfour.

'Bloody Balfour', as the Nationalists called him, adopted an equally aggressive policy at Westminster, where his mocking defiance of the Irish MPs played an important part in the recovery of Conservative morale from late 1887 onwards. Balfour's emergence as a 'star' was also important in diminishing the reputation and influence of the government's still dangerous backbench critic, Churchill.

Coercion confirmed Gladstone in his view that nothing now stood between Home Rule and hideous repression. 'Remember Mitchelstown' became a favourite Liberal war-cry. Indeed, the Liberal Leader soon convinced himself that the Irish, in making a 'modest and temperate demand for a self-government complete indeed but purely local', were behaving responsibly and that it was the *Conservatives* who were the dangerous troublemakers.[15]

The Liberals also managed to persuade many working-class leaders that they should give precedence to Ireland over all other issues because of the important principles of civil and political liberty that were at stake. On 13 November 1887 ('Bloody Sunday') the Metropolitan Radical Federation persisted in holding a protest rally in Trafalgar Square, despite a banning order by the Chief Commissioner of the Metropolitan Police: special constables were sworn in as reinforcements and serious rioting erupted, leading to the loss of two lives and some prominent arrests, including those of John Burns, the prominent labour leader, and a Radical MP, Cunninghame Graham. The Conservative government had already taken precautionary steps to quell civil disorder. Worried by (false) reports that an attempt was about to made on the life of the Queen at her Golden Jubilee, the authorities created the Special Branch, formed out of an earlier organization (the 'Fenian Office') based at Scotland Yard. In fact, the dynamite campaign conducted by Irish extremists had ended in 1885, but the atmosphere remained tense.[16]

In the long run, such a polarisation of opinion around the Irish Question had some advantages for Salisbury, because coercion erected an emotional barrier between the two 'Liberal' Parties. In the short run, however, it made for complications. Chamberlain, in particular, found it impossible to conceal his dislike of central elements in the government's Irish programme. Under pressure from his Birmingham supporters, he abstained on the second reading of the Crimes Bill—a gesture not sufficient to satisfy all his followers, four of whom returned to the official Liberal Party on 28 March. Chamberlain again broke ranks when he joined the Gladstonians in voting for an amendment to the government's 1887 Irish Land Bill—a measure which, in recognition of the severity of the agricultural depression, lowered the 'judicial' rents established

---

[15] Matthew, *Gladstone Vol. 2*, 310.

[16] B. Porter, *Plots and Paranoia: A History of Political Espionage in Britain, 1790–1988* (London, 1989), 102–10.

by the earlier Irish Land Act of 1881 but which did not, in its critics' eyes, go far enough. On both occasions Salisbury was saved by Hartington who, for all his grumbling, was determined to prioritize the safety of the Union by not giving any comfort to its enemies.

On the other hand, but for Chamberlain's pressure the ministry might not have moved to redress the grievances of the Irish tenantry at all. Salisbury privately called the 1887 Land Act 'the price we have to pay for the Union, and it is a heavy one'.[17] Indeed, faced by his exasperated backbenchers, Balfour had to redress the balance by 'proclaiming' the Irish National League in a move which provoked Chamberlain and five other Radical Unionists to follow Gladstone into the 'no' lobby.[18] Soon afterwards Salisbury prudently sent Chamberlain to Washington to mediate in a fishing dispute between the United States and Canada, an assignment which took him out of the country until March 1888.

But if the Unionists were taking risks with their strategy of coercion, the Liberal Leadership, with its commitment to a 'Union of Hearts' between Great Britain and Ireland, was also playing a hazardous game. For by investing so much political capital in Parnell, Gladstone was entrusting his party's fate to a mysterious and unpredictable politician who had problems of his own to surmount and the requirements of the Irish people to which to attend.

The Liberal–Irish alliance had come under strain as early as 1887, when *The Times* published a series of articles, 'Parnellism and Crime', providing evidence of Parnell's implication in some of the more violent episodes in the 'land war' earlier in the decade. Among its many lurid 'revelations' was a facsimile of a letter which seemingly showed Parnell (in opposition to his public declarations) expressing personal satisfaction at the Phoenix Park murders. The government, urged on by Chamberlain, established a Special Commission, which, it hoped, would decisively prove Parnell's guilt. Instead, in February 1889 defending counsel were able to show that the incriminating letter was a forgery—a blow not only to the reputation of *The Times* but also to the government, which had thrown all the resources of the state behind the prosecution.[19] Parnell's vindication therefore produced great rejoicing amongst Irish Nationalists and Gladstonian Liberals. Churchill, too, openly gloated over the government's discomfiture.

---

[17] J. P. D. Dunbabin, 'The Politics of the Establishment of County Councils', *Historical Journal*, 6 (1963), 239–40.

[18] Another 17 Liberal Unionists abstained, though Hartington rallied 47 Liberal Unionist MPs in support of the government.

[19] The Attorney-General, Sir Richard Webster, represented it before the Commission. The Special Branch had probably helped the prosecution as well.

In the wake of this debacle, morale on the Unionist benches sagged, and the government's majorities in 1890 fell to a dangerously low point—in one division it scraped home by only four votes. The ministry struggled through this crisis, saved by some efficient 'whipping' and by the industriousness of the pedestrian but respected Leader of the House, W. H. Smith, who despite ill-health doggedly persisted in his duty, winning the admiration of Salisbury, who found him 'straight'. However, adding to the government's difficulties was the cumulative effect of by-election defeats, which had reduced the Unionists' initial majority of 100 to 70.

Unionist fortunes then suddenly turned. In November 1889 the Irish Nationalist MP, William O'Shea, filed a divorce petition against Parnell for committing adultery with his wife Catherine. Parnell, who did not contest the case, stood exposed as an adulterer who, so the world was led to believe, had deceived and cuckolded one of his parliamentary followers.[20] This in itself would have done a lot to discredit the Irish Nationalist cause.

But the sequel was far worse. Abandoned by the Catholic clergy and by the majority of his former followers, Parnell lashed out violently against the Gladstonians. Despite having held amicable discussions about the details of Home Rule with Gladstone at the latter's home, Hawarden, as late as 18–19 December 1889, Parnell issued a manifesto in which he denounced his allies as 'English wolves' and damned, as a sham and an insult to the Irish race, the Home Rule settlement which a future Liberal government was likely to produce.

Though prepared shamefacedly to condone Parnell's sexual misconduct, the majority of Irish Nationalist MPs would not sacrifice all realistic prospects of achieving Home Rule out of concern for their Leader's wounded pride. But the damage had been done. The Gladstonian vision of a 'Union of Hearts' between England and Ireland never really recovered from the sordid revelations of the divorce court and from the still more sordid faction-fighting in Ireland which followed in its wake. In October 1891 Parnell died in the middle of a bitter by-election contest, but Nationalist divisions continued, with the majority faction, led by Justin McCarthy (though really dominated by John Dillon), locked in an implacable vendetta with the Parnellite minority, led by John Redmond.

Meanwhile agrarian agitation in Ireland was abating. By November 1889 the 'Plan of Campaign' had been broken and rural crime stood at a lower level than at any time since 1879. This gave Balfour the confidence to 'unproclaim' most of the country. He then went on to introduce measures designed to eradicate some of the social and economic discontents supposedly at the root of Irish

---

[20] To what extent were Chamberlain or other politicians involved in egging on O'Shea, whose wife's affair with Parnell he (and most of the political world) had known all about for at least five years? What *is* certain is that O'Shea had a financial motive for divorcing his wife at this time.

national feeling. When Smith died in October 1891 it was Balfour, the one clear ministerial success since 1887, who became Leader of the House, over the head of the unpopular Goschen, who had expected that post.[21]

The Union was still not entirely safe, but the likelihood of Home Rule being enacted steadily receded. The Liberals had won no fewer than ten seats from the Unionist parties between Parnell's vindication and the start of the divorce case: they won only another five in the remaining years of the second Salisbury government.[22] By late 1891 the ministry looked far more stable than it had been during its initial panicky years. True, ministers expected to lose the next general election, but they also thought that they had done enough to put a brake on Gladstone's mischievousness. At Westminster all talk of a 'centre party' had by now petered out: Churchill, his health and indeed his sanity seriously in decline, no longer inspired fear: and, most importantly, the Unionist alliance had stabilized.

Finally, with Ireland relatively tranquil, the policy vulgarly but mistakenly called 'Killing Home Rule With Kindness' was in full swing. Significantly, even a socially conservative Unionist such as Dicey had never denied that, behind the 'spurious' Irish Nationalist agitation, there lay deep grievances, mainly agrarian. These the government now found it safe to address.

Balfour's most successful innovation was the establishment of the Congested Districts Board, which provided public funds for the amalgamation of over-crowded agricultural units on the impoverished western seaboard, as well as for the construction of new roads, piers, and harbours. A Department of Agricultural and Technical Instruction was also set up, under the direction of Horace Plunkett, founder of the Irish Co-operative Movement. But the 1891 Land Purchase Bill, which sought to speed up further land sales, flopped for want of powers of compulsion. Another failure was the half-hearted Irish Local Government Bill of the same year, which disappointed all sides and had to be withdrawn.

Neither did Balfour succeed in constructing a viable Catholic Unionism in the South, which might have been the best protection in the long run for the Protestants throughout the country.[23] Had public money been found for the endowment of a Catholic university in Ireland, the government could then have outflanked Gladstone, whose first Home Rule Bill had denied a Dublin parliament the powers to take such an initiative. English Catholic supporters

[21] It was a sign of the times that Balfour was succeeded as Chief Secretary by a businessman, W. L. Jackson, a low-key appointment which suggested that Ireland no longer constituted a life-and-death political issue.

[22] The Liberals had won 14 by-election victories since 1887, culminating in triumphs in 1890 at Barrow and Eccles.

[23] R. Shannon, *The Age of Salisbury, 1881–1902: Unionism and Empire* (Harlow, 1996), 287–8, 291.

such as the Duke of Norfolk would also have been pleased. But the Parnell divorce case, by unleashing a flood of anti-Catholic and anticlerical feeling, scotched any such possibility.

In the short run, however, the abatement of the Irish crisis did at least leave the Salisbury ministry free to pursue a programme of mild social reform for the rest of the United Kingdom.[24] Partially but not entirely so, since the Irish situation set limits on what was politically feasible. For example, the Prime Minister had some sympathy with the cause of 'fair trade', while Balfour was attracted to the cause of bimetallism (which involved the establishment of a monetary system in which silver was placed on precisely the same footing as gold); but tampering with free trade, though it had the support of some sixty Conservative MPs,[25] was incompatible with co-operation with the Liberal Unionists—one of whose former members, the impeccably orthodox Goschen, now held the key post of Chancellor of the Exchequer. No Unionist from either party wanted to play into the Liberals' hands by giving them the 'dear food cry', and the wisdom of doing nothing reckless that might let Gladstone back into power and endanger the Union was obvious to them all.

In fact, Salisbury's greatest achievement was to have brought coherence and self-discipline to the disparate anti-Gladstonian forces.[26] A turning point came in the summer of 1888 when Chamberlain, the most independent-minded of the Liberal Unionists, was forced by Gladstonian aggression in his home town to set up a separate Birmingham Liberal Unionist Association.[27] By January 1891 Chamberlain and Salisbury were standing on the same platform at the first joint meeting of the two Birmingham Unionist parties, an occasion at which Chamberlain declared that he neither looked for nor desired Liberal reunion.[28] Meanwhile the differing factions within the Liberal Unionist Party were also growing closer to one another. When in December 1891 Hartington entered the Lords, having succeeded his father as the eighth Duke of Devonshire, Chamberlain assumed the Leadership in the Commons, and a partnership between the two men developed which, given their different backgrounds and political outlooks, worked surprisingly well.[29]

In fact, in the House of Commons a fairly stable two-party system had emerged by the end of the 1890 session, with cross-party voting and rebellions

---

[24] See Ch. 7.

[25] 48 from boroughs, 12 from counties (E. H. H. Green, *The Crisis of Conservatism: The Politics, Economics and Ideology of the British Conservative Party, 1880–1914* (London, 1995), 110).

[26] Shannon, *Age of Salisbury*, 342.

[27] R. Jay, *Joseph Chamberlain: A Political Study* (Oxford, 1981), 158.

[28] Ibid. 167.

[29] This helped cement the Unionist Alliance in other ways. Previously the Liberal Unionist Leader in the Lords had been Lord Derby, an ex-Conservative minister, who was not even on speaking terms with Salisbury.

against the whip becoming increasingly rare. At constituency level, it is true, friction between the two Unionist parties sporadically broke out over which had the reversion to a vacant seat, as at Warwick and Leamington in 1890. In early 1892 trouble also flared in East Worcestershire, where the Conservatives informed Chamberlain's son, Austen, that their support for him in the imminent by-election would depend upon his renunciation of Disestablishment. But at central level, Salisbury's shrewd employment of patronage (involving the distribution of chairmanships of important official inquiries as well as honours) kept the Liberal Unionists in good humour—to the benefit of the common cause.

In 1889 there was even talk, centring on disgruntled ex-Liberal intellectuals, of fusing the two Unionist Parties in order to avoid a damaging duplication of effort,[30] and a half-hearted attempt was actually made in 1890 to amalgamate the constituency committees of the two parties, but this was swiftly abandoned— much to the relief of the Conservative Chief Agent, Captain Middleton, who preferred to deal with the Liberal Unionists as a separate group. Nor did the Liberal Unionist Leaders show much enthusiasm for winding up their own party. Chamberlain, in particular, shrank from the prospect of dismantling his loyal Birmingham organization, and in any case he was now thinking of *transforming* Unionism by injecting some of his Radical passion into Conservatism, not of establishing a new National Party. Meanwhile Devonshire subordinated his own long-term ambitions to the goal of controlling Chamberlain, an objective which entailed the maintenance of a separate Liberal Unionist machine.

In May 1892 Salisbury for the first time held a joint meeting of the two Unionist front benches (previously he had dealt with his allies individually). By this time he had succeeded in his principal quest, which was, through survival, to have kept the Unionist Alliance in being and to establish it on a permanent basis—but without compromising the integrity of the Conservative Party itself.[31] Since the Conservatives were much the larger party, fusion, when it eventually came, would necessarily be on Conservative terms. For this reason alone, the Conservative Party owes Salisbury an enormous debt of gratitude.

In June 1892 Parliament was dissolved. During the July general election Home Rule failed to inspire the passions on mainland Britain that it had done in 1886—ominously for the long-term future of both Gladstone and Salisbury. The Conservatives fell back to 268 seats, but this still left them immeasurably stronger than they had been after the debacle of 1880, and, even without the

---

[30] Searle, *Country Before Party*, 39–40. Hicks Beach, too, favoured fusion—until Salisbury quickly brought him back into office, as President of the Board of Trade.

[31] P. Marsh, *The Discipline of Popular Government: Lord Salisbury's Domestic Statecraft, 1881–1902* (Hassocks, 1978), 137.

Liberal Unionists, they still held a majority of seats in England. The Liberal Unionists, reduced to forty-seven, suffered eighteen defeats, but they held their ground in their strongholds, Scotland and the West Midlands—which showed that, despite their recent abysmal by-election record, they were still a viable electoral force.[32]

The largest single group was the Liberal Party, which came back with 274 MPs (twenty-eight of them Welsh, fifty Scottish), which meant that, to form a government, it required the backing of the seventy-one Irish Nationalist MPs (the nine Parnellites could certainly not be relied upon). The Queen was depressed to learn that Gladstone would be her Prime Minister for a fourth time.

3. THE LIBERALS IN OFFICE, 1892–1895

The Cabinet which Gladstone formed in 1892 brought together elderly ministers with experience dating back to Palmerston's time (Lord Ripon) and young talent that was to mature over the following decades, notably H. H. Asquith, the new Home Secretary. The Prime Minister himself, weakened by a couple of recent physical mishaps, took on an immense task for someone of his age. The up-and-coming Scottish aristocrat Lord Rosebery became Foreign Secretary, to the Queen's relief. Five of the seventeen Cabinet Members were peers, fewer than in 1886, but the ministry still had a decidedly aristocratic tone, though leavened by the presence of professional men, writers, and one solitary businessman (A. J. Mundella). Morley returned to the Irish Office, and Harcourt became Chancellor of the Exchequer for the second time.

It had been assumed that the Liberals, when they next came to power, would prioritize Home Rule. Gladstone himself, in a famous phrase, had announced that he was 'fast bound to Ireland as Ulysses was to his mast'. He also managed to persuade many Liberals that Ireland was an 'obstruction' blocking the path to all other legislative reforms: indeed, by handing over Irish affairs to Irishmen in Ireland, Home Rule would—or so his son Herbert predicted—save at least a quarter of the Commons' time.[33]

However, there were early signs that this strategy was going astray, and even before the disastrous Parnell divorce case Gladstone was attempting to broaden the Liberal programme somewhat, a task that took on even greater urgency with the disappointing by-election results of 1890 onwards. The salience of the Irish Question had in any case stimulated national sentiment in both Scotland

---

[32] In the 1886 Parliament the Liberal Unionists had held only five of their seats in by-elections, sacrificing one to the Conservative Party and losing ten to the Liberal Opposition.

[33] D. A. Hamer, *Liberal Politics in the Age of Gladstone and Rosebery: A Study in Leadership and Policy* (Oxford, 1972), 134.

and Wales. In May 1886 a Scottish Home Rule Association was founded, with the Liberal MP for Caithness, Dr G. B. Clark, as its first President.[34] Opinion in Scotland was also 'ripening' on the issue of Scottish Disestablishment, so much so that in November 1891 the Liberal Leader, himself a Scottish Member, reversed his previous stand and risked the wrath of the Kirk by voting for a Disestablishment motion.[35]

It was this developing sense of the need to say something about non-Irish affairs which also explains why Gladstone should have given his (admittedly rather vague) blessing to the hotch-potch of policy commitments endorsed by the National Liberal Federation at Newcastle in 1891 (the so-called Newcastle Programme), though a desire to outmanoeuvre Chamberlain also played its part.[36] Even in 1891, then, the Gladstonian strategy of using Ireland to impose order on Liberal politics was being replaced by the idea of constructing a broad programme in which all the various 'faddists' and interests groups of which Liberalism was comprised could find a respected place.[37]

Then came the 1892 General Election. Gladstone, who had been hoping for a clear mandate, was so shocked by his lack of an overall majority that he initially proposed doing nothing except secure the assent of the House to the *principle* of Home Rule, while pursuing various administrative reforms; for it seemed a waste of time to formulate a complicated Bill which would inevitably founder in the Lords.[38] In this he was encouraged by both Harcourt and Rosebery, who urged the adoption of an 'English' or 'British' programme.

Morley, on the other hand, was horrified at such backsliding: 'The Irish are our masters and we had better realise it once', he realistically observed.[39] Spencer, a sincere if belated convert to the merits of Home Rule, joined him in pleading the cause of the Irish. Gladstone needed little pressing, and, with manic energy, set about drafting a second Home Rule Bill, while Rosebery and Harcourt sat apart on what they called 'the English bench'. On 13 February 1893 Gladstone moved its first reading in an oration of two-and-a-half hours— subsequently making no fewer than eighty separate speeches in its support.

---

[34] This acted as a pressure group within liberalism for Home Rule for Scotland until 1914 (J. Kendle, *Ireland and the Federal Solution, 1870–1921* (Kingston, Ont., 1989), 62).

[35] Hamer, *Liberal Politics*, 139.

[36] Gladstone picked and chose from among the items in the Newcastle Programme, refusing, for example, to support Welsh Disestablishment (M. Barker, *Gladstone and Radicalism: The Reconstruction of Liberal Policy in Britain 1885–1894* (Hassocks, 1975), 162). See also Shannon, *Gladstone: Heroic Minister*, 508–9.

[37] Hamer, *Liberal Politics*, 174.

[38] Barker, *Gladstone and Radicalism*, 235.

[39] P. Stansky, *Ambitions and Strategies: The Struggle for the Leadership of the Liberal Party in the 1890s* (Oxford, 1964), 3.

The Bill differed in some important respects from its predecessor. For example, the financial terms being offered to Ireland were far less generous than in 1886.[40] But, as previously, the main problem was what to do about Irish representation in the 'Imperial' Parliament. At an earlier meeting at Hawarden in 1889, the Liberal leaders had provisionally decided to retain a reduced number of Irish MPs—to the exasperation of those Liberals who saw the ejection of the Irish as Home Rule's most attractive feature. But Harcourt and Rosebery favoured retention, though for different reasons—Harcourt because he calculated that a Liberal government would need Irish votes to carry important domestic reforms, Rosebery because he dreaded giving any encouragement to the forces of Irish separatism.

As originally drafted, the Home Rule Bill stipulated that eighty Irish MPs (reduced from the earlier figure of 103) would sit in the 'Imperial' Parliament—but only when matters affecting Ireland were under consideration. How this would operate in practice was not at all clear,[41] and during the committee stage a new clause was inserted, allowing the reduced number of Irishmen back into Westminster on a *permanent* basis.

Despite the continuing split within their ranks, the Irish Nationalist MPs showed a remarkable self-discipline when the Home Rule Bill came before the House, staying mostly silent so as not to waste time. Ironically the guillotine, first introduced to overcome Irish obstructionism, was now used to circumvent Unionist sabotage. Three-quarters of the Bill's clauses were never discussed in the Commons at all. This provoked Chamberlain, in July 1893, into sardonic observations which caused tempers to flare: amid Liberal cries of 'Judas', fisticuffs broke out on the floor of the House. But an air of weary inevitability accompanied the progress of the Bill, which the Commons passed on 1 September by 307 votes to 267—only for the Unionist-controlled Lords to reject it contemptuously by the margin of 419 to 41. An excited mob cheered Salisbury through the streets as he made his way to his London home.

However predictable, the defeat of Home Rule left the Liberal government in a quandary. Gladstone wanted to dissolve and do battle against the Upper House on the issue of 'whether the people of the U.K. are or are not to be a self-governing people', but not a single minister supported him. Thwarted in his attempts to challenge Spencer's Naval Estimates, which he bitterly opposed,[42] Gladstone resigned, in rage and despair, though only after very considerable prevarication—a sour note on which to end an outstanding parliamentary career spanning sixty-one years.

---

[40] On this, see Matthew, *Gladstone, Vol. 2*, 337–8.
[41] For example, would the Irish MPs be allowed to vote on votes of confidence?
[42] See Ch. 8.

Gladstone had deliberately failed to groom a successor. In the event of the Queen asking his advice, he would, ironically in the circumstances, have recommended Spencer. As it was, the succession was bitterly disputed between Harcourt and Rosebery. Most Liberal MPs preferred Harcourt, but Rosebery, as well as being the Queen's favourite, also had the backing of the London press, the Scottish wing of the party, and, crucially, most members of the Cabinet, who had had more than enough of Harcourt's truculence.[43] On 3 March 1894 Rosebery kissed hands, leaving his rival, Harcourt, now Leader of the Commons, in a state of brooding discontent.

Although Home Rule was temporarily out of the running, Ireland continued to haunt British politics. At the very start of his premiership Rosebery made a bad blunder with his 'predominant partner' speech,[44] which particularly infuri-ated his touchy Welsh supporters, and played straight into the hands of Salisbury, who was amazed but gratified to find a Liberal Prime Minister echoing his own sentiments. Harcourt did not substantially disagree with his Leader's remarks, but thought the timing of their utterance a severe tactical mistake.

In this petty and poisonous atmosphere, the Cabinet struggled to devise a strategy. Rosebery initially hoped to follow Gladstone's lead by rousing the party in a campaign against the peers. But it was unclear whether he wanted to strengthen the Lords by reforming its composition, or whether he preferred the single chamber solution desired by the Radical wing of his own party. Eventually, at a public speech in Edinburgh on 17 March Rosebery plumped for a bicameral legislature. But nothing came of this venture because the Prime Minister had entirely failed to prepare his party, or even his Cabinet—evidence of the egotistical impulsiveness which had also been Gladstone's trademark, though unaccompanied by the 'People's William's' charismatic flair. Rosebery later floated the idea of joint conferences between the two Houses for the removal of deadlocks, but once again he failed to convince the Cabinet, which instead passed a resolution in favour of limiting the Lords' powers of rejection to one year and its powers of amendment to one submission.

While Salisbury stoutly defended the right of the Upper House to oppose a transient Commons majority, the general public failed to rally behind the Liberal government, no doubt because none of the measures mangled by the Lords (the Home Rule Bill included)[45] had much popular appeal: a rally in Hyde Park in August 1894 attracted a crowd of only 1,500 people. As a result, by 1895 the government had dropped the Lords issue completely.

[43] Even Morley briefly deserted Harcourt at a crucial moment, in the hope of securing promotion for himself.

[44] See Ch. 1.

[45] For other measures blocked by the Lords, see Ch. 7.

In a sense the Rosebery government, which stumbled on for fifteen unhappy months (from March 1894 to June 1895), never overcame the unhappy circumstances of its birth. Harcourt's 1894 Budget broke fresh ground in some respects,[46] but, no more than during Gladstone's last premiership, did the Liberals succeed in agreeing upon a 'constructive' programme of social reform.

Moreover, the Irish issue continued, indirectly, to distort Westminster politics. For example, Harcourt's efforts to combat the evils associated with heavy drinking through his 1894 Budget and his later proposals for 'Local Option' failed to satisfy the prohibitionists of the United Kingdom Alliance,[47] but annoyed the Irish Nationalists, over whom the distillery interests and the publicans exercised a considerable influence. Yet when, in his 1895 Budget, Harcourt tried to propitiate the Irish by remitting the previous year's spirits duty while leaving the beer duty intact, this was seen as favouritism towards the Irish—as was that country's exemption from the Local Option Bill.

The Opposition seized every opportunity to paint the Liberal government as indifferent to English interests yet over-eager to curry favour with the Irish, on whose votes they depended. For example, Morley's Evicted Irish Tenants (Ireland) Bill of 1894, eventually thrown out by the House of Lords by 249 votes to 30, was designed to help some of the 'victims' of the Plan of Campaign, but nothing comparable was done to help English farmers devastated by agricultural depression, who could only envy the special hardship grants given to Irish tenant farmers. The government's failure in its various abortive reform schemes to do anything about Ireland's over-representation could similarly be portrayed as a manifestation of the government's 'anti-national' proclivities. During the 1895 General Election campaign Chamberlain claimed that the country had been governed during the previous three years 'by a faction of disloyal Irishmen, of intolerant Welshmen, and of extreme teetotallers'.

An important expression of the growing exasperation with this style of government was the emergence of the 'Liberal Imperialist' group. Its origins can be traced back to the 'Articles Club', founded in 1889, of which R. B. Haldane was the wire-puller, Morley the mentor, Rosebery the leader, and Harcourt the *bête noire*.[48] The Liberal Imperialists were mainly young, ambitious politicians; some of them had already attained Cabinet office (Asquith, A. H. D. Acland, and H. H. Fowler), others, such as Haldane and Edward Grey, already seemed destined for great things. The real emotion driving the group forward was their eagerness to get away from Gladstone's

---

[46] See Ch. 7.

[47] See D. A. Hamer, *The Politics of Electoral Pressure* (Hassocks, 1977), 268–70.

[48] H. C. G. Matthew, *The Liberal Imperialists: The Ideas and Politics of a Post-Gladstonian Elite* (Oxford, 1973), 12–13. Morley was initially open to these new ideas, though he did not sustain it.

Home Rule obsession and Harcourt's negativity through a modernization of the party which, by highlighting moderate social reform and a commitment to Empire, would regain the centre ground that had been lost by Liberalism since 1886. What later became known as the 'New Liberalism' was another attempt to update the Liberal agenda.[49]

But however important for the future, both groups failed to revive the fortunes of the Rosebery government, which was eventually brought down, appropriately enough, by one of the special-interest groups that had been brought into existence by the salience of the Irish Question: the Welsh Nationalists.

The 'Welsh hunger for national dignity' had earlier found expression in the formation of a semi-autonomous Welsh group, vaguely modelled upon the Irish Nationalists. One of its brightest spirits, Tom Ellis, was later recruited into the Government's Whips' Office. But dissatisfaction mounted over the failure to carry a measure to disestablish the Church of Wales, culminating in four Welsh MPs, among them the newly elected Member for Carnarvon Boroughs, David Lloyd George, resigning the Liberal Whip: 'We have nothing to gain by subservience to the Liberal party, and ... we shall never get the English to do us justice until we show our independence of them', one of them bitterly declared.[50] In 1895 the Home Secretary, Asquith, did in fact give precedence to a new Welsh Disestablishment Bill,[51] but this, like Local Option, was never likely to pass through the House of Lords, and the government would have gained little from campaigning on an issue which aroused scant interest outside the Principality. Welsh Disestablishment, complained the Opposition, was in any case an assault on property rights that could not but undermine business confidence.

As morale on the Liberal benches plummeted, the government's position became increasingly precarious. On Gladstone's retirement, John Redmond and the Parnellite MPs had assumed full independence, which further reduced the Liberals' effective Commons majority, already dented by a succession of by-election defeats. The end came on 21 June 1895 when the War Secretary, Campbell-Bannerman, lost a snap vote on the Army Estimates (over the inadequate supplies of cordite). This was partly the result of slack whipping: two Liberal MPs (one of them Charles Dilke) voted against their own government, while no fewer than six ministers were absent unpaired. Significantly, several Welsh Liberal MPs also figured among the absentees and there was a

---

[49] See Ch. 7.
[50] Stansky, *Ambitions and Strategies*, 160.
[51] The government had sponsored a Bill in 1894 which they later dropped—it faced inevitable rejection in the Upper House.

poor turnout of Irish Nationalists, offended by Rosebery's recent attempt to set up a Cromwell Statue appeal.

Defeat on the 'cordite vote' gave Rosebery the excuse for which he was looking, and he promptly resigned, leaving Salisbury to form his own ministry in advance of a general election. This time Salisbury invited leading Liberal Unionists into his Cabinet. Bizarrely, Conservatives and Liberal Unionists had continued during the years of Liberal rule to sit on opposite sides of the House,[52] but their co-operation in resistance to the Second Home Rule Bill made the formation of a 'Unionist Coalition' a relatively uncontroversial gambit, for which Salisbury had already prepared the nervous Queen.

True, Chamberlain's attempts at bouncing the Conservatives into the espousal of an advanced social programme (for example, via a highly publicized article published in *Nineteenth Century* in November 1892) had recently caused some irritation; so, too, had what amounted to his announcement of a new Unauthorised Programme at Birmingham in mid-October 1894.[53] Further ructions broke out when two Liberal Unionists, one of them Chamberlain, voted in support of Welsh Disestablishment (another sixteen had been absent unpaired).[54] In early 1895 some sections of the Conservative press, led by the *Standard*, retaliated with a series of highly personal attacks on Chamberlain, which their hypersensitive victim much resented.

However, most Conservatives acknowledged that, in the fight against the second Home Rule Bill, Chamberlain had provided effective leadership in the Commons, showing his stature by taking on Gladstone in what developed into a titanic personal duel. Chamberlain, for his part, had meanwhile been tightening his grip over the Liberal Unionists in preparation for working with Balfour, who now mattered more to him than Devonshire, his titular Leader.

In fact, self-effacingly though he had behaved in 1886–7, Devonshire still entertained prime-ministerial ambitions. But Salisbury skilfully blocked off this option by forming a Coalition at breakneck speed without even attempting to negotiate over terms, hoping to bind the Liberal Unionists closely to him by treating their leaders with conspicuous generosity. No fewer than four Cabinet places went to Liberal Unionists: Devonshire became Lord President of the Council, with responsibility for Imperial Defence, Lansdowne went to the War Office, Henry James received a peerage and the post of Chancellor of the Duchy of Lancaster, and Chamberlain, who could have had the Treasury or the Home Office, startled Salisbury (who initially thought he had misheard

---

[52] Even more bizarrely, the Irish Nationalists sat on the Opposition benches, alongside the Conservatives!

[53] Chamberlain had more success in 'bouncing' the naturally cautious Devonshire.

[54] The Liberal Unionists also broke ranks over the Parish Councils Bill, on which see Ch. 7.

what was being said) by opting for the Colonial Office. Since Salisbury did not expect to win the forthcoming election outright, he may even have offered his allies a more favourable deal than the situation warranted—an action which later caused some resentment in Conservative circles.

As for senior Conservative politicians, Salisbury once again took the Foreign Office, Balfour returned as Leader of the House, and the latter's brother, Gerald, went to Dublin Castle as Chief Secretary. The fading Goschen, who had finally joined the Carlton Club in 1894, was sent to the Admiralty, while his former post as Chancellor of the Exchequer went to Hicks Beach, now largely recovered in health.

The General Election took place in July 1895 against a background of protracted rural and industrial depression. Outside Ireland the Home Rule question played an even smaller role than in 1892, with many Irish electors on mainland Britain deserting the Liberals for the Conservative Party, in protest against recent Liberal policies, which had threatened their church schools. In the event, the Unionists achieved a landslide victory. With 341 MPs, the Conservatives possessed an overall majority, but the Liberal Unionists also did well, their seventy seats almost bringing them back to the level of 1886 and giving them, for the first time, a secure urban base.

4. THE DISAPPEARANCE OF THE IRISH QUESTION?

Following their election victory the Conservatives certainly had much to crow about. Irish Nationalism had been quelled, seemingly for good, by a mixture of firm repression and sympathetic reform legislation. Gerald Balfour, the new Chief Secretary, was not even in the Cabinet—a sign that Ireland was now seen more as an administrative than as a political problem. The running Catholic grievance over not having their own university continued to fester; nevertheless, Gerald Balfour formulated a Land Purchase Act in 1896 which proved more successful than his brother's earlier 1891 measure, even though it had been heavily amended by a revolt in the Lords led by Lord Londonderry (who was later bought off by Cabinet office). Many Unionists, on the other hand, had all along believed in the healing powers of land purchase: 'French peasants', Dicey had written, 'were Jacobins until the revolution secured to them the soil of France';[55] it remained to be seen whether Irish peasants could similarly be turned into a conservative force. Another sign of the more relaxed mood was the passing of the 1898 Irish Local Government Act, which allowed the Irish Nationalists to capture most of the municipal seats in the Catholic South and

---

[55] Dicey, *Case Against Home Rule*, 139, 288.

West, but which could be seen as evidence that Ireland was returning to some sort of normality.

Indeed, though the Liberal Party could not quite bring itself to abandon Gladstone's commitment, few of its leading figures showed much stomach for a renewal of the old campaign. Ironically, it was Herbert Gladstone, the GOM's son, who had been the first to reveal his father's 'conversion', who effectively dropped Home Rule from the party programme when the country next polled in 1900.

Yet neither was all well with Unionism. In the wake of the 1895 triumph one Conservative MP pinpointed what was amiss when he complained that there seemed 'to be no cause on the carpet at all, barring perhaps poor old Temperance'.[56] The truth was that the unbeatable combination of Conservatives and Liberal Unionists had grown out of a common determination to resist Home Rule. 'Unionism' had been a fine rallying cry when Home Rule seemed possible of attainment, but it meant very little after Gladstone's retirement. For, if the Union was safe, what point was there in having a Unionist alliance? After 1895 fissiparous strains started to develop even within the ranks of Irish Unionism.[57]

There were, in fact, politicians on both sides of the Home Rule/Unionist divide who regretted the way in which Ireland had driven all other issues into the background. Indeed, many believed that it had separated people who were otherwise natural allies, creating in the process a reconfiguration of parties that was 'artificial' and 'unreal'.[58] Hence the sporadic attempts to 'reconstruct' the existing party system or even to bypass it entirely through the creation of a 'National Government'.

In all parties (bar the Irish Nationalist Party) there were also voices insisting that Ireland should not be allowed to distract attention from other equally— perhaps more—important issues.[59] Even Gladstone had intermittently paid some consideration to this viewpoint, while Rosebery and Harcourt, rivals in all else, were alike in being reluctant Home Rulers. Electoral considerations also came into play, since many Liberals feared that Gladstone had foisted a vote-losing issue onto his followers.

---

[56] Shannon, *Age of Salisbury*, 438.

[57] The Southern Unionists and Ulster Unionism began to develop in rather different directions, while in the north Protestant unity was also disrupted by the emergence of the tenant-right movement spearheaded by the Liberal Unionist MP for South Tyrone, T. W. Russell, which had a considerable appeal to Presbyterian farmers. Meanwhile the old feud between Parnellites and Anti-Parnellites continued and was not healed until 1900.

[58] Searle, *Country Before Party*, 33.

[59] Precisely such a claim was made by William Saunders, Radical MP for Walworth, in his 1893 pamphlet (J. Lawrence, *Speaking for the People: Party, Language and Popular Politics in England, 1867–1914* (Cambridge, 1998), 204).

For this very reason the Unionists showed a greater enthusiasm for keeping the Irish Question before the public's gaze. Even so, after 1895 most were convinced that the fight against Home Rule had been conclusively won. In politics nothing fails like success. By the late 1890s Salisbury and his friends were in danger of having worked themselves out of a job. What did Unionism now mean? It had no coherent political programme and no firm basis of class allegiance to hold together the disparate elements from which it had earlier been formed.[60]

That is why, with the Act of Union apparently secure, Chamberlain increasingly argued that Unionism would have to be redefined so as to embrace a 'union of social classes' and Empire Union—some sort of merger of the United Kingdom and its self-governing colonies. These two causes offered a plausible response to the wider problems besetting English society in the 1890s. But both spelt dangers to the kind of Conservative politics dear to the third Marquess of Salisbury.

---

[60] Shannon, *Age of Salisbury*, 423.

CHAPTER 6

The Social Question: Conflict and Stability, 1886–1899

1. THE CRISIS OF THE 1880s

While MPs were debating the merits of Home Rule, the economy was in the trough of a business slump. In 1885 the government had set up a Royal Commission on the Depression of Trade and Industry to examine the problem. Of the fifty Chambers of Commerce that responded to its request for information, thirty-eight replied that the industries in their area were in deep distress. With trade-union unemployment standing at over 10 per cent, workers took to the streets in angry demonstrations all over urban Britain. In the Trafalgar Square riots of February 1886, shops in Pall Mall and Piccadilly were robbed by a mob in broad daylight, producing a *grand peur* among the shopkeepers and others. 'After such a breakdown of police administration,' wrote Octavia Hill, 'one feels as if one *might* meet violence *any* where.'[1] As we have seen, further trouble flared up in the same place in November of the following year, leading to 'Bloody Sunday'.[2]

Though the forces of law and order were capable of containing casual street violence, there were many who feared the imminence of revolution. In 1883 Britain's first Marxist party, the Social Democratic Federation (SDF), had been founded, and in the unemployed riots of the late 1880s its leaders, for example, Tom Mann, played a highly visible role. Moreover, although Irish outrages on mainland Britain largely ceased after 1885, there were soon to be sporadic outbreaks of internationally organized anarchist terrorism, leading to incidents such as that of February 1894, in which Martial Bourdin accidentally blew himself up in Greenwich Park (the source of Conrad's later novel, *The Secret Agent*).[3]

---

[1] J. R. Walkowitz, *City of Dreadful Delight: Narratives of Sexual Danger in Late-Victorian London* (Chicago, 1992), 29.

[2] See Ch. 5.

[3] B. Porter, *Plots and Paranoia: A History of Political Espionage in Britain, 1790–1988* (London, 1989), 108–14.

Fear of revolution intermingled with concern at the revelation that in the centres of many big cities a way of life had been established which seemed completely at variance with the norms of 'civilization'. The source of these anxieties, in which pity mingled with fear, was the 'under-class' of casual labourers stranded in decaying city centres, such as London's East End. Andrew Mearns's *Bitter Cry of Outcast London* of 1883, which focused on this problem, encouraged many imitations—almost every town of any size was soon emitting its own 'bitter cry'.

The late Victorian middle classes also developed a fascination for the East End of London and its 'outcasts'—struck, as they were, by the paradox that at the very heart of the capital there existed people with lives as strange and exotic (in their eyes) as those of 'natives' in far-flung corners of the Empire. Hence the emergence in the mid-1880s of a new literary genre, the travel book which drew its readers' attention to the 'unknown' world that existed on their very door-steps and into which only the intrepid 'explorer' dared venture. For example, George Sims's *How the Poor Live* (1883) set out to guide the reader through 'a dark continent that [was] within easy walking distance of the General Post Office'.[4]

The parallels between the inner city and the world of the overseas savage received laboured treatment in 1890 in William Booth's *Darkest England and the Way Out*, with its comparisons between the alcohol-drenched districts of the East End and the swamps of the Equatorial forest. This tract had a title that mimicked the book written by the explorer Henry Stanley, *In Darkest Africa*, and had been largely ghosted by the journalist W. T. Stead. How lucrative could be the links between social reportage and sensationalism Stead had already discovered with his recent series of articles 'The Maiden Tribute of Modern Babylon',[5] which earned its author a brief gaol sentence, while pushing up the circulation of the *Pall Mall Gazette*, which had carried the lurid story. The *Bitter Cry of Outcast London* similarly borrowed from the techniques of the 'New Journalism' (through the use of capital letters and banner headlines), causing a similar stir with its suggestion that the overcrowding rife in the slum tenements was making incest commonplace.

On the East End of London a motley band of 'explorers' descended in the 1880s and 1890s, some openly proclaiming their identities, some in disguise, such as the American novelist Jack London, who dressed as a tramp so that he could report, first hand, on life in the 'spike'. Some of the 'travel' literature to which these incursions gave rise was frankly titillating. Indeed, part of the East End's fascination stemmed from its reputation as a milieu for shocking and

---

[4] Walkowitz, *Dreadful Delight*, 26–7. The genre can be traced back earlier, James Greenwood's tours of 'Low Life Deeps', for example, going back to the 1860s.
[5] See Ch. 2.

sordid crimes. Between 31 August and 9 November 1888 five prostitutes were brutally murdered in Whitechapel by a sadistic killer who almost immediately acquired the name of 'Jack the Ripper', events which drew to the area yet more sensation-hunting journalists and 'urban spectators', whose accounts conveyed an added dash of danger and excitement which readers were able to experience vicariously.

But, at its serious end, the literature of exposure exhibited a deep Christian concern: Mearns was running a city mission, and William (General) Booth had recently founded the Salvation Army, which purveyed an intensely Evangelical version of the Christian faith. Without casting doubt on the feelings of pity aroused by the distressing sights and smells that greeted them in the slums, it is questionable whether this literature of exposure would have been produced simply out of concern for the material well-being of the poor, the disadvantaged, and the exploited. The 'explorers' were shocked by the East End because they thought that it constituted a depraved environment in which it was desperately difficult (not impossible, since anything might be done with God's grace) for residents to lead decent, moral lives. The innocent, they alleged, were being 'contaminated' by close contact with the criminal; vicious, crushing poverty was driving onto the streets females who would otherwise have been virtuous; and overcrowding was leading to incest—incidentally, the latter danger was a very real one, a government survey of 1887 showing that 50 per cent of dockworkers and 46 per cent of costermongers were living with their families in only one room.[6]

However, social distress and its accompanying discontent were not confined to the urban areas. An agricultural depression had set in during the late 1870s, when a mixture of bad harvests, coinciding with the arrival of cheap grain from the prairie farms of North America, caused wheat prices to tumble from their average price of over 50s. a quarter in the 1870s to 23s. in 1894; other cereal prices followed suit. Unprotected by a tariff, arable farming experienced no real recovery until the outbreak of the Great War, though it picked up slightly after the late 1890s.

Against this background, the American agitator Henry George had made many converts during his highly successful visits to Britain in the early 1880s, when he had attacked the landlord monopoly and called for a single tax on land. In Scotland the crofters had risen up against their predominantly Liberal lairds. Meanwhile Gladstone's attempt to quell Irish agrarian agitation by ceding the '3 Fs' (fair rents, free sale, fixity of tenure) in his 1881 Irish Land Act had frightened landlords on the British mainland, who feared that the legislative precedents being established in Ireland would soon 'cross the water';

[6] A. S. Wohl, *The Eternal Slum: Housing and Social Policy in Victorian London* (London, 1977), 204.

and 'tenant right' was indeed making some progress among the English farming community. Could English society survive these multiple 'crises'?

2. AGRICULTURAL DEPRESSION AND RURAL SOCIETY

Those earning their living in the agricultural sector faced particular hardship. In 1894 wheat prices hit rock bottom, a mere 22s. 10d. a quarter, under half the level they had reached twenty years earlier. True, between 1873 and 1896 the *general* price level fell by about 40 per cent. But though this was more or less in line with the price-changes for oats and barley, wheat fell by about 51 per cent. This spelled disaster for many farmers.[7]

Earlier accounts of the agricultural depression may have painted too gloomy a picture because they drew so heavily upon the evidence put before the Royal Commission of 1879–82, the membership of which was dominated by large landowners with estates in the arable counties of the south and east, the areas hardest hit by recent price falls. In any case, even in the generally prosperous 1870s crops accounted for only about one-third of the value of all UK agricultural output (wheat alone a mere 8.4 per cent): the rest comprised wool, horses, eggs, poultry, and above all meat and milk.[8] Livestock farmers, in fact, were initially little affected by foreign competition and some actually benefited in a general way, since falling grain prices lowered the cost of home and imported cattle-feed by about 30 per cent. With real wage levels still rising, cheaper bread also boosted the purchasing power of the poor, who chose to spend more of their disposable income on protein-rich meat products. Soil permitting, many farmers had every incentive to switch over from arable to pasture, and many did so.

However, even in the livestock sector, foreign competition soon materialized. The invention of the refrigerated steamship removed the advantage which geographical distance had once given the British farmer, allowing first frozen, and then chilled, meat into the home market—notably, beef from Argentina and mutton from New Zealand. Farmers also came under pressure from Danish co-operatives, which by the end of the century were supplying the British breakfast table with cheap bacon and eggs.

Price falls in meat products, however, were not so dramatic as in cereals. This was partly because of consumer resistance: whereas the public soon became hooked on the light, fine-grained white bread produced from 'Manitoba hard no. 1',[9] imported meat, often clumsily frozen, did not compare in flavour

---

[7] R. Perren, *Agriculture in Depression, 1870–1940* (Cambridge, 1995), 9–10.
[8] Ibid. 10.
[9] A. Offer, *The First World War: An Agrarian Interpretation* (Oxford, 1989), 100.

with higher quality, home-killed produce. For many years traditional butchers (including co-operative stores catering for the more prosperous end of the working-class market) would not sell imported goods at all; this forced the Argentinean producers to set up their own retail outlets—notably, the River Plate Company.

There were also areas in which British farmers naturally monopolized the market, for example, liquid milk, a highly perishable commodity. Market gardening similarly flourished in areas such as Cornwall, where the balmy climate allowed early vegetables to be grown and then transported to distant urban areas along the comprehensive railway network. Fruit farming, too, expanded in the late nineteenth century, especially in Cambridgeshire, stimulated by the Chivers jam factory at Histon.[10]

Such developments have led some to decry the very notion of an agricultural depression and to talk of a painful but quite successful adjustment to new market conditions. There were also productivity gains during these years—registered, for example, in the increased per-capita output made possible by mechanization and other technical improvements.[11]

Yet there is something unconvincing about attempts to write off the contemporary literature of lamentation as special pleading or ignorance. After all, between 1886 and 1903 over 5 million acres of farmland fell out of (arable) cultivation, while labourers were drifting in droves to the cities or else emigrating.[12] Even in 1870 Britain was incapable of feeding herself; by the outbreak of the Great War she was importing over three-quarters of her cereals and some 40 per cent of her meat.

These developments significantly altered the balance between town and country. In Suffolk large tracts, once farmland, were converted to sport—gamekeepers were one of the few rural occupational groups to expand in the late Victorian and Edwardian period: Lord Iveagh employed seventy-eight of them on his Elveden estate. Rider Haggard was told by one of his Suffolk informants that some local landowners 'would be better off if they abandoned all attempts at agriculture, except such as might be needful to the preservation of partridges, gave notice to their tenants, and contented themselves with letting their shooting to South African millionaires'.[13] The countryside seemed

---

[10] A. Howkins, *Reshaping Rural England: A Social History 1850–1925* (London, 1991), 143, 147–8.

[11] Ibid., ch. 8. By the end of the century there were some 900 firms manufacturing agricultural equipment (A. Armstrong, *Farmworkers: A Social and Economic History, 1770–1980* (London, 1988), 112). See E. J. T. Collins (ed.), *The Agrarian History of England and Wales: Volume Seven: 1850–1914* (Cambridge, 2001).

[12] E. H. H. Green, *The Crisis of Conservatism: The Politics, Economics and Ideology of the British Conservative Party, 1880–1914* (London, 1995), 208; Howkins, *Rural England*, 171. Emigration, however, was no higher from the agricultural districts than from the big cities.

[13] H. Rider Haggard, *Rural England* (London, 1902), ii. 419.

a place where one spent, rather than earned, money. A severe psychological blow was thus delivered to British farming, from which it took decades to recover.

What, if anything, could have been done to arrest the decline? Agricultural protectionism was strong in Lincolnshire, where Harry Chaplin ('the Squire'), a prominent Conservative MP, provided vigorous leadership. But Britain had proceeded so far down the road of industrialization that a landlord-dominated Parliament never seriously considered adopting this 'solution'. In any case, cheap food particularly helped the poor, wherever they lived, because food absorbed a disproportionately high share of their income; it also indirectly helped industrialists by lowering labour costs.

Radical Liberals tended to blame the depression on an 'unsound' land system, and—even taking a narrowly economic view of the matter—they may have had a point. Home agriculture was at a disadvantage compared with the prairie farms of America, not simply because the soil was less fertile and units of production smaller, but because in Britain the land had quartered upon it a large leisure class in the form of resident landowners who drew rent but subcontracted its cultivation to tenant farmers, many of whom spurned dirtying their hands but delegated the sweaty work to their poorly paid labourers.

Controversy surrounds the issue of whether the landowners, who tradition-ally took responsibility for the improvement and upkeep of farmhouses and buildings and for the fencing and draining of the land, really 'earned' their rentals by performing such a role, and whether, by providing social, cultural, and political leadership, they indirectly rendered a valuable service to the entire nation. Equally controversial was the use of the land to sustain an Established Church at which many country people no longer worshipped. But the point is that overseas producers whose competition was undermining the livelihood of many British farmers were not burdened with similar overheads.[14]

How did the various classes who were still employed on the land, or who drew much of their income from it, fare during the years of depression? Farm labourers did well as consumers, gaining more from the supply of cheap food than they would have done from higher wages if tariffs on imported foodstuffs had been adopted. Moreover, in some districts the exodus from the land created labour shortages that were not entirely eliminated by the introduction of machinery, even causing a slight rise in wage-rates. Against a background of falling prices, this enabled the purchasing power of the average agricultural wage to increase, in real terms, by some 25 per cent.[15] Such improvements were

[14] Offer, *First World War*, Chs. 7–8.
[15] Armstrong, *Farmworkers*, 121.

most marked in counties that bordered large towns or industrial areas. By the Edwardian period the average weekly wage in Durham had climbed to 22s. 8d., whereas in isolated Wiltshire it remained stuck at 16s.[16] In general, however, farm labourers still formed an impoverished class; their share of farm income rose slightly in the 1890s, but it soon fell away once more.

The morale of agricultural labourers was also lowered by the virtual disappearance of agricultural trade unionism, following the period of short-lived success enjoyed by Joseph Arch's Agricultural Labourers' Union in the early 1870s. Arch, Liberal MP for Norfolk North-West in 1885–6 and from 1892 to 1900, proved useless as an advocate at this level, opening his mouth only to pour liquor down it. True, labourers' unions did linger on into the 1890s in Norfolk and Lincolnshire, but not until George Edwards's founding of the Farm Labourers' Union in 1906 was anything ambitious attempted. Even rural protest largely abated in the 1890s—unless activities such as poaching are accorded significance.

Contemporaries believed that it was overwhelmingly the young and the enterprising who escaped the monotony and the hopelessness of country life. Indeed, it was because farm labourers were perceived by outsiders as incapable of throwing up effective leaders of their own that urban-based Radicals set out in the 1890s to rescue them from social oppression. Middle-class politicians were soon followed by urban trade unionists and socialists. Unfortunately, these would-be friends often brought to their mission a condescending view of country people—who, far from being an undifferentiated bunch of yokels, formed a complex community, some members of which possessed highly specialized skills.

Although life was particularly harsh for agricultural labourers, it was far from easy for farmers, who bore the direct brunt of falling prices. With little more than a tenth of land being owned by a working farmer, rent reductions were essential if most were to survive. Such reductions did, indeed, occur in the distressed counties (the alternative would have been the abandonment of farms): on average, rents fell by more than a quarter between the mid-1870s and the mid-1890s, and by as much as 41 percent in the arable South-East. Even so, the statistics for bankruptcies show nearly 500 failures a year during the early 1890s, mainly, as one would expect, in the cereal-producing areas. And though it is arguable that this represents a relatively low failure-rate for agriculture as a whole, such figures take no account of farmers who quitted their tenancies in despair.[17]

---

[16] 1907 figures, in B. S. Rowntree and M. Kendall, *How the Labourer Lives* (London, 1913). But there was no *general* labour shortage (Armstrong, *Farmworkers*, pp. 137–8).

[17] R. Perren, 'Where was the "Great Agricultural Depression?" ', *Agricultural History Review*, 20 (1972), 30–45.

In these very difficult circumstances, it was those farmers who were alert to market signals and showed a capacity for grinding hard work who were most likely to survive, even prosper, though more was involved than mere entrepreneurial energy, since a farmer also needed support and sympathy from his landlord, plus luck—after all, not all soils could be converted at the drop of a hat from arable to pastoral farming, and in any case it was impossible to ask wheat-growers to metamorphose overnight into fruit-farmers. The 1890s was thus a time of considerable change in the countryside, involving a substantial turnover in personnel—large areas of Essex, for example, were taken over by hard-working Scottish immigrants who, relying on family labour, survived where their predecessors had not.

Statistics suggest that there was a sharp reduction in farmers' share of farm income between 1877 and 1885 and a perceptible improvement thereafter, but the variations between geographical areas and agricultural sectors make it difficult to draw general conclusions. Similarly with social behaviour. Many farmers were still in thrall to their landlord, but those who had successfully adapted to the new environment knew that they now had a much stronger bargaining position and tended, in consequence, to be less deferential to their 'superiors'. This may partly explain why 'tenant right' now mattered less to farmers than it had once done.[18] Significantly, however, farmers still found it difficult to put on a public show of *national* unity; not until 1907 were they able to form the National Farmers Union (NFU).

What, then, of the landowners? After 1885 this class experienced a greater relative decline in income from the land than did either farmers or agricultural labourers. The depression hit them in two ways. First, as we have seen, they were obliged to drop their rents. Given their fixed overheads and other burdens, especially family settlements, this meant an even greater fall in net revenue.[19] Landowners also suffered from a decline in the value of agricultural land—perhaps amounting to 60 per cent between 1875 and 1910. This, in turn, affected their traditional capacity to raise loans, using their estates as collateral.

In Ireland, where landowners had to endure the additional anxiety occasioned by a turbulent peasantry, the government effectively bought them out with a series of Land-Purchase Acts, which transferred ownership to sitting tenants, who then repaid the loans in the form of state annuities. But in England there was no such let-out. In fact, agricultural land was difficult to sell on any terms during the 1890s: 'Were there any effective demand for the

---

[18] Howkins, *Rural England*, 159–60. However, 'insubordinate' tenants were still vulnerable to the 'feudal screw'.

[19] The Duke of Devonshire was spending 17% of his disposable income on interest payments in 1874, 60% by 1880 (D. Cannadine, *The Decline and Fall of the British Aristocracy* (New Haven and London, 1990), 94).

purchase of land,' wrote the Duke of Marlborough in 1885, 'half the land of England would be in the market tomorrow.'[20] The political uncertainties arising from Harcourt's 'Death Duties Budget', which increased the burden on landed property, also contributed to the stagnation of the land market. Few large country houses were built after 1879—six a year during the 1890s, down from a peak of nearly forty in the early 1870s. Very seldom were such houses surrounded by an estate of over 2,000 acres, most of them having been commissioned by professional men and wealthy parvenus from the groceries and drinks trades, not by scions of old landed families.[21] On the other hand, substantial sums were sometimes made available for 'modernizing' old residences by the installation of electric lighting, lifts, and so on.

Large landowners with a geographical spread of estates came off best during the depression. The Earl of Derby was losing heavily during the 1890s on his Cambridgeshire properties, but breaking even in Derbyshire and doing very well in Lancashire, where he owned large tracts of land on the edge of Liverpool, Preston, and other towns. A dependence on agricultural rental alone could spell trouble: squires with medium-sized estates in counties such as Norfolk were sometimes reduced to renting out their residences to urban sportsmen during the season, or even closing them down altogether and moving to Italy or France, where the cost of living was cheaper. Other landlords entered the depression hopelessly encumbered with debts run up over preceding decades by overambitious drainage schemes, which had never looked likely to make a short-term profit, and by settlements and old debts. In this way the gap widened between impoverished landlords, many of them with smaller estates, and a 'plutocratic' class of super-rich landed magnates, often titled, for whom, with adjustments, a luxurious lifestyle was still available.

Among the latter was the Duke of Westminster who, apart from his Cheshire estates, held land in Mayfair from which he was said to be earning £1,500 a day—making him reputedly the richest man in England. The Devonshires, based upon Chatsworth, owed their prosperity to income from their stake in the burgeoning seaside town of Eastbourne and from their holdings in Barrow, a prosperous centre of the armaments industry and of shipbuilding. Similarly, the Duke of Northumberland derived enormous wealth from coal royalties; other landlords had the good fortune to draw canal dues or income from the railway companies which traversed their estates.

In the absence of these advantages, much could be gained from a more self-consciously businesslike approach to estate management. This process can be seen, for example, on the Earl of Leicester's vast 43,000-acre Holkham Estate

---

[20] Ibid. 110.

[21] In the last twenty years before the Great War only 8 out of 104 new country houses were built by old landed families (J. Franklin, *The Gentleman's Country House and its Plan* (London, 1981), 31).

in north Norfolk, where a shrewd husbanding of agricultural resources was accompanied by a policy of selling off outlying land and investing the proceeds in equities—a strategy facilitated by the Settled Lands Acts of 1882 and 1884. It is also a sign of the times that the Earl was not simply putting money into local enterprises such as railways, a commitment which had long been accepted as normal and natural, but also into foreign and imperial stocks, breweries, and financial companies; by the 1890s income from these sources matched the rentals on his Norfolk estates.[22] Another way in which big landowners could tap into an expanding capitalism was by accepting company directorships. By 1896 one-quarter of all peers were doing this—sometimes, as we will see, with disastrous consequences.

All this formed part of a wider development, whereby many landowners accepted the need to be more entrepreneurial. This occasionally found expression in their assuming direct responsibility for their estates and farming them on the most approved modern principles, as Lord Rayleigh did when he promoted his highly successful dairy enterprise, aimed at the lucrative London market. It could also take the form of 'rationalizing' an estate by (where possible) selling off 'surplus' land, regardless of tradition and sentiment. Some landowners, such as the Earl of Leicester, even took to disposing of 'bric-a-brac', that is to say, some of the treasures which their forefathers had accumulated in the form of priceless libraries and *objets d'art*. This formed the principal source of the personal fortune of the New York art dealer Joseph Duveen, whose rich American clients were able to take advantage of the English aristocracy's financial embarrassment—and greed.

The British aristocracy had traditionally been relatively open to entrants from commoner backgrounds. Earlier in the nineteenth century, however, it was adopting a more exclusive lifestyle, and this made all the more startling the apparently greater readiness of the holders of ancient titles to associate themselves with 'outsiders', even marrying them, as when Lord Rosebery joined his house with Hannah Rothschild—a development also seen in the escapades of pleasure-loving nobles with a penchant for actresses. Another channel through which American dollars engrafted themselves onto ancient British wealth was the much-trumpeted marriage between landowners with ancient titles and American heiresses—of which there were some spectacular, if untypical examples, notably the Duke of Marlborough's marriage to Consuelo Vanderbilt.[23]

[22] S. Wade Martins, *A Great Estate at Work: The Holkham Estate and its Inhabitants in the Nineteenth Century* (Cambridge, 1980), 62–4.
[23] M. E. Montgomery, *Gilded Prostitution: Status, Money and Transatlantic Marriages 1870–1914* (London, 1989), shows that British families entered into these marriages for a variety of reasons, of which the financial was only one.

On the other hand, two-thirds of sons of peers continued to marry into aristocratic or gentry families. Moreover, although one-tenth of British peers and sons of peers took American brides between 1870 and 1914, they mostly married into socially prestigious families; this suggests 'the growth of a trans-atlantic-cosmopolitan upper class' and a crumbling of national barriers rather than dramatic social change.[24]

All the same, there is evidence of a growing desire to keep the family estates intact, by hook or by crook. Indeed, to the dependants of some impoverished landowners, it seemed only proper that the son and heir should 'marry well', not in the sense of marrying his social equal, but of bringing much needed money into the estate. But this intensified preoccupation with money some-times stemmed less from economic adversity than from a liking for new luxuries (such as steam yachts, motor cars, and exotic holidays), and a deter-mination to find the means whereby to acquire them, following the lead set by the Prince of Wales (later King Edward VII). Landed society may thus have 'survived', but only by compromising the social values which had once distin-guished it from groups that were merely very wealthy.

It was as a reaction against this growing philistinism and materialism that a fashionable coterie, the 'Souls', sprang up in the late 1880s, revolving around Arthur Balfour, the future Conservative Leader. Its members, deliberately turning their backs on the field sports and gluttonous self-indulgence to be found, say, in the Marlborough House Set surrounding the heir to the throne, preferred to foster witty conversation, intellectual games, and a cult of friend-ship—flavoured by discreet, if irregular, sexual liaisons. Though predomin-antly aristocratic in composition, the 'Souls' welcomed 'outsiders' possessing wit or beauty: at the heart of the coterie were the daughters of the Scottish chemicals manufacturer Sir Charles Tennant, a social climber who had built a mock baronial castle to which he invited guests from the fashionable world.[25] 'Society', then, was becoming not only more heterogeneous in its composition (blending old and new wealth), but also more subdivided into different groups.

Yet, although the British aristocracy survived the agricultural depression in better shape than might have been expected, its social prestige and political influence may both have been weakened. For example, the more mercenary attitudes which it encouraged could on occasions undermine the unquestioning deference which it was accustomed to exact from the rest of society. When landowners, in self-pitying mood, cut back on their donations to local charities,

[24] Ibid., *passim*; F. M. L. Thompson, *The Rise of Respectable Society: A Social History of Victorian Britain, 1830–1900* (London, 1988), 105–7.

[25] On the 'Souls', see N. Ellenberg, 'The Souls and London Society at the End of the Nineteenth Century', *Victorian Studies*, 25 (1982), 133–60; A. Lambert, *Unquiet Souls: The Indian Summer of the British Aristocracy* (London, 1984).

as the Duke of Devonshire publicly threatened to do in the wake of the Death Duties Budget, they put their whole order at risk.[26] This can also be seen in the growing refusal of owners of important houses to allow visitors to see their parks and to inspect their artistic treasures, as they had done earlier in the century—even when organized crowds of sightseers began to descend on them, courtesy of the excursion train. With some exceptions, late Victorian aristocrats tended to draw defensively in upon themselves, either by turning visitors away or by charging them a 'realistic' entrance fee. No longer did they see themselves as 'custodians' of a 'national heritage'; rather were they determined to uphold what they saw as the rights of private property.[27]

On the other hand, though there were political dangers in this behaviour, it perhaps betokened a toughness in the face of adversity, a willingness on the part of aristocrats to fight to retain their privileges. As we have seen, landed society held on to its political position even after its economic base had begun to weaken; after 1888 it adapted, with equal success, to the advent of 'democracy' in the shires.[28] Meanwhile, however, many farmers struggled to survive, and 'Hodge' remained, as always, very near the bottom of the social heap.

3. INDUSTRIAL UNREST AND THE 'NEW UNIONISM'

Industry and commerce, as well as agriculture, were also passing through a period of painful transition. Between 1873 and 1896 the wholesale price index fell by some 40 per cent. These years (once known as the 'Great Depression') were also marked by falling profit margins and a slowdown in economic growth, which in turn gave rise to business troughs, such as the one that was causing such high unemployment and distress in 1885–6. (Moreover, in 1890 a further disaster was only narrowly averted when the prestigious financial house of Baring Brothers, which had overinvested in Argentinian securities, would have defaulted but for the concerted action of other leading banks, directed by the Bank of England.) For the first time foreign competition began to penetrate markets which British manufacturers had once thought theirs by right.[29]

A gloomy view of the British economy, then and subsequently, stresses technical backwardness and the unwillingness to invest in higher education or take it with sufficient seriousness, particularly science and technology (as distinct from the old artisanal virtues of 'rule-of-thumb'). Hence, an over-commitment to the old 'staples'—cotton, coal, and shipbuilding, at a time

---

[26] See Ch. 7.
[27] P. Mandler, *The Fall and Rise of the Stately Home* (New Haven, 1997).
[28] See Ch. 7.
[29] See Ch. 10.

when the industries of the 'Second Industrial Revolution' (e.g. chemicals and electrical goods), at which the Germans excelled, were growing in importance.

Moreover, many contemporaries worried over the prospect of Britain becoming a rentier economy, and feared that the City's expansion and the growth of the service industries was taking place at the expense of manufacturing, which contributed much more to the national wealth, defined in a wider sense. A new school of economic historians, influenced by similar trends in Germany, propounded a kind of neo-mercantilism, insisting, as Friedrich List before them had done, that free trade only benefited nations at a particular stage of their development, but on other occasions governments should seek to channel trade and investment in such a way as to promote the well-being of the citizenry through an enhancement of national power.

This led on to a further argument: that massive overseas investment was drawing capital into foreign enterprises which provided work for foreigners when it could have been utilized more fruitfully at home. As for the prosperity of the City, this was all well and good, but it did not generate employment for the working man in the way that labour-intensive manufacturing did—or so it was tendentiously argued. For a whole range of reasons, both strategic and social, the critics of the existing dispensation queried whether Britain could afford to see her manufacturing base contract, even if the statistics showed an overall growth in the national wealth.

Finally, it was argued that the rest of the world was not moving in the direction of free trade, as Cobden had once thought inevitable. By 1886 France, Germany, Russia, Austria, and the United States were all sheltering their key industries behind protective duties. As early as May 1881 the National Fair Trade League had been formed to campaign for a return to protection, and a range of struggling and declining industries started to align themselves with its critique of what would later be called unilateral free trade.[30] America's high McKinley tariff of 1891, which immediately impacted on Britain's exports of woollen goods, came as a particular shock, as did the Dingley tariff of 1897.

However, the system of free imports, though it may have threatened the livelihood of certain producer groups, benefited the consumer by cheapening the cost of food and so raising living standards, especially for the poorer classes. Since, indirectly, free trade also helped to lower labour costs, many industries derived a competitive edge over their foreign rivals, and this in turn generated further profits and employment.

With protection ruled out, some manufacturers reacted to their difficulties by forming trade associations which sought to secure collusive market power by controlling members' pricing and output—with mixed, and only tempor-

---

[30] See Ch. 7.

ary, success. A similar stratagem caught hold in the shipping industry: in 1900 the American banker J. P. Morgan sponsored the International Mercantile Marine (IMM), a cartel which brought together five transatlantic passenger lines and two German companies.

Manufacturers also believed that British businesses were being handicapped in international markets by restrictive practices ('ca'canny')—an anxiety later expressed in a series of articles, 'The Crisis of British Industry', published in *The Times* during the winter of 1901–2.[31]

Adding to the industrial tension was the spread of trade unionism to unskilled groups that had previously stood entirely outside the Labour Movement—a development dubbed by contemporaries 'the New Unionism'. In 1888 the match-girls at Bryant & May's, helped by the Fabian essayist Annie Besant, marched out of their factory—partly out of indignation at having a shilling compulsorily deducted from their meagre wages as a contribution to a statue of Gladstone![32] Next year the gasworkers, led by Will Thorne, forced the South Metropolitan Gas Company to reduce the working day for stokers to eight hours.

Most famous of all these industrial conflicts was the great dock strike of August 1889, from which the dockers emerged triumphant with their 'tanner' (i.e. an extra 6*d.* per week). The dignity shown by the striking dockers, and the remarkably good order which they maintained despite enduring considerable suffering, appealed to many middle-class sympathizers. Cardinal Manning, who anyhow had an interest in the well-being of the strikers, many of whom were Irish Catholics, eventually put himself forward as a friendly mediator—in the process earning much credit for the Roman Catholic Church as the working man's friend. What, however, really struck contemporaries as remarkable was that groups such as dockers could form stable unions at all—even if they relied upon officials from already well-established unions for many of their leaders (for example, the dockers' leader Ben Tillett had had to enlist the help of Tom Mann and John Burns from the ASE).

Employers were quick to launch a counter-offensive. Thus, the National Labour Association, run by William Collison, was supplying blackleg labour to employers engaged in a dispute with their workforce, probably with the backing of shipping and dock interests and other employers.

The short-lived boom of the late 1880s then burst, leading to a falling-away of trade-union membership and a reversal of many of the unions' recent gains. The 'new unions' thereafter supplied the trade-union movement with at most 14 per cent of its total membership, and those that survived, notably the National Union of Gasworkers and General Labourers, only did so by

---

[31] The theme had earlier been broached on 11 June 1900.
[32] Walkowitz, *Dreadful Delight*, 77.

conforming to the patterns of behaviour of the older, long-established organizations; the gasworks were anyhow easier to organize than, say, the docks, with their floating mass of casually employed workers.

By the end of the decade a trade recovery had set in, and manufacturers' order books were filling up once more. But industrial relations remained tense. At the centre of the unrest was a conflict over who controlled the processes of mechanization. Printing was particularly affected, with the introduction of lino-setting machines; also affected was boot and shoe manufacturing, which, except at the luxury end (centred on Norwich), was becoming factory-based, as in Leicester and Northampton. The process of deskilling destroyed the workman's pride and sense of independence, even in the case of the printers, who successfully insisted on controlling the new machines, though the work could now be performed by a typist.[33] Less fortunate still were the engineers. The Engineers Employers Federation (EEF), through which owners, nationwide, mobilized in a stand against disruption, broke the resistance of the Amalgamated Society of Engineers (ASE) by locking out its members in 1897. This dispute, which lasted almost half a year—quite the most significant of the decade—was called by the socialist journalist Robert Blatchford 'The Trade-Union Sedan'. ASE delegates saw the issue as one in which trade unionism itself might be wiped out altogether.[34]

The TUC undoubtedly exaggerated the capacity of employers, with their varied sectional priorities, to combine with a view to defeating the unions in industrial pitched battles. However, legal actions to curtail picketing and other union practices offered a far more immediate threat. Once this danger had been perceived, all trade unions, not just those of the unskilled, began taking an increased interest in political action.[35]

4. THE MARCH OF PROGRESS?

As producers, the unionized workforce was experiencing problems during the 1890s; but simultaneously, as consumers their prospects were brightening. Indeed, with prices falling while wages were still rising, real employment income per worker was growing by 1.71 per cent a year between 1882 and 1899—bringing about an improvement in average real wages of over a third during this period.[36] In addition, the new jobs that were being created tended

---

[33] Thompson, *Respectable Society*, 244.
[34] L. Barrow and I. Bullock, *Democratic Ideas and the British Labour Movement, 1880–1914* (Cambridge, 1996), 108, 97.
[35] See Ch. 7.
[36] C. Feinstein, 'What Really Happened To Real Wages?: Trends in Wages, Prices, and Productivity in the United Kingdom 1880–1913', *Economic History Review*, 43 (1990), 329–55. These figures are adjusted to account for the growth of salaried employment.

to pay more than those that were being destroyed. Finally, compared with earlier periods when rising wages resulted from increased overtime and higher wage-rates, the effect of deflation was to increase the disposable income of the housewife—thereby raising the level of domestic comfort.

Rising real wages in the closing decades of the century may also have led to improved diets, at least for better-off working-class families, who were now able to purchase a more varied range of foodstuffs, including more meat and less bread. Adulteration and poor food hygiene were also being tackled, following the passing of the 1872 Adulteration of Food, Drink, and Drugs Act—notwithstanding the problem of providing an uncontaminated milk supply to the big cities. The 'retail revolution' contributed to this process by raising general standards of reliability and purity.

Another indicator of 'social progress' was the per-capita fall in expenditure on alcohol. In England and Wales the per-capita consumption of beer peaked in 1875–9 at 32.2 gallons per annum, but then fell away in the 1880s, rose slightly in the 1890s, before continuing its downward path: in 1910–13 it was only 29.4 gallons.[37] Of course, the levels of alcohol consumption were still high by the standards of later decades, but there were signs that significant changes in social behaviour had taken place.[38] To put it another way, expenditure on alcohol dropped from over 15 per cent to under 9 per cent of the working-class family budget between 1876 and 1910.[39] This is usually explained, less by the temperance movement, than by the recent availability of new goods and services upon which surplus cash could be spent—many of which catered for women and children, not just for adult males.[40]

With increasing prosperity came a vast expansion of 'friendly society'[41] membership—up from 2,750,000 in 1877 to 5,600,000 in 1904, though multiple membership makes exact figures difficult to calculate; meanwhile their funds had risen even more dramatically, from £12,700,000 to £41,000,000.[42] By 1911 probably one-half of the male workforce belonged to a friendly society, a much higher proportion than belonged to a trade union. Like working men's clubs, the friendly societies quickly escaped the control of their original

[37] T. R. Gourvish and R. G. Wilson, *The British Brewing Industry 1830–1980* (Cambridge, 1994), 30.

[38] D. J. Oddy, 'Food, Drink and Nutrition', in F. M. L. Thompson (ed.), *The Cambridge Social History of Britain 1750–1950, Vol. 2* (Cambridge, 1990), 265.

[39] A. E. Dingle, 'Drink and Working-Class Living Standards in Britain', *Economic History Review*, 25 (1972), 611–12.

[40] See Ch. 14. But beer was also becoming more expensive in real terms, its price staying steady at a time of falling prices.

[41] Mutual aid organizations, with elaborate social rituals, many of them flaunting exotic titles such as the 'Ancient Order of Foresters' and the 'Independent Order of Rechabites'.

[42] P. H. J. H. Gosden, *Self-Help: Voluntary Associations in Nineteenth-Century Britain* (London, 1973), 91. See also P. Thane, *Old Age in English History: Past Experiences, Present Issues* (Oxford, 2000), 194–5.

middle-class patrons and by the end of the century had become an important source of working-class pride and respectability.

Other branches of self-help were also expanding: the number of Post Office savings accounts rose from 3,088,000 in 1881–5 to 5,776,000 ten years later.[43] By the turn of the century a mere 10 per cent of the population would have been without some protection against the vicissitudes of life, if only through subscribing to a locally managed burial society or doctor's club, or through taking out a policy with an industrial insurance company or 'collecting society'.[44]

The building society movement also participated in this trend: in 1894 3,351 societies had been registered since the Building Societies Act passed twenty years earlier.[45] Owner-occupation accounted for only about 10 per cent of residences before 1914, most middle-class families seeing no point in taking out a mortgage; so it may have been aspiring artisans and small tradesmen who most availed themselves of the building society, not just for depositing their savings but also for house purchases. Finally, there was the Co-operative Movement, which, as the societies relaxed their earlier credit restrictions, reached out way beyond the skilled working class—in 1881 it already had half-a-million members, but numbers then swelled to 2.1 million in 1905 and 4.6 million in 1920.[46] Again, the Co-operative Movement was more than simply a means of accumulating modest savings via the dividend, since it also played an important social, educational, and recreational role—women (through the Co-operative Women's Guild) were affected by this even more than men.

As self-help spread, the proportion of the population having recourse to the Poor Law significantly declined. The ratio of paupers to the total population of England and Wales had stood at 3.1 per cent in 1880, but fell in each successive half-decade: to 2.8 per cent in 1885, 2.7 per cent in 1890, 2.6 per cent in 1895, and 2.4 per cent in 1900 (after which there was a slow rise).[47] Changes in the criteria regulating relief can only have accounted for part of this decline.[48] By the end of the century anxieties about Poor Law costs were beginning to resurface, but the mid-Victorian fear of productive society being overrun by an army of parasites had effectively disappeared.

---

[43] Gosden, *Self-Help*, 239. The average total of deposits almost doubled within the same period: from £42 million to £83 million.

[44] Thompson, *Respectable Society*, 202.

[45] Gosden, *Self-Help*, 171.

[46] P. Johnson, *Saving and Spending: The Working-Class Economy in Britain 1870–1939* (Oxford, 1985), 67.

[47] S. and B. Webb, *English Poor Law History, Part II: The Last Hundred Years, Vol. II* (London, 1929; 1963 edn.), 1042.

[48] See Ch. 7.

Higher living standards were reflected in improved health statistics. For example, the crude death-rate slowly but steadily fell: from 20.5 per thousand in 1880 to 19.5 in 1890, to 18.2 in 1900—more rapidly for women than for men. Life expectancy at birth, which had been under 40 in the early Victorian period, stood at 41.9 in the early 1880s, and then rose to 45.5 in 1891, 48 in 1901, and 53.5 in 1911.

Unfortunately, the infant death-rate obstinately refused to come down: indeed, it rose quite sharply during the course of the 1890s, peaking in 1899 at 163 per thousand, before starting a fairly steady fall.[49] Puerperal fever was the principal killer of those under 1 year of age, but diarrhoea and dysentery also took a heavy toll, as did whooping cough, which accounted for 40 per cent of the deaths of those under 5.[50]

There were other blips in the narrative of medical progress. Diphtheria, though generally in decline, actually went up among the young after 1880, as school-attendance rates improved: for people of all social classes, schools remained distinctly dangerous places. Statistics also show a startling leap in deaths from cancer—though this might simply reflect diagnostic changes. In the absence of antibiotics, bronchitis and pneumonia, too, continued to be scourges.

Nevertheless, with the exception of infant mortality, there is clear evidence that, from however low a base, the population's health *was* improving, suggesting that urban living conditions, which certainly compared favourably with those in most other industrialized countries, had greatly improved in recent decades. Had it been otherwise, mortality would surely have been higher, given the population movement away from the rural districts.[51]

These improvements cannot have owed much to advances in medical treatment: the enhanced status of doctors is an interesting phenomenon in its own right, but it does not signify that 'medical interventions' became dramatically more effective in the late Victorian period.[52] True, the growing habit among GPs of referring patients, where appropriate, to a hospital, in which recent applications of anaesthesia and antisepsis permitted invasive surgery of a kind hitherto impossible, represented an important breakthrough. By the end of the century hospitals were no longer 'gateways to death'. Access also widened, with the rapid development from the 1870s onwards of workplace collections and 'Hospital Saturdays': by the late 1880s the latter were operating in more than

[49] See Ch. 11.
[50] J. Walvin, *A Child's World: A Social History of English Childhood 1800–1914* (Harmondsworth, 1982), 20.
[51] Thompson, *Respectable Society*, 116–17.
[52] See Ch. 16.

forty English provincial centres, giving their contributors an entitlement to hospital treatment.[53]

All the same, the main reason for the decline in mortality is to be sought, less in medical provision, than in the amelioration of the environment. For though there remained areas of putrefaction in the slum areas of all large cities, the powers given to medical officers of health to remove nuisances were having a cumulative effect. Also important was the passing by local authorities of by-laws, under the terms of the 1875 Public Health Act, which aimed at providing residences with piped water. Although quicker progress could have been made had so many municipalities not been obsessed with holding down the rates, by the late 1890s a clean and safe uninterrupted water supply was within reach of almost all sectors of the community.[54] Middens still survived in older build-ings, but by the late 1880s water closets were being installed in even the cheapest new housing, though more often outdoors than indoors; this made for much greater cleanliness—to say nothing of privacy.[55]

In consequence, diseases associated with dirt and impure water were gener-ally in retreat. Typhoid did not disappear until the 1920s, and a serious outbreak in Lincoln in 1904–5 resulted in 130 deaths. But typhus dropped to relatively insignificant levels after 1878—in 1886 it accounted for under 250 deaths in England and Wales, even though, as late as 1897, an epidemic broke out in Maidstone, with over 1,800 cases and 132 deaths in a population of 34,000. As for cholera, the last great epidemic had taken place in 1866.

Vaccination programmes were also proving their efficacy. In 1896 the National Vaccine Board reported that it had vaccinated nearly 100,000 people[56]—a highly unpopular course of action leading to widespread protest. But as a result, smallpox had been all but eliminated by the end of the century—the epidemic which broke out in Liverpool in 1902–3 was a relatively unusual occurrence.[57]

Of course, all these national statistics mask significant class variations. One's chances of survival and of enjoying good health still heavily depended upon whether one was living in an affluent or a deprived urban area. In Liverpool the contrasts were especially sharp: the death-rate in the 'Exchange' district stood at 36.9, in affluent Sefton Park at 9.9.[58] The infant death-rate was also generally

---

[53] S. Cherry, 'Hospital Saturday, Workplace Collections and Issues in Late Nineteenth-Century Hospital Funding', *Medical History*, 44 (2000), 470–1. Substantial sums were also raised through church collections ('Hospital Sundays').

[54] F. B. Smith, *The People's Health 1830–1910* (London, 1979), 228.

[55] M. J. Daunton, *House and the Home in the Victorian City: Working-Class Housing 1850–1914* (London, 1983), 258–62.

[56] Smith, *People's Health*, 164.

[57] P. J. Waller, *Democracy and Sectarianism: A Political and Social History of Liverpool, 1868–1939* (Liverpool, 1981), 84.

[58] Ibid. 163.

about twice as high among the working class as among the comfortably off.[59] Moreover, the damp and unhealthy accommodation in which hundreds of thousands of poor families were doomed to live directly contributed to many premature deaths, notably from tuberculosis (consumption). By 1900 mortality from this dreaded disease had halved since mid-century, but there were still 250,000 sufferers, making TB the main killer of the adult population; it also usually involved protracted periods of ill-health before death.

Similarly the highest mortality, unsurprisingly, continued to be found within those occupations employing manual labour—pottery workers and leadworkers being more at risk than any other group. Finally, grinding poverty was still a fact of life in the big cities, rising living standards notwithstanding. By the late 1880s voluntary societies were providing free or subsidized breakfasts for children arriving in school too hungry to concentrate on their lessons: of whom there were some 31,000 in London alone, according to a survey made in 1899.[60]

Yet class inequalities, though real, were frequently overlaid by regional and occupational variations. Thus 33.7 per cent of Gateshead's population were living in overcrowded conditions, but only 4.4 per cent of Blackburn's.[61] Similarly, in some towns rent levels rose so sharply as partially to cancel out cheaper food, as in York, where rent absorbed about 14 per cent of working-class income,[62] but this did not happen uniformly across urban Britain. Nor was it necessarily those occupations with low social status which presented the most dangers: among males aged 45 to 55, surgeons and GPs had a higher death-rate than farm labourers or domestic servants.[63]

In fact, belief in the 'healthiness' of the countryside was not merely a nostalgic myth: predominantly rural Ireland had consistently lower infant death-rates than England. This in turn may make us reconsider whether the 'retail revolution' was an unequivocal blessing. Irish labourers who subsisted largely on potatoes and buttermilk certainly ate more healthily than the English urban poor, who relied too heavily on the new white bread (from which most vitamins had been removed) and on sugar-rich substances which rotted the teeth (British consumers had the highest level of sugar in their diet of any people in the world). On mainland Britain, meals may have been becoming more 'appetizing', but they were not necessarily more nutritious. Indeed, some

---

[59] Smith, *The People's Health*, 65–9. The death-rate among the illegitimate also ran at about double the level of the legitimate.

[60] P. Hollis, *Ladies Elect: Women in English Local Government 1865–1914* (Oxford, 1987), 116.

[61] Daunton, *House and the Home*, 40–9.

[62] J. Lewis, *Women in England, 1870–1950: Sexual Divisions and Social Change* (New York and London, 1984), 26–7.

[63] A. S. Wohl, *Endangered Lives: Public Health in Victorian Britain* (London, 1983), 280–1.

of the new convenience foods were, on balance, positively harmful—for example, tinned condensed milk, which some poor mothers insisted on feeding to their babies.

But people in *all* social classes, not just the poor, were on diets that would seem unsatisfactory to a modern nutritionist: for example, too few vegetables were being consumed (vitamins not yet having been discovered). Finally, infant mortality and deaths in childbirth were still, by present-day standards, shockingly high even among the upper and middle classes: at a time when medical provision was still inadequate, wealth could not buy complete immunity.

5. THE SOCIAL EXPLORERS AND THE 'PEOPLE OF THE ABYSS'

Meanwhile changes in social circumstances, as measured by official statistics, were being accompanied by changes in the way in which poverty and deprivation were being conceptualized. In 1885–6 it was the plight of the 'underclass' in East London, the so-called denizens of 'Outcast London', which dominated the debate about poverty and disadvantage. Those who wrote on this topic eschewed a class vocabulary, since they did not think that the people they were studying were the real working class at all, but a demoralized residuum, many of whom were doing anything but work.

The same approach was adopted by the voluntary organization that saw itself as the main source of expertise on social problems, the Charity Organisation Society (COS), founded in 1869. The problem which the COS faced was the existence of hundreds of charities, of all shapes and sizes, some endowed, others raised by subscription for long-term purposes or to meet an immediate emergency—such as the Mansion House Fund launched by the Lord Mayor of London in 1886 to relieve the distress caused by unemployment. Although the true figures will never be known, it has been estimated that in London alone more money was being funnelled through the charities than was being spent on the navy—out of a combined income which exceeded that of many European states.

The COS activists thought this situation dangerous. Their view was that poverty (insufficiency of income) would be eliminated could society but eradicate 'pauperism' (a depraved attitude to life, leading to dependency). And so they set out to put down slackly run charities, to repress begging, as far as practicable, and to establish a clearing system which would enable charities to distinguish between deserving and undeserving cases, the latter being referred to the Poor Law authorities.

The principal COS leaders, among them Helen and Bernard Bosanquet, and its long-serving secretary, C. S. Loch, remained vocal in the debate on poverty well into the next century, and some of the techniques which the COS pioneered, such as case-work and their notion that social work was a 'profession' requiring training, were to exercise a profound influence over later generations. But the COS lost its domination of the debate during the mid-1880s. Intelligent, public-spirited men and women continued to be drawn into the organization, but many became disillusioned with the rigidity of the COS's ideology and moved on to other movements.

One such person was a protege of Octavia Hill, Samuel Augustus Barnett, vicar of St Jude's, Whitechapel, who annoyed the Society in 1890 by reading them a paper entitled 'The Faults of the COS' (it had never occurred to these good folk that they had any). Barnett was the moving spirit behind the Settlements Movement, which originated in London but spread to many other cities. The aim was to persuade idealistic young graduates (typically starting their careers but not yet married) to help the less advantaged, not by dispensing help and advice from above, but by living in their midst, as friends and neighbours. Toynbee Hall, in Whitechapel, was the most famous settlement house,[64] but all the major religious denominations soon had their own foundations, of which the most notable were Browning Hall in Walworth and Mansfield House in Canning Town (Congregationalist) and Bermondsey Settlement (Wesleyan Methodist).

The address given in 1883 by the Oxford history don Arnold Toynbee, after whom the Whitechapel Settlement was named, indicated clearly the philosophy which animated the movement: in it he begged the London poor to 'forgive' the middle class, saying that the best of that class henceforward would be only too willing to devote their lives to their 'service'. However, the 'sin' for which Toynbee was apologizing was not exploitation but neglect, and his hope was that the residents of a settlement would help their new-found friends, not just by raising their material living standards but also by running boys' clubs and providing cultural stimulation in the form of lectures and lantern-slide shows. In truth, the Settlements Movement had a profoundly condescending ethos: it did not aim at promoting equality but rather at community-building. 'The real and vital significance' of the settlement, Arthur Sherwell explained, lay 'in its suggestion of a spiritual idea, a new human relationship, the co-operation of all classes of society in a fellowship of sympathy and service that shall give head to the interests of all while preserving the freedom of each.'[65]

---

[64] Between 1884 and 1900 it attracted 102 residents; of 87 who can be traced, 52 came from Oxford (12 from Balliol), 27 from Cambridge. Their average stay was between one-and-a-half and two years (S. Meacham, *Toynbee Hall and Social Reform, 1880–1914* (New Haven, 1987), 44).

[65] Ibid. 80.

Barnett shared with the COS an intense dislike of the practice of handing out doles to unknown beggars. In the words of his colleague Sir Charles Trevelyan, the 'hand that has given and the hand that has taken have never felt the warm electricity of each other's touch'.[66] With some justification, the settlements have been dubbed manor houses for a new urban squirearchy.

However, this aspiration soon withered. The social gulf between young Oxford graduates and the East End poor was unlikely to be bridged by the 'practice of neighbourliness'. Instead, establishments such as Toynbee Hall soon came to resemble observation posts, from which a new breed of budding social scientists could observe the behaviour of the poor. Its sub-warden, the young William Beveridge, was able in this way to gather the data and impressions which later underpinned his important book, *Unemployment: A Study of Industry* (1907). In fact, Toynbee Hall functioned as a kind of finishing school for the next generation of social 'experts', civil servants, politicians, and academics: not only Beveridge, but also Sir Robert Morant, Hubert Llewellyn Smith, and Vaughan Nash all spent time in residence at Toynbee Hall—as, briefly, did Clement Attlee, the future Labour Party leader.

Yet the promotion of 'social science' did not necessitate prolonged residence in a settlement. This is evident from the career of Charles Booth (no relation of William), who launched his investigations into 'Life and Labour of the People in London' in April 1886, collecting data and information from whatever sources were available to him (school visitors proved to be especially useful), and supplementing this by brief sojourns in working-class lodgings in order to get 'colour'.[67] Booth famously concluded that 32 per cent of the inhabitants in the East End and 30.7 per cent of all Londoners were living in 'poverty'. And of those poor inhabitants whom he placed in Classes C and D, 13 per cent, according to Booth, owed their situation to 'questions of habit' (e.g. indulgence in drink), 19 per cent to 'questions of circumstance' (e.g. illness)[68], but no fewer than 68 per cent to 'questions of employment', which mainly meant irregular work and low wages.[69]

This finding was immediately disputed by the COS but seized upon by both socialists and radical social reformers, to whom it supplied seemingly objective

---

[66] G. Stedman Jones, *Outcast London: A Study in the Relationship between Classes in Victorian Society* (Oxford, 1971), 253.

[67] K. Bales, 'Charles Booth's Survey of *Life and Labour of the People in London 1889–1903*', in M. Bulmer, K. Bales, and K. H. Sklar (eds), *The Social Survey in Historical Perspective, 1880–1940* (Cambridge, 1991), 66–110.

[68] But also 'large families', which Booth clearly saw as something which just 'happened', like an epidemic disease.

[69] In the case of Classes A and B, a similar situation emerged: 14% 'questions of habit', 27% 'questions of circumstance', and 55% 'questions of employment', with the remaining 4% categorized as 'loafers'.

proof that poverty was a problem of society, outside the individual's control. In fact, Booth had not demonstrated anything of the kind. This was because his somewhat amateurish methodology (not until A. L. Bowley's investigation of 1912 was random sampling applied to such material) left open the possibility that most of those lacking work or in receipt of low and/or intermittent earnings were in some way 'defective', whether because of hereditary defects or because they had contracted 'bad habits'. In other words, by 'questions of habit', Booth merely meant *spending* habits. His findings could thus be interpreted in a variety of ways and probably served to confirm most readers in the views they already held.[70]

Nor did the impressive array of statistical tables mean that Booth had produced a dispassionate, 'objective', value-free study of poverty. On the contrary, his classificatory system had embedded within it some highly contentious moralistic presuppositions: thus members of his 'Class A' comprised prostitutes, criminals, vagrants, and other 'social deviants' of whom Booth happened to disapprove, and he was little more complimentary about 'Class B', the 'lower' elements of the casual poor, whom he wanted removed to 'Labour Colonies'.

Booth did, however, manage to convince himself that, in London at least, socialist invocations of 'the working class' were meaningless: he found within the community of manual workers so wide a range of incomes, expenditure patterns, and lifestyles that, far from forming a uniform class, he felt it necessary to distribute them between six different 'classes' (A to F, the latter comprising the highly paid respectable workers whom he so much admired). Some 30 per cent of Londoners might be living in poverty, but that left the rest living 'in comfort', including members of Classes E and F, the more affluent workers, who comprised 51.5 per cent of the total population. Moreover, amongst the 'poor' he distinguished between those who lacked a surplus of goods and those who were in 'want' or 'distress'. The imaginary map of London Booth presented was thus a place of many subtle gradations, not a contrast between 'palaces' and 'hovels', as earlier writers had implied.[71]

Moreover, Booth was free from the 'rural nostalgia' which affected so many of his middle-class contemporaries. He not only assumed without question that industrialization and urbanization were irreversible processes, but he also took an almost Dickensian relish in the panorama of London life, about which he wrote sensitively in the third series of his magnum opus, misleadingly entitled 'Religious Influences'. Booth had also achieved something very important in

[70] E. P. Hennock, 'Poverty and Social Theory in England: The Experience of the 1880s', *Social History*, 1 (1976), 67–91
[71] Walkowitz, *Dreadful Delight*, 32.

that he had largely de-sensationalized slum life, a useful counter to the melodramatic accounts which had preceded his own publications, showing in the process that even in working-class London not all was desperation and poverty.[72]

However, Booth's main legacy was the quantitative 'Poverty Survey', in which his most influential follower was Seebohm Rowntree, a member of the Quaker chocolate and cocoa manufacturers in York. There had been those predisposed to belittle Booth, arguing that London was a special case from which no wider generalizations could be drawn. However, York, a medium-sized northern town with a spread of manufacturing and service industries (it was also an important railway centre), seemed to be broadly typical. It was certainly not noted for being a sink of poverty and degradation, and when Rowntree began his investigations there, in the late 1890s, he did so at a time of relative trade prosperity. Yet Rowntree, too, came to the conclusion, eventually made public in *Poverty: A Study of Town Life* (1902), that 27.84 per cent of York's population were living in poverty, a figure startlingly close to Booth's, given the difference of their methodologies.

Rowntree, however, was responsible for two innovations, the absence of which had weakened Booth's work. First, he invented the concept of the 'poverty cycle', showing that a working-class family's fortunes were subject to wide fluctuations: relative affluence shortly after husband and wife had married, increasing financial difficulties as they brought children into the world, another brief period of comfort while the grown-up children were bringing additional income into the parental home, followed by a downturn when the children left to marry and set up homes of their own and the male breadwinner could no longer, through infirmity or illness, hold down a permanent job. Although Rowntree followed Booth in breaking up the working classes into a number of different categories (Classes A to G, in his case), the concept of the poverty cycle undermined Booth's probably fallacious notion that each of these classes inhabited a separate world: in other words, by presenting a moving film, instead of a series of static snapshots, Rowntree suggested to his readers that most working families could expect to move up and down these 'classes' at different stages in their life—hence, though only 28 per cent of the total population might be poor at any particular moment, a very much higher proportion would suffer this fate at some point in their lives.

---

[72] In his 'Religious Influences' series Booth displayed some of the 'anthropological' insights that were also present in the writings of Helen Bosanquet, Margaret Loane, and Lady Bell, who all tried to understand 'how social classes could be understood ("known") through their codes, conventions, habits, and mental horizons' (R. McKibbin, *Ideologies of Class* (Oxford, 1990; 1991 edn.), 167–9, 175). McKibbin sees 'a clear methodological tension in Booth's survey' between these two explanations of poverty.

Second, Rowntree made progress where Booth had stalled by distinguishing between 'self-induced' poverty and poverty brought about by external circumstances. Through a close examination of family budgets and of income levels (much easier to achieve in a smaller town such as York), Rowntree found that 9.91 per cent of the population were living in a state of 'primary poverty', meaning that their income was insufficient to maintain a family in a state of bare physical efficiency, however wisely it was expended (Rowntree turned to nutritionists to help him establish this point). Another 17.93 per cent were living in 'secondary' poverty, meaning that some 'misallocation' of income was taking place, though Rowntree, with greater generosity of spirit than Booth, argued that 'wasteful' expenditure covered not only over-indulgence in drink but perfectly meritorious activities such as taking children out on 'treats'. The extent of poverty thus appeared to be very much more extensive than had earlier been admitted. The wheel had come full circle, and the 'poor' and the 'working class' now had to be reintegrated once more—with important consequences for Edwardian policy-makers.

6. THE MAKING OF SOCIAL POLICY

But how, in the shorter term, did the new social knowledge affect policy-making? In general, it produced an upsurge of optimism. Booth had apparently demonstrated that the most degraded of London's poor (his Class A) constituted a mere 1.25 per cent of the city's population—'a disgrace, but not a danger', he had called them. And all available statistics indicated that, for most manual workers, living conditions were improving. More encouraging still, the habit of providence seemed to be growing.

There were further grounds for optimism. In 1901 the Criminal Registrar reported on 'a great change in manners: the substitution of words without blows for blows with or without words; an approximation in the manners of different classes; a decline in the spirit of lawlessness'.[73] One of the most remarkable features of this growth in public and private orderliness was the success of the police in the war against crime. During the 1890s the Metropolitan Police pioneered new techniques of surveillance and registration (finger-printing, for example) for dealing with what were now known as 'habitual criminals'.[74] One historian has concluded that 'the contest between law and the criminal was a wholly unequal one', with 'the balance of technological

[73] V. A. C. Gatrell, 'The Decline of Theft and Violence in Victorian and Edwardian England', in V. A. C. Gatrell, B. Lenman, and G. Parker (eds.), Crimes and the Law: The Social History of Crime in Western Europe Since 1500 (London, 1980), 241.

[74] S. Petrow, Policing Morals: The Metropolitan Police and the Home Office, 1870–1914 (Oxford, 1994), 79–93.

advantage' now lying 'with the law-enforcers', against whom 'criminals' had not yet erected adequate defences.[75] By the end of the century the police had also taken control of the streets, invading even the 'dark' areas where once they had feared to tread.[76]

As a result, the level of criminal activity probably dropped. The rate of trials for indictable crimes declined by 43 per cent from the early 1860s to the late 1890s, from 288 per 100,000 of the population to 164 in late 1890s.[77] This trend applied not only to larceny, but also to offences against the person. One explanation for this may be the growing disinclination to prosecute for minor offences, many of which were now resolved informally or by civil actions. Moreover, towards the end of the century nearly all offences (not just larceny) were made subject to summary jurisdiction (i.e. tried before petty sessions or the police courts). But both these changes may have occurred because crime did not provoke such hysteria as it had once done.[78]

Admittedly, serious property crimes, far from falling, actually increased after 1900, a trend that some contemporaries blamed on the emergence of 'the higher criminal'.[79] The statistics also show an increase in the incidence of sexual assault. This, however, may well reflect an increasing police intolerance of violence against women, as well as owing something to the Criminal Law Amendment Act of 1885 which, by raising the age of consent, necessarily created a new category of sexual offence.[80]

Despite the insecurity of the mid-1880s, society thus seemed to be basically stable. Rowdiness, drunkenness, and casual violence, too, had all probably abated since the 1870s. Significantly, the rate of trials for assaults on the police fell by 64 per cent between the late 1850s and the pre-war years, as did prosecution for drunkenness.[81] Greater law-abidingness, as much as police numbers, perhaps made the greatest contribution of all to this development.[82]

In this more relaxed atmosphere the courts were encouraged to impose shorter sentences on many categories of offenders. In the mid-Victorian period criminals had been regarded as highly dangerous men at war with society. But now, it seemed, they formed a very small group, and a declining one at that:

---

[75] Gatrell, 'Decline of Theft', 278, 336.

[76] D. Jones, *Crime, Protest, Community and Police in Nineteenth-Century Britain* (London, 1982), 177, for Manchester.

[77] Followed by a rise (Gatrell, 'Decline of Theft', 240, 281).

[78] Ibid. 290–1.

[79] Petrow, *Policing Morals*, 52.

[80] Similarly the Children's Charter of 1908, which permitted summary trial for indecent assaults on children under 16, later pushed up the total of indecent assaults (Gatrell, 'Decline of Theft', 289).

[81] Ibid. 289.

[82] D. Woods, 'Community Violence', in J. Benson (ed.), *The Working Class in England, 1875–1914* (Beckenham, 1985), 165–205.

down from 78,000 in 1869–70 to 31,000 in 1889–90.[83] The tendency was now to view habitual criminals as 'human wreckage', to use the title of a book published by Francis Peck, Chairman of the Howard League, in 1889: a class damaged by environment or by heredity (it was a curious feature of the 1890s that commentators saw no need to weigh the two factors against one another).[84] Their defining characteristics, according to the new band of experts, was not demonic strength but a congenital weakness, an inability to take responsibility for their own lives.

It was this assumption of pathological peculiarity which inspired books such as Havelock Ellis's *The Criminal* (1890), which popularized the notion (earlier propounded by the Italian criminologist Cesare Lombroso) of the criminal as resembling 'in physical and psychical characteristics the normal individuals of a lower race'. 'Criminal anthropology' had a wide credence. Sherlock Holmes's adversary, Moriarty, was described as possessing 'hereditary tendencies of the most diabolical kind' and having a 'criminal strain [running] in his blood'.[85] Admittedly, E. Ruggles-Brise, of the Prison Commission, believed that physical degeneration and bad social conditions *both* played a part in the formation of criminals.[86] But not until the appearance of Charles Goring's *The English Convict* in 1913, a book based on extensive empirical enquiry, were Lombroso's theories seriously discredited.[87]

Once the consumption of alcohol had started to drop, a 'medical' approach was also adopted towards drunkards. 'Inebriates' (a term first used by the law in 1889) seemed to be 'prisoners of their habit', defective human beings who required therapeutic management, not disciplinary action—especially if alcoholism, as the new social 'experts' claimed, was an illness, even a hereditary condition.[88] Hence the 1898 Inebriates Act, which permitted repeat offenders to receive distinctive treatment in special institutions.[89]

It was against this background that the Medico-Psychological Association pursued its investigations into 'abnormal psychology', out of which emerged T. S. Clouston's *Clinical Lectures on Mental Diseases* (1883; 6th edn. 1904) and Charles Mercier's *Psychology, Normal and Morbid* (1901). And though the Asylum Act of 1890 was drawn up with a view to protecting civil rights and

---

[83] M. J. Wiener, *Reconstructing the Criminal: Culture, Law, and Policy in England, 1830–1914* (Cambridge, 1990), 216–17.

[84] Hence, Gordon Ryland, in his *Crime: Its Causes and Remedy* (1889), could write: 'Two influences which determine above all others the amount of crime . . . to one or the other of which indeed all others may be ultimately reduced . . . [are] Heredity and Environment.' This is also true of Charles Booth.

[85] A. Conan Doyle, 'The Final Problem'.

[86] Wiener, *Reconstructing the Criminal*, 346–7.

[87] Goring demonstrated that in this respect there were no marked differences between convicts and university students!

[88] Wiener, *Reconstructing the Criminal*, 188.

[89] Ibid. 350.

preventing unlawful detention, between 1890 and 1914 the asylum population increased by more than 50 per cent.[90] By the end of the nineteenth century the numbers of those in county and borough asylums in England and Wales had soared to 74,000.

Another symptom of this interest in the 'unfit' was the growing use of the word 'feeble-minded', a term first used by Charles Trevelyan in an address to the COS in 1876. The word became increasingly employed to characterize the weak, the sickly, and the unfit—groups that would not have survived had the state not come to their support.[91] As a result, harsh punishments not only offended the sensibilities of bodies such as the Humanitarian League (founded in 1891 to protect children, animals, and prisoners), but also seemed, to most intelligent observers of the legal and penal systems, to be largely pointless. In the 1890s this new perspective on life, with its acceptance of diminished personal responsibility, was beginning to affect the operation of both the civil and the criminal law, penal policy, and, more slowly, judicial behaviour.[92]

For example, after 1880 successive Home Secretaries became increasingly unwilling to imprison children; those minors who did end up behind bars were also treated less harshly. The Probation of First Offenders Bill of 1887 allowed magistrates more alternatives to gaol when they sentenced juveniles, bailing became the norm for juveniles awaiting trial, and an Act of 1893 ended the automatic gaoling of juveniles before they went to a reformatory. By 1901 only eight children under the age of 12 were serving a prison sentence.[93]

The new approach to social problems was also modifying attitudes to the Poor Law. The policy of deterring the able-bodied from applying for relief was proving easier to implement now that the general standard of living had risen so substantially. But this increasingly left Boards of Guardians with the expensive task of coping with those suffering from various physical and mental illnesses, for whom treatment in an infirmary or an asylum seemed more appropriate than incarceration in a workhouse. The other main group of paupers consisted of the elderly, who, if in reasonably good health, were now mostly in receipt of outdoor relief.[94] Charles Booth was only the most prominent of those advocating that 'respectable' members of

---

[90] First Annual Report of Board of Control for 1914, 1915.

[91] H. G. Simmons, 'Explaining Social Policy: The English Mental Deficiency Act of 1913', *Journal of Social History*, 11 (1978), 388–90.

[92] Contractual liability based on free consent and tort liability based on personal fault slowly eroded: from the 1890s onwards a series of judgements whittled away or mitigated consensual obligation (Wiener, *Reconstructing the Criminal*, 202). Moreover, more and more categories of prisoners were exempted from penal servitude.

[93] Ibid. 293.

[94] In 1900 there were only 74,600 indoor paupers aged 65 and over, but 212,300 on outdoor relief. Booth found that 39% of East Enders over 65 were paupers (Thane, *Old Age*, 174).

this category should be taken out of the Poor Law entirely by being paid an old-age pension.

But though social policy was becoming more 'humane' in some respects, it was becoming harsher in others, since fewer people shared the COS's robust confidence in the capacity of all but the incurably sick to take charge of their own lives if only they made an effort. On the contrary, misfits, deviants, and incompetents, of various kinds, were increasingly identified as a problem of social administration that required custodial care and treatment at the hands of the relevant 'expert'—as much to protect society as to help the 'victims'. This dark vision of the world was to become more pronounced after 1900.

But, on balance, the 1890s was a time of optimism. The 'social crisis' of 1886–7 had disappeared by the end of Victoria's reign. The 'respectable' no longer dreaded an uprising of the dispossessed, and property seemed to be reasonably secure. Neither was there a return to the kind of blind panic which had gripped the country during the London garotting scare of 1862–3. What had come to pass, however, was not a harmonious, integrated society 'at peace with itself'. It makes more sense to use Harold Perkin's term: a 'mature class society', that is to say, a society within which each class accepted the institutionalized role assigned to it and sought to settle its differences with others through negotiation and compromise, not violence.

Finally, the 1890s was the decade in which all but a tiny unruly minority of the working class broadly accepted the right of appropriate authorities to regulate their lives: by 1888 it was being reported that the poor were ceasing to regard the sanitary inspectors as their class enemy, there was overwhelming parental compliance with the requirement that children attend school (except in times of emergency, for example, harvesting in rural areas),[95] and the role of the police was no longer openly challenged—except when they tried to interfere with the people's amusements (e.g. betting and drinking).[96] Indirectly, the path was being paved for a new age of social administration.

All of these developments had political consequences. True, Booth, along with most of his contemporaries, envisaged 'social science' and social enquiry as an *alternative* to politics, certainly an *alternative* to the clash of political parties, which he found tedious and disgusting: hence, perhaps, his failure to think clearly about how his proposed 'remedies' might be implemented—incarcerating members of his 'Class B' in Labour Colonies had never been a

---

[95] In the London School Board, the early 1900s was the crucial turning point: by 1906 88.2% of children were in regular attendance (D. Rubinstein, *School Attendance in London, 1870–1914: A Social History* (Hull, 1969), 111–12). See also Thompson, *Respectable Society*, 138.

[96] However, in poor districts the old cry 'Give it to the copper' could still sometimes be heard.

practical proposition. On the other hand, Rowntree, a much younger man, whose Quaker affiliations made him a natural Liberal (as was his father Joseph, the famous temperance reformer), assumed from the start that what he was doing was to supply politicians—reform-minded Liberals, in particular—with a new programmatic agenda. In this belief Rowntree was not mistaken.[97] For, like it or not, governments and Parliament were being increasingly sucked into a consideration of social questions—not least because of new political challenges.

[97] See Ch. 11.

CHAPTER 7

Politics and the Social Question, 1886–99

1. THE SALISBURY GOVERNMENT, 1886–1892

'Whatever happens will be for the worse, and therefore it is in our interest that as little should happen as possible', Salisbury once characteristically observed.[1] The new Prime Minister had spent most of his life under Whig-Liberal governments: only once since 1846 had the Conservatives won an overall majority of Commons seats (Disraeli's victory of 1874). This may explain why he was slow to read the runes of the recent election results: far from foreseeing the triumph of a new, more broadly based and popular Conservatism, he continued to hope for a return to the relative stability of the Palmerston era, when the Conservative Party's main function had been that of exercising restraint over demagogic Liberalism and 'democratic' excess.

But the fight against Home Rule did not allow Salisbury to follow his own instincts: his main priority had to be the conciliation of the various political groups that had coalesced in defence of the Union. On social issues, however, the Unionists by no means saw eye to eye. Chamberlain favoured the adoption of an advanced programme of 'construction', but the Liberal Unionist Leader, Lord Hartington, showed no such enthusiasm.

The Conservatives were equally split. Randolph Churchill's old 'Fourth Party' comrade, Sir John Gorst, now Financial Secretary of the Treasury, promoted the idea of the state as model employer and tried to revitalize Conservatism with ideas of social reform. But though these appeals were taken up by the chairman of the National Union, Sir Albert Rollit, a Hull shipowner, and by Arthur Forwood of Liverpool, Gorst was widely mistrusted in the parliamentary party.[2] The cause of Tory democracy may have appealed to younger Conservatives, but, at national level, it no more had the backing of the Conservative leadership than did advice from the rapidly failing Churchill.

---

[1] The observations, made in August 1887, in fact referred to the situation in the Balkans (A. Roberts, *Salisbury: Victorian Titan* (London, 1999), 435).

[2] R. Shannon, *The Age of Salisbury, 1881–1902: Unionism and Empire* (Harlow, 1996), 348–9, 360–2.

The government therefore steered a middle path. Salisbury felt that in a democratic age the Conservatives had no option but to sponsor a limited package of reforms. If the Conservatives failed to take the initiative, he warned his anxious backbenchers, the Liberals would soon confront them with much more unpalatable measures. Here the government's reliance upon the Liberal Unionists proved useful, because Salisbury could use this to persuade obdurate followers of the necessity of shifting ground.

On the other hand, Salisbury realized that if he wanted to entice former middle-class Liberal voters into an alliance based upon a strategy of 'resistance' to democratic excess, there was little point in going too far in wooing the working man. 'We have so to conduct our legislation that we shall give some satisfaction to both classes and masses', he patiently explained to Churchill in late 1886: 'This is especially difficult with the classes—because all legislation is rather unwelcome to them, as tending to disturb a state of affairs with which they are satisfied.'[3] Salisbury was not nearly as inflexible on social issues as his rhetoric sometimes suggested—for example, he wisely disassociated himself from the doctrinaire individualism of Lord Wemyss's 'Liberty and Property Defence League'. But he had good grounds for circumspection since, as well as managing his parliamentary party, he feared alienating important vested interests and frightening capital by flouting the 'laws' of political economy.

What reforms finally emerged from Salisbury's 'principled opportunism'? Outside Ireland, two major pieces of social legislation were enacted. In 1888 local government in the counties was at last transferred from the unaccountable magistracy to popularly elected county councils (necessary if increased exchequer grants were to be given to cover county expenses). This measure also involved the creation of the London County Council (LCC). And in 1891 the government effectively made elementary education free—an expensive innovation.

Backbench Conservative MPs disliked both measures, and Lord Carnarvon led a spirited resistance to the Local Government Bill when it reached the Lords. The creation of the LCC aroused even greater annoyance, particularly after the authority fell under the control of a metropolitan grouping calling itself the 'Progressive Party', which combined Radical Liberals with trade unionists and even Fabian socialists.[4]

Conservatives expected their government to pursue 'sound' financial policies. They were therefore delighted when the Chancellor of the Exchequer, George Joachim Goschen, built up a healthy budget surplus with his conversion of the National Debt in 1888. But this surplus had disappeared by 1892,

---

[3] J. P. D. Dunbabin, 'The Politics of the Establishment of County Councils', *Historical Journal*, 6 (1963), 251–2.
[4] See below.

partly as a result of the Naval Defence Act,[5] but also because of domestic commitments. State spending increased from £87.4 million in 1887 to £97.6 million in 1892, while the proportion of revenue raised by direct taxation continued to grow at the expense of indirect taxation. Backbench Conservatives stirred restlessly; they also disliked government-sponsored measures that pushed up the rates.

Yet were the Conservative reforms really as 'progressive' as grumpy Tory squires believed? The principal purpose of free education was to save church schools from financial collapse—the safest way of doing this once rate-aid had been rejected.[6] Similarly, the local government reforms, though something of a gamble, can be seen as a way of shoring up the authority of the local elites,[7] or else, as was claimed by C. T. Ritchie, the minister responsible for the measure, as a 'conservative' counter-balance to expanding state power. Salisbury later told Chamberlain that he had acted on the latter's views by adopting election rather than nomination as the guiding principle of his local government reforms—but he did not consult Chamberlain at the time.

The other social measures passed by the Salisbury government were something of a rag-bag. The Housing of the Working Class Act of 1890 gave local authorities compulsory powers to acquire land for housing development by borrowing from the Public Works Loans Commissioners and then letting out houses to working-class tenants; the latter, however, had to pay rent at market levels.[8] The Factory and Workshop Act of 1891, which some Conservative apologists presented as a bold piece of Disraelian social reform, was essentially no more than a consolidating measure.[9] More important were the Allotments Acts of 1887 and 1890 and the Small Holdings Act of 1892, which testify to a desire to outbid the Opposition by showing a solicitous concern for the farm labourer. But, despite urgent prodding from Jesse Collings, Salisbury was only with difficulty persuaded to give local authorities compulsory powers to acquire allotments,[10] while he successfully insisted on the absence of compulsion in the Small Holdings Act, which, as a consequence, became virtually a dead letter: less than 1,000 acres were acquired under its provisions over the following fifteen years.

---

[5] See Ch. 8.

[6] Chamberlain prudently absented himself from the vote extending free education to voluntary schools.

[7] See below.

[8] M. Fforde, *Conservatism and Collectivism, 1886–1914* (Edinburgh, 1990), 80.

[9] Shannon, *Age of Salisbury*, 358–9.

[10] Significantly, the Land and Glebe Owners' Association would have preferred action to have been taken by the landowners, without state intervention. Farmers, too, disliked the Acts, seeing them as an expensive way of benefiting the labourer.

Yet would a bold programme of social reform really have been the sure-fire vote-winner that its advocates claimed? Electorally, the Conservatives often performed best, not when advocating state-run welfare schemes, but when standing up in support of working-class leisure activities threatened by killjoy Nonconformists and faddists. For example, in the poor constituency of Wolverhampton West the Conservative MP, Alfred Hickman, built up a popular following, based upon a defence of Queen and Church and the right of the working man to pursue his pleasures free from external interference.[11] Salisbury was temperamentally unsympathetic to the culture of 'cakes and ale'—he certainly took no interest in 'manly sports'—but he entirely shared Hickman's hostility to the temperance reformers; people, he was convinced, could not be made moral by Act of Parliament. (This stance, of course, also brought the party welcome support from publicans and brewers.)

The defence of the Established Church, popular in some working-class quarters, was even more congenial to this pious High Anglican. In fact, despite the growth of Nonconformist Unionism, Salisbury went out of his way to help the Church—sometimes rescuing it from its own short-sightedness, as in an 1891 Bill which shifted the burden of tithe from occupier to owner in order to make the Church less politically vulnerable.[12] This kind of intervention had the additional advantage of costing the government nothing.

Here was Conservatism of a highly traditional stamp. A more serious contribution to its modernization lay in Salisbury's development of an efficient party machinery. At Westminster he relied upon the energy, tact, and good judgment of his Chief Whip, 'Bob' Akers-Douglas, a Kentish squire. Larger organizational matters were left in the competent hands of the Chief Agent, Captain Richard Middleton, the 'Skipper', who worked in close association with the Prime Minister's personal secretary, Schomberg ('Pom') McDonnell.

Underpinning the formal party organization was the Primrose League, founded in November 1883, with its bizarre mock feudal rituals. The League provided a forum in which middle-class members of the party could rub shoulders with landed society, thus helping to integrate the propertied classes in a common, Conservative-led front. But, despite its reputation for escapism and snobbery, the Primrose League was in many respects more modern in outlook than the Conservative Party itself. For example, many 'habitations' had a predominantly working-class membership, particularly in Lancashire; in 1900 Bolton's reached 6,000, a figure similar to the total paid-up membership

---

[11] J. Lawrence, *Speaking for the People: Party, Language and Popular Politics in England, 1867–1914* (Cambridge, 1998), Ch. 5.

[12] Fforde, *Conservatism and Collectivism*, 86. There was also the Clergy Discipline Bill in 1892. But Salisbury was no narrow sectarian: his Home Secretary, Matthews, was the first Roman Catholic to hold a Cabinet post.

of the most successful of the socialist societies, the ILP.[13] The League also provided an outlet for the political as well as the social energies of women, who comprised almost one-half of its total membership (some habitations had an exclusively female membership). Little wonder if the party conference should have come out in November 1887 in support of ceding the parliamentary franchise to women householders.[14] In general, then, the Primrose League, which claimed 1 million members by 1891, suggested the possibility of a more self-confident and populist Conservatism than its current leaders were willing to contemplate.

Chamberlain continued to urge the Salisbury government forward because he did not believe that a policy of 'resistance' would long suffice in a democratic age, and noisily claimed credit for its 'constructive' measures—foolishly, since, as Salisbury privately warned him, such language made it more difficult for the government to sponsor reform.[15] Balfour was the one senior Conservative who displayed an interest in Chamberlain's notions when these were put before him in January 1892.[16] But, again, Salisbury urged caution: if the Conservatives acted on Chamberlain's advice, he reminded Balfour, they would 'in so doing alarm a good many people who have always been with us'; 'these social questions', he gloomily predicted, were 'destined to break up our Party'.[17]

Equally contentious was protection, euphemistically dubbed 'Fair Trade'.[18] By the late 1880s this movement had won over about sixty Conservative MPs, led by Howard Vincent, one of the Members for Sheffield, where it enjoyed considerable support. Randolph Churchill, too, had briefly toyed with Fair Trade, and the National Union regularly carried favourable motions from 1887 onwards. Indeed, following the passing by the American Congress of the McKinley tariff, Salisbury himself, in a speech at Hastings in early 1892, declared that the present was an 'age of a war of tariffs', in which Britain had chivalrously but unwisely divested herself of her weapons.

But throughout the 1890s any move towards general industrial protection fell outside the realm of political possibility. Apart from anything else, it was unclear how, if at all, industrial protection could be combined with agricultural protection; in some respects the two movements wanted contradictory outcomes. Salisbury himself had prudently dissociated himself from tariffs on

---

[13] M. Pugh, *The Tories and the People, 1880–1935* (Oxford, 1985), 2.

[14] M. Pugh, *The March of the Women: A Revisionist Analysis of the Campaign for Women's Suffrage, 1866–1914* (Oxford, 2000), 113.

[15] The 1892 Allotment Bill was, in fact, one of the few measures where nagging by Chamberlain played a part in its adoption (Shannon, *Age of Salisbury*, 373).

[16] R. Jay, *Joseph Chamberlain: A Political Study* (Oxford, 1981), 177.

[17] E. H. H. Green, *The Crisis of Conservatism: The Politics, Economics and Ideology of the British Conservative Party, 1880–1914* (London, 1995), 131.

[18] See Ch. 6.

food or raw materials. Even so, his remarks at Hastings were thought to have cost his party votes; they also annoyed the Liberal Unionists (Chamberlain as much as Devonshire), to whom any questioning of free trade was still anathema.

And so, by the time that the Conservative ministry left office in 1892, it may have done enough to give the lie to Churchill's charge that the Tories were stupid and 'reactionary'. But no heroic legislative initiatives had been taken—wisely, from Salisbury's point of view, since, for the immediate future, cultivating 'Villa Toryism' offered much richer pickings.

2. THE LIBERAL MINISTRIES, 1892–1895

Despite their preoccupation with Irish Home Rule, the Gladstone and Rosebery ministries could claim some credit in the field of social legislation. This was partly because circumstances were driving the Liberals willy-nilly in a more radical direction. The Home Rule commitment had alienated both court and aristocracy. Moreover, many of the party's former wealthy backers had deserted the party in 1886—a source of anxiety to its fund-raisers.[19]

To what extent this trend encouraged the Liberal leadership to take a more sympathetic attitude towards working-class hardships, however, is not so clear. Gladstone famously alluded to the growing class divisions within British political life: the tendency for the 'classes' to take shelter within a selfish Unionism, leaving the Liberal Party to espouse the cause of the virtuous 'masses'. But his ambiguous language leaves one uncertain whether or not he *welcomed* this development.[20] In old age Gladstone gave a guarded welcome to the principles of trade unionism and even toyed briefly with payment for MPs.[21] Indeed, while remaining generally cautious in his observations about social legislation, Gladstone, mainly through his own personality and moral energy, became a hero to many politically conscious working men: the Gladstone pea was cultivated on many an allotment, and a lithograph of the great Liberal Leader adorned many a humble home. Even Keir Hardie, the socialist, participated in the cult.

Yet Gladstone continued to deplore the spread of 'materialism', and regretted the loss of the moderating influence once exercised by the great Whig families. Indeed, his gratitude towards those landed magnates who had stood

[19] M. Barker, *Gladstone and Radicalism: The Reconstruction of Liberal Policy in Britain 1885–1894* (Hassocks, 1975), 113.

[20] D. A. Hamer, *Liberal Politics in the Age of Gladstone and Rosebery: A Study in Leadership and Policy* (Oxford, 1972), 148.

[21] Barker, *Gladstone and Radicalism*, 91–4. He had taken a sympathetic stance over the dock strike, which, significantly, involved many trade unionists of Irish descent.

by the Liberal Party after the 1886 schism probably explains why so many of them received plum jobs: Rosebery the Foreign Office, Spencer the Admiralty, Ripon the Indian Office, Kimberley the Colonial Office, and so on. It was also symptomatic of Gladstone's essential conservatism that he should have been so eager to ingratiate himself with the Queen, despite the abominable treatment he continued to receive at her hands. Significantly, too, Gladstone disliked the early drafts of Harcourt's famous 1894 Budget: 'real property has more of presumptive connection with the discharge of duty than that which is ranked as personal', he declared; and he worried about the tendency of great estates to be bought up by 'neo-ploutoi', who did not share this sense of obligation.[22]

A similar ambiguity permeated the Liberalism which Gladstone represented. The Newcastle Programme adopted by the NLF in 1891 was in many ways an uncompromisingly Radical manifesto, but while some of its commitments (for example, Local Option[23] and Welsh Disestablishment) looked backward to an older Radicalism that took as its starting point the malignity of parson and publican, other items presaged the social democratic politics of the future, such as payment of MPs and employers' liability—though not the eight-hour day, which is the one reform that Labour badly wanted.

Yet how seriously did the Liberal Cabinet take these latter commitments? Despite its minority position, it could certainly claim credit for a number of useful reforms. The government's most ambitious measure, an Employers' Liability Bill, foundered in the House of Lords,[24] but parish councils, though emasculated in the Upper House, were established in 1894—a feeble attempt at revitalizing rural life through the introduction of 'democracy'.

Administrative action was one way of evading such obstruction from the peers. A. J. Mundella at the Board of Trade created an effective Labour Department, with important long-term consequences; A. H. D. Acland, Vice-President of the Council, was a vigorous Education Minister; and the War Secretary, Henry Campbell-Bannerman, introduced a forty-eight-hour week into all War Office factories—the Admiralty following suit in March 1894.[25] In 1894 Parliament established another precedent by limiting the hours that could be worked by railwaymen—admittedly to secure the safety of the travelling public rather than to help the workforce.

Yet the opposition to the ill-fated Employers' Liability Bill from wealthy and powerful Liberal employers had already shown what little room for

[22] Ibid. 250–1.
[23] Allowing local authorities to decide by ballot whether they wished to ban the sale of alcoholic drinks within their areas.
[24] Though Chamberlain had a case for saying that the Lords' amendments were reasonable and that the government's whole approach in the matter was misconceived.
[25] Barker, *Gladstone and Radicalism*, 256.

manoeuvre the Liberal government possessed. Later a Miners' Eight Hour Bill was effectively sabotaged by employer resistance within the party.[26] The reluctance of local caucuses to adopt working-class candidates, despite repeated high-minded injunctions from headquarters to do so, also alienated many erstwhile working-class sympathizers. In any case, most ministers did not wish to challenge head-on the older precepts of political economy, and a laissez-faire ethos remained strong in Liberal circles throughout the 1890s. For all these reasons, working-class radicals and moderate socialists who had initially been prepared to co-operate with the government gradually lost patience, Sidney Webb and Bernard Shaw, for example, issuing in November 1893 their famous article, 'To Your Tents, Oh Israel!', calling for separate labour representation.[27]

After Gladstone's retirement, the Liberals might have achieved more if the inherently difficult task of redefining the Liberal mission had not become hopelessly entangled with internecine squabbling. Rosebery, racked by insomnia and a prey to self-pity, became Prime Minister and party leader. But, as a peer in an overwhelmingly hostile Upper House, he found himself cut off from the mainstream of Liberal politics: well might he complain that leading a Liberal government from the Lords was like addressing a crowd through a megaphone with a pudding in its orifice. Moreover, his social position, coupled with his love of horse-racing, meant that, from the start, many of the more puritanical Nonconformists viewed him with intense suspicion.[28] Another weakness was that Rosebery's carefully cultivated image as a man of mystery led others to attribute to him convictions which he did not really hold. Finally, Rosebery's emergence as a leading 'imperialist' made him an intensely controversial leader of a party containing so many anti-imperialists.[29]

To have any chance of success, the Prime Minister needed to establish a loyal and co-operative relationship with Harcourt, now Leader in the Lower House. In the event, the relationship between the two men quickly deteriorated to the point where they could only communicate through third parties, often Asquith. Spencer's attempts at mediation met with a childish rebuff from Harcourt. 'I am not a supporter of the present government', its Commons Leader was wont to tell anyone who cared to listen.

Rosebery, coached by the young Scottish MP for Haddington, R. B. Haldane, intermittently showed some understanding of the nature of the

---

[26] However, in 1895 a Factories and Workshops Bill did pass.

[27] The article, first published in the *Fortnightly Review*, was incorporated in the following year into the Fabian pamphlet entitled *A Plan of Campaign for Labour*.

[28] But by no means all Dissenters, the leading Wesleyan, Robert Perks, being a great admirer of Rosebery's personality and imperialistic ideas.

[29] See Ch. 8.

emerging political order. For example, he had earlier been elected to the LCC for the City of London constituency, subsequently serving as its chairman. This gave him an air of modernity and brought him into contact with some of the personalities and ideas which dominated the metropolitan Progressives— an experience from which he might have learned much. Later, in the autumn of 1893, while Foreign Secretary, he successfuly mediated in the damaging coal strike, another harbinger of the future responsibilities which 'modern' govern- ments would find themselves assuming. But, for all his intelligence and eloquence, Rosebery lacked the stamina or the self-belief to develop this promising role—to the disappointment of his Liberal Imperialist admirers.

So much became apparent when Harcourt, who had stayed on as Chancellor of the Exchequer, produced his famous 1894 'Death Duties Budget', which treated landed estates on the same footing as personal property. This bold initiative brought out the reactionary streak in Rosebery's complex personality. In April 1894 he wrote his Chancellor a memorandum, protesting that the Budget would forfeit the support of the propertied classes and result in a 'horizontal division of parties'. In deference to Rosebery's complaints, Har- court softened the Budget's graduation scale, but he was scornful that the Prime Minister did not dare to bring his views to the attention of the full Cabinet and, with some justification, taunted him with being solely concerned with protecting his own pocket.

In retrospect Harcourt's Budget, which its author called a 'poor man's budget', seems to prefigure Lloyd George's later Financial Bill of 1909.[30] For, despite his failure to introduce a surtax, Harcourt raised the basic rate of income tax to 1s. 8d. in the pound, while extending relief by abatements and exemption to those at the lower end of the scale—an important step in the direction of a more progressive fiscal regime. Even more innovative were the amalgamated death duties, on a graduated scale, which removed the earlier distinction between personal and landed property—provisions which elicited howls of protest from many big landowners. Yet these duties were only intended to bring in £1 million in their first year and a revenue of £3.5 million thereafter. Over half of the new taxation in fact came from increased duties on beer and spirits, which annoyed Liberal brewers and distillers as well as many Irish Nationalist MPs.

Many Radical backbenchers urged Harcourt to be bolder. But the Chan- cellor's hands were tied by the heavy expenditure commitments incurred under the 1889 Naval Defence Act and by the further naval increases exacted by the Admiralty in late 1894. This deprived him of any scope for tax-cuts in

[30] For a fuller account, M. Daunton, *Trusting Leviathan: The Politics of Taxation in Britain, 1799–1914* (Cambridge, 2001), 244–53, 321–4.

1895—which happened to be election year. Such popular Radical ambitions as the institution of a 'free breakfast table' (the abolition of the regressive duties on tea and sugar) were thus frustrated.

Fiscal restraints also put paid to the prospect of initiating old-age pensions, another policy item which was rapidly gathering support on the Liberal backbenches. But, even if the opportunity to strike out in the kind of direction which Lloyd George was later to tread had been available, would Harcourt have taken it? During the 1894 Budget debates the Chancellor told the House: 'You have before you a future of ever-increasing expenditure—demands not only for the Army and Navy but for every kind of social reform.'[31] But the Chancellor usually gave the impression of being at heart more interested in the older sectarian Radical issues, especially Local Option, which continued to absorb much of his time; and temperance reform lacked appeal with the wider working-class electorate. In any case, the government's Local Option Bill, which applied to pubs but not to hotels and restaurants, could easily be characterized as a 'class' measure.

However difficult as a colleague, Harcourt remained popular with many Liberal MPs, who enjoyed his swashbuckling attacks on the Opposition, and he was behind much of what went well for the government. But he 'was essentially an unconstructive politician, and his instinct was usually to fall back on attack and negativeness',[32] even when this meant acting as a kind of opposition figure within his own ministry.

In this respect Harcourt epitomized much that was wrong about the Liberal Party as a whole. As early as June 1887 Chamberlain had attacked what he called the new Radical 'Nihilism', a charge which took on greater plausibility after the adoption of the Newcastle Programme, which many Liberals, too, later came to regret. Liberalism, so ran the indictment, had fallen under the control of 'faddists', of whom Henry Labouchere was only too typical. The Nonconformist pressure group the Liberation Society was thought to be wielding far too much influence, as were Radicals from the 'Celtic Fringe' with their increasingly strident challenge to metropolitan domination. Temperance reformers, through their excess of zeal and internecine squabbling, also did the party considerable electoral damage.

Liberal Imperialism was initially an attempt to remedy these weaknesses,[33] but from the start its adherents were vague about how their objectives were to be achieved. Greater progress in the reformulation of the Liberal creed was made by a different grouping, the so-called 'New Liberals', who set themselves

[31] D. Brooks (ed.), *The Destruction of Lord Rosebery: From the Diary of Sir Edward Hamilton, 1894–1895* (London, 1986), 16.

[32] Hamer, *Gladstone and Rosebery*, 189.

[33] See Chs. 5 and 9.

the task of updating the ideology of Liberalism by moving it away from its traditional anti-statism and its narrow concern with political rights, substituting a new concern for collective welfare and social justice—to be pursued, it was hoped, in co-operation with the developing Labour Movement. However, much of this activity remained subterranean, leaving the Liberal 'old guard' very much in control.

Liberal negativity damaged relationships with the party's working-class supporters when the country went to the polls in July 1895. Economic circumstances also operated to their disadvantage. Earlier in the year 8 per cent of trade unionists were out of work and agricultural prices stood only a little above their nadir. In Lancashire anger over the Government of India's decision to impose customs duties on the importation into India of cotton textiles led to many Liberal losses, while among English farm labourers and Scottish crofters alike there was a feeling of betrayal.[34] Against this background, Harcourt's panegyrics about the prosperity brought about by free trade rang very hollow.

A host of particular grievances told against the recent party of government. Morley lost many votes at Newcastle because of his opposition to the eight-hour day. By contrast, in other constituencies it was the backlash from the coalowners *opposed* to the recent attempts to impose an eight-hour day on their industry that cost the Liberals valuable votes.[35] In Lancashire, with its wealth of popular Anglican schools, many working-class electors deserted the Liberal Party for Unionism in protest at the Liberals' hostility to the Church. More important than any of these issues, in the eyes of many defeated Liberal candidates, had been the successful way in which the brewers, furious at the prospect of Local Option, had thrown their weight behind the Unionist forces.[36]

Finally, the appearance in the field of twenty-eight socialist candidates may, through a splitting of the 'progressive vote', have enabled the Unionists to defeat the Liberals in up to four seats.[37] Although coming at the bottom of the poll, the fact that these 'independents' had stood at all was a warning that the Liberals no longer had a monopoly claim on 'progressivism'.

[34] One Scottish Liberal backbencher had recently resigned the Whip in sympathy with the crofters. In England there was disappointment over the limited powers ceded to the parish councils, of which too much had been expected. Farmers in the barley-growing districts also disliked the prospect of Local Option.

[35] Barker, *Gladstone and Radicalism*, 149–50, 254.

[36] Of the nearly 500 English and Welsh seats, the drink trade was neutral in only five. W. S. Caine was one of several staunch temperance reformers who went down to defeat in 1895 (D. W. Gutzke, *Protecting the Pub: Brewers and Publicans Against Temperance* (Woodbridge, 1989), 122–3).

[37] Assuming that independent Labour candidates took twice as many votes off Liberal than off Conservative candidates, one can deduce that Tillett's intervention brought about the defeat of the Liberal in Bradford West and that the ILP was probably responsible for the Liberals losing a seat in each of the following double-member constituencies: Halifax, Newcastle upon Tyne, and Southampton. In addition, Hyndman of the Marxist SDF probably engineered the defeat of the Liberal at Burnley.

The Liberals might have fared better had their Leaders succeeded in finding a unifying theme. Moreover, the formation of the Salisbury government *prior* to the election deprived them of one of their strongest card: the claim that their opponents were fundamentally disunited. It was a sign of the Liberals' problems that they left 134 Unionist candidates unopposed, while only seventeen Liberal candidates did not have to face an opponent.[38]

In the event, the Unionists achieved a landslide victory. With 341 MPs, the Conservatives secured an overall majority. The Liberal Unionists also did well, their seventy seats almost bringing them back to the level of 1886 and giving them, for the first time, a secure urban base. On the other hand, despite winning 62 per cent of the Welsh and 53.9 per cent of the Scottish seats, the Liberals were reduced to only 177 MPs. A particularly striking feature of the election was the way in which the Unionists swept nearly all before them in the large metropolitan areas: only seventeen Liberal MPs (plus a solitary Irish Nationalist in Liverpool) were returned for the 114 seats contained within Greater London and the cities of Birmingham, Manchester, Liverpool, Sheffield, Leeds, and Glasgow.[39] Many former Liberal ministers suffered electoral humiliation: John Morley, Arnold Morley, Shaw-Lefevre, and G. W. E. Russell all lost their seats, and Harcourt, defeated at Derby, had to take refuge in the Western Division of Monmouthshire. Especially in London and Lancashire, but also throughout most of mainland Britain to a lesser extent, the Conservatives made startling gains.

Salisbury, who greeted the outcome of the 1895 Election with amazed relief, embarked on his premiership in a benign frame of mind. He had once feared that the newly enfranchised masses would use their vote to upset established institutions, but the result, he noted, had 'turned out exactly the other way'. In England popular government had come of age earlier than Salisbury had dreamt possible.[40] The Unionist outlook looked very rosy.

3. THE UNIONISTS AFTER 1895

Salisbury's third ministry was much richer in ministerial talent that his two earlier ones. The Liberal Unionist recruits brought new kinds of expertise to

---

[38] These figures include double-member constituencies where only one party candidate stood. Of the 134 Unionists left without a Liberal opponent, 13 were from Ulster and 8 were contesting university seats. The total would rise to 135 were one to include West Ham South, where the Conservative only had to face Keir Hardie, a Labour independent.

[39] Leeds was the only large city where Liberal MPs outnumbered their opponents (3 out of 5). But Birmingham was once again a Liberal-free zone, Manchester returned 1 out of 6, Liverpool 1 out of 9, Sheffield 2 out of 5, Glasgow 2 out of 7, and Greater London 8 out of 75.

[40] Speech to National Union, November 1895 (P. Marsh, *The Discipline of Popular Government: Lord Salisbury's Domestic Statecraft, 1881–1902* (Hassocks, 1978), 247).

the work of government, and nearly all the Conservative members of the Cabinet entered office with considerable experience. In association with their allies, the Conservatives were beginning to look the natural party of government, rather as the Whigs/Liberals had been in the middle years of the nineteenth century.

The Liberal Party, by contrast, seemed close to disintegration. On 6 October 1896 Rosebery, without consulting any other member of the Shadow Cabinet, resigned the leadership in a fit of pique.[41] The small and dispirited group of Liberal peers unanimously elected Lord Kimberley as their Leader, while Harcourt continued as Leader in the Commons. This arrangement did not last long. All the problems which had plagued the party in government continued to cause disruption, with disagreements over imperialism becoming particularly pronounced. Harcourt himself was generally identified with the 'Little England' wing of Liberalism; hence his decision to co-operate with his old friend Chamberlain, when an official inquiry was held into responsibility for the Jameson Raid,[42] not only seemed perverse but also served to undermine his reputatation for tactical astuteness. Perhaps realizing this, Harcourt and Morley, in a public exchange of letters in December 1898, announced their retirement to the backbenches.[43]

The Liberals found themselves in a quandary. Asquith, though mistrusted by some for his links with Rosebery and Liberal Imperialism, seemed by far the ablest man available; but, having recently acquired in Margot Tennant a wife with expensive habits, he did not wish to forego his large income from the Bar in order to concentrate on his Westminster responsibilities—clear evidence that he, for one, did not see the Liberals getting back into office in the near future.[44] In February 1899 the Commons leadership therefore went, almost by default, to the genial Scotsman Campbell-Bannerman, who had few enemies and was acceptable to almost everyone as a stopgap. Meanwhile Rosebery's friends and admirers still expected that great man of destiny to resume the Liberal Leadership before too long.

Over the next five years Salisbury's government suffered the usual crop of by-election defeats, its majority falling from 152 in 1895 to 128 by the eve of the 1900 Election. But the Liberals, demoralized, confused, and weakly led, did not look as though they were likely to oust the Unionists from power.

---

[41] He did so in response to Gladstone's recent call on the government to intervene on behalf of the Armenians against their Turkish oppressors, a course of action which aroused much enthusiasm in the country but which Rosebery thought hopelessly impracticable.

[42] See Ch. 8.

[43] Ostensibly in protest against the backing given to the government's actions in the Upper Nile by the up-and-coming Liberal Imperialist Edward Grey.

[44] Bizarrely, Balfour was persuaded to ask Asquith's wealthy father-in-law, Sir Charles Tennant, to give Asquith a larger allowance that would enable him to devote himself full-time to Liberal politics.

Paradoxically, however, the absence of an effective Opposition was by no means an unmixed blessing to Salisbury, since from the start the Conservative Parliamentary Party, with no serious external enemy to frighten it into cohesion, succumbed to gossip, grumbling, and factional intrigues. Perhaps, too, the efficiency of the Whips' Office deteriorated somewhat after 1895, following Akers-Douglas's promotion to the Cabinet (as First Commissioner of Works). 'A party triumphant out of doors but disaffected within', is how one historian has described the Conservatives in the late 1890s.[45]

Moreover, from the moment that Salisbury had published his list of ministers in 1895, many of his own backbenchers began complaining that the government had an 'exclusive' and 'clannish' tone to it. The *embourgeoisement* of Conservativism during the 1890s, manifested in the Party's success in urban middle-class districts and in a broadening of the social backgrounds of its MPs (under one-half of whom were now drawn from the landed classes), was certainly not reflected in the composition of Salisbury's governments, which remained as aristocratic as at any point in the nineteenth century.[46] Middle-class ministers such as Ritchie and W. L. Jackson did useful and important work, but they were essentially technocrats rather than statesmen and lacked leverage at the highest levels of government.[47]

With Salisbury cut off in the Lords, absorbed by his work as Foreign Secretary, the Cabinet also lacked effective central direction. Departmental ministers were left to go their separate ways. Some, such as Ritchie at the Board of Trade, won a reputation for competence, whereas others, such as Henry Chaplin ('the Squire') at the Local Government Board, proved to be liabilities.

The inexorable rise in public expenditure was another continuing worry. Largely unbeknown to the general public, the Treasury was under heavy pressure from a variety of quarters: from Chamberlain at the Colonial Office, from escalating expenditure on education and social welfare, and, not least, from the insatiable appetite of the Admiralty, struggling to preserve the 'Two-Power Standard' in a hostile world.[48] The result was that the country was

---

[45] Shannon, *Age of Salisbury*, 438.

[46] During the Salisbury and Balfour administrations, the landed classes supplied 23 of the 35 members of the Cabinet, and 22 of the 33 junior minsters—if one excludes the law officers who, obviously, were lawyers (J. P. Cornford, 'The Parliamentary Foundations of the Hotel Cecil', in R. Robson (ed.), *Ideas and Institutions of Victorian Britain* (London, 1967), 311).

[47] In any case, Balfour's earlier condescending verdict on Jackson in August 1891 is instructive: 'He justly inspires great confidence in businessmen; and he is that *rara avis*, a successful manufacturer who is fit for something besides manufacturing. A cabinet of Jacksons would [be] rather serious no doubt: but one or even two would be a considerable addition to any cabinet.' Jackson had, in the event, entered the Cabinet two months later as Balfour's successor as Chief Secretary, but no office was found for him in 1895.

[48] See Ch. 8.

reaching what one senior Treasury official called 'the limits of tolerable taxation'. Whatever they may have said in opposition, the Unionists were grateful for the existence of Harcourt's new death duties—which served to raise revenue out of which the landlords' rate problems could be eased.[49] Eddie Hamilton, Secretary to the Treasury, gloomily observed: 'Unless the brake is applied to the spending propensities of the State, the Government may ere long find themselves confronted with a choice of evils involving serious changes in our fiscal system, and consequently formidable Parliamentary difficulties.'[50]

Jubilee year (1897) happened to produce a bumper budget surplus, which led the usually pessimistic Chancellor, Hicks Beach, to predict that generations would pass before 'the British people reach[ed] again so high a level of widely diffused comforts, of financial ease both public and private, of social and political contentment, of class union, of world power, and of superiority to foreign rivalry and competition'.[51] But by 1899 the surplus had completely disappeared, to be replaced by an impending deficit of £4 million.[52]

To a remarkable extent, the agenda of the third Salisbury administration was dominated by foreign and imperial issues, by comparison with which its domestic record lacks interest. Hicks Beach at the Treasury displayed impeccable orthodoxy, sternly upholding free trade and blocking all attempts at currency reform, including bimetallism. The latter was an attempt to break free from the stranglehold of the gold standard by making silver as well as gold a unit of currency. Originating in India, bimetallism had the theoretical advantage of reducing debt burdens—which would have helped hard-pressed agriculturalists as well as distressed manufacturers. It enjoyed the backing of significant sections of the business world, as well as of several leading Conservative politicians, notably Balfour. But the bimetallist agitation effectively ended with the government's decision to put India on the gold standard in 1898, following its rejection of proposals from the American and French governments to establish an international bimetal standard.[53]

The dominant figure in Salisbury's Cabinet, insofar as it had one, was Arthur Balfour. But Balfour's judgement was by no means faultless: he blundered badly, for example, in an attempt to reorganize the educational system in 1896—the government's Bill had to be withdrawn after it had run into fierce opposition from all sides of the House, to be replaced during the

[49] Shannon, *Age of Salisbury*, 475–6.
[50] Diary entry of 24 July 1895, cited in A. Offer, *Property and Politics 1870–1914* (Cambridge, 1981), 211.
[51] Shannon, *Age of Salisbury*, 475.
[52] Brooks, *Destruction of Lord Rosebery*, 51.
[53] Green, *Crisis of Conservatism*, 115.

following year by a mere holding measure designed to bail out the floundering church schools.

Problems also beset the attempts at helping the Church of England: for example, the unpopular 1898 Benefices Act, which gave the clergy more autonomy, ran foul of the 'Protestant' crusade that had swept into its ranks many Conservative activists and MPs, especially in Liverpool, where indignant emotions had been whipped up by 'ritualist' irregularities and by Pope Leo XIII's dismissal in 1896 of the validity of Anglican Orders.[54] By contrast, traditional Conservatives broadly welcomed the Local Government Act of 1899, which split London into twenty-eight municipal boroughs in a move designed to neuter the 'subversive' LCC, though the Opposition condemned it as petty and vindictive.[55]

Another intensely partisan measure was the Agricultural Land Rating Act of 1896, which, through the provision of Exchequer grants, reduced the rateable value of agricultural land by one-half for poor rates and by three-quarters for general rates. The government hoped that the resultant savings would be passed on to farmers, about whose plight they had waxed eloquent in Opposition; but the immediate beneficiaries were the landowners themselves. The Liberals, with Harcourt to the fore, vigorously denounced this as a blatant bribe to the Conservative Party's natural supporters, the squires and the parsons, and Lloyd George alleged corruption—working out how much individual ministers stood to benefit (he concluded that the Cabinet as a whole would be better off by £2,250,000.)[56] More worryingly, the 1896 Act, which some agriculturalists thought insufficiently generous, infuriated many of the Party's urban supporters, provoking the MP for Stockport, George Whiteley, a cotton spinner, to cross the floor of the House.[57]

Both political parties were sympathetic in principle to the revival of British agriculture, the Conservatives because, for strategic reasons, they wanted the country less dependent on imported foodstuffs, while others, in all parties, thought the rural population sturdier, more patriotic, and more socially responsible than townees—a belief common throughout Europe. But, in the last analysis, even the Conservatives were not prepared to pay the necessary

[54] On Archibald Salvidge and Austin Taylor, one of the founders of the Layman's League, see P. J. Waller, *Democracy and Sectarianism: A Political and Social History of Liverpool, 1868–1939* (Liverpool, 1981).

[55] The Conservatives' 1895 victory had ensured the survival of the City Corporation, but the more radical ideas for emasculating the LCC were dropped under combined pressure from the civil servants and from Devonshire (K. Young, *Local Politics and the Rise of Party: The London Municipal Society and the Conservative Intervention in Local Elections, 1894–1963* (Leicester, 1975), 78–9).

[56] Green, *Crisis of Conservatism*, 139.

[57] Similar outrage greeted an 1899 Act which relieved clerical owners of tithe-rent charges of half their rates.

political or financial price. True, some public money was made available for the establishment of agricultural colleges. But although the privately organized Agricultural Co-operative Movement made significant strides in Ireland under the direction of Horace Plunkett, nothing comparable was done on mainland Britain, and probably it would not have achieved much anyway in the absence of the shelter provided by tariff walls—an important ingredient in the success of Denmark's co-operatives. Similarly, although the earlier establishment in 1889 of the Board of Agriculture and Fisheries had promised much, it soon got bogged down in carrying out such useful but mundane tasks as the enforcement of quarantine regulations.

More might have been done to revitalize the countryside but for the way in which the Home Rule schism had divided the ranks of the land reformers. After 1886 Joseph Chamberlain and Jesse Collings continued to sing the praises of smallholdings and allotments, and the Conservative government partly responded to their pressure. But, as Balfour noted at the time, whereas smallholdings aimed at converting the labourer into a farmer, allotments were merely a way of improving the labourer's way of life by affording him scope to supplement his income, while still remaining a labourer. In any case, because of inadequate powers, the various Smallholdings and Allotments Acts were largely ineffective.

Welfare legislation aimed at the urban poor was little more ambitious, the most notable failure being in old-age pensions, which by the late 1890s had become lost in a welter of inconclusive inquiries.[58] The Salisbury government's most enduring achievement was the 1897 Workmen's Compensation Act, the brainchild of Chamberlain, who for once was allowed out from the Colonial Office and given charge of a domestic measure. Abandoning the approach followed by the previous Liberal government, which had tried to impose obligations on employers (Employers' Liability), Chamberlain instead offered compensation to the injured workman out of government funds. True, Chamberlain only carried this measure by first agreeing to a long list of exceptions, including contracting-out provisions, many of them forced out of him by Middleton at Central Office and by wealthy and influential Conservative employers sitting on the Unionist backbenches, such as Gustav Wolff, MP for East Belfast. But an important precedent had been set, and the scope of the Workmen's Compensation Act was later broadened, in part by Chamberlain himself.[59] Meanwhile the Unionists had at least shown that, through a highly selective borrowing from Bismarckian social legislation, they too were capable

[58] Chamberlain, who had initially done so much to stimulate interest in this topic, similarly lost his way (J. Macnicol, *The Politics of Retirement in Britain 1878–1948* (Cambridge, 1998), 65–75).

[59] In 1900 Chamberlain brought agricultural labourers in under the scheme. The Liberal government further extended its provisions with their 1906 Act, on which see Ch. 11.

of initiating a 'constructive' solution to the practical problems of an industrial society.[60]

Yet were such legislative initiatives as urgent as had once been thought? The late 1890s saw their fair share of industrial disturbances,[61] but Salisbury's long-anticipated 'class war', it seemed, was not going to happen after all. To a traditional Conservative, the most comforting thing of all was the existence of a Conservative-dominated administration. Chamberlain was safely shackled for the time being, and now that he had stopped abusing landlords, dukes, and the Established Church and was directing his venom against foreigners, even traditional Conservatives were beginning to warm towards 'Joe'.

All the same, tension were growing between older Conservatives such as Salisbury and Hicks Beach on the one side, and the 'Radical Unionists' on the other. The fact is that the Conservatives' alliance with Chamberlain, though it had brought them considerable short-term gains, also carried risks. For Chamberlain, far from gravitating gradually towards Conservatism as Goschen had earlier done, retained strong Radical convictions, and Salisbury knew there was a danger that, over time, he might 'infect' younger members of the Conservative Party itself with his own enthusiasm for 'construction'.

Bearing in mind the nature of the Conservative Party, Chamberlain obviously stood no chance of persuading his new allies to go in for Church Disestablishment or secular education. But it was not beyond the realms of possibility that the Conservatives might be won over to the idea of embracing the interventionist state. Many young Conservatives, as well as Liberal Unionists, found this approach attractive. Whereas the older men still remembered with horror and disgust Chamberlain's 'ransom' speeches from the 1880s, when he was still the terrible Radical Jacobin, a younger generation realized that Britain was in decline as a Great Power and that the challenge of 'socialism' had been postponed but not averted by the party realignment of 1885–6. Chamberlain's solution to these difficulties was to broaden the meaning of Unionism so that it embraced a 'union of classes' and Imperial union as well as the defence of the 1801 Act of Union, a line which appealed strongly to many young Conservatives.

In 1895 Chamberlain knew that he lacked adequate support within the Conservative Party. That is why he opted for the Colonial Office, where he could direct his reforming energies towards the modernization of Britain's 'tropical estates'. But he was merely biding his time. The crisis into which the country was plunged with the outbreak of the Second Boer War in October

---

[60] However, for the differences between Chamberlain's scheme and the earlier German measure, see E. P. Hennock, *British Social Reform and German Precedents* (Oxford, 1987), 63–79. The latter required employers to enrol in a mutual insurance system administered by its members.

[61] See below.

1899 gave Chamberlain the opening he needed. As one phase of political life drew to an end, a qualitatively different one was about to take its place.

4. LOCAL POLITICS IN LATE VICTORIAN BRITAIN

Meanwhile, the lives of most British citizens were more affected by what was happening in local government than by events at Westminster and Whitehall. It depended on decisions at this level whether baths, washhouses, and libraries were built, bridges and highways properly maintained, slum housing cleared, and public-health measures vigorously prosecuted. School Boards decided the physical as well as the educational fate of many children, while the comfort and dignity of elderly people were often at the mercy of the Boards of Guardians.

Central government had initiated many of these policies, devolving responsibility for their implementation onto local authorities, partially compensating ratepayers for the resulting cost by the allocation of 'grants-in-aid', made conditional upon a regime of regulation and inspection. Such a control of the purse-strings made it difficult for a recalcitrant local authority openly to defy government.[62] But councils varied in the zeal with which they discharged their statutory obligations: the 1889 Adulteration Act was not seriously enforced at all in five counties.[63] Moreover, many of the activities carried out by local councils derived from permissive legislation or from private Acts. This left councillors free to decide on whether, for example, to establish their own library or to take over the running of the gas and water supply. No wonder that local government attracted idealistic men and (when allowed) women, who found in this arena a far wider field of public usefulness than was available to most backbench MPs.

The work of local government not only varied considerably from one locality to another but also varied between different *kinds* of authority. School Boards, for example, were unique in being elected by the so-called cumulative voting system, under which electors had as many votes as there were seats to be filled, with the option of casting all their votes for a single candidate.[64] This maximized the chances of representatives from various pressure groups who, even when included on a party 'slate' to give it balance, often felt primarily accountable to the particular 'constituency' which had returned them. Moreover, the absence of property qualifications made election to a School Board relatively cheap and trouble-free, encouraging candidates from a wide range of

---

[62] The most determined resistance was the policy of non-cooperation over the 1902 Education Act pursued by most Welsh county councils (see Ch. 10).

[63] J. P. D. Dunbabin, 'Expectations of the New County Councils and their Realization', *Historical Journal*, 8 (1965), 376.

[64] In other multi-member constituencies electors could not vote more than once for any candidate.

backgrounds. Secularists, anti-vaccinators, Orangemen (on Merseyside), Roman Catholics, women, and manual workers were all to be found on the larger School Boards, pursuing their own specific agendas.

The most important issue in School Board elections was religion, which generated intense sectarian rivalry. Politics structured in this way inevitably cut across parliamentary lines of division, since many Liberal Unionists were Dissenters. With Home Rule almost completely irrelevant to the conduct of local affairs (except in Liverpool), Liberal Unionists often co-operated with official Liberals.

The sectarian squabbling which dominated the debates of the larger School Boards infuriated many of the women councillors and 'labour' representatives.[65] The Fabian Annie Besant, first returned to the London School Board in 1888, was exasperated that so much time was being wasted on theological disputes—as when during the 1894 elections a dispute raged over whether children should be taught that Joseph was the father of Jesus. Instead she concentrated on the need to secure free schooling and worked hard to co-ordinate the work of the voluntary societies providing poor children with free breakfasts through the London Schools Dinner Association.[66]

Similarly, at Bradford Mrs Byles, elected in 1888 as an independent after having been denied a place on the Liberal slate, was largely instrumental in 1893 in appointing Dr James Kerr as Medical Superintendant of Schools—the first such appointment. Her policy was continued after 1894 by the middle-class socialist Margaret McMillan, who encouraged the Bradford Board to establish school nurses and school clinics, while also pressing for school feeding and special regimes for delicate and retarded children.[67] In 1902 McMillan moved back to London, as did Kerr, whom the London School Board made School Medical Officer on a *full-time* basis in the same year—another innovation. By the early 1900s some fifty local authorities had followed Kerr's pioneering work by instituting the medical inspection of their children.[68]

On Boards of Guardians things were also changing as the older COS preoccupation with stigmatizing pauperism came increasingly under challenge from an emerging alliance of Progressives, trade unionists, and women. These Guardians campaigned to humanize the Poor Law by improving workhouse diets (hitherto inferior in most areas to that provided in prisons), by boarding-

[65] The candidates put up by the Liverpool Trades Council in the 1888 elections ostentatiously campaigned on evening classes for workmen's children and the establishment of working men's scholarships to the local University College (Waller, *Democracy and Sectarianism*, 101).

[66] P. Hollis, *Ladies Elect: Women in English Local Government 1865–1914* (Oxford, 1987), 116, 119–20.

[67] Ibid. 183–4.

[68] C. Steedman, *Childhood, Culture and Class in Britain: Margaret McMillan, 1860–1931* (London, 1990).

out the children and having them educated in ordinary schools, by increasing the comforts and the dignity of the elderly, by making special provision for the feeble-minded and the disabled, and by setting up work schemes, as well as soup-kitchens, for the short-term unemployed. Such efforts gathered momentum after 1894, when the removal of property qualifications for Guardians encouraged more working-class candidates and also facilitated the election of women.[69] One such beneficiary was Mrs Pankhurst, returned on a 'Labour' ticket at Chorlton, near Manchester, in 1894.[70] Moreover, legislation dating from 1867 permitted the construction of rate-funded infirmaries; with London in the lead, most large towns began acquiring these facilities, which rapidly rivalled those offered in the voluntary hospitals. This was important, since after 1885 recipients of such relief no longer forfeited their right to vote.

By establishing secular parish councils, the Liberals' Local Government Act of 1894 also brought about change—even if some of the accompanying rhetoric describing it as a 'New Magna Charta' and 'Home Rule for the village' seems a little overblown.[71] Initially, at least, some of the poorer country people grasped their opportunity to right ancient wrongs by putting down the petty tyranny of farmer and clergyman. This particularly occurred in Norfolk, where George Edwards, a representative of the agricultural labourers, mobilized popular anticlericalism to good effect. Across the country as a whole, according to the calculations of the *Contemporary Review* in 1895, between a third and a half of the seats contested in the previous year were won by farmers, about a quarter by craftsmen. In Norfolk some parishes fell completely under the control of the labourers—provoking retaliation from parson and squire.[72]

Where the radicals took power, they concentrated on redirecting ancient charitable endowments for secular purposes, securing rights to common land, making provision for burials, and, crucially, creating allotments—the Fabians estimated that 1,500 of the country's 7,000 parish councils possessed allotments, amounting to some 52,000 holdings in all.[73] But after the initial excitement labourers and craftsmen lost interest, perhaps because they realized how limited were the councils' powers. Much of the enthusiasm had evaporated by the time the next elections took place, in March 1896, when two-thirds of all councillors were unopposed. Some of the smaller parish councils actually folded.[74] Apathy also engulfed the new Rural District Councils (RDCs)—not

---

[69] Hollis, *Ladies Elect*, 241: from 40 in London and 116 in the English provinces, to 86 and 716. The Act also abolished plural voting and ex-officio membership (i.e. magistrates).

[70] Ibid. 292.

[71] Lawrence, *Speaking For the People*, 207–8.

[72] Hollis, *Ladies Elect*, 360, 363–4.

[73] Most Radicals concentrated on the administration of charities and securing burial grounds for all, and, later, as depression intensified, campaigned on the land question.

[74] Hollis, *Ladies Elect*, 366, 370.

surprisingly, since they were little more than local Boards of Health and Boards of Guardians under a different name; many were captured by farmers whose main concern was with keeping down the rates.

Even in urban areas there was often a dearth of political excitement: A. L. Lowell's 1899 survey of 103 boroughs and urban districts showed that under a half of all seats were contested and that in thirteen towns no contest took place at all. This was sometimes because the social composition of the ward made the result a foregone conclusion, but in many cases particular candidates (prominent employers, for example) were accorded a 'right' to participation in local government.

Intense party rivalries were certainly not unknown in the town halls: the victorious party, for example, usually used its majority to fill all the vacant aldermanic seats. On the other hand, in many localities each of the parties was split over such issues as municipal trading and the provision of public services—some Liberal councillors being stern defenders of ratepayer interests, while Conservatives often pursued active, interventionist policies, 'Tory Democracy' having a resonance at local level which it seldom had in national politics. This could lead to a good deal of cross-voting in the council chamber. Then, too, the 'committee system' meant that, though the dominant party usually assumed the chairmanship of the most important committes, *all* councillors were involved in decision-making—resulting in a relatively consensual style of politics which some councillors, notably Fred Jowett of Bradford, found far more businesslike than Westminster's methods of operation.

Another brake on political partisanship was the necessarily technical nature of much local administration. In a speech of July 1896 Chamberlain compared the work of the great municipal corporations to that of a joint-stock company, in which the directors were represented by the councillors and the shareholders were constituted from the ratepayers.[75] This formulation gives an inadequate sense of the importance of officialdom. A strong-minded and energetic town clerk, such as Harcourt Clare in Liverpool,[76] accrued greater power than was wielded by even the strongest councillors. Other local-government 'experts', notably the medical officers of health, were also developing a strong sense of professional identity, with their own associations, journals, and conferences. As local government expanded, so did the potential for industrial unrest. In 1905 the white-collar union NALGO (the National Association of Local Government Officers) came into existence to protect the interests of clerical employees in the lower grades.[77]

[75] Offer, *Property and Politics*, 222.

[76] Waller, *Democracy and Sectarianism*, 118–19.

[77] S. D. Pennybacker, *A Vision For London, 1899–1914: Labour, Everyday Life and the LCC experiment* (London, 1995).

However, at a higher level councillors and their senior officials usually enjoyed a co-operative relationship. This was cemented by the Association of Municipal Corporations (AMC), established in 1872, which drew together town clerks, mayors, and councillors from all over Britain for regular exchanges of views. During the 1890s it became a highly influential advocate of urban interests. Serving as its Vice-President between 1880 and 1890 and as its President between 1890 and 1896 was none other than Albert Rollit, the prominent 'Tory Democrat'.

In the rural areas bureaucratization and professionalization were slower to develop. Here power and influence often remained in the hands of the established elites—to the disappointment of radicals and reformers. The 1889 elections threw up a regional contrast between the northern and eastern counties, where 'advanced Liberals' enjoyed some success, and the southern and western regions where the old magistrate class was largely left in possession of the field. Anti-magistrate feeling ran high in Wales, and also helped the Liberals to success in three English counties: Holland (Lincolnshire), the West Riding of Yorkshire, and Cumberland. But outside London, nearly one-half of all county councillors were magistrates, and many of the magistrates who suffered electoral defeat were then made aldermen—indeed, JPs comprised over one half of the aldermanic bench.[78]

Over much of rural England the old order thus survived almost intact, and arguably it was even strengthened as a result of its 'natural leaders' being given a new legitimacy through the opportunity to hold elected office. In East Sussex sixty-eight councillors owned between them 59,000 acres (twelve owning more than 1,000 acres each). The county council was usually chaired by the former chairman of quarter sessions or by a major landowning peer. Many landowners' agents joined them in the county hall: for example, Rowland Prothero, agent to the Duke of Bedford, was elected to Bedfordshire County Council in 1898. In 1911 over one-fifth of all county councillors and aldermen (outside London) were listed in the pages of *Walford's County Families*.[79] Admittedly, in an industrialized county such as Cheshire wealthy merchants and industrialists replaced the squires, many of them elderly ex-magistrates who gradually retired from public life. But this process took time.[80]

Not surprisingly, the enthusiasm which had attended the first county council elections, held in early 1889, soon evaporated. Even in 1889 only 54 per cent of electoral divisions were contested outside London (in part because

[78] Dunbabin, 'Expectations', 360.

[79] G. D. Phillips, *The Diehards: Aristocratic Society and Politics in Edwardian England* (Cambridge, Mass., 1979), 69, 74.

[80] J. M. Lee, *Social Leaders and Public Persons: A Study of County Government in Cheshire* (Oxford, 1963), 57.

of party pacts), but three years later the number of contests was halved. Even where elections took place, only 74 per cent of voters bothered to turn out in 1892, 62 per cent in 1892—a turnout very high by recent standards, but one significantly lower than that achieved in general elections.[81]

The one newly created local authority capable of generating lasting political excitement was the LCC—and not simply because it ran the capital. In 1892 the cautious ruling junta which included Rosebery lost power, giving way to a new grouping in which the Progressive leadership came under the control of the metropolitan Radical clubs, backed by T. P. O'Connor's London evening newspaper, the *Star*. The Progressives were a broad-based party. One faction, primarily concerned with 'moral improvement', led the LCC in an aggressive campaign to clean up the music halls (as well as to enforce safety measures in the theatres).[82]

But these traditional preoccupations were balanced by a commitment to civic improvement. Often working in conjunction with the revitalized vestries, the Progressive Party laid out parks and open spaces, created new swimming baths and washhouses, extended the public library service, and ran municipal housing schemes. Many of these activities employed direct labour from the council's Works Department on a forty-eight-hour week at trade-union rates—a cause dear to John Burns, himself a Progressive councillor. The LCC also stirred up controversy through its commitment to municipal trading (municipalities trading directly on the market by selling goods or services) and its attempt to equalize the rates in order to assist the poorer parishes. The rationale behind such activities was articulated by the Fabian Sidney Webb in his *London Programme*, published in 1892, the year of his election as a Progressive councillor for Deptford.[83] No wonder that an exasperated Salisbury should have denounced the LCC as a place where 'Collectivist and Socialist experiments were tried'.

However, trade-union representatives such as Burns and middle-class socialists such as Webb in no way controlled the Progressive Party, which was a broad populist alliance mainly concerned with advancing the interests of the community against local 'interests', notably the City Corporation and the monopoly suppliers in the utilities which the LCC was striving to bring under municipal control. Under its Leader, Sir John Williams Benn, who

[81] Dunbabin, 'Expectations', 353–79; Lee, *Social Leaders*, 61–2; Phillips, *Diehards*, 68, n. On turnout in general elections, see Ch. 4.

[82] See Ch. 14. The leadership of the Progressive Party eventually passed to the prominent Methodist minister Dr John Scott Lidgett (P. Thompson, *Socialists, Liberals and Labour: The Struggle for London 1885–1914* (London, 1967), 96).

[83] He held this seat until 1910, achieving considerable influence as the Chairman of its Technical Education Board: on which, see Ch. 10.

doubled up as Liberal MP for St George's, Tower Hamlets, the Progressives pursued objectives which seem to prefigure the work of the Liberal government after 1906.[84]

In fact, far from being socialists, the Progressives were running a municipalization project not so unlike the one which Chamberlain had spearheaded in Birmingham twenty years earlier; indeed, what the LCC was essentially engaged in doing was catching up with other self-governing municipal corporations in the creation of an urban infrastructure.[85] But the LCC was pushing forward with its schemes, some of them ostentatiously provocative,[86] at a time when many other cities, including Birmingham itself, had entered a more cautious phase of consolidation—hence the controversy.

But how were the LCC's expensive schemes to be funded? Here was a dilemma which, to a lesser or greater extent, bedevilled all local government. The domestic investment boom of the late 1890s stimulated suburban developments, requiring councils to spend more on roads, sewers, water, illumination, police stations, and schools.[87] As a result local-government expenditure soared, its share of total public outlay increasing from 38 per cent to 47 per cent between 1890 and 1913. Rates outstripped the rateable value of population, as well as population growth.

Poor Law expenditure also led to running battles. Following the Goschen Minute of 1869, and with the encouragement of the Charity Organisation Society, thirteen Poor Law Boards, including Manchester and Birmingham, had committed themselves to a total ending of outdoor relief to the able-bodied, with the consequence that by 1894 they had reduced the numbers in receipt of outdoor relief by 88 per cent, as against the national fall of 38 per cent.[88] Overall, the percentage of adult able-bodied paupers receiving outdoor relief fell from 83.4 per cent in the 1870s, to 77.8 per cent in the 1880s, to 76.2 per cent in the 1890s.[89]

But indoor relief did not come cheap, and changes in the workhouse regime, particularly the provision of improved medical facilities, meant that after many years during which Poor Law expenditure had risen more or less in line with

---

[84] A. M. McBriar, *Fabian Socialism and English Politics 1884–1918* (Cambridge, 1962), 224.

[85] Webb himself had pointed out, in the *Fabian Essays* of 1889, i.e. prior to the establishment of the LCC, that practically half of all gas consumers were supplied by public gasworks, which were to be found in 168 separate authorities; 65 local authorities had borrowed money for water supply, and 31 towns owned some or all of their own tramways (p. 83).

[86] As in the controversial scheme (later abandoned) for free municipal steamboats.

[87] Offer, *Property and Politics*, 231.

[88] Those on outdoor relief fell from 37.5 per thousand in 1871 to 17.2 by 1893 (M. J. Wiener, *Reconstructing the Criminal: Culture, Law, and Policy in England, 1830–1914* (Cambridge, 1990), 190). The Webbs suggested that needy able-bodied people, excluded in this way from outdoor relief, may simply have 'transferred themselves' to other categories, for example, the 'unemployed'.

[89] A. Digby, *Pauper Palaces* (London, 1978), 112.

the value of rateable property, in 1894 it began to soar upwards; this was the source of new anxieties, leading to the later establishment of the 1905 Poor Law Commission. Such financial embarrassments were exacerbated by the arrival of working-class Guardians after 1894. The socialist George Lansbury, elected for the poor metropolitan area of Poplar, saw himself primarily as a defender of the dependent poor: 'hang the rates!', was his watchcry.[90] This development did not surprise Salisbury, who had long been of the opinion that placing the administration of poor relief under democratic control was 'rather like leaving the cat in charge of the cream jug'.[91]

At municipal level many Conservatives—and some Liberals—made a defence of the ratepayer the centrepiece of their campaigns. These efforts became entangled during the 1890s with attacks on the extravagance and corruption thought to be inseparable from municipal trading.[92] In 1899 Lord Wemyss's Liberal and Property Defence League (or 'Liberty and License League' as its critics called it) published a book, *Dangers of Municipal Trading*; Leonard Darwin's *Municipal Trade* followed in 1903; and *The Times* gave the subject a wide airing in a series of articles in November 1902. The LCC's Works Department bore the brunt of the spleen of critics—some of whom had financial axes of their own to grind.[93]

Retrenchment, pure and simple, made for appealing election slogans. Curtailing municipal trading, however, proved to be more elusive. Radical Liberals were able to argue that the profits earned by municipal undertakings could be used to relieve the rates—essentially what Chamberlain's Liberals had done in Birmingham in the 1870s.[94] A mixed regime of private and public enterprise soon firmly established itself: by 1913 some 63 per cent of the country's tramway system was in municipal ownership, as was 81 per cent of electricity consumed.[95]

How to help the hard-pressed ratepayers split the community, not just on party, but also on rural–urban lines. The country areas, badly affected by the agricultural depression, called on the government to provide relief from central funds. The outcome, the passing of the Agricultural Land Rating Bill, provoked outrage in the towns. The Progressive paper *London* called the statute 'A Raid on London': 'Three hundred thousand pounds a year is the amount

[90] Hollis, *Ladies Elect*, 296.

[91] Salisbury to Cranbrook, 23 Nov. 1886, cited in Dunbabin, 'Establishment of County Councils', 241.

[92] Young, *Local Politics*, 51.

[93] Offer, *Property and Politics*, 234–8. The public figurehead of the movement was the banker, author, and Liberal Unionist MP Sir John Lubbock (made Lord Avebury in 1900).

[94] M. Savage, *The Dynamics of Working-Class Politics: The Labour Movement in Preston, 1890–1940* (Cambridge, 1987), 150–1.

[95] Waller, *Town, City and Nation*, 306.

which London will have to contribute to the agricultural interest', it complained.[96] Urban Conservatives were scarcely less enraged, some of them being
willing by the end of the decade to look sympathetically on the demand
emanating from the land-reform enthusiasts for the institution of site value
rating, aimed at winning back for the community the 'unearned income' being
pocketed by landlords lucky enough to hold land ripe for urban development.
The AMC actually sponsored a private bill on the subject in 1900, but there
was little likelihood of any government headed by Lord Salisbury responding
to such prompting.[97]

Faced by so many contradictory pressures, the hapless Unionist ministries
could think of nothing better than to ease the ratepayers' problems by giving
local authorities more central grants-in-aid: the amount of money disbursed in
this way actually doubled between 1887 and 1892.[98] Ironically, this transferred
the unresolved problem of local finance back to national government, unwittingly paving the way for the Liberal ministry's later reforms.

5. POPULAR POLITICS AND THE RISE OF LABOUR

The other open question was whether 'democracy' would lead to more working
men on elected bodies. Initially the omens did not look good. Though property
qualifications for municipal office had been removed in 1882, working men still
formed a tiny minority on even the biggest municipal councils: Birmingham's
had only three working men out of a total of sixty-four members in 1885–6,
only four out of seventy-two ten years later.[99] Working men had had a presence
on School Boards for much longer, and by abolishing plural voting and
property qualifications for Poor Law elections the 1894 Local Government
Act made possible the return of a trickle of working-class Guardians, as well as
allowing some farm labourers and artisans to get onto the new parish councils.
But only a few manual workers secured election to the first county councils,
Joseph Arch in Warwickshire and George Rix in Norfolk being two of the most
famous.[100] In 1885 the first working-class magistrates were *appointed*; but could
the working class, as a class, fight for its *own* emancipation?

This would not be easy. The working class, as we have seen, was internally
fractured along ethnic, religious, status, sectional, geographical, and gender
lines, and all these divisions operated against concerted political action.

---

[96] Offer, *Property and Politics*, 228.
[97] In 1901 Glasgow, the LCC, and Battersea all introduced similar measures (ibid. 230–1).
[98] Ibid. 201–2: from £4 million to £8 million.
[99] A. Briggs, *History of Birmingham, Vol 2: Borough and City, 1865–1938* (Oxford, 1952), 128. In
1895 46 of the 72 councillors were businessmen, 16 from the professions.
[100] Dunbabin, 'Expectations', 361.

Financial barriers were also important. The absence of payment for MPs before 1912 made it difficult for a working man to serve as an MP, unless, as in the case of the miners, his trade union was prepared to subsidize him. Becoming a councillor, too, was difficult, not so much because local-government service was unremunerated, but because meetings often took place in the middle of the working day: a standard demand in radical and labour programmes was that boards and councils should hold evening meetings.

Moreover, what was political action *for*? The politically conscious working class had traditionally oscillated between the strategy of banding together for mutual support in friendly societies, and attempting to improve their wages and conditions of work through industrial action organized by their trade unions.[101] Capturing the machinery of the state with a view to improving collective welfare services was a third possible option, but this kind of political involvement offered only hypothetical, long-term benefits.

Trade unionism was at the heart of working-class activism—so much so that when trade unionists *did* participate in elections their motivation was often narrowly 'economistic'. In Leicester, as in other towns, the trade-union-based socialists primarily wanted to secure better wages for manual council workers.[102] Similarly, the chairman of the selection committee picking candidates for the Bradford School Board elections wanted 'two staunch men' who were 'sound' on the 'Fair Contracts Question'; Margaret McMillan sympathized, but gently suggested that 'a word or two on educational matters might not be out of place'.[103] This exchange, which took place within the Bradford branch of the ILP, illustrates the tension that often developed between trade-union sectionalism and that wider concern with social injustice and suffering which so preoccupied socialists such as George Lansbury, who fumed over hungry schoolchildren and the treatment of the disabled and of the aged poor.

Socialism, which had first put down roots in Britain during the early 1880s, also disrupted working-class politics because its most active members were often not themselves manual workers—McMillan being a case in point. In the late 1880s, in particular, socialism and trade unionism gave the appearance of being alternative, rather than complementary, solutions to the problem of working-class 'servitude'. Henry Hyndman, who founded the first of the socialist societies, the Marxist Social Democratic Federation (SDF), in 1883,

[101] Savage, *Dynamics of Working-Class Politics*.

[102] B. Lancaster, *Radicalism, Co-operation and Socialism: Leicester Working-Class Politics, 1860–1906* (Leicester, 1987), 130.

[103] Steedman, *McMillan*, 38. A. G. Cook, put up by the London Society of Compositors for election to the London School Board, succeeded, with Headlam and Besant, in inducing Conservatives to impose trade-union rates on its contractors, the first council to do so (Thompson, *Socialists, Liberals and Labour*, 99).

openly despised trade unionism, dismissing it as a narrowly reformist movement which simply wasted the time, money, and energy of its working-class
activists. Many manual workers within the SDF, including Tom Mann and
John Burns, both prominent trade unionists, strongly disapproved of this line
and eventually severed their links with the organization. But their departure
left Hyndman and his cronies, notably Harry Quelch, in control of the central
organization.

The SDF, it is true, did build up a working-class following in some areas,
especially in London, where it tended to appeal to skilled craftsmen, many of
whom had grown up in Charles Bradlaugh's secularist movement, and also in
Lancashire, the only part of the country where it came near to establishing a
mass base. But the spectacle of the Old Etonian Hyndman, immaculately
dressed in frock coat, preaching revolution with the aid of well-chosen Latin
tags, could not but get under the skin of many class-conscious working men. It
was of long-term significance that Marxism should first have come to the
British working class in so disagreeably doctrinaire a guise.

During the 1880s there were other conspicuous middle-class socialists:
notably the artist and poet William Morris, leader of the Socialist League, a
breakaway from the SDF; and the vegetarian, sandal-clad anarchist Edward
Carpenter (author of the socialist anthem 'England Arise!'), a middle-class
drop-out who had abandoned his plans for a career in the Church so that he
could cultivate a smallholding in the Peak District with his working-class lover.
Socialism, presented in this way, was more an aesthetic rejection of the ugliness
of capitalism and its materialistic vulgarities than a movement tailored to
working-class needs.

The Fabian Society, founded in 1884, originated in an earlier body, the
'Fellowship of the New Life', which was also committed to a utopian commu-
nitarianism. But the Fabians replaced such sentimentalism with a hard-headed
'scientific' approach to social problems, also abandoning any romanticization of
the working class as such. The Society could not 'reasonably use the words
"bourgeois" or "middle class" as terms of reproach, more especially as it would
thereby condemn a large proportion of its own members', a Fabian pamphlet of
1896 declared.[104] The Fabian leaders—Sidney Webb, Graham Wallas, Hubert
Bland, and George Bernard Shaw—all came from the professional wing of the
middle class, and, as the Society's provincial branches fell away, it increasingly
functioned as a kind of metropolitan social research bureau, placing 'facts' at
the disposal of any political group which cared to study them, part of its famous
strategy of 'permeation'.[105] But though politically active trade unionists availed

[104] p. 7.
[105] See R. J. Harrison, *The Life and Times of Sidney and Beatrice Webb 1858–1905: The Formative
Years* (Basingstoke, 2000).

themselves of the Society's boxes of well-researched pamphlets, the Fabian leaders wanted to 'make socialists', not return more working men to Parliament. Significantly, the influential volume of *Fabian Essays*, published in 1889, contained no sustained discussion of trade unionism at all.

The turning point in the relationship between socialism and trade unionism came with the bitter 1892 Manningham Mill strike in Bradford, in the aftermath of which various local socialist societies, mostly with predominantly working-class memberships, came together in that town in January 1893 to form the Independent Labour Party (or ILP). The ILP's constitution made clear that it was a socialist organization, but, by adopting the title that they did, the founders signalled that their primary concern was to advance the cause of labour representation, to which socialist dogma would take second place. Like the Fabians, the ILP subscribed to a 'gradualist' philosophy, and its leaders sought to win power, locally and nationally, through the ballot box—thus differentiating themselves from Hyndman and Morris, who saw elections primarily as a platform for revolutionary agitation.

Moreover, by rejecting Marxism for an ethical socialism which accorded well with the Nonconformist beliefs and backgrounds of many of its adherents (especially in its home base, the West Riding), the ILP was able to attract intellectuals and artists such as the Scottish architect Bruce Glasier, who had earlier been greatly influenced by Morris. This approach also appealed to many women: indeed, the early ILP leaders were often husband-and-wife teams (the MacDonalds, the Snowdens, the Glasiers, the Pankhursts), though single women, such as Margaret McMillan, were also welcome. This contrasted with the mysogyny of the SDF—Quelch was a persistent and bitter opponent of women's enfranchisement.

Most important of all, the ILP, unlike its predecessors, quickly acquired a significant working-class base, though membership was highly regional in its concentration. The society fared best in towns with a stable population, particularly in those of the West Riding, but it soon expanded into South Wales, Clydeside, and other industrial districts. The organization tended not to attract the 'slummies'—who could anyhow not afford the membership dues and such obligations as the purchase of the society paper, the *Labour Leader*— but it successfully enrolled many skilled workers, often trade unionists, predominantly aged between 22 and 33 years.

Finally, the ILP leaders, 'pragmatic visionaries' such as Keir Hardie and Tom Mann, realized that, to capture power at local and national level, they would have to link up with the wider trade-union movement, whose resources in manpower and money they could never hope to rival. True, two of the society's up-and-coming men, James Ramsay MacDonald and the former excise officer Philip Snowden, felt an undertow of contempt for working-class politicians who had come up through the trade-union movement, in whom they found a lack of ambition and 'vision'. During the 1890s the ILP, by contrast, vigorously preached the 'religion of socialism', conversion to which meant replacing a life of selfish egotism by one devoted to 'fellowship': changing lives was thought to be essential if socialism was to have any chance of realization. But this 'idealism', racily conveyed in Robert Blatchford's best-selling *Merrie England* (1894), a reprint of articles he had earlier published in his weekly *Clarion*,[106] was usually married to a concern with the nitty-gritty of municipal government and to a support of trade unionists in their day-to-day industrial struggles. Indeed, most working-class members of the ILP were also members of their appropriate trade union.

But though socialism supplied a more coherent rationale for working-class independence than any that had yet emerged, many trade unionists took longer to win over to the socialist cause. Older men such as Thomas Burt, the veteran miners' leader, still revered Gladstone and believed that 'labour's' most realistic hope of success was to function as a 'group' within the wider Liberal Movement—something that made sense to miners because the geographical concentration of the coalmining industry enabled them to capture the nomination of winnable seats in their own heartlands. Old 'Lib-Labers', including Burt and Henry Broadhurst (the latter having served in Gladstone's third ministry), were joined by a younger generation of working-class politicians, including John Burns, the one-time SDF firebrand, who had been imprisoned for his part in the Trafalgar Square disturbances of 1887 but later made his own accommodation with the more powerful radical-liberal movement. Burns's outburst at the ILP conference against 'working-class housing, working-class boots, and working-class margarine' was partly jealousy at the emergence of a powerful rival in the person of Hardie (the two men intensely disliked one another). However, in the mid-1890s it was still far from certain that the formation of a new working-class party represented the best way forward for politically conscious manual workers.

Whereas in Germany industrialization had arrived late, in a sudden rush, bringing bitter class tensions in its wake, Britain's long-drawn-out 'industrial revolution' and step-by-step transition from oligarchy to democracy had allowed the creation of links between the classes, making possible the sort of 'Progressivism' that existed in London, where radical-liberals and moderate socialists could join forces. An avowed socialist, such as Sidney Webb, was still working with the LCC Progressives throughout the 1890s—and beyond. Had the local Liberal caucuses been more willing to adopt trade unionists as

---

[106] It sold over 2 million copies over the following fifteen years. Blatchford's paper, the *Clarion*, founded in 1891, soon acquired a circulation of 80,000 (J. F. C. Harrison, *Learning and Living 1790–1960: A Study in the History of the English Adult Education Movement* (London, 1961), 260).

candidates (Hardie had been rejected by the Mid-Lanark Liberal constituency party prior to a by-election in 1888), Labour's emergence as an independent force might have been still further delayed.

Another quite different obstacle to the formation of an independent Labour Party with strong trade-union support was the cult of 'independence'. In the late 1880s many trade unions were reluctant to have anything to do with party politics, partly because of divisions within their own ranks (many voted Tory, a majority doing so in some Lancashire towns), but also for ideological reasons. At national level, too, the TUC retained its policy of 'independence', as did many local trades councils. The cotton-workers' leader James Mawdsley (himself a Tory) bitterly attacked Labour politicians, while even a socialist such as Ben Tillett, the dockers' leader, welcomed the exclusion of politicians from the TUC in 1895.[107] To some trade unionists the ILP looked like interlopers, trying to capture their funds in support of an impractical sectarian programme lacking mass support—backed, it was sometimes alleged, by 'Tory gold'.

Nevertheless, trade-union hostility towards socialism began to abate during the 1890s, as trade unionism itself significantly changed. The eruption of the 'New Unionism' in the late 1880s made a contribution to the more militant mood. The leaders of these 'new unions', largely composed of unskilled workers, tended to sympathize with the cause of independent labour representation, and many of them were socialists—perhaps because, as new organizations, they were led from the start by a younger generation of official, and perhaps because the unskilled, less able to control their own labour markets, depended more on the sympathy of local police forces and councillors and upon a public framework of support.

However, the downturn in the economy in the 1890s quickly led to the contraction and even disappearance of many of the general unions, which had briefly flourished in the more propitious circumstances of 1887–9.[108] In any case, the notion of a simple polarity between 'old' craft unions and 'new' unions of the unskilled assumes a sharper distinction between skilled and unskilled labourers than actually existed.[109] The two largest blocs of unionized workers, those in textiles and in coalmining, certainly cannot be categorized in this way.

The miners varied in their political attitudes from one coalfield to another, but in the 1890s nearly all the county unions, out of which the Miners Federation of Great Britain (MFGB) was composed, supported the Liberal Party, even to the extent of securing the election of some of their officials as

---

[107] Lawrence, *Speaking for the People*, 253.
[108] See Ch. 6.
[109] See Ch. 3.

'Lib-Lab' MPs.[110] Some of these figures, notably the South Wales leader William Abraham ('Mabon'), MP for Glamorganshire, also practised moderation in the industrial field, preaching the virtues of collaboration and conciliation and basing their conduct on observance of the sliding scale (which linked wage rates to coal prices). Yet in general the miners, despite their Liberalism, enjoyed a reputation for industrial militancy—a reputation confirmed by the 1893 national coal strike. Thus Ben Pickard, the leader of the Yorkshire miners, combined toughness with an intense suspicion of the advocates of labour/socialism: Pete Curran, a senior official of the gasworkers, was stoned in the mining village of Wombwell when he ran as a socialist candidate in the Barnsley by-election of October 1897 against a popular local coalowner, who enjoyed the backing of the county union.[111] In retrospect such behaviour seems perverse, but at the time it made perfect sense: after all, as a result of physical concentration the miners were able to force their officials onto the local Liberal Party, and, possessing their own group of sponsored MPs, they saw little point in squandering their precious resources by furthering the parliamentary ambitions of other unions.

The changing temper in the trade-union movement really owed most to the radicalization of the older craft unions, which by 1895 had moved away from their earlier industrial strategies and Liberal affiliations, leaving Broadhurst a rather isolated figure. Indeed, precisely because they were at the cutting edge of technological change, the old craft unions were throwing up some of the most industrially and politically militant of all workers. The dock strike, for example, had given a prominent role to Burns and Mann, both members of the Amalgamated Society of Engineers (ASE), traditionally the most exclusive of all craft unions. Both men were also socialists—as, in fact, were many of the younger generation of unionists from the printing trades, such as George Roberts of the Typographical Association. The process whereby young militants replaced their elders on the union executive obviously took time, but a traumatic event such as the 1897 engineering lock-out assisted the process by radicalizing many skilled artisans.

As early as 1894 there were signs of a more militant temper at the TUC, which, at its Norwich Congress, passed a resolution in favour of the public ownership of the means of production, distribution, and exchange—the first time such a socialist commitment had been made. This event, given great publicity by the opponents of trade unionism, occasioned some anxiety about

---

[110] 'Lib-Lab', in this context, means that they were Labour representatives, because sponsored and financed by their lodge, but Liberals because they took the Liberal Whip on all issues which did not directly involve the affairs of the union.

[111] Curran came third with 9.7% of the poll, behind a Conservative as well as behind Joseph Walton, the Liberal.

the capture of the entire Labour Movement by the socialists. Nothing so dramatic had occurred. It was a snap vote, and the 'old guard' quickly re-established its control by banning from future congresses representatives who were not actively pursuing the trade or occupation of their sponsoring body, a palpable hit at Keir Hardie, once a coalminer but now a full-time socialist agitator, who was, as a consequence, debarred from future TUC meetings— though, paradoxically, Burns and Broadhurst were also excluded by this rule-change. At the same time, even the Lib-Labs, for all their scepticism about socialism, accepted other parts of the Labour programme, such as the state regulation of the working day and a minimum wage: indeed, celebration of May Day and the agitation for the eight-hour day had now become mainstream demands.

Most important of all, a series of adverse legal judgements seemed to be eroding the rights which trade unionists thought they had secured through the legislation of the 1870s: for example, *Temperton* v. *Russell* (1893) construed boycotting as 'a conspiracy to injure' and so liable to damages, and *Lyons* v. *Wilkins* (1896) restricted picketing to 'communicating information'.[112] This was a worrying trend which affected *all* trade unions, whether skilled, semi-skilled, or unskilled, particularly since it seemed to form part of a concerted 'employers' offensive'. Disillusionment with the Liberals and a mounting sense of insecurity were thus shifting allegiances: by the end of the decade even Lib-Labs such as John Hodge, secretary of the Steel Smelters, now saw some sort of Labour 'independence' as an inevitability.

Trade unionists' growing sympathy with socialism, whose adherents were multiplying within their own organizations, was complemented by the ILP's realization of its need for them. In the latter part of the 1890s the ILP enjoyed some limited, but growing, success in local elections: by 1900 it had fifty-one Guardians and sixty-six members of School Boards, and perhaps nearly 400 elected representatives in all. In alliance with the SDF it captured West Ham Borough Council in 1898, forcing the Liberals and Conservatives to unite against it.[113] Everywhere its members pressed for improved public services and a more humane treatment of the elderly, the sick, and the very poor—often in tandem with the 'ladies elect'.

But parliamentary success proved far more elusive. In the 1895 General Election the ILP put up twenty-eight candidates, all of whom finished bottom of the poll, securing about 8.8 per cent of the total vote in the seats they contested, a figure which is depressed by a handful of frivolous contests but boosted by the performance in West Ham South of Keir Hardie, who had been

---

[112] The case went to appeal, the final ruling going against the union in 1898.
[113] Thompson, *Socialists, Liberals and Labour*, 110.

given a straight fight against the Conservative by the local Liberals. Hardie, who lost his seat, rejoiced in the Liberal rout, but many Lib-Labs deprecated what they saw as the ILP's wrecking tactics; nor did all members of the ILP take Hardie's line.[114]

In fact, despite sporadic municipal success, the ILP found itself after 1895 up something of a cul-de-sac, much of the earlier enthusiasm and self-confidence having disappeared. In 1898 the journalist Tom Smedley commit-ted suicide after expressing discouragement over the poor attendances at his meetings: 'If socialism was not going to sweep all before it, life had nothing to make it attractive', he wrote.[115] As people of all classes in 1897 joined in triumphant commemoration of the Queen's sixtieth anniversary, the trans-formation of British society into a socialist commonwealth seemed far distant. ILP membership fell after 1895, recovered slightly until 1898, and then entered a steady decline which lasted until 1905.[116] Between 1896 and 1899 nearly one-half of all ILP branches simply disappeared.

The ILP faced a stark choice. Either it could combine with the rival SDF (from which the leadership was distanced partly by ideology but also by personal animosities) or, backpedalling still further on its socialism, it could seek to link up in some way with the more broadly based (but non-socialist) trade-union movement, hoping over time to permeate it with socialist values. A 'unity' campaign in 1898 revealed that the majority of ILP members, Blatchford to the fore, favoured the first of these options. The national council of the party thought otherwise, and sought instead to tap into the wealth and the mass membership of trade unionism.[117]

Those wishing to see a convergence between trade unionism and socialism seized their opportunity in 1899. Many trade unionists were already sufficiently worried about the long-term prospects of their movement to view, with greater sympathy than previously, the establishment of a separate working-class party. At its Congress in the autumn, Bill Holmes, a delegate of the Amalgamated Society of Railway Servants (locked in what proved to be a historic conflict with the Taff Vale Railway Company), successfully moved a resolution that called on trade unions, trade councils, and socialist societies to explore the possibility of establishing an autonomous Labour Party. Significantly, Holmes was an ILP activist. The vote was close

[114] Lawrence, *Speaking for the People*, 212, 214.
[115] S. Pierson, *Marxism and the Origins of British Socialism: The Struggle for a New Consciousness* (Ithaca and London, 1973), 249. On the earlier utopian phase, S. Yeo, 'A New Life: The Religion of Socialism in Britain, 1883–1896', *History Workshop*, 4 (1977), 5–56.
[116] D. Howell, *British Workers and the Independent Labour Party 1888–1906* (Manchester, 1983), 328–9.
[117] K. Laybourn, 'The Failure of Socialist Unity in Britain, c.1893–1914', *Transactions of Royal Historical Society*, 40 (1994), 160, 162–5.

(546,000 for, 434,000 against), but a meeting was duly arranged for the following February.

The various organizations which assembled in the Farringdon Street Memorial Hall to found the Labour Representation Committee (LRC) in February 1900 were, however, very unequal in strength. There were about 1,200,000 trade unionists affiliated to the TUC, about 25 per cent of adult males in the 'manual labour class'. By contrast, the socialist societies all had tiny memberships: the Fabian Society numbered under 1,000 (even including the provincial and university societies), the SDF claimed 9,000 (clearly an inflated figure), and the ILP 6,000. Even if one makes the generous assumption that for every card-carrying member of a socialist society there were another ten who broadly shared its ideals, this still represents a tiny minority of the adult working class. Working men and women were still associating themselves in much larger numbers with the two long-established parties.

Many labour 'leaders', a self-constituted elite, were anyway somewhat divorced from the bulk of manual workers as a result of their beliefs, ambitions, and lifestyle. In Wolverhampton hardly any of the 'labour' councillors lived in the poor districts of that town, 85 per cent of them having taken up residence in suburban wards.[118] This made it difficult for socialists to recruit among the poor: as one complained, 'the very people for whom we are working and toiling are our worst opponents—bitter and intolerant, unsympathetic and insolent, prone rather to live on charity than upon the rights of manhood and womanhood'.[119] One reason for this hostility was that, although socialists claimed to be *representing* the working class, they also wanted to *change* them—an ambiguity in their political approach which was to lead to some misunderstanding. The strength of working-class Conservatism was that it appealed to many manual workers by accepting them for what they were, 'vices' and all (a fondness for beer and having a flutter, for example).

The cause of independent labour was certainly much stronger in 1900 than it had been a decade earlier, but many obstacles lay ahead. Sidney Webb had glibly written in the *Fabian Essays*: 'So long...as Democracy in political administration continues to be the dominant principle, Socialism may be quite safely predicted as its economic obverse', notwithstanding a few 'freaks or aberrations'.[120] Britain was to experience many more freaks and aberrations than the pioneering socialists could possibly have foreseen.

[118] Lawrence, *Speaking for the People*, 35, 133.
[119] 1895, in K. Laybourn and J. Reynolds, *Liberalism and the Rise of Labour 1890–1918* (Beckenham, 1984), 319.
[120] p. 93.

CHAPTER 8

Uneasy Dominion: Britain Under Challenge, 1886–1899

1. INTRODUCTION

Englishmen may have been notoriously unwilling to accommodate themselves to foreign ways and foreign food. But though insular in this sense, late Victorian England was remarkably open to the rest of the world—exhilaratingly, perhaps dangerously so. Until 1905 the United Kingdom had virtually no restrictions on immigration, no exchange controls, and there were few barriers to the importation of foreign goods and commodities, customs duties being levied solely for revenue-raising purposes on a small range of goods, mainly spirits, tobacco, tea, coffee, sugar, and wine.

Economically this structure rested upon free trade and the gold standard, which, with sterling as the leading reserve currency, was the source of the prosperity of the City of London, the nub and organizing centre of the world trading system. Commodities, in bewildering variety and quantity, flowed in and out of such busy ports as Liverpool, Bristol, and Glasgow (the second city of the Empire). Most powerful of all these cosmopolitan marts was London, whose packed warehouses held riches that sharply contrasted with the poverty of the surrounding dockland: 'every day its workforce unloaded, sorted, stored, and catalogued goods with which otherwise they would never have come into contact because they were so poor.'[1]

2. OVERSEAS TRADE AND INVESTMENT

From a narrowly economic point of view, the system of free imports brought many benefits.[2] In a wider global perspective, however, it carried certain dangers. For it meant that Britain was dependent on overseas supplies, not only for over three-quarters of her cereals and 40 per cent of her meat, but also

---

[1] J. Schneer, *London 1900: The Imperial Metropolis* (New Haven and London, 1999), 44–5.
[2] See Ch. 6.

for many essential raw materials and semi-finished products (iron ore, tin, steel, chemicals, and dyestuffs). And to pay for these imports she needed to export heavily. More than three-quarters of the entire output of the cotton industry was sent abroad, along with almost a half of all manufactured woollen goods.[3] No other major industrialized country was so deeply involved in overseas trade, three-quarters of which took place with extra-European countries; her two emerging rivals, the United States and Germany, were very much more self-sufficient.[4]

Britain's export drive centred on the old staples of the first industrial revolution. In 1907 cotton manufactures and cotton yarn (valued at over £110 million) still headed the list, followed by coal (over £42 million), woollen goods and worsted yarn (over £34 million), machinery (almost £32 million), and new ships (over £10 million). Many parts of the country waxed fat on these industries: Lancashire, centre of the textile industry, alone employed over one million 'hands'. International trade and transportation also brought prosperity to the great shipbuilding yards of Tyneside, the Clyde, and Belfast, which supplied the world with about 60 per cent of its tonnage.

Yet during the late Victorian and Edwardian periods the country ran a significant trade deficit in 'visibles', the value of imports exceeding that of exports (including re-exports) roughly in the proportion of six to four. Before 1907 this deficit was more than bridged by 'invisible imports', which included the revenue generated by financial services such as insurance and banking, as well as the profits earned from shipping—Britain's merchant fleet still accounted for over one-third of the world's entire tonnage and carried one-half of all seaborne traffic.[5] Thereafter the trade balance was kept in the black by the returns on overseas investment, which surged after 1880.[6] Such dividends enriched the City of London, generating still more investment capital. Assets held abroad had risen to $4 billion by 1914.[7]

---

[3] A. Offer, 'Costs and Benefits, Prosperity and Security, 1870–1914', in A. Porter (ed.), *The Oxford History of the British Empire: Volume III: The Nineteenth Century* (Oxford, 1999), 695.

[4] In the late 1890s the UK's import trade per head of population was £9. 16s. 6d.: Germany's £4 10s. 7d., the USA's £2 1s. 11d.

[5] P. Burroughs, 'Defence and Imperial Disunity', in Porter (ed.), *British Empire: Nineteenth Century*, 334. This excludes another 5–9% supplied from other Empire countries (Offer, 'Costs and Benefits', 696).

[6] In fact, Britain's foreign direct investment far exceeded her portfolio investment because there were trading companies floated on the Stock Exchange that had acquired foreign assets. Total foreign investment in 1913 may have reached £4,000 million, yielding a 5% return (C. Feinstein, 'Britain's overseas investments in 1913', *Economic History Review*, 43 (1990), 293–4); T. A. B. Corley, 'Britain's Overseas Investments in 1914 Reconsidered', *Business History*, 36 (1994), 71–88).

[7] P. J. Cain, 'Economics and Empire: The Metropolitan Context', in Porter (ed.), *British Empire: Nineteenth Century*, 47.

What role did the United Kingdom's relationship with her overseas territories play within this elaborate international economic system? At the end of
the nineteenth century the British Empire embraced about a quarter of the
globe's population and covered some 12 million square miles, 4.25 million
square miles having been added during the previous three decades.[8] The
Empire's size and economic diversity encouraged the hope that, eventually, it
might become virtually self-supporting—a global state with the manpower and
material wealth to ensure its continued world dominance.

The problem with this scenario was that the various Empire countries varied
so greatly in the economic benefits that they conferred on the metropolis. India
dwarfed all others, accounting for nearly 40 per cent of Britain's colonial
exports; the Lancashire textile industry, in particular, depended heavily
upon the Indian market. After India, Britain's most important colonial trading
partners were all white settlements:[9] in descending order of importance, the
Australian colonies (united in the Federation of Australia in 1901), Canada,
Cape Colony and Natal, and New Zealand. Together these countries took in
about 46 per cent of British colonial exports and supplied her with 56 per cent
of her colonial imports. These latter included wheat and timber from Canada,
wool from Australia, frozen meat and dairy produce from New Zealand, and
minerals from Southern Africa. The richest of the South African Colonies was
the Transvaal, annexed to the British Crown in 1900, which, thanks to the
recent invention of blasting gelignite, was on the way to becoming the world's
largest single producer of gold.

By comparison, only a few British dependencies and protectorates (India
apart) had much economic significance. True, the Federated Malay States, a
British protectorate, contained extensive rubber plantations, which supplied
the raw material for a range of emergent industries (from cycle manufacturing
to contraceptives), as well as being rich in tin. Ceylon, where Lipton had
purchased a large tea estate, was displacing China as the source of Britain's
favourite beverage. Finally, Britain drew much of its palm oil from West Africa
and its cane sugar from the West Indian islands (though the West Indies were
in economic decline, as cheaper, subsidized sugar beet from Central Europe
rapidly displaced this product).

But many of the new dependencies had been acquired or were retained
primarily for their strategic value or from reasons of prestige: some were so

[8] The *Royal Primrose Atlas* of 1913 claimed that the Empire contained a population of 396 million,
outnumbering Germany and her colonies (71 million), USA (84 million), France and the French
Empire (93 million), Imperial Russia (130 million), and China (358 million) (R. Hyam, 'The British
Empire in the Edwardian Era', in J. M. Brown and W. R. Louis (eds.), *The Oxford History of the British
Empire: vol. IV: The Twentieth Century* (Oxford, 1999), 49).
[9] Though, of course, containing indigenous populations, of varying sizes.

poor that they came nowhere near covering the costs involved in their administration. Indeed, Britain's dependent territories in Africa and Asia in total accounted for only about 15 per cent of British colonial exports and 12 per cent of colonial imports (and a minuscule percentage of her total overseas trade). British traders operating in these regions might reap a comfortable profit, but the wider economy derived only a marginal advantage from their exertions. Nor, before the spread of high foreign tariffs in the 1890s, was it self-evident that the Union Jack needed to fly over a territory if British citizens were to trade with it.

The same applied to investment opportunities. Even in 1913 under one-half of Britain's capital outflow went to Empire countries, and only about one-third was doing so in the early 1890s: dependencies were the destination of a mere third of these totals.[10] The main recipient of British capital was the United States. Also important was South America, where British investors helped provide the infrastructure which enabled these developing countries to turn themselves into important sources of food for the British people, taking, in return, large quantities of British-exported goods. Well might Argentina, which enjoyed particularly close economic ties with Britain, be called a part of Britain's 'informal Empire' or even an 'honorary dominion'.[11]

Britain's visible trade revealed a similar pattern. Her most important overseas supplier was the United States (the source of the raw cotton consumed by the textile industry), followed by France, India, Germany, Holland, and Australia. Indeed, during the 1890s, as Britain sucked in increasing quantities of manufactured goods (mainly from Western Europe), the Empire's share in imports somewhat diminished.[12] Nor did Britain's overseas territories even dominate the supply of foodstuffs. Canada, Australia, and, in some years, India were major sources of wheat—but so, too, were the United States and Russia.[13] Similarly, though New Zealand and Australia provided British consumers with much of their meat—so, too, did Argentina. In fact, tea (87.3 per cent), wool (80.2 per cent), rubber (57.2 per cent), and oilseeds (53.3 per cent) were the only primary products, most of which were imported from the Empire.[14]

---

[10] In 1890–4 66% went to foreign countries, 24.7% to colonies of settlement, 7.2% to India, 2.1% to the other Dependencies. By 1910–14 these proportions were 61.4%, 28.9%, 4.6%, 5.2%.

[11] About one-half of Argentina's fixed assets were foreign-owned, mainly British-owned (P. G. Cain and A. G. Hopkins, *British Imperialism: Innovation and Expansion 1688–1914* (1993), 315).

[12] However, imports from Empire countries rose from 21.4% to 27% between 1870 and 1914.

[13] Though sources of supply fluctuated wildly from one year to another, the Empire's share of the UK's grain imports tended to increase in the years up to 1914; but it never exceeded 50%.

[14] Compare grains (35.3%), meat (24.7%), butter (19%) (Cain, 'Economics and Empire', 43). Colonies of settlement provided 54.6% of all colonial imports, India, 26%, other Dependencies, 19.4%. 24.9% of all imports came from Empire countries.

As a market for British exports, the Empire had greater importance. Imperialists were fond of pointing out that per-capita consumption of British goods was higher among the population of the self-governing colonies than among foreigners—proving that our kith and kin were our best customers. Indeed, between 1870 and 1914 the UK's share of overseas trade going to Empire countries as a whole significantly increased, from 22.7 per cent to 34.9 per cent, though most of this rise was concentrated into the 1870s. India was consistently her largest overseas market, absorbing about 12 per cent of total exports. Moreover, the metropolis enjoyed a massive trade surplus with the rest of the Empire; and this helped the UK avoid what might otherwise have been a serious balance of payments problem.[15]

On the other hand, foreign markets remained *in aggregate* far more important than all the British territories combined, supplying the metropolis with approximately three-quarters of her imports and taking two-thirds of her exports. After India, Britain's largest overseas markets were the United States and Germany.[16]

Government thus found itself in a dilemma. Salisbury briefly toyed with the idea of empire free trade, and an imperial *Zollverein* (i.e. a central customs union) had been advocated, first by the Fair Trade League and then by its successor, Howard Vincent's United Empire Trade League, founded in 1891. But, for all the Empire's emotional appeal, Britain's worldwide trading and investment links made any kind of imperial economic union difficult to achieve. With considerable justification, free traders argued that unfettered commercial activity, inspired by market signals rather than political imperatives, not only contributed to world peace but also underpinned Britain's prosperity. And though the Liberal Imperialists heatedly denied any incompatibility between Empire and free trade, Radical Liberals had a point when they warned that imperialist fervour, by encouraging the notion of an enclosed self-contained Empire, threatened to undermine the open global trading system which was the country's life-blood.

3. A GREAT POWER IN RETREAT?

Yet how secure, in reality, was this prosperity? Britain's heavy dependence on overseas-grown food meant that a hostile state which succeeded in cutting the sea lanes could starve the population into submission, since home agriculture

---

[15] Britain imported more from Argentina than from Australia, but exported less (Cain, 'Economics and Empire', 45).

[16] The USA was more important than Germany in 1885: by 1910 the positions had been reversed. Colonies of settlement took 50% of all exports to colonies, India 33.5%, and other Dependencies, 16.5%. 35.4% of all exports went to Empire countries (Cain, 'Economics and Empire', 35).

could only support the country for 125 days a year. Even minor privations, brought about by an interruption of food supplies, might, some thought, excite an unreliable working-class population into outbursts of disaffection.

There were two possible strategies for warding off these dangers: protection of home agriculture on the one hand, and maintaining a vast naval superiority on the other. In the 1890s only the second strategy was taken seriously.[17] Indeed, if Britain were to remain locked into an intricate trading system, based on international economic specialization, she really had no alternative but to 'rule the waves'.

Unfortunately the Royal Navy in the 1880s was in a highly unsatisfactory condition: retrospectively, Admiral Bacon identified 1888 'as marking the lowest level of efficiency of material that the British Navy had known since the middle of the eighteenth century'.[18] The wider public received some inkling of all this in September 1884, when W. T. Stead published in the *Pall Mall Gazette* a series of hard-hitting articles entitled 'The Truth about the Navy',[19] which questioned both the strength and the war-readiness of the British fleet. This sparked off an alarmist agitation, which enjoyed the backing of senior naval officers on the Board of Admiralty, one of whom, Charles Beresford, the Fourth Naval Lord, publicly voiced his discontents before resigning his post (in 1888).[20]

A bemused public was startled to learn that the Mediterranean Fleet was pursuing obsolete tactics and had no settled mobilization plan, and, furthermore, that it would need reinforcing from other seas should the country ever find itself at war with France. Naval matériel, too, was defective: a significant number of ironclads were still equipped with archaic muzzle-loading guns, while the more up-to-date breech-loaders had a nasty habit of discharging their missiles in the direction of their own gun crews. Not everyone shared *Punch*'s view that the situation was comical.

Could a navy so under-strength and ill-prepared even be counted on to protect the island realm from invasion? The possibility of such a catastrophe had been in the air ever since, in the aftermath of the Franco-Prussian War, a retired soldier, George Chesney, had written a fictional account of the Prussian army's invasion of England: *The Battle of Dorking* (1871). But it was the abortive 1882 proposal to build a Channel tunnel which generated the majority

---

[17] A. Howe, *Free Trade and Liberal England, 1846–1946* (Oxford, 1997), 194.

[18] A. J. Marder, *The Anatomy of British Sea Power* (Hamden, Conn., 1940), Ch. 8.

[19] One of Stead's informants was Hugh Arnold-Forster (see Ch. 10), another a young naval officer, John Fisher.

[20] In December 1888 Beresford also made a strong speech on the subject in the Commons. In both 1884 and 1888 a leading role in these naval war scares was played by the up-and-coming Liberal Unionist politician and defence expert Hugh Oakeley Arnold-Forster, author of *In a Conning Tower* (1888).

of the early invasion scares—scares in which the French were usually projected as the likely enemy. Typical of the genre was William le Queux's *The Great War in England in 1897* (1894), which by 1897 had already gone into fourteen editions.[21] (H. G. Wells brilliantly exploited the prevailing sense of vulnerability in his 1898 novella *The War of The Worlds*.)

Senior military officers fanned the flames for their own purposes. Colonel Maurice wrote *Hostilities Without Declaration of War* in 1883 and, three years later, the Director of Military Intelligence declared that London, the richest town in the world, lay at the mercy of the invader.[22] The alarmist speech in the Lords made on 14 May 1888 by the Adjutant-General, Garnet Wolseley, then galvanized the government into action: by 1892 some £68,000 had been spent on land fortifications around an allegedly defenceless London. In 1889 the War Secretary's military secretary was said to be planning on the assumption 'of our finding the French army on our breakfast tables with *The Times* tomorrow morning'.[23]

But navalists (with the Admiralty taking the lead) poo-pooed the possibility that a foreign enemy might evade the British fleet and land large numbers of troops on British soil. To the members of what they disparagingly called the 'blue funk' school, navalists such as Admiral Philip Colomb opposed sound 'blue water' doctrine, insisting that, so long as Britain commanded the sea lanes, all would be well, and that if she failed to do so, no amount of expenditure on the army would avert disaster because the country could quickly be starved into submission. These navalists gave the 'invasion scare story' their own idiosyncratic twist—as in the self-explanatory tale *Battle Off Worthing: Why The Invaders Never Got To Dorking* (1887), written by a 'Captain of the Royal Navy'.[24]

In 1889 the Conservative government came down on the side of the Senior Service by passing the Naval Defence Act, based on the principle that Britain should have a naval establishment 'on such a scale that it should at least be the equal to the naval strength of any two other countries'.[25] By the mid-1890s even the army had broadly accepted the validity of the blue water line on invasion.[26] Salisbury later summed up the situation with admirable brevity: 'We are fish.'

---

[21] W. J. Reader, *At Duty's Call: A Study in Obsolete Patriotism* (Manchester, 1988), 63.

[22] Ibid. 6.

[23] I. F. W. Beckett, 'The Stanhope Memorandum of 1888: A Reinterpretation', *Bulletin of the Institute of Historical Research*, 57 (1984), 246.

[24] C. D. Eby, *The Road to Armaggedon: The Martial Spirit in English Popular Literature, 1870–1914* (Durham, NC, 1987), 18–19.

[25] In the words of the First Lord of the Admiralty, Lord George Hamilton. See J. T. Sumida, *In Defence of Naval Supremacy: Finance, Technology, and British Naval Policy 1889–1914* (London, 1993), 13–15; Marder, *Anatomy*, Ch. 8.

[26] J. Gooch, *The Prospect of War: Studies in British Defence Policy 1847–1942* (London, 1981), 8.

But the Naval Defence Act created almost as many problems as it solved. For a start, the 'two-power standard', as it became known, encouraged the public in its belief that the country's security could be measured almost entirely in terms of large battleships—a delusion that was to prove almost impossible to dispel. In particular, the Act did not address the difficulty of how to protect the country's sea-borne commerce from a French 'guerre de course', which the French realized that the British would not be able to foreclose as easily as they had done during the Napoleonic Wars, because a close blockade of French ports was now impracticable thanks to the ever-increasing range and sophistication of the torpedo.[27] In 1896 the gravity of this threat increased when the French launched a new kind of commerce-raider, the 'Jeanne d'Arc' armoured cruiser, which carried face-hardened armour along its sides that were proof against fire from the batteries of any ordinary cruiser fast enough to catch her. In 1897 an alarmed Admiralty responded by launching its own 'Cressy' class of armoured cruiser. The naval arms race had gone up by yet another ratchet.

Maintaining a margin of naval superiority also necessitated significant financial sacrifices—partly because, unlike the army, the navy was a capital-intensive enterprise undergoing rapid technological change. The 1889 Naval Defence Act committed the country over the next five years to spending £21.5 million on ocean-going vessels, including ten battleships that were to be 'of the newest type and most approved design' (£5 million had also to be spent on improvements in fleet-support infrastructure). Five years later the Liberal ministry, at the insistence of Lord Spencer, the First Lord of the Admiralty, felt obliged to initiate yet another costly five-year rolling construction programme, this time devoted mainly to large cruisers and torpedo-boat destroyers. By the late 1890s design changes meant that battleships, too, were becoming ever more expensive to lay down.

True, the provision of a dominant navy was probably cheaper than an army designed to engage on equal terms with a major Continental power (indeed, running at about 3 per cent of national income, Britain's defence outlay was arguably lower than that of most other major European states).[28] All the same, naval expenditure between 1889–90 and 1896–7 increased by 65 per cent; in 1899 it topped £24 million, more than the cost of the army.[29] Goschen's debt

---

[27] The new gyroscopically controlled torpedo, perfected in 1900, allowed targets to be hit at about 2,000 yards (previously it had only been effective at 600 yards), forcing ships' batteries to increase their range.

[28] See discussion in J. M. Hobson, 'The Military Extraction Gap and the Weary Titan: The Fiscal Sociology of British Defence Policy 1870–1913', *Journal of European Economic History*, 22 (1993), 461–506. Using other measures some historians have reached very different conclusions; see, for example, L. E. Davis and R. A. Huttenback, *Mammon and the Pursuit of Empire: The Political Economy of British Imperialism, 1860–1912* (Cambridge, 1986), Ch. 5.

[29] Sumida, *Naval Supremacy*, 14–19.

conversion helped ease the pain as, later, did Harcourt's death duties.[30] Nevertheless prudent custodians of the national purse were appalled by what was happening. Gladstone resigned in 1894 in protest at the size of the naval estimates. By October 1901 the Conservative Chancellor, Hicks Beach, was warning the Cabinet that the Admiralty's demands would soon lead 'straight to financial ruin'.[31]

Nor, as the authors of the Naval Defence Act had once hoped, did these efforts even have the effect of deterring Britain's foreign rivals. On the contrary, the Royal Navy's relative advantage continued to erode. In 1883 Britain had boasted thirty-eight capital ships, as compared with the forty belonging to France, Russia, the United States, Japan, Germany, and Italy: by 1897 the ratio had slipped to 62 : 97.[32] It was particularly unfortunate, in the light of the two-power standard, that the next two naval powers were France and Russia, who formed an alliance with one another in 1894. In hindsight the odds of an effective Franco-Russian assault on the British fleet look small, but at the time there were agitators at home who believed that this might happen.[33] The emergence of Germany as a significant naval power after 1898 then magnified the Admiralty's problems by escalating the arms race. The global balance tilted still further against Britain, with Japan's rise to Great Power status in 1894–5 and the United States' in 1898, which meant that Britain no longer dominated the Pacific and the Western Atlantic Oceans.

During the 1880s the Admiralty had at least taken comfort from the thought that, such was Britain's industrial superiority, she could outbuild the dockyards of Europe. During the following decade this confidence evaporated. For, as other countries began to industrialize, Britain's early economic lead was being steadily whittled away: her share of world manufacturing output fell from 31.8 per cent in 1870 to 14 per cent in 1913. During the course of the 1890s German steel production outstripped Britain's—a particularly ominous development. Britain's share of world trade also fell between 1870 and 1913, from 24.9 per cent to only 14.1 per cent.[34]

Meanwhile the country was exhibiting other symptoms of relative decline. In 1886 the United Kingdom had a total population of about 36,300,000, rising by 1913 to a little over 45 million. However, the *rate* of population growth was

---

[30] See Ch. 7.

[31] H. C. G. Matthew, *Gladstone Vol. 2 1875–98* (Oxford, 1995), 351–5; Sumida, *Naval Supremacy*, 18–23; P. Smith, 'Ruling the Waves: Government, the Service and the Cost of Naval Supremacy, 1885–99', in P. Smith (ed.), *Government and the Armed Forces in Britain, 1856–1990* (London and Rio Grande, 1996), 21–52.

[32] P. Kennedy, *The Rise and Fall of the Great Powers* (New York, 1987), 209. See also A. Friedberg, *The Weary Titan: Britain and the Experience of Absolute Decline, 1895–1905* (Princeton, 1988), 153.

[33] Kennedy, *British Naval Mastery*, 179.

[34] Ibid. 189–90.

slowing down. Earlier in the century such a development would have been greeted with relief. Some contemporaries, among them the eugenist Montague Crackanthorpe, did indeed welcome the trend, wishing it could be taken further, on the ground that population growth inexorably led to war, famine, and disease. But by the late Victorian period the Malthusian nightmare, which decreed that the growth of food supplies was destined to lag behind any population increase, had been largely exorcised. The new fear was that the population was not increasing *fast enough* to keep pace with that of other foreign states (bar France). An obvious comparator was the Bismarckian Reich. In 1871 the population of a reunified Germany had already outstripped the United Kingdom by 9.2 million: by 1914 the gap had widened to 19.6 million. The military implications of this statistic would before long become very clear.

Only slightly less worrying was the fact that Britain was falling behind the United States. In the mid-1850s Britain and America had been states of roughly comparable size, but America then began to surge ahead. By the early twentieth century it already numbered over 77,500,000 inhabitants. Few were prepared to consider the prospect of an Anglo-American war, but American economic competition was formidable since the United States, along with many other natural advantages, possessed a home market appreciably larger than that of any of its European rivals except backward Russia.

It was this worry about Britain's limited population resources which led some imperialists to predict that she would follow the decline of Holland unless she succeeded in calling in the new world to redress the balance of the old—by somehow forging a more united state structure out of the disparate elements of her Empire. The quest for imperial consolidation thus proceeded more from a sense of weakness than from an aggressive bid for world domination.

Worse, just as Britain was losing her hegemony, the world was becoming, from her viewpoint, a much more dangerous place. It was Britain's misfortune that Bismarck, seeking to protect his annexation of Alsace-Lorraine in 1871 from French *revanchisme*, succeeded, to some extent, in diverting French ambitions outwards into areas where they conflicted with Britain's imperial holdings. This was easily achieved, since London and Paris had seriously fallen out over the invasion of Egypt in 1881: what had originally been planned as a joint expedition had then been conducted by the British alone at a moment when the French, preoccupied with domestic conflicts, lacked a government.

Bismarck screwed up the tension still further by belatedly launching Germany on a colonial policy in 1884, a course of action which immediately brought about a clash with Britain, particularly in Africa. The Berlin Conference of 1884–5 was only partially successful in defusing the resulting rivalries on that continent between the various European colonial powers.

Faced by mounting external challenges, the British government sought to formalize its relationship with many of its overseas 'clients'. This happened, for example, in Southern Africa, where in 1885 Sir Charles Warren was dispatched to annex Southern Bechuanaland[35] in order to prevent German South West Africa from expanding inland towards the Transvaal. Soon afterwards, in Eastern Africa, the activities of the German adventurer Carl Peters, in what is now Tanzania, quickly destabilized the status quo, leading to British annexations in Kenya and also to the establishment in 1891 of the British Central African Protectorate of Nyasaland (now Malawi). Germany's forward policy also precipitated a 'Scramble for the Pacific', at the end of which Britain, egged on by the Australasian colonies, emerged with a clutch of new territories: parts of New Guinea (1884), the Cook Islands (1888),[36] the Gilbert and Ellice Islands (1892), and the Solomon Islands (1893).

An even greater cause of concern was the seemingly relentless process of Russian expansion, made possible by a vast programme of railway construction. In the Far East this posed threats to the stability of a volatile region where all the great powers were struggling to secure trading concessions. In the Middle East Russian encroachments into northern Persia alarmed imperialists, who saw this as a threat to British domination of the Persian Gulf, so vital to the sea route to India. Most ominous of all was Russia's annexation of territory in Central Asia and the building of the Orenburg–Tashkent rail link, which brought her closer to Afghanistan and to India's North-West Frontier. Shortly before Salisbury took office in 1886, Britain and Russia had actually stood on the brink of war (thankfully averted) over the so-called Penjdeh incident, following the Russian defeat of an Afghan army.[37]

In fact, India, with its long land frontier, presented successive British governments with a nightmarish problem. Some 75,000 troops were permanently stationed in that country, as well as the 150,000-strong Indian Army. But in the event of a Russian invasion, 30,000 reinforcements would have had to be sent out from the United Kingdom—at least, that was the estimate made in 1892 by the Commander-in-Chief in India, General Frederick Roberts, who feared that any such incursion or even a military setback at the Russians' hands would trigger an internal rising.[38]

---

[35] Southern Bechuanaland became a Crown Colony, before later being transferred to the Cape.

[36] Transferred to New Zealand in 1901.

[37] Sensitivity over the security of India also played a part in Lord Randolph Churchill's action in annexing Upper Burma in 1885–6—though more with a view to forestalling the French, who had established a footing in nearby Indo-China.

[38] However, throughout the 1890s the War Office planned to counter such an invasion by launching amphibious attacks on the Russians, with the Indian Army adopting a defensive position (Beckett, 'Stanhope Memorandum', 245).

In two influential books, *The Influence of Sea Power upon History, 1660–1783* (1890) and *The Influence of Sea Power upon the French Revolution and Empire* (1892), Alfred Thayer Mahan, the American 'evangelist of sea power', argued that, during the previous 400 years, maritime states had achieved global dominance through their control of the seas. However, as the problem of Indian defence illustrates, continental powers with large, resource-rich heartlands could now, thanks to the 'railway revolution', project military force over vast distances more quickly than a maritime power could dispatch reinforcements by sea.[39] When Curzon, the Indian Viceroy, complained—not for the first time—that London was not opposing Russian expansionism with greater vigour, Salisbury wearily commented: 'He always wants me to negotiate with Russia as if I had 500,000 men at my back, and I have not.'[40]

What the British government *could* do was to protect the sea-routes to India. But here, too, ministers and defence experts apprehended danger—and from two quite distinct geographical areas. First, the British position at the Cape seemed threatened by the Boers' control of mineral wealth inland. In 1871 the Colonial Secretary, Lord Kimberley, had moved quickly to attach the newly discovered diamond fields of Griqualand West to Cape Colony, buying off a competing claim from the Orange Free State for £90,000. Far less easily handled were the consequences of the discovery of the deep gold reef in the Witwatersrand in the semi-independent state of the Transvaal in 1885–6—a development that threatened to tilt the balance in South Africa in favour of Afrikanerdom, so imperilling the future of the British naval base at Simonstown and the docking facilities at Cape Town.

Second, Britain's security depended on her dominance in the eastern Mediterranean, traditionally seen as the gateway to India. But this dominance was jeopardized both by the relative weakness of the Mediterranean Fleet and by the precariousness of Britain's hold on Egypt, through which passed the strategically important Suez Canal.[41] British traders, too, had a growing stake in the security of the Suez Canal Company—between 1880 and 1910 British tonnage passing through that waterway trebled. But could this vital strategic and commercial interest be preserved, given the policies of an embittered France who, it seemed, had set herself the objective of prising the British out of Egypt by fair means or foul?

So we are left with a paradox. The 1890s was an age of pomp, plumes, and vainglorious swagger. Britain was mistress of the greatest Empire that the

---

[39] This was the thesis argued by the geographer Halford Mackinder in his paper, 'The Geographical Pivot of History', published in the *Geographical Journal* (Apr. 1904).

[40] Earl of Ronaldshay, *The Life of Lord Curzon*, Vol. 2 (London, 1928), 206.

[41] Britain's dependence on Middle Eastern oil came later, after the conversion of the British fleet from coal to oil-fired turbines. See Ch. 13.

world had ever seen—an Empire which, at least to the superficial gaze, was at the very zenith of its power. The Diamond Jubilee of 1897, when 50,000 troops (a microcosm of the world's population) drawn from all round the Empire escorted the royal procession, aroused feelings of pride and complacency which united most citizens across the barriers of class. In the course of these celebrations a naval review was held at Spithead in June. British warships, over 165 in all, stretched out as far as the eye could see. This was the most powerful naval force that had ever been assembled in one place.[42]

But among the better-informed the Jubilee evoked mixed feelings, pride being tinged with foreboding: Kipling responded by writing his poem 'Recessional', a sombre warning of the transience of all political dominions. Thinking about the country's international position was also coloured by *fin-de-siècle* pessimism. Even Chamberlain, addressing the 1902 Colonial Conference, spoke of 'the weary Titan stagger[ing] under the too vast orb of its fate'.[43] Did the country possess the resources or even the will-power to defend the vast territories for which its government had assumed responsibility—obligations that were continuously growing in the 1890s, as more areas of the globe were painted red? Britain's seemed to be a serious case of what has since been called 'imperial overstretch'.[44]

In fact, neither the British government nor its people seemed to have its heart fully in the business of running an Empire, which they wished to accomplish at minimum cost and with a limited deployment of manpower. Hence, the proliferation during the 1880s and 1890s of chartered companies, which were given such vital governmental powers as the levying of taxes and the maintenance of internal order within their allotted territories.[45] But, as Salisbury recognized, in the long run this kind of 'imperialism on the cheap' was not sustainable. By the time that Goldie's outfit was bought out and Nigeria turned into a Crown Colony in 1900, the sole chartered company still in operation was Rhodes's British South Africa Company, its powers considerably clipped.

Yet because government still hesitated to assume full control over its Empire, the British continued to collaborate with assorted native princes, emirs, sultans, and chieftains. Indeed, the Indian Raj, with a population of nearly 300 million (about three-quarters of the inhabitants of the entire Empire), was being run, in practice, by no more than a couple of thousand

[42] Kennedy, *Naval Mastery*, 205.
[43] J. Amery, *The Life of Joseph Chamberlain: Volume Four 1901–1903* (London, 1951), 421
[44] P. Kennedy, *The Rise and Fall of the Great Powers* (New York, 1987).
[45] The North Borneo Company was the first chartered company to be established, in 1881, followed by Goldie's Royal Niger Company (July 1886), William Mackinnon's Imperial British East Africa Company (1888), and, fatefully, Rhodes's British South Africa Company (1889).

white officers serving with the Indian Army, plus some 2,000–3,000 white civil servants and police officers. Similarly, Frederick Lugard, appointed High Commissioner of Northern Nigeria in 1900, found himself ruling a vast territory, most of which had never been viewed by any European, with a civil staff totalling 104 and a military force of between 2,000 and 3,000 Africans, under a mere 200 British officers and NCOs (about one-third of whom were always on leave or sick).[46]

Indeed, it is arguable that the British Empire was something of a bluff, held together less by overwhelming force than by a mixture of cajolery and guile. From time to time 'emergencies' occurred: the Sierra Leone hut-tax revolt of 1897–8, for example, was crushed by the mobilization of superior military might, and punitive expeditions had to be launched against the Ashanti in the Gold Coast in 1896 and 1900. But Evelyn Baring (Lord Cromer), Viceroy of Egypt, correctly saw that the deployment of force denoted imperial failure.[47] Nor was armed suppression a risk-free operation now that modern European firearms had penetrated most areas of the globe.

The sense of vulnerability that this situation could engender was well captured by John Buchan in his novel *Prester John* (1910), where the narrator observes that in his fictional African territory 'there were five or six [natives] to every white man', leaving him with the feeling that he 'was being hemmed in by barbarism, and cut off in a ghoulish land from the succour of [his] own kind'. Away from the metropolis, this was often how the Empire was experienced by British 'colonials'.

4. THE PROBLEM OF IMPERIAL DEFENCE

If imperial defence imposed such financial burdens, why could the colonies and dependencies not make an appropriate contribution to its costs? India, it is true, did precisely that, supporting an army out of the taxes imposed upon its population. Indian troops were also frequently deployed abroad in campaigns that bore only indirectly, if at all, on Indian interests, most notably in the Sudan from 1896 to 1899.[48]

But it was quite otherwise with Britain's 'children', as Chamberlain called them. Between the 1860s and the 1890s Australia was arguably the wealthiest region in the world,[49] but its governments still looked to the metropolis for

---

[46] M. Perham, *Lugard: The Years of Authority, 1898–1945* (London, 1960), 27, 35.

[47] P. Burroughs, 'Imperial Institutions and the Government of Empire', in Porter (ed.), *British Empire: Nineteenth Century*, 178–9.

[48] M. Howard, *The Continental Commitment: The Dilemma of British Defence Policy in the Era of Two World Wars* (Oxford, 1971), 17.

[49] Offer, 'Costs and Benefits', 709.

protection. This had long been a source of irritation to British ministers. The 'presumptuous' demands of the Australian delegates at the 1887 Colonial Conference (held to coincide with the Golden Jubilee) particularly riled Lord Salisbury: 'It has a bad effect on my liver to think how these Australian colonists put upon us', he commented to Henry Holland, his Colonial Secretary.[50]

True, that same Conference did agree to establish an auxiliary naval squadron in Australian waters, towards which the Australian colonies offered to pay £126,000 p.a. and New Zealand £20,000. The squadron would come under the command of the Commander-in-Chief of the Australian Station, but only on the understanding that it would not be moved without the consent of the colonial governments.

This compromise satisfied neither side. The main difficulty was, that scarcely had the ink dried on the agreement than a new naval orthodoxy emerged (partly under the influence of Mahan's writings): naval force, it was now claimed, needed to be concentrated at crucial geographical points rather than being dispersed around the globe in a vain attempt to protect particular localities. Unfortunately the doctrine of 'One Sea, One Fleet' left the colonies without much to do other than contribute towards London's naval costs—without having any say in the Fleet's deployment. Little wonder if, at the 1897 Colonial Conference, only the Cape offered to help out in this way, by promising to donate a cruiser (which was later converted into an annual payment of £30,000). Obviously what the colonies wanted were coastal patrols in the vicinity of their more densely inhabited settlements—a desire mocked by the Admiralty as 'hugging the coastline'. The imperatives of imperial defence thus clashed with the Empire's 'political polycentrism'.[51]

In theory this difficulty could have been overcome by the establishment of a more politically united Empire, as demanded by the Imperial Federation League (IFL), founded in London in 1884, which aimed to strengthen the 'race' and unite the 'British Nation' through a federalization of the Constitution.[52] But although the IFL initially enjoyed the backing of prominent Liberals such as Rosebery, it folded in 1893—partly because its agenda blatantly favoured the United Kingdom at the expense of the white self-governing colonies, which had no desire to forfeit their hard-won autonomy or to become drawn into European quarrels. The 'islanders' were thus left, largely on their own, to sort out the problem of 'imperial defence'.

---

[50] A. Roberts, *Salisbury: Victorian Titan* (London, 1999), 464. The remark was occasioned by their apparent eagerness to involve Britain in a war with France over the New Hebrides.

[51] Burroughs, 'Defence and Imperial Disunity', 340–5.

[52] It was no accident that the subtitle of George Parkin's 1892 book *Imperial Federation* was 'the Problem of National Unity', or that F. P. de Labilliere's 1894 volume on imperial federation was entitled *Federal Britain* (J. E. Kendle, *Federal Britain: A History* (London, 1997), 56).

5. MODERNIZING THE ARMY

Against a background of almost continuous scares during the 1890s, the Admiralty began its long task of improving naval matériel, tactics, and morale—a programme that Jacky Fisher was to bring to fruition in the early years of the next century.[53] But the army faced no less of a challenge. For a start, what was the British army *for*? Some military thinkers argued that it might be needed one day to fight abroad, whether in defence of imperial territory or even against a great European rival. But no one yet seriously suggested that Britain should emulate the Continental example and adopt conscription: even compulsory military service for home defence had few advocates. It was mostly assumed that Britain's island situation and overseas commitments could be met by a small, voluntary army.

In fact, excluding the Indian establishment,[54] Britain's peacetime military strength barely exceeded 135,000 men—of whom about 30 per cent were on duty in colonial garrisons. Bismarck, who had at his back an army of nearly three-quarters of a million men, plus a reserve of four to five million, joked that if the British landed on German soil he would send off his police force and have the invaders arrested. Behind the army proper stood a number of poorly equipped and trained home-defence forces, numbering at most 100,000 men, principally the militia and the volunteers—forces which seemed to be serving a social, rather than a serious military, purpose.

In the late 1880s and 1890s the main aim of the reformers was not so much to boost numbers as to bring the army up to a higher level of professionalism. Yet formidable obstacles blocked their path. The first of these was the monarch, head of the army in more than a nominal sense, who could still mount a serious challenge to the authority of the Secretary of State for War, the latter not having anything like the free hand in determining policy enjoyed by other ministers. Significantly, the Commander-in-Chief of the army since 1856 was the Duke of Cambridge, the Queen's cousin (aka 'The Great German Sausage'), an obstinate defender of traditional practices. Perhaps the greatest single achievement of Henry Campbell-Bannerman was when, as Liberal War Secretary, he tactfully dislodged the 'Royal George' in 1895. This allowed Salisbury soon afterwards to install in his place Lord Wolseley, regarded at the time as the leader of the 'reform party' within the army.

The Duke of Cambridge, chairing a lecture to officers at Aldershot on the subject of foreign cavalry, had once declared: 'Why should we want to know anything about foreign cavalry? We have a better cavalry of our own. I fear,

---

[53] See Ch. 10.
[54] The two armies had been amalgamated in 1860, but soldiers whose memory went back before that date still entertained prejudices against the 'other side'.

gentlemen, the army is in danger of becoming a mere debating society.' This know-nothing philistinism presented enormous problems for those seeking to improve the standard of military education provided by the two military academies, Sandhurst (infantry and cavalry) and Woolwich (artillery and engineers). Although some improvements had been made from mid-century onwards, reformers struggled to make soldiering more like other professional careers.

But behind such obscurantism lay a much more complex situation. In contrast to nearly all the Continental states, the British officer corps was deeply rooted in the 'parent society'. Subalterns' basic pay, for example, was nominal—£95 16s. 3d. a year for an ensign, and only £365 for a lieutenant-colonel. These scales had been established in 1806 and were not to alter until 1 January 1914—providing an income which in no way covered the social costs of soldiering, where mess bills in fashionable regiments could be very high. Cavalry officers were anyhow required to provide their own horses and accoutrements, at very considerable expense (about £1,000). In some regiments it was established that an officer had to have a minimum independent income: £100 in line regiments, £600–700 in crack cavalry regiments.

Admittedly, throughout the century there were army officers, often from military families, who intended, from the start, to dedicate much of their adult life to military service, and the more successful of them provided the personnel who later secured promotion to the senior ranks. Successful generals were often well rewarded: Kitchener, as well as being made a peer, was given a grant of £30,000 following his victory at Omdurman (Wolseley had earlier received £25,000 for his Ashanti victory). Lower down the hierarchy, colonels could make a tidy profit out of clothing their regiments.

But such prizes were reserved for the few. For most British officers the acquisition of a commission represented a stage in the life of a 'gentleman', not a long-term commitment, and its main importance was as a confirmer of social status. Commissions, especially in the cavalry and in fashionable regiments of the line, were still heavily dominated by the scions of aristocratic and landed families; many officers came from Irish Protestant families, others from the South and South-West of England, another important military reservoir. By contrast, the 'scientific' branches of the army and the Indian Army were considerably less exclusive. But even at the end of the century only a small minority of military officers came from business, commercial, and industrial families.[55]

---

[55] E. M. Spiers, 'The Regular Army in 1914', in I. F. W. Beckett and K. Simpson (eds.), *A Nation in Arms: A Social Study of the British Army in the First World War* (Manchester, 1985), 39–42. The navy was more 'meritocratic'.

For many officers the main attraction of military life was social. During the season officers in some regiments expected to hunt twice a week. This could be defended as encouraging skills in horsemanship that contributed to a cavalry-man's efficiency—as could the playing of polo. But no such justification could be made of the time absorbed in social entertaining and in the performance of purely ceremonial duties. Many officers treated their units as though they were itinerant social clubs, containing all the complex social stratification found in civil society. Little wonder if both officers and men often felt a prime loyalty to their regiment, not to the army as a whole.

Looking anxiously at developments in Germany, Wolseley and the keen young officers whom he deliberately favoured,[56] realized the urgency of reform. These anxieties were not unconnected, perhaps, to the fact that these men had all been hardened in a succession of small, but gruelling, colonial wars (Wol-seley himself had commanded the troops at Tel-el-Kabir in 1882). Some Indian officers, notably General Roberts, hero of the earlier Afghan War, similarly saw the need for change—again, no doubt, because for them sol-diering was a calling that, at any time, might lead to actual fighting.[57]

And yet there were advantageous features in British 'amateurishness'. The pre-war British army was largely officered by precisely the same people who dominated social and political life in the counties, and were heavily represented in both Houses of Parliament and in government. Indeed, there was much overlap of membership: in 1898 35 per cent of all peers held commissions, and though the military interest in the Commons had shrunk following Speaker Brand's censure of officers on full pay serving as MPs (in 1898 there were only forty-one such MPs, thirty-six of them Unionists), many more Members had been commissioned at some stage in their lives.[58]

As a result, the British officer corps did not see itself as separate from civil society and so it posed no threat, unlike in so many Continental countries, to the authority of civilian government. 'Amateurishness' may have been a price that the Victorians were willing to pay for the safeguarding of their consti-tutional liberties. It is certainly significant that the promotion of a more career-minded group of officers into the higher commands of the British army in the 1890s gave rise to tension with the civilian government of a kind that the country had not experienced for generations. Thus, in his youth Wolseley had allied himself with the Liberals, whom he saw as fellow 'reformers' who could be forgiven their predilection for 'economy'. But in his Lords outburst in 1888 he publicly attacked the party system, which he called the 'curse of modern

---

[56] The so-called 'Wolseley Ring', with which he had first surrounded himself during the Ashanti War of 1873–4, included Evelyn Wood, Redvers Buller, and William Butler.

[57] Unfortunately Wolseley despised Roberts, who did not come from a prestigious landed family.

[58] G. Harries-Jenkins, *The Army in Victorian Society* (London, 1977).

England' (earning the rebuke of Salisbury), and in 1895 he proudly received a portrait of Bismarck, whom he now thought the greatest man alive, far superior to 'little politicians like Mr Gladstone'. Once installed as Commander-in-Chief, Wolseley chafed at civilian control and scarcely bothered to conceal his contempt for his superior, the Unionist War Secretary Lord Lansdowne, whom he dismissed as 'a cross between a French dancing master and a Jewess'.[59]

Charles Dilke, seeking a partial rehabilitation of his career following the divorce fiasco, and an able military correspondent, Spenser Wilkinson, came up with an ingenious solution to the problem of civil–military relations. They called for the creation in each service of a 'single responsible adviser', and for the transfer of control of the armed services from party politicians to the people as a whole, or to their MPs. In his minority note to the Hartington Commission Report, Lord Randolph Churchill endorsed a variant on this scheme. But most senior politicians dismissed it as a constitutional impossibility.

Similar difficulties surrounded the far more practical suggestion that Britain should establish a General Staff. Von Moltke's military triumphs in 1870–1 had certainly owed much to the existence within the Prussian army of a cadre of officers freed from routine administration and exercises so that they could focus on drawing up contingency plans for possible wars. An 1887 Select Committee praised what the Germans had done and noted that a General Staff had since been adopted by almost every other European state. Why, then, did the British hold back until 1905?

Traditionalists insisted that Germany's situation, as a great land power, differed significantly from that of Britain, an island state whose security was guaranteed by naval force and which was unlikely to find itself embroiled in a Continental war. The Hartington Commission of 1890[60] did indeed recommend that a General Staff be set up, but it also noted that such a body was basically incompatible with British constitutional practice, since it threatened to 'militarize' public life by giving dangerous powers to a group of officers with a vested interest in *provoking* war, under the pretence of preparing for the possibility of one.[61] Campbell-Bannerman, a Liberal of the old school, who served as War Secretary between 1892 and 1895, strongly subscribed to this view: 'Every minister', he observed in July 1890, 'may be ignorant of the technical details of the Department he administers, but he is presumed to have capacity for administration and public experience.'[62] Many Conservatives

[59] J. Symons, *Buller's Campaign* (1963), 4, 54.

[60] This body was set up after Admiral Charles Beresford's resignation and Wolseley's alarmist speech in the Lords.

[61] The Prussian general staff and command system were virtually independent of civilian ministers and of parliamentary supervision (W. S. Hamer, *The British Army: Civil–Military Relations 1885–1905* (Oxford, 1970), 40).

[62] Ibid. 152.

felt the same way. Salisbury himself had a well-known suspicion of the pretensions of 'military experts': 'If they were allowed full scope they would insist on the importance of garrisoning the moon in order to protect us from Mars', he wrote privately to Hartington.[63]

In 1895 the Commander-in-Chief was given some of the functions that might otherwise have gone to a Chief of Staff, including supervision of intelligence[64] and of the mobilization departments. He was aided in his work by a council composed of civilian and military personnel and by a subordinate Army Board, which concentrated on technical issues. But the various heads of department, though they had to consult with the Commander-in-Chief, were also answerable to the War Secretary—a confusing situation. Moreover, the British army still lacked a 'brain'.

A related issue, of only slightly lesser significance, was the establishment of machinery of government capable of overcoming the endemic rivalry of the two armed services. Wilkinson and other military reformers had been calling since the late 1880s for the establishment of a Defence Ministry. A modest step in this direction had been taken with the establishment of a Colonial Defence Committee (CDC) in 1885, which the Hartington Commission wanted to convert into a Cabinet Committee under the chairmanship of the Prime Minister.

In 1895 something along these lines eventually materialized. Building upon a recent initiative of the Rosebery administration, the new Unionist government set up a Defence Committee of the Cabinet, under the chairmanship of the Lord President of the Council, the Duke of Devonshire (the former Lord Hartington). However, the new body lacked the authority and the secretarial support it needed to make an impact: in 1900 an informed commentator could call it 'a joke and a very bad one'.[65] Well might the self-governing colonies, when accused of making little or no contribution to imperial defence, reply that there was no properly constituted and efficient body in London with which they could liaise. Given this unsatisfactory situation, it was imperative that the Foreign Office conducted its relationships with the other Great Powers in such a way that the country's military (and perhaps its naval) weaknesses were not exposed.

---

[63] September 1895, cited in Z. S. Steiner, *The Foreign Office and Foreign Policy, 1898–1914* (Cambridge, 1969), 28, n. 2.

[64] The office of Director of Military Intelligence (DMI) had been set up in 1886, that of Director of Naval Intelligence (DNI) in 1887. But the DMI presided over little more than an intelligence-gathering agency and had limited influence over the Secretary of State and his policy-advisers.

[65] Cited in G. R. Searle, *The Quest for National Efficiency: A Study in Politics and Political Thought, 1899–1914* (Oxford, 1971), 219.

6. SALISBURY AND THE FOREIGN OFFICE

During the late 1880s and 1890s Lord Salisbury, the Conservative Prime Minister, was almost continuously in charge of foreign policy. He took over the Foreign Office in January 1887, following Lord Iddesleigh's resignation,[66] and, except during the minority Liberal administrations when Lord Rosebery (1892–4) and Lord Kimberley (1894–5) briefly filled that post, he continued to hold it until October 1900.

Salisbury resumed the Foreign Secretaryship at a time of some difficulty, the disastrous diplomacy of the second Gladstone government having resulted, to all intents and purposes, in Gladstone's beloved 'Concert of Europe' uniting *against* Britain. Already an accomplished and experienced diplomat (he had served as Foreign Secretary between 1878 and 1880, and again during his caretaker government of 1885–6), Salisbury quickly restored Britain's prestige, earning the grudging respect even of Bismarck, who found him a wily and elusive negotiator.

Calm, sardonic, and pessimistic, Salisbury in many ways matched the spirit of the times. He did not, like Gladstone, assert the importance of moral principle in international life. His objective, in an increasingly dangerous world, was to protect essential British interests (the defence of the Raj against Russian incursions and the protection of the sea lanes to India through the Suez Canal and through the longer route via South Africa across the Indian Ocean), but to do so by preserving the peace and thus minimizing expenditure in the cause of domestic stability. To this difficult task Salisbury brought two great diplomatic skills. He clearly saw the interconnectedness between imperial issues and shifts in the European power game;[67] and he showed a remarkable aptitude for isolating whichever foreign power happened, at any moment, to be Britain's principal enemy (i.e. France before the Fashoda Crisis, the Boers in the run-up to the South African War).

Salisbury's tenure at the Foreign Office is often associated with the concept of 'splendid isolation'—a phrase popularized by Chamberlain, who picked it up from a remark made in the Canadian Legislature in 1896. In fact, Salisbury had no objection in principle to negotiating limited agreements with other European powers when he deemed these to be in Britain's interest, and he certainly did not believe it possible to disengage from the Continent. On the contrary, one of his principal achievements was the signing of two 'Mediterranean Agreements' with Italy and Austria-Hungary in 1887, which indirectly and loosely linked Britain to Germany, as well as shoring up British naval

---

[66] See Ch. 5.
[67] A point emphasized in J. Charmley, *Splendid Isolation? Britain and the Balance of Power 1874–1914* (London, 1999).

predominance in the eastern Mediterranean—which was seriously under threat. Though these agreements (the nearest thing to an alliance before 1914) lapsed in 1896, Salisbury continued with his policy of 'leaning to the Triple Alliance without belonging to it'. Meanwhile he placed his reliance on the navy, so that the country would be safe, with or without allies.

If on most other occasions Salisbury fended off overtures from the chancelleries of Europe with the argument that no British government could make a binding agreement with a foreign power which might be disowned at any time by a sovereign Parliament, this was because he saw no clear advantage in entering a treaty in circumstances currently prevailing: Russian and French hostility was a given fact, and Salisbury wisely resisted any attempt to draw the country into an alliance with Germany, which would have increased her vulnerability while bringing few, if any, compensatory gains—for Germany, Salisbury calculated, would not dare risk endangering its relationship with Russia by helping to pull British chestnuts out of the fire in Central Asia or the Far East, and could give little assistance to the British in Cairo.

Parliamentary difficulties, by contrast, inhibited Salisbury very little. The Commons had limited influence over foreign policy: the Mediterranean Agreements, for example, never came before MPs for their approval and inquisitive MPs were fobbed off with a near-lie. Insofar as there were disagreements over foreign policy, these took place within the Liberal Party, where a Radical 'Little England' faction (to which both Harcourt and John Morley were loosely allied) persistently questioned the legitimacy and utility of the British occupation of Egypt, and more generally, in the spirit of Cobden, denounced a policy of entanglements which threatened the peace of the world and necessitated damagingly high armaments expenditure, as well as speaking out, from time to time, on behalf of various native peoples suffering from British exploitation. But Rosebery, from the Liberal frontbench, was a committed advocate of 'continuity of policy', on the grounds that Britain would always be at a disadvantage in her rivalry with autocratically governed states such as Russia so long as foreign policy was allowed to become the plaything of party—as it had been, for example, during Gladstone's earlier assaults on 'Beaconsfieldism'.

In the House of Lords a cosy spirit of cross-party co-operation usually prevailed. Peers asked questions about foreign affairs diffidently, and Salisbury himself clearly believed that manifestations of curiosity were mischievous and even dangerous: in 1897 he rebuked Lord Kimberley, of all people, for being 'very inquisitive'.[68] If Salisbury chose to bring anyone into his confidence, that person was the Queen, who took an often well-informed interest in European

---

[68] R. Shannon, *The Age of Salisbury, 1881–1902: Unionism and Empire* (Harlow, 1996), 483.

affairs, in which she had a deep dynastic involvement—Kaiser Wilhelm II, who acceded to the German throne in 1888, was her grandson, and there was a more distant family connection with Tsar Nicholas of Russia. Contentious issues came to the attention of the Cabinet, but Salisbury's command of foreign policy was seldom challenged before 1898.

Salisbury conducted foreign policy in a very personal way: visiting diplomats often had to negotiate with him in the informal setting of his country residence, Hatfield House. Even his senior officials were allowed little latitude as policy-makers. Moreover, the Foreign Office itself bore no resemblance to a modern bureaucracy, staffed as it was, at its higher levels, by a small number of clerks, grouped into five administrative and four political departments, the latter containing the inner corps of about fifty men who made up the 'diplomatic establishment'. These men, and the Diplomatic Service attachés, came from a restricted social circle, mostly from families known to Lord Salisbury himself, and tended to be on Christian-name terms with one another. The Foreign Office, which had secured an exemption from the open competitive examinations imposed on the other Whitehall departments in the Order-in-Council of June 1870, was therefore staffed by a far more aristocratic personnel than was to be found in the Home Civil Service: one-half of all the successful Foreign Office candidates between 1898 and 1907 about whom information is available were Old Etonians, a proportion that actually rose during the Edwardian period. Members of the Diplomatic Service needed to have a private income.[69]

In practice, the British diplomatic corps did not differ markedly in social background from its European counterparts—indeed, one justification put forward by defenders of the status quo was that British prestige would suffer if the country's official representatives could not hold their own socially at diplomatic gatherings. In any case, from Palmerston's day onwards the Foreign Office had had its own internal examination procedures which, after 1892, were sufficiently rigorous to weed out the incompetent.

Nevertheless the aristocratic composition of the Foreign Office and the Diplomatic Service continued to attract hostility from Radicals who, using traditional Cobdenite arguments, alleged that foreign policy was being distorted by a 'feudal' clique who, cut off by birth and upbringing from an understanding of the requirements of a modern commercial society, positively welcomed diplomatic crises which justified their own existence, rather than pursuing a benevolent policy of intervention that would best preserve that world peace on which the happiness and prosperity of the British people ultimately depended. A variant of this complaint, and one with greater

[69] Steiner, *Foreign Office*, 173–5, 217–21.

justification, was that the Foreign Office, with its snobbish aversion to 'trade', undervalued the work of the middle-class Consular Service, to the detriment of British merchants and exporters.

For better or worse, the Foreign Office not only held aloof from other Whitehall departments but prided itself on its detachment from the vulgarities of everyday life. Historians have written about the 'official mind', a set of departmental principles and traditions which guided policy-makers and largely insulated them from external influences and unfamiliar ideas. True to the aristocratic ethos of the office, Salisbury and his advisers shuddered at the encroachment of democratic pressures into the diplomatic process and particularly feared that popular excitements, fanned by the new popular newspapers, would distort official policy. Rosebery partly shared this mistrust of 'enthusiasm', though he took more of an interest in the manipulation of public opinion—as behoved Gladstone's stage-manager during the Midlothian Campaign.

Salisbury, who knew that public opinion could not entirely be ignored, found himself on occasions pushed in directions he did not like by pressure groups within his own party, and also by an Admiralty which had captured the popular imagination. The formation of the Navy League in January 1895, for example, brought together a new breed of naval journalist with a politicized set of naval officers—a highly potent combination.[70] To what extent, then, was Salisbury really controlling events by the end of the decade? Were others setting the agenda and creating a new reality to which, with weary realism, he realized he had no option but to adjust?

Within his own government a serious challenge to the Salisburian approach came from Joseph Chamberlain after the latter's appointment as Colonial Secretary in 1895. Over the previous years Chamberlain had been advocating an approach to colonial affairs very different from Salisbury's, one that involved active government intervention with a view to developing Britain's tropical estates, a theme which he elaborated during the 1895 election campaign.

These sentiments were not, as Salisbury had once thought, mere rhetoric, for Chamberlain really did bring a new approach to the Colonial Secretary's work by treating the dependencies as economic propositions which could be made to pay handsomely, even if they needed pump-priming with Exchequer grants. As well as baling out the stricken West Indian islands, he succeeded in 1899 in persuading Parliament to authorize colonial loans worth about

---

[70] At the turn of the century the League's membership totalled 15,000 (Marder, *Anatomy*, 55). This figure, however, is small, compared with the German Navy League's 600,000 (F. and M. Coetzee, 'Rethinking the Radical Right in Germany and Britain Before 1914', *Journal of Contemporary History*, 21 (1986), 515–37).

£3 million, to be repaid at 3 per cent. True, Chamberlain's programme of state-aided development faltered because of Treasury parsimony, and perhaps because the great capitalists to whom he appealed did not respond quickly enough to his calls for co-operation.[71] Nevertheless, Lagos, British Guiana, Cyprus, and the Gold Coast particularly benefited from the existence of these new facilities.[72]

In many ways Joseph Chamberlain was a survivor from a fast-vanishing world in his faith that the importation into Africa and Asia of European technology and political practice (however brutally accomplished) would promote the modernization of these backward countries. While nearly all imperialists wanted to build railways and bridges, organize famine relief, supply medical services, and so on, there was an increasing emphasis on the impenetrability of non-European cultures. Chamberlain, by contrast, had a more robust confidence in the benefits of direct imperial involvement. He was particularly proud of his part in the establishment in 1899 of the London School of Tropical Medicine, which, by helping to reduce the risks from malaria and sleeping sickness, did much to open up West Africa to European penetration.[73] Nor were the self-governing colonies ignored, the Colonial Stocks Act of 1900 helping these settlements to improve their transportation systems and infrastructure.

However, what Chamberlain was doing at the Colonial Office also had implications for the more general conduct of British foreign policy. For the colonial and the foreign spheres could not neatly be separated. After all, British rule in Egypt, presided over by Lord Cromer, came under the supervision of the Foreign Office, since this was not a colony (it was declared a protectorate in 1914); the same applied to most of the newly acquired British possessions in central and eastern Africa, which came under the Foreign Office's 'Protectorates' division before being transferred to the Colonial Office between 1898 and 1905.

Moreover, Chamberlain's dogged defence of British colonial interests necessarily impinged upon the country's foreign policy. In West Africa the roots of the new departure can be traced back to the slump of 1890–4, when many businessmen, looking to the Empire for commercial salvation, had complained about the spread of foreign, mainly French, protectionism. Their representations received a sympathetic hearing from Chamberlain, who agreed that

---

[71] Arguably Chamberlain was ahead of his time, anticipating businessmen's need for crucial raw materials which Empire countries had in abundance (B. Porter, *The Lion's Share: A Short History of British Imperialism 1850–1983* (Harlow, 1975; 1984 edn.), 191–2). For protests from Hicks Beach and Edward Hamilton of the Treasury, see R. M. Kesner, *Economic Control and Colonial Development: Crown Colony, Financial Management in the Age of Joseph Chamberlain* (Westport, Conn., 1981), 205–6.

[72] M. Havinden and D. Meredith, *Colonialism and Development: Britain and its Tropical Colonies, 1850–1960* (London, 1993), 70–90.

[73] Similar institutions were soon founded at Liverpool and other British universities.

territories where the British had an interest should be brought under the authority of the Crown before they could be annexed by other European states and their markets effectively closed to British trade.

Trade rivalries of this sort—so different from the 'fair' competition envisaged by mid-Victorian Cobdenites—were often articulated in the fashionable language of Social Darwinism, with the struggle to control markets and defeat foreign competitors being presented as part of a larger 'struggle for existence', in which the 'unfit' would necessarily be driven to the wall. E. E. Williams's influential pamphlet *Made in Germany* (1896) further popularized the idea of foreigners malevolently filching Britain's markets—an impression already fostered by the Merchandise Marks Act of 1887. Foreign trade was thus coming to be seen as an extension of war by other means: F. A. Mackenzie's tract on transatlantic competition bore the significant title *The American Invasion* (1902).

Faced by French determination to create a great trans-Saharan empire, the government moved to ring-fence areas where British businesses had established themselves. Since most British traders in West Africa operated from the coastal strip, Whitehall was left with the tricky task of deciding how far back the interior boundaries of, for example, Sierra Leone and Gambia should be pushed.[74] Chamberlain also provided vigorous support for George Goldie's Royal Niger Company, a chartered company that had built up commercial interests many hundreds of miles down the Niger River. But this stance nearly landed the British in war with France in 1898; fortunately an agreement was reached with the Quai d'Orsay on 14 June, only a few months before the more serious clash between the two countries at Fashoda. Well might Salisbury privately grumble over the folly of going to war over a 'malarious African desert' (as he put it in October 1897).

Chamberlain had a complicated personality: he could play 'insider' politics as well as anyone, but he also liked to give the impression of being an 'outsider', bringing to a stuffy Whitehall establishment the vigorous, no-nonsense approach of an experienced businessman. In practice, Chamberlain was not a particularly efficient or 'businesslike' administrator, but this did nothing to detract from the impression, which was sedulously fostered by his press admirers.[75] And he did at least raise the profile of the Colonial Office in Whitehall.

Chamberlain also used the public platform to enhance his own authority both at home and abroad, specializing in a truculent, aggressive verbal response to any foreign threat. Characteristic was his reaction to the Kruger Telegram,[76] when he privately called on Salisbury for 'what is called an "Act of

---

[74] This was done in 1889 and 1891, respectively.

[75] R. V. Kubicek, *The Administration of Imperialism: Joseph Chamberlain at the Colonial Office* (Durham, NC, 1969).

[76] See below.

Vigour" ... to soothe the wounded vanity of the nation', adding: 'It does not matter which of our numerous foes we defy, but we ought to defy someone.'[77] Through his vivid and sometimes brutal language ('You can't make an omelette without breaking eggs' was how he justified the cruelties involved in imperial expansion), Chamberlain turned Britain's relationship with the outer world into a dramatic pageant for the entertainment and edification of the wider public.

Often identified with the so-called 'New Imperialism' (an expansionist, 'constructive' creed, as opposed to Salisbury's more defensive strategy), Chamberlain thus helped to create a 'new diplomacy', which many Foreign Office clerks found threatening. Moreover, there was an underlying difference of approach to Great Power rivalries. Salisbury and his associates saw Russia as Britain's main challenger and Germany, in the main, as a source of help. But Chamberlain, after initially flirting with the possibility of a German alliance, eventually became obsessed with the 'German menace'.

This difference of approach can perhaps be seen as one between 'Victorians' and 'Edwardians'.[78] The former group, exemplified by Salisbury and his Permanent Secretary at the Foreign Office, 'Lamps' Sanderson, wanted to keep defence estimates as low as possible and thought that there was little possibility of Britain's enemies ganging up on her. By contrast, the 'Edwardians', in whose numbers Chamberlain can be placed (notwithstanding his biological age), reacted with alarm to events since 1892, which suggested to their feverish minds the dangers of 'isolation'. This led them to a much more interventionist stance on foreign policy and a growing impatience with what they took to be the supineness of Salisbury. True, the Prime Minister viewed his Colonial Secretary with a modicum of tolerance, while Chamberlain too much respected the Prime Minister to launch a direct challenge to his authority. But eventually out of their disagreements there emerged a political schism that was to split the Unionist Alliance asunder.

A precursor of the trouble to come occurred in 1898, with Salisbury's failure to stop the Russian seizure of Port Arthur and its establishment of a protectorate over Manchuria. This led to Salisbury being challenged within the Cabinet and to an outburst of wider disaffection fomented by several newspapers, including *The Times*. The agitation was spearheaded by a group of Conservative backbenchers, notably Robert Yerburgh, MP for Chester, a cheerleader of the 'China Party', who called for a more bulldoggish response to foreign aggression in an area important to British trade. Curzon, who was particularly

---

[77] Charmley, *Splendid Isolation?*, 239.
[78] K. Neilson, *Britain and the Last Tsar: British Policy and Russia 1894–1917* (Oxford, 1995), 48–50.

scathing of Salisbury's attempts to foster 'a mutual temper of apathetic tolerance' between Britain and Russia, lent his support to the critics.[79]

In poor health, Salisbury temporarily ceded the Foreign Office to his nephew Arthur Balfour, who shared Chamberlain's view that Britain needed formal allies in an increasingly hostile world. Moreover, Salisbury's partial eclipse provided the Colonial Secretary with an occasion to carve out a foreign policy of his own. In May 1898 Chamberlain made his abortive overture to the German Ambassador, Count Paul von Hatzfeldt. He also delivered a number of ill-judged speeches, culminating in an effusion at Leicester in November 1899, when he spoke of the possibility of a triple alliance between 'the Teutonic race and the two branches of the Anglo-Saxon race'.[80] These initiatives, however, simply demonstrated Chamberlain's diplomatic ineptitude, and by the end of 1898 Salisbury's reputation had been restored by his triumph at Fashoda, an event to which we must now turn.

7. EGYPT SECURED

In the Far East Salisbury may have had little to show for his efforts, yet he had been generally successful in surmounting the two main challenges to British rule in the 1890s: in the Nilotic valley and in Southern Africa. Gladstone's occupation of Egypt had left Britain a disastrous legacy. Initially Salisbury had hoped to get out of that country altogether. But his emissary, Drummond Wolff, failed in 1887 to negotiate a withdrawal from Egypt which would have allowed the right of 're-entry' should a future threat to the Canal materialize— an idea unacceptable to Turkey and vetoed by France. By the time that France had moderated its opposition in 1889, the British position had hardened.

This hardening owed something to the imperialist commitment of Evelyn Baring (later Lord Cromer), but much more to a re-evaluation of Britain's attitude towards the eastern Mediterranean as a whole. In 1892 the Admiralty told Salisbury that the Royal Navy could not force the Straits and stop the Russians seizing Constantinople—an issue over which, only a decade or so earlier, Britain had been ready to go to war. Indeed, in the middle of the crisis created by the Armenian Massacres perpetrated by the Turks in 1895, Salisbury, hoping to send the Fleet through the Dardanelles to coerce the Sultan and block any Russian advance, found himself overruled in Cabinet and categorically told by the Admiralty that this was not possible. It was this episode that largely underlay Salisbury's famous public declaration of January

[79] D. Steele, *Lord Salisbury: A Political Biography* (London, 1999), 333–42.

[80] J. A. S. Grenville, *Lord Salisbury's Foreign Policy: The Close of the Nineteenth Century* (London, 1964), 281–3.

1897, to the effect that Britain might have 'backed the wrong horse' at the Congress of Berlin (when he himself had been Foreign Secretary). The possible 'loss' of Constantinople, however, seemed to matter less now that Britain controlled Cairo and the Suez Canal—an area far more crucial to the securing of the sea routes to India. The switch from Constantinople to Cairo thus necessitated a long-term presence in Egypt.

This commitment, which ensured the estrangement of France, had further implications. Baring and other 'experts' were adamant that the power controlling the upper waters of the Nile could destroy Egypt's fragile economy by cutting off, flooding, or diverting the course of that great river. In fact such an enterprise was probably not technically feasible, and Salisbury, normally a deflator of alarmism, may not have taken its prospect entirely seriously.[81] But that no European state should control Sudan and Uganda soon became an important objective of British foreign policy.

In 1888, partly with a view to protecting British and Indian commercial interests on the Zanzibar coast, Salisbury gave William Mackinnon's 'Imperial British East Africa Company' a charter and authorized it to extend its activities inland into what is now Kenya. Two years later the Foreign Office neutralized the German threat in this area by negotiating an agreement under which Britain ceded the island of Heligoland to the Germans in return for German recognition of Britain's Zanzibar protectorate and her claims to a paramount position in the Sudan and Uganda.[82]

By December 1890 Mackinnon's agent, Frederick Lugard, reached the Bugandan Court at Kampala, where the Church Missionary Society had had a presence since 1887. However, not until 1894 was the British Protectorate of Uganda established. This step was taken by Salisbury's successor at the Foreign Office, Rosebery. Despite considerable resistance from within his own Cabinet and party, Rosebery, aided by a vociferous campaign from the Church Missionary Society, successfully presented his policy as one that aimed to save missionary lives[83] and to stop the revival of the slave trade—even though its real purpose was to secure access to the headwaters of the Nile.

In March 1895 Edward Grey, the Liberal Under-Secretary at the Foreign Office, delivered a formal declaration in the Commons that Britain would regard as an 'unfriendly act' any attempt by the French to send an expedition

---

[81] D. R. Gillard, 'Salisbury's African Policy and Heligoland Offer of 1890', *English Historical Review*, 75 (1960), 631–53; J. Darwin, 'Imperialism and the Victorians: The Dynamics of Territorial Expansion', *English Historical Review*, 112 (1997), 636–8.

[82] By also recognizing Germany's rule in Tanganyika (now Tanzania) this Anglo-German agreement scuppered Rhodes' pipe-dream of a Cape-to-Cairo link, which Salisbury had never taken seriously.

[83] Bishop Hannington had been murdered in 1885, in a complex feud between Protestant missionaries, Catholic missionaries, and Muslims, aimed at controlling the Bugandan court.

to the Upper Nile. But Paris still refused to recognize that the Sudan, under the control of the dervishes ever since the failure of General Gordon's disastrous expedition in 1884–5, was a British sphere of influence.

Ignoring Grey's warning, the French army officer, Commandant Jean Baptiste Marchand led his intrepid force down the Congo towards the source of the Nile. Even before he could do so, the British government (with Salisbury now back at the Foreign Office) had begun the piecemeal reconquest of the Sudan. In 1896 General Kitchener (Sirdar, i.e. commander, of the Egyptian Army) moved south toward Dongola, at the head of an army of 8,200 British and 17,600 Egyptian and Sudanese troops, determined to achieve what had proved beyond Gordon's powers, the destruction of the dervishes (at the same time taking pressure off the Italians, who had recently suffered a disastrous defeat at the hands of Abyssinian forces at Adowa). The decisive engagement occurred at Omdurman, near Khartoum, on 2 September 1898, following which the dervish chief, the Khalifa, was killed.

The British victory was marred by the savagery of Kitchener's methods: 11,000 spear-wielding dervishes, many of them already wounded, were slaughtered by the deadly machine-gun,[84] and the Mahdi's tomb was destroyed, its disinterred remains being scattered about the ground—Kitchener briefly took possession of the Mahdi's skull and there was initially talk of converting it into an inkstand or a drinking cup. Such behaviour upset a young army officer called Winston Churchill, and later (in February 1899) it created uproar in London, where *The Times*, the Queen, and a number of Radical MPs expressed disquiet. Kitchener justified his brutality with talk of military necessity, but it seems equally likely that, by so decisively avenging Gordon's death, the British forces, in a cathartic act, were wiping out memories of an earlier painful humiliation. A grateful government rewarded Kitchener with a peerage, the Order of the Bath, and a grant of £30,000.

Later in the same month the long-awaited encounter between Kitchener's victorious army moving south and Marchand's expeditionary force moving north-east took place 400 miles upriver, at Fashoda. The two officers conducted an amicable exchange while their governments back home decided whether it was to be peace or war, with the fleets of both countries fully mobilized. It was French nerve which eventually cracked in February 1899, partly because, as the French Foreign Minister Delcassé acknowledged, 'we have nothing but arguments, and they have got troops', and partly because France belatedly recognized that their Russian allies had no intention of helping them in Africa. Salisbury, already under attack for his allegedly

---

[84] Compared with only 48 killed on the Anglo-Egyptian side. The Dervishes did, however, possess some field artillery (R. Kubicek, 'British Expansion, Empire, and Technological Change', in Porter (ed.), *British Empire: Nineteenth Century*, 265).

pusillanimous behaviour in the Far East, restored his reputation with a relieved Conservative Party and a delirious public opinion, whipped up by a provocatively belligerent press. The Sudan became a Protectorate, run by an Anglo-Egyptian condominium, and Egypt was henceforward safe from what was surely a non-existent threat.

8. PRELUDE TO THE SECOND BOER WAR

Another humiliation shortly to be avenged was the 1881 defeat at the hands of the Boers at Majuba Hill. This had been followed by the Pretoria Convention, which recognized the Transvaal as a self-governing state under the 'suzerainty' of the British Crown, whatever that might mean. The later London Convention of 1884, by omitting the word 'suzerainty', left it even more unclear what powers Britain retained over the Boer Republics, save that of ratifying or denying authorization of treaties with foreign governments.

This might not have mattered, but for the discovery of gold near Johannesburg in 1886 which, by changing the balance of power between Britons and Boers in Southern Africa, threatened to weaken Britain strategically in that crucial area. This posed problems for British businessmen and officialdom alike, since the gold reef was situated in the Afrikaner state of the Transvaal, whose President, Paul Kruger, used his new-found wealth to strengthen his military forces and to woo friendly European powers.

Into the Transvaal flowed prospectors, mining engineers, and financiers from all over the world, some German but most of them British.[85] By the mid-1890s these 'Uitlanders' numbered some 80,000. Also involved was Cecil Rhodes, who, not content with controlling the diamond production of the entire world through De Beers Company of Kimberley, had also (in 1887) established Consolidated Goldfields of South Africa, another powerful cartel.

Kruger's denial of voting rights to these immigrants, coupled with irksome (some said oppressive) forms of taxation, such as the state monopoly on dynamite, supplied the British government with a pretext for interference in the Transvaal, whose dangerously independent behaviour it was anxious to stop. London was particularly angry when Kruger began rerouting goods along the Delagoa Railway instead of sending them through the Cape, in a bid to free himself from British control (the 'Drifts Crisis')—though one of its consequences was to undermine the prosperity of that British colony, leading in the process to the estrangement of the Cape Dutch from their ethnic compatriots in the north.

---

[85] Between 60% and 80% of investment in the goldfields, too, was British (I. R. Smith, *The Origins of the South African War 1899–1902* (Harlow, 1992), 405).

It remains a moot point whether, left to their own devices, the capitalists of the Rand would have found a way of protecting their interests that did not involve an alliance with the British state.[86] But Rhodes was pursuing his own idiosyncratic project for controlling Afrikanerdom. Through the British South Africa (BSA) Company, first chartered in 1889, his Pioneers moved north of the Limpopo in 1890 into Mashonaland, lured by the prospect of gold which, under the British flag, would, he hoped, then be used to cancel out Kruger's advantage. This excursion led to the eventual annexation of these territories (later known as Southern Rhodesia), a mixture of guile and violence being used to secure the consent of the Matabele (Ndbele) and Mashona (Shona) tribes who lived there. In 1894, under the cover of the Anglo-Portuguese Convention of August 1890, Rhodes then pushed north of the Zambesi, where he carved out a new sphere for his company in what later became Northern Rhodesia—though, partly because of missionary objections, he failed in his original plan to control Nyasaland, which instead became a British Protectorate.

In 1895 the colonization of 'Zambesia' was further aided by the British government's annexation of Northern Bechuanaland (which became a High Commission Territory) and by the conferral on the Chartered Company of a strip of land, which included Mafeking, enabling Rhodes to link the Cape with these new territories. But no new Eldorado was discovered north of the Limpopo. Indeed, the shareholders of the British South Africa Company never drew a dividend until the 1920s.

Recognition of this failure encouraged Rhodes, Cape Prime Minister since 1890, to try to organize a coup in Johannesburg (where his brother Frank was one of the rebels), aided from outside by the forces of the BSA Company, led by its administrator, Dr Leander Starr Jameson—using the Bechuanaland strip as a jumping-off place. Chamberlain probably gave a guarded assent to these plans on the assumption that the raiders would only cross into the Transvaal following a 'spontaneous' rising of the Uitlander population.[87]

But the internal insurrection never occurred, and Jameson's 500 police were quickly rounded up by Kruger's army when they made their flagrantly illegal incursion in December 1895. Jameson was sentenced to a brief spell of imprisonment (which he served in Britain, having been handed over to the Crown), and Rhodes, momentarily disgraced, resigned the Cape premiership. The British government was covered in international obloquy, and Chamberlain,

[86] A. N. Porter, *The Origins of South African War: Joseph Chamberlain and the Diplomacy of Imperialism, 1895–99* (Manchester, 1980), 186–7 and elsewhere.

[87] Chamberlain's rashness contrasts with the behaviour of his two precessors, Knutsford and Ripon, who had both vetoed similar projects from Loch—in 1891 and 1894, respectively (J. Benyon, ' "Intermediate" Imperialism and the Test of Empire: Milner's "excentric" High Commission in South Africa', in D. Lowry (ed.), *The South African War Reappraised* (Manchester, 2000), 93.

who quickly disassociated himself from what had happened, was lucky that his career survived a parliamentary inquiry—thanks largely to his old friend Harcourt, now the Liberal Leader, who, though a member of the inquiry, gave him the benefit of the doubt by laying the entire blame on Rhodes, who accepted this as a necessary price to pay for the retention of his Charter.

The congratulatory telegram (the 'Kruger Telegram') which the German Kaiser sent Kruger in January 1896 also helped save Chamberlain, because it deflected attention from the criminal behaviour of the raiders and instead whipped up indignation over foreign interference in a recognized British sphere of influence—for the first, but not for the last, time 'patriotic' crowds attacked German shops. The imperialist party at home and in Southern Africa fêted Jameson as a hero, while the Kaiser's démarche strengthened British determination to lance the boil of Krugerdom.

In 1896, following the failure of the Jameson Raid, the BSA Company faced an uprising of the warlike Ndbele, which it savagely repressed. More serious for London in the long run was the way in which the Raid polarized the two white races in South Africa. In its wake the Boer Republics entered a defensive and offensive alliance, while the large Afrikaner population within Cape Colony, which had previously supported Rhodes's ministry, now grew increasingly suspicious of British designs.

With the star of the 'Colossus' in eclipse, the British government became drawn more directly into South African affairs. In 1898 it sent out as British High Commissioner a young Board of Inland Revenue official, Alfred Milner, who had earlier worked with Cromer at Cairo. Through the newly formed 'South African League', Milner worked to mobilize pro-British elements throughout Southern Africa, meanwhile sedulously using his many London contacts[88] to remove 'misapprehensions' at home about the gravity of the situation he faced. Milner's forward policy led to the deadlocked Bloemfontein Conference of June 1899.[89] Chamberlain had initially hoped that these talks would succeed, but Milner acted on the opposite assumption. Perhaps by the summer of 1899 neither of the white races in South Africa seriously contemplated compromise: all that mattered was the choice of an appropriate occasion to launch the long-awaited war.

The South African crisis provided a new dimension to the debate on British imperialism. In many other parts of the globe imperial expansion had been preceded by missionary endeavours. The relationship between missionaries and imperial officialdom in Africa and Asia was, admittedly, often a strained one. The missionaries incurred some mistrust for being well-meaning

[88] Notably such pressmen as as E. T. Cook and Edmund Garrett (ibid. 98).

[89] Intended to resolve the constitutional problem posed by the disfranchised Uitlanders, who after 1890 had to reside for 14 years before they could apply for naturalization.

busybodies, liable to destabilize the local societies within which they worked, thereby creating problems for others[90]—as, for example, when their zealotry contributed to the sanguinary Boxer Rising in China in 1900, during which the European legations in Beijing were besieged and many Europeans lost their lives.[91]

On the other hand, some missionary societies (the Church Missionary Society, for example) were advocates of imperial expansion, if only to forestall colonization by French Catholics. In any case, the British government usually felt obliged to come to the assistance of missionaries when their lives had become endangered. Nor were they above using this as a pretext for extending imperial rule (as in Uganda in 1891–4), when they favoured such a move for quite different reasons. But in the south of the continent imperialist apologists could not, as they had done in East Africa, mount a moral justification of British expansion in terms of extirpating Arab slavery or protecting the missionaries in their civilizing work.

Critics of imperialism had all along identified greed as a motivating force in British overseas expansion. Policy in Egypt, for example, could readily be ascribed to the pressure of the bondholders, anxious about their investments and eager to 'use' government to pull their chestnuts out of the fire. The controversial chartered companies, whose activities dangerously blurred the distinction between commerce and government, also encouraged conspiratorial interpretations, encapsulated in the slogan 'Stock Exchange Imperialism'. But nothing could have dramatized the role of economic interest groups in the formulation of governmental policy more vividly than the South African conflict.

Official propaganda, with some plausibility, sought to counter such hostility by representing the quarrel with Kruger as one over the extension of political rights to 'free-born' Englishmen. 'We seek no gold fields. We seek no terri-tory,' Salisbury publicly declared: 'What we desire is equal rights for men of all races, and security for our fellow subjects and for the Empire.' Kruger's obstinacy in denying his long-term residents the vote was understandable— he saw himself as engaged in the defence of his people's traditional way of life, threatened by foreign subversion. But his policy went some way in helping London to assume the moral high ground in the escalating conflict.

At the same time, it was difficult to present the Uitlanders and their financial backers as objects of sympathy or as plausible agents of the state. Some of their most prominent members were not even British by birth: Alfred Beit and

[90] See A. Porter, 'Religion, Missionary Enthusiasm, and Empire', in Porter (ed.), *British Empire: Nineteenth Century*, 222–46.

[91] In August 1900 an international force occupied Beijing, but not before 135 Protestant missionaries and 53 of their children had been killed, along with an even larger number of Catholic converts.

Julius Wernher, for example, were German-born. Their ranks also included self-made adventurers, such as the self-styled 'Barney Barnato', an East End Jew who committed suicide in 1896. Moreover, the wealthiest of the 'Randlords' had built up their empires by monopoly practices in Kimberley—Rhodes, for example, had established the dominance of De Beers by eliminating all competition and establishing what was effectively a cartel.

Nor did the government's claim to be wholly disinterested carry conviction. Sir Hercules Robinson, the former Governor of the Cape, had been a close friend of Rhodes and a director of his diamond company—indeed, he held shares in several of Rhodes's companies when helping him secure his charter. Lord Rosebery, an ardent imperialist, was another of Rhodes's friends; through his wife, Hannah Rothschild, he was also in close contact with Lord Rothschild, who, before the two men fell out in 1891, had been one of Rhodes's most important backers.[92]

True, anti-imperialist critics tended to overlook the commercial rivalries and differences of political perspective which prevented the mineowners from presenting a united front—differences which Kruger well knew how to exploit. British ministers were certainly not being manipulated by the mining companies in any simple sense. Moreover, Rhodes, who had never been well-disposed to the 'Imperial Factor', was positively eager, for self-interested reasons, to avoid the major war which Milner's diplomacy rendered likely. Yet, despite these cross-currents, it was all too easy to jump to the conclusion that British policy in South Africa was, if only indirectly, being propelled forward by a particularly unscrupulous kind of bucaneering capitalist, working to his own private agenda. Such a view was even held by Sir William Butler, the Irish-born Commander-in-Chief of British forces in South Africa.

Recognizing that this was the impression being conveyed, several senior Conservative ministers warned of the probable unpopularity of a war in South Africa in which Kruger did not unequivocally feature as the aggressor. Even Chamberlain felt some disquiet at Milner's 'forward' policy: engaging in war with the Transvaal, 'unless upon the utmost and clearest provocation', he warned in 1898, 'would be entirely unpopular in the country'. It was therefore fortunate, from the British standpoint, that Kruger should have issued his ultimatum to the British before the British could launch theirs, and then compounded the offence by summarily invading British territory.

Salisbury viewed the unfolding drama with mixed feelings. Having earlier expressed reservations about Milner's obduracy at the Bloemfontein Conference, he now wrinkled up his nose over the excesses of an intoxicated jingoistic public, and in a letter to Lord Lansdowne of 30 August 1899 wrote despondently of having to make a great military effort for 'people whom we despise and for territory which will bring no profit and no power to England'.

But this famous phrase is misleading if it is used to exonerate him from responsibility for the resulting war. For, at several crucial junctions, Salisbury threw his weight behind those seeking an unconditional victory in South Africa. He did so because, in the last analysis, he entirely shared Milner's view that what was at stake was a struggle to make sure that 'we not the Dutch are Boss'.[93] As early as March 1896 Chamberlain's junior minister, Lord Selborne, had stressed, in an important memorandum, that Britain would have to intervene directly to control the Transvaal because it was the natural commercial centre of the entire South African region. Salisbury essentially agreed with this view. It was also the position fervently, even hysterically, embraced by many Unionist politicians, at all levels, by the ultra-patriotic Primrose League,[94] by *The Times*, and by the Imperial South African Association, founded in 1896 'to uphold British supremacy and to promote the interests of British subjects in South Africa'—the latter a body manipulated by Milner through George Wyndham, Under-Secretary to the War Office, who was busily priming the London press.[95] In short, by 1899 South Africa was no longer seen primarily as a staging post on the long sea route to India: instead, the dispute over who controlled that area had escalated into a deadly fight for racial supremacy.

[93] His words, as cited in Selborne's letter to Milner, 27 July 1899 (Roberts, *Salisbury*, 725).

[94] For examples of the propaganda being put out both by Central Office and by the National Union, see Shannon, *Age of Salisbury*, 480–1. On the Primrose League, M. Pugh, *The Tories and the People 1880–1935* (Oxford, 1985), 87–93.

[95] This body, which also had the support of Rider Haggard, Rudyard Kipling, and Alfred Harmsworth, held 406 meetings and issued half-a-million pamphlets in 1899 alone (A. Davey, *The British Pro-Boers 1877–1902* (Tafelberg, 1978), 71).

CHAPTER 9

The Boer War, 1899–1902

I. PYRRHIC VICTORY?

The British entered the war in October 1899 determined to avenge Majuba, just as they had recently avenged Gordon's death. They did so in a spirit of blithe confidence. Moberley Bell, the manager of *The Times*, privately predicted that 'about the 15 December we shall have in South Africa a nice little Army & all the materials for a respectable war except the enemy'.[1] Few foresaw that the forces of two small pastoral republics, with a combined white population smaller than London's, would hold the British Empire at bay for over two and a half years, and that no fewer than 400,000 British troops would have to be put into the field before victory was secured.[2]

Unfortunately for the British, Kruger had used the period since the Jameson Raid to build up an impressive arsenal, as a result of which the Boer Commandos, equipped with modern Mauser 0.276 rifles, Krupp cannons, and French Creusot siege-guns, plus more ammunition than they immediately needed, were in many ways better armed than their British adversaries.[3]

Moreover, ministers and soldiers alike underestimated to a ridiculous degree the fighting capacity of the enemy, ignoring warning voices, such as that of Sir William Butler, the recent Commander-in-Chief in South Africa, whom Milner despised as a pro-Boer. Once again, as between 1879 and 1882, 'these hard-bitten farmers with their ancient theology and their inconveniently modern rifles', as Conan Doyle put it,[4] turned out to possess great equestrian skills and to be superb marksmen, able to pick off British officers at 1,200 yards or more. Their greater familiarity with the terrain over which the fighting took place also made them mobile and flexible in their tactics, compared with their ponderous adversaries. Most important of all, Boer morale was sustained by

---

[1] Moberley Bell to L. S. Amery, Oct. 1899.

[2] For a narrative of the war, I am particularly indebted to T. Pakenham, *The Boer War* (1979; 1992 edn.).

[3] Reserves were kept in hand for distribution to the Cape Dutch, should the latter rise in their support.

[4] A. Conan Doyle, *The Great Boer War* (London, 1901), 1.

the thought that they were engaged in a life-and-death struggle to preserve their distinctive culture.

When Kruger sent his commandos into the northern Cape and Natal on 12 October, he did at least help the British government by rallying public opinion behind the Union Jack. Yet his assault also gave him an immediate *military* advantage. True, a fortnight before the Boer attack Sir George White, heading a contingent of 10,000 men from the Indian Army, had been shipped over to Natal—arriving on 7 October, only in the nick of time to prevent the enemy marching unimpeded on its capital, Durban. Nevertheless, the Boers, who on mobilization had between 32,000 and 35,000 men, still decisively outnumbered the British, who could only put some 13,000 troops near the front line facing Joubert's 21,000 invaders: the 1st Army Corps, earmarked for service in South Africa in an emergency, did not set sail from Southampton until 14 October.

Under political pressure from Natal's Governor, Hely-Hutchinson, White decided against falling back on a defensive line south of the Tugela river, and sited his headquarters in the town of Ladysmith, which had unwisely been made the army's main base. Major-General Penn-Symons, in charge of the Natal Field Force, had already divided his men—basing some in Ladysmith, while he personally led an advance brigade to Glencoe, in Natal's exposed northern triangle.

Before the army corps could arrive from England, the Boers got in a series of telling blows. Penn-Symons was mortally wounded at the battle of Talana (20 October), and the Boers quickly overran Glencoe and Dundee, forcing the rest of the Natal Field Force to fall back on Ladysmith. The success of General French's cavalry at Elandslaagte (21 October) provided a brief respite, but an isolated column under Lieutenant-Colonel Carleton surrendered at Nicholson's Nek on 31 October, on the very day that White himself was losing the battle of Modderspruit (Mournful Monday). By the end of the month White and his force of some 15,000 men were trapped in Ladysmith.

Meanwhile, some 300 miles to the west, Boer forces had besieged the diamond town of Kimberley, imprisoned within which was none other than Cecil Rhodes. Another symbolic triumph for the Boers was their investiture of Mafeking, from which Jameson's raiders had set out three years earlier. Robert Baden-Powell, to whom Wolseley had given impractical orders to raise a force of irregulars to harass the Transvaal on its western flank, found himself faced, at least initially, by far superior numbers, and could do nothing but dig in with his Bechuanaland police and assorted 'loafers' until outside help arrived. Since the Boers had cut Mafeking's railway link to the south, he was likely to be in for a long wait.[5]

---

[5] T. Jeal, *Baden-Powell* (London, 1989), Ch. 6.

The British government appointed Wolseley's protégé, Redvers Buller, as Commander-in-Chief of British forces in South Africa. He arrived in Cape Town on the last day of October, followed on 18 November by the first contingent of a full army corps, plus colonial volunteers. The original War Office plan had been to advance along the central railway line from De Aar to Bloemfontein, capital of the Orange Free State, before striking into the heart of the Transvaal. Political circumstances, however, dictated a last-minute change of plan.

For in November the Boers had crossed in force into the Cape, which was defended by only 7,000 or so British troops. This threw Milner into a panic. Moreover, since the electoral defeat of Rhodes's party in 1898, the Cape ministry had been headed by the Afrikaner politician William Schreiner, whose administration adopted a neutral stance on the war. Even when some 10,000 Cape Dutch eventually joined the invading commandos, it was only with great difficulty that Milner secured permission to declare martial law in the most disaffected districts—and then not until late December 1900.

This was not the only problem facing the British authorities. Rhodes called hysterically for his own release and threatened to hand Kimberley over to the enemy unless the siege were quickly raised. Finally, weighing most heavily of all on Buller's agitated mind was a fear that White, marooned in Ladysmith, might be on the point of surrender.

Understanding clearly the likely political and domestic repercussions of abandoning White to his fate, and the symbolic importance of not allowing Kimberley (and Rhodes) to fall into Boer hands, Buller took the fateful step of splitting his army into three. He himself set off to rescue White in Natal. Lieutenant-General Methuen led the 20,000 men of the 1st Division along the route of the western railway towards Kimberley. And in the central theatre General Gatacre advanced to secure the Northern Cape.

All three forces met with sharp rebuffs. Methuen, after a couple of small but costly victories (Belmont and Graspan), walked into the trap set for him by de la Rey at the Modder river (28 November), where the Boers abandoned the kopjes and dug defensive positions into the mud, catching the British totally by surprise. The Boers then retreated to Magersfontein, where Methuen launched against them an ill-judged attack, following a night march over unreconnoitred ground (11 December). In the resulting carnage General Wauchope was killed, and his Highlanders, subjected to an ordeal which included being accidentally shelled by their own artillery, eventually took flight; 947 British soldiers were killed in this engagement.

The previous day (10 December) Gatacre, after another botched night march, had come to grief at Stormberg Junction, where 100 of his soldiers were killed and nearly 600 captured. This was a relatively minor setback. But on 15 December Buller suffered a major defeat when he crossed the Tugela and attacked the Boers at Colenso. So clumsily prepared was the attack that, despite enjoying a three-to-one advantage, Buller's men sustained some 1,139 casualties before being driven back across the river. The most mortifying aspect of Colenso was that, through a characteristic communications breakdown, the artillery had managed to get *ahead* of the infantry; as a result a whole battery was lost, despite heroic last-minute efforts to save the guns—which led to the award of seven Victoria Crosses.

Thus, in the space of a single week in December 1899—'Black Week', as it came to be known—the British experienced three defeats. At home the public, perhaps believing its own rhetoric about British invincibility, reacted with anger and disbelief. There had already been dismay over the large numbers of troops who had surrendered—hardened war correspondents viewed with incredulity the spectacle of Tommy Atkins's loss of nerve following Nicholson's Nek. Coming hard upon these humiliations, 'Black Week' was almost more than patriots could bear. To Cecil Rice, on diplomatic duty in Persia, life was 'a prolonged nightmare': 'the daily telegrams are a horror,' he confided to a friend, 'and waking in the morning or late at night is a terrible thing; one lies alone with a living and growing fear staring one in the face.'[6]

In the War Office all was consternation. Ministers could scarcely believe their eyes when they read a defeatist telegram dispatched by Buller in the aftermath of Colenso, which seemed to be calling on White to fire off his remaining ammunition and surrender at an opportune moment. Balfour and Lansdowne suppressed this telegram and, to Wolseley's dismay, promptly replaced Buller as overall commander with the 'Indian', General Roberts, who had been busily intriguing to secure this post—though his satisfaction, at this moment of triumph, was marred by news that his only son, Fred, had been one of those killed trying to save the guns at Colenso.

To meet the emergency, there came forward volunteers not just from British South Africa (numbering about 30,000), but from all over the white colonies of settlement—a remarkable display of imperial solidarity. By the end of the war 16,310 Australians, 6,051 Canadians, and 6,416 New Zealanders had seen service there. In addition several Indian princes made generous gifts, though Chamberlain turned down, on racial grounds, an offer of guides from the Malay States and of Hausa warriors from Nigeria, since this was supposed to be a 'white man's war'.[7]

[6] Spring-Rice to Chirol, 20 Dec. 1899, in S. Gwynn (ed.), *The Letters and Friendships of Sir Cecil Spring-Rice*, vol. i (London, 1929), 303–4.

[7] K. Jeffery, 'Kruger's Farmers, Strathcona's Horse, Sir George Clarke's Camels and the Kaiser's Battleships: The Impact of the South African War on Imperial Defence', in D. Lowry (ed.), *The South African War Reappraised* (Manchester, 2000), 188–9.

From within the United Kingdom itself men rushed to the colours. Among the most famous detachments was the City Imperial Yeomanry, which included thirty-four MPs and peers; there were also private companies, such as the Duke of Cambridge's Own, which consisted largely of 'gentlemen-rankers'. Public enthusiasm particularly centred on the City Imperial Volunteers (CIV), which was drawn from the Inns of Court, the Bank of England, and institutions such as Lloyd's.

Roberts arrived in Cape Town on 10 January 1900, bringing with him Kitchener as his Chief of Staff, to head a Field Force of over 40,000 men and 108 guns. Though Roberts, too, momentarily succumbed to the prevailing mood of pessimism, sending off a telegram every bit as defeatist as the one which had got Buller demoted, his spirits soon revived, and on 11 January he set off on a swift flanking march designed to take him to Bloemfontein, via Kimberley.

Buller was left to 'peg away' in Natal. With fresh reinforcements, he recrossed the Tugela in mid-January, only for part of his force, under General Warren, to blunder into the disaster of Spion Kop (24 January). Although British troops successfully stormed this hill, it turned out to be a death-trap, surrounded by higher eminences. After heavy shelling and bitter hand-to-hand fighting, the British retreated, having sustained nearly 1,100 casualties, 243 of them killed. Widely publicized photographs of dead soldiers strewn across the hill's ridge brought home to the British public, as nothing previously had done, the reality of modern war. Nor was this the end of Buller's agony, since Spion Kop was followed by another failed attack, this time at Vaalkrantz (5 February). Newspapers at home became really angry, more so than in the aftermath of 'Black Week', and what had once been thought of as a 'tea-time war' was now presented as an 'absent-minded war',[8] a terrible display of military incompetence.

Meanwhile to the west Roberts and Kitchener were embarking upon a bold gamble. To secure greater mobility, they doubled the number of their mounted infantry but skimped on the supplies needed to sustain them. Indeed, Kitchener's over-centralized transport arrangements soon led to muddle and, subsequently, to a serious shortage of supplies—a problem aggravated by the loss of the ox-wagon convoy containing medicines, bandages, and food following the Boer attack at Waterval Drift (15 February). This setback proved to be serious, but it was widely overlooked when later on the same day the exciting news came through that John French's cavalry had made a successful dash to relieve Kimberley.

Three days later Roberts and Kitchener trapped General Piet Cronje into abandoning the normal Boer tactics of harassment and flight for a full-scale

[8] The title of Captain Elliot Cairnes's 1900 tract.

stand-up fight at Paardeburg, north-west of Bloemfontein. On 27 February Cronje surrendered, along with 4,000 of his men. The following day Buller finally forced his way through into Ladysmith.

It was now that the shortage of fodder and other supplies for Roberts's Field Force began to take its toll. At Poplar Grove (7 March) French's horses were too exhausted to give chase to the retreating enemy, so missing the chance to capture Kruger. And when Roberts eventually occupied Bloemfontein on 13 March, he decided to rest his troops and reorganize his overstretched transport system (there was a chronic shortage of suitable remounts). Here the British suffered the horrors of an outbreak of enteric fever (typhoid), partly caused by troops drinking from the Modder river, heavily polluted by the corpses of men and horses deposited there by the recent battle. Almost 1,000 troops died in the epidemic, with which the Hospital Field Service was quite unable to cope. On 28 April William Burdett-Coutts described for *The Times* the terrible scenes being enacted before his eyes in language reminiscent of the dispatches which his great predecessor, William Russell, had sent in the winter of 1854-5, when British troops had rotted before Sebastopol.

A brighter note was sounded with the relief of Mafeking on 17 May, an event which a success-starved home population greeted with euphoria, turning its defender, Baden-Powell, into a national hero—and not entirely without reason, since 'B-P' had tied down some 7,700 Boers, almost a fifth of their total forces, at a crucial period in the war when Cape Colony south of Kimberley was almost denuded of defenders.[9]

Meanwhile in late April, the typhoid epidemic over, Roberts had resumed his advance. Meeting little opposition, he entered Johannesburg on 31 May and Pretoria on 5 June. Both towns were empty of enemy troops because the British authorities, in the mistaken belief that otherwise the Rand goldmines would be blown up, had been bluffed into allowing the Boers to withdraw their forces unmolested.

This was a fatal error. True, the British effected a quick conquest of all the major towns of the two Afrikaner republics before reaching Transvaal's eastern border at Komati Poort on 21 July, so cutting the Boers off from the outside world. But de Steyn, President of the Orange Free State, was intent on continued resistance and, ominously, a substantial number of enemy troops still operated behind British lines. Christiaan De Wet's earlier ambush of Major-General Broadwood at Sannah's Post (31 March) should have warned the British that the war was not yet won.

---

[9] The Boers arguably failed to press home their early advantage because the democratic nature of their military structures precluded the pursuit of bold, resolute policies: as a result, they tended to waste men investing towns which had symbolic significance for them, such as Kimberley and Mafeking, to the neglect of long-term strategic goals.

The warning was not taken. Balfour spoke blithely of 'the war now happily drawing to a close', and Chamberlain was equally sanguine. Parliament was dissolved, and the Unionists won the 'Khaki Election', held between 28 September and 24 October. Many of the troops returned home to a hero's welcome, the CIV triumphantly parading through London on 29 October. A month later, after handing over to Kitchener, Roberts set sail for England, where a grateful legislature voted him the sum of £100,000. All that remained to be done in South Africa, it seemed, was to mop up small pockets of resistance.

But as Buller realized, this was to misunderstand the enemy's psychology: the Boers cared little about the loss of their administrative and political centres, since their patriotism centred on their attachment to the countryside and to their farms. Milner's insistence on unconditional surrender merely added to the determination of the 'bitter enders' to keep up the apparently hopeless fight.

Faced by guerilla resistance, the British army deported its prisoners-of-war to St Helena, Bermuda, Ceylon, and India; Cape 'rebels', too, were harshly dealt with, some being shot. Before leaving South Africa Roberts had also initiated the policy, carried on by Kitchener, of burning farms thought to be harbouring or giving support to the commandos. Boer women and children made homeless in this way were herded into specially constructed 'concentration camps', some forty in all. Even in military terms this may have been a mistake since, although in the long run it perhaps undermined the commandos' will to resist, in the short run it freed them from assuming responsibility for their families and thus had the very opposite effect.

Poorly sited and provided with grossly inadequate hygienic facilities, these camps were soon swept by deaths caused by malnutrition and diseases such as measles, to which the Boers, leading healthy but isolated lives, had built up no resistance. Their children were, of course, particularly vulnerable. Emily Hobhouse, the sister of Leonard Hobhouse, a leader-writer for the *Manchester Guardian*, visited the camps between December 1900 and May 1901, and her exposure of the catastrophe received wide publicity. Milner privately blamed the situation on gross military mismanagement, but so rattled was he by Emily Hobhouse's activities that he had her arrested and deported when she attempted to return to South Africa in October 1901.

The War Office, aware of the damage being done to its reputation, commissioned Mrs Fawcett, heading a 'Ladies' Committee', to oversee conditions in the camps, and a number of prominent Englishwomen went out to South Africa on various philanthropic missions—among them Mary Kingsley, who died nursing Boer prisoners at Simonstown. But the alienation of the Afrikaner peoples was total. And no wonder, since, by the war's close, at least 20,000 deaths had occurred in the camps, about a quarter of all the women and children from the two former republics.[10] (No reliable statistics exist of the mortality among Africans, some 115,000 of whom had also been taken into 'protective custody'.)[11]

Kitchener was not entirely blind to the consequences of his actions. A prolongation of the war, he warned Milner, was futile, since in the end the two white races would have to share the running of the country. Indeed, as early as February 1901 Kitchener had informally met General Louis Botha in Middelburg to discuss possible peace terms. But Milner and the British Cabinet would countenance no concessions, and the fighting went remorselessly on.

Denied the compromise peace that he favoured, Kitchener pursued his 'scorched earth policy'—a policy which disgusted many of his own soldiers and weakened the public's support for the war effort, once it realized the methods that were being employed. An exasperated Milner pressed hard for an alternative strategy. He wanted to protect the British-occupied areas behind a defensive screen manned primarily by the South African Constabulary, and to start his programme of reconstruction within these enclaves—from which flying columns could pursue the commandos still on the run until the latter gave up hope and surrendered. Milner's plan would have allowed for a speedy reduction in the number of British troops in South Africa—an attractive proposition in the eyes of those ministers who shared Hicks Beach's dismay at the war's escalating costs. But Kitchener comprehensively triumphed over Milner in what became an increasingly bitter power struggle. The bottom line was that, after dismissing and demoting prominent members of the Wolseley circle, the Cabinet could not possibly sack its imperious Commander-in-Chief, for whom there was no plausible replacement.[12]

The war, in its final stages, lacked all shape and purpose. The British built blockhouses, constructed initially from stone, later from corrugated iron, linking them together with barbed wire in a defensive line which eventually stretched over 4,000 miles. From these strongholds the British conducted a series of 'drives' or 'sweeps' across the veldt in an attempt to trap and isolate

[10] Inevitably, the statistical estimates vary: E. M. Spiers, *The Late Victorian Army, 1868–1902* (Manchester, 1992), 311, gives a death-toll of 28,000, of whom 22,000 were under 16 years of age.

[11] Perhaps almost as many blacks as Boers died—though obviously not in the same proportions. Baden-Powell's treatment of the black population during the siege of Mafeking also continues to excite controversy.

[12] K. T. Surridge, *Managing the South African War, 1899–1902: Politicians v. Generals* (Woodbridge, 1998), chs. 6–7. On his return to London, Roberts replaced the angry Wolseley, while in October 1901 Buller was sacked from his Aldershot command for a foolish speech trying to explain away his notorious telegram to White—a speech mercilessly mocked by Hector Munro ('Saki'), in *The Westminster Alice* (which appeared in the *Westminster Gazette* between 25 July 1900 and 24 Jan. 1902).

the maddeningly elusive enemy. The British deployed the latest technological inventions: they maintained communications through the telephone and the cable, while powerful electrical illumination protected threatened buildings and installations. Despite all this, the commando leaders still retained the capacity not only to harass the British forces by ambushes, the derailing of trains, and such like, but even to launch the occasional attack deep into the heartland of British South Africa—as when Jan Smuts made a spectacular foray into the southern Cape in September 1901.

Finally the 'bitter enders' realized the futility of further resistance.[13] At Vereeniging, on 31 May 1902, the Boers surrendered and formally recognized the annexation to the British Crown of their two republics, first proclaimed in the summer of 1900. But to Milner's fury, Kitchener, with Chamberlain's backing, negotiated with the Boer commandos, thereby legitimizing their claims to be the political representatives of the Afrikaner peoples.[14]

In fact many, perhaps most, army officers—notably Kitchener's Chief of Staff, Ian Hamilton—had developed a grudging respect for their adversaries, and Kitchener himself was soon publicly calling the Boers 'a virile race and an asset of considerable importance to the British Empire'.[15] Indeed, the army leadership wanted to preserve the Boers as a counterbalance to what one officer contemptuously called the 'Johannesburg crew', with its 'money grubbing German Jews'. An embittered Milner realized that the British, for all their sacrifices, had not really secured their total predominance in South Africa.

And these sacrifices were very heavy. According to the later estimate of C. T. Ritchie, Beach's successor as Chancellor of the Exchequer, the War eventually cost £217 million, more than a quarter as much as the French wars which had lasted eight times as long.[16] About 22,000 troops died, and more than five times that number were wounded or incapacitated by disease. War memorials were soon being erected in towns and villages all over the land. On the major public schools the South African War had a particularly shattering impact: of the 300 former pupils of Clifton College who saw active service, forty-four never returned, a statistic recorded in the school's imposing memorial to the fallen dead, which features a knight in armour. Yet only a minority of soldiers had suffered a knightly fate: nearly two-thirds of all British fatalities were caused, not by wounds inflicted in battle, but by disease.[17]

---

[13] By this time many Boer farmers ('joiners') had thrown in their lot with the British authorities.
[14] Surridge, *Managing the South African War*, Ch. 8.
[15] K. Surridge, ' "All you soldiers are what we call pro-Boer": The Military Critique of the South African War, 1899–1902', *History*, 82 (1997), 582–600.
[16] B. Mallet, *British Budgets 1887–88 to 1912–13* (London, 1913), 199.
[17] The great war correspondent George Steevens died of fever at Ladysmith.

2. ON THE HOME FRONT

The Boer War volunteers who fought in South Africa may have comprised a mere 0.76 per cent of UK men of military age,[18] but this was a much larger number than had participated in the small colonial wars of recent decades. In addition, millions of citizens were vicariously caught up in the conflict. This was, in part, because events in South Africa were portrayed so vividly, not least photographically. Troops on both sides, as well as journalists, had access to the cartridge film first employed in the Pocket and Bullet Kodaks of 1896, supplemented, from 1900 onwards, by the cheap Brownie camera.[19] Thanks to the strong South African sunlight, the photographs taken were often of a remarkably high quality.

Moreover, through the bioscope, invented four years before the war's outbreak, music-hall audiences at home could see moving pictures from South Africa, shot by a new breed of professional photographer, of whom W. K.-L. Dickson (a naturalized American) was the acknowledged leader; however artificial and 'staged' much of this footage was, it gave the war a dramatically sharper immediacy.

The war also saw a vast outpouring of stories and poems, some of them written from the comfort of an armchair, but many emanating from soldiers on active service, drawn from all ranks (for by the turn of the century Tommy Atkins was generally literate). Even while the fighting was still raging, the immensely popular Arthur Conan Doyle wrote a history of the South African War, while Edgar Wallace was sending home colourful (and often fictitious) narratives for the delectation of readers of the *Daily Mail*.

Among the many accredited war correspondents who roamed South Africa were 'stars' such as Henry Nevinson of the *Daily Chronicle*, George Steevens of the *Daily Mail*, and Melton-Prior, famous for the drawings he supplied to the *Illustrated London News*. These men often exercised considerable political influence through their access to news and their control over its dissemination. How thin was the borderline between politics and reporting can be seen from the famous case of Winston Churchill, who, as well as filing reports for the *Morning Post*, used his personal experiences in South Africa (he was captured during a Boer raid on an armoured train before bravely eluding his captors) to boost his image and launch a political career. Similarly Burdett-Coutts, who

---

[18] W. J. Reader, *At Duty's Call: A Study in Obsolete Patriotism* (Manchester, 1988), 15. But this figure omits those who, out of patriotic ardour, joined regular army units. Perhaps 8.3% of males aged 18–40 were doing some kind of military service between 1899 and 1902, including involvement in the home defence formations (M. D. Blanch, 'British Society and the War', in P. Warwick (ed.), *The South African War: The Anglo-Boer War, 1899–1902* (Harlow, 1980), 229).

[19] The famous Spion Kop photos were taken by Boer photographers.

created a political sensation at Westminster with his revealing accounts of the typhoid epidemic, was a Conservative MP harbouring frustrated ambitions.

Image could thus be as potent as reality, particularly when it came to military reputations. Buller was popular with his men, of whose creature comforts he always took great care, but his contempt for pressmen and his heavy-handed methods of censorship cost him dear. Unable to present his own side of the story, he had no one else to do it for him, and so became widely depicted as a blundering buffoon. Roberts, by contrast, went out of his way to butter up the press corps and had a precocious understanding of the importance of what would later be called 'photo opportunities'; he also took care to keep pressmen away from unpleasant scenes such as the fever epidemic. In his poem 'Bobs', a powerful contribution to the 'Roberts myth', Rudyard Kipling said of his hero that 'he does not advertise'—in reality, the opposite was the case.

Younger members of the 'Roberts Ring', such as Colonel Ian Hamilton, helped spread the message to the waiting journalists—notably L. S. Amery, the military correspondent of *The Times*. This had fateful consequences, since Amery was later to write a semi-official history of the war in which he remorselessly contrasted Buller's abject failure with Roberts's triumphs—an account so powerful that only in recent years has it been challenged.[20]

A striking example of how heroic status could be achieved through press manipulation is provided by Baden-Powell, whose achievements at Mafeking, though not inconsiderable, became magnified in the public's imagination. 'B-P' had always had a somewhat childish liking for amateur dramatics, and his fame owed much to his instinctive recognition that the Boer War was a *spectacle*, played out on a global stage before an audience of millions.

The commercial world was quick to exploit the war's drama and excitement. Soldiers had, throughout the years of imperial expansion, featured prominently in advertisements, but during the war they were used in still greater numbers to promote every conceivable kind of product. One advertisement facetiously claimed that Roberts's advancing army had delineated the name 'Bovril' over the veldt; another drew a parallel between the Relief of Ladysmith and the relief of influenza sufferers who imbibed that beverage!

During the war's early stages 'khaki fever' raged throughout the land. Kipling's 'Absent-Minded Beggar', which Mrs Beerbohm Tree recited nightly and to which Arthur Sullivan wrote accompanying music, earned at least a quarter-of-a-million pounds for soldiers' wives and children. Sub-Kiplingesque bombast formed a staple of music-hall fare, a particular

---

[20] The pendulum may now have swung too far in the opposite direction: see Spiers, *Late Victorian Army*, 314, for an alternative view.

favourite being Will Dalton and F. J. Willard's 'A Hot Time in the Transvaal To-night':

> There is trouble in the Transvaal,
> And England wants to know
> Whether Mister Kruger or
> John Bull shall boss the show?[21]

Even Marie Lloyd sang her one and only patriotic song, though giving it a characteristically 'naughty' twist.[22]

Half-a-million people cheered off the 1st Army Corps as it embarked at Southampton,[23] and vast crowds lined the London streets when the CIV set off for war. People turned out, in even larger numbers, to greet the CIV on its return, a carefully stage-managed event, in which the troops followed very much the same route taken by the Queen on her Diamond Jubilee, before proceeding to a service at St Paul's Cathedral and finally ending up in the Guildhall, where the Lord Mayor greeted them with a patriotic speech.[24] Hysterical fervour also greeted the news of the lifting of the siege of Ladysmith and, later, the relief of Baden-Powell and his garrison at Mafeking.

Woe betide anyone who held aloof from this rejoicing: some Germans who refused to join in the Mafeking celebrations were assaulted.[25] Patriotic mobs also disrupted the lecture tour given in early 1900 by the Boer S. C. Cronwright-Schreiner. Prominent British 'Pro-Boers' who tried to hold public meetings were similarly given a rough ride.[26] When Lloyd George provocatively addressed a rally in Chamberlain's Birmingham, disorder broke out: one man was left dead, others were injured, and the speaker had to be smuggled out of the town hall disguised as a policeman.[27]

Attempts have retrospectively been made to distinguish between 'celebratory' and 'vindictive' crowds: the emotion being expressed on Mafeking night, it is claimed, derived from relief over liberation from danger, even perhaps from pleasure at the thought that the war would shortly be ending, rather than from raw jingoism—after all, few Britons (with the significant exception of the Irish Nationalists) wanted the British to *lose* the war, still less to suffer high casualties. As for 'vindictive' crowds, these, it has been argued, tended to be

[21] W. Van Wyck Smith, *Drummer Hodge* (London, 1978), 78.

[22] L. Senelick, 'Politics as Entertainment: Victorian Musical Hall Songs', *Victorian Studies*, 19 (1975), 176.

[23] Reader, *At Duty's Call*, 11.

[24] J. Schneer, *London 1900: The Imperial Metropolis* (New Haven and London, 1999), 28–34, 304.

[25] P. Panayi (ed.), 'Introduction', in *Racial Violence in Britain in the Nineteenth and Twentieth Centuries* (Leicester, 1996 edn.), 10.

[26] Significantly, however, protest meetings were largely left unmolested after 1900.

[27] Chamberlain's supporters were perhaps seeking revenge for similar acts of rowdyism which had been inflicted on Unionists by Radical mobs (J. Lawrence, *Speaking For the People* (Cambridge, 1998), 184).

orchestrated by politically motivated members of the lower middle class, not by ordinary working men.[28]

It may be significant, however, that contemporaries seldom drew such fine distinctions. John Burns, the Labour leader, thought his fellow countrymen to be 'khaki clad, khaki mad and khaki bad',[29] while J. A. Hobson and other Radicals bewailed what they saw as the prevailing mood of drunken jingoism to which all classes had succumbed. Anti-war socialists despairingly confessed that 'a very large number if not the majority of wage-earners have supported the plutocrats and murderers'.[30] In the arsenal and dockyard towns the war was particularly popular, even among trade unionists.

All the same, a sizeable minority of the population vehemently opposed the war, backed by C. P. Scott's *Manchester Guardian*, the *Morning Star*, the *Daily News* (from 1901 onwards), and assorted socialist journals. At the forefront of the agitation was the 'Stop The War Committee' (founded in January 1900). Both Keir Hardie and Ramsay MacDonald joined this organization, which was chaired by a former Methodist minister and minor novelist Silas Hocking, though its main inspirer was W. T. Stead, the former friend of Rhodes and one-time cheerleader for imperialism. But its emotive approach, epitomized by Stead's pamphlet *Shall I Slay My Brother Boer?*, was thought to have done a disservice to the anti-war cause. More influential were the Transvaal Committee and the South African Conciliation Committee, the latter being a meeting-place for high-minded Liberals such as John Morley, which met under the presidency of Leonard Courtney, a Liberal Unionist alienated by Home Rule but now returning to his old Liberal faith. Finally, there was the League Against Aggression and Militarism, inevitably called the 'lambs', a Radical Liberal body which included Lloyd George, Scott, and J. A. Hobson.

The opposition's case against the war was stated, at its simplest, in the resolution drafted by Lloyd George in February 1900, in which the war was denounced as 'a crime and a blunder, committed at the instigation of irresponsible capitalists'.[31] Also central to the pro-Boer creed was the conviction articulated by Keir Hardie, who said: 'You cannot build up an Empire of free peoples by force.'[32] Such criticisms of the government were often accompanied by an idealization of the enemy. The Boers, declared Edward Carpenter, were living a simple pastoral life, devoted to family, cattle, and farm, which

---

[28] On whether or not recruitment statistics demonstrate working-class enthusiasm for the war, see R. Price, *An Imperial War and the British Working Class: Working-Class Attitudes to and Reaction to the Boer War, 1899–1902* (London, 1972), and Blanch, 'British Society and the War', 210–38.

[29] Schneer, *London 1900*, 250.

[30] *Justice*, 11 Mar. 1900, cited in D. J. Newton, *British Labour, European Socialism and the Struggle for Peace, 1899–1914* (Oxford, 1985), 119.

[31] A. Davey, *The British Pro-Boers 1877–1902* (Tafelberg, 1978), 88.

[32] B. Porter, 'The Pro-Boers in Britain', in Warwick (ed.), *South African War*, 252.

compared favourably with Johannesburg, 'a hell hole of Jews, financiers, greedy speculators, adventurers, prostitutes, bars, gaming saloons, and every invention of the devil'; though the Boers may have had their 'faults', he wrote, the British were more *systematically* cruel[33]—a line of argument pursued with relish by Irish Nationalists.

Many pro-Boers, Labour and Liberal alike, also sounded an overtly anti-Semitic note. In *The War in South Africa* (1900), J. A. Hobson postulated corrupt collusion between the 'Goldbugs' of the Rand, London's Stock Exchange, and a 'bought' press. 'For whom are we fighting?', Hobson asked: 'a small group of international financiers, chiefly German in origin and Jewish in race', came his reply. This message was echoed in Hilaire Belloc's 'Lines to a Noble Lord' and in many of the utterances of Hyndman and Burns, the latter declaring that the British army 'had become in Africa the janissary of the Jews'.[34]

To his credit, Hobson went on to pen a more sophisticated interpretation of recent events in his book *Imperialism* (1902), which argued that imperial expansion was fuelled by the export of 'surplus' capital, for which the remedy lay in a redistribution of income and wealth at home, to the benefit of the poor and disadvantaged. Many socialists broadly accepted this thesis, though, unlike Hobson, they were more inclined to see imperialism as a natural manifestation of capitalism, not as a 'distortion' that could be corrected by appropriate governmental policies.

More immediately corrosive of 'khaki fever' was spreading disillusionment over the conduct of the war. Many soldiers in the field increasingly gave vent to their dissatisfaction in poems which lambasted incompetent generals and venal contractors, and proclaimed the futility and pity of war. Though personally uninvolved in the fighting, the London journalist T. W. H. Crosland penned verses, one of which, 'Slain', with its ironic invocation of the adage 'Dulce et decorum est pro patria mori', eerily foreshadows the work of the celebrated 'Great War Poets'.[35] Even Kipling, while never doubting the war's moral necessity, soon lost confidence in the military leadership—though, admittedly, his most scathing poems, such as 'Stellenbosch', were not published until the war had ended.

Why, then, given so much scepticism and hostility, did opposition to the Boer War prove so ineffectual, at least in the short term? Its Achilles' heel was

[33] D. Lowry, ' "The Boers were the beginning of the end"?: The Wider Impact of the South African War', in Lowry, *South African War*, 205; Newton, *British Labour*, 206.

[34] C. Holmes, *Anti-Semitism in British Society 1876–1939* (London, 1979), 67–76. Hilaire Belloc soon afterwards composed his novel *Emmanuel Burden* (1904), which features the sinister 'Mr I. Z. Barnett', with his 'hooked nose, thick lips, gross body and greasy curls'.

[35] Smith, *Drummer Hodge*, 112–14.

the lack of convincing leadership. At Manchester in January 1900 John Morley had denounced the war in a great speech that invited comparisons with John Bright's Crimean War phillipics, prompting Hardie to call on him to place himself at the head of the democratic forces. But Morley, immersed in his writing of the biography of Gladstone, then kept silent for nearly six months.

The 'troublemakers' faced another difficulty. Most Radicals attacked the war, not so much by subjecting it to a structural economic critique, as Hobson had done, but by launching *moral* attacks on what they saw as unadulterated evil: Morley himself, for example, had listed the various benefits which might flow from the war, before ending each item with the refrain, 'it will be wrong'. Yet, in taking this stand, the critics received little backing from the churches.

To no one's surprise, most Anglican clergymen rallied behind the Union Jack,[36] and the Wesleyan Methodists were almost equally bellicose. Old Dissent prevaricated. Prior to the outbreak of hostilities, the National Council of Free Churches had held prayer meetings for peace, but in March 1900 its organizing committee banned all discussion of the war. True, two famous divines, Dr John Clifford, a Baptist, and Silvester Horne, an Independent, bravely bore witness to the continuing vitality of the Nonconformist conscience, but they did not speak for their respective denominations—indeed, Horne was nearly dismissed by his irate congregation.

Greater resolution might have been expected from the Quakers, particularly in the light of their recent adoption of the 'peace testimony', which forbade inflicting injury on any human soul. Strengthened in these convictions by the discussions surrounding the 1899 Hague Peace Conference, many prominent members of the Society of Friends, including members of the Rowntree and Cadbury families, unequivocally denounced war, pride of Empire, and narrow popular patriotism.[37] But a significant minority of Quakers declined to follow this lead. The Primitive Methodists alone remained more or less united in opposing the war.[38]

Organized Labour, like mainstream Nonconformity, also opted for diplomatic caution, or cowardly silence—depending on one's point of view. The TUC officially maintained a position of neutrality on the war—partly because of the traditional assumption that questions of foreign policy and imperial defence lay outside the TUC's remit, partly because the leadership did not

[36] However, a minority of 'Christian Socialists', such as Conrad Noel, broke ranks with the hierarchy on this issue.
[37] T. C. Kennedy, 'The Quaker Renaissance and the Origins of the Modern British Peace Movement, 1895–1920', *Albion*, 16 (1984), 243–4, 246–7.
[38] G. Cuthbertson, 'Pricking the "Nonconformist Conscience": Religion Against the South African War', in Lowry (ed.), *South African War*, 169–87.

wish to pick a quarrel with those numerous rank-and-file trade unionists who had rushed to the colours.

Most class-conscious trade unionists and socialists, it is true, mistrusted Chamberlain and the government, hated militarism—which they saw as a deliberate attempt to distract attention from social reform—and inclined to the view that the war was a 'capitalist ramp'. A Lib-Lab such as John Burns, and Keir Hardie, the ILPer, could unite around this platform, though they agreed on little else. Indeed, when the executive of the Fabian Society decided not to make an official declaration on the war (in March 1900), this provoked the walkout of Ramsay MacDonald, George Barnes, Pete Curran, and others.[39] Robert Blatchford, the ex-ranker, predictably announced that in a national emergency he was a Briton first and a socialist second, and Hyndman, cross at the hypocrisy of Continental denunciations of the concentration camps, later sought to put a little distance between himself and uncritical pro-Boer effusions. But these were minority voices: the ILP and the SDF staunchly stood by their anti-war convictions.[40]

On the other hand, however vocal within their own organizations, the socialists' critique of the South African War was muted by their unwillingness to rock the boat while engaged in constructing the Labour Representation Committee.[41] Amazingly, the inaugural LRC Conference, held in February 1900, managed not to mention the war at all.

The most outspoken antagonists of the government's South African policy were the Irish Nationalists, who instinctively empathized with the Boers as fellow victims of imperialist aggression—ignoring the inconvenient fact that regulars of the Dublin Fusiliers were serving in South Africa as part of the Crown forces. An 'Irish Brigade', led by John MacBride, fought alongside the Dutch commandos, while at Westminster the Nationalist Party kept up a remorseless barrage of criticism. However, episodes such as that in which Irish MPs laughed and waved their order papers on being informed of Lord Methuen's defeat and surrender at Tweebosch in March 1902, merely made it that much more difficult for other would-be opponents of the government's policies to voice their discontents. The Boer War thus provided a powerful stimulus to Irish Nationalism in both its revolutionary and constitutional forms (the parliamentary party reunited under John Redmond in 1900); but at the

---

[39] Newton, *British Labour*, 134. The Society later issued an impish pamphlet, largely written by George Bernard Shaw, presenting the annexation of the South African republics as a progressive act because it signified the crushing of a backward oligarchy and a necessary step towards socialism and world government.

[40] Newton, *British Labour*, 135–6.

[41] See Chs. 7 and 10.

same time it set back the prospects of Irish Home Rule by reawakening anti-Irish feeling on mainland Britain.[42]

A responsible critique of the war, if there was to be one, could therefore only come from the Liberal Party. But were the Liberals in any fit state to provide this?

3. LIBERAL TROUBLES AND UNIONIST MUDDLES

Initially the Liberals could view their prospects with some optimism—even if, to ministers' surprise, the war had every appearance of being broadly popular. Yet anger at governmental mismanagement soon ran high, giving the main Opposition party much to exploit. Salisbury's failure to provide the country with decisive leadership and the government with central direction meant that Balfour, the Leader of the Commons, found himself playing the key role. But Balfour's badly judged speeches to his Manchester constituents in November 1899, when he said that he had no more idea than 'the man in the street' of the Boers' military preparations, brought down on his head a torrent of abuse. Salisbury fared little better when he addressed the Lords in January and March. Even Chamberlain, astonished at the turn that events had taken, momentarily lost much of his fire. The War Secretary, Lansdowne, was so discredited that some newspapers called for his impeachment, and it was left to his Under-Secretary, George Wyndham, to rally the party with a fighting speech to the Commons on 1 February.

The Liberals, however, were in even greater disarray. Campbell-Bannerman strongly disliked what he once called 'the vulgar and bastard Imperialism of ... provocation and aggression ... of grabbing everything even if we have no use for it ourselves', and he now accused Chamberlain, through his reckless policy of bluff, of precipitating an unnecessary war.[43] Yet although Campbell-Bannerman urged the long-term need for peace and reconciliation in South Africa, Kruger, by violently overthrowing Gladstone's post-Majuba settlement, had made it politically impossible for the Liberal Leader to defend the Boers, particularly while they were occupying British territory and when the war was going so badly for the British army. That is why, for all his open criticisms of the government, Campbell-Bannerman was one of the first senior Liberals—ahead of Asquith, for example—publicly to acknowledge the inevitability of an annexation of the two republics.

[42] Lowry, 'Beginning of the end?', 224.

[43] G. B. Pyrah, *Imperial Policy and South Africa 1902–10* (Oxford, 1955), 23; J. A. Spender, *The Life of Sir Henry Campbell-Bannerman* (London, 1923), i. 257–8.

'C-B', however, lacked the personal authority to impose this 'middle-of-the-road' policy on his followers. It did not go nearly far enough to attract doctrinaire pro-Boers such as Wilfrid Lawson, the temperance reformer, Henry Labouchere, and Lloyd George; yet, at the same time, it displayed insufficient warmth to the national cause to win the approval of the Liberal Imperialists, whose ranks included Asquith, Grey, Haldane, Fowler, and (more enigmatically) the former Leader, Rosebery.[44]

The depth of Liberal divisions became apparent on 19 October 1899 when Philip Stanhope, a Radical backbencher, moved an amendment to the address expressing 'strong disapproval of the conduct of the negotiations', an initiative which led to the humiliation of an open three-way split.[45] In February 1900 a craftily constructed vote of censure more or less held the party together,[46] but internal squabbling continued, exacerbated by the struggle to control the Liberal press. At the start of the war the Liberal Imperialists captured the *Daily Chronicle*, sacking its editor, H. W. Massingham, and abruptly changing its policy line. The 'pro-Boers' got their revenge when a syndicate, including Lloyd George and the Quaker cocoa-manufacturer George Cadbury, bought out the *Daily News* for £100,000 and replaced the imperialist E. T. Cook in the editor's chair by the 'Little England' Radical A. G. Gardiner.

Another three-way split within the Liberals' parliamentary ranks on 25 July[47] gave the Liberal Imperialists hope that the Leader whom they despised would shortly resign, allowing Asquith to take his place. This did not happen. But Liberal strife, combined with the belief that, following Roberts's entry into Pretoria, the war had effectively ended, stimulated Chamberlain to press for a dissolution, although Parliament still had two more years to run. Salisbury reluctantly acquiesced, privately complaining about Chamberlain's lack of 'character'. The General Election took place between 28 September and 24 October 1900. The Unionists were returned with a majority of 134 over all their opponents, eight seats fewer than in 1895 but slightly more than they had had on the eve of dissolution (132)—enough, at any rate, to secure their hold on government for years to come.

[44] See H. C. G. Matthew, *The Liberal Imperialists: The Ideas and Politics of a Post-Gladstonian Elite* (Oxford, 1973).

[45] The motion was defeated by 135 to 362, the minority comprising 43 Irish Nationalists, 2 Unionists, and 93 anti-war Radicals (among them Harcourt). Campbell-Bannerman and Asquith, along with 40 other Liberal MPs, abstained, but 15 (including Grey and Asquith) actually supported the government.

[46] Even so, two Liberals broke ranks by voting with the government, while another 22 abstained.

[47] Lawson's amendment to the Colonial Office List attracted 31 Liberals, but 38 supported the government (including Grey, Asquith, Haldane, and Fowler), and 42 abstained: Campbell-Bannerman tried to lead a walkout from the Chamber.

Historians, like contemporaries, have struggled to make sense of this confused contest. In some areas the election was totally dominated by the war, but in others South Africa took second place to other issues: in Glasgow, along with much of Western Scotland, the Unionists benefited from the capture of the Irish vote over the education issue, Liverpool was convulsed by the rights and wrongs of ritualism, while in other areas the agricultural depression took centre stage. The Unionists tended to do best in the big cities, dockyard towns, and armaments centres; the Liberals, however, more than held their own in many of the smaller market towns. In Scotland the government increased its representation from thirty-one to thirty-six seats, but in the Principality it fell back from eight seats to four.

The Unionist ploy of draping their candidates in the Union Jack similarly enjoyed mixed success. Some anti-war working-class candidates, such as W. C. Steadman in Stepney, went down to defeat, but others, such as Burns in Battersea and the LRC candidate, Richard Bell, in Derby, easily held off their assailants by campaigning hard on social reform: indeed, in the double-member constituency of Derby, the Unionist Geoffrey Drage, chairman of the Imperial South Africa Association, actually came bottom of the poll.[48] Pro-war Liberals fared slightly better than 'pro-Boers', but not by much:[49] Hedworth Lambton, who had heroically commanded the Naval Brigade at Ladysmith, failed to win Newcastle upon Tyne, despite the personal backing of Rosebery. Perhaps this was because Chamberlain had deliberately tarred all Liberals with the same brush through his notorious telegram to the effect that 'every vote given against the Government is a vote given to the Boers'—a message accidentally altered by a telephonist to read 'a vote *sold* to the Boers'.

Nevertheless, the war did affect the outcome of the election in one important respect. There were 161 uncontested Unionist victories (as against twenty-two Liberal ones) over the United Kingdom as a whole—compared with 122 in 1895 and a mere thirteen in 1906. This reflected the Liberals' difficulty in fielding candidates, which was in turn affected by the party's desperate financial straits, as many of its traditional wealthy backers continued to desert it. It is hard to believe that this state of affairs did not owe much to Liberal divisions over the war, and to the widespread perception that the party could not be trusted to run the Empire in a patriotic spirit.

Yet, despite winning a decisive electoral victory, the Unionist ministry looked far from healthy in late 1900. The Prime Minister was sunk in depression as he contemplated the tactics which had brought him a renewed term of office. The jingoism of the electorate signified, he privately mused, 'that the

---

[48] Price, *Imperial War*, 119.

[49] 29% of the former and 22.5% of the latter failed to be returned (figures reworked from Price, *Imperial War*, Ch. 3).

recent Reform Bills, digging down deeper and deeper into the population, ha[d] come upon a layer of pure combativeness', in which case the country had 'evil times before it'.[50] Nor were the Unionist Parties in much better fettle, as the grumbling over Salisbury's cliquish management of his government, first heard in 1895, started up once more. Meanwhile the press was screaming for the replacement of some of the 'old gang' with younger talent, with a view to reinvigorating the exhausted ministry.

But the reshuffle, when it was announced in early November, came as a disappointment. The embattled Lansdowne replaced Salisbury as Foreign Secretary, giving way to St John Brodrick, who soon became equally unpopular. The new First Lord of the Admiralty, Lord Selborne, proved over time to be one of the more successful promotees, later initiating, with Admiral Sir John ('Jacky') Fisher, a series of naval reforms which had profound long-term consequences; but in late 1900 commentators were more struck by the fact that Selborne was Salisbury's son-in-law, one of four close relatives of the Prime Minister to hold high office.[51] Wags referred to the government as the 'Hotel Cecil Unlimited'. Meanwhile Chamberlain remained at the Colonial Office, somewhat detached from the rest of his Cabinet colleagues, admired by many, but loathed by his political opponents.

The Liberal Imperialists particularly resented the unjust way in which Chamberlain had impugned their patriotism during the recent election:[52] 'Joe', Asquith privately observed, had 'the manners of a cad and the tongue of a bargee'. Chamberlain returned their contempt, making an exception only of Grey, and he was further angered when Liberal MPs from all wings of the party—Haldane in a prominent role—joined Lloyd George in December 1900 in attacking the Chamberlain family for benefiting from the allocation of war contracts in the so-called Kynochs Scandal.

But dislike of Chamberlain was not enough to hold together a Liberal Party which, over the following eighteen months, came close to disintegration. In March 1901 Grey and Haldane for the first time associated themselves with a factional grouping called the Imperial Liberal Council (ILC), established nearly a year earlier by the Liberal MP and prominent Wesleyan businessman Robert Perks. Liberal divisions deepened when Milner visited England on leave in late May. Grey joined the official delegation that met the High

---

[50] Salisbury to Cranbrook, 19 Oct. 1900, in A. E. Gathorne-Hardy, *Gathorne-Hardy, First Earl of Cranbrook* (London, 1910), ii. 374.

[51] As well as Selborne, the Cabinet contained two of Salisbury's nephews, Arthur Balfour and Gerald Balfour, the new President of the Board of Trade, while representing the Foreign Office in the Commons as Under-Secretary was his son, Lord Cranborne.

[52] Chamberlain's objective was probably the discrediting of Rosebery, whom he had every reason to fear.

Commissioner at Southampton, and he and Haldane fêted their old friend. John Morley, on the other hand, publicly denounced the High Commissioner as an 'imitation Bismarck', while Campbell-Bannerman privately fulminated over what he called '*religio Milneriana*', a disease he thought particularly likely to afflict Balliol men (C-B had been to Cambridge).

All these latent tensions were brought to a head by Emily Hobhouse's revelations of conditions in the South African concentration camps, to which Lloyd George had already alerted the Commons. At a dinner of the National Reform Union on 14 June, Campbell-Bannerman moved closer towards the pro-Boer backbenchers by using the phrase 'methods of barbarism' to describe British pacification policy. The Liberal Imperialists were shocked at this 'treacherous' attack on the army while a war was in progress (as were most soldiers), and a week later (20 June) Asquith publicly rebuked his Leader, an event which his delighted followers decided to celebrate by organizing a dinner in his honour at the Hotel Cecil on July 18.

In retrospect, this can be seen as the point at which the Liberals began their slow extrication from the abyss. On 9 July Campbell-Bannerman called a meeting of Liberal MPs at the Reform Club, where his leadership was unanimously confirmed, albeit on the understanding that each MP remained free to go his own way over policy. It also became clear that Liberal activists in the country overwhelmingly supported their Leader, as the meeting of the NLF at Derby in December later confirmed.

Even the organizers of the Asquith Dinner began to have second thoughts. They quietly dropped their original notion of sending out invitations to the Liberal Unionists, and Asquith, at heart a 'centrist' dragged by his friendships with Haldane and Grey into an artificially extreme position, privately reassured Campbell-Bannerman of his loyalty to the party. When the dinner finally took place, Asquith emphasized domestic reform 'as a question of social and Imperial efficiency', and did not enlarge on his disagreements with his Leader over South Africa.

The Asquith Dinner was anyhow overshadowed by the emergence of Rosebery. Two days earlier, in a public letter to the City Liberal Club, Rosebery had denounced the Liberal Party as an 'organised hypocrisy'. On the very day of the Asquith Dinner he elaborated on these observations in a speech to the club, in which he called on the Liberal Party to abandon its 'anti-national' proclivities and to adopt a 'clean slate', with a view to reconciliation with the Liberal Unionists. Meanwhile, Rosebery declared, he intended to 'plough his lonely furrow'.

Rosebery's motives for undermining Asquith are unclear. The 'man of mystery' may have been subconsciously jealous of Asquith's growing fame. But it is equally possible that, while expressing a general sympathy for his

Liberal Imperialist friends in the Commons, Rosebery was hoping to present himself to the wider public as the potential head of a 'national government'—an attractive scenario given the unpopularity of the two major parties. This possibility was frequently aired in journals such as the *National Review* and the *Nineteenth Century*, which noted that the old issues that had once divided the two main parties seemed to have lost their relevance—so much so that the Irish Question, around which the previous three elections had revolved, had scarcely figured at all in the 1900 campaign.[53]

This hypothesis would make sense of many of Rosebery's seemingly perverse actions. For example, at the start of the war he had formally severed his remaining ties with official Liberalism, instead choosing to make spasmodic appearances before the public with Delphic utterances in which the main themes were the need to achieve greater 'National Efficiency'. In particular, prompted by his admirer Haldane, Rosebery waxed eloquent on the need to apply 'business methods' to official life,[54] on the evils of the party system, and on the desirability of sending Kitchener to clean up the Augean stables of the War Office.

After the City Liberal Club speech, Asquith's friends no longer knew quite where they stood. While awaiting clarification, they embarked on an extended autumn speaking tour, and in October the ILC[55] was relaunched as the Liberal Imperialist League, with Grey as President, though Asquith still held aloof from what he clearly regarded as an intrigue. Meanwhile Sidney Webb, who had been drawn ever closer into Haldane's circle, published in the September edition of the *Nineteenth Century* an article, entitled 'Lord Rosebery's Escape from Houndsditch', in which, to Campbell-Bannerman's exasperation ('I fear I am too old to join that academy'), he called upon the great man to put himself at the head of those, from every party and class, who were crying out for a modern programme of social reconstruction, centred on increased efficiency in education and social policy.

Amid a flurry of speculation Rosebery then resurfaced with a big speech at Chesterfield (16 December), which Asquith and the other Liberal Imperialists attended in ignorance of the message about to be delivered. Much of what Rosebery said at Chesterfield about the Liberals' need to 'clean their slate' and abandon their 'fly-blown phylacteries' was by now familiar, as was the way in which he responded to Webb's promptings by dilating, though in very general terms, on the theme of National Efficiency. However, sensitive as ever to the

---

[53] G. R. Searle, *The Quest for National Efficiency: A Study in Politics and Political Thought, 1899–1914* (Oxford, 1971), Ch. 4.
[54] He had allowed his name to go forward as President of the Administrative Reform Association, set up with this as its objective.
[55] Its name had been changed in the late summer to the clumsy Liberal (Imperialist) League.

public's shifting moods, Rosebery surprised his audience by suggesting the possibility of a compromise peace in South Africa, following talks in a 'wayside inn'.

The Liberal Imperialist commoners trembled at the thought of the anger Milner must be feeling at Rosebery's advocacy of peace-feelers, but they were otherwise elated by Chesterfield. From their different standpoints Winston Churchill and Lloyd George joined in the applause. Even Campbell-Bannerman felt obliged to clarify Rosebery's views, sensing that their differences over South Africa might be narrowing. But when soon afterwards he called on Rosebery at his London home for an informal talk, he learned that the latter now saw Ireland as standing in the way of a harmonious reunion.

Campbell-Bannerman now openly threw down the gauntlet at the Leicester meeting of the NLF on 19 February 1902, asking whether Rosebery spoke 'from the interior of our political tabernacle or from some vantage ground outside', adding that he was not in favour of 'the doctrine of the white sheet' and would never apologize for Liberalism, least of all for Home Rule. Two days later Rosebery responded through a letter to *The Times*, saying that he remained 'outside his tabernacle, but not, I think, in solitude' at 'this moment of definite separation'.

Against this confused background, Rosebery's friends announced (26 February) that a new organization was to be launched, called the Liberal League (LL), with Rosebery as its President, and Asquith, Fowler, and Grey as Vice-Presidents, for the purpose of carrying out the Chesterfield policy—whatever that might be. But the deeper ambiguity remained: was the Liberal League merely a pressure-group *within* the Liberal Party, aiming at the protection and advancement of a particular set of policies, or was it meant to be the embryo of a new party or political grouping? The dropping of Home Rule would be an obvious first step towards reunion with the Liberal Unionists, and Rosebery, in a couple of big speeches at Liverpool and Glasgow, seemed to favour this development. However Asquith, though cautiously advocating the replacement of Gladstonian Home Rule by a gradualist 'step-by-step' policy, publicly affirmed his determination never to separate himself from mainstream Liberal politics.

Time was now running out for the Liberal Imperialists. The Peace of Vereeniging in late May removed the main bone of contention within the Liberal Party, and the Unionists were effectively imposing unity upon their opponents through their controversial Corn Duty (passed in early 1902), aimed at bridging the budget deficit, and their even more controversial Education Bill. At the Bury by-election on May 10 the Liberals took the seat from the Unionists on a 9 per-cent swing.

How close was the party to breakdown in the 1901–2 period? The Liberals undoubtedly had important differences, both over the conduct of the war and over the need to modernize their programme. But personal tensions cut across these disagreements. The actions of Haldane and Grey were largely inspired by contempt for Campbell-Bannerman's leadership. Personal friendships also explain why they were supportive of Milner, whose outlook was incompatible with *any* kind of Liberal politics, yet hostile to Chamberlain, whose backing they would have needed if a coalition of national unity had ever been formed.

Further complicating the situation was Rosebery, who managed to exert his peculiar magnetism over a wide array of politicians who otherwise had little in common. For example, he briefly had the endorsement of a section of the Fabian Society, which hoped to flesh out the slogans about National Efficiency with some hard-edged collectivist policies; but he was also a hero to the Wesleyans Perks and Fowler, whose primary allegiance was to Nonconformity and hence to precisely the kind of traditional sectarian politics from which National Efficiency was meant to offer an escape. In any case, Rosebery's morbid personality and long periods of withdrawal from active politics, punctuated by startling initiatives which he had not deigned to discuss in advance with any of his friends, made him an impossible leader.

But the Asquith circle showed little more resolution. Asquith had probably never intended to do more than 'permeate' the Liberal Party from within; Haldane and Grey, on the other hand, hovered between this strategy and some kind of political realignment, the precise nature of which they had never properly thought through.

And so, *faute de mieux*, the country had to put up with a further spell—perhaps another seven years—of discredited Unionist rule, with Salisbury, old beyond his years, determined to retain the premiership until the war had successfully finished.

Salisbury's government was not entirely barren of achievement between 1900 and June 1902, since these years saw the genesis of two great reforming measures: Balfour's Education Act of 1902 and Wyndham's Irish Land Act of 1903. Selborne was meanwhile launching an important series of naval reforms.[56] But it was in foreign policy that the most important initiatives were taken. Ministers were especially worried by the propaganda success enjoyed by the Transvaal's Foreign Secretary, Dr Leyds, in whipping up Anglophobia as he visited Continental Europe.

There were other grounds for concern. Never had the 'thin red line' been stretched thinner than in 1900.[57] Not only had troops been withdrawn from India and Egypt, but the United Kingdom itself was stripped of all but a single regular battalion, leading to renewed fears of an invasion. Stead returned to his

---

[56] See Ch. 10.

[57] R. Williams, *Defending the Empire: The Conservative Party and British Defence Policy 1899–1915* (New Haven and London, 1991), 9.

well-tried scaremongering tactics, suggesting in *The Review of Reviews* that 'all the German waiters in London, armed with cudgels and revolvers, would converge on Woolwich and seize the Arsenal'. In February Wyndham publicly called for 120,000 volunteers to guard the country against hostile raids,[58] and later in the year, hoping to influence the electorate as it went to the polls, the Navy League issued an inflammatory manifesto warning of 'a naval Colenso'.

Those perils, real or imaginary, gave fresh encouragement to those seeking an escape from 'isolation', the prospect of which had, in any case, come somewhat closer now that Salisbury had been replaced at the Foreign Office by Lansdowne. Chamberlain, in particular, renewed his efforts to secure an accommodation with Berlin.[59] But the Colonial Secretary's pro-German ardours rapidly cooled as a result of a bad-tempered series of public exchanges with the Imperial Chancellor, von Bülow, between October 1901 and January 1902. Even without these personal unpleasantnesses, it seems unlikely that any British government would have been prepared to pay the price which the Germans were demanding: an equality with Britain, which threatened the latter's maritime supremacy.

Yet for how much longer could this position of superiority be maintained? Naval expenditure was to rise by 80 per cent between 1897–8 and 1904–5, at a time when total expenditure rose by only 40 per cent. Even so, it was only with reluctance that the Cabinet, in October 1902, agreed to restore the two-power standard.[60] The new First Lord of the Admiralty, Selborne, was particularly worried by developments in Far Eastern waters, where Britain faced a threat from Russia which the Royal Navy, unaided, could no longer check. One solution to this difficulty was for Britain to enlist the support of the expanding Japanese fleet.

Herein lay the rationale for the signing of the Anglo-Japanese alliance in early 1902, which Selborne and Lansdowne rushed through the Cabinet before it was unveiled before an astonished Commons on 13 February 1902. Lansdowne admitted to his equally baffled fellow peers that the alliance represented a radical departure from the principles which had prevailed for at least a generation. However, only with the wisdom of hindsight does the alliance seem to mark the 'end of isolation', since Lansdowne, like Salisbury, was still thinking in terms of limited regional agreements: indeed, his primary aim had been to come to an arrangement with *Russia*, but the failure of this attempt in 1902 left the Japanese alliance as the only game in town.

---

[58] M. Howard, *The Continental Commitment: The Dilemma of British Defence Policy in the Era of Two World Wars* (Oxford, 1971), 21.

[59] e.g. in a speech at Leicester on 30 November 1899.

[60] N. A. Lambert, *Sir John Fisher's Naval Revolution* (London, 1999), 31–4.

There remained the necessity for a reconsideration of financial policy. Faced by the escalation of war-related expenditure, the elderly Chancellor, Hicks Beach, had to resort to drastic expedients. In his 1901 Budget he put a tax on refined sugar and, to the fury of the mining interests, imposed a levy of 1s. on exported coal. Income tax was raised by 2d. to 1s. 2d. in the pound, the Sinking Fund was suspended, and resort was had to more borrowing—in the end, to the dismay of Harcourt and other traditional 'economists', only 31 per cent of war-related expenditure was charged to income.[61]

Later in the year Hicks Beach spelt out to his Cabinet colleagues the implications of what he considered their irresponsible conduct: expenditure on education, the Post Office, colonial grants, and various grants-in-aid, to say nothing of the naval arms race, had created a financial crisis, even before the outbreak of the war.[62] The Chancellor warned that unless a stern resistance was offered to the wild demands for expansion and expenditure everywhere, the government would be obliged to undertake a complete overhaul of its fiscal policies, and he darkly hinted at the controversial possibility of revenue tariffs.

Salisbury sympathized, gloomily noting that 'we were in face of a Jingo hurricane, and were driving before it under bare poles'; he prophesied that there would be 'a Parliamentary explosion before long'.[63] Chamberlain responded rather differently: he drew attention to the fate that had befallen Randolph Churchill when he had tried to oppose the country's military and naval experts, and warned that 'any declaration of a "policy of economy" as a supreme object at the present time' would be politically risky.

In his 1902 Budget (April) Hicks Beach announced that there would be a deficit of nearly £27 million, if existing taxes were not raised or supplemented. So he suspended the Sinking Fund once more and added another penny to the income tax. In addition, this most orthodox of Chancellors found himself obliged to reimpose the registration duty on corn and flour, abolished by Lowe in 1869. Though Hicks Beach made it clear that he was only doing this for revenue purposes, the announcement of the Corn Duty was greeted with unseemly enthusiasm by the agricultural protection lobby ('well done, well done!', cried its spokesman, Howard Vincent). But an angry Liberal Party sensed a danger to free trade, as did many of his own ministerial colleagues. Nor were free traders reassured when Chamberlain, in a speech at Birmingham on 16 May, ominously referred to 'economic pedantry'.

---

[61] Mallet, *Budgets*, 171–3, 185–90, 199–202.

[62] Total expenditure rose from £92.2 million in 1886 to £100.9 million in 1895, to £112.3 million in 1898. Under the impact of the war it soared to £193.3 million in 1901 and to £205.2 million in 1902.

[63] Cited in P. Marsh, *The Discipline of Popular Government: Lord Salisbury's Domestic Statecraft, 1881–1902* (Hassocks, 1978), 309–10.

Thus, even before the war's conclusion, strains were showing in the alliance between Salisburian Conservatism and Radical Unionism. Fresh sources of taxation would have to be found if potentially unpopular economies were to be avoided; indeed, the ending of the wartime economic boom was shortly to give this quest an even greater urgency. Arthur Balfour, who replaced his uncle as Prime Minister on 12 July 1902, was clearly in for a difficult time, because the fiscal crisis that he had inherited made virtually inevitable a struggle for ascendancy between Chamberlain on the one side, and, on the other, the orthodox free traders within the Cabinet, now headed by C. T. Ritchie, Hicks Beach's successor as Chancellor of the Exchequer.

4. THE INQUEST

Long before the war petered out in anticlimactic fashion, an inquest had begun into the underlying causes of 'Black Week' and the country's subsequent humiliations. On first arriving in South Africa, Roberts had written: 'I was astonished beyond measure to hear of our utter unpreparedness . . . How could this have been permitted? And who is responsible?' Immediately hostilities ended, the government set up a Royal Commission of Inquiry (the Elgin Commission) to address all such questions.

Its report, which appeared in the summer of 1903, catalogued a succession of errors and muddles which, in other circumstances, would have been comical. At the outset of war there had been an almost total absence of maps of the ground over which the decisive engagements were to be fought. Some rifles were wrongly sighted, and there was an insufficiency of ammunition. The War Office initially possessed piles of red, white, and blue uniforms, quite useless for action on the veldt, but an inadequate supply of khaki. The understaffed and under-resourced Remounts Department failed to rise to the immensity of the challenge; the Royal Army Medical Corps broke down under pressure; and, at all levels, intelligence and staff work were inadequate.

Was this indictment just? George Wyndham, Under-Secretary at the War Office, had boasted at the war's outbreak that the army was 'more efficient than at any time since Waterloo'. In retrospect, there seems more truth in Amery's verdict that the 1899 army was 'nothing more nor less than a gigantic Dotheboys Hall'. Yet this, too, was an exaggeration. For example, the initial mobilization went like clockwork, and the Admiralty transported men and supplies over a distance of 6,000 miles without a hitch—confirming the Senior Service in a well-developed sense of its own superiority.

Moreover, the army's problems were aggravated by the government's blundering diplomacy, itself shaped by Milner's bellicosity. No minister, least of all Chamberlain, *wanted* all-out war, neither did the Cabinet or War Office

envisage a protracted conflict. Hence the shortage of ammunition and uniforms. Hence, too, the failure to foresee the logistical difficulties of moving
troops around such a vast area—initially the railway transport division consisted of one officer, the highly efficient Colonel Girouard, plus one batman,
one horse, and a groom.[64]

Milner and Cabinet ministers alike were scathing in private about military
incompetence: Goschen thought the army's conduct furnished 'a story of
imbecility and futility'.[65] Yet Lansdowne, the War Secretary, must take
much of the blame for what went wrong, as must 'that unmitigated cold-
blooded rude brute Hicks-Beach', as Jacky Fisher called him.[66] The provision
of adequate maps, for example, would have required a Treasury grant of
£100,000 and several years of survey work—Lansdowne, the War Secretary,
did not even try to secure the necessary funding.

Since the mid-1890s priority in expenditure had gone to the Navy.
The result, as General Brackenbury observed in a minute of 15 December
1899, was that Britain was 'attempting to maintain the largest Empire
the world has ever seen with armaments and reserves that would be insufficient
for a third-class Military Power'. Salisbury also had a point when, addressing the Lords in January and March 1900, he angered Hicks Beach by
lambasting the Treasury's parsimony and its irksome system of expenditure
controls.

Yet, to some intelligent observers of public life, all these governmental and
military failures and mishaps seemed symptomatic of a far deeper malaise, the
analysis of which was to preoccupy the political class for many years to come,
under the rubric of 'National Efficiency'.[67]

The war undoubtedly delivered a psychological shock, shattering national
complacency and creating an intensified sense of danger. 'Will Britain Last the
Century?', asked the up-and-coming journalist (and Joseph Chamberlain's
future biographer) J. L. Garvin. There was also much speculation about the
decadence and inefficiency which had earlier brought down the Roman
Empire, with whose fortunes Britain's ruling elite strongly identified. This
was the moral of Elliott Mill's anonymous pamphlet *The Rise and Fall of the
British Empire*, first published in 1905, which sold 16,000 copies in six months
and was to exert considerable influence over Baden-Powell, as he began
thinking about how to organize youth. But a more common reaction, articulated by Kipling in his poem 'The Lesson', published in *The Times*, was that

---

[64] It later expanded to several hundred officers and 5,000 men (Symons, *Buller's Campaign*, 138).

[65] R. Shannon, *The Age of Salisbury, 1881–1902: Unionism and Empire* (Harlow, 1996), 499.

[66] Fisher to Thursfield, 8 Jan. 1901, in A. J. Marder (ed.), *Fear God And Dread Nought, Vol. 1: The
Making of an Admiral 1854–1904* (London, 1952), 179.

[67] Searle, *National Efficiency*.

'we have had no end of a lesson, it will do us no end of good'. Yet what was this lesson supposed to be?

For those willing to take notice, events in South Africa gave insights into the grim nature of modern war. For example, smokeless cordite meant that soldiers sometimes had few glimpses of those firing on them: fighting, in other words, had become both more mechanical and more impersonal. 'In Natal war was divested of absolutely everything that once lent it meretricious glamour', wrote one war correspondent: 'no bright uniforms, no inspiring bands playing men into battle, no flags, no glitter or smoke or circumstance of any kind, but just plain primeval killing, without redemption, and with every advantage taken that international law allows.'[68]

The military academies did not subsequently use the South African conflict as a case-study because they shared the widely held view that the subjugation of Boer farmers on the vast open spaces of the veldt offered no preparation for engaging with another Great Power on mainland Europe.[69] Had they done so, they might have learnt a very useful lesson for the future: namely, that with the growing employment of barbed wire and trenches, the tactical advantage was swinging towards the defence.

On the long-term future of imperialism the war had a mixed impact. Amery waxed lyrical about how events in South Africa had demonstrated the importance of 'the vast reserve of power latent in the patriotism of the free nations which compose the British Empire', but, in doing so, he conveniently ignored the tensions which had already complicated the imperial relationship: Canada, for example, had declined to make any official contribution to an imperial war force because, in the words of her Premier, Wilfrid Laurier, this 'would entail an important departure from the principle of Colonial self-government', and risked his country becoming involved in that 'vortex of militarism' which was 'the curse and blight of Europe'.[70] Finally, the heavy cost of the war may have encouraged Chamberlain and his friends to think of bold fiscal initiatives designed to bring greater unity to the Empire, but it also played into the hands of those eager to prioritize 'economy' and to stamp on all such grandiose schemes.

Moreover, the reliefs of Ladysmith and Mafeking may have marked the climax of imperialist fervour. The innocent idealism of early 1900 could hardly survive the revelations of farm-burning and concentration camps. By the time of Vereeniging the wider public had, to some extent, lost interest in the war, which, significantly, hardly featured in the 1906 election: perhaps because

---

[68] D. Macdonald, *How We Kept the Flag Flying: The Story of the Siege of Ladysmith* (London, 1900), cited in Smith, *Drummer Hodge*, 163.

[69] Jeffery, 'Kruger's Farmers', 194–5.

[70] Ibid. 190.

Liberals did not want to remind voters of their former divisions, while Unionists did not want to remind them of their incompetent stewardship.

Arguably the war initiated very little, merely confirming contemporaries in views that they had long held. Mrs Fawcett, for example, believed that the publicity given to the disfranchised Uitlanders meant that women could not be denied the vote for much longer. There were, however, some unifying themes underlying the fashionable rhetoric of 'National Efficiency'. The failures on the veldt suggested that the nation was conducting its affairs by reference to a false system of values. In particular, the big public schools came under fire for elevating 'character' over scientific 'intelligence', as well as for their frivolous obsession with sport: 'More officers of the studious type are needed', wrote one commentator, but 'the right type cannot be got from the public schools'.[71] Nothing could have been more gallant than the conduct of most officers, but it was professional competence, not bravery alone, which won modern wars.

'National Efficiency' sometimes assumed populist forms. For example, the journalist Arnold White, in *Efficiency and Empire* (1901), thought that the war had exposed corruption in high places and the decadence of 'bad' smart Society, as it fell under the malign influence of 'plutocrats' and cosmopolitan Jews. Yet he also argued that, while he wanted to replace the traditional aristocracy of birth with a new aristocracy of merit, aristocracy was 'nothing more than the most efficient people in the nation, whose efficiency has been graded up by generations of training'. In short, 'National Efficiency' was less an attempt to democratize the British state or to institute *la carrière ouverte aux talents* than a movement for shaming the existing elite into modernizing itself before its members were swept away. In this context, Germany was frequently held out as a model for emulation—but also as a rival whose very efficiency threatened the Empire.

The National Efficiency 'movement' was mainly held together by an informal network of friends and acquaintances: its only institutional legacy, characteristically, was a dining club, the 'Co-Efficients', established in November 1902, whose original twelve members (including Haldane, Grey, Webb, and Amery) aspired to 'permeate' the state and reshape its policy agenda. National Efficiency is perhaps best seen as a 'benevolent conspiracy' hatched from within the political establishment for its own reinvigoration.

'National Efficiency' appealed to many different constituencies. The Webbs and other bureaucratic socialists used it as a cloak behind which to advance their own collectivist schemes of social reconstruction. Meanwhile many Liberals, anxious to escape the clutches of the Newcastle Programme, welcomed what they saw as a project of institutional modernization that was both progressive

---

[71] A. H. H. Maclean, *Public Schools and the War in South Africa* (1903), 6.

and patriotic. Yet 'National Efficiency' also became associated with the circle of young admirers forming around Milner, among them Amery and Garvin, who viewed 'efficiency' as a way of escaping from the sterility of adversarial politics through its fusion of imperialism and 'sound' patriotic social reform.[72]

The cross-party character of 'National Efficiency' was significant. For its advocates insisted that the old battles between Conservativism and Liberalism—even those between capitalism and socialism—meant little compared with the more serious battle now taking place between the forces of competence and incompetence. In short, to those who took this 'managerial' view of the world, 'expertise' and 'business methods' mattered more than principle.

This new approach had particular relevance to two areas of national policy: education and social welfare. Educational reformers (notably Haldane) drew the deduction that, if the country were to retain its international competitiveness, it must take a leaf out of Germany's book—modernize its secondary schooling and bring technology within the ambit of its university system.[73]

Second, the obsession with 'National Efficiency' fostered a view of men and women as resources, a kind of raw material that was being squandered through incompetence and neglect. In 1901 the journalist Arnold White pointed out that, at the Manchester recruiting station, three out of five recruits at the start of the war had had to be rejected because they failed to meet the army's already shockingly low physical standards. Rowntree made similar claims in *Poverty*, as did Major-General Sir John Frederick Maurice in two articles carried by the *Contemporary Review* (January 1902 and January 1903).[74]

These revelations sparked off a confused and often ill-informed debate about whether or not 'physical deterioration' was taking place, a debate which also engaged prominent doctors and the Inspector-General of Recruiting. The government responded by setting up the Royal Commission on Physical Training in Scotland and an interdepartmental committee of inquiry into physical deterioration, whose report in July 1904 helped influence later social policy, with its account of atrocious living and working conditions. The embryonic eugenics movement, to which White later attached himself, drew its own very different conclusions.

But, once again, the 'lessons' of the war proved to be ambiguous. For whereas to some commentators recent events in South Africa underlined the need for modernization, to others they encouraged nostalgia for a rural past.[75] Many

[72] At his departure banquet Milner claimed to be 'cursed with a cross-bench mind'.
[73] See Chs. 10 and 16.
[74] In all 32.9% men were rejected in 1899, 28% in 1900, 29.04% in 1901 (M. Hendley, ' "Help us to secure a strong, healthy, prosperous and peaceful Britain": The Social Arguments of the Campaign for Compulsory Military Service in Britain. 1899–1914', *Canadian Journal of History*, 31 (1995), 267).
[75] Surridge, 'All you soldiers', 582–600.

army officers admired the military prowess of their Boer adversaries and the youthful vigour of the colonial troops, from which impressions they were reinforced in their instinctive belief in the damaging consequences of urban life. This lesson was later rubbed in when England's rugby team suffered defeat at the hands of the visiting All Blacks from New Zealand in 1905: 'is our national physique declining?', one England player asked.[76]

Such anxieties about physical deterioration were to influence policy debates long after the excitement and anxiety of the Boer War had been half-forgotten. But, in narrowly political terms, National Efficiency achieved little of immediate significance. There was, admittedly, much loose talk about the desirability of establishing a 'National Government', but this ambition was doomed by Rosebery's ineptitude. In any case, with the ending of the war in the summer of 1902, intense party rivalry was about to resume.

[76] D. Andrews, 'Sport and the Masculine Hegemony of the Modern Nation: Welsh Rugby, Culture and Society, 1890–1914', in J. Nauright and T. J. L. Chandler (eds.), *Making Men: Rugby and Masculine Identity* (London, 1996), 131.

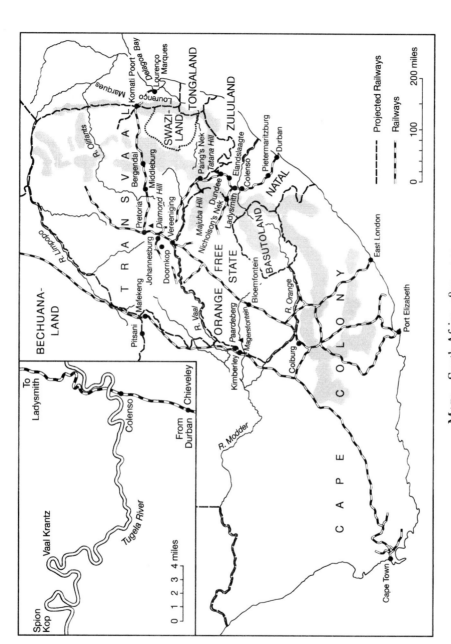

MAP: South Africa, 1899–1902

PART III

Edwardian England

CHAPTER 10

The Unionist Project, 1902–1905

Arthur Balfour was an unlucky Prime Minister. He had largely inherited his ministry from his uncle: fourteen of his nineteen Cabinet colleagues still retained their former posts. Hicks Beach's retirement necessitated one major change, the promotion to the Treasury of C. T. Ritchie. However, only two men joined the Cabinet for the first time: Balfour's friend George Wyndham, the Irish Secretary (now promoted to Cabinet rank), and Joseph Chamberlain's son Austen, who became Paymaster-General. Balfour thus found himself burdened with a stale ministry and a disgruntled party. There was also the prospect of future trouble from the elder Chamberlain, still recovering from a cab accident and none too pleased at the way his own prime-ministerial ambitions had been thwarted.

To his contemporaries Balfour often came over as an aristocratic dilettante. His many critics complained that he was too devoted to friends such as Wyndham; this cliquishness annoyed ambitious young MPs outside the charmed circle. But the malcontents included not only social outsiders but also the Prime Minister's cousin, Lord Hugh Cecil, leader of the rebellious 'Hughligan' faction to which Winston Churchill briefly attached himself. The all-pervasive presence of Balfour's trusted personal secretary 'Jack' Sandars, to whom even important business was often delegated, also bred resentment.

Influenced by ideas of 'National Efficiency', Balfour took a keen interest in state-funded science[1] and in the modernisation of education, co-operating across party lines with similar enthusiasts, notably his 'local' MP, the Liberal Imperialist R. B. Haldane,[2] who introduced him to the Webbs and their circle. These cross-party links, though often useful, further intensified the suspicions of the Conservative rank-and-file.

Finally, the Boer War had saddled Balfour with two major problems: a fiscal crisis and public alarm over the state of the armed services. The first gave rise to Chamberlain's tariff reform campaign which, as we will see, badly knocked

---

[1] His brother-in-law was the eminent physicist, Lord Rayleigh.

[2] Haldane represented Haddington, within the boundaries of which Balfour had his family seat, Whittingehame.

Balfour off course and made it difficult for him to keep his ministry afloat. On the other hand, in tackling issues of imperial defence, Balfour could boast considerable achievements during the two-and-a-half years he occupied 10 Downing Street.

International Relations

1. THE REORGANIZATION OF IMPERIAL DEFENCE

While the army was floundering on the South African veldt, the Senior Service had emerged from the war with some credit. But the navy did not subsequently sit on its laurels; on the contrary, the years of Balfour's government saw a massive programme of naval reform, presided over by the larger-than-life figure of Admiral 'Jacky' Fisher.[3] As Second Naval Lord (June 1902–August 1903), Fisher pushed through the so-called 'Selborne Scheme' (named after his political superior), which provided common entry and training for executive, engineering, and marine officers. This was part of Fisher's larger project aimed at producing a more meritocratic and less class-bound navy: 'The true democratic principle is Napoleon's "*La carrière ouverte aux talents!*" ', he later proclaimed.[4]

In October 1904, after serving as Commander-in-Chief at Portsmouth, Fisher returned to the Admiralty as First Sea Lord.[5] He secured the post, despite Selborne's reservations, because, at a time when naval expenditure was under acute pressure,[6] he was boasting that he could clearly see his way 'to *very great reduction* WITH INCREASED EFFICIENCY'.[7] One way of achieving this objective was by overhauling the Fleet Reserve through the establishment of the 'nucleus crew system', which ensured that ships in the reserve were manned with two-fifths of their normal complements, ready for expansion in a national emergency. With economy in mind, the Board of Admiralty also reorganized the fleets in late 1904 to produce a greater concentration of capital ships in home waters: there was to be a new Channel Fleet, based at Dover, and

---

[3] On the Fisher reforms, see A. J. Marder (ed.), *Fear God and Dread Nought: Vol. II: Years of Power 1904–1914* (London, 1956); J. T. Sumida, *In Defence of Naval Supremacy: Finance, Technology, and British Naval Policy 1889–1914* (London, 1993); N. A. Lambert, *Sir John Fisher's Naval Revolution* (London, 1999).

[4] Fisher to Esher, 5 Aug. 1910, cited in Marder (ed.), *Fear God and Dread Nought: Vol. II*, 334.

[5] Fisher assumed this title, which had previously been 'First Naval Lord'.

[6] Economy became all the more necessary after the Public Accounts Committee in 1904 had censured the raising of money by borrowing under the Naval Defence Acts (originally intended to improve only the naval infrastructure).

[7] Fisher to Thursfield, 5 July 1903, cited in Sumida, *Naval Supremacy*, 27.

a new Atlantic Fleet, based at Gibraltar. But Fisher abandoned the bases at Halifax and Esquimault, closed the Jamaica dockyards, and abolished the West Indian and North American squadrons.[8] One-hundred-and-fifty-four obsolete ships, 'too old to fight yet too slow to run away', were decommissioned 'with one courageous stroke of the pen', to use Balfour's own words. Vessels performing purely ceremonial or policing functions were scrapped.

Economy was also a leading consideration in Fisher's strong advocacy of the submarine. Ever since the French naval trials of 1899 the recognition had dawned that such underwater craft, armed with torpedoes, would revolutionize naval warfare by presenting a threat to all battleships and cruisers within their radius of action—a threat that no protective screen of destroyers could neutralize. An alarmed Admiralty decided in 1902 to build up its own flotilla. But it did so glumly, sensing that this new weapon of war would deprive the Royal Navy of future opportunities of operating a close blockade of enemy ports, as it had done during the Napoleonic Wars.

On the other hand, as Fisher was quick to grasp, the submarine significantly increased the security of an island state such as Britain, since, even if the main fleet had been defeated or lured away from home waters, flotilla defence, involving fast torpedo boats and submarines, would be more than adequate to deter an invader. This, in turn, meant that the army's defensive role could be reduced: Fisher gleefully predicted War Office economies which would bring down income tax to 3d. in the pound![9] Finally, submarines were cheap—a battleship cost twenty or thirty times as much—and, as Balfour noted, because they were invulnerable to attack from their enemy counterparts, they would not become obsolescent as speedily as surface vessels—another bonus in the eyes of 'economists'.[10]

Released from the obligation to patrol coastal waters, the submarine, Fisher believed, would liberate the Royal Navy to fulfil its traditional global mission. However, he advocated that this objective be met through the deployment of a new type of vessel that would combine the firepower of a battleship with the speed of an armoured cruiser—a hybrid to which he gave the name of 'battlecruiser'.

Although his name has been indelibly linked with the all-big-gun *Dreadnought* battleship, the keel of whose prototype was laid down on 2 October 1905, Fisher, ironically enough, had originally assigned a much greater significance to his *Invincible* battlecruisers, on which construction began a year

[8] M. Howard, *The Continental Commitment: The Dilemma of British Defence Policy in the Era of Two World Wars* (Oxford, 1971), 29–30.

[9] Lambert, *Fisher's Naval Revolution*, 81, 86. Fisher said: 'every battleship is open to attack by fast torpedo-craft and submarines' (p. 107).

[10] Lambert, *Fisher's Naval Revolution*, 65, 67, 89.

later. 'What is the use of battleships as we have hitherto known them?', he privately argued: 'NONE! Their one and only function—that of ultimate security of defence—is gone—lost!'[11] Indeed, he might well have suspended their construction entirely, had he not been overruled by his political chief, Selborne, who well understood how the public would take fright at the abruptness of this new departure. The Admiralty's Committee on Designs shared Selborne's unwillingness to put all its eggs into the battlecruiser basket. So Fisher was forced into a compromise which gave continuing pride of place to the battleship; and the battlecruiser, which only came into operation in 1908, was never built in the numbers that he had envisaged. Fisher may have had dictatorial proclivities, but on crucial issues he often failed to get his way.

Nevertheless the British Navy became a more effective fighting force during Fisher's stewardship. With the First Sea Lord's encouragement, Captain (later Admiral) Percy Scott improved gunnery standards, inaugurating a regime involving repeated target practice, as well as the use of modern, accurate range-finding instruments. Though the problem of fire-control was never satisfactorily resolved,[12] gone for ever were the days when naval commanders worried about getting their paintwork dirty!

Fisher's eccentric methods and personality made him many enemies. But he had the general support of Balfour and maintained a regular correspondence with the King, who treated him as a personal friend. Fisher also cultivated the support of the Navy League and of a band of devoted naval journalists, including Arnold White and editors such as J. L. Garvin, who were rewarded by being fed official information, often of a strictly confidential nature. Favoured politicians on both sides of the House were bombarded with effusive letters, usually written in coloured inks, peppered with exclamation marks, and invariably ending: 'please burn!' and 'yours till hell freezes!'

Fisher attracted controversy through his ruthlessness in promoting naval officers whom he knew he could rely upon to implement his policies—those in the 'Fishpond', as the saying went. This put an end to Nelson's happy 'band of brothers', and often made enemies even of sailors who had once largely been his allies. Prominent among the latter was Charles Beresford, second-in-command of the Mediterranean Fleet between 1900 and 1902, and later Commander of the Channel Squadron (1903–5), a naval officer whose carefully cultivated image of bluff seadog had brought him considerable popularity, which by 1904 had already earned him no fewer than four separate stints as a Conservative MP. With his political and 'Society' connections, Beresford emerged as the focal point of resistance for the naval traditionalists.[13]

---

[11] July 1904: Sumida, *Naval Supremacy*, 52. See also Lambert, *Fisher's Naval Revolution*, 92.

[12] See Sumida, *Naval Supremacy*.

[13] However, the most acute criticism came from Admiral Reginald Custance.

The Fisher era was thus marked by considerable turbulence. But it also resulted in very considerable achievements. The same could hardly be said of the army. This, though, was not for want of effort. In November 1900 St John Brodrick had entered the War Office so eager to proceed with his military reforms that, despite wiser first thoughts, he embarked upon them without waiting for an end to the fighting in South Africa. A committee of inquiry was already investigating War Office organization, and its report, issued in May 1901, paved the way later in the year for an expansion of the War Office Council and the Army Board and an amalgamation of the Mobilization and Intelligence Divisions. In March 1901 Brodrick took a far bolder step: he announced plans for creating six self-contained army corps on the German model, three of which, composed of regulars, were designed to fight abroad; the others, consisting of both regular and auxiliary units, would form a home defence force, to counter a possible invasion.[14]

This highly ambitious plan depended on the War Office attracting and funding an extra 11,500 recruits each year. Brodrick had originally hoped to hit this target by encouraging regulars to extend their three years of service— for example, by offering them increased pay. However, although he initially hoped that 75 per cent of regulars could be so persuaded, in the end only 22 per cent accepted the new terms. This doomed the scheme, since, from the start, the alternative of conscription had been ruled out—partly for political reasons but also because the army needed long-term recruits to man Britain's overseas garrisons. Another black spot on Brodrick's reputation was that during his regime military expenditure continued to rise, reaching a peak of £92.3 million in 1902, the last year of the war. Even in 1903 expenditure was still £69.4 million, three times higher than it had been before the outbreak of the South African hostilities: Hicks Beach and his successor, Ritchie, were loud in their complaints.[15]

To the unease of the whips, attacks on Brodrick, initially confined to the Cabinet, soon spread to the Unionist backbenches: on 12 March 1903 twenty-six Unionists voted with the Opposition, forcing the government into the desperate stratagem of wooing the Irish Nationalists, who were anxious to keep the ministry alive until the Irish Land Bill had been passed.[16] The War Secretary's proposals for home defence proved particularly contentious, since they involved raising the standards of the auxiliary forces; this provoked a

---

[14] R. Williams, *Defending the Empire: The Conservative Party and British Defence Policy 1899–1915* (New Haven and London, 1991), 11–21; E. M. Spiers, *The Late Victorian Army, 1868–1902* (Manchester, 1992), 327–8.

[15] Ritchie, in a memorandum to the Cabinet on 21 February 1903, warned that the present rate of military expenditure could not 'safely be continued'.

[16] Williams, *Defending the Empire*, 19.

rebellion among the Volunteer Colonels, about forty of whom, marshalled by Howard Vincent, sat in the Commons. The government was also being relentlessly harried by the twenty or so malcontents belonging to the 'Hughligans', most notably Jack Seely. Brodrick's army corps, they complained, were too small to fight in a European war but needlessly large for participation in the colonial conflicts they were more likely to face. In any case, Brodrick's plans scarcely got beyond the paper stage. The situation was well caught by the Opposition cartoonist who depicted Brodrick stumbling disconsolately around Salisbury Plain vainly searching for his army corps. In the reshuffle of October 1903 Brodrick, his reputation damaged by the recent Elgin Commission Report, was moved to the India Office.

It was a sign of the loss of confidence felt in all military men that Balfour originally wanted the War Office vacancy to be filled by Selborne, who was familiar with the widely admired board system at the Admiralty. Selborne declined the offer, as did several others,[17] but the post eventually went to H. O. Arnold-Forster, the Parliamentary and Financial Secretary to the Admiralty, another strong navalist. Indeed, Arnold-Forster had earlier commented in his diary that a good person to run the War Office might be Fisher himself— though he conceded that, were that to happen, 'the War Office would go mad!' Even so, the Admiral was prevailed upon to sit on a powerful three-man committee which Balfour set up in 1903 to reform the War Office.

This committee, which sat between November 1903 and February 1904, was chaired by Lord Esher, a member of the recent Elgin Commission, who combined an interest in military reform with a life of intrigue at the royal court, where he had served as Secretary to HM Office of Works between 1895 and 1902. In fact the Prime Minister, who was a personal friend, and the King had both tried to get him to take on the War Office. Esher declined because, as he frankly admitted to his son, he could not bring himself to sacrifice his 'independence' and ' "intimate" life', for a position which added nothing to the one that he then occupied.[18] Making up the 'triumvirate' was George Clarke, an army engineer who had earlier held a number of important posts including the secretaryship of the Hartington Commission, the secretaryship of the Colonial Defence Committee, and the governorship of Victoria.

Working with the remarkable haste that comes from knowing one's conclusions from the very outset, the Esher Committee made three key recommen-

---

[17] Nine men were considered, of whom five refused (3rd Viscount Chilston, *Chief Whip: The Political Life and Times of Aretas Akers-Douglas, First Viscount Chilston* (London, 1961), 313–20).

[18] 21 Sept. 1904. M. V. Brett (ed.), *Journals and Letters of Reginald Viscount Esher: Vol. 2 1903–1910* (London, 1934), 14. Esher made a habit of refusing offices and posts, among them the Under-Secretaryship for War in 1900, the Governorship of Cape Colony in the same year, and the Viceroyship of India in 1908.

dations. First, it advocated the abolition of the post of Commander-in-Chief (then held by Lord Roberts). Second, it urged the creation of an Army Council, modelled on the Board of Admiralty, on which the War Office ministers would be joined by four military members, with the First Military Member heading a newly constituted General Staff. Though accepted in principle by both Balfour and Arnold-Forster, and set up by an army order in January 1905, the General Staff did not become fully operational until October 1906, by which time the Unionists were out of office.[19]

This failure did not, however, too greatly disturb the Esher Committee, which envisaged a subordinate role for the General Staff on the ground that Britain was not a land power but relied primarily upon the navy to maintain her global empire. 'The German model is going to be our Frankenstein', Esher later privately complained.[20] Instead—and this was its third important recommendation—the committee proposed that the centre of defence planning should be the Committee of Imperial Defence (CID).

This was a body which Balfour had earlier created, in December 1902, after the two Service ministers, Selborne and Brodrick, had jointly approached him, declaring their inability to resolve the strategic differences between their respective departments. Balfour had responded by setting up a strong advisory Defence Committee, meeting under his own presidency, on which the Service ministers and their professional advisers could co-operate on an equal footing.

The Esher Committee now recommended the further strengthening of the CID by the addition of a Secretariat. Balfour agreed, appointing George Clarke as Secretary. Backed by Esher, Clarke argued that the CID should assume quasi-executive powers, gradually absorbing the planning and intelligence departments of War Office and Admiralty. Balfour warmed to this idea, and under his presidency the CID met over eighty times,[21] launching a series of investigations into the kind of complex strategic issues which required an input from more than one department.

None of this was welcome to Campbell-Bannerman, who, with some justification, dubbed the Esher Committee a 'Committee of Public Safety'. Moreover, the Opposition Leader continued to mistrust any augmentation of the role of military 'experts' and called for defence matters to be determined on the floor of the Commons: a view which Esher publicly dismissed as 'antediluvian'.[22] In fact the CID had, at least in theory, merely an advisory role, and it

[19] B. Bond, *The Victorian Army and the Staff College 1854–1918* (London, 1972), 221–3, explains the problems.

[20] Ibid. 220.

[21] Compared with the 44 times it was summoned during the years of Liberal rule between December 1905 and August 1914.

[22] G. R. Searle, *The Quest for National Efficiency: A Study in Politics and Political Thought, 1899–1914* (Oxford, 1971), 225.

was this which allowed military and naval officers to join the politicians in strategic discussions without technically infringing the prerogatives of Cabinet or Parliament. The CID thus provided a forum of co-operation between army and navy, while at the same time bridging the gap between political responsibility and military expertise and providing government with some protection from the buffeting of party politics. These advantages were well understood by the Liberal Imperialists, and, as the Balfour ministry slid to defeat in October 1905, Haldane was enlisted to provide reassurance of continuity.

In retrospect, Balfour's reconstitution of the CID can be seen as an important step in the professionalization of government: in December 1916 its Secretariat was transferred to the War Cabinet. At the time, however, the fate of the Unionists depended much less on what was happening to the CID than on whether Arnold-Forster could improve on the performance of his predecessor.

The new War Secretary entered office with a wide knowledge of defence issues and a strong commitment to fundamental military reform—both displayed in his 1900 pamphlet *The War Office, the Army, and the Empire*—and he quickly came up with a 'Scheme'. This involved not only the abandonment of Brodrick's army corps but also the abolition of the Cardwellian system of linked battalions. Instead, the army was to be divided between a short-term (three-year) home defence force of thirty battalions and a long-service (nine-year) army of 112 battalions for garrisoning India and the colonies and undertaking overseas operations.[23] Much of this foreshadowed Haldane's later army reforms.

Cocksure and tactless, Arnold-Forster unfortunately lacked Haldane's skill at man-management, and from the start he was treated by subordinates and superiors alike with a pitying condescension. The King, much interested in all things military, took offence at his War Secretary's ungracious manners, and Esher further worked to undermine his position at court. Indeed, Esher and Clarke used their position on the CID to sabotage the War Secretary's 'Scheme': in 1905, with Esher's help, Clarke fathered onto Balfour rival proposals of his own, which were printed on War Office stationery and dignified by the name of the 'Blue Paper'.

Arnold-Forster was also unlucky to have inherited the resentment felt by many soldiers at the high-handed behaviour of the Esher Committee, which, at the start of his term of office, had purged the War Office of all its existing senior military staff. Relationships did not improve thereafter. Before long Arnold-Forster was being openly defied by the military members of his new Army Council, who would take no responsibility for his proposed scheme.[24] One of

---

[23] Williams, *Defending the Empire*, 42–53.
[24] The War Secretary partly had himself to blame, having initially gone behind the Army Council's back.

the worst offenders was the incompetent first military member, Neville Lyttelton, who thwarted all attempts at dismissing him—an outcome not unconnected with the fact that he was the brother of Alfred Lyttelton, Chamberlain's successor as Colonial Secretary, one of Balfour's closest friends!

True, in October 1904 the Cabinet belatedly accepted the *principle* of long-term enlistments, and in June 1905 it went so far as to authorize an experiment in short-service recruiting.[25] But Arnold-Forster could make no serious headway within the Cabinet against the opposition of his two predecessors, Lansdowne and Brodrick, backed by Alfred Lyttelton; nor could he satisfy the Chancellor of the Exchequer's insistence that he bring army expenditure down from £29 million to £25 million.

Meanwhile, the War Secretary's clumsy attempts, in the interests of economy, at the amalgamation of the various voluntary forces[26] had aroused the wrath of MPs and peers representing the Militia, a long-established institution with deep roots in County Society (for example, Lords Salisbury and Selborne were both colonels in Militia regiments). In May 1904 twenty officers from the Auxiliaries went on a deputation of protest to the deeply worried Prime Minister.

Simultaneously Arnold-Forster was having to contend with the hostility of Lord Roberts who, following the publication of the Esher Committee Report, had vacated his position as Commander-in-Chief 'in a devil of a temper', and had had to be bought off with a place on the CID, plus a salary of £5,000 a year. In late 1905 Roberts was finally persuaded by Henry Wilson and other politically motivated middle-ranking officers to resign altogether from the CID, so that he could campaign for some kind of compulsory military service or training—as promulgated by the National Service League (NSL), established in February 1902, following the publication of George Shee's *The Briton's First Duty* (1901).[27] Roberts had already endorsed this idea in a speech at the Mansion House earlier in the summer. But compulsion in any form had, as yet, few supporters among Conservative MPs, nearly all of whom agreed with Balfour that, as well as being electorally suicidal, it was incompatible with the country's traditions and unsuited to the needs of a maritime power.

---

[25] See A. Tucker, 'The Issue of Army Reform in the Unionist Government, 1903–5', *Historical Journal*, 9 (1966), 90–100.

[26] The War Secretary was proposing to turn the Militia's best 60 battalions into short-service regular units ready for immediate overseas service, leaving the remaining 64 to be either disbanded or reformed to serve a purely defence role alongside the Volunteers and Yeomanry (Williams, *Defending the Empire*, 46).

[27] The NSL's programme was in constant flux, but in 1905 the League's formal demand was two months' compulsory training for males aged 18 to 22, to be supplemented by two weeks' annual training thereafter (ibid. 55); R. J. Q. Adams and P. Poirier, *The Conscription Controversy in Great Britain 1900–18* (Houndsmill, 1987), 10–16.

And so when Balfour left office, virtually nothing had been done to reform the army. Moreover, the legacy of the Boer War mishaps continued to haunt the ministry, as a series of reports from committees and commissions of inquiry came out, keeping alive the humiliating memories of 'Black Week' and damaging the reputations of politicians and administrators alike. At the Rye by-election in March 1903, the local Unionists were so demoralized by their party's record that they went into battle with the following campaign song:

> If we vote the muddlers out,
> We put bigger muddlers in.
> I shall vote for the present muddlers,
> And save a bigger sin.

(They duly lost.) In 1905 the Butler Report on the disposition of war stores was published—a damaging document which suggested that some senior army officers were corrupt as well as incompetent. No wonder that during the 1906 General Election campaign only one-third of Unionist candidates chose to make any specific reference to defence issues.[28]

Nonetheless, the overhaul of the War Office in the wake of the Esher Committee Report, the naval reforms, and the changes made to the CID between 1902 and 1905 have usually been held to Balfour's credit. The Prime Minister, who intellectually dominated the Cabinet, certainly had insights into the complexities of strategic planning which his two successors lacked. What, though, of the changes in British foreign policy, which should have constituted the context within which the ministry elaborated its strategic thinking?

2. THE END OF ISOLATION?

Though he perhaps underestimated the strength of isolationist feeling in America, Balfour had a far-sighted appreciation of the growing power of the United States, and worked hard to cultivate good relations with the Americans, building upon the Hay–Pauncefote Treaty of 1901, which had recognized the latter's naval dominance in the Western Atlantic.

But Balfour's main preoccupation was the menace to India implicit in Russia's railway development in Central Asia. 'The main purpose for which the army exists is not the defence of these shores, but the protection of the outlying portions of the Empire, and notably of India', Balfour declared.[29] No fewer than forty-three of Balfour's eighty-two CID sessions were largely

---

[28] A. K. Russell, *Liberal Landslide: The General Election of 1906* (Newton Abbot, 1973), 92.

[29] Feb. 1905, cited in Tucker, 'Army Reform', 94, n. 13.

devoted to Indian defence,[30] an obsession which few of the younger army officers shared.

Balfour's brooding over the Russian threat engendered in him something akin to pessimism. For the Prime Minister, like his uncle, did not believe that Russian expansion in Central Asia could be stopped militarily. The British government therefore did everything that it could to nip in the bud the confrontational policies of its headstrong Indian Viceroy, Lord Curzon—for example, disowning the latter in October 1904 over the Younghusband Mission into Tibet. Watchful diplomacy was instead the order of the day.

Balfour's stance on Russia was shared by Arnold-Forster and by his Foreign Secretary, Lord Lansdowne (a former Indian Viceroy). From the summer of 1903 onwards the latter was particularly anxious about the mounting tension in the Far East, where the conflicting claims of Russia and Japan in Manchuria threatened to escalate into war. Several members of the Cabinet wanted London to give strong backing to Britain's Japanese allies.

Lansdowne, however, still hankered after an accommodation with Russia over China and Central Asia, and the Foreign Office put much diplomatic energy into achieving this in 1903. St Petersburg, however, was no more responsive than it had been during the previous year.[31] Desultory exchanges with Berlin proved equally fruitless. Much greater success attended Lansdowne's attempts to improve relations with the French, a project which dated back to the spring of 1902, when he had opened conversations with the French Ambassador in London, Paul Cambon. The talks were resumed in October. Outstanding colonial differences, centring on Morocco, Newfoundland, and Egypt, dominated the agenda. The prospects of reaching a successful outcome increased during 1903, after King Edward had paid a successful visit to Paris and President Loubet had made a reciprocal goodwill visit to London soon afterwards.

Myth has it that these leisurely exchanges were then transformed by the mounting crisis in the Far East, which made the British much more eager for a settlement. In fact, Lansdowne nearly cancelled these talks at the last moment, showing that he attached relatively little importance to them. All the same, on 8 April 1904 the Anglo-French Entente was signed. Under its terms, the French agreed to underwrite Britain's position in Egypt, in return for which Britain, in a last-minute concession, recognized France's dominant role in Morocco. The Entente also contained secret clauses regulating the future disposition of these two 'colonies'. The only residue of Lansdowne's diplomatic efforts was thus an

---

[30] N. D'Ombrain, *War Machinery and High Policy: Defence Administration in Peacetime Britain 1902–1914* (Oxford, 1973), 62, n. 161.

[31] K. Neilson, *Britain and the Last Tsar: British Policy and Russia 1894–1917* (Oxford, 1995), Ch. 7, esp. p. 237.

arrangement with France—originally conceived as part of a bigger diplomatic edifice which was never, in fact, completed.

Meanwhile, on 8 February 1904 the long-foreseen Russo-Japanese War had at last begun. In Britain it produced an upsurge of sympathy for the Japanese, who were widely depicted as our Asiatic cousins and admired as another 'Island Race'. Beatrice Webb gushed in her diary about the wonders of *bushido*; H. G. Wells, in *A Modern Utopia* (1905), called his new governing elite the 'Samurai'; and Lord Rosebery claimed that the Japanese, with their collective discipline and self-reliance, furnished an inspiring example of 'National Efficiency'.[32]

Nevertheless, it is a testimony to ingrained racial assumptions that informed opinion in Britain should have been so slow to recognize that the Japanese were *winning*. Still obsessed with the alleged Russian threat, ministers watched with particular anxiety as Russia's Baltic Fleet lurched southwards en route to a rendezvous with its Pacific units in the Far East. In October 1904, off the Dogger Bank, a drunken Russian commander fired on some Hull trawlers, thinking them to be Japanese torpedo boats! An outraged public called for strong action, a majority in the Cabinet favoured war, and briefly the navy was placed on full alert.

Throughout this crisis Lansdowne displayed his usual cool common sense. The Russians furnished explanations and apologies, and the crisis passed. The Baltic Fleet steamed on to its nemesis at the battle of Tshushimo on 28 May 1905. Even before this momentous encounter, Port Arthur had been overrun by the Japanese army and riots in St Petersburg had forced the Tsar to summon the Duma. The scarcely conceivable had happened: Russia had been comprehensively defeated by an Asiatic power.

The Russian collapse provided the British with a number of unexpected windfalls. For the time being their imperial interests in India were safe from attack, while, at a stroke, the annihilation of the Russian fleet, until then the world's third most powerful navy, had increased Britain's margin of security, taking pressure off the naval budget. The diplomatic situation, too, was revolutionized. On 27 September the Anglo-Japanese Alliance was renewed, its scope being extended to India. It seemed that a new global order was emerging, one that linked together Britain, Japan, and—more indirectly—the United States.

The government, however, had misread the runes. For, preoccupied with securing their naval and imperial interests, Balfour and Lansdowne had been perhaps understandably inattentive to the impact which recent events had had on the balance of power in Continental Europe. The French Entente, for example, had been signed without reference to Germany: indeed, throughout

[32] Searle, *National Efficiency*, 57–9.

1903 and the early months of 1904 Lansdowne had seen no incompatibility between improved relations with Paris and the possibility of securing an Anglo-German accommodation. Nor did he fully understand how the destruction of Russia had indirectly weakened Russia's ally France, vis-à-vis Germany, thereby destabilizing the European order and creating new dangers for Britain herself.

German hostility, however, caused less surprise in the Admiralty. Selborne had first expressed alarm over the implications of Germany's 1900 Naval Law as early as November 1901, when intelligence reports had convinced him that the German Fleet was not designed for operations in distant waters. Since naval power was not essential for the protection of Germany's main supplies, which could easily be imported overland, what were the Germans up to? In his memorandum of 17 October 1902 Selborne gave his Cabinet colleagues an unambiguous explanation: 'I am convinced that the great new Germany navy is being carefully built up from the point of view of a war with us.'[33]

In the summer of 1903 Arnold-Forster visited Wilhelmshaven, from which he brought back a worrying account. Edward VII attended the Kiel Regatta in June 1904 and he, too, did not like what he saw: the return visit of the German Fleet to Plymouth the following month passed off in a sour atmosphere. In July 1904 *The Times*'s Berlin correspondent was writing of 'the readiness of the [German] fleet and the sleepless energy of the officers and men'.[34] Germany's very efficiency made her sudden arrival as a major naval power all the more threatening.

Selborne and his naval advisers began pondering the implications of these developments for the Two-Power Standard. The fear was that war with the Dual Alliance would leave Britain so weak as to be at the mercy of the rapidly growing German Fleet. Selborne therefore called for another £3 million to be added to the Navy Estimates, and later, in November 1904, Battenberg's committee recommended that Britain strive for a 10 per-cent margin of superiority over any possible combination of foreign navies—a standard officially adopted in late 1907.

However, it is only in retrospect that Fisher's appointment as First Sea Lord in October 1904 seems to signal the start of serious planning for a possible Anglo-German naval conflict. His regrouping of the British navy, producing a concentration of strength in, and close to, the North Sea, was not carried out with an exclusive eye to the German menace. Similarly, the development of a great naval base on the east coast, at Rosyth on the Firth of Forth, on which work now began in earnest, had been recommended by an Admiralty

---

[33] Cited in G. Monger, *The End of Isolation: British Foreign Policy 1900–1907* (London, 1963), 82.
[34] 1 July 1904. Marder (ed.), *Fear God and Dread Nought, Vol. II*, 108.

Committee as early as October 1902, purely on practical grounds (Rosyth's advantage was its proximity to the facilities and skilled workforce in the Glasgow region).[35] Far from being obsessed with Germany, Fisher's preference was for a Gibraltar-based strategy that would enable the Royal Navy to continue to play a global, imperialistic role.

Indeed, the Admiralty, despite its worries over Germany, still kept a watchful eye on the old enemy France: even in late 1904 it still had a contingency plan for attacking the French Fleet in the Mediterranean.[36] Selborne himself, in a memorandum of November 1904, coupled his worried remarks about the efficiency of the Germany navy with what must have seemed a truism: 'the French navy stands, as always, in the forefront.'[37] This stance was not entirely irrational since, even in late 1904, Germany was only the fourth or fifth naval power (depending on how one counted the vessels of the United States). Moreover, nearly all the recent technological innovations responsible for ratcheting up naval expenditure, from the armoured cruiser to the submarine, had been pioneered by the Marine Française, not at Wilhelmshaven. It was only the destruction of the Russian navy and mounting Franco-German hostility which left the expanding German fleet as Britain's most serious danger.[38]

The British public, however, was quicker to sound the alarm-bells. A. C. Curtis's *A New Trafalgar* (1902) features a surprise German naval attack against Britain, while Erskine Childers's exciting adventure yarn *The Riddle of the Sands*, published in the summer of 1903, describes how the Germans were planning a secret seaborne invasion of England from the Frisian coast while the bulk of the Royal Navy had been decoyed elsewhere.[39] Such invasion fantasies (there were to be many successors) alternated with loose talk about the desirability of a preventive attack on the German fleet before it had reached maturity. Journalistic effusions of this kind from Arnold White could readily be disowned by an exasperated Prime Minister. However, in late 1904 Fisher himself was talking (fortunately in private, and perhaps not very seriously) about 'Copenhagening' the German fleet, remarks which Arthur Lee, the Civil Lord of the Admiralty, repeated publicly, albeit in more diplomatic language,

---

[35] Lambert, *Fisher's Naval Revolution*, 34.

[36] S. R. Williamson, *The Politics of Grand Strategy: Britain and France Prepare for War, 1904–1914* (Cambridge, Mass., 1969), 16.

[37] Lambert, *Fisher's Naval Revolution*, 102, 104; R. F. Mackay, *Fisher of Kilverstone* (Oxford, 1973), 313–15.

[38] Sumida, *Naval Supremacy*, 59–60.

[39] Selborne was sufficiently alarmed by Childers's book to ask the Director of Naval Intelligence whether such an invasion scheme was feasible; he was told that it was not (C. Andrew, *Secret Service: The Making of the British Intelligence Community* (London, 1985), 37). The book went through ten impressions before 1914 (W. J. Reader, *At Duty's Call: A Study in Obsolete Patriotism* (Manchester, 1988), 69).

in February 1905. During the winter of 1904–5 an alarmed German government genuinely thought that it was about to be attacked.

The army, too, quickly cottoned on to the 'German threat'. In the summer of 1903 the CID had conducted a major inquiry into whether the navy was competent to protect Britain from a sizeable invasion. It concluded in the affirmative, and Balfour strongly endorsed its arguments in what was a crushing triumph for the 'blue-water' school of strategists.[40] On 9 March 1905 the Defences of London were officially abolished. However, most military men never really accepted the CID's verdict. Publicly they claimed that the fleet would be 'manacled' by its defensive responsibilities; privately, what galled them most was the suggestion that the army's sole role in home defence was coping with minor 'raids'. A number of keen, up-and-coming officers—men who prided themselves on being modern, 'thinking soldiers'—began to search for a new sphere of usefulness for the army.

The German 'threat' provided them with the strategic opportunity they craved. Some military men now began advocating the adoption of a system of military alliances in order that Britain could, at an appropriate moment, fight Germany in a Continental war: there was a difference, they contended, between preventing defeat and bringing a war to a decisive conclusion, for which a powerful army was needed.[41] They also wanted conscription, but had to conceal their ardour for this innovation behind a campaign for universal military service, which allegedly would have other advantages, such as toughening the physique and the character of the urban masses.

A Continental strategy thus began to take shape. Its leading advocate was Henry Wilson, who shortly afterwards, as Commandant of the Staff College between 1907 and 1910, made a detailed study of the battlefields of France and Flanders where he expected the next great European war would be fought, with Britain's full participation. Loosely attached to Wilson were young officers of whom much more was subsequently to be heard, such as William Robertson, James Grierson, and A'Court Repington,[42] as well as some of Roberts's younger protégés, notably French and Haig, two of the more successful Boer War commanders. As early as 1902 Robertson had argued: 'Instead of regarding Germany as a possible ally, we should recognize her as our most persistent, deliberate and formidable rival.'[43]

---

[40] This was the basis for the PM's statement to the Commons in May 1905.

[41] J. Gooch, *The Prospect of War: Studies in British Defence Policy 1847–1942* (London, 1981), 11. The point had earlier been made by Colonel Altham in his paper, 'The Military Needs of the Empire' (1901) (Howard, *Continental Commitment*, 35).

[42] Now military correspondent to *The Times*, after a scandal had led to his resignation from the army.

[43] Howard, *Continental Commitment*, 35.

Yet, oddly enough, within the Cabinet itself hostility to Germany was by no means universal. The one minister who, from an early stage, had treated an Anglo-German conflict as a strong likelihood was Joseph Chamberlain, still reeling from the failure of his earlier attempt to secure a German alliance.[44] Austen Chamberlain shared his father's view that it was in Britain's interest to convert improved relations with France into an anti-German front. But Lansdowne neither agreed with this position nor understood the emotions which underlay it.

In fact, the Foreign Secretary had first had his attention drawn to the strength of Germanophobia in the winter of 1902–3, when a joint naval operation with Germany to recover debts from the Venezuelan government had gone badly awry: German ships, without consultation, had opened fire, threatening to involve the British as well as themselves in hostilities with the United States. There was a public outcry, echoed at government level by Chamberlain. Rudyard Kipling registered the patriotic mood with a bilious diatribe against those who had tried,

> With a cheated crew, to league anew
> With the Goth and the shameless Hun![45]

Much more of this sort of language was to be heard over the next few years.

A few months later, in April 1904, Lansdowne was prevented from co-operating with Germany over a scheme to finance the Baghdad Railway because of the strength of popular hostility, fomented by another virulent press campaign, in which Chamberlain probably had a hand. Privately the Foreign Secretary lamented what he called an 'insensate outcry', but he bowed before the storm. Leopold Maxse, editor and proprietor of the right-wing monthly the *National Review*, was only one of a growing number of Fleet Street journalists who had 'Germany on the Brain'. The tariff reform campaign, too, had from the very start exploited the antipathy to Germans caused by their allegedly 'unfair' trading practices.

Germanophobia was also beginning to influence thinking within the Foreign Office itself. Admittedly, Lansdowne could count on the general support of his elderly Permanent Under-Secretary, 'Lamps' Sanderson, who had once tried to restrain his chief's pro-Germanism but now felt it necessary to counter the growing anti-German animus that was spreading all around him. The leader of this latter tendency was Francis Bertie, an Assistant Under-Secretary, who was convinced that Germany was 'false and grasping and our real enemy commer-

---

[44] Chamberlain, because he wanted quick solutions, was more easily discouraged than Salisbury, who saw all problems and situations as transient (J. Charmley, *Splendid Isolation? Britain and the Balance of Power 1874–1914* (London, 1999), 232).

[45] R. Kipling, 'The Rowers', in *The Years Between*.

cially and politically'.[46] Similar views were entertained by up-and-coming men such as Louis Mallet and Eyre Crowe. Bertie's main ally in the Diplomatic Service was Charles Hardinge, whose wife's position as one of the Queen's ladies-in-waiting gave the group easy access to the King, who increasingly shared their anti-German prejudices—though Edward's attitudes were largely determined by his fluctuating personal relationship with his cousin, the equally unstable Kaiser.

When, in 1903, Bertie left the Foreign Office for the Rome Embassy Hardinge briefly took his place, before becoming Ambassador to the Tsar in the following year. At the same time, in mid-1904, Bertie, enlisting the King's help, succeeded in getting himself transferred to the Paris Embassy, over Lansdowne's initial opposition. The final triumph of the Bertie–Hardinge axis came in 1905, when Lansdowne agreed to replace the ailing Sanderson with Hardinge, and shortly afterwards Mallet, on Hardinge's recommendation, was taken up by Lansdowne's successor, Edward Grey, as his private secretary. British foreign policy was about to take a much more overtly anti-German turn.

In the spring of 1905 even Balfour and Lansdowne found themselves driven into taking the German challenge more seriously, for on 31 March the Kaiser made his provocative landing in Tangier. Disturbed by Britain's Entente with France, but conscious of their own enhanced strength following the Russian collapse, the Germans felt that they could break the new Paris–London axis by challenging France's position in Morocco and exposing Britain's unreliability or ineffectuality as a friend.

Almost at once the Admiralty, alarmed by the Germans' demand for coaling stations in Morocco, adopted a defiant posture: 'this seems a golden opportunity for fighting the Germans in alliance with the French', Fisher told Lansdowne on 22 April. Once again the Foreign Secretary ignored the hot-headed advice he was receiving from the likes of Mallet. On 17 May he met the French Ambassador Paul Cambon and suggested that their two countries keep in close touch. An excited Cambon came away from this interview mistakenly supposing that the French were being offered a full-blown alliance. In fact, all that Lansdowne was trying to do was to prevent a rattled French government making terms with Germany over Britain's head.

The Foreign Office's worst fears were confirmed in early June when Delcassé, the French Foreign Minister, was forced under German pressure to resign his office. Though still anxious to limit their own commitments, the British now intensified their efforts to stiffen French resolve. German pressure

[46] To Mallet, 11 June 1904: Z. S. Steiner, *The Foreign Office and Foreign Policy, 1898–1914* (Cambridge, 1969), 66.

had thus produced the very thing that it was intended to avert: closer political co-operation between Britain and France, not just in colonial matters, but more generally on the European stage.

Behind the scenes other momentous events were taking place. In July the British government, for the first time, gave serious consideration to sending an expeditionary force to fight alongside the French, and a permanent CID subcommittee was actually set up to consider the technical problems involved in combined operations abroad. Though this body never met, events were acquiring a momentum of their own.

However, the CID was hardly in a position, as yet, to supply the government with a viable war plan. For a start, its creation had certainly not succeeded in resolving inter-Service rivalry. On the contrary, Fisher was still sticking to the idea of amphibious attacks on Schleswig-Holstein, to the increasing derision of the War Office (Arnold-Forster privately dismissing it as simply 'ridiculous').[47] In fact, in October the Director of Military Operations specifically reversed an earlier War Office decision to back a Baltic expedition—on the ground that it would be too risky to send troops through mined coastal waters. Ominously, military war games had taken place in April and May on the premise that British troops might instead have to fight on the Continent in alliance with France.

When the Unionists left office in December 1905 the Moroccan Crisis remained unresolved, with an international conference about to meet at Algeçiras to sort out the Great Powers' competing claims. Balfour's legacy to his successors was therefore a mixed one. Britain, though stronger than she had been for some time as a global, imperial power, faced a difficult situation in Europe—a situation which, briefly, grew even more fraught when a friendly meeting between the Tsar and the Kaiser at Bjorko in late May 1905 threatened to bring together her two most embittered foes in a Continental alliance. Though that danger quickly passed, Britain *was* being drawn into an anti-German bloc, something which Lansdowne clearly regretted but seemed powerless to avert.

A similar uncertainty clouded strategic thinking. The CID had provided the British government with a planning mechanism of which much more might have been made. The navy was indeed in a stronger position, even taking into account the recent expansion of the German fleet. On the other hand, the army remained unsure of its role and largely unprepared for any of the contingencies currently under discussion.

Is it right to claim that Balfour had presided over a fundamental shift in British foreign policy? Addressing the United Service Institution on 27 June 1904, Edward Grey, the Liberals' foreign-policy expert, was already hailing the

---

[47] D'Ombrain, *War Machinery*, 61.

end of 'splendid isolation', whose time, he argued, had now well and truly passed. Grey's assessment may have been correct; but few Unionist ministers saw things in this black-and-white way. Lansdowne had been an accomplished Foreign Secretary, whose coolness under fire had served his country well, while Balfour had displayed an interest in strategic planning which few modern Prime Ministers could match. But the overwhelming impression left by the two men is that of sleepwalkers stumbling into a Continental entanglement which had originally been very far from their thoughts.

The Domestic Front

I. THE 1902 EDUCATION ACT

After his resignation Balfour publicly questioned whether the new Foreign Secretary, Edward Grey, for all his capacity and patriotism, could preside over a foreign policy that equalled Lansdowne's. But he could hardly be so bullish about the outgoing government's record in domestic affairs, which gave the impression of stumbling from one disaster to another. This is true even of the Education Act of 1902, a measure which won him posterity's plaudits but did his government little good at the time.

Ministers had been working on this measure since late 1901. Given the continuance of the war, they would probably have left education entirely alone, but for the mess created by the Cockerton Judgement of 1901,[48] which had thrown into doubt the legality of the so-called 'higher grade schools'—the educational establishments run by the School Boards which catered for pupils aged 12 and even older. Emergency legislation had been rushed through Parliament allowing these schools to operate for another year. But what then?

The minister with departmental responsibility was John Gorst, who commanded little support in the Commons. So in December 1901 a Cabinet Committee was appointed to hammer out a new Education Bill. Its members quickly resolved that all post-elementary education should be put under a committee of the county and county borough councils—the authorities currently in charge of technical education.[49] But why not go further and transfer the work of the School Boards to these education committees, thus bringing both elementary and secondary education under the same 'unitary' authority? After all, as Gorst had reminded Devonshire in December 1900, School Boards

---

[48] The House of Lords upheld the judgement reached in Queen's Bench in 1900, which in turn upheld the previous year's decision by the district auditor, T. B. Cockerton.

[49] Since 1890 technical education had been subsidized out of the so-called 'whisky money': tax revenue originally earmarked to compensate brewers and publicans for forfeited liquor licences; intense temperance pressure eventually forced the government to abandon these licensing proposals.

were 'a modern anomaly in Local Government, which would never have been created if county councils had existed in 1870'.[50] Much overlapping, confusion, and waste would disappear once these ad hoc authorities were wound up. Some ministers, however, still hesitated to stir up this particular hornet's nest.

There were also divided counsels within the Cabinet Committee about what, if anything, to do with the ailing church schools, some 14,000 in number, where over one-third of all children were still acquiring their 'three Rs'. Traditional Conservatives had long wanted public money to be used to save these predominantly Anglican schools from financial collapse. Indeed, the Whips' Office warned Balfour that his backbenchers would explode in anger if he sidestepped this problem by confining his measure to secondary education. Even the Liberal Unionist, Devonshire, a member of the Cabinet Committee, agreed that something would have to be done for the voluntary schools. Yet Salisbury and Chamberlain—an unlikely combination—urged caution: the former fearful of destroying the independence of the church schools, the latter only too aware of the Nonconformists' likely objections.

Once ministers had resolved to pursue a broader measure, Chamberlain desperately searched for ways of averting sectarian strife. Nonconformist opposition, he initially suggested, would be lessened if church schools were simply given an increased Exchequer grant rather than rate aid. Ironically, the hideous expense of 'Joe's war' ruled out such a solution. This left the government with no alternative but to put the church schools on the rates. Chamberlain was only mollified when, at the suggestion of Devonshire, the government resolved that the new local educational authorities (LEAs) would have the 'option' of taking over elementary education (including the church schools in their locality) but would not be *compelled* to do so: with the likely consequence that in strongly Nonconformist parts of the country this part of the educational system would not operate.

Yet this concession, however politically prudent, threatened to create a crazy administrative patchwork quilt—without fundamentally propitiating the Bill's critics. That point was soon grasped by Balfour, who, working in conjunction with Robert Morant, a ruthlessly ambitious civil servant at the Board of Education, decided that boldness was the best policy. On 9 July he therefore encouraged the House, at committee stage, to vote down the 'Local Option clause'—a fateful move which unfortunately took place at a time when Joe Chamberlain was in hospital following his cab accident.[51] Showing exceptional

---

[50] R. Betts, *Dr Macnamara 1861–1931* (Liverpool, 1999), 143. It also made administrative sense to link the educational authority to the local rating authority.

[51] The Clause was taken on a free vote, with Austen Chamberlain, significantly, voting to retain the status quo. Liberal MPs were also split—mainly over the amendment's other consequence, the transferral of all Board schools.

determination, as well as his customary agility in debate, Balfour then pressed ahead with his Bill, which was passed by the Commons under closure in December.

In its final form, the 1902 Education Act had a pleasing clarity of purpose. It made it mandatory on the new LEAs to organize educational provision at *all* levels—elementary, secondary, and technical—in the process taking financial responsibility for the cost of the secular instruction that the church schools offered. The huge London School Board, with its more than 500 schools catering for half-a-million pupils, was temporarily reprieved, but the other 2,650 or so Boards were swept away, their place being taken by some 350 LEAs.[52] To many reformers the ending of the dual system and the establishment of a 'unitary' educational body was welcomed as a long-overdue measure of administrative rationalization.

Moreover, National Efficiency advocates had long hankered after less democratic accountability and more expertise: the LEAs, they believed, would not only shield education from direct popular control but could also co-opt 'experts' of various kinds. This is the main reason why, breaking ranks with his party, Haldane supported the 1902 measure, as did the Webbs. A similar coalition came together once more in 1903, when the machinery of the 1902 Education Act was extended to London.[53]

Yet, especially in the big cities, powerful vested interests had grown up around the School Boards, most of them controlled by Radicals who were hardly likely to be attracted by arguments about more efficiency and less accountability. Campbell-Bannerman and James Bryce, the Liberal Party's educational pundit, openly advocated the retention of the School Boards. So, unanimously, did the Parliamentary Committee of the TUC. And so, understandably, did the Women's Local Government Society's most politically active women: after all, about 370 women were currently sitting on these bodies, whereas they were still debarred from serving on county councils and county borough councils. (This difficulty was later overcome, in part, by requiring LEAs to co-opt women with relevant expertise.[54])

But the controversy caused by the abolition of School Boards was as nothing compared with the furore surrounding the granting of rate aid to church schools. The Irish Nationalists supported the move, because it safeguarded

---

[52] Boroughs with populations over 10,000 and urban districts with populations over 20,000 were also made LEAs. Some have questioned whether this was much of an improvement (P. J. Waller, *Town, City and Nation: England 1850–1914* (Oxford, 1983), 271).

[53] Haldane and the Webbs successful worked for a broadening of the Bill, so that the LCC was given full powers.

[54] P. Hollis, *Ladies Elect: Women in English Local Government 1865–1914* (Oxford, 1987), 128–30. By 1907 women comprised some 7% of LEA members, but they found it difficult to make a mark, now that they were no longer directly elected.

the position of the Catholic schools in England and Wales—which was where most Irish immigrant children were educated. But two groups (with overlapping membership) were enraged: Nonconformists, who objected to paying for the upkeep of schools promoting a creed to which they had strong conscientious objections; and 'democrats' who, campaigning under the banner of 'no taxation without representation', denounced the use of public money to bale out schools that were not under full public control.

Balfour declared himself puzzled that there should be such anger about rate-aid, when grants from *central* government had been paid to church schools for generations without, of late, eliciting much protest. In any case, the 1902 Act gave the LEAs a statutory right to minority representation on the governing boards of those voluntary schools in receipt of public funds, as well as control over their provision of purely secular instruction; moreover, following the passing, on a free vote, of an amendment tabled by the Conservative back-bencher Colonel Kenyon-Slaney, even religious instruction would in future be the responsibility of the school managers, not the parish clergyman. But nothing could soften Nonconformist anger: in June the National Council of Free Churches publicly declared that Nonconformity faced 'a crisis more serious than any that [had] arisen . . . since 1662 and the Act of Uniformity'.[55]

In Wales, Lloyd George stirred up a rebellion against the Act, which coincided with a powerful revivalist movement: most local authorities in the Principality threatened to ignore the measure, forcing the government to intervene directly (through a Default Act). In England the protests were only slightly less furious. Militant Dissenters, following the lead of the Baptist minister Dr John Clifford, refused on principle to pay that share of the rates that they deemed likely to go to church schools: some of these 'passive resisters' suffered distraint of their property, and a few were prepared to embrace imprisonment.[56]

In this sharply polarized conflict the Unionists found themselves at a disadvantage. Angry over the Kenyon-Slaney clause, Lord Hugh Cecil and other members of the High Church party complained that the Education Act was unfair to *them*: they feared—rightly, in the long run—that its provisions would result in Anglican schools being effectively nationalized and deprived of their distinctive sectarian features. Also critical were some Conservatives representing agricultural constituencies, such as Harry Chaplin and F. C. Rasch, who fretted over the prospect of increased local expenditure.[57]

---

[55] S. H. Zebel, *Balfour: A Political Biography* (Cambridge, 1973), 120.

[56] More than 34,000 summonses in 1903–4. By the start of 1904 there had been 7,324 summonses against resisters and 329 distraint sales of resisters' goods.

[57] Rasch, MP for Chelmsford, was one of two Conservative MPs voting against the Bill on its second reading.

The Unionist Nonconformists, too, were up in arms—but for diametrically opposed reasons. Their leading spokesman, Chamberlain, also had grounds for feeling betrayed over the disappearance of the optional clause. Indeed, in October he came under attack from within his own Liberal Unionist organization in Birmingham and needed all his eloquence and prestige to face down his critics. Privately Chamberlain warned ministers that Liberal Unionist voters, many of them Nonconformists, were deserting the Unionist government in droves, and he predicted that they would not easily be won back.[58]

Meanwhile the Liberal Opposition, identifying itself with Dissent, promised to repeal what it saw as nothing more than a Voluntary Schools Relief Act devised by the Church party. As well as being active in his native Wales, Lloyd George achieved national prominence by making highly personalized attacks in the Commons on the Prime Minister and excoriating the latter's attempt to 'rivet the clerical yoke on thousands of parishes'. Other leading Liberals, though more cautious in their language, took broadly the same line. Haldane, in his support of the Act, was a lonely figure. The other Liberal Imperialists, Asquith, Grey, and even Rosebery (pressurized by his two Methodist friends, Henry Fowler and Robert Perks) assailed the measure as keenly as did the Radical wing of the party. A series of by-election triumphs (notably at North Leeds on 30 July) indicated that the Liberals were on to a winner.

Balfour's bid to rectify the failures of the English educational system was eventually vindicated. When the Liberals returned to office at the end of 1905, they found Balfour's settlement very difficult to overturn—and not just because of the hostility with which the House of Lords greeted their counter-proposals. For Balfour had surely been right in his decision to incorporate the church schools, on tightly defined terms, into an orderly local educational system. Building new secular schools to replace them would have been intolerably expensive; expropriating them, a violation of property rights quite unacceptable to mainstream Liberal opinion.

In fact, the 1902 Education Act led to positive improvements in voluntary schooling—which is why it received a guarded welcome from some members of the National Union of Teachers, including its former President, the Radical MP Dr Macnamara.[59] The Act also made possible a dramatic improvement in the provision of secondary education. By 1914 over 1,000 secondary schools had been created under the Act, 349 of them for girls. Central schools started in London in 1911, providing vocational education of a lower standard, and from 1913 onwards there were junior technical schools, designed to provide skills

---

[58] Even at parliamentary level, Liberal Unionist cohesion had been gravely weakened. Not only had Devonshire and Chamberlain pursued divergent lines, but the amendment removing the Optional Clause had actually been moved by a Liberal Unionist backbencher, Henry Hobhouse.

[59] Betts, *Macnamara*, ch. 8, esp. pp. 162–3, 165–7.

needed in local industries. Belatedly Britain also began to develop a system of university education more closely resembling that found on the Continent.[60]

But politically the 1902 Education Act was an unqualified disaster. For a start, it left Chamberlain disgruntled. When the Colonial Secretary set off in November 1902 on his tour of South Africa to oversee the reconstruction of the conquered Boer republics, he was already in an aggrieved mood; and his temper did not improve when, on returning in mid-March of the following year, he found the government in poor shape, with its 1903 Bill extending the 1902 Education Act to London under fierce fire in the Commons. Moreover, in January the Liberals, campaigning hard on the education issue, had won a sensational by-election victory at Newmarket, which they captured on a 10 per-cent swing. Two months later they secured an even bigger swing of 18 per cent to take the hitherto impregnable seat of Rye. Chamberlain's discontent mingled with other grievances in a way that changed the face of British politics: he launched the tariff reform movement, thereby challenging the primacy of free trade and opening the way to the introduction of tariffs for protectionist, preferential, and revenue-raining purposes.

2. THE GENESIS OF TARIFF REFORM

Tariff reform broke upon a startled political world, yet it had been a long time a-brewing.[61] Calls for the protection of British industries from 'unfair' competition had not abated since the 1880s—and were being skilfully exploited by advertisers.[62] In April 1902 Ernest Williams, author of the notorious *Made in Germany* (1896), attempted to create a 'Fiscal Reform Association', against a background of hysteria about foreign penetration of the home market—this time more centred on America than Germany. Moreover, politicians with long memories had not forgotten that in 1895 Chamberlain, challenged in the Commons, had suggested that old-age pensions could be paid for 'by an import duty on wheat'. Such a duty now existed.[63]

Intermittently Joseph Chamberlain had also indicated his sympathy for closer economic ties within the Empire, notably in two speeches in March and June 1896 shortly after becoming Colonial Secretary. Closer trade relations had also figured on the agenda of the 1897 and 1902 Colonial Conferences. But

---

[60] See Ch. 16.

[61] See Ch. 8.

[62] Buttercup Metal Polish urged consumers to 'help home trade' by purchasing its product, which would give them a superior polish and also provide employment to a large number of home workers (*The Lady*, 1 July 1897: cited in L. A. Loeb, *Consuming Angels: Advertising and Victorian Women* (Oxford and New York, 1994), 53).

[63] R. A. Rempel, *Unionists Divided: Arthur Balfour, Joseph Chamberlain and the Unionist Free Traders* (Newton Abbot, 1972), 19.

when Chamberlain broached the issue of an imperial *Zollverein* (customs union) at the 1902 Colonial Conference, he had gathered little support from the assembled delegates. Instead, Wilfrid Laurier, the Canadian Premier, reminded him that in 1897 Canada had unilaterally cut its tariff on imported British goods by 25 per cent and three years later by 33 per cent; he now asked whether the British could not make a reciprocal gesture to this 'generous offer'. Chamberlain did his best: at the Cabinet of 19 November, just before leaving for South Africa, he seemed to have squeezed out of his colleagues a provisional agreement to give Canada a preferential advantage on the corn registration duty.

However, in Chamberlain's absence Ritchie, egged on by his Treasury officials, prepared a counter-attack. In early 1903 he informed Balfour that he would resign rather than allow the long-term future of free trade to be prejudiced by any preferential arrangement. In mid-March, a fortnight after Chamberlain's return to England, the Cabinet formally upheld Ritchie's position. Afraid of further offending the Canadians, Chamberlain urged the total repeal of the corn duty—which Ritchie was more than happy to do. The Cabinet attempted to appease the angry Colonial Secretary by telling him that he could reopen the fiscal problem at some future date. This compromise might just possibly have secured peace, had not Ritchie (ironically, a one-time protectionist) then made a doctrinaire defence of free trade in his Commons statement on 23 April—in clear breach of the spirit of the recent Cabinet agreement.

Chamberlain reacted to this provocation. On 15 May he made a controversial speech at the Bingley Hall in Birmingham in which, through a series of rhetorical questions, he challenged the premises of free trade and called for the closer economic unity of the Empire. To compound the confusion, this was the very day on which Balfour was defending the abolition of the corn registration duty to a disappointed agricultural deputation headed by 'Squire' Chaplin.

Chamberlain still had only the haziest notion of what he wanted to achieve. All the same, friend and foe alike were electrified by the Birmingham speech. L. S. Amery, the military correspondent of *The Times*, later likened it to Luther's challenge to the authority of the Church of Rome at Wittenberg. Liberal politicians were equally quick to appreciate the significance of an initiative which they had been predicting for several months.

Events then unfolded rapidly. A week later Chamberlain spoke in the Commons, widening his demands to include not only preferences but also social reform, a measure of agricultural protection, and the safeguarding of manufacturing industry against unfair practices, including dumping, exporting commodities at below the cost of production to ruin overseas competition— implying, moreover, that in all of this Balfour agreed with him.

The Unionist Party split wide open, as Chamberlain's allies and opponents prepared for a fight. On 20 June Chaplin moved an amendment condemning the government for its repeal of the corn duty, and four days later 130 MPs attended a meeting to discuss the furtherance of preferential trade within the Empire. Meanwhile the so-called Unionist Free Fooders, who included not only Beach and Ritchie but also younger 'Hughligans' such as Churchill, Seely, and Lord Hugh Cecil, began their counter-offensive.

Balfour tried to head off the split by a series of delaying moves designed to blur the edges of the ideological divisions within his party.[64] In a Commons statement on 9 June he declared that he personally had 'no settled convictions' on the matter, but urged that preference be treated as an open question for the time being. His Cabinet colleagues were ordered to maintain silence while further enquiries were conducted.

Despairing of receiving objective advice from Treasury officials, Balfour turned to Llewellyn Smith at the Board of Trade and to a young economist, Percy Ashley.[65] In the autumn the Prime Minister produced a paper, *Economic Notes on Insular Free Trade*, in which he acknowledged that the protectionist policies of Britain's trading partners necessitated a reconsideration of the case for free trade and argued for 'liberty of fiscal negotiation' and a possible resort to retaliation against countries whose tariffs were unreasonably high. A Cabinet meeting of 13 August discussed this document. But it also had before it a confidential 'Blue Paper', in which Balfour provisionally accepted the theoretical case for preferential tariffs but made it clear that this was not yet within the realm of practical politics. Balfour had thus subtly changed his stance, turning his government from one of fiscal *enquiry* into one committed to fiscal *change*, albeit at some indeterminate point in the future.

The following month Balfour secured a breathing-space by ridding his Cabinet of 'extremists' of both wings. When Chamberlain announced his desire to leave the government to conduct a propaganda campaign in the country in support of his big idea, Balfour encouraged him to do so. However, he did not reveal this news to his intransigent free trade colleagues, Ritchie, Balfour of Burleigh (the Scottish Secretary), and Lord George Hamilton (the Indian Secretary). All three ministers resigned, leaving office on 6 October, the same day as Chamberlain's departure.

In the resulting reshuffle, Austen Chamberlain was made Chancellor of the Exchequer, a step which further unsettled the orthodox free traders and left the wider world uncertain about quite what deal, if any, Balfour had struck

---

[64] A. Sykes, *Tariff Reform in British Politics 1903–1913* (Oxford, 1979), 54.

[65] Balfour bypassed Mowatt completely, but consulted Hamilton who, though a free trader, was more circumspect.

with his former Colonial Secretary. Balfour's less than straightforward conduct troubled the elderly Duke of Devonshire, who, uncomfortable at being separated from the other free-trade ministers, joined them on the backbenches a week later, despite the entreaties of the Prime Minister, who was much disconcerted by the loss of so respected a colleague. At least the Unionist government had survived, after a fashion. But Balfour's political machinations had saddled him with a reputation for sophistry which he never succeeded in shaking off.

Chamberlain's own programme, hitherto obscure, became much clearer when, free from the responsibilities of office, he made his key speech at Glasgow on 6 October, in which he called for a duty on corn not exceeding 2s. a quarter (with an exemption for maize), a corresponding tax on flour, and a small tax of about 5 per cent *ad valorem* on imported meat and all dairy produce except bacon. All these duties were to be levied on foreign but not on colonial imports. There was mention of further colonial preferences on wine and perhaps on fruit. To offset the cost to the consumer, the existing taxes on tea, sugar, coffee, and cocoa were to be lowered. Finally, Chamberlain recommended the adoption of duties averaging 10 per cent on all foreign manufactured goods.

What was this programme designed to achieve? 'For my own part,' Chamberlain told Devonshire in September 1903, 'I care only for the great question of Imperial Unity. Everything else is secondary or consequential.'[66] However, imperial preferences, the only practical way forward, required the United Kingdom to impose duties on food, in particular corn, since these were the main products imported from the self-governing colonies—in their absence, the United Kingdom had nothing upon which it could give the colonies a preference. This challenge to the historic Peel/Cobden settlement of 1846 involved considerable political risks.

Chamberlain hoped to minimize the risks by offering sops to the working-class electorate. On 21 May, goaded by Lloyd George, Chamberlain specifically linked the cause of old-age pensions to the adoption of a revenue tariff,[67] but a month later he was already having second thoughts. For if the food taxes were indeed, as he claimed, so modest that they were unlikely to affect the cost of living, could they really generate enough revenue to fund such an expensive initiative? The idea of a tariff-funded pension scheme never quite disappeared from the agenda, but it soon receded into the background. Instead, Chamberlain opted for 'compensations', including a remission of existing excise duties on such articles of common consumption as sugar and tea, which bulked

---

[66] Cited in E. H. H. Green, *The Crisis of Conservatism: The Politics, Economics and Ideology of the British Conservative Party, 1880–1914* (London, 1995), 186.

[67] In fact, the future tariff reformer Edward Goulding had earlier introduced a Private Members' Old Age Pension Bill in March 1902, to be funded by a revenue tariff (Green, *Crisis of Conservatism*, 249–50).

disproportionately large in the working man's budget—a move towards the old Radical goal of a 'free breakfast table'.

But such a fiscal readjustment would, by itself, have created a significant budget deficit: hence the inclusion in the Glasgow Programme of the average 10 per-cent duty on manufactured goods. Protective tariffs were anyhow attractive in their own right, because they allowed Chamberlain and his followers to stress the greater security of employment which the working man could expect from the adoption of his scheme—the origins of the later propaganda cry, 'Tariff Reform Means Work For All'. Duties on foreign manufactured imports also held considerable potential appeal to hard-pressed industrialists bearing the brunt of foreign competition in home markets. Finally, these duties seemed to meet the prevailing cry for retaliation against countries indulging in unfair practices such as 'dumping'.

In an attempt to secure 'a scientific tariff ... which [would] not add a farthing to the burden of the taxpayer',[68] Chamberlain created his own Tariff Commission, upon which sympathetic businessmen were invited to serve. Under the direction of its able secretary, the economic historian W. A. S. Hewins, formerly the Director of the London School of Economics, this fifty-nine-member body embarked on the long-drawn-out enterprise of collecting information from a wide range of industries, including agriculture, on the basis of which it could propose the appropriate tariff levels. This, it was hoped, would revive the British economy, currently in recession.

As the tariff reform campaign developed, Chamberlain increasingly used what he apologetically called the 'squalid argument', invoking the plight of whatever distressed industries were located in the place where he happened to be speaking: 'Sugar has gone; silk has gone; iron is threatened; wool is threatened; cotton will go! How long are you going to stand it?'.[69] Although Chamberlain deliberately avoided the offensive label 'protectionism' which his opponents were trying to pin on him (he preferred the more progressive-sounding phrase 'tariff reform'), his movement increasingly assumed a protectionist character.

This impression was strengthened by the conduct and composition of the Tariff Reform League, created on 13 July 1903, initially without Chamberlain's personal imprimatur.[70] Although chaired from 1905 onwards by the wealthy

---

[68] A. Marrison, *British Business and Protection, 1903–1932* (Oxford, 1996), 34.

[69] Speech at Greenock, 7 Oct. 1903.

[70] For a time he preferred to work through his own Birmingham Tariff Committee, renamed the Imperial Tariff Committee, of which he was President. In fact, a so-called 'Protection League' had come into existence a day prior to the Bingley Hall speech, established in total ignorance of what Chamberlain was about to say, if Powell Williams, its organizer, is to be believed. This soon became the Imperial Tariff League, and later, on 21 July 1903, the Tariff Reform League (F. Coetzee, *For Party or Country: Nationalism and the Dilemmas of Popular Conservatism in Edwardian England* (New York, 1990), 46).

Northumbrian landowner Lord Ridley, most of its members were well-established businessmen, attracted by its commitment to 'the defense and development of the industrial interests of the British Empire'.[71]

Yet, whatever his opponents might allege, Chamberlain had no intention of allowing businessmen to capture tariff reform—any more than businessmen were prepared to be so captured.[72] Rather, he saw himself as pursuing a political project which far transcended economic considerations. Chamberlain believed that the future lay with great empires: Britain would decline to the level of Holland if, through failure to unite her scattered territories, she remained merely an offshore island—size really did matter.

Chamberlain also felt that the Unionist government was in difficulties because it lacked a 'constructive' programme: Unionism needed to be revitalized now that Irish Home Rule was dormant, perhaps dead. In its absence, the Liberals and the recently founded Labour Representation Committee were gaining ground through a variety of demagogic sectional appeals. The tariff, Chamberlain hoped, would neutralize this pernicious 'anti-national' strategy by uniting *all* classes in support of the Empire and in opposition to the 'foreigner'.

Such a stance intensified the prevailing mood of xenophobic nationalism, already present in contemporary politics—witness the campaign culminating in the 1905 Aliens Act, which aimed at curbing the influx of Jews from Eastern Europe. 'Britain Expects That Every Foreigner Should Pay His Duty', declared the unionist journalist Leopold Maxse, one of Chamberlain's most fervent supporters. Tariff Reform League leaflets regularly featured predatory foreigners, often Germans ('Herr Dumper'), sometimes Americans (with sinister portrayals of 'Uncle Sam'), along with derogatory depictions of cosmopolitan financiers, British or otherwise, who were often given markedly Semitic characteristics.

But tariff reform also had a more constructive side. For Chamberlain and his 'whole hog' supporters were convinced that anti-socialism and the defence of property rights (even xenophobia) could not, by themselves, bind the urban masses to the institutions of the state. The trick was to devise a programme which would not frighten capital out of the country but also had popular appeal.

---

[71] Green, *Crisis of Conservatism*, 64–6. Some also argued that trusts and syndicates promoted efficiency (p. 226).

[72] The Association of Chambers of Commerce persistently refused to declare itself publicly, on the ground that this controversial party issue threatened to disrupt the organization's unity and might even provoke secessions. Also significant is the failure of both Tariff Reform League and the Tariff Commission to attract major subscriptions: the former was spending no more than £14,000 in 1906, and the latter's income dwindled from a peak of £10,364 in 1904 to barely £3,000 in 1912 (F. Coetzee, 'Pressure Groups, Tory Businessmen and the Aura of Political Corruption Before the First World War', *Historical Journal*, 29 (1986), 840–1).

The intellectuals of the Chamberlainite discussion group, the 'Compatriots Club', which included Garvin and Amery, were particularly keen on this objective. Amery, for example, wanted a pamphlet to be written which would show that 'trade unionism and our movement are really one and the same thing: that unionism defeats its own ends if it only keeps out the home "blackleg" but pays no heed to the foreign blackleg'.[73] Chamberlain took a similar line: 'You cannot have free trade in goods, and at the same time have protection of labour.' Agriculturalist, manufacturer, and working man, he claimed, had a common interest in regenerating national production and in opposing those 'unpatriotic' Cobdenite cosmopolitans who affected to see no difference between foreigners and our own kith and kin.

Naturally the free traders fought back. Invoking a harmonious world order in which each country specialized in the goods and services to which it was naturally adapted, their propagandists associated their cause with that of universal peace—which they claimed a return to protection would threaten. But the tariff reformers countered these traditional arguments by claiming that the best way to avoid war was to prepare against its eventuality. Adopting the moral high ground, they further accused their opponents of sacrificing all that made life meaningful on the altar of 'cheapness'.

Faced by traditional arguments about the 'Big Loaf' and the 'Little Loaf', Chamberlain was obliged to walk a tightrope. He promised that a possible rise in the price of bread would be offset by his various 'compensations'. He also argued that 'the British Empire was acquired by sacrifice' and could only be maintained by sacrifice. At the same time, closer Imperial Union, he claimed, would *in the long run* provide the country with a secure imperial market, benefiting the employer's profits and the workman's wages and job prospects.

More fundamentally still, tariff reformers met the free trade emphasis on consumer interests by appealing to 'producers'. They portrayed agriculture and industry alike as important sources of national and imperial strength. Indeed, central to the tariff reform case was the prediction that, as a consequence of free trade, the manufacturer and producer were fast disappearing, leaving Britain as 'a nation of middlemen and consumers', its economy too beholden to a parisitic City of London, which provided the population with little employment.

Most professional economists continued to speak out on behalf of the latter groups: fourteen 'professors' sent a letter to *The Times* on 15 August 1903, solemnly refuting Chamberlain's 'erroneous opinions' and warning of 'the injury which the British consumer would receive' if free trade were aban-

---

[73] Cited in Green, *Crisis of Conservatism*, 262.

doned.[74] But the tariff reformers responded to this manifesto with sneers against doctrinaire pedants in thrall to abstractions which blinded them to the changes taking place in the real world. They rallied to their support economic *historians* such as William Cunningham, Sir William Ashley, and W. A. S. Hewins, all of whom were soaked in a German economic tradition which emphasized factors of production, viewed from the standpoint of the nation.

3. DRIFTING TO DISASTER

A deep fissure rapidly opened up within Unionism, one which cut clean across the line of demarcation between Conservatives and Liberal Unionists, each party being *internally* divided. For example, Chamberlain and Devonshire, the two leading Liberal Unionists, took diametrically opposite sides in the fiscal dispute. On 12 December 1903 Devonshire went so far as to advise Unionist electors not to vote for any candidate who favoured food taxes, a more extreme step than any Liberal had taken during the recent period of internal squabbling. Chamberlain responded by forcing Devonshire's resignation from the reorganized Liberal Unionist Association.

Though proportionately more were drawn from the Liberal Unionist than from the Conservative Party, the 'free fooders' came from all quarters of Unionism.[75] Numbering at their peak some sixty-five MPs, they included elder statesmen such as Goschen, James of Hereford, Ritchie, and Devonshire, all of them stern upholders of 'economy', but also younger MPs such as Churchill, with more 'progressive' social views. What held the group together was a perceptive understanding of the unpopularity of food taxes and a sense of *noblesse oblige* towards the working-class consumer (particularly evident in an old Whig such as Devonshire). In addition, many Conservatives from landed backgrounds despised Chamberlain, whom they depicted as a vulgar materialist, indifferent to the interests of Church and Constitution and to the finer traditions of Conservatism: the Birmingham politician was nothing other than an 'alien immigrant', sneered Lord Hugh Cecil.

Balfour's own position was subtly different. He, too, saw very clearly the crudity of the tariff reform programme and the electoral dangers with which it threatened his party. As Conservative Leader, Balfour was also highly conscious of the damage which Peel had done to Conservatism in 1846 by his

---

[74] 'In the days of Protection,' opined Hamilton, 'producers were more powerful than consumers. Nowadays consumers are the more powerful and will remain so' (A. Howe, *Free Trade and Liberal England, 1846–1946* (Oxford, 1997), 230).

[75] Of 83 identifiable Unionist Free Traders, 60 were Conservatives, 23 Liberal Unionists (Rempel, *Unionists Divided*, p. 95).

precipitate adoption of fiscal change. As he explained to Devonshire on 27 August 1903, the Unionist Alliance was the custodian of 'a great many all-important interests, besides those immediately affected by our fiscal policy'; jeopardizing these interests through internal divisions would be nothing short of a national disaster.[76] At the same time Balfour had little patience with the doctrinaire free-trade creed espoused by the likes of Ritchie.

The Prime Minister therefore tried to devise a middle path between the two extremes, in the hope of buying time. At Sheffield, on 1 October 1903, he advocated the tariff as a retaliatory device which could be used in trade negotiations to promote the cause of true, worldwide free trade. Later, at Edinburgh on 3 October 1904, he added that, if returned to power after the next election, he would summon a Colonial Conference which, should it agree on a scheme of imperial preferences, could then submit it to the people at the election after that. Balfour thus relegated colonial preference to the distant future by surrounding it with a number of hard-to-achieve conditions. Admittedly, at the Albert Hall on 2 June 1905 the Prime Minister did concede that preference was 'the most urgent of all the great constructive problems with which we have to deal'; but the 'double-election pledge' remained.

Attempts to hold this line frequently came under challenge, not least from the Chancellor, Austen Chamberlain, who, torn between personal loyalty to the Prime Minister and filial devotion, constantly nagged Balfour behind the scenes to adopt a more 'advanced' position. The free fooders, on the other hand, used their direct personal access to Balfour in an attempt to forestall any such move.

Within the Commons a bitter struggle to control the Unionist Party soon developed. The free fooders, outnumbered approximately two to one by Chamberlain's avowed followers,[77] were at a disadvantage from the outset. Hicks Beach (who, as Balfour once rightly observed, had the 'manners of a pirate and the courage of a lady governess'), refused to give a firm lead, fearing to inflict serious embarrassment on the government. Ritchie, Goschen, and Devonshire, in their different ways, were little more effectual. The free fooders also lacked a national organization that could rival the Tariff Reform League: the Unionist Free Food League, created in July 1903, and its successor, the Unionist Free Trade Club, were predominantly parliamentary bodies. They thus fell dependent on the Free Trade Union, an umbrella organization which was ostensibly non-party but in fact controlled by the Liberals.

In late 1903 desultory talks took place between Devonshire and Rosebery to explore the possibility of creating some new 'centre' grouping, a venture on

---

[76] Cited in Sykes, *Tariff Reform*, 47.
[77] Herbert Maxwell was able to mobilize 112 tariff reform MPs in March 1904.

which Churchill was especially keen. Nothing came of this. Equally abortive were later communications over a possible electoral pact between the wider body of Unionist free fooders and the Liberal Party. Here the main stumbling-block was the 1902 Education Act, with which many of the Unionist free fooders—notably Devonshire—had been prominently associated. In any case, by early 1904 Campbell-Bannerman, the Liberal Leader, had deduced from recent by-election results that his party did not need to compromise its principles by doing any such deal. Isolated and marginalized within the Unionist Party, seventeen free food MPs, including Churchill and Seely, eventually crossed the floor of the House: eleven did so before 1906. The rest, including Lord Hugh Cecil, were left stranded.

The Unionist free fooders were further undermined by the attacks which tariff-reform fanatics launched against them in their own constituencies. A secret society called the 'Confederates' took a mysterious part in such activities; so did local branches of the Tariff Reform League, which numbered some 250 by July 1905, with a heavy concentration in the Midlands, London, and the South-East.[78] By 1905 these tactics had destroyed several prominent free fooders, including Ritchie, who, disowned by his Croydon constituency party, decided not to stand at the next general election.

Conservative free fooders indignantly complained that they were being deselected for failing to subscribe to policies which did not even form part of the official Unionist programme. But Balfour, to whom they appealed, showed little sympathy and refused to intervene on their behalf, giving the excuse that the constituency associations were autonomous.

The relationship between Balfour and Chamberlain also began to deteriorate from 1904 onwards. The 'whole hoggers' protested that the Unionist cause in its entirety was being compromised by the Prime Minister's overly cautious behaviour: free trade could only be vanquished, they contended, by bold and open defiance, not by equivocation, studied ambiguity, and rhetorical evasion.

This, though, was partly bluster. By 1905 Chamberlain privately accepted that the Unionist Party would lose the next general election, but he hoped to reconstruct Unionism in opposition around his own programme: 'all my efforts and hopes are directed to the election after next', he told a friend.[79] Yet this stratagem was being wrecked by Balfour's remarkable tenacity in defying the odds and clinging to office—where, the Prime Minister prided himself, he was doing important 'national' work. Meanwhile, Conservative officials viewed Chamberlain's factionalism and 'treachery' with bitterness and fear, the government Chief Whip, Acland-Hood, suspecting—with some

[78] Coetzee, *For Party or Country*, 64–6.
[79] Sykes, *Tariff Reform*, 80.

reason—that the 'Birmingham crowd' were plotting to suborn and capture Conservative Central Office itself.

By 1905 the Unionist Party was in a state of almost open civil war. Ever since May 1903 the Liberals at Westminster, turning the tables on their former tormentors, had moved a succession of motions designed to cause splits in the Unionist ranks. In late March 1905 Balfour led his followers out of the House to avoid a damaging division; but this made him look not only cowardly but also ineffectual, since he was defied by thirty-five free fooders who voted with the Liberal Opposition. In the country at large the 'whole hoggers' continued to make progress: in both 1904 and 1905 tariff-reform motions were passed by the National Union at its annual conference. The nadir was reached at Bristol on 21 November 1905, when Chamberlain insolently attacked Balfour's personality and policy: 'No man was ever led successfully to battle on the principle that the lamest man should govern the march of the army.' It was this humiliation which effectively persuaded Balfour and his government to resign.

4. A DOOMED PROJECT?

The main reason for the electoral unpopularity of tariff reform was never in doubt. In August 1903 Harmsworth commissioned 'Walking Inquirers' for the *Daily Mail* in a pioneering exercise in opinion-polling. They interviewed 2,000 people, one-fifth of whom had never heard of Chamberlain's programme, but the rest were overwhelmingly hostile towards it, largely because of the prospect of increased food taxes, or 'stomach taxes' as they were called in Harmsworth's papers. As Balfour had earlier warned Chamberlain, in Britain 'the prejudice against a small tax on food [was] not the fad of a few imperfectly informed theorists', but 'a deep-rooted prejudice affecting the large mass of voters'.[80]

The Chamberlainites hoped to defuse the dear-food scare by pointing out that the price of bread would not necessarily rise in the bakers' shops if the corn duty succeeded in replacing foreign sources of supply (such as the United States, Argentina, and Russia) by colonial countries (for example, Canada and Australia), whose produce would continue to enter the United Kingdom duty-free. But this involved a leap into the unknown, which opponents depicted as a reckless gamble with the people's food. (It did not help the tariff reformers that working-class standards of living were higher in Britain than in Germany and other European protectionist countries.) Indeed, Chamberlain's talk about 'compensations' seemed to concede that the cost of bread and perhaps meat probably *would* rise.

---

[80] Cited in Coetzee, *For Party or Country*, 57.

All attempts to mobilize working-class support for fiscal change therefore faltered. An offshoot of the TRL, the Trade Union Tariff Reform Association, never acquired a genuine identity of its own, while the TUC repeatedly passed motions critical of Chamberlain, on one occasion calling on its members to resist tariff reform 'as you would a malignant disease'.[81] Even socialists, who agreed in principle with attacks on the fetish of 'cheapness' and the cult of unbridled market competition,[82] would have nothing to do with tariff reform: partly out of personal suspicion of Chamberlain's character and motives, but also because they disliked the regressive nature of the food taxes. Early on in his campaign, Chamberlain had declared that he was content to leave himself in working-class hands: 'You are the judges. You are the Caesar to whom I appeal.'[83] Although some working-class supporters did indeed rally to his banner in areas such as the West Midlands, by and large 'Caesar' gave tariff reform a decisive 'thumbs-down'.

Herein lay the most important reason for the failure of Chamberlain's project. But it was also weakened by its own internal contradictions, to which Asquith skilfully drew attention. As Edward Hamilton of the Treasury had noted in his diary in late 1902, those who were attracted by the prospect of retaliation tended to be different people from those who were inspired by imperial preference. Indeed, retaliation, if successful, would have lowered tariff barriers between the United Kingdom and its foreign trading partners, whereas preferential tariffs were intended to increase the volume of trade taking place within the Empire—an outcome more likely if European and American tariffs remained high.[84] Moreover, as William Ashley conceded in his respected study *The Tariff Problem*, duties of between 40 per cent and 75 per cent might have been necessary to counter a determined dumping campaign from abroad—way above the average 10 per-cent duty on imported manufactured goods which Chamberlain had advocated in his Glasgow Programme.[85]

So although rhetorical flourishes against the nefarious conduct of 'Herr Dumper' continued to make effective platform propaganda, retaliation, as such, soon began to recede into the background, partly for all the reasons given above, and also because this was a policy that had become too closely identified with Balfour.

[81] K. D. Brown, 'The Trade Union Tariff Reform Association, 1904–1913', *Journal of British Studies*, 9 (1970), 141–53. In September 1905 the TUC affirmed its support for free trade by 1,253,000 to 26,000.

[82] F. Trentmann, 'The Transformation of Fiscal Reform: Reciprocity, Modernization and the Fiscal Debate Within the Business Community in Early Twentieth-century Britain', *Historical Journal*, 39 (1996), 1005–48.

[83] Sykes, *Tariff Reform*, 57.

[84] Coetzee, *For Party or Country*, 56.

[85] Marrison, *Business and Protection*, 31.

Imperial preferences initially seemed to offer more promise, if only because they exuded a nobility of purpose which went some way towards offsetting the pejorative emotions aroused by the spectacle of greedy manufacturers clamouring to secure a sectional advantage. But the Liberal Imperialists were not alone in asking whether the Canadian 'offer'—the basis of the reciprocity idea—had any realistic prospect of producing greater Empire unity. After all, protectionist interests in Canada were so strong that a preferential system was unlikely to yield significant economic benefits to the mother country. In fact, nothing dealt Chamberlain's confidence a greater blow than his gradual realization that Laurier's seemingly 'generous' offer was not really generous at all.[86]

Moreover, Chamberlain's vision of Empire was a very restricted one. For example, Curzon rightly suspected that the tariff reformers, with their emotional affinities for their kith and kin in the colonies of settlement, had forgotten India, whose place in their scheme of things never became entirely clear.[87] More fundamental still was the objection that the Empire depended ultimately on ties of sympathy, which haggling over tariffs might put at risk, especially if the working man came to feel that the cause of Empire required him to make 'sacrifices' which would imperil his already precarious standard of living.

Nor was the working-class consumer alone in wondering whether imperial preference constituted a good bargain. One of the oddities of the tariff campaign was that it attracted so much support from the agricultural protection lobby and, more generally, from the landed interest.[88] But, as Chamberlain privately conceded to Devonshire in September 1903, it was 'ridiculous to suppose that 2/-a quarter on corn would restore prosperity to agriculture', especially since colonial produce (corn as well as meat) would continue to enter duty free.[89] As Chamberlain also observed, 'the farmers might possibly support [the corn tax] as drowning men [would] catch at a straw', many of them also hoping that the revenue from a tariff might be used to reduce agricultural rates—something which Chamberlain finally agreed to do in July 1905.[90] In truth, however, it mattered little to the Lincolnshire wheat-growers, whom

[86] The tariff reformers later had more joy from their alliance with Arthur Deakin, the Australian Prime Minister, but this only partly offset their disappointment with Laurier.

[87] A point strongly voiced by John Morley: E. H. H. Green, 'The Political Economy of Empire, 1880–1914', in A. Porter (ed.), *The Oxford History of the British Empire: Vol. III: The Nineteenth Century* (Oxford, 1999), 365.

[88] Howe, *Free Trade*, 239.

[89] At Welbeck in August 1904 Chamberlain suggested a 2s. duty on wheat, barley, and rye, a 5% *ad valorem* duty on meat and dairy produce, and an unspecified duty on flour.

[90] In its *Agricultural Report* the Tariff Commission later recommended an additional 1s. duty on colonial corn, which would have retained the colonial preference while giving home farmers some relief. But the exact status of this recommendation remained unclear, and it disappeared from the official programme entirely in 1910 (Green, *Crisis of Conservatism*, 187, 213–14).

Chaplin was trying to help, whether they were undercut in home markets by prairie farmers from the United States or from Canada. As for low-paid agricultural labourers largely reliant on shop-supplied produce, they would probably have suffered more from rising food prices than almost any other group in the community.

For sectors of manufacturing industry, also, putting too many eggs in the imperial basket seemed a dubious proposition. As Ritchie had earlier reminded the Cabinet, foreign countries currently took more than twice as much of our exports as were sent to the colonies, measured by value.[91] Admittedly, recent decades had seen a growing proportion of UK exports going to colonial destinations, and the per-capita consumption of British goods was also higher in the colonies than in those foreign countries which traded heavily with Britain. But the enormous expansion of Empire trade in recent decades had helped fuel quite unrealistic optimism about its long-term potentialities. For example, was Canada really on the way to matching its neighbour to the south in population and in economic resources, as some tariff reformers believed?

Arguments about the greater security and dependability of colonial markets carried little more conviction, since, although there was no likelihood that British territories would go to war with one another, hostilities with a European power might result in a cutting of the sealanes: the United Kingdom's markets and sources of supply would then be equally at risk whether they were located in New Zealand or in Argentina. Theoretically, national security might have been enhanced if the United Kingdom had grown more of the foodstuffs it needed to feed its teeming population. But that objective, even if feasible, would have been totally incompatible with Chamberlain's imperial project.[92]

Another obstacle confronting Chamberlain was that some of Britain's major industries were doing very well out of the global free-trade system: notably the Lancashire textile industry, which drew the bulk of its raw material from a foreign country (the United States), and exported most of its finished products to foreign destinations. Admittedly, Lancashire heavily relied upon the Indian market, but India remained largely unaffected one way or another by Chamberlain's scheme. On 21 July 1903 a joint meeting in Manchester of employers' representatives and trade-union officials proclaimed 'that the great cotton

---

[91] Cited in Sykes, *Tariff Reform*, 34. Perhaps it was imperial preference, rather than retaliation, that turned business opinion back to Free Trade (F. Trentmann, 'The Strange Death of Free Trade: The Erosion of the "Liberal Consensus" in Britain, *c.*1903–32', in E. Biagini (ed.), *Citizenship and Community* (Cambridge, 1996), 237).

[92] But only by following Germany's example and supplementing natural manure with synthetic fertilizers could Britain have come anywhere near to meeting her population's demand for food. The Royal Commission on Food Supply, set up in 1903, reported in 1905 that it would not be practical even to depend on a combination of home and imperial grain supplies.

industry of the United Kingdom [owed] its pre-eminence to and [could] only be maintained by the policy of Free Trade'.[93]

Shipbuilding and coal were similarly dependent on foreign markets, and shipbuilders were also conspicuous 'consumers' of raw or semi-finished goods (iron and steel) which had largely been imported—some said 'dumped'—from abroad. Moreover, 'cheap food' probably helped industrialists by lowering manufacturing costs, which gave them a competitive advantage over most of their foreign rivals. Finally, free trade, on balance, undoubtedly contributed to the prosperity of Britain's burgeoning financial services sector: Chamberlain's opponents frequently drew attention to his difficulty in securing any representatives from the City to serve on his Tariff Commission. In short, Britain was so intertwined into a global system that a retreat into 'Fortress Empire' was impossible—except at the cost of reduced living standards and levels of economic activity that no sane politician could accept.[94]

But there may be an even simpler explanation for the failure of the tariff reform movement to mobilize British industry in the way some of its advocates favoured. Despite alarmist talk about an 'economic' crisis precipitating national decline, in fact the British economy was in too healthy a state during the Edwardian period for the tariff reformers to have succeeded. It was certainly unfortunate for Chamberlain that the three general elections of the early twentieth century all occurred when trade was on an upswing, making it easy for the Liberals to mock him as an 'economic Jeremiah'.

Finally, what difficulties the British economy *was* facing (for example, in the new science-based industries) could be tackled in a multitude of ways. Many Liberals argued that protection and the existence of 'safe' imperial markets might simply lead to the feather-bedding of uncompetitive industries, whereas, to quote the words of a Liberal Imperialist pamphlet, what was really needed was 'Efficiency not Tariffs'—in other words, improved technical education (which was also Balfour's favoured solution). The chemical manufacturer Sir John Brunner (a staunch Liberal and a free trader) advocated yet another approach, calling for a policy of 'state development' particularly geared to improving the country's infrastructure—for example, by a revival of the canal system. In short, at an economic as well as at a political level, the case for tariff reform was shaky, and it is little wonder that it failed.

---

[93] P. F. Clarke, *Lancashire and the New Liberalism* (1971), 96–7.

[94] However, aligning whole industries on one side or another of the fiscal divide according to whether they would have benefited from free trade or protection is hazardous. Most industries were subdivided in complex ways along product and market lines: for example, cotton merchants showed a stronger commitment to free trade than did textile manufacturers. Nor was the City by any means unanimous on the fiscal question: many stockbrokers favoured tariff reform, while shippers and bankers did not (Marrison, *Business and Protection*, Ch. 2).

5. THE END OF THE UNIONIST ASCENDANCY

Balfour's ministry never recovered from the crisis which Chamberlain had provoked, and a sequence of shocking by-election defeats presaged the electoral disaster which was to overwhelm the Unionist parties when the country eventually went to the polls in January–February 1906. Even the hitherto hyper-efficient electoral machine started to run down, with the resignation of 'Captain' Middleton in the middle of 1903—his successor, Captain Wells, proving an inadequate replacement.

Moreover, Balfour's government became peculiarly accident-prone. Many of the mishaps which undermined its reputation were especially upsetting because they affected the relationship between the Prime Minister and those who had once been his closest friends. For example, George Wyndham had had a great success with his Irish Land Purchase Act of 1903, which made Exchequer subsidies available for the transfer of whole estates from landlord to tenant—a measure which irrevocably changed the structure of Irish rural society. But in 1904 Wyndham carelessly allowed his name to be associated with a controversial plan of 'devolution' that was being pushed by his Permanent Under-Secretary, Antony MacDonnell, himself an Irish Catholic. In the ensuing uproar Wyndham was forced to resign, and his office given to Walter Long, who returned to the more obdurate Unionism from which it had seemed that Balfour's government was breaking free.

The imperial arena, too, seemed to be particularly strewn with banana skins. When Chamberlain left the government, the Colonial Office was offered to Milner, who turned it down. The post was then accepted by Balfour's long-term friend Alfred Lyttelton, who found himself promoted beyond his abilities. His poor judgement was exposed in 1903 over the issue of 'Chinese Labour'. Anxious to establish the Crown's dominance in the Transvaal, Milner desperately wanted to encourage a mass influx of British settlers into the Rand, something which would only happen if its goldmines could quickly be brought back to full production. But the orginal 'Kaffir' force had dispersed during the recent war—hence the call for indentured Chinamen to be brought in as unskilled labourers. Chamberlain, sensing the political dangers, had vetoed the plan; Lyttelton, considerably in awe of Milner, sanctioned the Chinese Labour Ordinance on 10 February 1904.

'Chinese Labour' soon ran into fierce resistance. Within South Africa it was attacked by spokesmen for the white miners, angry at cheap Asiatic competition. Some trade unionists at home echoed their complaints. But these economic fears became swamped by highly moralistic protests over what the Opposition was soon calling 'Chinese Slavery', in which pity for the plight of Chinese labourers living very restricted lives within compounds combined with horror over the sexual implications of separating so many adult men from their wives and womenfolk.

In March 1905 Milner returned from South Africa, to be replaced by Selborne, whose post at the Admiralty was filled by the colourless Lord Cawdor. But there remained another twist to the South African story. In August 1905 the Colonial Secretary was amazed to learn that, shortly before his retirement, Milner had permitted the overseers to flog their Chinese labourers—an illegal act which seriously angered Balfour, who already had more than enough troubles with which to contend.

The Chinese Labour affair finally broke the ties of friendship and sympathy between Milner and his Liberal Imperialist friends. When the Opposition moved a vote of censure on 21 March 1904, only Haldane was prepared to speak out in the High Commissioner's support. Chinese Labour also played a prominent role in the 1906 General Election, where Liberal posters depicting manacled Chinamen were particularly effective because they appealed to humanitarian compassion, while at the same time playing upon the visceral dislike which many Britons felt for 'Orientals'.

India, too, was a source of proconsular trouble. The Viceroy, Lord Curzon, had repeatedly shown an unwillingness to accept that the Government of India must ultimately be subordinate to London, and the Cabinet grew increasingly weary of his complaints that his great work on the Subcontinent was passing unappreciated at home. Curzon eventually engineered his own downfall when, ignoring good advice, he insisted on having Kitchener appointed as Commander-in-Chief of the Indian Army, apparently because he thought that the greatest proconsul of the day deserved to have as his colleague the most famous soldier in the world.

In late 1902 Kitchener arrived in India. But the two autocrats were never likely to work well together, and almost at once Kitchener demanded the abolition of the Military Member's department, which came under Curzon's direct control. Both sides appealed to London, but Kitchener, making good use of his friendship with Lady Salisbury, proved to be the more skilful intriguer. The Indian Secretary, Brodrick, eventually came down in Kitchener's favour— probably a wrong decision, had the issue been resolved on its merits—but getting even with the exasperating Curzon seems to have been what determined the outcome. Curzon resigned his post in August 1905, and when he returned to London, no member of the Cabinet joined the friends who had gathered on Charing Cross Station to welcome him home; nor was the ex-Viceroy given the earldom which he expected. This falling-out was all the more poignant in that Balfour, Brodrick, and Curzon had once been good friends and fellow 'Souls'.

In its dog days Balfour's government could still claim credit for carrying several important pieces of legislation, but most were highly controversial and probably did the ministry more harm than good. For example, the Licensing Act of 1904 attempted to deal with the problem caused by an excessive number of licensed premises, but on terms so favourable to the publicans that the Opposition could plausibly claim that their opponents were in the pockets of the drink trade—another black mark in the Nonconformists' books.[95] The Aliens Act of the following year, which ended immigrants' automatic right of asylum, also caused ructions, antagonizing Jews of all kinds, against whom it had mainly been directed, and offending libertarians in all parties. Churchill, now a Liberal MP, threw himself with particular vigour into the anti-restrictionist movement, for which his reward was a nomination as Liberal candidate for the constituency of North-West Manchester, in which there was a sizeable and well-organized Jewish vote. As for the Unemployed Workmen's Act of 1905, though it set a number of important precedents,[96] it reached the statute book too late to revive the government's fortunes.

The Unionists' discomfiture was the Liberal Party's opportunity. Already brought closer together by the 1902 corn registration duty, the Liberals now largely buried their earlier differences in opposition to the Education Act. This meant that although talk of centrist combinations lingered on, adversarial party politics once more became the order of the day.

But it was tariff reform that gave the Liberals the election cry which would later bring them back to power. In Campbell-Bannerman's words, from the very start 'all the old war-horses [were] snorting with excitement'.[97] Even Haldane, along with nearly all the other Liberal Imperialists, came out for free trade. Rosebery and Grey briefly wobbled, but Asquith was free trade's most influential advocate, following Chamberlain around the country and challenging the latter's often dubious statistics and logic.

True, the Liberal revival pre-dated the Birmingham Speech, and the Unionists' by-election record actually improved in late 1903: 'whole hog' candidates surprisingly held Dulwich and Lewisham in December, in the wake of the release of Devonshire's potentially damaging letter. But after another comfortable win at Ludlow later in the month, the Unionists suffered a succession of terrible by-election humiliations.[98] All the same, the Liberals

---

[95] The Act compensated owners who were denied a renewal of their on-licences (except for misconduct)—albeit out of a fund to which brewers and other licensed property-owners had contributed (D. W. Gutzke, *Protecting the Pub: Brewers and Publicans Against Temperance* (Woodbridge, 1989), 155). Temperance reformers, and their Liberal supporters, denied that any such compensation was justifiable.

[96] See Ch. 11.

[97] J. A. Spender, *The Life of the Right Hon. Sir Henry Campbell-Bannerman* (London, 1923?). ii. 97

[98] Three of the six swings of over 10% registered during Balfour's premiership actually came before the Birmingham speech. But many of the Liberals' greatest successes in 1904–5 occurred in constituencies which had been uncontested in 1900 and for which swing cannot therefore be calculated: Norwich (Jan. 1904), St Albans (Feb. 1904), Oswestry (July 1904), Brighton (Apr. 1905), Whitby (June 1905), and Barkston Ash (Oct. 1905).

had fared so poorly in recent years that they still did not believe they could win the next general election. And this, in turn, was to influence the way they responded to the political aspirations of the Labour Movement.

6. THE FORGING OF THE PROGRESSIVE ALLIANCE

The Labour Representation Committee (LRC), which emerged from the meeting at the Memorial Hall, Farringdon Street, on 27 February 1900, was an artfully devised compromise which brought together the socialists (or at least the ILP), who supplied it with leadership and energy, and the trade unions, which contributed the money and manpower.[99] Organizationally, the LRC was a loose-jointed federal body, to which the three main socialist societies (Fabians, ILP, and SDF) and interested trade unions could all affiliate. It thus contained socialists but did not embrace an official commitment to socialism. The constitution owed much to the tactical skill of Keir Hardie, whose amendment adroitly steered a middle path between the SDF's socialist purism and the Lib-Labs, who wanted a mere trade-union pressure group. But if the LRC was more than a pressure group, it fell some way short of being a fully-fledged party such as the Irish Nationalists—notwithstanding the claim of its founders to have been inspired by Parnell's example.

Initially the LRC received very little outside attention. In the 1900 election Hardie had been returned in a strange contest as an LRC-sponsored candidate for the double-member borough of Merthyr,[100] while Richard Bell, a railwaymen's official whose views closely resembled those of the old Lib-Labers, won the railway town of Derby, another two-member constituency—again, in harness with a Liberal. But the other thirteen LRC candidates, put forward at the last moment, came bottom of the poll, even though several enjoyed the advantage of a straight fight against the Unionists.

At first many of the big trade unions held back. But in July 1901 the five Law Lords confirmed the Taff Vale Judgement, which made unions financially responsible for the 'tortious' acts of their agents.[101] After Balfour had publicly refused to introduce legislation 'to give trade-union funds the protection they [had] had for thirty years', Ramsay MacDonald, the Secretary of the LRC, circularized the trade unions, pointing out that their very existence was at stake, which made a Labour party in Parliament 'an immediate necessity'.[102] By

---

[99] For its origins, see Ch. 7.
[100] The Conservatives did not put up a candidate, and, though the Liberals ran two candidates, one had unpopular views on the war and was deserted by many of his own supporters.
[101] N. McCord, 'Taff Vale Revisited', *History*, 78 (1993), 243–60. Another judgement in 1901, *Quinn* v. *Leathem*, declared boycotting to be illegal.
[102] F. Bealey and H. Pelling, *Labour and Politics, 1900–1906* (London, 1958), 77.

early 1903 the LRC had affiliated to it 127 unions, with a combined membership of 847,315. These advances more than outweighed the decision of the SDF to disaffiliate, in protest against Labour's refusal to accept the doctrine of the class war. Another important step in the consolidation of the new party was taken when a resolution was passed at its Newcastle Conference in 1903 authorizing the imposition of a financial levy (1*d.* a member) in order to establish a central fund for the contesting of elections and the subsidizing of future MPs (who were promised a maximum salary of £200 p.a.). MacDonald was later to impress upon the Liberals the significance of the fact that the LRC allegedly had at its disposal a fighting fund of £100,000—a significant bargaining chip in the discussions concerning an electoral pact.

In the North-East Lanarkshire by-election in September 1901 most Liberals voted for the socialist miner, Robert Smillie,[103] rather than for Cecil Harmsworth, a Liberal Imperialist and an outspoken supporter of the current war, but the split Liberal vote meant that the Unionist candidate was able to capture this safe Liberal seat with 42.5 per cent of the vote. The Liberals drew the necessary deduction from the debacle. When, in August 1902, a vacancy occurred in Clitheroe, in the Lancashire textile district, they stood aside for D. J. Shackleton, a textile-union official, who was returned unopposed. Similar self-abnegation allowed Will Crooks, sponsored by the Woolwich Trades Council, to capture the Conservative seat of Woolwich in March 1903, a feat that would almost certainly have been beyond an official Liberal candidate. Two months later a triangular clash at Barnard Castle threatened disaster but, fortunately for both 'progressive parties', victory went to the President of the Ironfounders Union, Arthur Henderson, a moderate who had once been agent to its deceased Liberal MP.

So by the summer of 1905 the LRC, as well as making some progress at municipal level in towns such as Preston and Leicester, had also boosted its representation from two MPs to five. But this had only been achieved by putting forward candidates from the trade-union side of the party so as not to frighten traditional Liberal voters. The price was paid by socialists such as Snowden, who was persuaded to withdraw from Clitheroe in favour of David Shackleton, even though the latter's union had only affiliated to the LRC a few months before polling day. Another prominent ILPer, Bruce Glasier, who never succeeded in landing a winnable seat, had good grounds for his private complaint: 'we are all— those who teach the faith—held to be a bit disqualified these days.'[104]

Such a development followed logically from the LRC's founding constitution, which had prudently distinguished between the importance of independence and the futility of isolation. The stated objective was the establishment of

---

[103] Sponsored by the Scottish Workers Representation Committee, not by the LRC.
[104] Glasier to Hardie, 15 May 1903, Bealey and Pelling, *Labour and Politics*, 150.

a distinct Labour Group in Parliament, who shall have their own Whips, and agree upon their policy, which must embrace a readiness to co-operate with any party which for the time being may be engaged in promoting legislation in the direct interest of labour, and be equally ready to associate themselves with any party in opposing measures having an opposite tendency.

This coded language implied approval for a policy of cautious co-operation with the Liberal Party, provided that Labour's separate organizational identity was not threatened.

What other line could the LRC conceivably have taken? Men such as Shackleton and Henderson were still working-class Liberals in all but name. There was even a considerable rapport between the ILPers and the Radical wing of the Liberal Party, strengthened by their recent opposition to the Boer War. Moreover, most trade unionists and socialists hated the 1902 Education Act. Significantly, Henderson was a Methodist lay preacher, while Snowden, though an agnostic, came from a Dissenting background. Both men also shared in that strong puritanical vein which found expression in temperance—hence their hatred of the 1904 Licensing Act which, according to the critics, had privileged the drink trade. Later, almost all trade unionists and socialists opposed tariff reform, partly on 'dear food' grounds, partly because they so intensely mistrusted Chamberlain and the business interests which had rallied to his fiscal banner.

Finally, in London habits of co-operation had become established between moderate Labour and Radical Liberalism through the Progressive Party.[105] London was also the home of the National Reform Union, within which the converging traditions of Labour and Liberalism effortlessly merged. In addition, at an intellectual level there existed the metropolitan discussion group the 'Rainbow Circle', where Radical Liberals such as Hobson and 'liberal' socialists such as the Fabian Edward Clarke met in a friendly atmosphere to explore a common agenda.[106] True, outside London class divisions kept the two forces apart, but few of the militant ILPers genuinely believed that there was *nothing* to choose between the two 'capitalist' parties. MacDonald, in *Socialism and Society* (1905), may have claimed that socialism was destined to supplant Liberalism, just as modern Liberalism had displaced old Whiggery, but he saw them as being nourished by the same soil, and he reciprocated the belief cherished by many advanced Liberals that there could be 'good fellowship' between the two wings of the army of Progress.

This provides the background to the negotiations which began in the spring of 1903 between MacDonald, Secretary of the LRC, and Herbert Gladstone,

---

[105] See above.

[106] M. Freeden (ed.), 'Minutes of the Rainbow Circle 1894–1924', *Royal Historical Society: Camden Fourth Series*, 38 (1989).

the Liberal Chief Whip. In fact, Gladstone delegated the detailed discussions to one of his officials, Jesse Herbert, whose salary was being paid by George Cadbury, a strong believer in Liberal–Labour co-operation.[107] Though not ratified until September (in the unlikely setting of the Leicester Isolation Hospital), these negotiations had already developed a certain momentum *before* Chamberlain delivered his Birmingham Speech, when the Liberals still had only a dim premonition of the electoral triumph just around the corner. Thus, in early March 1903 Jesse Herbert had impressed on his boss that an electoral agreement with Labour might spare the Liberals the expenditure of £15,000 and deprive the government of ten seats. By the end of 1903, with rich businessmen flocking back to the party, this inducement would have been less tempting, but by then the fateful step had been taken.

The Gladstone–MacDonald agreement was essentially an informal, secret understanding between the Leaders of the two parties that each would use influence during the forthcoming election to prevent the running of 'wrecking candidates' whose intervention would risk handing over a seat, on a minority of votes, to the Unionist enemy. It was provisionally agreed that in twenty-three seats Labour should be given a free run, another five being 'adjustable': but, significantly, none was a seat which the Liberal Party currently held or could be confident of winning.[108]

The 'pact' had to be kept secret. Many Liberal notables were suspicious, especially in those parts of the country, such as the West Riding, where the ILP was strong and had been pressing them hard in local elections. Labour, too, had good grounds for caution. Its constitution bound it to 'independence', and the National Executive Committee had on more than one occasion nearly expelled Bell for appearing on Liberal platforms. Moreover, two groups within the LRC were wary of moving too close to the Liberal Party: working men whose prior allegiance lay with the Conservative Party, as in parts of urban Lancashire; and socialists who, already feeling sidelined, were constantly on the lookout for evidence of betrayal. Though MacDonald was prepared to defy his critics in order to establish for Labour a foothold inside Westminster, he dared not take too many risks.

In the January 1904 by-election at Norwich the local branch of the ILP almost upset the apple-cart by running a local printer, George Roberts, against both Liberals and Unionists. Fortunately for all concerned, Roberts came a bad third, which meant that the Liberals, who easily took the seat, could later afford to show magnanimity. Broad co-operation therefore continued, and was

---

[107] Cadbury was also making donations to Hardie.

[108] To be precise, of these 28 seats, 20 were held by Unionists, 2 by Labour. There were also 6 double-member constituencies, in which the Liberals held only one of the seats (in four cases sharing with a Unionist, in two cases with Labour); 13 of the 28 seats were in double-member constituencies.

cemented by the Caxton Hall Agreement of 1905, which warded off the prospect of working-class candidates sponsored by the LRC challenging Lib-Lab candidates, or vice versa. Moreover, on both sides of the party divide there was a general disposition in favour of electoral co-operation—which was just as well, since the two sets of Leaders could only use persuasion and subtle pressure on their local followers. Unsurprisingly, the arrangement worked best in double-membered constituencies, it being much easier to persuade activists to stand down one of two candidates than to abandon the fight altogether.

7. DEFEAT

Freed from serious risk of attack on their flanks, the Liberals now consolidated their position. Campbell-Bannerman's precarious position became more secure. His co-leader, the respected Earl of Kimberley, died in 1902, to be replaced by Lord Spencer, a very sick man who was obviously out of the running as a potential Prime Minister. Although the leading Liberal Imperialist commoners had still not reconciled themselves to the prospect of a Campbell-Bannerman ministry, Rosebery had impressed upon them in late 1903 that he did not see himself as a contender. Against this background, Asquith, Haldane, and Grey met at the latter's fishing lodge, Relugas, in early September 1905, where they provisionally agreed not to serve under Campbell-Bannerman unless they received the high offices to which they felt themselves entitled (the Treasury, the Woolsack, and the Foreign Office respectively), and, even more crucially, unless Campbell-Bannerman agreed to accept a peerage, leaving the Leadership in the Commons to Asquith.

On matters of policy, rather than personnel, however, the two wings of the party were coming closer together. By 1905 the 'step-by-step' policy towards Irish Home Rule, which Asquith and Grey had been espousing since the autumn of 1901, entered the official programme—Campbell-Bannerman and even Morley being by now prepared to postpone a Gladstonian settlement in the interests of winning the next general election. Redmond, the Irish National Leader, reluctantly accepted this deferral when Campbell-Bannerman put it before him at a private meeting on 14 November—partly because he basically trusted Campbell-Bannerman and knew that full-scale Home Rule was not then a realistic proposition, besides which, anything was better than the Walter Long regime.[109]

In November 1905 Balfour decided that he could hold his ministry together no longer. But instead of dissolving Parliament he opted for resignation,

---

[109] F. S. L. Lyons, *John Dillon* (London, 1968), 280–1.

hoping that the policy divisions within the Liberal Party would become apparent to the public before the country polled. This characteristically ingenious ploy nearly worked. True, Asquith had always been a reluctant conspirator, and he now refused to play his part by presenting his Leader with an ultimatum, having no wish to sacrifice his claims to the Treasury or to jeopardize party unity at such a delicate moment. But Rosebery, badly out of touch and unaware that the other Liberal Imperialists were co-authors of the 'step-by-step' policy, publicly denounced Campbell-Bannerman's presentation of it in a speech to his constituents on 23 November—exposing the fault-line within Liberal Imperialism between those who wanted to demote Irish Home Rule and those who really wanted to abandon it outright. Rosebery's action unsettled Grey, who went to see C-B, 'all buttoned-up and unwilling to undo a single button', rudely ordering him to take a peerage. However, fortified by his wife's advice of 'no surrender', Campbell-Bannerman called the Liberal Imperialists' bluff. Asquith gratefully accepted the Treasury, along with the Leadership of the House, while Grey and Haldane were silenced by being offered the posts of Foreign Secretary and War Secretary.[110] The Liberal Leader thus became Prime Minister without forfeiting his Commons seat.

Campbell-Bannerman's ministry is usually regarded as a very strong one. Morley was moved from his old Irish Office berth (which was given to James Bryce) and made Indian Secretary. Among promising young men brought into government for the first time were Lloyd George, the new President of the Board of Trade, and John Burns, who became President of the Local Government Board. Churchill was appointed Colonial Under-Secretary, a more important post than it sounded, since his superior, the administratively astute but politically lightweight Lord Elgin, was a peer, somewhat removed from the fray. Thus, by the time polling opened in January 1906 the Liberals were able to present the country with a united face.

[110] It is a sign of Campbell-Bannerman's confidence that he first offered the Foreign Office to Lord Cromer, who turned it down: Grey was only his second choice.

The Transition to Liberal Rule, 1906–1908

1. THE 1906 GENERAL ELECTION

The Liberals, with 400 MPs (twenty-four of them 'Lib-Labs'), won an overwhelming victory in the 1906 General Election, reducing the Unionists to a paltry 157 seats. Balfour was defeated in his Manchester constituency, and only three of his outgoing Cabinet ministers were returned to the new House of Commons.[1] In greater Birmingham and in the Black Country Unionism showed greater resilience, and this strengthened the position of the Chamberlains, Joseph and Austen, both of whom survived the flood. 'Orange' Liverpool and protectionist Sheffield also largely kept faith with the Unionists.

But otherwise impregnable Conservative seats—Cheltenham, Eastbourne, even Chelsea—were captured by Liberal candidates, many of whom had simply stood to keep the old flag flying. The swing to the Liberals manifested itself across the 'nations': in Ireland most of the seats, eighty-two in all, predictably went to the Irish Nationalists, but the Liberals won 67 per cent of English and 83 per cent of Scottish seats, as well as all but one of the Welsh seats. The Liberals enjoyed success throughout the entire social spectrum: they even managed to take sixteen of the forty-five most middle-class urban and suburban English constituencies, fourteen for the first time.[2] As Chamberlain observed to Mrs Asquith, 'What a smash!'

The first-past-the-post system grossly exaggerated the Liberals' predominance in 1906; as opponents were quick to point out, the Liberals had secured only 49 per cent of the total vote. But this statistic is misleading, because it ignores the fact that twenty-seven Liberal candidates were elected unopposed, twice the number of unopposed Unionist candidates; neither does it take account of the intervention of the Liberals' 'ally', the LRC, which secured twenty-nine seats.[3]

The existence of the pact contributed to the scale of the Unionist defeat, especially in the North-West, where the LRC made gains in an area of traditional Conservative strength and Liberal weakness: the Unionists, who

---

[1] Austen Chamberlain, Akers-Douglas, and Arnold-Forster; defeated were the two Balfours, George Wyndham, Alfred Lyttelton, St John Brodrick, A. E. Fellowes, and Walter Long.

[2] i.e. since their creation in 1885.

[3] One of the miners' candidates, J. W. Taylor, joined the LRC immediately after the election.

had held eight of the nine seats in Manchester and Salford in 1900, lost them all in 1906, six to the Liberals, three to the LRC.[4] Yet even without this assistance the Liberals would still have won a comfortable victory. By endorsing the pact, the Liberals had therefore given Labour a toehold inside Parliament which, in retrospect, seems a grave mistake—even at the time it aroused misgivings among many provincial Liberals.

However, from the Liberal viewpoint there was much to record on the profit side of the balance sheet. First, the splitting of the progressive vote had been avoided—except in Scotland, to some extent, where the pact did not apply.[5] Second, many Labour sympathizers, deprived of a candidate of their choice, presumably voted for a Liberal, with whose party Labour was clearly in some kind of informal alliance. Finally, although the LRC men may not have been as moderate as Jesse Herbert claimed, the pact did contribute to the marginalization of socialism within the LRC, since it further encouraged the party to present itself in ways that traditional working-class Liberals would find reassuring.

As for the LRC (now renamed the Labour Party), the pact brought both benefits and dangers. In the long run it fettered Labour's effective independence, except at a formal organizational level. But it also gave them twenty-nine seats, of which only four had involved a fight with a serious Liberal opponent;[6] significantly, eleven of their successes occurred in double-membered boroughs where Liberals and Labour had each put up a single candidate. By contrast, nearly all the LRC-sponsored candidates who tried to go it alone were defeated. After 1906 Labour MPs sat on the Opposition benches—where else could they have found room to sit?—but a realization of their electoral dependence on the Liberals made it hard for them to operate as a genuine Opposition party, even though the pact itself had formally ended. Keir Hardie, newly elected as chairman of the Parliamentary Labour Party, was in for a difficult time.

In these circumstances Balfour's verdict—'We are face to face (no doubt in a milder form) with the Socialist difficulties which loom so large on the Continent'[7]— seems a wild exaggeration. It is more realistic to see the Liberal victory as reflecting disgust with a Unionist Party that had offended too many interest

---

[4] There was a 13.1% swing against the Unionists in the North-West, compared with a 10.5% swing in mainland Britain as a whole.

[5] Labour intervention actually led to the Liberals losing two seats to the Unionists which they had held in 1900: Govan, and Lanarkshire, North-West. And in Glasgow, Camlachie, it almost certainly stopped the Liberals from winning.

[6] Two of these victories came in Scotland, to which the Lib–Lab pact did not apply; another was in the double-member seat of Merthyr, where Hardie again pushed one of the Liberal candidates into third place; only Fred Jowett in Bradford, an ILP stronghold, successfully took on the two main parties.

[7] B. E. C. Dugdale, *Arthur James Balfour*, vol. 2 (London, 1936), 20.

groups. Discarding all pretence of political neutrality, Dissenting ministers lined up behind the Liberals during the 1906 General Election: Whitefields Tabernacle, the famous Congregational Church in the Tottenham Court Road, was surrounded during the campaign by large Liberal Party hoardings, and some Nonconformist clergy went on motorized tours of the country on its behalf.[8] Disgusted by the 1902 Education Act, many Dissenters, alienated by Home Rule in 1886, now returned to their ancestral home—fulfilling Chamberlain's earlier prediction.

Other 'interests' also came out in opposition to Unionism. Trade unionists resented the late government's failure to introduce legislation restoring their former powers following the Taff Vale Judgement. Jewish voters took exception to the Aliens Act of 1905. Despite the shelving of Home Rule, Irish residents in mainland Britain had every incentive to replace a Unionist by a Liberal ministry—though many supported Labour, especially where the Liberal candidate was not a 'tried friend'. The Liberals made much of the Unionists' 'broken promises' and, employing the populism they normally affected to despise, cynically exploited the 'Chinese Slavery' issue— *Reynolds's Newspaper* calling Chamberlain 'the Rt. Hon. Chowseph Chamerstein' and the Tories 'the pro-pigtail party'.[9]

However, the main issue in the election campaign was undoubtedly free trade versus protection, on which Unionist divisions were all too evident. Devonshire repeated his advice to voters to subordinate party loyalty to the defence of free trade, as did St Loe Strachey, editor and proprietor of the influential Liberal Unionist weekly the *Spectator*. Equally seriously, eleven tariff reformers found themselves challenged by a free fooder.[10] One of these clashes occurred at Greenwich, where Lord Hugh Cecil, standing as an Independent Unionist, split the Unionist vote and let the Liberals in to a hitherto secure Conservative seat.

The Liberals, on the other hand, were able to unite their followers across the boundary of class. Free trade made a strong populist appeal ('the big loaf and the little loaf'), but it also enjoyed considerable business support. Symbolic was Churchill's capture in 1906 of the North-West Division of Manchester, the very heart of Lancashire's commercial district. The 'consumerist' emphasis in free-trade propaganda also appealed to women, who, despite not themselves having the vote, may have exercised influence

[8] The Free Church Council advised all Nonconformists to vote for the candidates and the party soundest on education, temperance, Welsh Disestablishment, and Chinese Labour.

[9] J. Lawrence, *Speaking for the People: Party, Language and Popular Politics in England, 1867–1914* (Cambridge, 1998), 223.

[10] R. A. Rempel, *Unionists Divided: Arthur Balfour, Joseph Chamberlain and the Unionist Free Traders* (Newton Abbot, 1972), 109.

over their male relatives. The Women's Free Trade Union, an offshoot of the Free Trade Union, mobilized many Unionists and anti-suffragists as well as Liberals in what the *Women's Weekly* called a 'women's election'.[11]

The place of social policy in the Liberal campaign was more ambiguous. In defending free trade, the Liberals could claim to be defending working-class living standards. But, despite a groundswell of support for social reform among the rank-and-file, the party's candidates still had traditional Radical causes closest to their hearts. An analysis of Liberal election addresses reveals that 69 per cent of them mentioned 'Poor Law reform and pensions', but in order of rank this issue only came seventh, behind references to free trade, amendments to the Education Act, the reform of Irish government, licensing reform, Chinese Labour, and Tory misuse of its 1900 mandate.[12] The leadership acted with even greater circumspection. In late 1904 Herbert Gladstone had had difficulty in getting C-B to formulate a policy on unemployment,[13] and a year later the latter would still not commit himself on social policy other than making vague promises to 'colonise the land', a leading theme in his pre-election Albert Hall rally. The Liberal peer Lord Crewe had warned Campbell-Bannerman in November 1905: 'The Liberal party is on its trial as an engine for securing social reforms ... It has to resist the ILP claim to be the only friend of the workers.'[14] But even Lloyd George was still taking the line that, before acting on old-age pensions, the government must first put the 'national finances in spick and span order'. The old Radical slogan of 'retrenchment' overshadowed any recognition of the need for a publicly financed welfare programme.

Shortly before going out of office Balfour had set up a Royal Commission on the Poor Laws, the membership of which extended across a wide ideological range: from old-fashioned COS pedants such as Helen Bosanquet at one extreme, to trade unionists and Beatrice Webb at the other.[15] Candidates from all parties expected that the Poor Law would soon be tackled, but it suited the Liberal leaders to wait until the commission got round to submitting its report—which was likely to take a couple of years, at the very least.

---

[11] A. K. Russell, *Liberal Landslide: The General Election of 1906* (Newton Abbot, 1973), 177; A. Howe, *Free Trade and Liberal England 1846–1946* (Oxford, 1997), 259–60.

[12] Unemployment legislation came fourteenth (at 41%).

[13] J. Harris, *Unemployment and Politics: A Study in English Social Policy 1886–1914* (Oxford, 1972), 219–20.

[14] Cited in N. D. Daglish, 'Robert Morant's Hidden Agenda?: The Origins of the Medical Treatment of Schoolchildren', *History of Education*, 19 (1990), 141.

[15] Perhaps a reward for the Fabians' support for Balfour's educational work.

2. THE LIBERALS IN OFFICE: THE EARLY YEARS

The Liberal Parliamentary Party that assembled in euphoric mood in 1906 contained a higher percentage of Dissenters than at any time since the Bare-bones Parliament in the seventeenth century: no fewer than 157 Liberal MPs belonged to one of the various Nonconformist churches. Hardly surprisingly, then, the new ministry gave pride of place to measures designed to meet the sectarian grievances of their hard-core supporters.

The 1906 parliamentary session was dominated by an Education Bill which aimed at fundamentally revising Balfour's 1902 settlement. Its main provision was a tightening of public control over church schools receiving rate aid. In these 'transferred' schools religious tests were to be abolished, and, though religious teaching might be given twice a week, this could no longer be done by regular members of staff. The President of the Board of Education, Augustine Birrell, himself the son of a Baptist minister, felt private unease about a measure that the Anglican Church was bound to see as a provocation, but Lloyd George and a majority in the Cabinet were determined to get even with their old adversaries.

Forced by closure through the Commons, the Education Bill was amended out of recognition in the Upper House, where the Archbishop of Canterbury organized fierce resistance. Moderates on both sides sought a compromise, but negotiations in December between Crewe (Leader of the Lords), Asquith and Birrell on the one hand, and Balfour, Lansdowne, and Cawdor on the other, failed to break the deadlock, and the government decided to drop the entire Bill rather than accept amendments that undermined its central purpose.

The Liberals, with their fresh mandate, fulminated against the behaviour of the unelected Upper Chamber, but the ministry held back from dissolving on an issue which they knew had little popular appeal. Indeed, in the North-West the Bishop of Manchester had earlier organized a vast rally of supporters of the Anglican schools: some 10,000 Lancashire men, filling thirty-three excursion trains, descended on London during the Whit Wakes to express their anger. However, such loyalty to the institutional position of the Church was not widespread, impatience over sectarian squabbling being a more common popular reaction to Birrell's Bill and the antagonism it had excited.

More worryingly for the government, the Bill had underlined the precariousness of the Liberal–Irish Alliance. With Lord Ripon, the solitary Catholic in the Cabinet, playing a prominent part, the government had tried to appease the Irish Nationalists by inserting into the Bill a clause the effect of which was to provide more favourable terms for Catholic schools in the urban areas of England and Wales—which, of course, were heavily used by the Irish community. But this attempt to drive a wedge between their Anglican enemies and their Irish Nationalist allies miscarried: the Free Church Council demanded the withdrawal of the offending clause (in the Commons Sir Robert Perks was especially truculent), and the Irish voted against the Education Bill on its second reading. Birrell, who soon afterwards moved to the post of Chief Secretary for Ireland, realized that there was a lot of fence-mending to be done in this quarter.[16]

Failure also attended two further legislative measures to change Balfour's Education Act, both of them brought forward in 1908—to the great disappointment of militant Dissenters, some of whom persisted in witholding part of their rates. The Liberals sought to deflect this anger by blaming the situation on the House of Lords. The Upper House also caused outrage by rejecting the 1908 Licensing Bill, another attempted reform which was greatly cherished by the temperance party, many of them Dissenters.[17]

In 1907 the Campbell-Bannerman Resolutions, passed by the Commons,[18] had already supplied a warning that the government would not indefinitely submit to the mangling of its measures by an unelected and partisan Upper Chamber. But the government prudently ruled out a trial of popular strength on an issue such as temperance which commanded little enthusiasm: indeed, in March 1908 the Unionists won a rowdy by-election in Peckham on a huge swing (47 per cent), during which the 'trade' alleged that the government was both trying to deprive the working man of his glass of beer and also threatening the thousands of small shareholders created by the recent flotation of many brewery companies.[19] As the People's Budget was shortly to reveal, temperance also played badly in Southern Ireland, where the Nationalist Party enjoyed close links with the distillery industry and with publicans.

Traditional Radical attacks on brewers, publicans, and parsons, on the other hand, did on the whole facilitate co-operation between the Liberal and Labour Parties. Indeed, after 1906 there were proportionately more Nonconformists on the Labour than on the Liberal benches: 67 per cent compared with 39 per cent. The PLP broadly supported the Education Bill, in part because of its commitment to the principle of democratic control.[20] It similarly supported the

[16] See Ch. 12.

[17] The Bill aimed to reduce the number of licensed premises, in return for compensation deemed quite indequate by the vested interests, and also made provision for Local Option referenda (D. W. Gutzke, *Protecting the Pub: Brewers and Publicans Against Temperance* (Woodbridge, 1989), 167). It therefore appealed to both the prohibitionists of the United Kingdom Alliance and to restrictionists who primarily sought a diminution of licensed retail outlets.

[18] See Ch. 12.

[19] On the mobilization of the shareholders, see Gutzke, *Protecting the Pub*, 225–8.

[20] However, a 'conscience clause' had to be introduced into the party's constitution to accommodate its Irish Catholic members. Labour would have preferred a purely secular solution to the educational difficulty.

Licensing Bill: indeed, many leading Labour MPs, on both the trade-union and ILP side of the party, believed in temperance reform, because, while rejecting the idea that drink was the prime cause of working-class poverty, they did not see how a working class stupefied with alcohol could ever successfully fight for its own emancipation.

All the same, the Liberals' fortunes were closely aligned with Nonconformity, as Labour's were not. Yet after 1908 there was growing Nonconformist disillusionment with the Liberal ministry, which offered them little by way of legislative redress. Lloyd George retained his Vice-Presidency of the Liberation Society, but his mind had switched to wider social issues.

The government did, nevertheless, have some success: its handling of the South African problem, for example, proved particularly popular with its backbenchers.[21] Campbell-Bannerman himself also enjoyed the trust of most members of his parliamentary party, even his old Liberal Imperialist adversaries gradually admitting that he had captured the tone of the new House as thoroughly as he had misjudged the mood of the old one. So much became apparent when 'C-B' effortlessly swatted aside the attack launched on his government by Balfour, who, on his return to the Commons at a by-election in March 1906, found his sophisticated dialectics on the fiscal question dismissed with the contemptuous phrase, 'enough of this foolery!' Liberal morale was also boosted by the manifest disarray of the depleted Unionist Opposition, still at sixes and sevens over the fiscal issue, and by Joseph Chamberlain's virtual disappearance from public life, following a severe stroke in July 1906.

Yet, despite its crushing Commons majority, the government had comparatively little to show in the way of legislative achievement when, in late 1907, its popularity started to plummet in the wake of a business recession which brought about high unemployment. Between the summer of 1907 and the spring of 1908 the government lost five by-elections, two in rather odd circumstances to a Labour or socialist candidate in Jarrow and Colne Valley, in July 1907, and three to a Unionist Party now rejuvenated by its discovery that unemployment could be exploited with the cry 'Tariff Reform Means Work For All!'[22] The government had to show that its commitment to free trade and a free labour market was compatible with decent living conditions for the mass of the people. Ominously, as many as seventy Liberal backbenchers voted for one or other of Labour's Right to Work Bills, the first of which, in 1907, had actually been introduced by a Radical, Whitwell Wilson, one of the *Daily News* journalists. In short, by the spring of 1908 the Liberal government faced a serious crisis of morale.

[21] See Ch. 13.
[22] Opposition by-election successes continued throughout 1908 and early 1909.

At this delicate moment the dying Prime Minister resigned. Shrewd but idle, Campbell-Bannerman had proved more successful than his many critics could possibly have imagined, but he was an old man in poor health, who had spent much of his time in office watching by the bedside of his sick wife, who refused to be nursed by strangers, and had largely been content to leave policy-formation to more forceful colleagues. It was time for a new start. This was provided by Asquith, his unchallenged successor, who travelled to Biarritz to kiss hands in April 1908.

This necessitated a ministerial reshuffle, the first since the Liberals' advent to power.[23] Lord Elgin was brutally sacked and replaced at the Colonial Office by the up- and-coming Leader of the Lords, Lord Crewe (Rosebery's son-in-law), on whose judgement Asquith came increasingly to rely. Other old-timers were put out to grass: the dotty Lord Tweedmouth, First Lord of the Admiralty, was replaced by Reginald McKenna, and in October Lord Ripon, who had once served under Palmerston, also departed—offended at being asked by Asquith to use his influence with the Catholic Church to call off a eucharistical procession through the capital.

In came Winston Churchill, the new President of the Board of Trade, replacing Lloyd George, an effective and surprisingly pro-business minister who now found himself promoted to the post of Chancellor of the Exchequer. Some promising junior ministers also got their first taste of office, notably C. F. G. Masterman, the writer and social investigator, who became Parliamentary Under-Secretary at the Local Government Board under John Burns (a distinctly unhappy experience). Another promising young politician, Herbert Samuel, Under-Secretary to Herbert Gladstone at the Home Office, was soon afterwards brought into the Cabinet (in June 1909).

This reshuffle altered, perhaps deliberately, the balance of power within the government. Already changes were occurring at lower echelons of power. In 1906 almost the entire staff of the *Daily News* had been returned, along with thirty-one Progressive councillors;[24] other newly elected Liberal MPs had once resided in Toynbee Hall and other settlements. There were thus between twenty-five and forty committed 'Social Radicals' on the backbenches eager to support the new departure. The old Radicalism survived, not least the preoccupation with the abuses of landed privilege; but there was henceforward a commitment to collectivist welfare, aimed at improving the lives of the urban poor. A new era of welfare politics had begun.

---

[23] In January 1907 Bryce had been removed to the Washington Embassy, to be replaced at the Irish Office by Augustine Birrell, whose position as President of the Board of Education was filled by Walter Runciman. Two months later Harcourt junior entered the Cabinet as First Commissioner of Works.

[24] H. V. Emy, *Liberals, Radicals and Social Politics, 1892–1914* (Cambridge, 1973), 101–2.

CHAPTER 11

The Liberal Party and Social Welfare Politics

1. THE LIBERAL WELFARE REFORMS

Retrospectively, the pre-war Liberal government's main claim to fame rests on the extraordinary number and variety of welfare reforms that it sponsored. Yet, in the aftermath of the 1906 General Election, ministers probably had no more idea than the general public that such a major initiative was in the offing.

The government's early activities were certainly modest. In 1906 it took over a Private Member's Bill that allowed local authorities to raise the rates by another halfpenny in the pound to subsidize school meals for needy schoolchildren, and the following year it established a system of school medical inspection. In the autumn of 1906 the Chancellor of the Exchequer, Asquith, and his Chief Secretary, Reginald McKenna, set their officials to work on the feasibility of an old-age pension scheme; however, not until the spring of 1907 did ministers commit themselves to take action on this long-debated reform.[1] Appeasing their own Nonconformist supporters still took priority over all else.

With the change of Prime Minister in April 1908, the tempo of reform dramatically quickened. The crucial breakthrough came with the carrying of the Old Age Pensions Act of 1908. As it emerged, significantly amended after scrutiny in both Houses of Parliament, this measure conferred a weekly pension of up to 5s. on all British citizens aged 70 or more (based on a sliding scale) whose annual income fell below £31 10s.[2] About 490,000 people drew a pension on 1 January 1909. This number was relatively low, since disqualified from entitlement were recipients of any poor relief except medical assistance since 1 January 1908 (this knocked out a quarter-of-a-million old people). Certain categories of criminal, and those who were deemed guilty of 'habitual failure to work according to [their] ability, opportunity, or need, for [their] own maintenance or that of [their] legal relatives' were also excluded. But this latter

---

[1] On the background to old-age pensions legislation, P. Thane, *Old Age in English History: Past Experiences, Present Issues* (Oxford, 2000), 206–11.

[2] After amendment in Committee, citizens earning £21 p.a. or less were allocated the full 5s. those earning between £21 and £31. 10s. 00d. p.a. between 1s. and 5s., on a sliding-scale basis.

provision—the so-called 'industry test'—proved impossible to implement, and after the Poor Law disqualification had lapsed in March 1911, the pension population rose to over 1 million, about 40 per cent of the relevant age-group.[3]

In late 1908 Lloyd George's problems in finding extra money to cover old-age pensions expenditure coincided with an upsurge in the naval estimates, following the agitation for increased naval spending, and with the problem caused by falling tax revenues—a consequence of economic recession. The Chancellor declared that he faced a prospective deficit of £16 million, though he perhaps exaggerated its size for political reasons. Against this background Lloyd George introduced his famous 'People's Budget' of 1909, whose constitutional implications will be considered in the next chapter. Aside from the politically contentious but financially insignificant land taxes (designed to raise only £500,000 in 1909–10), the Budget stipulated a hike in the standard rate of income tax from 1s. to 1s. 2d. in the pound and the introduction of a 'super-tax' on incomes exceeding £5,000 at a rate of 6d. on every pound over £3,000. Death duties were also stiffened. Finally there were increases in the duties imposed on beer, spirits, and tobacco, a rise in stamp duty and in licensing duties, and two new taxes: one on motor vehicles, and a 3d. per-gallon petrol duty.

Even before the House of Lords had precipitated a constitutional crisis in the autumn of 1909 by rejecting his Budget, Lloyd George made further important commitments. Challenged in the Commons about how he proposed to help other disadvantaged groups not included in his old-age pensions scheme, the Chancellor announced the impending introduction of a great measure of National Insurance, this time based on compulsory contributions, which would embrace the sick, the disabled, and the unemployed.

Throughout late 1909 and 1910, a year dominated by two general elections, the ministry planned its National Insurance Act. It was really two separate Bills which, for technical reasons, had been amalgamated. Part One, the health insurance scheme, the handiwork of Lloyd George, covered all insured workers between the ages of 16 and 70 earning £160 p.a. (the income-tax threshold) or less. In return for contributions of 4d. a week from men and 3d. from women (plus contributions from employers and the state), it provided the insured worker, when sick, with a weekly out-of-work benefit of 10s. for men and 7s. 6d for women for the first thirteen weeks of sickness, then 5s. for the next thirteen weeks.[4] For the long-term sick there was a disability benefit of 5s. In addition, the Act covered the cost of medical treatment from a panel doctor—that is to

---

[3] J. Macnicol, *The Politics of Retirement in Britain, 1878–1948* (Cambridge, 1998), 155–62; Thane, *Old Age*, 226–7.

[4] Nothing, however, was paid out for the first three days.

say, from a list of doctors available to treat those covered by the insurance scheme. Two further fringe benefits were tagged on: a maternity benefit of 30s. to defray the cost of childbirth (almost entirely absorbed by hiring an attendant), and a sanatorium benefit in aid of those suffering from tuberculosis. The scheme came under the control of a newly created body, the National Health Insurance Commission (Joint), with subordinate commissions for Ireland, Scotland, and Wales. Day-to-day administration was devolved upon so-called 'approved societies', friendly societies, insurance companies, or trade unions, in which the insured were invited to enrol. A 'deposit' scheme was established by the Post Office to cater for the residuum who failed to join, or were turned down by, these voluntary bodies. The 'approved societies' received a state subvention which handsomely covered their outgoings.

Part Two of the National Insurance Act was created by Winston Churchill, the President of the Board of Trade. Unlike Part One, it was restricted to only about $2\frac{1}{4}$ million men, employed in a handful of trades susceptible to cyclical or seasonal job losses, mainly building and engineering. Insured workers qualified for an unemployed benefit of 7s. per week for a period of up to five weeks in any one year (after the first week of unemployment). The scheme was largely administered through the trade unions, acting as approved societies, but it also made use of the Labour Exchanges, set up under the Board of Trade in 1909, which supplied the mechanism that could test whether an applicant was genuinely seeking work. Like Part One of the National Insurance Act, unemployment insurance was funded from three separate sources: a compulsory contribution of $2\frac{1}{2}d$. each from employer and employee, plus a subvention from the state. The National Insurance Act reached the statute book in the autumn of 1911.

Other, lesser pieces of legislation became law between 1908 and 1910. In 1908 the coalminers had their working day reduced to a maximum of eight hours. In 1909 Churchill set up a national network of Labour Exchanges, designed to match supply and demand in the labour market. In that same year he also took charge of the Trade Boards Bill, under which machinery was set up to regulate wages in four casual and notoriously sweated industries, including box-making, lace-making, and tailoring, where some 200,000 (mainly female) workers had found it impossible to protect their own interests by trade-union action—workers, employers, and representatives of the state enjoyed equal representation on each of these trade boards.[5]

---

[5] S. Blackburn, 'Ideology and Social Policy: The Origins of the Trade Boards Act', *Historical Journal*, 34 (1991), 43–64. Some think its prime motive was to tackle prostitution on the one hand, and high infant mortality on the other—not to give proper reward to women's work (J. Lewis, *Women in England, 1870–1950: Sexual Divisions and Social Change* (New York and London, 1984), 200–1).

After 1911 the government's attention became deflected from social policy. Miners' minimum-wage legislation was enacted in 1912,[6] and the establishment on a semi-public, semi-private foundation of Lloyd George's Land Campaign presaged further major reforms. But these reforms were aborted by the outbreak of the Great War.[7] All the same, an extraordinarily ambitious programme of welfare legislation had materialized between 1908 and 1912.

2. RATIONALE FOR LEGISLATION

How to explain this flurry of activity? The most plausible explanations include: the need to fend off the challenge of Labour; pure humanitarianism; the search for electoral popularity; considerations of National Efficiency; and a commitment to a modernized version of welfare capitalism.

From the outset, the Liberals had certainly shown an anxiety to throw 'sops' at the Labour interest, as Campbell-Bannerman put it.[8] The most striking example of this came in March 1906, when the Prime Minister adopted a TUC-sponsored Bill. This measure, which completely freed the trade unions from all corporate liability arising out of an industrial dispute, displaced a Bill dealing with the Taff Vale Judgement based on the recommendations of a recent Royal Commission Report, that his own law officers had earlier introduced.

Another such 'sop' was the 1906 Workmen's Compensation Act, which built upon Chamberlain's 1897 reform by extending its scope to another 6 million workers and by allowing claims to be made, not only for accidents, but also for certain specified industrial diseases. Even the *Labour Leader* conceded that this was 'about as bold a [Bill] as a British capitalist administration could be expected to bring forth'.[9]

Greater controversy surrounded the 1908 Miners' Eight Hours Bill, for which the MFGB had been campaigning for some forty years. Several prominent Liberal capitalists took exception to this violation of the laws of political economy. Nor did it please all miners. In the North-East, where the average working day had already fallen *below* eight hours, the colliers were less than enamoured of a government initiative which threatened to worsen their conditions of employment.[10] Elsewhere miners were disappointed that, as amended

---

[6] See Ch. 12.   [7] See Ch. 12.

[8] Campbell-Bannerman to Asquith, 21 Jan. 1906, cited in B. B. Gilbert, *The Evolution of National Insurance in Great Britain: The Origins of the Welfare State* (London, 1966), 203. He meant both the Labour Party and the old 'Lib-Lab' contingent, between whom there was now a quite amicable relationship.

[9] H. A. Clegg, A. Fox, and A. F. Thompson, *A History of British Trade Unions Since 1889* (Oxford, 1964), 395, n. 6.

[10] Their discontent later sparked off the Durham miners' strike of 1910, arguably the start of the Great Labour Unrest.

by the Lords, the Bill excluded 'winding times', leaving them, in practice, to work for nine or even ten hours a day. The Eight Hour Bill also encouraged the coal-owners to divide the entire day into three eight-hour shifts, which interfered with customary working practices and forced miners onto a rota system that involved them in 'unsocial hours'. This should have taught ministers a salutary lesson: social reform would not always be universally popular with its recipients.

The one direct contribution to 'social reform' made by Labour came about when the government took over the Private Members' Bill, introduced by the Labour MP William T. Wilson, authorizing rate-aid for school meals. But most of those who voted for Wilson's Bill seem to have regarded it primarily as an *educational* measure: after all, there was something absurd about providing, at public expense, tuition from which some pupils were physically incapable of benefiting.

In fact, the feeding of schoolchildren well illustrates the complexity of welfare politics. Labour politicians, though sponsoring the 1906 Bill, by no means dominated the campaign to secure this reform. Margaret McMillan of the ILP, whose work in Bradford was vigorously publicized by Fred Jowett, MP for that city, made a great impact.[11] But so did the Liberal MP Thomas Macnamara, a prominent figure in the NUT, working closely with the 'Tory Democrat', Sir John Gorst. The campaign also enjoyed the backing of the medical press, which stressed the national importance of the 'food factor' and pointed to the precedent set by France, where the predominant motive had been fear of underpopulation. The establishment of a school meals service thus brought together an unlikely alliance of Labour politicians, medical experts, educationalists, Liberal reformers, and Tory democrats, each working to a somewhat different agenda. Argumentative stratagems were adopted that seemed appropriate to the audience being addressed. Macnamara himself, for example, once unblushingly claimed that public subsidies for starving children would be 'first-rate imperialism', and Labour MPs often mischievously made the same point.[12]

The humanitarian impulse was more directly operative in the campaign against 'sweating'. In 1906 the Liberal *Daily News* organized an exhibition of sweated goods, which attracted over 30,000 visitors and enjoyed widespread backing: from imperialists such as Milner, social-reforming Radicals, and the Women's Fabian Group. Under pressure from the all-party National Anti-Sweating League, for which Lady Dilke became the leading spokesman, the

[11] J. Welshman, 'School Meals and Milk in England and Wales, 1906–45', *Medical History*, 41 (1997), 9. On McMillan, see Ch. 7.

[12] J. Stewart, 'Ramsay MacDonald, the Labour Party, and Child Welfare, 1900–1914', *Twentieth-Century British History*, 4 (1993), 121.

government set up a Select Committee, whose report the Home Secretary, Herbert Gladstone, largely followed in preparing what later became the Trade Boards Act.

In the case of old-age pensions, humanitarianism, informed by social science, was once again the predominating motive. After all, no one stood in *fear* of the elderly poor or saw them as a decisive factor in military or industrial efficiency. Despite being, by objective measurements, less likely to be in distress than younger age-groups,[13] the elderly poor excited considerable pity; besides which, it was realized that a state measure of relief would also take financial pressure off their children (as well as off local government). Significantly, many backbenchers who lobbied the government to introduce a pension scheme had already had experience of settlements work[14] or had made personal first-hand studies of the problems of the poor. The same applies, to some extent, to National Insurance. Charles Masterman, a High Anglican, author of *The Condition of England* (1909), played a key role in its formulation and implementation, while Lloyd George emotively presented himself as a driver in the Red Cross ambulance corps, coming to the rescue of the sick and the destitute.

But there was more to the Liberal government's involvement in the politics of social welfare than either a desire to curry favour with the Labour interest or mere benevolence. Lloyd George, for example, was well aware of how social reform might restore the party's electoral fortunes and spike the campaigns of the socialists on one flank, and the tariff reformers on the other. 'It is time we did something that appealed straight to the people—it will, I think, help to stop the electoral rot, and that is most necessary', he told his brother in May 1908 while steering his Old Age Pensions Bill through the House.

The scheme's main defect, in the eyes of its critics, was the high qualifying age: most manual workers did not reach the age of 70 and had dropped out of the labour market many years earlier, as Radical Liberal backbenchers and Labour MPs bitterly complained. Indeed, the National Committee of Organized Labour for Promoting Old Age Pensions, set up by Charles Booth with trade-union backing in May 1899, wanted a starting-age of 65,[15] while the

---

[13] Rowntree's study of York demonstrated that those aged 5–15 were the poorest age-group, with 37.58% in poverty, compared with only 21.39% of those aged over 65 (B. S. Rowntree, *Poverty: A Study of Town Life* (London, 1901; Nelson edn.), 442–4).

[14] See Ch. 6.

[15] Sir William Lever's Private Member's Bill, passed by the Commons in 1907, had also had a 65-years threshold. In 1899 the President of the Wolverhampton Trades Council advocated a 5s. pension at the age of 65, 'but only on condition that they had insured against sickness and funeral expenses for a certain period in a friendly or trade union society', and it was the Conservatives who pressed for universality (J. Lawrence, *Speaking for the People: Party, Language and Popular Politics in England, 1867–1914* (Cambridge, 1998), 149).

TUC itself had recently passed a resolution in favour of pensions at 60. All the same, by providing substantial cash benefits quite outside the unpopular Poor Law, old-age pensions created an enormously important precedent. Indeed, such was their popularity that Balfour was furious when the Liberals implied that the Unionists would repeal them if they got back to office.

National Insurance, on the other hand, turned out to be unpopular because it required compulsory deductions from the wage-packet. The Conservative leadership, initially supportive, soon went over to the attack, and the government had to recruit paid lecturers to preach the word. However, the Liberals may not have understood in advance how contentious National Insurance would be. Nearly all the government's major measures were *intended* to be popular.

Electoral considerations, however, sometimes jostled with other motives, not least 'National Efficiency'. 'There is a tremendous policy in Social Organisation', Churchill told Asquith, in a hectoring letter of December 1908:

The need is urgent and the moment ripe. Germany with a harder climate and far less accumulated wealth has managed to establish tolerable basic conditions for her people. She is organised not only for war, but for peace. We are organised for nothing except party politics.[16]

More influenced by National Efficiency arguments than was his newfound ally Lloyd George, Churchill for a while (in 1908) drifted into the Webbs' camp, telling Sidney that he would 'find the door of my room open whenever you care to come', and inviting him to 'feed me generously from your store of information and ideas'.

Better social organization would, some Liberals sincerely believed, improve the country's international competitiveness, particularly in its struggle for domination with Germany. In fact, visits to Germany formed an indispensable part of the education of all Edwardian social reformers, ministers, government officials, academic 'experts', and trade unionists alike. Lloyd George in 1908 was only the most conspicuous visitor; others included William Beveridge, William Braithwaite, and several trade-union delegations. However, the British did not blindly imitate earlier German achievements: attitudes to Germany usually involved a blend of revulsion, admiration, and emulation.[17] Perhaps Germany's main importance was that its social welfare schemes made it that much more difficult for British Conservatives to offer a blanket condemnation of everything the Liberal ministry was trying to do: after all, no one had ever accused Bismarck, the author of his country's great social insurance measures, of being a sentimental philanthropist, indifferent to *raisons d'état*!

[16] Cited in P. Addison, *Churchill on the Home Front 1900–1955* (London, 1992), 74.
[17] E. P. Hennock, *British Social Reform and German Precedents: The Case of Social Insurance 1880–1914* (Oxford, 1987).

Some ministers, notably Churchill, also believed that social legislation would strengthen national solidarity in a dangerous world. Labour Exchanges, for example, were viewed by their creators as a matter of commercial organization quite as much as an attack on the scourge of unemployment—hence their sponsorship by the Board of Trade. Even Lloyd George, whose incitement of the working-class audience attending his meeting at Limehouse in the summer of 1909 laid him open to his opponents' accusation that he was a 'socialist', can also be found, faced by a business audience, putting the case for social reform in 'business terms', stressing that increased profits would accrue from a contented workforce integrated into the fabric of existing society. But, as often as not, such talk was rhetorical, designed to neutralize opposition. As for Churchill, his statist vision never occupied the ideological centre-ground of Liberalism: the Mastermans, who knew him well, were not alone in thinking that much of the 'aboriginal Tory' still clung to him.

In any case, though electoral considerations might not have been everything, Lloyd George and most other Liberal ministers had a firm grasp of electoral reality, and this dictated that, to be popular, their new welfare schemes must not be contaminated by association with the hated workhouse. That is why nothing significant was done to reorganize, still less to abolish, the Poor Law, as the Webbs were demanding. Indeed, as more and more categories of the 'deserving poor' were accorded special treatment, ministers were the more tempted to leave the Poor Law largely alone, as a useful, but no longer very important, safety-net for the residuum.

If the pragmatic Lloyd George was animated by a big idea of any kind, it was probably the urgency of helping the respectable working man by replacing his lost income when, through some misfortune (illness, accident, old age, unemployment), he fell out of the labour market. But he was determined to do this in a way that bypassed the guardians. The Webbs could not, or would not, understand this basic point. In attacking the inadequacies of National Insurance, they made many pertinent points: the scheme did not, as they rightly said, cover dependent wives and children nor meet the cost of hospital treatment (except the anomalous sanatorium benefit). The Webbs wanted, instead, to establish a unified health service, a demand which the Labour Party officially backed in 1911. But Lloyd George had never originally envisaged his (perhaps misleadingly entitled) National Health Scheme as a health service at all, its medical benefit having been thrown in at a comparatively late stage. This explains why, at least initially, maternity benefit was paid direct to the insured worker (even when this person was the husband):[18] after all, the costs of childbirth fell mainly upon the household's bread-earner, usually a man.

---

[18] In 1913 the Women's Cooperative Guild got maternity benefit paid to the wife.

The Webbs devised their own counter-proposal for the 'break-up' of the Poor Law and the redistribution of its services among specialized committees of the county and borough councils, supplemented by a National Plan to 'organise the labour market'. But this never held much attraction for the Liberals. For a start, it would have involved heavy expense[19] and bureaucratic investigations into the lives of the poor and needy—hardly conducive to the government's popularity. Fortunately the Poor Law Commission, when it reported in February 1909, produced a majority and a minority report, and this allowed a relieved government to shelve the entire issue. In fact, despite some support from their old friends Haldane and Robert Morant, Permanent Secretary at the Board of Education, plus the backing of highly placed government health officers (notably George Newman, Chief Medical Officer at the Board of Education, and Arthur Newsholme at the Local Government Board), the Webbs never commanded the influence of which they boasted; Haldane was now isolated in the War Office, remote from social issues; and John Burns, at the Local Government Board, felt intense hostility to the Webbs and all their works, as, to a lesser extent, did Asquith himself, who saw them as tiresome busybodies.

Nothing more annoyed the Webbs than the fact that social insurance gave the insured worker an entitlement to benefit if he met the conditions laid down in the scheme—without the need for any investigation into the circumstances which had led to his destitution and without the guarantee of any reformation of behaviour. But, from the Liberals' point of view, this avoidance of 'coercion' was actually its most attractive feature.

Rowntree's 'poverty cycle' had already suggested that poverty was an affliction that affected most working-class people at certain stages in the family cycle, and was not confined to a 'submerged tenth'. Similar deductions could be drawn from Beveridge's pioneering research into the problem of unemployment and underemployment, which demonstrated that a high percentage of the unemployed were craftsmen, thrown out of work by a trade depression, who then found it difficult to switch jobs but would have nothing to do with special relief works. If unemployment could hit, in this almost random way, people so very different in their circumstances and morals, the incarceration of the so-called 'unemployables' in Labour Colonies, as recommended by Charles Booth and others, no longer seemed as appropriate as a comprehensive insurance scheme. Churchill, who had by now freed himself from the tutelage of the Webbs, took the point, observing in late 1909 that insurance, which embodied the magic of averages, obviated the need for any inquest into a recipient's

---

[19] Both Reports also required a fundamental overhaul of local-government finance. See below.

character.[20] And herein lay the importance of the Liberal welfare reforms: that they replaced the old demoralizing system of doles with a new set of citizen entitlements.

3. CREATING AN IMPERIAL RACE?

The Liberal reform programme was not confined to providing a network of protection against the harsh vicissitudes of life. Intersecting this programme was a larger movement, involving the Liberal government but also others, which aimed at combating 'physical deterioration' and laying the foundations for a vigorous and healthy 'imperial race'. It was devised as a response to three different problems: first, the refusal of the infantile death-rate to decline;[21] second, the alarming recruiting statistics during the Boer War, which suggested a civilian population too enfeebled to carry the burdens of Empire; and third, clear evidence that differential fertility was bringing about a situation in which, according to Karl Pearson, 'the fertile, but unfit, one-sixth' of the population was about to reproduce one-half of the next generation, a trend which, according to the alarmists, threatened 'race suicide' and Britain's disappearance as a world power.

The Interdepartmental Committee set up by the Unionist government soon concluded that there was no evidence supporting the hypothesis of 'physical deterioration' and racial degeneration. Nor did it believe that urbanization necessarily led to 'impaired vitality': after all, over recent decades life-expectancy had improved while urbanization was proceeding apace. Nevertheless the committee, comprising many medical experts as well as educationalists, uncovered in the course of its investigation a mass of poverty, sickness, and squalor calculated to deepen public alarm; its report, published in 1904, itemized a long catalogue of proposals, including the provision of school meals and state medical inspection of schoolchildren, as well as measures to reduce smoke pollution, improve working conditions in factories, and, generally, to ameliorate the urban environment. Such social reforms, the committee recommended, should be complemented by a programme of physical training (much along the lines that had recently been suggested by the Royal Commission into Physical Training (Scotland)). Leaders of youth movements, town planners, the pioneers of garden cities, educationalists, doctors, and social workers could all find material in the committee's report from which to draw encouragement.

[20] However, despite Churchill's famous remarks, for financial reasons workmen who had been discharged for misconduct *could* be excluded from benefit: 50,000 such claims were dismissed during the first two years of the scheme (J. Harris, *Unemployment and Politics: A Study in English Social Policy 1886–1914* (Oxford, 1972), 314).
[21] See Ch. 6.

Others were not so easily persuaded that physical deterioration was not taking place, and blamed differential fertility for what was happening. These fears intensified when, in 1904 and 1905, the scientific polymath Sir Francis Galton, a cousin of Charles Darwin, delivered two influential papers to the Sociological Society in London, suggesting that the time might now be ripe for further investigations into what he had earlier (in 1883) called 'eugenics', which he later defined as 'the study of the agencies under social control that may improve or impair the racial qualities of future generations either physically or mentally'.

This led to two developments: first, the creation of the Eugenics Laboratory attached to London University under the charge of Galton's young friend and future biographer, the biometrician, Karl Pearson; and second, the foundation in the winter of 1907–8 of the Eugenics Education Society,[22] whose London branch had built up its membership by 1914 to just under one thousand, a membership weighted towards professional men, especially doctors.

Caleb Williams Saleeby, an early pioneer of eugenics, popularized the notion that the new 'science' could be divided into two complementary sections: 'positive eugenics', that is, encouraging healthy parents to have large numbers of offspring; and 'negative eugenics', the attempt to arrest what soon became known as the 'multiplication of the unfit'—preferably by persuasion, but if need be by bringing defective adults into custodial care so that they could not reproduce themselves.

Eugenists varied very much in their sophistication, but since most tended, when talking about the 'unfit', to conflate hereditary physical and mental illnesses with low wages and low social status, it is hardly surprising that their movement quickly developed into a forceful (albeit fallacious) assault on the premises which underlay the Liberal welfare programme: fit income-tax payers, claimed the eugenists, were limiting their families because of the pressure of taxation, itself the consequence of the mistaken policy of helping the unfit to propagate their kind. These developments, they argued, threatened the survival of the British race. 'I demand that all sympathy and charity shall be organised and guided into paths where they will promote racial efficiency, and not lead us straight towards national shipwreck', wrote Pearson.[23] Whom should we believe, one eugenist asked: Lloyd George, a demagogue lamentably ignorant of science, or agriculturalists who, by selective breeding, had dramatically improved their livestock?

Admittedly, social reformers and eugenists did not always confront one another in quite so stark a way. Some 'reform eugenists', Saleeby included,

---

[22] Galton originally disapproved of the Society, and it was only with reluctance that he later agreed to serve as its President.

[23] *The Scope and Importance of Eugenics* (London, 1909), cited in D. Mackenzie, *Statistics in Britain 1865–1930: The Social Construction of Scientific Knowledge* (Edinburgh, 1981), 86.

wished to establish a concordat between the two programmes. Conversely, some intellectuals from both the Liberal intelligentsia and the Fabian Society (notably George Bernard Shaw and the Webbs) took a sympathetic interest in eugenics, which they hoped to incorporate as a minor component within their own reform programmes. Many individuals peregrinated between the hereditarian and environmental camps,[24] while the crusade against 'racial poisons' such as alcohol and syphilis,[25] and efforts to control alleged antisocial menaces (for example, 'white slave traffickers', vagrants, and feeble-minded mothers), drew support from social reformers and eugenists alike.

Moreover, however idiosyncratic the practical conclusions to which it gave rise, eugenics had certain things in common with other aspects of contemporary 'social hygiene'. In both cases there was a tendency to redefine social policy in biological and medical terms and to trust in a 'dynasty of experts' supposedly elevated above partisan controversy. Also common to both groups was a fascination with 'planning', even when this meant overriding parental wishes and decisions. Lord Rosebery declared that 'in the slums and rookeries [of our great cities] an Imperial race cannot be *reared*' (my italics);[26] this, of course, carried different connotations from the language of the eugenists, who talked about *breeding*. But underlying both was a conception of human beings, not as citizens (still less as God-created possessors of an immortal soul), but as a biological species, subject, as were other members of the animal kingdom, to the processes of regeneration and decay.

Germ theory, by encouraging a search for the causation of specific diseases, contributed to the new scientism. In particular, the impact of bacteriology, which from the 1890s onwards exploited new, more powerful microscopes, seemed to suggest that dirt did not in itself create disease and that the solution therefore required changes in behaviour: better personal hygiene, more intelligent child-rearing, and so on. Emphasis thus switched away from the Victorians' concern with large-scale sanitary engineering—a project now largely, though not entirely, completed—to the promotion of the health of individuals and to the control of common infections spread by social contact through personalized medical services. And this, in turn, involved a novel way of scrutinizing *bodies*, especially those of children and of women.[27]

---

[24] G. Jones, *Social Hygiene in Twentieth Century Britain* (Beckenham, 1986), 11–12. Newman was sympathetic to eugenics, though Newsholme was a fierce opponent.

[25] Mrs Gotto, the EES Secretary, helped set up the Society for Combating Venereal Disease, which led to the establishment of the Royal Commission which sat from 1913 to 1916.

[26] Glasgow University Rectorial Address, 16 November 1900, *Miscellanies* (London, 1921), ii. 250.

[27] Armstrong claims that the body came to be the subject of 'various techniques of detail which analyzed, monitored and fabricated it': the imposition of adult will upon human bodies through feeding, medical inspection and treatment, and the infliction of physical pain (T. Armstrong, *Modernism, Technology, and the Body: A Cultural History* (Cambridge, 1998)).

Infant welfare, approached from this perspective, gave rise to two important public-health developments, both aimed at the saving of babies' lives.[28] Even before the Boer War public-health officers and doctors had expressed disquiet over the existence of untrained midwives, many of them posing a danger to both mother and child. But Bills dealing with this problem failed to reach the statute book in 1890 and 1899, and it was only after the 1902 Midwives Act that unregistered (and untrained) midwives were debarred from practice. The Midwives Act of 1905 further strengthened this move towards professionalization—even though midwifery never became a self-regulatory profession such as medicine, and untrained midwives still outnumbered trained ones.[29] We have to fight against 'race-deterioration and race-degeneration', wrote Emilia Kanthack, a midwife instructor, in 1907: 'we want not only to keep babies *alive*, but we want them to be healthy young animals.'[30]

The second important manifestation of this new concern with infant health was the movement to improve the milk supply. Medical experts, debating allegations about 'physical deterioration' in the wake of the Boer War, were almost unanimous in their belief that much of the high infant mortality (primarily deaths from diarrhoea, the second largest killer)[31] resulted from contaminated liquid milk, the feeding of babies with unsuitable forms of tinned milk (particularly the separated, sweetened, and machine-skimmed variety, which contained too much carbohydrate and insufficient fat), and the use of dirty feeding bottles.[32] (Dried milk powders only became available on the eve of the Great War.) It was observed that in hot summers, when bacteria multiplied in milk, infant-mortality figures sharply rose.

Doctors and social workers urged working-class mothers, if at all possible, to increase their children's survival chances by breastfeeding them. For those who could not do this, milk depots were set up in the early years of the century (based on the 'gouttes de lait' in Paris). However, these never really caught on: the pasteurized milk they provided was too dear (at 4*d.* a quart), while collecting it and returning the bottles to the depot proved to be too inconvenient for many hard-pressed mothers.

Soon after the Liberals' advent to power the emphasis therefore switched to infant clinics and health visiting. Alys Russell, wife of the philosopher Bernard Russell, set up the first School for Mothers in St Pancras in 1907 following a

---

[28] See below.   [29] Lewis, *Women in England*, 198.

[30] D. Dwork, *War is Good For Babies and Other Young Children: A History of the Infant and Child Welfare Movement in England 1898–1918* (London and New York, 1987), 160.

[31] The infant death-rate from diarrhoea peaked in 1900 but still accounted for 28% of infant deaths in 1911, after which it fell away.

[32] The *Daily Chronicle* ran a seven-part series on 'Milk and Disease' in 1904. Full-cream milk was safer, though it quickly deteriorated after the tin had been opened.

visit to Belgium, which had taken a lead in these activities, and a Mothers' and Babies' Welcome was established so that babies could be weighed and advice given on the best methods of feeding. Similar clinics soon sprang up all over the country (by 1918 1,278 maternity and child-welfare centres were in existence, 578 depending on voluntary effort[33]); many of them also put on lectures and classes and offered subsidized meals to pregnant and nursing women.

This work was supplemented by domiciliary visiting. Health visitors, who were often sanitary inspectors and usually women, had been appointed by the more enlightened local authorities since the late 1890s. They were increasingly joined in their work by an army of middle-class female volunteers. Such home visiting was more easily effected after the enactment of the 1907 Notification of Births Act, a permissive measure speedily adopted in most of the large cities, which required births to be notified to the Registrar within a period of thirty-six hours.[34] When George Newman wrote in 1913 that infant mortality was 'mainly a question of motherhood and ignorance of infant care and management', this was symptomatic of the Edwardian fashion for blaming these domestic tragedies upon what one MOH called 'maternal mismanagement'.[35] Cynics have also noted that, whereas doing something fundamental about the disadvantages suffered by working-class mothers would have been very expensive, the dispensing of good advice came cheap!

As a result, subjects were increasingly inserted into the school curriculum with a view to turning out 'good wives and little mothers'. Scant emphasis had been given to this in the early years of the School Boards,[36] but the Inter-Departmental Committee into Physical Deterioration thought this a regrettable omission and called, in its report, upon the education authorities to combat girls' ignorance of household affairs, hygiene, and nutrition, and inadequate mothering skills. In 1905 the Board of Education responded to the report by insisting that domestic science should have a practical content, and Morant, in his 1906 Code, declared that 'the reaction against excessively domestic and feminine types of training ha[d] already gone too far'.[37] Moreover, in 1910 the Liberal backbencher Christopher Addison, himself a medical man, introduced a Bill that, if passed, would have required all elementary schools to give introduction in infant care to girls over 12 years of age.

---

[33] C. Dyhouse, 'Working-Class Mothers and Infant Mortality in England, 1895–1914', in C. Webster (ed.), *Biology, Medicine and Society, 1840–1940* (Cambridge, 1981), 77.

[34] 113 authorities had adopted it by March 1908, and the LGB ordered all metropolitan boroughs to do so in 1909.

[35] J. Lewis, *The Politics of Motherhood: Child and Maternal Welfare in England, 1900–1939* (London [c.1980]), 65; Dyhouse, 'Working-Class Mothers', 88.

[36] See Ch. 2.

[37] Lewis, *Politics of Motherhood*, 90.

The tone of class condescension underlying many of these initiatives is obvious, as is the scarcely concealed desire to turn out a large reservoir of well-trained domestic servants. But the infant-welfare movement was predicated on the belief that 'mothercraft' was far from natural and, in any case, was much too important to be left entirely to the vagaries of individual mothers—whatever their class. Interestingly, middle-class girls attending secondary school and going on into higher education were themselves coming under growing pressure to study 'mothercraft'. After 1905 higher elementary and secondary schools were required to differentiate the girls' curriculum from that offered to boys, by providing 'a practical training in home duties applicable to the circumstances of their own homes' in the case of girls.[38] In 1906 the Board of Education pressurized even the Girls Public Day Schools Company into introducing housewifery into the syllabus. This development was particularly welcomed by many eugenists, who deplored the way in which modern education was encouraging intelligent girls to develop career ambitions, to the detriment of their racial responsibilities.

Many 'advanced' reformers joined in the campaign to turn motherhood into woman's central vocation by dramatizing its wider public significance. 'People rear children for the State and the future', H. G. Wells declared; 'if they do that well they do the whole world a service, and deserve payment just as much as if they built a bridge or raised a crop of wheat.'[39] This was in support of the Fabian call for the 'endowment of motherhood': a combination of family allowances and publicly financed infant-welfare clinics which, it was claimed, would encourage 'fit' parenthood.[40]

Some followers of this cult of 'maternalism' clearly hoped to halt women's advancement by imprisoning them within the home and teaching them to see the whole meaning of their lives as 'guardians of an Imperial race'. The President of the Local Government Board, John Burns, like many other male trade unionists, feared married women as cheap competitors in the labour market. Addressing the first Conference on Infant Mortality in 1906 (another was held in 1908), he declared: 'We have got to restrict married women's labour as often and as soon as we can', since this was responsible for infant mortality and rickety anaemic children, broken homes, unhappy fathers, 'idle and loafing husbands', and low wage-rates.[41] Many MOHs took a similar line,

---

[38] In 1908 the Board allowed girls over 15 to drop science in favour of an approved course in a domestic subject, while the 1909 Regulations for Secondary Schools suggested that they might substitute such courses 'partially or wholly for science and for mathematics other than arithmetic' (C. Dyhouse, *Girls Growing Up in Late Victorian and Edwardian England* (1981), 165).

[39] *Independent Review*, Nov. 1906.

[40] See Fabian Pamphlet no. 149, *The Endowment of Motherhood* (1910), by Henry D. Harben.

[41] Such utterances may also indicate a downward dissemination of traditional middle-class ideals about a woman's proper place.

even though much contemporary evidence, including an official report commissioned by Herbert Gladstone in 1907, showed that infant mortality was actually lower among mothers in employment than among those not industrially employed, perhaps because working mothers were able to raise living standards for their families by supplementing their incomes.

During the Edwardian decade articulate, politically active women could not agree among themselves over the desirability of mothers working: Margaret Bondfield opposed it, Mary MacArthur asserted a woman's right to choose, while Mrs Fawcett stressed the improvements brought about by the additional income.[42] The teaching of 'mothercraft' also divided the promoters of girls' education, as did the attempt on the eve of the Great War to raise the scientific status of 'household science' at university level.[43]

However, although perhaps holding back women's advancement by stressing their functions as wives, house-managers, and mothers, the new social politics in some ways empowered them, not least by creating novel openings in paid work—as health visitors, female school officers, midwives, and nurses (another expanding profession), all of these occupations being subjected to higher standards of training and competence.[44] By 1909 there were already between 200 and 300 salaried health visitors, and ten times that number of voluntary workers.[45]

The 'feminization of politics', resulting from the new emphasis on the importance of the mother and child, also played its part in promoting the political emancipation of women. Significantly, women were given the vote and membership rights on county and borough councils in 1907, where many of them specialized in this kind of welfare work—for which they saw themselves as eminently qualified, local government service being, in their view, a kind of 'compulsory philanthropy' or 'municipal housekeeping'. Moreover, as Parliament and government increasingly concerned themselves with health issues, women's claims to the parliamentary vote became harder to resist.

From whatever motives, many Edwardian women were more than happy to co-operate with the maternalist cult: 'Our children are a valuable asset to the nation, and the health of the woman who is doing her duty in rearing the future race should have a claim upon the national purse', one said.[46] Even the Eugenics

---

[42] P. Hollis, *Ladies Elect: Women in English Local Government 1865–1914* (Oxford, 1987), 435; Lewis, *Women in England*, 23–4, 34, 50.

[43] King's College for Women started a three-year course in 'Home Science and Economics' in 1908.

[44] The LGB in 1909 decreed that in the LCC area health visitors should have a medical degree, be fully trained nurses, hold a certificate from the Central Midwives Board or a health visitor's certificate from a local authority, or have appropriate experience. These provisions were extended to the rest of the country in the Maternity and Child Welfare Act of 1918.

[45] Hollis, *Ladies Elect*, 436–7. Lady inspectors had also been operating since 1893.

[46] Dwork, *War is Good For Babies*, 165.

Education Society proved surprisingly attractive to women: they comprised 48.7 per cent of its total membership in 1914;[47] the organization was also being run on a daily basis by a very efficient female Secretary, Mrs Sybil Gotto.[48]

'Radical' women, who disliked the eugenists' obsession with 'breeding', nonetheless valued the child-welfare movement: in 1911 the Women's Labour League opened a clinic of its own at North Kensington, in memory of Mary Middleton and Margaret MacDonald. A body such as the Women's Co-operative Guild invariably put greater stress on the *mother*'s health than most male MOHs were doing, but it too called for the maternal health movement to be extended.

The premise that 'mothercraft' was too important to be left to the unaided exertions of mothers can also be seen in the public support given after 1906 to school meals and to the development of a school medical service. Increasingly education came to be seen as an important medium of socialization, a place where children were taught 'good manners, kindliness to and consideration for others, and self-control'.[49] For slum children school dinners often provided an intro-duction to the use of a knife and fork.[50] The school also functioned as a laboratory for social investigation: this was one of the underlying reasons for Parliament's establishment of school medical inspection in the Education (Miscellaneous Provisions) Act of 1907, the measure being particularly supported by MPs who wanted an accurate anthropometrical survey of the population in order to establish conclusively whether or not physical deterioration was taking place.

However, exploiting the revelation of widespread ill-health that school medical inspection had uncovered, Newman and Morant subsequently created a school medical service (usually under the authority of the MOH, assisted by a female nurse). When referrals to the local hospitals proved too costly and complicated, school clinics rapidly became the norm—following the example of Germany, Austria, Switzerland, and the United States, where clinics already existed in large numbers. Margaret McMillan established the first school clinic in London in 1908, and by the end of 1913 the Board had sanctioned 260 clinics in 139 local authority areas.[51]

[47] I. G. Brown, 'Who Were the Eugenicists? A Study of the Formation of an Early Twentieth-Century Pressure Group', *History of Education*, 17 (1988), 301. But they numbered only 8 out of 41 Council members in 1914.

[48] Karl Pearson's assistant, Alice Lee, from her recording of cranial measurements of male and female scientists in Dublin, showed that no connection existed between skull capacity and intellectual ability. Yet she and her colleague, Ethel Elderton, nevertheless emphasized women's role as wives and mothers (R. Love, ' "Alice in Eugenics Land": Feminism and Eugenics in the Scientific Careers of Alice Lee and Ethel Elderton', *Annals of Science*, 36 (1979), 145–58).

[49] Newman, cited in P. Horn, *The Victorian and Edwardian Schoolchild* (Avon, 1989), 87.

[50] Ibid. 87–8.

[51] B. Harris, *The Health of the School Child: A History of the School Medical Service in England and Wales* (Buckingham, 1995), 64.

All this represented a dramatic departure from existing practice: in 1905 Sir John Gorst had secured a Commons majority for the subsidized feeding of schoolchildren, but the outgoing government had delegated this task to the Poor Law authorities. When the old-fashioned A. V. Dicey attacked the feeding of schoolchildren by rhetorically asking 'why a man who first neglects his duty as a father and then defrauds the State should retain his full political rights?', he drew attention to the way in which social legislation was changing traditional concepts of parental responsibility. However, few Edwardian social reformers shared Dicey's misgivings. No longer so concerned about state invasions of the home, Parliament now happily passed legislation such as the 1908 Children's Act, which empowered the authorities to cleanse verminous children and to place children deemed at risk into safe custody, as well as ending imprisonment for juveniles and stopping them from entering pubs and being sold cigarettes. The title of Gorst's book, *Children of the Nation*, epitomizes the way in which the young were being reconceptualized. H. G. Wells announced that one of the discoveries of the age was that of the state as 'Overparent', ready, if need be, to interpose itself between parents and children to promote the future of the nation and the race.

Interestingly, however, the ILP and mainstream Labour were more cautious: anxious to uphold the family, both were careful not to do anything that smacked of the 'state maintenance of children', as advocated by the Marxist SDF.[52] That is why the Bill authorized local authorities to retrieve the cost of the school meal from parents who were deemed capable of paying—with the result that only children from very poor families were fed gratis.

In any case, to what extent was the Liberal government itself influenced by the concern to debate 'national deterioration'? Its three chief Medical Officers of Health, Newman at the Board of Education, Newsholme at the Local Government Board, and Leslie Mackenzie at the Scottish Local Government Office, with the approval of their ministerial superiors, vigorously promoted many of the new public-health strategies. Yet the government did not commit itself whole-heartedly to these initiatives. It was voluntary bodies, in association with enlightened local authorities in the big cities, which largely took the lead in promoting the health of women and children. In 1905 (i.e. *prior* to legislation) forty-eight LEAs in England and Wales were already making some provision for the medical inspection or supervision of schoolchildren,[53] and fifty-five of the seventy-one county boroughs were organizing school meals.[54]

---

[52] Stewart, 'Child Welfare', 105–25. Blatchford, too, advocated the institution of communal child-care, a solution favoured by some radical women suffragists (Lewis, *Women in England*, 239).

[53] Horn, *Schoolchild*, 84.

[54] However, outside the large urban areas not much was being done (J. S. Hurt, *Elementary Schooling and the Working Classes, 1860–1918* (London, 1979), 105).

This pattern of activity continued after 1907, notably through the Children's Care Committees, which brought together school managers, voluntary organizations such as the NSPCC, health visitors, settlement workers, and GPs. And even the local authorities were often motivated by considerations of economy. For example, some LEAs may well have calculated that treating children suffering from body lice and ringworm (the latter treated by X-rays) would cost less than losing part of their annual grant through absenteeism.[55]

Central government continued to betray an even greater anxiety over incurring additional financial burdens. Initially the only central support given to the infant clinics took the form of grants from the Board of Education in support of lecture courses. Not until 1914, on the very eve of war, did the Local Government Board offer grants in support of maternity and child-welfare services. Again, it was only in June 1914 that the government made the Education (Provisions of School Meals) Act compulsory, removed the halfpenny rate limitation, and allowed feeding during the school holidays, for which it gave the local authorities grants-in-aid by way of reimbursement. Partly as a result of this cautious approach, even in 1911–12 only 131 of 322 LEAs in England and Wales were providing a school meals service, and of these seventeen depended entirely upon voluntary contributions and another nineteen used rate-aid solely for administrative purposes.[56]

The development of a schools medical service also brought out the mean side in the Liberal government. From the start, the County Councils Association had complained that government was imposing new responsibilities upon local authorities without contributing to their cost. The Liberals' response in 1909 was to agree to the passing of a Private Member's Bill, introduced by a Conservative MP, Walter Guinness, which allowed local authorities to 'charge the parent of every child in respect of any treatment provided for that child such an amount not exceeding the cost of treatment as may be determined by the Local Education Authority'. The LEAs, however, found that this scarcely brought in enough money to cover their administrative expenses. It was only later, in the spring of 1912, that government stepped in to pay a medical treatment grant, which it extended a year later to cover the costs of inspection. Such caution contrasts markedly with the Liberals' bold embrace of a compulsory old-age pensions scheme.[57]

As for eugenics, to this the Liberal government prudently gave a wide berth. Churchill briefly flirted with it when he gave consideration to the possibility of using Röntgen-rays to sterilize mental defectives—a proposal which, ironically, went much further than the EES leadership was prepared to go. In 1908

[55] Ibid. 132.   [56] Horn, *Schoolchild*, 86.

[57] J. D. Hirst, 'The Growth of Treatment Through the School Medical Service, 1908–18', *Medical History*, 33 (1989), 318–42.

the government did respond to the scare about the spread of feeblemindedness by setting up a Royal Commission on the subject. This paved the way for the Mental Deficiency Act of 1913, under which those deemed to be feebleminded could be brought into custodial care and then sexually segregated. The measure was strongly supported by both the EES and by Mrs Dendy's National Association for the Welfare of the Feebleminded: it was these two societies combining in 1912 to bring in their own Bill which forced the government to produce a measure of its own. But it is doubtful if government or Parliament saw this as a step towards the 'sterilization of the unfit': the measure could also be defended at the time on the grounds of the protection it afforded to a pitifully vulnerable class of people, as well as holding out the hope that Poor Law expenditure and crime would ultimately be reduced.[58]

There was indeed a larger trend towards the 'medicalization' of social policy in Edwardian Britain, with a whole range of social 'problems'—for example, race, criminality, hereditary illness, alcoholism, poverty, and sexual deviance—being 'biologized'. But this process had begun before the Liberals came to power and would doubtless have continued under any party regime. In 1914 a measure for the restraint of inebriates (the Inebriacy Bill) was deferred because of the war, but in the previous year the government had made compulsory the local authority implementation of the provisions of the Elementary Education (Defective and Epileptic Children) Acts, first passed in 1899 for special education.[59] This formed part of the movement towards categorizing 'social inefficients' and providing them with appropriate institutional treatment—again to the approval of the EES.[60]

On the other hand, although leading MOHs proudly pointed out that falling infant mortality was due to a decline in deaths in the post-neonatal (1–12) months, rather than in the neonatal death-rate, which they took to mean that the unfit were *not* being kept artificially alive, the broad thrust of their approach to social policy remained what it had always been, an environmentalist one. Even Newman and Mackenzie, and still more Newsholme, recognized the primacy of poverty in producing ill-health, and were not solely concerned with combating maternal ignorance and inefficiency.[61]

A leading Liberal minister such as Lloyd George was never enamoured of medical and scientific experts (witness his quarrel with the medical profession

---

[58] The contribution of eugenics is downplayed in M. Thomson, *The Problem of Mental Deficiency: Eugenics, Democracy, and Social Policy in Britain c.1870–1959* (Oxford, 1998), esp. 298–304.

[59] The 1913 Act created special schools for these groups.

[60] Earlier, in 1889, the Royal Commission on the Blind, Deaf, and Dumb had drawn attention to the danger of pauperism unless these people received an appropriate education, which led to the 1893 Elementary Education (Blind and Deaf Children) Act, making it obligatory for local authorities to provide an 'efficient and suitable' education for the handicapped.

[61] Dwork, *War is Good For Babies*, 133.

over health insurance), and he was seldom tempted, as even many Fabians
were, to discuss the British population in biological terms. Churchill (about to
become a father) pressed for the inclusion in the People's Budget of rebates to
income-tax payers with small children (the so-called 'brat')—which could just
conceivably be presented as a measure of 'positive eugenics', on the ground
that income-tax payers were likely to possess greater physical and mental
efficiency than the vast majority of the population who paid no direct taxes at
all. But though talk about rearing an imperial race gave the Liberals some
support from unexpected quarters after 1906 and, through the child and
mother welfare initiatives, did make an impact on the British people in the
opening decade of the century, it was always marginal to the Liberals' own
reforming project. And it is to some of the consequences of their major social
reforms that we must now turn.

4. THE POLITICAL LEGACY OF WELFARE REFORM

In organizational terms the Liberal welfare reforms were something of a hotch-
potch. Old-age pensions were established by the Treasury and administered
via the Post Office. Part One of the National Insurance Act involved the
setting-up of what would today be called a new quango, while the Board of
Trade, which had, perhaps surprisingly, supplanted the LGB as the principal
health and welfare department, ran Labour Exchanges and unemployment
insurance. In the crucial matter of funding, ministers also made up policy on
the hoof. Having vigorously denigrated the principle of compulsory insurance
when pushing through old-age pensions, they then turned to the German
model of social insurance in their later legislation—because old-age pensions
had proved so expensive. The Cabinet seldom debated social policy and its
wider implications. Asquith ran his government on a loose rein, leaving the
initiative to individual ministers, the more energetic and ambitious of whom
(notably Lloyd George and Churchill) then presented their colleagues with
schemes for rubber-stamping.

Political ambition and political necessity drove some ministers forward
faster than the administrative infrastructure allowed. For example, the Treasury officials who planned old-age pensions took copious evidence from what
was already being done in other countries (Germany, Denmark, New Zealand,
etc.), but their calculations were amateurish—they did not even consider the
way in which the country's changing age-structure would affect future financial
liabilities. Health and invalidity insurance, which turned into a fiendishly
complex measure the likes of which no previous government had attempted,
was undertaken in an equally lighthearted manner, under the leadership of that
master of improvisation, Lloyd George. Characteristically, the broad outlines

of the measure were hammered out by the Chancellor, his officials (including Braithwaite, hot-foot from an inspection of German social insurance), and other advisers, on Nice Pier in January 1911. The Bill which later received the Royal Assent bore only a slight resemblance to its prototype.

This was for a very important reason. In embarking on welfare legislation, the government did not, as in most of its traditional operations, have the field entirely to itself, since other agencies were already at work: private charities, self-help organizations such as friendly societies and trade unions, commercial bodies such as insurance companies, and professional men such as the GPs, who traded their specialist expertise in return for fees.

At local government level, co-operation between voluntary bodies and public authorities may have presented few problems. But at national level ministers faced an acute dilemma. The government was acting because it knew that a sizeable section of the poor, through poverty or irregularity of earnings, could not get themselves adequately covered from a private source. It thus faced a choice among four possible strategies. The state could press ahead with its own schemes and damn the vested interests, perhaps minimizing opposition by setting benefits at a low enough level to give individuals an incentive to take out private cover (which is what largely happened with old-age pensions). Second, it could buy out the vested interests, as a preliminary to running its own comprehensive state scheme—for example, by nationalizing the industrial assurance industry. But this would have been politically impossible, since the 80,000 insurance agents had a strong organization and were well placed to influence public opinion; it would also have been financially ruinous, as Lloyd George realized when he learnt to his horror, in the course of 1910, that it would cost £30 million to buy out the insurance companies. Leaving the vested interests alone and simply plugging the gaps (as had been done in the 1870 Education Act) was a third possibility, but in that case why should prudent workers consent to be taxed to fund a scheme for the remnant? This left the government with no option but to adopt the fourth strategy, namely, subsuming the private agencies into the public sphere—hence, the invention of the 'approved society'.

This arrangement, in turn, powerfully influenced the shape of the government's welfare reforms. Ministers were able to organize old-age pensions on a non-contributory basis because neither the friendly societies nor the insurance companies covered the 'risk' of old age (the Foresters and the Manchester Unity each ran a superannuation scheme, but both badly flopped).[62] The more intelligent friendly society leaders, for all their ideological aversion to state intervention, could see advantages in the government taking sole responsibility for this

[62] On the friendly societies, see Ch. 6. Most societies provided a concealed old-age pension for their elderly members in the form of extended sickness benefit.

area of welfare provision. The United Ancient Order of Druids was the first society to support non-contributory state pensions in 1897,[63] but by 1908 most of the large societies favoured co-operation with the government, though many called in vain for friendly society or trade-union benefits to be excluded from the income limit.

However, a quite different situation prevailed with health and invalidity insurance, where government competition directly threatened both voluntary and commercial agencies with ruination. Realizing this, Lloyd George quickly grasped the importance of incorporating the friendly societies into his own measure—something he favoured in any case, since, like most Radical Liberals, he admired the work which these self-help groups were doing and wanted to help them. But at this point the insurance companies, seeking opportunities to promote their own lucrative life-assurance business and worried at the prospect of the introduction of 'death benefits', determined to muscle in on the government's scheme. This became a matter of some urgency when, for political reasons, the government dropped its proposed widows' benefit and used the savings to double sickness benefit from 5s. to 10s. a week, making the state scheme a really serious competitor.[64]

More effectively organized and led than were the amateurish friendly societies, the insurance companies eventually forced Lloyd George to turn National Insurance inside out to meet their institutional needs. Originally the government had proposed that the approved societies be subjected to the democratic control of their own members. But a giant insurance company such as the Prudential would have needed to hire the Albert Hall to do this, and, in practice, the situation would probably have been exploited by its collectors, who had their own effective trade union. The insurance companies got their way and 'democratic control' disappeared from the Bill. Kingsley Wood, a lobbyist for the 'Combine', the insurance industry's trade association, memorably observed in 1910: 'we have got LG there (putting his thumb on the desk) and we shall get our own terms!'[65] Lloyd George, determined to have *any* scheme of national insurance on the statute book rather than admit failure, sacrificed the friendly societies, provoking the resignation of Braithwaite, the civil servant originally in charge. Friendly society membership went into speedy decline.

Another threat to National Insurance emerged from the medical profession, many of whose senior members were also animated by party feeling:[66] in 1912

---

[63] Thane, *Old Age*, 200.

[64] Gilbert, *National Insurance*, Chs. 6–7, provides a full and clear account of Health Insurance.

[65] 22 May 1911. H. N. Bunbury (ed.), *Lloyd George's Ambulance Wagon: Being the Memoirs of William J. Braithwaite 1911–1912* (1957: Bath, 1970), 168.

[66] The President in 1912 was James Barr, a Vice-President of the EES. On doctors' hostility to women's demands, B. Harrison, *Separate Spheres: The Opposition to Women's Suffrage in Britain* (London, 1978), 59–68.

26,000 GPs, fearful of losing their professional autonomy, announced that they would take no part in the scheme. Fortunately for the government, the British Medical Association (BMA) overplayed its hand, and Lloyd George was able to isolate the well-paid consultants on its executive by raising the capitation fee to a level which poorly paid GPs found too tempting to resist, and by issuing veiled threats about how impecunious Scotsmen might have to be employed in a state-organized medical service if the medical profession proved recalcitrant. Doctors' fees had increased during the 1880s, but a quarter were still earning less than £195 p.a. in 1913–14, so their eventual acceptance of health insurance is understandable.[67] By January 1913 GPs were rushing to sign up as panel doctors, and the government's scheme, covering 12,700,000 persons, was safe.

But although the BMA lost membership as a result of its mishandling of the situation, the doctors had successfully exacted their price from the government, in that, whereas the friendly societies had previously been able to set rates of contribution and doctors' fees, the approved societies could no longer submit the GPs they employed to lay control. As a result, the medical profession emerged from the battle to establish National Insurance with greatly increased prestige and authority.[68]

'So many private interests were trying to sting the new proposals to death', Braithwaite later wrote of National Insurance: 'The history of the bill is how they were bought off, conciliated, and, in a very few instances, over-ruled.'[69] But ministerial dependence on voluntary agencies and commercial organizations came about, not only because the latter were too powerful to be ignored or bypassed, but also because, in their various ways, they constituted a repository of knowledge and expertise which the state was anxious to tap. In the early years of Liberal rule the civil service was still too small in numbers and too dominated, in its higher ranks, by 'generalists' to feel competent in handling these new welfare initiatives. Significantly, it was the Board of Trade which quickly moved to the centre of government planning—perhaps because, since the establishment of its Labour Department in 1893, it was employing economists and boasted a sophisticated statistical division and so had better access to relevant data than did rival departments such as the Local Government Board.

This was important since, to draft bills and oversee their implementation, the new welfare work required administrators with the kind of talent that had been discouraged by the Northcote–Trevelyan reformers: strong-minded individuals who were 'programme-driven', rather than routine administrators—or, to put it another way, 'problem-orientated rather than career-orientated'

[67] J. Lewis, 'Providers, "Consumers", the State and the Delivery of Health-Care Services in Twentieth-Century Britain', in A. Wear (ed.), *Medicine and Society: Historical Essays* (Cambridge, 1992), 321.
[68] Ibid. 327. [69] Bunbury (ed.), *Lloyd George's Ambulance Wagon*, 161.

officials.[70] Such a man was Robert Morant, who, working with his MOH friends, had pressed ahead with the establishment of a School Medical Service, before being transferred to the National Health Insurance Commission, which he chaired.[71]

A similar role was played in the Board of Trade by its Permanent Secretary, Hubert Llewellyn Smith, a former resident of Toynbee Hall[72] with a lifetime's commitment to social science and statistical research (he had been the Board's original Labour Commissioner). The case of William Beveridge is also interesting. Like Morant, a one-time resident of Toynbee Hall, where he had served as sub-warden between 1903 and 1905, Beveridge had acquired a reputation as the leading expert on Labour Exchanges, the subject on which Beatrice Webb got him to give evidence to the Poor Law Commission. When Churchill was thinking of starting a Labour Exchange scheme but uncertain how to do it, Beatrice pressed on him the 'boy Beveridge', who thus found himself, at the tender age of 29, head of the Labour Exchanges Division at the Board of Trade.

The early twentieth century thus saw a revolution in government, leading to a civil service which was both broader in its composition and greatly enlarged. At lower administrative levels, too, there was a need to co-opt outside talent, bypassing the usual channels of appointment, as in the case of the managers of Labour Exchanges. Career civil servants were ill-fitted to fill these posts, so, using a competitive interview, followed by a qualifying examination, the Board of Trade succeeded in recruiting men from a wide array of backgrounds, including trade-union leaders and businessmen, as well as a number of odd-balls, among them a retired Polar explorer and an American gold speculator who claimed to have 'run a labour exchange in Chicago, with a revolver provided as part of the office equipment in the drawer of his desk'.[73]

This whole process aroused strong partisan controversy. In October 1912 the new Conservative Leader, Bonar Law, alleged that the Liberals, through ruthless exploitation of their powers of patronage, were creating a new spoils system, on the American model. By the spring of 1914 the civil service numbered over 167,000, and ministers admitted that 5,387 permanent and 10,510 temporary extra civil-service posts had been created in consequence of legislation passed by the Liberal government: health insurance alone absorbed over 2,000 civil servants, the Board of Trade had expanded to nearly 2,500, and valuers were being employed in their hundreds on land valuation, often on

[70] R. Davidson and R. Lowe, 'Bureaucracy and Innovation in British Welfare Policy 1870–1945', in W. J. Mommsen (ed.), *The Emergence of the Welfare State in Britain and Germany 1850–1950* (Beckenham, 1981), 268.
[71] Morant had by then made himself unpopular with the teachers' unions (the Holmes Circular).
[72] See Ch. 6.   [73] J. Harris, *William Beveridge: A Biography* (Oxford, 1977), 157.

temporary contracts. Moreover, 2,133 permanent and 9,387 temporary civil servants had been dispensed from sitting an open competitive examination.

Profiting from this ministerial largesse were some prominent trade-union leaders, who were given administrative offices which paid a salary well in excess of anything that they could otherwise have earned: for example, Richard Bell, dismissed in disgrace by the railwaymen's union, was appointed superintendent of the Labour Exchanges at a salary of £400 p.a., while David Shackleton, Keir Hardie's successor as chairman of the PLP, was made a Labour Adviser at the Home Office in 1910. Winston Churchill was particularly alert to the advantages of 'managing' Labour in this way. By 1913 places had been found over the previous six years at the Board of Trade for 117 active union workers (at a combined annual salary of £25,240), for 124 in the National Insurance Departments (£33,700), forty-eight at the Home Office (£13,600), and another eighty-five on Labour Exchanges (£34,800).

As well as precipitating changes in the ethos of Whitehall, Liberal social policy changed the relationship between government and Parliament. Everyone had had a say about the shape of old-age pensions, but the battle over National Health Insurance largely took place behind closed doors or on the floor of the House, and involved technical amendments moved by spokesmen for one or other of the various interested parties (470 amendments were disposed of under closure, without discussion, on a single day—30 November 1911). Lloyd George once silenced an angry conference between his officials and representatives of the trade unions and friendly societies by telling them: 'at the present moment we are making law.'[74]

More fundamentally, social welfare brought the state into a new relationship with the general public by blurring the division between the state and civil society—a reversal of a century-old trend, which had seen a concentration of authority in the hands of a largely autonomous state. Titled ladies initially declared their refusal to 'stick stamps for Lloyd George' (i.e. to administer health insurance for their domestic employees). However, this short-lived 'revolt' was more than mere farce: the state was now intruding into citizens' lives in quite unprecedented ways, and one did not have to follow Hilaire Belloc in his diatribes against the 'Servile State' to see dangers in this trend.

Social reform also necessitated drastic changes in the public finances. Between 1890 and 1910 the cost of local government expenditure on social services increased from £19.4 million to £60.2 million. But the failure to overhaul local government finance, which would have been an immensely complex and politically hazardous undertaking, meant that the main financial

---

[74] Gilbert, *National Insurance*, 382.

burdens fell upon central government through the grants-in-aid it made to the municipalities.[75]

Initially the Liberals had hoped to make space for new welfare initiatives by rigid 'retrenchment', particularly in the armed services. In their first two years in office they enjoyed some success in this endeavour. The overall budget fell to £143.4 million in 1908, a lower figure than at any stage since the outbreak of the Boer War. This was largely thanks to the happy accident of reduced naval expenditure, following the collapse of the Russian navy in 1905.[76] Admiral Togo, it has jokingly been said, deserves to be honoured as one of the architects of the British welfare state. But after this windfall the naval arms race with Germany drove up expenditure once more: the navy's share of the budget rose from 22.7 per cent to 24.1 per cent between 1906 and 1914, and the overall budget went up to £156.9 million in 1910 and to £184 million in 1913.[77]

Failing an accommodation with Germany, what was to be done? As early as 1907 a Cabinet memorandum admitted that social reform, if persisted in, 'must entail heavy additional expenditure'; the country refused 'any longer to drink itself out of its financial straits', it claimed, and so, 'unless the whole system of taxation [was] to be recast', the solution could only be found in an increase of direct taxation.[78]

Old-age pensions provided the catalyst, because their cost turned out to be much higher than the Treasury had foreseen: from the £6–7 million estimated by Asquith in April 1907, they were absorbing £12,500,000 by 1914. One reason for this was that politicians from all wings pressed amendments on the government as the original Bill passed through Parliament, mostly with the effect of increasing its total cost—including the end of the unpopular reduced benefit for married couples (7s. 6d. a week) and the introduction of a sliding scale. Moreover, in Ireland, where statistics of birth registration were chaotic or inadequate, many claims must have been fraudulent, since 98.6 per cent of the Irish population aged 70 and more drew a pension, compared with 44.7 per cent in England and Wales.[79] Nor did later events bear out the hope that the cost of old-age pensions could significantly be recouped from reduced outlays elsewhere: Poor Law expenditure in England and Wales stayed almost static

---

[75] There were 8 million ratepayers, as compared to just over 1 million income-tax payers, of whom 800,000 received rebates (J. Harris, 'The Transition to High Politics in English Social Policy, 1880–1914', in M. Bentley and J. Stevenson (eds.), *High and Low Politics in Modern Britain* (Oxford, 1983), 78 and n. 59).

[76] Naval expenditure fell from £36.8 million in 1905 to £31.1 million in 1908.

[77] Defence costs increased from 26.1% to 29.9% between 1905 and 1913, those on 'social services' (including education and Poor Law) from 28.3% to 33%.

[78] H. V. Emy, 'The Impact of Financial Policy on English Party Politics Before 1914', *Historical Journal*, 25 (1972), 139.

[79] Gilbert, *National Insurance*, 227.

between 1909 and 1914, at £12,300,000, though the numbers on outdoor relief fell dramatically. The Unionist Opposition, now regrouping under the tattered banner of tariff reform, taunted ministers by alleging that free-trade finance stood on the edge of collapse.

This context explains why Lloyd George was prepared to risk political unpopularity by building checks and safeguards into his original old-age pension scheme (often under cover of upholding the moral status of the respectable poor).[80] It also explains the paradoxical situation of Unionists joining with Labour and dissident Radical MPs in striking out these restrictions: they clearly hoped in this way to provoke a financial crisis.

A few stern ideologues, such as Harold Cox of the Cobden Club, the leaders of the Charity Organisation Society (COS),[81] and the elderly Liberal Unionist jurist A. V. Dicey, continued to contest the very principle of social legislation. But few frontbench parliamentarians did likewise. Significantly, once the Liberals had launched old-age pensions, none of their rivals dared attack the policy head-on. Instead, the battle raged over the means by which the necessary revenue was to be raised. Some Opposition MPs, disliking a government measure which drew funding out of general taxation, pressed the case for compulsory social insurance, on the German model. But most followed Balfour's lead and advocated a revenue tariff,[82] so as to 'broaden the basis of taxation'.

Eventually the government, in its National Insurance Act, agreed to adopt a compulsory insurance scheme, but, far from introducing a revenue tariff, the Liberals boldly went for the opposite stratagem, placing the emphasis on direct taxes (income tax and death duties). As a result, whereas in 1906 customs and excise duties and stamp duties had accounted for 45.6 per cent of government revenue, this proportion had fallen to 41.5 per cent by 1909 and to 37.8 per cent in 1913. During the same period the income-tax share rose from 20.4 per cent to 21.7 to 22.4 per cent, and the death-duties share from 11.2 per cent to 12.1 to 13.3 per cent.[83]

Moreover, direct taxes, which were levied disproportionately on the well-to-do, were then made even more 'progressive' through the application of the principles of differentiation and graduation. Asquith, a more adventurous Chancellor than his cautious demeanour suggested, had established an

[80] Similarly the Unemployment Insurance scheme guarded against 'malingering' by the 'five-to-one' rule: the insured worker needed to work for five weeks to earn an entitlement to one week's payment—a rule which simultaneously combined financial prudence with a principled stand against the work-shy.
[81] Very different from the COS was the City Guild of Help, created in Bradford in the autumn of 1904, which numbered 70 branches by 1911, with more than 8,000 members, some of them working-class. The Guild was especially strong in the northern cities.
[82] See Ch. 10
[83] The remaining revenue came from Post Office income, etc.

important new fiscal principle in his 1907 Budget when he differentiated for income-tax purposes between earned and unearned income, with the latter taxed at a higher rate. Lloyd George carried the process further: for example, though the People's Budget raised the standard rate of income tax to 1s. 2d. in the pound, for earned incomes below £3,000 the rate remained at 1s., while at the upper end a 'supertax' was applied to incomes over £5,000. It was this method of revenue-raising, rather than social reform itself, which generated the anger directed against the government by pressure-groups such as the recently created Anti-Socialist League. In many ways the 1914 Budget was even more 'radical' than the more famous 'People's Budget' of 1909, since it applied the principle of graduation for the first time to the whole range of *earned* incomes.

Moreover, budgets themselves now became politicized in an unprecedented way. For example, the 'People's Budget' was important in that, even more than Harcourt's Budget of 1894, it showed that a Finance Bill could also be an instrument of social policy. Tagged on to it were provisions for a Road Fund and a Development Fund, the latter giving rise to a Development Commission, with responsibility for scientific research and education, experimental farming, forestry schools, rural transport, co-operative marketing, and land reclamation, all of which were to be financed out of government money distributed through the local authorities.[84]

What were the party-political implications of these developments? Some Unionist backbenchers, eager to steal the Radicals' thunder, developed their own agenda, not least the Unionist Social Reform Committee, established under F. E. Smith in 1912, which contained sincere reformers such as J. W. Hills, an ally of the Webbs. The Opposition also adopted its own land programme, aimed at the multiplication of small property owners. But, in general, the Conservative Party fell back on a negative set of responses—to the unease of many of Joseph Chamberlain's followers.

On balance, the adoption of social welfare probably revitalized the Liberal Party, broadening its appeal and giving it a new urgency and relevance. At the same time, the writings of 'New Liberal' intellectuals such as J. A. Hobson, L. T. Hobhouse, and H. V. Massingham (editor of the *Nation*) provided a theoretical underpinning to what Lloyd George and Churchill were doing. Liberals did not discard their traditional belief in 'individuality', but its meaning was extended by a sophisticated exploration of the interdependence of citizens and the society of which they were members.[85] Arguably this meant that the old Gladstonian creed gave way to a new 'social democratic' vision that

---

[84] But the initiative had to come from local authorities. As a result, little had been done by 1914.

[85] On the 'New Liberals', see P. Clarke, *Liberals and Social Democrats* (Cambridge, 1978); M. Freeden, *The New Liberalism: An Ideology of Social Reform* (Oxford, 1978).

proved capable of meeting the class needs of the working-class electorate and of sidelining the challenge from Labour. In the 1910 General Elections, as Herbert Samuel noted, the Liberals held on to, even in some areas extended, their gains in working-class constituencies (especially in the North)—though at the cost of frightening away the middle classes in the Home Counties and the agricultural constituencies.

But the Liberals ran considerable risks in pursuing such a strategy. After 1906 middle-class defence groups sprang up all over the land, with publications such as *The Bitter Cry of the Middle Classes* (1906). In 1907, making a stand on economy and fighting with slogans such as *Its [sic] Your money we want!*, the Municipal Reformers (the old Moderate Party) wrested control of the London County Council (LCC) away from the Progressives.[86] Outside London, too, anxieties over high public expenditure did much to weaken the traditional relationship between Dissent and Liberalism. In 1907 Robert Perks founded the Nonconformist Anti-Socialist Union, and the following year Perks's old hero, Lord Rosebery, emerged from semi-retirement to denounce old-age pensions as destructive of the Empire. A notable feature of the 1910 elections was the reluctance of many Nonconformist ministers to back the Liberals openly, as in 1906; those who did so sometimes provoked wealthy chapelgoers into walking out.

In fact, Lloyd George, however 'populist' his rhetoric, had no intention whatever of alienating those capitalists who formed an indispensable element in the party's constituency of supporters, both through their financial subventions and through their contribution to the Liberals' claim to be a 'national' party that transcended class and creed. What Lloyd George was seeking was an alliance of all 'productive' workers against idle landowners and rentiers, so *preventing* a drift into the kind of class politics which had recently all but destroyed Liberalism in Germany.[87]

But even within the Cabinet the Chancellor had critics, who suspected that the supposedly redistributive features of the 'People's Budget' would create a defensive combination of all property-owners, facilitated by the promise of the tariff reformers that, if they held power, the 'foreigner' would pay for social improvement and national defence, not the hard-pressed income-tax payer. In Cabinet Loulou Harcourt predicted that the 1909 Finance Bill would bring about 'the triumph of tariff reform', and the wealthy shipowner Walter Runciman, the President of the Board of Education, subjected Lloyd George's

---

[86] K. Young, *Local Politics and the Rise of Party: The London Municipal Society and the Conservative Intervention in Local Elections 1894–1963* (Leicester, 1975), 89–93.

[87] G. R. Searle, 'The Edwardian Liberal Party and Business', *English Historical Review*, 98 (1983), 26–60.

proposals to sustained and detailed criticism.[88] Runciman's father, President of the Northern Liberal Federation, later gave up his office in protest at the Government's 'socialistic' finance, one of several prominent Liberal businessmen to voice their disquiet. The hostility of the City of London could be discounted (the City had long been a Conservative stronghold), but the alienation of prominent northern manufacturers was much more worrying.

Significantly, as many as seventy of the Liberal MPs who declined to stand again in the 1910 General Elections were thought to be disgruntled over the Budget. Even after 1910 the Parliamentary Liberal Party contained MPs critical of the whole drift of government policy. Notable is the 'Cave', mainly though not exclusively composed of businessmen grouped around the Liverpudlian shipowner Richard Holt, which later succeeded in inflicting a serious defeat on clauses of Lloyd George's 1914 Budget.[89] Through its rhetoric as much as through its policies, the 'advanced' wing of Radicalism was pushing more cautious Liberals further than they were willing to go. A class realignment of politics threatened, which was likely, in the long run, to bring the Conservative Party, however battered and demoralized, new supporters—a more promising tactic than trying to oubid the Liberals, as the Social Reform Group was trying to do.

From the Liberal viewpoint, these risks might have been worth incurring if their welfare initiatives had proved capable of blunting the appeal of the Labour Party. But class-conscious, politicized working men had always had ambivalent feelings about social reform. The *Nation*, for one, was puzzled and disappointed at the absence of 'any large, insistent public policy' in TUC programmes and its preoccupation with more narrowly sectarian issues, while Chiozza Money claimed, with some justification, that in 1906 the Liberals could boast more avowed collectivists than Labour.[90] What the 1906 Trades Disputes Act shows is that organized Labour, far from welcoming an extension of state power, still preferred to work within a voluntary framework. Indeed, right up to 1914 and way beyond, the TUC consistently rejected any suggestion of, for example, compulsory arbitration—in the name of its great mantra, free collective bargaining.

True, more Labour than Liberal candidates in 1906 advocated social reform, but significantly, it bulked less prominently in their addresses than the need for increased working-class representation and the repeal of Taff Vale. The main theme in the official manifesto was that Labour was entitled to the same representation and privileges as were enjoyed by 'landlords, employers,

[88] B. Murray, *The People's Budget 1909/10: Lloyd George and Liberal Politics* (Oxford, 1980), Ch. 6.
[89] I. Packer, 'The Liberal Cave and the 1914 Budget', *English Historical Review*, 111 (1996), 620–34.
[90] H. V. Emy, *Liberals, Radicals and Social Politics 1892–1914* (Cambridge, 1973), 142, 176.

lawyers, brewers, and financiers'. In January 1910 once again more Labour candidates referred to social reform, many implying that old-age pensions would never have reached the statute book but for the presence of the PLP. But National Insurance split the Labour and socialist ranks. The trade-union wing of the party, allied with Ramsay MacDonald, who became the chairman of the PLP in 1911, gave their more or less grudging backing to what the Liberals were doing; but the Fabian Society and most members of the ILP opposed a measure which was fiscally regressive, in that compulsory contributions from the insured meant that the low-paid were bearing a disproportionate share of the scheme's cost. Socialists had always oscillated between the view that social reform was a stepping-stone to socialism and the view that it constituted a dangerous alternative to socialism. The latter view now significantly gained ground, this time with the additional charge (levied, in particular, by George Lansbury's *Daily Herald*) that Liberal welfare politics were a sinister ploy for 'incorporating' working-class activists into the bourgeois state: 'thousands of men have found social salvation for themselves—by a system under which the capitalist seeks to rivet more and more firmly the shackles of slavery upon the workers'.[91]

Working-class attitudes to state welfare are difficult to pin down. Social reform was certainly not a simple response to 'pressure from below'; indeed, arguably the Liberals were adopting 'a state-centred' approach, in which 'the state itself shape[d] the sorts of demands put on it and even the array of interests articulating grievances and voicing demands'.[92] Working men and women (if such generalizations are permissible) seem to have differentiated, pragmatically, between the measures from which they thought they would derive direct benefits and those which appeared coercive or inquisitorial.[93] Thus old-age pensions were generally popular—even if ironic cheers sometimes greeted public references to a measure which was seen as excessively 'mean'. On the other hand, trade unionists could only with difficulty be induced to accept Labour Exchanges (which aroused the suspicion that they might be strike-breaking organizations), while even Lloyd George privately admitted that National Insurance, involving compulsory deductions from the wage-packet, had contributed to his party's by-election defeats in 1912–13— despite his populist cry that the working man was getting 'ninepence for fourpence'. Finally, it was a misfortune that, soon after the implementation of the Liberal welfare measures, real wages began to fall, a development which

[91] George Lansbury, 'Socialists and Socialism', *Daily Herald*, 13 Jan. 1913.
[92] J. E. Cronin, 'The British State and the Structure of Political Opportunity', *Journal of British Studies*, 27 (1988), 204.
[93] See P. Thane, 'The Working Class and State "Welfare" in Britain, 1880–1914', *Historical Journal*, 27 (1984), 877–900.

sparked off massive working-class unrest, making nonsense of the hope that social reform would lead to greater social stability.

There was another defect to Liberal social policy. After the miners had belatedly affiliated to the Labour Party in 1908 (the last of the large manual trade unions to do so), the Liberal Parliamentary Party was almost entirely devoid of working-class MPs. The commercial, financial, and industrial interests, comprising approximately one-third of the parliamentary party, more or less held their own, despite the anxieties occasioned by social reform, but the group benefiting most from the departure of the old 'Lib-Labs' was the professional middle class, particularly that sector of it which drew its living from journalism, academia, and social investigation. It was from this social grouping that the 'New Liberalism' drew most of its impetus. Many of the Social Radicals inside the Commons (Masterman, for example) came into politics from precisely this background. The spirit of Liberal welfare legislation was essentially 'paternalistic', its practitioners being not rebels, but 'repenters'. As 1906 had shown, the main demand of the Labour Movement had all along been for 'Labour representation': class-conscious working men wished to exercise greater influence over their own lives. Could the Liberal welfare schemes, however benevolent the feelings that inspired them, satisfy this basic need? And did they succeed in raising the condition of the people to any significant extent?

5. HEALTH AND WELFARE IN EDWARDIAN BRITAIN

The most dramatic sign of improvement in the nation's health was the startling fall in the infant death-rate between 1899 and 1914: down from 163 to 105 per thousand live births, a 35 per cent fall. Campaigners in the infant and maternal welfare movement were delighted: Newsholme claimed that 185,722 infant lives had been saved since the start of the century.[94] But it seems unlikely that infant clinics and pre-natal care alone could have accounted for more than a small part of this decline, which probably owed more to a general improvement in living standards, coupled with a weakening in the ferocity of certain infectious diseases. After all, only a small proportion of women and children came into contact with the health visitors.

Health visitors were, anyhow, viewed as a mixed blessing by those into whose homes they often barged uninvited, since many were tactless and caused offence.[95] Similarly, the introduction of homecraft lessons into the school syllabus was often resented by girls, who found it a complete waste of time. Others, too, have argued that the growing 'professionalization' of domestic and

[94] Lewis, *Politics of Motherhood*, 28.   [95] Ibid. 106–7.

maternal advice networks depreciated the experience and help of neighbours and grandmothers, upon which poor mothers had traditionally relied—which ironically weakened an important source of working-class 'self-help'.[96]

School inspection and the creation of a school medical service did undoubtedly lead to health improvements, in no way more obviously than in a decline in the number of children found on inspection to be verminous: in London schools down from one-third in December 1904 to less than a twentieth in 1912.[97] By 1914 children often received free eye-tests (though parents were usually expected to pay towards the cost of the spectacle frames), and X-ray treatment for ringworm was also being provided in the larger cities. The schools, too, participated in the vigorous assault on tuberculosis by sending infected children to open-air schools, where many made a rapid recovery. Even so, George Newman could still report in 1913 that 50 per cent of children had bad teeth, 10 per cent were carrying vermin, 10 per cent were suffering from seriously defective vision, and 5 per cent had defective hearing.[98]

But, as with school attendance, it took time for the benefits of a school medical service to be appreciated. Sick children were initially often expected to attend hospitals at some physical distance from their homes, involving parents in loss of earnings as they accompanied them to the treatment centres; moreover, some treatments, such as the removal of tonsils and adenoids without the aid of anaesthetics, could be exceedingly uncomfortable and distressing, as was the drilling of a carious tooth by a foot-operated drill (the electric drill did not make its first appearance until 1908).[99] Children given the 'green card' and sent home with infestations of body lice (often picked up from fellow pupils) suffered acute humiliation, as did their parents. Neither was the provision of school meals a source of universal satisfaction. The breakfasts and lunches might keep starvation at bay, but they were sometimes so repellent (greasy soup was a staple) that children rejected them, while some working-class parents resented being charged for them (in default of which they could be sent to court).

Moreover, the Children's Care Committees which assessed parental charges contained, *inter alia*, COS veterans who basically disapproved of free 'handouts', and from a concern to prevent parents neglecting their responsibility towards their offspring, tried to limit access to this facility. In this they had the sympathetic support of some Board of Education officials, such as Selby-Bigge, Morant's successor as Secretary to the Board of Education.[100]

---

[96] For the contemporary critique of welfare policies by the feminist Anna Martin, see E. Ross, *Love and Toil: Motherhood in Outcast London 1870–1918* (Oxford, 1993), 196–7.

[97] Hurt, *Elementary Schooling*, 133.   [98] Horn, *Schoolchild*, 90.

[99] Hurt, *Elementary Schooling*, 140.

[100] J. Hurt, 'Feeding the Hungry Schoolchild in the First Half of the Twentieth Century', in D. J. Oddy and D. S. Miller (eds.), *Diet and Health in Modern Britain* (London, 1985), 174.

Social welfare was most popular when it involved a minimum of intrusion into the lives of the recipients. This explains the popularity of old-age pensions, once it had become clear that no serious attempt would be made to enforce the 'industry test'.[101] Unlike other contemporary welfare measures, old-age pensions also had the effect of strengthening the family by providing a financial incentive to children to take in elderly parents who might otherwise have had to enter the workhouse—though this could lead to inter-generational friction.[102] Before 1909 over a third of those in receipt of poor relief in England and Wales were elderly; so, not surprisingly, outdoor relief among the over-seventies almost disappeared thereafter: there were 138,223 such recipients in 1910, but only 8,563 in 1913, though this was partly due to the pre-war economic boom.

However, for poor elderly people without children prepared to accommodate them in this way, there still remained only the workhouse, whose inmates diminished in numbers only slightly—from 57,701 to 49,207 between 1910 and 1913.[103] Responding to the spirit of the age, many guardians, especially females, sought, with some LGB encouragement, to make workhouse conditions less oppressive. In some enlightened Unions flowers bedecked the wards, occupational therapy schemes were introduced, and the whole environment became more 'homely'.[104] One historian has written of 'the deconstruction' of the workhouse, as group after group of paupers with special needs was accorded special treatment, often outside the workhouse itself: children, for example, were increasingly 'boarded out' or placed in special homes.[105]

Some Poor Law authorities ran separate infirmaries, providing nearly 41,000 beds in 1911 (twice as many as were located in the voluntary hospitals[106]), and many of these places were used by non-paupers who saw them as an efficient municipal hospital. To meet the growing demand, more and more medical staff had to be employed.[107] The number of Poor Law nurses increased from 3,000 to 7,600 between 1893 and 1913.

On the other hand, mortality inside Poor Law infirmaries still ran at double its level outside. As for the general mixed workhouse, still the only resort for many vagrants, alcoholics, and mothers of illegitimate children, this still filled the respectable poor with dread. Nor was there much prospect of the Poor Law being fundamentally altered or abolished—indeed, such a prospect had actually receded between 1906 and 1914.

---

[101] However, such criteria were commonplace in friendly society and trade-union benefit schemes.
[102] Lewis, *Women in England*, 54.
[103] Gilbert, *National Insurance*, 229.
[104] Hollis, *Ladies Elect*, 283–6.
[105] Ibid. 284.
[106] Lewis, 'Providers', 321.
[107] S. Cherry, *Medical Services and Hospitals in Britain, 1860–1939* (Cambridge, 1996), 48.

One reason for this lies, as the Webbs bitterly acknowledged, in the introduction of National Insurance in 1911–12. Here was a welfare measure which never enjoyed as much favour as old-age pensions. Employees tended to resent the compulsory deduction from their wages, employers the costs and the extra paperwork to which they were subjected. Meanwhile a minority of class-conscious socialists, joined by bourgeois libertarians such as Hilaire Belloc, fulminated against National Insurance, which they interpreted as the forcible imposition upon the workers of a state system which regimented them, subjected them to bureaucratic regulations, and discouraged them from taking responsibility for their own fates, either individually or through collective trade-union action. A similar mistrust of Labour Exchanges, initially seen by many trade unionists as a sinister strike-breaking device, took a long time for ministers to remove, if indeed they ever did so: only one-third of vacant situations in the insured trades were being filled in this way in 1913 since most trade unionists preferred to rely on their own union's information service. By contrast, in the last year of peace, when unemployment was generally low, over 23 per cent of insured workers claimed unemployment benefit.

Health insurance was also well used, particularly by insured female workers, whose high level of claims shocked Whitehall into setting up a committee of investigation in 1914 (the explanation surely lies in the unequal distribution of nourishing food within the family, and inadequate health care and rest shortly before and after childbirth). Under National Insurance there were about 850 insured workers per panel doctor, but this is an average: the maldistribution of doctors meant that the profession continued to be centred on London, the prosperous suburbs and spas, and markets towns. In the poorly serviced industrial areas, individuals often got little more than a sick-note and a bottle of medicine. Moreover, it has been calculated that 9 million out of the 12 million workers originally included in the National Health Insurance scheme were already members of self-help societies offering medical benefits, only about one-half of them in registered societies, so that the Act did not greatly widen access to medical care.[108] Indeed, in many ways National Health Insurance was really club practice writ large, but with one important difference: the loss of lay control over the medical profession—which represented a defeat for the working-class consumer.

Moreover, even after the passing of the National Insurance Act there were still gaping holes in medical provision. The dependants of insured workers were excluded unless extra cover had been taken out on their behalf. Nor did the scheme meet the cost of hospital treatment—hence, the continuing growth of

---

[108] In 1900 there were already over 4 million friendly-society members eligible for medical care, and another 9 million for sickness benefit.

'Hospital Saturdays', whereby working men paid out a penny a week in return for admission tickets to the hospitals to which they had been subscribing. Poor people needing protracted attention could not usually afford doctors' fees and were driven back upon the charitable dispensaries or the out-patient departments of voluntary hospitals (which increasingly means-tested their applicants).

The scale of untreated illness can be gauged both from the continuing popularity of spiritual healing and herbal remedies,[109] and also from the vast and heavily advertised trade in patent medicines, which made up about a quarter of all advertisements in some journals and an even higher proportion in the religious press. (The *British Medical Journal* opined that quack remedies particularly appealed to Nonconformists.) There were even potions on the market which claimed to be suitable for any complaint 'from whatever cause arising'![110] Doubtless no one died from swallowing 'Dr Williams' Pink Pills for Pale People' (aimed at anaemic girls?),[111] still less from an addiction to 'Beecham's Pills' ('Worth A Guinea A Box'). But other concoctions contained ingredients that were more or less harmful—a scandal satirized by Wells in *Tono-Bungay* (1908). Under pressure from the BMA, the House of Commons in 1912 set up a Select Committee of Inquiry which, reporting on the very day that Britain declared war on Germany, spoke of 'a tissue of fraud and falsehood' never before 'disclosed to any Parliamentary Committee in either House'.[112]

On the other hand, for the more affluent medical provision did improve in many ways. Though the ratio of GPs to population in England and Wales improved only slightly between 1881 and 1911, private nursing homes and hospitals sprang up to cater for the lower middle class. Indeed, hospitals generally were now better financed and serviced: for example, the nursing profession expanded significantly during the Edwardian decade—from 64,209 in 1901 to 77,055 in 1911. There was also a growth in the number of childrens' hospitals, pioneered by Great Ormond Street, founded in 1852. Hospitals, especially the voluntary hospitals, were increasingly being seen as curative institutions, rather than as isolation and detention centres. (However, for tuberculosis, a major cause of fatalities, isolation in sanatoria constituted the main form of treatment before 1914, and municipal institutions were still being constructed for the *containment* of infectious diseases.[113])

---

[109] Ross, *Love and Toil*, 176–8.
[110] D. Vincent, *Literacy and Popular Culture: England 1750–1914* (Cambridge, 1989), 105–6; M. Saks (ed.), *Alternative Medicine in Britain* (Oxford, 1992).
[111] Vincent, *Literacy and Popular Culture*, 114.
[112] However, many of these advertisements appeared in the BMA's own journal!
[113] P. Weindling, 'From Infectious to Chronic Diseases: Changing Patterns of Sickness in the Nineteenth and Twentieth Centuries', in Wear (ed.), *Medicine in Society*, 314. Infectious illnesses

The 1890s and the Edwardian period are sometimes seen as a time of so-called 'epidemiological transition', in which the old killer epidemics (cholera, typhus, etc.) became less devastating, heart disease and cancer more so. This may partly be explained by the availability of new diagnostic aids, which made it possible to identify chronic and degenerative ailments, leading to a switch of interest from 'social' to 'biological' disease.[114] But, apart from the use of salversan, an arsenic compound for controlling syphilis, advances in medical knowledge did not necessarily lead to immediate therapeutic improvements: for example, 'tuberculin' therapy did not work. Paradoxically, it was better housing and diet which dramatically reduced the incidence of TB, *before* antibiotics became widely available in the late 1940s.

The falling death-rate is thus largely attributable to the improved environment brought about by several decades of public-health reform. But the extent of this 'progress' can easily be exaggerated. The implementation of sanitary and factory legislation varied considerably from one part of the country to the other. London may have acquired an impressive sewerage system between 1858 and 1865, but (to take a particularly bad case) in Manchester two-thirds of its working-class inhabitants lived in houses which still had the pail system, ash-boxes, or a privy midden as late as 1911.[115]

The Town Planning Act of 1909 for the first time linked public health to the layout of towns and to the development of urban transport systems. It also gave the LGB power to order local authorities to prepare and submit town-planning schemes and to replace their slums with new working-class housing (the 1890 Housing Act had merely been permissive). But little progress had been made on either front by 1914. Liverpool, the English town which possessed most municipal dwellings, accommodated only 1.31 per cent of its total population in this way. Indeed, the 'People's Budget', by precipitating a slump in the building industry, made existing overcrowding worse.[116] As for planning, this remained 'a totem of collectivist ideologues', but achieved little before 1914,[117] Birmingham being the only major city to formulate an ambitious and coherent plan. Privately organized 'garden cities' and a handful of industrial estates established by benevolent employers for their workforce (Bourneville, Port Sunlight, Earswick, etc.) did, it is true, raise living standards in some areas, but only a minority of the population benefited.

were made notifiable under an adoptive Act in 1889 and the law became compulsory in 1899 (E. Fee and D. Porter, 'Public Health, Preventive Medicine and Professionalization: England and America in the Nineteenth Century', in Wear (ed.), *Medicine in Society*, 270).

[114] Weindling, 'From Infectious to Chronic Diseases', p. 309. Also, see Ch. 16.

[115] A. S. Wohl, *Endangered Lives: Public Health in Victorian Britain* (London, 1983), 97–8.

[116] 117,000 houses had been built in the five years before 1909, only 70,000 in the following five years—mainly because of the unsettling effect of the land-value duties (Murray, *People's Budget*, 298).

[117] P. J. Waller, *Town, City and Nation: England 1850–1914* (Oxford, 1983), 172.

Similar gaps between intention and achievement can be seen in relation to state-sponsored schemes of protection at work, which scarcely impinged upon some occupational groups, even after the passing of the 1901 Act which consolidated the various Factory and Workshop Acts. On the eve of the war most workshops, which considerably outnumbered factories, remained largely out of reach of the law.

As we have seen, the rural population seems, at first glance, to have enjoyed much better health than most urban workers.[118] But mortality statistics give little indication of people's morbidity and standards of living. In fact, Rowntree's investigation into the condition of farmworkers in 1912–13 revealed grinding poverty and hardship, rural housing being particularly deplorable. Their wage-rates remained amongst the lowest in the country (averaging under 18s. a week), which meant that in only five counties did their total income lift them above the poverty line; laying off without pay in bad weather and during the winter months also forced most farmworkers to depend upon extra payment at harvest time and upon supplementation from other members of their family. It has been calculated that 70 per cent of agricultural workers' income went on food, with only 2 per cent of it being disposable. The Liberal government, as we will see, was trying to tackle this particular social problem after 1913, but its Land Campaign was cut short by war before changes to rural Britain could seriously begin.

Poverty was endemic among urban labourers too. It would take decades to eradicate the suffering revealed in the surveys of Mrs Pember Reeves and of the Women's Co-operative Guild. Moreover, it was unfortunate that, after several decades of sharply rising real wages, the standard of living of wage-earners levelled off in the inflationary years after 1910. Workers stuck in the same job actually experienced a decline, and this neutralized many of the benefits brought about by social policy.[119]

Even where mortality was concerned, Edwardian Britain also remained deeply divided by class. The Registrar-General's report for 1911 showed an excess mortality of Class V (unskilled working class) over Class I (the higher professions) of 41 per cent in the first month of life, 92 per cent among babies aged between one and three months, 142 per cent between three and six months, 165 per cent between six and nine months, and 183 per cent between 9 and 12 months.[120] Marked differences in height between schoolchildren from different backgrounds made it seem that the social classes consti-

---

[118] See Ch. 6. Wohl, *Endangered Lives*, 280–1.

[119] C. Feinstein, 'What Really Happened to Real Wages?: Trends in Wages, Prices, and Productivity in the United Kingdom, 1880–1913', *Economic History Review*, 43 (1990), 329–55.

[120] Lewis, *Politics of Motherhood*, 67.

tuted, as it were, quite separate 'races'—a perception taken literally by the eugenists.[121]

Moreover, although much of this was happening as a result of global economic changes which the government of the day could do little to influence, the Liberals' fiscal policies were only modestly redistributive, despite Opposition cries of 'socialism'. The poor directly benefited from Asquith's remission of the sugar duties in 1908, but the main gainers from Lloyd George's more famous Finance Bill of the following year were probably middle-class people on modest incomes, not manual workers, who were hit disproportionately by rises in the beer and tobacco duties. As for National Insurance, this was a very regressive way of funding a welfare service, as opponents of the measure complained at the time: workers earning 18s. a week found themselves paying over 10 per cent of their meagre income in indirect taxes and contributions, better-paid artisans on 35s. per week only 3.65 per cent.[122]

The wider purpose of social policy was to spread contentment by removing much of the uncertainty that haunted working-class life, thereby reducing class conflict. Beveridge, for example, saw social insurance as a 'means of promoting social cohesion and of harmonizing the warring forces unleashed by the free market'. He argued that, quite apart from the material benefits flowing from social reform, it was desirable to bring private associations into intimate contact with the State, and vice versa.[123]

However, if the Liberals' prime concern really was the stabilization of capitalism, only a minority of businessmen, outside the ranks of the party faithful, believed that this would happen. True, in 1906 the Birmingham Chamber of Commerce was taking an intelligent interest in German social insurance, but even once-friendly businessmen soon became alarmed at the costs which social policy seemed to be imposing upon industry. Charles Macara, a cotton baron who set up the Employers' Parliamentary Association in 1911, was more representative of his class in his attacks on the Liberal welfare programme and his insistence on the need for cost-cutting in the face of foreign competition.[124]

Moreover, employers soon began to worry that social policy was a disincentive to hard work, since many insured workers retained their membership of friendly societies, and the benefits derivable from this source, plus National

---

[121] A study carried out by Dr F. E. Larkins, Assistant MOH for Warwickshire, showed that the average weight of children aged 13–14 was nearly 100 pounds to parents earning over 25s. a week, but only 71 pounds if parents earned between 12s. and 14s. (*Medical Officer*, 17 Dec. 1910, cited in J. Bourke, *Working-Class Cultures in Britain 1890–1960: Gender, Class, and Ethnicity* (London, 1994), 13).

[122] P. Thane, *The Foundations of the Welfare State* (Harlow, 1982), 96.

[123] Harris, *Beveridge*, 95, 101.

[124] R. Hay, 'Employers and Social Policy in Britain: The Evolution of Welfare Legislation 1905–14', *Social History*, 2 (1977), 435–55.

Insurance benefits, meant that a workman in periods of sickness suffered only a very small loss of income. Little wonder that businessmen preferred to run their own private schemes, such as the Foreman's Mutual Benefit Society set up by the Engineering Employers' Federation.

George Askwith, the government's Labour Commissioner, pointed to another weakness in Liberal social legislation when he complained that Labour Exchanges institutionalized 'the division of classes into two camps', so helping to 'form a prop to the class war'.[125] Paradoxically, though hoping to reduce class conflict, the Liberals through their policies may unwittingly have institutionalized it—thereby precipitating a wider crisis.

[125] G. R. A. Askwith, *Industrial Problems and Disputes* (1920), 278.

CHAPTER 12

The Years of 'Crisis', 1908–1914

1. INTRODUCTION

In retrospect, the Liberal government's welfare reforms look the most significant part of its legislative programme, but a scrutiny of the postbags of
Liberal politicians suggests another perspective. The claims of Nonconformity
may have been pushed into the background within the first few years of Liberal
rule (Asquith drifted away from his roots under the influence of his smart,
Society-loving wife—the symbol of his move away from Dissent was noted),
but other traditional Liberal concerns by no means disappeared after 1908.
Lloyd George, the author of National Health Insurance, also saw himself
as the scourge of the aristocracy, in direct descent from John Bright and
Chamberlain.

If anything, the Radical assault on 'feudalism' actually intensified in the
immediate pre-war years. This was because, since 1886, there had been a
significant bifurcation in the social profiles of the two major parliamentary
parties.[1] The Unionists continued to be dominated by 'officers and gentlemen',
most of them public-school and Oxbridge educated. Liberal MPs, on the other
hand, came from much more diverse social and educational backgrounds, and a
mere 5 per cent of them can be classified as 'landowners'.[2]

True, Liberal Cabinet ministers were socially more exclusive than the parliamentary party as a whole. For example, tradition dictated that the Foreign
Office be run by a landed gentleman—hence the selection of Edward Grey.
Moreover, in order to maintain some sort of a ministerial presence in the Upper
Chamber, Campbell-Bannerman and Asquith turned to the handful of landed
aristocrats who, true to the traditions of progressive Whiggery, had kept faith
with Liberalism, men such as Lords Elgin, Carrington, Tweedmouth, and

---

[1] Cf. Ch. 4.

[2] Some 55% of Unionists elected in the December 1910 election had been at a public school, as
against 21 per cent of Liberals, while 47 per cent of Unionists had attended either Oxford or Cambridge
University, compared with only 29 per cent of their Liberal counterparts. Liberal MPs were also over
twice as likely as Unionists to have graduated elsewhere (mainly from London and the Scottish
universities).

Crewe, who all received high office. Yet, even in the Lords, many ministers were former MPs ennobled for political services. These included not only the Lord Chancellor, Lord Loreburn, but also John Morley and Haldane, who became viscounts in 1908 and 1911, respectively. As for the Liberal Cabinet, a clear majority of ministers, Campbell-Bannerman and Asquith included, were indisputably middle class.

Also significant is the fact that the pre-war Liberal ministries encompassed all the national groupings of mainland Britain. Seven of Campbell-Bannerman's original Cabinet of sixteen were Scotsmen, and government positions were also found for Welshmen and Jews.[3] Moreover, many famous Liberals who were English by birth sought safe seats north of the Border—the two Fife constituencies, for example, were represented by Augustine Birrell and Asquith, while Churchill, after his by-election defeat at North-West Manchester, moved to Dundee. The prominence within Liberalism of politicians from the 'Celtic Fringe' annoyed most Conservatives, although, ironically, both Balfour and Bonar Law were Scottish. England, Leo Maxse once declared, was a country governed by Scotsmen, plundered by Welshmen, and kicked by Irishmen. The Unionists, by contrast, took a pride in being a predominantly English party.

If the Conservatives after 1906 saw themselves as a traditional elite under siege, the Liberals' self-image was that of outsiders, up against an entrenched establishment. Both sides were reinforced in their prejudices by the dispute over the composition of the county magistracy.[4] Nominations to these positions were made by the Lord-Lieutenant, invariably a major landowner.[5] But by 1907, as a result of the 'flight of the Whigs' following Gladstone's espousal of Home Rule, only six of the forty-three English Lord-Lieutenants were Liberals. To compound the problem, the final decision as to who should fill the magistrates' bench rested with the Lord Chancellor, and that dignitary during the ten years of Unionist rule had been the jovially cynical Lord Halsbury, who appointed almost no Liberals. As a result, by 1906 Tory magistrates greatly outnumbered Liberals in most rural areas—by 214 to 10 in Shropshire, to take one notorious example. Yet Loreburn, Halsbury's Liberal successor, was reluctant to redress the imbalance by 'positive discrimination'[6]—to the fury

---

[3] Campbell-Bannerman, Loreburn, Elgin, Haldane, Tweedmouth, Bryce, and Sinclair, later joined by McKinnon Wood. Lloyd George was Welsh, Samuel and Isaacs Jewish.

[4] J. M. Lee, 'Parliament and the Appointment of Magistrates, The Origin of Advisory Committees', *Parliamentary Affairs*, 7 (1959), 85–94; C. H. E. Zangerl, 'The Social Composition of the County Magistracy in England and Wales, 1831–1887', *Journal of British Studies*, 11 (1971), 113–25; G. D. Phillips, *The Diehards: Aristocratic Society and Politics in Edwardian England* (Cambridge, Mass., 1979), 60–8, 74–6.

[5] In 1907 35 out of 43 were peers. A not dissimilar situation prevailed even in Scotland and Wales: at most 2 out of 13 Lord-Lieutenants in Wales, and probably only 8 out of 32 in Scotland were Liberals.

[6] However, in 1906 Loreburn abolished the £100 property qualification for county magistrates.

of his own backbenchers. Eventually, in 1911, the government transferred the right of nomination to newly established local advisory committees, on which the Lord-Lieutenant did not necessarily sit. Predictably, the Conservatives shrilly denounced this initiative, and the agitation which had preceded it, as a plot to 'job the magistracy'.

The county bench was not the only political arena in which the Liberals felt themselves disadvantaged. Edward VII, admittedly, showed greater sympathy to the Liberals than his mother had done: his trusted confidant, Lord Esher, and his Secretary, Lord Knollys, both had easy access to the Liberal leadership. All the same, the Liberals were in a minority at court, and after George V's accession Asquith's government had to deal with a generally unfriendly monarch. Liberals were also poorly represented in the higher reaches of the armed services and the diplomatic corps, and were generally mistrusted by senior members of the Anglican hierarchy.

However, the main institutional barrier to the Liberal Party was, of course, the House of Lords itself, still predominantly a bastion of landed privilege, within which, despite using their powers of patronage to 'promote' their wealthy backers, the Liberals remained heavily outgunned. In December 1908 only 102 peers were taking the Liberal whip, as against 459 Unionists and forty-two crossbenchers—a reverse image of the relationship between the two parties in the Lower House. And when Balfour observed at Nottingham in January 1906 that 'the great Unionist Party should still control, whether in power or whether in Opposition, the destinies of this great Empire', ministerialists read into his words a none-too-subtle threat to use the Lords to overthrow contentious Liberal legislation.

In fact, for several decades the Upper House had been developing a theory of 'plebiscitary democracy'—that is, asserting its right to hold up controversial Bills until they had received the explicit endorsement of the electorate. But, apart from the obvious objection that this vetting power was exercised only when the Liberals held office,[7] its practice seemed unmistakably partisan after 1906, when the Liberals had so clear a majority in the Commons.

In the event, the Unionist-dominated Upper Chamber rejected or wrecked ten Liberal Bills sent up to it between 1906 and 1909 and, during the same period, amended no less than 41 per cent of the legislation it scrutinized. True, the Lords took care not to tamper with government Bills for which a prior mandate had been secured—the Trades Disputes Act, for example, reached the statute book unamended. But they mercilessly slaughtered what they

---

[7] During Balfour's premiership the Lords amended only 16 of the 107 Bills sent up to them and rejected none (J. Ridley, 'The Unionist Opposition and the House of Lords, 1906–1910', *Parliamentary History*, 11 (1992), 247–8).

regarded as 'faddist' measures, especially if these had been inadequately debated in the Commons. Measures designed to help the Nonconformists fell into such a category; so did the government's attempt in 1906 to end plural voting.[8]

But the main struggle between the two Houses took place over the land question. A hostility to landed privilege was widespread within both the Liberal and the Labour parties. In 1906 68 per cent of Liberal candidates had mentioned land reform in their manifestos, and 280 members of the new House, under the chairmanship of J. H. Whitley, were soon urging the government to turn promise into performance.[9]

The land reformers were a motley crowd. Some 130 of them belonged to the Land Nationalisation Society. Others, colourfully marshalled by Josiah Wedgwood, took their lead from Henry George and advocated the destruction of the 'land monopoly' by subjecting real property to the 'single tax'. Yet another group, responding to disgruntled West Country farmers, sought to strengthen 'tenant right' (a weak Bill along these lines became law in 1906). Different again was the panacea of the 'land colonizers', who took up the old cry for more smallholdings and allotments—seen by its advocates as a partial solution to the unemployment problem.

In 1908 the government succeeded in steering a Smallholdings and Allotments (England and Wales) Bill onto the statute book—only for it to be stymied by the county councils, most of them Conservative-controlled, which, despite having been given powers of compulsory purchase, had acquired by 1914 a mere 155,000 acres for rental. Meanwhile the Upper House had twice destroyed Bills for the valuation of land in Scotland (in 1906 and 1907) before, in 1908, throwing out the Small Landholders (Scotland) Bill, which would have extended the scope of the Crofters Acts to all the Scottish counties. Even the relatively uncontroversial Irish Land Act of 1909, an extension of Wyndham's earlier measure, suffered amendments in the Lords, perhaps because it was seen as a sop to the Irish Nationalists.

There was, however, a seemingly simple key to unlocking the land problem. In the 1906 election no fewer than 52 per cent of Liberal candidates had mentioned the taxation of land values, supported, on this issue, by the Labour Party which, interestingly, urged the need to relieve overburdened ratepayers. Asquith, at the Treasury, was not unresponsive to this pressure, but his early attempts to separate site value from hereditaments were blocked by his cau-

---

[8] The Lords argued that, if plural voting were to end, the anomaly of Irish 'over-representation' ought simultaneously to be removed—a condition which the Liberals were obviously unwilling to meet.
[9] A. K. Russell, *Liberal Landslide: The General Election of 1906* (Newton Abbot), 65; H. V. Emy, 'The Land Campaign: Lloyd George as a Social Reformer', in A. J. P. Taylor (ed.), *Lloyd George: Twelve Essays* (1971), 42.

tious Treasury officials. And there the matter might have rested, but for the rise of Lloyd George, an instinctive (albeit muddle-headed) land reformer with a visceral hatred of landlords derived from boyhood memories of the arrogant alien class which had held sway in rural North Wales.

Lloyd George's 1909 Budget[10] included four new land taxes. The first imposed a halfpenny in the pound duty on the capital value of undeveloped land, the second placed a similar duty on undeveloped minerals,[11] the third was a 10 per cent reversion duty, and the fourth a 20 per-cent tax on the unearned increment of land values. These taxes, combined, were forecast to bring in a mere £500,000 in 1909–10, but they served another two functions: first, ministers fondly (though mistakenly) supposed that they would release more cheap land for building and industrial development; and secondly, they provided a justification for the land-valuation provisions, which were also part of the Budget—to the delight of the Liberal land reformers, all of whom needed valuation as the starting-point for the realization of their own pet projects.

In framing the Budget, neither Lloyd George nor the Cabinet as a whole deliberately set out to provoke the Upper House; Lloyd George was looking, rather, to gain the initiative with a measure which would circumvent the obstructive Lords. However, no tears were shed by ministers when on 30 November, to their surprise, the Lords flouted a parliamentary convention of over 150 years' standing by rejecting the Finance Bill by 350 votes to seventy-five[12]—thereby precipitating a general election, held in January of the following year.

2. THE CONSTITUTIONAL CRISIS

Why did the Conservative leadership embark on this risky course, against which they had been warned by many of their veterans, including Lord Cromer and other prominent free fooders?[13] They did so partly because they believed that land was being unfairly singled out for discriminatory treatment out of partisan malice—an impression reinforced by Lloyd George's own rhetorical extravagances. But, of course, many Conservatives also had their own private agendas. They resented income-tax increases and the introduction of the 'supertax', but they could hardly attack higher taxation as such while

[10] B. K. Murray, *The People's Budget 1909–10* (Oxford, 1980); A. Offner, *Property and Politics 1870–1914* (Cambridge, 1981), ch. 22; M. Daunton, *Trusting Leviathan: The Politics of Taxation in Britain 1799–1914* (Cambridge, 2001), 364–6.

[11] This, however, was amended in Committee to a 5% duty on the rental value of the rights to work such minerals.

[12] After Balfour had announced this publicly at the Bingley Hall on 24 September.

[13] Among them Lord St Aldwyn, the former Hicks Beach, Lord James of Hereford, and Lord Balfour of Burleigh.

simultaneously berating the government for not building more battleships; and so they focused on the 'unfairness' of the land taxes and on the inappropriate way in which the land-valuation clauses had been included in a Finance Bill.[14]

Even so, Balfour and Lansdowne (the Opposition Leader in the Lords), who were both essentially cautious men, would probably have avoided the political dangers of rejection had they not been under strong pressure from three different sources: from the landowners themselves; from a City angrily opposed to 'socialist finance'; and, not least, from the tariff reformers, eager for a showdown with the government and determined to demonstrate that no free-trade budget could meet expanding expenditure. Many peers also allowed themselves to be rattled by Lloyd George, whose moderation in the Commons contrasted with the violence of his platform speeches: at Limehouse on 30 July he cunningly identified landlords as a class with the House of Lords as an institution, and in Newcastle later in the year he likened the aristocracy to cheese (the older it was, the higher it smelt).

Yet the Liberals, too, faced very real difficulties over the rejection of the Budget, which had led to a general election in which their chances of victory, though improving throughout the summer, were still far from assured. In any case, if they won, how would the government curb the Lords' powers? A Cabinet Committee, chaired by Lord Loreburn, had considered this very subject in 1907, and recommended that future deadlocks be resolved by the Commons meeting a Lords' delegation in joint session—an arrangement known misleadingly as the 'Ripon Plan', though its principal authors were Asquith and Crewe. However, Campbell-Bannerman, foreseeing the grave disappointment of most Liberal backbenchers, quashed this report, and instead sponsored the so-called 'C-B Resolutions'. These stipulated, first, that the Lords had no power to tamper with a Finance Bill; second, that the House of Lords' absolute veto should be replaced by a suspensory veto, so that a Bill passed by the Commons in three successive sessions within the lifetime of the same parliament would automatically receive the royal assent, even if it failed in the Lords (this later became known as the 'veto policy'); and third, that parliaments should in future run for five years, not seven. The Commons overwhelmingly endorsed these resolutions on 24 June 1907.[15]

However, complicating the constitutional issue was the question of the future of Ireland. True to their electoral promises, the Liberals had not tried to introduce a Home Rule Bill during the 1906 Parliament. Instead, the new Irish Secretary, James Bryce, relying heavily on his controversial Permanent

---

[14] N. Blewett, *The Peers, the Parties and the People: The General Elections of 1910* (1972), 72–5.

[15] C. C. Weston, 'The Liberal Leadership and the Lords' Veto, 1907–10', *Historical Journal*, 11 (1968), 508–23.

Secretary, Antony MacDonnell, drew up a devolutionary measure, which was inherited by Augustine Birrell when Bryce left Britain for the Washington Embassy in early 1907.[16] The Irish Councils Bill, however, fell foul of the Irish Nationalists, who objected, as they had consistently done since 1884, to any 'concession' which gave even the smallest appearance of being an alternative to a full Home Rule settlement. The Bill had therefore to be withdrawn.

Birrell subsequently tried to mend fences with John Redmond and John Dillon by sponsoring the 1907 Evicted Tenants Act and by establishing in 1909 a national (Catholic-dominated) university in Ireland. But mutual suspicion was still hanging heavily in the air when the government introduced its Budget, which met a distinctly frosty reception in Ireland, where the distillery interests and the publicans, both strong supporters of Redmond's party, disliked the prospect of more expensive liquor licenses and higher spirit duties (the government's revenge for the recent destruction of its Licensing Bill). As a result, Redmond's followers voted against the Budget on its second reading—which, of course, they had the luxury of doing, knowing that this would not actually imperil the government.

Then, on 30 November 1909, Redmond upped the stakes by demanding, via Morley, that the Cabinet reactivate Irish Home Rule. Here was an unwelcome message since, by 1909, the 'union of hearts' had largely died, the attitude of most Liberals to Home Rule being, at best, 'a stoical spirit of obligation'.[17] For Ireland was steadily drifting apart from mainland Britain, largely because land purchase had created there a race of peasant-proprietors which had no serious counterpart on mainland Britain. In addition, Ireland was experiencing a 'devotional revolution', marked by the growing wealth and self-confidence of the Catholic Church, allied to a new pride in the country's Gaelic past. This heady cultural revival was beginning to affect political life. In 1907 Redmond came under pressure to take a more assertive line from the Young Ireland branch of the United Ireland League, some of whose members sympathized with Arthur Griffith's recently founded Sinn Fein party.[18] The Nationalist Leader may also have been aware of the re-emergence of Fenianism, as the old Irish Republican Brotherhood (IRB) began recruiting among the young.

But, in the short run, the more immediate threat to Redmond's position was posed by the breaking-away from mainstream Irish Nationalism of almost a

---

[16] P. Jalland, 'A Liberal Chief Secretary and the Irish Question: Augustine Birrell, 1907–1914', *Historical Journal*, 19 (1976), 421–51.

[17] P. Jalland, *The Liberals and Ireland: The Ulster Question in British Politics to 1914* (Brighton, 1980), 25.

[18] The Irish Councils Bill was also unpopular with the Catholic Church, which feared increased secular control over Irish education. In the Bill's aftermath, the Chief Whip, Sir Thomas Esmonde, resigned his post, and another Nationalist MP resigned his seat.

dozen MPs, led by Tim Healy and William O'Brien. Operating from their base in County Cork, these two veteran mavericks founded the All-For-Ireland party, the defining characteristic of which was a scepticism about the Liberal Alliance and a willingness to work out a deal with sympathetic Unionists—as had happened prior to the Wyndham settlement. This made some sense since, on social and economic policy, as well as on education, the Unionists arguably had more to offer. Feeling himself under threat from these diverse sources, Redmond had no option but to play it tough in his dealings with the Liberal government.

The January 1910 General Election was dominated by the Budget and the propriety of the Lords' behaviour.[19] This benefited the Liberal Party, since the Budget enjoyed general Labour approval; indeed, the Opposition were prone to claim Snowden as its real author, a flattering suggestion which that 'sea-green incorruptible' scarcely troubled to refute. In reality, Labour would have preferred stiffer taxes, along with the total abolition of the House of Lords, but they were prepared to accept the 'veto policy' as a first step.

Against this background, there was an informal renewal of the Gladstone–MacDonald pact. True, a complication had arisen over the belated decision of the miners, in 1908, to affiliate to the Labour Party, a decision which some elderly Lib-Lab MPs—Thomas Burt in Morpeth, for example—continued to defy. The question of who would have the reversion of such seats when these men died or retired was to create future trouble. However, discussion between the two sets of leaders kept the number of contests between Liberals and Labour down to only twenty-seven.[20]

The result of the January 1910 election mildly disappointed all sides. The Liberals were reduced to 275 seats, only two more than the Unionists, which meant that they lost their overall majority, though they could count on the general support of Labour, with its forty MPs, and, more problematically, on most of the eighty-two Irish Nationalists.[21] At least the Liberals were not swept out of office, as had recently looked likely. Yet, ominously, Nonconformity failed to rally to the Liberals quite as it had done in 1906. Admittedly, some deeply committed Dissenters relished the fray, seeing in it many historic symbolic overtones; as the electorate polled, the ghosts of Laud and Strafford stalked the land. But many of their co-religionists could not overcome their disappoint-

---

[19] For the two general elections and the Constitutional Crisis generally, see Blewett, *The General Elections of 1910.*

[20] Financial difficulties produced by the Osborne Judgement (see below) had little impact on these negotiations, although it led the miners to put up fewer candidates in December. In none of the clashes between Liberals and Labour was the Labour candidate successful.

[21] The election gave Redmond 71 reliable followers: 8 belonged to the All-for-Ireland League, and another 3 pursued their own independent line.

ment with the government's failure to remove their education grievance, while others were becoming uneasy at the general drift of the government's social and economic policies.[22]

Despite these cross-currents, the Liberals held on to most of their northern urban seats: they even won back North-West Manchester, which Churchill had lost in the 1908 by-election. And though the Conservatives advanced slightly in Wales,[23] in Scotland the government registered a further gain. By contrast, the Liberals fell back heavily in the suburban areas of Greater London, in the shires, and in the market and cathedral towns—leading Lloyd George to talk, privately, of the growing schism between 'the progressive North' and 'the semi-feudal south'.[24]

The Unionists similarly enjoyed mixed fortunes. On the one hand, they could take some comfort from the thought that they had recovered well from their 1906 humiliation. In a fair world Balfour might have been given more credit for this. On the other hand, the Opposition had not done well enough to regain power, and Asquith's ministerial team looked set to stay in place for many years to come.

The Unionists' one hope was that the combined forces of the 'Home Rulers' could somehow be broken up. And here they could see a chink of light. For, unbeknown to his backbenchers, Asquith had gone into the General Election with no guarantee that the King would use his prerogative to create enough peers for the government to pass a Bill embodying the 'C-B Resolutions' through the Upper Chamber—a failure later revealed by Asquith in a halting statement to the Commons on 21 February. Worse still, it was becoming apparent, from a scrutiny of their public speeches, that some leading Liberals, Grey to the fore, hankered after the so-called 'reform' option—that is to say, the policy of changing, not the powers, but the composition of the Upper House through a dilution of its hereditary element. 'We cannot inspire (electoral confidence) by patching up working arrangements either with the Labour or Irish parties or with both', Grey privately warned Asquith, adding that 'the so-called C-B plan' was 'open to the charge of being in effect a Single Chamber plan'. Instead, Grey advocated 'a new Second Chamber, much smaller in size than the House of Commons . . . based upon the democratic elective principle, with if desired a minority of distinguished members'.[25] Churchill and Herbert Samuel broadly concurred with this analysis.

[22] See Ch. 11.

[23] They won 2 seats. With Labour representation increasing from 1 to 5, the Liberals fell back from 33 to 27.

[24] P. Jalland, 'United Kingdom Devolution 1910–1914: Political Panacea or Tactical Diversion?', *English Historical Review*, 94 (1979), 767.

[25] Grey to Asquith, 7 Feb. 1910, cited in Blewett, *General Elections of 1910*, 149.

But such a prospect dismayed many Liberal backbenchers and the Labour Party. It also antagonized the Irish Nationalists, who, in addition to their disgust at ministerial backsliding under enemy fire, could envisage no reformed Upper House that would be a friend to Home Rule. Redmond therefore announced a policy of 'no veto, no budget', demanding that the veto would have to be removed in the current session if the Irish were to support the Finance Bill. The government could not capitulate to this ultimatum without loss of face. But the Irish Nationalists also faced a dilemma. If they went too far, they risked bringing down the only government likely to grant them Home Rule: yet what point was there in keeping in office a ministry that was not going to resolve the constitutional deadlock in ways which made Home Rule possible?

A fascinating alternative scenario now presented itself. If the Irish defied the government and co-operated with the Unionists, they could bring Asquith down on the second reading of the reintroduced Budget, forcing the King to ask Balfour to form a caretaker ministry, pending a fresh dissolution. But what if the Unionists were then to dig in by stitching up a deal with the Irish Nationalists, involving, perhaps, a measure of devolution forming part of a wider scheme of Home-Rule-All-Round? Such an outcome would have been more than welcome to the O'Brienites, and some Redmondites could also see advantages in working with the British party that controlled the Upper House.[26]

Some Unionists, including recent fire-eaters such as Garvin, began to urge their leaders to give serious consideration to this option. A readiness to abandon principle in order to enjoy the fruits of power came into their calculations, of course, but there were also more substantial reasons why the Unionists might re-examine their blanket opposition to Home Rule. For Ireland, it could be argued, had changed so dramatically since Gladstone's day as a result of Wyndham's land settlement that it was no longer unsafe to give its inhabitants a wide measure of self-government: 'would not an Ireland under Federal Home Rule on the Quebec model', reasoned one senior Unionist, 'send a solid *majority* of Conservatives to help defend in the Imperial Parliament nearly all we care for?'[27]

Many Unionists also understood that the blocking of Irish national claims was fomenting bad blood between Britain and the United States, as well as sowing dissension in Australia and Canada, which also had sizeable and politically influential Irish communities. Finally, many 'imperialists' saw

---

[26] For the debate among Unionists, see A. M. Gollin, *The Observer and J. L. Garvin 1908–1914* (London, 1960), chs. 6–8.

[27] J. Turner, 'Letting Go: The Conservative Party and the End of the Union with Ireland', in A. Grant and K. J. Stringer (eds.), *Uniting the Kingdom?* (London, 1995), 267.

merit in Federal Home Rule (even if this involved concessions to nationalist Ireland), provided that it was formulated in a way compatible with a later federalization of the Empire—muddled thinking, maybe, but many Conservatives were reasoning along these lines. And though federating the Empire would presumably have necessitated a written constitution, even this was beginning to appeal to some Unionists, who despaired of ever capturing power under the existing rules.

In the event, things never developed along these lines. On 13 April the Cabinet resolved not to alter the Budget—'to purchase the Irish vote by such a concession would be a discreditable transaction', it piously said. But next day Asquith announced in the Commons that veto resolutions would immediately be introduced into both Houses of Parliament; were the Lords to reject them, he added, the King would be asked to agree to a mass creation of Liberal peers prior to the next general election. This statement satisfied the Irish Nationalists, to whom the advancement of Home Rule had always mattered more than liquor licenses and excise duties. They accordingly voted for the Budget when it came up for its second reading. So the government prevailed—but only by effectively allowing the Irish to dictate the terms of a future constitutional settlement. For this they were roundly condemned by their opponents, Balfour accusing ministers of 'eating dirt'.

Little wonder if many Liberals in the summer of 1910 took a pessimistic view of their situation. True, the Budget was approved by the Commons on 27 April, the Lords allowed it through on the following day,[28] and the measure received the royal assent on the day after that. So far, so good, from the Liberal viewpoint. But the Liberals now found themselves having to work with the Irish to carry the Parliament Bill. Then, with the government still dependent on the lesser parties for a working majority, it could only be a matter of time before they would feel obliged to introduce a third Home Rule Bill.

Many Liberals, at all levels of the party, dreaded such an outcome. Indeed, some no longer wanted to have anything to do with Home Rule. The recent estrangement between the Liberals and the Irish, particularly over education, had killed Lloyd George's former enthusiasm for the measure, while Asquith had long been a lukewarm Home Ruler. Finally, the Liberal Cabinet had little stomach for a bitter, partisan struggle which threatened to annihilate the normal civilities of political life and to precipitate a national crisis. Would such a conflict benefit the Opposition? Many frontbenchers suspected that it would.

At this crucial moment, on 6 May, Edward VII died, to be succeeded by George V. This provided a convenient opportunity to call for what Milner's

---

[28] In deference to the popular will, as expressed in the recent General Election, the Opposition peers merely abstained when the Budget again came before them.

journalist friend F. S. Oliver emotively dubbed a 'Truce of God'—a political ceasefire ostensibly aimed at protecting the inexperienced young monarch at the very start of his reign. Feelers were put out between the two frontbenches, who agreed that the Speaker should chair a conference at which attempts would be made, behind closed doors, to resolve the impasse.

The participants at the Constitutional Conference, which held its first meeting on 17 June, were, on the Liberal side, Asquith, Lloyd George, Lord Crewe (Leader of the Lords), and Birrell, Chief Secretary for Ireland (testifying to the way in which constitutional and Irish affairs had already become intertwined).[29] The Opposition delegation consisted of Balfour, Austen Chamberlain, Lansdowne, and Lord Cawdor. As important as who participated in the conference was the decision to exclude the minor parties. The Irish Nationalists, in particular, could do no more than hope that Birrell would keep a watching brief over their interests. Activists from the main parties similarly sensed betrayal, and as far as the government's supporters were concerned, these suspicions were more justified than they realized. For in the secrecy of the conference the Liberal leaders put forward for discussion, not a version of the C-B Resolutions, but the Cabinet Committee's earlier recommendation of joint sessions—a scheme quite unknown to the wider public.

The 'Ripon Plan' did at least provide an acceptable basis for negotiation. The Opposition responded by advocating that all legislation should be categorized in one of three ways. Financial Bills, they conceded, should be exempt from amendment or rejection in the Lords, provided that safeguards were introduced against 'tacking'—introducing into a Money Bill provisions beyond its natural scope. Ordinary legislation could then be dealt with along the lines of the Ripon Plan. However, the Unionists insisted that a third category of 'organic' or 'constitutional' legislation required more stringent safeguards, namely, a referral to the electorate in the form of a referendum.

The conference held twelve sessions between June and late July, then adjourned for a summer break. It resumed again in early October. Controversy revolved around two issues. The first was the exact definition of the number of peers that would sit in joint sessions, a figure that would have to be adjusted to take account of the size of the governing party's Commons majority. This important matter was never resolved. Still more contentious was the issue of what measures should be defined as 'constitutional'. Under this rubric both sides agreed to group any Bill that modified or abolished the monarchy or the Established Church, as well as any future measures redefining the relationship between the two Houses of Parliament. The sticking-point was whether it

---

[29] J. D. Fair, *British Interparty Conferences: A Study of the Procedure of Conciliation in British Politics 1867–1921* (Oxford, 1980), ch. 4; Weston, 'Lords' Veto', 523–37.

should also cover an Irish Home Rule Bill, as demanded by the Opposition. Even here Birrell showed a disposition to compromise, but Lloyd George would not surrender the point[30]—no doubt because he feared that Home Rule might be defeated in a referendum, leaving Liberal ministers at the mercy of a bitterly estranged Irish Nationalist Party, which would then waste little time in turning them out.

However, strongly partisan though he was within the Constitutional Conference,[31] Lloyd George's fertile mind was playing with other possibilities. The Chancellor calculated that, if the Liberals were to break with their Irish allies, this could only be done with safety by joining forces with the Unionists! In August, in the calm of his native Criccieth, he dictated a memorandum in which he advocated the formation of a coalition between the two main parties, using the managerial language beloved of the National Efficiency advocates: 'the time', he announced, 'has arrived for . . . bringing the resources of the two Parties into joint stock in order to liquidate arrears which, if much longer neglected, may end in national impoverishment, if not insolvency.'[32]

Lloyd George quickly took a few friends into his confidence, among them Churchill, a lifelong advocate of 'national politics', who responded with enthusiasm, and the Mastermans, who expressed principled doubts. But he did nothing further until the leaders returned to London for the reconvened conference in early October. Lloyd George then secretly approached Balfour, to whom he had increasingly felt attracted, and arranged a tête-à-tête, employing as his intermediary Churchill's friend F. E. Smith, the Conservative MP for the Walton division of Liverpool. Balfour was given to understand that the Liberals were preparing a whole series of concessions—over the tariff, the adoption of conscription, even over Ireland—in the interests of a national settlement. Balfour also learnt that Lloyd George wanted him to be Leader of the House of Commons, with Asquith relegated to the Lords (a reverse-action replay of Relugas!)

Meanwhile, Lloyd George was circulating to favoured ministers the text of his August memorandum, followed by a second one, dated 29 October. Both documents minimized the concessions being offered to the Opposition but emphasized the need for a bipartisan approach to issues such as National Insurance. Asquith subsequently gave his conditional consent to what he clearly regarded as a hare-brained scheme—he might have displayed rather

---

[30] He did, however, concede that, on one occasion, a Home Rule Bill might have to await a general-election endorsement.

[31] It is, however, amazing that Lloyd George should privately have agreed that no provisions should be attached to a Finance Bill which provided benefits for a particular class.

[32] On the Secret Coalition Talks, G. R. Searle, *The Quest for National Efficiency, 1899–1914* (Oxford, 1971; new edn., London, 1990), ch. 6; Gollin, *Garvin*, ch. 7.

less *sang froid* had he known of the plans for his own effective demotion! Yet it is probable that all the Liberals who were consulted understood that the coalition plan presupposed the watering-down of Home Rule; even the August memorandum, for example, hinted at the need for a federal solution of the Irish difficulty as part of a wider scheme for the better organization of the Empire.

The senior Conservatives were divided over Lloyd George's proposals—insofar as they understood them. Austen Chamberlain, conscious of his father's earlier flirtation with Home-Rule-All-Round, took a sympathetic interest. Other Unionists 'in the know' were even more eloquent in praise of Lloyd George's scheme. The unprincipled Smith thought that Lloyd George was coming over to the Unionist side, and to secure this was quite prepared to ditch the Irish extremists of both wings, including the Orangemen who formed part of his own party. Meanwhile Garvin, true to his belief in national government, took it upon himself to press Lloyd George's offer on Balfour.

But the Opposition Leader remained far from convinced, unerringly putting his finger on the contradictions in the federal scheme. Nor, given his past history as an implacable foe of Irish nationalism, did he need his former whip, Akers-Douglas, to remind him of the dangers of playing the part of Sir Robert Peel—the former Conservative Leader who, by espousing a historic fiscal compromise, had split his party from top to toe. Balfour's veto proved decisive, and by late October Lloyd George's private initiative was dead.

This breakdown also marked the beginning of the end of the Constitutional Conference, which had been proceeding in parallel with the secret coalition talks, the two sets of negotiations involving an overlapping, but not identical, cast of players. On 10 November the newspapers baldly announced that the conference had collapsed, and all the combatants returned to battle stations, the delegates having earlier bound themselves not to divulge what negotiating positions had been adopted there. As for the secret coalition talks themselves, these remained a secret to all but a handful of politicians until after the Great War—though they did generate some confused rumours. (How impressive that the lid could be kept on such explosive stuff!)

The search for a compromise settlement aborted, Asquith went back to the King for another dissolution, and this time sought a royal guarantee that, in the event of the Liberals winning the forthcoming election and seeing their Parliament Bill thrown out by the Upper House, sufficient Liberal peers would be created to swamp the Opposition there. The request was unusual, in that the King was being asked to bind himself to a course of action on some future occasion. George V also disliked Asquith's demand that, once given, the so-called 'contingent guarantees' would not be mentioned by the Liberals during the election campaign—a ploy adopted to protect the King's name from being bandied about in public, but which the simple-minded 'sailor king' disliked on the grounds that he had never before been ashamed of his behaviour and saw no need to act furtively now.

At the royal court George V received conflicting advice about how he should act. His personal secretary, Arthur Bigge, confirmed the King in his initial wish to turn Asquith down, but Lord Knollys (Edward VII's former secretary) advised acceptance, and carried the day by a piece of subterfuge. Knollys knew that, in the current situation, Balfour was prepared to take Asquith's place as a caretaker Prime Minister—a development which might later have tilted the electoral scales in the Unionist Leader's favour. But, thinking it necessary to deceive the monarch in order to save the monarchy, Knollys withheld this vital information. The King therefore gave way on the 'contingent guarantees', and on 18 November Asquith was able to announce the dissolution of Parliament.

The second 1910 General Election, which lasted from 2 to 19 December, focused primarily on constitutional reform. The Unionists campaigned on the basis of the so-called Lansdowne Resolutions, a version of the Ripon Plan modified to suit their own case which the Lords had endorsed on 24 November. The Opposition also publicized the imminent threat to the Union by denouncing Redmond, who in the autumn had gone with other Irish politicians on a lecture tour of the United States, netting $100,000 in the process. The 'Dollar Dictator', Unionists alleged, was now presuming to give orders to the British government—an accusation which privately made many Liberals, too, feel uneasy.

The December 1910 Election brought about few surprises. The only real difference from January was that Labour put up fifty-six rather than seventy-eight candidates, so keeping clashes between the two progressive parties down to eleven.[33] In another important development Balfour, under pressure from Lord Derby and other Lancastrian free fooders, promised to submit a future tariff-reform budget to a referendum in a gesture of apparent even-handedness. This last-minute decision dismayed Austen Chamberlain, all the more so since it did not, in the event, produce the intended Unionist breakthrough. True, as many as fifty-seven seats changed hands,[34] but each of the major parties returned to Westminster in early 1911 with 272 MPs—the Liberals having lost one seat overall, while the Unionists gained three.

The constitutional crisis now moved quickly to its climax. The Parliament Bill was reintroduced into the Commons, where it passed all its readings to the accompaniment of rowdy scenes, and went up to the Lords, where the Opposition planned to defeat it. Only on 20 July 1911 did the government

---

[33] Labour did not win a single triangular contest.
[34] Compared with the state of the parties on the eve of dissolution.

formally announce that the King had already given the 'contingent guaran-tees'—an announcement which, in view of ministerial silence during the recent election campaign, caught the Unionist leadership on the hop.[35] On his next appearance in the Commons Asquith was shouted down by infuriated Unionist MPs shouting 'Traitor' and 'Who Killed the King?', an organized demonstra-tion in which Lord Hugh Cecil and F. E. Smith took a prominent part. Privately many members of the Opposition condemned the new King for having allowed himself to become the Liberals' pawn: the monarch was a 'natural' ally of the Unionists, and they regarded Asquith's legerdemain with unabated bitterness.

The situation was slipping out of the Unionist leadership's control. Balfour and Lansdowne reluctantly concluded that their followers should abstain on the Lords' second reading of the Parliament Bill, their reasoning being that such a tactical retreat would leave them in control of an Upper House that still retained the power to delay a future Home Rule Bill—whereas defiance might result in Home Rule becoming law within the year. But a section of the party, declaring their willingness to die in the last ditch, disobeyed their leaders and rallied around the banner of the 85-year-old Lord Halsbury. For Balfour this spelled danger, because the 'ditchers' included not only 'backwoodsmen', such as Lord Willoughby de Broke, but also the Shadow Chancellor, Austen Chamberlain, Wyndham, Carson, F. E. Smith—even his own cousin's hus-band, Lord Selborne. A section of the Unionist press also came out in open revolt, headed by Maxse, who ran a lively campaign under the slogan of 'Balfour Must Go' ('BMG').

When the Lords held their fateful vote on 10 August (in the middle of a heatwave, which did not improve tempers), most Unionist peers followed the advice of Balfour and Lansdowne. Even so, a mass creation of Liberal peers (a provisional list had already been prepared) would still have been necessary, had not the bishops and twenty-nine Conservative peers (the so-called 'Judas Group'), rallied by Lord Cromer, voted *for* the government, on tactical grounds.[36] The Parliament Bill passed by 131 votes to 114.

This humiliating three-way split ended Balfour's long reign, though, oddly enough, Lansdowne, who had performed feebly throughout the crisis, sur-vived. After Walter Long and Austen Chamberlain, the rival contenders for the leadership, had effectively cancelled one another out, Balfour's place went to a rank outsider, Andrew Bonar Law, who, by another oddity, had recently been a

---

[35] Though Balfour had privately been forewarned on 7 July, his supporters knew nothing of the guarantee.

[36] Lord Newton, who himself abstained, also took a part in the early stages of the crisis (D. Southern, 'Lord Newton, the Conservative Peers and the Parliament Act of 1911', *English Historical Review*, 96 (1981), 834–40).

'Hedger' rather than a 'Ditcher'. Balfour's fall, however, owed comparatively little to his tactics during the constitutional crisis—where he had had little room for manoeuvre—but really represented a vote of no-confidence in a man who, having led his followers into three successive election defeats, resolutely refused to pander to what he characteristically dismissed as 'the Music Hall attitude of mind' exhibited by Diehards, as right-wing Tories became known.

The Parliament Bill duly became law in the autumn of 1911. Its provisions largely followed the lines of the 'C-B Resolutions', the main innovation being a preamble which raised the possibility of a later reconsideration of the Lords' composition—a token concession to the 'reform' group within the Cabinet. The Unionists fumed at the government's behaviour, claiming that the country was under the sway of what they variously dubbed a 'Single Chamber Dictatorship', a 'Regicide Government', and a 'revolutionary junta'. Ministers had 'lost the right to that implicit obedience that can be claimed by a Constitutional Government', said Bonar Law.[37]

The Liberals, of course, saw things quite differently. The Lords' rejection of the Budget, Asquith had solemnly informed the Commons on 2 December 1909, was 'a breach of the Constitution and a usurpation of the rights of the Commons'. Yet the Opposition did have a point in their protests over the Budget's valuation clauses, which had been blatantly 'tacked' on to a Finance Bill in the hope of giving them immunity from rejection in the Lords—these clauses would almost certainly have been disallowed by the Speaker under the terms of the 1911 Parliament Act. Similarly, Asquith was asking the King in 1910 to do something unprecedented over the 'contingent guarantees'. Finally, the Liberals had largely overturned a bicameral legislature without replacing it with anything other than vague promises of a reconstituted Second Chamber.

However, when all is said and done, the Opposition seemed to be offering the greater threat to that 'ancient constitution' for which they professed such affection. Ever since Lord Newton's Bill of 1907, some peers had shown an interest in reforming their own Chamber by introducing an elected element. This idea also underlay the resolutions tabled in 1910 by the crossbencher Lord Rosebery, to which Lansdowne had initially objected, but had then supported when they came before the Lords on 17 November 1910. Another manifestation of the desire of many Conservatives to 'modernize' the Constitution, at the same time as putting obstacles in the path of their opponents, was their sudden conversion to the referendum, a new-fangled device which Asquith, ever a stickler for legal precedents, declared totally incompatible with a parliamentary system of government.

[37] At Caernarvon, 11 Dec. 1913.

Thus charges were met with counter-charges. In the end it all boiled down to political judgement. The weakness of the Unionist case for a reconstituted Second Chamber stemmed from the difficulty they had in agreeing upon a precise scheme, some peers favouring self-selection from within their own ranks, some direct election, some nomination, and some a mixture of all these methods. Meanwhile other Unionists, including Halsbury, failed to see how the House of Lords could possibly be improved—hence their enthusiastic adoption of the alternative proposal of the referendum. Lansdowne's reform scheme was thus, of necessity, a muddled compromise. The fact that it was then passed by the Lords in a single session, after a debate of only three hours, could also be cited as proof of the insincerity of its promoters. Certainly insufficient time had been allowed before the December election to sell so startling a proposition to the voters.

The Liberals, too, had their strategic differences, but they eventually united around a version of the C-B Resolutions, with which informed electors would already have been familiar. Moreover, here was a settlement which, in some ways, went with the grain of constitutional development, as the Unionist counter-proposals did not. Against this background, Asquith was the ideal party leader. A shrewd politician who, in the end, accepted the unavoidability of what his more zealous parliamentary followers were demanding, he could plausibly present himself as a cautious lawyer upholding venerable constitutional traditions, while defying the revolutionary subversion offered by his opponents. At a time of national emergency, in which the whole constitution was in the melting-pot,[38] the Liberals thus reaffirmed the country's commitment to parliamentary government and rejected the alternative concept of plebiscitary democracy. Some reformers of a later generation have regretted that this rare opportunity to modernize the British state was not seized. But what Asquith was offering seemed at the time, even to many of the government's critics, much the safer bet.

3. CRISIS IN IRELAND

It was in this feverish atmosphere that the government introduced the third Home Rule Bill.[39] Its final form emerged after important discussions in Cabinet

---

[38] A Royal Commission was also considering the possibility of 'electoral reform', i.e. changes to the first-past-the-post voting system—a reform favoured by certain individuals in all parties, though, predictably, disliked by Asquith. Many backbench MPs were members of the Proportional Representation Society, and there was still greater support for the AV in 'progressive circles' (M. Pugh, *Electoral Reform in War and Peace 1906–18* (London, 1978), ch. 1).

[39] On the government and Ireland, Jalland, *Liberals and Ireland*; on the Irish Nationalists, F. S. L. Lyons, *John Dillon: A Biography* (London, 1968), chs. 10–12.

Committee over how the Bill was to affect the rest of the United Kingdom. Lloyd George cautiously confined himself to a modest scheme for setting up Commons grand committees in which the members of England, Scotland, and Wales could deal with their own particular 'regions'. But Haldane and Grey strongly favoured linking Irish Home Rule to some larger scheme of Home-Rule-All-Round. Churchill went further, proposing a separation between the imperial Parliament and local assemblies. This would have pleased many of the Liberal Party's Scottish supporters: D. V. Pirie, an enthusiastic Home Ruler, thought that as many as sixty of Scotland's seventy-two MPs wanted to have their own parliament in Edinburgh, and, of these, some also championed United Kingdom devolution on its own merits.[40] The Welsh remained largely preoccupied with Disestablishment, but E. T. John, soon to be elected as Liberal MP for East Denbighshire, launched a campaign for Welsh Home Rule in August 1910.

Where, however, would England fit into 'Home-Rule-All-Round'? Churchill boldly advocated the division of the United Kingdom into ten or twelve separate provinces, each with its own 'legislative and administrative body', which in Scotland, Wales, and Ireland would assume parliamentary form, while the various English 'provinces' would each have an assembly. The Irish parliament, he proposed, would be set up immediately, the other assemblies in the following year. The government's constitutional experts shot this blueprint down in flames, and, when Churchill later floated it publicly in a speech to his Dundee constituents in September 1912, Maxse, mocking this attempted resurrection of the 'Heptarchy', sarcastically asked why England should be cut into pieces, when no significant number of her inhabitants had asked for it, simply as part of a tacky deal with the 'disloyal' Irish. In the event, all such schemes—even Lloyd George's—were abandoned, mainly because, as Birrell explained, the Irish resented anything that denied the uniqueness of their own national grievance.

'Federalism' continued to attract those individuals in all parties who craved a compromise over Ireland, and Asquith himself, when introducing the Home Rule Bill, declared his measure to be merely a first step towards wider devolution. But the opportunity to provide Britain with a formal constitution in which power passed downwards to its constituent national components was not taken in early 1912. Such an exercise would in any case have been exceedingly difficult, for, as Colin Matthew argues, the British Constitution was an accumulation of conquests, bargains, Crown prerogatives, and common law, which had always worked by convention: 'any attempt at devolution was therefore bound to be a messy business, for it was very hard to devise an

---

[40] Jalland, 'United Kingdom Devolution', 763.

intellectually systematic plan when the constitution whose powers were to be devolved was not systematically stated in law.'[41]

Another area of contention was whether special provision needed to be made for Ulster. This was becoming far more important than when the earlier Home Rule Bills had been drafted, if only because, once most of the Ascendancy landlords in the South and West of Ireland had sold up, the Opposition were bound to emphasize the Ulster difficulty. Ulster was in any case becoming socially, economically, and culturally increasingly distinct from the rest of Ireland—though of course the third of its population belonging to the Catholic-nationalist community cherished their links with their compatriots in the South. Finally, in 1910 the Ulster Unionist Council (UUC) had brought in as its Chairman the Southern Unionist Edward Carson, MP for Dublin University—a man who, with his considerable contacts on both sides of the Irish Sea,[42] was likely to prove a formidable adversary.

To propitiate the Ulster loyalists, Lloyd George and Churchill proposed in Cabinet on 6 February 1912 that the predominantly Protestant counties should be allowed to contract out of Home Rule, but Crewe and Asquith persuaded their colleagues against such an approach. As a result, the Bill which went before the Commons treated Ireland as an entity, and when in June 1912 a backbench Liberal MP, Agar-Robartes, proposed a resolution allowing the four heavily Protestant counties of Armagh, Antrim, Down, and Londonderry an opt-out, the government mobilized its parliamentary following to turn the scheme down. Even so, five Liberal MPs rebelled and another sixty-two abstained. Agar-Robartes also won the tactical backing of the Opposition, which hoped to embarrass the government and wreck its plans. Carson, for one, still thought that, without the Protestant heartlands, Home Rule could never be made to work.[43]

Under the terms of the Parliament Act there seemed nothing else that the Unionists could do other than delay Home Rule—unless, that is, they could force the government into seeking a mandate specifically on the Irish issue, the objective they had recently pursued at the Constitutional Conference. Because Home Rule had historically been a vote-loser, Asquith was never going to comply; he could also cite constitutional propriety as a cloak behind which to conceal his pursuit of party advantage. But what if the King could be frightened into believing that, with the Upper Chamber neutered, only a royal veto stood between the country and 'single chamber despotism'? At a tense meeting in May 1912 Bonar Law told a red-faced George V that he had

[41] H. C. G. Matthew, *Gladstone Vol. 2 1875–98* (Oxford, 1995), 249.

[42] He had been Solicitor-General in the Balfour ministry.

[43] Churchill's Dundee speech obviously strengthened the case for special treatment for Ulster: if England could be subdivided, why not Ireland?

the choice either of accepting the Home Rule Bill or of dismissing his ministers and choosing others who would support him in vetoing it—'and in either case, half your subjects will think you have acted against them'.[44] The King was sufficiently alarmed to urge his Prime Minister to compromise, but wisely declined to pursue the veto option.

The Opposition then fell back on their second line of defence: fomenting rebellion within Ulster itself. In September 1911 the UUC announced that a 'Provisional Government' would be set up to take over the running of the Province in the event of Home Rule becoming law; and twelve months later, in an impressively melodramatic ceremony at Belfast Town Hall, the Ulster loyalists, headed by Carson, signed a Solemn League and Covenant to which, in a single day, 80,000 pledged themselves. Soon afterwards the UUC created a paramilitary body, the United Volunteer Force (UVF), to defend what it saw as its sacred constitutional birthright.[45]

Bonar Law, a Presbyterian with Ulster connections, had no difficulty in identifying with Ulster loyalism. At Blenheim in July 1912 he declared that there was 'no length of resistance to which Ulster would not go', and in this and other speeches he seemed positively to be inciting his audience to armed rebellion. However, like Carson, the Conservative Leader did not really want armed conflict, his primary concern being to pressurize the Cabinet (by frightening the King) into a suicidally premature dissolution. He also wanted to reunite his fractured party by concentrating on an issue where little separated them.[46]

This was especially necessary in the aftermath of another bout of party infighting over the tariff. In November 1912 Bonar Law and Lansdowne, under pressure from the ardent tariff reformers, had announced the abandonment of the referendum pledge. This provoked outrage from the free food members of the party, to appease whom Law effectively dropped the food taxes in the following month.[47] This second volte-face occasioned such an uproar that the two Leaders actually proffered their resignations, and only withdrew them on receipt of a 'round robin' in January 1913 signed by all but six

[44] H. Nicolson, *King George V: His Life and Times* (London, 1952), 200–1.

[45] P. Buckland, *Irish Unionism, II, Ulster Unionism and the Origins of Northern Ireland 1886–1922* (Dublin, 1973); A. T. Q. Stewart, *The Ulster Crisis* (London, 1967).

[46] R. Blake, *The Unknown Prime Minister: Life and Times of Andrew Bonar Law* (London, 1955), chs. 7, 9–13; D. G. Boyce, 'British Conservative Opinion, the Ulster Question and the Partition of Ireland, 1912–21', *Irish Historical Studies*, 17 (1970–1), 89–112; P. Murphy, 'Faction and the Home Rule Crisis, 1912–14', *History*, 71 (1986), 222–34; J. Smith, ' "Bluff, Bluster and Brinkmanship": Andrew Bonar Law and the Third Home Rule Bill', *Historical Journal*, 36 (1993), 161–78; S. Evans, 'The Conservatives and the Redefinition of Unionism, 1912–21', *Twentieth Century History*, 9 (1998), 11–15.

[47] Law said that food taxes would not be imposed until the colonies had negotiated an acceptable deal with London, which might mean that they would never be imposed at all.

members of the parliamentary party, pleading with them to stay on. Ireland, at least at first, seemed to offer a welcome distraction from these embarrassments. Moreover, what Asquith caustically called 'the new style' was Bonar Law's way of putting distance between his own leadership and that of his discredited predecessor, Balfour.

Why did the government not defuse the whole issue by offering its opponents a concession over Ulster from the very start, as Lloyd George and Churchill had earlier urged? They did not want to alienate Redmond and Dillon. Irish Nationalists still thought of Ireland as a seamless garment (almost to the very end, 'an Irish parliament, an Irish executive and the integrity of Ireland' was their cry).[48] Ministers also had to take into account the interests of the sizeable Catholic minority within Ulster, led by Jo Devlin, the Nationalist MP for Belfast West. In Whitehall there was undoubtedly an underestimate of the strength of popular feeling among the Protestants of the north-east, and ministers were only too willing to accept the view of Redmond and Dillon that the whole loyalist movement was nothing more than a grotesque bluff. In any case, the Bill's exceedingly complex financial arrangements, devised by Samuel, made any kind of future exclusion very difficult to achieve—which suggests that the problems of Ulster were far from the forefront of ministerial minds in early 1912. Nor were ministers helped to form a realistic assessment of the situation by Dublin Castle intelligence, which was still mainly focused on former Fenian terrorists who offered little immediate threat.

On the other hand, the Liberals knew that sooner or later they would probably have to give ground over Ulster. As early as 1912 the Cabinet agreed to inform the Irish leaders that the government held itself free 'to make such changes in the Bill as fresh evidence of facts, or the pressure of British opinion, may render expedient', including special arrangements for the Ulster counties. But the Liberals did not want to play this card too soon, for fear of disheartening their own supporters and encouraging the Opposition to raise the stakes by issuing yet further demands. Under the new parliamentary timetable the Home Rule Bill would have to make three circuits through Parliament, and neither side would start bargaining in earnest until the third circuit had been reached.

A similar reluctance to make concessions inhibited the Opposition. Carson, for example, initially saw Ulster as a battering-ram to destroy Home Rule. The danger he ran was that, by concentrating so heavily on Ulster, he would tacitly be abandoning the southern Unionists, while the Unionist Party as a whole would find the ground cut away from under its feet should the government

---

[48] They did concede the possibility of the Ulster counties enjoying limited autonomy within a Home Rule framework: what was known as 'Home Rule Within Home Rule'. However, the Ulster Unionists regularly rejected this suggestion.

ever seriously meet the Ulstermen's demands. In fact, in October 1913 the southern Unionists and the Ulstermen did agree to go their separate ways. However, the southern Unionists dreaded anything that smacked of partition, be it temporary or permanent—even Home Rule in a united Ireland would have afforded them better protection. Early 1914 therefore saw a rally of the southern Unionists, protesting against their abandonment, and this made an impact because, though numerically small, they enjoyed many personal and social contacts with mainland Conservatism—their Leader, Lord Midleton, was the former Conservative War Secretary, then known as St John Brodrick, and their ranks included no less a grandee than Lord Lansdowne, a great Kerry landlord.[49]

Nevertheless, by late 1913 the prospects of a compromise settlement began to strengthen. Brushing aside the ineffectual Birrell, who for some months had been distracted by his wife's declining health, Lloyd George effectively took on the role of Irish Secretary. The Chancellor was cross that Ireland should be distracting attention from his Land Campaign, and probably shared the regret expressed by the *Nation*, mouthpiece of the New Liberal reformers, that so much time was being devoted to 'questions which were ripe for settlement twenty years ago'.[50]

Lloyd George consequently suggested an ingenious compromise aimed at speedily resolving the crisis: each Ulster county could opt out of Home Rule but would automatically be included after a period of three years; this meant that the Unionists would have an opportunity of testing Home Rule's popularity in a general election and, if that were the will of the British people, could repeal the Bill in its entirety before Ulster came under the sway of a Dublin parliament.[51] On 22 February 1914 Redmond reluctantly accepted this arrangement as the price to be paid if Home Rule were to become law at all—only to be told a fortnight later that the opting-out period had now been extended to six years.

Even this did not satisfy Carson and the Ulstermen, whose public position, staked out in their Commons vote in January 1913, was for a 'clean cut' of the entire nine-county Province of Ulster—including Donegal, Monaghan, and Cavan, in which the Catholics formed a clear majority. Incidentally, had Carson got his way, Ulster would have contained so many Catholics that democratic rule might have eluded the Unionists—in January 1913 the Nationalists actually took a majority of parliamentary seats in the Province

---

[49] P. J. Buckland, 'The Southern Unionists, the Irish Question and British Politics, 1906–14', *Irish Historical Studies*, 15 (1966–7), 228–55.

[50] Cited in Jalland, *Liberals and Ireland*, 30.

[51] Lloyd George cunningly calculated that the UUC would find it impossible to keep its organization and armed force in being for this length of time, in readiness for an 'emergency' that might never arise.

after Londonderry City had changed hands in a by-election.[52] Aware of the danger, Carson was soon privately admitting his readiness to limit his demands to the six counties of Antrim, Armagh, Down, Londonderry, Fermanagh, and Tyrone.

However, still bitterly contentious were two issues: was exclusion to be temporary or permanent, and should voting take place across the entire area of 'statutory Ulster' or on a county-by-county basis? The Unionists demanded the clean cut because they would otherwise lose Fermanagh and Tyrone, which had large Protestant minorities whom it was politically impossible to abandon. The wondrous symmetry that governed Irish politics meant, of course, that the Irish Nationalists had to demand county option.

Churchill, blowing hot and cold over Ulster, invited Austen Chamberlain on to his Admiralty yacht in September 1913, where he invoked the 'lost opportunity' of the secret coalition talks in an attempt to cajole the Unionist leaders into a compromise settlement—but in vain. Three rounds of talks then took place between Asquith and Bonar Law from October to December 1913, followed by another two between Asquith and Carson from December 1913 to January 1914. The Prime Minister came away from these meetings with the wry satisfaction of knowing that Carson, for all his bravado, occupied an even more difficult position than himself. However, no agreement was reached—to the relief of English Unionists such as Walter Long and Leo Amery, who had long been suspicious of the Ulster exclusion idea because it implied the inevitability of Home Rule for the rest of Ireland.

As far as Westminster politics was concerned, the aim of both party Leaders was to put themselves in the most favourable light before mainland public opinion by manoeuvring their opponents into apparently unreasonable conduct. But in Ireland itself a grimmer game was being played out. At first the loyalist members of the UVF had drilled with broomsticks, to widespread amusement. But a succession of purchases in the European arms market, culminating in the audacious Larne gun-running of April 1914, soon wiped the smile off its opponents' faces. Numbering some 90,000 men, with officers largely drawn from retired British army officers, the UVF developed into a serious military body, complete with motor divisions, a medical and a nursing corps, and signallers—in fact, with almost all the elements of a modern army, except heavy artillery and aerial support.[53] Heading it was a retired Indian army officer, Lieutenant-General Sir George Richardson, who had been strongly recommended for the post by Lord Roberts.[54]

---

[52] The victor was, unusually, a Liberal.

[53] However, there was a relative shortage of ammunition, and some military historians think the UVF was more potent as a political symbol than it would have been if called upon to fight.

[54] I. F. W. Beckett (ed.), *The Army and the Curragh Incident 1914* (London, 1986), 6.

From within the War Office, the Director of Military Operations, General Sir Henry Wilson, himself an Ulsterman and a virulent Unionist, provided help and encouragement to the UVF. Lord Milner secretly raised a guarantee fund for 'officers in the Army who decide[d] to resign rather than violate their consciences'.[55] More openly, working through the Union Defence League, Milner organized a British Covenant, which eventually attracted 2 million signatories who bound themselves to take 'any action' that might stop Home Rule becoming law; Lord Roberts, A. V. Dicey, and Rudyard Kipling were among its many famous and wealthy supporters. Willoughby de Broke's British League for the Support of Ulster and the Union, supported by 100 peers and 200 MPs, kept up the pressure. The press even carried unofficial advertisements for patriots willing, should the need arise, to fight side by side with the UVF. The prospect of violence was welcomed by many Diehards, who thought that the shedding of 'good red blood' might be the only way to shake the British population out of its complacent lethargy.[56]

The presence of the UVF did at least prevent further communal rioting of the kind that had erupted in Belfast in early 1912. To Carson and Bonar Law this was important, since both knew the revulsion that was felt for such behaviour on mainland Britain. In fact, no sectarian killings occurred at all after 1912, which compares starkly with the violence accompanying the two earlier Home Rule Bills. But the emergence in November 1913 of the Irish Volunteers, over which the Nationalist leadership had less than total control, suggested that a more militant phase of Irish Nationalism was beginning; the prominent role in its creation played by Gaelic Leaguers such as Eoin Mac-Neill, and the presence in the movement of the Irish Republic Brotherhood (IRB), was even more ominous.

In March 1914 the British government lost any chance of reimposing order in Ireland with the so-called Curragh Incident, following a botched attempt by the War Secretary, Jack Seely, and Churchill, the First Lord of the Admiralty, to reinforce arms depots in Northern Ireland. Churchill, the prime mover in the affair, had already raised the temperature with a bellicose speech at Bradford on 14 March. He now ordered a battle squadron to Lamlash, near Belfast, fuelling Unionist fears of an impending 'Ulster pogrom'. Sixty officers of the 3rd Cavalry Brigade stationed at the Curragh, near Dublin, led by Brigadier-General Hubert Gough, took advantage of the option given them by the Commander-in-Chief in Ireland, Sir Arthur Paget, and resigned their commissions rather than take part in operations in Ulster.[57] The government

---

[55] Ibid. 5.

[56] G. Searle, 'The "Revolt from the Right" in Edwardian Britain', in P. Kennedy and A. Nicholls (eds.), *Nationalist and Racialist Movements in Britain and Germany Before 1914* (London, 1981), 27.

[57] Officers domiciled in Ulster were told that they could 'disappear' while the operation was in progress.

refused to accept these resignations, but Seely promised Gough in writing that the army would never be used to quell opposition to a Home Rule Bill. The Cabinet promptly cancelled this concession, causing Sir John French, the CIGS, and Sir John Ewart, the Adjutant-General, to resign their offices, followed by Seely.[58] Asquith temporarily took charge of the War Office.

With senior military personnel still seething with discontent (the disaffection had even spread to the navy), the government feared (perhaps mistakenly) that, as an instrument for enforcing its Irish policies, the army was a broken reed. Indeed, Bonar Law no longer saw any necessity for using the Unionist majority in the Lords to amend the Army Annual Act, the stratagem to which the Unionist leadership had reluctantly agreed.[59] Another legacy of the Curragh Incident was acute mistrust between civilian politicians and senior officers, a mistrust which was to distort strategic planning once the Great War broke out: ominously, one of those caught up in the 'Incident' was the Director of Military Training, Major-General Sir William Robertson—of whom, more anon.

From the Liberals' point of view, the events of March 1914 made the search for a compromise all the more necessary. Compromise also attracted senior Unionists, frightened about what the future might hold. The 'Federalists' had already made yet another attempt to push their favoured panacea, following the release of the Loreburn Letter, a public letter in which the former Lord Chancellor urged a federal solution of the Irish question, in September 1913; this gave rise to a flurry of inconclusive discussions in early 1914. Then in July the Speaker convened the Buckingham Palace Conference, to which were summoned Irish Nationalist representatives as well as Unionist delegates from both parts of Ireland, along with members of the two frontbenches. But this conference soon broke down over the future of Fermanagh and Tyrone: each side, having made as many concessions as it dared, was unwilling to go the final mile.

The situation was now as follows: the Home Rule Bill was about to receive the royal assent. The government had introduced an Amending Bill, offering temporary exemption to each county in Ulster, but this had been amended out of recognition in the Upper House.[60] Asquith informed the King that he

---

[58] With some justification, the Opposition suspected that Seely had been scapegoated. Interestingly, the two principal culprits, Churchill and Paget, both retained their posts.

[59] The idea had originated with Lord Hugh Cecil. However, the stratagem, which was supported by many moderates and lawyers, was not aimed at a total paralyzing of the army (J. Smith, ' "Paralysing the Army": The Unionists and the Army Annual Act, 1911–1914', *Parliamentary History*, 15 (1996), 191–207).

[60] This, as Jalland argues (*Liberals and Ireland*), constitutes an argument against the government's tactical decision neither to include special terms for Ulster in the original Home Rule Bill nor to accept amendments during its first circuit, which would have brought the entire package under the protection of the Parliament Act.

therefore intended to restore county option in a new Amending Bill, but this time, instead of automatic reinclusion at the end of a fixed term, there would have to be a second referendum in the affected counties. Such an arrangement, barely acceptable to the Orangemen, would, if publicly announced, have been greeted with fury in nationalist Ireland and would probably have undermined Redmond's authority, to the benefit of his Republican adversaries.

These manoeuvrings took place against a background in Ireland of communal unrest, with bloodshed threatening to break out in the border areas and in cities with mixed populations, notably Belfast. The tension increased still further with the clash at Bachelor's Walk near Dublin on 26 July, when British troops, having vainly tried to intercept an arms shipment to the Irish Volunteers, fired on the crowd that was baiting and throwing stones at them, killing three and injuring another thirty-eight. No wonder that Asquith privately expressed relief when the outbreak of the Great War temporarily put an end to his Irish nightmare.

Could the Liberal government have done more, either by moving quickly to defuse the Ulster protests or by cracking down on what bore every indication of being treasonable dissent? Basically, the government found itself torn in two directions. It risked alienating 'middle England' and offending sections of its own backbenchers if it denied to the Ulster loyalists the right of self-determination (in this case, the right to remain an integral part of the United Kingdom) that it had acknowledged when asserted by their Catholic neighbours to the south, and it would have been politically suicidal to allow British troops (even had they been willing to obey orders) to fire on Union-Jack-waving 'loyalists'. Agar-Robartes, a Cornish landowner with many Wesleyans among his constituents, was not alone in instinctively sympathizing with the plight of his fellow Protestants in Ireland.

On the other hand—and this seems to have been what particularly motivated Churchill, a moderate at heart—the Liberals disliked retreating in the face of violence and the threat of violence, and in this they were wholeheartedly backed by the Labour Party, which otherwise affected to be bored by the never-ending Irish dispute. Last but not least, the Liberals could see the political dangers of breaking with the Nationalist Party, on which they largely depended for their continuance in power.

Why, in that case, did the government not crack down more quickly on the UVF before it had become a formidable force? This would not have been easy. Initially the UVF had been licensed by local magistrates, which gave the force a semblance of legality. In any case, the government could hardly move against a local firebrand without taking some notice of Carson and Bonar Law, but the latter's arrest would have provoked an Opposition walkout from the House, neutralizing Asquith's trump card, his possession of a parliamentary majority.

Even so, when all allowances have been made, it is hard to exonerate the government from the charge of having let things drift: an embargo on the further importation of arms into Ireland was not imposed until 1 December 1913. Perhaps, neither for the first nor the last time, Asquith simply failed to comprehend the passions which were being unleashed in Ireland, still less the extremes to which the Opposition were prepared to push their objections to Home Rule. In the absence of a firm prime-ministerial lead, the restless Churchill was tempted to launch his own 'freelancing' escapades.

On mainland Britain the Irish Question might have been more easily contained had it not been for the legacy left by the passing of the Parliament Act. Like Welsh Disestablishment (another contentious issue pitting the Commons against the Lords), Irish Home Rule was being discussed in an atmosphere of intense bitterness and mutual suspicion. For the first time since the seventeenth century the country genuinely confronted civil war, not because of sharp policy divisions between the two major parties—these formed a normal feature of party strife—but because the Opposition did not wholeheartedly accept the legitimacy of the *institutional arrangements* which had emerged during the years of Liberal rule.

4. THE ISSUE OF CORRUPTION

This denial of the legitimacy of Liberal rule was strengthened by the Opposition's belief that Asquith's ministry was incorrigibly 'corrupt'.[61] Unionists reckoned, in part, that the Liberals were pursuing a treacherous policy of conciliating Irish nationalism because they could not bear to be parted from their ministerial salaries—supported by backbenchers who, since the introduction of payment of MPs in 1912, had a similar pecuniary interest in sustaining Asquith in power.

These accusations were accompanied by the wider charge that the party system itself had become corrupt, a belief which by 1912 had spread far beyond the circle of Hilaire Belloc, G. K. Chesterton, and his brother Cecil, who had argued this case with bilious vehemence in their book *The Party System* (1910). However exaggerated the indictment, the Liberals had largely brought it upon their own heads by trading honours for contributions to the party funds. The rot had started with Campbell-Bannerman's Patronage Secretary, George Whiteley (already disliked by Unionists as a party turncoat), who converted the £20,000 he had inherited from his predecessor to £514,000 before retiring in June 1908. His successor, the Quaker Jack Pease, did not fundamentally alter

---

[61] On 'corruption', see G. R. Searle, *Corruption in British Politics, 1895–1930* (Oxford, 1987), chs. 5–10.

Whiteley's dubious fund-raising methods, but it was under the next Patronage Secretary, the Master of Elibank, a shrewd and unscrupulous Scottish laird, that the issue of honours trafficking threatened to engulf the government in scandal. Elibank was responsible for the award of a record number of peerages—fifteen in 1910, twenty-two in 1911 (admittedly, a Coronation year), and ten in 1912—and for a similar inflation in the award of baronetcies, up from thirteen in 1910 to twenty in 1912.

The Conservative leadership, however, shrank from attacking the government too fiercely because it knew that it had skeletons in its own cupboard, not least the barony which had been awarded in mysterious circumstances to Alfred Harmsworth in Balfour's outgoing honours list. This is probably why Bonar Law and Lansdowne did so little to help Lord Selborne when the latter tried to uncover Liberal malpractices. Well might the frontbench show caution, since the Unionist whip, Acland-Hood, had continued to promise honours to potential subscribers to the fund, building up a tidy 'nest egg' of over £300,000 by 1911—though this meant that 'a year's peerages [had been] hypothecated'. The Unionist Leadership realized that, if it pressed its case against Liberal ministers too far, it ran the risk of counter-exposure. Significantly, both sets of managers resisted the mounting calls for the auditing of party funds.

Something similar occurred during the Marconi Scandal of 1912–13. This complicated affair centred around the actions of three ministers: Lloyd George; Rufus Isaacs, the Attorney-General; and the Master of Elibank, who all bought shares in the American Marconi Company, whose Chairman, Godfrey Isaacs, was Rufus Isaacs's brother; Elibank made an additional purchase out of the Liberal Party funds. What made these speculative transactions particularly reckless was that they took place while the Postmaster-General, Samuel, was in the process of awarding a contract to the English Marconi Company for the building of a chain of telegraph stations linking together different parts of the British Empire; this laid the three ministers open to the charge of insider trading. True, the English and the American Marconi companies were technically separate, allowing Lloyd George to deny in a statement to the Commons in October 1912 that he had bought any shares in 'this company'. In fact, however, the English Company had a holding in the American Company, interlocking membership linked them at directorship level, and both used the same patent, so that their share price tended to rise and fall simultaneously. The evasiveness of the peccant Liberal ministers when their assailants began to close in on them, Asquith's determination (whether noble or cowardly) to stand by his colleagues, and the blatant partisanship shown by the Liberal members of the Select Committee of Inquiry set up to get to the bottom of this murky affair—all did great damage to the personages involved, especially to Lloyd George. 'The idol's wings are a bit clipped', Asquith privately remarked.[62]

But though most Conservatives would have been delighted to bring down Lloyd George, Bonar Law rather liked the Chancellor, with whom he sometimes played golf, so he did not make too much of the 'scandal'. More startling was the appearance of F. E. Smith and Carson as counsel for Rufus Isaacs (the three men knew one another well from the circuit), when he sued a French newspaper which had unwittingly libelled him. The real running over Marconi was therefore left to the Belloc–Chesterton crowd, now grouped together with the likes of Arnold White in the National League for Clean Government, and figures on the fringes of the Conservative Party, such as Maxse of the *National Review* (collectively known to posterity as the 'Radical Right'). Maxse, who had earlier made fun of the relationship between the Right Honourable A. J. Foozle and the Right Honourable H. H. Boozle, was confirmed in his suspicion that the party fight at Westminster was little more than a put-up job.

The Marconi Affair generated a considerable body of anti-Semitic prejudice, directed not only at the Isaacs brothers, but also at the blameless Herbert Samuel, whose sole offence was being a wealthy Jew. Anti-Semitism was even more blatant in the contemporary 'Indian Silver Scandal' involving Edwin Montagu, Under-Secretary at the India Office, and his cousin, the Liberal backbencher Stuart Samuel, elder brother of Herbert. But the ravings of Belloc's *Eye-Witness* (later renamed the *New Witness*) should not be accorded too much importance. Most Marconi muckrakers had their sights trained on Lloyd George and Elibank, and what drove the agitation forward was anger at the alleged propensity of ill-bred Radicals to use public office for personal enrichment.

Hypocrisy constituted the other main theme in the attacks on Liberal 'corruption'. This emerged very powerfully in the response to Lloyd George's Land Campaign, which was launched by the Chancellor at Bedford in October 1913. The campaign sought to revolutionize rural life by providing a minimum wage and improved housing for the agricultural labourer, as well as securing tenure and 'fair rents' for the farmer through the establishment of Land Courts.[63] But what infuriated the landowners was that the Land Enquiry Committee had sought information about the private circumstances of individual members of their class, and this, coupled with the land-valuation exercise, convinced them that they were the victims of a vendetta.

In October 1912 twenty-eight Unionist MPs decided to retaliate by setting up the 'Radical Plutocrats Enquiry' (RPE). Warmly backed by the *National*

---

[62] R. Jenkins, *Asquith* (London, 1964), 253.

[63] A report on urban land appeared in 1914.

Review and other right-wing papers, this shadowy organization encouraged sympathizers to write in with scandalous titbits about the antisocial behaviour of Radical landlords who closed footpaths, rode roughshod over their poor neighbours and dependants in the pursuit of sport, and generally engaged in 'swank'. The enquiry then broadened out into attacks on 'cosmopolitan millionaires', wealthy Liberal businessmen who allegedly evaded their social responsibilities and tried to push the burden of taxation on to the hard-pressed landlords. 'Tax 'EM: Liberal Plutocrats Who Could Bear Georging. NO LAND—BUT TONS OF MONEY', screamed the *Daily Express*. Maxse to the fore, the organizers of the RPE also launched bitter attacks on the hypocrisy of Liberal ministers who wept crocodile tears over the sufferings of the poor, while ostentatiously 'living it up' in Brighton or on the French Riviera—a telling hit at Lloyd George, or '£loyd George', as the wits now designated him.

Like other 'Radical Right' escapades, the RPE had something of the character of a black joke. More orthodox Conservatives expressed their unease: Pretyman, the agriculture spokesman, told Maxse that he found the project 'distasteful', while others warned against sinking to the low, sneaking methods of their opponents. The enquiry soon petered out. But for a while it had had a certain importance by exposing some of the ambiguities of Edwardian Liberalism—in particular, the contradiction between the party's reliance on a small number of wealthy business backers and its claim to be a 'people's party'.

The agitation perhaps had a still wider significance. From the 1890s onwards moralists had been shaking their heads over the phenomenon which they called 'plutocracy', a useful term that identified a new class of very rich people, drawn indiscriminately from landed society and the financial world, who led lives of unbridled and vulgar luxury.[64] At the start of the century Arnold White had inveighed against the 'bad, smart set', to which, he boldly hinted, the Prince of Wales (the future Edward VII) belonged, as well as his rich Jewish friends such as Ernest Cassel. Indeed, in many ways the new King admirably symbolized all the things that the moralists disliked, with his rackety sexual life, his addiction to luxuries of all sorts, his friendliness with American women, and his restlessness.

Edward's great love of motoring helped make the motor car a symbol of the new 'plutocracy', as it dashed along the un-tarmacadamed roads showering humble villagers with dust—witness the depiction of 'Toad' in Kenneth Grahame's *Wind in the Willows* (1908). Admittedly the tone of the court changed when Edward was succeeded by George V, whose simple family life recalled an earlier age of Victorian respectability. But the corrosive influence of plutocratic values was not so easily effaced.

---

[64] J. Camplin, *The Rise of the Plutocrats: Wealth and Power in Edwardian England* (London, 1978).

Also under attack were the so-called 'cosmopolitan financiers'. This term often served as a code word for 'rich Jews', but it carried the further implication that because capital, unlike land, was mobile and could easily be moved across national frontiers, the financier was necessarily devoid of patriotism. Cassel, a naturalized Briton, had been born in Hamburg, something which his many critics would not allow him to forget once the Great War had broken out. The influence of international finance was particularly resented by doctrinaire tariff reformers, who called for the development of national industry and lamented the emergence of a rentier economy.

But, of course, a hedonistic lifestyle was not confined to Liberals on the make, nor was 'finance' exclusively linked to the Liberal Party—indeed, Cassel, though he kept a low political profile, was donating considerable sums of money to the Tariff Commission. Insofar as the Conservatives were heavily implicated in the world of plutocracy, they had to be careful about what language they used in attacking their opponents. Nor could they have been unaware that the foremost critic of international finance earlier in the century had been the Radical J. A. Hobson, and that currently its most effective spokesmen was the maverick Hilaire Belloc, who had actually sat as a Liberal MP between 1906 and 1910.

In fact it was socialists who seized most eagerly upon the subversive potential of the attacks on plutocracy, because this afforded them countless opportunities to contrast the self-indulgence of the very rich (now increasingly visible, thanks to photography) with the wretched lives of the poor. It also put ammunition at the disposal of left-wing critics of the Lib-Lab pact. For example, those impatient of the restraints imposed by the Progressive Alliance, such as Lansbury of the *Daily Herald*, drew attention to the way in which the Labour MP on the Marconi Select Committee, James Parker, had cravenly joined the Liberals in trying to cover up for the incriminated ministers. In short, while many Conservatives believed that the Liberals were corrupt because they were parvenus, militant socialists lambasted them for being members of a capitalist party embedded in a corrupt economic order. Thus was the revolt from the right paralleled by a revolt from the left.

5. THE GREAT LABOUR UNREST

At the parliamentary level Liberals and Labour continued to co-operate quite harmoniously, especially after Ramsay MacDonald became chairman of the PLP in 1911.[65] Labour were also kept relatively docile in the aftermath of the Osborne Judgement of December 1909, when the Lords, in their judicial

---

[65] None of his predecessors, George Barnes, Arthur Henderson, or Keir Hardie, had been particularly happy in that role.

capacity, had ruled that financial donations to a political party did not count as a legitimate trade-union activity as defined by the Trade Union Amendment Act of 1876—a ruling which threatened to destroy the Labour Party's financial base.[66]

In the summer of 1911 MacDonald therefore struck a bargain with Elibank: the PLP would support the government over National Insurance, in return for which its financial plight would be eased by the introduction of payment of MPs. In 1911 legislation was accordingly passed conferring a salary of £400 p.a. upon all non-ministerial MPs. However, it is a sign of how much the Liberals took Labour for granted that not until 1913 did they get round to passing the Trade Union Act, to deal directly with the situation which the Osborne Judgement had created—a delay they explained by invoking 'parliamentary congestion'. Moreover, because of deep-seated Liberal objections to a *compulsory* level, Labour did not get the simple reversal of Osborne that it wanted.[67] Instead, the Trade Union Act authorized trade unions, whose members had agreed on a ballot to support a political party, to do so through a specially constituted political fund from which individual members were free to contract out.

MacDonald meanwhile was having great difficulties in keeping his side of the bargain. Most Labour MPs followed his lead and supported the National Insurance Bill, but Snowden, Lansbury, Fred Jowett, James O'Grady, and Will Thorne all voted against it. The rebels, most of them ILPers,[68] called instead for the abolition of the Poor Law along lines laid down by the Webbs, and for the adoption of 'true' socialist policies.

MacDonald's increasingly conventional conception of the necessity for party discipline also annoyed many of his followers. In its early years Labour had resisted the notion that it was a party at all, and even after 1906 some of its MPs still refused to canvass, seeing this as an infringement of the voter's freedom of conscience. Nor did all Labour MPs hold Commons procedure in much reverence.[69] The Labour Party's informal electoral understanding with the Liberals was a further bone of contention. All these discontents were forcefully articulated by Victor Grayson, who won Colne Valley as an 'independent socialist' at a by-election in July 1907, and then used his position in the

[66] M. Klarman, 'Parliamentary Reversal of the Osborne Judgement', *Historical Journal*, 32 (1989), 893–924; Klarman, 'Osborne: A Judgement Gone Too Far?', *English Historical Review*, 103 (1985), 21–39.

[67] Churchill's earlier Bill of 1911 had been withdrawn in the face of Labour hostility, only to be reintroduced, substantially unchanged, a year later.

[68] See previous Chapter. Thorne and O'Grady had both been sponsored by their trade unions (the Gasworkers and the Furnishing Trades, respectively), but they were also lifelong socialists—Thorne being an ex-SDFer.

[69] See Ch. 7 for Jowett.

House to disrupt Commons debates so as to draw attention to the plight of the unemployed—rather as Hardie had done earlier in his career.

In 1909 disaffected elements within the ILP joined Grayson and the ever-critical Blatchford in rallying behind *Let Us Reform the Labour Party*, the so-called 'Green Manifesto'. Ben Tillett, the trade-unionist firebrand, gave them his support, arguing that it would be much better for socialists to face defeat fighting for their principles than to risk betrayal by their political enemies. By persuading the ILP's 1909 annual conference to refer back that section of the executive's report which dealt with its parliamentary activities, the rebels provoked Snowden, Hardie, Glasier, and MacDonald into resigning from the party's National Council; the resignations were only retracted when a chastened conference gave them a vote of confidence.

Though he lost his seat in January 1910, Grayson continued to be a thorn in the side of the party leadership. In August 1911 he resigned from the ILP, calling for socialist unity, and led a number of disgruntled ILP branches into a union with the SDF; but the outcome of this initiative, the British Socialist Party (BSP), amounted to little more than the old SDF under a new name.[70] Ruined by drink, Grayson emigrated to New Zealand and disappeared.

The leadership of the Labour left then passed to George Lansbury, who combined his MP's role with the running of the *Daily Herald*, which had been launched as a strike sheet during a printers' dispute in 1911 before being relaunched as a daily on 15 April 1912. Combining the literary talents of the young Oxford don G. D. H. Cole and William Mellor with the vitriolic class-conscious cartoons of Will Dyson, the *Herald* soon boasted 50,000 to 150,000 subscribers and probably twice as many readers, quite overshadowing the Labour Party's official organ, the worthy but dull *Daily Citizen*.

Lansbury resigned his seat in November 1912 to fight a by-election as an 'independent' in protest against Labour's attitude towards the suffragette hunger-strikers, but also in order to dramatize his objections to MacDonald's particular brand of Fabian gradualism.[71] Lansbury was defeated, but he continued to wield considerable influence in the Labour Movement through the '*Herald* League', some twenty branches of which were founded in July 1914 alone. Lansbury was important because he linked the older socialist language of 'independence' to the libertarian assault on welfare politics being spearheaded by Belloc and the Chesterton brothers, but also because he espoused the cause of the militant strikers who were beginning to challenge cautious trade-union officialdom.

---

[70] K. Laybourn, 'The Failure of Socialist Unity in Britain, c.1893–1914', *Transactions of Royal Historical Society*, 40 (1994), 168–71.

[71] See below.

For, running parallel with the controversies that were agitating parliamentary Labour was the dramatic industrial upheaval known as the 'Great Labour Unrest'.[72] In 1909 the total number of working days lost in stoppages had been only 2,690,000. It then rose in the following years to 9,870,000, 10,160,000, and 40,890,000 in 1912 (a record), before stabilizing at just under 10 million for the remaining pre-war period. What characterized the 'Great Labour Unrest', especially in 1911–12, was the occurrence of a small number of very big strikes, conducted on both sides with great bitterness and obduracy, which, because they were located in key industries, made a huge impact on the wider community.

One of the earliest of these large-scale conflicts involved coalminers in the Rhondda Valley, where, because the easy seams had been exhausted and output per head was lower than elsewhere, a contentious restructuring of labour practices was taking place. On 1 September 1910 the Cambrian Combine locked out its men at the Ely pit over what should be the rate of pay in a newly opened seam. The conflict widened to cover the issue of 'abnormal places', and later became linked to the miners' growing demand for a minimum wage. By the time that the Cambrian miners had returned to work, defeated, nearly a year later, 3 million work days had been lost.

While the Cambrian dispute was still unresolved, members of Havelock Wilson's Sailors and Firemen's Union struck in June 1911, first in Southampton, then in almost every other major port. Loosely co-ordinated by the newly created National Transport Workers Federation (NTWF), a weak grouping of some thirty largely autonomous organizations, the dispute rapidly spread to dockers and carters, bringing chaos to the waterfront—rather as had happened in 1889. The employers' organization, the Shipping Federation, was caught by surprise, and the seamen won a series of stunning victories over wage-rates and manning scales. So did the dockers, their hands strengthened by the adhesion to their strike on 29 July of the London members of Tillett's Dock, Wharf, Riverside, and General Workers Union.

Then, in mid-August 1911, some of the Liverpool employees of the Lancashire and Yorkshire Railway walked out, precipitating an official national rail strike. The leaders of the four main unions involved wanted to give the conciliation boards that had been set up in 1907 the power to confer pay awards, and they also hoped to coerce the employers into recognizing their organizations. On 19 August Lloyd George's dramatic intervention[73] succeeded in getting the strike called off on terms broadly favourable to the unions (a royal comission was set up to investigate the men's grievances against the

---

[72] H. A. Clegg, *A History of British Trade Unions Since 1889: Vol. II: 1911–1933* (Oxford, 1985), Ch. 2.

[73] See below and Ch. 13.

1907 agreement)—but not before Tom Mann, who had arrived in Liverpool as secretary of the district committee of the NTWF, found himself leading a sympathetic strike of all the transport workers in that city, a strike which soon acquired a momentum of its own, pulling in waterside workers in other ports, such as Hull and Cardiff.

A period of relative tranquillity then set it, broken only by a stoppage of the cotton weavers between December 1911 and January 1912. But a month later the Miners Federation of Great Britain (MFGB) came out in support of the 'five and two', that is to say, a minimum wage-rate of 5s. a shift for men and 2s. for boys. The strike, potentially the most serious to date, lasted about five weeks and had a serious knock-on effect: large numbers were laid off in the railway and transport industries and swathes of manufacturing were effectively shut down: particularly badly affected were the potteries, where 80 per cent of the workforce found themselves unemployed.[74] 'This coal strike is the beginning of a revolution', Grey confided to a friend.[75] A shaken Asquith rushed through Parliament a Miners' Minimum Wage Act, which went some way to meeting the strikers' demands by creating wage boards empowered to set regional minima, but not a national one; the miners were balloted and turned the deal down, but the MFGB executive nevertheless called the strike off, on the ground that less than two-thirds of the membership had endorsed its continuation.

Scarcely had the national coal strike ended than 100,000 dockers in the Port of London came out once more. This time the employers were well prepared and, with dockers in other ports failing to rally to the Londoners' support and with the sailors and firemen also holding aloof, Tillett's men stood little chance of success: they were forced back to work in August, their union membership depleted by 15,000, having forfeited most of their recent gains.

The following year, 1913, saw a record number of strikes, 1,497 in all. Unlike the stoppages of the two preceding years, most were relatively small-scale affairs, scattered across a wide range of industries—with one notable exception. In the autumn serious trouble flared in Dublin, where the newly founded Irish Transport and General Workers Union (ITGWU) became drawn into a series of conflicts with the town's major employer, William Martin Murphy (who was also an Irish Nationalist MP). The ITGWU's general secretary was 'Big Jim' Larkin, an inspirational but febrile leader, who whipped his followers into a frenzy of excitement as he carried his fiery cross through the local slums (some of the worst in Europe). The conflict began with Murphy sacking ITGWU men from his paper, the *Independent*. The

---

[74] Unemployment temporarily rose to 11.3% at the end of March, though it soon fell back.

[75] Grey to Katharine Lyttelton, 8 Apr. 1912, in G. M. Trevelyan, *Grey of Trevelyan* (London, 1937), 176–7.

dockers then retaliated by boycotting the paper's distributors; this was in breach of an agreement with the port companies, which now entered the fray. On 3 September, after fighting had broken out between union and non-union men on the Dublin tramways, Murphy persuaded 400 of his fellow employers to lock out all members of the ITGWU. The bitter dispute dragged on for almost half a year, ending in a comprehensive defeat for the union.

Ireland was, in many ways, a place apart, and no one was surprised when serious violence occurred in Dublin—notably between 30 August and 1 September, after which Larkin was arrested and imprisoned (though soon afterwards released on bail). But violence, to a lesser or greater extent, marked nearly all the industrial conflicts of the 1911–14 period. Coal strikes were traditionally quite peaceful affairs, if only because blackleg labour could not easily be imported and, as a future miners' leader once memorably observed, 'you can't cut coal with bayonets'. However, during the Cambrian dispute in November 1910 public order broke down in Tonypandy, where a mass meeting of miners trying to win over the safety men ended with rioters attacking and looting Jewish-owned shops.[76] Churchill, the Home Secretary, sent in police reinforcements followed by troops,[77] but before calm could be restored one striker had been killed and over 500 injured.

Equally ugly scenes were enacted in the transport industry and on the waterfront, where union density was traditionally low and the threat of blacklegging high. On 13 August 1911 the Riot Act had to be read in Liverpool, where sectarian fighting briefly added to the mayhem; in the resulting disturbances over 200 people were injured and there were two fatalities, one a policeman. The Home Office received hysterical appeals from local mayors, backed by Lord Derby, who roundly declared that this was no ordinary riot but that 'a revolution was in progress'. The government responded by dispatching a warship to the Mersey, where it anchored off Birkenhead with its guns trained on Liverpool.

By late 1911 some 2,300 troops were stationed on Merseyside. Another large force, under the command of Major-General Nevil Macready, was dispatched to South Wales, where it behaved like an army of occupation. On 18 August a train driven by blackleg labour at Llanelli came under attack from rioters, who assaulted the driver and knocked him unconscious; the troops responded by shooting two men dead. Revolutionary turbulence spasmodically affected other industrial areas, too, often taking the form of attacks on property and threats of sabotage. George Askwith, the Board of Trade's Labour Commissioner, was perturbed to hear a meeting of striking dockers in Hull interrupted by cries from the audience of 'let's fire the docks', and a councillor who had been in

---

[76] Jews were also driven from their shops in Ebbw Vale in the summer of 1911.

[77] See A. M. O'Brien, 'Churchill and the Tonypandy Riots', *Welsh Historical Review*, 17 (1994), 67–99

Paris during the Commune said that the events in that town reminded him of those tempestuous times.[78] Even more common was looting, to contain which magistrates (encouraged by the Home Office) swore in special constables. This heightened tension still further.

At times the country appeared to be on the verge of civil war. In early 1912 Mann and Guy Bowman were imprisoned under the Incitement to Mutiny Act of 1797 for publishing a 'Don't Shoot' leaflet addressed to troops. Another revolutionary journal, the *Syndicalist*, carried an article in January 1912 entitled 'Learn to Shoot Straight'. Even Tillett, addressing his union in 1912, urged members to 'protest against violence, with violence',[79] though his words were not perhaps meant to be taken literally.

What also gave the industrial disputes of these years an exhilarating, or alarming, character (depending on one's point of view) was the unprecedented employment of the sympathy strike. Disruption tended to flicker back and forth between different industries, often in defiance of the union leadership—as happened in Liverpool, where railwaymen, in contact with waterfront workers, initially came out on a wildcat strike, which was only later declared official. Indeed, workers sometimes downed tools as a gesture of solidarity with fellow workers, and only *then* framed their own demands, demands which often struck outsiders as being either 'unrealistic' or imprecise. When Askwith, on a mission of conciliation, visited the port of Hull in the summer of 1911, he was upset not only by the spectacle of 'women with hair streaming and half nude, reeling through the streets, smashing and destroying', but also by the absence of anyone with whom he could negotiate, the men having disowned their accredited officials.[80]

'The new-fangled strike is less of a haggle, far more of a display of temper', declared H. G. Wells. Frightened observers were often driven back upon metaphor. *The Times* ascribed the unrest to a psychological malady: 'LABOUR AGITATION GONE MAD', ran its headline of 16 August 1911. Some likened what was happening to the spread of a contagious fever or to a fire that had flared out of control. More prosaically, others simply blamed the sweltering heat.

The spirit of rebellion could take the most unlikely of forms. It briefly disrupted professional football, and threw the music halls into confusion.[81] In

---

[78] G. R. A. Askwith, *Industrial Problems and Disputes* (London, 1920), 150.

[79] Report for 1912, cited in A. Bullock, *The Life and Times of Ernest Bevin: Vol I: Trade Union Leader, 1881–1940* (London, 1960), 35.

[80] Askwith, *Industrial Problems*, 148–50.

[81] R. Holt, *Sport and the British: A Modern History* (Oxford, 1989), 298. Joseph Bevir Williams's Amalgamated Musicians' Union staged a strike in 1907, and it needed Askwith to step in as an arbitrator to impose a settlement upon the provincial halls in 1912 (C. Ehrlich, *The Music Profession in Britain Since the Eighteenth Century: A Social History* (Oxford, 1985), 147–8, 173, 182). For other trouble in theatreland, see M. Sanderson, *From Irvine to Olivier: A Social History of the Acting Profession in England, 1888–1983* (London, 1984), 103–7.

1911 schoolchildren came out 'on strike' in sixty-two towns and villages, though the most famous of such episodes, the one occurring in April 1914 in the Norfolk village of Burston, was really an expression of indignation against the tyranny of the local clergyman, and was linked to a new 'rebellion of the field' involving the normally apathetic agricultural workers.[82]

More than anything else, it was an intense class-conscious anger which turned what might otherwise have been a disconnected set of industrial disputes into what had the appearance of a Worker's Rebellion. 'The class war is the most brutal of wars and the most pitiless', declared Tillett: 'Capitalism is capitalism as a tiger is a tiger; and both are savage and pitiless towards the weak.'[83] Such feelings proved strong enough to vault over both religious differences and ethnic and linguistic divisions.[84]

Syndicalism was sometimes blamed for this upsurge of class hatred. Syndicalism was a version of socialism which totally rejected the Fabian concept of the neutral state and defiantly preached the necessity of class warfare.[85] Its advocates contended that the working class must unite across the boundaries of craft, industry, and geographical district, until eventually the point was reached where it could overthrow the capitalist order by an apocalyptic 'general strike'—the necessary prelude to the inauguration of a workers' republic in which ultimate power would rest, not with a nationalized board, but with workers at the point of production, 'workers' control' being the declared objective. Syndicalism shared with anarchism a commitment to 'spontaneity', perhaps partially under the influence of George Sorel's book *Reflections on Violence*, which idealized a rank-and-file that was supposedly pure at heart though misrepresented by reactionary and out-of-touch Labour 'bureaucrats'. Syndicalism was also closely allied with 'industrial unionism', the creed elaborated by the American labour leader Daniel De Leon, which called for new industrial unions, containing skilled and unskilled alike, to work alongside existing organizations ('dual unionism').

But although the Great Labour Unrest superficially looks like a manifestation of these beliefs, probably no more than 2,000 militant workers formally subscribed to them. The newspaper of the British syndicalists admitted that, of the strike leaders in 1911–12, few had ever pronounced the word 'syndicalist' and not 5 per cent of them knew what it meant. Yet self-avowed syndicalists *did*

---

[82] A. Howkins, *Poor Labouring Men: Rural Radicalism in Norfolk 1870–1923* (London, 1985), 115–16. In the Burston school strike, pupils, backed by their parents, came out in support of one of their teachers, Tom Higdon, who had been dismissed from his post at the behest of the local vicar. Higdon's offence was that, as well as being a socialist, he sat on the executive of the village branch of the Agricultural Labourers' Union.

[83] Bullock, *Bevin, Volume I*, 35.

[84] Though it could not neutralize native antipathy to the Chinese in South Wales.

[85] B. Holton, *British Syndicalism 1900–1914* (London, 1976).

occupy a number of important positions in the trade-union movement. Their best-known leader was the veteran socialist agitator Tom Mann, who in 1910 returned to England from Australia via America, where he had encountered De Leon's organization, the 'International Workers of the World' (IWW), before travelling with a fellow socialist, Guy Bowman, to Paris to study the ideas and practices of the French syndicalists.[86] In September Mann set up the Industrial Syndicalist Education League in Manchester, and soon afterwards was popularizing his new beliefs in strike-torn Liverpool, where his paper, the *Transport Worker*, had a circulation of 20,000.

Moreover, in South Wales syndicalism had powerful backing from the Unofficial Reform Committee, whose leader, Noah Ablett, composed the influential *The Miners' Next Step* (1912), which inspired a younger generation of miners disillusioned with the cautious approach of the executive of the South Wales Miners Federation (SWMF).[87] Larkin, too, was an instinctive syndicalist, while his lieutenant in Dublin, James Connolly, had been deeply involved in the Socialist Labour Party (SLP), an industrial unionist organization with a strong presence on the Clyde that had been founded in 1903 as a breakaway from the SDF.

'Dual unionism''s only triumph was the creation of the Building Workers' Industrial Union, amongst the leaders of which were several prominent De Leonites, such as Jack Wills. This bitterly class-conscious union was involved in an unsuccessful five-month struggle with the London builders, which occupied much of 1914. But syndicalists were active in the Amalgamation Movement which tried, through the organization of a shop stewards' movement, to break down the divisions between competing unions in engineering, where the traditional boundary between craftsman and labourer was being increasingly eroded by technological advance. Mann, an engineer by trade, actually managed to secure 25 per cent of the poll when standing in 1913 for the presidency of the Amalgamated Society of Engineers (ASE), hitherto a preserve of 'labour aristocrats'.

The emergence in the same year of the National Union of Railwaymen (NUR), which brought together all the rail unions bar the standoffish footplate workers (of the Associated Society of Locomotive Engineers and Firemen) and the railway clerks, was also a victory, of sorts, for 'amalgamation'. But practical rather than theoretical considerations provided its underlying rationale: significantly, its first Political Secretary was the very moderate Labour MP for

---

[86] De Leon was the leader of the Socialist Labor Party. He played a role in the IWW after its foundation in 1905, but was eliminated as a presence by 1908. His advocacy of political action was decisively rejected by the anarcho-syndicalists of the IWW.

[87] Ablett was a member of the Plebs League, set up in late 1908 by Ruskin College and Central Labour College students to propagate the revolutionary socialist message.

Derby J. H. ('Jimmy') Thomas, who made little attempt to pass himself off as a socialist of any kind. In short, although syndicalists supported industrial unions for ideological reasons, the few amalgamations of the period would probably have taken place regardless. Besides which, the most striking outcome of the Great Labour Unrest, as in 1888–9, was the spread of general unions embracing the unskilled across a range of industries, not the organization of the proletariat on an industry-by-industry basis. However, although syndicalism as a coherent, self-conscious movement achieved little before 1914, it was more influential as a 'mood'.

What underlay the discontents upon which the syndicalists tried to capitalize? Changes in the structure of world trade lay at the source of many industrial disputes. Foreign competition had intensified during the early twentieth century as traditional export markets contracted, and this sharpened the determination of employers to 'speed up' and 'drive' their workforce: for example, by the use of piecework in engineering and of subcontracting in the building trades. Such a development was accelerated by the replacement of smaller, family-owned firms by larger corporations, such as the Cambrian Combine, whose salaried managers were less prone to adopt a paternalistic attitude towards their men. In particular, after 1910 industrial life was increasingly invaded by 'scientific management', or 'Taylorism' as it was often called (after F. W. Taylor, the American engineering consultant). This involved the breaking-down of jobs into their component parts and the basing of piece-rates upon a system of incentives. Craftsmen found the new approach irksome, because it destroyed their control over the work process and largely bypassed collective bargaining. Another grievance was the growing subdivision of labour, which tended to throw up new management hierarchies, with their own recruitment schemes, blocking the upward mobility of the ambitious artisan.

Such pressures were particularly intense in industries such as the railways, where rising costs could not automatically be recouped by higher charges to the consumer, since freight rates were regulated by government. Coalmining also experienced problems, caused in part by the exhaustion of the easy seams and in part by the increased costs imposed upon it by government (for example, through eight-hour-day legislation); even though profitability remained buoyant in the coal industry, employers were tempted to meet these difficulties through a strict control of the wages bill, which formed as much as 80 per cent of their total operating costs. Not all these employer initiatives were successful; some were actually counter-productive. But nearly all groups of manual workers *thought* that their conditions of employment were deteriorating, and trade unionism fuelled the resulting discontent.

Employer pressure did not always take the form of coercive labour practices. It also encouraged a move to establish nationwide conciliation schemes, along the lines of the famous Brooklands Agreement of 1893, under which joint procedures were agreed for adjusting wages and resolving disputes; the sixty-four conciliation and arbitration boards in place in 1894 had grown to 325 by 1913.[88] This development enjoyed the backing of successive governments. Indeed, the Conciliation (Trade Disputes) Act of 1896, which replaced earlier, ineffectual legislation, empowered the Board of Trade to put itself forward as a mediator in industrial disputes, which it increasingly did after 1906: some 10 per cent of all industrial stoppages, affecting 25 per cent of workers engaged in strikes and lockouts, were settled in this way between 1906 and 1914.[89] Even though a new body, the Industrial Council, created in 1911, was usually ignored by both sides, Askwith, representing a supposedly neutral government, played an important role as an abitrator, in pursuit of which he encouraged the consolidation of moderate and 'responsible' trade unionism within a voluntary framework.

But such official interventions were fiercely resented by class-conscious socialists—understandably so, since they more often served the interests of the employers than those of their workforce. Well might the ILP call the Conciliation Act 'the most effective device by which the trade union movement [had] been humbugged by the dominant class'.[90] Moreover, the practice of conciliation drew trade-union executives willy-nilly into the function of labour management, and this often caused strain with rank-and-file activists, who complained that the union's democratic procedures were being flouted. Hence the abuse hurled at labour bureaucrats by militant workers who, in turn, were attacked by their own leaders for indiscipline and demagoguery. Larkin, a one-time official of James Sexton's Liverpool-based Dockers' Union, became a spokesman for these rank-and-file dissidents, directing his ire especially at Sexton himself, who had additionally laid himself open to attack as a result of his sybaritic lifestyle and his matiness with Lord Derby.

Paradoxically, another cause of worker discontent was the introduction of state welfare legislation. True, many shopworkers, Post Office employees, and clerks responded to the National Insurance Act by joining trade unions, which could also function as 'approved societies'. The Workers' Union (founded by Mann in 1898, but now led by the moderate Labour MP Charles Duncan) was the fastest-growing of all trade unions because it vigorously took up the claims of workmen caught up in the scheme's intricacies.[91] But welfare legislation

---

[88] V. Gore, 'Rank-and-File Dissent', in C. Wrigley (ed.), *A History of British Industrial Relations 1875–1914* (Brighton, 1982), 67.

[89] R. Davidson, 'Government Administration', in C. J. Wrigley (ed.), *A History of British Industrial Relations 1875–1914* (Brighton, 1982), 168.

[90] Davidson, 'Government Administration', 169.

[91] H. Pelling, *Popular Politics and Society in Late Victorian Britain* (London, 1968), 154–5.

sometimes directly provoked industrial conflict. For example, the Durham coal strike of 1910, the first major dispute of the Great Labour Unrest, was a protest over the implementation of the eight-hour day, which, by disrupting the traditional shift system, had interfered with normal family life.

Straightforward economic considerations also came into play. Most workers already had plenty of reasons for discontent with their low pay, but this was exacerbated after 1900 by the tendency of prices to rise faster than wages, as the international terms of trade turned against Britain. Whereas living standards had significantly improved during the latter quarter of the nineteenth century, real wages were now being checked and even pushed back. Between 1900 and 1910 trade-union efforts to maintain the living standards of their members had been inhibited, first by the Taff Vale Judgement, and then, after the passing of the 1906 Trades Disputes Act, by the sharp recession of 1908–9, when unemployment probably exceeded 9 per cent.[92] Then, in 1910, trade prosperity returned, causing unemployment to plummet—not to rise above 3.3 per cent until the outbreak of the Great War.

This created the classic conditions for trade unions to expand their membership, which rose from just over 2,500,000 in 1910 to over 4,100,000 in 1914, and to launch an aggressive push for higher wages. It can be no coincidence that 1913, the year that witnessed most strikes, was also the year when unemployment fell to its lowest point since 1899, only 2.1 per cent. Most strikes between 1910 and 1914 were successful, only one in seven ending in outright defeat for the union, and by 1914 average real wages had caught up with the rising cost of living—though some groups, notably the miners, did fall behind. But whatever the outcome, underlying nearly all of these stoppages was the workers' demand, in the face of employer pressure, that a 'living wage' be the first charge on industry—in other words, that wages should determine prices, not the other way round. Hence the unpopularity of labour leaders who continued to stick to older conciliation devices such as sliding-scale agreements.

All the same, on mainland Britain union officials generally kept control over their rank-and-file critics. For example, nationalization, denounced in *The Miners' Next Step* as a form of state capitalism, remained the favourite option among organized workers and won overwhelming support at the 1912 TUC Congress.[93] Moreover, in 1914 the limits of the 'sympathetic strike' were reached when British trade unions refused to go beyond providing humanitarian aid to the Dublin workers (they raised a fund eventually totaling £94,000 and sent a food ship). Larkin called in vain for an embargo on all goods going to

---

[92] For the pressure on real wages, see Ch. 11.

[93] Carried by 1,693,000 to 48,000 (B. C. Roberts, *The Trade Union Congress, 1868–1921* (London, 1958), 253).

Dublin, and when he once again denounced the British trade-union leaders for their cowardice, a special conference held in December condemned him for these 'unfair attacks'. In particular, Thomas, the railwaymen's leader, savaged by Larkin as 'a double-dyed traitor', was supported by his members, who were tired of constantly being asked to make sacrifices for other unions, the actions of which they were powerless to determine.

Before 1914 the syndicalist wave was starting to turn. However, before doing so it had thrown the socialist world into turmoil, opening up a profound ideological division between the advocates of workers' control and those who continued to cling to an older sense of popular sovereignty and community. The ILP, which had always viewed trade unionism as a narrow and unintelligent expression of sectional selfishness, had even less time for syndicalism, a creed which, if Snowden was to be believed, reduced men to the status of mere producers, ignoring their other roles as consumers and as citizens—a line of argument also pursued by the Webbs. Hyndman, too, despised syndicalism and eventually managed to stop its proponents seizing control of the BSP—but only after a series of ructions and expulsions which saw the membership of that society drop from 40,000 in 1912 to 13,500 a year later.

'Direct action' and 'workers' control' threatened the Parliamentary Labour Party even more profoundly. For syndicalists were scornful of the compromises of party politics and parliamentary institutions: Tillett, catching the new mood, called them 'a farce and a sham', while the *Daily Herald* had a Westminster column entitled 'the House of Pretence'. The PLP, many of whose leaders doubled up as union officials, hit back. In 1911 four Labour MPs, one of them Henderson, tabled a bill which would have made strikes illegal unless thirty days' advance notice had been given,[94] and during the Dublin lockout Labour MPs actually put themselves forward as 'impartial' mediators between the two sides—to Larkin's predictable fury. Clynes, the one-time firebrand of the Gasworkers Union, gave another reason for the PLP's mistrust of syndicalism when he observed in 1914 that 'too frequent strikes caused a sense of disgust, of being a nuisance to the community'.[95]

The Great Labour Unrest impacted even more dramatically on Labour's political partner, the Liberal Party. Even an advanced 'New Liberal' such as Hobhouse saw the advocacy of class conflict as the negation of all that he held dear—social harmony, consensus resulting from reasoned discussion, and so on. Lloyd George spoke for most Liberals when, in March 1908, he declared his antipathy to all strikes and lockouts: 'The weak goes to the wall whether he

---

[94] R. Miliband, *Parliamentary Socialism: A Study in the Politics of Labour* (London, 1961; 1964 edn.), 35.
[95] Ibid. 38.

has justice at his back or not', he said, while hardship was visited upon workers in allied trades and on 'women and children, the weak, the feeble, the aged'.[96] As always, Lloyd George's sympathies were with the poor, not with the organized working class as such.

The events of 1910–14 also challenged the Liberal Party's claim to be a 'national party' capable of harmonizing capital and labour. More immediately, it triggered off sharp disputes within the Cabinet. Churchill called for an inquiry into the 'causes and remedies' of industrial unrest, of which he took an alarmist view:

a new force has arisen in trade unionism, whereby the power of the old leaders has proved quite ineffective, and the sympathetic strike on a wide scale is prominent. Shipping, coal, railways, dockers etc. etc. are all uniting and breaking out at once. The general strike 'policy' is a factor which must be dealt with.[97]

On the other hand, Sydney Buxton, the President of the Board of Trade, urged patience and caution, rightly seeing that industrial relations would only be inflamed still further if attempts were made to regulate them by law.[98]

Indeed, some ministers were so eager to have the major strikes settled that they recklessly put themselves forward as mediators. Thus Lloyd George, pleading patriotic necessity during the Agadir Crisis, managed to have the national rail strike called off after he had banged the heads of the two sides together. Dockland proved less amenable to this sort of interventionism, but John Burns's finest hour came in August 1911, when he helped the Labour Department of the Board of Trade to secure an agreement in the Port of London, his former stamping-ground. But the trick could not always be pulled off. In the dockers' strike of 1912 no fewer than four ministers, one of them Lloyd George, made bungled attempts to intervene in the Port of London dispute—earning Askwith's justifiable contempt.

The 1912 miners' strike similarly revealed the fault-lines within Liberalism. Lloyd George and Buxton would have been happy to cede the 'five and two', as would Edward Grey, who actually proposed (privately) that the coalowners be indemnified by the Treasury for the consequential loss to the tune of one-quarter of a million pounds—a suggestion which the Prime Minister promptly squashed. Churchill, on the other hand, wanted the miners to be 'taught a lesson'. These disagreements extended into the parliamentary party. When the government's compromise Bill was going through committee stage, the Labour Party put down an amendment in favour of the 'five and two' which attracted

---

[96] C. J. Wrigley, *David Lloyd George and the British Labour Movement* (Hassocks, 1976), 59–60.

[97] R. S. Churchill, *Winston S. Churchill: Young Statesman 1901–1914* (London, 1967), 379.

[98] Ministers (and the Opposition frontbench) considered, only to reject, the legal enforcement of contracts.

the support of forty-five Liberal backbenchers (plus one Conservative who had wandered into the wrong lobby!). It thus needed the Opposition to save the government from defeat.

The Liberal government sought to maintain its 'neutrality' during the Great Labour Unrest, but in doing so merely alienated both sides. In some ways government found it easier to coerce the employers than it did their workforce, as the railway companies and the coalowners ruefully discovered. On the other hand, the government's responsibility for maintaining law and order and ensuring the uninterrupted supply of food to 'innocent' members of the public was often interpreted as a manifestation of hostility to the trade-union movement. It was an impression fortified by memories of the 1911 Tonypandy incident and by what Mrs Masterman called Churchill's 'whiff-of-grapeshot' attitude. When this resulted in deaths at Llanelli in 1911, the fury of the Labour Party knew no bounds: 'the men who have been shot down have been murdered by the Government in the interests of the capitalist system', raged Hardie in his pamphlet *Killing No Murder*. The day after the Llanelli incident Churchill authorized the moving of troops around the country during the rail strike without first receiving a requisition from the civil authorities.[99] Another sinister feature of the Great Labour Unrest, in socialist eyes, was the broad bipartisanship that developed at Westminster, with the Conservative Opposition generally supporting the government in its stand against working-class 'extremism' (in marked contrast to its hostility to the government on all matters Irish).

Nor did it help the 'Progressive Alliance' that many of the employers at the centre of these industrial disputes were themselves prominent Liberal politicians and activists: for example, D. A. Thomas (the future Lord Rhondda), until December 1910 MP for Merthyr Tydfil, was head of the Cambrian Combine and thus a prominent target for the hostility of trade unionists, who compared him (unfavourably) with the Tsar of Russia. Also hated was the Chairman of the Port of London Authority, Lord Devonport, another one-time Liberal MP (and junior minister). In 1912 Tillett led the striking dockers on Tower Hill in public prayer: 'Oh God, strike Lord Devonport dead!'

The Great Labour Unrest also impinged on the Liberal Party by 'radicalizing' many trade unions. For example, the MFGB was the last of the major manual unions to switch to Labour, which it only did in 1908–9; yet by 1912 the membership had elected as its national president the Scottish miners' leader Robert Smillie, a lifetime member of the ILP. Even the Agricultural Labourers' Union in Norfolk, once closely allied to Radical Liberalism, had

[99] J. Morgan, *Conflict and Order: The Police and Labour Disputes in England and Wales 1900–1939* (Oxford, 1987), 54–6.

largely broken free by 1914, after a series of bitter clashes with Liberal farmers. These developments would in time transform the Labour Party itself, making a co-operative relationship with the Liberals increasingly difficult to sustain. Hence the paradox that the syndicalist 'mood', hostile to all forms of parliamentary politics, probably left as its main legacy the desire to create a more effective, militant, and independent Labour Party.

Another consequence of the Great Labour Unrest was a rise of over 60 per cent in trade-union membership between 1910 and 1914.[100] After the passing of the Trade Union Act in 1913, this meant that the Labour Party's income also increased, because only a tiny number of trade unionists chose to contract out of the political levy. Flush with funds, Labour was able to develop its local organization. A remarkable feature of these years was the spontaneous appearance of what, to all intents and purposes, were divisional Labour parties— anticipating the structural changes later agreed to at the end of the Great War. The London Labour Party, for example, was founded in May 1914.[101]

Improved organization and healthier finances in turn stimulated a rush of new parliamentary candidacies, even though this meant contesting a constituency currently held by a Liberal. Between 1912 and the outbreak of war the Labour Party was involved in no fewer than fifteen triangular contests, a testimony to its newfound ambition to break free from the restraints of the 'Lib-Lab pact'. True, Labour came bottom of the poll in every single case, but the setback may not have been as serious as appears at first sight, since many of these by-elections took place on the Midlands coalfield, where working-class Liberalism remained exceptionally strong, while in other cases Labour was contesting a constituency for the first time.

Therefore, the Progressive Alliance was in a precarious state in 1914. In a sense the two parties needed either to move closer together or to drift further apart. The case for doing the former was very compelling: as a result of their by-election rivalry, the two parties had allowed the Unionists to win five seats on a minority of votes cast.[102] Moreover, were Labour aggression to provoke the Liberals into running their own candidates against sitting Labour MPs, the PLP might, in Snowden's view, be reduced to barely half-a-dozen Members. The reform of the Conservative machine instituted by Bonar Law after 1912,

---

[100] That is, members of unions affiliated to the TUC. Perhaps surprisingly, the militant miners did not make significant gains, and the membership of the SWMF actually declined. Part of the union expansion is attributable to the provisions of Part 1 of the National Insurance Act: the Shop Assistants, for example, almost trebled their membership between the end of 1911 and the end of 1912 (H. Pelling, *Popular Politics and Society in Late Victorian Britain* (London, 1968), 153).

[101] R. McKibbin, *The Evolution of the Labour Party 1910–1924* (Oxford, 1974), Ch. 2.

[102] There were five constituencies, won by the Liberals in a straight fight in December 1910, in which the Conservative majority at a later by-election was less than the Labour vote. In addition, the Conservatives won Derby North-East as a result of a Liberal intervention.

with Arthur Steel-Maitland installed as Party Chairman, made it quite likely that the Opposition would win the forthcoming general election. The breakdown of the Progressive Alliance would still further have boosted Bonar Law's chances—a prospect which alarmed Liberals and mainstream Labour alike.

Against this background, Elibank sounded out MacDonald in October 1912 (several such hints had been dropped earlier), as to whether he might be prepared to serve in a Liberal government, even though 'a proper coalition . . . was impossible as yet'. Then, in March 1914, with the storm-clouds gathering over Ulster, Lloyd George offered MacDonald a new electoral pact, an agreed programme for implementation after the next election, and, if Labour desired it, representation in the Cabinet. The offer was discussed at the NEC on 17 March, but Hardie killed it off by leaking the story to Fenner Brockway, editor of the *Labour Leader*, who raised it, with Snowden's support, at a flabbergasted meeting of the ILP Conference at Easter: MacDonald had to deny his involvement.[103] More hopeful were the efforts being made to trim to modest dimensions the number of Labour candidates standing at the next general election so as to preserve the anti-Unionist front. As many as 170 Labour candidates had been provisionally selected by 1914, but nothing like that number would actually have stood.[104]

By contrast, at the level of local politics, where the main struggle usually revolved around the level of rates needed to pay for municipal services, the Labour and Liberal parties were often at one another's throats, even in a town such as Norwich, where the 'Lib-Lab pact' had operated smoothly in all three parliamentary elections. Indeed, formal anti-Labour pacts were already well established in 1913 in a number of towns, such as Leeds. In 1913, its peak year before the Great War as far as municipal politics was concerned, Labour contested 123 English and Welsh municipalities (London excluded) and saw 171 of its 426 candidates elected, of whom, significantly, only twenty had been returned unopposed, while of the rest at least 30 per cent had been opposed by Liberals, Progressives, and Municipal Reformers.[105] Could the animosity engendered in such contests be prevented for ever and a day from spilling over into the sphere of national politics?

The Gladstone–MacDonald electoral arrangement of 1903, originally envisaged as a short-term expedient, had lasted much longer than its creators had intended. But the very existence of the pact suggests that the 'New Liberalism'

---

[103] D. Marquand, *Ramsay MacDonald* (London, 1977), Ch. 8.

[104] McKibbin, *Evolution of Labour Party*, Ch. 3; D. Tanner, *Political Change and the Labour Party 1900–1918* (Cambridge, 1990), 325–37.

[105] M. G. Sheppard and J. Halstead, 'Labour's Municipal Election Performance in Provincial England and Wales, 1901–13', *Bulletin of the Society for the Study of Labour History*, 39 (1979), 39–62. For a salutary warning about exaggerating Labour's advance on the basis of a faulty analysis of election statistics, see D. Tanner, 'Elections, Statistics, and the Rise of the Labour Party, 1906–1931', *Historical Journal*, 34 (1991), 893–908.

had in no way blocked Labour's advance. Indeed, the two parties were only able to co-operate as effectively as they did because they made an appeal to different social constituencies. The Labour Party still operated from a restricted geographical base, nearly all its parliamentary and municipal candidates coming from the industrial areas of Scotland, Wales, and the North of England, plus a few in or near the East End of London. In none of these areas was the Liberal Party particularly strong.

However, at a more fundamental level Labour's appeal rested on its claim that working-class electors had a right to be represented by men of their own class—a claim which 'advanced' social policies could do nothing to deflect. Many Labour activists had come by 1914 to reject the Liberal Party, not for what it was doing, but for what it was.

True, working-class Liberalism had not disappeared as a force by 1914; it was strong on some coalfields and still commanded the loyalty of the likes of Walter Osborne, Secretary of the Walthamstow branch of the Amalgamated Society of Railways Servants, a head porter at Clapton, whose objection to having to pay money into the Labour Party had precipitated the famous judgement which bore his name.[106] When the trade unions balloted their members in 1913–14 over whether or not to establish a political fund, sixty out of sixty-three unions agreed to do so, but in many of these the minority vote was quite high—for example, 43 per cent of the miners, 44 per cent of the weavers, and 38 per cent of the engineers, the figures in all cases being of votes cast (many workers not participating in the ballot)—probably a reflection of the survival of old Lib-Lab allegiances and, to a lesser extent, of working-class Toryism (though some votes might have come from revolutionary socialists who thought the Labour Party a waste of time). Nor should we underestimate the capacity of many Labour politicians, especially those from its socialist wing, to offend potential working-class supporters with their patronizing didacticism: the coarse-grained Jimmy Thomas, so popular with his Derby constituents, being a notable exception.

On the other hand, there is strong evidence supporting the view that younger working men tended to be more critical of Liberalism and more willing to give Labour its chance than older men, who were more firmly set in their ways. In coalmining the greatest militancy was to be found among semi-skilled workers, including the pitboys, who would have been the chief beneficiaries of the 'five and two', not the hewers who had once dominated the MFGB: the former mostly did not yet have the vote, but it would only be a matter of time before they did so.[107]

---

[106] Though, ironically, the judgement went much wider than he had intended, damaging Lib-Lab MPs like Bell and Burt as well as Labour stalwarts like Henderson.

[107] R. Church, 'Edwardian Labour Unrest and Coalfield Militancy, 1890–1914', *Historical Journal*, 30 (1987), 841–57.

6. THE WOMEN'S REVOLT

Also driving the two parties of progress further apart, despite the determination of both sets of leaders to patch up an accomodation, were the activities of the Women's Labour League and the Women's Co-operative Guild (WCG), which on the eve of the war were beginning to reach out to the very poor in ways that were not tainted by the craft exclusiveness and the concern for 'respectability' shown by an earlier generation of (male) Labour leaders.[108] The growing assertiveness of women, in other words, represented another challenge to the traditional political assumptions on which Liberal political rule had long rested. How did the Liberals respond to this new challenge?

Despite the foundation in 1897 of the National Union of Women's Suffrage Societies (NUWSS) under the presidency of Millicent Fawcett,[109] the issue of women's suffrage seemed to have gone to sleep after the excitement of earlier decades: no Bills or resolutions at all came before the Commons between 1897 and 1904. But the end of the Boer War opened up new possibilities. The initiative came, not from the NUWSS executive—still little more than a cross between a debating society and a genteel pressure group—but from one of its affiliated provincial bodies, the North of England Society, which during the late 1890s had tried to shed its image of middle-class gentility by campaigning hard among the female textile-workers of Lancashire. Two of its most striking leaders, Esther Roper and Eva Gore-Booth, came from well-to-do backgrounds—the former had graduated from the Victoria University, the latter was the daughter of a prominent aristocratic Irish landowner—but both were interested in the vote as a way of improving the conditions of working-class women, several of whom emerged as effective campaigners in their own right, among them Selina Cooper and Ada Nield Chew. In 1901 and 1902 the Society presented the Commons with a petition signed by over 66,000 women factory-workers, and its pressure persuaded the NUWSS Convention, meeting in 1903, to sponsor a parliamentary candidate at the next general election[110]—a tactical innovation suggesting that the NUWSS was about to embark upon a far more active campaign.

Then, on 16 March 1904, the Commons passed a pro-suffrage resolution by 184 votes to 70, a very wide margin[111]—though this was, admittedly, no more than an abstract expression of opinion. The pro-suffrage cause was then

---

[108] J. Lawrence, *Speaking for the People: Party, Language and Popular Politics in England, 1867–1914* (Cambridge, 1998), 157–60.

[109] See Ch. 2.

[110] Standing in Wigan in 1906, Thorley Smith came 1,370 votes behind the victorious Conservative, but 305 ahead of the Liberal.

[111] In 1897 a Private Member's Bill had been carried on second reading by 230 to 159.

boosted by the 1906 Liberal landslide, which Mrs Fawcett thought had brought into the House as many as 400 sympathetic MPs. The general election also introduced another new phenomenon: aggressive heckling from women, impatient with what they saw as the tortuously slow progress being made by the cause. It emanated from a breakaway group from the North of England Society, the Women's Social and Political Union (WSPU), which had been founded in October 1903 by Emmeline and Christabel Pankhurst, the widow and daughter of Dr Richard Pankhurst, a pioneering member of the Manchester ILP. At first the WSPU relied heavily upon the ILP, and much of its early membership was drawn from the ranks of Lancashire textile girls—notably Annie Kenney, who always introduced herself as 'a factory girl and a trade unionist'.

In the summer of 1906 the WSPU moved its headquarters to London, after which it largely severed its links with its erstwhile working-class supporters (whom the Pankhursts now saw as little more than demonstration fodder), and also with the ILP, from which the Pankhursts resigned the following year. Campaigning under slogans aimed at the well-to-do, such as 'Tax Paying Women are Entitled to the Parliamentary Vote', the WSPU quickly acquired a reputation for social and political conservatism: Katherine Glasier, a prominent ILPer, sneeringly referred to it as the 'Society Woman's Political Union'.[112]

The WSPU deliberately set out to dramatize by direct action women's disadvantages, instead of simply petitioning Parliament and acting through the agency of male sympathizers. The resort to publicity-seeking stunts (lively barracking, protesters' chaining themselves to railings, etc.) did indeed raise the profile of women's suffrage. A turning-point came on 23 October 1906, when ten WSPU members were arrested and briefly imprisoned in Holloway after a scuffle outside Parliament. In the ensuing protests the NUWSS leadership, still smarting at the way in which Campbell-Bannerman had amiably brushed aside its representations on 19 May, played a full part. Indeed, Mrs Fawcett, in an open letter to *The Times* in October 1906, generously acknowledged the way in which the WSPU's activities had given a fillip to *all* the pro-suffrage organizations.

For at this stage there was still a considerable membership overlap between the WSPU and the NUWSS. Nor were the two organizations yet employing radically different methods.[113] For example, in February 1907 the NUWSS

[112] S. Holton, *Feminism and Democracy: Women's Suffrage and Reform Politics in Britain 1900–1918* (Cambridge, 1986), 37. See J. Park, 'The British Suffrage Activists of 1913: An Analysis', *Past & Present*, 120 (1988), 147–62.

[113] M. Pugh, *The March of the Women: A Revisionist Analysis of the Campaign for Women's Suffrage, 1866–1914* (Oxford, 2000), 181–7.

organized a major suffrage procession in London (the 'Mud March'), involving 3,000 followers. But the WSPU soon displayed a greater aptitude for stage-managing such events: in July 1908 almost half-a-million people are said to have attended its rally in Hyde Park, upon which 30,000 marchers converged.

The 'suffragettes', as the militants were soon being called (the term originated with the *Daily Mail* in early 1906), acquired a reputation for pursuing shockingly new modes of agitation, but in a way they were simply continuing with the tactics long favoured by male Radicals: asserting their legitimacy by laying claim to public space, interrupting and haranguing prominent politicians, and forcibly putting questions from the floor. (Liberal politicians tried to neutralize these methods by holding ticketed meetings.) However, this departure from conventional feminine decorum often provoked equally vigorous protest from male crowds.

To avoid mob retaliation some suffragettes turned to stone-throwing in order to get themselves arrested—the first such episode occurred, spontaneously, in June 1908. Then, if imprisoned, they went on hunger strike.[114] This was an unprecedented form of protest: militant Irish nationalists, for example, had never yet employed it.[115] The baffled Home Secretary, Herbert Gladstone, eventually responded, in late 1909, by authorizing force-feeding—an invasion by male doctors of the female body, which, like the earlier enforcement of the Contagious Diseases Acts, aroused widespread disgust. Some of the 'political prisoners', such as Lady Constance Lytton, suffered permanent damage to their health.[116] Such judicial 'torture' ('brutal outrages upon defenceless women', one Liberal called it) also created martyrs for the cause, which in turn attracted new members into the WSPU.

However, although the NUWSS continued to speak out strongly against official cruelty, not all women suffragists approved of WSPU activities. As early as October 1906 Esther Roper privately confessed that her working-class friends were 'shrinking from public demonstrations', because they disliked being 'being mixed up with and held accountable as a class for educated and upper class women who kick, shriek, bite and spit'.[117] The calmly rational Mrs Fawcett, too, disliked the sensational posturing and the millenarian language increasingly affected by the militants, and she was even more appalled when the WSPU's 'calculated and limited threats to public order' spilled over into

---

[114] This form of protest was initiated by Marion Wallace Dunlop in July 1909.

[115] It was to become central to non-violent political struggle, practised by Gandhi, and later by the IRA in Northern Ireland—with variable success.

[116] Lady Lytton had a heart murmur, which led to her being leniently treated until she posed as a working girl, 'Jane Warton'. Some male sympathizers were also force-fed.

[117] J. Liddington and J. Norris, *One Hand Tied Behind Us: The Rise of the Women's Suffrage Movement* (London, 1978), 56.

actual criminal conduct and damage to property: its call on 'the lowest class of London toughs' to 'rush' the House of Commons in October 1908 struck her as despicable. But Mrs Fawcett only came out as an open critic of these methods when it was reported that a member of the Women's Freedom League (WFL), a breakaway from the WSPU, had thrown acid in a polling booth at the Bermondsey by-election of October 1909.[118] Militant and constitutional suffragism thereafter drifted into mutual antagonism.

Meanwhile the WSPU was stepping up its harassment of prominent Liberal ministers such as Churchill, whose earlier support for women's enfranchisement rapidly cooled as a consequence! Such tactics seem perverse, given that a clear majority of Liberal MPs supported votes for women, unlike the parliamentary Unionist Party which was predominantly hostile. This is why the NUWSS, many of whose leaders were prominent members of the Women's Liberal Federation (WLF), persevered for so long in trying to work with the Liberal Party. But the Pankhursts believed, perhaps correctly, that Mrs Fawcett was living in the past with her trust in the possibility of successful initiatives from private backbenchers. The lesson taught by recent changes in Commons procedures (Balfour's imposition of the 'railway timetable', for example)[119] was that only *governments* could carry major legislative measures—a lesson which the NUWSS itself belatedly recognized in 1912. In the WSPU's eyes, this put the onus on the Liberal ministry to meet the women's demands, and its failure to do so convinced them that ministers were fundamentally hostile—for which they should be punished until they repented the errors of their ways or acknowledged the expediency of surrender.

Unfortunately, the Liberal government, like the Opposition, was paralyzed by its internal divisions. In fact, the years between 1908 and 1914 threw up the paradoxical situation in which, while Balfour and Bonar Law were mildly sympathetic to the principle of women's suffrage but could not—or would not—do anything about it because their parliamentary followers were predominantly hostile, the Liberals, a broadly pro-suffrage party, were led by Asquith, an out-and-out opponent.

Moreover, even though the antis were undoubtedly in a minority both within the parliamentary Liberal Party and in the Commons as a whole, they believed so strongly in the merits of their case that they could not easily be overridden. Hostility to votes for women remained essentially what it had always been: a mixture of misogyny and chivalry.[120] But the more stridently women advanced their claims and the closer they came to success, the greater

---

[118] In fact, the incident in question had been misrepresented: see L. E. N. Mayhall, 'Defining Militancy: Radical Protest, the Constitutional Idiom, and Women's Suffrage in Britain, 1908–1909', *Journal of British Studies*, 39 (2000), 365–6.
[119] See Ch. 4.   [120] See Ch. 2.

the misogyny displayed by their male opponents and the more determined their will to resist.

Not that anti-suffragist prejudice was by any means confined to men. Few harsher critics of the 'women's righters' existed than Margot Asquith, who fully shared her husband's prejudices. Indeed, in July 1908 the Women's National Anti-Suffrage League was founded, to encourage prominent women to come out and say why they did not want or deserve the vote. Paradoxically some of these anti-suffrage women, notably the formidable Gladys Pott, did much to undercut their own arguments by showing impressive skill as organizers and public speakers.

Female 'antis' did at least act as a brake on the more misogynistic of their male colleagues. Refusing to go along with arguments which emphasized women's alleged biological incapacity, they instead stressed the need for women to cultivate their own particular talents within the domestic sphere, which they took to include local government. This claim was so uncontroversial that few voices were raised against the 1907 Act which belatedly conferred on women the right to sit on county councils. In September 1911 the novelist Mrs Humphry Ward, a prominent 'anti', formed the Local Government Advancement Committee to encourage women to take advantage of these opportunities. But the distinction between local and national government was becoming increasingly meaningless: 'The raising of children, the advancement of learning and the promotion of the spiritual', argued Beatrice Webb, 'are, it is clear, more and more becoming the main preoccupations of the community as a whole.'[121]

A less nuanced resistance to women's suffrage was put up by the Men's Committee for Opposing Female Suffrage (founded in December 1908), jointly run by two eminent ex-imperial proconsuls, Lords Cromer and Curzon, which trotted out all the by-now familiar arguments. In October 1910 this organization amalgamated with the women 'antis' to form the National League for Opposing Woman Suffrage—within which the male and female organizers soon developed a considerable contempt for one another! Despite these crosscurrents, there was general agreement among the antis about their objectives, a strong determination to stop change, and a robust confidence that the general public was on their side—hence their calls for a referendum, a call which, significantly, all the suffrage societies opposed.[122]

[121] J. Lewis, *Women in England, 1870–1950: Sexual Divisions and Social Change* (New York and London, 1984), 97.
[122] The referendum, as suffragists understood, would of course only have elicited the opinion of male voters. Contemporaries divided on the question of how widespread was the support among adult women, each side to the argument conducting research which happened to support its own convictions!

By contrast, many male supporters of women's suffrage were fair-weather friends, unprepared to take huge risks by standing up for their beliefs—particularly if this might endanger other reforming causes to which they attached greater importance. The Irish nationalists, in particular, feared that the suffrage issue might bring down the government, so imperilling the prospects of a Home Rule settlement. Such half-hearted advocacy could not but play into the hands of the upholders of the status quo. It also perhaps justifies the strategy of the WSPU, which was quick to recognize that male sympathy would not be likely to lead to legislation so long as women's claims were given such low priority at Westminster.

Even so, the intellectual argument over enfranchisment had largely been won by 1906, and women would probably have gained the vote before 1914 but for two other difficulties. First, the suffrage movement was still backing limited Franchise Bills which, by simply removing sexual discrimination, would have enfranchised only propertied widows and spinsters, who numbered little more than a million—effectively, the local government franchise. No one had a harsh word to say about widows, but privileging spinsters was less popular, even with female suffragists—the prominent trade unionist Margaret Bondfield 'deprecated votes for women as the hobby of disappointed old maids whom no one had wanted to marry'.[123]

Miss Llewelyn Davies's Women's Co-operative Guild, whose membership consisted overwhelmingly of wives and mothers, accordingly started advocating the inclusion of married women in any suffrage measure. Such pressure stimulated the Liberal backbencher W. H. Dickinson into adopting an amendment, which made provision for the wives of householders aged 25 and older, as well as female householders themselves, to be enfranchised, some 6 million women in all. The NUWSS executive, on the other hand, initially objected to this formula because it entailed a franchise qualification which did not apply equally to both sexes (men's right to vote being unaffected by their marital status).

A second stumbling-block to the adoption of the original Suffrage Bills stemmed from the widely held, if erroneous, belief that such limited measures would benefit mainly the well-to-do.[124] Many prominent Conservatives, such as Balfour and his Cecil relatives, found such a restriction positively attractive.[125] But it alienated most Liberal and Labour MPs, who wanted a thoroughgoing

---

[123] Liddington and Morris, *Hand Tied Behind Us*, 231.

[124] The first Conciliation Bill, for example, would have enfranchised only 1 million women and was framed in a way which made it impossible to broaden in committee—which is why Lloyd George voted against it.

[125] Balfour and Bonar Law later voted for the first Conciliation Bill, on which see below.

democratization of the electoral system, in which all adults would be given the vote.

It is true that Keir Hardie, joined by Snowden, continued to back a limited Suffrage Bill as a step in the right direction, assuring doubters that women currently holding the municipal franchise were predominantly working class.[126] On the other hand, old-fashioned trade unionists tended to be suspicious of the 'bourgeois' equal-righters, whose pioneers had once been so hostile to factory reform,[127] while in 1904 the LRC effectively sidelined the women's demands by coming out for adult suffrage.

Of course, it was theoretically possible to combine an agitation against both class privilege and sexual injustice. Margaret Bondfield, Mary Macarthur, and the WCG certainly thought so—hence their support for the People's Suffrage Federation, which enjoyed the enthusiastic backing of most members of the PLP, notably Arthur Henderson, as well as of many radical Liberals. But, in espousing this line, the PSF antagonized the main body of women suffragists, in the WSPU and NUWSS alike. Mrs Despard was not alone in suspecting that adult suffrage was merely a mask for sexual prejudice. The suffragists also feared, with good reason, that such attempts at democratization would, in practice, lead to the establishment of adult *male* suffrage, setting their own cause back by decades. Finally, as a furious Lady Betty Balfour put it, 'no-one want[ed] an equality which [would] put women in a majority'.

All these divisions of opinion were replicated within both the Cabinet and the Parliamentary Liberal Party. Though individuals often moved from one camp to the other under the influence of extraneous events, three broad factions can be identified. A minority, led by Asquith, did not wish to give women the parliamentary vote on any terms whatever. In Cabinet Asquith could rely on the support of Harcourt, Samuel, Pease, and, increasingly, Churchill. Ominously for the women, Pease and Harcourt were the ministers later entrusted with dealing with other aspects of franchise reform.

The second faction was composed of 'equal rights suffragists', led by the Foreign Secretary, Edward Grey, who called for an immediate removal of sexual discrimination as a matter of principle. But a third faction, the 'democratic suffragists', to which Lloyd George was loosely attached, favoured the women's cause but would not back a measure which created further social injustice and threatened the future long-term prospects of their party, as limited Suffrage Bills seemed likely to do. According to the journalist H. N. Brailsford, there were some seventy to eighty Liberal MPs, otherwise

---

[126] The plausibility of such claims is examined in Pugh, *March of the Women*, 199.

[127] The SDF was a hotbed of anti-suffragism—its theoretician, Belfort Bax, was the author of *The Fraud of Feminism*.

good friends of the cause, who felt this way.[128] The result of the three-way split was gridlock.

Asquith's prevarications and the onset of the constitutional crisis meant that women's suffrage played only a peripheral role in the two General Elections of 1910—there were three suffrage candidates, but they gathered only 696 votes between them. However, a petition calling for female enfranchisement did attract 280,000 signatories, and after January some 323 MPs were said to favour the cause. Against this background a truce was declared by the WSPU, allowing sympathizers from all parties to come together to form the Conciliation Committee, chaired by a Conservative, Lord Lytton, Lady Constance's brother. Under the guidance of Brailsford, who kept in close touch with Mrs Fawcett, this committee produced a Private Member's Bill which basically offered the municipal franchise—to the general approval of both the NUWSS and the WSPU. This measure received a Commons endorsement of 299 to 189 votes, but Parliament was dissolved before the matter could proceed further.

The truce then broke down with a vengeance on 18 November, 'Black Friday', when women who attempted to rush the Palace of Westminster received rough treatment at the hands of an over-zealous constabulary, many women being punched and having their hair pulled and breasts punched.[129] Mrs Fawcett again deplored police brutality, but privately railed against 'those idiots [who] go out smashing windows and bashing ministers' hats over their eyes', a criticism she repeated, slightly more diplomatically, in the organization's journal, *Common Cause*.[130]

After the December election another truce was called, allowing a second Conciliation Bill to pass through the Commons, this time by an even wider margin (255 to 88). But within the Liberal Cabinet the measure aroused the hostility not only of the doctrinaire antis but also of Lloyd George. Believing that 'the Conciliation Bill would, on balance, add hundreds of thousands of votes throughout the country to the strength of the Tory party', Lloyd George was privately advocating in September 1911 that the 'Liberal Party ought to make up its mind as a whole', either to 'have an extended franchise which would put working men's wives on to the Register as well as spinsters and widows' or to 'have no female franchise at all'.[131] The Chief Whip assured the Chancellor that the party's agents broadly backed his stance.

---

[128] L. P. Hume, *The National Union of Women's Suffrage Societies, 1897–1914* (Brighton, 1982), 111.

[129] The police, drawn from the East End, were inexperienced at handling suffragette demonstrators, and were perhaps trying to avoid arresting them by pushing them back.

[130] Hume, *National Union*, 92.

[131] Lloyd George to Elibank, 5 Sept. 1911, in J. Grigg, *Lloyd George: The People's Champion 1902–1911* (London, 1978), 297–8; the Report submitted to Elibank summarizing the views of the agents in P. Rowland, *The Last Liberal Governments: Unfinished Business 1911–14* (London, 1971), 90–2.

Faced by these difficulties, Asquith announced on 7 September 1911 what he hoped would be a broadly acceptable solution: the government would introduce its own measure to abolish plural voting and to reform the registration system (a move that would have taken the country a long way towards adult manhood suffrage), to which women's suffrage amendments could then be tabled and taken on a free vote at committee stage. The NUWSS cautiously welcomed the initiative,[132] but the WSPU reacted with fury, particularly Christabel Pankhurst, who increasingly saw herself as locked in a personal vendetta with Lloyd George. Riled by WSPU heckling, the Chancellor responded in kind, defiantly declaring at Bath on 24 November that these 'anti-Liberal women' had been 'torpedoed'. The truce broke down once more.

But militancy was now becoming counter-productive. On 1 March 1912 the WSPU for the first time attacked private property, and three days later went on the rampage in Knightsbridge. Police feared that an attempt would be made to assassinate Lloyd George, and Herbert Gladstone set the Special Branch to monitor the 'extremists'.[133] These 'outrages' helped destroy the third Conciliation Bill, which the Commons rejected by 208 votes to 222 on 28 March: twenty-six MPs (sixteen Liberals, ten Conservatives) who had pledged themselves to support the Conciliation Bill in fact voted against it, while sixty-six moved from abstention to opposition and another forty from support to abstention.[134]

But equally important in causing the Bill's defeat was a switch of support by the Irish MPs, stirred up by Churchill and by the mischievous 'Loulou' Harcourt into voting against a measure which they thought was destabilizing the Liberal ministry on the eve of a Home Rule settlement. (The militants' response, on 18 July, was to throw an axe into a carriage driving Asquith and Redmond through Dublin on a Home Rule demonstration.) Nor did it help that, when the crucial vote was taken, many friendly Labour MPs were away from Parliament, absorbed by the national coal strike.

More serious from the government's point of view was the reaction of the National Union, which, despairing both of any future Private Member's Bill and of Liberal goodwill, took the momentous decision of turning towards the Labour Party. This made a kind of sense, since Labour at its annual conference in January had resolved, over the opposition of the still-recalcitrant miners,

---

[132] Lloyd George had assured them that the government Bill would be introduced first. If none of the women's suffrage amendments passed, its advocates would have a second chance to carry the day with another Conciliation Bill, for which the government would find space. In fact, the two legislative measures came before the Commons in reverse order.

[133] Hume, *National Union*, 132; B. Porter, *Plots and Paranoia: A History of Political Espionage in Britain, 1790–1988* (London, 1989), 131.

[134] Hume, *National Union*, 137–8.

that while supporting adult suffrage, no franchise measure which excluded women would be acceptable.[135] The NUWSS therefore decided in May that it would support Labour candidates at by-elections (plus a few 'tried friends' from the Liberal Party) and would fund such campaigns through a semi-autonomous body, the Election Fighting Fund (EFF). Ironically, a few weeks later, in October, the WSPU moved in the opposite direction, declaring all-out war on Labour candidates, be they friend or foe, as punishment for keeping the Liberals in office.

The National Union's volte-face caused consternation among those of its members with a lifelong attachment to Liberalism (for example, Eleanor Acland, who was also a member of the executive of the WLF), and it provoked some resignations. As for Labour, MacDonald was jealous of his Party's autonomy and did not want to have his relationship with the Liberals damaged by his new female allies. However, Henderson and Arthur Peters, the party's agent, soon concluded an agreement with the NUWSS.

Of course, none of this manoeuvring would have mattered one way or the other if Asquith's compromise had given the suffragists the prize which they craved. However, on 27 January 1913, in response to a question from Bonar Law, the Speaker ruled that all four of the women's suffrage amendments tabled to the government's Franchise and Registration Bill were invalid because they fundamentally altered its scope and meaning. Asquith was privately amused at this latest turn of events ('the Speaker's *coup d'etat* has bowled over the Women for this session—a great relief'). But he also thought the Speaker's decision to be a 'wrong' one.[136]

The angry suffrage societies saw things very differently. Christabel Pankhurst maintained that there had been collusion between the Prime Minister and the Speaker, while in February 1913 her militant followers smashed the orchid house at Kew, set a railway carriage alight, and bombed Lloyd George's house.[137] Two months later the stiff-necked Home Secretary Reginald McKenna brought in the 'Prisoners' Temporary Discharge for Ill-Health Bill', better known as the 'Cat and Mouse Act' of 1913, under which hunger-strikers could be released on health grounds but later rearrested unless they gave pledges of future 'good behaviour'.

Following the Speaker's ruling, the government had no option but to withdraw the Franchise and Registration Bill in its entirety, instead offering

[135] M. Pugh, 'Labour and Women's Suffrage', in K. D. Brown (ed.), *The First Labour Party 1906-1914* (London [*c*.1985]), 246-7.

[136] Jenkins, *Asquith*, 249-50. Historians differ over the propriety of the Speaker's action, and also over the issue of whether any of the four very different women's suffrage amendments before the House would have attracted a majority of votes, had a vote ever been taken.

[137] Hume, *National Union*, 193.

facilities to a Private Member's Suffrage Bill. But the latter, introduced by
W. H. Dickinson, was lost by forty-eight votes, largely because, enfranchising
as it did wives of householders as well as those holding property under their own
name, it was so 'democratic' that few moderate Conservative suffragists would
support it, and also because the Irish were now overwhelmingly hostile.[138]

The WSPU drifted into futility. Emily Wilding Davison died, throwing
herself under the King's horse during the Derby of 1913. A vast crowd of
sympathisers, moved by her bravery, attended her funeral, but many contemporaries were exasperated by the gesture. No longer content with largely
symbolic gestures of protest, the suffragettes stepped up their campaign,
carrying out actions which seriously threatened life and property. The slashing
of Velasquez's *Rokeby Venus* in the National Gallery and attempts to horsewhip
Liberal politicians in public places and even on the golf course—all these
'outrages', however comprehensible they might be as manifestations of disappointment and frustration, had the effect of distracting attention from the
merits of the women's case and making it appear predominantly a 'law and
order' issue. Most worrying of all were indiscriminate arson attacks on pillar-
boxes and empty properties of all kinds, which did damage amounting to nearly
half-a-million pounds.[139] That no one was killed owed more to luck than
careful planning.

Always autocratic in their methods of running their organization, Emmeline
and Christabel Pankhurst increasingly stamped upon all internal dissent.
Charlotte Despard and Teresa Billington-Greig, two of the ablest of the
WSPU's original leaders, had been driven out as early as September 1907,
when Emmeline and Christabel Pankhurst unilaterally suspended the constitution and assumed direct personal control. 'The split' produced another
organization, the Women's Freedom League, to which perhaps one in five of
the original WSPU membership defected. The devoted Pethick-Lawrences
were banished in 1912, and even the younger daughter, Sylvia Pankhurst, still
inconveniently loyal to her socialist convictions, was effectively expelled,
whereupon she formed her own organization in the East End of London (the
East London Federation for Women's Suffrage), which campaigned on a range
of women's issues, not just their exclusion from the vote. Though still flush
with funds, WSPU membership plummeted.[140]

---

[138] 145 Liberals and Radicals, 35 Labour, 13 Irish, and 28 Conservative MPs supported it: 76 Liberals
and Radicals, 54 Irish, and 139 Conservatives opposed. Some of the Conservative supporters insisted
that the Bill be narrowed down at Committee stage so that it accorded with the Conciliation Bill.

[139] Over £450,000, according to figures in A. Rosen, *Rise Up Women! The Militant Campaign of the
Women's Social and Political Union 1903–1914* (London, 1974), chs. 16, 18.

[140] In October 1913 the Union stopped giving statistics of new members: but they had steadily
declined from 4,459 in 1909–10 to only 923 in the first 8 months of 1913–14 (ibid. 211). No *full* list of
members was ever published.

Directing the agitation from her exile in Paris, to which she had escaped in disguise, Christabel Pankhurst broadened her indictment of patriarchal values. Despite the courageous service rendered by male 'friends' such as F. W. Pethick-Lawrence (the suffragette Emmeline's husband),[141] there had from the start been a strain of hostility within the WSPU to men per se, a prejudice of which Mrs Fawcett strongly disapproved. Completely rejecting both the 'equal franchise' thesis and arguments about there being a beneficial complementarity between male and female roles, Christabel now presented men as essentially *wicked*—all the world's problems, she claimed, were God's or Nature's retribution for men's unbridled sexuality.[142] In her pamphlet *The Great Scourge and How To End It* (1913), she warned women that between 75 per cent and 85 per cent of men had acquired gonorrhoea before marriage and so were better avoided: 'Votes for Women, Chastity for Men', was her new cry. Indeed, when the head of Special Branch, accompanied by a police doctor, visited Mrs Pankhurst to see if she was fit enough to be rearrested under the Cat and Mouse Act, he was greeted by women shouting not only 'Cowards', 'Pigs', 'Dogs', and 'Brutes', but also 'Syphilis' and 'Gonorrhoea'.[143]

Such effusions embarrassed the long-suffering members of the NUWSS, as well as confirming opponents in their view of women as being too emotional to take a full place in public life. Brutal things were said about the 'physiological emergencies' which allegedly denied women the use of their reason for much of their adult lives—the very point which the physician Almroth Wright had earlier made in a notorious letter to *The Times*. There was also much sneering at the expense of mentally unbalanced spinsters. (Of the WSPU women still active in 1913 and 1914, almost two-thirds were unmarried.[144])

Such developments complicated the task of those Liberal ministers sympathetic to the cause of women's enfranchisement. As Lloyd George said to a deputation in February 1914, the position was 'quite hopeless as far as this Parliament is concerned', since 'militant members have made it almost impossible for those Liberal leaders who are in favour of women's suffrage to address meetings in support of it'.[145] Asquith did make some vaguely encouraging

[141] In 1912 he had served a nine-months' prison sentence for 'conspiracy'. He was also the organization's Treasurer.

[142] Christabel was here drawing upon a line of argument already well developed by 'radical feminists'. For example, the actress Cicely Hamilton had earlier dealt with the dangers of marriage in *Marriage as a Trade* (1909) (L. Bland, *Banishing the Beast: English Feminism and Sexual Morality 1885–1914* (Harmondsworth, 1995), 245–6).

[143] Porter, *Plots and Paranoia*, 131.

[144] 63% in the fiscal year 1913–14, compared with 45% in 1906–7. All 23 WSPU organizers listed in *The Suffrage Annual of 1913* were unmarried (Rosen, *Rise Up Women!*, 210). Park finds 64.6% of the WSPU activists listed in the *Women's Who's Who* were unmarried, compared to 46.8% of those from the NUWSS (Park, 'Suffrage Activists', 159).

[145] Rowland, *Unfinished Business*, 295.

noises to a deputation from Sylvia Pankhurst's East End supporters in 1914, but for the time being (until the next election at least) women's suffrage was dead, though a Plural Voting Bill was shortly destined to reach the statute book.

The suffragettes' methods were simply inept. The WSPU's violence never reached a point at which ministers were genuinely intimidated (as distinct from being very annoyed); yet it did more than enough to antagonize the public and weaken the women's cause. It was, anyhow, illogical to demand the parliamentary vote while undermining parliamentary institutions. (More sensible was the WFL's policy of passive resistance—including a boycott of the 1911 Census and the refusal to pay the dog licence.)[146] Well might Mrs Fawcett call the militants 'the most powerful allies the antisuffragists have'.[147]

Yet, despite the counter-productive antics of the WSPU, the *medium-term* prospects for women's suffrage were far from hopeless. After all, the Liberal Cabinet had compelling reasons for trying to resolve a dispute which had the capacity to tear both party and government apart. 'It would be appalling', Churchill privately wrote, 'if this strong Government and Party... was to go down on Petticoat politics.'[148] Moreover, Liberals at all levels had been troubled in their consciences about force-feeding; on the eve of the January 1910 election the issue led two of the party's most famous journalists, Brailsford and Henry Nevinson, to resign from the *Daily News* in protest. And though the subsequent Cat and Mouse Act may have been effective in prising many suffragettes away from militancy,[149] it lost the Liberal Party the moral high ground—a situation skilfully exploited by women protesters who were quite prepared to play the chivalric card when it suited their convenience.

In particular, the WLF, on which so many MPs had come to rely for assistance at election time, was thrown into crisis: 'Look at the bitter injured feelings of the women Liberals', wrote one member to Lloyd George in October 1913: 'they are leaving in shoals, and joining the only party honestly pressing women's suffrage [ie Labour].'[150] Between 1912 and 1914 sixty-eight local branches of the WLF folded and 18,000 members were lost.[151]

The government had also to contend with a much-strengthened NUWSS. This organization was undergoing a remarkable transformation, as a younger generation of women worked their way into the leadership and new recruits

---

[146] Pugh, *March of the Women*, 184–5.

[147] Hume, *National Union*, 179.

[148] Churchill to Elibank, 18 Dec. 1911, cited in D. Morgan, *Suffragists and Liberals: The Politics of Woman Suffrage in Britain* (Oxford, 1975), 87.

[149] Pugh, *March of the Women*, 208–10.

[150] Holton, *Feminism and Democracy*, 119.

[151] Pugh, *March of the Women*, 143. Disillusionment among female Liberal activists led to the formation of the Liberal Women's Suffrage Union.

flocked to join. The Society's membership had already steadily risen from 5,836 in 1907 to 21,571 in 1910;[152] it then rocketed (by about 1,000 a month in 1913) until, on the eve of the war, its supporters numbered nearly 100,000, one-half of them fully paid-up members. The NUWSS in 1913 had 460 branches (as against the WSPU which had only ninety),[153] as well as its own journal, *The Common Cause*, ably edited by Helen Swanwick. Arguably the most impressive of all pre-war demonstrations was the Society's 1913 'Pilgrimage', when supporters, after a week's march, converged on London from all over the country. Moreover, NUWSS activists now did not spurn paper-selling and street-chalking—even though in so doing they often incurred violence from opponents who mistook them for members of the WSPU.

Political attitudes were also changing. The pro-Labour policy of the NUWSS had been adopted by Mrs Fawcett and other members of its executive largely for tactical reasons—to pressurize the Liberals into changing their policy on the suffrage question. That is why the NUWSS continued to lobby friendly Liberal ministers, while simultaneously negotiating with the Conservatives. Yet many of the new recruits believed in a suffrage–Labour alliance for its own sake, since they saw the sex barrier and the class barrier as twin manifestations of monopoly and privilege. This was particularly true of a younger group of middle-class women, which included the Society's Secretary, Kathleen Courtney, Helen Swanwick, and Catherine Marshall (the Parliamentary Secretary from 1911 onwards).

The adoption of the Election Fighting Fund (EFF) also made it easier for the Society to employ hardened working-class activists such as Ada Nield Chew, either on a full- or part-time basis. Although still middle class in ethos, the NUWSS now had a genuine industrial base, causing once-hostile working-class groups such as the miners to drop their opposition to its programme. In September 1913 the TUC unequivocally passed a pro-suffrage motion.

Whether the NUWSS's Labour 'alliance' would have proved effective in the long run, however, is another matter.[154] Before the outbreak of war the NUWSS, through its fighting fund, intervened on Labour's behalf in eight three-cornered fights, four of which the Liberals lost. It also encouraged Labour to put up candidates for the forthcoming general election against a number of hated Liberal antis, including Harcourt and Pease. But,

---

[152] Hume, *National Union*, 57, 95.

[153] Pugh, *March of the Women*, 211. The WFL had 61 branches.

[154] Lansbury wanted the PLP to vote against *every* Liberal measure until women were enfranchised. When he stood with the Society's support at the Bromley by-election in November 1912, he lost his seat in a straight fight against a Conservative—not helped by the ostentatious support he had attracted from the WSPU.

understandably, the policy was not universally popular among the NUWSS membership and could not have been sustained indefinitely.[155] Nor, despite the EEF, was Labour willing to attack the Liberals except in constituencies which it had its own reasons for fighting.

All ultimately depended on how the Liberals themselves read the situation. The Labour–NUWSS alliance had inflicted some damage on the government, but would ministers have felt sufficiently threatened by it to have entered the forthcoming general election committed to some form of women's suffrage? War broke out before the crucial decision had been taken.

Yet though the parliamentary franchise for women was not secured before the outbreak of the Great War, its advocates had several achievements to their credit. For example, the NUWSS succeeded in persuading many former opponents and neutrals that full political enfranchisement would not 'unsex' women or threaten family life and conventional morality. The WSPU activists went further, challenging with reckless courage older concepts of femininity and asserting women's right to choose their own way of life, without prior male approval or co-operation.

Finally, working for the cause, through whichever suffrage organization, often engendered among its participants a joyful sense of camaraderie and a heightened self-confidence, sharpened through a common exposure to danger and ridicule. Active involvement in the suffrage campaign thus gave many women a new sense of the solidarity of their sex—a transforming experience which, for many, probably meant far more than the mere prospect of acquiring the parliamentary vote.

7. THE STRANGE DEATH OF LIBERAL ENGLAND?

Writing in 1935, George Dangerfield noted that there were certain common elements in the various challenges that faced Liberalism on the eve of the Great War. Ulster loyalists, physical-force Irish nationalists, syndicalists, and suffragettes were all in revolt, not only against the authority of Parliament, but also against contemporary notions of 'respectability'.[156]

Indeed, each group (with the exception of the Irish republicans) self-consciously sought to subvert the image which others held of it: Ulster loyalists declared rebellion, right-wing Conservatives proclaimed revolution, syndicalists contemptuously dismissed the stereotype of the honest, respectable labourer so painfully built up during the late Victorian years, and women claimed their rights in ways which were totally at variance with accepted

---

[155] Its most articulate opponent was Eleanor Rathbone.
[156] G. Dangerfield, *The Strange Death of Liberal England* (London, 1935).

codes of feminine behaviour. All of these movements exhibited a strain of moral absolutism: compromise was rejected, as was the liberal culture of 'government by discussion', and even reason itself. Little wonder if that epitome of the bourgeois liberal virtues, Asquith, could not get the measure of any of the protests.

But was there anything more than an underlying 'mood' linking these movements? Larkin and Connolly, obviously, provided a junction between working-class militancy and uncompromising Irish nationalism. There was also a loose alliance between revolutionary socialism and Sylvia Pankhurst, whose East London Federation had links with the *Daily Herald* League.[157] On the other hand, the WSPU spurned the mainstream Labour Movement as an ally of the hated Liberal government, and it was left to the constitutionalists of the NUWSS, soaked in liberal values, to make common cause with the Labour Party.

Nor did women suffragists have anything in common with the right-wing rebels. The Ulster loyalists, like the Irish nationalists, saw the women's cause as a distraction, and Carson himself was an 'anti'. True, the ranks of the Diehards contained a few friends of women's suffrage, such as Lord Selborne and Lord Willoughby de Broke, but these were a minority: significantly, one of the main planks in Maxse's attack on Balfour in 1911 was that the Conservative Leader had not disassociated himself sufficiently from other members of his 'cranky' Cecil family who favoured giving women the parliamentary vote.

The Ulster loyalists and working-class militants were even more obviously at one another's throats. Socialists might initially have deplored the amount of attention being given by mainstream politicians to the age-old Irish dispute, but the possibility of a coup directed by right-wing army officers against a policy approved by the Commons frightened all wings of the Labour Movement: Labour MPs repeatedly challenged the double standard whereby the forces of law and order showed leniency to the Carsonites, while cracking down so harshly on the suffragettes.

There may be some substance in the view that, between 1910 and 1914, the country was experiencing a 'crisis of the state', caused by a questioning of the legitimacy of all established authority. The government itself briefly worried about the strategic implications of the union embargo on the movement of foodstuffs during the 1911 dock strikes.[158] On the other hand, the Home Office continued to take the view that the prime responsibility for law and order during industrial disputes rested with local police authorities, while the Special

---

[157] This was the reason for her expulsion from the WSPU. On this and other links between the militant wing of the suffrage movement and the socialist rebels grouped around Lansbury, see Holton, *Feminism and Democracy*, 127–9.

[158] D. French, *British Strategy and War Aims, 1914–16* (London, 1986), 86.

Branch (though monitoring the suffragettes) took little interest in the Labour Movement. Indeed, the authorities still had very little concept of 'political crimes', that is to say, activities that were criminal simply because they were politically subversive.[159]

In any case, by the summer of 1914 voices of moderation were beginning to reassert themselves, except perhaps in Ulster, where the cautious Carson had lost control of events to local 'hard men'. In nationalist Ireland Redmond might have been under pressure, but he moved quickly to place himself at the head of the recently established Irish Volunteers movement and was still the hero of the hour. Meanwhile the militant wing of the suffrage movement had landed itself in a cul-de-sac from which only the war would extricate it.

The greatest threat to the stability of government came from the Labour Movement. During 1913–14 the first tentative steps were taken to create a 'Triple Alliance', linking the NUR, the MFGB, and the National Transport Workers Federation, and if all three of these unions had simultaneously terminated their agreements with their employers they could certainly have shut down much of the country's economic life; Basil Thomson, a colonial lawyer and prison governor, who became Secretary of the Prison Commission and then Assistant Commissioner of the Criminal Investigation Department,[160] viewed this development with alarm and thought that only a European war could save Britain from revolution. However, the 'alliance' was never ratified before 1914, and it was, in any case, little more than a gigantic bluff—a way of securing 'bloodless victories' for the working class. In practice, the union leaders' prime objective was to spread and thus minimize the suffering which members of each constituent union inevitably incurred when another came out on strike. It is even arguable that the Triple Alliance signified less a revolutionary bid for power through the preparation of a 'general strike', than an attempt by the union leaderships to avert stoppages and avoid industrial chaos by strengthening their position vis-à-vis a militant rank-and-file.[161]

By 1914 the Great Labour Unrest seemed to have abated, except for the London building strike, which affected 40,000 men, and a local dispute on the Yorkshire coalfields. By badly overplaying his hand, Larkin had helped restore the authority of traditional union leaders, and the syndicalist 'moment' had largely passed. Industrial disruption might possibly have broken out if the Yorkshire and Scottish miners, each with outstanding wage-claims, had succeeded in involving their 'allies' in the transport and railway industries in their cause. But later developments were to show the difficulties of orchestrating

[159] Porter, *Plots and Paranoia*, 131–5.
[160] B. Thomson, *The Scene Changes* (London, 1937), 234–44.
[161] G. A. Phillips, 'The Triple Alliance in 1914', *Economic History Review*, 24 (1971), 55–67.

trade-union action in this way—action for which men such as Thomas had absolutely no stomach.

It is even possible that the Liberals might have won the general election soon to take place (by 1915 at the latest)—especially if Labour, fearful of a Conservative return to power, had continued to prune its candidacies. After all, Bonar Law was hardly a welcome prospect as a future Prime Minister.

What destroyed many features of Liberal England, not least the Liberal Party itself, was the Great War. To what extent did the shadow of hostilities contribute to the febrile state of politics between 1910 and 1914? As we shall see, invasion scares heightened tension and contributed to the ferocity of Opposition attacks on a 'pacifist' government that was allegedly neglecting national defences. The international scene also played a part, probably a subordinate one, in Lloyd George's dreams of a national coalition in 1910 and in the later attempts to close ranks in the face of a common enemy. Yet the fact that such an outcome could even be envisaged would suggest that the country was not standing on the brink of civil war in 1914.

In one way, and in one way only, were domestic discontents and the perilous international situation linked. Much Diehard truculence originated in a strong sense of the aristocracy's importance as a hereditary military caste.[162] If war ever did break out, which seemed quite likely, the virtues of the aristocracy, which Lloyd George had mocked with amused scorn, would play an important part in national salvation. Denigrating aristocracy as a decaying social formation presupposed, as Herbert Spencer had earlier put it, that military society had given way to industrial society, in which individuals and communities no longer sought to resolve their differences by violence. That, however, was clearly not the international world which Britain confronted in the summer of 1914.

---

[162] In March 1914 De Broke introduced a Bill to conscript the sons of the upper classes (R. J. Q. Adams and P. Poirer, *The Conscription Controversy in Great Britain 1900–18* (Houndsmill, 1987), 47).

CHAPTER 13

The Road to War

The Liberal landslide victory of 1906 had swept into the Commons many MPs who hoped, above all else, that the new government would decisively break with the foreign and imperial policies of Balfour's discredited regime. These Radicals took reassurance from Campbell-Bannerman, who, during the election campaign, had struck an authentically Liberal note, excoriating the recent growth of armaments and arguing that Britain's role was 'to place itself at the head of a league of peace'.[1]

On the other hand, Edward Grey had earlier stated (in May 1905) that foreign policy should not be a matter of party controversy and, in a powerful speech at the City of London on 21 October, the Foreign Secretary-to-be advocated 'continuity of policy'.[2] Lansdowne responded by welcoming Grey as his successor and privately offering him help.[3] Another Liberal Imperialist, R. B. Haldane, had been involved in the outgoing Unionist ministry's changes to the Committee of Imperial Defence (CID)—changes designed to secure its survival if and when the Liberals assumed office.[4] Which Liberal faction would prevail?

1. IMPERIAL POLICY

The arena in which Liberal policy was first publicly tested was South Africa. On 21 March 1906 Liberal backbenchers, baying for the blood of the hated Lord Milner, were countered by the Colonial Under-Secretary, Winston Churchill, who carried through the House a motion intended to provide

---

[1] A. J. A. Morris, *Radicalism Against War 1906–1914: The Advocacy of Peace and Retrenchment* (London, 1972), 25.

[2] K. M. Wilson, *The Politics of the Entente: Essays on the Determinants of British Foreign Policy, 1904–1914* (Cambridge, 1985), 17; G. W. Monger, *The End of Isolation: British Foreign Policy 1900–1907* (London, 1963), 260.

[3] Wilson, *Politics of the Entente*, 19.

[4] Lord Esher, along with Sir John French, was made a permanent member of the CID after a meeting at Buckingham Palace in early October. The meeting also set up two subcommittees which the new government could not easily terminate.

some protection for the former High Commissioner; but, whether by accident or design, he did this in a condescending speech, urging his followers, in their moment of triumph, to show generosity to a man who had 'ceased to be a factor in public life'. This insulting treatment of a person whom *The Times* called 'one of the greatest and most devoted of England's public servants' enraged the Unionist Party and offended the King. But, significantly, none of Milner's old Liberal Imperialist friends spoke out in his defence. An emotional chasm opened up between the two sides of the House that was never entirely to close.

Throwing over the legacy of the hated Milner, however, proved to be less easy. Despite Liberal denunciations of indentured Chinese labour as 'slavery', the government quickly discovered that it had no legal right to cancel contracts that had already been signed, some as recently as November 1905—except by incurring a huge bill for compensation. The indentured labour system had therefore to be phased out—against a background of Opposition taunts at the Liberals' hypocrisy. Moreover, the new Colonial Secretary, Lord Elgin, had to work with Milner's recently appointed successor, Lord Selborne, the one-time Unionist minister—not until 1910 were the Liberals able to appoint their own High Commissioner, Herbert Gladstone.

However, morale on the Liberal benches significantly rose when the government boldly reversed its predecessors' policy towards the conquered Boer colonies. The so-called Lyttelton Constitution had merely promised 'representative institutions leading up to self-government'—presumably so that the Boer provinces would be completely 'anglicized' before the British relaxed their control. But the Cabinet swiftly resolved to replace this unsatisfactory halfway house with immediate 'responsible' government, Campbell-Bannerman persuading it to scrap the Lyttelton Constitution altogether.[5] A constitution drawn up on the basis of white manhood suffrage came into operation in the Transvaal in December 1906; the Orange Free State received a similar settlement six months later.

The Liberals portrayed what they had done, in typically Liberal language, as an act of reconciliation, designed to win over the allegiance of former enemies by extending to them the hand of trust and friendship. In fact, privately Liberal ministers were not so confident that their magnanimous, but risky, policy would succeed. Yet succeed it did, at least in the short run—so much so that, through the South Africa Act of 1909, the government was later able to unite the two former Afrikaner republics with Cape Colony and Natal in a new Union of South Africa.[6] When the South African Premier, Louis Botha, the

---

[5] On the myths surrounding this episode, R. Hyam, *Elgin and Churchill at the Colonial Office 1905–1908: The Watershed of the Empire-Commonwealth* (London and New York, 1968), 124–36.

[6] The new state formally came into existence the following May.

former Boer commando, took his country into the Great War on Britain's side, the Liberal gamble seemed to have been vindicated.

Yet, as the Liberals were well aware, the price paid for this achievement was the sacrifice of the black peoples of South Africa, since only 'British subjects of European descent' could sit in the Union Parliament and an explicit colour bar continued to apply to the electoral registers of the Transvaal and the Orange Free State. True, some 'coloureds' could still participate in Cape elections, but they made little impact in the new white-dominated state. The Liberal government salved its conscience by retaining direct control over the native protectorates of Swaziland, Bechuanaland, and Basutoland. But, though it regretted the South African colour bar, it acknowledged that without this 'essential compromise' the 'Union would be smashed'.[7] Two Liberal ideals had thus come into conflict in South Africa, self-government on the one hand, and the duty to protect native rights on the other. Fatefully, the government gave priority to the former.

In the dependencies of Africa and Asia the Liberals displayed a similar mixture of benevolence and timidity. Whatever its opponents might have feared, the Liberal ministry certainly had no intention of giving away the Empire. Yet neither did it have any well-thought-out development plan. The Liberal years therefore saw a process of muddling along, policy being generally shaped by the exigencies of time and place and by the recommendations of the 'men on the spot'. In some colonies positive steps were taken to develop local resources: Churchill, Under-Secretary at the Colonial Office from 1905 to 1908, became a keen advocate of railway extension, especially in Uganda. 'Loulou' Harcourt, Colonial Secretary from November 1910 to 1915, shared these enthusiasms, but like his predecessors was severely constrained by the Treasury's tight-fistedness. Elsewhere the government relied more on 'indirect rule', as in Northern Nigeria, where such methods had been elevated into something resembling an ideology by its Governor, Sir Frederick Lugard. In fact, British officials and ministers remained generally chary of grandiose schemes of 'westernization', believing that 'natives' resented being hustled— even though a new generation of educated Africans was beginning to emerge who found 'indirect rule' patronizing and even distasteful because its effect was to freeze an unjust status quo.

Perhaps the Liberals were more sensitive to the needs of protecting the welfare of native peoples than the Unionists had been. The Aborigines Protection Society—which amalgamated with the Anti-Slavery Society in 1909— kept up pressure on them to do so, backed by some of the government's own

---

[7] B. Porter, *The Lion's Share: A Short History of British Imperialism 1850–1983* (Harlow, 1975; 1984 edn.), 209.

backbenchers, including the veteran Sir Charles Dilke. Ministers also took notice of the immense support generated by the Congo Reform Association, which graphically exposed the cruelties practised by agents of King Leopold in that mineral-rich part of Africa. In 1909 the Belgian government responded to international outrage by taking the Congo out of the hands of the King and placing it under state control. (One reason why British officials so disliked Chinese labour was that it weakened their own protests against King Leopold's practices.)

Fearful of imitating the worst features of the Congo regime, the Colonial Office generally discouraged the leasing of territory to entrepreneurs with exclusive territorial privileges: William Lever, for example, was denied in 1907 the concessions he requested in West Africa for the extraction of palm oil to be used in his soap manufactories (he eventually got what he wanted in the Congo!) Instead, the Liberal government encouraged peasant cultivation, in association with free commercial activities—as advocated by the Liverpudlian shippers who, significantly, played a prominent part in the Congo Reform Association.

But if the Liberals were suspicious of 'monopolists', they had little confidence in white settlers and in settler governments. Their views were shared in the Colonial Office, where one senior official prophesied that the Empire would eventually be destroyed, not by 'natives', but by 'the white colonials, who would bring this about by their sheer stupidity, brutal insensitivity to non-European races, and parochial inability to view any problem either in its essential wider Imperial perspective or within the overriding realities of international relations'.[8] But ministers were restricted in what they could do. In 1907 Elgin tried to stop the Government of Natal executing twelve Africans who had been subjected to a highly irregular trial. But, faced with the threat of resignation from the entire Natal ministry, he soon gave way. The Natal authorities (dubbed by Churchill the 'hooligans of the Empire') then went on to provoke a serious rebellion headed by the Zulu chief Denizulu—a tragic and bloody episode which, once again, the Liberal government proved powerless to prevent.

Policy towards 'natives' was equally half-hearted. On the one hand, Churchill publicly promised 'to advance the principle of equal rights of civilised men irrespective of colour', and professed a heavy-handed kind of paternalism towards the 'backward peoples' under British care; on the other hand, he insisted on the need for 'a careful patient discrimination between different classes of coloured men', privately expressing his hope that the African would

[8] R. Hyam, 'The British Empire in the Edwardian Era', in J. M. Brown and W. R. Louis (eds.), *The Oxford History of the British Empire: Vol. IV: The Twentieth Century* (Oxford, 1999), 57.

wear clothes, so that he would become in time 'less crudely animal'.[9] Significantly, when Lord Crewe's circular of 1909 warned colonial administrators that they could be punished if they formed liaisons with native women, this was partly a well-meaning attempt to protect vulnerable people from exploitation (following the Silberrad case),[10] but also an expression of the view that the authority of an imperial race would suffer from too familiar a relationship with its charges.

Almost entirely ignorant of the societies over which they presided, ministers did little in practice to achieve that equality under the Crown, regardless of race, for which some Labour and Radical backbench MPs were beginning to contend. For example, although the Colonial Office, joined on this issue by the Government of India, supported Gandhi's protests at the maltreatment of Indians in Natal, it lacked the means, and perhaps the stomach, to intervene.

Things were somewhat different in India itself, which was entrusted in December 1905 to John Morley, whose initial appointment raised the hopes of the moderate Congress leaders. Delighted that they now had the opportunity of working with Gladstone's biographer and a student of Burke, educated Indians looked forward to a further instalment of liberal political reforms, along the lines earlier pioneered by Lord Ripon (Viceroy 1880–4), now Lord Privy Seal. One of Congress's leaders, Gopal Krishna Gokhale, on visiting London was speedily accorded an appointment with Morley, who showed a sensitive understanding of the need to offer concessions to moderate nationalists if the growing band of militants was to be marginalized. Morley also accepted the need for some institutional reforms.

However, Morley's tenure at the India Office disappointed his would-be Indian admirers. True, the Secretary of State did succeed in cajoling Lord Minto, the Viceroy he had inherited from the Unionists, into associating himself with a moderate reform package. The Morley–Minto reforms, finalized in 1909, extended the role of Indian representatives on the Imperial Legislative Council and the provincial councils (on the latter, some were now elected), and allowed for the appointment of an Indian to both the Secretary of State's Council in London (the post went to Gokhale) and to the Viceroy's Council in Calcutta.

But, addressing an unsympathetic audience in the House of Lords (to which he had been 'promoted' on Asquith's ascent to the premiership), Morley denied that his innovations were designed to pave the way for Indian self-government; he merely hoped that they would import the *spirit* of British

---

[9] Hyam, *Elgin and Churchill*, 359, 375.
[10] Silberrad was a colonial official in East Africa whose sexual relationships with a succession of native women had occasioned a scandal.

constitutionalism into Indian affairs and create a more harmonious relationship
between governors and governed. In private the Indian Secretary was even
more pessimistic, saying that there could be 'no progress in the East' since
progress was 'bound up with Christianity'.[11]

In any case, Morley cancelled out any good that his concessions might have
achieved by refusing (at Minto's request) to reconsider the ending of Curzon's
partition of Bengal, which had infuriated the Congress leadership. This refusal
strengthened the hands of 'extremists' such as Bal Gangadhar Tilak and Lal
Lajpat Rai, who poured scorn on the policy of begging concessions from the
British government. They organized a boycott of British goods and of the
British authorities in protest against the partition, and later withdrew temporarily from Congress itself. Passive resistance soon gave way to bombings and
assassinations, to which Morley, despite his abhorrence of Bismarckian (and
Milnerian) methods, responded with a battery of repressive measures, including the draconian Press Act of 1910 and the deportation and imprisonment of
militant nationalists. A similar pattern of concession and repression was currently being pursued by Cromer's more liberal successors in Egypt.

Perhaps surprisingly, a 'sounder' Liberal policy in India was instituted when
Morley and Minto were replaced in November 1910 by Lord Crewe and his
new Viceroy, Lord Hardinge (previously Permanent Under-Secretary at the
Foreign Office). During the King's visit to India for the 'Durbar' in 1911,
Hardinge announced the revocation of the Partition of Bengal. This volte-face,
however, was accompanied by the removal of the Indian capital from Calcutta
(in Bengal) to Delhi, a move highly unpopular with educated Hindu nationalists, many of them Calcutta residents. Congress leaders also viewed the elevation of Delhi as a further sop to the Muslims, for whom Morley had earlier
created a separate electoral roll.

But such a policy of 'divide and rule', unpopular with the Hindu leadership
of Congress, did not really appease the Muslims, who in 1906 had formed their
own organization, the All-India Muslim League. The Muslims were becoming
increasingly restless over the failure of the Raj to protect the Ottoman Empire.
From the start they had resented the Entente with Russia,[12] Turkey's long-
standing enemy, and such anxieties assumed hysterical proportions during the
Balkan Wars of 1912–13, when it briefly seemed possible that Istanbul might
fall to the 'infidel'.

Britain's long-term intentions towards India remained unclear in 1914. In
February 1912 the Indian Under-Secretary, Edwin Montagu, a Jew who
empathized with the yearning of educated natives for recognition and respect,

---

[11] S. E. Koss, *John Morley at the India Office, 1905–1910* (New Haven, 1969), 136.
[12] See below.

had publicly interpreted one of Hardinge's recent dispatches as meaning that the British government aimed, in the long run, at provincial self-government for India within a federal state. But Montagu was promptly contradicted by his superior, Crewe. It was left to the parliamentary Labour Party, and in particular to the ILP leadership, to press the case for a true democratization of British rule in India—causing a grateful Congress in 1911 to offer Ramsay MacDonald its presidency, an offer which, on Morley's advice, the Labour Leader refused.[13] The Liberals thus fell between two stools: their policies had aroused the suspicion of 'old India hands', not least Lord Curzon (who, as Minto once privately complained, could never forgive his successors for replacing him), while failing to secure a substantial body of Indian support.

The Liberals made a more distinctive impact in the imperial field in their handling of the 'colonies of settlement'. Decisively rejecting Chamberlain's earlier attempt to turn the Empire into a more centrally directed state, fenced off by tariffs from the external world, the Liberal ministry acted on the assumption that the Empire was a free association of self-governing states, held together by bonds of commerce, kinship, and friendship.

At the Colonial Conference of 1907 Churchill stole the headlines and infuriated the Opposition when he turned down the colonial premiers' demand for imperial preference by declaring that his government had 'banged', 'barred', and 'bolted' the door on a policy which, he warned, risked creating an 'anti-Colonial Party' in the United Kingdom, dedicated to the destruction of the Empire. Milner and other indignant 'race patriots' tried to offset such 'anti-imperial' language by ostentatiously courting their favourite 'colonial', the Australian Premier Alfred Deakin. But by and large the colonial delegates, very touchy about their own autonomy, accepted that the mother country must be left equally free to pursue fiscal policies which had recently been massively endorsed by her own electorate.

In 1907 ministers humoured the white colonies by creating a separate Dominions Department[14] within the Colonial Office, to which a new 'Imperial Secretariat' was loosely attached. India, as in earlier conferences, was merely represented by 'assessors' from the India Office, on the ground that, not enjoying its own elected government, it could only be represented by nominees of the British government. It was also agreed in 1907 that 'Imperial Conferences', as they were now to be called, should convene every four years, with the British Prime Minister acting as ex-officio president.[15]

---

[13] B. Porter, *Critics of Empire: British Radical Attitudes to Colonialism in Africa 1895–1914* (London and New York, 1968), 313.
[14] The self-governing white colonies were designated 'dominions' for the first time.
[15] J. E. Kendle, *The Colonial and Imperial Conferences, 1887–1911* (London, 1967), chs. 5–6.

Useful co-operation resulted from such consultative gatherings. For example, at a subsidiary conference on defence held in 1909, the military forces of the self-governing colonies agreed to associate themselves with the Imperial General Staff, with a view to ensuring standardization of equipment, training, and staff procedure—an initiative which proved invaluable after 1914. Colonial premiers and defence ministers were also permitted to sit on the CID while passing through London.

Naval defence proved to be more troublesome. As the arms race with Germany intensified, the British government increasingly resented the negligible contribution which the self-governing colonies were making to imperial defence. Yet the colonies were reluctant to make regular contributions to the Exchequer, partly because they did not wish to be involved, willy-nilly, in a European war which only marginally affected their interests, and partly because they understandably resented the Admiralty's policy of withdrawing ships from distant oceans to concentrate on the North Sea, a policy which gathered further momentum after 1909.[16]

At times of crisis some colonies made gestures of solidarity: the naval scare of 1909, for example, prompted the New Zealand and Australian governments into making the Admiralty a gift of a battle cruiser each, and in 1912 the Malay States funded a Dreadnought—all these vessels being built in British yards. But, significantly, when the pro-British Conservative, Sir Robert Borden, replaced Laurier as Canadian Premier in 1912, he was unable to get his parliament to implement his promise to donate three Dreadnoughts— confirming Fisher's earlier (privately stated) view that the Canadians were 'an unpatriotic, grasping people, who only stuck by us for the good they [could] get out of us'.[17]

Colonial self-assertiveness was matched by an impatience with imperialist rhetoric within the ranks of the government's own supporters. In 1908 the new House of Commons symbolically turned down by sixty-eight votes the idea of officially recognizing Empire Day—to loud Irish and Labour cheers. Given this political context, the Liberal ministry was wise to move cautiously. The best way to unite the Empire, it believed, was to improve communication between its component parts. Ignoring his opponents' gibes about the abandonment of free trade, Lloyd George at the Board of Trade went ahead in 1907 with a scheme to pay a subsidy to mail packets plying between British territories (the 'All-Red Route'). Five years later the government embarked upon the

---

[16] In 1909 Canada and Australia were permitted separate 'fleet units', on the understanding that they would come under Admiralty control in the event of a major war. Grey later warned the Dominions that British loss of control of the seas would scupper the Empire.

[17] P. O'Brien, 'The Titan Refreshed: Imperial Overstretch and the British Navy Before the First World War', *Past & Present*, 172 (2001), 159.

construction of an imperial network of telegraph stations—the origins of the ill-fated Marconi Affair.

These were modest measures, but they achieved more than anything that was likely to emerge in the near future from the grandiose schemes of their opponents. In any case, imperial idealism was effectively discarded by the Unionist Party when, in 1913, it dropped the food taxes that were an essential component of any system of imperial preference. Even more futile was the empty constitution-mongering of Milner's young friends in the 'Round Table Circle', who hankered after a process of political centralization that no self-governing colony could possibly have tolerated.

In fact, the Liberals were well justified in their belief that what held the mother country and her white colonies together was less 'machinery' than the spontaneous, undirected activities of their populations. Between 1900 and 1913 the overall share of British exports going to the Empire fell slightly, but in textiles and iron products it rose significantly—from 39.7 per cent to 43.9 per cent, and from 36.7 per cent to 48.2 per cent, respectively.[18] India remained Britain's second-largest market (after Germany)[19], and UK exports to Canada, Australia, New Zealand, and South Africa also stayed very buoyant, rising from 11.4 per cent of total exports in 1902 to 14 per cent in 1913.[20] True, the tightening of Canada's links with its great neighbour to the south meant that she became less dependent on the mother country.[21] Yet the reverse did not apply. Indeed, as Australia increased its acreage devoted to cereals and Canada developed for the first time into one of the world's great granaries, Britain was actually drawing more of its imported wheat (nearly one-half) from the colonies in 1913 than it had done in 1902 (about one-fifth).

The white colonies, and indeed other parts of the Empire, also shared in the great capital export boom which immediately preceded the war, though not, of course, to the exclusion of foreign countries. Australia, New Zealand, South Africa, and Canada greatly benefited from the investment, at low rates of interest, which Britain was exceptionally well placed to provide, helped by the Colonial Stocks Act of 1900.[22] Finally, emigration to the colonies picked up pace in the immediate pre-war years: between 1910 and 1913 alone over half-a-million people from the United Kingdom started a new life in Canada, as it embarked upon the big expansion of its prairie farming. Such developments

---

[18] P. Cain, 'Political Economy in Edwardian England: The Tariff-Reform Controversy', in A. O'Day (ed.), *The Edwardian Age: Conflict and Stability 1900–1914* (London and Basingstoke, 1979), 50.

[19] Third, if re-exports are included, which would put the USA into first place.

[20] A. Offer, *The First World War: An Agrarian Interpretation* (Oxford, 1989), 264.

[21] G. S. Graham, 'Imperial Finance, Trade, and Communications, 1895–1914', in E. A. Benians, J. Butler, and C. E. Carrington (eds.), *The Cambridge History of the British Empire: Vol. III: The Empire-Commonwealth 1870–1919* (Cambridge, 1959), 481–2.

[22] See Ch. 8.

probably contributed to that deepening of imperial sentiment which induced all the white colonies to offer Britain their support in August 1914.

At the same time, the Colonial Office lost the importance that it had briefly assumed under Chamberlain. The flamboyant Churchill gave it a high profile, but he was suspected of using his stay there primarily to advance his own career—he was certainly very keen to be transferred to another post (not simply promoted) when Asquith became Prime Minister. Churchill was, in any case, subordinate to Lord Elgin. The latter, a former Indian Viceroy and a sound administrator, largely lacked political contacts and talents and was terrified of public speaking—probably the main reason why Asquith unceremoniously sacked him in April 1908. Elgin's successor, Lord Crewe (1908–10), had much greater influence at Cabinet level, but he was doubling up as Leader of the Lords, which reduced the time that he could devote to his departmental duties. Crewe's successor, Harcourt (1910–15), was more effective, but he was not a minister in the top flight. The appointment of such men indicates the low priority which Campbell-Bannerman and Asquith accorded to imperial affairs. The attention of the Liberals was more focused on domestic issues and on the European balance of power. However, imperial and European policy could not entirely be divorced, and Indian defence constituted an important point of intersection between them.

2. THE FORMATION OF THE ANGLO-RUSSIAN ENTENTE

How best to defend the Raj without incurring prohibitive costs was a problem which immediately confronted Campbell-Bannerman's ministry. It did so because Russia had recovered from its defeat at the hands of Japan with surprising rapidity, and its railway construction programme was bringing its agents steadily closer to Afghanistan, Tibet, and the Gulf.[23]

In 1907 a subcommittee of the CID, meeting under Morley, reached the ominous conclusion that, in the event of a Russian attack on India, 100,000 troops would have to be sent there in the first year of war; Lord Roberts warned that an additional half-a-million men might later be needed.[24] For a Radical ministry pledged to economy, this was a deeply disturbing prospect. What to do? Britain's ally, Japan, did not wish to help out in India, nor, understandably, did the India Office want her to do so. Given ministerial hostility to the

---

[23] The Gulf's importance was soon to be enhanced by the navy's conversion of its battleships from coal- to oil-fired turbines, a momentous decision which in turn led to the government's purchase of a stake in the Anglo-Persian Oil Company in August 1914.

[24] Kitchener had earlier fixed on a figure of 300,000–400,000 (M. Howard, *The Continental Commitment: The Dilemma of British Defence Policy in the Era of Two World Wars* (Oxford, 1971), 19).

Japanese treaty, the one part of Lansdowne's legacy of which few senior Liberals approved,[25] the only other option was to come to terms with Russia, a course of action which Grey had been advocating as early as 1895, and which had another powerful champion in Sir Charles Hardinge, Grey's Permanent Under-Secretary and until recently British Ambassador at St Petersburg.[26]

The likelihood of such a rapprochement improved when the German government, piqued by its setbacks at the Algeçiras Conference,[27] blocked all financial help to Russia, precipitating the fall of Witte's pro-German regime in May 1906. Grey encouraged (though he would not underwrite) a Barings' loan to Russia, and this was enough to create a more friendly atmosphere in which diplomatic talks could go forward between Isvolskii, the new Russian Foreign Minister, and Hardinge's successor at St Petersburg, Sir Arthur Nicolson.[28]

These negotiations nearly became derailed by events within Russia. A renewal of anti-Jewish pogroms in 1906 led to hostile questions in the House. Then, on 16 June 1907, Tsar Nicholas dissolved the second Duma, a development to which Campbell-Bannerman responded with the cry: 'La Douma est morte, vive la Douma!' The Tsar cancelled the proposed visit of the Russian fleet to Britain the following month. However, despite an outcry in the Liberal press, the Foreign Office stood by its guns, strongly supported by Morley.

The Anglo-Russian Entente, finalized in August 1907, was the sort of understanding for which Lansdowne had vainly been searching earlier in the century. Its main significance was that it allowed the two imperial powers to square their Asian differences. Russia recognized that Tibet fell under Chinese control, while the British, for their part, withdrew from the Lhasa Convention;[29] the two countries agreed to confer over Afghanistan; and Persia was effectively divided between a Russian sphere of influence in the north, a British zone in the south fronting the Gulf, and a central zone which was allocated to the Shah of Persia.

The Russian Entente was anathema to the Government of India, and former officials, including Curzon, lined up to denounce it. Of course the Entente was predicated on Russian 'good behaviour', and in that sense was 'an act of faith'.[30] Was that faith, as Curzon thought, misplaced? As early as October 1908 critics

---

[25] Monger, *End of Isolation*, 286.
[26] P. M. Kennedy, *The Rise of the Anglo-German Antagonism 1860–1914* (London, 1980), 284.
[27] See below.
[28] K. Neilson, *Britain and the Last Tsar: British Policy and Russia 1894–1917* (Oxford, 1995), 267–74.
[29] In 1903 Sir Francis Younghusband, in defiance of the government, had forced the Tibetans to sign a convention making that country virtually a British protectorate.
[30] Wilson, *Politics of the Entente*, 82.

complained that the Russians were not controlling their agents in Persia, and by 1912 similar concerns were being expressed about their encroachments in Mongolia, Tibet, and Chinese Turkestan.[31]

The Anglo-Russian rapprochement landed Grey in much domestic trouble. Initially many backbench Liberal MPs had been prepared to give the Entente a fair wind, impressed by Morley's strong advocacy of it and conscious of the saving in armaments expenditure which it promised to bring. On the other hand, cosying up to the Tsarist regime had, from the start, elicited bitter protests. In the summer of 1908 some Liberal and Labour Members voiced their opposition to the King's meeting with Nicholas II at Reval so vehemently that the Radical MP Arthur Ponsonby was denied an invitation to attend the annual Buckingham Palace garden party—as were Victor Grayson and Keir Hardie.[32]

Radical anger deepened over revelations of developments in Persia. By 1910 Professor E. G. Browne was revealing through the columns of the *Manchester Guardian* how the Russians were undermining the constitutional forces in that country.[33] Supported by Curzon, the Radicals blamed the British Foreign Secretary for not preventing such 'outrages' as the Russian-inspired sacking of Morgan Schuster, the American Consul in Tehran. In 1912 the Radicals, cheered on by Scott of the *Manchester Guardian*, filled Covent Garden Opera House to protest against British collusion in the 'virtual dismemberment of this unhappy country'. Ponsonby, Philip Morrell, and Brailsford wanted to end the Russian Entente entirely, and were even prepared to involve Germany in Persia to save it from British and Russian bullying.[34]

Yet, by and large, Grey stood by the Russian Entente. He did so, partly because it was difficult to see how else, except at prohibitive expense, Britain's long land frontier in India could be safeguarded. But wider considerations were also involved, since, from the start, the Entente had amounted to much more than the local colonial arrangement which Morley had envisaged: it also had a European dimension. In February 1906 Grey had written privately of his impatience 'to see Russia re-established as a factor in European politics'.[35] Britain's coming-to-terms with Russia, France's alliance partner, was thus valued by the Foreign Secretary as an essential element in his pursuit of a 'balance of power', which would offset Germany's Continental dominance.

---

[31] Ibid. 83.
[32] Labour moved a reduction of the Foreign Office vote by way of protest.
[33] Morris, *Radicalism Against War*, 257.
[34] H. Weinroth, 'Radicalism and Nationalism: An Increasingly Unstable Equation', in A. J. A. Morris (ed.), *Edwardian Radicalism, 1900–1914* (London, 1974), 221–2.
[35] Howard, *Continental Commitment*, 33.

3. THE HARDENING OF THE ANGLO-FRENCH ENTENTE

Unlike his mentor Rosebery, Grey had long been suspicious of Germany. As we have seen, he also strongly favoured following the policies of the outgoing Unionist government. When he took office, in the middle of the first Moroccan crisis, Grey probably believed that he was doing precisely that. However, encouraged by his permanent officials, Grey gave British diplomacy a far more anti-German twist than Lansdowne and Sanderson would have countenanced. He also put a much greater emphasis on Continental, as distinct from imperial, considerations. For example, the British now accepted Germany's acquisition of a port on the Moroccan coast, an issue over which the Admiralty had been prepared to fight a war only a few months earlier. But although Grey, looking at the issues on their merits, had initially wanted the French to make concessions and had briefly backed a compromise solution put forward by the Austrian government, his principal objective was to stiffen French resolve, thereby upholding the Entente, which he clearly valued for its own sake. By the time the Algeçiras Conference ended on 7 April, the Germans had been forced into an ignominious retreat.

It is a telling indication of Grey's extreme sensitivity to French susceptibilities that in October 1907 he should have threatened resignation if the War Office sent the band of the Coldstream Guards on a visit to Germany, when it had earlier turned down an invitation from the French military![36] Grey took this absurd line because he feared that, were Britain once to allow France to fall under German domination, she herself would become isolated and vulnerable. This view was shared by nearly all of his senior officials, the most Germanophobe of whom, Eyre Crowe, composed the famous memorandum of 1 January 1907 which sought to uncover in the events of the previous decade a calculated plan of aggrandizement on the part of the Reich—a memorandum that took on more significance in retrospect than it had at the time, but which shows the way the tide had begun to flow in higher diplomatic circles.

This anti-German outlook also coloured the attitudes of the War Office and the Admiralty, especially when the naval arms race began in earnest from 1907 onwards. The German government made more enemies by sabotaging the 1907 Hague Peace Conference, on which Campbell-Bannerman had pinned many hopes. The Foreign Office had never shared the Prime Minister's optimism, and took some pleasure from the breakdown of the conference: 'Bülow has come into the open, and we know where we are', Grey complacently observed.[37]

In February 1908 *The Times*'s military correspondent Colonel Repington revealed that the Kaiser had sent a personal letter of remonstrance about the

---

[36] Monger, *End of Isolation*, 299.
[37] Kennedy, *Anglo-German Antagonism*, 443.

size of Britain's naval estimates to the First Lord of the Admiralty, Lord Tweedmouth; this revelation further stimulated anti-German sentiment. Relationships worsened again after the Kaiser had given an ill-judged interview with the *Daily Telegraph* on 28 October (supposedly cleared in the German Foreign Ministry), in which he presented himself as a friend of Britain, vainly trying to soften his subjects' anti-British animus.

Faced by the 'German menace', most of Grey's advisers would have liked Britain to convert the French Entente into an alliance: Nicolson forcefully advocated this in 1909 and 1912, as did Francis Bertie, the Ambassador in Paris; and in February 1914 many prominent figures within the Foreign Office urged that Russia, too, be brought within such an alliance.[38] But Grey resolutely refused, justly pointing out that 'alliances, especially Continental alliances, [were] not in accordance with our traditions'.[39] Paul Cambon, the French Ambassador in London, was time and again fobbed off with this argument.

What really held Grey back was his realization that no Liberal-dominated House of Commons would countenance a thorough going Continental entanglement. But he also feared that too open a commitment to France might encourage in Paris the spirit of *revanchisme*:[40] in other words, peace would be better preserved if, while generally supporting the French, the British kept the Quai d'Orsay guessing. But Grey's position was even more complex than this, in that he seems on occasions genuinely to have shared the desire of his own backbenches to treat the French Entente as a model for a similar agreement with Germany. He was certainly prepared to negotiate with Berlin on subsidiary issues—though, crucially, not if this threatened a rupture with Paris. Thus Grey was walking a tightrope: pursuing a policy that was not wholly unacceptable to his peace-loving party, while taking due notice of the warnings being pressed upon him by his professional advisers.

4. THE STRATEGIC DILEMMA

Superimposed upon this difficulty was an acute strategic dilemma. How were the armed services to be prepared to fight Germany, should the need arise? Ideally this problem should have been tackled on its merits, but this did not happen because, from the moment they assumed office, the Liberals were so intent on reducing armaments expenditure. This pressure for economy

[38] Churchill and Henry Wilson wanted a defensive pact that also included Belgium and Denmark, an arrangement quite unacceptable to Belgium (D. French, *British Strategy and War Aims, 1914–16* (London, 1986), 12).

[39] Wilson, *Politics of the Entente*, 42.

[40] In March 1913 he told Bertie that Britain 'can be no party to France precipitating a conflict for the revanche' (S. R. Williamson, *The Politics of Grand Strategy: Britain and France Prepare for War, 1904–1914* (Cambridge, Mass., 1969), 330).

exacerbated the perennial competition for funding between War Office and Admiralty, which in turn distorted the whole process of military planning.

Well aware of the financial constraints, Haldane was determined to keep the cost of the army below £28 million—indeed, it was this figure, rather than any true military strategy, that dictated the size of the military force he set about creating. Bringing military expenditure down from the levels reached under the Unionists also helped him immensely when he came to steer his Army Bill through the Commons.[41]

But Fisher at the Admiralty dared not pursue a finance-driven policy of this kind; nor, given the public's irrational belief that security could be measured simply by the counting of large battleships, would the political heads of his Department allow him to do so. In 1906, admittedly, no problems had arisen, the improved international situation (in particular, the recent annihiliation of the Russian navy) allowing him to cut back on the Cawdor Programme he had inherited from the Unionists, so that only two, not four, Dreadnoughts were laid down in that year—no small matter, since each extra Dreadnought cost £2 million. The Admiralty's policy of concentrating ships in home waters, essential to the naval principle of 'command of the seas', also had the happy consequence of producing economies.[42]

However, the Admiralty balked when Asquith, the Chancellor of the Exchequer, tried to lop off a Dreadnought from the following year's programme. A fierce Cabinet row was only averted when Haldane intervened with the proposal that the building programme be made contingent on the outcome of the Hague Conference. When the Conference collapsed, the third battleship was duly built.

As Anglo–German relations deteriorated, the rivalry between the two armed services intensified. In May 1908, encouraged perhaps by Fisher, the two Radical 'economists', Churchill and Lloyd George, sought a reduction in the size of the force Haldane was organizing for overseas operations, which Churchill thought 'dangerous and provocative'.[43] Helped by Esher and the King, Haldane fought off his assailants. But Lloyd George threatened Esher in June that 'no reduction in Army Estimates next year means no Dreadnoughts'. As Esher observed: 'This is bounce.'[44]

The Radicals' attempt to curb the Admiralty's expenditure in 1909 coincided with reports, partly emanating from H. H. Mulliner, Managing Director of the

---

[41] In 1905 the Army Estimates exceeded £29 million: by 1907 they had fallen to under £28 million, by 1909 to under £27 million, after which they rose slightly to just over £28 million in 1913.

[42] There was another phase to this process in 1909 (Williamson, *Grand Strategy*, p. 239), and again in 1912.

[43] Ibid. 99.

[44] 26 June 1908, in M. V. Brett (ed.), *Journals and Letters of Reginald, Viscount Esher, Vol. 2 1903–1910* (London, 1934), 326.

Coventry Ordnance Works, that Germany was secretly accelerating its ship-building programme, stockpiling items that would otherwise cause bottlenecks in the construction programme[45]—a worrying development, given that Germany could now outbuild the Royal Navy through her capacity to manufacture heavy gun mountings. The Admiralty, headed since the previous May by Reginald McKenna, who had succeeded the semi-senile Tweedmouth, demanded that six new Dreadnoughts be built in response. The Radicals in the Cabinet dug in their heels at four. But the discovery later in the year that the Austrian and Italian navies were laying down more capital ships afforded the government a way out. In Churchill's famous words, 'the Admiralty demanded six Dreadnoughts, the economists offered four, and we eventually compromised on eight'.

The outcome seemed to be a vindication of the Opposition. For with the total collapse of naval bipartisanship, the Conservatives were now vigorously attacking Liberal parsimony: 'We Want Eight and We Won't Wait' was their slogan. In fact it soon transpired that the Dreadnought gap, pointed to by the government's critics, did not exist: the Germans had been honest when they denied that any acceleration was taking place. No matter: the Admiralty had won a famous victory.

What, however, was the Admiralty proposing to do with its naval forces, should Britain find itself at war? In the interests of state security, Fisher, the First Sea Lord, refused to divulge his precise plans, but his thinking seems to have been this. A concentration of British vessels in home waters would force Germany into surrender by imposing an economic blockade which would eventually flush Tirpitz's numerically inferior High Fleet out of harbour, after which it would be sent to the bottom of the sea in a re-enactment of Trafalgar. The Admiralty also played with the idea of using the navy in a series of amphibious assaults against North Germany. In 1906–7 the Royal Naval College was making secret preparations for obstructing the Elbe, bombarding the Baltic Ports, launching large-scale raids between Kiel and Memel, and even capturing a German or Dutch island, perhaps Borkum.

Although it is questionable whether Fisher himself believed all these oper-ations to be feasible,[46] most naval officers were agreed that land fighting should mainly be left to their allies, while Britain maintained control of the seas and harnessed its economic strength. Money spent on a large army, they thought, would not only be squandered, but every pound devoted to this purpose would be subtracted from the navy, on which the Empire's safety ultimately depended; the Secretary of the CID from 1912 onwards, Maurice Hankey, a Royal Marines officer, believed that 'if every man had military training the

[45] F. Coetzee, *For Party or Country: Nationalism and the Dilemmas of Popular Conservatism in Edwardian England* (New York, 1990), 108–9.

[46] N. A. Lambert, *Sir John Fisher's Naval Revolution* (London, 1999), 180–1.

nation would lose its perspective on the vital importance of sea power'.[47] Instead of getting bogged down in the affairs of the Continent, Britain should, navalists thought, be basing defence policy around the Empire and developing closer links with the United States.[48]

Haldane at the War Office, on the other hand, was pursuing a completely different strategy. Its origins go back to the first Moroccan crisis. In December 1905 the CID had called a series of conferences to decide what action Britain could take were it to be involved in a Franco-German war. The General Staff 'gatecrashed' these discussions, hoping to develop them into the kind of military entente with France that had been on its mind since earlier in the year. In mid-December General Grierson, the Director of Military Operations, made contact with Colonel Huguet, the French Military Attaché in London, and the military conversations began in earnest—conversations which assumed that, in a Franco-German war, British troops would be sent to the Continent to reinforce France's left flank.

On 9 January 1906, with the general election campaign in full swing, Grey at last learned what was afoot. Mistakenly thinking that these talks had been sanctioned by the Unionists, he let them proceed. Haldane, the new War Secretary, indicated his approval a few days later. On 10 January Cambon tried to find out what political significance the talks had in the eyes of the British government; Grey replied that, in his personal opinion, public opinion 'would be strongly moved in favour of France', but only the Cabinet could give a binding answer.[49]

With the election over, Grey for the first time sent the Prime Minister and Lord Ripon, the Leader of the Lords, an edited dispatch of his exchanges with Cambon, but this document made no reference to the actual staff talks,[50] though Haldane may later have given 'C-B' a somewhat fuller verbal account. The Anglo-French military exchanges then resumed on an official basis. But only a handful of ministers had any knowledge of the commitments that were being made on their behalf. Even Grey's misleading dispatch was not brought by the Prime Minister and Ripon to the attention of the Cabinet when it met on 31 January.

Grey's willingness to act behind the back of most of his colleagues[51] has often been censured, and unfavourable comparisons drawn with Lansdowne's conduct. But the Prime Minister's behaviour was also questionable. He had

[47] Wilson, *Politics of the Entente*, 41.

[48] Perhaps significantly, Hankey's parents were Australian, his wife South African (Offer, *First World War*, 266).

[49] Monger, *End of Isolation*, 269.

[50] J. Charmley, *Splendid Isolation? Britain and the Balance of Power 1874–1914* (London, 1999), 335.

[51] Grey was more frank with Colonial delegates than he was with his own Cabinet.

1. The Diamond Jubilee procession passes through Trafalgar Square, 1897

2. London congestion, 1912. The junction between Holborn and Kingsway is crowded with both horse-drawn and motorized traffic. The entrance to the underground station can be seen on the corner

3. An advertisement of 1900 plays on the social aspirations of rich and poor

4. The Lobby of the House of Commons, 1886, from the *Vanity Fair* Christmas
Supplement of 1886. The foreground group includes (left to right) Joseph Chamberlain,
Charles Stewart Parnell, William Gladstone, Lord Randolph Churchill, and
Lord Hartington. John Bright stands third from the left

5. A Sunderland slum area, 1889

6. The motor car as both status symbol and fashion accessory—the actress Ethel Oliver goes motoring, *c.*1910

7. HMS *Dreadnought* 1909. This picture clearly illustrates the size
and modern technology associated with this ship

8. Native stretcher-bearers carry the wounded at the Battle of Colenso (15–16 December, 1899)

9. Mafeking Night, 18 May 1900. Crowds in Central London celebrate the relief of Mafeking

10. Children in the street in London's Whitechapel, August 1911

11. Workers were only too aware of the contrasts between rich and poor, as is shown by the banner carried in this unemployment march in London, 10 October 1908

12. Ulster Day, 1 September 1912. Lord Charles Beresford, F. E. Smith, and Edward Carson lead the protest rally to City Hall, Belfast, for the signing of the Covenant against Home Rule

17. A working-class treat: families are taken on a Bank Holiday excursion, c.1895

Russell and Sons.]
ASTON VILLA'S FIRST GOAL IN THE LAST CUP FINAL.

18. Aston Villa score a goal against Newcastle United, 1904

19. Blackpool, *c.* 1903, with the Blackpool Tower in the distance

20. The music hall, Lambeth, *c.*1900—a large audience has gathered
for the last performance of the night

21. Letchworth Garden City, November 1912. Note the space given over to allotments and the Arts and Crafts style of the houses

22. Ernest Rutherford's room at the Cavendish Laboratory, Cambridge

23. Birmingham University buildings

24. In Manchester Flora Drummond and Phyllis Ayrton greet David Lloyd George and introduce him to a group of enthusiastic women munitions workers, September 1918

25. Trench warfare, c.1916. German prisoners act as stretcher-bearers near Bourton Wood

26. 'Women's Work': switchboard operators at the new telephone exchange at Euston, London in February 1915

already written to Ripon, saying that he disliked 'the stress laid upon joint preparations', which came 'very close to an honourable undertaking', and, on a visit to Paris shortly afterwards, he told an angry Clemenceau that 'he did not think that English public opinion would allow of British troops being employed on the Continent of Europe', a harsh message which Grey subsequently tried to soften.[52] Yet this was as far as Campbell-Bannerman was prepared to go to bring his Foreign Secretary to heel.

Almost certainly the Prime Minister thought it wiser not to communicate the gist of the talks to either the Cabinet or the party, knowing that both were split from top to bottom on this sort of issue. The Liberal government was in any case largely run on departmental lines, leading to a compartmentalization of policy, in foreign as in domestic matters. Nor did Campbell-Bannerman or his successor, Asquith, ever give international relations the sustained attention they had received under Balfour. As for Grey, a politician with an almost bottomless capacity for self-deception, he seems to have consoled himself with the thought that, since the military conversations were merely contingency exercises initiated by experts, his Cabinet colleagues could legitimately be left in ignorance. However, not only was the Cabinet sidelined: so, too, was the CID; even Esher only learnt the details of the staff talks in late 1908, and the Admiralty was kept entirely in the dark.

Meanwhile, Haldane had succeeded by 1907 where Arnold-Forster had signally failed: he had put together a package of army reforms which enjoyed the initial backing of the General Staff. He then slipped his plans effortlessly through the Cabinet, to the amazement of Campbell-Bannerman, who had rather hoped that his old adversary would fail. Traditionalists were soothed by a return to the old Cardwellian system of 'linked battalions'. But the centre-piece of Haldane's scheme was his creation of the British Expeditionary Force (BEF), which comprised about 150,000 men, divided between six infantry divisions and a cavalry brigade.[53] The old Militia was partly converted into a Special Reserve to replenish losses, while the Yeomanry and the Volunteers became a new home defence force, the Territorial Army, organized at county level by the Lords-Lieutenant.

Haldane was an uncommonly boring public speaker. This gift served him well when he presented a somnolent Commons with his Army Bill in 1907. Given the failure of his own War Secretaries, Balfour, a personal friend, thought it indecent to deny the Liberals their opportunity, while Radical backbenchers mainly directed their fire against peripheral features of the scheme, such as the governmental funding of school cadet corps and rifle

[52] Monger, *End of Isolation*, 325.
[53] Only 50,000 of these soldiers were 'in the colours', the others being reservists.

clubs and the employment of the 'feudal' Lords-Lieutenant.[54] Remarkably enough, few MPs (or indeed Cabinet ministers) asked what the BEF was *for*.

In all probability, the BEF was initially seen by its authors as a 'general purpose' army which could be employed as a strike-force in any part of the globe where British imperial interests were threatened, including, of course, India. Significantly, Grierson, the one member of the Army Council to know about the Anglo-French military conversations, did not play a very important role in the BEF's creation.[55] But one of its possible functions was intervening on the Continent, should this be necessary to counter German aggression. And, with Haldane's approval, this became its *predominant* role once Henry Wilson had moved from heading the Staff College to become Director of Military Operations (DMO) in 1910. Another stone had been laid in the edifice of the Continental strategy—a strategy that was obviously at complete variance with Admiralty thinking.

Which of the two competing approaches made the greater sense? As the military camp argued, it was certainly difficult to see how Germany could be defeated by naval power alone. Esher himself conceded that France's naval superiority in 1870–1 had not saved her from occupation, and that Napoleon had been defeated at Waterloo, not Trafalgar. Long before the British navy had starved the German population into submission, the Germans might have captured Paris, forcing the French to surrender—unless the French received military support.

On the other hand, the Continental strategy also possessed fatal flaws. Fisher got to the heart of the matter when he observed to Esher in May 1908: 'The Army is too big for a little war, too little for a big war!'[56] Germany possessed eighty-four divisions, France only sixty-six. Well might the Kaiser later observe: 'Excuse my saying so, but the few divisions you could put into the field could make no appreciable difference.'[57]

At first the Continental strategists were reduced to arguing that British intervention would at least provide a fillip to French morale.[58] But a more subtle justification was later offered by Henry Wilson. From his frequent discussions with French staff officers, Wilson eventually came to the (erroneous) conclusion that when the German army invaded France it would stay

---

[54] Morris, *Radicalism Against War*, 92.

[55] More important was William Nicholson, Quartermaster-General from 1905 to 1907 and the Chief of the Imperial General Staff between 1908 and 1912 (J. Gooch, *The Prospect of War: Studies in British Defence Policy 1847–1942* (London, 1981), 111).

[56] 5 May 1908, in Brett (ed.), *Esher: Vol. 2*, 309.

[57] In March 1911. Wilson, *Politics of the Entente*, 27.

[58] Hardinge, for example, privately admitted in May 1908 that Britain could never send an expedition of more than 150,000 men while Continental armies were counted by millions (Williamson, *Grand Strategy*, 102–3, 169).

below the line of the Meuse, attacking on a line from Liège to Verdun, so as not to commit a major infringement of Belgian neutrality. Since the road system would only accommodate fifty-one German divisions, the arrival of six British divisions alongside, say, forty French divisions might indeed tilt the military balance.

However, the cunning Wilson only half-believed his own theories, which also rested upon the questionable assumption that the next European war would be a short one. In private he was admitting that the six divisions, which was all that Britain could offer, were 'fifty too few'. The logic of the Continental strategy, as Fisher realized from the start, thus pointed to conscription.

Conscription, however, was politically impossible to promote. True, it had the backing of most regular army officers, who viewed the part-time soldiers of the Territorials with derision.[59] But, whereas on the Continent compulsion could be justified in terms of the need to defend the national territory, Britain was a predominantly maritime state. Most Liberals, moreover, had very strong ideological objections to any kind of military compulsion, seeing the voluntary principle as being inextricably bound up with other priceless liberties, such as freedom of assembly and of speech. They also knew that conscription would be both expensive and hideously unpopular.

Even the National Service League (NSL), under the presidency of the venerated Lord Roberts, dared not admit that one reason why it wanted compulsory military service was to allow the British army to operate on the Continent.[60] Instead, backed by Repington and Lord Lovat, Roberts engineered another 'invasion scare'.[61] He was helped by Balfour, who had not personally retracted his former 'blue-water' doctrines but who now argued that the strategic and political situation had changed since the last CID Invasion Inquiry in 1904 (when France, not Germany, was still thought to be the most likely enemy). In November 1907 the government agreed to set up another CID investigation—before which Balfour himself made a distinguished appearance.

However, there were two fatal defects in the NSL's line of argument. First, if the fleet could not secure Britain's coastline, might not the obvious solution be to spend more money on the Royal Navy, rather than drawing up contingency

---

[59] One of Haldane's few supporters was General Ian Hamilton, and even he admitted to Lady Roberts that almost the whole General Staff favoured 'conscription on the pure Continental basis'. Hamilton, however, headed a faction of army officers who prized the voluntary system because they thought it would produce a military force with greater attacking élan (C. Howard, *Continental Commitment*, 39–40).

[60] Howard, *Continental Commitment*, 39.

[61] R. J. Q. Adams and P. Poirier, *The Conscription Controversy in Great Britain 1900–18* (Houndsmill, 1987), 34.

plans that assumed its failure? Second, if the government really could be persuaded that a threat of all-out invasion existed, the natural response would be to hold back a significant part of the BEF. But this would scupper the planning of the Continentalists.[62]

In the event, the Invasion Inquiry, which lasted from 22 November 1907 to 28 July 1908, broadly vindicated the Admiralty's assertion that, largely thanks to Britain's flotilla defence, nothing more need be feared than small raids involving a maximum of 70,000 invaders, to contain which two regular divisions would be used, but only until such time as the 'Terriers' were battle-trained.[63]

Despite this qualified triumph, Fisher's days were numbered, as his enemies multiplied. The First Sea Lord's increasing obstinacy had earlier alienated his old friend George Clarke, who fell out with him in 1906 over the Admiralty's refusal to co-operate with the CID: Clarke was moved to the vacant governorship of Bombay in August 1907. Less easily quashed was Fisher's old enemy Admiral Charles Beresford, still smarting from the Admiralty's decision to relieve him of his command of the Channel Fleet a year early. Beresford threw the Senior Service into turmoil by publicly alleging that, due to Fisher's stewardship, the navy was not in a state of war-readiness. After Tweedmouth had failed to mediate between the two admirals, Asquith headed an inquiry which largely exonerated Fisher, though in rather tepid terms—Fisher being censured, for example, for his failure to establish a naval war staff.

Fisher was simultaneously coming under attack from the Big Navy lobby, whose spokesmen alleged that he was taking a reckless gamble with the country's safety by truckling to the cheese-paring Radicals. The result was that, led by a barrister, Horton-Smith, and the defeated Liberal Unionist candidate for Rushcliffe, Harold F. Wyatt, a militant faction broke away from the Navy League in the winter of 1907–8 to found the Imperial Maritime League. The new organization was backed by Beresford, who was in fact playing a dirty game, privately assuring Lloyd George that he would work for the Liberals as First Sea Lord were Fisher to be sacked!

A far more dangerous enemy was Haldane, Fisher's one-time admirer, who may behind the scenes have been fomenting Beresford's agitation and helping Repington over the Invasion Inquiry. In 1908 'that soapy Jesuit, Napoleon B. Haldane', as the old admiral now bitterly called him, persuaded Asquith to authorize a CID inquiry into the Military and Naval Needs of the Empire. This investigation, which occupied three sessions between 3 December 1908

---

[62] Alternately, to throw resources behind the Territorials, which would have run counter to the whole thrust of NSL propaganda.

[63] Williamson, *Grand Strategy*, 98; Gooch, *Prospect of War*, 13.

and 23 March 1909, inevitably showed up the divergent strategies being pursued by the two Service Departments. Though Esher loyally supported him, Fisher failed to establish the feasibility of the Admiralty's plan to use the army as 'a projectile to be fired by the Navy'.

Even now Fisher refused to concede defeat. But Haldane had identified the chink in the First Sea Lord's armour: his failure to create a naval war staff. In late 1909 the government used this issue to force Fisher into retirement. His successor, Admiral Arthur Wilson, promised to work with the War Office in ferrying the BEF to the Continent. But in practice he did little to honour his promise.

5. GREY UNDER CHALLENGE

Higher naval expenditure had meanwhile impacted on Edward Grey at the Foreign Office, since alarmed Radicals, dismayed at the government's failure to honour its election pledges to curb swollen armaments budgets, began pressing hard for a rapprochement with Germany—a project which they would have favoured even more had they known how close Britain had come to war with Germany in November 1908, over the so-called Casablanca Incident.[64]

The Foreign Office professionals were not keen to open communications with Berlin, and Bertie, in Paris, sometimes disobeyed instructions in his anxiety to stop them. But from late 1909 onwards Grey no longer had quite as much freedom of manoeuvre as he had earlier enjoyed. On 20 January 1911 a Cabinet Committee was therefore set up to oversee the Anglo-German negotiations, a body which included Morley, Crewe, and Walter Runciman, as well as Asquith and Grey. Also emerging as a formidable critic of the whole drift of Britain's foreign policy was the Lord Chancellor, Lord Loreburn.

The Anglo-German naval talks opened in 1910, and more or less continued up to the time of the Haldane Mission of 1912.[65] Unfortunately, throughout these complex negotiations the two sides never really budged from their starting-points. Grey sincerely wanted to call a halt to the arms race.[66] But the Germans insisted as their price for doing this that Britain sign a neutrality pact. In January 1912 Harcourt, McKenna, Lloyd George, Loreburn, and Jack Pease all favoured making this concession.[67] But, though the Foreign Office was

[64] This incident was caused by the German consul in Casablanca, who tried to conceal deserters from the Foreign Legion. McKenna was told to have the fleet in readiness, and Esher noted in his diary that 'it looked like war' (Kennedy, *Anglo-German Antagonism*, 444).

[65] The objective of Haldane's mission was to explore the possibility of trading off British naval supremacy for a promise to help Germany acquire more colonies and give them assurances against future aggression.

[66] Grey feared that the patience of the British taxpayer was being strained by its cost.

[67] Wilson, *Politics of the Entente*, 29.

prepared to promise that Britain would not take part in any unprovoked attack on Germany, it would not agree to breaking its close accord with the French by agreeing to neutrality. As Grey put it to Nicolson at the time of the breakdown of the Haldane Mission, 'although we cannot bind ourselves under all circumstances to go to war with France against Germany, we shall also certainly not bind ourselves to Germany not to assist France'.[68] Nor would Berlin consent to alter its latest naval law. The naval arms race therefore continued, pushing the Admiralty's budget up to £48,800,000 by the summer of 1914.

In the middle of these Anglo–German talks London and Berlin nearly came to blows when the Germans, in the middle of 1911, once again challenged France by sending a gunboat, the *Panther*, to the Moroccan port of Agadir. Initially the British were undecided how to react. Bertie and other Germanophobe diplomats wanted full support to be given to the French, but Grey, for internal political reasons, had to move more cautiously. Loreburn bluntly warned the Foreign Secretary on 25 August against military intervention on the Continent in what he described as 'a purely French quarrel', adding that such an action could only be carried through the Commons 'by a majority very largely composed of Conservatives and with a very large number of [the] Ministerial side against you', which meant that 'the present government would not carry on'.[69]

Fortunately for Grey, he received on this occasion support from the one-time Little Englanders, Churchill and Lloyd George. Churchill had for some months been absorbed by the drama of the developing Anglo–German conflict. Lloyd George's crossing of sides seems more surprising, but Esher had shrewdly observed in his diary as early as February 1909 that the Chancellor, 'in his heart, [did] not care a bit for economy, and [was] quite ready to face Parliament with any amount of deficit, and to "go" for a big Navy', since he was 'plucky and an Imperialist at heart'.[70]

In the summer of 1910 Lloyd George, in his secret coalition memorandum, had advocated that Britain adopt the Swiss militia system, based on compulsion; and thereafter, like Churchill, he was a secret conscriptionist. However, all this was unknown to the wider public, so that it came as a great shock to them, and of course to the German government, when, after consultations with Grey and Asquith but acting behind the back of the Cabinet, the Radical Chancellor made his famous speech at the Mansion House on 21 July, warning Berlin not to leave Britain out of account in its handling of the Moroccan question. It was this speech which persuaded the German government to back down once more.

---

[68] Williamson, *Grand Strategy*, 262.

[69] Morris, *Radicalism Against War*, 295. Loreburn later discovered that the Unionist Leaders had indeed been asked for their support (Wilson, *Politics of the Entente*, 31).

[70] 12 Dec. 1909, in Brett (ed.), *Esher, Vol. 2*, 370.

The Agadir Crisis brought to a head the strategic differences between War Office and Admiralty, which were thrashed out at the CID on 23 August. Henry Wilson trounced his naval namesake, whose emphasis on *close* blockade and amphibious action in the Baltic amazed and confounded even his own departmental chief, McKenna. Moreover, for the first time, the full extent of the War Office's commitment to the French army was revealed—a commitment recently extended by an 'accord' of 20 July 1911, according to which the six infantry divisions and one division of cavalry would disembark at Rouen and Le Havre, assembling in the Arras–Cambrai–St-Quentin area.[71]

Contrary to received opinion, the War Office's 'triumph' was not total. Hankey came away from the 23 August meeting convinced that the Admiralty's case had *not* been overthrown. This was because Henry Wilson had been challenged by Churchill, who shared the view of many military experts—including Sir John French, the soon-to-be appointed CIGS—that the BEF should be sent directly into Belgium, where, it was hoped, it could safeguard the Channel Ports and operate, in a semi-independent role, in conjunction with the navy.

Yet so 'puerile' (Asquith's private epithet) was Arthur Wilson's performance at the CID meeting that it was easy, for the moment, to overlook these cross-currents. The crucial outcome of the meeting was that the indolent Asquith felt obliged to move McKenna, too closely identified with the views of his professional advisers, to the Home Office; ominously, McKenna went protesting his continued opposition to the military entente with France. Haldane, who had earlier flirted with the idea of heading a new Ministry of Defence, now put himself forward as McKenna's successor. Asquith, after some hesitation, ruled this out on the ground that Haldane's recent translation to the House of Lords made it politically undesirable—but really in order to avoid inflicting too deep a humiliation on the Senior Service. Instead, he decreed that McKenna and Churchill should swap posts.

Churchill took charge at the Admiralty in October 1911, and immediately set up several interdepartmental committees to organize troop transportation to the Continent. In June 1912 Haldane replaced Loreburn on the Woolsack. The War Secretaryship passed to Haldane's former Under-Secretary Jack Seely, who, by a happy chance, was an old friend of Churchill's from their 'Hughligan' days. Thereafter inter-service co-operation improved,[72] especially once Churchill had further distanced himself from Arthur Wilson's fantasies by replacing a close blockade with an observational one (and in the summer of

[71] Williamson, *Grand Strategy*, 174–6.
[72] Between August 1913 and May 1914 Churchill and Seely worked effectively together on mobilization through the body called the 'High Level Bridge'.

1914 with a distant blockade), so closing down the possibility of amphibious operations against Germany.

But although, by and large, the War Office's Continental option had, belatedly, been chosen in preference to the Admiralty's plans, even after August 1911 there were still divided counsels. This became apparent during the third Invasion Inquiry of January 1913–May 1914 (by which time the threat of aerial attack had also come into the equation), when, ironically, it was the *Admiralty* which emphasized the risk of invasion, perhaps wanting to keep at least one division back in order to hamper the Continental strategists.[73]

In theory the CID could have done more to resolve these inter-service disagreements. But Clarke's attempt to make this body the planning centre for the Empire had not survived his departure as Secretary in October 1907. His two successors, Captain Ottley (1907–12) and then Captain Maurice Hankey, denied the sort of support which Balfour had once given Clarke, concentrated on ensuring the body's survival by avoiding controversial issues, unless the Prime Minister commanded otherwise, and devoted themselves instead to a series of technical issues, many of them devolved upon subcommittees: between April 1912 and the summer of 1914 there were fourteen such ad-hoc bodies, as well as the standing Overseas, Home Ports, and Air committees.[74] Full meetings of the CID degenerated into farce, with Asquith allowing up to thirty members to debate issues in a strategic vacuum.[75] In short, the CID's withdrawal from the consideration of larger strategic issues (Esher was fobbed off in 1912 with the establishment of a strategic subcommittee) meant that planning remained in the hands of the two Service Departments.

All this was to lead to future problems. Meanwhile Agadir had also created dissension on the domestic front. For the August 1911 meeting of the CID had been blatantly packed; no invitation, for example, had gone out to Morley, Harcourt, or Esher, all opponents of Continental entanglements. Tipped off by the aggrieved McKenna, the dissident ministers soon learned of what had happened at the meeting, not least the secret military conversations. They insisted on bringing the matter up at two tense Cabinet meetings, held on 1 November and 15 November. At the latter they pressed a resolution to the effect that 'no communications should take place between the General Staff and the Staffs of other countries which can, directly or indirectly, commit this country to military or naval intervention', and that 'such communications, if they relate to concerted action by land or sea, should not be entered into

---

[73] Williamson, *Grand Strategy*, 308.

[74] N. D'Ombrain, *War Machinery and High Policy: Defence Administration in Peacetime Britain 1902–1914* (Oxford, 1973), 265.

[75] Ibid. 121. However, it is arguable that Britain's CID, for all its faults, offered a forum for strategic discussion unavailable elsewhere (J. Keegan, *The First World War* (London, 1998), 31).

without the previous approval of the Cabinet'.[76] The resolution was adopted by fifteen votes to five, the minority consisting of Asquith, Grey, Haldane, Lloyd George, and Churchill.[77]

But still no clear course of action emerged. Grey published the innocuous 'secret' clauses of the 1904 Entente, along with an assurance to the House that the Liberals had not made any additions to them. Henceforward the Foreign Office had to behave with greater caution. In January 1912 the Cabinet kept up the pressure, this time insisting that 'anything which passed between experts ... was not to be taken as prejudicing the freedom of decision of the Government'.[78] However, the Foreign Office took the Cabinet resolution of 15 November to cover only new guarantees, not the continuation of existing ones, and Asquith, albeit without enthusiasm, was soon privately reassuring Grey, Haldane, and Churchill that the military exchanges with the French should not be terminated.[79] Indeed Henry Wilson, whose contempt for civilian politicians (or 'Frocks' as he called them) was increasing minute by minute, actually tightened his links with the French General Staff, producing arrangements far more detailed than those between Austria-Hungary and Germany or between France and Russia.[80]

Moreover, in 1912, following the breakdown of the Haldane Mission, the Admiralty decided to withdraw many of Britain's capital ships from the Mediterranean, leaving its eastern waters to be protected only by her cruiser squadrons at Malta and by the French navy.[81] This move was intended to complement the French decision, reached independently in 1906, largely to withdraw from the northern reaches of the English Channel. Though such a naval division of responsibility made sense from the viewpoint of preparing for a war with Germany in alliance with the French, it alarmed the Radical 'pacifists', who feared that Britain would incur an obligation which might draw her ineluctably into war. They even declared a preference for higher naval expenditure to make Britain independent of foreign powers—a stand they were soon to rue! This brought them into an incongruous alliance with

---

[76] Howard, *Continental Commitment*, 47–8.

[77] Grey called the requirement to secure the prior approval of Cabinet 'a little tight', a phrase he later deleted. But Asquith, on 5 September 1911, had already had second thoughts, privately warning Grey that the military talks were 'rather dangerous, especially the part which referred to possible British assistance', and urging that 'the French ought not to be encouraged in present circumstances, to make their plans on any assumptions of this kind'.

[78] Wilson, *Politics of the Entente*, 29.

[79] Grey had told Asquith: 'It would create consternation if we forbade our military experts to converse with the French. No doubt these conversations and our speeches have given an expectation of support. I do not see how that can be helped' (Williamson, *Grand Strategy*, 197, 204).

[80] Z. S. Steiner, *Britain and the Origins of the First World War* (London and Basingstoke, 1977), 198.

[81] Howard, *Continental Commitment*, 48. Some historians believe that the agreement with France was designed to reassure Paris in the wake of the Haldane Mission (French, *Strategy and War Aims*, 10).

imperialists in whose eyes the Mediterranean remained crucial to the maintenance of Britain's position as a global power: 'Adieu to the sea command of
Great Britain until after the next war', lamented Esher: 'perhaps, then, for
ever.'[82] A horrified Roberts asked how Britain was to defend India, while the
War Office complained that Britain's garrisons in Egypt, Cyprus, and Malta
were also being jeopardized—to which Churchill replied that it would 'be
v[ery] foolish to lose England in safeguarding Egypt'.[83]

Attacked in Cabinet by an angry McKenna, Churchill beat a partial retreat,
finally agreeing to a confused compromise, hammered out at the CID on 4 July
1912. This ruled that, subject to maintaining 'a reasonable margin of superior
strength ready and available in home waters', there should be 'available for
Mediterranean purposes, and based on a Mediterranean port, a battle fleet
equal to a one-power Mediterranean standard, excluding France'.[84]

To pacify its own Radical members, the Cabinet also felt it necessary to
clarify the relationship with France. This was the origins of the Grey–Cambon
letters of 22–3 November 1912, which advocated joint consultations should
either government have 'grave reason to expect an unprovoked attack by a third
Power, or something that threatened the general peace', but which made it
plain that the governments would not necessarily be bound by the plans of their
General Staffs.[85] As opposition to the Continental entanglement built up
among Liberal backbenchers, the Prime Minister gave a series of evasive,
even misleading, statements in the House about the true extent of Britain's
commitment to the French—to the dismay of Cambon.[86]

Yet the Radicals, although numerically dominant inside the Cabinet in
November 1911, failed to stop, or even reverse, Grey's foreign policy. This
was partly because they naively read too much into the verbal formulae by
which the Foreign Secretary sought to appease his critics. But the Radicals also
lacked effective leadership once they had been deserted by Lloyd George and
Churchill. The Lord Chancellor, Loreburn, Grey's most persistent antagonist,
had offended too many of his own backbenchers over the magistrates' question.[87] The elderly Morley was hypersensitive and petulant ('Priscilla' was what
Campbell-Bannerman called him behind his back), and worked poorly with
others. McKenna, the one-time advocate of a big navy, seemed too blatantly

---

[82] Britain, he lamented, would be like Rome, dependent on its foreign legions (Williamson, *Grand
Strategy*, 278).
[83] 6 May 1912: ibid. 267.
[84] Howard, *Continental Commitment*, 49–50.
[85] Williamson, *Grand Strategy*, 297.
[86] See his answers to Lord Hugh Cecil on 10 March 1913 and to Byles and the King soon afterwards
(ibid. 330–1).
[87] See Ch. 12. In November 1911 Loreburn had suggested to Morley and Harcourt that all three
should resign—but the other two would not do so (Morris, *Radicalism Against War*, 299).

motivated by personal animosities. John Burns, it is true, had all the right opinions ('Splendid Isolation: No Balance of Power: No Incorporation into a Continental System'), but was held in scant respect by his colleagues. After Loreburn had left the government, an embittered man, the leadership of the anti-Grey faction in the Cabinet devolved on the Colonial Secretary, Harcourt, who, though able, was mistrusted as an intriguer.

Disaffection, however, was not confined to the Cabinet but rippled outwards throughout the party, where, as the risk of Continental war increased in late 1911, the mood hardened against the 'policy of the ententes'. In November 1911 more than eighty MPs came together to form a Liberal Foreign Affairs Committee, under the chairmanship of Noel Buxton, the Balkans expert, with Arthur Ponsonby serving as its Vice-chairman. Meanwhile another Liberal MP, Philip Morrell, had created a 'Radical Foreign Affairs Group' to mobilize support outside Parliament, while the veteran Lord Courtney led his own group, which included L. T. Hobhouse and a former MP, Sir John Brunner, who had been elected on 23 November 1911 as President of the National Liberal Federation.

The most extreme of the Radical critics was E. D. Morel of the Congo Reform Association, who had become convinced that the Foreign Office's reluctance to give him wholehearted backing in his campaign against King Leopold's atrocities stemmed from its unwillingness to offend the French and Belgian governments, on whom its anti-German strategy depended.[88] In *Morocco in Diplomacy* (1912), Morel lambasted Britain's secret diplomacy and called for Anglo-German co-operation in the destruction of the Congo rubber monopoly and the cession to Germany of land in Africa.[89]

Many Radical backbenchers also railed against the 'mad' expenditure on naval armaments, for the escalation of which Britain seemed primarily responsible; after all, 'it was not Germany that built the first Dreadnought'. Some Radicals also believed that Britain had been at fault in clinging to the 'barbaric relic' of capture at sea at the 1907 Hague Conference,[90] while others blamed the Admiralty for insisting on the right of blockade, which had allegedly forced the Germans to build up their own navy.[91]

---

[88] See his article in the *Nineteenth Century* in November 1911.

[89] C. A. Cline, 'E. D. Morel: From the Congo to the Rhine', in Morris (ed.), *Edwardian Radicalism*, 241. Like many colonial 'experts', Morel saw Germany as a 'civilized' nation—with a far better record than most other European peoples, certainly better than that of Britain's current 'allies'.

[90] A stance in which Loreburn found himself with some unlikely allies, since many commercial interests, and the MPs representing them—for example, F. E. Smith, a Liverpudlian MP—also wanted this reform (G. H. S. Jordan, 'Pensions Not Dreadnoughts: The Radicals and Naval Retrenchment', in Morris (ed.), *Edwardian Radicalism*, 173–4).

[91] This was a somewhat unfair criticism, given the government's willingness to curtail this right by ratifying the Declaration of London (which it only failed to do because of persistent opposition in the Lords).

However, the campaign against bloated armaments expenditure soon ran into difficulties. For, like their hero Richard Cobden, few Edwardian Radicals challenged the government's insistence that Britain should retain its control of the seas, many of them developing in consequence 'contradictory love–hate feelings towards the navy'.[92] And on the issue of whether the navy's margin of safety really was at risk, they found it difficult to counter the claims of the experts. So, when Asquith made his solemn statement to the Commons on 16 March 1909, outlining the grounds for the Admiralty's concern, the Radical dissidents 'scattered like sheep': whereas 143 MPs had signed the February protest, only twenty-eight actually voted against the government.[93] Even the *Manchester Guardian* and *Westminster Gazette* belatedly acknowledged that spending more on the navy might be preferable to co-operation with the French, leading to conscription[94]—a point made by McKenna to the Cabinet on 24 June 1913.

Moreover, the tug of party loyalty proved very strong. Even doctrinaire Radicals were sometimes unwilling to criticize the government over its 'armament madness' because of their approval of the 'People's Budget' and their commitment to free trade and Irish Home Rule. Ominously, Lord Courtney's Committee soon closed for lack of membership and funds.[95] In addition, although generally trusted by the Opposition, Grey remained in many ways an authentic Liberal, using a rhetoric of peace and conciliation which harmonized well with the Liberal mind. This made many Radicals blame those aspects of British foreign policy they disliked not on the Foreign Secretary himself but on his 'reactionary' advisers—though such observations were unfair on Grey, who was nobody's tool.

What also contributed to harmony inside the Liberal Party was the seeming improvement in international relations following the fright over Agadir. Admittedly, on the Continent the military arms race accelerated as the Germans passed their Army Bills of 1912 and 1913 and the French their Three-Year Law in July 1913. The continuing build-up of Russian strength also convinced many in Berlin that they might have to fight a 'preventive' war while they still had a reasonable hope of victory.

Yet in 1913 Grey successfully prevented a widening of the Balkan War by convening a conference in London, where he played a skilful mediatory role, in close conjunction with the Germans. This episode annoyed the French and the

---

[92] Jordan, 'Pensions Not Dreadnoughts', 165.

[93] Moreover, not all Liberal MPs were 'doves' when it came to naval expenditure: on 19 February 1908 82 of them asked the Prime Minister to guarantee 'complete efficiency' in imperial defence and deprecated reckless naval economies (Morris, *Radicalism Against War*, 157–8, 128).

[94] Williamson, *Grand Strategy*, 272.

[95] Morris, *Radicalism Against War*, 269.

Francophiles within the British Diplomatic Corps,[96] but it produced a renaissance in Grey's reputation within his own party.

Taking advantage of the improved international atmosphere, Harcourt then pressed ahead with his quest for an accommodation with Berlin over the Baghdad Railway and the future disposal of the Portuguese colonies. The British had never had any principled objection to helping Germany build up its colonial empire—especially if this involved giving away bits of other countries' territory! As Grey had observed to Bertie in July 1911, 'it really doesn't matter to us who owns tropical territory that we do not want for ourselves'.[97] Though never ratified, these Anglo-German talks calmed the financial markets (Cassel was deep in discussion with German bankers over the Baghdad Railway) and gave the Radicals fresh heart.

Admittedly, the ongoing naval arms race continued to cause irritation between London and Berlin, as well as domestic difficulties for the British government. In March 1912 Churchill officially confirmed what had for several years been Admiralty practice: the abandonment of the Two-Power Standard for one of 60 per cent superiority over Germany in Dreadnoughts. But even this more modest target was proving difficult to hit. Hence, following the failure of his suggestion to the Germans of a 'naval holiday', Churchill put forward naval estimates in March 1914 totalling almost £50 million.[98] This provoked opposition within the Cabinet, where the Radical ministers were joined once more (and for the last time) by Lloyd George, understandably concerned, as Chancellor, to curb mounting public expenditure. Asquith skilfully bided his time until some sort of a consensus had developed, and in the end Churchill got his way—partly because no one questioned the need to outbuild the German navy, partly because Churchill reminded his critics that the Admiralty's liabilities had been increased by their recent revolt over his Mediterranean policy.[99]

Even so, in early May 1914 Arthur Nicolson could privately observe that he had not seen the international scene so calm in years.[100] The Anglo-German relationship appeared almost sunny.

---

[96] Williamson, *Grand Strategy*, 330.

[97] Wilson, *Politics of the Entente*, 10.

[98] The Admiralty had not been helped by the Canadians reneging on their promise to donate a battleship.

[99] Williamson, *Grand Strategy*, 320. In the longer term, however, Churchill could only have kept within his spending limits by substituting battleships with submarines, as the retired Jackie Fisher was urging him to do.

[100] S. R. Williamson, 'The Origins of the War', in H. Strachan (ed.), *The Oxford Illustrated History of the First World War* (Oxford, 1998), 15.

6. INVASION SCARES AND SPIES

Yet such complacency was in stark contrast to the marked antipathy to Germany which had long gripped a significant sector of the British population. Indeed, no one who read the newspapers could have been blind to the possibility that Britain might soon be fighting the Germans. During the years of Liberal rule 'invasion scare' literature came rolling off the presses in ever greater quantity, Germany nearly always being designated as the enemy. The most famous, William Le Queux's *The Invasion of 1910*, was serialized in the *Daily Mail* before appearing in book form. The very titles of other books in this genre convey their atmosphere and contents: *When the Eagle Flies Seaward* (1907), *When England Slept* (1909), and *When William Came: A Story of London Under the Hohenzollerns* (1913, written by 'Saki'). P. G. Wodehouse's spoof, *The Swoop! or How Clarence Saved England: A Tale of the Great Invasion* (1909), in which a heroic boy scout single-handedly saves his country from the simultaneous invasion of eight foreign armies (joined by the Swiss navy carrying out a dastardly attack on Lyme Regis), won more admirers from a later generation of readers than it did from contemporaries.

Northcliffe was only one of many newspaper proprietors who realized that these stories were commercially profitable, insisting on Le Queux altering the invading route of the German army so as to boost the *Mail*'s circulation in the towns through which it passed. It is to be assumed that many readers enjoyed being made to have their flesh creep: *The Invasion of 1910* appeared in twenty-seven languages and sold over 1 million copies. The invasion stories also testify to the enhanced sense of vulnerability on the part of many Britons. The 'scaremongers' deliberately played on these fears for political reasons, genuinely believing that an unpatriotic Liberal ministry had cynically endangered national safety. Nor were their campaigns without public consequences: in preparing *The Invasion of 1910*, Le Queux received help from Lord Roberts and H. W. Wilson, the naval correspondent, both of whom wanted to work up a public agitation in support of their Invasion Inquiry. Three years later Major Guy Du Maurier's West End play *An Englishman's Home* proved an effective recruiter for the Territorial Army: the War Office shrewdly set up a recruiting booth in the theatre's foyer to catch the converted before their ardour cooled—30,000 volunteers came forward in the first seven weeks of the production.[101]

After 1909 the grammar of alarmism was extended by the emergence of the 'air threat'. Balloons had long been used by all the European armies: they had performed a useful reconnaissance role in the Boer War (the clear, still atmosphere of South Africa made them particularly effective). However,

---

[101] C. Andrew, *Secret Service: The Making of the British Intelligence Community* (London, 1985), 53.

when balloons started to be fitted with internal combustion engines, a potentially dangerous new weapon of war emerged. The invention was most thoroughly exploited by the Germans, who, profiting from the inventiveness and the determination of Count Zeppelin, equipped their armed service with a fleet of airships capable of overflying southern England and returning to their bases—as early as July 1908 an L24 had travelled a distance of 240 miles, staying airborne for twelve hours.[102]

The Admiralty was keen to acquire its own airships for the purpose of surveillance—though its prototype, the *Mayfly*, had to be written off after being blown against the door of its shed on 24 September 1911.[103] But the patriotic press was soon speculating on the possibility that 'Zeppelins' might support an invasion of England. More realistic were fears of bombs being dropped on battleships or military/naval installations, or even used to kill and demoralize the civilian population. H. G. Wells was ahead of the pack with his fantasy *The War in the Air* (1908), which featured a fleet of German airships, each as large as an ocean liner.

These alarming possibilities led to periodic outbreaks of paranoia. On the night of 14 October 1912 there were numerous reports of noise from an aerial engine over Sheerness (an important dockyard on the Isle of Sheppey); an Admiralty investigator concluded that a Zeppelin might indeed have overflown the town, though the German government issued a categorical denial. Like later hysteria about UFOs, the Zeppelin scares fed on popular suggestibility. Though some of the 'sightings' were engineered by hoaxers, such innocuous phenomena as a farm labourer at night time wheeling a barrow, with light attached, along the brow of a hill could give rise to rumours of an enemy visitation. An exasperated Northcliffe tried in vain to get his newspapers to adopt a more responsible and dignified line on the subject.

The air threat took on new dimensions with the rapid development of heavier-than-air flying machines, following the American Wright brothers' famous flight on 17 December 1903. By 1909 there were no fewer than three different British societies concerned with aspects of aerial flight, one dealing with the technicalities of aviation, one aimed at sportsmen, and a third, the Aerial League of the British Empire, an educational and propaganda organization. Whether aeroplanes would ever get the better of airships, and if so, how quickly, was a matter on which the experts disagreed: airships presented easy targets for attack and were not very manoeuvrable, but the early aeroplanes had very short ranges, some being capable of little more than brief hops across the fields, and they could not operate at all at night or when visibility was poor.

---

[102] A. M. Gollin, *The Impact of Air Power on the British People and Their Government, 1909–14* (Houndmills, 1989), 2.

[103] No more airships were commissioned by the Admiralty.

Northcliffe, however, quickly realized the aeroplane's very considerable military potential, and stimulated its development by the award of prizes to airmen who accomplished record-breaking feats: this provided the occasion for Blériot's flight across the Channel on 25 July 1909, after which it was clear to all that England 'was no longer an island'.[104] However, it tended to be Frenchmen, flying French-designed machines, who carried off these prizes: for example, the London–Manchester race was won in April 1910 by Louis Paulhan, beating off a plucky challenge from an Englishman, Claude Grahame-White. In aeroplanes, as in airships, Britain, despite its swelling rank of pioneers, seemed always to come off second-best. Lloyd George, visiting the Reims air show in August 1909, told the press that 'as a "Britisher" ', he felt 'rather ashamed that we were so completely out of it'.[105]

The campaign against the government and the War Office for not taking the air menace with sufficient seriousness was not entirely disinterested. Civil aviation was still a distant possibility, so the new breed of manufacturer (most of whom had started off making motor cars) depended on procurement orders from the Service Departments. The outcry against the government was also taken up by an increasingly desperate Opposition: the Parliamentary Aerial Defence Committee may have begun as an all-party organization (its Chairman, Arthur Lee, the former Civil Lord of the Admiralty, was a Conservative; its Vice-chairman, Cecil Harmsworth, Northcliffe's brother, a Liberal), but the organization began harassing the government in the spring of 1910 and had gone over to an all-out attack by 1913.

The critics' case was a cogent one. Haldane at the War Office was never entirely convinced that the aeroplane had much utility except for reconnaissance (for which purpose he initially preferred the airship); in this profound misapprehension he was encouraged by his grumpily outspoken CIGS, 'Old Nick', William Nicholson. Haldane also took a dim view of the capacity of practical engineers (the Wright brothers included), seeing them as mere 'empirics'.[106] The War Secretary preferred to rely on a committee of academic scientists, headed by Lord Rayleigh, working in conjunction with the National Physical Laboratory;[107] this, he believed, was the only way of putting aviation on to a truly scientific footing.

---

[104] This was the famous phrase first used by Northcliffe about Saintos-Dumont's flight of 23 October 1906.

[105] Gollin, *Air Power*, 91.

[106] They were, admittedly, a bizarre bunch. Their ranks included the exotic American Samuel Franklin Cody, who had earlier been a cowboy, gold prospector, and 'wild west' theatrical showman, before being employed by the War Office from 1905 to 1909. He died in an air crash in 1913. See H. Driver, *The Birth of Military Aviation: Britain, 1903–1914* (London, 1997).

[107] See Ch. 16.

However, Haldane's approach meant that in the short run British airpower lagged some way behind that of other European states. Only in 1912, with Haldane no longer at the War Office, did the government eventually establish the 'Flying Corps', with a military and a naval wing. In June 1914 the latter broke away to form the Royal Naval Air Service, at the behest of Churchill, who had from the start shown a keen interest in the possibilities of aviation.

But long before then the public had become anxious. At the Hendon Air Display of 12 May 1911, one of the many events of this kind attracting huge crowds and massive newspaper (and cinema) coverage, Grahame-White created a sensation by accurately dropping a 100-pound sandbag onto the outline of a battleship whitewashed on the grass from the height of 2,000 feet—an exploit which left one of the spectators, Admiral Fisher, visibly shaken.[108] In June 1914 Admiral Percy Scott emerged from retirement to argue in *The Times* that command of the seas was passing from surface battleships to submarines and aeroplanes, a prophecy made earlier in the *Daily Mail* by H. G. Wells.

Some Liberal newspapers continued to decry the alarmism of the scaremongers, but even they were changing their tune by 1913. Warnings that Germany was 'mistress of the air' and that an aerial assault could leave London looking 'like a last year's buzzard's nest'[109] had now to be taken seriously. In 1912 the government belatedly took urgent measures to protect its communication systems, ammunition dumps, and naval dockyards from possible air attack, and after 1913 armed guards were stationed at key installations: arsenals, munitions factories, magazines, and oil tanks. Fortunately, the Germans believed British defences to be much more sophisticated than they actually were.[110]

The new sense of vulnerability made many Britons not only fearful of assaults from without but nervous about the enemy within, since invasion, whether from a foreign army or from the air, might well be aided by the presence of a fifth column—as Le Queux argued in his tale *Spies of the Kaiser* (1909). In 1908 Roberts claimed that there were nearly 80,000 potential German troops in England.[111] The following year Haldane had to respond in the Commons to the rumour (whose author, interestingly, was an elderly *Liberal* MP) 'that there [were], in a cellar within a quarter of a mile of Charing Cross, 50,000 stands of Mauser rifles and 7,500,000 Mauser cartridges'.[112] The newspapers filled with stories of German waiters cycling around the countryside, presumably mapping out an invasion route on behalf of the fatherland. Some of these stories were set up by practical jokers, others gained currency

[108] Gollin, *Air Power*, 172.   [109] Ibid. 18.
[110] Gooch, *Prospect of War*, 14–15.   [111] Coetzee, *Party or Country*, 107.
[112] Howard, *Continental Commitment*, 38.

from the likes of Le Queux, who enjoyed an entirely unwarranted fame as a master spy-detector.

A 'spy fever' was soon in full swing, centring on German waiters, barbers, and tourists who happened to live in the vicinity of telephones, telegraphs, railway lines, and bridges on the East Coast and near London.[113] Suspicion later settled on any German near the coast who might be in a position to guide enemy forces or help U-boats or Zeppelins by showing lights. There were even fears that 'German money', aimed at the economic sabotage of the country, lay behind the industrial disturbances of the immediate pre-war years.[114]

Churchill, as Home Secretary, was convinced from an early stage of the reality of the spy menace. In June 1910 his Department drew up a new Official Secrets Act, which Seely, with cross-party backing, later rushed through both Houses of Parliament on a single Friday afternoon (18 August 1911) when the House was half empty, in the middle of the Moroccan crisis—and also, perhaps significantly, while the country was in the throes of the rail strike. The Bill, which the Attorney-General claimed contained 'nothing novel in principle', was ostensibly concerned with the unauthorized divulgence of official documents (a reinforcement of the D-notice system reached with newspaper proprietors earlier in the year),[115] but it also broke new ground by placing the onus on the accused to demonstrate their innocence—in contrast to the 1889 measure which it replaced, where the prosecution had had to prove 'intent'.[116] Only nine Labour and three Liberal MPs voted against the Bill, though it was precisely the sort of measure of which the Commons had previously been wary.[117]

Churchill also instigated the compilation, with the help of local police forces, of a list of 'aliens' from probable enemy countries: nearly 29,000 names had been placed on the register by July 1913.[118] The exercise had to be kept unofficial because the Liberal-dominated House would not countenance any interference with the principle of free political asylum.[119] Churchill's introduction of the 'general warrant system',[120] which made it easier for the police to

---

[113] D. French, 'Spy Fever in Britain, 1900–1915', *Historical Journal*, 21 (1978), 357.

[114] Andrew, *Secret Service*, 72–3.

[115] The War Office scheme provided for a liaison between the two Service Departments and press representatives. In 1906 and 1908 attempts to institute press censorship had been blocked by the Newspaper Society.

[116] Andrew, *Secret Service*, 63.

[117] B. Porter, *Plots and Paranoia: A History of Political Espionage in Britain, 1790–1988* (London, 1989), 127–8; Andrew, *Secret Service*, 58–60.

[118] Porter, *Plots and Paranoia*, 127. However, the War Office believed that there were some 75,000 enemy aliens living in Britain when war broke out (p. 129), Andrew, *Secret Service*, 60–1. French claims 28,380 names were on the register, 11,100 being Germans or Austro-Hungarians ('Spy Fever', 360).

[119] French, 'Spy Fever', 359: Churchill's Aliens Bill of 1911 had had to be withdrawn.

[120] Andrew, *Secret Service*, 61.

intercept and open the correspondence of suspects, marked another small stage in the direction of a Continental-style police state.

Initially the War Office failed to take the issue of foreign spies seriously— rumours of their existence did certainly tend to follow the storylines of popular invasion-scare literature. But Le Queux successfully hoodwinked the Director of the military operations counter-intelligence section (MO5), Lt.-Colonel James Edmonds, and in 1909 even the usually imperturbable Haldane felt that, along with much obvious nonsense, the spy stories contained enough substance to warrant official investigation. A 'Secret Service Bureau' was set up by a subcommittee of the CID in August 1909, which soon divided between MO(t), for domestic counter-espionage (the forerunner of MI5) and another body for covert intelligence-gathering abroad.[121]

MO(t), under its hard-working officer Captain Vernon Kell ('K'), never uncovered the network of German spies who were making preparations for the invasion of Britain—not surprisingly, since no such network existed. But it did identify a number of German agents who were gathering intelligence for Berlin, rather incompetently, at British ports and dockyards.[122] Five spies were arrested under the terms of the new Official Secrets Act and put on trial, and a list of another twenty-two German agents was also fortuitously uncovered, though 'K' cunningly kept the suspects under surveillance until, on the first day of the war, all bar one were rounded up. All the same, even in 1914 MO5(g), as it had now become, had acquired a staff of only three officers, one barrister, and seven clerks, aided on occasions by the Special Branch, which by August 1914 was employing 114 officers—some of them based on British ports.[123]

Meanwhile what later became known as MI6, under Commander Mansfield George Smith-Cummings ('C'), was organizing a rather amateurish spy ring in Germany in the hope of getting advance warning of an enemy 'bolt from the blue'. 'C' went on several expeditions to Germany, heavily disguised, and later declared that it was all 'capital sport!'.[124] These escapades had little practical significance, but along with 'spy fever', they suggest that the country was experiencing what one admiral perceptively called 'a state of war without present violence'—what would later be known as a 'cold war'.[125]

---

[121] Porter, *Plots and Paranoia*, 127. On the tortuous history of MI5, so named in October 1917, see D. Hiley, 'Counter-Espionage and Security in Great Britain During the First World War', *English Historical Review*, 101 (1986), 635–61).

[122] Porter, *Plots and Paranoia*, 128–9.

[123] Ibid. 135. In June 1913 the Special Branch and CID came under the control of Basil Thomson.

[124] Andrew, *Secret Service*, 76.

[125] Admiral Troubridge in February 1912, cited in Williamson, *Grand Strategy*, 265.

7. A MILITARIZED SOCIETY?

Although by comparison with most European countries Britain remained a remarkably unmilitaristic society, it did not differ as markedly from Germany in 1913 as it had done in the 1890s. One consequence of the Boer War alarms and the scares about invasion had been the spread of rifle clubs and cadet corps. The latter were especially prominent in the big public schools, where by the Edwardian decade they had even begun to erode the dominant position once held by team games. By a special army order of March 1908 Haldane organized these bodies into what became known as the Officer Training Corps (OTC), giving them official recognition and a War Office subsidy and attaching them to the appropriate Territorial division. Thus did Haldane appeal to the 'militarism' of the upper middle classes, as he himself put it, and use it to reinforce the government's scheme of army reform. By 1914 there were about 20,000 schoolboys and 5,000 undergraduates enrolled in the OTC.[126]

Haldane had originally hoped to introduce rifle training into elementary schools. This would have aroused less antipathy than compulsory military training, perhaps because it seemed an extension of the by now well-established principle of compulsory education.[127] But, following Labour and Radical protests, the government desisted. The schools patronized by working-class children were thus protected from the 'virus' of militarism. However, it was far different in the big public schools, many of which received visits from Lord Roberts, who propagandized tirelessly on behalf of the National Service League. The notion that a gentleman might have a call to serve his country, even to die for it, was thus put into the heads of many impressionable middle- and upper-class youths.

Roberts tried hard to get away from the anachronistic image attached to army life by conjuring up a vision of a citizen's army in which peer and ploughboy would discover a common citizenship—the theme of Kipling's short story 'The Army of a Dream' (c.1908). Compulsory military training, argued the spokesmen for the NSL, would also lead to social improvement by taking sickly working-class youths out of the slums, putting them under canvas for two months, and giving them good, wholesome food, as well as inculcating habits of self-respect and self-control which would make them better workmen when they returned to civilian life—more servile, said the critics. Milner told Maxse in February 1907: 'even if they never fought, the trained people would still prevail in *peace* by virtue of its greater grit and all-round efficiency.'[128]

[126] W. J. Reader, *At Duty's Call: A Study in Obsolete Patriotism* (Manchester, 1988), 89.

[127] Adams and Poirier, *Conscription Controversy*, 47; D. J. Newton, *British Labour, European Socialism and the Struggle for Peace, 1899–1914* (Oxford, 1985), 351.

[128] Adams and Poirier, *Conscription Controversy*, 19.

These were also the goals of the various youth movements which flourished in Edwardian Britain, all of them propagating their own particular version of 'manliness'—of which the complement was the fostering among girls of skills in motherhood and home-making. However, the older youth movements, many of them pioneered by the great apostle of Empire Lord Meath, struggled to turn themselves into mass organizations. Similarly, the Boys Brigade and its imitator, the Church Lads' Brigade, both proponents of muscular Christianity, expanded only slowly: membership of the former stuck at around 60,000, being heavily concentrated in Scotland.

Into this gap moved General Baden-Powell, the great popular hero of Mafeking. With Haldane's encouragement, 'B-P' retired from his post as commander of the Northumbrian Division of the Territorial Army in 1910 to devote himself full-time to the training of youth. Earlier, between 27 July and 9 August 1907, he had held his first experimental camp on Brownsea Island in Poole Harbour, trying out the various rituals, pastimes, and organizational structures which would characterize his Boy Scouts Movement, founded the following year. By the outbreak of war the Scouts numbered over 150,000, nearly two-and-a-half times the size of the next most successful youth movement, the Boys Brigade.

'Scouting', as B-P presented it, was not a straightforward expression of militarism,[129] but it possessed some obvious military features, especially in its early years before it had surprised its founder by mushrooming into an international movement. The original editions of *Scouting for Boys* preached an uncomplicated conservative message of honour, duty, loyalty, and self-control. Boys were told to learn from the example of the 'young Romans who lost the Empire of their forefathers by being wishy-washy slackers without any go or patriotism in them', and warned against 'politicians' who tried to save money by making the navy and army smaller.

Not surprisingly, many of the early scoutmasters were serving or retired army officers, as were one-half of the members of the executive committee of the Boy Scouts' Governing Council; two of the latter combined this position with a prominent role in the National Service League, while another, Sir Edmund Elles, was an active recruiter for the Territorials. These militaristic influences provoked an exodus from the movement, led by Sir Francis Vane, who set up his own 'National Peace Scouts'—to be followed later by the colourful John Hargrave, founder of the 'Kibbo Kift Kindred'. When war broke out, the scouts 'did their duty' by delivering messages, guarding reservoirs, running canteens, and, revealingly, looking out for spies.[130]

---

[129] See below.
[130] Some 150,000 ex-scouts joined the armed forces, of whom 10,000 were killed.

Characteristically, Baden-Powell, in launching his movement, had over-looked the fact that half of all 'youths' were female. Many girls found the outdoor activities of the Scouts highly exciting, and initially they were allowed in as members (6,000 or so had joined by 1909)—only for poor B-P to find himself accused by the editor of the *Spectator* of sponsoring a 'mad scheme of military co-education'! His sister Agnes was promptly drafted in to organize the 'Girl Guides' on suitably feminine lines. If anything, the patriotic propaganda element in the Guides was even more pronounced than in the Scouts, lessons being provided, for example, on how girls could prepare themselves for colonial life, should this prove to be their destiny.

Neither the Scouts nor the Guides managed to reach down to the poorest strata of society. Apart from anything else, the cost of the uniform proved prohibitively high for the parents of the urban poor, and the emphasis on 'thrift' was also unhelpful; in some towns the Scouts were mocked, even attacked, as they patrolled through the streets. All the same, the Scout Movement, with its strong appeal to the lower middle class, successfully mobilized large numbers of young people, especially in London and the Home Counties, in ways previously thought impossible of achievement. H. G. Wells, who had earlier toyed with the idea of incorporating elements of military instruction into a scheme for the compulsory training of youth, providing a militia for home defence (as had other leading Fabians: the Webbs thought that mandatory military drill would be a useful antidote to the 'sottishness' of youth),[131] was impressed by B-P's work: 'I liked the Boy Scout,' he wrote in *The New Machiavelli* (1911), 'and I find it difficult to express how much it mattered to me, with my growing bias in favour of deliberate national training, that Liberalism hadn't been able to produce... anything of this kind.'[132]

To counter 'slackness' and to keep warm the embers of patriotism among adults, a number of nationalistic leagues were also founded. The oldest was the Navy League, from which more 'extreme' elements broke away to form the Imperial Maritime League in 1907–8. The former had a membership of 21,500 in 1908, a figure which rose to 100,000 in 1912, and to about 126,000 a year later—completely overshadowing its upstart rival, whose supporters numbered only about 1,500,[133] though these included famous figures such as Kipling, Beresford, Gwynne of the *Morning Post*, and its President, Lord Willoughby

---

[131] Adams and Poirier, *Conscription Controversy*, 19; A. M. McBriar, *Fabian Socialism and English Politics 1884–1918* (Cambridge, 1962), 130. But the Fabians did not favour removal from civil life or forced sojourns in barracks.

[132] H. G. Wells, *The New Machiavelli* (1911; Penguin edn. 1946), 245–6.

[133] Coetzee, *Party or Country*, 138, 143–4. The IML was reduced to soliciting Indian princes for support. Like other patriotic organizations, the Navy League contained a sizeable female membership. See also F. and M. Coetzee, 'Rethinking the Radical Right in Germany and Britain Before 1914', *Journal of Contemporary History*, 21 (1986), 522.

de Broke, the Diehard peer. But even the Navy League's membership paled by comparison with that of the German Navy League, which at its peak in 1913 had 331,910 members.[134] This difference may partly reflect the fact that the German people needed to be persuaded of the importance of sea-power, as Britons did not. All the same, the two British organizations took nothing for granted, awarding prizes, holding exhibitions and displays, and encouraging the observance of Trafalgar Day and Empire Day.

Meanwhile the NSL had set itself a more difficult mission. True, it enjoyed some success in questioning whether the Territorial Army would, at any time in the foreseeable future, be fit to fulfil its allotted role. The 'Terriers' were supposed to be building up into a force of some 300,000 men, but the recruiting drive petered out after 1910 with the onset of good trade and low unemployment: by 1912 they were about 50,000 men short of their target, and very deficient in equipment.[135]

Yet the political class proved resistant to NSL propaganda: in no pre-war vote did more than 177 MPs vote in favour of any kind of Conscription Bill. The wider public were even harder to persuade of the merits of compulsory military training. The membership of the NSL may have risen throughout the years of Liberal rule: from about 10,000 in 1907, to 21,500 by the end of 1908, to 43,000 in 1909, 62,000 in 1910, and to 96,526 in 1913.[136] But these enthusiasts were almost certainly unrepresentative of the population as a whole.

The problems confronting the conscriptionists were dramatized by the Stratford by-election, held in May 1909, when the Liberal MP, Captain Kincaid-Smith, applied for the Chiltern Hundreds and stood for re-election as an Independent on the NSL's platform. But though prominent Conservatives such as Milner, Curzon, and F. E. Smith strongly supported compulsory military service (Curzon was one of the NSL's Vice-Presidents), Balfour refused to give Smith a free run against the official Liberal candidate—partly because, as we have seen, he doubted conscription's necessity and believed that Haldane's Territorial Army should be given a fair wind, but also because he thought it would be electoral suicide to embrace so controversial an objective.[137] And so the local Conservatives adopted a candidate who subscribed to tariff reform, which was part of their official programme, while opposing compulsory military service, which was not.[138]

---

[134] The income of the British leagues was also small: in the case of the Navy League, only £7,814 in 1913! (Coetzee, *Party or Country*, 142–3.)

[135] Williamson, *Grand Strategy*, 91, 304. In September 1913 they were still short of 1,893 officers and 64,778 other ranks (P. Simkins, *Kitchener's Army: The Raising of the New Armies, 1914–16* (Manchester, 1988), 18–19).

[136] Adams and Poirier, *Conscription Controversy*, 23, 17.

[137] Lansdowne privately thought some form of compulsory service to be 'inevitable', but ruled it out as too unpopular for his party to embrace (Adams and Poirier, *Conscription Controversy*, 23).

[138] See Coetzee, *Party or Country*, 116–17.

The outcome was a Conservative victory, with Kincaid-Smith relegated to third place with a paltry 479 votes. It was events such as this which encouraged the 'Plague On Both Your Houses' stance adopted by many in the patriotic leagues. Well might Roberts privately complain in 1912 that the Conservatives 'were as much to blame as the Liberals' for the fact that Britain still lacked 'a National Army'.[139]

Yet the Conservative and Unionist Party, for all its limitations, seemed, from this perspective, to be 'persuadable' in a way that the Liberals were not. Of the 105 MPs sympathetic to the NSL after 1910, only three supported the government.[140] As for the Imperial Maritime League, it had been opposed from the very start to the Navy League's non-party stand: how could it stay neutral when, as one of its activists, Fred Jane, alleged, the Liberal government had 'cut the Navy down because of a few dirty little Radical and Socialist supporters'?[141] Even the Navy League felt impelled to intervene on the Unionist side in the Peckham by-election in March 1908.[142] The Aerial League of the British Empire later made the same transition.

Did such protests against the indifference or cowardice (as they saw it) of the British government elicit a significant popular response? The electoral evidence is ambivalent. The decision of the Unionists to associate themselves with the 'Big Navy' cry paid dividends at the Croydon by-election of 29 March 1909, held in the middle of the 'We Want Eight and We Won't Wait' scare, when their candidate retained the seat on a significantly increased share of the vote. The ploy was repeated, with the full approval of Balfour, at the two 1910 General Elections; it undoubtedly helped the Unionists in January to capture the naval dockyards of Portsmouth, Chatham, and Devonport, on huge anti-government swings,[143] and it also contributed to the defeat of the Labour MP Will Crooks at Woolwich, the site of a big Royal Ordnance factory.[144] But these were merely local triumphs. Over the country as a whole scaremongering was not an obvious vote-winner in working-class areas: outside the dock towns and armament centres, loyalty to the principles of trade unionism, combined with a commitment to traditional liberal values such as free trade and a voluntary army, remained the dominant political positions.

---

[139] Adams and Poirier, *Conscription Controversy*, 40, 23.

[140] Wilson, *Politics of the Entente*, 54. However, its founder, George Shee, had been a Liberal Imperialist.

[141] Coetzee, *Party or Country*, 79. Ironically, by 1913 it had come to despair of *both* parties, thus returning to the 'non-party' position, which it had come into existence to oppose! (p. 144).

[142] Coetzee, *Party or Country*, 85.

[143] 19.8%, 17.2%, 8.2%, respectively, compared with a national swing of 4.3%. Even in southern England the swing seldom exceeded 10%.

[144] On a 15.2% swing, compared with 5.6% in Inner London as a whole. However, Crooks did regain the seat in December.

8. FEELING IN THE COUNTRY

The British people had been bombarded for many years before 1914 by blood-curdling warnings of the German menace, and the air had been heavy with talk of war—sometimes idealized as an antidote to effeminacy. War, declared one patriotic pamphleteer, was 'the Great Flail that threshe[d] the wheat from the chaff' and thus made for 'the ethical advance of the race'.[145]

Yet militarism, as an ideology, by no means swept all before it. Even those who applied the rhetoric of Social Darwinism to the phenomena of international life did not necessarily do so in order to glorify war. Many, including L. T. Hobhouse, subscribed to a version of that creed which saw competition in the modern world as in the process of being elevated from the military sphere to the intellectual one: international rivalry, it was argued, was increasingly taking the form of a contest between opposing ideas, theories, and ideals. Biologists who thought that their discipline had implications for public life tended, in any case, to deprecate warfare. The eugenists, for example, saw fighting as racially harmful ('dysgenic') because it tended to kill off a disproportionate number of the mentally and physically fit—only the latter being likely to present themselves for service under a voluntary system of recruitment, with the sickly being unlikely to pass a medical examination whatever recruitment system was in place.

Nor, in any case, should invasion scare stories necessarily be cited as evidence of widespread militarism. Saki's *When William Came* offers a warning of the dire consequences of national complacency and softness. But lurid predictions of war could also serve as warnings of how horrible war might be, as in the case of *The War in the Air*, in which European (and American) civilization is 'blown up'. The predominant message in this literature was 'wake up!' But wake up to what? In Wells's story old Tom draws the final conclusion: 'You can say what you like. It didn't ought ever to 'ave begun.'[146]

The ambiguities of 'patriotism' are also apparent in the Boy Scouts Movement. B-P was a professional soldier imbued with many of the values of his class, but in other respects he was unorthodox—for example, in his preference for operations which required small groups to assume maximum discretion and to observe the minimum of military formality. Indeed, B-P's success owed much to his avoidance of the dreary emphasis upon military drill which had so limited the success of Meath's endeavours. Even the scout uniform (scoutmasters and boys both wore shorts) was deliberately chosen for its unmilitary connotations. Prudently, in the second edition of his *Aids to Scouting*

---

[145] The words are those of a fictional character in a novel by Maud Diver (Reader, *At Duty's Call*, 23).
[146] H. G. Wells, *The War in the Air*, 389.

Baden-Powell toned down his admonitory passages on threats to the Empire, and by 1911 the section on 'national deterioration' had disappeared entirely. The *Headquarters' Gazette* of November 1910 bluntly declared: 'essentially ours is a Peace organization.'

Obviously B-P was heavily influenced by his public-school background and military experiences, but he was an eclectic thinker who also drew heavily upon (and arguably plagiarized) Ernest Thompson Seton's romantic woodcraft movement, itself loosely based on the lore and rituals of the American Indians. Boys probably joined the Scout Movement in such large numbers because its founder, who had never quite grown up, had an instinctive understanding of what boys and youths enjoyed: the camaraderie of the camp, the games, and the cult of the open air being the chief attractions. Even among the young, naive, uncritical patriotism was probably not particularly widespread.

One could, in any case, be patriotic and have a mistrust of Germany yet still view the prospect of an Anglo–German war with dismay. British businessmen, in particular, were well aware that Germany remained Britain's second-largest customer (after India), while Britain relied upon Germany for a range of raw materials and manufactured items which she could not easily procure else-where—for example, dye stuffs (needed for the khaki uniforms of British troops!), optical glass, steel bars, pig iron, as well as huge consignments of beet-produced sugar, which ministered to her people's sweet tooth (West Indian cane sugar was vastly more expensive). Moreover, the great pre-war boom contrasted sharply with the depression of the 1890s which had earlier fuelled anti-German business sentiment. Whatever the tariff-reform Jeremiahs might say, in 1914 the British economy was still flourishing—why put all this at risk by going to war?

True, some industrialists stood to gain from increasing international tension, notably British businessmen locked in direct competition with their German counterparts. Thus, bitterness over the popularity of German pianos provoked the trade magazine *The Pianomaker* in 1913 into making its own declaration of 'war'—the start of a campaign which culminated in the Guildhall School of Music parting with its Bechsteins![147] The Tariff Reform League contributed powerfully to this perception of Germany as a national threat by providing hostile depictions of 'Herr Dumper' and presenting Anglo–German trade competition as a kind of war to the death.

The emerging industrial-military complex surrounding the aviation industry (which had few alternative customers) had an even more direct stake in the armaments race, which brought in lucrative government orders. So, to a degree, did shipbuilding and some sectors of heavy industry, represented on the Liberal

---

[147] C. Ehrlich, *The Piano: A History* (Oxford, 1990, new edn.), 152.

benches by the likes of Christopher Furness, chairman of Palmer's Ship-building and Iron Co. Ltd., and Sir Charles McLaren, head of John Brown & Co.[148]

On the other hand, in the chemicals and the machine-tools industries, where product specialization had spontaneously occurred, a complementary relation-ship developed between the two countries. Moreover, with their more highly developed financial sector, the British were sometimes able to provide capital for German firms—the rationale behind the proposed Baghdad Railway agree-ment. This was only one of a number of commercial relationships that were developing in the early twentieth century: by 1914 over one-half of pre-war international producer cartels were Anglo-German.[149]

There was thus no single business viewpoint on international relations. But, on balance, London's fragile position as a financial centre and its exceptionally heavy dependence on international trade made most British businessmen averse to the dangers and uncertainties that war would entail. Indeed, so interconnected was the world trading system that Norman Angell was inspired to write his influential book *The Great Illusion* (1910), which argued that advanced capitalist countries would be brought economically to their knees within months, if not weeks, of the outbreak of a major war.[150]

Some conservatives, it is true, believed that war would stabilize British society: one old military buffer thought that 'a good big war might do a lot of good in killing Socialist nonsense and would probably put a stop to all this labour unrest'. But more common was the fear that war would lead to social revolution.[151] Even without war, the staggering rise in naval spending, up from a little over £62 million in 1906 to £72.5 million in 1913 (a 33 per cent increase), was widely thought to have brought the country to the very limits of its taxable resources.[152]

9. THE CHALLENGE OF THE PEACE MOVEMENT

Because Britain *did* embark on war with Germany in 1914, it is easy to overlook how widespread Germanophilia had recently been. Much of this admiration of Germany sprang from the prestige enjoyed by her science, philosophy, and

---

[148] Jordan, 'Pensions Not Dreadnoughts', 176. In pursuing this cause they found themselves at one with trade-union leaders such as John Jenkins, MP for Chatham (by trade a shipwright), and Charles Duncan, MP for Barrow (an engineer).

[149] Steiner, *Origins of First World War*, 63.

[150] An earlier elaboration of this theme was I. S. Bloch's *Is War Now Impossible?* (1899).

[151] Wilson, *Politics of the Entente*, 12, 14.

[152] Though in fact, at about 3% of GDP, British defence spending does not seem excessive. On the other hand, it was only a little lower than that of Germany—widely, if erroneously, portrayed as a hothouse of militarism.

music.[153] Bertrand Russell was not alone in combining these sentiments with a condescending dismissal of France's supposedly inferior intellectual life. Anglo-German ties were also strengthened by the fact that so many Britons and Germans were studying at each other's universities—among them the young Germans at Oxford who were being funded by Rhodes scholarships.

Indeed, Britain possibly enjoyed a greater variety of contacts with Germany than with any other country, particularly in all matters affecting social policy.[154] Whatever tensions may have crept into their relationship, British socialists had close dealings with the German Social Democrats—more so than with other European socialist delegations. The links between Christians in the two countries were also extensive: 'the fighting Quaker', J. Allen Baker, a Liberal MP, was only one of many Dissenters working amicably with German religious leaders.

As the prospect of war increased, strenuous efforts were made on both sides of the North Sea to maintain friendly communications. The Anglo-German Union Club, dating back to May 1905, was soon afterwards joined by the Anglo-German Conciliation Committee, which held a public meeting on 1 December that attracted an audience of 2,000. There was also the Anglo-German Friendship Committee, formed by the banker Lord Avebury and the elderly Lord Courtney, which ran its own newspaper and had the approval of Sir Frank Lascelles, the British Ambassador in Berlin from 1896 to 1908, and Count Paul Metternich, the German Ambassador in London.[155] Municipal officials and Chambers of Commerce, too, exchanged friendly visits. Although such manifestations of Anglo-German solidarity could be interpreted as a defensive response to the deteriorating relationship between the two countries, the vitality of organizations such as the Friendship Society was remarkable—nothing quite like it had sprung into existence to offset Anglo-French estrangements in the late 1890s.

Liberals queued up to proclaim the affinities between the German and British peoples. According to the National Liberal Federation, Germany was 'a country with which we have no real ground of quarrel, but, on the contrary, many powerful ties of race, commerce and historic associations'.[156] Its President, the chemical manufacturer and ex-Liberal MP Sir John Brunner, felt particularly strongly on this subject.[157] As war loomed in 1914, Norman Angell and his friends, banded together in the Neutrality League, declared: 'wedged

---

[153] See Ch. 15 and 16.

[154] See Ch. 11.

[155] Kennedy, *Anglo-German Antagonism*, 287; Cline, 'Morel', 242–3; Morris, *Radicalism Against War*, 223. Morel, however, stayed away from the 'banquets and amiable speeches' of the Anglo-German Friendship Society once he learnt that its members did not wish to probe the precise understandings underlying the Anglo-French entente (Cline, 'Morel', 243).

[156] Morris, *Radicalism Against War*, 305.

[157] S. Koss, *Sir John Brunner: Radical Plutocrat 1842–1919* (Cambridge, 1970), 260.

in between hostile States, highly civilised, with a culture that has contributed greatly in the past to western civilisation', Germany was 'racially allied to ourselves and with moral ideals largely resembling our own'.[158]

True, not all Radicals were so Germanophile: many had been disillusioned by the behaviour of the German delegates at the second Hague Conference. Even so, like Massingham, editor of the *Nation*, they usually drew a distinction between the reactionary *government* in Berlin and the German *people*, with whom they saw no reason to quarrel. This was a line commonly taken in the Liberal press, notably in C. P. Scott's *Manchester Guardian*, which consistently called for Anglo-German reconciliation and lambasted those who sought to sow needless discord between the two countries.

The socialists of the ILP broadened the attack to cover militarism in all its forms. Hardie viewed even the Territorial Army as a 'thinly disguised form of conscription', and, together with Snowden and with the backing of some Radical-Liberals, he spearheaded an agitation in 1913–14 against arms manufacturers, the so-called 'merchants of death'. In books such as G. H. Perris's *The War Traders* (1913), these critics pointed to the interchange of funds and ideas between Nobel's Explosives Co. and the German Powder Group, going back to 1880s, and sought to demonstrate that an 'international arms trust', not Germany, posed the real threat to the country.[159]

However, not all socialists took this line. After 1902 the SDF ceased to be affiliated to the Labour Party, and so it was no more than a minor irritant to the likes of Hardie when, during the first Moroccan crisis, its maverick leader Hyndman issued a call for Britain to come to France's aid, and when later, in 1908, he published articles drawing attention to the German danger.[160] Contemptuous of the ILP's 'bourgeois pacifism', the SDF even advocated the establishment of a citizen militia—albeit a proletarian body free from military law, in which officers would be democratically elected by their own men.[161]

More disruptive of socialist unity was the 'defection' of the ex-ranker Robert Blatchford, the most gifted socialist journalist of his day. Not only did Blatchford write a series of inflammatory articles declaring an Anglo-German

---

[158] Kennedy, *Anglo-German Antagonism*, 459.

[159] C. Trebilcock, 'Radicalism and the Armament Trust', in Morris (ed.), *Edwardian Radicalism*, 182, 195. However, though exchanges of weapons designs and market-sharing agreements between the big armaments firms across national frontiers were not uncommon, the 'dynamite monopoly' was highly unusual, and no single monolithic trust existed—largely because the government, as the sole customer, had such a strong hand to play (pp. 195, 184–5).

[160] Newton, *Struggle for Peace*, 147–50, 199. Hyndman and Quelch had little liking for the German socialist movement, thinking it incapable of restraining the Reich's militarism. Hyndman also believed that peace propaganda was a tactical mistake, since it might simply encourage the Prussian military to wage a war of aggression (p. 329).

[161] Ibid. 160–2.

war all but inevitable and calling for conscription and military aid to France, but he sent these articles for publication to the *Daily Mail*, which held them back for release until the general election campaign began in earnest on 13 December 1909.[162]

In the attempt to stop the drift to war, the mainstream Labour Movement was also unreliable. True, in September 1907 the TUC forbade trade unionists to join the 'Terriers', 'as they are thereby liable to be called out in times of industrial disputes to quell and possibly shoot down their fellow workers'.[163] But although all but one Labour MP (Will Crooks, MP for Woolwich, a persistent offender) had followed the agreed party line and voted against Haldane's Army Bill, another three trade-union-sponsored MPs were unable to vote because they were on a tour of Switzerland at the NSL's expense, investigating that country's citizen army system.

Moreover, the trade unionists often reduced their socialist allies to despair by treating most aspects of foreign policy as none of their business. Thus the Parliamentary Committee of the TUC decided in 1905 to have nothing to do with the British National Committee of the Second International.[164] Hardie and his friends were thus left to fight on alone in 1913 in their attempt to persuade the unions to use the strike weapon to stop the country going to war.

What, though, of the wider public? All one can say is that those whom Maxse contemptuously dubbed the 'Potsdam Party' were probably outnumbered by 'jingoes'.[165] Thus, a Radical pamphlet such as Morel's *Morocco in Diplomacy*, despite its later fame, sold very few copies, whereas Le Queux's books went through numerous editions. Significantly, most national newspapers in the Edwardian era, including the best-selling *Daily Mail*, leant to the Conservative side in politics and adopted a warmly martial tone. So, although there was no widespread enthusiasm for war, neither did it appear as if the anti-war movement, whether Radical-Liberal or Labour in origins, would be strong enough to halt one should a real crisis develop.[166]

---

[162] Adams and Poirier, *Conscription Controversy*, 21. He later changed his mind about conscription after observing the army's behaviour during the Great Labour Unrest. The articles were reissued in August 1914 as a pamphlet, entitled *The War That Was Foretold* (Reader, *At Duty's Call*, 73).

[163] Newton, *Struggle for Peace*, 163.

[164] The International's recent campaign against 'revisionism' made all but Marxists feel unwelcome—very offputting for the vast majority of Labour Party members, who did not consider themselves to be socialists of any kind (Newton, *Struggle for Peace*, 344).

[165] A 'miscellaneous assortment of ex-Ambassadors on the stump, Cocoa Quakers, Hebrew journalists at the beck and call of German diplomats, soft-headed Sentimentalists, snobs hypnotised by Hohenzollern blandishments, cranks convinced that their own country is always in the wrong, cosmopolitan financiers domiciled in London to do "good work" for the Fatherland' (cited in Koss, *Brunner*, 252–3).

[166] On the peace movement, see M. Caedel, *Semi-Detached Idealists: The British Peace Movement and International Relations, 1854–1945* (Oxford, 2002), and P. Laity, *The British Peace Movement, 1870–1914* (Oxford, 2002).

10. CRISIS

Such a crisis eventually occurred on 28 June 1914, when the Austrian Arch-duke Ferdinand was assassinated by a Serbian terrorist in the Bosnian capital of Sarajevo.[167] Twenty-five days later the Austrian government issued Serbia with a humiliating ultimatum and, backed by Germany, prepared for war. On 30 July the Russians ordered a general mobilization in support of their Serbian allies. On 1 August Germany declared war on Russia. France seemed set to honour its treaty obligations to Russia.

Initially the Serbian cause was unpopular in Britain. The demagogue Horatio Bottomley demanded that country's annihilation, and even the Con-servative *Daily Telegraph* denounced what it called the Serbian 'plot' at Sarajevo.[168] But the British Cabinet, rather slowly dragging its attention away from Ireland,[169] was from the start more aware of the larger European dimen-sions of the developing crisis.

Grey initially hoped to localize the conflict, as he had done during the recent Balkan wars. As late as 1 August he told Cambon that Britain was under no obligation to the French because of the latter's alliance with Russia, about which he was uninformed, and, briefly, he went so far as to inform Berlin that Britain would remain neutral if Germany promised not to attack in the West. An agitated Henry Wilson, joined by the Conservative backbencher George Lloyd, alerted Conservative leaders to the possibility that the government might desert the French.[170]

An angry Cambon protested, telling the British government that it was at London's 'request that France had moved her fleets to the Mediterranean, on the understanding that we undertook the protection of her Northern and Western Coasts'. This was not an entirely accurate account of the origins of the naval agreement. All the same, there was a high level of co-operation between the British and French navies—higher than prevailed between their armies, because the former had a truly integrated command structure. Finally, though eager not to give the French undue encouragement for fear of making war more likely, Grey was already too far committed to the French to abandon them in their hour of need.[171]

---

[167] For a full account of these events, see K. Wilson, 'Britain', in K. Wilson, *Decisions for War, 1914* (1995), 175–208.

[168] Morris, *Radicalism Against War*, 382.

[169] On 23 July, *after* the assassination at Sarajevo, Lloyd George was still assuring the Commons that Britain's relations with Germany were 'very much better than they were a few years ago' (Hansard, 5th ser., vol. 65, 727–8: 23 July 1914).

[170] Williamson, *Grand Strategy*, 351–2.

[171] Grey privately observed to Nicolson, 'Yes, but he has nothing in writing' (Wilson, *Politics of the Entente*, 144).

Yet within the Cabinet a majority favoured Britain staying out of the war, even after it had become apparent that Grey's attempts at mediation were being sabotaged by Berlin's determination to stand by Austria-Hungary and engineer a Balkans showdown. Asquith declared, 'I shall stand by Grey in any event', but initially, aided by Samuel, McKenna, and Crewe, he was mainly preoccupied with finding a compromise that would hold his government and party together.[172] The Liberal press, too, was decidedly against war; so was the Foreign Affairs Committee, though Asquith, Grey, and Churchill urged silence upon it.[173] Indeed, as Asquith reported to Venetia Stanley on 2 August: 'a good $\frac{3}{4}$ of our own men in the H. of Commons are for absolute non-interference at any price.'[174]

The turning-point came on Sunday 2 August. At the first of two meetings held on that day the Cabinet resolved that the government could not be indifferent to German naval action in the Channel. The 'war party' was also stiffened by the arrival of a letter of patriotic support from Bonar Law and Lansdowne,[175] the significance of which was that, if the Liberal ministry collapsed through internal dissension, those favouring intervention would be able to form a coalition with their Unionist opponents—an important consideration in the Cabinet's gradual abandonment of the 'peace option'. The drift towards war was gathering momentum.

At the second meeting of 2 August the Cabinet edged further in this direction, most ministers agreeing that a 'substantial violation' of Belgian neutrality would compel intervention—even if Belgium joined in on the side of the Germans![176] Then, on 4 August, the German armies crossed the Meuse, although the Belgian government had already declared its determination to resist. The British ultimatum demanding a German withdrawal expired at 11 p.m. (Greenwich Mean Time) on that day. Britain was at war: a momentous commitment to which the Cabinet itself had never assented.[177]

How many Liberal ministers would resign in protest? It was the Belgian issue which was decisive in allowing Lloyd George to part company with the other 'pacifists'—a course of action which, privately, he already favoured. But for other ministers the letter from the Conservative leaders probably mattered more. Jack Pease, the Quaker President of the Board of Education, noted in his diary: 'The PM is anxious we should see this thing through as a Party and does

---

[172] Ibid.

[173] Kennedy, *Anglo-German Antagonism*, 459.

[174] M. and E. Brock (eds.), *H. H. Asquith: Letters to Venetia Stanley* (Oxford, 1982), 146.

[175] Egged on behind the scenes by Milner.

[176] Kennedy, *Anglo-German Antagonism*, 461–2. This was not a totally implausible scenario: as late as July 1914 the Belgian army had been carrying out manoeuvres to repel an Anglo-French, as well as a German, invasion (Williamson, *Strategies*, 333).

[177] Wilson, 'Britain', 201.

not want a Coalition and says he wants as many of his colleagues to stay with him as he can get so as not to go outside the Party.'[178] In the event, Beauchamp and Simon caved in at the last minute, leaving Morley and Burns as the only members of the Cabinet to resign.[179] Churchill was exhilarated as he contemplated the stupendous drama in which he hoped to play a heroic part. But most other Liberal ministers, not least Grey, entered hostilities with a very heavy heart.

Did the British have any alternative but to intervene? Given internal political pressures, the Entente system had been a necessary compromise, but one of its consequences, as Churchill neatly put it, was that Britain had incurred 'the obligations of an alliance without its advantages and above all without its precise definitions'. That is why the conversion of the two Ententes into alliances had been advocated by most senior Foreign Office officials and (from 1912 onwards) by the Opposition frontbench.

As far as the Liberal government was concerned, the crucial element in the French Entente was the military understandings which had grown up around it.[180] True, ministers repeatedly declared that the military and naval conversations were mere contingency plans which left Cabinet and Parliament free to decide on policy when issues of peace and war arose. Grey had told the Dominion PMs in May 1911: 'we are not committed by entanglements which tie our hands. Our hands are free.' He even claimed that, by engaging in thorough planning which made a Continental option possible, the government's freedom had actually been widened.[181] But Esher's earlier observations in March 1913 were very much to the point: 'Of course there is no treaty or convention, but how we can get out of the commitments of the General Staff with honour, I cannot understand.'[182]

The military and naval conversations made Britain's entry into the war significantly more likely—but not inevitable. In 1914 Britain's naval superiority was beyond doubt: she had twenty Dreadnoughts to Germany's thirteen, twenty-six pre-Dreadnought battleships to Germany's twelve, and twice as many cruisers.[183] This freed her from any serious risk of invasion (for which the Germans had, in any case, laid no serious plans). But this does not necessarily mean that in the long run Britain would have benefited from holding aloof. For example, breaking with Russia might again have put Britain's Asiatic Empire at

---

[178] Wilson, *Politics of the Entente*, 141.
[179] Along with C. P. Trevelyan, Parliamentary Secretary at the Board of Education.
[180] In 1914 the British and Russians had also embarked upon naval conversations with one another. However, these had more political than strategic significance.
[181] Wilson, *Politics of the Entente*, 86.
[182] Williamson, *Grand Strategy*, 331.
[183] Steiner, *Origins of First World War*, 98.

risk.[184] Moreover, as Tweedmouth had noted as early as November 1906, diplomatic isolation could also have resulted in a situation in which, on some future occasion, all the major naval powers would range themselves against Britain, a threat she was already not strong enough to counter unaided.[185]

The real importance of the staff talks is that, once the decision to intervene had been made for political reasons, they dictated the form that such intervention would take. This, in turn, meant that Britain was drawn into a protracted land campaign in France and Flanders, for which in many ways she was quite unprepared.

True, Hankey, operating on a shoe string budget, had successfully compiled what later became known as the 'War Book', a carefully prepared document giving each ministry precise instructions about what action it should take in the first few days of hostilities. But, as was true of other aspects of British policy, this exercise was valuable only in the short term. Crucially, British plans were predicated upon the war being short. Should it prove otherwise, the British had done little to prepare for the creation of a mass army: it would take six months to bring the 'Terriers' up to war readiness, besides which its members had individually to consent to serving abroad.[186] Nor had plans been adequately laid for economic mobilization. Perhaps ministers and opinion-formers like J. M. Keynes were too ready to believe Angell's prognostications. The City was certainly eager for Britain to stay out of the European conflict: a near panic swept the Square Mile (the acceptance houses were close to collapse) once the realization dawned that this might not be possible.[187]

It is symptomatic of the government's unpreparedness for the war upon which they were about to embark that even so crucial a matter as devising a scheme of marine insurance had never been brought to completion—largely because the Treasury would not foot the bill. Cost-cutting in the years following the Boer War also meant a drop in munitions expenditure of one-third between 1905–6 and 1912–13. This necessitated a rundown of manpower and machinery in the government's own ordnance factories, and forced private manufacturers to diversify into other areas, such as bicycles and motor-cycles, since the Liberal ministry did not realize the need, by spreading orders, to keep in being an arms industry capable of expansion should hostilities ever break out. As a result, not only was the army's stock of munitions in August 1914 grossly inadequate for even its current requirements, but scant

---

[184] This is the (exaggerated) thesis of Wilson, *Politics of the Entente.*

[185] Though he added that the Admiralty 'cannot base their plans upon the shifting sands of any temporary and unofficial international relationships' (Monger, *End of Isolation*, 310).

[186] Adams and Poirier, *Conscription Controversy*, 32.

[187] Lord Rothschild later tried to get *The Times* to change its campaign for intervention (Kennedy, *Anglo-German Antagonism*, 453–9).

consideration had been given to the issue of how to expand supply in a national emergency.[188]

Finally, the country's leaders lacked any real imaginative grasp of the ordeal which the British people were about to experience. In the course of his influential address to the Commons on 3 August, Grey declared: 'if we engaged in war, we shall suffer but little more than we shall suffer if we stand aside.'[189]

---

[188] D. French, *British Economic and Strategic Planning 1905–1915* (London, 1982), 43–7.

[189] Steiner, *Origins of First World War*, 210.

PART IV

Leisure, Culture, and Science

CHAPTER 14

The Pursuit of Pleasure

1. TIME FOR PLAY

We are a nation at play. Work is a nuisance, an evil necessity to be shirked and hurried over as quickly and easily as possible in order that we may get away to the real business of life—the golf course, the bridge table, the cricket and football field or some other of the thousand amusements which occupy our minds.

(Arthur Shadwell, 1907)

According to the 1911 census, actors and chefs were the occupational groups which had grown fastest during the previous decade, while two of the most rapidly expanding towns were Southend and Bournemouth. Many Edwardians, clearly, were not only making steel and preparing for the possibility of war, but were also having a lot of fun.

The rise of real wages by one-third in the final two decades of the nineteenth century allowed all but the very poor to do more with their lives than struggle for bare survival. But this increase in disposable income would have been of limited benefit had it not been accompanied by an expansion of the time available for what contemporaries often referred to, rather disapprovingly, as 'play'.

In the early 1870s unionized workers negotiated a set of voluntary agreements which made the nine-hour day the norm over much of manufacturing industry. Further gains were secured by parliamentary enactment. The 1874 Factory Act reduced the working week of textile operatives to 56.5 hours, another hour being later shaved off by an Act of 1892.[1] Anxious to 'afford an example to private employers throughout the country', as Campbell-Bannerman put it, the minority Liberal administration of 1892–5 went further when it accepted a parliamentary 'Fair Wage' motion, effectively ceding the eight-hour day for ordnance and dockyard workers employed by the Admiralty

---

[1] H. Cunningham, 'Leisure and Culture', in F. M. L. Thompson (ed.), *The Cambridge Social History of Britain 1750–1950: Vol. 2: People and Their Environment* (Cambridge, 1990), 282–3.

and War Office—an objective which the Labour Movement wished to make a national legal requirement.

In 1897 the Webbs were already calling the eight-hour day 'the Natural Day', though in fact it did not become so until after the Great War. However, the significance of the TUC's involvement in the agitation for a shorter working week was that it showed how organized Labour now valued leisure for its own sake. These demands formed part of a wider 'civic gospel', which acknowledged that working men and women were citizens as well as 'hands', and had psychological needs (relaxation, rest, pleasure) that could only be satisfied outside working hours.

What was at stake here was not simply a total reduction in the length of the working week, but rather a changed attitude to time itself. The trend from the 1870s onwards was to draw a sharper differentiation between the hours that employees owed to their employer and the hours that could be devoted to their private affairs. Here the breakthrough had occurred in the 1870s when Midlands employers had traded off a shorter working week, involving freedom on Saturday afternoons, for a commitment to greater regularity of timekeeping: expensive machinery could not be run at anything like optimum capacity if the workforce continued to follow the tradition of honouring 'Saint Monday' and in other ways taking time off whenever they felt the urge.[2]

In practice, 'Saint Monday' did not disappear as quickly as many employers would have liked: for example, it remained rife in coalmining well into the next century. Nor could greater time-discipline be applied to occupations such as agriculture, where demand for labour fluctuated seasonally, still less to the not inconsiderable ranks of casual labourers. But such irregular work-patterns were now often portrayed as pathological: Charles Booth, for example, labelled the dockers and other poor Londoners who comprised his 'Class B' a 'leisure class' whose ideal was 'to work when they like and play when they like'—something of which he clearly disapproved.

Even socialists began to change their attitudes. Ruskin had earlier preached that all work should be a creative activity and the source of deep psychic satisfaction. Such beliefs were transmitted via William Morris and Edward Carpenter to the Edwardian Arts and Crafts Movement[3] and also to a younger generation of socialists. But the Fabians, more hard-headedly, accepted that manual labour in an industrial society was largely drudgery, from which 'freedom' could only be secured by giving people spare time during which they could do exactly as they pleased.[4]

---

[2] D. Reid, 'The Decline of Saint Monday, 1766–1876', *Past & Present*, 71 (1976), 76–101.
[3] See Ch. 15.
[4] A. M. McBriar, *Fabian Socialism and English Politics 1884–1918* (Cambridge, 1962), 161.

The commercial purveyors of amusements, too, relied upon this sort of 'freedom' because they needed to plan their activities ahead. For example, watching sporting events was not in itself new; what characterized the late Victorian period was the compression of sporting encounters into a short time-span which allowed them to take place regularly and frequently, as in football, where games were scheduled weekly during the season.[5] By the 1890s, if not earlier, most workers could count on having the Saturday afternoon off as of right. Had it been otherwise, professional football, as a spectator sport, could hardly have developed. Many of the original League teams came from the factory districts of Lancashire and from the industrial areas of the Midlands, perhaps because most factory operatives stopped work at Saturday lunchtime; in the London area, where casual work was still widespread, the professional game only developed some ten or fifteen years later.

Bank Holidays, dating from legislation in 1871 and 1875, denoted another new development: the creation of secular days of leisure. As their name suggests, these had been primarily envisaged by their originator, Sir John Lubbock, as a way of providing relief for overworked bank clerks and other white-collar employees, and at first they were not popular with manual workers, who complained that they were receiving no payment for their enforced leisure. However, twenty years later many towns were virtually at a standstill during the August Bank Holiday: in the 1890s half-a-million Londoners each year took advantage of it to visit the coast or the countryside, though it was less observed in the northern industrial districts, where traditional wakes and feast holidays had largely survived.[6]

Some large employers, keen to promote industrial welfare and good labour relations, organized their own annual works outings: the brewing firm of Bass was commissioning eighteen trains to take his 10,000 workers (arranged in hierarchical order) from his Burton brewery for a day out at Blackpool during the 1890s. Longer holidays were less easily arranged. True, work ground to a halt during the Lancashire 'Wakes Weeks', when in the course of the summer all the factories in a particular town closed for a whole week to avoid the piecemeal disruption caused by casual abstentions—the main reason for the remarkable expansion of late Victorian and Edwardian Blackpool.[7] Though the cotton industry was a special case, Brunner Mond, Lever Bros, and the Gas Light & Coke Company started to grant their workforce an annual holiday, albeit without pay, during the 1880s and 1890s.

[5] Cunningham, 'Leisure and Culture', 310.

[6] J. K. Walton and R. Poole, 'The Lancashire Wakes in the Nineteenth Century', in R. D. Storch (ed.), *Popular Culture and Custom in Nineteenth-Century England* (London, 1982), 100–24.

[7] Blackpool had more than doubled in size between 1891 and 1901, though its growth slowed down during the following decade (J. K. Walton, *Blackpool* (Edinburgh, 1998), 46).

2. THE ROLE OF RELIGION

The one block of time in which most workers were released from the tyranny of toil was, of course, Sunday—not entirely released since, to the dismay of the Lord's Day Observance Society (LDOS), some paid labour did take place on that day, a practice legitimized by the Anglican Church, which made exceptions for works of necessity as well as for works of piety and charity. This rule had never been easy to interpret, and even Anglican bishops, to say nothing of Members of Parliament, continued to disagree over whether 'rules of perfection' should be *imposed* on the mass of humanity.

Whether sanctioned by the Church or not, in late Victorian Britain a reduced rail service operated on Sundays (though when trains crashed, Sabbatarians saw this as a sign of God's displeasure); pubs stayed open, despite the efforts of the Central Association for Stopping the Sale of Intoxicating Liquors on Sundays; and journalists and printers worked to ensure that newspapers were available on every day of the week. Such practices drew together in an improbable alliance doctrinaire adherents of 'laissez-faire', Jewish traders, groups of workers whose livelihood depended upon Sunday working, and poor families for whom the Sunday markets provided a convenient way of buying household provisions.

But the Sabbatarians, strong in Nonconformity and on the Evangelical wing of the Established Church, agitated tirelessly for the statutory prohibition of all Sunday working, and regularly brought in Private Member's Bills to restrict it. Nor did they entirely lack support within the working-class community—institutionalized in the Working Men's Lord's Rest Day Association, founded in 1860. Several Labour leaders during the 1880s and 1890s, such as William Abraham (a Calvinistic Methodist), Ben Pickard (a Wesleyan teetotaller), and John Hodge (a Scottish Presbyterian), were chapelgoers, but their aversion to Sunday working derived not only from conscientious scruple; it also reflected the anxiety of the men they represented not to work what would later be called 'unsocial hours'. In 1912 a number of prominent Labour MPs introduced a 'Weekly Rest Day Bill', designed to cover all workers. But, significantly, though Richard Bell of the Amalgamated Society of Railway Servants favoured legislative restrictions on the services which the railway companies could run on a Sunday, he was prepared to settle for time-and-a-half pay by way of compensation.

Such a trade-union response made the LDOS uneasy: one of its spokesmen denounced 'this determination to settle the whole matter on the basis not of Divine Law but of personal convenience, with a flavouring of humanitarian sentimentality'.[8] The decisive showdown between doctrinaire Sabbatarians and

---

[8] J. Wigley, *The Rise and Fall of the Victorian Sunday* (Manchester, 1980), 163.

those who advocated Sunday as a 'day of rest and leisure' took place in March 1896, when Parliament, on a free vote, authorized by 178 to 93 the Sunday opening of national museums and art galleries: a long-standing demand of bodies such as the National Sunday League and the more recently founded Sunday Society. The British Museum, the National Gallery, and the South Kensington museums shortly afterwards opened their doors to the public on Sunday afternoons.[9] But Edwardian Middlesborough was more typical: shops, theatres, and libraries all stayed shut, leaving local people with a choice between the numerous public houses and six music halls showing films.[10]

Those who strove to keep the Sabbath holy did so because they feared that otherwise the churches would be emptied. In fact, Sunday worship had never been universally observed: the 1851 religious census had shocked the pious by revealing that about one-half of all those adults who could have attended a place of worship on 'census Sunday' had not in fact done so, though this avoidance of church and chapel applied more to men than to women—a marked gender division that has continued to the present day.[11] Nothing so ambitious as the 1851 census was ever repeated. But in 1886–7 the Nonconformist paper the *British Weekly* undertook a survey of London, as did the *Daily News* in 1902–3, and both revealed a pattern of continuing decline: churchgoing in Inner London, which had stood at just under 30 per cent in 1851, was down to 28.5 per cent in 1886–7, and down again to 22 per cent in 1902–3 (excluding twicers).[12]

The *Daily News* census also appeared to demonstrate that churchgoing, as in 1851, was still class based, the ratio of worshippers to total population being 36.8 per cent in the wealthy suburban districts, 22.7 per cent in other middle-class areas, 16 per cent in districts containing the skilled working class, but only 11.7 per cent in the slums.[13] Yet, interestingly, the most dramatic falls between 1886 and 1902 occurred in London's suburban and upper-class districts, where attendance declined by a third.

Possibly the 'crisis of faith', observable in the smaller proportion of the population coming forward for ordination and in the well-documented histories of prominent intellectuals such as Mark Rutherford and Leslie Stephen, may have contributed to the waning prestige of Christianity among these relatively affluent people. On the other hand, 'doubt' cannot provide the

[9] Ibid. 147–8.
[10] Lady (Mrs Hugh) Bell, *At The Works* (London, 1907), 132.
[11] 61% of churchgoers in London, according to the 1902–3 Census in London, were females, though women in general comprised 54% of the population.
[12] H. McLeod, *Class and Religion in the Late Victorian City* (London, 1974), 237.
[13] Ibid. 27, 237. But for a critique of this, and similar interpretation, see C. G. Brown, *The Death of Christian Britain* (London, 2001), 150–6.

main explanation for the level of church-attendances. Significantly, the 'atheist mission' had failed to make mass converts: the National Secular Society peaked in the mid-1880s, boosted by Charles Bradlaugh's refusal to take an oath on election to the Commons, but even so its membership numbered no more than 1,883 in 1882–3.[14] Among the very poor (except the Irish) there was widespread indifference to official religion, and some scepticism over doctrines such as the existence of Hell (though missionary reports suggest much confusion and ignorance on these matters), but little disposition to challenge the Bible story head-on or to disparage its central ethical claims. Charles Booth noted that a Hall of Science in the East End stood as deserted as the churches: 'the people want[ed] neither religion nor its antidote. All they wanted was to be left alone.'[15] Thus militant unbelief was relatively rare, probably rarer than in the 1840s and 1850s, especially once 'secularism' (agnosticism) had come under challenge from the new 'religion' of socialism.[16]

Socialism itself enjoyed an ambiguous relationship with orthodox religious beliefs. Marxism, admittedly, was subversively critical of Christianity. However, the type of socialism that made the swiftest progress, the ethical socialism of the ILP, was soaked in Christian feeling and language: Philip Snowden's most popular address bore the title 'The Christ That Is To Be'. R. J. Campbell, a friend of Keir Hardie and a member of the Finsbury branch of the ILP, could call socialism 'a swing back to the gospel of the Kingdom of God'.[17]

The Labour Churches, started in 1891 by a disillusioned Unitarian minister, John Trevor, eventually became little more than an excuse to hold political meetings on a Sunday, but the initial success of the experiment suggests that, in the 1890s especially, socialism was most effective when presented as an extension of the Sermon on the Mount. Many leading Labour politicians of this generation were themselves regular chapelgoers. Others were Anglicans, mainly adherents of the 'High Church' tendency, where, as in the Revd Stewart Headlam's Guild of Saint Matthew, the profession of 'Christian Socialism' was not uncommon.

All of this makes the proposition that religion was 'in decline' a highly dubious one, much obviously depending upon what meaning is attached to this vague phrase. Church attendances in London had always been poor, but other industrial towns recorded even lower figures: an unofficial census of 1881

---

[14] A slight underestimate, because it ignores the provincial branches. On secularism, see E. Royle, *Radicals, Secularists and Republicans: Popular Freethought in Britain, 1866–1915* (Manchester, 1980), D. Nash, *Secularism, Art and Freedom* (Leicester, 1992).

[15] Cited in C. F. G. Masterman *The Condition of England* (London, 1909), 116.

[16] Home visitations of Liverpool by the Free Churches in 1911 revealed few avowed secularists or atheists.

[17] In *Christianity and the Social Order* (1907), cited in K. Robbins, *History, Religion and Identity in Modern Britain* (London, 1993), 143.

showed its level as being 27.1 per cent in Bradford, 24.2 per cent in Nottingham, and 23 per cent in Sheffield. On the other hand, this same survey showed church attendances running as high as 40 per cent in Bristol, more or less where it had been in 1851.[18] In fact, church attendance continued to grow until 1906, though not as a percentage of the total population, while the levels of church *membership* in England and Wales probably peaked during the Edwardian decade.[19] Moreover, such statistics cannot tell the whole story, since they omit, for example, revivalist and 'tea-and-experience' meetings (more a feature of urban than of rural life), and take no account of those missionary activities which were so striking a feature of the late Victorian period.[20] In any case, head-counting exercises, intrinsically fraught with difficulties, hardly provide an index of the intensity or the sincerity of Christian belief.

Despite some doubts among the intelligentsia, the doctrinal challenge to Christianity in 1886 was therefore weak. The churches faced no substantial rivalry from other faiths: in 1903 26,612 men, women, and children attended the London synagogues for Passover, but Judaism attracted few who were not ethnically Jewish. Indeed, the English population may have been more imbued with Christian values in the late Victorian period than at any previous period as a result of the 1870 Education Act and the making compulsory of elementary education, which familiarized all children with the rudiments of the Christian faith.[21]

These educational developments in turn liberated the Sunday schools from the need to impart the 'three Rs', leaving them free to inculcate the faith. Sunday schools were valued even by working-class parents who themselves seldom set foot in church or chapel—perhaps, as the cynics said, because this gave them a few hours of privacy in which to conduct their marital relations, perhaps because they thought attendance at the schools would teach their children 'discipline'. Be that as it may, Sunday-school membership trebled between the 1860s and 1906, by which time it embraced some 80 per cent of the 5–14 age group.[22]

But though Christianity was certainly not being abandoned, one can discern a certain change of temper. Many churches devoted an excessive amount of their time to fund-raising to pay for the vast building programmes of earlier decades, and this 'religion of bricks and mortar' perhaps reflected a diminution of zeal. Moreover, some clergy were weakening the severity of the Christian

---

[18] H. E. Meller, *Leisure and the Changing City, 1870–1914* (London, 1976), 79–80.
[19] Brown, *Death of Christian Britain*, 163–4.
[20] See Ch. 3.
[21] J. Harris, *Private Lives, Public Spirit: A Social History of Britain 1870–1914* (Oxford, 1993), 178.
[22] However, worried at evidence of decline, some Sunday schools increasingly turned from indoctrination to 'nurture' (S. J. D. Green, 'The Religion of the Child in Edwardian Methodism', *Journal of British Studies*, 30 (1991), 398).

faith in order to make it more generally palatable, substituting for the 'God of Judgement' the less frightening figure of the 'Suffering Servant'.[23] A typical Edwardian phenomenon was the Pleasant Sunday Afternoon movement, launched by the Nonconformists, which mingled mild edification with communal hymn-singing and good-natured sociability. And for many suburbanites religion now provided an agreeable aesthetic experience, centred upon flowers, music, and personal kindliness—again betokening an unwillingness to make Christianity too difficult and demanding. Notable, too, is the tendency of churchgoers to attend a place of worship less frequently.[24]

All of these developments seem to have impacted upon the observance of Sunday. Even in those homes where Protestantism continued to be warmly professed, the grim atmosphere so memorably described by Dickens in *Little Dorrit* thirty years earlier had been considerably softened. Sunday obviously remained for most Christians a special day, to be marked by the wearing of one's best (usually uncomfortable) clothes and by a ban on frivolous games and on the reading of all but religious books, as well as by attendance at church or chapel. But, above all, Sunday was becoming a day consecrated to family visiting and entertainment, often involving domestic music-making on piano, accordion, or mandolin (not necessarily confined to hymns or sacred compositions). Such occasions were often recalled in later years as times of exceptional happiness by the children who had experienced them.

But many late Victorian Christians, having attended a religious service, now felt free to spend the rest of the day in a more relaxed fashion: only a minority still believed secular enjoyment to be intrinsically sinful. Significantly, Sunday papers in 1900 sold in approximately double the number of dailies.[25] Another popular pleasure was strolling on a Sunday afternoon through the local park, perhaps to listen to a brass band. True, the LDOS denounced Sunday newspapers and saw the devil's handiwork even in Salvation Army bands, but extremism of this sort largely isolated it from mainstream society. By contrast, several prominent Catholic and Anglo-Catholic clergymen came out as critics of joyless puritanism: in 1895 the High Churchman Canon Barnett organized Sunday concerts and lectures in the East End, and served, for a time, as President of the Sunday Society.[26]

---

[23] Edmund Gosse, looking back during the Edwardian decade on the religious convictions of his father in the 1850s and 1860s, found it 'very extraordinary for a man, so instructed and so intelligent as he, to dwell so much on the possible anger of the Lord, rather than on His pity and love' (*Father and Son*, (1907), 155).

[24] It has been argued that this development may have led to an under-representation of the size of the churchgoing population (Brown, *Death of Christian Britain*, 151).

[25] Cunningham, 'Leisure and Culture', 312.

[26] Wigley, *Victorian Sunday*, 139.

Higher up the social scale, too, sabbatarian inhibitions were being discarded. Among the aristocracy there was a rage for weekend house-parties, in which token Christian observance did little to interfere with worldly pleasure. Even the Prince of Wales, having fulfilled his duty by attending morning service, felt free to spend the rest of the day on his pleasures, even playing cards—though he did so privately, in the vain hope of avoiding public censure. Contemporary moralists saw this as simply one more manifestation of the new hedonism particularly associated, during the new reign, with the 'plutocracy'—a hedonism which also found expression in a love of yachts and motor cars and in a weakness for all kinds of conspicuous luxury.

Such delights were confined to a small minority. Those of more modest means, however, could partake of the cycling craze of the 1890s, which took many young men and women out of the cities on enjoyable Sunday explorations of the surrounding countryside (and also allowed socialists to spread their message to the agricultural worker). Others took excursions on horse-drawn brakes. Thus, while many of the non-religious still clung to the notion that Sunday should be a 'quiet day', and decorum generally prevailed in the streets, for others Sunday was becoming merely a part of a weekend which stretched, largely uninterrupted, from midday on Saturday until the start of Monday morning.

As for that section of the urban working class largely detached from organized religion, life on Sundays went on as it had long done. Booth portrayed the situation in working-class London as follows:

[The people] get up at nine or ten . . . [when they are to be seen] at breakfast half-dressed or lounging in the window reading Lloyd's Weekly Newspaper. After they are washed and dressed the men wait about until the public-houses open, and then stay within their doors till three o'clock when they go home to dinner, which meanwhile the women have been preparing . . . After dinner the men, if they have drunk much, may go to bed, but the better sort take a stroll. In the evening the young people pair off for walking out, while the elders may perhaps go to a concert or Sunday League lecture.[27]

As is obvious from this account, the preparation of the Sunday lunch, the grandest meal of the week, meant that, for the wife at least, the Sabbath could be no time of rest—which had to be postponed to the evening of Monday, 'Mother's Day'.[28]

What about the role of the churches in organizing the leisure time of the people on other days of the week? Organized religion was still the centre of a

---

[27] A. Fried and R. Elman (eds.), Charles Booth's London (1969; Harmondsworth 1971 edn.), 253.

[28] The importance of preparing the Sunday lunch also explains why in most working-class Protestant denominations women were more inclined to attend the evening service (Brown, Death of Christian Britain, 160–1). See also E. Ross, Love and Toil: Motherhood in Outcast London, 1870–1918 (Oxford, 1993), 37–9.

dense and intricate network of voluntary clubs and associations: Dissenters could, if they so wished, participate in a different chapel-based social activity, serious or light-hearted, on every day of the week. Children and youths were particularly well catered for, with Sunday-school outings (held out of term-time on a weekday) providing many poor children with their only chance of going on an excursion. In *Anna of the Five Towns* (1902), Arnold Bennett's depiction of 'the treat' depicts the children marching in procession to the special train which takes them to the beauty spot in the countryside, where games are arranged and a grand tea served. Boys' and girls' clubs also flourished, while after 1907 most Scout and Girl Guide troops were affiliated to church or chapel. But Christianity did not provide comfort, enjoyment, and stimulation only for the young and deprived: in the new suburban districts church and chapel rescued many a housewife from a life of isolation and boredom by involving her in a range of activities, from philanthropic good works to the flower-arranging classes beloved of the Mothers' Union.[29]

Though some of these enterprises had a specifically Christian content, others resembled 'loss leaders'. This was especially true of the attempt to retain the institutional allegiance of young men and women who might otherwise have drifted into 'bad company'. For example, the Christian laity (more rarely the ministers of religion) set very high store by the encouragement of organized games. Many famous soccer clubs, which later turned professional, originated in a Sunday school or a church or chapel.[30]

So what was happening was less an erosion of traditional Christian beliefs than a watering-down of religious practice, as the churches sought popularity by making their peace with an increasingly secular society. For many late Victorians and Edwardians, Christianity was becoming privatized—turned into a kind of Sunday hobby, drained of public or political significance, something clearly apparent in the provision of 'amusements' which, even when notionally under church control, now often served no real moral purpose, but had a great deal to do with 'having a good time'.

3. RATIONAL RECREATION

This growing hedonism not only diluted the mission of the churches, it also struck at the roots of what contemporaries called 'rational recreation'.[31] Throughout the nineteenth century the mainly middle-class advocates of this

---

[29] F. M. L. Thompson, *The Rise of Respectable Society: A Social History of Victorian Britain, 1830–1900* (London, 1988), 252.

[30] See below.

[31] For the whole issue of 'rational recreation', see the pioneering study, P. Bailey, *Leisure and Class in Victorian England* (London, 1978).

creed had tried to discourage, even suppress, older forms of plebeian culture, particularly pastimes that involved cruelty (cock-fighting, for example) or that had associations with heavy drinking and gambling. In their place they sought, often with limited success, to establish 'improving' activities such as lectures and lantern-slide shows, visiting art galleries and museums, and enjoying the amenities offered by the often recently acquired public parks and botanical gardens. Churches and chapels were at the forefront of these efforts, and continued to be so until the outbreak of the Great War.

These endeavours linked up, in complex ways, with the 'culture of self-improvement', centred mainly upon better-paid, better-educated workmen anxious to associate themselves, individually and as a class, with the onward march of 'Progress'. This intellectual ambition found outlet in the establishment of a myriad of improvement societies, reading circles, dramatic societies, and musical groups.[32]

As this working-class involvement increased, so the quest for 'rational recreation' underwent a slow transformation. By the end of the century the earlier stress on the need to combat the ignorance and barbarism of the poor had given way to a far more optimistic vision—that of a society reintegrated through a shared cultural heritage. Canon Barnett, for one, believed that 'simpler living and higher thinking would bring rich and poor nearer together', united by a shared pride in 'Libraries, Art Galleries, good music, University teaching', and he wanted to make these blessings of civilization accessible to all.[33]

The civic leaders organizing such cultural projects came from diverse social backgrounds: they included ministers from most of the mainstream churches (though not those appealing to humbler strata of the population, such as the Salvation Army and the Bible Christians, who generally preferred to concentrate on evangelism); public-spirited landowners; successful businessmen eager to win social approval by dignifying and 'beautifying' the cities in which they had made their fortunes; and 'progressively minded' professional men and their wives.

A novel feature of the 1890s was the willingness of some municipalities, benefiting from the greatly increased revenue generated by recent economic growth, to put public money into cultural ventures, such as sponsoring musical concerts[34] and erecting impressive buildings to house their library collections.

---

[32] J. Rose, *The Intellectual Life of the British Working Classes* (New Haven and London, 2001), 58. More on these autodidacts is to be found in Ch. 16.

[33] Meller, *Leisure and Changing City*, 99–100.

[34] By the 1890s 'music on the rates' was a feature of seaside resorts such as Eastbourne as well as of large towns like London and Sheffield (D. Russell, *Popular Music in England, 1840–1914* (Manchester 1987), 37–8).

More often, however, public authorities acted in co-operation with private individuals. For example, Bristol acquired a museum and a public art gallery between 1895 and 1905; the museum owed its existence to the generosity of a past mayor, while money for the construction of the gallery came from its leading industrialist, W. H. Wills, the tobacco magnate, with running costs funded out of the interest derived from another private bequest.[35]

Private agencies also took the lead in making provision for adult education, another key component in the culture of 'rational recreation'. Toynbee Hall (an undenominational but essentially Christian organization) offered its East End neighbours in the 1890s an exhausting array of lectures, classes, reading parties, and musical lessons. Along with the churches, the older universities, too, now acknowledged a wider social responsibility, and from the 1870s onwards tried to reach out to adults otherwise debarred from pursuing a formal higher education by offering them extension courses—in so doing, sowing the seeds of future university colleges, many of which in time acquired their own charter. 'The peak year was 1891–2, when Oxford and Cambridge together provided 722 courses attended by nearly 47,000 people.'[36] Albert Mansbridge further widened access to learning by establishing the Workers' Education Association (WEA) in 1903, which achieved the difficult feat of linking the Co-operative Movement, run by its working-class members, to the new university colleges and to the wider extension movement.[37]

These activities did not always benefit those for whom they had been specifically designed. Edward Carpenter, an early extension lecturer, expressed disappointment that many of his pupils 'were of the "young lady" class', not manual workers: in fact, the latter comprised only between one-quarter and a fifth of all extension students in Yorkshire between 1885 and 1902.[38] The WEA, aided in many localities by the new LEAs, enjoyed greater success by giving ambitious working men access to talented tutors later to have famous careers in the Labour Party, notably R. H. Tawney and Arthur Greenwood, then a young economics lecturer at Leeds University. Militant class-conscious socialists, who later went on to found the Plebs League and the Central Labour College, feared that socialism was being undermined by a movement which placed conventional educational ideals before political propaganda—though there is no evidence that the disinterested pursuit of knowledge and beauty did have these political consequences.[39] On the other hand, the WEA's success testifies to a working-class thirst for knowledge and self-improvement which had earlier been stimulated by bodies such as the ILP and which was also

[35] Meller, *Leisure and Changing City*, 66–8.

[36] J. F. C. Harrison, *Learning and Living 1790–1960: A Study in the History of the English Adult Education Movement* (London, 1961), 243.

[37] Ibid. 261–6.   [38] Ibid. 236–7.   [39] Rose, *Intellectual Life*, Ch. 8.

catered for in some areas by local co-operative societies, which ran not merely vocational courses but also ambitious programmes of classes in mathematics, foreign languages, science, and music.[40]

The adult education movement was often bedevilled by tensions between those offering well-intentioned provision from above and intelligent artisans and working women trying to exercise direct control over their own lives. This sort of tension eventually wrecked the Adult School movement in Yorkshire, inspired by Quakers such as the Rowntrees, which tried to reach out to the working classes with a message of 'fellowship' and 'service'. But such difficulties were less damaging than the tendency to overestimate the energy and inclination of most workers for serious study. Instructive here is the fate of the Institute of Working Men's Clubs (CIU), which in the mid-1880s possessed more than half-a-million members.[41] By the end of the century the movement had broken free from upper-class patronage, only to degenerate into what critics (perhaps unfairly) saw as little more than a collection of drinking clubs.[42]

Insidious fleshly pleasures could also creep up almost unobserved on organizations which the established elites continued to dominate. For example, by the 1880s even middle-class temperance leaders realized that, if the allure of the public house were to be overcome, alternative 'attractions' must be provided. Hence temperance coffee houses began to spring up in all the major urban centres. But it soon became clear that drinking coffee would not, in itself, entertain the working man for an entire evening. Newspapers and books were accordingly made available on their premises; these were later supplemented by billiard tables, until the coffee-house proprietors eventually became drawn into the entertainments business. This process was particularly marked in the case of the Band of Hope, which many teenagers joined, not because they had been converted to a lifetime's abstention from the 'Demon Drink', but because they wanted to take advantage of its club facilities, not least those for organized sport. The Young Men's Christian Association (YMCA) went down a similar path: by the Edwardian period it was deeply involved in the business of organizing holidays and excursions at home and abroad and of providing sports facilities. To be sure, this might be harmless fun, but it was not quite what had been envisaged by the Nonconformist worthies who had founded the YMCA way back in 1844.

The economist W. S. Jevons wrote in 1878: 'Among the means towards a higher civilization, I unhesitatingly assert that the deliberate cultivation of

[40] P. Gurney, *Co-operative Culture and the Politics of Consumption in England, 1870–1930* (Manchester, 1996), esp. Ch. 2.

[41] Thompson, *Respectable Society*, 326.

[42] For an account of working-men's clubs in Bradford, one of the centres of the movement, see, P. Jennings, *The Public House in Bradford, 1770–1970* (Keele, 1995), 227–30.

public amusements is a principal one . . . popular amusements [being] no trivial matter but one that has great influence on national manners and character.'[43] A half-century of commitment to 'rational recreations' had done much to bring a more respectable tone to English social life—though, as we will see, many highly disreputable pastimes, new and old, still flourished. But by the turn of the century Canon Barnett's vision of a cultural renaissance already looked unrealistic.

Yet a minority of cultivated working men self-consciously eschewed 'vulgarity'. Though museums and art galleries held little popular appeal, the free libraries were well used by working men and women between 1886 and 1914. True, their progress had been slightly disappointing, mainly because the 1*d.* rate set in the permissive legislation of 1855 was not raised until 1919, making it difficult for municipalities to acquire buildings and to build up book stocks.[44] As late as 1896 forty-six districts with populations of over 20,000 still had not adopted the Act, London's parishes being particularly backward in this respect—hence the importance of the Carnegie Bequest, which stimulated the establishment of 225 libraries in England and Wales between 1897 and 1913, by which time the service was available to nearly two-thirds of the population.[45] However, although rooms were set aside for the exclusive use of ladies, the fastidious still shrank from the coarse language and odour of the vagrants attracted into the public library by its warmth and comfort,[46] and the middle classes preferred to use the subscription libraries, of which the doyen was Mudie's (whose 1 guinea subscription could be relied upon to keep out most manual workers), joined in 1900 by Boots Book-Lovers' Library.

Who exactly used the free libraries? In Bristol in 1891 the largest groups comprised schoolboys and students (one-third), artisans (10.8 per cent), 'assistants' (9.8 per cent), and clerks (7.6 per cent). The unskilled, predictably, were less interested in books: only 1.9 per cent of the Bristol users were labourers, 1.8 per cent errand boys.[47] Lady Bell, enquiring into the reading habits of Middlesborough workers during the Edwardian years, found that 4.5 per cent of the population borrowed a book from the free library, these being mainly 'the better class of workmen', not 'the very poor'.[48] Her house-by-house survey also reveals that some 31 per cent of working-class adults took reading seriously, 54 per cent did some light reading, while the rest were indifferent or

---

[43] Cited in Meller, *Leisure and Changing City*, 15.
[44] Following the original Act of 1850, which sanctioned only one halfpenny.
[45] R. D. Altick, *The English Common Reader: A Social History of the Mass Reading Public, 1800–1900* (Chicago, 1957), 227–8; R. Williams, *The Long Revolution* (London, 1961), 170.
[46] Altick, *Common Reader*, 238.
[47] Worked from table in Altick, *Common Reader*, 237.
[48] Though to this should be added the use of a small library connected with the ironworks, and another to a workmen's club (Bell, *At The Works*, 163–4).

hostile. Women tended to show less interest than men, several saying that they lacked the opportunity, or, more bluntly, that reading was a total waste of time.[49]

What was being read? High-minded contemporaries lamented the great popularity of 'fiction', which accounted for between 65 per cent and 90 per cent of the 30–40 million books being lent out by public libraries by the end of the century[50] ('I've got to open a Free Library somewhere', one novelist makes a cynical upper-class character say: 'You know the sort of thing that happens— one unveils a bust of Carlyle and makes a speech about Ruskin, and then people come in their thousands and read *Rabid Ralph, or Should He Have Bitten Her?*[51]). However, it should be noted that 'fiction' included poetry and drama as well as novels. Lady Bell found that the author most often mentioned by her respondents was Mrs Henry Wood, *East Lynne* being a particular favourite.[52] Moreover, a 1904 survey of Lancashire shows that working-class houses usually had on their shelves the Bible and Bunyan's *Pilgrim's Progress*, as well as a scattering of children's Sunday school prizes.[53]

A faint residue of the earlier culture of self-improvement can be seen in the fact that Lord Northcliffe, the newspaper proprietor, was also producing books in his 'Home Educator' series. But by the start of the twentieth century a new hedonism was in the air. H. G. Wells caught the mood accurately in his portrayal of Mr Polly, who reads, not to improve himself, but for fun. For every working man studying Shakespeare or attending lectures on Herbert Spencer there were now a hundred following the fortunes of their football team, attending the music hall, reading light-hearted newspapers or magazines, or enjoying themselves by the seaside.

4. RISE OF THE LEISURE INDUSTRY

It was during the 1880s that a distinctively organized 'leisure industry' first emerged, aimed at the exploitation of the new mass market. The process was evident over a wide range of social life. For example, the music hall had originated in the 'sing-songs' attached to public houses, whose proprietors wanted additional attractions to induce customers to consume their beer. But after 1886 many of the halls became grouped into highly profitable theatre chains, nationwide in their scope. The most successful of the new impresarios, Richard Thornton, Edward Moss, and Oswald Stoll, eventually came together in 1900 to form a syndicate, 'Moss Empires', based on ten separate companies

---

[49] Ibid. 162–6.   [50] Altick, *Common Reader*, 231, 239.
[51] 'Saki' (H. Munro), 'The Unbearable Bassington' (*Collected Works*, (London, 1980), 638).
[52] Bell, *At The Works*, 166.   [53] Altick, *Common Reader*, 246.

with fourteen music halls, with a capitalization of over £1.5 million: between 1902 and 1908 the syndicate paid an average of nearly 22 per cent to its shareholders.[54] By the early 1890s about 45,000 people a night were crowding into London's thirty-five biggest halls.[55] Sumptuous variety theatres such as the Coliseum, built in 1904 by the great theatre architect Frank Matcham, could seat an audience of over 2,000, with standing room for another 500,[56] as could another outstanding Matcham building, the Olympia, Liverpool, opened with a flourish for Moss Empires in 1905.[57]

The early twentieth century was the heyday of extravagant theatrical spectacle, based upon all manner of technological gadgetry. The Coliseum, for example, had a revolving stage, while the London Hippodrome (designed by Matcham for Moss and Stoll), which opened on 15 January 1900, had a stage that could retract, uncovering a water tank into which elephants slid down along an inclined plane.[58]

Some halls continued to play to a predominantly working-class public, but the larger ones, such as the London Pavilion (opened in 1885), aimed at a more heterogeneous audience; others, for example, the 'Empire', also attracted a raffish and aristocratic set, which included the Prince of Wales. This social mix was made possible by a differential pricing policy: customers could gain entry for as little as 6d., but the very best seats might cost as much as 2 guineas.[59] As the theatres expanded, the nature of the entertainment they provided altered. In place of the old intimacy between performer and audience, customers were now kept at bay by a proscenium arch, which, with its safety curtain, served as a protection against theatre fires. Performers became 'artistes', the most successful of whom (Dan Leno, Little Tich, Charlie Chaplin, Marie Lloyd, Vesta Tilley) could command earnings of up to £20,000 a year. Moreover, such 'stars' were often employed on a 'turns' system which took them to several halls in a single night—a system which meant that there could be no ad-libbing

---

[54] M. Sanderson, *From Irving to Olivier: A Social History of the Acting Profession in England, 1888–1983* (London, 1984), 117; C. Ehrlich, *The Music Profession in Britain Since the Eighteenth Century: A Social History* (Oxford, 1985), 168; T. C. Davis, *The Economics of the British Stage 1800–1914* (Cambridge, 2000), 176–7, 268.

[55] Thompson, *Respectable Society*, 323. Nationally, there were about 500 halls in all.

[56] Sanderson, *Acting Profession*, 124.

[57] Matcham built an astonishing number of theatres, including the Hippodrome, Palladium, and the Victoria Palace in London, the Grand Theatre and the Tower Ballroom in Blackpool, and Buxton's Opera House.

[58] B. M. Walker, *Frank Matcham: Theatre Architect* (Belfast, 1980), 75–6. The Coliseum's revolving stage caused a disaster in 1906, when a stunt re-creating Derby Day led to the accidental death of the jockey Fred Dent (pp. 76–7).

[59] P. Summerfield, 'Patriotism and Empire: Music-Hall Entertainment, 1870–1914', in J. M. Mackenzie (ed.), *Imperialism and Popular Culture* (Manchester, 1986), 23. At the Coliseum in April 1912 prices ranged from 6d. for the balcony to 1 guinea for a private box (Walker, *Matcham*, 27).

because it disrupted the timetable. The transformation of the old music hall into a kind of variety theatre was further speeded up after 1890 by the installation of fixed seats and the removal of food and drink from the auditorium. Some of the new halls, among them the 2,000–3,000 seater established in Bristol during the 1890s, were alcohol-free from the very start.[60]

This disassociation of entertainment from drinking also characterized a radically new leisure institution, the cinema. Most of the early films were 'newsreels'—for example, the record of the 1896 Derby which was projected onto a screen twenty-four hours after the race at the Alhambra Theatre, one of London's leading music halls. In no time the cuckoo was taking over the nest: ten of Middlesborough's music halls were showing films on the cinematograph by 1914. But specially designed picture palaces, of which the Balham Empire was the first, were also being constructed—luxurious buildings, softly lit and furnished with plush carpets and gilt mirrors. By 1914 there were, in all, between 3,500 and 4,000 picture palaces, with a capitalization of approximately £11 million.[61] Most highly educated people still saw the cinema as an ingenious toy, even as a bit of a joke: Asquith, visiting a picture palace for the first time in 1911, is said to have laughed heartily and to have continually made loud, 'witty' comments about what he was watching.[62]

The large audiences that flocked to the cinema and the major music halls came from far and wide, something that was only possible because of the efficiency of the public transport system. Cheap and efficient transport, between as well as within cities, was even more essential to the development of spectator sport, which assumed the geographic mobility of players. This was particularly the case with football, which staged nationwide competitions with the FA Cup,[63] started in 1871–2, and later with the Football League. Many spectators, too, wanted to watch away games (football 'special' trains were 'a regular feature by the early 1880s'[64]), while huge crowds converged annually on London, usually from the north, on Cup Final Saturday.

Team games promoted the 'nationalization of leisure' in a more fundamental way. For example, the modern form of association football (soccer) dates from the codification of its rules at Cambridge in 1848 and again in 1863 (the year when the Football Association was founded), the original purpose being to

---

[60] J. M. Goldby and A. W. Purdue, *The Civilisation of the Crowd: Popular Culture in England, 1750–1900* (1984), 174.

[61] Thompson, *Respectable Society*, 332; Cunningham, 'Leisure and Culture', 311: P. J. Waller, *Town, City and Nation: England 1850–1914* (Oxford, 1983), 101.

[62] A. R. Ubbelohde, 'Science', in S. Nowell-Smith (ed.), *Edwardian England, 1901–1914* (Oxford, 1964), 239.

[63] The Scottish Cup began as early as 1874, but the most successful Scottish team, Queens Park (of Glasgow), continued for many years to take part in the FA Cup, reaching the finals in 1885.

[64] T. Mason, *Association Football and English Society 1863–1915* (Brighton, 1980), 146.

enable former public-school pupils to play one another when they met at university or in 'old boy' matches. The game then rapidly spread throughout most of urban Britain, promoted by the churches, which saw it as providing much-needed discipline and exercise for slum children, and by employers such as Arnold F. Hills, owner of the Thames Ironworks and founder of West Ham United, who thought that fit and healthy workers would be more efficient and productive.[65] Most of today's big clubs originated in these years, either with a church or chapel (Aston Villa, Fulham, Barnsley), or as works' teams (Arsenal, Liverpool, Coventry City, Manchester United, as well as West Ham).

However, in the late 1870s and early 1880s the game began to break away from the patronage of the social elites. A symbolic moment occurred in August 1877, when the working-class members of the football club attached to Christ Church, Bolton, broke with the local vicar and walked out into a nearby pub, from which they re-emerged as Bolton Wanderers. Clubs rapidly proliferated: by the end of the decade there were 203 in Liverpool alone, most of them autonomous.[66] So rapid an expansion created problems of where teams were to play, since most municipal parks had been set out in the mid-Victorian years as places in which to walk, with games-playing discouraged.[67] Like many other towns, Bristol, which had established a swimming bath in 1884, then had to offer public land suitable for other sports by laying out recreation grounds.

The next stage in the development of football came when the bigger clubs restricted casual access to their matches by enclosing the playing area and charging entrance fees. From this revenue, the ambitious northern clubs started to make furtive payments to imported players, many drawn from Scotland. In 1886 the FA finally accepted the inevitable and legalized professionalism. This led quite logically to the institution of the Football League two years later: clubs which were saddled with heavy wage bills could not afford to rely upon the lottery of a knock-out competition such as the otherwise highly successful FA Cup, and needed a regular fixture list which could sustain spectator interest and generate income throughout the season.

By the 1890s most of the features of the modern professional game were well established. The leading clubs followed the example of the music halls and floated themselves as limited liability companies, the equivalent of Moss and Stoll being men such as the cotton manufacturer William Sudell, who founded Preston North End and played an important role in pioneering the professional game.[68]

[65] C. Korr, 'West Ham United Football Club and the Beginnings of Professional Football in East London, 1895–1914', *Journal of Contemporary History*, 13 (1978), 211–32.
[66] R. Holt, *Sport and the British: A Modern History* (Oxford, 1989), 151.
[67] Ibid. 151–2.
[68] Waller, *Town, City and Nation*, 103.

Just as Matcham's grand buildings were needed to stage the new kind of variety theatre, so expensive, purpose-built stadiums, such as Stamford Bridge (1905), Old Trafford (1908–9), and Highbury (1913), came into existence to accommodate the growing crowds. Though First Division matches initially attracted average gates of under 5,000, in 1905–6 they were averaging over 13,000 and in 1913–14 23,100.[69] During the Edwardian years some 6 million paying customers were going through the turnstiles to watch Football League matches, with a weekly turnover of £300,000–£400,000 (the League had by now increased from twelve to twenty clubs and had acquired a Second Division).[70] International contests between the 'home countries' could attract crowds of 80,000 or more—with tragic consequences when a stand collapsed during a Scotland versus England match at Ibrox Park, Glasgow, in 1902. In 1901 a record crowd of 113,000 attended the Cup Final—admittedly an unusual occasion, this being the only time before the war when the Cup was won by a London club, Tottenham Hotspur.[71]

With a standard entry charge of 6d. for big matches (3d. for non-League games), football fell comfortably within the means of better-paid workers, including miners, who were fanatical fans, though it would have been rather expensive for the casual poor.[72] A Football League ruling of 1890 stipulated a minimum entrance charge of 6d. for adult males, and this remained the case until 1920.[73] Ex-public-school pupils quickly lost interest in the game once it had become thoroughly professionalized and switched their allegiance to the rugby union code. But the early stands had reserved places, at higher prices, for tradesmen, small businessmen, and the like,[74] so there was a certain amount of social mixing—albeit at a distance.

In 1891 448 players were registered with the Football League, but numbers had reached about 5,000 by the Edwardian period.[75] What of their pay? In 1900 the League introduced a maximum weekly wage of £4, raising it to £5 in 1909—about double what a skilled industrial worker could earn, bringing top players within the income-taxpaying bracket and making them objects of envy to their fans,[76] though most players earned considerably less than the maximum. Benefit matches could also bring in sums as high as £500. Signing-on

---

[69] W. Vamplew, *Pay Up and Play the Game: Professional Sport in Britain, 1875–1914* (Cambridge, 1988), 63.

[70] Holt, *Sport*, 161. In 1909 1 million people watched soccer each Saturday afternoon (N. Tranter, *Sport, Economy and Society in Britain, 1750–1914* (Cambridge, 1998), 17).

[71] Waller, *Town, City and Nation*, 105.

[72] This can be demonstrated by an analysis of those injured in the Ibrox Park disaster, though this was a more expensive international fixture (Holt, *Sport*, 159–60).

[73] Mason, *Association Football*, 150.

[74] Holt, *Sport*, 160.

[75] Ibid. 292; Tranter, *Sport, Economy and Society*, 21.

[76] Holt, *Sport*, 288. Manchester City were fined in 1905 for breaching these rules (p. 294).

bonuses were limited in 1891 to £10, but the limit was often exceeded, and other inducements were frequently offered. The public reacted with amazement when Alf Commons transferred from Sunderland to Middlesborough in 1905 for £1,000, but it was the club, not the player, which principally benefited from the sale. Indeed, the PFA came into existence in 1907 to protect its members from managerial exploitation—and almost immediately found itself embroiled in a serious 'industrial dispute'.[77]

But though many boards of directors treated their players rather as most bosses treated their workforce, professional football did not operate in a free market, since the maximum wage and stringent transfer regulations prevented players from maximizing their earnings. One historian sees the Football League as 'a kind of non-profit-making cartel in which the power of the largest clubs was limited by the smallest',[78] but its rules can also be viewed as an indirect stratagem on the part of the clubs for maximizing *their own* profits by equalizing the playing strengths of the teams and thereby sustaining spectator interest.

And yet football was never a particularly profitable enterprise: the two top First Division sides of 1904–5, Newcastle and Everton, each made an operating profit of £5,000, but only six of the sixty-two leading clubs paid shareholders any dividend at all in 1908–9, a dividend which the FA had in any case restricted to 5 per cent.[79] This probably mattered little, since shareholders did not expect to become rich out of football, and neither did the directors, most of them small businessmen from the retail and food-and-drink sectors, who largely sought their reward in civic recognition and personal satisfaction.[80] Nevertheless, professional football, in many of its aspects, had become thoroughly commercialized by the Edwardian period, a situation underlined when Oxo ran an advertisement claiming that Manchester City, cup-winners in 1904, had drawn strength from its product.[81]

All of these developments understandably depressed the gentlemen who had pioneered the game. A compelling case could be made for *playing* football, on the ground that it promoted physical health and inculcated the virtues of 'team-spirit', 'character', and 'fair play'; simply *watching* others play for money seemed to betoken idleness and 'loafing'.[82] The *Economist* in 1913 declared that it would be 'far better that England, which has always been the recognised champion of pure amateurism, should be the last in every contest than we should descend to the commercialisation of our amateur sport'.[83]

[77] Holt, *Sport*, 298.   [78] Ibid. 285.   [79] Ibid. 283.

[80] Ibid. 284. But when club shares were pitched at £1 or less, working men subscribed to them in significant numbers (Mason, *Association Football*, 39–40).

[81] Waller, *Town, City and Nation*, 104.

[82] However, more continued to play soccer than to watch it—there being perhaps 10,000 players at the turn of the century (Cunningham, 'Leisure and Culture', 316).

[83] Vamplew, *Pay Up*, 2.

Many middle-class contemporaries also worried about the assembly of large crowds and the hysteria thereby engendered. The monthlies in the 1890s carried solemn articles on 'The New Football Mania' and 'The Football Madness'. John Burns agreed, saying that he did not like the sight of so many young lads 'developing the wrong end of their anatomy', and expressing anxiety about the all-male atmosphere: 'where women and children were not, there was the beast.' The spectator sports also came under suspicion because they were associated with drinking (unreasonably, since a big match usually emptied the pubs) and with gambling (a more reasonable fear, since by 1913 some 2 million football pools coupons may have been issued nationally[84]). Football hooliganism constituted another problem: the *Leicester Mercury* reported 137 'incidents' between 1885 and 1914, many involving verbal abuse, as well as pitch invasions, the hurling of missiles at players, and fights between spectators.[85] How typical such behaviour was remains unclear, but all agreed about the emergence of an 'unsportsmanlike' ethos which favoured winning at all costs; as boards of directors realized, fans certainly wanted to support a successful team.

No other sport was as thoroughly commercialized as soccer. Cricket, allegedly the 'national game', had a much longer history and managed to blend the old amateur tradition with the new professionalism by having 'players' and 'gentlemen' in the same team, while socially segregating them.[86] The legendary W. G. Grace, arguably the most widely recognized figure of his day after Queen Victoria, spanned the gulf between the two worlds. He both batted (as befitted a gentleman) and bowled (which was the player's role), scoring 54,896 runs at an average of 39.55 and taking 2,864 wickets. A medical practitioner outside the season, 'WG' qualified as an amateur, but he charged appearance fees ranging from £20 to £36, made money out of writing four bestselling books, and drew about £9,000 from his benefit match in 1895. He also displayed an intense desire to win, by fair means or foul—perhaps one reason for his popularity with a wider national audience not entirely taken in by the pretensions of the amateur code. By comparison, most of the 200 or so professional cricketers operating in 1910[87] could count themselves lucky if they earned even £3 a week in the summer and reduced wages in winter, supplemented by a one-off 'testimonial', which averaged about £816 in the 1890s.[88]

Cricket drew sizeable crowds, though not as large as soccer's: an average of 14,000 people attended first-class cricket matches between 1891 and 1910, after

---

[84] M. Clapson, *A Bit of a Flutter: Popular Gambling and English Society, c.1823–1961* (Manchester, 1992), 165. The first football pool may be one advertised in *Athletics News* in 1889. In the 1880s and 1890s guessing competition were also being run by the newspapers (Mason, *Association Football*, 181).
[85] Holt, *Sport*, 332. [86] See Ch. 3. [87] Tranter, *Sport, Economy and Society*, 20.
[88] Holt, *Sport*, 288–9.

which numbers fell. The county championship, started in 1873, gave backbone
to the season, but by the Edwardian period the greatest excitement was that
surrounding the games played by visiting 'test' (international) sides: 40,000
spectators watched Yorkshire play Australia in 1902. The entrance fee of 6d.,
the same as for soccer, was low enough to be affordable by many working men,
but matches which stretched over several days, during the week as well as on
Saturday, would cost a workman dear in lost wages. Warwickshire's county
ground at Edgbaston (in Birmingham) became a limited liability company. But
most of the patrons who subsidized the county sides showed scant commercial
flair or interest. The game's wider popularity therefore depended (even more
than did soccer's) on newspaper coverage: street urchins who seldom if ever
attended a first-class match, let alone played the game, often had an encyclo-
pedic knowledge of averages and form. In fact, all classes seem to have brought
to cricket that passion for statistics, for the precise measurement of achievement, which was one of the characteristics of the age.[89]

Rugby followed yet another path. A dispute over how to deal with 'shama-
teurism' led to the great schism of 1894, culminating in the establishment of
the breakaway Northern Union. The new body initially required its players to
have a source of income outside the game and merely legalized 'broken time'
payments. But 'Rugby League', as it soon became known, soon developed into
a fully professional game, with strong working-class support in parts of the
industrial North, leaving 'Rugby Union' to reign unchallenged in the South.[90]

Horse-racing was different again, because, unlike the major spectator sports,
it relied partly on aristocratic patronage (from the likes of Lord Rosebery, Lord
Derby, and not least members of the royal family),[91]and partly on the income
generated from gambling and from stud fees. Between 1891 and 1913 investment in bloodstock increased from £3 million to £7–8 million, by which time
stud fees of 300 guineas were not unusual.[92] However, racing's development
paralleled that of soccer and cricket in other respects. 'Spectating' gave way to
'consumption' as the major courses were enclosed and the public charged for
admission.[93] In the 1890s regular crowds of 10,000–15,000 were attracted to the
big races. By this time the sport had assumed a commercial character. For
example, Sandown Park, originally a partnership, became a limited liability
company in 1885, with issued share capital of £26,000; Haydock Park (the first
course to be enclosed) followed suit in 1898; and Newbury Racecourse opened

[89] W. F. Mandle, 'W. G. Grace as a Victorian Hero', *Historical Studies*, 19 (1980), 355.

[90] In the Scottish Lowlands and in South Wales Rugby Union was also popular, though playing a
social role in each which differentiated it from the English game.

[91] The Prince of Wales's Derby winners in 1896, 1900, and 1909 (when King) contributed to his
popularity.

[92] W. Vamplew, *The Turf: A Social and Economic History of Horse Racing* (London, 1976), 47.

[93] Vamplew, *Pay Up*, 73–4.

in 1906, with share capital of £80,000.[94] Though the Jockey Club restricted returns to shareholders to 10 per cent, racing could be profitable to all concerned, not least to the top jockeys, who were perhaps the best paid (and most lionized) of all professional sportsmen, capable of earning £35,000 in the course of their careers and over £5,000 each season; most successful of all was Fred Archer, who rode 246 winners in 1885 and then plunged the nation into grief by shooting himself the following year.[95]

However, not all sports moved inexorably towards professionalism. Lawn tennis, which became enormously popular as a participatory activity among middle- and upper-class youth, did indeed draw large crowds to its big tournaments (Wimbledon dates from 1877), but it did so without succumbing to commercialism. Golf differed in having professional players, but it, too, was mainly a participatory sport, based upon a rapidly expanding network of private clubs—about 1,200 in England alone in 1912.[96]

Some sports actually moved in the opposite direction. Pedestrianism, in which professionals had always taken part, gave way (except in a few areas, such as Sheffield) to the newly codified sport of athletics, organized by the appropriately named Amateur Athletics Association (AAA), founded in 1879. Interestingly, athletics (perhaps because it outlawed betting) did not usually attract such large crowds as pedestrianism had once done.[97] The exception to this was London's staging of the Olympic Games in 1908, when 300,000 spectators assembled to watch 1,500 competitors drawn from nineteen different nations. But the Olympic movement, inspired by the Frenchman Baron de Coubertin, adhered fanatically to an amateur code—a code which owed more to the ethos of the English public school than it did to the customs of ancient Greece. Moreover, some sports, for example, rowing, largely *lost* their former wide appeal to the spectating public, while in boxing the growth of the amateur game followed rather than preceded the popularity of its professional version: the ABA was not founded until 1880, and amateur boxing only became a popular working-class sport in the 1890s.[98]

There was another arena in which competing for money was taboo: female sport. In 1895 the *Girl's Home Companion* singled out tennis, croquet, golf, cycling, and cricket as outdoor games in which female involvement was now thought normal and proper: by 1914 hockey, archery, badminton, and gymnastics could have been added to this list. Few were the private girls' schools that did not now employ a specially trained games mistress. Women could also

[94] Ibid. 57, 4.   [95] Holt, *Sport*, 304–5.

[96] J. Lowerson, *Sport and the English Middle Classes 1870–1914* (Manchester 1993; 1995 edn.), 125.

[97] Professional contests, however, coexisted with the new amateur-run sport well into the twentieth century, attracting considerable bets (Holt, *Sport*, 184–5).

[98] Tranter, *Sport, Economy and Society*, 19.

play sport at college, while some enlightened employers provided facilities for their female, as well as their male, workforce. Indeed, a handful of sports-women achieved national fame, notably Lottie Dodd, who won Wimbledon in 1887. But even when a sport was being run, nationally, by its own Ladies' Association, this was always done on an amateur basis.[99]

All the same, contemporaries were correct to identify a general trend towards sport as a spectacle, to be 'consumed' passively, often at second-hand through the press. Thus horse racing, closely associated with gambling, relied upon the tips and news service provided by the *Sporting Life*, founded in 1859, a paper which boasted a circulation of 300,000 in the 1880s. All forms of sport, including racing, also featured in the sports pages of the national and provincial press, being particularly prominent in the 'evenings'. From 1872 onwards 'Extel' was supplying a results service for the horse-racing industry; by the 1880s telegraph installations, too, had appeared in all the big cricket grounds. Finally, from the late 1880s onwards, aided by the growing use of the telephone, football 'specials' spread to almost every moderately sized town: printed on pink paper, these sports editions ('pink 'uns') had become by the 1890s 'as much a part of the cultural scene as the gas lamp and the fish and chip shop'.[100]

Simply as an economic phenomenon, the development of sport merits attention, as it may have accounted for some 3 per cent of the total gross national product. By the end of the century, even leaving aside those who played games for their living, sport provided employment for thousands, particularly in the manufacture and sale of sports equipment. On the eve of the Great War about £600,000 was being spent each year on golf, mainly on golf balls, now being made by a rubber-strip machine (superseding the older gutta-percha ones). The firm of Slazenger, makers of tennis rackets, which converted into a public company, amassed annual profits of £50,000. Another success story was that of Wisdens, which founded its cricket-ball factory at Tonbridge in 1890 and later diversified by producing the famous cricket annual.[101] In fact, sports books soon established themselves as a recognized branch of the publishing trade: the various volumes in the Badminton series, for example, appeared between 1885 and 1914. Sport also gave an enormous fillip to the newspaper industry and to the railway companies, and became

[99] See C. Parratt, *More Than Mere Amusement: Working-Class Women's Leisure in England 1750–1914* (2001), K. E. McCrone, 'Play up! Play up! And Play the Game! Sport at the Late Victorian Girls' Public Schools', in J. A. Mangan and R. J. Park (eds.), *From 'Fair Sex' to Feminism: Sport and the Socialization of Women in the Industrial and Post-Industrial Eras* (London [c.1987]), 97–129, and for the opportunities for middle-class females, Lowerson, *Sport and English Middle Classes*, 203–30, and Ch. 2.

[100] Mason, *Association Football*, 193.

[101] Tranter, *Sport, Economy and Society*, 21, 33, 76–7.

inextricably intertwined with an important new manufacturing industry, bicycle-making—which explains why its leading firms were so willing to sponsor cycle races.

Late Victorian Britain did, indeed, 'teach the world to play' by codifying and developing most of today's leading sports. Other European countries were slow to follow in Britain's wake—and wisely so, according to some contemporary commentators. Kipling launched a diatribe during the Boer War years against the national obsession with sport, lambasting 'flannelled fools at the wicket' and 'the muddied oaf at the goal': he wanted youth to devote its leisure to the manly art of rifle-shooting.[102] P. G. Wodehouse entered the debate from a quite different angle with his satirical novel *The Swoop!*, which portrays invading armies marching across England while its inhabitants placidly get on with their games of golf, and the sad tidings appear on newspaper placards sandwiched between the latest county cricket scores.

More common than warnings about the danger of military defeat were fears of economic decline and national decadence. Arthur Shadwell, visiting the Rhineland in 1905, had his fear confirmed that games-playing was sapping his countrymen's 'national efficiency' when he came across a football match between Düsseldorf and a neighbouring industrial town that was being watched by a crowd of only sixty-five: the Germans, he deduced, had more important things on their minds. Modern Britain, others felt, was going the way of ancient Rome, whose citizens, in their period of decadence, preferred to be 'artists and sportsmen by proxy', and so hired 'a team of gladiators' to do what they lacked the energy to do for themselves.[103]

5. 'I DO LIKE TO BE BESIDE THE SEASIDE'

Passivity also increasingly characterized behaviour on the seaside holiday, the popularity of which steadily increased throughout the late Victorian period. Fashionable spas, it is true, still attracted wealthy valetudinarians, 75,000 visitors entering Bath's Pump Rooms in 1913.[104] But by the 1870s the seaside had largely displaced the spa, and the pleasures that it offered were drawing in not only those who could comfortably afford to take a week's holiday on the coast, but also poorer people on day excursions, especially during the August Bank Holiday.

---

[102] R. Kipling, 'The Islanders': published in *The Times* in Jan. 1902.
[103] A disillusioned Hills, founder of West Ham United, in 1899: C. Korr, 'West Ham United and the Beginning of Professional Football in East London, 1895–1914', *Journal of Contemporary History*, 13 (1978), 220.
[104] Waller, *Town, City and Nation*, 134.

Paid holidays, already common in white-collar occupations, were only enjoyed before 1914 by a few manual workers (some railwaymen, for example), though workers' clubs sprang up to help families save for this purpose.[105] Despite these difficulties, Booth and Rowntree's researches suggest that 75–80 per cent of working-class families could afford occasional seaside excursions: 2 million trippers visited Blackpool in the 1890s, nearly 4 million by 1913.[106] By 1911, such had been the recent improvement in living standards, some 55 per cent of the population were making day trips to the seaside, while another 20 per cent were booking holiday accommodation there. By the end of the century there were as many as forty-eight large coastal resorts with a combined population of 900,000; travel guides listed as many as 200 resorts in all.[107] In 1901 the permanent residents of these towns may have comprised one in twenty-five of the country's total population—a figure that excludes visitors, who probably outnumbered them by fifteen or twenty to one during the high season.[108]

As the seaside holiday became 'democratized', problems arose of how people of different classes should coexist. The wealthy had several options. They could flee the masses by patronizing areas which were difficult to reach by train or otherwise remote, such as Cornish fishing villages, or they could take themselves off to such exotic locations as the Alps and the French Riviera. Those with social pretensions but less money could only preserve their gentility by studiously avoiding 'vulgar' places such as Blackpool and Skegness. Some resorts colluded in these aspirations by deliberately discouraging day-trippers, who were often unruly. More common was the adoption of municipal by-laws which led to a kind of 'social zoning' within particular towns: thus, unfashionable Margate had its own exclusive quarter in Cliftonville,[109] while Brighton was adjoined by Hove, Blackpool by Lytham St Anne's, and so on. Torquay's exceptionally mild climate enabled it to flourish as a winter resort—another way of keeping up the social tone.

Which resorts flourished owed much to sheer accident. Once-promising seaside towns, such as Bootle and Swansea, were destroyed by industrial encroachments; others found a new role for themselves by attracting a large residential population of rentiers or by becoming, at least in part, 'overspill' towns inhabited by commuters (for example, Southend and Brighton). Some resorts proper were quite highly planned, but most of these developments happened willy-nilly.

[105] Waller, *Town, City and Nation*, 141   [106] Thompson, *Respectable Society*, 291–3.
[107] Waller, *Town, City and Nation*, 131, 135, 137.
[108] J. A. R. Pimlott, *The Englishman's Holiday* (London, 1947), 172–3.
[109] Blackpool, too, had its exclusive, middle-class enclaves.

Good railway connections were obviously a *sine qua non* for seaside towns wishing to tap the day-tripper and mass market, though the railway companies more often followed than created new resorts. But, to be worth visiting, a resort also required 'amenities', which meant heavy investment either from private landowners (for example, the Earls of Radnor in Folkestone or the Dukes of Devonshire in Eastbourne),[110] or from a combination of municipal and private enterprise. Commercial companies and entrepreneurs sank vast sums of capital into piers, luxury hotels, theatres, and concert halls. Blackpool acquired its Tower in 1891–4 and its Grand Theatre in 1894, and later used electrical power to launch its famous 'illuminations' in 1912.[111]

As in other areas of leisure, private enterprise was supplemented by publicly funded initiatives. Thus Brighton Corporation built a 3-mile protected sea-front and an aquarium in 1901.[112] Other municipalities involved themselves in the laying-out of promenades and, crucially, as in the case of Bournemouth, the provision of sporting facilities such as a golf course and bowling greens.[113] An important innovation was made by Blackpool, which in 1879 secured the power to levy a rate to advertise itself, the only pre-war British town to do so.[114]

All of these developments portended a subtle shift of tone. Sea-bathing and swimming remained important, but they now came under challenge from more sedentary activities. 'Rational recreations', too, became edged to the margins of the seaside holiday. The study of local flora and fauna could still be pursued by those with an interest in such things, just as devout holiday-makers could attend a church service on Sunday if they chose. But the seaside scene now featured pierrot, Punch and Judy, and 'black and white minstrel' shows, donkey rides, 'what the butler saw' peep-shows, the consumption of 'rock', the wearing of silly hats, and of course sport, in both its participatory and spectating modes. Typical of the new style was 'Spanish City', opened in Whitley Bay in 1904, with its music-hall entertainments, funfair attractions, and 'Empress Ballroom' (dating from 1910), modelled on Moorish architecture at Granada! The pretence that a trip to the coast had an educational purpose or was necessarily connected with recuperation from illness[115] wore increasingly

---

[110] D. Cannadine, *Lords and Landlords: The Aristocracy and the Towns, 1774–1967* (Leicester, 1980), Part 3.

[111] Walton, *Blackpool*, ch. 4. Some years earlier, in 1878, there took place the first football match to be floodlit (by electric light), at Bramall Lane, home of Sheffield United.

[112] Waller, *Town, City and Nation*, 143.

[113] Tranter, *Sport, Economy and Society*, 64. In 1890 Bournemouth pioneered the establishment of a municipal golf course (Lowerson, *Sport and English Middle Classes*, 134)

[114] Waller, *Town, City and Nation*, 140.

[115] However, some resorts such as Worthing actively sought to attract the sick and the hypochondriacal by emphasizing the healthiness of the local air, ozone being an Edwardian discovery.

thin. Holidays had become hedonistic, secular, and detached from all vestiges of religion in a way that had not been so half-a-century earlier.

6. FORBIDDEN PLEASURES

To focus on the changing face of recreations in late Victorian and Edwardian Britain is to miss the many continuities linking past to present. In the rural areas, particularly, much of the old order survived. For example, fox-hunting (largely an eighteenth-century 'invention') had its devotees in all classes, though court, aristocracy, and the nouveaux riches were tending to desert it for other field sports, notably shooting, where improvements in firearms and the adoption of the *battue* system were responsible for the horrendous mechanical carnage which disfigured the immediate pre-war years. Trout angling was also popular, driving up the cost of rental on favoured stretches of water, especially in Scotland.[116]

Cruelty of a socially more disreputable kind continued in the form of plebeian rural sports such as cock-fighting (strictly illegal) and dog fights (specifically banned in 1911), as well as hare-coursing and ratting (the latter enjoying some aristocratic backing). In urban areas of Lancashire, too, the traditional sports of wrestling and 'purring' (shin-kicking) survived into the new century, along with 'knur-and-spell' (a game involving hitting a small ball with a special bat as far as possible), which also flourished in South Yorkshire. But most ancient games had radically to modernize themselves if they were to survive, as had notably happened earlier in the century, when Scottish merchants revived golf at the very time when the old clans which had once nurtured the game were collapsing.

'Pugilism' and unorganized street brawls were slow to die out, but bare-knuckle boxing declined in the 1890s, giving way to the modern version of the sport based upon the 1867 Queensberry Rules. Boxing still constituted a world in which criminals and rakish aristocrats often rubbed shoulders, but with the establishment of the National Sporting Club in 1891 and the introduction of the Lonsdale Belt in 1909, it was achieving a kind of respectability.

Many other games, notably darts (which, in its modern form, dates from the very end of the nineteenth century), quoits, billiards, dominoes, and skittles were essentially pub-based activities, and that takes us on to our next theme. Publicans had arguably been the first of the occupational groups to discern the public's need for entertainments, and, though some of the new sports passed them by, in general they successfully adapted to the new recreational patterns. Thus publicans sometimes made land available for playing sport (this being the

---

[116] Holt, *Sport*, 57.

origin of the White Hart Lane ground used by Tottenham Hotspur), while many professional sportsmen, especially boxers, often set up as publicans on their retirement. Traditional hobbies such as flower- and vegetable-growing (increasingly popular with working men) were also based upon the public house. 'Singing-rooms', where the performers might be either professional or amateur, were another well-used amenity.

By the end of the nineteenth century the well-to-do mainly drank in their clubs or purchased alcohol at the off-licence or from their wine merchant for consumption in the privacy of their homes. Despite this, the public house remained by far the most important of all social centres, providing rooms for many trade-union and friendly-society meetings, as well as hosting a variety of entertainments—sometimes of a disreputable kind, since some pubs were the haunts of prostitutes. Quite apart from these extras, drinking and smoking were still, for most working-class males, the most popular of all 'pastimes', far more popular than any of the spectator sports. It is often overlooked, too, how many women had access to the pleasures and dangers of alcohol: Rowntree's investigation of York revealed that adult males comprised slightly under half of those entering pubs in slum areas, women about one-third, the remainder being children, presumably accompanying a parent; moreover, women convicted for drunkenness in Britain in the 1880s were 50 per cent more likely than men to be 'habitual offenders'.[117]

Despite the recent downward trend in alcohol consumption,[118] the turnover in beer, wine, and spirits amounted, even in the Edwardian period, to about £170 million, while, as pipe-smoking gave ground to the cigarette, tobacco sales soared from £13.5 million in 1870 to over £40 million in 1913; expenditure on booze and 'baccy could absorb one-third of a labourer's wages, about the same as he was paying in rent. No wonder that in 1905 seventeen of Britain's fifty-two most heavily capitalized companies should have been involved in brewing, and that heading the list should have been the Imperial Tobacco Company.[119]

Pubs dominated the urban landscape. The ratio of inhabitants per 'on' licensed premises ranged in provincial towns from 222 in Southampton to 575 in Leeds. In London in 1898 drinking outlets were more densely concentrated still—one for each acre in the City.[120] Most working-class

[117] F. Finnegan, *Poverty and Prostitution: A Study of Victorian Prostitution in York* (Cambridge, 1979), 153.

[118] See Ch. 6.

[119] P. L. Payne, 'The Emergence of the Large-Scale Company in Great Britain, 1820–1914', *Economic History Review*, 20 (1967), 539–42.

[120] B. S. Rowntree, *Poverty: A Study of Town Life* (1901; Nelson edn.), 364; on London, B. Harrison, 'Pubs', in H. J. Dyos and M. Wolff (eds.), *The Victorian City, Images and Realities, Vol. 1* (1973; 1976 edn.), 163.

neighbourhoods, everywhere in Britain, possessed at least one corner pub, its gas flares sending out at night a welcoming pool of light into the surrounding streets. Towards the end of the century these homely venues were being supplemented in the city centres by palatial new establishments, garishly decorated with ornate mirrors and gold-leafed ornaments, large enough to hold a hundred customers or more.

The threat of a legislative reduction in the number of licensed premises continued to bulk large in party political controversy.[121] But even temperance reformers increasingly recognized that one reason for the ubiquity of pubs was that they satisfied a wide array of legitimate social needs, for example, by functioning as hotels, eating places, resting areas for travellers and commuters, and commercial rendezvous. In any case, was their influence entirely evil? Like his father Joseph, a leading temperance reformer, Seebohm Rowntree was a committed abstainer, but when, one Saturday evening in May 1901, he went on a tour of York public houses, he was 'very forcibly' struck by 'their social attractiveness', particularly by the warmth, comfort, and friendly atmosphere, which, he realized, must be powerfully appealing to workers 'after a day's confinement in factory or shop'. Charles Booth had earlier found the scene in the ordinary working-class London pub 'comfortable, quiet, and orderly'.[122]

Most artisans had long contended that moderate drinking was quite compatible with 'respectability', as they understood that term; alcohol, they insisted, only caused harm if taken in excess. Educated middle-class opinion increasingly shared this conviction: 'I do not think that a moderate consumption of drink is in any way wrong on the part of the working man', Joseph Chamberlain told an official inquiry.[123] Drunkards ('inebriates') were now seen less as moral reprobates than as sufferers from a kind of disease in need of custodial care and medical treatment.[124] A social survey suggested that there were a million abstainers in 1899.[125]

Towards other addictive substances, including tobacco, the late-Victorian generation seems to have taken a surprisingly relaxed attitude. The *Lancet* endorsed Ogden Cigarettes, and the *Illustrated London News* in 1900 opined that, 'used with due moderation Tobacco is of value second only to food itself'.[126]

---

[121] See Chs. 10, 12.

[122] D. Dixon, *From Prohibition to Regulation: Bookmaking, Anti-Gambling, and the Law* (Oxford, 1991), 54.

[123] P. Thane, *Old Age in English History: Past Experiences, Present Issues* (Oxford, 2000), 165.

[124] See Ch. 6.

[125] According to Joseph Rowntree and Arthur Sherwell: T. R. Gourvish and R. G. Wilson, *The British Brewing Industry 1830–1980* (Cambridge, 1994) 35.

[126] L. A. Loeb, *Consuming Angels: Advertising and Victorian Women* (Oxford and New York, 1994), 78. The earlier anti-smoking campaign had largely lost its momentum by the end of the century, censure focusing on under-age smoking (M. Hilton, *Smoking in British Popular Culture 1800–2000* (Manchester, 2000), esp. Ch. 7).

Neither was the recreational use of drugs a matter of pressing concern to the late Victorian and Edwardian generation. True, the 1868 Pharmacy Act, tightened up by a subsequent measure of 1908, bracketed opium with poisons, limiting its sale to professional pharmacists. However, the police did not seriously enforce this legislation, and left largely undisturbed the opium dens in the major seaports catering for sailors, Chinese settlers, and an assorted crowd of sensation-seekers.[127] Cocaine and hashish were also in circulation and attracted a certain following among the denizens of the Bohemian subculture. But such exotic substances seldom spread far beyond these limited circles— though Rosebery, as well as taking sulphonal to counter his insomnia, occasionally pepped up his speeches by sniffing cocaine![128]

Meanwhile attempts by British reformers to curb or ban the international opium trade proceeded apace, and doctors and pharmacists conducted their own technical debates about the medical value and danger of various drugs. (Strangely enough, doctors initially hailed heroin[129] not only for its undoubted medicinal properties, but also as a safer alternative to opium.) A similar insouciance was displayed towards patent medicines: laudanum, to quieten crying babies, was freely available at chemists' shops, 'Godrey's Cordial' being the brand leader.

The authorities only became seriously alarmed about domestic drug use during the First World War, when faced by what seemed a dangerous cocaine 'epidemic' among soldiers on leave. Out of this panic there eventually emerged the 1920 Dangerous Drugs Act.[130] But it would be anachronistic to talk of the existence of a 'drugs scene' before 1914, and alcohol, for good or ill, still had no serious competitor as a narcotic.

As gross and bestial drunkenness began slowly to diminish, attitudes to alcohol grew somewhat more liberal. But the opposite was the case with gambling, the incidence of which seems to have steadily increased in the late Victorian period. The main reason for this was the expansion of a racing industry, backed by punters who seldom if ever attended a race meeting in person but who relied for their betting activities upon the starting prices carried by the electric telegraph, a service widely available after 1890. Moreover, most late Victorian newspapers, to say nothing of the sporting press, gave extensive coverage to racing and employed their own resident 'tipsters', for example, 'Robin Goodfellow' of the *Daily Mail* and 'Scout' of the *Daily Express*—though public librarians sedulously pasted these items out before

---

[127] V. Berridge, *Opium and the People* (1981; 1987 edn.), for this and the next two paragraphs.

[128] R. P. T. Davenport-Hines, *The Pursuit of Oblivion: A History of Narcotics* (London, 2001), 130.

[129] Heroin, a more powerful, synthetic form of morphine, itself a derivative of opium, was first manufactured by the German chemists working for Bayer in the 1890s.

[130] Berridge, *Opium*, 249–5, 262–4.

making papers available to their readers. In this way, ironically, growing literacy may actually have promoted the betting habit—which, if one testimony is to be believed, gave manual workers an incentive to master the art of reading![131]

The result of all this was a moral panic about gambling, which led to the establishment in 1890 of the National Anti-Gambling League (NAGL) and to a profusion of articles and books, notably *Betting and Gambling: A National Evil* (1905), edited by Seebohm Rowntree, which contained essays by J. A. Hobson and Ramsay MacDonald among others. The 'betting mania' came under attack for a variety of reasons. Businessmen blamed it for Britain's faltering economic performance, instancing slack work and lost production; Nonconformist divines joined Anglican bishops in calling on the people to forsake their sinful ways; social reformers lambasted an 'irrational' pastime which they believed underlay much poverty and crime; and Arthur Henderson spoke for many Labour MPs when he declared gambling 'to be a greater foe to labour than all the forces of capitalism'.[132] Rowntree summed up the indictment: gambling, he declared, 'ruins sport, checks industrial development, postpones social progress, destroys the character of the gambler, ruins yearly thousands of homes, lowers the whole tone of social life'.[133]

According to those with a taste for sociological explanations, betting, in its various forms, was also a symptom of the hysteria engendered by the unnaturalness of urban life. Masterman claimed that the big cities were inhabited by 'a weak-kneed, narrow-chested, listless breed',[134] and Reginald Bray described townees as people of 'a quick, artificial intelligence' and 'an excitable disposition'; betting was thought to stimulate, though it could never satisfy, this craving for excitement.

Acts of 1853–4 had already given the police powers to close betting shops and gaming houses, though there was nothing to stop, say, the Prince of Wales's set from playing roulette and baccarat for very high stakes in their country houses—as dramatized in the 1891 Tranby Croft affair. On-course betting had always been allowed, but the exact status of betting outside the special racecourse enclosures was not entirely clear-cut, and became even more confused after a series of contradictory court rulings from 1896 onwards.[135] Parliament responded by establishing the 1901–2 Lords Select Committee,

---

[131] R. Roberts, *The Classic Slum: Salford Life in the First Quarter of the Century* (London, 1971; 1973 edn.), 164.

[132] Dixon, *Prohibition*, 73.

[133] Ibid. 73, 69.

[134] C. F. G. Masterman, 'The Social Abyss', *Contemporary Review*, 81 (1902), 60.

[135] For this complicated episode, see Dixon, *Prohibition*, and S. Petrow, *Policing Morals: The Metropolitan Police and the Home Office, 1870–1914* (Oxford, 1994), 254–7.

whose report of the following year formed the basis of the 1906 Street Betting Act—a private measure introduced by Lord Davey, a Liberal peer, which enjoyed the government's blessing. Under this draconian measure (for which the NAGL, steered by its energetic secretary John Hawke, had lobbied hard), all off-course betting was effectively criminalized, forcing bookmakers, supported by a minor army of touts, 'runners', and 'look-outs' or scouts (the latter often children), into engaging in elaborate games of cat-and-mouse with the police.[136] Some magistrates later tried to apply the Act to gamblers themselves, though this was not the intention of its original authors, who hoped that education and 'moral suasion' would eventually convince the latter of the error of their ways—a mission pursued after 1906 by Cadbury's Society for the Suppression of Gambling.

Although the 1906 Act remained on the statute book, largely unamended, until 1960, many of its original champions soon had second thoughts. Because of their duty to suppress minor street disorders (drunkenness, vagrancy, loitering, children playing on the King's highway, and so on),[137] the police were already none too welcome in many working-class neighbourhoods, and they now had the additional task of enforcing a measure so unpopular that it virtually united whole communities against them. In some large cities the police showed great zeal, particularly in Manchester, 'the capital of gambling', where 387 bookmakers and their agents were prosecuted in 1911 alone. But in 1908 the Royal Commission into the Metropolitan Police was already reporting, ominously, that some policemen were taking bribes in return for tipping off bookmakers about forthcoming raids. Abuses of this kind were certainly taking place in Preston that very year.[138]

In the face of a serious threat to its livelihood, all sections of the racing industry rallied in self-defence. They were helped by the fact that betting on horses, a minority interest at the start of the nineteenth century, 'had become among the most common of British male leisure activities by 1914', with large swathes of the middle class showing as much enthusiasm for the turf as did those above and below them in the social scale.[139] The racing fraternity could also count on the support of aristocratic Tory 'sportsmen', who clearly preferred the working man to have his flutter (or to drink himself silly, if that is what he wanted to do), rather than to immerse himself in literature from which

---

[136] There were maximum fines of £10 for the first offence, £20 for the second, £50 or six months imprisonment with hard labour for a third. For gambling as a street activity in working-class Salford, A. Davies, *Leisure, Gender and Poverty* (Buckingham, 1992), Ch. 6.

[137] Leaving aside offences under the Vagrancy Act, these amounted to 15–20% of all arrests by the late nineteenth century (Thompson, *Respectable Society*, 331).

[138] Clapson, *Flutter*, 65.

[139] M. Huggins, *Flat Racing and British Society 1790–1914: A Social and Economic History* (Manchester, 2000), 232 and ch. 3.

he might pick up 'subversive' ideas. In 1901 Lord Salisbury, himself no 'sportsman', came to a similar conclusion about the inclusion of betting news in newspapers, saying: 'I cannot conceive a state of society in which that kind of censorship of the Press would be tolerated.'[140]

Another defender of gambling was Horatio Bottomley, proprietor of the weekly *John Bull*, who attached himself to the National Sporting League, set up earlier in 1902. Having ignominiously failed in his attempt to license bookmakers and register their offices, he fell back upon inciting 'the working men of England' to rebel against the 'prevailing wave of puritanical and namby-pamby, goody-goody legislation', which 'struck at those fundamental principles of self-reliance and robust manhood which made the English race what it was'.[141] Bottomley's agitation against well-to-do prigs who gambled on the Stock Exchange, while attempting to curtail the innocent pleasures of the people, probably inflicted some damage on the Liberal government of the day.[142] And for once it is hard not to sympathize a little with the loud-mouthed populist: after all, the Street Betting Act was a blatant piece of class discrimination, even more so than the various curbs being brought forward by temperance reformers for 'controlling' the drink trade.[143] By 1914 many socialists were revising their view of the authoritarian paternalism which was spreading under that piece of legislation.

Whatever the state of the law or of public opinion, the fact remains that, in total, huge, though unquantifiable, sums of money were being expended on gambling—covering not just horse-racing but also other sporting encounters, games of cards, newspaper prize competitions, even casual street games of pitch-and-toss. As many as 80 per cent of the adult population may have been betting regularly in 1914.[144]

However, the NAGL, a minority interest group that could not even claim to speak for the middle class, went too far in its lamentations.[145] Probably about twenty times as much money was being spent on beer than on gambling in the early twentieth century.[146] In any case, most punters placed small wagers: before 1914 the customary stake on a horse was 6*d.* or a shilling, and

---

[140] Dixon, *Prohibition*, 158–9.

[141] Clapson, *Flutter*, 33. There was also a Sporting League (1894), an Anti-Puritan League, and a Turf Guardian Society (Dixon, *Prohibition*, 123).

[142] Ironically, Bottomley himself was a Liberal MP between 1906 and 1911, until his local association washed its hands of him; he resigned because of bankruptcy the following year.

[143] In fairness to the NAGL, it had initially favoured a less class-biased Bill, but realized that only a measure bearing down on the working classes was feasible.

[144] R. McKibbin, 'Working Class Gambling in Britain, 1880–1939', *Past & Present*, 82 (1979), 154.

[145] For evidence suggesting that the NAGL was losing momentum before 1914, see Huggins, *Flat Racing*, ch. 8.

[146] P. Thompson, *The Edwardians: The Remaking of British Society* (London, 1975), 201.

working-class women who liked a flutter—so one well-placed observer claims—could not comprehend a sum larger than £5.[147] Such expenditure may have been wasteful, but it was unlikely, by itself, to bring a family to ruin.

Nor were working men and women compulsive gamblers of the kind memorably delineated by Dostoevsky. On the contrary, most did their best to eliminate risk by pitting their wits and deploying their knowledge of horses in such a way as to maximize their chance of a modest return. Trapped as the poor were in a cycle of credit and debt, this sort of small-scale betting may have been no more irrational than, say, their penchant for burial insurance, which bit deeply into working-class incomes to little economic purpose.[148]

Anxieties about gambling were paralleled by the agitation of social purity crusaders to stamp out all sexual impropriety. At an official level the 1886–1914 period was one marked by extreme prudishness, following the panic about sexual vice which had culminated in the passing in 1885 of the Criminal Law Amendment Act.[149]

Every year between 1885 and 1914, under the terms of this Act, an average of 1,200 brothels were suppressed, the police being particularly zealous in Sheffield, Leeds, and even more so in Liverpool, where the National Vigilance Association (NVA) took control of the Council in 1890, in alliance with temperance reformers and sympathetic Liberals.[150] Paradoxically, these efforts merely pushed more prostitutes and their pimps out onto the street—just as attempts to stop off-course betting had done with respect to bookmakers and their agents. In London in 1905, at the height of the police crackdown, as many as 944 females came before the courts charged with having sexual intercourse in the open air.[151] But the police soldiered on, encouraged by a new pressure group, the Public Morality Council, founded by Bishop Creighton of London in 1901 (its deputy chairman was William Coote, the leading spirit of the NVA), and later by James Marchant's Forward Movement.[152] Another contribution to the clean-up of the city was made by men who patrolled the streets with a view to frightening off the prostitutes' male clients—'moonlighting', as it was called.[153]

The government responded to the repressive mood by passing the Vagrancy Law Amendment Act in 1898, which, among other things, outlawed the practice of living off immoral earnings. Interestingly, of those subsequently

---

[147] McKibbin, 'Working-Class Gambling', 155, 163.

[148] Betting and burial insurance, each in its way, may have provided emotional satisfaction: but that is another issue (McKibbin, 'Working-Class Gambling', 161).

[149] See Ch. 2.

[150] E. J. Bristow, *Vice and Vigilance: Purity Movements in Britain Since 1700* (London, 1977), 154, 161–2. The UK was out of step in these matters with Europe, most of which had legalized and regulated 'vice' systems.

[151] Ibid. 168–9.   [152] Ibid. 165, 219.   [153] Ibid. 162–3.

arrested in London for this offence, as many as a quarter were foreigners, mainly French, Germans, Belgians, and immigrant Jews—the existence of so many Jewish prostitutes and pimps giving urgency to Constance Battersea's rescue mission.[154]

Awareness of 'foreign' involvement in the vice trade in turn gave rise to the pre-war crusade against 'white slavery', a vague phrase which was sometimes used to cover almost any instance of female prostitutes being abetted by a third party, whether they had been entrapped or were simply seeking their freedom. Nevertheless Scotland Yard set up a White Slavery Bureau to control the alleged evil, and suffragists and suffragettes used the issue to great polemical effect. Swept by a tide of emotion following W. T. Stead's drowning on the *Titanic*, Parliament decided to honour his memory by passing the 1912 Criminal Law Amendment (White Slavery) Bill, one clause of which authorized the flogging of men on a second conviction for living off immoral earnings, and another the arrest of suspected procurers.[155]

The repression of 'vice' naturally extended to a clampdown on pornography, a shady trade which centred, as it had done for most of the nineteenth century, on London's inaptly named Holywell Street, off Fleet Street.[156] The Obscene Publications Act of 1857 gave magistrates and police wide powers to confiscate obscene prints and books and to prosecute their vendors, but in the late Victorian and Edwardian years the authorities were kept up to the mark by the NVA, which not only gathered information to help the police, but also, on occasions, initiated its own prosecutions.

Unfortunately for the moral crusaders, improved technology and commercial growth often indirectly helped their enemies. Thus pornographers, who had been quick to exploit photography, could now also employ the 'mutoscope' to transmit obscene images.[157] Faster communications and modern marketing devices, too, were enlarging the scope of their activities. In 1889 an Indecent Advertisements Act (a measure actually drafted by the NVA's legal subcommittee) was passed, aimed at the trade in pornographic material—and also in abortifacients.[158]

The greatest of all the difficulties faced by the sexual purity lobby arose out of the internationalization of the vice trade. Many of the entrepreneurs dealing

---

[154] Ibid. 170, 173.

[155] Ibid. 191–2.

[156] For an analysis of the responses to mid-Victorian Holywell Street, L. Nead, *Victorian Babylon: People, Streets and Images in Nineteenth-Century London* (New Haven and London, 2000), 161–89.

[157] Bristow, *Vice and Vigilance*, 218.

[158] D. Thomas, *A Long Time Burning: The History of Literary Censorship in England* (London, 1969), 285.

in erotic and obscene literature and photography lived in Belgium or France, whence they posted off their wares to their British customers[159] (rather as operators of racing sweeps, football betting, and other lotteries later transferred their businesses to Switzerland)[160]. Thus the self-styled Charles Carrington (né Paul Ferdinando) published, from his base in Montmartre, vast quantities of erotica, including the pornographic classic *My Secret Life* and other books, some of which he falsely claimed to be older works of scholarly interest. The British police, using legislation recently passed in 1908 regulating the sending of obscene material through the post, sought to cut off the flow of such material into Britain by collaborating with their French counterparts, but not entirely successfully—the two sides failing, for example, to agree on whether the portrayal of pubic hair was 'obscene'.[161]

Anything even mildly risqué now came under attack. For example, in the Edwardian period there was a craze for picture postcards, 800 million being handled by the Post Office in 1908 alone.[162] In 1906 the Liverpool magistrates began cracking down on the stationers who sold 'naughty' items, forcing the Newsagents' Federation and the Postcard Traders' Association to set up a scheme of self-regulation.[163] The vigilantes also panicked Mudie's and W. H. Smith's into not only banning all offensive books but also, from 1909 onwards, into an attempt to pre-censor any volume which they might stock.

The 'moral purity' crusade, led by the NVA, took absolutely no account of the new insights into sexual behaviour purveyed by writers such as Havelock Ellis. The difficulty of differentiating between 'obscenity' and serious, though controversial, works of scholarship and literature led in time to a changed relationship between authority on the one hand, and writers and artists on the other, especially in respect of the censorship of drama.[164]

In fact, the late Victorian theatre had largely shaken off its former reputation for licentiousness and immorality—though old-fashioned Dissenters (and W. T. Stead) would take longer to be convinced of this. Actors themselves increasingly came from professional middle-class backgrounds, with a public-school or university education, actresses from families of 'good' stock. This was partly because such people instinctively understood the social mores of the

---

[159] The Post Office Protection Act of 1884 enabled anyone who had received obscene material through the post to complain to the postal authorities, which could then apply to the Home Secretary for a warrant to open letters.

[160] Dixon, *Prohibition*, 168.

[161] Bristow, *Vice and Vigilance*, 221.

[162] The picture postcard first appeared in 1870, costing a halfpenny. After 1902 one could write on the same side as the address, leaving the reverse for the photograph (D. Vincent, *Literacy and Popular Culture: England 1750–1914* (Cambridge, 1989), 46).

[163] Bristow, *Vice and Vigilance*, 217, 220–1.

[164] See Ch. 15.

characters they would have to impersonate in fashionable plays, which tended to have modern upper-class settings.[165]

At the same time changes in theatre design were encouraging more 'polite' behaviour on the part of the paying public. A succession of serious fires in the 1860s had led to the construction of new purpose-built theatres, sometimes erected on island sites, with multiple entrances, a safety arrangement which also made it possible to segregate different kinds of customer. Moreover, the pit and gallery, previously the source of much popular rowdiness, were now often abolished or diminished, as at the Haymarket, to make room for more seats in the stalls, whose respectable clientele was thus brought much closer to the stage. The 1880s also saw the introduction of new ticketing arrangements which necessitated fixed seating; this meant that the audience no longer roamed around the theatre while performances were in progress, and that on arrival most members of the public had to queue, a social habit which grew to be much commoner thereafter. By the end of the century it had even become acceptable for women to attend matinées at suburban theatres.[166]

However, the most popular form of theatrical entertainment, the music hall, took much longer to establish its respectability, partly because of the unashamed vulgarity with which it sang the praises of 'boiled beef and carrots' or serenaded the luxurious delights of champagne. Social purity campaigners also mistrusted the halls because of their traditionally close links with the drinks trade (much to the disgust of temperance reformers, such as F. N. Charrington of the NVA) and with prostitution. The first problem was largely overcome by installing fixed seating, the latter by constructing new theatres which did not have 'promenades', and banishing prostitutes from those promenades which still existed. Despite these changes, prostitutes continued to be in evidence in some of the smaller halls until at least the outbreak of the Great War.

Music halls were quite independent of the Lord Chamberlain's Office[167] but came under the control of the local authorities. This meant, in London, that after 1889 a committee of the LCC was the regulatory authority, empowered to make rulings, not only on issues of safety, but also on matters pertaining to social morality. Ominously, six of the twenty-one members of this committee in the 1890s happened to be connected with the NVA, one of them being Charrington himself.[168]

The content of the 'acts' performed on the music-hall stage soon became a subject of contention, stirred up from the outside by Mrs Ormiston Chant and

---

[165] Sanderson, *Acting Profession*, 18–19.
[166] Cunningham, 'Leisure and Culture', 298.
[167] Though in 1911 the Office's jurisdiction extended to music-hall 'sketches', which often featured straight actors.
[168] Bristow, *Vice and Vigilance*, 209.

her Social Purity League. The vigilantes were particularly incensed when, in late 1893, Charles Morton introduced living statuary or 'tableaux vivants' into his halls; this apparent display of nudity caused deep offence, nor were the critics entirely mollified when they learnt that the nudity was in fact being simulated by performers wearing flesh-coloured body-stockings ('maillots').[169] Mrs Chant and her friends also rose up in arms over obscene jokes, though they were baffled over how to proceed in the face of the widespread resort to innuendo and double-entendres: 'there was an unwritten language of vulgarity and obscenity known to music-hall audiences, in which vile things can be said that appear perfectly inoffensive in King's [sic] English', observed one disapproving journalist.[170]

In 1889 the LCC put six halls on probation and revoked the licences of another three, only returning them when their managers gave promises of future good behaviour. The following year it appointed thirty-three inspectors to monitor events. The big proprietors realized that they could not afford the bad publicity and the loss of revenue that might result from offending the authorities, and Stoll, anxious to attract family audiences, was soon fining any of his artists who overstepped the mark. A system of self-regulation thus developed, which the cinema industry was shortly to follow when it set up the British Board of Film Censors in 1912.

At the same time leading public figures, including Lord Rosebery, the LCC's first chairmen, realised how unwise it was to harass music-hall performers over minor peccadilloes or breaches of good taste. That audiences fiercely resented all attempts at moral censorship was clear from the delight with which they greeted acts which lampooned Mrs Chant and others of her ilk. Charrington may never have revised his opinions about the 'music hells', as he called them, but in 1912 King George V more accurately reflected the public mood of the day when he attended the Royal Command performance which featured nearly all the famous music-hall stars—bar Marie Lloyd, who was not invited, doubtless because she had perpetrated one double-entendre too many. The music hall, it seemed, had finally acquired the royal seal of approval.

7. HOBBIES

Many late Victorian and Edwardian amusements, however, took forms that were neither educational nor heavily commercialized, and certainly fell under

---

[169] See also Lucy Bland, *Banishing the Beast: English Feminism and Sexual Morality 1855–1914* (Harmondsworth, 1995), 105–8; T. C. Davis, 'Indecency and Vigilance in the Music Halls', in R. Foulkes (ed.), *British Theatre in the 1890s* (Cambridge, 1992), 111–31.

[170] P. Bailey, 'Conspiracies of Meaning: Music-Hall and the Knowingness of Popular Culture', *Past & Present*, 146 (1994), 158.

no imputation of immorality. Though presumably giving satisfaction to those who pursued them, they met with little approval and excited little disquiet, perhaps because, being home-centred or 'private', they often escaped public attention altogether. These were the interests which contemporaries called 'hobbies'—a term for which, significantly, there seems to be no real equivalent in other European languages.[171]

Some hobbies were heavily concentrated in particular regions or among particular occupational groups. For example, miners were famously attached to pigeon-fancying,[172] and, like railwaymen, also took a great pride in their gardens. (Gardening might well have been even more popular but for the inadequate supply of allotments in urban areas before 1914.) In the North-East working men devoted themselves fanatically to the breeding of whippets as well as of pigeons, Norwich formed an intense attachment to the canary, while all over England angling took people away from the crowded city centres: by the end of the century there were some 20,000 registered anglers in Sheffield alone.[173]

Such activities tended initially to be organized around local societies, but in the 1890s many had acquired their own national federations, as well as the 'special interest' magazines which did so much to give their followers a sense of collective identity. One journal, *Hobbies*, tried, unusually, to cater simultaneously for a range of recreational interests: how varied these could be is clear from its opening number of October 1895, which carried articles covering a number of different sports, photography, stamp collecting, and several handicrafts, including fretwork and ironworking.[174]

The development of the safety machine and the invention of the pneumatic tyre in the late 1880s gave rise to yet another popular leisure activity, this time one which spanned the social classes: cycling. Though membership of the Cycling Touring Club (CTC) had declined to only 15,000 by the outbreak of the Great War, at its peak in the late 1890s it numbered 60,000,[175] with some 750,000 machines being produced annually. Downturn in demand later in the decade drove several cycle firms (for example, Humber, Swift, Rover, Sunbeam, and Morris) to switch production to motor cars. But whereas motoring remained a rich man's hobby, the bicycle could be afforded by better-off working men, especially since easy terms were readily available.[176] People from all social backgrounds relished the freedom which the bicycle provided

[171] R. McKibbin, 'Work and Hobbies in Britain, 1880–1950', in J. Winter (ed.), *The Working Class in Modern British History* (Cambridge, 1983), 129.

[172] Holt, *Sport*, 187.   [173] Ibid. 188–9.   [174] McKibbin, 'Hobbies', 128–9.

[175] Holt, *Sport*, 195.

[176] D. Rubinstein, 'Cycling in the 1890s', *Victorian Studies*, 21 (1977), 57–8. In the 1890s the *Clarion* was selling them to members of its own cycling clubs for as little as £8, and prices subsequently fell. Cheap second-hand machines were also available.

for exploring the countryside, individually and in the company of a small groups of friends (of mixed sex). Cycling, incidentally, happened to be one of the few 'sports' of which socialists unequivocally approved: the Fabian leaders, Shaw, and the Webbs were converts, and even the Marxist SDF sold its own 'liberty' model to members at a cheap price made possible by bulk-purchase.[177]

The late Victorian period was also a golden age for amateur music-making. Pianos were sold in increasing numbers, until by 1914 there were somewhere between 2 million and 4 million of them in British homes, about one for every ten to twelve members of the population, with the cheaper models finding their way into such humble abodes as miners' cottages.[178] Sheet music, particularly of popular music-hall songs, sold in huge quantities for family performance.

Choral singing, enormously popular in all classes, flourished in the textile districts of Lancashire and Yorkshire, Cornwall, and in South Wales, while large amateur choirs also made an indispensable contribution to prestigious musical festivals such as the Three Choirs, the Norfolk and Norwich Triennial, and the Birmingham Festival. By 1914 there were also some seventy-five musical competition festivals, where the main emphasis fell on choral music.[179] Finally, there were between 700 and 1,000 brass bands dedicated to taking part in competitions, the most successful of which were drawn from the industrial towns and villages of northern England, among them the famous Black Dyke Mills Band. Thousands of enthusiasts crowded to hear these amateur musicians when they performed at concerts or vied for prizes at such venues as the Crystal Palace and Belle Vue, Manchester.[180] Brass bands also provided the inspiration behind many compositions of the period.

It is sometimes said that the drive for 'rational recreations' succeeded in marginalizing the old 'disreputable' popular pastimes, only itself to fall victim to the new commercial leisure industries. In fact, the social history of late Victorian England cannot quite be fitted into this neat explanatory framework. For a start, the distinction between respectability and impropriety had never been clear-cut, different individuals and social groups having their own, somewhat different notions of what these terms meant, and by the turn of the century the boundary-line was becoming even harder to draw.

Hard-core pornography found few defenders. But, outside the milieu of the chapel, Mrs Grundy increasingly became a figure of fun. By the Edwardian

---

[177] Ibid. 47–71. Graham Wallas and C. P. Trevelyan taught the Webbs, Shaw, and Samuel to cycle (A. Offer, *Property and Politics 1870–1914* (Cambridge), 348).

[178] Ehrlich, *Music Profession*, 91. The price of music and of musical instruments also fell substantially. Fine French violins could be bought for between £5 and £15. Piano scores of *Messiah* cost 21s. in the 1830s, 1s. fifty years later (pp. 101–3).

[179] Russell, *Popular Music*, 41 and Ch. 10.

[180] Ibid., ch. 9. In all there may have been between 30,000 and 40,000 amateur wind bands.

period few would have fainted away in disapproval on hearing a rendition of that well-loved ditty 'Stop Yer Tickling, Jock!'; indeed, the 'knowingness' of the music hall had by then united people from *all* social classes with the performer in a 'conspiracy of meanings'.[181] Nor is it any accident that the saucy Marie Lloyd was perhaps the best loved of all music-hall stars. Similarly, respectable working-class families (along with many middle-class men and women) saw nothing reprehensible in having a mild flutter, while artisan culture had never been hostile to the pub. In other words, though many working men and women had firm views about 'respectability', the ideal they followed was one generated within their own class, not superimposed upon it by others.[182]

Some middle-class reformers tried to discipline their social inferiors by using leisure as an instrument of 'social control', but working people showed a remarkable capacity to create their own culture independent of external direction or tutelage, selecting from others what they found congenial and rejecting the rest, the outcome being 'neither the submission of subordinate groups to new standards nor an untrammelled celebration of class identity'.[183] Middle-class do-gooders, Labour politicians, parsons, publicans, leisure impresarios—all, in their different ways, if they were to enjoy any success, had to recognize that the wider public was determined to 'have a good time'.

Thus Nonconformist newspaper proprietors, such as the Cadburys and the Rowntrees, who attempted to drop racing news from their titles quickly restored them as sales plummeted.[184] Similarly, socialists who tried to establish a proletarian counter-culture and berated the working man for his vulgarity succeeded only in isolating themselves from the class they aspired to represent.[185] For reasons other than commercial gain, mainstream politicians, too, prudently fell into line with popular tastes, MPs and mayors often 'kicking off' at important football matches and aristocrats being keen to be photographed with the local team. The royal family followed suit: Edward VII became patron of the Football Association in 1902 and George V attended the 1914 Cup Final, the first monarch to do so. Royal patronage of this vulgar spectacle (for so *Times*-reading folk then saw soccer) was also significant as an acknowledgment that regular indulgence in 'amusements', of one kind or another, had become an indispensable and valued part of national life.

---

[181] Bailey, 'Conspiracies of Meaning', 167.

[182] Cunningham, 'Leisure and Society', 301–2.

[183] Ibid. 335; Thompson, *Respectable Society*, 297.

[184] Dixon, *Prohibition*, 156–7.

[185] C. Waters, *British Socialists and the Politics of Popular Entertainment, 1884–1918* (Manchester, 1990).

CHAPTER 15

Art and Culture

I. THE MARKET FOR ART

The expansion of the popular entertainments industry formed merely a part of a wider growth in the market for cultural productions and artefacts of all kinds. Between the censuses of 1881 and 1901 the number of authors, editors, and journalists rose by 81 per cent, that of musicians by 69 per cent—a trend which continued, at a slightly less hectic rate, during the following decade.[1] More rapid still was the expansion of the acting profession: the number of actors and actresses almost trebled between 1881 and 1911 (to over 18,000). Meanwhile theatres, museums, galleries, and concert halls all proliferated. In 1914 300 playhouses were still in operation, quite apart from the numerous 'palaces of variety' and cinemas.[2]

Demand for printed material also soared. Newspaper circulation doubled between 1896 and 1906 and then doubled again by 1914.[3] Indeed, publishing of all kinds flourished in response to a popular interest in books and in their authors which may have been proportionately greater in late Victorian and Edwardian Britain than at any time before or since.[4] The annual issue of book titles, which had been a mere 2,600 in the 1850s, reached 6,044 in 1901 and 12,379 by 1913,[5] helped by a steep fall in book prices after 1900 (despite the general adoption of the 'net book scheme' in 1899).[6] To meet the voracious demands of readers, the public library service expanded: between 1896 and 1913 both the number of public libraries and their stock and issues approximately doubled.[7]

---

[1] Number of authors, editors, and journalists rose from 3,400 in 1881 to nearly 6,000 in 1891, about 11,000 in 1901, and to nearly 14,000 in 1911: musicians from 25,500 to 38,600 to 39,300 to 47,110.

[2] W. Bridges-Adams, 'Theatre', in S. Nowell-Smith (ed.), *Edwardian England, 1901–1914* (Oxford, 1964), 372.

[3] R. Williams, *The Long Revolution* (London, 1961), 203–4.

[4] J. Gross, *The Rise and Fall of the Man of Letters: Aspects of English Literary Life Since 1800* (1969; 1973 edn.), 221.

[5] Williams, *Long Revolution*, 170.

[6] R. D. Altick, *The English Common Reader: A Social History of the Mass Reading Public, 1800–1900* (Chicago, 1957), 316.

[7] D. Hudson, 'Reading', in Nowell-Smith (ed.), *Edwardian England*, 309.

What did these developments mean? Some observers triumphantly discerned manifestations of progress, but others feared that cultural standards were slipping and warned that more meant worse. George Gissing's novel *New Grub Street* (1891) features a high-minded writer (an idealized portrayal of its author) who is constantly worsted by unscrupulous rivals, determined to provide 'the world's vulgar' with all that it could comprehend: 'good, coarse marketable stuff.' In Gissing's pessimistic view, the once noble art of literature had been dragged down into a branch of trade, as profit-hunting businessmen exploited the unsophisticated 'quarter-educated' readership thrown up by the Education Acts. In his final book, *The Private Papers of Henry Ryecroft* (1903), Gissing's self-pity spills over into total contempt for the democratic masses. This, in time, became a common stance. Authors and painters who claimed to be producing works primarily for posterity went so far as to treat their current unpopularity as a badge of merit.

In music and drama things necessarily differed, in that these were performance arts which had no existence without a live audience—the gramophone, still in its infancy, was treated mainly as a toy. Even so, the movement in favour of a national theatre, which gathered momentum after 1906, was predicated on the assumption that 'serious' plays, whether classical or modern, faced a threat from the twin perils of commercialism and the public's fickleness. As the playwright Henry Arthur Jones put it, there was a pressing need 'to distinguish and separate our drama from popular amusement' by establishing 'a national repertory theatre where high and severe literary and artistic standards may be set'.[8]

In retrospect, this contempt for commercialism seems exaggerated. Many landed aristocrats no longer had the means, or even the inclination, to act as patrons of the arts, leaving a vacuum to be filled by the cultivated businessman. Thus the country owes the Tate Gallery of Modern Art, established in 1897, to a donation from the prosperous sugar refiner Sir Henry Tate. F. J. Horniman, a philanthropic tea merchant and Liberal MP, made an equally 'princely gift to the people' in 1902 when he drew upon his wealth to set up the Horniman Museum in South London. And the Edwardian expansion in the public library service might never have happened but for the lavish building programme funded by Andrew Carnegie, a Scotsman who had emigrated to the United States and made a fortune out of his Pittsburgh steelworks.

Other businessmen proved to be discerning lovers of art, collecting paintings and commissioning buildings that set new standards of excellence—and this at a time when many landowners seemed mainly concerned with selling off the artistic 'bric-a-brac' (library collections as well as paintings) which their more

---

[8] J. Woodfield, *English Theatre in Transition* (London [c.1984]), 100.

discriminating ancestors had amassed.[9] Music, too, benefited, though less directly, from accumulated business wealth: Thomas Beecham, a younger son of the owner of Beecham's Pills, inheriting the means to subsidize new operatic productions which would never have been commercially viable—and emerging, in the process, as one of Europe's leading conductors.

Nor was the wider public as incapable as Gissing supposed of appreciating important contemporary art. Despite the initial failure of *The Dream of Gerontius* at its first performance at the Birmingham Music Festival in 1900, Edward Elgar soon acquired an immense following: his First Symphony (1908) received a hundred performances in little over twelve months (some of them, admittedly, abroad), and won the acclaim of British audiences nation-wide. Britain was in the process of shaking off its unjustified reputation abroad as the 'Land Without Music', a development confirmed by the success of the London Promenade Concerts, which were inagurated in 1895 under the baton of Sir Henry Wood and soon became a popular national institution, drawing in large crowds every summer.[10]

Moreover, it was still possible for serious writers to earn a healthy income with their pens. Kipling became a wealthy man, while the novels of H. G. Wells, Arnold Bennett, and John Galsworthy quickly went through innumerable editions. Meanwhile West End audiences warmed to J. M. Barrie's whimsical little comedies, *Quality Street* (1902), *The Admirable Crichton* (1903), and *What Every Woman Knows* (1908), and Somerset Maugham, initially sponsored by the elitist Stage Society, went on to achieve popularity in the commercial theatre. By present-day standards poetry, too, was reaching a remarkably wide reader-ship. *Georgian Poetry, 1911–12*, the first of the annual anthologies brought out by Winston Churchill's private secretary Eddie Marsh, sold 15,000 copies, its successor volume 19,000. Old poetry did even better: Palgrave's *Golden Treasury*, first published in 1861, was reissued in 1907 and went through twelve reprintings (and yet another edition) before the end of the Great War.

In fact, the boom in the sale of cheap reprints of the 'classics' was a striking feature of the years around the turn of the century. As so often, W. T. Stead was the first to identify a gap in the market with his 'Penny Novels', which boiled famous books down into one-sixth or one-eighth of their original length. To these so-called 'Penny Steadfuls' he added his series of 'Penny Poets', which sold nearly 5 million copies.[11] George Newnes adopted the same formula

[9] A notable exception is the Wallace Collection, given to the nation by the widow of the Anglo-Irish landowner Sir Richard Wallace (F. M. L. Thompson, *The Rise of Respectable Society: A Social History of Victorian Britain, 1830–1900* (London, 1988), 266).

[10] The Carl Rosa Opera company, started in the 1870s, was in full spate in the 1890s, taking opera to provincial middle-class audiences.

[11] Altick, *Common Reader*, 314–15.

in 1896 when he launched his 'Penny Library of Favourite Books'. Other major publishing houses pursued a slightly different strategy, concentrating on reprints that cost slightly more but were far better produced. 'Collins's Classics', started in 1903, sold 80,000 copies at a shilling a volume within the first six months. The 'World's Classics', which Oxford University Press took over from Grant Richards in 1909, also flourished, one volume being the best-selling Palgrave.[12] But it was Joseph Dent, a naive missionary for culture, who proved to be the most successful of all these publishers: starting with the handsomely produced 'Temple Shakespeare' series (illustrations by Walter Crane), he went on, with his editor Ernest Rhys, to create the stylish 'Everyman's Library' in February 1906. Produced in batches of fifty titles and selling at what Dent called the 'Democratic Shilling', the Everyman's series caught on like wildfire—so much so that by August the firm had to expand into a new factory, located, appropriately enough for so idealistic a venture, in Letchworth Garden City.[13]

Moreover, cultural pessimists notwithstanding, the audience for artistic productions before 1914 remained in many ways startlingly unstratified. In the immediate pre-war years many leading actors regularly appeared on the music-hall boards: Beerbohm Tree, knighted in 1909, took it in his stride when he had to follow a performing seal act and was enjoined by the call-boy to ''Urry up, 'Erbert'.[14] Adeline Genée, the first ballet dame, danced at the Alhambra, while the great Russian ballerina Anna Pavlova was another regular music-hall entertainer, sharing the bill with the likes of Harry Lauder. Indeed, ballet only extricated itself from popular entertainment and became a serious 'art form' following successive visits from the Diaghilev Company from 1911 onwards. Such was the catholicity of the bandsman's taste that by the 1890s a brass-band concert might feature 'serious' symphonic and operatic arrangements (Wagner enjoyed a certain vogue) jostling cheek by jowl with popular dances and light-hearted operetta.[15] As for Elgar's music, 'wonderful in its heroic melancholy' to quote Yeats, this leapt over all the boundaries: his masque *The Crown of India*, composed to celebrate the Indian Durbar, was being performed on the stage of the Coliseum in 1912, sandwiched between comic turns, performing animals, and showings on the bioscope. This could be

---

[12] Hudson, 'Reading', 312.

[13] Gross, *Man of Letters*, 227–31; Altick, *Common Reader*, 317. However, the works published were mainly out of copyright—which, in conjunction with the high price of new books, contributed to the gap between popular literary taste and the work of the avant-garde (J. Rose, *The Intellectual Life of the British Working Classes* (New Haven and London, 2001), ch. 4).

[14] M. Sanderson, *From Irving to Olivier: A Social History of the Acting Profession in England, 1888–1983* (London, 1984), 126.

[15] D. Russell, *Popular Music in England, 1840–1914* (Manchester), 174–94. A similarly wide range of musical material characterized the choral repertoire.

construed as a 'debasement' of art, but it also suggests a willingness of popular audiences to open themselves to forms of entertainment of some sophistication.

The difficulties of cultural categorisation are dramatically illuminated by the career of Arnold Bennett. Despised by posterity for his frank expositions of how to make writing pay and for his undisguised liking for the yachts and champagne which such success might bring, Bennett was also arguably the most discerning critic of his age, as well as the creator of two of its greatest novels, *The Old Wives' Tale* (1908) and *Clayhanger* (1910), novels which seem totally at variance with the crudely materialistic philosophy which he at other times espoused. Bennett makes a nonsense of any attempt to differentiate between 'high brows', 'middle brows', and 'low brows'.

It is true that briefly, during the 1890s, writers seemed to be deliberately cutting themselves off from the public by huddling together into coteries such as the Rhymers' Club, and communicating with their select readership through little magazines such as the *Yellow Book* and the *Savoy*. But the phenomenon quickly passed, and Edwardian cultural life was enlivened by rumbustious public arguments, part literary, part political, between celebrities (H. G. Wells, Bernard Shaw, Hilaire Belloc, G. K. Chesterton), played out before large audiences. It would certainly be hard to find a *less* elitist writer than Chesterton, whose regular weekly column in the *Daily News* positively exuded a spirit of childlike optimism. Chestertonian high spirits, in fact, were but one manifestation of that Edwardian propensity to present politics, literature, even religion as something of a 'lark'. This, after all, was an age which took delight in jokes, pranks, sparkling paradoxes, and general playfulness—the age not only of Chesterton but also of Shaw, self-appointed jester to the nation, of Max Beerbohm's witty caricatures, and of E. C. Bentley's 'clerihews'.[16] Many artists, however 'serious' their message, spared no effort to make their writings 'fun'—and succeeded in winning an appreciative audience by doing so.

Yet Gissing may have been right to point out that too high a price was being paid for this achievement. The press expansion of the 1890s, for example, largely rested on the popularity of evening papers which sold on their coverage of sport and gave comparatively little room to serious politics and current affairs. The first daily newspaper whose circulation reached the 1 million mark, just before the outbreak of the Great War, was Northcliffe's *Daily Mirror*, originally a woman's paper which was later relaunched as a picture tabloid.[17] By comparison, greatly respected papers such as the *Manchester Guardian* and the *Westminster Gazette* had tiny circulations. The transfer of power within Fleet Street from journalists and editors to those who financially controlled

[16] Brilliantly described in J. Rose, *The Edwardian Temperament, 1895–1919* (Athens, Ohio, 1981), ch. 5. E. C. Bentley's *Biography for Beginners* first appeared in 1905.

[17] Williams, *Long Revolution*, 205.

newspapers (exemplified in the Northcliffe Press), also gave rise to concern in literary circles.

Moreover, trashy romances and adventure yarns tended to dominate the best-selling lists during the Edwardian decade. A case might perhaps be mounted on behalf of, say, Baroness Orczy's *The Scarlet Pimpernel* and Edgar Wallace's *The Four Just Men* (1906), but few would now want to defend on literary grounds the ephemeral volumes produced by Guy Thorne, Elinor Glyn, or Jeffery Farnol. By contrast, E. M. Forster's *A Room With A View* (1908) had sold only 2,312 copies by 1913, and *Howards End* (1910) only 9,959, while the audience for late Henry James novels and those by Joseph Conrad remained, for many years, select but very small.[18]

A survey of public-library holdings paints a similar picture, revealing, as it does, that the most popular author was M. E. Braddon, followed by Mrs Henry Wood, Emma Worboise, Marie Corelli, Mrs M. W. Hungerford, and Ouida, of whom only Mrs Wood would now be considered to possess any great literary merit.[19] Art collectors showed little more discernment. Walter Sickert's top price for a painting in 1912 was only 60 guineas, while other artists, ignored by posterity or little valued by it, such as Frank Brangwyn, could command prices over fifty times higher.[20]

Ambitious theatrical directors, too, could easily come unstuck: Charles Frohman lost heavily in attempting to establish a repertory at the Duke of York's Theatre, though his plays included Galsworthy's *Justice*, Granville Barker's *The Madras House*, and Shaw's *Misalliance*. Indeed, by the 1890s even Gilbert and Sullivan had gone out of favour, not just because their formulae now seemed somewhat old-fashioned, but also perhaps because Gilbert's satire and verbal cleverness were proving too taxing for a public which flocked, instead, to performances of flimsy musical comedies such as Sidney Jones's *Gaiety Girl* (1893) and *The Geisha* (1896), followed in the next decade by Edward German's patriotic operetta *Merrie England* (1902).[21]

So the situation of the arts in late Victorian and Edwardian Britain was in many ways a confused one. A major artist such as Elgar had no difficulty in achieving fame, popularity, and wealth, but many others struggled to do so and some scarcely tried. 'Give them what one wants oneself', wrote Henry James privately about his readers: 'it's the only way: *follow* them and they lead one by a grand straight highway to abysses of vulgarity.'[22] Indeed, by the outbreak of

---

[18] Hudson, 'Reading', 315.

[19] Ibid. 310–11.

[20] J. Russell, 'Art', in Nowell-Smith (ed.), *Edwardian England*, 337–8.

[21] D. Cannadine, 'Gilbert and Sullivan: The Making and Un-Making of a British "Tradition" ', in R. Porter (ed.), *Myths of the English* (Cambridge, 1992), 19.

[22] Henry James to Mrs Florence Bell, 7 Feb. 1890, in P. Horne (ed.), *Henry James: A Life in Letters* (London, 1999), 219.

war the concept of the artist as misunderstood genius, persecuted or ignored by the wider society, had become widespread. Under the baleful influence of Nietzsche, some writers, notably Wyndham Lewis and D. H. Lawrence, went further, lashing out furiously against a stupid populace which, subsisting on tinned foods, seemed incapable of any kind of refinement. In 1908 Lawrence was privately fantasizing about 'a lethal chamber as big as the Crystal Palace' in which these hideous creatures could be painlessly annihilated.[23]

Such extremism was not untypical of what has since become known as 'modernism', which was coterie art with a vengeance. The journals promoting avant-garde art all had tiny circulations: even the *New Age*, far more successful than most, had a circulation averaging little more than 3,000, operated at a loss of over £1,000, and often could not pay its contributors.[24] True, the Georgian poets still commanded a huge audience, but the modernists were about to demolish it, destroying, in the process, the mass audience for poetry itself. The artist as rebel and outcast was about to isolate himself from the wider society.

But artists were also alienating 'officialdom' in its various guises, not just the general public. In 1913 a new word came into currency, the 'intelligentsia', a word denoting the existence of a gap, not only between the avant-garde and the democratic masses, but also between the artistic community and those authorities who claimed to be the guardians of conventional middle-class taste. How had this latter division occurred?

2. ART AND MORALITY

Deeply embedded in the country's Protestant culture was a belief in the primacy of the word. This encouraged the view that the artist's role was to provide a narrative, preferably one imparting an improving moral lesson. Not only novelists, but also painters and sculptors, were expected to pursue this objective—hence, the popularity in the mid-Victorian years of the 'genre picture', often bearing a literary title, or paintings illustrating a biblical theme. This sort of didactic moralism—'Hebraism', Matthew Arnold had earlier dubbed it—led naturally to the position taken by the gentleman chairing a Moral Crusade meeting in November 1908, who said that 'he would destroy even the best form of art if he believed it was inimical to true morality'.[25]

Music became enveloped in a similar ethos. The Revd H. R. Haweis's *Music and Morals*, which had gone into its twentieth impression by 1903, argued that

---

[23] J. Carey, *The Intellectuals and the Masses: Pride and Prejudice Among the Literary Intelligentsia, 1880–1939* (London, 1992), 12.
[24] W. Martin, *The New Age Under Orage: Chapters in English Cultural History* (Manchester, 1967), 25–7.
[25] S. Hynes, *The Edwardian Turn of Mind* (London, 1968), 289.

music produced healthy thoughts and that musicians were embodiments of virtue, except for 'a large number of very low-class foreigners, with foreign habits and very foreign morals [who] have unhappily taken up their abode in England'. Significantly, the late Victorian musical scene was dominated by oratorios, attendance at which became, for some, a kind of pious duty,[26] though it must also have given stern Protestants, whose faith still barred them from setting foot in a theatre, an outlet for their natural love of drama. Whatever the explanation, Handel's *Messiah* and Mendelssohn's *Elijah* received countless performances. As for modern compositions, few works sold as many copies of sheet music as John Stainer's *Crucifixion* of 1887, which quickly carved out a cherished place for itself in Anglican devotions.

William Morris challenged all these orthodoxies by propounding a rather different aesthetic vision: art, he contended, should bring pleasure and dignity to its creator while at the same time being *useful*. Hating machine production, Morris sought to unite art and the handicrafts, the fateful division between which he traced back to Renaissance times. Herein lay the inspiration for the later Arts and Crafts Movement.[27]

Morris's idealization of the world of the medieval guild could be made compatible with Christianity, but for Morris and such like-minded friends as Walter Crane it led instead to a utopian belief in the capacity of socialism to 'heal' society by reintegrating useful labour with artistic self-expression. Yet, social rebel though he was, Morris did not subvert established views about the relationship between art and morality; he redefined them. A good society was one in which human beings could achieve fulfilment through the making of useful and beautiful objects: artistic and moral excellence were thus one.[28]

A far more radical challenge to Victorian moralism came from the Aesthetic Movement. Whereas Morris had stayed faithful to Ruskin's injunction to be 'true to nature', the aesthetes insisted on art's autonomy. Walter Pater, echoing Charles Baudelaire, famously declared that 'all art constantly aspires towards the condition of music'.[29] The painter James McNeill Whistler developed this idea, provocatively giving his portraits and landscapes titles such as 'Symphony in White' and 'Nocturne'. In his famous 'Ten O'Clock Lecture' of 20 February 1885, full of characteristic persiflage, the 'Butterfly' went further, mocking the notion that art 'elevates': on the contrary, he insisted, art was 'selfishly occu-

---

[26] C. Ehrlich, *The Music Profession in Britain Since the Eighteenth Century: A Social History* (Oxford, 1985), 67–8.

[27] See below.

[28] S. K. Tillyard, *The Impact of Modernism 1900–1920: Early Modernism and the Arts and Crafts Movement in Edwardian England* (London, 1988), 22–4.

[29] Significantly, by the end of the century a reaction set in against the oratorio, taking the form of the symphony concert, where the music that was performed was 'pure'.

pied with [its] own perfection only—having no desire to teach—seeking and finding the beautiful in all conditions and in all times'. Oscar Wilde later spelt out boldly what this meant for the writer: 'There is no such thing as a moral or an immoral book. Books are well written, or badly written. That is all.'[30]

For all his outspoken attacks on commercialism and the banalities of middle-class life, Wilde possessed a superb gift for *self*-promotion, marketing himself as a kind of latter-day Regency 'dandy', a work of art made flesh. Indeed, as one critic puts it, in Wilde's case 'duplicity was sincerity, artifice was art, the pose was the person and the mask was the man'.[31] Sporting his green carnation, Wilde flatly rejected that adulation of 'Nature', to which Ruskin had recently imparted fresh life, declaring in one of those witty aphorisms with which he delighted his admirers that fogs 'did not exist until Art invented them'.

The egotistical Wilde saw the artist as a godlike creator, above good and evil, whose duty it was to cultivate and refine rare and exquisite sensations, after the manner of Des Esseintes, the hero of Huysmans's novel *A Rebours* (1884). But such a quest necessarily led, as it had earlier done with Baudelaire, to the deliberate transgression of conventional moral boundaries, both in word and in deed. A telling contemporary skit on Wilde has its aesthete-hero declare: 'To sin beautifully . . . as I have sinned for years, is one of the most complicated of the arts.'[32] Contemporaries called this 'decadence'.

A sense of evil, of perversity, of the forbidden and the corrupt, certainly hangs like a heavy perfume around the *Yellow Book*, the house-magazine of the decadent group, which John Lane launched in 1894 under the imprint of the Bodley Head. No one captured its spirit more powerfully than the talented Aubrey Beardsley (or 'Aubrey Weirdsley', as *Punch* called him), whose disturbing, erotic pen-and-ink drawings conveyed through their sinuous lines intimations of cruelty and vice, well exemplified in his early illustration to Wilde's *Salomé, J'ai baisé ta bouche Iokaanan—j'ai baisé ta bouche*,[33] or the grossly voluptuous *Fat Woman* of 1894.[34]

In his best-selling book *Degeneration* (1895), the Hungarian Max Nordau portrayed aesthetes, Europe-wide, as clinical degenerates; he also advanced the theory that the *fin de siècle* portended the death of civilization itself. In reality it was the 'decadent moment' that was dying. In 1895 Wilde became an early victim of Labouchere's 1885 amendment. Found guilty of homosexual conduct, he was despatched to Reading Gaol and thence to exile in France. The

---

[30] Preface to *A Portrait of Dorian Gray*.   [31] Tillyard, *Impact of Modernism*, 56–7.

[32] Robert Hitchens, *The Green Carnation* (1894), cited in ibid. 58.

[33] Published in the *Studio*, Apr. 1893.

[34] On Beardsley, see P. Raby, *Aubrey Beardsley and the Nineties* (London, 1998), S. Calloway, *Aubrey Beardsley* (London, 1998), J. H. Desmarais, *The Beardsley Industry: The Critical Reception in England and France, 1893–1914* (Aldershot, 1998).

actor-manager George Alexander, who had successfully promoted several of Wilde's plays, immediately cut all ties with him, and his work remained unperformed during the remainder of his lifetime—though revivals started soon after his premature death in 1900. Others felt the backlash of Wilde's disgrace. Beardsley was barred by John Lane from contributing further to the *Yellow Book*, which folded two years later; he was then employed by Leonard Smithers's *Savoy*, but died in 1898, aged only 25, shortly after being received into the Roman Catholic Church and having ordered the destruction of all his 'obscene drawings'.

'Bohemia' had sounded a rather jolly place in Gerald Du Maurier's best-selling novel, *Trilby* (1894), set in Paris's Latin Quarter in the 1850s. However, 'Bohemian' life in 1890s London turned out to be more sordid than romantic. The dedicated pursuit of dissipation led to the early deaths of what W. B. Yeats later called the 'Tragic Generation' of poets and writers: as well as Beardsley (a victim of tuberculosis), Ernest Dowson died in poverty, aged 33; Lionel Johnson fractured his skull in a fall off a bar stool in the Green Dragon, Fleet Street, aged 35; John Davidson drowned himself off a Cornish cliff. Arthur Symons, it is true, lived on into his eighties, but spent much of his latter years in an asylum.

Others broke away from the 'decadent' circle. W. E. Henley, the journalist and minor poet who had participated in the Rhymers' Club, bitterly denounced Wilde and formed what Ford Madox Hueffer (later Ford) was to call the 'physical force school' of literature, surrounding himself with his circle of 'young men' (the so-called 'Henley Regatta'), who tried to outrival one another in manly bombast. Henry Newbolt stoutly declared that the public demanded that the artist 'shall chant to them ... their own morality, their own religion, their own patriotism'.[35] And a swashbuckling patriotism was what the 'young men' willingly supplied to those caught up in the excitement and drama of the Boer War—as did Kipling, who had himself once been attached to the Rhymers' Club. Another one-time member of the coterie, W. B. Yeats, now immersed in Irish politics, noted the sharp change of mood: 'Henceforth nobody drank absinthe with his black coffee; nobody went mad; nobody committed suicide; nobody joined the Catholic Church or if they did I have forgotten.'[36]

However, aestheticism did not entirely disappear in the late 1890s. It re-emerged soon afterwards, albeit in a less provocative guise, with the

---

[35] P. Brooker and P. Widdowson, 'A Literature for England', in R. Colls and P. Dodd (eds.), *Englishness: Politics and Culture 1880–1920* (Beckenham, 1986), 128.

[36] J. M. Hone, *W. B. Yeats, 1865–1935* (2nd edn., 1962), 179. Other 'decadents' joined, or had always been members of, the Catholic Church: for example, Lionel Johnson, and Francis Thompson, author of the tortured religious poem 'The Hound of Heaven'. On the other hand, Protestantism was flatly incompatible with the new aesthetic creed.

Bloomsbury Group, a salon established by the four children of the grand old man of Victorian letters Sir Leslie Stephen, who died in 1904. Virginia, who married Leonard Woolf, and Vanessa, who married Clive Bell, devoted themselves, respectively, to writing and painting. Their brother Thoby recruited into the coterie several clever young men whom he had met while at Cambridge, mostly one-time members of the secret society, the 'Apostles'[37]—notably the brilliant economist John Maynard Keynes, a Fellow of King's College, and the waspish Lytton Strachey, who later became famous for his debunking book *Eminent Victorians* (1918). The painters Clive Bell and Duncan Grant (Strachey's cousin), and the art critic Roger Fry also became drawn into the charmed circle, to which E. M. Forster was more loosely attached.

Bloomsbury drew its philosophical inspiration from the Cambridge philosopher G. E. Moore, who argued in *Principia Ethica* (1903) that 'by far the most valuable things, which we know or can imagine, are certain states of consciousness, which may be roughly described as the pleasures of human intercourse and the enjoyment of beautiful objects'.[38] This creed, more aesthetic than ethical, was later elaborated by Roger Fry, who declared (with greater finesse than Wilde) that the artist's aim was 'not to imitate life, but to find an equivalent for life'.[39]

The high valuation set by Bloomsbury on 'personal relationships', unconstrained by conventional moral codes, encouraged homosexual relationships, platonic and otherwise. There was much risqué talk about 'the higher sodomy'. Meanwhile Keynes, Strachey, and Grant were conducting a complicated triangular flirtation. But such goings-on took place in private. In 1913–14 E. M. Forster wrote a novel celebrating homosexual love, *Maurice*, but he told a friend that it would be unpublishable 'until my death or England's' (it was indeed only published posthumously, in 1971). He had to be content, in *A Room With A View* (1908), with denigrating English prudishness and parochialism and with celebrating spontaneity, the naked human body, and 'the holiness of direct desire'. Such oblique language was unlikely to cause widespread scandal.

Admittedly, even more 'dangerous topics' were sometimes broached by late Victorian and Edwardian writers, many of whom—even though the impact of Freud was still to be felt—had become increasingly aware of the precarious situation of the rational individual, threatened from within and without by dark and sinister forces impossible to acknowledge in polite society; an awareness

[37] See W. C. Lubenow, *The Cambridge Apostles, 1820–1914* (Cambridge, 1998).

[38] Rose, *Edwardian Temperament*, 41. Such a position had earlier been staked out by Walter Pater, who also influenced Oscar Wilde.

[39] Cited in J. Berthoud, 'Literature and Drama', in B. Ford (ed.), *The Cambridge Guide to the Arts in Britain: Vol. 8: The Edwardian Age and the Inter-War Years* (Cambridge, 1989), 82.

deepened by books such as the psychologist James Sully's *Illusions* (1881), which dealt with dreams and hallucinations, and by the writings of C. S. Myers, who by the mid-1880s had developed the concept of the 'subliminal self' and was talking about how 'hidden in the deep of our being is a rubbish-heap as well as a treasure-house'.[40]

The theme of the divided self is treated overtly in Robert Louis Stevenson's *Dr Jekyll and Mr Hyde* (1886)[41] and in Bram Stoker's Gothic fantasy *Dracula* (1897); it also emerges in Conan Doyle's *The Hound of the Baskervilles* (1902). Far more disturbing is Conrad's *Heart of Darkness* (1902), which shows its central character, Kurtz, driven 'by the awakening of forgotten and brutal instincts, by the memory of gratified and monstrous passions'. To a lesser or greater extent, all of these books contained shocking material, but they evaded public controversy, perhaps because of the subtle way in which their subversive elements were presented—perhaps, too, because order, of a kind, is restored in their closing pages.

Nevertheless, such writers needed to proceed with caution, since the puritanical National Vigilance Association (NVA) remained very active right up until the outbreak of the Great War, showing scant ability to discriminate between works that were disturbing but serious, and those that sought merely to titillate. Well might Shaw call the Society's secretary, the fervently evangelical William Coote, 'in artistic matters a most intensely stupid man and on sexual questions something of a monomaniac'.[42] Artists far less provocative than Wilde (or even Conrad) thus ran very real risks, ranging from criminal prosecution to having their books banned by the circulating libraries, themselves under acute pressure from the moral crusaders.

The Irish novelist George Moore, an early victim of the latter kind of informal censorship, had responded by penning a pamphlet, *Literature at Nurse* (1885), in which he pleaded for the novelist's liberty 'to write as grown-up men and women talk of life's passions and duties', but his plea fell on deaf ears, the libraries later refusing to stock his greatest novel, *Esther Waters* (1894).[43] A far worse fate befell the publisher Henry Vizetelly, who

[40] F. M. Turner, *Between Science and Religion* (New Haven, 1974), 104–33. On Myers, see Ch. 16.

[41] Jekyll perceives 'that man is not truly one, but truly two...I learned to recognise the thorough and primitive duality of man: I saw that of the two natures that contended in the field of my consciousness, even if I could rightly be said to be either, it was only because I was radically both...It was the curse of mankind that these incongruous fagots were thus bound together—that in the agonised womb of consciousness these polar twins should be continuously struggling. How, then, were they dissociated?' (R. L. Stevenson, *Dr Jekyll and Mr Hyde, the Merry Menand, and Other Tales* (London, 1925), 48–9).

[42] E. J. Bristow, *Vice and Vigilance: Purity Movements in Britain Since 1700* (London, 1977), 118.

[43] D. Thomas, *A Long Time Burning: The History of Literary Censorship in England* (London, 1969), 469–72; Bristow, *Vice and Vigilance*, 257.

had had the courage to bring out Moore's *A Mummer's Wife* (1885) in a cheap edition. This made him a prime target for the NVA, which got its revenge a few years later when it twice prosecuted him for publishing novels by Émile Zola, whose frank treatment of sexuality had caused widespread offence; the second trial of 1889 ended in the publisher receiving a three months' prison sentence.[44] This verdict, followed by Vizetelly's death shortly afterwards, delighted most Nonconformists: the *Methodist Times* called 'Zolaism' 'a disease', and argued that no one could read Zola's books 'without moral contamination'.[45] (Gladstone likewise thought *La Terre* 'the most loathsome of all books in the picture it presents'.)[46]

Even Thomas Hardy encountered opposition from the morally censorious: he had difficulties in getting his *Tess of the D'Urbervilles* (1891) published in an unexpurgated edition, and faced such hostility over *Jude the Obscure* (1895) (the Bishop of Oxford wanted it burnt) that he subsequently abandoned novel-writing altogether for poetry. True, Hardy benefited from the emergence of a 'radical' international public that deliberately dissociated itself from a 'conformist' mainstream and eagerly sought out socially critical works. However, it may be significant that the Hardy revival of the Edwardian years centred upon early pastoral novels such as *Under the Greenwood Tree* (1872)—*Tess* and *Jude* were largely ignored.

A feature of Edwardian writing was the quest to break down the barrier between the material and the sacred, the body and the soul. This gave rise to the kind of 'sacramentalized sexuality' most powerfully expressed by D. H. Lawrence, but which was also present in many other contemporary novels, where sexual fulfilment outside marriage often did *not*, as in Victorian fiction, invariably bring down death or lasting disgrace on their 'erring' female characters.[47]

Sooner or later scandal was bound to attach itself to one of these novels. In the event the storm raged around H. G. Wells's *Ann Veronica* (1909), which contains a sympathetic portrait of a young woman who opted for 'free love' (the plot was loosely based upon one of Wells's own amorous escapades). St Loe Strachey of the *Spectator* led the campaign against this book, alleging that it suborned the institution of the family and hence the authority of the state. In the wake of the dispute, the Circulating Libraries' Association was panicked into making a formal announcement in December 1909 that its members would handle nothing that was 'likely to prove offensive to any considerable section of our subscribers'.

---

[44] The second trial also involved two novels by Guy de Maupassant and one by Paul Bourget.

[45] Cited in the NVA's *Pernicious Literature* (1888), 24. Samuel Smith, Liberal Member for Flintshire and an ally of the NVA, helped to instigate Vizetelly's first prosecution.

[46] R. Shannon, *Gladstone: Heroic Minister 1865–1898* (Harmondsworth, 1999), 474.

[47] e.g. Helen Schlegel in E. M. Forster's *Howards End*.

James Joyce had meanwhile run into a slightly different kind of opposition—nervousness on the part of a printer, who effectively delayed the publication of his collection of short stories *Dubliners*, so that, although completed in 1906, it did not come out in its original form until June 1914. A year later D. H. Lawrence was prosecuted for obscenity following the publication of his novel *The Rainbow*. 'The atmosphere of this island', thought Arnold Bennett, 'is enough to choke all artists dead.'[48]

Painters and sculptors, too, could easily bring down moralistic wrath upon their heads if they blatantly disregarded conventional notions of sexual decorum. Thus Jacob Epstein created a furore in 1908 with his majestic frieze fronting the British Medical Association's new headquarters in the Strand, which depicted the naked human body.[49] Walter Sickert was meanwhile shocking the public with his depictions of low-life subjects, as in his 'The Camden Town Murder' series and in his music-hall paintings.[50] Even dancing could cause an uproar, as happened in 1908 with the ballet *The Vision of Salomé*, in which Maud Allan performed, bare-legged, in a loose Greek gown.

Drama faced a more direct peril, since an official working under the Lord Chamberlain, the 'Examiner', had to license all plays for public performance in London. Actors and managers rather liked this arrangement since it freed them from uncertainty, the sudden prohibition of a production by a prurient local authority being what they most dreaded. They were, in any case, anxious to affirm the theatre's new-won respectability, recently endorsed by the royal seal of approval.[51] (The conferral of a knighthood in 1895 on the great actor-manager Henry Irving set a trend: by 1914 another six actors had been similarly honoured.) But playwrights saw censorship as a threat to their livelihood, not least because of the often arbitrary nature of the Examiner's judgements. It also put an obstacle in the path of those wishing to experiment with new theatrical forms.

Just as the novels of Zola had aroused acute controversy, so the theatrical world was convulsed by the plays of Henrik Ibsen. The Norwegian was enthusiastically promoted by his translators, Havelock Ellis and William Archer (who was also an influential theatre critic), and the artistic avant garde immediately took him up. But in other quarters Ibsen's work was greeted with incomprehension and moralistic rage. *A Doll's House*, first produced in

---

[48] Thomas, *A Long Time Burning*, 220.
[49] It was defaced and virtually destroyed thirty years later.
[50] R. Cork, 'The Visual Arts', in B. Ford (ed.), *Guide to Arts*, 158.
[51] Queen Victoria had a great liking for theatre, but during her widowhood expected it to be performed in the privacy of the royal palaces. Edward VII also loved the theatre and often attended public performances.

unadapted form in England in June 1889, threw the country into a state of 'moral epilepsy', according to Archer.[52] This prefigured the row two years later over *Ghosts*, a play which disturbed even some of Ibsen's own sympathizers when they first read it, because they feared that its subject matter (syphilis) made it impossible to stage. Even Arthur Jones, author of several commercially successful 'social problem' plays, such as *The Profligate* (1889), spoke out against 'a school of modern realism which founded dramas on disease, ugliness, and vice'.[53] In general, though, the battle-lines were clearly drawn: between the 'Ancients', led by Clement Scott, drama critic of the *Daily Telegraph*, and the 'Moderns', whose ranks included not only Archer but also younger men such as Shaw.[54]

In fact, moderately sized West-End audiences *were* soon watching nearly all of Ibsen's plays, including *Ghosts*—but only thanks to the efforts of J. T. Grein's Independent Theatre (1891–8) and later of the Stage Society (1899–1914), organizations which sidestepped the 'Examiner' by putting on private performances paid for out of membership subscriptions rather than by ticket purchase at the theatre door.[55] This method was also used for the first performances of Shaw's early plays which treated, in that spirit of 'comic irreverence' which soon became his hallmark, such 'taboo' subjects as brothel-keeping, in *Widowers' Houses* (1893), and prostitution, in *Mrs Warren's Profession* (1894).[56]

But a showdown with the Examiner could not indefinitely be delayed. It occurred in 1907, when licences were unexpectedly withheld from two plays, one of which, Harley Granville Barker's *Waste* (which touched on the theme of abortion), its author had been planning to produce at the Royal Court Theatre. A letter was printed in *The Times* on 29 October 1907, over the signature of almost every Edwardian writer of any note (bar Kipling), protesting against 'the menace hanging over every dramatist of having his work and the proceeds of his work destroyed at a pen's stroke by the arbitrary action of a single official neither responsible to Parliament nor amenable to law'. In February 1908 J. M. Barrie led a deputation of writers to see the Home Secretary.

The following year a Joint Select Committee on Censorship opened its hearings, the most prominent witness being Shaw himself, who set out to make censorship look ridiculous, though in the short run his impish jokes may

---

[52] Woodfield, *Theatre*, 37.

[53] Hynes, *Edwardian Turn of Mind*, 176.

[54] Woodfield, *Theatre*, 16.

[55] The altruistic Grein also put his personal wealth at the Society's disposal.

[56] J. Bertoud, 'Literature and Drama', in Ford (ed.), *Guide to Arts*, 94. In *The Sanity of Art*, a counterblast to Nordau, Shaw defended the right of the artist 'to utter sedition, to blaspheme, to outrage good taste, to corrupt the youthful mind, and, generally, to scandalize one's uncles' (cited in C. Baldick, *Criticism and Literary Theory 1890 to the Present* (London, 1996), 23).

have backfired. In November the committee recommended that theatrical censorship be made optional rather than compulsory—a compromise broadly acceptable to the Dramatic Committee of the Society of Authors, which thought it 'a notable advance on anything of the kind that has appeared before'. But the government, immersed in the constitutional crisis, did nothing.

The status quo inconvenienced not only 'straight' theatre, but also opera, which also fell under the Examiner's control. For example, it proved difficult for Beecham to produce Richard Strauss's *Salomé*, the libretto of which violated nearly all the current taboos: its text, which derived from Wilde's play (originally written in French, now translated into German), was based on a biblical story to which a sadomasochistic twist had clearly been given. The opera eventually went ahead at Covent Garden in 1910, but only after the producer had agreed to call St John 'The Prophet', and replaced his severed head with a cloth which vaguely resembled a 'bedaubed tea-tray'. Even so, the opera created a scandal—Strauss's music, which many opera-goers found cacophonous, adding to the offence. Beecham also had trouble with the Lord Chamberlain later in the year over his production of Strauss's next opera, *Elektra*, and then over *Rosenkavalier* in 1913, when the Examiner insisted on the removal of the bed from the stage production![57]

Richard Strauss and his backers, like Wilde a decade earlier, enjoyed upsetting the puritanical bourgeoisie. The position of the proponents of the 'new drama', by contrast, was more complex. Like Wilde, they insisted on the artist's right to treat whatever subject matter he pleased—or, rather, they insisted on the *playwright's* prerogative to do so, since these were the years which saw a transition from an 'actors' theatre' to a 'writer's theatre'.[58] However, whereas Wilde had had no sympathy with the literary treatment of 'social problems' ('No artist has ethical sympathies... All art is quite useless'), Shaw and Granville Barker, like their hero Ibsen, were didactic moralists of a sort, eagerly exposing contemporary evils from which the hypocritical middle class would have preferred to avert its gaze.[59] In other words, the practitioners of the new 'theatre of ideas', most of whom were Fabians,[60] had a greater commitment to 'art for life's sake' than to the pursuit of art as an end in itself.[61] Shaw was particularly contemptuous of pure aestheticism.[62]

---

[57] Hynes, *Edwardian Turn of Mind*, 237–8.

[58] Shaw, in particular, took a firm command over the way actors performed his plays, a trend seen earlier in the somewhat similar authorial control exercised by Gilbert and Sullivan over the D'Oyly Carte company.

[59] Yeats, significantly, disliked Ibsen's work.

[60] e.g. John Galsworthy, author of *Strife*.

[61] To quote Holbrook Jackson's phrase.

[62] In *Man and Superman* he flamboyantly asserts the superiority of 'the life force' over the poetic temperament, portraying Hell as an aesthetic paradise: 'Music is the brandy of the damned.'

Nevertheless, for the time being this issue took second place to the controversies surrounding theatrical censorship, a system which seemed distinctly anomalous once playwrights (starting in 1891 with Pinero and Jones, followed by Shaw) began to publish their plays in volumes which often included works that had been refused a licence. This gave the wider public an opportunity to form its own judgement on the intelligence and good sense shown by the Lord Chamberlain's Office, and to compare the plays which had fallen under its ban with the succession of vulgar French farces which officialdom regularly licensed. As a result, the Examiner between 1895 and 1911, G. A. Redford (a former bank manager), became, among the intelligentsia, nothing short of a figure of fun.[63] Neither did intellectuals respect his successor, who proudly announced that the British were 'not an artistic nation', and that its people did not know 'good art from bad'.[64]

On the very eve of the Great War, it is true, a more tolerant attitude can be discerned: the new Examiner appointed in 1913 immediately let through plays which his predecessors had unhesitatingly vetoed. It was a sign of the changing times that *Ghosts*, of all plays, was being publicly performed in London for the first time in the summer of 1914 (Britain was the last European country to stage it), along with Maeterlinck's *Monna Vanna*, long banned for its suggestions of nudity and rape.

The problematic relationship between art and the state can nowhere be better illustrated than through an examination of the problems caused by Tennyson's death in 1892. His obvious successor as Poet Laureate would have been Algernon Charles Swinburne, but Gladstone, the Prime Minister, adjudged his poetry to be 'bad and terrible'.[65] The post therefore remained unfilled until 1896, when Salisbury sprang one of his little jokes on the British people by appointing Alfred Austin. The verses which this minor writer and Conservative journalist produced in celebration of events such as the Jameson Raid and the death of Queen Victoria were immediately appreciated for what they were: masterpieces of unintentional comedy. Salisbury later said that he gave Austin the Laureateship 'for the very best reason, because he wanted it'. But who else could he have chosen? Rudyard Kipling was too controversial a writer (and, over the next decade, became steadily more so), as, in another way, was Henley. Robert Bridges, who succeeded Austin in 1913, cut a less ludicrous figure, though he is now best remembered as the friend and patron of

---

[63] Redford later became the censor for the film industry, announcing that he hoped 'to keep the tremendous number of cinema theatres throughout the country clean and free from any stigma even of vulgarity'.

[64] Hynes, *Edwardian Turn of Mind*, 240.

[65] Shannon, *Gladstone, 1865–98*, 531. William Morris was sounded out by a member of the Cabinet, with Gladstone's approval, about whether he would accept the post, but he refused (J. W. Mackail, *The Life of William Morris* (London, 1899; 1901 edn.), 288).

Gerard Manley Hopkins. The major poets of the day were too difficult or too 'private' to play the public role which this office demanded.

Artistic contempt for officialdom extended beyond state functionaries to embrace other figures of authority, including leading academicians. For example, painters had little regard for the Trustees of the National Gallery, who had refused the gift of a Dégas in 1904 and declined to exhibit Sir Hugh Lane's magnificent collection of modern paintings, many of them by French Impressionists.[66] Artists also had a quarrel to pick with the leadership of the Royal Academy (RA) over the latter's bungling of the Chantrey Bequest of 1875, under which money had been left 'for the purpose of forming and establishing a Public National Collection of British Fine Art in Painting and Sculpture executed within the shores of Great Britain'. Unfortunately, the RA squandered this money on pretentious rubbish drawn from its own exhibitions, ignoring the work of nearly all the major artists of the day: for example, it let Whistler's portrait of his mother go to Luxembourg for the paltry sum of £120. In 1904 the art critic, D. S. MacColl, aided by Lord Lytton, mobilized the art world in protest—but with little immediate success.[67]

Impatience with the Academy had brought about the secession of most of the talented younger artists as early as April 1886, when the New English Art Club was founded. Some of the rebels, including George Clausen, later returned to the fold, but Sickert continued to hold aloof, and from about 1905 onwards reaffirmed his independence of academies of all kinds by holding his famous Saturday afternoon 'no jury' exhibitions for young artists from his studio at 19 Fitzroy Street. This formed the prelude to the establishment in 1910–11 of the Camden Town Group, centred upon four talented young artists, Spencer Gore, its president, Robert Bevan, Charles Ginner, and Harold Gilman, but also including Sickert, its inspirational leader, and Augustus John, Duncan Grant, and Wyndham Lewis, among others.[68] Such coteries multiplied on the eve of the war.[69]

Prudishness in 1914 may have been slightly on the wane. Significantly, the attempt at informal censorship made by the circulating libraries in 1909 had provoked a strong reaction from the Society of Authors, one of whose spokesmen indignantly protested (in the spirit of Gissing) that no artist should have to take his orders from a tradesman. More to the point, many subscribers, their curiosity aroused, began asking for the very books that had been banned. Theatregoers, too, seem to have become more broad-minded than they had been ten years earlier. In short, the moral crusaders were beginning to meet

[66] Hynes, *Edwardian Turn of Mind*, 325.
[67] D. Farr, *English Art, 1870–1940* (Oxford, 1984), 340–5.
[68] Russell, 'Art', 343–4: Farr, *English Art*, 197.
[69] See below.

determined consumer resistance. But meanwhile the conventionally minded members of the public were having their notions about 'art' shaken by another assault on their sensibilities, this time from the proponents of what posterity would call 'modernism'.

3. REALISM AND MODERNISM

In 1910 Fry organized at the Grafton Gallery an exhibition of 'Manet and the Post-Impressionists'. This was the occasion when, if Virginia Woolf is to be believed, 'human character changed'. The critical response to the exhibition, which attracted 20,000 visitors over a two-month period, was mixed: not all reviewers were hostile, but many reacted with incredulity and anger. One 'stout elderly man', confronted by Cézanne's portrait of his wife, 'went into such convulsions of laughter...that his companion had to take him out and walk him up and down in the fresh air'.[70] Philip Burne-Jones, son of the Pre-Raphaelite Sir Edward Burne-Jones, opined that the show was 'a huge practical joke organised in Paris at the expense of our countrymen'.[71] No wonder that the wider public, which had as yet scarcely come to terms with the Impressionists,[72] and whose elderly members had been brought up on the academic art of Lord Leighton and the scented soap of Sir Lawrence Alma-Tadema, was baffled by these strange paintings which flouted all conventional laws of perspective and anatomy.

But to Fry herein lay the merit of Post-Impressionism. In March 1908 he had hailed Cézanne as greater than Monet, because the former's work left 'far less to the casual dictation of natural appearance', eschewing, as it did, visual realism for 'significant form', a concept he elaborated the following year in his *Essay in Aesthetics*.[73] Fry's Bloomsbury friend, Clive Bell, put it like this: 'We have ceased to ask, "What does this picture represent?" and ask instead, "What does it make us feel?" We expect a work of art to have more in common with a piece of music than with a coloured photograph.'[74] Cheap cameras had brought exact pictorial reproduction (albeit usually in monochrome) within the means of any citizen capable of stumping up 5 shillings—the cost of the 1900 Box Brownie. As a result, many painters lost interest in accurate representations of the external world and turned their attention instead to an exploration of deeper psychological truths.

---

[70] I. Dunlop, *The Shock of the New: Seven Historical Exhibitions of Modern Art* (London, 1972), 120.
[71] Hynes, *Edwardian Turn of Mind*, 328–9, 331.
[72] A major collection of Impressionist art was mounted in London in 1905, though by this time Impressionism had become old-fashioned in France.
[73] Russell, 'Art', 348.   [74] Cork, 'Visual Arts', 160.

Yet the gallery-going public still greatly preferred, say, the glossy, highly finished portraits of the American John Singer Sargent, whose flattering portrayals of the rich and fashionable won him popular success, along with the (in many ways unjustified) contempt of the avant-garde.[75] But further shocks lay in store for the conventionally minded, with the eruption between 1910 and 1914 of Cubism, Futurism, and Vorticism, all of which offered new ways of perceiving the world that broke radically with literal representationalism.

Nothing quite as startling as this occurred in literature, but here, too, there was a rejection of naturalism. In the 1890s many poets from the Rhymers' Club, such as Arthur Symons, had been deeply influenced by French Symbolism, which insisted on 'the mystical and sometimes occult power of the symbolic imagination to gain access to an underlying, but superior, reality'.[76] Yeats, who saw poetry as an 'ecstatic escape' from the mundane world, insisted that it be kept entirely separate from what he dismissively called 'rhetoric'— discursive meditations on life, politics, or indeed anything that was not contained within the poem itself.[77]

The rejection of 'exteriority' as something fixed and given took longer to make its impact upon the writing of novels, though when it did, more than one writer's reputation underwent a profound re-evaluation. For example, through the regular column which he contributed to the *New Age* between 1908 and 1911, Arnold Bennett had eloquently pleaded the cause of the 'modern' novel, as exemplified in the work of its great French and Russian masters. But Bennett later found himself mocked by those who found the plots of *The Old Wives' Tale* (1908) and *Clayhanger* (1910) depressingly deterministic and complained that their punctilious scene-setting was overloaded with fussy detail.

By contrast, the later novels of Henry James and the writings of Joseph Conrad were based upon a non-representational aesthetic, characterized by authorial self-consciousness and irony. 'Art *makes* life, makes interest, makes importance', James exclaimed to H. G. Wells, in their famous exchange of views of 1915. In *The Wings of the Dove* (1903) it sometimes seems as though James's characters have read the novels in which they exist.[78] Conrad, too, dispensed with the device of an all-seeing, omniscient narrator, instead presenting the events which he chronicled from a variety of different perspectives, none of them authoritative.

---

[75] Unfair because it ignored the irony and acute perception of character which underlay Sargent's best work, as well as his adventurous use of colour and brush-strokes (Farr, *English Art*, 64).

[76] Brooker and Widdowson, 'A Literature for England', 122.

[77] Baldick, *Criticism and Literary Theory*, 27.

[78] J. Fletcher and M. Bradbury, 'The Introverted Novel', in M. Bradbury and J. McFarlane (eds.), *Modernism: A Guide to European Literature 1890–1930* (Harmondsworth, 1976), 397.

Not only was the 'truth' of the novel thus called into question by this process of narrative introversion, but so, too, was the integrity of the human personality. The 1913 edition of Sigmund Freud's *The Interpretation of Dreams* may only have been on sale to 'Members of the Medical Scholastic, Legal, and Clerical professions', but through Maurice Eder's articles in the *New Age* many of its ideas were coming into wider circulation.

This was only one way in which the older kind of neo-Darwinian determinism, which had influenced writers as diverse as Zola, the early George Moore,[79] and Thomas Hardy, began to be replaced by new ways of exploring interior states of mind. The attack on determinism and 'fatalism' really originated in the 1890s,[80] and was powerfully reinforced by Samuel Butler's novel *The Way of All Flesh*, which was published posthumously in 1903 to great acclaim. Enthusiastically propagated by Shaw (notably in *Man and Superman*), Butler's message involved the rejection of Darwinian natural selection for a 'Vitalist' philosophy which postulated the existence of a 'Life Force' that was striving, throughout the entirety of creation, to achieve 'higher organization, wider, deeper, intenser self-consciousness, and clearer self-understanding'.[81] The resulting 'cult of life' inspired a whole series of 'life novels', tracing an individual's heroic efforts to shape his own destiny: Lawrence's *Sons and Lovers* (1913), Joyce's *A Portrait of the Artist as a Young Man* (1914), Somerset Maugham's *Of Human Bondage* (1915), and Wells's *Tono-Bungay* (1909) are only the most famous. The notion that the novel should reflect 'life' in being 'open-ended' in turn gave rise to the 'stream of consciousness' novel: on the eve of the Great War Joyce was working on the early drafts of his epic work *Ulysses* (1922), while Woolf had finished *The Voyage Out* in 1913, though it was not published until 1915. Such experimentation unsettled readers through strangeness of form even more than earlier writings had challenged them through their 'scandalous' subject matter.

Once again, drama pursued its own, slightly different path. Only in Ireland, under the influence of Yeats, did poetic, symbolic drama become firmly established. In London, by contrast, the running was made by Shaw and Granville Barker, who advocated a 'natural' subject matter and a 'natural' acting style (involving carefully rehearsed ensembles). But this constituted a reaction against the bombastic productions beloved of the great Edwardian actor-managers which, with their amazing 'effects', were, in some respects, naive attempts to mimic the realism of the 'bioscope'.[82]

---

[79] Compare his early *A Mummer's Wife* (1885) with the later 'vitalist' *The Lake* (1905).

[80] Note the popularity of the swashbuckling Henley's lines: 'I am the master of my fate; | I am the captain of my soul'.

[81] Rose, *Edwardian Temperament*, 74–80.

[82] Ibsen's later plays, significantly, were less naturalistic than symbolic.

The difference of approach appeared most starkly in stage interpretations of Shakespeare. The great actor-managers—Henry Irving at the Lyceum, who died in 1905, and his principal successor, Beerbohm Tree at His Majesty's— continued to present Shakespeare in a heavily edited form, partly in order to pamper their 'stars', but also because their prime concern was realistic spectacle. For example, in Tree's lavish 1910 production of *Henry VIII*, 47 per cent of the text was cut to make space for what the *Era* called 'not so much a drama as a moving panorama of the period'.[83] Such florid extravaganzas were not uncommon: his *Midsummer Night's Dream*, for example, had live rabbits running around the stage; his *Richard II* live horses.

But many discerning theatregoers now sneered at Tree. For the new trend was towards a restoration of Shakespeare's full text (again a privileging of author over actor and producer) and a return to the staging conventions prevalent in Shakespeare's own day. Thus Ellen Terry's son, the theatrical producer Edward Gordon Craig, insisted on symbolic scenery and bright lighting effects, while the designer William Poel broke fresh ground by employing a three-tiered apron stage instead of a proscenium arch. Many of these innovations came together in the brilliant 'post-impressionist' Barker–Lillah McCarthy productions of *The Winter's Tale*, *Twelfth Night*, and *A Midsummer Night's Dream*, staged at the Savoy between 1912 and 1914, with Elizabethan airs supplied by Cecil Sharp. These fast-moving interpretations had a severe simplicity which contrasted with the 'bloated realism' that still prevailed in mainstream theatre.

The preference for a sparse, pared-down style affected other kinds of writing: the convoluted sentences of Henry James's late novels attracted the mockery of Wells in *Boon* (1914), and provoked even James's brother William to remonstrate: 'Say it *out*, for God's sake and have done with it.'[84] Such impatience, all too often, sprang out of a partiality for an unlovely telegraphic kind of journalese.

In other art forms the search for a stylized simplicity encouraged an interest in a variety of non-European cultures. For example, the composer Gustav Holst learned enough Sanskrit to be able to translate, without a crib, from the Veda, out of which emerged his *Veda Hymns* (1907–8) and his starkly ritualized chamber opera *Savitri* (1908), which employed only three main singers and a dozen instrumentalists—a work so startling unconventional that it did not receive a professional performance until 1921. A similar interest in oriental 'spirituality' (usually contrasted with western 'materialism') underlay the vogue for theosophy, popularized in her post-Fabian phase by Annie Besant

---

[83] M. R. Booth, *Victorian Spectacular Theatre, 1850–1910* (Boston, 1981), 134–5, 154.
[84] Rose, *Edwardian Temperament*, 146.

and by Edward Carpenter, that weathervane of turn-of-the century 'advanced' thought. Epstein's sculpture *Maternity* also owed its inspiration to Indian examples.

Such cross-cultural influences became commonplace among contemporary artists and sculptors anxious to escape the tyranny of western perspective. For example, Japanese art, of which Whistler had been an early promoter, continued to have its admirers. Gauguin later focused attention on Oceanic culture, in which he discerned a childlike spontaneity,[85] and this encouraged Epstein to make a study of carvings from that region in 1912–13. Epstein and Eric Gill also drew upon African carvings as inspiration for their sculpture. Such developments won the whole-hearted approval of the Vorticists (a group including Wyndham Lewis, the sculptor Gaudier-Brzeska, and Ezra Pound) who called, in their manifesto *Blast* (July 1914), for the adoption of a visual language as abstract as music which would incorporate the primitive and primordial.

The 'modernists' by no means discarded tradition in its entirety—on the contrary, older cultural myths and legends often dominated their work, as in the case of the two American immigrants Ezra Pound and T. S. Eliot, and, even more explicitly, in Joyce's *Ulysses*. Pound declared that he reverenced Dante, Villon, and Catullus, while expressing 'different degrees of antipathy or even contempt' for Milton, the Victorians, and 'the softness of the "nineties" '.[86] This brusque rejection of Victorian models and conventions in favour of the Middle Ages and Ancient Rome was but one manifestation of a frenzied search for the 'new'—a search which led to the foundation of a rapid succession of 'movements', no sooner formed than rent by schism. Thus the Canadianborn painter Wyndham Lewis, who had once been attached to the Camden Town Group, later exhibited in the Second Post-Impressionist Exhibition in late 1912, before quarrelling with Fry and taking up Futurism, which on the eve of the war he then abandoned for 'Vorticism'. Will Dyson well captured the hectic atmosphere of this period in his cartoon 'Progress', in which one painter, a 'Post-Elliptical Rhomboidist', says dismissively of another's work: 'Him a modern, Bah! He paints in the old-fashioned manner of last Thursday!'[87]

The reaction against Europe's recent cultural legacy expressed itself differently in each art form. By and large British architecture remained stylistically

---

[85] Fry opined that 'the untaught child is artistically in a state of grace' (Rose, *Edwardian Temperament*, 187).

[86] Cited in Baldick, *Criticism and Literary Theory*, 40. Ford Madox Ford, however, was important in recruiting Yeats, a poet of a much older generation, to the modernist project, as well as promoting the 'modernist' credentials of James and Conrad.

[87] 'Progress', illustrated in Martin, *New Age*, 191.

conservative, few buildings, for example, featuring exposed steel.[88] But poetry saw the wider adoption of *vers libre*, music the abandonment of tonality. The point is that the British public was being asked to revise its artistic preconceptions as never before. Lovers of the Georgian poets found themselves simultaneously confronted with Pound's 'Imagist' verses and with the Eliot poems soon to be gathered into the *Prufrock* collection. What can it have been like for concert-goers, whose musical taste had been formed by Brahms and Dvořák and by domestic renditions of Grieg's *Lyric Pieces* (those 'pink bonbons filled with snow', as Debussy called them),[89] to sit through Arnold Schoenberg's *Five Orchestral Pieces*, which Wood conducted at a 'Prom' in 1912, or to hear Igor Stravinsky's *Rite of Spring* in July of the following year?

In fact, it seems that after the brouhaha surrounding the 1910 Post-Impressionist Exhibition, London audiences largely took these latest provocations in their stride, though perhaps more from stunned politeness than a sense of approval. Audiences in other European capitals often showed less tolerance. Thus the Promenaders may have hissed Schoenberg's revolutionary music, but *The Rite of Spring* was not accompanied by riots in London, as it had been on its Paris premiere. The new art would never capture the following enjoyed by Dickens, Tennyson, and Millais, but perhaps Virginia Woolf was right in thinking that human character really had changed in 1910.

4. THE NATURE OF 'ENGLISHNESS'

But did this mean that England had been 'successfully invaded from the Continent' during the final months of peace?[90] It certainly seemed so to those of a paranoid disposition, who condemned both 'immorality' in art and the revolutionary new aesthetic by grumbling that such 'savagery' was 'un-manly' and 'un-English'.

The accusation was undeniable in one sense. Few of the truly innovative 'modernists', with the exception of D. H. Lawrence, *were* English.[91] The great Glasgow-based architect and designer Charles Rennie Mackintosh was Scottish. An astonishingly high proportion of the most notable writers of the day were Irish, many of them 'expatriates', either living largely in London, as

---

[88] A. Service, *Edwardian Architecture* (1977). Among the few 'modernist' buildings of distinction were Voysey's Sanderson Wallpaper Factory in Chiswick (1902–3) and John Burnet's Kodak Building in Kingsway (1910–11).

[89] The composer dubbed 'the most popular musician in the home life of England since Mendelssohn' was given an honorary degree by Oxford University in 1906 (Ehrlich, *Music Profession*, p. 93). But Forster damns the aspiring clerk, Leonard Bast, in *Howards End*, by having him play Grieg—and badly at that!

[90] Hynes, *Edwardian Frame of Mind*, 345.

[91] Confusingly, Lawrence's verses regularly appeared in the early numbers of *Georgian Poetry*.

Wilde and Shaw did, or, like Moore and Yeats, dividing their time between London and their native land. Joyce, ever the loner, left Dublin in 1904 for exile in Trieste, where he settled in early 1905. The great Irish cultural revival, centred upon the Abbey Theatre in Dublin, mounted productions of new plays by Moore, Yeats, Lady Gregory, and J. M. Synge, several of which were quickly taken up by the subscription theatre movement in London.

Outside the British Isles, the United States provided English cultural life with much of its creative input, going back to the arrival of Whistler in 1859 and Henry James in 1876.[92] In the immediate pre-war years many other Americans followed suit. Epstein, a New York Jew, took out British nationality in 1907, having earlier disembarked in London while returning home from Paris. In 1908 Ezra Pound took up residence in the metropolis more deliberately, thinking it to be America's true cultural capital. His friend T. S. Eliot, after postgraduate research in Oxford, decided to settle in England seven years later. Another influential transatlantic immigrant, Wyndham Lewis, came from Canada. The most exotic of the outsiders attracted to England was the Polish-born Joseph Conrad, who did not even hear her language spoken until he was 23 years old.

Those artists who *were* English tended to look abroad for their models. The cultural traffic was not all one-way: Beardsley's drawing style, popularized by magazines such as the *Hobby Horse* and *Studio*, helped turn 'Art Nouveau' into an international phenomenon; the Arts and Crafts Movement, too, was speedily taken up abroad, notably by the *Deutscher Werkbund*. But in England self-consciously 'modern' artists spent much of their time berating their fellow-countrymen for insularity and philistinism, holding up for their emulation the pioneering developments taking place on the Continent, with Wagner, Nietzsche, Zola, and Ibsen serving as their chief icons.[93]

France played a more important role than all the other European countries combined. One critic has noted that 'at times it seemed that literary London was populated by natural Parisians who could not quite summon up the cross-channel fare'.[94] George Moore and Arnold Bennett drew heavily upon their personal knowledge of recent and contemporary French writing, not least Flaubert and Zola. Wilde, who actually wrote his play *Salomé* in French, shamelessly copied Baudelaire and Huysmans, while the poets of the Rhymers' Club (Yeats, Dowson, Symons, and Johnson) were all heavily influenced by the French Symbolists Rimbaud and Mallarmé.

---

[92] Also Sargent in 1895.

[93] These writers were at the heart of a 'pre-modernist' cosmopolitanism in the 1890s, distinct from a later phase, centred on Eliot, Pound, Virginia Woolf, and Post-Impressionism.

[94] M. Bradbury, 'London 1890–1920', in Bradbury and McFarlane (eds.), *Modernism*, 174.

Painters owed the French an even greater debt. Whistler had pursued his studies in Paris, which also attracted ambitious young men, eager to master their craft, such as Wilson Steer. Walter Sickert, the nearest thing to an Impressionist painter that England ever produced, became a close friend and admirer of Dégas, and, before settling permanently in England in 1905, spent many years in Dieppe, where an important Anglo-French artistic colony developed. In fact, the main task of England's self-appointed avant-garde became one of explaining to a bemused English public what modern French painters were doing.

Before the outbreak of the Great War France's only European rival as a cultural centre was Russia, which impinged powerfully on people's consciousness between 1910 and 1914—thanks largely to the visits, from 1911 onwards, of the Diaghilev Company, which not only revolutionized English people's conception of ballet (the great dancer Nijinsky made a particularly vivid impression), but also introduced to London audiences the music of Stravinsky and the costumes and decor of Leon Bakst. At the same time Arnold Bennett was awakening the literary world to the importance of Russian writing, much of it still largely unknown, and encouraging the translation and publication of Chekhov and Dostoevsky, to go alongside the already familiar works of Tolstoy and Turgenev. On the eve of the war there was a positive craze for all things Russian.

It could be argued that great art, by definition, knows nothing of national frontiers and is, in that sense, always international. But, as the Great War approached, art was acquiring a new kind of cosmopolitan identity. Many writers benefited from the tightening-up of international copyright laws, which meant that they no longer financially depended on the success of their work with a particular national audience. Similarly, with dwindling support from the general public in any one country, like-minded painters and sculptors formed international coteries. Thus, whereas the first Post-Impressionist Exhibition in London was devoted to French painters (Van Gogh and Picasso being, as it were, Frenchmen by adoption), its successor in 1912 brought together artists not only from France (Matisse was the new star), but also from Russia and England—the latter drawn mainly from the Camden Town and Bloomsbury groups (including Vanessa Bell, Fry, Gore, Duncan Grant, Henry Lamb, Wyndham Lewis, and Stanley Spencer).

Simultaneously Epstein, a truly international figure, was forming friendships in Paris with Modigliani, Picasso, and with the French sculptor Henri Guadier-Brzeska, who followed him back to London. Futurism had as its leader the Italian Filippo Marinetti (though his early writings were in French), and Cubism and Vorticism were both international styles—even if the Vorticists tried, rather unconvincingly, to pass themselves off as an English-led resistance movement. No wonder that by 1914 the wording of the Chantrey Bequest looked so outmoded: its creator had hoped to establish a national school of modern painting and sculpture, but the contemporary visual arts had long since become part of a wider international movement—as, to a lesser extent, had literary modernism.

The situation of music was different. In 1886 English musical life was still dominated by Germany, which supplied it with most of its celebrated conductors and soloists. Thus, when Charles Hallé died in 1895, he was replaced, after a short interval, by Hans Richter from the Vienna Opera, a regular visitor to these shores. It is not surprising that the two leading composers of the 1880s and early 1890s, Hubert Parry and Charles Stanford (the former of Welsh ancestry, the latter Irish), saw their principal mission as being that of bringing English music up to the standards of composition and performance that prevailed in Germany and Austria.[95]

Moreover, when a native composer of undoubted genius did emerge, in the person of Edward Elgar, he developed an idiom which, though highly personal, owed much to Brahms and Wagner, which may partly explain why its importance was so quickly acknowledged in Germany—among others, by Richard Strauss and by Richter, who conducted several Elgar premieres. In the British context Elgar was a 'modern' composer, whose achievement it was to connect England once more to the Continental mainstream. But, with his Germanic idiom and the ardent Catholic faith which underlay his greatest work, *The Dream of Gerontius* (set to a version of Cardinal Newman's rambling poem), Elgar seems an unlikely embodiment of the 'spirit of England', which was how he eventually came to be viewed. How was this reputation achieved?

National pride may partly supply the answer. Elgar's reputation was also shaped by his willingness to be associated with great patriotic occasions. The *Imperial March* of 1897, which was included in the State Concert commemorating the Diamond Jubilee, marked the start of Elgar's unofficial reign as music laureate, a position later confirmed when King Edward VII, on hearing the first performance of the *Pomp and Circumstance Marches* in 1901, suggested that the Trio of no. 1 be set to words—which the composer did the following year in the 'Coronation Ode', to a text by A. C. Benson.[96] Thus was born 'Land of Hope and Glory', England's second national anthem. Elgar cemented the relationship with monarchy and the state by dedicating his Second Symphony of 1911 to the memory of Edward VII and by writing music for George V's

---

[95] Parry was Director of the Royal College of Music from 1884 to 1918, its Professor of Composition being Stanford (1883–1924). Parry was also Professor of Music at Oxford University, 1900–8, Stanford holding the equivalent position at Cambridge from 1887 to 1924.

[96] When first performed, on 22 October 1901, during the Boer War, 'the people simply rose and yelled', as Elgar proudly noted.

Delhi Durbar (and later in aid of the war effort). Official recognition followed: a knighthood in 1904, the Order of Merit in 1911. Only after the war, by which time the exuberant patriotism of the Edwardian era had become something of an embarrassment, did music critics emphasise the 'pastoral' elements in Elgar's music, supposedly the result of his Worcestershire roots.

Even more problematic was the national identity of Frederick Delius, son of an immigrant German Bradford wool merchant, who until 1904 called himself 'Fritz'. After a short spell as a businessman in Florida, Delius trained for a musical career at the Leipzig Conservatory,[97] and then travelled widely over the Continent (visiting Grieg in Norway, for example), before settling down in a village near Fontainebleau with the woman he later married, the German artist Jelka Rosen. Delius's greatest work, *The Mass of Life* (1904–5), was set to words by Nietzsche and received its first complete performance in London in June 1909 under the baton of Beecham, a lifelong devotee, after sections had earlier been premiered in Munich. Delius was as detached from mainstream English life as Elgar became integral to it: 'Did you say English music? Well, I've never heard any', he once characteristically observed.[98] Yet other, mainly younger, composers found the Teutonic legacy a suffocating burden. Gustav Holst, in his student days, 'ate and drank Wagner and took in huge draughts of Wagner with every gasp of air he breathed', according to his daughter Imogen. Like his friend Ralph Vaughan Williams, Holst only acquired his own voice after he had found a new source of inspiration—in England's newly discovered folk music.

Contrary to received wisdom, the English folk-music revival preceded that celebrated moment in 1903 when Cecil Sharp had a Somerset gardener, the aptly named John England, sing for him the ballad 'The Seeds of Love'. The Folk Song Society had actually been founded in 1898, and five years earlier Lucy Broadwood and J. A. Fuller-Maitland had published their anthology *English Country Songs*—itself the culmination of the work of a group of pioneering folk-song publications in the late 1880s and early 1890s, in which the field collector Sabine Baring-Gould was a leading figure. But the energetic Sharp soon became the unchallenged organizer of the folk-music movement, working after 1905 with Mary Neal, who in 1910 established the Espérance Guild of Morris Dancers.

Sharp aimed at rescuing native melodies and ballads, which went back, he believed, to time immemorial, from the threatening onward march of urban

---

[97] Elgar had also wanted to go there, but lacked the means.
[98] M. Kennedy, 'Music', in Ford (ed.), *Guide to Arts*, 117. Operas by Stanford and by Ethel Smyth were also premiered in Germany.

music-hall songs. But, in a spirit of unabashed patriotism, he also saw this quest as a means of spreading among schoolchildren a love of their own national music, a love which he thought was currently being stifled by a 'cosmopolitan' education system 'calculated to produce citizens of the world rather than Englishmen'.[99]

Sharp also saw his own personal crusade as leading to a wider national revival. 'Since the death of Purcell', he argued, 'the educated classes ha[d] patronised the music of the foreigner, to the exclusion of that of the Englishman', most obviously in opera, the music of which was sung in a foreign tongue, but also in the concert hall, where programmes were dominated by the performance of 'European' composers. 'We must leave it to [the younger generations] to restore English music to its rightful position— to do for our country what Glinka and his followers did for theirs.'[100] It remained unclear whether folk music really did offer a solution to this state of affairs. The highly influential music critic Ernest Newman, a great Wagnerite, pertinently challenged Sharp to say whether Elgar would have been a better composer had he been acquainted with traditional English folk songs. Elgar himself privately thought not, exclaiming 'I write the folk-songs of this country'.

On the other hand, Elgar notwithstanding, the folk revival did lay the basis for what is often called an 'English Musical Renaissance'. Thus Vaughan Williams, who began collecting folk songs in Essex shortly after his friend Sharp had set to work in Somerset, found in the modal inflections of this music the material for later large-scale works, such as the folk opera *Hugh the Drover*, written between 1911 and 1914. Vaughan Williams's other inspiration was Tudor music, with which he had become closely acquainted while editing the *English Hymnal* between 1904 and 1906—at a time when the *Fitzwilliam Virginal Book* (1899) had already been published, though the massive *English Madrigal Book* series only started in 1913. This influence was most directly displayed in his *Fantasy on a Theme of Thomas Tallis* of 1910.[101]

Vaughan Williams did not entirely spurn Continental models, his harmonic idiom, for example, having been heavily influenced by the lessons he received from Maurice Ravel in Paris. The 'London Symphony', completed in its first

---

[99] G. Boyes, *The Imagined Village: Culture, Ideology and the English Folk Revival* (Manchester, 1993), 77.

[100] A. Howkins, 'The Discovery of Rural England', in Colls and Dodd (eds.), *Englishness*, 69–70; Boyes, *Imagined Village*, 45.

[101] Vaughan Williams was also inspired by the histories of his friend G. M. Trevelyan (D. Cannadine, *G. M. Trevelyan: A Life in History* (1992; 1993 edn.), 9).

version just before 1914, is an eclectic work, showing traces of Debussy, Stravinsky's *Petrushka*, and (no doubt to Sharp's dismay) snatches of music-hall song, as well as folk music. But it was the folk music which enabled Vaughan Williams to compose with a marked national inflection—just as it helped Holst, George Butterworth (who was killed during the Great War before he could develop his full potential), and the Australian Percy Grainger.[102]

Folk revivalism, with a strongly patriotic hue, was not confined to music and dancing, but also influenced literature. In both cases its impetus partly derived from a desire on the part of Englishmen to keep up with the 'Celts'. Sharp, for example, urged his fellow-countrymen to attend to their own heritage and not be content to follow the lead of other peoples: 'English songs for English children, not German, French, or even Scottish or Irish.' This formed merely one aspect of the English backlash against the assertive claims of the other British nations, manifested, for example, in the cultural nationalism of the Irish, and in the establishment during the 1880s of the Welsh Eisteddfod in its modern form. Such rivalry forms the background to the late Victorian reformulation of the Arthurian legends, which resulted in King Arthur being wrenched out of his original 'British' (i.e. Cornish or even Welsh) context and 'reinvented' as a perfect English gentleman. So successfully was this done that Celtic nationalists eventually abandoned all claims to Arthur. This allowed English patriots to hold their heads high, believing that they possessed a native mythology that ranked with the Homeric legends and surpassed the epic myths of most other modern European nations (including those of Siegfried and the Nibelungs').

Those who felt little attraction to the chivalric world of the Knights of the Round Table could turn instead to a more popular, even democratic, mythic figure in the person of Robin Hood—whose value to English nationalists was not only that he supposedly operated in Sherwood Forest, the very 'heart of England', but that he could also be presented as an 'Anglo-Saxon', bravely protecting the ancient liberties of the people against the Norman occupiers.[103] Increasingly English national identity was being expressed in racial terms, with culture as its principal mode of transmission.

Meanwhile the scholarly volumes compiled by the Early English Text Society offered testimony to a newfound pride in the country's linguistic heritage. This pride also took other forms, including the opening of the National Portrait Gallery in 1896, and the start of work on the *Dictionary of*

---

[102] It was Grainger who provided Delius with the Lincolnshire folk song which was later reworked into *Brigg Fair* (1907), though, characteristically, this work received its first performance abroad.

[103] S. L. Barczewski, *Myth and National Identity in Nineteenth-Century Britain: The Legends of King Arthur and Robin Hood* (Oxford, 2000).

National Biography, the first series of which, edited by Leslie Stephen, came out between 1885 and 1901.[104]

The impulse to commemorate great national figures extended from statesmen and scholars to eminent 'men of letters'. In 1885 an article in the *Daily News* drew attention to the absence in England of anything like the threepenny series of books in Germany celebrating its great literary heroes. The response was the launching of Cassell's 'National Library', followed by the 'Men of Letters' series, which, as edited first by Leslie Stephen and then by Edmund Gosse, provided a kind of national literary pantheon.[105] Quiller-Couch's *Oxford Book of English Verse* (1900) and the *Cambridge History of English Literature* (launched in 1907) also helped to stimulate a more intense awareness of the country's literary achievements. Little wonder that by 1914 'English Studies' had established itself as an important academic discipline in all the major British universities; the recently founded English Association could call the subject 'our finest vehicle for a genuine humanistic education'.[106]

A new pride in the English language was another characteristic of the years around the turn of the century. Opinion divided between those who stressed the current language's derivation from 'Anglo-Saxon' (or 'Old English', as it was now often called), and those who argued that the modern language and literature of England owed much more to the classical world than to Beowulf. But both sides could agree with the purpose underlying James Murray's *New English Dictionary* (later renamed the *Oxford English Dictionary*), which, according to its 1888 preface, aimed, 'by the completeness of its vocabulary and by the application of the historical method to the life and use of words', to 'be worthy of the English language and English scholarship'. Moreover, this authoritative project, by helping to standardize 'correct usage', was intended to help unify the nation both socially and geographically, while at the same time recovering and preserving the riches of the linguistic past.[107]

Though most 'modernist' writers had scant sympathy with such nostalgia, a sophisticated interest in defining the essence of 'Englishness', in a more general sense, became an important aspect of Edwardian cultural life. Many writers

---

[104] The National Portrait Collection had been established earlier, but its present home was only completed in 1896. The *DNB* was initially edited by Leslie Stephen, joined in 1890 by Sidney Lee, who took over the project in 1891.

[105] S. Collini, *Public Moralists: Political Thought and Intellectual Life in Britain* (Oxford, 1991; 1993 edn.), 356–7; Gross, *Man of Letters*, 106–8.

[106] See Ch. 16; B. Doyle, 'The Invention of English', in Colls and Dodd (eds.), *Englishness*, 102–10.

[107] Collini, *Public Moralists*, 352; T. Crowley, *The Politics of Discourse* (London, 1989), esp. 110. The *English Dialect Dictionary*, begun in 1898, was a self-conscious counterpart to 'correct' linguistic forms (Collini, *Public Moralists*, 353). Some late Victorian and Edwardian grammarians indignantly denied that dialect was 'an arbitrary distortion of the mother tongue', but others took it as axiomatic that 'English' denoted 'the English of the present time as spoken, written and understood by educated people' (Crowley, *Politics of Discourse*, 139, 147).

brought to this quest moral and political categories such as freedom, natural-
ness, and spontaneity, which they then sometimes juxtaposed with Teutonic
'order'—as when Rupert Brooke, in his famous poem 'Grantchester' (1913),
compares Berlin's regimented tulips with the 'English unofficial rose', blowing
in Cambridgeshire's 'unkempt' hedgerows.

Not dissimilar is the passage in Forster's *Howards End* in which Margaret
Schlegel, brought up sharply against her German cousins' abstract cast of
thought, meditates upon her own sense of identity, which, she realizes,
grows out of a particular place, the wych elm of an old country house. Indeed,
to Forster, the countryside represented civilization's only safeguard against the
creeping 'red rust' of suburbanization and the intrusions of the motor car,
symbol of the restless modern world of 'telegrams and anger'.

Many contemporaries shared this conviction that 'Englishness' itself was
bound up with the peace and stability that mainly belonged to its landscape,
within which were contained all the continuities of national life. It was precisely these sentiments that E. V. Lucas evoked in the opening lines of his
poem 'The Old Country':

> Oh England, country of my heart's desire,
> Land of the hedgerow and the village spire.[108]

5. PASTORALISM

'Pastoralism' of this kind was part of a wider social phenomenon: a revulsion
against the ugliness, squalor and unhealthiness of large towns, resulting in an
idealization of country life, and in various attempts at getting people 'back to
the land'. Such aspirations were widely held, though people of different
political persuasions gave them their own distinctive twist. Thus many traditional Tories hoped to preserve as much as possible of the older hierarchical
social order, centred upon the 'Big House'. Reforming Liberals, in complete
contrast, wanted to reclaim the land for the common people who (they thought)
had been robbed of their rightful inheritance. Finally, Robert Blatchford and
many other socialists could only envisage a social rebirth, leading to a harmonious commonwealth, if this took place within a predominantly rural/agricul-
tural setting.

Indeed, some utopian socialists went so far as to seek a cultural revolution on
the basis of rural revivalism. The kernel of this creed lay in the writings of John
Ruskin and William Morris. Some socialists were also influenced by the

---

[108] E. Rhys (ed.), *The Old Country: A Book of Love and Praise of England* (London, Everyman edn.,
1917). However, the last two stanzas of this four-stanza poem nostalgically evoke the sights and sounds
of London.

communitarian theories of Tolstoy and of the Russian anarchist Prince Kropotkin, author of *Fields, Factories and Workshops* (1898). Drawing together the loose threads of this diffuse movement was Edward Carpenter, who, after settling in 1882 on a smallholding at Millthorpe, south of Sheffield, emerged as the chief spokesman and model for a whole generation of rural 'colonists'.

Carpenter's anti-industrialism formed but one aspect of his rejection of the complexities of conventional middle-class society, which he ruthlessly dissected in *Civilisation: Its Cause and Cure* (1889). In writing this book, Carpenter naturally drew upon the work of earlier socialist thinkers, but he was also strongly influenced by two American writers. From the pantheistic poetry of Walt Whitman he derived the inspiration for his own epic poem *Towards Democracy* (1889), and from Henry Thoreau's *Walden* (first published in England in 1886), an account of its author's retreat into a life of self-sufficiency in the woods of New England, he gained powerful insights into how to practise the 'simple life', an idea which he did more than anyone in England to popularize.

G. K. Chesterton may have had a point when he quipped that more genuine simplicity could often be found in the man who ate caviare on impulse than in one who ate grape-nuts on principle—the pursuit of a simple life necessitating the adoption of elaborate strategems which sometimes only the possession of a private income made possible. All the same, it is understandable that in the late Victorian and Edwardian periods some prosperous middle-class rebels should have rejected for something radically different the rigid codes of etiquette, the rich, over-lavish meals, and the heavy, constricting attire which were *de rigeur* in conventional society.

On first arriving at Millthorpe, Carpenter symbolically discarded his dress clothes in favour of loose-fitting, comfortable garments. Soon afterwards he adopted the Indian hand-made sandal, which became almost part of the 'simple-lifer''s uniform. Morris himself had worn soft blue cotton shirts which were smock-like in appearance, but most simple-lifers, on both hygienic and aesthetic grounds, preferred the sanitary woollen shirt and knitted leggings, based on the principles of Gustav Jaeger of Stuttgart, who had argued that wool, unlike cloth made from vegetable fibres, allowed noxious gases emanating from the body to evaporate.[109] This fashion spread way beyond the ranks of the 'back to the land' utopians—being espoused, for example, by Shaw. Agricultural labourers, who had long since abandoned the old-fashioned smock, were often frightened when they came across these strangely clad intruders! Meanwhile many younger women, braving social ridicule, embraced

---

[109] The British Jaeger Clothing Company was successfully established in 1883 (J. Marsh, *Back to the Land: The Pastoral Impulse in England, from 1880 to 1914* (London, 1982), 191).

the principles of the Rational Dress Society, founded in 1881, dispensing with a hat while in the open air and, more daringly still, discarding their stays.

The pursuit of the 'simple life' often involved other radical departures from convention, such as nudism and *al fresco* sex, while Carpenter saw it as offering an opportunity for developing new kinds of affectionate relationships with his various working-class male friends. Sexual experimentation, however, was a minority pastime. Far more common was the principled rejection of tobacco, alcohol, and even caffeine, along with the adoption of a vegetarian diet. Carpenter himself subsisted on 'wholesome' dinners, comprising oatmeal, an egg, some cheese, and a little fruit.[110] Most simple-lifers favoured vegetarianism purely on health grounds, but others also advocated it in the name of 'animal rights', a cause which extended to attacks on hunting and vivisection as well as the rejection of meat-eating.[111]

Logically enough, the simple-lifers, wishing to insulate their children from the corruption and artificiality of contemporary civilization, had their own distinctive educational ideas—to meet which there emerged experimental schools such as Abbotsholme, situated in rural Derbyshire, which was founded in 1889 by Cecil Reddie, a one-time member of the Fellowship of the New Life and a disciple of Carpenter. Such institutions dispensed with all but the minimum of formal discipline and deliberately created a non-competitive environment in which, for example, school prizes and competitive games were disallowed. At Abbotsholme (an all-boys establishment) the pupils wore 'rational clothes' (a Norfolk jacket, soft woollen shirt, and knickerbockers), and devoted much of their day to outdoor activities, such as working on the school farm, while their leisure hours were often given over to the acquisition of a handicraft and to participating in folk-singing and dancing. The boys were also taught not to be ashamed of their bodies—hence the custom of nude bathing.[112]

As for the agrarian communities themselves, these fell into two main categories. Doctrinaire socialists mostly favoured communal living, and a number of experimental colonies on these lines sprang into existence—such as the one at Whiteway in the Cotswolds (still extant), which was linked to the Fellowship of the New Life and at various times enjoyed the support of Ramsay MacDonald, Olive Schreiner, her lover Havelock Ellis, as well as the ubiquitous Carpenter. However, such communes rarely survived long in the face of the strained relationships which quickly developed among the 'com-

---

[110] Ibid. 20.

[111] Thus Henry Salt, the founder in 1891 of the Humanitarian League, edited the vegetarian journal *Humanity*, and also the magazine *Animal Rights*, founded in 1892 (ibid. 196; Rose, *Edwardian Temperament*, 63–4).

[112] This proved impossible in the breakaway institution Bedales, which admitted girls as well as boys (Marsh, *Back to the Land*, 210–11).

rades'. More successful, both socially and economically, was the movement to set up family-based smallholdings. These concentrated mainly on bee-keeping, fruit- and poultry-farming, and the growing of fresh vegetables, sometimes amalgamating to form larger enterprises, such as the Methwold Fruit Farm Colony in Norfolk, which was run by the 'escapee', R. K. Goodrich, a London businessman in an earlier incarnation.[113]

It required great courage and persistence to exchange a comfortable urban job for this tough and precarious existence. Fortunately, for those deficient in such qualities who were nevertheless attracted by rustic simplicity, more comfortable alternatives were at hand. The poet Edward Thomas, a London Welshman, was only the most famous of the many late Victorians who, after reading the nature writings of Richard Jefferies, embarked upon a lengthy exploration of rural England—in Thomas's own case, Wiltshire and other areas within what he called the 'South Country'. By the end of the century rambling had become, for many people from all but the poorest sectors of society, a positive obsession. Thus Leslie Stephen founded the 'Sunday Tramps', which was later rejuvenated by the historian G. M. Trevelyan—a 'terrific walker', like his friend Bertrand Russell.[114] Other contemporaries, such as Edward Grey, sought Wordsworthian consolation in wild mountainous scenery.[115]

Cycling and motoring, both modern modes of transport, could not so readily be assimilated into this kind of 'transcendentalism'. On the other hand, Nature-worshippers could, if they chose, acquire a gypsy van and horse and then set off on romantic wanderings along the 'open road'. In fact, in the New Forest, gypsy vans could be hired by the week—which suggests that the joys of caravanning were by no means confined to Augustus John and his family, to Edward Thomas, and to the fictional Mr Toad.

An even less arduous entry into Arcadia was available to those able to purchase or rent a country cottage, if only as a weekend retreat. Ideally such a cottage should have a thatched roof and roses climbing around its porch, and be situated in a spectacularly lovely landscape—such as the Cotswolds, which were 'discovered' in 1895 when the actress Mary Anderson settled in Broadway, drawing in visitors such as Barrie, Elgar, Edmund Gosse, Henry James, and Augustine Birrell.[116] Several colonies of agriculturalists and craftsmen soon settled in this picturesque area. Others preferred the more rugged scenery of the Southern Cotswolds—home not only to the Whiteway colony, but also to

---

[113] Ibid. 113–14.
[114] A. Offer, *Property and Politics 1870–1914* (Cambridge, 1981), 334–5.
[115] Forster treats this theme with ironic sympathy in *Howards End*, through his portrayal of the downtrodden clerk Leonard Bast, who sets out on a nocturnal rustic ramble that will enable him to watch the sun rising above the Surrey Hills—only to find the experience cold and wet.
[116] Marsh, *Back to the Land*, 30.

the furniture workshops of Ernest Gimson and the Barnsley brothers, who based themselves on the remote village of Sapperton, outside Cirencester. (For escapees of more modest means and ambitions makeshift freehold dwellings, costing only a few pounds, were beginning to spring up on small, dispersed plots of land, particularly in Essex, at Pitsea, Laindon, Billericay, and Rayleigh.[117])

Such socio-economic experiments and leisure patterns might seem irrelevant to a consideration of culture, but in fact a strong connection existed between them in the minds of those who had learned from Ruskin, Morris, and Carpenter that true art was not a commodity but formed an integral element in personal and social wellbeing. For if art and lifestyle were indeed one, then the smallholder, dressed in floppy hat, woollen shirt, knickerbockers, and sandals, was making an artistic 'statement', quite as much as Oscar Wilde had earlier done when sporting his green carnation.

Rural nostalgia, however, did more than encourage particular patterns of living. It also influenced artistic design and subject matter, most obviously in Helen Allingham's pretty-pretty watercolours of country cottages, in Kate Greenaway's drawings featuring 'demure country maids in bonnets and bows, set in neat gardens or rustic interiors',[118] and in the iconography of the illustrator Walter Crane. Books poured off the printing presses singing the praises of rural England, its landscapes and its peoples, of which Edward Thomas's *The South Country* (1908) is perhaps the most sensitive. Amateur naturalists quietly furthered the cult, as can be seen from Edith Holden's *Country Diary of an Edwardian Lady*, while the members of photography clubs set off from the cities to capture charming village scenes for posterity: for example, the Photographic Survey of Warwickshire, 'Shakespeare-Land'. The rural revival influenced creative writers in a more indirect way. A. E. Housman, a Cambridge classics don, wrote 'pseudo-folk ballads set in a mythical Shropshire countryside'.[119] And on the eve of the Great War the 'Georgians' were turning out countless 'poems about country cottages, old furniture, moss-covered barns, rose-scented lanes, apple and cherry orchards, village inns, and village cricket', poems which soon made a powerful nostalgic appeal to soldiers on active service.[120]

Pastoralism also gave rise to the romanticization of the life of the gypsy and the traveller. George Borrow's books *Lavengro* (1851) and *The Romany Rye*

[117] These developments date back to the 1890s (D. Hardy and C. Ward, *Arcadias for All: The Legacy of a Makeshift Landscape* (London and New York, 1984), 194–5).

[118] Marsh, *Back to the Land*, 143–4.

[119] W. Mellers and R. Hildyard, 'The Edwardian Age and the Inter-War Years', in Ford (ed.), *Guide to Arts*, 16.

[120] J. Reeves (ed.), *Georgian Poetry* (London, 1962), p. xv.

(1857), little noticed when they initially appeared, only caught on in the late Victorian and Edwardian periods. But Robert Louis Stevenson's *Songs of Travel* (1893) enjoyed almost instant popularity, being set to music by Vaughan Williams (first performed in 1904) and generously anthologized in E. V. Lucas's *The Open Road* of 1899, 'a garland of good or enkindling poetry and prose fitted to urge folk into the open air', which by 1922 had gone into its thirty-first edition.[121] Another contribution to the genre was W. H. Davies's *Autobiography of a Super-Tramp* of 1908. Davies's fellow Georgian, John Masefield, was meanwhile providing a nautical version of Stevenson's travel verses in his well-known poem 'Sea Fever'—yet another hymn of praise to the ecstasy which human beings could experience when in naked contact with the elemental forces of nature.

In the case of some writers, Nature-worship merged into a mystical pantheism. For example, E. M. Forster and his friend Goldworthy Lowes Dickinson promulgated a kind of Hellenic paganism, intimating that, among the trees and meadows, there still lurked the Great God Pan—clearly visible to those sufficiently clear-sighted. On the eve of the war the young Cambridge coterie the 'New-Pagans', which included Rupert Brooke, also subscribed to this sort of vision. Another of its manifestations was the anthropomorphism which shaped so much of the children's literature of the age, notably Kenneth Grahame's *Wind in the Willows* (1908) and the tales of Beatrix Potter (the first, *Peter Rabbit*, published in 1901), works which from the start gave as much delight to adults as to the young.[122]

At a more practical level, 'rural nostalgia' gave rise to three significant cultural developments: 'conservationism', the 'arts and crafts' movement, and a changed attitude to architectural design.

During the closing decades of the nineteenth century conservation organizations proliferated. The Society for the Protection of Ancient Buildings (SPAB) came into existence in 1877, the National Footpaths Preservation Society in 1884. Most famous of them all, the National Trust for Places of Historical Interest and Natural Beauty, to give the body its full name, was established in 1895, primarily to buy up scenic landscapes threatened by developers—rather than to purchase historic aristocratic houses, as it increasingly did after the Great War.[123] Before 1914 'conservationism' enjoyed little prestige. Nevertheless, the National Trust made a number of significant acquisitions, among them a stretch of the Lake District much cherished by Ruskin,

---

[121] M. A. Crowther, 'The Tramp', in Porter (ed.), *Myths*, 107.

[122] Rupert Brooke claimed to have seen Barrie's *Peter Pan*, his favourite play, no fewer than ten times (C. D. Eby, *The Road to Armaggedon: The Martial Spirit in English Popular Literature, 1870–1914* (Durham, NC, 1987), 213).

[123] Offer, *Property and Politics*, 339–40; Marsh, *Back to the Land*, 58.

while the SPAB fought doughtily to get access for the general public to the Stonehenge site.[124]

These developments were paralleled by attempts to preserve, revive—and even invent!—dying folk customs. Richard Jefferies had earlier initiated the vogue for books devoted to country lore. His example was followed by the naturalist W. H. Hudson, the founder in 1897 of the magazine *Country Life*, with his best-known work, *A Shepherd's Life* (1905). George Sturt, a wheel-wright from the small Kentish market town of Faversham, writing under the nom de plume of 'George Bourne', sought, in *Change in the Village* (1912) and *The Wheelwright's Shop* (1923), to record the rhythms of speech and traditional wisdom of his neighbours before they were irrevocably destroyed by urban encroachment.

The folk song and folk dance revival, presided over by Sharp and Mary Neal, reveals with great clarity what these amateur rural anthropologists hoped to achieve. In Sharp's view, the old men and women whose songs he was transcribing were the remnants of an ancient 'peasantry', which still clung to a music which was 'transparently pure and truthful, simple and direct in its utterance', and free from 'the taint of manufacture, the canker of artificiality'.[125] Its preservation, like the revival of maypole dancing, excited the folklorists because it seemed to be opening a door 'into a new country, which is yet as old as Merrie England'.[126]

Reviving the old village crafts also proved an exciting challenge. The Peasant Arts Society, founded in 1898, established itself in Haslemere, where it trained local girls in traditional craft skills (such as lacemaking), followed by tea and folk songs and dances (Sharp was a paid-up supporter).[127] Its most successful venture was the creation of a homespun weaving industry (later relocated in Letchworth). As in contemporary Ireland, the cult of the peasant, advanced by bodies such as the Peasant Arts Fellowship, which held its first meeting in London in February 1912, served a variety of contradictory causes. To an eccentric democratic Radical such as G. K. Chesterton (and also to the Hammonds), it meant liberating the common people from bondage to their aristocratic oppressors. To Sharp, by contrast, it offered a reassuring message of social harmony in a turbulent world, since, as he explained, 'the culture of the Folk was a heritage common to all—it was the product of the race, not of the working class'.[128] Finally, Kipling's 'Hobden the Hedger' and Edward Thomas's 'Lob' symbolized historical continuity and

---

[124] See Marsh, *Back to the Land*, 53.
[125] Ibid. 79.
[126] Boyes, *Imagined Village*, 63.
[127] Marsh, *Back to the Land*, 167.
[128] Boyes, *Imagined Village*, 36.

also an outlook on life refreshingly free from the taint of modern 'consumerist' values.

The folk revival had much in common with the Arts and Crafts Movement: both admired William Morris and desired to escape machine production. But the latter's membership was more restricted, consisting largely of professional architects and designers who hoped to earn their liveilihood in more satisfying ways, while at the same time revolutionizing society. Arthur Mackmurdo's Century Guild, dating from 1882, was the first of several such ventures.[129] Most notable of them all was the Guild and School of Handicraft, founded in 1888 by London artist-craftsmen who went on to acquire premises in White-chapel, where a variety of traditional crafts were practised. In 1902 its dominating figure, the architect C. R. Ashbee, a former Toynbee Hall resident who had been greatly influenced by Carpenter, took the bold decision to move out of London into the small Gloucestershire town of Chipping Campden, where the craftsmen acquired premises in a disused silk mill.[130] In 1908 the Guild went into liquidation, but re-emerged as a trust which, supported by a small-holding, aimed at 'the encouragement of Craftsmanship in conjunction with Husbandry, with a view to enabling Craftsmen and their families to live a healthier and more reasonable life in the country'.[131] Meanwhile, to the south, Gimson and the Barnsleys continued to oversee the production, at Kenton & Co., of honest, handmade furniture, designed so as to be both severely functional and 'true' to the materials out of which it was constructed.

Unfortunately, however beautiful they might be, the guildsmen's handmade pottery, furniture, and metalwork stood no chance of displacing factory goods, which were much cheaper. Moreover, as Ashbee later admitted, his own group's move from London to the Cotswolds was probably a mistake, since, although costs of production were lower there, the craftsmen were turning their back on their consumers, mainly urban connoisseurs with the money to indulge their 'good taste'. Another difficulty lay in the 'unfair' competition which these professional craftsmen soon came under from (to use Ashbee's term) 'dear Emily'—that is, from amateur ladies who had profited only too well from the classes run by institutions such as Lethaby's Central School of Arts and Crafts, founded in 1896. Worse still, many commercial firms, such as Liberty's, began turning out, by mechanical means, cheaper imitations of the products being created in the craft workshops. Between 1908 and 1911 even Ashbee, partly under the influence of the American architect Frank Lloyd

---

[129] e.g. the Arts and Crafts Exhibition Society, founded in 1886, which gave the movement its name, and the Birmingham Guild of Handicrafts (1895).

[130] Since the Guild was run on co-operative lines, the move had to be agreed to on a show of hands.

[131] Marsh, *Back to the Land*, 150.

Wright, came to acknowledge that machinery was here to stay and could, imaginatively employed, create objects of beauty.[132]

Yet, despite its commercial failure, the Arts and Crafts Movement did succeed in instituting something of a revolution in design by popularizing new decorative styles—lighter, clearer, simpler, more 'natural' in appearance and feel than most earlier commercial wares. Just as 'rational dress' was a healthy reaction against the heaviness and pomposity of the conventional clothing under which many women had long been smothered, so something similar was happening across the entire field of the applied arts—and also in architecture.

In fact, as John Betjeman has noted, turn-of-the-century English architecture presented two quite contrasting styles. On the one hand there was 'Edwardian Baroque', a mélange of historical idioms, marked by formal grandiloquence and brash ostentation. In the hands of Norman Shaw, most of whose work pre-dated 1890, this style had given rise to noble buildings such as New Scotland Yard (1888). But by the start of the new century it had become somewhat coarsened and debased. Aston Webb typified 'Edwardian Baroque', with such edifices as the Admiralty Arch, the Royal Naval College, Dartmouth, Birmingham University, the Victoria Memorial, and the refronting of Buckingham Palace. Perhaps its most extreme manifestation was the vast, domed Ashton Memorial at Lancaster of 1906 (designed by John Belcher and J. J. Joass), which the wealthy lineoleum manufacturer Lord Ashton erected in honour of his late wife.

Many younger architects, influenced by Philip Webb, a socialist and friend of William Morris, would have no truck with such pomposity. This group, which included C. F. A. Voysey, W. R. Lethaby, and M. H. Baillie Scott, mainly designed small-scale, suburban houses for the professional man of taste, or simple country residences, based upon traditional farmhouses and cottages—buildings, in other words, which, by using local materials, 'sought to blend into, rather than dominate, the landscape'.[133] This architectural style was often accompanied by the vogue for 'wild' gardens, in lieu of the regimented beds of geraniums and suchlike which an earlier generation had admired.[134]

Admittedly, the greatest architect of the age, Sir Edwin Lutyens, was at home with both these styles. The monumental grandeur of New Delhi and,

[132] G. Naylor, *The Arts and Crafts Movement: A Study of its Sources, Ideals and Influence on Design Theory* (London, 1971), 170–7. Compare his Morrisonian *Craftsmanship and Competitive Industry* (1908) with *Should We Stop Teaching Art?* (1911).

[133] M. J. Wiener, *English Culture and the Decline of the Industrial Spirit 1850–1980* (Cambridge, 1981: 1982 edn.), 66.

[134] As espoused by William Robinson, author of *The Wild Garden* (1870) and *The English Flower Garden* (1883). Among the garden designers who favoured this style was Gertrude Jeykll.

later, of the Cenotaph shows him the master of the grand manner, while his delicate country houses, such as Heathcote, Ilkley, fit squarely within the alternative tradition of unpretentious rusticity.

But it was the small-scale, 'cottagey' style to which the town planners turned in the early twentieth century when they created Letchworth, the first of England's garden cities. Its inspirer was Ebenezer Howard, with his visionary concept of a marriage between town and country, combining the finest qualities of each, a vision outlined in his influential book *Tomorrow: A Peaceful Path to Real Reform* (1898), reissued three years later as *Garden Cities of Tomorrow*. Letchworth's organization and financing have already been described.[135] As models, Howard was greatly influenced by earlier housing developments such as Port Sunlight (1888) and especially Bourneville (1895), with its planned environment and the provision of gardens in which tenants could grow their own vegetables.[136] Letchworth incorporated many of the ideals and practices associated with the cult of the 'simple life'. The consultant architects were Raymond Unwin, a former member of Morris's Socialist League, and Barry Parker, a Fabian adherent of the Arts and Crafts Movement. They opted for a vernacular style which allowed for a mix of housing types, while avoiding expensive, pompous dwellings on the one hand, and cheap, skimpy accommodation on the other. Unwin and Parker, following Howard's general ground-plan, also favoured low housing density, which enabled land to be generously allocated for the purposes of gardening and working a smallholding, to which the planners attributed quasi-mystical powers. Letchworth was soon exercising an influence far and wide, partly through Unwin's own writings, *Town Planning in Practice* (1909) and *Nothing Gained by Overcrowding!* (1912). Many of its features were subsequently replicated—initially in Hampstead Garden Suburb, to which Unwin largely transferred his attention in 1906—and, later still, in countless inter-war private housing developments, as well as in France.

When Edward Carpenter visited Letchworth Garden City, he must have found much to please him. The residents on three occasions voted to stay loyal to their much-mocked teetotal pub, the Skittles Inn, so called after the skittles alley which was one of its social amenities. There was a Food Reform Restaurant and a Simple Life Hotel to cater for vegetarian visitors. Other well-established appurtenances of the simple life followed. The arrival in the town of Carpenter's old friend from Millthorpe, George Adams, meant that a heavy demand for home-made sandals could readily be met. Many other handicrafts also flourished: the Letchworth Morris Men achieved national fame, the local

[135] See Chs. 3, 11.
[136] S. Meacham, *Regaining Paradise: Englishness and the Early Garden City Movement* (New Haven and London, 1999).

school had country dancing on its PT timetable, and there was a community centre for practitioners of the New Life, 'Cloister Garth', where residents, many of them followers of the Tolstoyan guru John Bruce Wallace, slept in hammocks in a roofed room otherwise open to the elements.[137]

And yet Letchworth Garden City never came anywhere close to achieving self-sufficiency. Howard had originally envisaged a population of up to 32,000 inhabitants on a 6,000-acre site, but by 1914 its numbers had only reached 9,000, and the town was only saved by London's northwards expansion during the war. Even in its early days many residents were commuting daily to London, thanks to a good rail service. Some firms from elsewhere, it is true, relocated to Letchworth, including Dent the publishers and W. H. Smith's binding department, but ironically, one of the largest sources of employment in this Mecca of the simple lifers was the Spirella Company Ltd., makers of 'High Grade Corsets', a British subsidiary of an American company—though a firm with a justified reputation for employer benevolence.[138]

Letchworth generated affection among most of its residents, who found it a pleasant place in which to live,[139] but to those who yearned after a completely new way of life (a total breach with urban civilization, no less) it was obviously a disappointment. As for its immediate successor, Hampstead Garden Suburb, this was avowedly nothing more than an appendage to the 'Great Wen'. The quest for the simple life nonetheless changed British society, though not by reviving rural England nor by encouraging a significant drift back to the land. Indeed, why should it have done so? It was never self-evident that handicrafts such as luxury bookbinding and printing or metalwork required a rustic setting for their revival, nor did all the craftsmen themselves think so—whereas Gimson had a deep affection for the actual countryside, Ashbee was more in love with it as an idea.[140]

Nor did one have to set out into rural England in order to enjoy the comfort of loose-fitting, informal dress, or to adopt a new dietary regime. In fact by 1894 there were as many as fourteen vegetarian restaurants in London alone, and another five in Manchester, to say nothing of numerous vegetarian guest-houses and food stores. Growing consumer demand even provided the spur to the invention of a new meatless gravy based upon yeast-extract, 'Marmite', which was launched by the Marmite Food Company in a disused malthouse at

---

[137] Marsh, *Back to the Land*, 233, 238; Meacham, *Paradise*, ch. 6.

[138] Marsh, *Back to the Land*, 234.

[139] However, some working-class residents defiantly disclaimed all 'pretence to intellectual culture' and the social veneer that went with it, and the alcohol ban led to a regular Saturday night exodus to the public houses of nearby Hitchin (Meacham, *Paradise*, 135–7).

[140] M. Greensted, *The Arts and Crafts Movement in the Cotswolds* (Stroud, 1996), 55.

Burton-on-Trent in 1902—to the approval of the Vegetarian Society.[141] A commercialized capitalism thus adapted itself to at least *some* facets of the lifestyle of the artistic rebels, though many of the latter would have construed this as abject defeat, not as a qualified victory.

Meanwhile the Morrisonian vision lived on through the activities of the Guild Socialists, a society founded in 1904 by A. J. Penty, whose creed was most clearly formulated in the writings of Father J. N. Figgis, who advocated a pluralistic association of groups, each, like a medieval guild, with its own privileges and responsibilities, encompassed within an organic corporate state. Drawing upon Ecclesiasticus (38: 39) for their motto ('They shall maintain the fabric of the world, and in the handiwork of their craft is their prayer'), the Guild Socialists carried through into the inter-war years what was a quintessentially Edwardian search for a spiritual synthesis between artistic creativity and human fellowship.[142]

6. CONCLUSION

Cultural life in late Victorian and Edwardian England did not follow a single trajectory. Its vibrancy, rather, stemmed from the jarring of contradictory impulses. Some artists, in their approach to their public, preached that art lay within the grasp of Everyman; others went out of their way to make their work so difficult that it could be appreciated only by a small minority. Some rejoiced in urban living, the artificiality of which they saw as mirroring art itself; others denounced the city as an abomination and presented the country-side as a veritable Arcadia. Some proclaimed that they were serving the cause of an English national revival; others dismissed patriotism as insularity and proclaimed their allegiance to an international brotherhood. Even within the same author the commitment to 'efficiency'[143] often jostled with a spirit of levity and a love of 'fun'. And in all the arts, a delight in swagger, in heavily upholstered luxury, and in flamboyant spectacle confronted the cult of natural-ness and simplicity: Aston Webb versus Voysey, Elgar versus Vaughan Williams, Beerbohm Tree versus Gordon Craig, and so on.

If there be a unifying theme in late Victorian and Edwardian culture it is the pursuit of 'many-sidedness'. In the vacuum left by the decay of orthodox Christian belief, artists reached out for a vision of the world which would, they hoped, reunite its seeming opposites by harmonizing body and soul, work

---

[141] Marsh, *Back to the Land*, 199–200. The process of using the yeast that is a by-product of the brewing industry owed its origin to the German chemist, Justus Liebig. Marmite, rich in B vitamins, was later found to have dietary merits (e.g. as an antidote to beriberi).

[142] Rose, *Edwardian Temperament*, 60–1.

[143] See Ch. 16.

and play. Although their 'solutions' differed radically, they could at least agree over the necessity of reconciling the outer and the inner life, thereby restoring harmony and integrity to human existence.[144] A similar impulse is discernible in contemporary science and learning.

[144] Rose, *Edwardian Temperament*, 201–7.

CHAPTER 16

Science and Learning

1. THE AGE OF DISCOVERY

In few periods has technology so dramatically altered people's lives as between 1886 and 1914. Evidence of change was visible in the homes and streets of every English community. In the mid-1880s the carriage of persons and goods across urban areas was still taking place almost entirely on foot or by horse. Gottlieb Daimler's invention in 1885 of the internal combustion engine soon put an end to that.[1] In 1914 the unmistakable odour of horse-dung was still impregnating the atmosphere: in fact, the number of working horses had probably reached its peak of 3,500,000 in 1902. But the future of transport clearly lay with the new machines that were crowding the streets of all the big cities. Yet this development formed only part of a much wider transport revolution.

Britain's merchant marine had embarked on the transition from sail to steam during the 1860s, but her foreign trading partners were slower off the mark. Only 21.4 per cent of all boats entering and clearing British ports in 1886 possessed their own engines. The 1890s marked the decisive turning-point. By the end of the century steam vessels accounted for over nine-tenths of all registered tonnage.

Moreover, marine steam transport was itself changing. In 1884 the British engineer Charles Parsons developed the first efficient steam turbine, which, after 1897, began to replace the reciprocating engine on steam-driven vessels.[2] Equipped with these new engines, the Dreadnought battleships, first launched in 1906, could cruise at 21 knots. The passenger liner *Mauretania*, which made her maiden voyage the following year, was powered in a similar way, enabling her to cross the Atlantic in a mere five days at speeds often exceeding $24\frac{1}{2}$ knots—compared with the upper cruising limit of 17 knots which was all that

---

[1] See Ch. 3.

[2] The first ship to be fitted, a small boat called the *Turbinia*, raced through the assembled fleet at Spithead in 1897, demonstrating its superior speed (T. Coleman, *The Liners: A History of the North Atlantic Crossing* (London, 1976), 57).

the fastest ship in the Cunard fleet could achieve in 1882. Technology was also taking mankind into realms hitherto unexplored. Between 1898 and 1905 Royal Navy shipyards were building submarines—useless for ordinary transportation, but a formidable new weapon of war. The conquest of the strange world beneath the ocean was quickly followed by the even more remarkable conquest of the air, first by airships and then by aeroplanes.[3]

The resulting shrinkage of the world was further advanced by amazing inventions which permitted people to communicate with one another over great distances. By the 1880s the British people had long been familiar with the telegraph. But a new device now pressed itself on their attention: the telephone, patented and demonstrated in Philadelphia in 1876 by the Edinburgh-born American, Alexander Graham Bell. In 1880 the Post Office created the United Telephone Company to integrate Bell's system with that of his rival, Thomas Edison (another American), and by the end of the century, with the spread of 'stations' (as the early exchanges were called), two-way communication between cities became possible: London was linked to Birmingham in 1890.

Equally miraculous seemed to be the transmission of messages by radio waves. The 'wireless', in a recognizably modern form, dates back to Heinrich Hertz's demonstration of 1887, when a long-distance message was broadcast, by morse code, using a spark generator which had then to be received by a 'coherer'. Several British scientists, including the physicist Oliver Lodge, helped develop the new technology. Then, in 1896, the Italian inventor Guglielmo Marconi, rebuffed by the Italian government, brought his experimental apparatus to England where, later that year, aged only 22, he took out his first patent. In 1900 the Marconi Wireless Telegraph and Signal Company (renamed Marconi's Wireless and Telegraph Company later in the year) was floated with a capital of £100,000. The efficacy of Marconi's system became apparent in 1901, when a message was successfully transmitted across the Atlantic, from Newfoundland to Cornwall. Progress accelerated after 1904, when John Ambrose Fleming invented the thermionic valve to replace the clumsy 'coherer'.

Few understood initially what these new gadgets portended. Why install telephones to relay messages, some asked, when a good postal and telegraph service already existed and when messenger boys could be hired so cheaply? It was widely believed that the telephone was little more than an amusing toy, one that would enable people to listen to a play, an opera, or a concert from the comfort of their own homes! However, by the turn of the century most large public offices and commercial establishments (though not the Bank of England)

[3] See Ch. 13 and below.

had installed a telephone, as had some adventurous wealthy householders. The number of subscribers rose from 45,000 (0.12 per cent of the population) in 1890 to 210,000 (4.51 per cent) ten years later, before doubling again by 1905.[4]

The wireless almost immediately established its credentials. Though the Post Office initially showed little comprehension of its potentialities, the Admiralty, which had for several years been looking for an efficient system of offshore communication, quickly took it up: radio sets were put through an experimental trial in the 1899 naval spring manoeuvres. The wider public later realized wireless's importance after its use, in spectacular circumstances, to catch the murderer Crippen when he tried to escape to America in 1910, and again, two years later, when the doomed *Titanic* was able to alert other ships to her plight. By 1914 Jellicoe's Grand Fleet had become reliant for its system of central command upon radio transmission—likewise the country's embryonic air defences. The wireless's future as a public entertainment medium, however, was still not widely foreseen.[5]

These technological changes heralded the beginning of the end of the Carboniferous Age, when coal dominated the industrialized world. The railways still relied totally upon coal, and so, before 1912, did the British navy. But thereafter, in stages, the turbine engines of its great battleships were converted to oil, a fuel which had been adopted a year earlier for many submarines and destroyers. In initiating this development the Admiralty was taking something of a gamble. Britain possessed coal reserves aplenty, but had to look abroad for the new fuel. However, the risks were thought to be worth taking: oil increased the fleet's radius of action by 40 per cent for the same weight of coal, and allowed battleships to travel at 24 rather than 21 knots—a decisive advantage.

Another break with the dominance of coal came with the invention of the internal combustion engine, which ran on a refined petroleum called 'petrol' (a new word, borrowed from the French *pétrole*). Then, a decade later in 1897, the German inventor Rudolph Diesel devised the compression-ignition engine which bears his name: after 1910 such engines began to be installed in ships, soon proving their worth in submarines. (Diesel-powered lorries did not make an appearance until the early 1920s.) Electricity, too, was harnessed to traction: many urban tramway systems and London's underground railway underwent electrification during the 1890s.[6]

In fact, the most important single development of the 1880s was arguably the bulk generation of electricity. By the end of that decade there had sprung up

---

[4] A. Briggs, *Victorian Things* (London, 1988), 388.

[5] Another of Edison's inventions of the late 1870s, the phonograph (in 1887 renamed the gramophone), was also misunderstood, being seen as, essentially, an educational medium and as a mechanism for recording 'historic' speeches or public events, not as a way of transmitting music.

[6] See Ch. 3.

massive power stations driven by Parsons's steam turbines, many of them established by the American-owned Westinghouse Company, based at King's Cross in London.[7] Progress was not as swift in Britain as in the United States, partly because so many firms and muncipalities had earlier invested heavily in gas plants. Nevertheless, electric lighting soon became commonplace—thanks to the invention of an effective light-bulb made from carbon filaments. In 1881 its two main inventors, Edison and his rival, the English chemist Joseph Wilson Swan, combined to form the Edison and Swan Electric Light Company, and commercial expansion rapidly followed. By the end of the century many towns had electric street lighting. Electrical illumination was also shedding a new kind of glamour (very different from the old gas flares) over theatres and shop-window displays. During the 1890s Blackpool exploited the new technology by constructing its brightly lit promenade, Gigantic Wheel, and Tower.

Electric lifts, a popular feature of the big department stores, found their way into the palatial residences of the very wealthy, such as 'Cragside', the newly designed country house of Sir William Armstrong, the great armaments manufacturer.[8] Sebastian de Ferranti, the inventor of the alternator, went further, installing a thermostatically controlled central heating system in his Derbyshire home. The transatlantic liners, very much in the forefront of technological advance, quickly followed suit: the *Campania*, launched in 1893, was fitted with electric light throughout, and that great floating hotel the *Titanic* had electric lifts.

The widespread *domestic* utilization of electricity, however, still lay at some distance in the future. Most homes before 1914 were still being lit either by paraffin lamps or by gas—following the 1885 design of an effective incandescent mantle. Gas fires could be bought, but heating still derived overwhelmingly from coal. (Electric fires were being installed in some well-to-do homes, but as late as 1912 an advertisement still felt it necessary to warn their owners not to 'use a poker' on the appliance!)[9] As for cooking, a lively debate developed after 1890 over the respective merits of the coal-fired range and the gas-stove: the latter, though efficient in many respects, was unfortunately liable to explode. In 1908 the American James Spangler, using one of his wife's pillows as a dustbag, invented the electrically driven vacuum cleaner, selling his patent soon afterwards to the Hoover Company. But before 1914 the plentiful supply of domestic servants largely obviated the need for such labour-saving appli-

---

[7] However, Edison designed the first central electric power-station in England, at Holborn.

[8] In 1880 he had set another trend by installing 'Swan' lights (M. Girouard, *The Victorian Country House* (New Haven and London, 1979), 306–7).

[9] H. C. Long, *The Edwardian House: The Middle-Class Home in Britain 1880–1914* (London, 1993), 100.

ances, nor had the small electric motor yet been brought to perfection. House-wives had to wait at least until the 1920s before they could savour the delights of domestic refrigerators and of electrically powered washing machines,[10] dish-washers, and cookers.

The *industrial* applications of electricity, on the other hand, proceeded more quickly. Electrical power was installed in some of the larger mills during the 1890s and in the light manufacturing industries, and by 1910 the enterprising Britannia Colliery at Monmouth was employing electricity for ventilation, pumping, lighting, and coal-cutting. Moreover, as well as being an important new industry in its own right, electricity soon spawned many others. For example, after 1886 modern electrolytic methods were used in the extraction of aluminium (a metal essential to the production of automobiles and aircraft), as well as in the refining of magnesium, sodium, zinc, and nickel. This brought into existence a new branch of manufacturing industry, electro-chemicals.

Chemicals comprised the other main component in what is sometimes called the Second Industrial Revolution. Laboratory-based science gave rise between 1880 and 1914 to the discovery of a wide range of new, or vastly improved, chemical products: synthetic drugs such as aspirin, artificial fertilizers, viscose (a man-made fibre of the kind later called 'rayon'), and various plastics, notably celluloid (used for shirt collars and for film[11]), and bakelite, patented by the American Leo Baekeland in 1908.

2. TECHNOLOGY AND SCIENCE

Such technological innovation often originated with 'ingenious mechanics', following up their ideas privately or in the workshops that employed them. For example, the revolutionary advances in naval construction presided over by Admiral Fisher were hatched in the minds of engineers who possessed consid-erable 'hands-on' experience, but not necessarily any specialized scientific qualifications. Many of the pioneers of the aeronautical industry, too, emerged from the frenzy of activity surrounding the cycle boom of the 1890s.[12] (The Wright brothers themselves had once run a sales-and-repair cycle shop, an experience which gave them a close familiarity with the operation of spoked wheels and gears.) After the invention of a workable internal combustion engine, many small British firms making bicycles (Morris, Austin, Triumph, Swift, Sunbeam) moved into the manufacture, first of 'motor bikes', and then of automobiles, or 'motor vellocipedes' as they were sometimes called. From

---

[10] The pre-1914 machines were operated by hand.

[11] A. R. Ubbelohde, 'Science', in S. Nowell-Smith (ed.), *Edwardian England, 1901–1914* (Oxford, 1964), 244. Plastics were also necessary for insulating electrical wires.

[12] Following John Boyd Dunlop's development of the pneumatic rubber tyre in 1888.

there it was but a short step to the construction of aero-engines and aircraft, a transition made by, among many others, John Siddeley, who supplied engines to the Royal Flying Corps and later to the RAF during the Great War.

R. B. Haldane was sniffy about the likes of Wilbur Wright, who had not studied science at an advanced level and possessed only a smattering of mathematics.[13] But practical mechanics achieved far more for aeronautics, at least in the short run, than did the government's own committee of university-based scientific experts (headed by the esteemed Lord Rayleigh).

At the other end of the spectrum to the practical engineer stood amateur-gentlemen (many of them clergymen), in a tradition that stretched back to the foundation of the Royal Society in the late seventeenth century. The Penzance Natural History and Antiquarian Society, established in 1839, was thriving during the Edwardian years: evidence that the older kind of 'natural philosophy' was still flourishing in some localities at the end of the nineteenth century.

Despite his hostility to clerical pretensions, even the 'inventor' of eugenics Francis Galton, Darwin's cousin, can be said to have emerged from this world. Not only did he largely fund his investigations from his own private means, but he was also able, in the course of a long life, to make important contributions across a wide range of the human and physical sciences—biology, psychology, meteorology, fingerprinting, statistics, comparative anthropology, and much else besides.

The continued existence of polymaths such as Galton meant that, in the late Victorian period, the natural sciences still had not become so specialized as to be inaccessible to the intelligent layperson. True, most statesmen and politicians had received a classics-dominated education which acted as a barrier to their understanding of contemporary science, but there were several notable exceptions to this rule. Lord Salisbury, for example, installed a private laboratory in Hatfield House, where he carried out intrepid experiments in chemistry that often terrified his family and guests! Salisbury's nephew Balfour, whose bent was for theoretical disquisition rather than empirical investigation, took an even better-informed interest in contemporary science. Significantly, his younger brother Frank was an eminent comparative embryologist, and his sister's husband, Lord Rayleigh, was the Cavendish Professor, a Nobel Prize winner, and the discoverer (in 1895) of the gas Argon; yet Rayleigh once declared that he was severely tested in scientific discussion with his political brother-in-law. Similarly Haldane, whose brother 'Johnny'[14] was a distinguished physiologist, could converse learnedly on advanced scientific topics.

[13] R. Wohl, *A Passion for Wings: Aviation and the Western Imagination, 1908–1918* (New Haven and London, 1994), 10. Wright's experiments with gliders led him to the discovery of 'wing warping' in 1900—necessary for the stability of flight—and in 1903 he added a propeller.

[14] John Scott Haldane, father of the controversial inter-war biologist J. B. S. Haldane.

Nor are these isolated cases. Significantly, only 28 per cent of the members of the Royal Society in 1881 held a university post, another 13 per cent being applied scientists; all the rest (59 per cent) were 'friends' of science or wealthy amateur practitioners of one sort or another.[15]

Yet the closing decades of the nineteenth century did see the start of scientific research in a recognizably modern form: that is to say, group research, based upon laboratory or controlled field experiments, undertaken by professional investigators working for scientific institutes or university departments. This development was far advanced in Germany, especially in chemistry, where university staff often enjoyed close links with the commercial companies that subsidized them. In medicine, too, German laboratory-based science was firmly established, leading to a series of important advances. For example, in 1895 Wilhelm Röntgen, Professor of Physics at Würzburg University, discovered X-rays—or Röntgen rays, as they were first known—and in 1910 Paul Ehrlich successfully synthesized 'salvarsan 606', a chemotherapeutic drug that offered a cure for syphilis. By contrast, Britain's own greatest contribution to medical knowledge during this period resulted from painstaking empirical fieldwork of a traditional kind, carried out in a colonial setting: Sir Ronald Ross's identification of the mosquito as the source of malaria.

But in Britain, too, the links between advanced research methods and applied science were drawing closer. Thus Charles Parsons, the inventor of the turbine, had studied science at Trinity College Dublin and at St John's College, Cambridge, while Osborne Reynolds, the inventor of an effective turbine pump, patented in 1887, held the chair of civil engineering at the Victoria University of Manchester, where the famous Whitworth Engineering Laboratory was housed from 1885 onwards. Pioneers of the radio industry, such as Marconi, were also 'hybrids', though of a different kind—being neither practical electrical engineers nor university-educated scientists. Nevertheless, Marconi would not have made such progress but for his co-operation with Ambrose Fleming, the Professor of Electrical Technology at University College, London, who served as his company's scientific adviser. Finally, though privately funded R&D was comparatively rare in Britain before the Great War, it was not unknown: for example, in 1900 Brunner-Mond's United Alkali Company created one of the country's first sophisticated laboratories for analytical chemistry.[16]

Both applied and pure scientists were meanwhile beginning to group themselves into something resembling a professional occupation: by 1914 the

---

[15] Ubbelohde, 'Science', 223.

[16] In 1894 Alfred Mond also made a lavish donation in support of the Davy–Faraday Laboratory for physical chemistry at the Royal Institute (R. Macleod, 'Resources of Science in Victorian England', in P. Mathias (ed.), *Science and Society*, (London, 1974), 160–1).

proportion of the Fellows of the Royal Society who earned their living from science, as academics or as applied scientists, had risen to 78 per cent, compared with 41 per cent in 1881. Conversely, the percentage of Anglican clergymen within the membership steadily fell from almost 10 per cent in mid-century to little over 3 per cent by 1899, as 'men of science', eager to establish their professional autonomy, pushed the gentlemen-naturalists to the sidelines, often employing a sharply anticlerical rhetoric as they did so.[17]

This process of professionalization particularly affected the biological sciences. Operating in a milieu very different from that of the young Galton, British biologists in the early 1900s were investigating the laws of particulate inheritance (opened up by the rediscovery in 1899 of the Abbé Mendel's work) through controlled experiments, whose results were then communicated to scientists across the world through specialized journals and academic conferences. William Bateson, author of *Mendel's Principles of Heredity* (1909), coined the word 'genetics' to describe this new scientific discipline. In 1908 Cambridge University created for him a new Chair of Biology, which a little more than a year later he vacated for the directorship of the John Innes Horticultural Institute at Merton Park—soon to achieve fame for its large-scale plant-breeding programmes. Bateson realized that these experiments would in time (though not as quickly as most eugenists believed) lead to the unlocking of the mysteries of human genetic makeup.

Of equal long-term significance to the human race was the scientific research being conducted in Cambridge University's Cavendish Laboratory, under Professor J. J. Thomson, its Professor of Experimental Physics, famous for his discovery of the electron. Building upon the earlier work of Henri Bequerel and of the Curies (who had discovered radiation in 1900), Thomson and his pupils were among the leading pioneers of nuclear physics (as well as of electronics). A defining moment came in 1902, when the New Zealand-born Ernest Rutherford (then at McGill University, Montreal) collaborated with Frederick Soddy (at Glasgow University) to produce the paper in which the theory of the atomic disintegration of matter was first outlined. In 1907 Rutherford returned to England to a post at Manchester University, where he was joined five years later by the great Danish physicist Niels Bohr, before eventually succeeding to Thomson's Cavendish Chair in 1919. Meanwhile Soddy, at Glasgow, was discovering, and naming, isotopes. All this highly theoretical work had enormous practical potential. For, as Sir William Ramsay reminded the British Academy in 1911, the world's existing stores of energy were not unlimited. Might it not eventually

---

[17] F. M. Turner, *Contesting Cultural Authority: Essays in Victorian Intellectual Life* (Cambridge, 1993), 187. Galton, Spencer, and Huxley, for example, were all prepared to challenge head-on the authority of the Church and of Scripture.

prove possible to liberate the stored-up energy in matter so that it could be placed at the service of mankind?

3. BRITAIN'S INTERNATIONAL PERFORMANCE

Even before 1886 ideas were crossing national frontiers, through personal travel and academic interchange as well as via the printed word. Hardly a British organic chemist of any note can be found who did not complete his education in Germany, before returning to pass on to his pupils what he had learnt abroad of modern laboratory-based research. But applied science was also an international project in a more profound sense. Marconi, enticed to these shores by Sir William Preece, Chief Engineer at the Post Office, retained his Italian citizenship and went 'home' to die at Rome, though he had spent most of his working life in England, where his main company was registered.[18] British industry owed much to immigrants: the distinguished chemical manufacturer Ludwig Mond was a German Jew, whose naturalized son Alfred (later the first Baron Melchett) joined up with John Brunner (a scientist of Swiss extraction), to create the largest alkali company in the United Kingdom, at Winnington in Cheshire—the nucleus of what later became ICI. In addition, foreign firms (Siemens, Daimler, Westinghouse, Edison-Bell) established subsidiary companies in Britain, while foreign manufacturing licences were acquired by Britons, as when Sir William Mather, the Manchester-based engineer (part-German educated), acquired the British rights to the Edison dynamo. Committed internationalists rejoiced at such developments: science and technology, they believed, were acting as a force for harmony and co-operation between all the advanced industrial nations. But others pointed to the way in which Germany, behind tariff walls and with patent protection, was building up powerful new science-based industries, upon which the British might later have to depend. Worryingly, some of these industries had great strategic importance.

In two areas of manufacturing in particular, Britain's relative backwardness soon caused alarm bells to ring. The first was motor-car production. During the 1890s French manufacturers such as Peugeot had successfully exploited Daimler's patent, establishing an early lead in the production of high-performance, luxury motor cars. After 1903 the French were overtaken by American manufacturers, who mainly concentrated on volume production—the brand leader being the Ford Motor Company's hugely successful Model T.[19] British firms

---

[18] He also set up a subsidiary company in the USA, thereby unwittingly precipitating the Marconi Scandal: see Ch. 12.
[19] Ford opened a subsidiary at Trafford Park, Manchester, in 1911.

slightly increased their share of an expanding world market during the pre-war decade, thanks to the success of the Wolseley Motor Company and the launch of the 'Morris Oxford' in 1913, but they still lagged behind the French, to say nothing of the Americans—whose production was four times that of all European countries combined. Britain, which had once pioneered the railway, was a net importer of motor cars in 1914. (Most British taxis before 1914 were Renaults.) And this backwardness arguably had a knock-on effect on the related aeroplane industry, which, initially, was as much dominated by French manufacturers such as Voisin, as it was by French aviators—many of whom, Blériot included, were also engineers and designers.

In fairness, Britain's poor performance in automobile and aeroplane construction could hardly be blamed on shoddy design or inadequate technical education.[20] The designer of Britain's first four-wheel petrol-driven car, Frederick Lanchester (trained at Finsbury Technical College), went on to adumbrate the vortex theory of sustenation, the basis of the modern science of aerodynamics.[21] Similarly Rolls-Royce, which became a public company in 1906, quickly established its credentials as a maker of high-quality engines, both for automobiles and for aeroplanes. The Americans, starting off with the crushing advantage of a huge, buoyant home market, pulled ahead of the British in motors, not because of their superior technological inventiveness, but through their ruthless pursuit of modern industrial methods of mass production, involving the interchangeability of parts, a systematic division of labour, and the assembly of standardized components.

In chemicals, on the other hand, there is a much stronger case for the view that inadequate scientific and technical education was responsible for Britain's relative international failure. During the mid-Victorian period it had been a British chemist, W. H. Perkin, who had first extracted an aniline dye from coal tar (the famous mauve), but his discoveries were not exploited by his fellow countrymen and an important new industry was allowed to pass to Germany, from whom the British were purchasing 80–90 per cent of their artificial dyestuffs in 1914. This was a national misfortune, since coal-tar crude formed the basis of many new chemical substances, not merely dyes. One of its by-products, benzene, could be converted into phenol, an ingredient of the drug 'aspirin' that was later developed by the great German chemical firm the Badische Anilin-und-Soda-Fabrik (BASF); another by-product, toluene, was used in the manufacture of the high explosive TNT.

Continental advances in organic chemistry affected Britain's national interests in another important way. The high agricultural yields needed to feed the

---

[20] On the eve of the Great War Bristol University established a chair of Motor-Car Engineering.
[21] H. Driver, *The Birth of Military Aviation: Britain, 1903–1914* (London, 1997), 14–15, 17.

expanding populations of the industrialized European countries required a heavy input of artificial fertilizer. At the start of our period this mainly came in the form of natural nitrates, which had to be imported in bulk from Chile. The German chemist Fritz Haber, realizing the riskiness of such dependence at a time when Britain still controlled the world's sea lanes, led a team which devised a way of fixing nitrates from the atmosphere. The process also permitted the conversion of ammonia (used in fertilizers) into nitric acid, an important ingredient in both high explosives and propellants.[22] After 1905 BASF developed an effective operating process, which by 1914 could turn out 250 tons of nitric acid daily. Britain did not acquire similar plants until after the war.[23]

It was also ominous that, although in chemicals Britain still enjoyed an internationally competitive advantage in some product lines, many of these were located in the technically backward parts of that industry. For example, most British alkali manufacturers (Brunner-Mond being the significant exception) continued to rely on the antiquated Leblanc process for extraction, which in Germany had long been abandoned.

Yet the impression that in science and technology as a whole Britain was failing would be misleading. Through Thomson, Rutherford, and Soddy, Britain played a leading role in theoretical physics; British biologists were similarly to the fore in genetical research. In electrical engineering the Germans had achieved a dominant position, and the Americans may have had the edge in other branches of engineering; but Parsons's turbine was one of the wonders of the age, while in marine design Britain still led the world. Moreover, during the decade before 1914 Marconi, from his base in England, was building up a telecommunication system which quickly eclipsed the Danish Poulsen[24] and the German Telefunken systems, his only serious rivals. It has been calculated that between 1876 and 1900 14.2 per cent of all significant inventions throughout the world were of British origin.[25] This was a not inconsiderable achievement. But was it good enough for a country that aspired to global predominance? Around the turn of the century many Britons thought not. What is more, the pessimists had a ready explanation for what they saw as the country's faltering industrial and commercial performance: the failure to invest adequately in pure and applied science. Germany's work-chemists, it

---

[22] Ubbelohde, 'Science', 233.
[23] Haber was intensely aware of the relationship between science and warfare: he later developed the first of the poison gases used in the Great War.
[24] In 1898 Valdemar Poulsen also invented the magnetic tape, but it was scarcely exploited before 1914.
[25] D. Edgerton, *Science, Technology and the British Economic Decline 1870–1970* (Cambridge, 1996), 65.

was said, outnumbered Britain's roughly in the ratio of three to one, as well as being trained to a much higher level.[26] Did the country have the will to close this gap?

4. THE 'ENDOWMENT OF RESEARCH' MOVEMENT

Warnings about the dangers to the state from the neglect of scientific knowledge were not new. They had first been raised following the 1867 Paris Exhibition, at which British manufacturers won prizes in only ten out of ninety categories of wares. Disappointment at this outcome contributed to the founding two years later of the scientific journal *Nature*, whose editor, the astronomer Norman Lockyer, used it as a weapon in his long campaign for greater public funding for science. The annual meetings of the British Association, hosted each year by a different city, provided another influential public platform for the likes of Lockyer, Henry Roscoe, Lyon Playfair, T. H. Huxley, and Professor E. Ray Lankester. The industrial depression of the 1880s gave an added fillip to the 'endowment of research' movement: the National Association for the Promotion of Technical Education was founded at precisely this time, in 1887, with Huxley launching the new organization with a stirring speech.

In fact, Britain's facilities for imparting scientific and technology instruction, which filled Huxley with such anxiety, had improved significantly since, say, 1870, when they had indeed compared poorly with those in almost every other industrial state. By 1886 there were colleges of science and advanced technology at Manchester (Owens College), Leeds (the Yorkshire College of Science), Sheffield (Firth College), Birmingham (Mason College), and Liverpool (University College), as well as lesser foundations in Southampton, Exeter, Newcastle, Bristol, Nottingham, and Reading.

Nor were the ancient universities unaffected by the demands for more and better science. Oxford University, admittedly, failed to rise adequately to the challenge: it had a reputable record in physiology, zoology, and comparative anatomy, but was weak in physics and did not introduce engineering as a degree subject until 1907–8. Crucially, Oxford's Natural Science School expanded very slowly, with the result that by 1910 little over one-tenth of the University's graduates were scientists, compared with one-third of Cambridge's.[27]

---

[26] 4,500 compared to 1,500–2,000 (Ubbelohde, 'Science', 220).

[27] It has been argued that Oxford 'missed out' by failing to go for growth because of an absence of empire-builders among its science professors (J. Howarth, 'Science Education in Late-Victorian Oxford: A Curious Case of Failure', *English Historical Review*, 102 (1987), 334–67). See also J. Howarth, ' "Oxford for Arts": The Natural Sciences, 1880–1914', in M. G. Brock and M. C. Curthoys (eds.), *The History of the University of Oxford: Volume VII: Nineteenth-Century Oxford, Part 2* (Oxford, 2000), esp. 458–9.

Perhaps because of its traditional strength in mathematics, Cambridge embraced science with positive enthusiasm, 'modernizing' its course offerings and investing heavily in research. Indeed, with the establishment of the Cavendish Laboratory in the early 1870s Cambridge acquired one of the world's greatest research centres in physics. It also built up impressive facilities in other branches of the natural sciences, including chemistry, where one of the professors was Sir James Dewar, inventor of the vacuum flask, quinoline, and cordite.[28]

As a result, by the end of the century Cambridge's Natural Sciences Tripos (founded in 1851) had emerged as the most popular of all the triposes, overtaking its two nearest rivals, Mathematics and Classics. In 1892 Huxley privately conceded that 'a very good scientific education [was] to be had at both Cambridge and Oxford, especially Cambridge now'.[29] Nor was applied science neglected. James Stuart had established laboratory-based engineering at Cambridge as early as 1875, and his successor, Sir Alfred Ewing, launched the Mechanical Sciences Tripos in 1894. Although engineering at Cambridge attracted comparatively few students before 1914, it possessed from the start a highly practical orientation.[30]

How were these innovations funded? Cambridge University, as well as running effective appeals directed at its rich alumni, took good advantage of the terms of the 1877 Oxford and Cambridge Act, which allowed the partial transfer of money held by wealthy colleges for the establishment of new scientific chairs.[31] The local science colleges could not call upon such resources. Instead they were mainly kept afloat, in the early years, by fee income and by grants from sympathizers, most of them local businessmen concerned to effect a closer connection between manufacturing processes and advanced scientific knowledge.[32] Then, in 1889, an important precedent was set when the Treasury initiated a system of grants-in-aid to universities and university colleges (most of the English provincial institutions having attained the latter status).

In fact, the last two decades of the nineteenth century saw a marked expansion of higher education. Statistical returns (if they are to be believed) suggest that between 1881 and 1891 the full-time student population in England rose from 4,950 to 9,463 in the provincial university colleges, and, more modestly,

---

[28] Though he spent most of his time in London, at the Royal Institute.

[29] T. W. Heyck, *The Transformation of Intellectual Life in Victorian England* (London, 1982), 113. Perversely, he sent his own son to Oxford, much the inferior of the two universities in respect of science, though it had a higher social and political prestige.

[30] 36 took the Tripos in 1910.

[31] Though only after the changes in Cambridge's 1882 statutes, and even then much depended upon the co-operation of the colleges (Macleod, 'Resources of Science', 136). On Oxford's failure to adopt a similar system to Cambridge's, see Howarth, 'Oxford for Arts', 486–7.

[32] P. Alter, *The Reluctant Patron: Science and the State in Britain* (Oxford, 1987), 35–59.

from 5,610 to 6,550 at Oxford, Cambridge, Durham, and London—an overall increase of nearly 52 per cent. Throughout the following decade student numbers continued to rise, though more moderately (by 11.4 per cent). Much of this expansion was concentrated in vocational, technological, and scientific studies. As a result, by 1900 the lacunae in the country's provision of scientific education were already well on the way to being filled. However, the clamour for more state recognition of science did not abate. The setbacks of the Boer War and the attendant calls for greater National Efficiency spurred the 'science lobby' to yet further efforts. Lockyer had long wanted Oxford and Cambridge to be converted into purely research institutions, with generous state funding; Karl Pearson had similar ambitions for London University, which he envisaged as being run by its professoriate, on the German model.

Such claims, when they had first been raised some twenty years earlier, had exasperated a public still unaccustomed to the tendency of scientists to 'urge the social utility of science when asking for public money, but [to] defend the social autonomy of science while spending it'. The constant invocation of all things German had also provoked irritation, Grant Allen, the popular novelist, fulminating in 1887 against 'our bookish educators of the new school', who had 'conceived the noble ambition of turning us all into imitation Germans'.[33]

Moreover, even many scientists, especially those of an older generation, feared the emergence of 'scientific deaneries', staffed by official appointees responsible to no one—as Huxley put it.[34] Could government really be trusted to promote disinterested research and avoid the temptation to push placemen and sycophants into these state-funded posts, as had notoriously happened with the Regius Chairs at Oxford and Cambridge? J. J. Thomson raised another objection when, in 1913, he passionately warned Cambridge's Senate that acceptance of state money would lead inexorably to state control.[35]

But after 1900 such cautionary voices were overborne by noisy pleas for the 'endowment of research'. Dewar, in his presidential address to the British Academy in 1902, argued that the 'the claims of science . . . no longer require[d] the begging box', insisting that the state had to 'recognize in science one of its elements of strength and prosperity'.[36] In 1900 Germany, it was claimed, was spending over six times as much as England on university science and technology departments.[37] Action was imperative.

---

[33] Macleod, 'Resources of Science', 112, 154.

[34] Heyck, *Transformation*, 110–11.

[35] Apropos the suggestion that Cambridge seek a grant to support medical education. In any case, Thomson and Rutherford were both notoriously reluctant to acquire expensive apparatus, preferring to run the Cavendish on a shoestring (C. Brooke, *A History of the University of Cambridge: Vol. 4, 1870–1990* (Cambridge, 1993), 97, 176–7).

[36] Ubbelohde, 'Science', 217.

[37] M. Sanderson, *Education and Economic Decline in Britain, 1870 to the 1990s* (Cambridge, 1999), 19.

In reality, the British state *was* funnelling large sums of money into scientific projects, in the concealed form of expenditure on the armed services. For example, at the Admiralty, Henry Jackson, a science-minded naval officer, in his desperation to acquire an effective system of offshore communication, was effectively subsidizing Marconi's development of the radio.[38] But Lockyer, the editor of *Nature*, took no interest in such under-the-counter subsidies, and in October 1905 he created a new body to press his case, the British Science Guild (BSG): to 'bring home to all classes the necessity of making the scientific spirit a national characteristic which shall inspire progress and determine the policy in affairs of all kinds'.[39] 'Our universities must become as much the insurers of the future progress as battleships are the insurers of the present power of States', Lockyer declared. A number of prominent politicians jumped on to the bandwagon, Haldane, for example, agreeing to serve as the BSG's first president. But would *governments* be prepared to pay out the public money which most scientists said that they needed?

Since 1882 government had allocated an annual grant of £3,000, which the Royal Society then disbursed to successful applicants, mainly with a view to covering the equipment costs of individual researchers. In addition, from 1894 onwards money from the Royal Commission for the Exhibition of 1851 was used to set up imperial fellowships for scientific research: one of the first of these was awarded to Rutherford.[40] But the sums involved in these initiatives were trifling.

Balfour genuinely wanted to do more, but his government was initially hamstrung by the necessity of reining in public expenditure, which had risen alarmingly as a result of the Boer War. However, in 1900 the government set up the National Physical Laboratory (NPL), which was funded by the Treasury though administered by the Royal Society. The new institution, partially modelled on the Physikalisch-Technische Reichsanstalt in Berlin, was given the objective of 'standardizing and verifying instruments' and determining 'physical constants', but it soon began to widen its brief. By 1914 the NPL was in receipt of an annual public grant of £30,000. Wealthy industrialists, too, helped out: the South African mineowner Julius Wernher provided £10,000 for extensions to the NPL's metallurgical laboratory, and Sir Alfred Yarrow donated £20,000 for the building of a test tank for model ship constructions.[41]

---

[38] The Admiralty bore much of Marconi's R&D costs by giving his equipment a free trial on Royal Naval vessels. But its deal with Marconi (an initial grant of £6,000 for radio sets and annual royalties of £3,200) in the long run proved financially highly beneficial to both sides (R. F. Pocock, *The Early British Radio Industry* (Manchester, 1988), 172–3).

[39] *Nature*, 72 (1905), 585.

[40] Macleod, 'Resources of Science', 160–1.

[41] Edgerton, *Science, Technology and the British Economic Decline*, 42; Ubbelohde, 'Science', 232; Alter, *Reluctant Patron*, 138–49.

The Balfour government also increased the state funding of universities and university colleges. When Austen Chamberlain became Chancellor of the Exchequer in the autumn of 1903, he overhauled the system of grants-in-aid, as a result of which these sums significantly increased—a trend which continued under his Liberal successors. Grants-in-aid, which had amounted to a mere £57,000 in 1903, stood at about £120,000 in 1909 and at £185,000 in 1914. On the eve of the war some 50 per cent of university income was being met out of public funds, if local authority contributions are also taken into account.[42] Though this public money was ostensibly given in support of university *teaching*, university-based *researchers* indirectly benefited.

This increased level of funding was needed, not least to meet a new wave of university expansion. In 1899 England possessed only five universities proper: Oxford, Cambridge, Durham, the federal University of London, and Victoria University (a northern examining board servicing Owens College, Manchester, and colleges at Liverpool and Leeds).[43] England's ratio of universities to total population, at 1 per 6.16 million, was thus very low: Scotland, Wales, and even Ireland were all better served, let alone Germany and Switzerland.

Then, between 1903 and 1905, the Victoria University was broken down into its constituent elements, giving rise to three new universities at Liverpool, Manchester, and Leeds. Fully chartered universities were also fashioned out of Mason College at Birmingham in 1900 (the first of the civic universities), Firth College at Sheffield in 1905,[44] and Bristol University College in 1909. In other words, within a decade the number of English universities precisely doubled. There were also University Colleges at Newcastle (affiliated to Durham), Nottingham, Reading, and Southampton.

London University, too, was drastically overhauled in 1900, when it became a teaching as well as an examining body. Hitherto its prestige had largely derived from King's College (an Anglican body) and the rival University College, which catered for Dissenters and freethinkers.[45] But the London

---

[42] The 1902 Education Act made it obligatory, instead of optional, for the LEAs to spend their 'whisky money' on technical education, while for the first time the county boroughs were given powers to aid 'education other than elementary' without restriction. As a result, on the outbreak of the Great War just over £100,000 p.a. was being spent by the English and Welsh local authorities on university education.

[43] Scotland was better provided, with its four ancient universities of Edinburgh, Glasgow, St Andrews, and Aberdeen. The University of Wales received its royal charter in 1893, and had affiliated to it colleges in Cardiff, Swansea, Aberystwyth, and Bangor.

[44] See D. Smith, *Conflict and Compromise: Class Formation in English Society 1830–1914: A Comparative Study of Birmingham and Sheffield* (1982), 215. Firth College amalgamated with the technical school and medical school to become the Sheffield University College in 1897. Its application for a charter was granted in 1905, but only on condition that all its statutes and ordinances be submitted to the three northern universities for their approval.

[45] UCL did not formally become incorporated in London University until 1905.

School of Economics (LSE), founded by the Webbs in 1895 out of a private bequest, became increasingly important after 1900, while the Imperial College of Science (created out of the Royal School of Mines, the Royal College of Science, and the City and Guilds College), which opened its doors to students in 1909, was proudly acclaimed as London's 'Charlottenburg'—after the great Technical High School in Berlin. Both these new colleges became affiliated to the much-reinvigorated London University.

Yet what did all this expansion mean? The 'endowment of research' lobby continued to insist that, despite all of these improvements, Britain still lagged shamefully behind Germany, especially in technological training. But the Anglo-German comparisons which it favoured were often misleading. Germany had a binary system of higher education in which the Technical High Schools (though they could award their own degrees after 1899) were institutionally separate from universities proper. Britain, by contrast, chose to include higher technological and vocational subjects within an integrated university system, where they rubbed shoulders with the pure sciences, the natural sciences, and the humanities. British technological education was different from Germany's, but not necessarily inferior.

It has also been calculated that, in the early twentieth century, the proportion of the British population attending university (1.2 per cent) fell short of that of Germany (1.47 per cent) or France (1.65 per cent).[46] But the differences were not very great, and in any case, was like being compared with like? In 1913–14 there were 18,228 full-time students in England, over 42 per cent of them in Oxbridge, but in the new civic universities and university colleges full-time students were outnumbered by part-timers. The university extension movement also enrolled thousands of students. The statistics, in other words, might be presented so as to put English higher education in a much more favourable light. The same applies to technical education, where many skilled workers continued to acquire the knowledge that they needed from apprenticeships, supplemented by instruction at evening classes in technical colleges, not through the pursuit of full-time educational qualifications—an arrangement which most British employers heartily endorsed.

Businessmen were not, as a class, indifferent to university education as such, and sometimes their intervention helped shape its development. Lavish bequests from Andrew Carnegie,[47] the millionaire steelmaster, and Lord Strathcona, the shipping magnate, eventually persuaded Chamberlain that his beloved Birmingham University must directly serve the economic needs of

[46] Cited in M. Sanderson, 'The English Civic Universities and the "Industrial Spirit", 1870–1914', *Historical Research*, 61 (1988), 101–2. The figures for the USA are between 2% and 4%.

[47] The Carnegie Trust, founded in 1901, with an endowment of £2 million, devoted half of its income to providing Scottish universities with scientific equipment, the other half to assisting students.

its region: hence the endowment there of a mining department and of a School of Commerce, under the direction of William Ashley, who later became prominent as a tariff reform apologist. Similarly, in 1901 Lord Rothschild, by heading a fundraising appeal, helped the Webbs to convert the LSE into something resembling a Continental polytechnic: that is to say, an advanced college for the training of the administrative elite and senior business managers.[48] Cajoled by Haldane and Rosebery, great 'Randlords' such as Julius Wernher later gave munificent donations towards the establishment of Imperial College (though their own businesses would not benefit therefrom). Meanwhile the other civic universities continued to profit from employer largesse, as they had done in their 'college of science' days. Thus Muspratt Brothers, the chemical manufacturers, built and equipped Liverpool's new chemical laboratories in 1906, and in the pre-war period Manchester was receiving, on average, gifts and bequests amounting to £30,000 a year, mainly from local businessmen.[49] Yet it is not clear how much practical assistance industry derived from these educational developments. Leaving aside chemicals (a somewhat special case), no clear-cut link can be traced between improved industrial competitiveness and the provision of technical education. For example, in Britain the steel industry lost ground badly in world markets, although Sheffield University was famous for the excellence of its metallurgical engineering. Yet cotton remained highly competitive until 1914 and beyond, despite having a largely uneducated (though highly trained) workforce at all levels.[50]

This may explain why the agitation for improved scientific education came primarily from scientists, educationalists, and politicians rather than from actual manufacturers, most of whom attached greater importance to training on the job. Interestingly enough, at the start of the century nearly three-quarters of all chemistry graduates in employment were earning their living from schoolteaching rather than in industry, where their expertise was not always valued. This situation was understandably an irritant to professional scientists, and they had other reasons for dissatisfaction. The impetus behind the movement to create new university institutions in England had never had as its sole purpose the promotion of science, still less the assistance of industry. Even Chamberlain had initially hoped to create in his home city a 'real' university, dedicated to pure scholarship, thinking that the narrowly technical and vocational training supplied by the old Mason College was derogatory to Birmingham's status. Such feelings of civic pride also mattered to many

---

[48] Hutchinson, its benefactor, had wanted the School to promote socialism, as Bernard Shaw kept reminding Webb.

[49] For further details, see M. Sanderson, *The Universities and British Industry 1850–1970* (London, 1972).

[50] Manchester University lacked a cotton textile department.

businessmen: the Brunners, for example, gave a large sum of money to Liverpool University in order to promote, *inter alia*, Egyptology and archaeology![51]

Canon Hastings Rashdall's pioneering work on the medieval university, which he turned into a lecture that was often delivered to public audiences, may have familiarized the Edwardian generation with the notion that even the most respectable of universities could legitimately meet practical vocational needs, as Bologna, Paris, and Oxford had done 700 years earlier. But the old snobbish aversion to 'practical' subjects survived (as, indeed, it did in Wilhelmine Germany). Medicine, it is true, was treated as a special case—nearly a quarter of full-time students in the big civic universities in 1914 were located in faculties of medicine. Law's academic credentials, too, went unchallenged. But the training of undergraduates for careers in commerce and industry was still widely thought to be detrimental to a university's prestige.

In any case, some of the new English university colleges and universities had been heavily influenced by the earlier university extension movement, in which science had played a subordinate part. In 1913–14 arts students comprised 36.4 per cent of all full-time students at Birmingham, Leeds, Sheffield, Liverpool, and Manchester. Moreover, over one-fifth of all university students in the Edwardian period were women, of whom the majority were preparing for a career in schoolteaching through a study of subjects such as history, English and modern languages. Thus, even within the civic universities, the physical sciences and technology, though important, were by no means dominant.[52] As for the ancient universities, the spectacular scientific achievements of Cambridge must be placed alongside turn-of-the-century Oxford University (probably closer to the centre of social and political authority):[53] as many as 90 per cent of male and 95 per cent of female Oxford finalists still sat their examinations in the arts schools.[54]

At the level of secondary education, too, the progress of the natural sciences was uneven. The Clarendon Commission and the Schools Inquiry Commission of 1861–4 had earlier found that, of the 128 schools they examined, only fifteen had room for practical scientific work and only eighteen devoted even four hours a week to the subject.[55] By the end of the century much had changed.

---

[51] But physical chemistry and economic science also benefited.

[52] In Edinburgh, and still more Glasgow University, the number of engineering students increased sharply during the Edwardian period, though the status of the traditional faculties of medicine and law still retained their dominance north of the border.

[53] Oxford (4,025) and Cambridge (3,679) between them comprised 42.26% of all full-time students in English universities. Manchester was the only other university whose numbers exceeded 1,000.

[54] B. Harrison (ed.), *The History of the University of Oxford, Vol. VIII: The Twentieth Century* (Oxford, 1994), 59.

[55] Ubbelohde, 'Science', 227.

Most public schools now offered adequate opportunities for the study of science to those boys whose parents desired it, and in the 'modern' side of such schools, set up to prepare pupils for the army entrance exams, both mathematics and the natural sciences bulked large. Moreover, a few public-school headmasters, notably H. G. Wells's great hero F. W. Sanderson of Oundle, proselytized eagerly on behalf of science, investing in laboratories and workshops and encouraging pupils to conduct their own scientific investigations. In Manchester Grammar School, another institution with a high reputation in science, there were no fewer than five masters teaching chemistry alone.

But none of this amounted to a genuine curricular revolution in the country's most prestigious schools. The committee appointed by Asquith during the Great War to inquire into the position of the natural sciences in the educational system, concluded in 1919 that there was still 'no general recognition of the principle that science should form an essential part of secondary education', and that the establishment of 'modern' sides in the public schools had 'had the unforeseen result of forming an excuse for the neglect of science on the classical side'.[56] Science-trained headmasters were still very rare, and even masters highly sympathetic to science often shied away from defending its practical utility, preferring to argue that, properly taught, science 'trained the mind' no less effectively than other subjects contributing to a traditional 'liberal education', while some still defended science by claiming that its study taught 'reverence' for God-the-Creator.

In addition, in most of the publicly funded secondary schools which mushroomed in the wake of the 1902 Education Act scientific instruction took second place to the objective of supplying a good general education, upon which specialized technical and vocational courses could later be grafted if needed. Indeed, Sir Robert Morant, the influential Permanent Secretary at the Board of Education, a classics-trained product of Winchester and New College, Oxford, has often been criticized for discriminating against technical schooling. This is unfair, since Morant was the creator between 1905–6 of the Junior Technical School and he also authorized the continuation of some Central Schools, which had a 'practical', commercial orientation. On the other hand, with his 1904 Regulation, Morant compelled the new LEA-funded grammar schools to devote eight hours a week to English, history, geography, and languages, one of which (if two were studied) had to be Latin. His main legacy was thus to stop early specialization in the sciences and to reinforce that traditional emphasis on the virtues of a liberal education which ultimately derived from the practices of the country's most eminent public schools.[57]

---

[56] T. W. Bamford, *The Rise of the Public Schools* (London, 1967), 277.

[57] The 1914 School Certificate regulations required students to pass in three groups: English subjects, foreign languages, and science and mathematics (Smith, *Conflict and Compromise*, 253).

In short, as the new century dawned, science had not really cast off its former Cinderella-status. It might now be attracting more funding, but it still lacked prestige. Indeed, just as many artists felt themselves to be unappreciated by the wider public and persecuted by authority, so scientists and engineers complained about being socially marginalized and misunderstood. The quarrelsome Professor Ray Lankester went further. Addressing the York meeting of the British Academy in 1906, he railed at 'the trifling with classical literature and the absorption in athletics', as, in 1914, did *Nature*, which likewise saw the country as being 'governed almost entirely by the literary spirit'.[58] As for the British Science Guild, not content with insisting upon state-funding for science as a national duty, its leaders also spent much time arraigning politicians, statesmen, and civil servants for their ignorance of science and neglect of the scientific method. The indictment was echoed by the eugenics movement, which quickly developed a strain of authoritarian elitism, totally dismissive of party politics and of democratic government.

Whether deliberately or unwittingly, members of the 'science lobby' in late Victorian and Edwardian Britain thus displayed an eager concern for professional self-advancement, not just in the obvious sense of laying claim to public resources that would fund their own careers,[59] but also in redefining the national interest in such a way as to privilege the specialized kinds of knowledge and expertise of which they were the exclusive guardians. This approach to the world—'technocracy', it might be called—developed into an important strand in the country's wider culture.

5. ATTITUDES TO SCIENCE AND TECHNOLOGY

It was H. G. Wells who emerged as the popular prophet of technocracy. A grammar-school boy of humble origins, who had started life as a draper's assistant, Wells then became a schoolteacher, winning a scholarship to the Normal (i.e. Teachers' Training) College at South Kensington, where he studied science under T. H. Huxley, among others. Through his profuse literary outpourings Wells then set himself up as a kind of seer, claiming to be able to identify in the majestic processes of scientific discovery the source of those fundamental social and economic changes of which he believed legislators and ministers to be woefully ignorant. Wells's vision was most explicitly laid out in *Anticipations* (1901), *Mankind in the Making* (1903), *A Modern Utopia* (1905), and *New Worlds for Old* (1908), all of which became great commercial

---

[58] Ubbelohde, 'Science', 221; Turner, *Contesting Cultural Authority*, 216.
[59] Lockyer, employed at what was in effect a state-endowed solar physics observatory, was open to the accusation that he stood to gain pecuniarily from 'the endowment of research'.

successes—*Anticipations*, for example, running through seven editions in its first year of publication.

Wells, quite as much as any aesthete, felt a profound contempt for the democratic masses: the 'Dull' and the 'Base' was how he characterized them in *A Modern Utopia*. His admiration was reserved for the scientist-engineer, whom he saw as the dynamic (albeit often undervalued) element in all modern societies. In *Mankind in the Making* Wells predicted that such people might eventually evolve into a new 'Samurai', a benevolent but autocratic caste fated to dominate the world—part of his wider interest in securing a 'government by experts', that familiar fantasy nurtured by the quest for 'National Efficiency'. This ruthless technocratic creed (so different from the florid medievalism of the utopian prophecies in William Morris's *New From Nowhere* (1890), written little more than a decade earlier[60]) offered a powerful critique not only of 'sentimental democracy', but also of the squalor, muddle, and waste which Wells portrayed as the defining characteristics of modern capitalism—notably in his novel *Tono-Bungay* (1909).

Such an appeal for order, regulation, and discipline attracted many members of the Fabian Society, which Wells joined in 1902. However, in 1908, defeated in his attempt to overhaul the Society, he cut loose from it. The bitter schism had many causes, among them the mutual exasperation which had grown up between Wells and the Fabian 'Old Guard', who had initially patronized the insecure young man but who later, led by Shaw, moved skilfully to neutralize his growing threat to their authority. The Webbs' disapproval of Wells's sexual philandering further embittered their relationship.[61]

But Beatrice Webb also had a serious intellectual difference of opinion with Wells, who, she felt, was in error, not so much because of his idealization of science, as because of his over-narrow conception of it. 'A world run by the physical science man straight from his laboratory is his ideal', she privately complained: 'he does not see that specialised faculty and knowledge are needed for administration exactly as they are needed for the manipulation of machinery or forces.'[62] In other words, Wells lacked any understanding of social organizations and of the professionalism needed to run them.

No one could deny that Wells had many dazzling insights into the technological future: he foresaw the tank ('land cruiser') and the use of aerial warfare aimed at the demoralization of civilian populations. But the Webbs

---

[60] This book was written to answer the American socialist Edward Bellamy's *Looking Backward* (1888), which portrays a technocratic utopia of the kind that Morris loathed.

[61] See Ch. 15. Wells retaliated against the Webbs' criticisms of him in his novel *The New Machiavelli* (1911), where they are cruelly caricatured as the 'Baileys'.

[62] S. Hynes, *The Edwardian Turn of Mind* (London, 1968), 100.

correctly noted that these were mere intuitions, not the result of systematic, methodical enquiry.[63]

Yet futuristic technology still had about it, in many people's minds, an aura of adventure and romance—an aura well captured in the stories of the French science-fiction writer Jules Verne. Manned flight, in particular, provided a powerful stimulation to the poetic imagination, inspiring artists all over Europe to try to capture its essence—though, paradoxically, to express their sense of wonder they were often driven back upon traditional tropes such as the classical legend of Icarus.[64] In a way the very fragility of pre-war aircraft and submarines contributed to contemporaries' enchantment, since it seemed that the human beings who operated such machines were mystically uniting their lives with the worlds of the fish, the marine mammals, and the birds. Even the advance of electricity was greeted, in some quarters, with near-ecstasy: it 'would restore our large cities to their old habitable beauty and healthfulness before the smoke-demon destroyed the vegetation and blackened the sky', enthused Oliver Lodge.[65]

Moreover, the feelings of awe which the new technology could inspire also provided many writers, notably Rudyard Kipling, with a new kind of material. Like Wells, Kipling intensely loved machinery (he was an early owner of an automobile) and admired engineers. He also wrote a number of short stories featuring advanced technology—some of it yet to be invented! These included 'Wireless' (1903), in which mastery of the aether has permitted time-travelling, 'With the Night Mail' (1904), about an aerial crossing of the Atlantic, and 'As Easy as A.B.C.' (1912), in which an international company of telephonists takes over the world.[66] Even more daring was his 1895 tale 'The Ship That Found Herself', in which the various parts of a ship's machinery converse with one another.

Modern technology also gave rise to a new, distinctively modern aesthetic— for example, T. E. Hulme's and the American poet Ezra Pound's commendation of Imagism, with its hard, sharp, *metallic* imagery. Somewhat similar was Filippo Marinetti's 'Futurism', which celebrated speed, violence, and machinery, at the heart of which stood that very modern hero-figure, the aviator (represented in Britain by the dashing Claude Grahame-White). Indeed, fascination with machinery was widespread among the pre-war avant-garde. 'I look upon *Nature*, but I live in a *steel city*', proclaimed David

[63] Hynes agrees with the Webbs that Wells's social prophecies merely extrapolated from current scientific trends and that he '*use[d]* science as authority for social and political predictions', without bothering to supply evidence, logic, or proof.

[64] Wohl, *Passion for Wings*, esp. ch. 4.

[65] W. P. Jolly, *Oliver Lodge* (London, 1974), 51–2.

[66] R. Kipling, *A Diversity of Creatures* (1917).

Bomberg, one of a group of painters (including Edward Wadsworth and William Roberts) who often gave human beings jagged edges which made them resemble machines. Jacob Epstein brought this fusion of machinery and art to an apotheosis in the early version of his sculpture 'Rock Drill', which actually includes in its structure this superficially unprepossessing piece of equipment.

But machinery-worship was not without its disturbing aspects. For whereas the scientist had once been humbly proud, through 'natural religion', to celebrate God-the-Maker, the modern scientist-engineer now took pride in his *own* godlike role, as the master of the world, on sea, land and in the sky.[67] Many Christians found such claims offensive. Gladstone professed himself to be a 'believer in the harmony between science and religion', but his secretary noted that 'he shuns anything which seems to give an additional lustre to scientific discoveries that may run counter to the Bible and its teachings'.[68] The old antagonism between the Darwinians and the Christians had still not entirely died down: in 1894 even Salisbury, in his presidential address to the British Academy, brought down on his head the wrath of Karl Pearson for suggesting that the theory of natural selection conflicted with what was known about the earth's changing temperatures.[69] Others took issue with science's 'materialism', Ruskin going so far as to oppose the new physical laboratory that was built at Oxford in 1884, on the ground that it was a desecration of the spirit of that noble university.[70]

Such hostility to natural science is encountered less frequently after the mid-1890s, but a mistrust of *scientists*, often portrayed as a sinister 'priesthood', persisted in certain working-class circles and among educated feminists. Doctors bore the brunt of this hostility, largely as a result of the way in which they had earlier supported the operation of the Contagious Diseases Acts. Many prominent suffragists also opposed vivisection and vaccination, both of which were eliciting strong, organized protests right up until 1914 and beyond.[71] Far from science being intrinsically benign, many self-professed humanitarians saw much in its practice which was barbarically cruel.

Nor were all of Wells's readers entranced by his vision of a scientific future dominated by technological wizardry. Indeed, such was the revulsion it was capable of inspiring that several Edwardian 'dystopias' were published in the pre-war years. Perhaps the best-known of these is E. M. Forster's story 'The

---

[67] Turner, *Contesting Cultural Authority*, ch. 4.
[68] R. Shannon, *Gladstone: Heroic Minister 1865–1898* (Harmondsworth, 1999), 285–6.
[69] D. A. MacKenzie, *Statistics in Britain 1865–1930* (Edinburgh, 1981), 81; A. L. Kennedy, *Salisbury, 1830–1903* (London, 1953), 243–4.
[70] Macleod, 'Resources of Science', 154.
[71] On anti-vaccination, see D. Porter and R. Porter, 'The Politics of Prevention: Anti-Vaccinationism and Public Health in Nineteenth-Century England', *Medical History*, 32 (1988), 231–52.

Machine Stops' (1908), which shows people, perpetually underground, living isolated lives and communicating with one another only electronically. This nightmarish story, Forster later said, had been written as 'a reaction to one of the earlier heavens of H. G. Wells'. The Webbs's somewhat different view of a scientifically regulated future, laid out in Sidney's ponderous, bureaucratic prose, excited little of this fear and revulsion. Nevertheless, it left many with distinct feelings of discomfort and unease: feelings which G. K. Chesterton, for one, sought to exorcise in his playful depiction of a Fabian idealist 'who went mad and ran about the country with an axe, hacking branches off the trees whenever there were not the same number on both sides'.[72]

Yet the most common response to science was neither unqualified idealization nor abuse, but ambivalence. For example, although George Bernard Shaw, like his fellow Fabians, subscribed to the cult of the expert, he held a whole variety of 'heretical' opinions: delighting in Nietzsche and Bergson, favouring the Lamarckian theory of the inheritance of acquired characteristics rather than Darwin's 'mechanistic' theory of natural selection (*Man and Superman*, 1903), scoffing at the authority of doctors (whose claims to be able to cure disease, he told readers, should be treated as one would treat the claims of fortune-tellers[73]), and adopting many of Carpenter's accoutrements of the new life, from rational dress to vegetarianism.[74] In *Man and Superman* Shaw also has fun at the expense of the Wellsian engineer, who here appears in fictional guise as 'Enry Straker.

Even Wells himself can be cited in support of the contention that science aroused feelings of deep ambivalence. Certainly the note of chirpy optimism characteristic of much of Wells's discursive writings is at variance with the mood of his imaginative fiction. This is especially true of the early 'fables', where the futuristic adventure story pioneered by Verne is turned to much darker purposes. Thus, in Wells's terrifying *The Island of Dr Moreau* (1896), the story of an evil vivisectionist whose creations turn violently against him (an echo of Stevenson's earlier *Dr Jekyll and Mr Hyde*), natural selection runs backwards. In other works Wells's own deep-seated social fears are given 'scientific' validation: for example, the doltish proletariat are transmuted into the 'Morlocks' in *The Time Machine* (1895). A black misanthropy also manifests itself in the recurrent images of mass destruction, gloatingly portrayed, in *The War of the Worlds* (1898) and *The War in the Air* (1908).

---

[72] G. K. Chesterton, *The Napoleon of Notting Hill* (1904), 12.

[73] Preface to the *Doctors' Dilemma* (1906)—mainly, it is true, a diatribe against private medicine, but also scathing about vivisection and vaccination.

[74] Shaw declared in 1909 that he belonged to a generation which believed fervently in science and still did so, though 'at the moment we are passing through a phase of disillusion' (Hynes, *Edwardian Turn of Mind*, 132).

Imaginative enough to envisage the possibilities inherent in the release of nuclear energy, Wells also foresaw the destructive potential of atomic bombs in *The World Set Free* (1914). It is almost as though he wished annihilation on those stupid enough to ignore his advice and disregard his warnings.[75] An even deeper pessimism underlies the closing pages of *The Time Machine*, in which, far into the distant future, the only object to be discerned on the face of the earth, under the black sky, was 'a round thing, the size of a football perhaps', with trailing tentacles: 'it seemed black against the weltering blood-red water, and it was hopping fitfully about'. No blithe late Victorian optimism here.

6. SCIENCE AND SPIRITUALITY

There is another, quite different sense in which science, and hostility to science, strangely intermingle in turn-of-the-century thought. Belief in the 'paranormal' was widespread from the 1880s onwards. Mysticism of this sort engaged the sympathy of many artists, writers, and would-be religious gurus, and of many 'serious' scientists too. The leading figure in the Society for Psychical Research (SPR), established in 1882, was Frederick Myers, an Oxford-trained philosopher who, having lost his Christian faith, sought a new kind of religion that could reassure him that death did not lead to extinction—'the discovery by scientific methods of a spiritual world'. Myers was joined in his quest by a number of leading scientists and 'friends' of science, to whom the paranormal presented a set of hypotheses that could be proven or disproven by the normal methods of investigation. Balfour, normally thought of as an icy rationalist, was a central figure in the SPR, serving as its President in 1894. He was followed by William James, the American psychologist,[76] who in turn gave way between 1901 and 1903 to the eminent physicist Oliver Lodge, then Principal of Birmingham University. An even more eminent physicist, Lord Rayleigh no less, was also a member.

The Society for Psychical Research took its commitment to scientific methods seriously, conducting experiments and attempting to verify otherwise inexplicable phenomena, before writing up its conclusions, in a scholarly idiom, in its *Proceedings* and *Journal*. In particular, the Society went to great lengths to differentiate its own investigations from the credulity and charlatanry associated with the table-rapping brigade; it even sent one of its members all the way to India to expose Madame Blavatsky, the theosophist. In short, the Society's objective was emphatically not the repudiation of modern science

---

[75] However, in this tale Wells also imagines that the human race is shocked by the devastatation of such a war into accepting the necessity for world government.

[76] His brother, Henry, showed an indebtedness to the work of the Society when writing 'The Turn of the Screw'.

but, to quote Myers' own words, its 'expansion' to the point where it could 'satisfy those questions which the human heart will rightly ask, but to which Religion alone has thus far attempted an answer'. His book, *Human Personality and Its Survival of Bodily Death* (1886–7), goes some way to explaining why psychical research was taken seriously by so many scientists. In its two vast tomes, Myers deals at exhaustive length with somnambulism, automatic writing, hypnotism, hysteria, and dual personality. All of these issues were also of central concern to the emerging discipline of psychoanalysis, in which 'science' was sometimes difficult to disentangle from imaginative fantasy.[77]

The participation in the Society's work of Oliver Lodge, a specialist in radio transmission, supplies another clue to its success. Lodge was acutely aware that scientists were engaged in uncovering a series of mysterious but powerful 'forces', quite invisible to the naked human senses: not just radio waves, but also magnetism, electricity, X-Rays, and radiation. Who could say that telepathy and other psychic phenomena might not perhaps be emanations of some other, yet imperfectly understood, 'spiritual' energy?

Indeed, matter itself was disintegrating under the scrutiny of the physicist Max Planck, whose Quantum Theory of 1900 (stimulating the later work of Albert Einstein), overturned the old stable Newtonian universe in which nature was assumed to observe regular and predictable laws—leading later to Heisenberg's principle of 'indeterminacy'. Wells captured the spirit of the new science when, in *Tono-Bungay*, he introduced 'quap', a radioactive substance which spread like a disease—'an elemental stirring and disarrangement, incalculably maleficent and strange'. Just as psychoanalysis was fragmenting the human personality, so the paradigm of the physical sciences was changing, with the discrediting of positivism. The Victorian version of matter, declares one historian, had suddenly become 'as obsolete as Genesis'.[78]

Edward Carpenter triumphantly hailed the glorious revolution. Writing in 1912, he lumped together microbes with radioactivity, radio waves, hypnotism, 'the subliminal consciousness', and telepathic communication, all of which, he believed, supported his contention that 'the subtlest forces and energies, totally unmeasurable by our instruments, and saturated or at least suffused with intelligence, are at work all around us'.[79] On the eve of the Great War there no longer seemed to be a clear-cut boundary separating scientific understanding from the spiritual domain—from religious mysticism, dreamlike trances, the occult, and the play of the artistic imagination.

The undermining of Victorian positivism by these developments in nuclear physics was thus already beginning to make some sort of an impact on

---

[77] F. M. Turner, *Between Science and Religion* (New Haven and London, 1974), 126. See also Ch. 15.
[78] Hynes, *Edwardian Turn of Mind*, 136.
[79] Ibid. 137.

intellectual debate even before 1914. Moreover, by pure happenstance, the new understanding of matter being propagated by theoretical physicists harmonized quite well with the dominant school of philosophy in turn-of-the-century Britain, that of 'Idealism'.

The Oxford-based 'Idealists', led after T. H. Green's premature death in 1882 by F. H. Bradley and Bernard Bosanquet, drew their inspiration from the German philosophers Kant and Hegel. This involved them in a flat repudiation both of the British utilitarian tradition and of the kind of scientific naturalism which Herbert Spencer was promulgating.[80] Self-realization, argued the Idealists, was a moral imperative, not a matter of calculating self-interest, and human beings could only achieve this state, as citizens, through participation in a spiritualized common life, of which the state was the ultimate expression. It was an approach which, in L. T. Hobhouse's hands, marked a decisive break with the older individualism.[81]

But Idealism also offered a distinctive view of human nature. Mankind, claimed its spokesmen, were free, self-directing agents, not pieces of machinery to be understood in psycho-biological terms.[82] This in turn meant that philosophy, far from being restricted to an analysis of the knowledge generated by the physical and social sciences, possessed its own particular knowledge. It was consciousness, or 'spirit', which shaped the material world, not vice versa.

In an important article of 1885, James Ward, a psychologist from Cambridge University, similarly upheld the priority of mind over nature. Psychology's emancipation from theology and metaphysics, Ward argued, could not be measured by the extent to which it conformed to the methods and conceptions of the physical sciences, and it was certainly not to be approached exclusively through a study of the brain and the nervous system. Like the Idealists, Ward denied that science alone generated true knowledge, instead asserting that there was a spiritual dimension to natural phenomena and that psychology's task was to provide a space for spontaneity, freedom, and creativity, so restoring purpose and worth to the universe.[83] More immediately, Ward's work caught the attention of the American psychologist William James, who was working along similar lines. In his influential book *The Principles of Psychology* (1890), James presents 'mind' as a self-activating and creative entity. Human

---

[80] In this respect, at least, they were in agreement with G. E. Moore, on whom see Ch. 15.

[81] However, Bosanquet, a pillar of the COS, did not draw Hobhouse's Radical conclusions, preferring to emphasize the family and civic responsibility.

[82] L. S. Hearnshaw, *A Short History of Psychology, 1840–1940* (London, 1964), 119.

[83] Some of these insights were later developed by Henri Bergson, whose 'vitalist' philosophy, transmitted through George Sorel, made a contribution to pre-war syndicalism. See Ch. 12. Bergson also participated in the deliberations of the Society for Psychical Research.

beings, he argues, need to believe more than can be rationally proven—hence the centrality of the 'will' in his 'pragmatic' philosophy.

Many theologians took heart from these various demolitions of the older materialistic certainties. In 1889 an influential Anglo-Catholic collection of essays, *Lux Mundi* ('The Light of the World'), edited by the Christian Socialist Charles Gore, had aroused controversy by accepting the conclusions of German biblical criticism and by abandoning the doctrine of a 'special creation' out of deference to Darwinian evolutionism. But Idealism suggested ways in which Christians could avoid being trapped by this sort of scientific naturalism. Miracles, for example, ceased to be a 'problem' if it could be shown that the world itself was intrinsically miraculous.[84]

However, it should be emphasized that, for the most part, the interest in seemingly non-rational behaviour, whether of individuals or of crowds, represented a broadening of the scientific project, not a repudiation of it. Whether the investigators were probing the 'occult', the realm of the subconscious, crowd hysteria, the customs of primitive tribes, or the role of instinct or religion in securing social cohesion (all topics of interest around the turn of the century), they expected to find rational explanations—even if unconventional ones. To acknowledge, in Balfour's words, that there were 'things in heaven and earth not hitherto dreamed of in naturalistic philosophy', scarcely betokened a descent into obscurantism and unreason, even if Karl Pearson thought otherwise.[85]

7. SOCIAL SCIENCE

Mechanistic models, whether of physical phenomena or of human behaviour, were not as pervasive in 1914 as they had been thirty years earlier. Idealist philosophy, later supplemented by developments within the physical sciences themselves, had seen to that. However, the extent of the reaction against positivism can easily be exaggerated. Karl Pearson, in his popular book *The Grammar of Science* (1892), was still confidently presenting 'the scientific method' as 'the sole gateway to the whole region of knowledge', its material being 'coextensive with the whole life, physical and mental, of the universe'. 'Sociology', in Pearson's classification, featured merely as a subdivision of 'Psychology', which in turn was a subdivision of 'Biology'.[86] This particular schema did not go unchallenged, but nearly all those who sought to place

---

[84] A. Quinton, 'Thought', in Nowell-Smith (ed.), *Edwardian England*, 281.

[85] Hynes, *Edwardian Turn of Mind*, 142. On Pearson's attacks on Balfour, see Mackenzie, *Statistics*, 89, and L. S. Jacyna, 'Science and Social Order in the Thought of A. J. Balfour', *Isis*, 71 (1980), 11–34.

[86] K. Pearson, *The Grammar of Science* (London, 1892; 1900 edn.), 15–24, 526–7.

'Social Science' on a surer footing broadly agreed that the physical sciences furnished them with the appropriate model to follow.

Indeed, despite all the censures emanating from philosophers and theoretical psychologists, the gap between the natural sciences and the study of human behaviour narrowed appreciably between 1886 and 1914. The medical laboratory had for some years been instrumental in providing a scientific analysis of the human body, giving rise to new fields of study such as bacteriology. Now human beings were being increasingly subjected to a much wider kind of investigation and measurement—carried out, not just by anthropologists and ethnologists on their expeditions to 'primitive' peoples, nor even by dispassionate observers of modern industrial society such as Booth and Rowntree, armed with their notebooks and carefully constructed questionnaires. For, like the lower animals, mankind was now being enticed away from its 'natural habitat' and scrutinized within the controlled environment of the psychological laboratory: one of a number of 'technologies of surveillance' being developed in these years.[87]

In 1884 Francis Galton set up, at his own expense, an anthropometric laboratory in London, in association with the International Health Exhibition, at which, in return for the payment of 3d., visitors could have their height, weight, and reaction times accurately measured—an experience for which over 9,000 people volunteered.[88] The British Academy supported this work with a small grant, and Galton was thus furnished with the extensive collection of human measurements which he then analysed in his important book *Natural Inheritance* (1889), an early attempt to determine the relative importance of nature and nurture. Karl Pearson continued this line of research in his own Eugenics Laboratory (now called the Galton Laboratory), which was set up in 1909.

But psychology as an experimental science really took off in Britain for the first time in 1897, when James Sully established an important psychological laboratory at University College, London, and W. H. R. Rivers acquired his more modest premises at Cambridge. True, the subject thereafter expanded less rapidly in Britain than in contemporary Germany and the United States. All the same, by 1914 small psychological laboratories were functioning in a number of universities: notably at Cambridge, London, Liverpool, Manchester, Edinburgh, and Glasgow.

The data generated by psychological laboratories cried out for more sophisticated methods of quantitative analysis than had traditionally been employed

---

[87] S. Sturdy and R. Cooter, 'Science, Scientific Management, and the Transformation of Medicine in Britain *c*.1870–1950', *History of Science*, 36 (1998), 421–66.

[88] When the Exhibition closed, the testing apparatus was transferred to the South Kensington Museum. Unfortunately, most visitors would not take their shoes off, so their height had, in part, to be guessed.

by the Victorian statistical societies, and Galton (with his motto, 'Whenever you can, count') devoted much of the latter part of his life to meeting this need. His 1885 paper 'Co-relations and their Measurement' marks an important stage in the development of modern statistics, which in the course of the 1890s also threw up such now-familiar concepts as 'correlation coefficient' and 'regression'. W. F. R. Weldon, an eminent marine zoologist (who died of pneumonia in 1906, aged only 46), came up with the concept of negative correlation and formulated the theory of multiple correlation, while Pearson invented the terms 'normal curve' and 'standard deviation'. In 1901 these two men launched the journal *Biometrika*, which pioneered 'biometry', the application of advanced statistical methods to the study of variability in humans, animals, plants, and (obviously) in Weldon's marine specimens. Needless to say, the driving force behind Pearson's biological work (to which, interestingly, he had come relatively late in life via a study of history) was the advancement of his eugenical project.

The same can be said of another product of laboratory-based psychology: intelligence testing. In 1904, inspired by Galton's *Inquiries into Human Faculty* (1883), Charles Spearman, a retired army officer of independent means studying in Leipzig, wrote his seminal paper ' "General Intelligence": Objectively Determined and Measured', which, using a method which later became known as factor analysis, distinguished between 's', a measurement of specific and particular skills, and 'g', which allegedly measured an underlying 'general' intelligence, so accounting for the overlapping scores between the various specific abilities measured. The basis for a new discipline, 'psychometry', was thus laid.

Five years later the young Cyril Burt, recently appointed to a lecturing post in psychology at Liverpool University, co-authored another famous article, 'Experimental Tests of General Intelligence', the importance of which lay in its pioneering use of written group tests of intelligence. Burt went on (between 1913 and 1915) to revise the 'Binet–Simon Scale', which the two French educationalists of that name had devised to separate defective from normal children.[89] In pre-war Britain, too, the original impetus may have come from a concern to identify and make special provision for mentally defective children,[90] though, as we have seen, intelligence tests were soon being applied to so-called 'social inefficients' (prostitutes, criminals, etc.), in the belief that this would confirm the prevalent theory that 'the unfit' comprised people of 'tainted stock'.

Psychometry made further progress when, in 1911, the German psychologist William Stern came up with the concept of an 'Intelligence Quotient' (or

[89] 1905, revised in 1908, with the introduction of an age scale, and again in 1911.
[90] G. Sutherland, *Ability, Merit and Measurement: Mental Testing and English Education, 1880–1940* (Oxford, 1984), 55. See Ch. 6.

IQ), which involved dividing a person's mental by his/her chronological age and then multiplying the number by 100.[91] This in turn suggested the possibility of a meritocratic educational policy, which would discount all forms of environmental conditioning. Engineering such a policy became Burt's own primary mission, especially after 1913, when he was appointed (on Spearman's recommendation) as the first psychologist to the LCC.[92]

Advanced statistical methods, it seemed, could also be applied to *social* life, just as psychologists were using them to illuminate *individual* human behaviour. Thus A. L. Bowley, a pioneer of the sample survey, brought a new rigour to the analysis of official quantitative data[93]—notably in his *Livelihood and Poverty*, published in 1915 but largely completed before the outbreak of war. The Superintendent of Statistics at the General Register Office, T. H. C. Stevenson, was meanwhile engaged in lifting demography to a much more sophisticated level.

Meanwhile economics was being similarly transformed—thanks, in part, to F. Y. Edgeworth, Professor of Political Economy, first at King's College, London, and then at Oxford, who made several important contributions to statistical theory. Nor is it any coincidence that Alfred Marshall, whose majestic *Principles of Economics* (1890) established him, in the world's eyes, as 'the first great economist *pur sang*' (to use J. M. Keynes's later phrase), had once studied for the Mathematical Tripos—as had Keynes himself. Indeed, when Marshall, in his inaugural lecture in 1885, urged that the scientific basis of economics be strengthened, he meant that it should become more mathematical—in contrast to what he saw as John Stuart Mill's 'literary' approach.[94]

But Marshall also helped to place 'economics' on a scientific footing by establishing its autonomy. This meant warding off an attempted takeover bid from the 'historical economists' or economic historians, led in Cambridge by his adversary, the politically committed William Cunningham. It also meant disentangling it from the older subject of political economy. Marshall's triumph came when, in 1903, he persuaded Cambridge University to create a separate Economics Tripos. Thereafter he strove to maintain a proper distance between economics, as a scientific discipline, and the world of political decision-making. Indeed, so austere was his conception of his field that he positively discouraged all but a few dedicated undergraduates from

---

[91] This IQ was then often equated, erroneously, with Spear's 'g'—in which Binet, incidentally, did not believe (Sutherland, *Ability, Merit and Measurement*, 127).

[92] See below.

[93] Compared, say, with the earlier investigations of Charles Booth.

[94] J. Maloney, 'Marshall, Cunningham, and the Emerging Economics Profession', *Economic History Review*, 29 (1976), 445.

studying it. A. C. Pigou, who succeeded Marshall in his Cambridge chair in 1908, went even further in safeguarding its position of mathematical rigour and ethical and political neutrality.[95] Thus, although some universities in 1914 were still calling economics 'Political Economy', its subject matter and approach had been transformed. London University registered this all-important change as early as 1901, when it authorized the LSE to offer a B.Sc. (Econ.) degree, the first of its kind in Britain.

Economics, as reshaped by Marshall, enjoyed the advantage over most other branches of the social sciences in being a very difficult subject, with a severely defined body of knowledge. The same, to a lesser extent, was true of geography, which Halford Mackinder, Reader at Oxford University between 1887 and 1905, was doing more than anyone else to restructure.

The attempt to provide a comprehensive scientific understanding of *society as a whole* proved, however, to be far more problematic. The word 'sociology' had earlier been coined by the French theorist Auguste Comte, and then popularized on this side of the Channel by J. S. Mill and, more particularly, Herbert Spencer. But when the newly formed London Sociological Society held a series of meetings in 1904 and 1905, hoping to agree upon a common methodology, all Babel broke loose—not surprisingly, since these gatherings attracted Idealists, Spencerians, Fabians, Eugenists, New Liberals, members of the COS, and many more besides, each group pressing its own distinctive terminology. All could agree with Beatrice Webb's contention that 'what we have to do is to apply the scientific method to the facts of social life'.[96] But that left unresolved what 'scientific method' *was*.

Those, such as Sir Edward Brabrook, who believed strongly in social statistics, soon despaired of the new organization and fell back upon the long-established Royal Statistical Society. Meanwhile Galton and Pearson, in the name of eugenics, were contending for a social science rooted in the study of biological inheritance; they, too, largely withdrew in disgust when their approach was rejected. Another would-be guru who was quickly isolated was the Social Darwinist Benjamin Kidd, whose best-selling book *Social Evolution* (1894) had already outlined a 'sociology' which stressed the role of religion in suppressing the individualistic 'rationalism' which he saw as detrimental to the well-being of the social organism as a whole.[97]

[95] S. Collini, D. Winch, and J. Burrow, *That Noble Science of Politics: A Study in Nineteenth-Century Intellectual History* (Cambridge, 1983), 336–7. Also see below.

[96] S. M. D. Otter, *British Idealism and Social Explanation: A Study in Late Victorian Thought* (Oxford, 1996), 136.

[97] D. P. Crook, *Benjamin Kidd: Portrait of a Social Darwinist* (Cambridge, 1984).

This left two main contending parties. The first group centred around Victor Branford, a great admirer of the Scottish civic planner Patrick Geddes, who, inspired by the French geographer Le Play, saw sociology as a branch of 'civics'.[98] This definition led to the development of an 'urban sociology', which focused not only on the city but also on the region and the conurbation—an approach which, whatever its other limitations, usefully contributed to the emerging theory and practice of town planning.

If any victor can be said to have emerged from these confused debates it was the 'New Liberal' L. T. Hobhouse, who held an evolutionary view of society while insisting on the centrality of social and cultural, rather than biological, inheritance.[99] In 1907 Hobhouse was appointed to the first chair in Sociology at a British university, the Martin White Chair at London.[100] A year later he assumed the editorship of the new *Sociological Review*. Then, in 1909, the LSE sponsored, under his direction, a new Department of Sociology.

Yet Hobhouse did not dominate sociology, even at London. For, in the very year in which he became a professor, there appeared Graham Wallas's *Human Nature in Politics*, an impressive demonstration of the contribution which social psychology could make to the emerging subject.[101] Moreover, under the direction of the Webbs,[102] the LSE had already started to mount a variety of severely vocational options in social administration. For example, its Railway Department ran a course for railway managers, part funded by the railway companies, and after 1906 there were also classes specifically designed for army officers (one of Haldane's many bright wheezes). In 1912 the LSE created a separate Department of Social Science and Administration, under E. J. Urwick, following its takeover of the hitherto independent School of Sociology.[103]

Thus, even before 1914 sociology in Britain was splintering, the most significant rift being between those engaged in 'practical' social reform on the one hand, and, on the other, those, such as Hobhouse, whose ambitious attempt to synthesize moral philosophy and social analysis ultimately led to a kind of 'top-down' theorizing that was anathema to the 'practical' men and women.[104] Such divisions partly explain why sociology did not become a generally accepted academic subject in Britain until after the Second World War.

---

[98] The group's members attempted to trace the evolutionary process through which human being changed their environment, starting off with family and community and ending with cities.

[99] 'Progress is social not racial', he repeatedly argued (*Social Evolution and Political Theory* (1911)).

[100] Soon afterwards another chair was awarded to the Finnish-born E. A. Westermarck, though he was really a comparative anthropologist.

[101] Wallas was appointed Reader in Political Science at London in 1912.

[102] Sidney Webb was Chairman of the Governors at LSE.

[103] The latter had been set up in 1903, originally to promote the ethos and methods of the COS.

[104] P. Abrams, *The Origins of British Sociology, 1834–1914* (Chicago, 1968), 148–9.

8. THE TRIUMPH OF ACADEMIA?

In the confusion surrounding the birth of sociology, one salient feature stands out: the *academic context* in which it occurred. Throughout the nineteenth century there had been no shortage of thoughtful writing about social questions, some of it scholarly, but the last place from which one would have expected it to emanate would have been a university. In 1903 Herbert Spencer died, the Englishman whose ambitious 'Synthetic Philosophy' had bequeathed to modern sociology much of its conceptual furniture, with terms such as 'function' and 'structure' borrowed from the biological sciences. A proudly independent man, Spencer had never held a university post at any time in his long life. Compare his career with that of Spearman, the retired army officer: scarcely had his important work on intelligence appeared than London University conferred on him a Readership, with the Grote Chair in Mind and Logic following five years later.

The word 'science' has a variety of meanings. To some it denotes the utilization of intellectual techniques such as statistics, others think that it rests upon a particular methodology (e.g. positivism). But it also signifies a particular way of *knowing*, involving empirical observation and experimentation, the division of labour, and classification. Such impersonal procedures were acquiring increased prestige around the turn of the century, as the investigative processes they validated were successfully applied to social administration, to government, and (rather more tentatively before 1914) to the management of business corporations.[105] As the Webbs well understood, this conception of science also had significant implications for how knowledge itself should be organized. The result was that after 1880 science and scholarship came to be restructured as discrete academic 'disciplines', each along professional lines.

Thus psychology broke free from philosophy ('mental and moral sciences') and laid claim to being 'entirely an empirical science, divested alike of theological and of metaphysical assumptions'.[106] In 1901 the professional credentials of its practitioners were underpinned by the foundation of the British Psychological Society, which on the eve of the war took over responsibility for the *British Journal of Psychology*, which Ward and Rivers had launched ten years earlier. Like other academic disciplines, psychology quickly subdivided: neuropsychology, child psychology, socio-psychology, and industrial psychology had all become recognized intellectual specialisms by 1914. Psychiatry

---

[105] Sturdy and Cooter, 'Transformation of Medicine', 421–66.

[106] Hynes, *Edwardian Turn of Mind*, 148. The quotation comes from the opening number (1904) of the *British Psychological Journal*, which by 1914 had come under the control of the British Psychological Society.

and psychoanalysis found it more difficult to achieve scientific respectability. However, Freud's disciple and friend Ernest Jones founded the London Society of Psycho-analysts and set up as a consultant in London in 1913, the year in which papers were read to the Birmingham meeting of the British Association on Freud's theories of dreams and of the subconscious.[107]

Such a process of subdivision also occurred in the organization of the British Association, which set up six new Sections between 1884 and 1921: Anthropology (H) in 1884, Physiology (I) in 1893, Botany (K) in 1895,[108] Education (L) in 1901, and Agriculture (M) in 1912, while experimental psychology, recognized as a subsection of Physiology in 1906, became a Section in its own right (J) in 1921. The universities followed a parallel course. Cambridge University, a fairly conservative institution, though not inflexibly so, already had in 1885 Triposes in eight subject areas: Mathematics, Classics, Moral Sciences, Natural Sciences, Theology, Law, History, and Oriental Languages.[109] By the time war broke out it had another three: Medieval and Modern Languages (1886), Mechanical Sciences (1894), and Economics (1903), while within the first of them a new academic specialism (English Language and Literature) was developing, though it was not given its own Tripos until 1919.

The formation of new academic 'disciplines' thus affected the humanities as well as the natural and social sciences. The institutionalization of 'English' as a distinct subject throws a particularly revealing light on the process. Gladstone could never see why English literature should be studied in universities at all; this was not just because he deemed its texts inferior to the great writings of the ancient world, but because he also thought that something which was part of every intelligent person's cultural inheritance need not be formally taught. In the 1880s, however, a decline in the popularity of classics led to a search for a more accessible literature, which could similarly be used for the purpose of elevating 'character'. English literature, freed from the encumbrance of philology, seemed to fit the bill. During the 1880s 'English', long established in London University, spread like wildfire in the provincial colleges. In 1893 Oxford recognized it as a degree programme.[110]

A different trajectory was followed by history, which had established a niche for itself in the older universities rather earlier: Cambridge's History Tripos

---

[107] Jones's *Papers on Psychoanalysis* (1912) and Bernard Hart's much-reprinted *The Psychology of Insanity* (1912) also popularized key Freudian concepts, though the latter also drew on theorists like Janet (Hearnshaw, *Psychology*, 106–7).

[108] Botany separated off from Zoology.

[109] Strictly speaking, the Oriental Languages Tripos was not founded until 1895, but it was created out of two earlier Triposes, Semitic Languages and Indian Languages, created in 1878 and 1879, respectively.

[110] Though no student sat the Oxford Final Honour School in that year and only four did so in the following year!

dates back to 1875, Oxford's Final Honour School in that subject to 1872.[111] Numbers then steadily rose, until by 1914 history had become the most popular of all subjects in the two ancient universities, displacing the Natural Sciences at Cambridge and 'Greats' at Oxford. Despite this success, it still had difficulty in validating its credentials as an exact scholarly discipline.

In 1886 the *English Historical Review* was founded, edited by Mandell Creighton, the Dixie Professor of Ecclesiastical History at Cambridge. Creighton was best known as the author of the *History of the Papacy during the Period of the Reformation*, a scholarly opus which deliberately avoided the picturesque.[112] Rather than pursue a wider popularity, historians such as Creighton chose to emphasize, as their German counterparts were doing, the importance of historical *research*, focusing especially on such technical aspects as the editing of texts. When J. B. Bury, in his Cambridge 1903 Inaugural Lecture ('The Science of History'), proclaimed that history was 'simply a science, no less and no more', he was signalling a new approach to historical study.

Why did such academic specialization, along supposedly scientific lines, occur? Some think that the increase of knowledge led to its growing subdivision, and so to departmentalization. But more plausible is the claim that the dynamic was provided by a desire for professional advancement on the part of university tutors and lecturers, an expanding occupational group.[113] By 1919–20 there were already 2,277 full-time university teachers in Great Britain—excluding Oxford and Cambridge, which formed a world apart.[114]

Some historians and sociologists have interpreted these changes as forming part of a unilinear process, whereby knowledge of all kinds slowly but inexorably passed from clerics to laymen, from well-informed amateurs to specialized professionals, and from men of letters to scholars. Some such shift obviously occurred between, say, 1870 and 1970, with many of the crucial changes falling within the years 1886–1918. For example, in 1909 R. Douglas Laurie, a zoologist at Liverpool University, initiated the discussions which were to culminate in 1919 in the establishment of the Association of University Teachers (AUT), while just before the outbreak of the Great War the government set up a superannuation scheme for the profession.[115]

However, the late Victorian and Edwardian period can better be seen as a time of transition, in which many elements of an older cultural world coexisted

[111] Both had earlier linked history with law.
[112] Heyck, *Transformation*, 149.
[113] See the observations on the relationship between the 'marginal revolution' and the academic institutionalization of economics in Maloney, 'Marshall, Cunningham', 451.
[114] H. Perkin, *Key Profession: The History of the Association of University Teachers* (London, 1969), 49.
[115] FSSU (Federated Superannuation System for Universities).

with the new professionalism. For a start, in 1914 academic institutionalization still had a long way to run. Influential literary critics, in particular, were still as likely to be found outside academia as within it. Thus the prolific George ('King') Saintsbury only secured a university teaching post, the Chair at Edinburgh, in 1895, in his fiftieth year, having spent most of his earlier life as a literary journalist, while Edmund Gosse was Librarian to the House of Lords from 1904 onwards. Most leading critics were self-employed reviewers and columnists—notably the ex-don Andrew Lang (with his regular 'At the Sign of the Ship' column in *Longman's Magazine*), to say nothing of free spirits such as Arnold Bennett and G. K. Chesterton, or the hard-to-categorize Havelock Ellis.[116]

The same is true of history, many of whose leading practitioners (with serious works of scholarship to their name) were still earning a living with their pen rather than depending on an academic stipend. G. M. Trevelyan, for example, was awarded a Fellowship at Trinity, Cambridge, in 1898, the first such award to be made, and the following year he turned his doctoral dissertation into a book, *England in the Age of Wycliffe*. However, what seemed to be developing into a conventional 'modern' academic career abruptly ended in 1903 when Trevelyan left Cambridge for London, where he helped found the *Independent Review*. A steady stream of books then appeared, some of them on conventional historical themes: *England Under the Stuarts* (1904), for example, and the great trilogy on Garibaldi, published between 1907 and 1911. But Trevelyan also felt free to write a study of George Meredith. Not until 1927 did Trevelyan return to Cambridge, where he succeeded Bury as Regius Professor—an ironical succession, since, in *Clio: A Muse* (1913), he had given memorable expression to the view that history, far from being a 'science' as Bury had asserted, was better approached as a branch of humane literature.[117]

Yet Trevelyan's is not an isolated case. Many of the leading historians of the day used their position as 'public' authorities to instruct their wide circle of readers on the way in which the past cast light on modern social and political preoccupations. Thus the Webbs found time, in the midst of careers devoted to public administration and political intrigue, to chronicle the development of institutions of local government, while the Hammonds analysed the social consequences of industrialization in *The Village Labourer, 1760–1832* (1911)—J. L. Hammond combining this work with editing the *Speaker* from

---

[116] In his Oxford lecture, 'The Functions of Criticism', David Nichol Smith observed that the leading critics of the day (Bradley, Raleigh, Saintsbury, etc.) were now academics, in contrast to the Victorian age of independence (C. Baldick, *Criticism and Literary Theory 1890 to the Present* (1996), 59). These observations were premature.

[117] D. Cannadine, *G. M. Trevelyan: A Life in History* (London, 1992).

1899 to 1906. The enlargement of citizenship and political enlightenment meant much more to these 'public historians' than did scholarly precision and the perfection of 'technique'.[118]

Even within the university system, there was resistance to academic professionalism. Given the expansion of the curriculum taking place between 1886 and 1918, it was perhaps inevitable that the first generation of teachers in many of the new disciplines were 'late entrants' who had been trained in other fields. This sometimes resulted in an enhanced scholarly rigour and originality. No one would seriously claim that Marshall and Keynes were handicapped as economists because, when students, they had read Mathematics at Cambridge, nor that the legal and constitutional historian F. W. Maitland (Downing Professor of the Laws of England, 1888–1906), arguably the greatest historian of his age, suffered as a result of his legal education.[119] A. C. Bradley (who did *not*, contrary to general belief, think it fruitful to enquire into how many children Lady Macbeth had)[120] still commands respect on the basis of his lecture series, published in 1904 as *Shakespearean Tragedy*, at a time when he was holding the Chair of 'Poetry' at Oxford University; but Bradley had read 'Greats' as a student, and had then specialized in philosophy (he edited T. H. Green's *Prolegomena to Ethics*), before pursuing an academic career as a teacher of English Literature. Such disciplinary cross-fertilization could do nothing but good.

On the other hand, the sudden emergence of new subjects sometimes risked enthroning the plausible amateur. This happened particularly in English Literature. For example, Bradley's predecessor in the Poetry Chair had been the ludicrous W. J. Courthope, assistant editor of the *National Review* and a bombastic nationalist of limited discernment. Similarly, Walter Raleigh, Merton Professor of English Literature at Oxford from 1904 onwards, for all his organizational flair, was essentially an imaginative writer manqué and a dilettante, who failed to develop his occasionally acute insights and came to despise his own 'effeminate' critical role; in 1916 he gave up his Oxford Chair in relief, taking on what he regarded as the more rewarding post of official historian of the RAF.[121] At Cambridge an even odder situation developed. The first King Edward VII Professor of Literature (the chair was founded in 1910–11) was A. W. Verrall, an elderly obscure classicist, who died within a few months of

---

[118] V. Feske, *From Belloc to Churchill: Private Scholars, Public Culture, and the Crisis of British Liberalism 1900–1939* (Chapel Hill, NC, and London, 1996).

[119] Indeed, Maitland was never part of the Cambridge History Faculty, though he contributed 14 articles and 22 reviews to the *English Historical Review*. He held a specially created chair in Legal History, but his few students were reading law, not history.

[120] Baldick, *Criticism and Literary Theory*, 46.

[121] On Raleigh's organizational skills, D. J. Palmer, 'English', in Brock and Curthoys (eds.), *University of Oxford: Volume VII*, 406–11.

his appointment. His successor, Sir Arthur Quiller-Couch, ripened into a lovable 'character' and became a popular lecturer (though, perhaps, not entirely so with the women in his audience, whom he pointedly ignored). Best known through his earlier editorship of the *Oxford Book of English Verse*, 'Q' was the quintessential belle-lettrist—he had never before held any kind of academic post, and perhaps received the Cambridge Chair from Asquith as a reward for working for the Liberal Party in his native Cornwall!

In fact, within Oxford and Cambridge (still by far the largest of the English universities) the ideals of German scholarship were by no means universally embraced. This was partly because the new emphasis on research seemed to threaten that great achievement of the mid-Victorian years, the competitive examination. Educational 'modernization' also became entangled in the long-standing tension between the colleges and the university authorities.

What this meant for the development of Oxford history is illustrated by the quarrel which broke out in 1904, when the new Regius Professor, C. H. Firth, used his inaugural lecture to launch a heated attack on the superficiality of the History School, which, he alleged, produced 'journalists, politicians and well-informed men' but did 'not train historians'. The tutors (led by their dominant figure, A. L. Smith) vigorously responded, arguing that teaching was a skilled profession in its own right and that history, along with other subjects contained within the Faculty of Arts, embodied 'ideals of humane and liberal education'. By and large the tutors remained in control. Few undergraduates attended Firth's programme of Advanced Historical Training, while between 1897 and 1914 only thirty-six history candidates read for the newly established B.Litt. degree.[122] Lord Curzon, Oxford's Chancellor, clearly endorsed these priorities: 'Education is one thing and the spirit of inquiry is another', he declared in 1908.[123]

It was to escape such attitudes that the distinguished medievalist T. F. Tout left Oxford in 1890 for Manchester, where he constructed a very different kind of syllabus, one which featured a special subject based on the analysis of original sources and an undergraduate dissertation. The Manchester degree programme was a success insofar as, out of the eighty students who passed through the History School between 1905 and 1914, six later taught in a university or college, a high percentage; even more became schoolteachers (48.7 per cent of the men, 80.62 per cent of the women).[124] But Oxford and Cambridge were not trying to turn out a well-trained cadre of full-time

---

[122] P. R. H. Slee, *Learning and a Liberal Culture: The Study of Modern History in the University of Oxford, 1800–1914* (Manchester [c.1986]), 146–7; R. N. Soffer, 'Modern History', in Brock and Curthoys (eds.), *University of Oxford: Volume VII*, 370–2. Oxford had established two minor research degrees, the BSc. and BLitt., in 1895; Cambridge a DSc. and Litt.D. in 1883 (R. Simpson, *How The PhD Came to Britain* (London, 1983), 56, 62–3).

[123] Slee, *Learning and a Liberal Education*, 134.   [124] Ibid. 159–60.

historians so much as a governing national elite: 25 per cent of the Oxford students who graduated in history in the late-1890s were still going into the Church, 15 per cent into law, and 9 per cent into politics, the civil service, or local government, leaving only 17 per cent to pursue careers in any kind of teaching.[125] (No wonder that the Ph.D. was not adopted in British universities until the end of the Great War, and then mainly in response to the inability of British nationals to complete their studies in Germany or America).[126]

Though standards of proficiency in history teaching undoubtedly improved between 1886 and 1918 (encouraged by informal groupings such as the 'Junior Historians' at Cambridge from 1911 onwards),[127] the isolation of the professoriate from both college tutors and from most students permitted the survival in the ancient universities of an older ethos, not unlike that surrounding the classics, in which history was valued for its contribution to the formation of character and the fostering of a sane patriotism.

The same was even more true of literary studies. From the very start, keen advocates of 'English', such as the cantankerous lecturer John Churton Collins, had urged the universities to take it in hand before it fell victim to flaccid dilettantism on the one hand, and philosophical pedantry on the other.[128] As things worked out, the subject, if anything, veered towards the former: it certainly became *less* specialized and technical, once the mid-Victorian preoccupation with Anglo-Saxon and philology had been supplanted by an emphasis on the civilizing power exerted by great works of imaginative literature.

In many ways English Literature thus went against the grain of academic development: in the emerging social sciences, as well as in the natural sciences, the tendency was rather to make academic study more stringent, austerely scholarly, and difficult. Yet even in the social sciences the move towards strict 'scientific objectivity' was checked by a traditional commitment to the furtherance of human progress.

This desire to serve humanity did not always find expression in 'benevolence'. Anxieties about the irrationality of the crowd (articulated, in different ways, by Graham Wallas, William McDougall, and W. B. L. Trotter, author of *The Instincts of the Herd*, 1908–9) led to the search for ways to stabilize society by

---

[125] Ibid. 125. On the careers of Balilol history graduates, see R. N. Soffer, *Discipline and Power: The University, History, and the Making of an English Elite, 1870–1930* (Stanford, 1995).

[126] Perkin, *Key Profession*, 35. Many universities gave higher research degrees to distinguished scholars. For the complicated story, see Simpson, *PhD*.

[127] Brooke, *University of Cambridge*, 235–6.

[128] S. Potter, *The Muse in Chains: A Study in Education* (London, 1937), 190. Yet the first holder of the Merton Chair in English Language and Literature, established in 1885, was A. S. Napier, a specialist in German philology (J. Gross, *The Rise and Fall of the Man of Letters: Aspects of English Literary Life Since 1800* (London, 1969; 1973 edn.), 193–4). Collins later acquired a chair of his own at Birmingham University (Baldick, *Criticism and Literary Theory*, 24).

bringing 'dangerous' social elements under the control of the appropriate 'experts'. Such a quest reached its logical culmination in the programme of 'negative eugenics', in which many social scientists participated—not only the eugenists themselves, but many psychologists who made a study of 'deviance', social 'pathology', and the danger allegedly posed by 'the multiplication of the unfit'.

Yet this was only one side of the Edwardian intellectual scene, which also had its sunnier aspects. Marshall, berated by Cunningham for assuming the fixity of human nature, in fact placed the study of economics within an evolutionary framework which postulated a kind of moral progress: indeed, he could write optimistically about the emergence of a new kind of 'economic chivalry', in which people, instead of being driven by pecuniary motives, would increasingly act out of a sense of 'honour'. Economics was thus, in Marshall's eyes, becoming less a science of wealth-creation than one of welfare-promotion, a formula which allowed ample scope for the play of ethical forces. Even the Webbs, for all their somewhat brutal talk about the need to regulate the affairs of the 'average sensual man', were optimists at heart—indeed, the reason why they were so willing to allot so much power to their beloved 'experts' was precisely because they could never quite understand how this power might be employed cruelly or for the experts' own self-aggrandizement.[129]

The concept of 'progress' also remained at the centre of social thought because of the continuing popularity of Social Darwinism, still dominant in anthropology, politics, and branches of psychology as well as in sociology. According to Hobhouse, humanity passes through three stages of development, from kinship, to authority, and finally to the attainment of 'citizenship'—a schema which allowed him to equate moral with intellectual progress and to locate both within an evolutionary framework, thereby underpinning his 'New Liberal' convictions.

In 1907 the young philosopher Bertrand Russell took issue with these assumptions in an article in the *Independent Review*, where he argued that a moral standard could not be *deduced* from the evolutionary process since it depended on external factors. Such a rejection of a particularly British kind of moralism was later to become almost an orthodoxy of the social sciences, whose practitioners came to view different societies as 'working systems', to be understood purely in their own terms.[130] But such historical and cultural relativism was more a feature of the post-war world than it was of the Edwardian period.[131]

[129] See R. Soffer, *Ethics and Society in England: The Revolution in the Social Sciences, 1870–1914* (Berkeley, 1978), 168.

[130] Pitt-Rivers, for example, converted from evolutionary theory to functionalism.

[131] J. W. Burrow, *Evolution and Society: A Study in Victorian Social Theory* (Cambridge, 1966), 276. Neither was there any scope for moral relativism in Idealism.

Before 1914 few social theorists had yet withdrawn so far into their special-isms as to lose contact with the ethical assumptions that largely governed public life. On the contrary, in Jose Harris's words, they continued, almost without exception, to believe 'that a major purpose of social science was the promotion of public virtue', and that 'moral character, active citizenship and "public spirit" were the indispensable building-blocks of a well-ordered soci-ety and a virtuous state'.[132] This vision clearly owed much to the traditions of Oxford, of which Hobhouse himself was a product, in that it sought to foster civic worth and national leadership quite as much as the encouragement of 'modern' conceptions of research.

In any case, for many pre-war scholars ethical and political impartiality proved rather elusive goals. Thus Lord Acton, Regius Professor of History at Cambridge from 1895 until his death in 1902, true to his semi-German ancestry, hymned the praises of a scrupulous impartiality which he tried to impose on contributors to the *Cambridge Modern History*, of which he was the first editor. But, stout Liberal Catholic that he was, he scarcely practised what he preached, all his own (very scanty) writings being imbued with an ardent belief in liberty, freedom of conscience, and moral rectitude; he was no more disinterested than his polemical predecessor, Sir John Seeley. Significantly, Acton largely owed his Chair to his long-standing friendship with Gladstone, who may have awarded it to him as a consolation prize after he had been denied (by Morley's veto) the Cabinet office for which he had shamelessly asked in 1892.[133]

In contemporary Germany Max Weber was bewailing the inability of social scientists to gain access to political power, but in Britain his counterparts experienced exactly the opposite fate.[134] Many aspiring scholars deserted their research for careers in social reform or politics—for example, the first two Directors of the LSE, W. A. S. Hewins, the economic historian, and the geographer Halford Mackinder left within a few years of their appointment to serve as Unionist MPs in support of tariff reform.

And yet, when all due allowance has been made for these mid-Victorian 'residues', a qualitative change *had* taken place in intellectual life between 1886 and 1918. Growing disciplinary specialization, like the proliferation of other professional associations, had undoubtedly promoted an advance in the organ-ization of knowledge, leading to mankind's greater capacity to control the natural and social environment. However, a cultural price had to be paid for this 'progress'.

---

[132] J. Harris, *Private Lives, Public Spirit: A Social History of Britain 1870–1914* (Oxford, 1993), 250.
[133] He had been fobbed off, at the time, with a lordship-in-waiting at the court, where he had endeared himself to the Queen.
[134] Abrams, *Origins of Sociology*, 148–9.

Among the victims were the clergy, who largely lost their central position in scholarship and learning, especially at the ancient universities. Earlier in the nineteenth century 92 per cent of Oxford Fellows were in Holy Orders, but between 1881 and 1900, as a result of the earlier relaxation of conditions governing Fellowships, the proportion had fallen to 31 per cent, and continued to decline. Yet during the same period the proportion of Fellows going into a university teaching career rose from 13 per cent to 57 per cent.[135] A new lay profession was thus emerging quite outside the ambit of the Established Church. Some clergymen, it is true, could still be found combining their scholarly work with their clerical vocation: Creighton became Bishop of London in 1897, and Cunningham, for many years vicar of Great St Mary's, Cambridge, was eventually made Archdeacon of Ely in 1908. But such men were now a minority even within their own university. As for the new civic universities, these had, from the start, been entirely secular institutions.

Secularization also affected the student body. In the middle of the nineteenth century one-half of all Balliol undergraduates went into Holy Orders, but by the 1890s only one in twenty-five was doing so.[136] The fact that bright young men now tended to avoid the Church as a career in turn affected the public schools: only 27 per cent of their teachers were clergymen by 1886; fewer still, 20 per cent, by 1890.[137] And although in the public schools it remained common to have a clergyman as headmaster (about 60 per cent of Headmasters' Conference schools did so in 1903), the scholarly calibre of these men seems to have declined: Edward Lyttelton, headmaster at Eton, had only secured a Second Class degree and struggled as a teacher of very able boys[138]—in painful contrast to the situation only a few decades earlier, when public school headmasters included some of the most eminent classical scholars in the land.

Academic specialization was also undermining the capacity of even the most well-read layman to keep abreast of developments in contemporary scholarship. In 1870 most areas of learning outside mathematics and the physical sciences could quite easily be mastered by the intelligent citizen—though philosophical Idealism, admittedly, presented a severe problem to those

[135] A. J. Engel, *From Clergyman to Don: The Rise of the Academic Profession in Nineteenth-Century Oxford* (Oxford, 1983), 286.

[136] Heyck, *Transformation*, 183. On the principal careers of Oxford men graduating in the late nineteenth century, see M. C. Curthoys, 'The Careers of Oxford Men', in M. G. Brock and M. C. Curthoys (eds.), *The History of the University of Oxford: Volume VI: Nineteenth-Century Oxford, Part 1* (Oxford, 1997), 477–510, esp. 503.

[137] In 22 leading schools. In ten 'great' schools, 40.3% were ordained in 1880, 28.7% in 1889, 13.13% in 1906 (J. R. de S. Honey, *Tom Brown's Universe: The Development of the Victorian Public School* (London, 1977), 308).

[138] Ibid. 317.

unwilling to master its esoteric language. But thereafter difficulties multiplied, particularly as a result of the intrusion of statistical complexity into the social sciences. 'When I turn over the pages of *Biometrika*,' confessed George Bernard Shaw, a man not noted for his humility, 'I am out of my depth at the first line.'[139] In economics the marginal productivity theory of distribution, which Marshall and others were developing in the 1890s, proved similarly difficult to comprehend. Philosophy, too, became largely inaccessible to all but the cognoscenti, following Russell's marriage of advanced mathematics and logic in *Principia Mathematica*, co-authored with A. N. Whitehead in 1910–13.

J. A. Hobson, a man with a grievance who felt that his heterodox economic opinions had debarred him from a university teaching post, wrote an article in 1893 railing at the way in which an academic class, consisting of 'prig, pedant, and specialist', was enjoying 'an artificially protected and specialised form of intellectual life'.[140] University staff, charged the critics, were turning themselves into a new kind of priesthood, custodians of an arcane body of knowledge unintelligible to the general public, to whom they were in no way accountable.

Such criticisms were unfair, in that many university teachers gave generously of their time and expertise to the University Extension Movement and, after 1903, to assisting the Workers' Educational Association, which had a highly democratic ethos.[141] But this did not alter the fact that those debarred from all forms of academic education were increasingly at a disadvantage. Before 1880 it had been widely assumed that knowledge and science were open to all able men (and women?) of perseverance. Indeed, Herbert Spencer's earlier appeal to intelligent working men and women had rested on the hope that a mastery of his 'Synthetic Philosophy', however tough the going, would suffice to unlock all the mysteries of the universe. But by the time of his death the 'Synthetic Philosophy' had been so discredited in academic circles that it could no longer be treated as a talisman—though Spencer retained a large popular following in the United States.

It was the plebeian autodidacts of the spiritualist and secularist societies, however, who found themselves most comprehensively stranded by the new structure of learning. The spiritualists, who had always insisted on the capacity of ordinary men and women to control their own bodies without recourse to the mumbo-jumbo of official medicine, believed in the 'democratic intellect'. In 1865 one of their leaders had spoken of creating a 'People's University',

---

[139] B. Shaw, *The Doctor's Dilemma, Getting Married, and The Shewing-Up of Blanco Posnet* (London, 1911), p.lxxiii.

[140] He also wrote of 'a corporation, a clique, or a coterie for purely intellectual purposes' (Heyck, *Transformation*, 185, 228).

[141] See Ch. 14. Not all university extension classes, however, were taught by university staff: the most popular teacher of economics was the Revd Philip Wicksteed, a Unitarian minister.

which would teach physiology, phrenology, social science, psychology, anthropology, cosmology, and, of course, spiritualism. Though this ambition was never realized, the spiritualists set up 'Lyceums' in many towns: in 1910 these numbered 210, with a registered membership of over 10,000. The Lyceums, however, catered mainly for the needs of children and young people, rather in the role of an alternative Sunday school—the larger educational project quietly lapsed.[142]

Admittedly, the socialist societies and other working-class organizations kept alive the older tradition of educational self-help, up until 1914 and even beyond.[143] But 'science', in its widest sense, changed its character once it ceased to be the common property of all well-read citizens and became entangled in the acquisition of formal educational qualifications. A situation was being created in which the 'man in the street' was supposed to defer to accredited expertise. Knowledge itself was thus more hierarchically organized in 1914 than it had been thirty years earlier, which in turn led to new forms of social stratification.

It is significant that James Murray's *Oxford English Dictionary* (1888) was the first in which the word 'intellectual' appeared as a noun: 'a person possessing or supposed to possess superior powers of intellect'—so ran the definition.[144] By 1914 it could be assumed that such people would very probably have been university-educated—a truly novel state of affairs.

[142] L. Barrow, *Independent Spirits: Spiritualism and English Plebeians 1850–1910* (London, 1986), 194–210.
[143] See Ch. 14.
[144] Heyck, *Transformation*, 236.

PART V

The Great War

CHAPTER 17

The Great War: The Loss of Innocence, 1914–1916

1. 'ALL OVER BY CHRISTMAS?': AUGUST–DECEMBER 1914

As ministers made their way through cheering crowds to hear Asquith tell an enthusiastic Commons that Britain was at war with Germany, they sensed that they enjoyed the backing of most of their fellow countrymen. 'Peace resistance' melted away almost overnight. The ILP directed a greeting of sympathy 'across the roar of the guns' towards its German comrades, but the international solidarity of the working class proved to be little more than a slogan. Ramsay MacDonald, critical to the end of Grey's foreign policy, resigned as Chairman of the Parliamentary Labour Party, to be replaced by Arthur Henderson, who, like his counterparts abroad, voted war credits and offered the government his patriotic support. Most suffragists, the WSPU as well as the majority of the NUWSS, rallied behind the war effort. Though reservations abounded, those who harboured them deemed it prudent, for the time being, to maintain a public silence.

Party rancours took longer to abate—if indeed they ever fully did so. Churchill, radiant with happiness over his chance of playing a leading role in 'this glorious delicious war', as he described it to Margot Asquith, had already sounded out the Opposition Leaders about their readiness to join Liberals in a 'National Government', only to be rebuffed for his pains. How strained the relationship between the two major parties still was became apparent in mid-September when Bonar Law led his followers out of the Commons, in protest at the way in which the government had placed the Irish Home Rule and the Welsh Disestablishment Bills on the statute book, albeit with the proviso that they would not come into operation until the war had ended. Nevertheless an all-party electoral truce was quickly put into place,[1] and the Opposition Leaders offered the Asquith ministry general support from the backbenches.

[1] The truce expired in January 1915 and was thereafter renewed on a monthly basis. In December 1915 a Bill was introduced to extend the life of Parliament for a year—a time-limit reduced in committee to 8 months.

The government was also given a non-partisan character that it would otherwise have lacked when Balfour helped persuade Lord Kitchener to fill the office of War Secretary—in place of its temporary occupant, the Prime Minister. Changes were soon afterwards made at the Admiralty. The elderly Lord Fisher was recalled as First Sea Lord, though without the powers exercised by Kitchener, who had a Cabinet seat—a discrimination that rankled—while command of the Grand Fleet was transferred from Sir George Callaghan to the pessimistically conscientious Admiral Sir John Jellicoe.

Kitchener promptly used his immense prestige to appeal for 100,000 volunteers aged 19–30 in an all-party campaign: even John Redmond, the Irish Nationalist Leader, participated in its work. The resultant rush to the colours surprised, even embarrassed, the War Office. In the first month of war 300,000 men came forward, with a daily peak of 33,000 being reached on 3 September.[2] Struggling to equip, clothe, and train so vast a horde,[3] the authorities raised the minimum height of recruits by three inches on 11 September, before lowering it at the end of October and restoring it to its former level on 14 November. What animated this military ardour, which gripped men of all social classes, remains unclear.[4] Even more mysteriously, if the war was indeed to be 'all over by Christmas', as almost everyone bar Kitchener predicted, there would hardly be a need for a mass army which could not take the field until well into 1915, at the very earliest.

On 5 August a subcommittee of the Cabinet, the War Council, decided to send the British Expeditionary Force (BEF) to France at once. However, at a Cabinet meeting on the following day Kitchener insisted that for the time being only four divisions should go there, the other two being held back, ostensibly to guard against the possibility of invasion, but perhaps also to preserve the social peace.[5] The navy, which Churchill had put on a war footing as early as 1 August, rose to the occasion, and 120,000 troops were transported across the Channel within ten days, without a single loss of life.[6]

But where precisely should the BEF assemble? Sir John French, the Commander-in-Chief, favoured a rear concentration of troops in Amiens, and even broached the possibility of an Antwerp-based expedition (the 'Belgian option'), the better to safeguard the Channel ports. This dismayed Sir Henry Wilson,

[2] N. Ferguson, *The Pity of War* (Harmondsworth, 1998), 198.

[3] In January 1915 the new battalions had only 400 rifles, half their proper allowance (J. M. Bourne, *Britain and the Great War 1914–1918* (London, 1989), 159).

[4] See Ch. 20.

[5] Ferguson, *Pity of War*, 167.

[6] On 20 August a fifth division was released, a sixth followed in early September, and a seventh, formed from troops from South Africa, arrived in the middle of September (H. Strachan, *The First World War: Volume One: To Arms* (Oxford, 2001), 206).

who feared that all his plans were about to be set aside. But on 12 August French and Kitchener reluctantly agreed that the BEF, in accordance with Wilson's mobilization scheme, should proceed south-east from Boulogne towards Maubeuge, just outside the Belgian border, where it would operate on the left wing of the main French force. This decision, duly ratified by the War Council, had three momentous consequences: it placed the BEF smack in the path of the advancing German armies;[7] it left the northern Channel ports unprotected; and, though few realized it at the time, it effectively meant 'the surrender of independent military initiative by Great Britain'.[8]

Meanwhile, in accordance with the Schlieffen Plan, the Germans were attacking France through Belgium and Luxembourg in a sweeping movement aimed at encircling Paris. Anxious to avoid the nightmare of a war on two fronts, they hoped to crush the French in the west within forty-two days of mobilization, before the cumbersome Russian army had time to assemble on Germany's eastern border and launch an offensive of its own. Simply in military terms, the odds were heavily stacked against Germany's success: funnelling vast numbers of troops so quickly along the inadequate road systems of France and Belgium could scarcely be accomplished within the tight time-scale, nor was allowance made for the possibility of even the smallest resistance, such as that offered by the Belgian army when it mounted its brave defence of the forts at Liège and Namur. However, what gave the Germans an outside chance of victory was the folly of the French, who, following Joffre's Plan XVII, hurled their main armies into Lorraine, where they sustained huge losses. France's 5th Army, under General Lanrezac, was left to counter the main German thrust. Alongside it stood the small BEF.

Advancing northwards from Maubeuge, Sir John's force stumbled into the German 1st Army at Mons (23 August). Here 75,000 British soldiers engaged fourteen enemy divisions, comprising about 300,000 troops in all, in an area covered in mines, factories, and slag-heaps. The British demonstrated their proficiency at rapid rifle fire (fifteen rounds a minute), and also showed that they had learnt something from the Boer War about the importance of defensive entrenchment by digging in by the Mons–Condé canal. The BEF thus helped to slow down the Germans' outflanking movement.[9] But though sustaining casualties of only 1,600, many fewer than Germany's, the BEF,

---

[7] Too eager to co-operate with the French General Staff, Henry Wilson had uncritically accepted the view of the French Commander, General Joffre, that the Germans would attack along a route that ran south of the River Meuse. In fact, the Schlieffen Plan decreed that the German armies would advance *north* of the Meuse. This exposed the BEF to maximum danger.

[8] W. J. Philpott, *Anglo-French Relations and Strategy on the Western Front, 1914–1918* (Basingstoke, 1996), 8–12.

[9] T. Wilson, *The Myriad Faces of War: Britain and the Great War 1914–1918* (Oxford, 1986: Cambridge, 1988 edn.), 41.

unsupported by the French forces to its right, was so heavily outnumbered that it had no option but to beat an orderly retreat to the south.

Shedding their packs and greatcoats, the 'Old Contemptibles' covered a distance of some 200 miles in thirteen days, in blazing heat which caused many to drop out. The 1st Battalion of the Gloucestershire Regiment averaged 16.5 miles a day, marching an astonishing 23 miles on 27 August. The II Corps, under Smith-Dorrien, was subjected to an additional ordeal when it was forced, on 26 August, to fight a rearguard action at Le Câteau, where, before being extricated by the French cavalry, it lost 8,000 men, more than Wellington had lost at Waterloo.[10] The survivors who escaped to relative safety along the cobbled streets of nothern France were dazed with exhaustion, their boots filled with blood.

If the feet of the troops were bruised, so were the feelings of their Commander-in-Chief, who had been nursing a grievance over Lanrezac's failure to keep him informed about the French army's movements when it had retreated from the River Sambre, at the very moment of the engagement at Mons. An ill-tempered meeting with the French generals at St Quentin on 26 August (at which no one could speak the other's language fluently except Henry Wilson) added to the inter-Allied discord. Indeed, Sir John briefly contemplated withdrawing the BEF to below the Seine, on the far side of Paris, transferring his stores from Rouen to Le Havre, or even leaving France altogether in order to refit. Kitchener, arriving in France in a destroyer, saved the Entente by summoning French to the Paris Embassy (2 September) to convey the Cabinet's instruction that he stay in the line, 'conforming to the movements of the French Army'. Yet did this mean, as Joffre supposed, that he could in future treat the British as a subordinate auxiliary force? Or was the BEF ultimately an independent army responsible only to its own government, as Sir John maintained? The issue was never to be satisfactorily resolved.

Yet even as the Allies fell into disarray, the Schlieffen Plan was unravelling. The German advance had already fallen behind schedule when, on 28 August, the Commander of the 1st Army, von Kluck, decided, with his General Staff's approval, to change his line of advance, moving *east* of Paris, with a view to cutting the capital off from the main body of the French forces, instead of sweeping around it from the west, as Schlieffen had stipulated. This last-minute change of plan not only marked the end of the attempt to encircle the French Army, it also exposed the German flank to the counter-attack being prepared by Joffre, who had, only in the nick of time, pulled in reinforcements

---

[10] J. Keegan, *The First World War* (London, 1998), 113. More British troops were killed than in any battle since the seventeenth century: A. Gregory, 'Lost Generations: The Impact of Military Casualties on Paris, London and Berlin', in J. Winter and J.-L. Robert (eds.), *Capital Cities at War: Paris, London, Berlin 1914–1919* (Cambridge, 1997), 88.

from the east (the newly constituted 6th Army) to check the advance of the Germans, who were daily getting drawn further away from their main supply lines.

In the decisive battle of the Marne (4–9 September), Joffre threw thirty-six divisions against fewer than thirty very weary German divisions, quickly opening up a gap, 35 miles in width, between the enemy's 1st and 2nd Armies. The BEF was initially resting 10 miles in the rear, but, revitalized by the arrival of four fresh brigades, it moved forward into this gap, in support of the French armies, following an emotional appeal to Sir John from Joffre—and in accordance with his Cabinet instructions. The Germans, worsted in the Battle of the Marne, in which the British necessarily played a relatively minor part, pulled back to the Aisne, where they dug in on 14 September, the French and British troops hard on their heels. From then until 27 September the antagonists launched bloody but inconclusive assaults against one another.

There followed the episode known as the 'race to the sea', in which each side attempted to turn the other's flanks, attempts which soon petered out for want of space upon reaching the North Sea to the west and the Swiss border to the east. During these manoeuvres Churchill, with his insatiable love of adventure and publicity, arrived in Antwerp in early October to direct the Royal Marines and sailors from the Royal Naval Division, who had earlier arrived there by train to bolster the Belgian defenders; this melodramatic escapade succeeded in holding up the German advance for a crucial few days. Meanwhile (and of much greater significance), the BEF in late September had successfully spirited itself away under the noses of the Germans, in order to take up new positions to the north and west in Flanders, nearer to their home base.

They did so just in time to participate in the first battle of Ypres (8 October–22 November). Here 60,000 British troops (which now included the 7th Division, composed of regulars from overseas) desperately held the line in the face of the German assault, despite being heavily outmanned and outgunned. The Germans suffered the greater losses, but of the Regulars of the original BEF less than half survived unwounded, and nearly one-third died: from the crack 7th Division only 2,500 men and fifty officers were still operational a month later. By the end of the year the British had lost at least 30,000 men, a small number indeed compared with the half-million or so casualties sustained by the French, but Sir John, a veteran of relatively small-scale colonial wars, was horrified—as well he might be, since these casualties were at least three times higher than the General Staff's pre-war estimate.[11]

---

[11] D. French, *British Strategy and War Aims, 1914–16* (London, 1986), 68.

So, on the Western Front 1914 ended in stalemate, the combatants separated by fortified lines which stretched over 475 miles. The British, who were holding about 35 miles of this line, which included the notorious Ypres Salient, found themselves jammed between the Belgians and the French on one side, and the main bulk of the French army on the other. The Schlieffen Plan had obviously failed: indeed, during 1915 the German General Staff were to operate it in reverse, holding ground in the west and concentrating their main attacks in the east against the now fully mobilized Russian armies. Worryingly for Berlin, the Germans were reaching the zenith of their man-power resources, while the Allies were only beginning to harness theirs. On the other hand, the German army remained in occupation of most of Belgium and a large slice of north-west France, where much of its mining and heavy industry were located.[12] This gave the Central Powers, almost to the end of the war, the strategic initiative. Henceforward the French objective was self-evident: liberation of the national territory. But what should the British be doing?

Oddly enough, the British Cabinet still did not realize that it had made an irrevocable commitment to Continental warfare. On the contrary, it believed that all it had done was to engage in an amphibious operation that could be terminated at will. After all, the British way in warfare had traditionally sought to exploit the country's greatest asset, dominance at sea. Indeed, the Admiralty shared with the wider public an expectation that the war would speedily be won in a new Trafalgar, with the Grand Fleet sending the upstart German navy to the bottom of the ocean.

But the German navy stayed bottled up in harbour, its commander, Vice-Admiral Reinhard Scheer, knowing that the British had maintained a decisive margin of superiority in Dreadnought-type battleships—twenty-four to thir-teen.[13] There were, admittedly, two early engagements, the first off Heligoland on 28 August 1914 and the second at Dogger Bank on January 1915 (when, through a chapter of accidents, Beatty lost his chance to destroy Hipper's battle cruisers), but neither involved the main battle fleets, and the Germans only ventured forth on another five occasions during the whole of 1915. The British, for their part, had no means of forcing the German fleet to come out and fight, the electromagnetic mine and the torpedo making the enforcement of a close blockade too hazardous. The Admiralty was thus left with no option but to rely on a distant 'contraband' blockade, policed from the Scottish bases at Rosyth, on the Firth of Forth, and Scapa Flow, in the Orkneys. A distant blockade of this limited kind would gradually exert pressure on the German economy, but

---

[12] As a result of the German occupation, France had lost 50% of her coalfields and 64% of her iron.
[13] The British were also laying down another 13 new vessels, Germany only 10. In fact, Scheer struck a middle course between Tirpitz's recklessness and the Kaiser's ultra-caution.

not for many months to come. Had the Schlieffen Plan succeeded, Britain's naval superiority would have counted for naught.[14]

The immobility of the German fleet freed its Zeppelins to go on bombing raids over England, while U-boats were similarly released to counter the British blockade by attempting to establish a blockade of their own through the destruction of merchant vessels. On 20 October 1914 a British steamer was sunk, and in February 1915 the Germans declared the area around Britain a war zone—a portent of danger to come.

Nevertheless, in retrospect, Britain's containment of the German High Fleet can be seen as a strategic victory. It not only permitted the safe passage of the BEF to France but, with support from the Japanese navy, ensured the equally safe transportation of troops from India, Australia, and New Zealand to Europe, Asia Minor, and Africa. Britain and her Allies thus had a geographic mobility which the Central Powers could never match. But if this was a victory, it did not feel like a particularly glorious one to the patriotic general public.

The Admiralty's frustration at being confined to the role of chaperone to the army was increased by its failure to stop German hit-and-run raids: Yarmouth was bombarded on 3 November, Scarborough, Whitby, and Hartlepool on 16 December. More worrying still was the German adoption of a 'guerre de course', spearheaded by Admiral von Spee's squadron, led by the *Scharnhorst* and the *Gneisenau*, originally based in the Pacific. Japan's entry into the war on the Allied side in late August caused von Spee to move his commerce-raiding operation into the South Atlantic, where he not only preyed on British merchant shipping but also succeeded in trapping Admiral Cradock's squadron at Coronel, off the coast of Chile, on 1 November, sinking two of its ships, the *Monmouth* and *Good Hope*, with the loss of 1,600 sailors. It was Britain's first naval defeat for a hundred years. Fisher dispatched two of his beloved new battle cruisers, *Invincible* and *Inflexible*, to the South Atlantic to deal with the danger. On 8 December Admiral Sturdee duly ran von Spee down and, with his superior speed and firepower, annihilated the German squadron at the battle of the Falklands Islands. But the whole episode had shown up what was to prove one of Britain's most serious naval weaknesses: Fisher's neglect of ordinary cruisers, whose replacement, the Dreadnought-type battle cruisers, were so expensive to build that they did not exist in sufficient numbers.

A disappointed public put pressure on the Liberal ministry to achieve some sort of naval success, anywhere and by any means. Asquith told Churchill it was 'time he bagged something, & broke some crockery'[15]—advice the impetuous First Lord was only too eager to act upon, especially since, after the

[14] Which is why Schlieffen despised seapower and took so slighting a view of the German navy itself (Keegan, *First World War*, 33).
[15] Wilson, *Myriad Faces*, 110.

Falklands encounter, he felt the navy was free to adopt an aggressive role. Fisher, still dreaming of an amphibious Baltic operation, briefly converted Churchill to his impractical notion of seizing the island of Borkum off the German coast.[16] A maritime strategy was also advocated by some Liberal ministers, such as the Home Secretary, Reginald McKenna, who was anxious to avoid a protracted Continental entanglement. But to have diverted resources from home waters at this juncture would have been an act of reckless desperation, playing into the hands of Scheer, whose waiting game was predicated upon the British forfeiting their advantage in capital ships through a series of piecemeal engagements and accidents. Nor was this a total impossibility, since Britain's margin of naval superiority *was* being gradually eroded. In October a brand new battleship, the *Audacious*, sank when it hit a mine off Northern Ireland,[17] and though no further mishap of this kind befell a modern battleship for the rest of the war,[18] no one could have foreseen this at the time.

The jittery mood within the Admiralty also owed something to the fact that, on only the third day of the war, a light cruiser, the *Amphion*, had been destroyed by a mine with the loss of 150 officers,[19] while on 22 September a U-boat had sunk another three elderly cruisers. Moreover, during October two Dreadnoughts had not quite been completed and another four were undergoing repairs (the fact that the Grand Fleet spent far more time at sea than its German counterpart was significant here). For a while, during November, the British superiority in Dreadnought battleships fell to the narrow margin of 17 : 15, and in battle cruisers to 5 : 4. No wonder that Jellicoe, acutely conscious that he was indeed the 'only man on either side who could lose the war in an afternoon', pursued an ultra-cautious policy and exercised a highly centralized system of command over his Grand Fleet.

However, the temptation to engage in distant operations remained strong, and was increased with the entry of Turkey into the war on the side of the Central Powers. In late August the Admiralty had requisitioned, with offers of compensation, two Dreadnoughts that were being built for the Turkish fleet: one of which, renamed *Agincourt*, became, with its twelve 14-inch guns, the most heavily armed ship in any European navy.[20] This angered the Turkish government. What swayed the balance was the escape of the German battle cruiser *Goeben* and the light cruiser *Breslau*—for which Churchill was unfairly

---

[16] The First Lord also favoured an amphibious raid on Zeebrugge (French, *British Strategy*, 66).

[17] It was there because Scapa Flow itself was still deemed insecure (J. Terraine, 'The Substance of the War', in H. Cecil and P. H. Liddle (eds.), *Facing Armageddon: The First World War Experienced* (London, 1996), 6).

[18] On 1 January 1915 an old battleship, *Formidable*, was sunk in the Channel by a U-boat.

[19] Terraine, 'Substance of War', 5.

[20] Keegan, *First World War*, 281.

blamed. The two ships proceeded to Constantinople, where they handed themselves over to Turkey, which, falling increasingly under German influence, joined the war on the side of the Central Powers in late October.

On 11 November Sultan Mehmed V declared holy war on Britain. The British responded by making Egypt a British Protectorate and rushing troops from India to its defence—in time to repel a Turkish attack on the Suez Canal in February 1915. In the longer run Turkey's intervention presented the British with both a danger and an opportunity. For although many ministers worried over the threat posed by pan-Islamism to their dominance of the Near and Middle East, the widening of the war also suggested to many Britons the possibility of acquiring gains outside Europe or on its peripheries, while allies were left to fight on mainland Europe—a very traditional scenario.[21] But as the fighting on the Western Front died down towards the end of 1914, Britain's future role in the war was still unclear.

2. THE END OF THE LIBERAL MINISTRY, JANUARY–MAY 1915

The crucial decisions were made in a series of War Council meetings in January 1915, when ministers debated what use they intended to make of their new armies. Lloyd George favoured pulling out altogether from France and Belgium and launching operations in Syria (against Turkey) and in Salonika (against Austria-Hungary): was it not possible, he asked, 'to get at the enemy from some other direction, and to strike a blow that would end the war once and for all?'[22] 'Are we really bound to hand over the ordering of our troops to France as if we were her vassal?', he pondered.[23] A similar posture was struck by Churchill, who protested at the spectacle of British troops 'chew[ing] barbed wire in France'. The War Council's Secretary, Maurice Hankey, a Royal Marine, not an army officer, sympathized with this viewpoint, suggesting action against Turkey in alliance with Greece and Bulgaria, though without specifying exactly where and how.[24]

But those who later became known as the 'westerners' had a powerful case to make against such a strategy. The Central Powers, they argued, enjoyed the advantage of interior lines of communication, which meant that the Germans could always, if necessary, rush troops to reinforce their allies faster than the

---

[21] As an imperial power, Britain also had an incentive to capture Germany's colonies to prevent them from becoming hostile bases for the German navy—though this task was largely devolved onto the Japanese and Dominions governments.

[22] Lloyd George seemed to be mainly concerned to sponsor a feasibility study of a Balkans expedition (Wilson, *Myriad Faces*, 105).

[23] In a letter to Churchill of Jan. 1915 (Bourne, *Great War*, 149).

[24] Wilson, *Myriad Faces*, 104.

British could transport men through mine- and U-boat-infested seas to distant theatres of operation. Such arguments were reinforced by the Admiralty's reluctance to move its more powerful ships away from home waters while the German High Fleet remained undefeated.

Even if the 'easterners' could have agreed on precisely where they wanted to concentrate the British effort, these considerations would have been cogent. Austria and Turkey were in truth not, as they loosely claimed, 'props' of the German Reich—rather the contrary. There were indeed geopolitical considerations which supported action in the east, the defeat of Serbia having opened a direct line of communication between Berlin and Constaninople which menaced Britain's position in Egypt, the Middle East, and India. But many proponents of what A. J. P. Taylor has called 'cigar butt strategy' fundamentally wanted cost-free successes, as Churchill admitted in a moment of rare common sense, when he reminded Fisher in January: 'Germany is the foe, and it is bad war to seek cheaper victories and easier antagonists.'[25]

Sir John French cut even deeper to the heart of the matter when he reminded ministers that 'in the western theatre a German victory would be decisive', and that a 'crushing defeat' of the French 'would be very dangerous and embarrassing to our own safety'.[26] True, Kitchener personally favoured a policy of passive defence in the west, using the new armies in areas such as the eastern Mediterranean, until they were ready to take part in a big push in 1917, by which time the other powers would have fought themselves to a standstill.[27] But Britain had entered the war to honour its treaty obligations to the Belgians and to prevent France from being crushed; it would therefore have to play its part in ejecting the invader. In any case, the French still doubted how committed the British were to their cause—understandably, in view of the great disparity between the casualties which the two countries had incurred— and French susceptibilities had to be soothed. On 13 January the War Council accordingly resolved to persevere on the Western Front, but to review its options in the spring if a stalemate had developed.[28]

This was a somewhat inconclusive verdict. It certainly did not quash entirely the possibility of diversionary exercises in other theatres. Indeed, one such exercise was about to begin at Gallipoli. The origins of this ill-fated escapade reflect credit on none of the major actors: Churchill should not be made to shoulder the entire blame. Kitchener, more than any other minister, set the ball rolling when, responding to an appeal of 2 January from St Petersburg, he floated the idea of an operation against Turkey which would relieve pressure on

[25] Gilbert, 'Strain of Office', 35.
[26] Wilson, *Myriad Faces*, 106.
[27] G. Cassar, 'Kitchener at the War Office', in Cecil and Liddle (eds.), *Facing Armageddon*, 38, 41.
[28] Wilson, *Myriad Faces*, 107.

the hard-pressed Russians in the Caucasus and perhaps open a supply route to them via the Black Sea—an operation, he added, which could easily be cancelled if it was not going well. The fact that Britain currently had no surplus of supplies and ammunition to send to her ally did not apparently cross his mind. Nor were there 150,000 troops available for the amphibious expedition which Kitchener was envisaging.

Churchill met this difficulty by contending that a naval force of older battleships could, with the minimum of ground troops, force the Straits and sail through to menace Constantinople, causing the Turkish government to leave the war. The scenario was implausible, not least because ministers, in their anxiety to entice other Balkan states (Greece, Bulgaria, and Romania) to join the Allies, had been promising them large chunks of Turkey's European territory. The War Council on 10 January had in any case agreed to accept Russian claims to Constantinople and the Dardanelles, provided that 'both we and France should get a substantial share of the carcass of the Turk'.[29]

Meanwhile, encouraged by the French government, there was talk of landing troops in Salonika: indeed, on 9 February Kitchener actually persuaded the War Council to send the 29th Division there. When the Greek government vetoed this idea,[30] voices were raised in favour of sending this fresh military consignment to Gallipoli instead—were they to be needed. Throughout these confused debates the Prime Minister, Asquith, provided no clear direction to his colleagues. Nor, in the absence of a Chiefs-of-Staff system such as was instituted during the Second World War, did ministers have anyone to turn to for expert and disinterested advice.[31] Into this policy vacuum Churchill pressed ahead with his own pet scheme, Fisher sometimes offering him encouragement and sometimes issuing warnings. On 13 January the War Council instructed Vice-Admiral Carden, the officer in charge of Britain's naval forces in the eastern Mediterranean, to 'take' the Gallipoli Peninsula, though at the same time warning him against hurried action that involved the risk of 'heavy losses'. Carden's understandable hesitations were brushed aside by the overeager Churchill, who, in the aftermath of the Dogger Bank, felt that the danger of diverting warships to the eastern Mediterranean was not now so great.

The initial attempt to force the Straits on 19 February, in which the British were joined by French ships, enjoyed an immediate diplomatic success: the Greeks offered troops, the Bulgarians broke off their negotiations with Germany, and the Italians drew closer to the Allies (they joined the war as full participants in May). But, as soon became apparent, it was hazardous, perhaps

[29] Ibid. 119.
[30] The Greeks wanted the prize of Constantinople, which had already been promised to Russia.
[31] Gilbert, 'Strain of Office', 36.

impossible, for minesweepers to clear a path for the battleships through the minefields in the face of fire from concealed Turkish shore batteries—even had the navy silenced the forts, it could not permanently have knocked out the mobile howitzers. The attack launched on 18 March by Carden's replacement, de Robeck, proved to be—as the Admiral himself admitted—'a disastrous day': three ships, one French and two British, were sunk, and others damaged or put out of action. Within a few hours de Robeck had lost nearly one-third of his fleet.

On 22 March the wholly naval operation was called off, and General Ian Hamilton was hurriedly commissioned to take charge of a military force of one British division, plus a contingent of French soldiers and troops from Australia and New Zealand (the 'Anzacs'), with the aim of capturing the Gallipoli Peninsula and silencing the Turkish guns. Seldom has an expedition of such difficulty been so ill-prepared, perhaps because the Turks were not thought of as a first-class military power but as an inefficient, backward despotism. Kitchener, now obsessed with the possible loss of prestige throughout the Orient which would follow a British reverse or withdrawal, pressed ahead without consulting his General Staff.[32] Hamilton, given only one-half of the men that Kitchener had earlier deemed necessary, did not even possess up-to-date maps of the terrain that he had been ordered to occupy.

On 25 April Allied troops landed—the small French contingent on the Asian side of the shore, the 29th Division at Cape Helles on the southern tip of the peninsula, and the Anzacs further north—on the wrong beaches, as it happened. The operation lacked the essential ingredient of surprise: most of the Turkish defenders were waiting for their assailants, and the British naval bombardment, by itself, proved incapable of overwhelming the enemy's trench defences. Some men got ashore unopposed, but most were raked with fire. On V Beach, off Cape Helles, the sea turned crimson with blood. Of 950 Lancashire Fusiliers involved in this theatre, 500 hundred were killed or wounded in desperate fighting, which resulted in six VCs being awarded. In all, 2,000 Allied casualties were incurred. To the north, the Anzacs, displaying almost unbelievable heroism, succeeded in establishing a beach-head, but soon became trapped on the steep and rocky hillsides. They, too, sustained about 2,000 casualties. It had taken only a few hundred stubborn Turkish defenders (led in the north by Mustapha Kemal) to inflict this carnage.

Over the next few weeks the situation did not improve. In the south the first battle of Krithia (28 April) achieved little, and the attempted offensive of 6 May met with no greater success. Two days later Hamilton was told by the War

---

[32] Cassar, 'Kitchener at the War Office', 42. 'The effect of a defeat in the Orient would be very serious. There could be no going back. The publicity of [Churchill's earlier jubilant] announcement has committed us' (French, *British Strategy*, 80).

Office that, although there was no more ammunition, it was 'important to push on'.[33] From their great ships the sailors watched helplessly the scenes of heroism and suffering unfolding before them. Then, in the course of May, the navy lost several of its ships to torpedoes and German U-boats. Fisher, who had been upset by the detachment of a Queen Elizabeth battleship from the main fleet to reinforce the flotilla assembling off Mudros, recalled it on 14 May. A fortnight later the *Majestic* sank, whereupon all the big ships were promptly pulled back well away from the peninsula—to the dismay of the troops, whose 'sense of abandonment was acute'.[34] At home the aftershocks contributed to the fall of Asquith's Liberal government on 25 May.

Meanwhile Britain's main offensive on the Western Front was faring little better. An earlier Anglo-French meeting had agreed that in the spring the two countries would co-ordinate their attacks on the shoulder of the Ypres Salient, the French advancing in Champagne, supported by the British at the north at Aubers and Vimy Ridge, where they hoped to cut the German supply lines.

The British action at Neuve Chapelle (10–12 March) began well enough. The Germans were initially caught by surprise, Sir John's attacking force of 60,000 men having been brought up to the lines without detection. The opening bombardment, employing 340 guns, though puny by later standards, was also unprecedented. But the operation, which had been programmed like clockwork, soon lost momentum—partly because of rigidity and overcentralization. The leading assault force was refused permission to exploit the opening which had been achieved in the initial attack, Sir John's allocation of the reserves was faulty, and the artillery continued to shell enemy positions no longer occupied. The Germans were thus given time to regroup and counter-attack. By the time the assault was called off the British had captured Neuve Chapelle itself, but not the strategically important Aubers Ridge which lay behind the village—still less the city of Lille. The reputation of the BEF as a serious fighting force had been restored, but for modest territorial gains it had sustained some 13,000 casualties, about double those of the Germans. The accompanying French offensive in Champagne similarly petered out.

In late April it was the turn of the British to be caught by surprise. On 22 April, to disguise the transfer of German troops to the Eastern Front, Falkenhayn launched an offensive in the vulnerable Ypres Salient, employing chlorine gas for the first time. The British held firm but, unusually, sustained more casualties conducting a defensive operation than did their assailants: 60,000 (plus another 10,000 among the French), compared with Germany's 35,000.

---

[33] Wilson, *Myriad Faces*, 137.

[34] G. Till, 'Brothers in Arms: The British Army and Navy at the Dardanelles', in Cecil and Liddle (eds.), *Facing Armageddon*, 173–5.

The employment of gas, not to disable the enemy temporarily (as with tear gas) but as a killing agent, was greeted by the British with intense indignation. The Canadians, who had suffered hideously from this 'unsporting' conduct, allegedly killed some of their German prisoners-of-war in reprisal. However, although the resort to large-scale chemical warfare, masterminded by Fritz Haber in association with IG Farben, was initiated by the Germans, the British, overcoming their revulsion, quickly followed suit. A gas unit was created under Major Charles Howard Foulkes, which initially used chlorine but soon developed the far more deadly phosgene, before in January 1916 learning to mix the two gases in equal proportions in a compound called 'White Star'.[35]

In the month following the second battle of Ypres the Allied armies resumed the offensive. On 9 May the British attacked at Aubers Ridge. The French, advancing shortly afterwards at Vimy Ridge, enjoyed limited success, but the British operation was a disaster. The opening artillery bombardment left the enemy wire largely uncut, the result of poor gunnery and faulty ammunition. The attack was called off on the second day, with 9,500 casualties. The pattern was repeated at Festubert on 15–16 May. Though the initial night attack was an effective innovation, showing the importance of surprise, the Germans quickly plugged the gap in their defences and by 25 May the fighting died away, with another 16,500 casualties having been incurred for little purpose.

Sir John French, by now on very bad terms with Kitchener, blamed his failures on a shortage of ammunition. In the aftermath of Aubers Ridge he briefed the military correspondent Colonel A'Court Repington, who relayed the story to *The Times*, which published it on 14 May under the headline 'Need for Shells'.[36] Next day the government was shaken by the Gallipoli fiasco, Fisher walking out of the Admiralty. The Asquith ministry now faced its greatest crisis since the advent of the war.

Hitherto the Prime Minister, having steered an all-but-united Cabinet and Party into the war, had generally commanded the nation's confidence. The embittered Opposition Leaders, it is true, privately continued to blame the Liberals for the inadequacy of their preparations. The backbench Unionist Business Committee, wishing to put more 'ginger' into the parliamentary Opposition (formed January 1915, initially with twenty-five members), was more outspoken, while the Conservative press hounded unpopular ministers such as Haldane, and called for tougher measures against aliens.[37] But Kitchener's prestige shielded the ministry from more serious attacks, besides which it remained unclear what alternatives were to hand. Unionist backbenchers in

[35] D. Richter, 'The Experience of the British Special Brigade in Gas Warfare', in ibid. 355.
[36] Cassar, 'Kitchener at the War Office', 42.
[37] M. Pugh, 'Asquith, Bonar Law and the First Coalition', *Historical Journal*, 17 (1974), 813–36.

general favoured attacking the government if this could be done without offending the patriotism of the electorate. Bonar Law, on the other hand, knew the risks of precipitating a general election in the midst of a national emergency. Moreover, it was obvious that no government could steer the country through the war and preserve national unity from outside the Liberal Party. For the moment, therefore, Asquith seemed the indispensable man.

An alternative strategy was the creation of a 'national government'. This was being openly advocated by a handful of maverick MPs, mainly Liberals, and also enjoyed the backing of some newspapers, notably Garvin's *Observer*. But Churchill was one of the few ministers to favour a coalition government. From the Opposition, the semi-detached Balfour (with valuable experience gleaned from his earlier presidency of the CID) regularly attended War Council meetings, but among frontbench Unionists Austen Chamberlain was unusual in wanting to save the ministry from the troubles that lay ahead by joining it. Walter Long spoke for most of his colleagues when he privately said that he hated the thought of 'our good fellows sitting with these double-dyed traitors'.

The Prime Minister found the political problems confronting his government in many ways less intractable than those that had bedevilled it during the last few years of peace. Thus, when in March 1915 a continuing feud between McKenna and Lloyd George threatened to destabilize the government, amid rumours that the Prime Minister himself faced a possible putsch from either Churchill or Lloyd George himself, Asquith had little difficulty in reasserting his authority.

The main problem centred on how to expand munitions production. In late 1914 the BEF could only fire six rounds per gun per day.[38] Attempts to improve this situation generated tension between Kitchener and Lloyd George, who quickly emerged as the most formidable critic of the War Office's inefficiency and dilatoriness. But even this problem seemed well on the way to resolution, with the establishment of a Munitions Committee of which Lloyd George was a leading member—the first step in stripping the War Office of its powers to supply ordnance.

However, a party administration was ill-equipped to run a long-drawn-out war. So the ministry's position, though seemingly impregnable, was in fact nothing of the kind. Its collapse came very suddenly. The 'Shells Scandal' hit the government hard, deeply angering Asquith who, acting upon Kitchener's reassurance that all was well, had delivered an ill-advised speech at Newcastle on 20 April, which contained an absurdly over-optimistic assessment of the munitions situation.[39] Fisher's scandalous walkout from the Admiralty had

---

[38] Keegan, *First World War*, 147.
[39] Cassar, 'Kitchener at the War Office', 42.

simultaneously created a crisis of confidence in the way in which the war was being run. 'Patching' no longer seemed enough.

On 17 May a worried Bonar Law, unsure of his ability to keep his own restless backbenchers under control, paid a visit to Lloyd George who, in an outburst, said that 'the situation was altogether intolerable'. The two men agreed on the necessity of coalition, and promptly presented Asquith with what may have been an ultimatum. Asquith fell in with their wishes—perhaps because his Chancellor's brusque move had knocked some of the fight out of him; more probably because he wanted to extend the electoral truce and avoid a general election.[40] The French–Repington 'plot', originally intended to bring down Kitchener, had thus resulted in the destruction of Asquith's Liberal administration.

Could Asquith have soldiered on? With approximately three times more Conservative than Liberal MPs serving at the Front, and with the general support of the Irish Nationalists and the PLP, the ministry still commanded a comfortable parliamentary majority: which is why Cabinet ministers, suddenly confronted with a prime-ministerial request for their resignations, reacted with amazement, and why Asquith later struggled to explain his actions to his parliamentary followers.[41] From the Liberal viewpoint, coalition represented a serious setback, not least because almost one-half of all ministers would have to step down to make way for their political opponents. Some Liberals had even deeper forebodings: one of the victims of the governmental reconstruction, Charles Hobhouse, observed in his diary: 'The disintegration of the Liberal Party is complete. We shall not return to power for some years.'[42] Things were to be worse than that: never again would the Liberals wield power alone.

Yet it is difficult to see how Asquith's Liberal ministry could have continued indefinitely: the nation's troubles required a ministry far more broad-bottomed than one composed of members of a single political party—albeit one including the by-now much diminished Kitchener. Even opponents of the innovation such as Curzon were half-convinced of its inevitability.

Asquith handled the reconstruction unwisely. Angry over Kitchener's conduct, he initially thought of replacing him with Lloyd George. The imprudence of such a course was soon shown when the Northcliffe Press's attacks on 'K' led to angry scenes—the *Daily Mail* being burnt on the floor of the Stock Exchange and suffering a sharp fall in circulation. Seen

---

[40] Asquith's relationship with Venetia Stanley had also ended five days earlier, in distressing circumstances, when she announced her engagement to Edwin Montagu.

[41] Only Grey and Crewe were given advance warning. Asquith later claimed, disingenuously, that a parliamentary debate might have frightened off the Italians.

[42] E. David (ed.), *Inside Asquith's Cabinet: From the Diaries of Charles Hobhouse* (London, 1977), 247.

at close quarters, Kitchener did not inspire trust: his taciturnity, his unwilling-ness to take civilian politicians fully into his counsels, and his weaknesses as an administrator, deriving from his reluctance to delegate, his propensity for improvisation, and neglect of planning (allowing, for example, the General Staff to disband)—all of this suggested that he was 'the wrong man in the wrong place'. But, as Margot Asquith famously observed, he remained 'a great poster', and, as such, at least for the time being, was unsackable.

Asquith therefore left Kitchener where he was, but further diminished his powers by placing Lloyd George at the head of a newly created Ministry of Munitions. This made it theoretically possible for Bonar Law to be sent to the Treasury, as Asquith had originally intended; but, giving way to party preju-dice, he decided that no tariff reformer should hold this sensitive office, which accordingly went to the orthodox McKenna (whose wife, Pamela, was one of the Prime Minister's favourites). Bonar Law, argued out of Munitions by Lloyd George's Celtic eloquence, was fobbed off with the Colonial Office. Indeed, the one Conservative to hold a post centrally concerned with the war effort was Balfour, who became First Lord of the Admiralty in place of the indignant Churchill, who was demoted to being Chancellor of the Duchy of Lancaster. The Liberals also received the lion's share of the lesser ministerial offices. Asquith had undoubtedly pulled a fast one over the old enemy, but the grumbling sense of dissatisfaction which this created on the Unionist side of the House was to weaken his Coalition during the troubled months that lay ahead.

Two other consequences of the May Crisis require notice. A Cabinet seat was found for Arthur Henderson, nominally as President of the Board of Education but in reality as a 'labour troubleshooter'—an increasingly import-ant role, given the government's important relationship with the trade-union movement as it gradually placed the economy on a war footing. Labour thus entered government for the first time—an important milestone. The Irish Nationalists would have joined them there but for the fact that John Redmond, faithful to his party's principles, refused to accept office in a Westminster ministry with Home Rule still unachieved. The Nationalists thus faced the galling spectacle of Carson being made Attorney-General—giving him privileged access to the very centre of power. This, plus the fact that the establishment of the Coalition had deprived the Irish of their pivotal control of the Commons, was shortly to have serious consequences for their party—and, indirectly, for the fate of their Liberal allies. In the early summer of 1915, however, the new ministerial team had more pressing problems on their minds.

3. TROUBLED DAYS, MAY–DECEMBER 1915

In July 1915 the new Cabinet agreed that 'the western theatre was the principal one for our efforts'.[43] But the Gallipoli commitment could not immediately be liquidated. Rejecting Kitchener's advice, it was resolved to mount a second landing on the peninsula—indeed, when Ian Hamilton asked for an additional three divisions, he was surprised to be offered five.[44] On 7 August troops were landed at Suvla Bay, 20,000 of them under cover of darkness, but, ineptly led by the timorous and long-retired General Stopford, they took far too long to break out from the beaches to capture the surrounding hills. A detachment did later fight its way through to the highpoint of Chunuk Bair, from where it could look down on the Dardanelles; however, mistakenly shelled by its own side, it was forced to retire. Many troops made even less progress and stayed trapped in shallow enclaves, powerless to advance against a determined enemy that took full advantage of terrain ideally suited to defensive operations.

At this point the whole expedition should have been wound up. But flaws in the machinery of government, already obvious during Asquith's Liberal ministry, blocked intelligent strategic planning. On 7 June 1915 the War Council was replaced by another Cabinet subcommittee, the Dardanelles Committee (showing how preoccupied the government was with events in that theatre of war), but, despite having Hankey as its competent Secretary, it lacked executive authority. Membership steadily grew until it numbered fourteen, and the decision-making process foundered, since members who found themselves outvoted could always appeal to the authority of the full Cabinet—a body dubbed by Carson '22 gabblers round a table with an old procrastinator in the chair'.[45]

These strategic disagreements, which proved so difficult to resolve, by no means invariably followed party lines. For example, whereas many Conservatives, including Bonar Law, favoured a withdrawal from Gallipoli, Lord Curzon, invoking his authority as a former Indian Viceroy, passionately insisted that this would lead to a collapse of British prestige throughout the East. Nor was the dispute simply one between 'easterners' and 'westerners', because the former were split between those who wanted to press on at Gallipoli and those who favoured opening an entirely new operation from Salonika to aid Serbia—whose plight worsened in August when its neighbour Bulgaria (encouraged by Germany's recent capture of Warsaw) finally entered the war on the side of the Central Powers, primarily with the purpose of seizing from Serbia parts of Macedonia which it had gained during

[43] Wilson, *Myriad Faces*, 266.
[44] Cassar, 'Kitchener at the War Office', 43.
[45] French, *British Strategy*, 102.

the Second Balkan War.[46] The Greek government, which had a treaty with Serbia, asked the Allies to send 150,000 men into the Balkans.

The French showed interest in the invitation, as did certain members of the British government, notably Lloyd George, who was joined on this issue by Bonar Law and Carson (a trio that was to combine, with explosive effect, in the following year). On 5 October an inter-Allied force accordingly embarked for Salonika, but by the time it arrived there the pro-Allied Greek premier, Venizelos, had been overthrown by King Constantine, who was friendly towards Germany. Despite the withdrawal of the Greek government's offer and its retreat into neutrality, the Allied troops landed there regardless, violating Greek sovereignty—a move which, whatever Lloyd George's denials, bore an uncomfortable resemblance to Germany's earlier violation of Belgium.

The landings took place too late to save the Serbs, the remnants of whose army straggled across Montenegro into neutral Albania, and thence by ship to Corfu. Carson promptly resigned (complaining in his resignation speech of 12 October about the machinery of government), while Lloyd George broke out furiously against Kitchener, whom he held responsible for neglecting to double the carrying capacity of the single-track railway from Salonika to Nish, 250 miles to the north—perhaps unfairly, given the logistical problems presented by the wild, mountainous terrain. All this being water under the bridge, most British ministers advocated withdrawal from what Asquith called 'a wild goose affair',[47] but at an inter-Allied conference held in Calais in December Lloyd George was joined in opposing evacuation by the French government, acting from purely internal party-political motives. So, to the amusement of the Central Powers, a large Anglo-French army remained in the malaria-ridden swamps of Macedonia, where some units suffered 100 per cent losses from disease. Sarrail's attempts to break out in the spring of the following year achieved little, 5,000 British soldiers being killed or wounded: two of the six British divisions, plus their equipment, were later removed. It would be many months before the 'Gardeners of Salonika' managed to dig themselves out of this particular hole.

Yet, if the Salonika Expedition did nothing to change the balance of forces in the Balkans, the diversion of troops to this theatre did at least spell the end of the Gallipoli adventure. In October Hamilton was sacked, to be replaced by General Monro, whom Kitchener went out to meet, initially with some vague notion that he himself might become a kind of generalissimo in the Near East. By November Monro was urging evacuation, a course of action with which Kitchener at last agreed, though Curzon and Churchill continued to fight a

---

[46] Despite the fact that the British and French, desperate to avert a Bulgarian intervention, had secretly promised Sofia help in appropriating the territory of its Serbian ally!

[47] Wilson, *Myriad Faces*, 272.

rearguard action against it in Cabinet. A freak winter storm which flooded the
trenches, drowning many soldiers, clinched the issue. Between 28 December
1915 and 8 January 1916 80,000 men were brought back to the ships and away
to safety, without a single loss of life. It was a successful end to a disastrous
campaign, which had cost the Allies some 265,000 casualties, the brunt of them
borne by the 29th Division and by the Anzacs.

The winding-up of the Gallipoli Expedition was accompanied by important
political and administrative changes. Asquith at last moved to reform the
machinery of government, setting up (on 2 November), in lieu of the now
defunct Dardanelles Committee, a new War Committee of six members—
though it soon developed the weaknesses that had crippled its predecessors.[48]
Asquith had originally proposed to leave the Conservative Leader out of this
inner group, before Bonar Law indignantly asserted his right to a place there.
But the Prime Minister did succeed in omitting Churchill, who immediately
resigned from the government and went off to France to join his battalion;
Curzon, another opponent of evacuation, was also dropped.

The War Office, too, was in the process of being reorganized. Kitchener
returned to London on 30 November to find that the Prime Minister had
installed a new Chief of the General Staff, William Robertson, with considerably enhanced powers: the latter insisted that he was to be 'the one authoritative channel' of military advice to Cabinet, to have direct access to field
commanders, and to be free from routine departmental administration. All
this was laid down 'in a document more like a draft treaty between two
sovereign powers than a memorandum a military subordinate might properly
send to a Secretary of State'.[49] Kitchener, by now largely stripped of his say in
matters of strategy, offered his resignation, which Asquith refused.

Events on the Western Fron were meanwhile proceeding badly. The first of
what was to be a number of inter-Allied conference took place at Chantilly on 7
July. The Cabinet, with Sir John French in attendance, had four days earlier
agreed to defer Britain's big push until 1916, but Joffre, alarmed at the prospect
of the Germans switching back troops from the Eastern Front in the course of
the following year, vigorously protested.[50] Kitchener, worried about the plight
of Russia as well as about French suspicions, was persuaded of the need for
swift and immediate action: 'We must make war as we must; not as we should
like', he philosophically observed. So, essentially for political reasons, another
offensive was planned to begin on 25 September.

The British army was now very unlike the BEF which had disembarked in
France just over a year earlier. The few survivors from 1914 had been supple-

---

[48] Its membership soon stabilized at 9 and by 1916 had climbed to 11.
[49] French, *British Strategy*, 162.
[50] The British agreed to extend their line to the Somme, a clear sign of the changing balance of forces.

mented by the arrival of Territorial units, troops from the Dominions and the first of Kitchener's New Armies, still raw and inexperienced, which had begun arriving in May and June. Sir John now commanded two armies, the first of which, under Douglas Haig, was assigned the task of spearheading the attack at Loos, just south of Aubers Ridge.

This area had been chosen mainly because of its proximity to the French army's operations. In a strictly military sense it had little to recommend it. British troops would have to fight their way across open ground against an enemy sheltering in the industrial landscape. As Kitchener made clear to his unhappy Commander-in-Chief, he had to expect 'very heavy losses indeed'. Haig himself saw only one way of achieving a breakthrough over this unpropitious terrain: the offensive would be preceded by releasing gas over the German lines—and, thanks to cunning concealment, the British gas attack did indeed catch the Germans by surprise. But because the offensive had been scheduled for a specific day, there was no guarantee that the wind conditions would be suitable. In the event some of the gas, when released from its canisters, drifted back into the British trenches. Whether, on balance, it helped or hindered the British assault remains unclear. In any case, gas could not cut barbed wire, towards which the infantry advanced in serried ranks, to be mown down by German machine-gunners. Units which broke through into enemy trenches failed to make further advances, partly because they lacked efficient hand-grenades, but also because French mishandled the disposition of the tactical reserves. For slight territorial gains, British troops were slaughtered, many of them raw recuits who had only landed in France a fortnight earlier. The following day (26 September) Haig personally made the disastrous decision to renew the attack, needlessly sacrificing yet more lives. The operation spluttered on until early October, by which time the Germans had clawed back most of the territory they had earlier lost leaving 16,000 British soldier killed and 25,000 wounded.[51] The French infantry, attacking in Champagne, suffered a similar fate.

In the wake of Loos recriminations broke out between Sir John French and Haig, of whom the Commander-in-Chief had become increasingly jealous and resentful. When French sought to minimize his own share in the catastrophe by sending home a dispatch which misstated the time at which Haig had taken control of the reserves, his ambitious subordinate threw aside all restraint. Haig told the King on his visit to the Front in late October that Sir John was 'a source of great weakness to the army, and no one had confidence in him any more'[52]—which was no more than the truth, though it might have been more

---

[51] The 7th Northants went into battle the day after landing at Boulogne (Bourne, *Great War*, 159).
[52] Keegan, *First World War*, 310.

dignified of Haig not to draw attention to his own superior qualifications for the post. Characteristically Kitchener, who had long felt that French should be sacked,[53] now had second thoughts about doing so. But on 17 December the indignant Commander-in-Chief was prevailed upon to submit his resignation, and Haig duly took his place. Kitchener himself, though almost equally discredited, stayed on as a figurehead War Secretary. Strategy had passed into the hands of the Robertson–Haig partnership, where it was to be located for the next twenty-five months.

Kitchener's legacy, however, lived on in one very important respect. In July he had committed the government to work towards a seventy-division army, thereby doubling its current size—a momentous decision, the implications of which were never adequately explored at the time.[54] However, as enlistments slowed down during 1915 and casualties mounted, it became problematical whether this ambitious target would ever be met without resort to compulsion. After Loos Kitchener, hitherto a voluntaryist, began to shift his position, but, loyal to the last towards Asquith, he allowed himself to be persuaded by the Prime Minister that it was premature to move in this direction.[55] Those who favoured conscription, most of them Conservatives, had long fumed at Kitchener's willingness to provide a fig-leaf over what they saw as the Liberal Party's pusillanimity, and by the autumn of 1915 they broke cover and began openly agitating for compulsion—an initiative which threatened to rend the Coalition ministry asunder. The conscriptionists railed against what Lord Esher called 'the Principle of Unequal Sacrifice', insisting that all citizens had a duty to serve the nation in its hour of peril.[56]

But the anti-conscriptionists mounted a multipronged attack on their opponents. The state did not have the moral authority over life and death, they claimed—indeed, the resort to conscription would undermine the very purpose of the war, which they saw as a crusade against Prussian militarism.

The two Liberal ministers directly concerned with economic management, McKenna at the Treasury and Walter Runciman, the President of the Board of Trade, supplemented these warnings by questioning whether a seventy-division army could be *afforded*. 'Our ultimate victory is assured', McKenna claimed, 'if, in addition to our naval and military activities, we retain unimpaired our power to assist in financing, supplying and carrying for the Allies':

---

[53] Sensing this, French had employed Freddie Guest to spread malicious rumours about the War Secretary!

[54] The figure was subsequently reduced to 67.

[55] Cassar, 'Kitchener at the War Office', 44. On 8 October 1915 Kitchener asked for 35,000 men a week until the end of 1916, way above the 5,000–10,000 McKenna was prepared to concede (French, *British Strategy*, 130).

[56] Terraine, 'Substance of War', 4.

adopting conscription was the only way in which the war could be lost.[57] Runciman was convinced that the country faced possible bankruptcy, which was only being staved off by running up deficits with the United States.

Yet such arguments were really directed against the Continental strategy, perhaps even against Britain's very participation in the war, and it was rather late in the day to question the desirability of either. Asquith, who never doubted the wisdom of the decision the country had taken in August 1914, thus found himself in a particularly difficult situation. His instinct was to leave issues of strategy to professional soldiers, but how could he then deny the military high command the extra resources which it claimed were imperative for victory?

By mid-October, if not earlier, Asquith had seen that sooner or later compulsory military service would have to be adopted. But to a late stage he held back. He did so, partly because even the 'patriotic' wing of the Labour Movement, including respected figures such as Henderson, feared that military conscription might lead to industrial conscription and, still worse, an erosion of trade-union rights that would then be difficult to reverse once the national emergency had passed. Any move towards the adoption of the programme of the National Service League, Asquith knew, could thus easily imperil the 'industrial truce' so essential to the success of Britain's war effort. Compulsion would also be exceedingly unpopular at nearly all levels of the Liberal Party, thereby fracturing that national unity by which Asquith set so much store.

What complicated the situation still further was that, while some Conservatives such as Balfour doubted the wisdom of compulsion, some senior Liberals favoured it—indeed, Churchill had broached it in Cabinet as early as August 1914, to the irritation of his colleagues. But by the late summer of 1915 Churchill was joined in his advocacy by Lloyd George, whose successes at the Ministry of Munitions had given him an authority in the country which transcended peacetime party loyalties. Increasingly the Welshman found himself working in close association with senior Conservatives on the conscription issue. Indeed, in a much-publicized speech in Manchester in June he alarmed his own civil service advisers by going beyond even the NSL's programme,[58] and advocating the right of the state to direct labour wherever it saw fit: 'When the house is on fire, questions of procedure or precedents or etiquette and time and division of labour disappear.'[59] This merely increased Labour opposition to the compulsory raising of troops. Lloyd George's increasing restlessness also challenged the Prime Minister's credentials and opened up fissures in the Coalition.

---

[57] Bourne, *Great War*, 145; French, *British Strategy*, 121.
[58] Now under the presidency of Lord Milner.
[59] Lord Beveridge, *Power and Influence* (London, 1953), 127–8.

In early August, faced by these contradictory pressures, Asquith set up
a War Policy Committee under the chairmanship of Lord Crewe, to examine
manpower and resources—a committee on which, characteristically, conscriptionists and anti-conscriptionists were neatly balanced. The following
month, again playing for time, he placed a conscriptionist, the Conservative
Lord Derby, in charge of a scheme whereby men not yet in the colours were
invited to 'attest' their willingness to serve in the army if called upon to do so,
on the understanding that married men would not be taken up until all the
eligible bachelors had first been conscripted. The initiative helped stimulate a
rash of weddings (the marriage-rate hit a peak of 19.4 in 1915, compared
with 15.7 in 1913, before falling in 1917 to an all-time low of 13.8), but
otherwise it had a disappointingly small effect on recruitment. On 20 December Derby issued his final report, which indicated that there were still 318,533
single and 403,921 married men 'actually available' who had yet to come
forward; only 1,150,000 of 2,179,231 single men of military age had as yet
come forward.[60]

On 27 December Lloyd George threatened to resign if compulsion were
not adopted. But Asquith had already decided that the time was ripe for
forcing the issue. On 29 December he cajoled the Cabinet into accepting the
principle of compulsory service for unmarried men and widowers aged 18
to 41, and a Military Service Bill on these lines soon afterwards came
before Parliament. As he had so often done in the past, the Prime Minister
skilfully assuaged the anxiety of his colleagues. McKenna and Runciman
did not carry out their threatened resignations, after Asquith had agreed
to set up yet another inquiry into the optimum size of the army. The
Home Secretary, Sir John Simon, was left to stage his lonely act of self-
immolation. More importantly, the Labour Movement, which had been holding an emergency conference on the subject, bowed to the fait accompli,
once Asquith had given them reassurances about the retention of the tribunals
set up under the Derby Scheme and safeguards for conscientious objectors.
The Commons voted through the Bill by 403 to 105, the minority consisting
of sixty Irish Nationalist, eleven Labour, and thirty-four Liberal MPs.
The country in general proved to be readier to accept the necessity of 'sacrifice'
than many of its political leaders, as the conscriptionists had always said
would be the case. The Bill became law in January 1916: a further Act,
covering married men, would follow four months later. Britain was now fully
at war.

[60] R. J. Q. Adams and P. P. Poirier, *The Conscription Controversy in Great Britain 1900–18* (Basingstoke, 1987), 134–5.

4. JUTLAND AND THE WAR AT SEA

Britain still retained the advantage of commanding the ocean lanes. Germany's only exit to the open sea lay through a narrow corridor between Holland and Denmark, since mines had effectively blocked the westward passage through the Channel; yet, moving northward into the waters separating Britain and Norway, the High Fleet immediately came under the surveillance of the British navy, stationed at Rosyth and Scapa Flow. Indeed, in the entire course of war perhaps only a few hundred German ships escaped the northern blockade. The Royal Navy had the additional advantage of having fortuitously captured German naval code-books at the very start of the war,[61] and this made possible a sophisticated cryptological service in the Admiralty Old Building, 40 OB, which intercepted the radio messages of which the Germans were making excessive use. This allowed the movements of the German fleet to be monitored—the Germans realized that something was amiss, but attributed the leakage to espionage. In matériel, too, the British retained the whip-hand. By 1916 the destruction of German raiding cruisers, the withdrawal from Gallipoli, and the strengthening of the Allies' position in the Mediterranean following Italy's entry into the war had all contributed to the restoration of the Royal Navy's decisive lead: in April the ratio stood at 31 : 18 in modern battleships, 10 : 5 in battle cruisers. This goes far towards explaining Germany's resort to submarine attacks on Allied merchant shipping.

Prior to 1 February 1915 only one British merchant ship had fallen victim to U-boats, as against fourteen that were sunk by mines and fifty-one by surface raiders. This was because, initially, the U-boats attacked on the surface, and since they were unable to capture enemy vessels or to take their crews on board, the informal rules of war required their commanders to give the merchant ship due warning so that the crew could make its escape—a procedure which laid the U-boat open to retaliation. However, as Fisher had long predicted, the Germans then moved over to unrestricted warfare, attacking merchant shipping with torpedos from beneath the surface—a practice which Britain denounced as barbarous, because merchant seamen were conventionally thought of as non-combatants. Outrage mounted in May 1915 when the ocean liner *Lusitania* was sunk, with the loss of 1,201 passengers, 129 of them Americans. (The liner is now thought to have been carrying explosives as well as passengers, though the U-boat commander probably did not know this at the time.) The British navy could find no defence against this menace, and in August

---

[61] In August 1914 the German light cruiser *Magdeburg* went aground in the Baltic with signal books and key—the Russians passed the information on to their allies. In October another code was seized from a German steamer interned in Australia, and later that month a third code-book, used by admirals at sea, was dredged up in the nets of a fishing boat!

1915 forty-two ships were sunk (five without warning), more than could be built. Fortunately, two months later submarine warfare was called off in the seas around Britain's western coast and in the Channel—out of concern for the feelings of neutral powers, the United States in particular. Significantly, this self-denying ordinance did not apply to the Mediterranean, where few American lives were at risk.

This left Scheer with limited options. In April 1916 he authorized the bombardment of Lowestoft, but his main hopes still depended on luring a detachment of the Grand Fleet into battle on terms favourable to Germany. Yet since, unbeknown to Scheer, the intelligence-gathers at 40 OB would always be able to eavesdrop on such plans, the British had it within their power to catch the Germans in their own trap. This essentially is what happened at the battle of Jutland (31 May–1 June 1916)—an encounter which 'could have occurred at any time in the war, [but], by the same token, [might] never have occurred at all'.[62]

As Scheer set out on 31 May with sixteen battleships and five battle cruisers, Jellicoe, with his twenty-eight Dreadnoughts, had already left Scapa Flow; so had eight battleships stationed further south at Cromarty, along with Beatty's Battle Cruiser Fleet, which consisted of six battle cruisers and the super-Dreadnoughts of the 5th Battle Squadron. The Germans were steaming towards probable annihilation. However, a breakdown of communications at the Admiralty, where the Operations Division's staff officers mistrusted the intelligence emanating from 40 OB, let them off the hook. Thinking that Scheer was still in harbour, Jellicoe sailed south slowly, to conserve fuel—which meant that his ships were too far from the main German fleet at the very moment when Beatty's force was perilously close.

Nevertheless, in the course of the so-called 'run to the south' Beatty duly made contact with his opposite number, Hipper. This exchange resulted in the blowing up of the *Indefatigable* and the *Queen Mary*, the occasion of Beatty's famous remark, 'There seems to be something wrong with our bloody ships today'. However, albeit at the cost of losing another of his battle cruisers, Beatty did succeed in drawing Hipper, Scheer's ships in his wake, towards the main body of Jellicoe's Grand Fleet—'the run to the north'.

For a brief moment Scheer seemed doomed. But, performing a smart 180-degree manoeuvre, the Germans escaped under cover of the smoke, mist, and worsening light, helped by Jellicoe's over-cautious decision to turn away out of range of an imaginary force of German torpedo boats. Then, for a brief moment, Scheer got on the wrong side of the Grand Fleet once more, but with night descending he managed to break through the

[62] Wilson, *Myriad Faces*, 283.

British lines and make a dash back to port—Jellicoe's force had inadequate searchlights and star shells, and was neither equipped nor prepared for night fighting. The first great sea battle of the war had come and gone in a flash, with the main engagement lasting a mere twenty minutes. There was to be no encore.

The British seemed to have come off worse in material terms, losing three battle cruisers, four armoured cruisers, and eight destroyers, whereas the Germans lost only a battle cruiser, a pre-Dreadnought battleship, four light cruisers, and five destroyers—though their ships arguably suffered more damage and were unable to take to sea for several weeks. In terms of human life the balance of advantage heavily favoured the German side: 6,094 British seamen died, against only 2,551 Germans.

However, in retrospect, the battle of Jutland, by confirming British control of the seas, can be seen as a strategic Allied victory. The High Fleet never again left harbour in such numbers, allowing Britain to continue its ruthless blockade.[63] Scheer's outing has justly been dubbed 'an assault on the gaoler, followed by a return to gaol'.[64] In desperation, the Germans stepped up their U-boat campaign,[65] which had reopened in the spring of 1916 but had once again been suspended following the sinking in May of the cross-Channel steamer *Sussex*, with loss of American lives. After Jutland desperation drove the Germans to disregard such probable diplomatic repercussions. Indirectly, the outcome of Jutland thus contributed to America's belated entry into the war.

Yet Jutland did not feel like a victory at the time, but rather was an acute disappointment to a public conditioned to expect a repeat of Trafalgar. The mishandling of the situation by Balfour, the First Lord of the Admiralty, meant that the most pessimistic construction was generally read into the naval encounter. 'Heavy and Unaccountable British Losses', ran the headline in the *Daily Express*. The sinking four days later (5 June) of HMS *Hampshire*, which hit a mine off the Orkneys and went down, taking Lord Kitchener to a watery grave, intensified the gloom. Public confidence in the Admiralty perceptibly declined, and in November the First Sea Lord, Admiral Jackson, was replaced by Jellicoe, while Balfour, his political superior, survived only on borrowed time.

How blameworthy were the naval authorities? The inquest conducted by posterity has proved inconclusive. Jellicoe was undoubtedly the blameless

---

[63] There were to be only three later sorties into the North Sea, in August and October 1916 and in April 1918, never with a view to engaging the Grand Fleet.

[64] Keegan, *First World War*, 296.

[65] The new type of U-boat was capable of operating as far away as the USA: nowhere could the mercantile marine now operate in safety.

victim of a communications muddle;[66] on the other hand, he is open to criticism for not acting more intelligently on the basis of what he *could* see and hear. Some have gone further, arguing that Jellicoe's system of rigid centralization had destroyed initiative lower down the command chain. However, Jellicoe cannot reasonably be arraigned for being over-cautious. If he set his heart like stone against any division of the fleet, this was because he knew that the cost of a British naval defeat far exceeded the possible benefits that would have followed a crushing victory, good though the latter would have been for morale.[67] His successor, the dashing Beatty, later pursued an almost identical strategy.

The British navy, too, suffered from several deficiencies, nearly all of them dating back to the years of the Fisher reforms. For example, if, as Jutland suggested, there was a need for improved reconnaissance, this was because Fisher's new battle cruisers had been designed with a capacity to engage with battleships rather than to use their speed to escape, a function for which traditional cruisers were better suited. The Grand Fleet was also weakened by a shortage of destroyers to provide it with a protective screen—hence Jellicoe's exaggerated concern about a possible torpedo attack. The design failures of British ships have also attracted attention, some historians seeing this as emblematic of the country's technological inferiority to Germany, whose domination of the optical glass industry certainly gave her the advantage in range-finding equipment—though this was aggravated by Beatty's inaccurate gunnery in the early stages of the conflict. The German ships also enjoyed better armour protection. But the main difference in matériel was that the Germans had divided the hulls of their ships into watertight compartments, making them less likely to flood, and, learning from an earlier mishap at the Dogger Bank, had also realized the dangers of leaving loose cordite between the magazine and turret, where it could be ignited by a flash travelling down the turret. Nearly all the British losses were caused by such explosions.

The authorities moved swiftly to rectify this serious defect, while also extending the system of director firing with a view to improving the accuracy of the navy's gunnery. Communication problems remained, but after Jutland 40 OB was allowed to interpret as well as decode the data it amassed, thereby

---

[66] Though communications had been revolutionized by radio-telegraphy, it was still impossible to transmit voice signals, only morse, and decoding it and transmitting it to the bridge took 10–15 minutes—adequate for strategic purposes, not for battle plans, which relied on flag signals, often hard to see in poor light or when obscured by smoke (Beatty's signal officer being incompetent). When battle was drawn codes could have been dispensed with by having a receiver on the bridge—but this was not done because 'the "culture" of the signal flag had fleets in its grip' (Keegan, *First World War*, 283). The German fleet's manoeuvring system was less complex, and so required fewer hoists.

[67] Some historians have argued that, if victorious, the Grand Fleet could have opened a Baltic offensive, so averting the Russian Revolutions!

reducing the chances of the misunderstandings which had assisted Scheer's lucky escape. In short, for all the disappointments of Jutland, and despite the worries surrounding the continuing threat to merchant shipping, the Royal Navy entered 1917 more strongly placed than it had been twelve months earlier. However, it had long been apparent that the war was not going to be won solely at sea.

5. THE SOMME CAMPAIGN

An inter-Allied conference, meeting at Chantilly in early December 1915, had agreed that a series of co-ordinated Allied offensives would take place during the following year—a decision which received the qualified approval of the War Committee on 13 January. However, the British contribution was bound to be very different from anything that had been envisaged even twelve months earlier. For in early 1916 Kitchener's New Armies were beginning to arrive in numbers on the Western Front: soon there would be six of these armies, each consisting of five divisions, in addition to eleven regular divisions and twenty-eight divisions formed out of the Territorials. The Cabinet Committee on the Co-ordination of Military and Financial Effort, in its final report in February, planned on putting sixty-two divisions into the field by June—not counting the units earmarked for home defence.[68]

Kitchener's game plan had been to turn Britain in this way into a major military force, so that she could play the leading role in the final offensive against the Central Powers which he thought would occur in 1917—a role which would enable her to dictate the peace, if need be, against the wishes of her Allies, whom he continued to mistrust. Kitchener had not foreseen the rapidity with which the French and Russian armies would exhaust themselves as a result of the futile offensives of 1915. Even before 21 February 1916, when the Germans launched their violent assault on the French fortress town of Verdun with a view to bleeding the French army dry, it had become apparent that Britain would soon become the dominant partner on the Western Front, and would have to take a full part in the fighting much earlier than originally planned. The need to take pressure off the beleagured French at Verdun later added to the pressure on London to sanction its own major assault. Indeed, though still numerically larger than Britain's, the French army had already had much of its fighting spirit sapped.[69]

Some British ministers, including Lloyd George and Balfour, remained sceptical, but the military high command willingly embraced its new role,

[68] French, *British Strategy*, 175.
[69] Philpott, *Anglo-French Relations*, 86.

though for a variety of somewhat different reasons. Robertson, an increasingly dominant figure as CIGS, believed that an offensive would lead to an attrition of manpower favourable, on balance, to the Allied cause; on 31 March the General Staff suggested to Kitchener that if they could inflict [permanent] casualties on the Germans at the rate of 150,000 men a month, the enemy would be forced to sue for peace after another ten months or so, even if the Allies sustained comparable losses.[70] Robertson assured the War Committee on 30 May: 'there was no idea of any attempt to break through the German lines, it would be only a move to *degager* the French.'[71] Haig, on the other hand, favoured an offensive more because he believed in the possibility of achieving a decisive breakthrough—provided the offensive had been preceded by an appropriately severe artillery barrage.

Both arguments have since been subjected to sustained criticism and ridicule, often by those unwilling to recognize the dilemma which the British faced. The navy did not enjoy the kind of superiority that would have permitted a major diversionary exercise of an amphibious nature—nor was the point lost that the earlier expeditions to Gallipoli and Salonika had not forced the Germans to make any kind of response. Indeed, in a way the situation on the Western Front was the very reverse of the situation at sea: having seized the strategic initiative, all that the Germans had to do in France and Flanders was to stay put, thereby imposing on the Allies the task of finding some way to eject them. Doing nothing was not an option, not least because it would once more have sown doubts in French minds about the seriousness of Britain's contribution: Lloyd George privately observed that the French thought 'that they are making all the sacrifices and we are endeavouring to preserve our trade and carry on as usual'.[72] But neither was the 'offensive attrition' favoured by Robertson and by some of Haig's own commanders, notably General Rawlinson, politically attractive, since 'bite and hold', that is to say, conquering and retaining small parcels of German-held land, would have been costly in lives while holding out little prospect of immediate victory, and perhaps 'offensive attrition' was a contradiction in terms.[73]

But the constraints of alliance politics meant that Haig could not stage in 1916 the kind of offensive that he wanted, which would have been in Flanders.[74] Instead, Joffre persuaded him to take over more of the French line and

[70] French, *British Strategy*, 185.
[71] Ibid. 201.
[72] Lord Riddell, *War Diary, 1914–1918* (London, 1933), 168: 1 Apr. 1916.
[73] Kitchener was never clear how attrition would work if the Entente had to attack—could one attack heavily fortified positions and still kill more Germans than one's own losses? (French, *British Strategy*, 201).
[74] Philpott, *Anglo-French Relations*, 114–26.

to attack on the Somme at the point where the two Allied armies met. Haig gave way, true to his policy of acting 'on General Joffre's "General Instructions" as if they had been Orders, but [retaining] absolute freedom of action as to how I carried them out'[75]—further influenced by the French promise to help with a co-ordinating attack further south.

But even before the Somme offensive began, events had conspired to derail it. The intensity of the fighting around Verdun meant that only six French divisions eventually participated in the battle, less than one-seventh of those envisaged at Chantilly.[76] More worrying still, it soon became evident that the terrain over which Haig was planning to throw his new armies presented formidable difficulties. Advance raiding parties reported that the Germans had prepared sophisticated defences, burrowing deep into the chalky soil, where they constructed bunkers safe from even the heaviest of bombardments. Nevertheless, as so often before and since, events had already acquired their own momentum. On 7 April Haig was authorized by the British government to concert an offensive with the French. The big push was about to start.

The first day of the Somme (1 July 1916) has been thought the greatest disaster in the long history of the British army. The troops of Rawlinson's 4th Army, many of them raw and inexperienced men (including the Ulster Division, the UVF in uniform),[77] had been led to believe that the preliminary artillery bombardment would obliterate the enemy defences, leaving them with little to do but march into abandoned trenches. Some successes were registered in the southern sector.[78] But, over the Front as a whole, although the bombardment lasted a full week and used up a million shells—unprecedented at this stage in the war[79]—the weight of ordnance was not nearly enough. Moreover, two-thirds of the shells were shrapnel, rather than high explosive; the artillery still lacked an effective graze fuse for cutting barbed wire; many shells detonated in the ground, throwing up the barbed wire and making it even more difficult to traverse; and up to a third of the shells, hastily produced by the Ministry of Munitions, did not explode at all. The barrage and a preliminary explosion of mines *before* the assault also removed all element of surprise.

---

[75] W. Philpott, 'Haig and Britain's European Allies', in B. Bond and N. Cave (eds.), *Haig: A Reappraisal 70 Years On* (London, 1999), 136.

[76] Bourne, *Great War*, 51. But as a result of Verdun, French contributions were drastically scaled down, from 22–6 to 13 divisions.

[77] The New Armies were not trained for battle: 'Six of the eleven Fourth Army infantry divisions which attacked ... on 1 July 1916 had no previous experience of battle' (Bourne, *Great War*, 160).

[78] G. Sheffield, *Forgotten Victory: The First World War: Myths and Realities* (London, 2001), 135–6, 139.

[79] Rawlinson commanded 1,437 guns, 427 of them heavy, and ammunition allowing for the firing of 150,000 rounds a day, 5,000 by night (Terraine, 'Substance of War', 12).

After the barrage had ended, soldiers from nineteen British and three French divisions went 'over the top', advancing at walking speed, at intervals of two or three paces—only to meet a hail of machine-gun fire which stopped most of them from even reaching the largely uncut barbed-wire defences. Half of the first wave of attackers had become casualties within thirty minutes.

By the end of 1 July the British had incurred 60,000 casualties, one-third of them dead; whole battalions were all but wiped out. German losses probably ran at about one-tenth of this total. Haig confided in his diary that the casualties could not 'be considered severe in view of the numbers engaged, and the length of front attacked',[80] but a terrible failure the first day had proved to be. Only three of the thirteen villages that formed the objective had been captured, representing a shallow advance of about 1 mile over a 3-mile front.

Nothing daunted, Haig opened up a new stage in the offensive on 14 July when, against Joffre's advice, he moved the point of the offensive further south. Attacking on a narrower front, he succeeded in capturing Longueval Ridge, an operation in which Rawlinson made skilful use of the creeping barrage; but the failure of the cavalry to exploit his success allowed the Germans to consolidate once more. A further attack near Aubers Ridge in Flanders at the end of the month was a total fiasco. Piecemeal attacks followed throughout the summer, and, as the Germans counter-attacked, the 'body count' no longer told so heavily in the enemy's favour. But the government was becoming anxious, as well it might, at the scale of British casualties.

The fighting on the Somme dragged on into September, when the most notable development was the first appearance at Flers of thirty-six British tanks—nearly all of which quickly broke down. By the end of the month the crest of the ridge which the Allies had hoped to capture on 1 July had mostly fallen into their hands. The weather broke on 2 October, after which the campaign no longer had much point, but Haig continued to pound away until, on 19 November, the offensive was finally called off. The Allied armies had advanced no further than 7 miles during four-and-a-half months of savage fighting. These paltry gains could be seen for their true worth when, early in the following year (25 February—5 April), the German army, under new command, began implementing a strategy of defence in depth and gave ground on the Western Front, falling back on a new defensive line (the 'Hindenburg Line') that would prove exceptionally difficult to breach.

It is all too easy to blame Haig for what had gone wrong. The fact is that the technology of war continued to operate against attacking forces. Machine-guns, stationed in trenches protected by barbed wire, gave defenders a massive advantage. To have any chance of a breakthrough the army needed to launch a

---

[80] R. Blake (ed.), *The Private Papers of Douglas Haig 1914–1919* (London, 1952), 154.

heavy artillery bombardment, but, even if successful in cutting the wire and neutralizing the defenders, this forfeited the advantage of surprise, enabling reinforcements to be rushed to the threatened spot. Even when a breakthrough was made, there was no means of exploiting it. In the early months of fighting troops were still utterly dependent on horses to transport them, once trains had brought them to the frontier: in fact, the ratio of horses to men in most armies in 1914 was 1 in 3.[81] Tanks, which moved at an average speed of only 2 m.p.h. and were prone to mechanical failure, were little more effective than the cavalry, though of course they were better protected against machine-gun fire than horses could ever be. Nor had any army yet found a way of co-ordinating the artillery and the infantry. If the infantry, under cover of an artillery bombardment, did make initial progress, this merely took it beyond the support of the gunners (who feared to go on firing for fear of hitting their own troops)—leaving them very vulnerable to machine-gun fire directed from deeper defensive positions.

Underlying all of these difficulties was the fact that 'communications consistently lagged behind weaponry'.[82] Wireless was being quite effectively utilized by the navy, but the army's 'trench set' radio required twelve men to carry it. For reconnaissance the army heavily depended on receiving photographs taken from aeroplanes, but unfortunately once ground battle was joined the air-crews were less effective—even after the early 75-pound wireless sets mounted in aeroplanes had been replaced in the autumn of 1915 by Sterling sets weighing under 20 pounds, linked to ground receiving stations that were in communication with the artillery. And so, in John Keegan's words: 'Generals were like men without eyes, without ears and without voices, unable to watch the operations they set in progress, unable to hear reports of their development and unable to speak to those whom they had originally given orders once action was joined.'[83] It would be 1918 before many of these difficulties were solved.

What, if anything, had the battle of the Somme achieved? It arguably helped the French by relieving the pressure on Verdun. But Haig's boast that he had kept occupied German troops that would otherwise have gone to the Eastern Front had less justification: in fact, even while the Somme offensive was taking place German troops were being switched to that theatre.

The main defence of the Somme offensive was the attritional argument favoured all along by Robertson but increasingly stressed by Haig, too. Since the different armies compiled casualty figures on a different basis, 'body counts' are fraught with difficulty, but the best guess is that the French lost

[81] Keegan, *First World War*, 83.
[82] R. Holmes, 'The Last Hurrah: Cavalry on the Western Front, August–September 1914', in Cecil and Liddle (eds.), *Facing Armageddon*, 284.
[83] Keegan, *First World War*, 365, 347.

194,451 men, the British 419,654, and the Germans over 600,000. Thus the losses sustained by the two antagonistic blocs were approximately equal. However, the Central Powers, with their smaller manpower resources, could arguably less well afford such losses (which included some of their more effective officers), and although Germany's fighting capacity had not yet been seriously undermined, she entered 1917 in a relatively weakened state, while the British had—albeit at a terrible price—vindicated their claim to have transformed themselves into a major military power.

For a brief while, in the summer of 1916, Allied policy-makers could even permit themselves a spasm of optimism, disappointment over the Somme campaign being more than offset by jubilation at the success of the Russians during the June Brusilov offensive, when between one-third and one-half of the Austrian army were killed or captured within less than a week. Robertson was writing privately on 9 August: 'The general situation is now better than it has ever been since the beginning of the war. The Entente are winning on all fronts and losing nowhere.'[84] Grey thought the Germans would seek an armistice by October.

The optimists took further heart when, on 17 August, Romania, impressed by the Brusilov offensive, finally succumbed to Allied blandishments and signed the Treaty of Bucharest, which offered her Austrian territory in Transylvania and parts of Hungary should she enter the war on the Allied side—which she duly did ten days later. But Romania had jumped off the fence at entirely the wrong moment. The Central Powers counter-attacked, little support was forthcoming from either the Russians or from Sarrail's forces in Salonika, and Romania was quickly overrun, the capital Bucharest being occupied on 6 December. The British sabotaged some of the Romanian oil-wells, but the Central Powers now had access to a million tons of oil and 2 million tons of grain—a vital factor in Germany's ability to prolong the war.

6. BACKGROUND TO THE DECEMBER 1916 CRISIS

It would have been surprising if the twin disappointments of Jutland and the Somme had not undermined the public's confidence in the British government's conduct of the war—even before the disaster of Romania's collapse, which proved to be the last straw. In non-European theatres, too, the war was going badly in 1916. Admittedly, in Egypt Sir Archibald Murray was advancing cautiously across the Sinai peninsula, initially to secure the Suez Canal, but later with the intention of stirring up an Arab revolt against the Turks, in conjunction with Sherif Hussein.[85] On the other hand, disaster struck the

---

[84] French, *British Strategy*, 204, 210.
[85] Wilson, *Myriad Faces*, 381.

British operation in Mesopotamia (modern Iraq). In November 1914 Britain had assigned the 6th Indian Division to Abadan Island to protect the valuable oil installations—and to assert British power in the region. After capturing Basra (22 November 1914), the strengthened expeditionary force, under Major-General C. V. F. Townshend, advanced up the Tigris in the hope of pulling off the prestigious coup of occupying Baghdad. But Townshend, moving recklessly ahead of his supply lines, was halted by Turkish resistance at Ctesiphon (25 November 1915), before falling back on Kut, which he reached on 3 December. Cut off from his base, Townshend and his 13,000 men eventually surrendered on 29 April 1916, despite an attempt to rescue him which resulted in a further 23,000 casualties.[86] Over two-thirds of the British prisoners-of-war, who were brutally treated by the Turkish army, failed to survive their captivity.

London, shocked by this humiliation, promptly took over responsibility for the Mesopotamian campaign from the India Office. But the Asquith government was shaken by the defeat, and in July the Prime Minister was forced to accept the establishment of a Commission of Inquiry into what had happened in Mesopotamia, as well as one into the Gallipoli fiasco—a sign of its declining political authority.

On 5 June Kitchener's death at sea made a major impact. As news seeped through, the big London stores closed for the rest of the day, and flags on public buildings flew at half-mast. The semi-mythical status of Kitchener can be seen from the hysteria which attended his demise. Since his body was never found, rumours abounded that the great hero had miraculously survived the disaster and would in due course return to save his people. Others alleged that Kitchener's death had been brought about by occult forces or, more specifically, that he was the victim of the 'Hidden Hand', a pro-German cadre of traitors in high places who had betrayed the movement of the *Hampshire* to Berlin.

All of this signified the disappearance of the earlier optimism and idealism, and its replacement by a sour xenophobia and by the sort of atrocity-mongering which had already been given a certain legitimacy the previous year by the credulous Bryce Report.[87] In this atmosphere it was easy to whip up venom against the 'enemy within', which found outlet in attacks on the properties and persons of German nationals or, indeed, of anyone with a German-sounding name, including the likes of Sir John Brunner, whose family in fact came from Switzerland. Zeppelin raids over London and other major cities, against which British air defences seemed powerless, created additional anger—which gave an opening to the pioneering aviator Pemberton Billing, who successfully ran

---

[86] Wilson, *Myriad Faces*, 379.   [87] See Ch. 19.

as an Independent, backed by the demagogue Horatio Bottomley, in the Hertford by-election of 10 March 1916. In the House Billing demanded aerial retaliation against German cities, while also exploiting, often in wild language, a range of grievances, from profiteering to the supposed machinations of the 'Hidden Hand'.[88]

The resulting political fallout damaged the anti-war ILP (a cartoon has the Kaiser awarding the Iron Cross to 'Keir von Hardie'), but it also affected the Liberal Party, many of whose prominent members (the 'Potsdam Party') stood accused of not having reacted to the German threat before 1914 with sufficient vigour—an accusation which had already cost the hapless Haldane his Cabinet office when Asquith had earlier formed his coalition government. A further impression of Liberal weakness was conveyed by the circumstances surrounding the passing of the second Military Service Bill, which extended compulsion to all men aged 18 to 41, regardless of marital status. An angry Commons, meeting in secret session on 27 April, blew away the elaborate safeguards contained within the government's original Bill, forcing Asquith into an ignominious retreat. Twenty-seven Liberal MPs voted against the revised measure on its second reading in a final, futile defence of the voluntary system.[89]

As if this crisis were not enough for the beleagured premier, compulsion in England coincided with the oubreak of the Easter Rising in Ireland. The long-serving Irish Secretary, Augustine Birrell (a close friend of Asquith's), resigned amid complaints from Unionists that he had ignored the threat to Dublin Castle posed by Irish Nationalist extremists because of his over-eagerness to co-operate with the Home Rule leaders John Redmond and John Dillon. The repression which followed the Easter Rising, involving the imposition of martial law, the shooting of sixteen of Sinn Fein's leaders, and the prosecution and execution of Roger Casement, did little to appease these right-wing critics, but in the medium run it demoralized and weakened the Liberal ranks. Backbench Liberal MPs joined the Irish Nationalists in protesting against the government's harsh actions. Henceforward the Nationalists consistently failed to support the government in the division lobby—in the ultimately vain hope of reasserting their credibility with their own constituents.

The Easter Rising also damaged the Liberal Party in a more subtle way, by driving Asquith and Lloyd George (and their respective admirers) further apart. Sent to Ireland in the wake of the Rising to search for a political solution, Lloyd George came up with a shaky plan for conceding Home Rule to Ireland,

---

[88] G. R. Searle, *Corruption in British Politics 1895–1930* (Oxford, 1987), Ch. 11.

[89] The measure was carried by 328 votes to 36. The minority comprised 26 Liberal, 9 Labour, and 1 Irish MP, in addition to which there were two tellers, one Liberal and one Labour.

with an opt-out clause for Ulster. Since this agreement had only been reached by Lloyd George's conveying to Carson and Bonar Law the impression that partition would be permanent and to Redmond and Dillon the promise that it would be temporary, the deal would sooner or later have unravelled; but before it could do so Asquith withdrew his support in the face of opposition from Lansdowne, who, as a Southern Unionist, naturally found such a constitutional arrangement complete anathema. (Another Unionist minister, Lord Selborne, had already resigned.) Asquith's seeming weakness figured in a growing body of complaints being compiled by such friends of Lloyd George as Christopher Addison, his Parliamentary Under-Secretary at Munitions, who in turn had contact with the forty or so 'patriotic' Liberal backbenchers who had earlier come together (in January 1916) to form the Liberal War Committee.

By now Lloyd George was rapidly assuming a position from which he could effectively challenge the Prime Minister. When the death of Kitchener in June created a vacancy at the War Office, the Minister of Munitions, elbowing aside Bonar Law's feeble challenge, insisted on the post for himself. Asquith's wife Margot despairingly wrote in her diary: 'We are out: it can only be a question of time now when we shall have to leave Downing Street.'[90]

Lloyd George became War Secretary on the eve of the Somme offensive, far too late to halt it even had he wanted to do so. Stripped of most of his authority by the previous year's reorganization of the War Office, which had concentrated strategic authority in the hands of Robertson, Lloyd George could only watch helplessly the events unfolding on the Western Front. On 11 October he briefly shared in the prevalent view that victory was nigh, issuing his defiant 'Knock-Out Blow' speech in response to US President Wilson's half-hearted attempt at mediation—in the process alienating still further many Liberals of a more traditional cast of mind.

But Lloyd George had no confidence in either the tactics or the strategy underlying the policies of the military high command, and as the losses from the Somme mounted, grumbled that he was merely a butcher boy, rounding up men for the abbatoir. Amid worrying news from Romania, Lloyd George visited the Front in mid-September, where he expressed views sharply critical of GHQ. However, Haig, belying his pose as a bluff, apolitical soldier, had always been adept at keeping in touch with sympathetic pressmen, and, duly prompted, Northcliffe, Strachey, and Gwynne warned the government against interference, the latter most notably in the *Morning Post*'s editorial of 26 September. Robertson also blocked Lloyd George's blatant attempt to sideline him by sending him off on a mission to Russia, saying that he was not prepared to leave the country so that the War Secretary could 'play "hankey-pankey" behind his back'.[91] Balked in this direction, the War Secretary sought another way round Robertson's roadblock by advocating major reforms to the machinery of government.

The ensuing political drama unfolded against a grim background. The realization that Germany possessed much greater resilience than had been supposed at the start of the year presented the government with the dilemma of how to raise the manpower necessary for future campaigns. On 21 November the War Committee agreed to another comb-out, and a week later the military members of the Army Council peremptorily demanded that every man up to 55 years of age be placed at the disposal of the government—in other words, the adoption of industrial conscription. On 30 November another meeting of the War Committee, under pressure from Lloyd George and Edwin Montagu, the Minister of Munitions, accepted the necessity for this desperate measure—and even raised the age-limit to 60. Lloyd George suggested that a committee be set up to prepare the appropriate legislation, and its chairmanship was allotted to Montagu.[92]

But Runciman, who had not been present at that meeting, immediately sent Hankey a stiff note of protest, declaring himself adamantly opposed to any further extension of state controls.[93] Quite apart from their concern about the threat to civil liberties, he and McKenna had long warned that the cost of combining the role of a great military power with that of paymaster and financier to the Allies would eventually prove too great. In half a year's time, McKenna was predicting, Britain would be completely dependent financially on the United States.[94] Alarmingly, on 28 November 1916 America's Federal Reserve Board advised investors not to lend any more money to the belligerents. So worrying was this situation that Lord Lansdowne, the elderly Minister Without Portfolio, submitted to the Cabinet a memorandum in which he argued that the country was bankrupting itself and bleeding its population dry in pursuit of grandiose objectives that had never been adequately defined.

No other minister exhibited such defeatism, most agreeing with Bonar Law that bankruptcy was preferable to defeat. However, were the government finally to abandon all attempt to fight the war against the Central Powers on limited liability principles, it would face formidable difficulties for which it was ill-prepared, its political credit being almost as precarious as its finances. Ministerial authority had been crumbling more or less steadily throughout

---

[91] French, *British Strategy*, 232–3.

[92] Adams and Poirier, *Conscription Controversy*, 186.

[93] S. Roskill, *Hankey: Man of Secrets, Vol. 1: 1877–1918* (London, 1970), 322.

[94] J. Turner, *British Politics and the Great War: Coalition and Conflict 1915–1918* (New Haven and London, 1992), 127.

the year, and the Prime Minister, devastated by the death of his eldest son Raymond on the Somme in mid-September, now cut a forlorn figure.

Moreover, added to Irish disaffection and Liberal divisions was mounting unrest in the Conservative Parliamentary Party. On 7 January 1916 Carson, released from the responsibilities of government, had taken on the chairmanship of the Unionist War Committee, founded the previous month, with a membership of approximately 150 members. This body became the main mouthpiece of those calling for an entirely new kind of political leadership— a call endorsed by the group surrounding Lord Milner, one of whom, Geoffrey Robinson, was editor of *The Times*.

The butt of Carson's attacks was less the much-derided Asquith than the Party Leader, Bonar Law, trapped within a so-called National Government in which he exercised limited influence. The precariousness of Law's position was brutally revealed in the so-called Nigerian Debate of 8 November, when Carson challenged the Colonial Office's policy for disposing of captured enemy assets in Nigeria. Though the government won the parliamentary vote, only seventy-three Unionists, many of them office-holders, supported Bonar Law, the Colonial Secretary, while sixty-five entered the lobby with Carson. Asquith was clearly not the only party leader whose job was now on the line.

With the Canadian-born press lord and backbench Conservative MP Max Aitken acting as go-between, Bonar Law countered this peril by moving closer both to Carson and Lloyd George. On 25 November the 'triumvirate' met for the first time and agreed upon a scheme for streamlining the machinery of government by creating a small inner council, which could meet at regular intervals, under Lloyd George's chairmanship. The following day Bonar Law presented this proposal to the Prime Minister, who politely turned it down, as he was again to do when Lloyd George pressed on him a modified version of the same idea on 1 December. Asquith declared his objection to any administrative change that would derogate from the authority of the full Cabinet, but, as he was later to put it, his prime anxiety, understandably enough, was that executive power might transfer itself to Lloyd George, leaving him a prime minister only in name.

On 2 December Lloyd George thereupon sent Bonar Law a historic letter, saying 'the life of the country depends on resolute action by you now'. But Bonar Law faced problems within his own party, mainly with senior Conservative ministers (the '3 Cs': Curzon, Austen Chamberlain, and Robert Cecil), who felt that their Leader had identified himself too closely with Lloyd George, whom they still deeply mistrusted. On the morning of Sunday, 3 December, they summoned Bonar Law to a meeting, which ended confusingly with them all signing a letter to Asquith calling on him to resign, on the ground that the government, as constituted, could not go on; meanwhile they offered their own resignations. But this letter also contained disapproving references to a leak about the proposed reorganization which had appeared in that day's *Reynold's News*, a paper edited by Lloyd George's long-term friend and associate Henry Dalziel. Historians have long puzzled over whose side the '3 Cs' thought they were on.

In the afternoon Bonar Law met Asquith to communicate the gist of this somewhat self-contradictory message—but he did not hand over the letter itself. Asquith was possibly taken aback; in any event, he decided to meet his critics halfway. In the evening Asquith and Lloyd George rapidly agreed on the outlines of a constitution for the new 'War Committee', though who should serve on it presented difficulties yet to be faced. Briefly, it seemed as though yet another governmental crisis had been surmounted.

However, on the following day *The Times* carried a clearly politically in-spired article, describing the new machinery of government in terms highly disparaging to Asquith. This article, it is now clear, had been prompted by Carson, but Asquith's suspicions were drawn towards Lloyd George, long mistrusted and feared for his press machinations and for his friendly relation-ship with Northcliffe. On the advice of his Liberal colleagues, Asquith broke off the dialogue with Bonar Law and Lloyd George and tendered his resigna-tion to the King—an act which automatically entailed the end of his ministry. Montagu, torn between personal affection for Asquith and admiration for Lloyd George's talents, continued his desperate search for a resolution of the breach, but all the other senior Liberal ministers unequivocally threw in their lot with the Prime Minister. There is some evidence that Asquith hoped that by acting in this way he might succeed in reimposing his authority and bring his treacherous Welsh colleague to heel; if so, this was a delusion which few senior Liberals shared.

The King then called a conference of all the party Leaders, plus Balfour and Lloyd George, which assembled at Buckingham Palace but failed to resolve the impasse. His next step was the logical one of commissioning Bonar Law, now Leader of the largest parliamentary grouping, to form a new ministry. Bonar Law, aware of his personal unfitness for the role, went ahead reluctantly, hoping that Asquith might not find it beneath his dignity to serve under him in some such prestigious office as that of Lord Chancellor—so preserving national unity. Asquith, however, would not consent to such a demotion. This forced the King to turn to Lloyd George, who thus found himself, by default, on the verge of the premiership. Starting off with the aim of subordin-ating Robertson to civilian control, Lloyd George had inadvertently brought about the fall of Asquith.

CHAPTER 18

The Great War: Tragedy and Triumph, 1916–1918

1. TURNING OVER A NEW LEAF?

Lloyd George, his hand strengthened by his powers of patronage, managed to form a ministry with surprising ease. The much-criticized Balfour, who had earlier submitted his resignation as First Lord of the Admiralty, was won over with the offer of the Foreign Office—despite being thought of as the Conservative who stood closest to Asquith. The other leading Conservatives, the '3 Cs' included, also decided that their patriotic duty required them to join the new government, as did Arthur Henderson, the Labour Leader, who at a late stage transferred his allegiance from Asquith to Lloyd George. Lloyd George's position was also strengthened by Addison's timely announcement on 6 December that 136 Liberal backbenchers 'had definitely promised support' were the Welshman to form an administration (the true number was probably between forty and fifty!)[1] Yet, on the debit side, all the senior Liberal ex-ministers followed Asquith on to the backbenches—Montagu in agony of spirit, most of the others with relief. Only Liberal politicians of the second rank, such as Addison, were willing to be prominently associated with the new government.

This left Lloyd George, though allegedly heading a 'National Government', dangerously dependent on Conservative support. He tried to offset this disadvantage by constructing an inner 'War Cabinet' of five members (Bonar Law, Curzon, Milner, and Henderson, as well as himself), which broke with Asquithian precedent by largely ignoring the claims of party. True, Bonar Law, the new Chancellor of the Exchequer and Leader of the House, owed his elevation to the fact that he was the Conservative Leader. But Henderson was included less because he was chairman of the PLP than because he supposedly possessed influence over the unionized factory workers. Curzon, an important fish to land, was selected because of his knowledge of foreign and imperial affairs, and a berth was found for Milner who, as an accomplished bureaucrat,

---

[1] J. M. McEwen, 'Lloyd George's Liberal Supporters in December 1916: A Note', *Bulletin of the Institute of Historical Research*, 53 (1980), 265–72.

had much to contribute to a government committed to comprehensive planning. (Interestingly, the third member of the 'Triumvirate', Carson, was made First Lord of the Admiralty, outside the War Cabinet—even though his inclusion within the inner sanctum had recently been pressed upon a highly disapproving Asquith!) Placed at the disposal of the War Cabinet were Maurice Hankey and his secretariat.

Lloyd George's advent to power gave a temporary lift to morale. Of course, many traditional Liberals looked with suspicion on the new ministry, as did most socialists, trade unionists, and Irish Nationalists. But, given the emergency, what was the alternative? Barbara Hammond, doyenne of the New Liberalism, put it well when she privately noted: 'the Asquith regime means certain & moderate disaster; the Ll.G. either absolute disaster or success.'[2] This was why many right-wing Conservatives, who before 1914 were the bitterest of Lloyd George's critics, now welcomed the change. For the first time, they thought, the country was being led by a man who would have the courage to break free from the shackles of the discredited party system and do whatever was necessary, however unconventional, to win the war.

Yet it is easy to exaggerate the extent of the changes brought about by the new regime. Despite the dropping of Runciman and McKenna, it certainly did not signify the replacement of Freedom by Control. For Lloyd George immediately tied his own hands by making a number of concessions without which he could probably not have formed a ministry at all. For example, Labour's co-operation required more than simply giving office to leading trade unionists (as well as Henderson, George Barnes and John Hodge were put in charge of the new Ministries of Pensions and of Labour). Even before Asquith's fall, Henderson and Hodge, reversing an earlier decision, reported that trade-union leaders would not accept industrial conscription, so Montagu's draft National Service Bill, agreed to in principle by the outgoing ministry, was not proceeded with. True, a Ministry of National Service was created in December 1916, but Lloyd George's appointee as its first Director-General, Neville Chamberlain (Austen's half-brother), was given a muddled brief and denied executive authority—a recipe for disaster.

Lloyd George further handicapped himself by assuring the Conservatives that not only would he not reinstate Churchill but that he did not intend to interfere in military strategy and would not remove Haig or Robertson—in earnest of which Lord Derby, the 'soldier's friend', was appointed War Secretary, although he was generally thought to possess 'the brains of a tomtit'.[3] This proved to be the greatest limitation of all. Lloyd George's determination to

[2] P. Clarke, *Liberals and Social Democrats* (Cambridge, 1978), 185.
[3] D. French, *The Strategy of the Lloyd George Coalition, 1916–1918* (Oxford, 1995), 19.

alter the machinery of government stemmed from his wish to assert civilian control over GHQ. 'Haig does not care how many men he loses,' the Premier was privately declaring: 'He just squanders the lives of these boys. I mean to save some of them in the future . . . I am their trustee.'[4] The Prime Minister was also concerned to economize on human lives because he understood the finite extent of the nation's manpower resources, and knew that the morale of the people would eventually snap if stretched too far. But how was this new policy to be implemented while Robertson, a man quite impervious to Lloyd George's charm, remained in office, his powers intact?

Arguably the best way to head off what Lloyd George later called 'hetacombs of slaughter' would have been to accept the attempt at mediation which President Wilson launched in December 1916. But the new administration had been formed with a view to more vigorously prosecuting the war: significantly, Lansdowne was the one Conservative serving in Asquith's Coalition to be dropped from office in December.[5] Ministers therefore greeted with relief Berlin's refusal to agree even to unconditional Belgian independence, a stance which effectively sabotaged any prospect of a compromise peace.[6] The war would go on.

2. GAMBLING ON NIVELLE

Yet Lloyd George's changes in personnel and improvements to the machinery of government could never by themselves resolve the cruel dilemmas which had led to Asquith's downfall. In November 1916 the French Chamber, in secret session, had resolved 'that France [was] bearing more than her fair share of the war, and that her allies should be called upon to make greater sacrifices in the common cause'.[7] This put pressure on the British to humour their French ally by fully participating in a new military offensive.

Lloyd George's initial hope was that, baited with the promise of more Allied equipment, the Italians might be persuaded to bear the brunt of the fighting in 1917: the matter was discussed at the Rome Conference in January, but Cadorna, the Italian Commander-in-Chief, would have none of it. The Prime Minister's next move was even more surprising. He had been impressed by Joffre's successor, General Nivelle, who, visiting London, expounded in

---

[4] In January 1917: see T. Wilson and R. Prior, 'British Decision-Making 1917: Lloyd George, the Generals and Passchendaele', in H. Cecil and P. H. Liddle (eds.), *Facing Armageddon: The First World War Experienced* (London, 1996), 95.

[5] On Lansdowne, see Ch. 17.

[6] T. Wilson, *The Myriad Faces of War: Britain and the Great War 1914–1918* (Oxford, 1986: Cambridge, 1988 edn.), 439–40.

[7] French, *Lloyd George Coalition*, 53–4.

fluent English his master plan for winning the war—to be achieved by a massive preparatory artillery barrage which would entail minimal Allied casualties. The French Government had already underwritten this plan. Lacking confidence in Haig, Lloyd George resolved to subordinate him to Nivelle's command, an idea which he sprang upon his astonished military advisers at a meeting held in Calais on 26–27 February—a meeting ostensibly held to discuss the railway congestion that had been caused by a shipping accident which blocked Boulogne harbour for twenty-six days during December and January.

Lloyd George fatally overreached himself. Robertson threatened resignation, Lord Derby and the King were beside themselves with rage, and Haig, who mistrusted Nivelle even more than he mistrusted most Frenchmen, communicated his objections to Conservative sympathizers such as Austen Chamberlain and Walter Long. Faced by the prospect of the ministry's collapse, the indispensable Hankey was authorized to negotiate a compromise: Haig's subordination to Nivelle, it was now agreed, would only be for the forthcoming offensive, and Haig would retain responsibility for the troops in his own sector and have a right to appeal to London if he thought his army endangered. Even so, Haig's reluctant compliance with this arrangement was only given when he was assured that, should Nivelle fail to achieve his promised breakthrough, British troops would later be transferred north for an offensive in Flanders aimed at relieving the Channel ports—a notion provisionally accepted by the War Cabinet on 13 March.

Through his incompetent deviousness, Lloyd George had thus got the worst of all possible worlds. Robertson and Haig, by no means agreed over strategy, closed ranks to ward off further 'interference' and, as a result, civil–military relations, already strained by an unauthorized press release from Haig's GHQ earlier in February, sank to an all-time low. Worse still, attempts to create an effective inter-Allied command were set back for many months. Indeed, Anglo-French military relations perceptibly worsened in early 1917, so much so that in March Nivelle had the effrontery to ask Lloyd George informally to sack Haig and replace him with Gough! Finally, the British government had half-committed itself to another major offensive later in the year—the one thing that Lloyd George was most anxious to avert.

'I do hope [Nivelle] will not fail,' wrote Lloyd George's mistress, Frances Stevenson, 'for D [i.e. Lloyd George] has backed him up against Haig, & it will rather let D. down if he proves to be a failure.'[8] Unfortunately, the reckless gamble did indeed fail. Before Nivelle's offensive had even begun, the German

---

[8] 10 Apr. 1917: A. J. P. Taylor (ed.), *Lloyd George: A Diary by Frances Stevenson* (London, 1971), 150.

army, forewarned by the capture of detailed French military plans, had adroitly pulled back to a more easily defended position, the Hindenburg Line. This reduced still further the chances of success for Nivelle's overambitious scheme since, by shortening their line by 25 miles, the Germans released between twelve and twenty additional divisions—some of which, Haig feared, might soon attack the BEF in Flanders. Though the latter did not happen, the Nivelle Offensive, launched on 16 April, was a total catastrophe which cost 29,000 French lives (proportionately more than the British had lost on the Somme), and sparked off widespread mutinies. On 15 May Nivelle was replaced as French C.-in-C. by Philippe Pétain, who partially restored his troops' morale by promising no more bloody offensives. Despite holding two-thirds of the Allied line, the French were to stay largely on the defensive for many months to come.[9]

Meanwhile, on 9 April, ahead of Nivelle's main thrust, Haig had mounted his diversionary attack at Arras. The offensive showed that at least some of the lessons of the Somme had been learnt. Troops approached the Front through tunnels, and a modicum of surprise was also achieved by shortening the duration of the opening barrage—even though three times as much ordnance was employed as had been fired off before the Somme.[10] The BEF was also better equipped: it now possessed such devices as the '106 fuse' for destroying barbed wire, and gas shells, propelled by Liven's gas projector.

The first day of Arras was a triumph for the British forces, which, under Allenby, advanced some three-and-a-half miles, the greatest distance any army had progressed since the Western Front had succumbed to stalemate; 9,000 German prisoners were also taken. Among many heroic exploits, Byng's Canadian Corps captured the Vimy Ridge in only a couple of days. However, as well as poor weather (the offensive began in a snowstorm), the fighting at Arras was bedevilled by all the problems which had earlier caused promising initiatives to peter out. The cavalry proved unable to make rapid progress over broken ground, nor were the tanks much more effectual; moreover, over-rigid centralized planning meant that by the time the offensive was renewed on 23 April the Germans had had time to rush in reinforcements. When fighting stopped in June the enemy had incurred over 100,000 casualties, but the BEF had lost even more men, perhaps 150,000: the highest casualty rate per day during any British offensive.[11] Haig made Allenby carry the can: soon afterwards the luckless commander was dispatched, in semi-disgrace, to Palestine.

[9] Until they went into action near the Chemin des Dames on 23 October. Pétain, at Paris on 4–5 May, promised support for Haig's summer offensive, but was unable to deliver.

[10] J. Keegan, *The First World War* (London, 1998), 350; Wilson, *Myriad Faces*, 349.

[11] G. Sheffield, *Forgotten Victory: The First World War: Myths and Realities* (London, 2001), 159.

3. THE UNRESTRICTED U-BOAT CAMPAIGN

These disheartening events took place against the background of a worsening
of the situation at sea. The Allies' dismissal of the German 'Peace Note' had
provided Berlin with a pretext for resuming unrestricted U-boat warfare on
1 February, with a view to starving Britain into submission within six months.
This objective had become more practical since the launching in June 1916 of a
new type of U-boat, which could reach as far as the east coast of America.
Improved torpedoes also facilitated more underwater attacks—Germany's
response to the Royal Navy's use of Q-boats[12] and its arming of merchant
vessels. The U-boat menace was reinforced by the existence of German
destroyer and patrol boat flotillas operating out of Flemish ports—which
briefly closed the Channel to merchant ships and troop transports. As early
as 9 November 1916 Runciman had warned that 'a complete breakdown in
shipping would come before June 1917', and his prediction seemed about to
become true.

Germany planned to sink 600,000 tons of Allied shipping a month. In April
it actually exceeded that target, sinking more than 850,000 tons, over a quarter
of all ships leaving British ports. Some neutral shipping was also frightened
away from British waters, while, by stepping up U-boat attacks in the Mediterranean, the Germans forced commerce with the Far East and Oceania to
take the long route around South Africa. Fatalities among merchant seamen
rose from 1,225 during the whole of 1916 to 3,833 in the first half alone of
1917.[13] Of more pressing concern was the depletion of Britain's wheat stocks,
which fell to a dangerously low point in April, the month when the country
seemed closest to defeat.

But the Germans had to pay a heavy price for such successes. In late 1916
Anglo-American relations were at a low ebb, in part because of the operation of
the British blockade, in part because of London's lukewarm response to
President Wilson's attempts at mediation. However, sympathies in Washington began to shift after 25 February, when the Foreign Office passed on to
Wilson a transcript of the 'Zimmerman Telegram', which revealed the German
government's promise to Mexico that, should war break out between Germany
and the United States, it would help the Mexicans secure land in Texas if they
joined in on the side of the Central Powers. Then, on 18 March, U-boats sank
three American merchant ships without warning. This outrage won over the
waverers in Washington.

The United States declared war against Germany on 7 April—admittedly,
as an associated power, not as an ally—thus putting unlimited credit at the

---

[12] Armed decoy vessels used as an anti-submarine weapon.
[13] Wilson, *Myriad Faces*, 431.

disposal of Britain and France. This, in turn, enabled the British to switch their imports of wheat from Australia to the United States, which, because it was geographically nearer, saved valuable tonnage. The Allies were also strengthened by the co-operation of the American navy, which had the second-largest fleet of modern battleships in the world. Finally, there was the prospect of American troops arriving in Europe en masse some time in the course of 1918.

But could Britain and France hold out that long? The Germans were gambling on winning a decisive victory long before then, and this outcome seemed a distinct possibility after February, when a revolution in St Petersburg overthrew the Tsar, leaving a major question-mark over Russia's willingness or capacity to stay in the war.

In reality, the odds had always been weighted against the chances of Germany forcing Britain to surrender by naval pressure alone. Only in April 1917 did the U-boats reach their target of destroying 600,000 tons of merchant shipping a month. Moreover, the German navy never had enough vessels to fulfil its objectives: between January 1917 and January 1918 Germany built eighty-seven new boats, but lost seventy-eight.[14] Losses of matériel and trained manpower still further reduced the effectiveness of the U-boat campaign. On the other hand, although, from May 1915 onwards, wireless direction-finding enabled a U-boat's movements to be plotted right across the North Sea,[15] the Board of Admiralty in early 1917 was declaring its impotence in the face of the new menace.

The most effective form of defence eventually proved to be the organization of merchant shipping into convoys protected by the Royal Navy—a system already employed to transport coal and other supplies to France. Its wider adoption, however, was delayed because Carson and Jellicoe (First Lord of the Admiralty and First Sea Lord respectively), reinforcing each other's temperamental pessimism, overestimated the number of escorts necessary and did not believe that merchant seamen, operating a range of diverse craft, had the skill or the discipline required to sail in convoy. Nor did Hankey at first find it easy to interest Lloyd George in this solution. Eventually, on 30 April, amid the deepening crisis, the Prime Minister threw his weight behind a change of policy—by which time most senior naval officers had come to accept the inevitability of convoys. Soon afterwards Carson was replaced as First Lord by Eric Geddes, a dismissal camouflaged by the former's 'promotion' to the War Cabinet.

---

[14] N. Ferguson, *The Pity of War* (Harmondsworth, 1998), 283.
[15] Otherwise the hydrophone was only operable over a few hundred yards.

The first convoy set sail from Gibraltar on 10 May, all of its seventeen ships reaching British ports without loss. By the end of the year more than half of Britain's overseas trade was being conducted under convoy, with a loss-rate of under 1 per cent. Leaving aside the Mediterranean, between February and October 1918 nearly 49,000 merchant ships sailed in convoy, only 120 of them being sunk by U-boats, whereas 357 vessels not in convoy *were* sunk.[16] Moreover, under Geddes's vigorous direction, more mines were laid and more aircraft and airships devoted to anti-submarine patrols, as a result of which the destruction of U-boats steadily mounted. These successes engendered a new mood of confidence at the Admiralty, which received a further boost when, on Christmas Eve, Geddes sacked Jellicoe, replacing him as First Sea Lord by Admiral Wemyss. 'One obstacle to a successful war is now out of the way', commented one naval insider.[17]

By 1918 it had become evident that the U-boat menace had been contained, with Germany unable to build submarines faster than Britain rebuilt sunk tonnage. Even so, this success would have arrived too late, had the government not acted decisively on the home front to make optimum use of scarce resources. The hero of the hour was the Director of Shipping, a former shipowner, Joseph Maclay, who not only instigated a vast shipbuilding programme but also reorganized the docks so as to cut the delays involved in 'turning-round' (unloading and reloading cargo).

At the same time the government was driven into intervening in agricultural production. A committee set up by Asquith the previous year had already recommended guaranteed prices for cereal producers, but opposition from landowners had led to its proposal being shelved. Under pressure of circumstances these powers were now enshrined in the Corn Production Act, passed in August 1917, which also imposed controls on agricultural rents and wages. The government also took direct responsibility for the first time for the distribution of foodstuffs. Lloyd George's original Food Controller, the wholesale grocer Lord Devonport (formerly Hudson Kearley, a Liberal backbench MP), had become something of a laughing-stock, with his promotion of 'meatless days' and his attempts to institute an impractical scheme of 'voluntary rationing'. He was replaced in June 1917 by Lord Rhondda, who was given powers to control almost all aspects of food distribution and sales—setting a process in motion that was to culminate the following year in a centrally imposed rationing scheme.

Voluntaryism was thus finally buried, not in December 1916 when Lloyd George became Prime Minister, but in the summer of the following year, when

---

[16] Wilson, *Myriad Faces*, 633.
[17] J. M. Bourne, *Britain and the Great War 1914–1918* (London, 1989), 70.

the threat of starvation forced the government to discard its former inhibitions—though whether an Asquith-led ministry containing the likes of McKenna and Runciman would have responded as effectively to the crisis is highly problematical.

The need to release more men to work in the shipbuilding industry and in agriculture added fresh urgency to the work of manpower planning. Neville Chamberlain, at the Ministry of National Service, became the scapegoat for failures which really stemmed from the Prime Minister's own earlier timidity. He was replaced in August by Eric Geddes's brother, Auckland Geddes, who, like Rhondda, was given the clear mandate and enhanced powers that had been denied to his predecessor.

But manpower policy needed to be accompanied by policies designed to appease labour and ensure its continued support of the war effort. So much became apparent in the spring of 1917, when war-weariness and a succession of niggling grievances led to a partial breakdown of the industrial truce. Many munitions workers came out on strike on 21 March, followed by engineers at Rochdale in April. By May trouble had spread to forty-eight towns, involving 200,000 men, with the loss of 1,500,000 working days.[18] The disturbances, spearheaded by shop stewards, were mainly caused by the government's decision to abolish the trade-card scheme and to extend 'dilution' to private work (the breaking-down of skilled craft procedures into a series of simpler operations that could be performed by unskilled or semi-skilled merchinists, many of them women); the unrest, in other words, was mainly economic and sectional in origin, not an expression of revolutionary aspirations.[19] (Significantly, the Labour Party Conference in January had endorsed the 'fight to the finish' by a large majority.) However, the government took fright—understandably so, given the interest being taken by many Labour activists in current developments in Russia. On 3 June a number of prominent socialists summoned a conference at Leeds, at which a resolution was passed calling on the workers to follow the Russians' example and form soviets in their localities. There were some faint intimations that the spirit of rebellion might even reach the armed forces: in June the Home Counties and Training Reserve Branch of the Workers and Soldiers Council assembled at the unlikely location of Tunbridge Wells.[20]

The government's response took the form of meeting many of the strikers' practical demands, while isolating and repressing the extremist elements among the leadership. It also set up a Commission on Industrial Unrest,

---

[18] Bourne, *Great War*, 209.

[19] French, *Lloyd George Coalition*, 86.

[20] D. Englander and J. Osborne, 'Jack, Tommy and Henry Dubb: The Armed Forces and the Working Class', *Historical Journal*, 21 (1978), 604.

which uncovered a wide range of discontents within working-class communities, such as rising food prices and rents and indignation over alleged profiteering, as well as the friction caused by the imposition of dilution. In July Lloyd George made a significant gesture towards removing these discontents by upgrading the Reconstruction Committee which had been operating since the previous March and turning it into a fully fledged ministry—with the partial purpose of stiffening flagging morale by holding out to unionized workers the prospect of extensive social reforms as a reward for patriotic co-operation in the war effort. This new body was placed under the control of Addison, moved sideways from Munitions, where he had antagonized many important union leaders.

At the same time Lloyd George moved to broaden the political base of his ministry. Ever since the formation of the new government Lloyd George's friends had been watching Asquith with some anxiety and suspicion. As Liberal Leader, the former Prime Minister still had the capacity to destabilize his successor's ministry. And so, on 28 May, Lloyd George's friend, the Lord Chief Justice Lord Reading, sounded Asquith out on his willingness to join the government in any capacity except that of Premier. Asquith refused to rise to the bait, telling Reading that Lloyd George had 'incurable defects, both of intellect and character, which totally unfitted him' to head a government.[21] Undaunted, Lloyd George then sought to attach other prominent Liberals to his ministry. In July, at the same time as 'promoting' Carson, he replaced Addison at the Ministry of Munitions with Winston Churchill, to the fury of most Tories, and made Edwin Montagu Indian Secretary, to the almost equal indignation of many independent Liberals, who bitterly resented Montagu's 'desertion'.[22]

4. THIRD YPRES AND CAMBRAI

All of these domestic mishaps were overshadowed in the summer of 1917 by the issue of whether or not Haig would be allowed to have his 'show' in Flanders. This momentous decision was about to be made by the newly created War Policy Committee—essentially the War Cabinet, minus Henderson but with the addition of Jan Smuts, the South African Minister of Defence. By this time an almost unstoppable momentum had built up behind the project. Its starting-point had been the Admiralty's agonized confession the previous November of its powerlessness to protect the merchant fleet, and its recommendation of a

---

[21] J. Turner, *British Politics and the Great War: Coalition and Conflict 1915–18* (New Haven and London), 212.

[22] Montagu replaced Austen Chamberlain, who had resigned following the publication of the Commission into the Mesopotamian fiasco, for which he bore ministerial responsibility.

military operation to capture the Belgian U-boat bases.[23] Haig's original plan involved a breakout from the Ypres Salient, to be accompanied by an amphibious attack on the coast, aimed at the German-held bases of Blankenberghe and Ostende.[24] The War Policy Committee, meeting on 20 June, was attracted by this proposal.

In truth, Haig had always wanted to fight in Flanders, and this for two important reasons. First, there was a clear military advantage in driving the Germans from the heights overlooking the death-trap of the Ypres Salient.[25] Second, this was terrain which the Germans dare not abandon (for fear of losing control of the vital railway link between Menin and Ostende and of being ejected from Belgian territory); since their lateral communications were no more than 10 miles in some places from the front line, the Germans would have to stand and fight. To Robertson, who favoured an attritional strategy, this was an especially powerful recommendation. British ministers agreed that the aim should be, not the breaking of the German line, but 'wearing down and exhausting the enemy's resistance'.

Haig himself also genuinely believed that the forthcoming offensive offered the prospect of a breakthrough which might end the war before the close of 1917—'one last push'. He told Henry Wilson in early June that 'he was quite sure that another 6 weeks' fighting & the heart of the Bosches would be broken',[26] a view he reiterated to Robertson: 'The German was now nearly at his last resources.'

Robertson, though sceptical of this view, shared Haig's impatience over Lloyd George's fascination with minor theatres of war. Moreover, both men disbelieved in waiting for the Americans—in part because they feared that France might surrender before the Americans arrived,[27] but also because they had a well-founded suspicion that Wilson was thinking of dictating a peace settlement along lines which ran counter to British imperial interests. More visceral emotions also came into play. The summer of 1917 marked the point at which the BEF indisputably replaced the French army as the main force on the Western Front, and Haig relished the prospect of fighting his own campaign, free, for the first time, from French restraints.

Robertson, always the more cautious of the two, warned Haig not to oversell his operational plans but to come up with arguments which would assuage the

[23] French, *Lloyd George Coalition*, 50.
[24] G. Till, 'Passchendaele: The Maritime Dimensions', in P. H. Liddle (ed.), *Passchendaele in Perspective: The Third Battle of Ypres* (London, 1997), 84.
[25] Wilson, *Myriad Faces*, 459.
[26] French, *Lloyd George Coalition*, 112.
[27] By March 1918 only 318,000 Americans were serving in France, though by August numbers were expected to rise to 1,300,000.

War Cabinet's fear of another futile bloodbath. On his visits to London in June, Haig accordingly emphasized that his campaign would proceed step by step, that it would 'commit me to no undue risks, and [could] be modified to meet any developments in the situation'.[28] These words did much to remove the doubts of the War Policy Committee.

Its members, Milner and Smuts in particular, were also concerned about the likely reaction of Britain's allies to a strategy of inaction. Initially the worries centred on Russia, which Milner visited in January, and these worries increased after the fall of the Tsarist regime two months later. Indeed, the failure of Brusilov's new offensive in June–July even led Lloyd George to start playing with the idea of a compromise peace with Germany, at Russia's expense.[29]

But, in the planning of Ypres, Russia counted for less than France. Here the cause for concern was only marginally the situation created by the French mutinies. In fact, Pétain partially concealed from Haig the gravity of what had happened to the French army, while Haig in turn did not pass on all that he knew to London. (Fortunately for the Allies, the German government, too, knew little of what had happened and so did not seek to exploit its advantage.)

The volatile state of French politics in mid-1917, however, preoccupied British ministers considerably more. The fall of the Briand ministry three months earlier had led the British to worry lest their old bugbear, the pro-German Joseph Caillaux, was about to take power—indeed, not until Clemenceau became Premier in November were the French led by someone committed to outright victory.[30] Action somewhere, anywhere, seemed unavoidable: 'The option of not playing was unavailable to the British government. And Flanders was the only game in town.'[31] The British were discovering that their new role as the dominant Alliance partner was restricting their freedom of manoeuvre almost as much as their subordinate status had done in 1915 and early 1916.

Yet why did Lloyd George confine himself to an expression of scepticism and doubts, and not use his authority to overrule a Commander-in-Chief in whose honesty as well as capacity he had so little confidence? Admittedly, the Prime Minister interrogated Haig closely when he appeared before the War Policy Committee between 19–21 June, and once again suggested prioritizing

---

[28] In similar vein, he told the War Policy committee that 'it would be possible for me to discontinue the advance if and when it appears that the means at my disposal are insufficient to justify further effort' (French, *Lloyd George Coalition*, 111–12).

[29] Asquith publicly attacked the idea in a speech at Leeds on behalf of the NWAC, and GHQ leaked to the public its view that Germany could be defeated on the Western Front even without Russian help (J. Turner, 'Lloyd George, the War Cabinet, and High Politics', in Liddle (ed.), *Passchendaele*, 21).

[30] One month after coming to office Clemenceau removed Caillaux's parliamentary immunity, neutralizing this threat to the Allied war effort.

[31] J. Bourne, 'The World War Context', in Liddle (ed.), *Passchendaele*, 12.

Italy, while waiting for the Americans. But, following the collapse of the Nivelle Offensive, Lloyd George had momentarily lost much of his customary self-belief. At the War Policy Committee meeting of 21 June he explicitly conceded 'that the responsibility for advising in regard to military operations must remain with his military advisers'.[32] Finally, on 16 July, the War Policy Committee, with Lloyd George demurring, agreed on the go-ahead, provided that Haig adopted a step-by-step policy and did not allow his campaign 'to degenerate into a drawn out, indecisive battle of the "Somme" type'.[33]

Even before third Ypres proper began, the BEF had shown the spectacular achievements that might be gained by such methods. On 7 June General Plumer carried out a textbook assault on Messines Ridge, 5 miles south of Ypres. The attack, meticulously prepared by his Chief of Staff, Tim Harington, was prefaced by exploding under the German trenches nineteen mines, containing a million pounds of high explosive—the noise of which could clearly be heard in Downing Street. The 2nd Army, with tanks to the fore, then made unprecedented advances, with scant resistance from the demoralized enemy.

Unfortunately, the main part of the offensive, already put back by Arras, was then further delayed by almost eight weeks, giving the Germans time to make their preparations. These included employing concrete pillboxes and bunkers, some inside derelict buildings—more effective than entrenchments in this low-lying, boggy terrain—and dividing their troops into two separate formations, a trench garrison and counter-attack divisions in the rearward battle zone. To overcome these obstacles the BEF deployed a massive artillery barrage, fired off from 2,299 guns, one to every five yards, a barrage that employed four times the number of shells fired off during the prelude to the Somme.[34] But one consequence of this was the destruction of Flanders's intricate drainage system, turning the countryside into a quagmire. Although 136 tanks led the initial assault, they could no more make rapid advance over this terrain than the luckless infantry, many of whom were drowned in flooded shell-holes. These horrors were accentuated by unusually rainy weather in early August; September was dry and sunny, but the rains returned with a vengeance in October.

Tactically, the BEF showed much greater imagination and versatility than it had done at the Somme. This can be seen from its initial, relatively small losses: only 35,000 casualties, some of them French, before 3 August. But third Ypres, which in any case was more a succession of eight separate battles than one single operation, suffered from strategic incoherence, with Haig and

[32] Wilson, *Myriad Faces*, 463.
[33] French, *Lloyd George Coalition*, 120.
[34] Keegan, *First World War*, 385.

(initially) Gough harbouring ambitious ideas of a breakthrough, while Plumer and Rawlinson set greater store by 'bite and hold'. For this confusion Haig must, of course, bear ultimate responsibility.

On 23 August it was agreed that a landing on the Belgian coast would not be feasible. Five days later Haig, recognizing that the war would *not* after all be over by Christmas, switched the centre of gravity of his operations from Gough's 5th Army to the 2nd Army, commanded by Plumer, who set himself strictly limited objectives. Even so, the resulting battles—notably Menin Road Ridge (20–7 September), Polygon Wood (26 September–3 October), and Broodseinde (4 October)—proved very costly in lives.

The British government was perhaps initially misled by the optimistic accounts emanating from GHQ, but belatedly it made a feeble attempt to call Haig to book. On 4 September the Commander-in-Chief returned to London to justify the continuation of the offensive, and later in the month the War Policy Committee reconvened for the first time since the start of the campaign.[35] The Prime Minister contemplated making a personal intervention, but was persuaded by Milner not to do this on the ground that GHQ would 'defend their position by engaging the sympathies of the Opposition and the Press'. Robertson, too, was now in some danger; however, Lloyd George was warned that if he dismissed his CIGS, Balfour, Cecil, Carson, and Curzon might resign in sympathy.[36] Hence, although the Prime Minister was soon comparing the current offensive unfavourably with Nivelle's, he was powerless to halt it.

Soon afterwards the heavy rains returned. Even the offensive-minded Gough urged that the fighting be called off, there being nothing further to be gained now that Plumer had taken control of parts of the Ypres Ridge. But Haig obstinately persevered, perhaps misled by John Charteris, his Intelligence Chief, who consistently told him a tale of how the Germans were 'used up'. The German troops, however, were not the only ones to suffer. Many British divisions fell seriously below strength, and problems of drunkenness and psychological disorders became increasingly apparent, leading to such incidents as the riot at the base camp of Étaples in September (mainly directed at the unpopular 'Red Caps', the military police). This explains Haig's growing reliance for spectacular assaults on Anzacs and the Canadian Corps, whom he subjected to a succession of terrifying ordeals. Indeed, it was the Canadians' capture of the tiny village of Passchendaele on 6 November which marked the effective end of the campaign.

---

[35] Wilson and Prior, 'British Decision-Making 1917', in Liddle (ed.), *Passchendaele*, 97.
[36] B. Bond, 'Passchendaele: Verdicts, Past and Present', in ibid. 485.

On 12 November Haig formally called off his offensive. After nearly three-and-a-half months of fighting the BEF had advanced no more than 10,000 yards, failing to reach all of the objectives that had been set for the *first day*. True, the Ypres Salient had been flattened out, but the German railway line remained uncut, the U-boat bases were never even remotely threatened, and the great breakthrough had not materialized.

Haig later argued that Pétain had urged him to extend the fighting into the autumn to relieve pressure on his own mutinous troops, but no evidence for this claim has ever emerged: on the contrary, the French military favoured a passive strategy on the Western Front, pending the arrival of the Americans en masse in 1918. Moreover, far from wishing to 'protect' the battle-weary French troops, Haig was eagerly (though vainly) trying to get them to participate on his behalf. Nor did the Russians greatly benefit from the BEF's exertions, the German high command being sufficiently relaxed to switch six divisions to the east, partly to counter the Kerensky Offensive and partly to assist the Austrians.

The defenders of third Ypres are on somewhat firmer ground in presenting the battle as a success in attritional terms. However, the absence of reliable casualty statistics makes it difficult to draw up an accurate balance-sheet. Most historians agree that about 70,000 British troops were killed and over 170,000 wounded, amounting to perhaps 275,000 casualties in all, if the Messines operation is included—a horrendous total but less so than that from the Somme, which lasted only slightly longer but had resulted in 419,000 casualties. But what of the enemy? By their obstinacy in launching counter-offensives to recover lost ground, the Germans probably suffered losses that were only slightly lower—say, 220,000.

As an exercise in 'Boche Killing', third Ypres hardly seems an unqualified success: the best that can be said is that *both* sides fought themselves to a standstill.[37] True, Germany, with fewer manpower resources than the Allies, could less afford casualties on the scale that Haig had inflicted upon them in 1917. On the other hand, the Germans had another army in the east which they were about to redeploy on the Western Front, an advantage which the British lacked.

Moreover, German troops, buoyed up by their success in knocking out Russia, were far from being the demoralized rabble depicted by Charteris. So much became apparent when Haig—surprisingly, given the circumstances—authorized General Byng to launch yet another attack, this time to the south at Cambrai.

---

[37] Ibid. 482. Compare the more optimistic account in Sheffield, *Forgotten Victory*, 176–80.

Byng's surprise assault showed for the first time the full potential of the tank, over 300 of which went into action on 20 November, equipped with 'fascines', bundles of brushwood, which acted as a bridge over the enemy trenches. But this was not the only tactical innovation. For the first time the British employed a sophisticated system of artillery 'registration', that is to say, 'registering the deviation of each [gun] from a norm by electrical means'—so obviating the need for a lengthy preliminary bombardment.[38] Smokescreens and dummy smokescreens added to the surprise. The tank assault succeeded in breaching the Hindenburg Line in several places, and the BEF advanced nearly four-and-a-half miles, neutralizing two whole German divisions for the loss of only 5,000 men. In Britain church bells were rung in celebration.

However, the momentum of the attack could not be sustained, partly because, to achieve surprise, so few reserves had been brought up close to the line, and partly because the cavalry, which was anyway brought into action too late in the day, struggled to make progress over a battlefield that was still littered with barbed wire. The co-ordination between tanks and the infantry also left much to be desired. Finally, many tanks quickly broke down, while others, with their limited visibility, passed enemy machine-gun emplacements by instead of destroying them. A week after the initial assault, all that the British had done was to trap themselves in another salient.

Then, on 30 November, the Germans counter-attacked, regaining nearly all of the ground they had earlier lost. When fighting ended on 7 December the British had suffered another 45,000 casualties (about the same number as the Germans), including about one-third of their tank crews. Two-thirds of the tanks had also been knocked out.[39] For Haig and GHQ, however, the real humiliation of Cambrai was that it gave the lie to their claim that they had broken the fighting spirit of the German army during third Ypres, a point not lost on 'patriotic' pressmen who, for the first time, started to voice public criticisms of the British Commander: on 12 December *The Times* called for Haig's removal, reflecting Northcliffe's more general disillusionment over the way the war was being conducted.

Lloyd George, emboldened, saw an opportunity for making a clean sweep of the military high command, but Derby threatened resignation and the Prime Minister drew back, perhaps thinking that for the time being he had quite enough on his plate in reorganizing the Admiralty. Haig consequently survived, but only after he had agreed to dump Generals Kiggell and Charteris, the two most notorious members of his staff.[40]

---

[38] Keegan, *First World War*, 396.   [39] Wilson, *Myriad Faces*, 492.
[40] General Launcelot Kiggell was Haig's Chief of Staff.

As for Robertson, Lloyd George had already worked out a plan for outmanoeuvring him. At an inter-Allied conference which met at Rapallo on 5 November, he took the lead in setting up a Supreme War Council, based at Versailles, under the control of the British, French, and Italian Prime Ministers and the American President, with a view to more effectively co-ordinating future Allied offensives. The pretext for this initiative had been the catastrophic defeat of Cadorna's Italian army at Caporetto in October. To Robertson's dismay, 200,000 British and French troops were diverted from the Western Front to shore up the Italians. Ominously for Robertson, the British government had meanwhile started to provide itself with alternative sources of military advice: in particular, Henry Wilson, a long-time critic of Haig's, was made Britain's Representative on the new Versailles Council.

However, there were political risks in such actions. Many Conservative backbenchers, including the ex-minister Austen Chamberlain, could be counted upon to resist any civilian encroachment into military affairs. These malcontents were soon to find a formidable spokesman in Carson, that perpetual loose cannon, who resigned in January 1918 in protest at the government's attempts to find an Irish Settlement. Equally worrying to Lloyd George was the stance of Asquith, who, after staying at Haig's headquarters for two days, spoke out in the Commons on 19 November in support of the principle of military 'independence'.

As 1917 drew to an end, the one encouraging development was the success of Allenby's forces in Palestine. On Christmas Eve Allenby entered Jerusalem— the 'present' for the British people that Lloyd George had so ardently hoped for. Britain, it seemed, would emerge from the war with an enhanced imperial role in the Middle East. Yet this assumed that she would at least avoid defeat on the Western Front, which, with the arrival of American troops taking place so slowly, could by no means be taken for granted.

5. CRUMBLING MORALE

By the summer of 1917 the strain of three years of total war was beginning to be felt, with the government facing a series of challenges to its authority, not least in Nationalist Ireland. In the absence of conscription, Ireland was enjoying considerable prosperity, largely as a result of the insatiable demand for its agricultural products. But disaffection with British rule mounted apace.

In January Sinn Fein reorganized itself on a more obviously republican basis, under the presidency of Eamonn de Valera, spared because of his American ancestry from the death which had been meted out to most of the other commanders who fought in the Easter Rising. In the course of 1917 Sinn

Fein took four seats off Redmond's Irish Nationalists in by-elections, starting
with North Roscommon in February, where the victor was Count Plunkett,
father of one of the executed signatories of the Easter Proclamation. In July de
Valera himself was returned for East Clare—a seat made vacant by the death of
John Redmond's brother Willy, who had died in action in France the previous
month.[41]

On coming to office Lloyd George had set up the Irish Convention, in the
vain hope that the Irish people, if left to their own devices, might reach a
negotiated settlement which the British government could then underwrite—
failing which, the Irish issue would at least have been kept off the national
political agenda for many months. But the Convention was boycotted by Sinn
Fein and viewed with deep suspicion by the Ulster Unionists. True, an
unlikely troika consisting of John Redmond, the Southern Unionists (led by
Lord Midleton, the former St John Brodrick), and the Irish Catholic bishops
managed to agree on the outlines of a settlement. But the compromise they
came up with, all-Ireland Home Rule with safeguards for the Protestant
minority, was even less acceptable to the loyalists as a whole than it would
have been before the war. In December the Convention broke down, amid
republican derision, and such was Ulster Unionist anger that Carson stormed
out of the government in January 1918.

A disaffected Labour Movement was a more immediate cause for concern.
Industrial unrest abated from May onwards as a result of the government's
timely concessions, but events in Russia continued to have a disturbing impact
on British working-class activists. Admittedly, the hot air generated by the
Leeds Convention amounted to very little (despite alarming Britain's security
services), but how best to react to the fall of Tsardom created a raft of
problems. In fact, the first Russian Revolution met with a mixed reaction on
the left: some had their faith in the international brotherhood of the working
class revived, but others, relieved at no longer being allied to a discredited
autocracy, cherished the hope that Kerensky's 'democratic' regime would give
fresh impetus to the war effort. Consequently, when signs multiplied in the
summer of 1917 that Lloyd George was contemplating a deal with the Central
Powers at Russia's expense, this elicited protests not only from the usual
quarters (the military leadership, for example), but also from Asquith, who
spoke out publicly against the prospect at Leeds in November, and from many
Labour activists, who were equally aghast.

But could Russia be persuaded to stay in the war at all, in the face of food
shortages, intense war-weariness, and Bolshevik subversion? The pro-war

---

[41] Other victors were Joseph McGuiness in Longford South in May and William Cosgrave in
Kilkenny City in August.

Henderson, visiting Petrograd in the summer on behalf of the War Cabinet, learnt at first hand how difficult it would be to sustain the 'democratic forces' (i.e. Kerensky's party) there. He therefore dropped his earlier hostility to the proposal, emanating from the Socialist International, that a conference should be held at Stockholm at which delegates from both military blocs as well as neutrals were be present. Henderson now felt that the British Labour Party ought to attend, so that it could defend the 'idealism' of the Allies' war aims in face-to-face encounters with German and Austrian socialists on the one hand, and Russian revolutionary defeatists on the other.

Unfortunately, the Prime Minister was moving in the opposite direction, and so when Henderson, with MacDonald and Wardle, set off for Paris to press his arguments on his French comrades (arguments which he repeated at a specially convened Labour Conference on 10 August), Lloyd George chose to interpret this as a breach of collective responsibility, and excluded him from the War Cabinet which discussed his 'delinquency'—the famous 'door mat incident'. Henderson resigned, and though his place was filled by another Labour man, George Barnes, who had proved a highly successful Minister of Pensions, the events of August 1917 marked the point at which Labour gradually began to disengage from Lloyd George's administration—for example, at the end of the year it declined to ratify the electoral truce.[42]

However, none of this signified hostility to the war itself; indeed, at a second Labour Conference, held on 22 August, a vocal minority of delegates, including the miners' delegates, were sharply critical of Stockholm.[43] It is also significant that, even before the government had decided to withdraw the Labour delegates' passports, Havelock Wilson's Sailors' and Firemens' Union had resolved not to transport them to their destination—evidence of the existence of a strongly 'jingo' element even within the organized Labour Movement. (The seamen, of course, were bitter and angry over the heavy casualties they were sustaining at the hands of the German U-boats.)

In fact, during 1917 overt opposition to the war came less from the socialist world than from the middle-class radicals who dominated the leadership of the Union of Democratic Control (UDC). Founded in August 1914 to promote the principle of the democratization of foreign policy, this pressure group was persuaded by its most energetic leader, E. D. Morel, to adopt as its immediate objective the securing of peace by negotiation. The UDC's campaign was particularly directed at the ILP and at the trade-union movement. In August 1917 Morel was arrested, then convicted and imprisoned for violating the

---

[42] See Ch. 20.
[43] The majority in favour of Stockholm fell sharply, in part because of the prior decision to exclude the ILP.

Defence of the Realm Act: his specific offence being the transmission of two of his publications to someone living in neutral Switzerland. On his release from prison in January, this one-time Liberal parliamentary candidate took the plunge and joined the ILP. But the UDC had meanwhile found another ally of sorts, albeit in a most unlikely quarter—Lord Lansdowne, whose 'Letter' was published in the *Daily Telegraph* on 29 November; this manifesto, essentially a revamp of his earlier Peace Note to the Cabinet, made the case for a negotiated settlement on both economic and humanitarian grounds. The elderly Unionist peer, who had not entertained a progressive thought for decades, suddenly became, to his own astonishment, a hero to the idealistic and revolutionary left.

But although, for the first time since August 1914, it had become possible for opponents of the war to make their case publicly, the strength of the anti-war movement needs to be put into perspective. British security agencies had an obvious vested interest in exaggerating its importance—as have latter-day historians with socialist sympathies. Yet between October 1916 and April 1918 none of the five 'Peace by Negotiation' by-election candidates made any impact—between them securing a mere 16 per cent of the total vote.[44] Compare this with the achievement of the veteran maverick Labour politician Ben Tillett, who, on a pro-war platform, romped home in the Salford North by-election of 2 November in a straight fight with a Liberal.

Indeed, the main beneficiaries from the crumbling of the patriotic front were right-wing xenophobes, not the idealistic left. In August the archetypal 'Diehard', Brigadier-General Page Croft, Conservative MP for Christchurch, founded a new political grouping, the 'National Party', whose manifesto promised 'the eradication of German influence' and an end to corruption in all its manifestations, including honours trafficking. This oblique accusation that Lloyd George, far from being a 'national' statesman, untarnished by the abuses of the party system, was in fact perpetuating some of these abuses in a new, more extreme form, was one of several indications that many of the Diehards were beginning to lose confidence in the Prime Minister. Yet Croft's National Party (of which Conservative Central Office naturally disapproved, though it was strongly backed by right-wing papers such as the *Morning Post*) occupied a peculiar political position in 1917 and early 1918: it oscillated between criticizing Lloyd George and claiming to bolster him against the bunch of carping 'Mandarins' in his entourage.

Perhaps for this reason, the National Party refrained from running any independent candidates during the war itself. But no such inhibitions were

---

[44] The most successful, by far, was W. Bland, who secured some 26% of the vote at Keighley in April 1918.

felt by the right-wing xenophobes who grouped around Pemberton Billing and the bombastic fraudster Horatio Bottomley. As casualty lists mounted in the war zones, and amid the panic spread by the raids of German 'Gotha' bombers (first launched against Folkestone on 25 May before being extended to London), the search intensified for the 'enemy within', variously identified as pro-Germans, aliens, Jews, sexual perverts, and those who were allegedly sapping national morale and sabotaging the war effort.

The heady brew of sexual innuendo and patriotic abuse was most explicitly present in Pemberton Billing's 'Vigilante' group, impresarios of the politics of paranoia, whose candidates secured over 30 per cent of the vote in the Islington East by-election on 23 October 1917 and over 42 per cent at Finsbury East the following July—the latter contest coming soon after the notorious Pemberton Billing trial, which opened in late May 1918, and which, not coincidentally, occurred at another moment of intense national danger.

6. PLANNING FOR 1918

As it took stock of its position at the start of the new year, the government was dismayed by the slowness with which the Americans were arriving in Europe—it seemed that only about half-a-million US troops were likely to be in France by June. This dilatoriness was partly explained by General Pershing's unwillingness to incorporate his troops into existing French or British units, but ministers and GHQ harboured suspicions about the ulterior motives of the 'Associated Power'.

American procrastination provoked widespread exasperation in London and Paris, because the Allied leaders realized that the balance of advantage had momentarily tilted, very sharply, in favour of the Central Powers. In November Lenin had seized power, and the Bolsheviks then sought to extricate Russia from the war on any terms, however humiliating: an armistice was accordingly signed on 15 December, leading to the Treaty of Brest-Litovsk, ratified on 3 March 1918, under which Poland, the Baltic provinces, parts of the Ukraine, Finland, and the Caucasus were transferred from Russia to Germany—territory three times the size of Germany, which contained one-quarter of the previous Russian population.[45]

The Germans were now in a position to plunder this enormous area as well as to seize the Allied stores at Archangel and Murmansk. The British government also feared that, in conjunction with the Turks, Berlin might succeed in expanding south-east into Asia Minor, creating a powerful empire in that region which would menace Britain's position in India—a threat taken with

---

[45] Keegan, *First World War*, 368. The rest of the Ukraine was allocated to Austria-Hungary.

great seriousness by imperialists within the Cabinet such as Milner and Curzon. Even Haig raised no serious objection when the government, in January, sent a military mission to the Transcaucusus under Major-General Dunsterville with instructions to organize local resistance to the Central Powers.

The corollary of this approach was that Britain would stay largely on the defensive on the Western Front in 1918. Indeed, the government had less confidence that the war would be over within the next twelve months than it had had at the start of 1916 and 1917.[46] The decisive battle, ministers now thought, would have to be deferred until 1919, perhaps until 1920.

Ministerial caution was reinforced by the country's acute manpower shortage. Between January and November of the previous year Britain had suffered nearly 790,000 casualties, leaving the army seriously under strength.[47] Haig warned that unless he was given 250,000 Category A men at once and 50,000 each month until June his infantry divisions would be 40 per cent below establishment. But, as the Ministry of National Service, under the firm direction of Auckland Geddes, had already pointed out, the army's requirements had to be balanced against a multitude of competing demands. In early December a new Committee on Manpower was set up, consisting of the Prime Minister, Curzon, Barnes, Smuts, and Carson, with Hankey as its secretary. It resolved to give priority to the navy and air force, followed by shipbuilding, airplane and tank manufacture, food production, and timber production and food storage: the army's needs came bottom of the list. Instead of the withdrawal of 600,000 Category A men from civilian life to serve in the BEF, which is what the army wanted, it was promised only 100,000.

Protests from GHQ and the Army Council were countered with the argument that resources could better be devoted to building up the country's arsenal in the form of aircraft, tanks, machine-guns, and Stokes' mortars. This strategy was particularly favoured by Winston Churchill, the Minister of Munitions, who remarked: 'Machines save life, machine-power is a substitute for man-power.'[48] To increase the relative firepower of each division, the government also forced Haig to reduce his divisions from twelve infantry battalions to nine and to disband two of his five cavalry divisions. Aided by their technological superiority, the BEF, so the War Cabinet ruled, could safely stay on the defensive until 1919.

Haig, however, retorted: 'The Campaign of 1919 may never come.'[49] In other words, there was the danger that, taking advantage of Russia's defeat, Germany would be able to deploy its eastern army in France and Flanders,

[46] Wilson, *Myriad Faces*, 545.   [47] French, *Lloyd George Coalition*, 180.
[48] Ibid. 182.   [49] Ibid. 182.

breaking the Allies there before the United States had fully mobilized. Indeed, some members of the General Staff now sounded a note of alarm about the vulnerability of Haig's position. However, these alarms were hardly consistent with Haig's earlier confidence—in December he had actually turned down Lloyd George's offer to relieve soldiers exhausted in the recent fighting. Haig's declining credibility in turn reduced the influence of Robertson, who was unable to prevent the dispatch of 190,000 Category B men to Italy between January and March.

In January, over Robertson's protests, the Supreme War Council established a 'general reserve', controlled by an executive committee under Foch. Haig defied the Prime Minister, saying that he would resign if ordered to release men to fill this force.[50] However, the general who ended up resigning was not, in fact, the Commander-in-Chief. For on 16 February Lloyd George offered Robertson the option of either going to Versailles as the British Military Representative or else staying on as CIGS but with much reduced powers. Robertson refused both offers and withdrew to the relatively unimportant office of head of Eastern Command—a droll posting for so staunch a 'westerner'. His place was taken by Henry Wilson, whose voluble wit was much more to the taste of the Prime Minister than Robertson's dour taciturnity, though it is arguable that he was less efficient than his predecessor and only slightly more willing to fall in with the War Cabinet's plans—'Wully Redivivus', Lloyd George was soon calling him. Haig, who had not raised a finger to save Robertson, survived, despite a half-hearted attempt in March to replace him with Plumer—whom Hankey privately dismissed as equally stupid! The Commander-in-Chief was about to be put to the supreme test.

7. 'BACKS TO THE WALL'

On 21 March Ludendorff unleashed his storm-troopers against Gough's 5th Army in a deliberate gamble which held out the promise of a quick victory. At the commencement of this assault ('Operation Michael') the Germans had 192 divisions in the west, as against the Allies' 178, but in the actual battle area their superiority was far more pronounced, since 28 of the 42 miles of line that Gough was holding had only recently been taken over from the French, and had never been properly strengthened. In any case, though the British had recently improved their attacking tactics, they had neglected to adopt the sophisticated methods of defence-in-depth perfected by the Germans.[51]

[50] Wilson, *Myriad Faces*, 548.
[51] Ibid. 557. This would in any case have been difficult for Gough, since behind him ran the heavily cut-up terrain of the old Somme battlefield, which the British had occupied after the German withdrawal a year earlier.

Moreover, the 5th Army was seriously below strength:[52] many battalions had recently been disbanded, to be replaced by new units consisting of young, inexperienced troops: others were still recovering from the ordeal of third Ypres.

The Germans' devastating opening barrage shook the resolve of Gough's overstretched forces, which also had to endure the release of tear gas over their trenches, followed by waves of the far more deadly phosgene (a blistering mustard gas). Seventy-six crack German divisions, scarcely visible in the heavy mist, then bore down on the weakened British lines. By evening the BEF had not only lost a large quantity of guns, but 7,000 infantrymen had been killed, 10,000 had been wounded, and a staggering 21,000 taken prisoner,[53] these casualties amounting to about one-third of Gough's original force. Some units fought back bravely, inflicting significant casualties upon the enemy,[54] but in other parts of the Front men surrendered en masse. In a single day the Germans captured over 98 square miles, to a depth of four-and-a-half miles, virtually the same extent of territory as had earlier fallen to the British during the entire Somme offensive. More to the point, Ludendorff's offensive succeeded in punching a 4-mile hole in Gough's line, separating him from the 3rd Army on his left and the French army on his right, and bringing German troops to within 12 miles of Amiens.[55] On 23 March the Kaiser gave German schoolchildren a 'victory' holiday.

Initially Haig had paid little attention to Gough's pleas for help, preferring to concentrate his reserves in Flanders and Arras, the most important strategic parts of his Front, where he expected the Germans shortly to deliver their main attack. This was a risky option, but at least the British army had not experienced a Caporetto, and though Gough himself was dismissed on 28 March, the 5th Army soon rallied, creating new lines of defensive entrenchments.

The emergency drove the Allies into co-operating more effectively with one another. Pétain, primarily concerned with the defence of Paris, belatedly sent Haig six divisions, with the promise of more to come. Foch, by contrast, was insistent that the Allies must fight in front of Amiens. His resolution impressed British and French ministers, who, at their meeting at Doullens on 26 March, charged him with the task of co-ordinating the operations of the British and French armies; at Beauvais, on 3 April, they went further, making the pugnacious Frenchman Generalissimo, though since his powers were ambiguous and he had no staff, this decision betokened a hardening political resolve rather

---

[52] By mid-March the 5th Army was holding a massive 42–mile front with only 11 divisions in the line and wholly inadequate reserves.
[53] Keegan, *First World War*, 429–30.
[54] The Germans lost over 10,000 dead, 29,000 wounded.
[55] By 5 April they had reached Amiens's outskirts.

than the start of a radically new way of conducting operations—to the relief of Haig, who still had no intention of jeopardizing the independence of the BEF. At home Lloyd George strengthened his grip by moving Derby to the Paris Embassy and replacing him, on 18 April, by the much more substantial figure of Milner.

Meanwhile the German offensive was beginning to lose momentum, largely because of Ludendorff's chief weakness: a propensity to pursue short-term tactical advantage at the expense of an overall strategic plan. By switching his attack on 28 March to Arras, which, along with Vimy Ridge, was successfully defended by the strong British 3rd Army, Ludendorff certainly blurred the focus of the operation. Heavy losses among German elite formations, and the ill discipline of some German troops, who gorged themselves on captured Allied stores, also slowed down the advance. Most important of all, the attackers were advancing too far ahead of their supply lines and reinforcements, while the British, however demoralized, were falling back on theirs. The Germans' last attempt to capture Amiens took place on 4–5 April; it failed, amid a spirited counter-attack from Anzac troops.

On 9 April Ludendorff replaced 'Operation Michael' with 'Operation George', an attack in Flanders directed against Horne's 1st Army and Plumer's 2nd Army. Once again the initial assault was successful: the Portuguese troops in that theatre ran away and the British were driven back over the Messines Ridge. Characteristically Haig, who had responded calmly to Gough's earlier travails, reacted with alarm to this threat to the Channel ports. On 11 April he issued his famous 'Backs to the Wall' order. ('Where's the —— wall?', asked the men.)[56] Foch at first refused to send up any reserves, thinking that the British problems were containable, but, helped by the Belgian army, the BEF narrowly held out. Indeed, by deliberately abandoning Passchendaele to shorten his line, Plumer cleverly trapped the Germans in a dangerous salient. By 25 April 'Operation George' was aborted, with heavy German casualties.

Between late May and the middle of July Ludendorff changed his point of attack yet again, this time threatening Paris by throwing troops against the French army. Five British divisions, brought south to recuperate at Chemin des Dames, a supposedly quiet section of the line, got caught up in the ferocious fighting, during which the Germans briefly reached Chateau-Thierry, less than 40 miles from the French capital. But the Americans, now arriving in France at the rate of 250,000 a month, helped staunch the advance, most notably on 18 July, during the second battle of the Marne, when General Mangin led a telling Allied counter-attack.

[56] J. C. Dunn, *The War the Infantry Knew 1914–1919* (London, 1938; 1994 edn.), 468.

On that same day Ludendorff cancelled his projected new offensive in Flanders. The gamble of the Spring Offensive had failed. By 7 August the retreating German armies had returned approximately to the point from which they had started, depleted by ruinously high casualties (some quarter-of-a-million all told), including many of their most highly trained troops, who were quite irreplaceable. The odds had swung back decisively to a likely Allied victory.

8. LLOYD GEORGE'S TRIUMPH

Although Haig had been momentarily taken aback by 'Operation Michael', he was about to surprise his detractors by showing not only resolution but skills in generalship in which he had earlier seemed singularly deficient. Lloyd George, too, reacted calmly and courageously in adversity—unlike his new CIGS, whose volatile temperament inclined him to panic.

In fact, the Prime Minister had had a difficult time since the start of the year. The Bolsheviks' mischievous release of the 'Secret Treaties' signed between the Allies had unsettled even moderate Labour and Radical opinion by apparently confirming the UDC's view that the war was being fought for selfish and imperialistic ends. (In fact, most of these treaties were primarily intended to prevent a future quarrel between the Allies once victory had been secured, but this was a subtle point that few could grasp.) The British government badly needed to restore confidence in the war effort through a public formulation of a credible set of war aims.

This provides the background to Lloyd George's important address (largely drafted by Cecil and Smuts), delivered, significantly, to a trade-union conference on 5 January, which declared Britain's objectives as being: the restoration of Alsace-Lorraine, self-government for the peoples of the Habsburg Empire, the 'unification' of Italy and Romania, the placing of Germany's former colonies under governments acceptable to their inhabitants, reparation for the victims of war crimes, and the establishment of an international organization to secure a peaceful post-war world.[57] Lloyd George's manifesto closely resembled the document recently passed by an Inter-Allied Conference, which was in turn based upon the UDC's recent 'Four Points'; it also overlapped, in many places, with President Wilson's idealistic 'Fourteen Points', promulgated three days later.[58] Those wishing to be so convinced could read into Lloyd

---

[57] D. Stevenson, *The First World War and International Politics* (Oxford, 1988), 191–3. Lloyd George declared independence for Poland to be 'desirable', but claimed that the break-up of the Habsburg Empire was 'no part of our war aims'.

[58] But there were some important differences, notably about the freedom of the seas, which Wilson proclaimed but which Britain was determined to resist.

George's words proof that the British government was animated by lofty ideals, from which humanity as a whole would benefit.

Simultaneously Lloyd George moved to cover his right flank against his critics in the 'patriotic' press. In early February he put Lord Beaverbrook, the proprietor of the *Daily Express*, in charge of the Ministry of Information, which was soon chock-a-block with seconded newspapermen. But the dangerous Northcliffe was the fish the Prime Minister really wanted to land. The 'Napoleon of Fleet Street', however, had already publicly turned down an offer of the Air Board the previous November—a mischievous act which precipitated the resignation of its current incumbent Lord Cowdray, who was unaware that his post was being hawked around in this way.[59] Instead, Northcliffe's brother, Lord Rothermere, was appointed Air Secretary on 26 November, a post he held until 26 April of the following year. Then, in February, Northcliffe finally consented to serve the government, not indeed as a minister (this would have compromised the independence of his newspapers), but as the Director of Propaganda in Enemy Countries.

Unfortunately, from Lloyd George's point of view, most Conservative backbenchers took a dim view of the press lords, and their unhappiness burst into the open on 19 February when Austen Chamberlain, in a stinging intervention in the Commons, spoke of 'an atmosphere of suspicion and distrust' caused by the inclusion of so many pressmen in government. On the same day the Unionist War Committee passed a resolution calling for a ban on newspaper proprietors holding public office so long as they retained control of their journals. Next month Lloyd George personally appeared before the Unionist War Committee and impishly suggested that 'Beaverbrook had been selected Director of Propaganda because he was an unscrupulous ruffian', and that Northcliffe was 'ideal for sowing, in enemy countries, distrust of the Government and lack of confidence in the General Staff'![60] Amid laughter, the 'rebellion' died away. However, on 18 April Lloyd George shrewdly brought Austen Chamberlain back in from the cold, putting him straight into the War Cabinet—on the same day on which, backed by Bonar Law and Milner, the Prime Minister at last got rid of Derby. Of his heavyweight Conservative critics, only Carson was still at large.

By this time Lloyd George was the beneficiary of an upsurge of patriotism stimulated by the German Spring Offensive, which led to a rallying behind the government at a time of national peril. On the industrial front, trade disputes died down (only 15,000 days were lost in strikes in April), productivity soared,

---

[59] Cowdray became one of Lloyd George's bitterest enemies, and subsequently pursued a vendetta against him through J. A. Spender's *Westminster Gazette*, in which he had a large financial stake.
[60] G. R. Searle, *Corruption in British Politics, 1895–1930* (Oxford, 1987), 321–2.

and in some heavily unionized areas such as the South Wales coalfields men rushed to enlist. As the Ministry of Munitions worked flat out to replace lost matériel, workers everywhere forewent their Easter holidays: by the end of March Churchill could tell the War Cabinet that nearly 2,000 new guns would be supplied by 6 April.[61]

Finding the men to reinforce Haig's armies was more difficult, but not as contentious as might have been expected. Two divisions from Palestine and one from Italy were promptly switched to the Western Front, while the government rushed a new Military Service Act through Parliament, reducing the minimum age limit to 17½, raising the maximum limit to 50 (55 in the case of doctors), and drastically curtailing rights to exemption. As a concession to the right wing of the Conservative Party and to the Ulster loyalists, the War Cabinet also included in the measure powers, by orders-in-council, to extend compulsion to Ireland.

The latter provision threw Ireland into uproar. Nationalists of all stripes united in passionate protest: on 18 April the Mayor of Dublin summoned a meeting at the Mansion House, which was attended by all the Irish Nationalist Leaders (including the Sinn Feiners) plus a representative of Irish Labour. A declaration was drafted, presented at the church doors of every parish the following Sunday, pledging signatories to 'resist conscription by the most effective means at our disposal', and the Irish TUC called a one-day strike on 23 April, observed almost everywhere except Belfast. In the face of these protests the government made no attempt to impose conscription on Ireland, because this would have tied down more British soldiers than the measure could possibly have raised—even if accompanied, as it was, by the sweetener of the promise of immediate Home Rule. To cover its own confusion, the government claimed to have discovered a 'German plot' implicating Sinn Fein, most of whose leaders (minus Collins and Brugha) were summarily arrested and interned (17 May). This, in turn, merely enhanced Sinn Fein's popularity and accelerated the decline of the Irish Nationalist Party, which had enjoyed a mild recovery at the start of the year, beating off the Sinn Fein challenge in two by-elections, one of them caused by John Redmond's death in March.[62] But henceforward Britain's hold on Ireland became very tenuous.

On mainland Britain trouble might have been expected from militant trade unionists such as the engineers. The Labour Movement had balked at the somewhat less draconian measure passed in early February, which facilitated 'bulk release' by cancelling many occupational grounds for exemption[63]—a

---

[61] Wilson, *Myriad Faces*, 576.

[62] In another by-election, at Tullamore, a Sinn Fein candidate was returned unopposed. Redmond was replaced as party leader by John Dillon.

[63] All male munitions workers under 25 were henceforward liable for conscription.

measure which trade-union resistance soon turned into almost a dead letter. Yet the Military Service (no. 2) Act of April was given a relatively easy ride. For, despite much evidence of war-weariness, the public mood remained broadly favourable to a continuation of the fighting. Practical grievances abounded, but the government succeeded in defusing many of them—for example, by extending rationing to a variety of commodities, including most foodstuffs.

But though the government was in some ways strengthened by the German Spring Offensive, Lloyd George himself was vulnerable to one particularly damaging accusation: that he had put the BEF at risk by deliberately starving it of men in the course of his vendetta against GHQ. The military correspondent A'Court Repington made precisely this allegation in the *Morning Post* on 8 April, prompting the Prime Minister to declare in the Commons the following day that the British army had been stronger in January 1918 than it had been the previous January, a reassurance repeated shortly afterwards, with a flourish of statistics, by Ian Macpherson, Under-Secretary at the War Office. But these figures were in turn queried by Major-General Maurice, the recently retired Director of Military Operations, who, in defiance of military discipline, sent a letter to the press on 7 May in which he effectively accused the government of wilfully misleading the House. Asquith, who had consistently deprecated political 'interference' in the running of the war, pressed for an inquiry by a Select Committee.

In the so-called Maurice Debate, held on 8 May, the Prime Minister routed his parliamentary enemies in a brilliant but unscrupulous speech, in which he claimed—correctly—that his original statistics had actually been provided by Maurice's own department; what Lloyd George did *not* say was that the War Office had later sent him another set of figures, correcting the earlier errors,[64] in a document which he had almost certainly seen.

The complex rights and wrongs of the 'Maurice Affair' continue to fascinate historians, but for the MPs who attended the debate of 8 May the choice was very simple. Lloyd George was offering them a judicial inquiry into the substance of Maurice's allegations, but was treating Asquith's motion in support of a Select Committee as one of 'no confidence' in the government. Asquith, perhaps out of a misplaced sense of parliamentary propriety, had refused to withdraw this motion. MPs would thus have to decide whether they really wanted a change of regime or not. In the event, the government came through this crucial challenge to its existence, by 293 votes to 106.

These voting statistics, however, reveal two rather different stories. The first is the unwillingness of Conservative MPs to oppose the government—only one

---

[64] e.g. they incorrectly included 86,000 troops that had been sent to the Italian Front.

actually did so. Carson had hoped otherwise, but after attending a meeting of
the Unionist War Committee earlier in the day, he ruefully accepted that its
members were not prepared to defy a Prime Minister they considerably
mistrusted if this risked returning the discredited 'Squiff' to 10 Downing
Street. So long as Lloyd George retained the support of Bonar Law, he had
no reason to fear further disaffection on the Conservative benches.

The second story was one of Liberal division. Asquith had drawn into the
lobby with him nine Labour MPs and no fewer than ninety-eight Liberals
(including tellers)—as against the seventy-one Liberal MPs, many of them
office-holders, who rallied behind Lloyd George. One did not have to possess
prophetic powers to see in this outcome the germs of a later Liberal schism. In
fact, a group of Liberal backbench snipers had been challenging the government for quite some time—for example, over the imposition of Indian tariffs
on imported cotton, and more recently, over Irish conscription.[65] But this was
the first time that Asquith had joined them—puzzlingly enough, since,
whereas on previous occasions the dissidents could claim to be standing up
for sound Liberal principles, no such claim could be made for the rebellion of 8
May. 'What is Genl. Maurice to us, or are we to Genl. Maurice?', asked one
Liberal.[66] Others expressed disquiet over the Liberal Leader's apparent willingness to support an act of military insubordination.

If Asquith's limp parliamentary performance during the Maurice Debate
hardly restored MPs' confidence in his leadership qualities, neither did it boost
his popularity in the country at large. Indeed, soon afterwards Asquith, his wife
Margot, and his closest friends had to endure the wildest of libels in the famous
Pemberton Billing trial, which opened towards the end of the month. Billing
and his witnesses created outrage in some quarters, amusement in others, by
alleging that Asquith, his wife, and many of their personal friends featured
among the names of 40,000 sexual 'perverts' contained within a German 'Black
Book' that was being used to blackmail them into sabotaging the British war
effort. As A. J. P. Taylor notes, it is significant, however, that Lloyd George
was never exposed to the public pillorying visited upon so many members of
the 'establishment'—indeed, one witness explicitly said that the Prime Minister was 'doing his best' to stop patronage abuses, even though he had 'a hard
job'.[67] It is also significant that, in defiance of every principle of justice, the jury
should have acquitted Billing of libel—to the noisy approval of the jingo mob.

Meanwhile Lloyd George, who had trembled for his future at the start of the
Maurice Debate, now had the comfort of knowing that he enjoyed secure

[65] E. David, 'The Liberal Party Divided, 1916–1918', *Historical Journal*, 13 (1970), 515–18.
[66] R. Douglas, *History of the Liberal Party, 1895–1970* (London, 1971), 115.
[67] Searle, *Corruption*, 260–4.

parliamentary backing—something which had never previously been tested. It also enabled his Patronage Secretary, Freddie Guest, to distinguish, more clearly than before, between Liberal friend and foe (even if some eighty-five Liberal MPs had prudently abstained or absented themselves from the Maurice Division). This was important to Lloyd George, since a new electoral reform measure, the Representation of the People Bill, had finally reached the statute book, making it possible to dissolve Parliament later in the year.

Yet the preparations for a 1918 general election, which gathered momentum from the summer onwards, still rested on the premise that it would be a wartime election, held to allow the British people to decide who was best equipped to take the country to victory. And victory, the War Cabinet still thought, would not happen before the start of the New Year.

9. FORWARD TO VICTORY

Haig thought differently. On 8 August (later dubbed by Ludendorff 'the black day of the German army'), General Rawlinson led a mass Anglo-French attack, spearheaded by several hundred tanks, including the latest model, the 'whippet'.[68] On this day alone, though the British suffered 9,000 casualties, 15,000 German soldiers were taken prisoner. From 21 August to 25 September the British armies attacked all along the Somme. Victory followed victory. On 29 August the New Zealand component of Byng's 3rd Army entered Bapaume, a prize which had eluded Haig during the Somme Offensive, and Monash's Australians (of the 4th Army) took Peronne on 2 September, another astounding feat. To the south, on 12 September the Americans won a striking victory at the St Mihiel salient, south of Verdun, taking 15,000 prisoners.

Responding to Foch's cry, 'Everyone to battle' (26 September), the British, French, Belgian, and American troops pushed home their advantage against a weakening enemy, whose soldiers had started to surrender in droves. Ludendorff attempted to consolidate for the winter behind the Hindenburg Line, but this, too, immediately came under attack, with Haig for the first time employing mustard gas. On 29 September the North Midlanders crossed the Canal du Nord, a seemingly impregnable part of this defence system, using collapsible boats and life-belts. In front of the Allies there now lay open country. A day earlier Ludendorff had reached the conclusion that an armistice must urgently be sought.

Still the Allied offensive rolled on. On 17 October the 5th Army liberated Lille. Amid mounting domestic chaos, a new German government, with Prince

---

[68] Precise estimates differ: Keegan, *First World War*, 440; Wilson, *Myriad Faces*, 430; Bourne, *Great War*, 534.

Max of Baden as Chancellor, dismissed Ludendorff from his command (26 October). On 9 November the Kaiser abdicated, and two days later, at the very moment when the British were entering Mons without encountering any serious resistance, Berlin appealed to President Wilson for a peace based on his Fourteen Points. An armistice was duly signed on 11 November.

Meanwhile Germany's allies were faring no better. The Italians managed to avenge Caporetto by crushing the Austrian army at Vittorio Veneto on 23–4 October—helped by small contingents of British troops who had been there since late 1917. The war even became mobile in Macedonia: on 15 September Franchet d'Esperey broke out of Salonika and led a dramatic cavalry drive towards Skopje, forcing the Bulgarians to surrender a fortnight later—on terms which the French did not deem it necessary to discuss with their British (still less their American) allies.

In the Middle East, by contrast, it was the British who largely held the whip-hand. Allenby's advance northwards through Palestine, aided by friendly Arabs, had brought him by late September to Megiddo, where he decisively defeated the Turkish army; on 30 October the Turks signed an armistice at Mudros. Soon afterwards British forces in Mesopotamia reached Mosul, shortly before receiving the Turkish surrender on 21 November.

How was it that the fortunes of war had turned so suddenly and so dramatically? The Royal Navy could claim some credit for the Allied victory, in that its blockade had gradually throttled the German economy, contributing to the deprivation which eventually destroyed civilian morale. True, the Royal Navy never succeeded in knocking out the U-boat bases—the nearest it got to doing this was Roger Keyes's Zeebrugge Raid of 23 April 1918, which was a gallant failure. On the other hand, the U-boat campaign had clearly failed to achieve its ojectives, and this was confirmed by Germany's abortive last-ditch attempt to disrupt Allied convoys in May. His other options blocked off, Admiral Scheer planned to break the Allied stranglehold by a do-or-die assault on the Grand Fleet on 30 October, only to be defied by German sailors who mutinied. The Royal Navy had totally triumphed, albeit in circumstances which exuded an atmosphere of anticlimax.[69] The German crewmen, bottled up in Kiel Harbour, would have been well aware of the suffering and discontents of the civilian population. The German military were more insulated from these developments, but they, too, cannot have been entirely unaware of the crumbling of morale on the home front.

The mass troop surrenders of late 1918 suggest that the German army was also disheartened by the seemingly limitless supply of fresh American troops

[69] P. Liddle, 'Britons on the Home Front', in H. Cecil and P. Liddle (eds.), *At The Eleventh Hour: Reflections, Hopes and Anxieties at the Closing of the Great War, 1918* (Barnsley, 1998), 61–2.

and by the imbalance of resources between the two military blocs. Even at the commencement of Ludendorff's Spring Offensive, the Germans were outgunned by the BEF alone in nearly all areas of munitions, since they possessed only a handful of tanks (10 compared to 800) and were also inferior in aircraft (3,670 to 4,500) and in guns (14,000 to 18,500).[70] As the American economy was gradually put onto a war footing, these disparities could only widen.

We have seen that Churchill viewed the conflict as an 'engineer's war', in which Allied technology and ingenuity in weapons design would prove to be the decisive factor. Churchill was correct in his perception that the nature of the Great War had changed almost beyond recognition since August 1914. Whereas, in those early months, the elite troops of the BEF had gone into battle relying on their skills in musketry and looking vaguely like gamekeepers (some officers had led their men forward by flashing their swords!), by 1918 Haig was presiding over the most highly mechanized army the world had ever seen, an army reliant on 'a vast force of specialists and technicians closer in spirit to the world of mass production'.[71] Not without reason has the Great War been called the 'first industrial war'. Haig may have served his military apprenticeship as a cavalry officer devoted to the lance, but by September 1918 there were only three cavalry divisions serving on the Western Front (comprising about 1 per cent of BEF, compared with 7.72 per cent in August 1914), where they were quite overshadowed by the Tank Corps and by an independent air force, both of them recent innovations which the Commander-in-Chief, to his credit, had consistently backed.[72] As for the artillery, in 1918 it comprised twice the number of men enlisted in the entire BEF in 1914.

Yet technological inventiveness, by itself, could not guarantee a speedy victory—as can be seen from the fact that gas by 1918 was being used to harass the enemy, but was no longer considered a war-winning device. Consider, for example, the case of the tank, which the Germans made very little effort to develop. Here the Allies had a massive superiority, which they put to good use in August at Amiens. But subsequently they were only once able (on 29 September) to place 100 or more tanks in the field, so prone were these machines to break down and so high was the mortality among their specialized crews (one-third of all officers and men of the Tank Corps became casualties during the last ninety-six days of the war). Although tank performance

---

[70] Keegan, *First World War*, 422. By 1918 Britain had a 30% superiority in guns, 20% in planes. The Germans were particularly deficient in airpower, motorized transport, and tanks (though they pioneered chlorine gas, flame-throwers, trench mortars, and steel helmets) (Ferguson, *Pity of War*, 260, 290).

[71] J. Bourne, 'The British Working Man in Arms', in Cecil and Liddle (eds.), *Facing Armageddon*, 341.

[72] The cavalry had grown by 80%, the infantry by 469%, the artillery by 520%, the engineers by 1,429%, and the army service corps by 2,212%.

improved substantially in late 1918, even the faster 'whippets', with a maximum speed of 8.3 m.p.h., were still not a war-winning weapon.

Arguably a greater contribution to the Allied victory was achieved through their dominance of the skies. In 1918 the 5th Army alone had 180 aircraft acting in its support. Technology in this area was changing even more rapidly than in the case of the tank. As a consequence, the advantage repeatedly swung from one side to the other. But by 1918 Britain and France had the edge, allowing them to reconnoitre the battlefield with impunity, aided by balloons, with telephone wire fixed to a tethering cable. Aircraft could also provide occasional tactical support for the infantry and launch raids on enemy supply lines, communication centres, and reserves.[73] Moreover, at the end of 1918 Trenchard, the 'father' of the RAF, was well advanced in his plans to launch bombing raids deep into Germany. However, the war ended before the effectiveness of this strategy could be tested. So in this area, too, technological superiority was not decisive.[74]

If the ultimate denouement on the Western Front occurred more quickly than most informed observers had predicted, this was mainly because the BEF, still the largest of the Allied armies fighting in France and Flanders, had emerged in 1918 as an infinitely more effective military body than it had been at third Ypres and Cambrai. For this improvement Foch bore only a small responsibility, since the Generalissimo's role was more that of a cheerleader than that of overall commander. Indeed, Haig continued to behave as though he enjoyed virtual autonomy, telling Foch that he was 'responsible to [his] Government and fellow citizens for the handling of the British forces',[75] and probably deferring to him less than he had once done to Joffre. This did not particularly displease Lloyd George who, despite his fondness for French generals, soon came to see that the offensive-minded Foch was as careless of human lives as any of his own commanders had ever been.

More important to the Allied victory was a change in tactics, many of them pioneered by the British army. Paradoxically, this change owed something to a realization that the Great War was *not* simply an engineer's war. In 1916 and 1917 primacy had been accorded to the artillery, who were supposed to blast the enemy to smithereens, allowing the infantry to walk unopposed into their positions. By 1918 high-calibre ordnance had greatly increased the artillery's destructive power, and the creeping barrage had been much refined, notably by the Australian commander General John Monash, a civilian engineer before

[73] Bourne, *Great War*, 170.

[74] On the war in the air, see J. H. Morrow, Jnr., *The Great War in the Air: Military Aviation from 1904 to 1921* (Shrewsbury, 1993); M. Paris, *Winged Warfare: The Literature and Theory of Aerial Warfare in Britain, 1859–1917* (Manchester, 1992).

[75] Wilson, *Myriad Faces*, 594.

the war. Enormous strides had also been made in counter-battery fire, which, utilizing flash-spotting, sound-ranging, and aerial observation, largely dispensed with registration, so contributing an element of surprise.

But the new emphasis was on a sophisticated co-ordination, through wireless telegraphy (a two-way radio had become available during 1918), of the various military branches—artillery, infantry, machine-guns, tanks, gas, and aeroplanes—all melded into a single 'weapons system'.[76] Moreover, to take part in this new, more mobile kind of fighting, the infantry were now much better trained, thanks in large measure to the input of the recently appointed Inspector-General of Training, Sir Ivor Maxse.[77] This was essential since, rather than simply relying on artillery support, the infantryman now went into battle armed with Lewis guns, grenades, rifle-grenades, and mortars.

The implementation of the tactics of 'fire and manoeuvre' in turn entailed a departure from the massive, centralized battle-plans, masterminded from GHQ, that had earlier characterized Haig's command. Now individual army corps commanders had to show greater initiative and flexibility. More important, the offensives of 1918 were, for the first time, genuinely attritional in the sense that they aimed, not at capturing pre-set objectives, but at breaking the German army. Hence the fighting took place across a very wide front, with the centre of attack repeatedly switching from one area to another, before resistance solidified and the enemy could deploy his reserves and counter-attack. These were the tactics which, under Haig's increasingly confident command, eventually wore down the resistance of Germany's once highly formidable army and achieved victory.

On 11 November, at 10.55 a.m., Lloyd George made a short statement outside 10 Downing Street: 'At eleven o'clock this war will be over. We have won a great victory and we are entitled to do a bit of shouting.' Those present responded by singing 'God Save The King', and, against a background cacophony of church bells ringing and cannons firing, jubilant crowds spilled onto the streets and gathered around Buckingham Palace. Street parties were held up and down the land. However, for many the dominant emotion was relief, and the happiness of others was undercut by the agony of bereavement. In Nationalist Ireland reactions were predictably mixed.[78]

Yet, at the heart of government, the mood was one of relief but not of euphoria or triumphalism. Ministers, who had only recently been tiring their brains over how best to conduct the campaign of 1919, still scarcely grasped the

---

[76] Ibid. 586.

[77] P. Griffith, 'The Extent of Tactical Reform in the British Army' in P. Griffith (ed.), *British Fighting Methods* (London, 1986), 1–22.

[78] For the variety of responses, see P. Liddle, 'Britons on the Home Front', in Cecil and Liddle (eds.), *Eleventh Hour*, ch. 5, esp. p. 81.

magnitude of Germany's defeat. Not until 2 November were ministers informed, through Room 40 OB, of the mutinies that had immobilized the High Fleet, and not until 8 November did they learn that soviets had been established in many of the larger German cities. Similarly, the General Staff worried, almost to the last moment, that the German army would decline the humiliating armistice terms that were on offer. In fact there seems, in retrospect, a compelling case for the Entente to have invaded Germany and imposed even harsher terms[79]—a denouement that would at least have killed off at source the later myth of a 'stab in the back'.

However, this would have been a risky stratagem, since the retreating German army might well have recovered its stomach for a fight once Allied soldiers had set foot on German soil. As it was, both War Cabinet and the military authorities were only too happy to settle, once they learnt that Berlin had accepted the armistice conditions. For, in truth, by November 1918 the British were almost at the end of their tether.

The fact is that the battles of late 1918 had resulted, for the British, in a daily loss of men (3,645) higher than had been earlier sustained on the Somme or at third Ypres.[80] Indeed, it has been argued that between August and October 'the Germans achieved a killing surplus over the British rivalled only by the period of the Battle of the Somme'.[81]

It had not been easy for the British to replace these losses. Further drives in midsummer to 'comb out' men from manufacturing industry had led to a succession of industrial disputes (the patriotic fervour of the spring now forgotten). A strike of woodworkers took place in the aircraft industry in late June. Even more serious was the unrest in the Midland engineering shops, where attempts to reimpose the hated leaving certificate provoked a 'down tools'—in the face of which the government effectively retreated. By late 1918 the War Cabinet was scraping the bottom of the barrel in its search for army drafts. As one historian has noted, from the British point of view the war ended 'not a day too soon'.[82]

Haig himself was well aware of these manpower problems. After all, about one-third of the British troops rushed out to reinforce him in the wake of the German Spring Offensive had been raw, inexperienced lads, under 19 years of age. This explains why, in the course of 1918, he so frequently relied for the most daring of his assaults on Canadian and Anzac units. Meanwhile, over the Western Front as a whole, the fresh 'doughboys' from across the Atlantic,

[79] Some soldiers, surprised by the sudden cessation of fighting, wanted to press on into Germany and give the Germans a taste of their own medicine (ibid. 55–6).
[80] John Terraine, cited in Bourne, *Great War*, 173.
[81] Ferguson, *Pity of War*, 300.
[82] Bourne, *Great War*, 187. On civilian disaffection, see Ch. 20.

whom Pershing grouped in August into the 1st American Army, were playing an ever-more important role.[83]

Britain's game-plan had once been to conserve its military forces, so that at the peace conference it could dictate terms not only to the defeated enemy but also to its exhausted allies, but this plan had clearly gone awry. Instead, Britain's military establishment had peaked in 1917, shortly before the Arras Offensive, when Haig was commanding sixty-two divisions containing one-and-a-half million men; by the end of the war this total had dropped to fifty-nine (numerically smaller) divisions, and if the war had gone on into 1919 the number would have fallen still further, to between thirty-nine and forty-four divisions, as Henry Wilson had warned Haig in July. In relative terms, too, the British army was declining by the month, as the American arrivals steadily altered the balance of power within the Entente.[84]

In July 1917 President Wilson had told his emissary Colonel House (in the strictest confidence, of course): 'England and France have not the same view with regard to peace that we have by any means. When the war is over we can force them to our way of thinking because by that time they will, among other things, be financially in our hands.'[85] Things had very much come to pass as Wilson had predicted. By late 1918 the British relied almost totally on American credit to stay in the war, having amassed total debts to the United States of about £1,000 million. Nor was this all. Much of Britain's overseas investment portfolio had been liquidated to pay for the war, the National Debt had risen over elevenfold, valuable overseas markets had been lost (some permanently, it later transpired), while tax levels were, by pre-war standards, astoundingly high: the standard rate of income-tax, for example, stood at 6 shillings in the pound, an eightfold increase. All of these burdens were inexorably piling up, week by week—another reason why the government was so eager to clinch the 11 November armistice deal.

In some respects, it is true, Britain emerged the stronger from its four-year ordeal. The British Empire had expanded to its greatest ever extent, largely as a result of the collapse of the Ottoman Empire, which allowed London to establish effective control over both Palestine and Mesopotamia (Iraq).[86] The conflicting promises that had been given to France, to the Hashemite

[83] But there were many effective units drawn from the UK, such as the 12th Division (P. Simkins, 'Co-Stars or Supporting Staff: British Divisions in "The Hundred Days" ', in Griffith (ed.), *British Fighting Methods*, 50–69).

[84] French, *Lloyd George Coalition*, 272. The BEF numbered 1,800,705 men in 1917, only 1,763,980 in 1918; it held 123 miles of line in February 1918, but only 88 in May (K. Simpson, 'The British Soldier on the Western Front', in P. Liddle (ed.), *Home Fires and Foreign Fields* (London, 1985), 145).

[85] French, *Lloyd George Coalition*, 64–5.

[86] Conquered German colonies in Africa and the Pacific were later effectively annexed, under a League of Nations trusteeship, by the white Dominions in their vicinity with the exception of German East Africa (Tanganyika), which passed under UK control.

Kingdom, and to the Zionists (promised Palestine as a 'national home', in the Balfour Declaration of November 1917), would shortly turn the Middle East into a source of trouble as well as a strategic and economic asset. But all of these difficulties lay in the future.

On the other hand, even before the formal surrender of the Central Powers, the War Cabinet was in the grip of a new nightmare. 'Our real danger now is not the Bosches but Bolshevism', was how the CIGS summed up the ministerial discussion of 10 November.[87] This was a relatively new perception. As recently as 22 July the Prime Minister had told the War Cabinet that it was 'none of Britain's business what sort of government the Russians set up, a republic, a Bolshevik state or a monarchy'. Yet before the end of the year the Allies were, in effect, involved in a confused war of intervention against Lenin's regime—although, in Britain's case, this had come about almost by accident.[88]

When Haig, in the autumn, had advised against a continuation into 1919 of the fight against Germany, he had based his case on the prediction that such a policy would leave that country 'at the mercy of Revolutionaries', adding that there was the additional risk of disorder later spreading to France and England.[89] The War Cabinet shared these fears, which had recently been fuelled by a series of industrial disputes, some of which had clear political undertones or implications—not least the police strike which was called in London in late August, before it was harshly broken by the authorities. Even Basil Thomson, the Assistant Commissioner of the Metropolitan Police, in his fortnightly reports to the Cabinet could find no real evidence of a slackening of support for the war in working-class communities, but fears as to the spread of Bolshevik-style 'revolutionary defeatism' were not so easily allayed.

Nor were ministers, and their allies on the right, the only ones expressing anxiety about the possibility of revolutionary subversion. Arthur Henderson explicitly declared that the new-style Labour Party, with its commitment to socialism via Clause 4, was intended to function not only as the enemy of 'Reaction', but also as an instrument for the democratic reform of society— Britain's last chance of demonstrating that she had no need for revolution on Lenin's model.

---

[87] French, *Lloyd George Coalition*, 277–8.

[88] In the summer of 1918 the Allies had moved to extricate Czech prisoners of war, trapped on the Trans-Siberian Railway, so that they could serve on the Western Front. They then got drawn into backing the White Russians, who were also supporting the Czechs. By the end of the year Britain found herself supporting 'counter-revolutionary' forces in southern Russia. She also had her own force in North Russia, under General Ironside, organizer of the Slavo-British Legion—legacy of a mission of marines, who had landed in Murmansk on 4 March to prevent this naval base, and its stores, falling into the hands of the Germans via their Finnish allies.

[89] French, *Lloyd George Coalition*, 277.

Henderson did at least view the future with confidence, thinking that Labour was exceptionally well placed to take advantage of the extension of the franchise brought about by the recent Representation of the People Act. Many Conservatives were not so sure that they could, in the long run, successfully reach out to the new voters. As for Lloyd George, on the very eve of the election he privately thought that things would come out 'all right': 'I shall be very surprised if we are beaten', he told his wife, adding that he would be 'content' if the government had a majority of over 120.[90] In the event, the 'Coupon Election' confirmed the Prime Minister in office by a landslide, with 415 more MPs than Labour, the largest of the Opposition groups.[91]

Yet the usually ebullient Welshman, addressing a public meeting at Manchester on 12 September, foresaw 'atmospheric disturbances in the social and economic world' against which his own country could not entirely be insulated. Another cause for anxiety was his apprehension that Britain at the time of the Armistice differed profoundly from the Britain that had so blithely embarked on hostilities. In what ways had four years of war reshaped the identities of the English people?

---

[90] Letter of 13 Dec., in K. O. Morgan (ed.), *Lloyd George Family Letters 1885–1936* (Cardiff, 1973), 188–9.

[91] Bar Sinn Fein, which declined on principle to take up its seats.

CHAPTER 19

The Patriotic Experience

I. THE EXPERIENCE OF WAR

Throughout the British Empire as a whole more than 900,000 military personnel were killed, died of their wounds, or went missing during the Great War; 723,000 of these came from the British Isles (1.5 per cent of the pre-war population). These figures do not include those who died after the Armistice from war-induced wounds or disease, nor those who died in the Spanish 'flu epidemic that wreaked such havoc between 1918 and 1920, killing more people around the world than died in the war itself.

Despite these horrendous fatalities, the 1921 census revealed a 2.4 per cent *increase* in population since 1914: the United Kingdom's inhabitants now numbered 47,168,000, as against 46,048,000 before war broke out. How could this possibly be? In large part it was because the war stopped emigration—indeed, between 1914 and 1918 there was a net inflow of population. This particularly affected Ireland, whose population for the first time since the Famine ceased its secular decline and actually registered a 0.5 per cent increase. The population of England and Wales also rose—from 36,967,000 in 1914 to 37,932,000 in 1921, up by 2.6 per cent.[1]

Natural increase would almost certainly have brought about even sharper rises, had not the birth-rate declined substantially during the war: comparing 1910–14 with 1915–19, it fell by 25 per cent in England and Wales, by 16.2 per cent in Scotland, and by 10.9 per cent in Ireland.[2] One historian calculates that this resulted in a wartime 'deficit' of 600,000 births in England and Wales alone.[3] These 'lost lives' were partly compensated for by the 'baby boomlet' of 1920, when the birth-rate rose to 25.5 per thousand, just above its pre-war rate (24.1 in 1913), before resuming its long-term downward path. The sum result of all of these contradictory social movements was that, although war-related

---

[1] In Scotland a 2.8% increase.
[2] Comparing the 1910–14 years with 1915–19.
[3] J. M. Winter, *The Great War and the British People* (London, 1985), 253.

deaths slowed down England's population growth, they did not bring about a population decline.

Moreover, international comparisons suggest that, demographically, Britain escaped relatively lightly from the horrors which the Great War inflicted. Of British males in the age range of 15–49, some 6.3 per cent were killed; in England and Wales the percentage would have been slightly higher.[4] But these figures, however appalling, do not approximate to those of Serbia, which had almost a quarter (22.7 per cent) of its males of combatant age wiped out. Most other Allied countries, too, sustained a heavier death-toll: France and Romania lost proportionately over twice as many of their young men (13.3 per cent and 13.2 per cent, respectively), and even Italy fared worse. So did all the Central Powers, Germany's proportional losses (12.5 per cent) being almost double Britain's.[5]

But statistical exercises of this kind would have offered scant consolation to the 160,000 British wives who found themselves prematurely widowed and to the more than 300,000 children who were left fatherless.[6] The agony of loss was sharpened by the circumstance that some 5 per cent of those presumed dead never had their bodies recovered. About 20,000 British servicemen died in German prisoner-of-war camps from ill-treatment, starvation, and disease (particularly dysentery); those captured by the Turks suffered, if possible, an even worse fate. Thousands more died from injuries so horrific that identification was impossible. These 'disappearances' encouraged many of the bereaved to go on hoping, against all the odds, that their loved ones would eventually reappear.

Some turned in their anguish to spiritualism, whose phenomenal growth in popularity during and after the war provides moving testimony to a deep-seated urge to deny the finality of death. Conan Doyle, who lost his son, his brother, and his brother-in-law, found relief in this way, as did the physicist Oliver Lodge, who depicted his son's posthumous life in 'Summerland' in a much reprinted book, *Raymond*.[7] Something was done to ease the material suffering of widows through the payment of war pensions: by 1921 239,000 allowances were being paid to soldiers' wives and 395,000 to soldiers' children.[8]

---

[4] The British figure is depressed by the inclusion of Ireland, which did not have conscription imposed upon it. See below.

[5] The Russian statistics are unreliable, and estimates vary according to whether or not the Great War is elided with the subsequent Civil War. Of the other major combatants, Belgium escaped surprisingly lightly (2%), while the USA entered the war too late to lose more than a small percentage of its males aged 15–49—only 0.4%. The Central Powers were harder hit: Bulgaria (8%), Austria-Hungary (9%), and Turkey (14.8%).

[6] J. M. Bourne, *Britain and the Great War 1914–1918* (London, 1989), 178, 198. This resulted in a rise in the proportion of widows per 1,000 members of the population from 38 to 43.

[7] J. Winter, *Sites of Memory, Sites of Mourning: The Great War in European Cultural History* (Cambridge, 1995; 1996 edn.), 59–62. Lodge had long been interested in the paranormal: see Ch. 16.

[8] S. Pedersen, 'Gender, Welfare and Citizenship in Britain During the Great War', *American Historical Review*, 95 (1990), 1005.

As a result, there were proportionately fewer widows in employment after the war than there had been before it (47 per cent instead of 66 per cent).[9] But grief was less easily assuaged. After the Armistice some 12 per cent of widows died within a year, 14 per cent reported seeing a ghost of a loved one, and 39 per cent said that they still felt their husband's presence.[10]

While the fighting was in progress, the process of grieving was eased by the establishment of street shrines, which sprang up in all British cities from August 1915 onwards.[11] Civic war memorials and church monuments later played an important part in the rituals of remembrance, as did the Allied war graves in France and Belgium, visits to which became for the bereaved a kind of pilgrimage.

Coming to terms with injury generated a different kind of anguish. At least 1,600,000 British servicemen were wounded or fell seriously ill during the war. Before the introduction of the steel helmet in 1915, serious head wounds were common. The effects of gas attacks inspired even greater horror. Protective measures succeeded in dramatically reducing the incidence of such injuries in the war's final couple of years; even so, in the 1920s there were 40,000 hospital inmates who were partially blind. Another 65,000 were being treated in mental hospitals for the newly designated condition called 'shell shock'. In fact, some 6 per cent of all those drawing disability pensions were suffering some sort of psychological damage.[12] The total number of war pensions disbursed by the Ministry of Pensions during the 1920s amounted to about $3\frac{1}{2}$ million. Moreover, there were many who, although they did not qualify for a pension, were scarred for life, among them the returning POWs, who had been at the bottom of the food chain while in custody.

For later generations the dominant image of the Great War has been one of futile carnage, an image heavily dependent on a one-sided reading of a handful of poets such as Wilfred Owen, Siegfried Sassoon,[13] Isaac Rosenberg, and Robert Graves—later reinforced in the 1960s by books such as Leon Woolf's *In Flanders' Fields* and by the anti-war theatrical satire *Oh, What A Lovely War!* To quote one exasperated modern historian, the Great War has thus

---

[9] T. Wilson, *The Myriad Faces of War: Britain and the Great War 1914–1918* (Oxford, 1986: Cambridge, 1988 edn.), 722.

[10] G. J. DeGroot, *Blighty: British Society in the Era of the Great War* (London, 1996), 224.

[11] A. Gregory, 'Lost Generations: The Impact of Military Casualties on Paris, London and Berlin', in J. Winter and J.-L. Robert (eds.), *Capital Cities at War: Paris, London, Berlin 1914–1919* (Cambridge, 1997), 89.

[12] D. Winter, *Death's Men: Soldiers of the Great War* (London, 1978), 252; D. Englander and J. Osborne, 'Jack, Tommy and Henry Dubb: The Armed Forces and the Working Class', *Historical Journal*, 21 (1978), 599; J. Bourke, *Dismembering the Male: Men's Bodies, Britain and the Great War* (1996; 1999 edn.), ch. 1.

[13] Sassoon's attitude to the war was complex. He subsequently disowned his anti-war letter of protest to *The Times*, published on the eve of third Ypres (Bourne, *Great War*, 220, 226–7, 231).

become fixed in the minds of posterity 'in predominantly literary terms as a black hole or national trauma—a gap in history—redeemed and rendered meaningful for them only by disenchanted memoirs and the poetry of pity'.[14]

Interestingly, however, it was not until the late 1920s that this interpretation achieved wide currency. C. E. Montague may have set the trend with his *Disenchantment* (1922), but the new orthodoxy really established itself in 1929, the year which saw the publication of Robert Graves's *Good-Bye To All That*, R. C. Sherriff's *Journey's End* (a successful West End play, made into an early 'talkie' in 1930), and, in Germany, Erich Remarque's *All Quiet On The Western Front*.

The Great War did indeed inspire a great literary outpouring, particularly of poetry: 2,225 poets whose work was published between 1914 and 1918 have been identified, 523 of them women, but very few expressed sentiments similar to those found in the familiar canon. The most popular poet at the time was John Oxenham, who celebrated heroism and sacrifice, the most common of all poetic themes. Rupert Brooke's collected poems, too, remained popular throughout the war. There was even a revival of idealistic verse in the aftermath of the German Spring Offensive.[15] Nor, as we shall see, did all combatants descend into disillusionment and despair, still less into a 'modernist' rhetoric. (To heal the pain of bereavement, efforts to commemorate the dead more often than not found expression in 'traditional' forms, whether romantic or Christian.[16])

Is it possible to generalize at all about what it was like to 'experience Armageddon'? About 84 per cent of Britain's servicemen were employed in the army, most of them serving on the Western Front. But the force of over 2 million men which Haig was commanding in 1918 included vast numbers of military personnel who never 'went over the top'. One-third of a million men were exclusively occupied in supplying the BEF.[17] As well as transport and communications, the medical services, civil engineering, and the labour corps all absorbed considerable manpower. Indeed, as the BEF expanded, the percentage of combatants steadily fell: from 83.9 per cent at the start of war to only 64.84 per cent at its end.[18] Interestingly, the military branch which grew most rapidly during these years was the Army Service Corps.

[14] B. Bond, 'British "Anti-War" Writers and Their Critics', in H. Cecil and P. H. Liddle (eds.), *Facing Armageddon: The First World War Experienced* (London, 1996), 829.

[15] Bourne, *Great War*, 226; D. Hubbard and J. Onions (eds.), *Poetry of the Great War: An Anthology* (London, 1986).

[16] Winter, *Sites of Memory*.

[17] N. Ferguson, *The Pity of War* (Harmondsworth, 1998), 352.

[18] K. Simpson, 'The British Soldier on the Western Front', in P. Liddle (ed.), *Home Fires and Foreign Fields* (London, 1985), 145.

Never before or since had the British put into the field such a gigantic force. In 1918 it comprised, as well as military personnel, 404,000 animals, 31,770 lorries, 7,694 cars, 3,532 ambulances, 14,464 motor-cycles, 6,437 guns, 1,782 aircraft, and vast quantities of stores.[19] Keeping this organization operational required staff work of a high order; in the difficult circumstances it was quite efficiently performed. Particularly impressive was the work of the Medical Service Corps. In fact, the Great War stands out from earlier conflicts (notably the recent Boer War) in that deaths from illness and disease were outnumbered by battlefield deaths in the ratio of 1 to 15: in the past the balance had been the other way round, usually about five deaths from disease to every man killed or dying from his wounds. Although 'trench foot' (and venereal disease) immobilized large numbers, various sanitary precautions limited the damage, while an innoculation programme proved successful, at least on the Western Front. Behind the lines the recent discovery of anaesthetics, early experiments in blood transfusion, and rapid improvements in plastic surgery all contributed to a relatively high recovery rate (particularly from gas attacks).

Moreover, as science and technology were increasingly utilized, the nature of warfare changed. By 1918 the BEF, with its bureaucratic structures, had taken on something of the character of a gargantuan factory. (French and Haig may have been cavalry officers, but, contrary to popular preconceptions, the cavalry comprised only 1.01 per cent of the BEF in late 1918.) In specialized units such as the newly formed Tank Corps and Machine Gun Corps, men dressed and behaved more like industrial workers than traditional soldiers.

Nevertheless the infantry remained to the end the largest single element in the army, over one-half of all combatant troops, and the popular view of the war does not err in presenting the infantrymen of the BEF as those facing the greatest risk of death and injury.[20] Over one in four were wounded, one in eight was killed—a casualty rate of nearly 40 per cent. But in envisaging the life of the infantryman, it is misleading to focus upon a few dramatic, but in some ways untypical, episodes, such as the horrendous fighting which marked the first day of the Somme or the end of third Ypres. (The equally sanguinary 'forgotten battles' of 1918 have not, until recently, aroused so much interest— perhaps because a competent Haig leading his armies in a series of more-or-less successful offensives does not fit into the conventional picture of the war's character.)

In fact, only about two-fifths of an infantryman's time was spent in the front line, and participation in major battles occurred even less frequently.[21] For long

---

[19] Bourne, *Great War*, 177.
[20] Over 91% of officer casualties were incurred on the Western Front.
[21] Bourne, *Great War*, 352.

periods he was on leave or in the rear, resting in places such as Poperinge. Tedium and discomfort, punctuated by moments of sheer terror, formed the lot of most infantrymen. War gives 'relaxation and jollity and mere boredom their place alongside hardship & bloodshed', according to one perceptive officer who saw much active service: fighting 'in the battle zone between antagonists of equal tenacity and resource is prolonged drudgery ... but drudgery with fearful moments: and, as in everyday life, there is very much that is trivial, or seems so'.[22] For many 'Tommies' the principal fight was one waged against cold, waterlogged trenches, lice, and rats—the main concerns being food, clean water, and cigarettes.

When infantrymen, fortified by rum, went over the top, many of them experienced panic, but others felt exhilaration—surviving letters and memoirs show a vast array of attitudes on this, as on other, subjects. It seems that some soldiers (in all armies) killed with relish, with a view to avenging the deaths of former pals or to vindicate the honour of their battalion. Others found satisfaction in the very act of killing—this was 'the dirty secret that dared not be uttered after the war if combatants were to settle back to their calm civilian life, unbrutalised'.[23] It is a gross simplification to see soldiers as mere sacrificial victims. Moreover, innocent expressions of enthusiastic patriotism often crop up in officers' correspondence even in the war's latter stages. Writing home from France on 29 August 1917, Old Etonian Christopher Tennant could declare: 'This is a great adventure and I am enjoying it' (five days later he was killed).[24] Another junior officer exclaimed in July 1918: 'By Jove I am proud of our British Empire.'[25] Among NCOs and privates, the predominant stance was one of stoicism, tinged with black humour.

Of course, the personal feelings of ordinary infantryman were of no interest to the British military authorities, which operated a disciplinary regime arguably more severe than any other army's bar the Italian. Between August 1914 and March 1920 over 300,000 soldiers were court-martialled, mostly for relatively trivial offences, of whom 270,927 were convicted. But only 3,080 were sentenced to death,[26] and a much smaller number, 346 (excluding Indians), had their sentences confirmed and carried out. Contrary to popular opinion, those who faced the firing squad were, in most cases, guilty of desertion while on active service. Another thirty-seven had committed murder,

---

[22] J. C. Dunn, *The War the Infantry Knew 1914–1919* (1938; 1994 ed.), p. xxxiii.

[23] J. Bourke, 'The Experience of Killing', in P. Liddle, J. Bourne, and I. Whitehead (eds.), *The Great World War 1914–45: Volume 1: Lightning Strikes Twice* (London, 2000), 306.

[24] D. Winter, *Death's Men*, 130.

[25] P. Liddle, 'British Loyalties: The Evidence of an Archive', in H. Cecil and P. H. Liddle (eds.), *Facing Armageddon*, 524.

[26] Most served lesser punishments such as detention, fines, Field Punishment no. 1, and reductions in ranks.

and only eighteen were executed for cowardice in the face of the enemy. (Nearly one-half of those executed had committed a serious offence for at least a second time.[27])

The ratio of military police (the intensely unpopular 'Red Caps') to armed servicemen increased in the latter stages of the war, but the indiscipline which they faced, especially in the winter of 1917–18, mainly took the form of drunkenness and other petty offences. Small things could rile: for example, the West Kents briefly mutinied, complaining that their boots were unfit to wear. (On the other hand, the fact that the British army was relatively well clothed and fed prevented the outbreak of the sort of serious disaffection that, at various stages in the war, incapacitated the French, Russian, and German armies.) There was some malingering, leading to a cat-and-mouse game with the authorities, some self-mutilation, and—more worryingly—a desertion rate of 10.26 per cent p.a.[28] But, although morale was sometimes low, discipline in the BEF never broke down (the one major army, bar the American, of which this could be said), and most men, even in appalling circumstances, performed their duty more or less uncomplainingly.

Nor, except when the 5th Army's positions were overrun in the spring of 1918, did British soldiers surrender in droves. This may in part have been because surrendering was a highly dangerous ploy, one which often led to death, whether by accident or design.[29] But too much weight should not be attached to fear or coercion: for ordinary soldiers the main concern seems to have been not to let down one's 'mates', a sentiment naturally strong in the original 'Pals' Battalions' (units formed locally, or from a single workplace). Private Surfleet, in action at the Somme, later took pride in the reflection that, despite his intense nervousness, he could now 'look the rest of the lads in the face and claim to be one of them'.[30]

Of course, fighting in the Great War was not confined to land operations. The Royal Navy lost one in sixteen of its officers and men: 43,244 souls in all. Death could come suddenly, 'out of the blue', overwhelming an entire ship: for example, 1,200 sailors, most of them reservists, died with the sinking of three cruisers in the North Sea in September 1914.[31] Naval engagements came few and far between, to the frustration of most ratings. But stress was the constant

[27] J. Peaty, 'Haig and Military Discipline', in B. Bond and N. Cave (eds.), *Haig: A Reappraisal 70 Years On* (London, 1999), 196–222. These figures relate to all soldiers, not only to those operating on the Western Front, but 322 were executed in that theatre. For a different interpretation, see G. Oram, *Worthless Men: Race, Eugenics and the Death Penalty in the British Army During the First World War* (London, 1998).

[28] Englander and Osborne, 'Jack, Tommy and Henry Dubb', 595.

[29] Ferguson, *Pity of War*, ch. 13.

[30] Wilson, *Myriad Faces*, 361.

[31] Gregory, 'Lost Generations', 73.

companion of the blockade-enforcers, who spent long spells at sea in conditions of acute discomfort.[32] Such operations, however important to the war's outcome, did not lend themselves to dramatic re-enactments.

Airmen, by contrast, from the start attracted attention in the press because they seemed to be participating in an older kind of war, one marked by individual heroism and gallantry: Lloyd George called them 'the knighthood of the war, without fear and without reproach'.[33] A particular glamour surrounded such 'aces' as the pilot Lanoe Hawker, who received a posthumous Victoria Cross after being killed on 23 November 1916 in a duel with his German counterpart, Manfred von Richthofen, flying the much superior Albatros.[34] In fact, although fatalities among air-crew were exceptionally high, 8,000 of the 14,166 pilots who died did so in training accidents in the United Kingdom.[35] The rapid turnover in air-crew was also expedited by 'breakdowns', many of them caused by terror at the prospect of death by burning—a dreadful fate which pilots shared with members of the tank crews.

However it was experienced, by land, sea, or air, the Great War marked for life those who had fought in it. It also isolated the military in many respects from civilian society, all too often coming between ex-soldiers and their uncomprehending wives. 'Patriotic versifiers' vilified civilian 'shirkers', newspapermen, and pacifists, but so, too, did Sassoon, whose savage satires took in many more targets than the bungling staff. Those on active service were often dismayed, on revisiting 'Blighty', to discover life apparently going on much as usual. Not until the spring of 1915 were professional football matches and most race meetings suspended,[36] and even in 1917 and 1918 the affluent could still be seen guzzling at their clubs and restaurants. Music halls may have lost custom, but their place was taken by the expanding cinema, which did a booming wartime trade—part of the Americanization of popular culture during the war. 'Are you forgetting there's a war on?', some patriots indignantly asked.

Yet military and civilian life, though separated in some respects, also reacted upon one another in a multitude of ways. The army, for example, was

---

[32] On the risks and privations, no less acute, facing merchant seamen, see T. Lane, 'The British Merchant Seaman at War', in Cecil and Liddle (eds.), *Facing Armageddon*, 146–59.

[33] J. H. Morrow, Jnr., *The Great War in the Air: Military Aviation from 1909 to 1921* (Shrewsbury, 1993), 365.

[34] Wilson, *Myriad Faces*, 372.

[35] Ibid. 364. Another estimate gives 16,623 casualties, of which 6,166 were killed or died, 7,245 wounded or injured, 3,212 missing or interned, perhaps more than half of pilots (Morrow, *Great War in the Air*, 367). Only one in fifty members of the RFC/RAF died (Winter, *Great War*, 72–3), but that was because only a small minority of them actually flew.

[36] However, the 1915 Cup Final, won by Sheffield United, was blacked out by the papers, which after December 1914 only gave the football *scores* (J. Winter, 'Popular Culture in Wartime Britain', in A. Roshwald and R. Stites (eds.), *European Culture in the Great War: The Arts, Entertainment, and Propaganda, 1914–1918* (Cambridge, 1999), 339).

transformed by Kitchener's recruiting campaign and by the later introduction of conscription, which created a citizen's army—to the disapproval of Henry Wilson, who, like many professional officers, dismissed Kitchener's new units as 'ridiculous and preposterous' (as well as being a waste of manpower, since they would need a full two years to be properly trained). Behind such gibes lay a deep fear of the subversive implications of creating mass armies. Remember that, even before conscription, 2,400,000 men had joined the army of their own volition, ten times the regimental strength of the regular army in 1914.[37]

As a result, the number of officers expanded from 28,060 in 1914 to over 229,316 by the end of the war,[38] and this expansion, plus the heavy losses among the original officer corps, necessitated the giving of commissions to 'temporary gentlemen'—some, it is true, were public-school types recruited from the OTCs, but increasingly the new officers were drawn from those who, in peacetime, would have been rejected on social grounds.[39] Duff Cooper found that his fellow cadets in the Household Guards Officer Cadet Battalion included a shoemaker, a window-dresser from Sheffield, and a bank clerk with a cockney accent. The change in social tone was particularly marked in such technological branches of the army as the Machine Gun Corps, the Tank Corps, and the Gas Corps, new formations without any regimental tradition behind them. Artillery and engineering officers, likewise, needed to display technical proficiency, rather than 'character'.[40]

Neither, with safety, could the private soldiers in what was effectively a citizen army be 'broken in' to accept the brutally harsh discipline that had regulated the pre-war army, especially those who had responded to the call of patriotic duty in the early months of the war. It was thus deemed prudent to relax, somewhat, the infliction of unpopular penalties such as 'Field Punishment no. 1', under which miscreants were tied to carriage wheels. Moreover, many units took a perverse pride in being *un*-military in their dress and demeanour.[41] Australian troops had a particular reputation for being insubordinate, but the Australian government refused to allow their men to be subjected to the death penalty—except for murder. No wonder that old-style

---

[37] Winter, *Great War*, 27.

[38] K. Simpson, 'The Officers', in I. F. W. Beckett and K. Simpson (eds.), *A Nation in Arms: A Social Study of the British Army in the First World War* (Manchester, 1985), 88.

[39] The original phrase denoted non-regulars, but later applied to those brought up outside the usual officer class; 212,772 of the 229,315 combatant commissions awarded between August 1915 and December 1918 went to temporary, territorial or special reserve officers, (M. Petter, ' "Temporary Gentlemen" in the Aftermath of the Great War: Rank, Status and the Ex-Officer Problem', *Historical Journal*, 37 (1994), 136, n. 32).

[40] Ibid. 137.

[41] Jay Winter opines that the troops 'never left home; they brought it with them in their imagination as cultural baggage which saw most of them through the worst of what they had to face' (Winter, 'Popular Culture', 333).

army officers yearned for the time when the war would end, so that they could get on with the good old profession of soldiering!

But if military life became invaded, to some extent, by civilian values, civilian life was simultaneously becoming 'militarized'. Although the Great War saw nothing like the blurring of the boundary between civilians and military that characterized the Second World War, ordinary citizens became exposed to the kind of danger that had never before affected a country not actually in process of invasion. Merchant seamen, dodging the U-boat blockade, were performing much the same function as the members of the Royal Navy assigned to protect them: 14,287 of them (including fishermen) paid with their lives, about one-third the number of fatalities incurred by the Royal Navy. The workforce employed in the munitions industry, including many women, also ran the risk of injury, disfigurement, and even death—most spectacularly in the Silvertown disaster of January 1917, which killed seventy workers, this being only the worst of a number of explosions in munitions works. Naval bombardment of coastal towns and the bombing raids of first Zeppelins, and then of Gotha airplanes might, within the wider context of the war, have been little more than an irritant, but they nevertheless caused more than 1,000 deaths and three times as many injuries.[42] In a single Gotha attack on London, 162 civilians died and 432 were hurt, Liverpool Street Station being the main target.[43] Like the shelling of seaports, these events showed that civilian status no longer conferred immunity. Panicky Londoners took refuge in tube stations, and some East Enders decamped to Brighton. 'It's no business to happen here you know, it's no business to happen here', complained one Londoner.[44]

Nor was this all, since, as we will see, civilian life became increasingly regimented and controlled the longer the war went on.[45] Indeed, the military model came to penetrate the way society was perceived, and even affected the processes of scientific research. For example, in their work on aspects of gas warfare, physiologists came to share with military thinkers 'a view of the war itself as an experimental enterprise, in which new techniques of warfare were continually being developed and tested, and in which the line of demarcation between the laboratory and the battlefield was increasingly blurred'.[46]

---

[42] 51 Zeppelin and 57 Gotha raids were responsible for 1,413 deaths and 3,407 injuries, the Gotha raids being much the more lethal (DeGroot, *Blighty*, 200). Winter gives an estimate of 1,266 civilian deaths, including those sustained in bombardments (*Great War*, 71).

[43] Wilson, *Myriad Faces*, 509.

[44] Ibid. 511.

[45] See Ch. 20.

[46] S. Sturdy, 'War as Experiment: Physiology, Innovation and Administration in Britain, 1914–1918: The Case of Chemical Warfare', in R. Cooter, M. Harrison, and S. Sturdy, *War, Medicine and Modernity* (Stroud, 1999), 74.

2. NATIONAL IDENTITIES

The war affected all parts of the United Kingdom, but it impinged upon them in somewhat different ways. In the voluntary phase of recruitment, the Scottish people showed themselves to be marginally the most patriotic of all Britons: 26.9 per cent of males in the 15–49 age-bracket enlisted, as against a comparable figure of 24.2 per cent for England and Wales.[47] This may explain why, by the end of the war, they had suffered a significantly higher mortality rate (10.9 per cent) than had the inhabitants of the other 'kingdoms'.[48] Moreover, Scottish regiments soon acquired a reputation in enemy circles for being especially tough and ferocious.

However, in the Highlands a different approach to recruiting sometimes proved necessary. Thus Macdonald of Clanranald, a chieftain of Jacobite stock, chose to remind his audience of how 'Butcher' Cumberland and his German troops had brutally suppressed their ancestors in 1745, before pointing out that 'the Germans by their behaviour in Belgium and other places ... are showing that they are quite as brutal now as Cumberland and his men were then'.[49]

In Wales, too, patriotic sensitivities had to be massaged. True, the industrial workers in South Wales, like their counterparts in England and Scotland, rushed to the colours in the war's early stages. But in North Wales recruiting was initially very slow, perhaps because this area lacked a tradition of military service. A furious Lloyd George forced a reluctant Kitchener to agree to the appointment of Nonconformist chaplains and the use of Welsh on parade and in barracks; he also involved popular Welsh-speaking notabilities in the recruiting campaign, an effort to make the army responsive to the needs of a mass democracy which many regular officers saw as a deplorable act of 'politicization'.

Lloyd George also played the nationalist card skilfully. In his famous Queen's Hall speech in mid-September he lambasted Prussian arrogance by singing the praise of 'little 5-foot-5 nations', and drawing parallels between gallant little Belgium and Israel—but also, by implication, between Belgium and Wales, the victim of big, bullying England.[50] Welsh national pride was further mobilized behind the war effort on 1 March 1915 (St David's Day),

[47] Winter, *Great War*, 11. P. E. Dewey, 'Military Recruiting and the British Labour Force During the First World War', *Historical Journal*, 27 (1984), 216, shows that by July 1915 24% of Scottish males had enlisted, compared with the UK average of 20%.

[48] By the war's end, however, only 41.4% of Scotland's young males had served in uniform, compared to 46.2% of those in England and Wales—probably because so many exempted occupations were concentrated in southern Scotland.

[49] E. A. Cameron and I. J. M. Robertson, 'Fighting and Bleeding For the Land: The Scottish Highlands and the Great War', in C. M. M. Macdonald and E. W. McFarland (eds.), *Scotland and the Great War* (East Linton, 1999), 84.

[50] J. Grigg, *Lloyd George: From Peace to War 1912–1916* (London, 1985), 164. See his famous address to London Welshmen on 21 September hoping to see a 'Welsh Army'—in which the 'race who faced the Normans for hundreds of years in a struggle for freedom' could prove their mettle.

when Lloyd George inspected the North Wales Brigade at Llandudno, the troops wearing in their cap or through their shoulder straps 'the leek of old Wales'.[51] Such exploitation of national feeling seems to have achieved its desired objective. By the end of 1914 enough Welshmen had come forward to establish the 38th (Welsh) Division (another innovation which Kitchener had initially tried to block),[52] and six months later Welsh enlistment exactly mirrored that of mainland Britain as a whole.

As so often, the odd man out was Ireland. With Redmond controversially placing his Irish Volunteers at the disposal of the government and taking an active part in the recruiting campaign, enlistment from the Emerald Isle was initially quite brisk: some 44,000 Irishmen came forward in 1914, 46,000 in the following year. Predictably, the highest provincial rate of recruitment was supplied by Ulster, where Carson had thrown the UVF behind the war effort. Yet, while Kitchener allowed the Ulstermen to use the red hand of Ulster on their colours, plunging Redmond into 'a fine frenzy', he foolishly refused to concede the right of the Southern Irish Division to employ its own emblem, the harp—which makes it all the more surprising that as many as 57 per cent of all Irish recruits were Roman Catholics.

However, in August 1914 the British government was worried enough about Ireland's volatile politics to hold back two of the BEF's six divisions, and although these fears for a time seemed to be misplaced, the Asquith coalition wisely exempted Ireland from the provisions of the two Military Service Acts of 1916. The emergence of a separatist brand of republican nationalism in the aftermath of the Easter Rising then reduced the flow of volunteers to a trickle (19,000 in 1916, 14,000 in 1917, and fewer than 11,000 in 1918). Many patriots on mainland Britain, especially Conservative politicians, fumed at the privileges being accorded to Irish 'slackers', but the mere threat to extend conscription to Ireland in the spring of 1918 threw the South into uproar, even moderate Catholic bishops castigating this as an outrage that should be resisted by all means compatible with the law of God. The Irish people were thus never subjected to conscription, and, as a result, only 12.3 per cent of Irish males of serviceable age entered the armed forces—about a quarter the proportion coming from the rest of the United Kingdom.[53]

All the same, at least 200,000 Irishmen (including the regulars) fought in the Great War—the exact number is impossible to calculate, especially if one

[51] C. Hughes, *Mametz: Lloyd George's 'Welsh Army' At The Battle of the Somme* (Gerrards Cross, 1979 and 1982), 22–4. Meanwhile the newly formed Welsh Guards mounted guard at Buckingham Palace, while the Welsh emblem was flown over the Chancellor's residence. Well might the *Daily News* refer to 'what may be termed the new Welsh nationalism'.

[52] C. Hughes, 'The New Armies', in Beckett and Simpson (eds.), *Nation in Arms*, 115.

[53] This does not include Irish volunteers resident in other parts of the UK (Winter, *Great War*, 28).

broadens the enquiry to include Irishmen resident in mainland Britain.[54] Irish units, of both denominations, distinguished themselves in the fighting, suffering very high casualties in the process: the 10th Irish Division of Kitchener's 1st Army lost three-quarters of its men at Suvla Bay in August 1915, and the 36th Division (incorporating much of the old UVF) was slaughtered on the opening days of the Somme.[55] Among the estimated 30,000 or so Irish casualties was John Redmond's brother and fellow MP Major Willie Redmond, killed in action on the Western Front in June 1917. Yet the fact that the subsequent by-election was won by De Valera shows how detached from the war effort the Nationalist section of the community had by then become.

In short, although the war initially held out some promise of a more amicable relationship between Ireland and England, it ended by driving the two countries irrevocably apart. Unfortunately, it also intensified the divide within Ireland between the Protestant North-East and the rest of the country (Dublin and Belfast celebrated the Armistice in very different ways[56]), and even sowed dissension within the Irish nationalist community itself. For example, many Dublin women whose men were serving at the Front reacted with hostility to the 'treacherous' behaviour of the Easter rebels, while William Kent, the brother of Eamonn, one of the Rebellion's leaders, was later killed fighting with the Royal Dublin Fusiliers.[57]

Amongst those who actually served in the armed forces, the experience of war began by heightening national consciousness through the engendering of more-or-less friendly rivalries. One Irish regular soldier who had spent his boyhood playing Irish chieftains dealing death and destruction to the Sassenach, contrasted the bravery of his Irish battalion with what he saw as the cowardice of the English. Similar observations can be found amongst Scottish regiments: 'Holy God what did those damned English do but turn back.'[58] In fact, until forced by the nature of trench warfare to abandon their kilts, the Scottish units ('devils in skirts', the Germans called them) made a conspicuous parade of their nationhood—in the process annoying not only the Tommies but also the Catholic troops of the 16th (Irish) Division.[59]

---

[54] The higher figure of 400,000–500,000 ignores the presence of non-Irishmen in many Irish divisions (D. Fitzpatrick, 'Militarism in Ireland, 1900–1922', in T. Bartlett and K. Jeffrey, *A Military History of Ireland* (Cambridge, 1996), 388–92).

[55] The 16th Division suffered similarly at Ypres and during the German Spring Offensive.

[56] See Ch. 18.

[57] G. Till, 'Brothers in Arms: The British Army and Navy at the Dardanelles', in Cecil and Liddle (eds.), *Facing Armageddon*, 163.

[58] Wilson, *Myriad Faces*, 56, 59, 260–1.

[59] For this hostility, which was of course sectarian in nature (the Scottish troops were predominantly Protestant), see D. Gill and G. Dallas, 'Mutiny at Etaples Base in 1917', *Past & Present*, 69 (1975), 101.

Local identities proved to be very useful for recruiting purposes (they figured prominently in the 'Pals' Battalions', as well as helping to stimulate Welsh enthusiasm for the war). Admittedly, not all military units were composed exclusively of the national or regional groups which gave them their name. When the 15th Battalion of the Welsh Regiment (Carmarthenshire) first left for France, 21 per cent of its personnel came from England.[60] Cockney and other regional English accents could also be heard in many Scottish and Irish regiments. But, at least in the short run, the introduction of conscription may actually have reinforced national identities: for example, before the war only 10 per cent of the Welch Fusiliers (satirically dubbed the 'Birmingham Fusiliers'), were actually Welsh, but this proportion had risen to about 50 per cent in 1917.[61]

On the other hand, the rapid expansion of the army after the carnage of the Somme and third Ypres inevitably led to a muddling together of different nationalities and regional groupings, just as it blurred the original distinction between regular, Territorial, and service battalions. Englishmen, for example, had to be drafted in to replace the heavy losses sustained by the Irish units. The War Office may have actually encouraged such a process in order to minimize the impact of casualties on local communities. Unfortunately, some soldiers, surrounded by virtual strangers, felt that the camaraderie which had sustained them in the earlier stages of the war had been dissipated. In any case, the overall effect was to submerge national feelings and county identities alike within a more integrated concept of Britishness. At leadership level, the army had from the start been a pan-British institution: Robertson epitomized the outspoken Yorkshireman, but Kitchener and French were southern Irish Protestants, Henry Wilson an Ulsterman, and Haig a Scot—a situation which provoked a self-pitying whinge from John Hay Beith, author of *The Oppressed English* (1917).

Among the civilian population, too, the war led, on balance, to a weakening of national feeling. For the disruption of economic life led to widespread geographic mobility, with women migrating at a rate of 5,000 a month from their homes to munitions areas, many of which, by the end of the war, had been dispersed so as to remove dangerous plants from proximity to the city centres.[62] The largest of such complexes was that surrounding the National Factory at Longtown, near Gretna in Scotland, which drew in thousands of labourers from far and wide, many of them Englishmen. Similarly, many Scotsmen moved south of the border in search of well-paid war work.

---

[60] Hughes, 'New Armies', 116.   [61] Dunn, *Infantry*, p. xxxviii.
[62] Wilson, *Myriad Faces*, 719.

Such population movements need not, in themselves, have led to a waning of national feeling. However, as we shall see, dilution and other industrial innovations raised serious issues of principle that concerned factory workers throughout Britain, uniting them across the boundaries of nationality. Admittedly, the Clyde to some extent hoed its own row after the summer of 1915. But the general effect of industrial upheaval was to sharpen class consciousness in ways that operated to the advantage of the Labour Party, an organization which (Keir Hardie notwithstanding) had never shown much sensitivity to national susceptibilities. True, Plaid Cymru was founded in 1925, followed by the Scottish National Party three years later, but it would be decades before either became a force in the land. For one of the war's most important legacies (leaving Ireland to one side) was that the national question lost its pre-war importance—and did not recover it until the late 1960s.

But this more integrated sense of British nationality formed merely one element within an enlarged imperialist consciousness. In August 1914 the King declared war on Germany in the name of the entire Empire as well as on behalf of the United Kingdom's subjects, but this elicited no significant protests in the self-governing colonies of Australia, New Zealand, and Canada. In South Africa, it is true, the declaration triggered off an Afrikaner revolt led by de Wet, Christoffel Kemp, and Salomon Maritz, but the 11,000 rebels were quickly overpowered by 30,000 loyalists, directed by the one-time Boer commandos Botha and Smuts.[63] From all parts of the white Empire recruits rushed to the colours, even if French Canadians[64] and Irish Australians tended to hold aloof, and in Canada it was those who had been British-born who were most likely to enlist.[65]

In July 1916 New Zealand adopted conscription, as did Canada seventeen months later. In two separate referenda, the first held in October 1916, the second in December 1917, the Australian electorate rejected the proposition that they should follow suit, as their belligerent Premier, 'Billy' Hughes, was urging them to do. All the same, 413,000 Australians eventually enlisted, some 30 per cent of all their eligible males. Proportionately this was a slightly greater contribution than that made by the 629,000 Canadians (27 per cent of those eligible), though smaller than that of the 129,000 New Zealanders (40 per cent), the most ardently pro-British of all the Dominions; 136,000 white South

---

[63] Wilson, *Myriad Faces*, 100.

[64] The French Canadians, around 35% of the population, contributed only 5% of the Canadian Expeditionary Force (R. Holland, 'The British Empire and the Great War, 1914–1918', in J. M. Brown and W. R. Louis (eds.), *The Oxford History of the British Empire: Volume IV: The Twentieth Century* (Oxford, 1999), 126).

[65] Only 51% of the total Canadian Expeditionary Force had been born in Canada (S. Constantine, 'Britain and the Empire', in S. Constantine, M. W. Kirby, and M. B. Rose (eds.), *The First World War in British History* (London, 1995), 266).

Africans also rallied to the support of the mother country. This meant that the white Empire was providing some 1,307,000 troops to the Allied cause.[66]

Initially the main contribution of the colonial troops lay in mopping up German colonies in their vicinity. For the loss of fewer than 100 lives (no more than was often incurred in a single trench raid on the Western Front), the South Africans took German South-West Africa; they also participated in the fighting in Tanganyika. Meanwhile the Australians were ousting Germany from Papua, and the Solomon Islands and the Bismark Archipelago; the New Zealanders were doing likewise in Samoa.

But colonial troops also participated in theatres of war very distant from their homes. The Anzacs may have suffered in vain at Gallipoli, but they went on to play an important role on the Western Front: from 1916 onwards five Australian divisions joined the BEF, as did four Canadian divisions and one from New Zealand. Arguably the most skilful general to emerge on the Allied side, Sir John Monash, had been an Australian engineer before 1914. Haig thought the Dominions troops his finest (he particularly admired the New Zealanders), and, partly because they were relatively fresh, they were increasingly used during 1918 for the BEF's most dangerous and difficult offensives. For this they paid a high price. The Canadians sustained 42,000 casualties in the last four months of the conflict, while the Australians and New Zealanders incurred a heavier death-rate among mobilized men during the war than did the United Kingdom itself.

Although its Muslim population was unsettled by hostilities against Turkey, India, too, participated in the war. In the autumn of 1914 one-third of all British troops in France were either Indian or drawn from Indian garrisons, but, operating in a strange climate far from home, they were not thought to have distinguished themselves there, and by the end of 1915 the two Indian divisions were withdrawn. However, the ill-fated Mesopotamian expedition, launched by the Government of India, consisted in its early stages entirely of troops from the Indian Army, most of them 'natives'. In addition, nearly 50,000 Indians fought in Africa, where they were instrumental in the eventual defeat of Lettow-Vorbeck.

In all, 827,000 Indians were mobilized during the war, enabling British troops in East Africa, Egypt, and Palestine to be moved to the Western Front.[67] Moreover, desperate to replenish its military losses, the War Cabinet increasingly turned its eyes with longing in the course of 1918 to this vast manpower reserve in the East. Lloyd George spoke publicly of India as the

---

[66] Many of these colonial troops served abroad: 76,184 white South Africans, 458,218 Canadians, 331,814 Australians, and 112,223 New Zealanders (ibid. 260).

[67] Brown, 'Empire and Great War', 117, 121–2.

'bulwark of Asia', eliciting a promise of half-a-million extra Indian troops, but the war ended before this promise could be redeemed—to the relief of Curzon, a cautious traditionalist, who wanted to limit India's military involvement.

A parallel debate took place concerning the wisdom of employing African troops. British and French colonial administrators in Africa warned against allowing European quarrels to spill over onto their continent, but this did, to some extent, happen. For example, the King's African Rifles, drawn from detachments from Sierra Leone, Nigeria, the Gold Coast, and Gambia, combined with French Senegalese troops to capture Togoland. Some 56,761 African troops also took part in the East African campaign, as did thousands of 'natives' in the largely conscripted carrier and labour forces, among whom mortality was particularly high.[68] True, Haig doubted the ability of Africans to perform well in Europe, but by 1918 many were participating on the Western Front as members of the Labour Corps.[69] African troops might have been used in even greater numbers, and more generally, if the war had not ended when it did.

Nor was the imperial contribution to the war confined to the raising of troops. The Government of India donated £100 million towards its costs, but in economic terms the greatest assistance was rendered by Canada, which supplied the mother country with millions of bags of flour at the start of the war, as well as making an important industrial contribution: one-third of the BEF's munitions in 1917–18 were Canadian-made.[70] (Less helpful was the offer of a supply of coconuts from the Marakei people of the Gilbert Islands!)[71] Indeed, all parts of the Empire, whether Crown Colonies or self-governing, helped the British government to stay in the war by placing their resources at its disposal, while simultaneously denying them to the Central Powers. British-controlled Africa was an alternative source of supplies for raw materials obtainable only with difficulty elsewhere—for example, wool from Kenya.

Yet although the Great War provided an awe-inspiring spectacle of imperial solidarity, it also set off centrifugal forces. In particular, the experience of Gallipoli helped to create a more powerful sense of Australian nationality, through the celebration of Anzac Day (25 April). Indeed, Australian republicans still invoke Gallipoli as evidence of England's willingness to squander Australian lives in a squalid imperial war on the other side of the globe.

Nor were relationships between British and colonial troops, when they found themselves in close proximity to one another on the Western Front,

---

[68] Constantine, 'Britain and the Empire', 261.
[69] The Labour Corps also included Egyptians, Indians, West Indians, Cape Coloured, Mauritians, and Fijians, as well as 92,000 Chinese 'coolies' (Constantine, 'Britain and the Empire', 261).
[70] Holland, 'British Empire and Great War', 118.
[71] Constantine, 'Britain and the Empire', 263.

entirely amicable. The devil-may-care informality of the 'diggers' grated on many British soldiers, though the Scots perhaps got on better with them than the English.[72] In fact, ill-discipline landed the Australian troops in a number of serious scrapes. Allenby sent them home from Egypt in disgrace, and their misbehaviour extended beyond the Armistice, with 'illegal absentees' still marauding through areas behind the line.[73] Haig admired the Australians' fighting prowess, but worried that these rough-hewn democrats were putting 'revolutionary ideas' into Tommy's head.[74]

More generally, the relative affluence of the colonial troops often stirred up resentment: the Canadians, for example, were paid a dollar a day, while British privates were drawing a miserly shilling. In some English units there was also a suspicion that colonial exploits got more press publicity than they themselves could ever command. Incredulity greeted Monash's later claim that the Australian Corps, comprising less than 10 per cent of the total strength of the BEF, had seized almost a quarter of all German prisoners and guns captured by the British armies.[75]

The precise status of the Dominion troops also generated some ill-will. At the start of the war General C. Bridges, Inspector-General of the Australian Military Forces, had wanted to create a separate Australian Division, but this idea did not appeal to the Army Council. Instead, Australian units were at first merged with British formations. In November 1917 the five Australian divisions were reconstituted as a separate corps. Even then they came under the command of an Englishman, General Sir William Birdwood, who tended not to promote Australians to staff posts. Other Dominion troops found themselves in a similar situation. For example, the Canadian Corps which so distinguished itself at Vimy Ridge was commanded by Julian Byng, another English officer. The South Africans occupied an even more subordinate position: so heavy were their losses in March–April 1918 that the South African Brigade was merged with the 9th Scottish Division.[76]

At governmental level similar problems arose. The Committee of Imperial Defence had the potential to develop into an institution through which colonial governments could contribute to policy-making, but it was suspended in August 1914. And though the Canadian Premier, Borden, was invited to a Cabinet meeting in July 1915, he was not told much, nor was the Australian, Billy Hughes, on his visit in March 1916.

[72] Gill and Dallas, 'Mutiny at Etaples', 99–100.
[73] A. Ekins, 'Australians at the End of the War', in H. Cecil and P. Liddle (eds.), *At The Eleventh Hour: Reflections, Hopes and Anxieties at the Closing of the Great War, 1918* (Barnsley, 1988), 160.
[74] Englander and Osborne, 'Jack, Tommy and Henry Dubb', 601.
[75] Ekins, 'Australians at End of War', in Cecil and Liddle (eds.), *Eleventh Hour*, 157.
[76] Holland, 'British Empire and Great War', 129–30.

Lloyd George, however, was aware of the danger of Dominion resentment and, not before time, acted to stop it getting out of control. He accordingly established the Imperial War Cabinet, which held fourteen meetings between March and May 1917, and Smuts stayed on in London, where he became a key figure in the inner circle directing the war. The work of this body was complemented by the Imperial Conference, meeting under the presidency of the Colonial Secretary, Walter Long. In 1917 the Government of India, along with the self-governing colonies, was invited to participate in this Conference, in contrast to what had happened in 1907; moreover, two Indians came over to London in Delhi's delegation.[77] This innovation paved the way for the Montagu Declaration of August 1917, in which the Indian Secretary, Edwin Montagu, brushing aside Curzon's protests, promised that after the war India would be given greater powers of internal self-government.

The cumulative effect of the various initiatives that took place under the Lloyd George regime were significant. 'Before December 1916', concludes one historian, 'Britain was at war, assisted by her Empire; subsequently the Empire was at war, orchestrated by Britain much as a *primus inter pares*.'[78]

The war stimulated imperial consciousness in a further way. Turkey's entry into the conflict on the side of the Central Powers immediately transformed the war's nature and purpose, so far as London was concerned. Before the end of 1914 Britain, fearing a Turkish attack, had established a Protectorate over Egypt, where a large base was built at Suez. From here British troops later set off to conquer Palestine, an adventurous project in which they were assisted by Bedouin forces, working with the mysterious Colonel T. E. Lawrence, himself the source of much subsequent romanticization of 'Arabia'.

Old imperialist juices flowed again: 'give me Jerusalem as a Christmas present for the British people', Lloyd George told Allenby; and when the latter entered that city on 9 December 1917, the bells of Westminster Abbey were rung for the first time.[79] Through their involvement in Mesopotamia as well as Palestine, the British ended the war as the dominant power in the Middle East. Indeed, at the end of 1918 the Empire was at the zenith of its territorial extent. How could pride in the Empire not have been stimulated by such events? The war's other legacy, a consciousness of shared sacrifice, also strengthened the imperial bond: it is no accident that the Armistice silence, soon to become the central act of remembrance, originated as a South African ceremony, first observed in Cape Town in 1916.[80]

[77] Holland, 'British Empire and Great War', 123.
[78] Ibid. 125.
[79] Ibid. 134.
[80] Devised by the South African magnate Sir Percy Fitzpatrick (B. Nasson, 'Armistice 1915 and 1918: The South African Experience', in Cecil and Liddle (eds.), *Eleventh Hour*, 222).

3. PACIFISTS, PATRIOTS, AND JINGOES

But though there was indeed 'an imperialization of the British polity under the stress of war', such developments took second place to a single-minded desire to defeat Germany. Self-appointed publicists—poets, journalists, university lecturers, and churchmen—invested this objective with deep spiritual significance. Writing to *The Times* in late 1914, the Poet Laureate, Robert Bridges, assured readers that the conflict was 'manifestly a war between Christ and the Devil'. Most church leaders agreed: the Bishop of London, A. F. Winnington-Ingram 'the Bishop of the Battlefields', in his Advent sermon of 1915, hailed the war as 'a great crusade', nay, 'A HOLY WAR', in which the killing of Germans was necessary 'to save the world'.[81] Another cleric, Canon Holmes, similarly linked God's Will with the *patria*:

> Fight for the colours of Christ the King,
> Fight as He fought for you;
> Fight for the Right with all your might,
> Fight for the Red, White, and Blue.[82]

A more secular justification was advanced in academia. In *Why We Are At War: Great Britain's Case* (1914), a group of Oxford historians declared that Britain was fighting 'in the noblest cause for which men can fight', 'the public law of Europe, as a sure shield and buckler of all nations, great and small, and especially the small'.[83] Some intellectuals who before 1914 had been admirers of German 'Kultur' stood firm by their earlier allegiances, suggesting that there were 'two Germanys', an older civilized one as well as the brutal militaristic polity which had unleashed war on Europe.[84] But other academics, including Walter Raleigh, now declared that they had never been enamoured of German scholarship and openly rejoiced at the prospect of an escape from the tyranny of the German footnote![85]

Lloyd George, a subscriber to the 'two Germanys' view, nevertheless presented warfare itself as a purifying force. At the Queen's Hall, on 19 September 1914, he declared:

We have been too comfortable and too indulgent, many, perhaps, too selfish, and the stern hand of Fate has scourged us to an elevation where we can see the great

---

[81] Ferguson, *Pity of War*, 208–9.

[82] A. Marrin, *The Last Crusade: The Church of England and the First World War* (Durham, NC, 1974), 182.

[83] S. Wallace, *War and the Image of Germany: British Academics 1914–1918* (Edinburgh, 1988), 60–2. Less temperate was Ramsay Muir's *Britain's Case Against Germany* (1914).

[84] H. Strachan, *The First World War: Volume One: To Arms* (Oxford, 2001), 1126.

[85] Wallace, *Image of Germany*, 36. At Oxford the Lecturer in German had his salary halved, to make more space for the teaching of French and Italian Literature (Winter, 'Popular Culture', 345).

everlasting things that matter for a nation—the great peaks we had forgotten, of
Honour, Duty, Patriotism, and, clad in glittering white, the great pinnacle of Sacrifice
pointing like a rugged finger to Heaven.[86]

A commonplace of patriotic rhetoric was the claim that the soldier who laid
down his life for his country had made the 'Great Sacrifice', for which the
model was Christ's crucifixion.[87]

Only slightly less exalted in their language were those to whom the war was a
'great game'. For example, many soldiers, in the early phases of the war,
presented 'hunting the Germans' as a jolly, exciting field sport. Even more
common was the invocation of the values learned on the public-school cricket
field. The creator of 'Raffles', the writer E. W. Hornung, expressed it thus in
his poem 'Lord's Leave' (1915):

> Better the cricket here; yet some who tried
> In vain to win a colour while at Eton
> Have found a place upon an England side
> That can't be beaten.[88]

Jessie Pope, prolific purveyor of patriotic uplift in the Northcliffe Press
(innocently unaware of double-entendres), drew a similar analogy:

> Our cricketers have gone 'on tour',
> To make their country's triumph sure.
> They'll take the Kaiser's middle wicket
> And smash it by clean British cricket.[89]

Those who preferred the winter game took inspiration from the famous case of
Captain Nevill, who kicked a football into no-man's land and invited his men to
follow, having offered a prize to the first of his platoon who dribbled a ball into
the German positions—a prize that, not surprisingly, was never claimed.[90]

Though probably only a minority of contemporaries shared these extravagant views, it would be a mistake to dismiss them out of hand. For there is no
getting round the fact that, at least initially, the war was exceedingly popular.

---

[86] Grigg, *Lloyd George*, 166.
[87] Bourne, *Great War*, 230.
[88] Soon afterwards his son was killed at the Front (M. Tozer, 'A Sacred Trinity—Cricket, School,
Empire', in J. A. Mangan (ed.), *The Cultural Bond: Sport, Empire, Society* (London, 1992), 19–20).
[89] 'Cricket—1915', in D. Hibberd and J. Onions, *Poetry of the Great War: An Anthology* (London,
1986), 57–8.
[90] C. Veitch, 'Play up! Play up! and Win the War!: Football, the Nation and the First World War
1914–15', *Journal of Contemporary History*, 20 (1985), 363. The 1st Battalion of the 18th London
Regiment went into action at Loos led by men kicking a football (T. Mason, *Association Football and
English Society 1863–1915* (Brighton, 1980), 255). An officer in charge of a bombing patrol, writes home
of '*new Hand-bombs*—glorious things, just the size and weight of a *Cricket Ball*!' (Tozer, 'Sacred
Trinity', 20).

Even after the initial rush to the colours, men were still coming forward at an average of almost 128,000 a month, and only in late 1915 did the numbers seriously trail away. Almost $2\frac{1}{2}$ million men eventually volunteered to fight.

Motives for enlisting were various. Some men caved in to employer pressure, which was also exerted later against munitions workers who refused to attest.[91] Others may have panicked in the wake of the brief but sharp rise in unemployment that occurred in August and September 1914.[92] There were also those who simply failed to grasp the enormity of the decision they were taking and saw enlistment as a bit of a 'lark'. Many would presumably have found it difficult to assign a precise cause to their conduct. However, it would be unduly cynical to downplay the role of patriotic duty—misguided or otherwise. Can it have been a coincidence that recruitment peaked at the very moment when the German army seemed to be threatening Paris?

Patriotism, admittedly, had its limits. In late 1914 and early 1915 men joined the Territorials in considerable numbers, opting for home rather than imperial service; in March 1915 the War Office had to plug this particular bolt-hole by stopping direct recruiting into the Territorials, and later the Military Service Acts of 1916 obliged all members of that force to take the Imperial Service obligation.[93] The War Office also harboured suspicions of those who, having enrolled in auxiliary groups called Voluntary Training Corps (VTCs), then swaggered around in uniform while claiming that their work and family obligations prevented them from joining the colours. Nor was the desire of the craft unions to preserve their exemption from military service animated purely by a desire to protect trade-union privileges. In other words, many so-called 'shirkers' clearly did *not* embrace the prospect of an early death when called upon to make the 'supreme sacrifice'—which is hardly surprising! But a prudent spirit of self-preservation seldom denoted actual disapproval of the war.

Significantly, all those organizations that castigated Britain's involvement fared badly with the public. The ILP experienced mass resignations when its leaders refused to back the voting of war credits; and though MacDonald and even Hardie held back from out-and-out opposition to the war, by late 1918 membership had fallen to less than 35,000. Moreover, when Hardie died his Merthyr seat was captured in the resulting by-election in November 1915 by a jingo Labour man, C. B. Staunton, who, with strong backing from the South

---

[91] B. Waites, *A Class Society at War: England 1914–1918* (Leamington Spa, 1987), 189–90.

[92] DeGroot, *Blighty*, 47.

[93] I. Beckett, 'The Territorial Force', in Beckett and Simpson (eds.), *Nation in Arms*, 135–7. Those who refused imperial service would be forced to resign, if officers, or else discharged—in either case, becoming liable to conscription. The 1916 Acts also removed from pre-war Territorials the right to be discharged at the end of their term of engagement.

Wales miners, easily beat the official Labour candidate. No wonder that individuals hostile to the war on the whole kept their heads down.

Pockets of dissidence did, of course, exist. In December 1916, in response to Bethmann-Hollweg's peace-feelers, the British peace movement presented a petition to the new Prime Minister calling for a negotiated end to the fighting, which was signed by over 200,000 individuals.[94] But when 'Stop-the-War' candidates entered the electoral arena they performed poorly, attracting far fewer votes than maverick jingoes whose complaint was that the war was not being conducted with sufficient ferocity. The British Socialist Party (BSP), the only established political party to call for an immediate end to hostilities, had a mere 6,435 members in 1917. As for revolutionary defeatism, this was virtually non-existent on mainland Britain, except in Glasgow, where its main spokesman was John Maclean—nationalist Ireland predictably provided more fertile soil for this political position. Even militantly class-conscious Clydeside shop stewards on occasions suspended industrial action so as not to embarrass the Allies on the eve of an important offensive. And, as we have seen, the German Spring Offensive led to a renewal of the industrial truce and sparked off a new outburst of heated patriotism across the entire social and political spectrum.

Moreover, although it later staged a mild recovery under the leadership of the Revd Herbert Dunnico, a Baptist minister, the Edwardian 'peace movement' all but disintegrated in August 1914; the President of the Peace Society, Jack Pease, member of a distinguished Quaker family, actually stayed on in government as President of the Board of Education.[95] In fact, by 1917 between one-quarter and one-third of all eligible Friends had enlisted,[96] in defiance of the Quakers' 'peace testimony', which affirmed the sanctity of human life. All the same, despite many defections, the Society of Friends provided money and leadership to all of the organizations which, in one way or another, held out against the prevailing bellicose clamour.

The 'pacifists' were, in any case, a highly disparate group, divided over some very fundamental issues. For example, some adherents objected to all wars, others only to the current one. The Quakers, the Christadelphians, and the members of the oecumenical Fellowship of Reconciliation (founded in January 1915), took their stand on Christian principle. Socialists, by contrast, were more inclined to argue that the working class had nothing to gain from a military contest being fought by the 'ruling classes' in pursuit of imperialist interests. Of the latter, some later demonstrated through their enthusiasm for

[94] K. Robbins, *The Abolition of War: The 'Peace Movement' in Britain 1914–1919* (Cardiff, 1976), 114.

[95] M. Ceadel, *Semi-Detached Idealists: The British Peace Movement and International Relations, 1854–1945* (Oxford, 2002).

[96] Robbins, *Abolition*, 31–3.

Russia's new Bolshevik government that they were more than willing to condone the use of violence, if harnessed to a revolutionary agenda.

Moreover, antagonism between working-class socialists and the 'middle-class peace men' ('dirty dogs', one trade unionist called them) was never far below the surface. As F. W. Hirst, the financial pacifist, found in late 1917 and early 1918, it proved equally difficult to engineer an alliance between Lord Lansdowne and the Labour Movement—not least because 'Lansdowne wanted peace to conserve the old order: radicals and Socialists wanted peace in order to change it'.[97]

Finally, 'pacifism' encompassed what, in reality, were three logically distinct political strategies: stopping the war ('peace by negotiation'); defending the position of the conscientious objecters; and making plans for a new international order from which war would be banished. In some respects these campaigns happily complemented one another; on the other hand, many protesters subscribed to one or two of them, but not to all three. For example, although the Union of Democratic Control, with its commitment to wresting jurisdiction over foreign policy from diplomats and politicans and entrusting it to 'the people',[98] implied a strong criticism of Grey, it did not actually exclude from membership those who felt that, once hostilities had broken out, the government should be supported in its policies. Morel himself really did loathe the war in all its aspects, as well as holding Grey personally culpable for it, a case he argued in his 1916 pamphlet *Truth and the War*. But Henderson, a founder member of the UDC's General Committee, went on to serve as a wartime Cabinet minister. Indeed, the UDC programme was later, in large measure, adopted by the official 'pro-war' Labour Party, and parts of it eventually became incorporated within the government's own War Aims.

The idea of a League of Nations similarly brought together those who opposed the war and those who went along with it. In May 1915 a League of Nations Society grew out of the activities of an earlier group, headed by Lord Bryce. Though its original officers were mainstream Liberal politicians, it soon attracted intellectuals highly critical of the war project, such as G. Lowes Dickinson, H. N. Brailsford, and J. A. Hobson. But from June 1918 onwards the Society's activities were being paralleled by the League of Free Nations, chaired by the classical scholar Gilbert Murray, whose executive included J. A. Spender, H. G. Wells, and two prominent associates of Lloyd George, David Davies and Charles McCurdy, backed by such ultra-patriots as Garvin. After difficult negotiations, the two organizations united on 10 October to form the 'League of Nations Union', at a meeting chaired by Edward Grey—of all

[97] Ibid. 152   [98] See Ch. 18.

people. By this time Lloyd George and President Wilson, albeit in vague language, were underwriting the idea of a 'League of Nations', and there was even a League of Nations section inside the Foreign Office. No wonder pacifists proper quickly began to harbour doubts about the whole concept, particularly when the suggestion was made that the League needed to be given 'sanctions' to enforce its will.

The one unequivocally anti-war organization to emerge in Britain was the No-Conscription Fellowship. Founded in late 1914 by Clifford Allen, an ILPer who had earlier been the general manager of Labour's newspaper the *Daily Citizen*, this was an organization of young men pledged to resist all war service. It drew support from the ILP (Snowden, Fenner Brockway, Dr Alfred Salter), the Society of Friends (Edward Grubb), and from the radical intelligentsia (Bertrand Russell), as well as benefiting from the organizational skills of its secretary Catherine Marshall, formerly of the NUWSS. Once conscription had been introduced, the Fellowship provided protection for the 16,500 men who had declared their unwillingness to enlist on grounds of conscience (whether political or religious).

In fact, the tribunals, to which most of these men were referred, gave some form of exemption to over 80 per cent of the 'conscientious objectors', while 90 per cent accepted an alternative form of national service—either in the Non-Combatant Corps, or as part of the Home Office scheme, or in some other activities deemed by the tribunals to be helping the war effort. This left some 6,000 men who refused to accept the tribunals' authority, of whom a hard core of 1,298 'absolutists' received custodial sentences, often accompanied by great hardship: ten died as a result of their prison treatment, and others suffered a deterioration in their health, among them Allen, who had never been a fit man.[99] The 'conchies', as they were derisively called, were further stigmatized under the terms of the 1918 Representation of the People Act by being denied the vote for five years (starting in 1921), unless they could prove that they had performed wartime work of national importance. Civil servants who had been absolutists were refused readmission to their old posts.

Britain was the only combatant nation, apart from the United States, which so much as recognized the existence of conscientious objectors during the Great War. But the amendments to the Military Service Acts which made provision for their special treatment (moved by the Quaker MPs Arnold Rowntree and Thomas Edmund Harvey) were poorly drafted and open to differing interpretations from the local tribunals, and this led to some harsh

---

[99] Bourne, *Great War*, 212. Cf. J. Rae, *Conscience and Politics* (Oxford, 1970), 226–7: only 9 or 10, which out of total prison population of some 1,200 COs over three years was a lower death-rate than for prisoners as a whole.

decisions. But the sufferings of the small number of 'absolutists' such as Stephen Hobhouse, who obstinately (or courageously) courted martyrdom by refusing to co-operate with the authorities in any way, has rather obscured the fact of their atypicality. The largest single bloc of COs consisted of 1,400 Christadelphians, who rested their case on a literal reading of the Bible, not on any kind of political argument: these men, more passive than pacifist, did not appear before the tribunals at all, and provided they were not forced to observe military discipline, were quite happy to do other kinds of war-related work, including even employment in munitions factories.

By the end of 1917 the leaders of the No-Conscription Fellowship (whose membership peaked at about 5,500) privately acknowledged that their movement was up a cul-de-sac; no one felt more bitter about this than Russell, who took over its chairmanship during Allen's imprisonment. Internal wrangling went along with growing state repression. Russell, whose stand on the war had already cost him his Fellowship at Trinity College, Cambridge (an act of petty vindictiveness), was sent to prison for six months in 1918 for publishing 'seditious' material, rather as Morel had been in September 1917.

But, as has justly been observed, the courage of these dissenters has been more honoured by posterity than it was by their contemporaries: indeed, the hostility which they engendered may, paradoxically, have stiffened the resolve of the majority of their countrymen to see the war through to its conclusion.[100] In any case, the total number of conscientious objectors amounted to only 0.33 per cent of the men in uniform: Parliament and government was amazed that conscription had encountered so little opposition. Moreover, the dissenters often ruefully conceded the absurdity of their position, with socialists invoking the international solidarity of a working class which existed only in their imaginations, while the radical democrats were proposing that the safeguarding of peace should be in the hands of a 'people' who, to quote MacDonald, were 'ready to dance around bonfires to heap them up and to fan them into flames'.[101]

In fact, officialdom had much less to fear from outright opponents of the war than from 'troublemakers' within the industrial working class. The Special Commissioners investigating Industrial Unrest in 1917 uncovered great dissatisfaction over alleged profiteering, high rents, and food shortages. But this dissatisfaction was grounded in a desire for 'fair play' and the not-unjustified suspicion that necessary sacrifices were not being equitably spread across the community. Even that inveterate conspiracy-theorist Basil Thomson of Scotland Yard grudgingly accepted as much, informing the War Cabinet in late 1918 that, despite much 'grousing', the working class was still fundamentally loyal.

---

[100] Bourne, *Great War*, 212–13.   [101] Robbins, *Abolition*, 63.

After a spell spent in 'Blighty' consorting with the likes of Bertrand Russell, Siegfried Sassoon published his famous 'protest' in *The Times*. But disaffection among serving officers and men never seriously threatened Britain's capacity to keep on fighting. In early 1918 the Calais censor, worried lest news of shortages at home might be affecting military morale, made a careful examination of the letters which troops were sending home and found a great deal of grumbling on the food question, but, like an earlier survey by the Directorate of Secret Intelligence held in mid-September 1917, discovered no sign of serious disaffection with the war effort as such.[102] Very few servicemen, however warweary, wanted the fighting to be called off in circumstances where Germany could claim a victory.

Critics of the war, then and since, have ascribed this sort of acquiescent patriotism to the manipulation of the gullible masses by the government's propaganda agencies. It is certainly true that the Parliamentary Recruiting Committee (PRC), which drew together MPs from all the parties, including the Irish Nationalists and mainstream Labour, worked tirelessly to get across its message, eventually sending out 50 million posters and other publications, as well as hosting countless rallies, some 340 of which were addressed by the demagogue Horatio Bottomley. This must have had some effect. However, it is worth noting that the first, dramatic surge in recruiting actually took place before the PRC was established.

In fact, the government was slow to see the importance of propaganda or even to accept its legitimacy. The three presidents of the PRC happened to be Asquith, Bonar Law, and Henderson, but the organization itself purported not to be an 'official' one. The government's first direct initiative was taken in secret, when in September 1914 it established a bureau at Wellington House, under C. F. G. Masterman, which it entrusted with presenting the Allied case. But Wellington House directed its early propaganda almost entirely at public opinion in the *neutral* countries, especially the United States. Moreover, its approach was austerely intellectual and elitist, and largely took the form of encouraging and subsidizing the likes of Arnold Bennett, Conan Doyle, Galsworthy, Thomas Hardy, Masefield, Newbolt, G. M. Trevelyan, and H. G. Wells—famous literary figures who were expected to put a high-minded gloss on Britain's war activities.[103]

Admittedly, at its second meeting, on 7 September, Wellington House brought together most of the prominent national newspaper editors; this

---

[102] Earlier the War Office and the Ministry of Food had sent out teams of speakers to France to remove troops' 'misunderstandings' (Waites, 'The Government of the Home Front and the "Moral Economy" of the Working Class', in Liddle (ed.), *Home Fires*, 190).

[103] All these writers, and more besides, attended the initial meeting on 2 September; Kipling and Quiller-Couch, though not present, indicated their support.

presaged a new phase in the propaganda campaign. But press management, for many months to come, was still mainly a matter of ensuring that newspapers did not unwittingly divulge important information to the enemy. Hence the establishment of the Press Bureau, under the direction of, first F. E. Smith, and later of Lord Buckmaster. But this organization could only recommend prosecutions to the Service Departments if it thought that DORA regulations had been infringed,[104] and most newspaper proprietors and editors found its sporadic interventions irksome and even counter-productive. In practice, the press largely censored itself: Northcliffe, for example, did not divulge the movements of the BEF until it had safely arrived at its destination, and he never allowed his papers to criticize the Gallipoli campaign, however much he may have fumed in private. For this reason, the 'D-Notice' system, which was later introduced to warn newspapers off 'sensitive' topics, was only sporadically employed.

There were indeed a few occasions when Whitehall stepped in because it felt that press comment was mischievously undermining civilian morale. Thus the Conservative *Globe* was suppressed in November 1915 for printing a story about Kitchener's alleged resignation (to the delight of Liberals), while exports of the *Nation* were suspended in April 1917 (to the delight of Conservatives). Later the *Morning Post* and its correspondent, Repington, were each fined £100 for revealing details of the general reserve scheme.[105] By the end of the war some ministers, Auckland Geddes, for example, had also become adept at getting their point of view over to the public by means of selective leaks to the London newspapers.[106] But Fleet Street never became 'controlled' in any systematic way.

This may have been because several ministries had been quick to develop their own information services. Yet it is surely significant that a separate Department of Information, under John Buchan, was not set up until February 1917, and it only became a full ministry, under Beaverbrook, a year later. Worried, perhaps unnecessarily, by what it saw as flagging morale, the government also established a National War Aims Committee in June 1917, for the better co-ordination of existing work; this body issued propaganda literature, and sponsored speeches designed to shame the 'shirkers' and dissenters, while praising the 'sacrifices' being made by the patriotic.[107]

By the middle of the war state propaganda had progressed way beyond anything that could have been envisaged in August 1914. No longer much

[104] C. Lovelace, 'British Press Censorship During the First World War', in G. Boyce et al., *Newspaper History From the Seventeenth Century To the Present Day* (London, 1978), 310–13.
[105] Ibid. 313.
[106] K. Middlemas, *Politics in Industrial Society: The Experience of the British System Since 1911* (London, 1979; 1980 edn.), 131.
[107] Bourne, *Great War*, 203–4.

concerned with influencing the 'thinking classes', the Department of Information now made use of a wide variety of populist devices, including pamphlets, posters, and, increasingly, film. The Ministry of Information later had a Cinema Branch, which produced 700 propaganda films in all, and boldly employed the latest technology available.

But how effective was such propaganda in generating support for the war? The confused responses to the government-sponsored film *The Battle of the Somme* illustrates the difficulties that the government faced. Released in August 1916 and shown in cinemas all round the country, this famous film possibly achieved attendances of 20 million in the first six weeks, reaching over half of the domestic population.[108] Its most famous scene, that of Tommies going over the top, is now known to have been faked—though probably not with a view to deceive. Yet, by the standards of the day, the film provided civilians with a grippingly realistic view of trench warfare: indeed, its shots of dead soldiers (most of them Germans) led to an animated public debate about whether or not such horrors should be gawped at from the comfort of a cinema seat. Partly because of its novelty value (later films in roughly the same idiom enjoyed far less success), *The Battle of the Somme* clearly involved the civilian population emotionally in what was happening on the Western Front; but, at the same time, it elicited reactions so diverse that its main impact may simply have been to confirm members of the audience in whatever view of the war they had originally held.

In some respects official propaganda could even be a self-defeating activity. For example, the Ministry of Information perhaps had, on balance, a divisive impact, thanks to the unsavoury reputation of its director, Lord Beaverbrook. Many Conservatives seem to have been less worried about the spread of industrial unrest and pacifism than they were about the emergence of a newfangled agency whose real purpose, they suspected, was the entrenching of Lloyd George in power. Others feared that, by stuffing his Ministry with pressmen, Beaverbrook represented a threat to the independence of Fleet Street—one of those essential liberties which the British had ostensibly gone to war to protect. More fundamentally still, propaganda was often attacked for being somehow 'un-English'—significantly, the British always spoke about 'Information', not 'Propaganda'.[109] Faced by all of these protests, Lloyd George promised to dissolve the Ministry of Information almost the minute that war ended—and this was one of the promises that he kept.

[108] N. Reeves, 'Through the Eye of the Camera', in Cecil and Liddle (eds.), *Facing Armageddon*, 782–4.
[109] S. Badsey and P. M. Taylor, 'The Experience of Manipulation: Propaganda in Press and Radio', in P. Liddle, J. Bourne, and I. Whitehead (eds.), *The Great World War 1914–45: Volume 2: The Peoples' Experience* (London, 2000), 49.

But, for very much the same reasons, many pressmen were reluctant to jump into bed with ministers and their officials. Northcliffe, in particular, proved very hard to 'anchor', and only belatedly agreed to take on public office, not wanting to destroy the reputation of his newspapers by appearing as a government stooge. Of course, like other influential figures in Fleet Street, Northcliffe had always been available to politicians and soldiers who wished him to render them help. In particular, Haig—belying his pretence of being a simple, 'unpolitical' soldier—had quickly become adept at buttering up pressmen, Gwynne of the *Morning Post* and Maxse of the *National Review* being only two of the prominent editors who could generally be relied upon to present the view of the world that was entertained at GHQ.

But Northcliffe had learnt, from his disastrous attempt to drive Kitchener from office in May 1915, that he dare not get seriously out of step with his readership. If the press generally took a 'patriotic' line—for example, by avoiding pictures of dead soldiers, by giving a rosy account of British offensives, or by castigating pacifists and slackers—this was because it thought this to be the commercially and ethically right line to take. Patriotic propaganda was thus usually more effective when undertaken by freelances—be they pressmen, bishops, dons, or poets.

In any case, it is arguable that German behaviour constituted the most effective propaganda agency of all. In the early months of the war the German invasion of Belgium, the barbaric treatment of Louvain, and the naval bombardment of East Coast towns all created intense indignation. This set a pattern, in that, whenever it seemed that enthusiasm for the war was flagging, the German army or government did something to confirm the British population in its belief that it was engaged in a righteous cause: for example, unprecedented barbarisms such as the use of gas at first Ypres and the Zeppelin and, later the Gotha, aerial bombing raids on civilian targets. Unrestricted U-boat warfare, leading to the deaths of so many civilian passengers and merchant seamen, created particular anger—not least among Havelock Wilson's Seamen's Union, the most fiercely anti-German of all labour organizations. Finally, many of those in Britain who had started to look favourably on the idea of a compromise peace reassessed their position after seeing the brutal terms which a triumphant Germany had imposed, first upon Romania, and then, even more dramatically, upon Russia through the Treaty of Brest-Litovsk.[110]

The sinking of the *Lusitania* in May 1915 sparked off serious anti-German rioting in many towns, particularly in Keighley, where law and order broke down for several days. No further disturbances occurred on quite this scale,

---

[110] Keegan may be right to call the Great War a civilized war, but that is only by comparison with the Second World War, the horrors of which could not have been foreseen at the time.

but renewed anti-German outbursts followed the death of Kitchener, which was popularly blamed upon German saboteurs, and again after the Gotha air raids of July 1917, which left fifty-seven dead and 193 injured in north London. When tempers became thus badly frayed all foreigners were liable to be attacked, amongst them Russian Jews, unfairly accused of evading military service.[111] An atmosphere also developed in which rumours of entirely fictional German 'atrocities' could quickly spread—for example, the widely believed story that the Germans had set up 'corpse-converting' factories. Many of these rumours received an undeserved credence from the slapdash methods and gullibility of the 1915 Commission of Inquiry into alleged German atrocities in Belgium, headed by James Bryce, a Gladstonian Liberal and a former university teacher of whom better might have been expected.[112]

Frustrated that the war was not moving swiftly towards an Allied victory, many people in Britain gave a partial backing to the rabble-rousers—men far less scrupulous than Bryce. Leading the mob was the former MP (and arch-swindler) Horatio Bottomley. In his journal *John Bull*, on 15 May 1915, he declared a 'blood feud' against the Germans, arguing that 'you cannot naturalise an unnatural beast—a human abortion—a hellish freak. But you *can* exterminate it.' The Germans (or 'Germ-huns', as he preferred to call them), should, he said, wear distinctive badges and be deported.[113] This sort of Germanophobia developed into a belief in the existence of a mysterious conspiracy, the 'Hidden Hand', linking Berlin to traitors sheltering on British soil. Ellis Powell of the *Financial Times* gave voice to this fantasy, and so did the incorrigible Arnold White. Swelling the chorus of hatred were Emmeline and Christabel Pankhurst, who in October 1915 renamed their paper *Britannia*, and then, in November 1917, founded the 'Women's Party', an organization which had little to say about women but a great deal to say about the beastliness of Germans. In short, patriotism was now being measured by the virulence with which the enemy was attacked and vilified, individually and collectively.

Early victims of such paranoia were those of German descent or those with German-sounding names. Naturally Lord Battenberg had to resign his post of First Sea Lord, and, ironically, there were those, including the Pankhursts, who also called for the sacking of Eyre Crowe because of his German connections.[114] Those in high social positions were also vulnerable. Edward VII's old

---

[111] C. Holmes, *Anti-Semitism in British Society 1876–1939* (London, 1979), 126–36. Although in places the police did little to control the rampaging mobs, in general they upheld law and order, while the judiciary acted fairly and firmly in sentencing.

[112] P. Panayi, 'Anti-German Riots in Britain During the First World War', in P. Panayi (ed.), *Racial Violence in Britain in the Nineteenth and Twentieth Centuries* (Leicester, 1996 edn.), 65–91.

[113] Ibid. 73.

[114] On Crowe, see Ch. 13.

friend Ernest Cassel, born in Hamburg, was one of many wealthy Jews pressurized into issuing 'Loyalty Letters' to *The Times*. Ridiculous charges were brought against the likes of Sir John Brunner (a man of Swiss descent), who stood accused of signalling to the German fleet from his home at Overstrand on the north Norfolk Coast. The conduct of Sir Edgar Speyer, who, along with the German side of his family, really did show sympathy for the Central Powers, gave a rough justification to such attacks on the 'cosmopolitan financiers'.

The other targets of jingoistic hatred were prominent Liberals who, it seemed, had shown insufficient awareness of the German danger before 1914 and were thought to be soft on Germans. In the early months of the war the Conservative leadership took advantage of the atmosphere created by the likes of Arnold White in the *Daily Express* to harass the Home Secretary, McKenna, for not arresting enemy aliens wholesale. And when the first Coalition was formed in May, Bonar Law succeeded in excluding from office Haldane, who had been pilloried in the right-wing press and libelled in outrageous ways—this lifelong bachelor was said, for example, to have a secret German wife, which was nonsense (though was it entirely sensible of him to have called his dog 'Kaiser'?) After the change of regime in December 1916 Asquith himself came under fire (*Britannia* called him on one occasion 'the flunky and toady and tool of the Kaiser'),[115] while his unpopular wife Margot was accused of playing tennis with German POWs and sending them hampers from Fortnum & Mason![116]

Even had it wanted to, no British government could have entirely ignored the often hysterical anti-German mood, which was sustained by the publication of books such as John Buchan's best-seller *The Thirty-Nine Steps* (1915). On the outbreak of war British intelligence agencies swiftly rounded up twenty-two German agents; twelve of the thirty-one Germans who fell into the state's hands were eventually executed. Another 201 people were detained on suspicion of being in contact with the enemy. To deal with such problems, MI5 was formed in January 1916 out of earlier intelligence bodies.[117] Meanwhile fears of sabotage gave rise to a force of special constables who guarded bridges, tunnels, gasworks, and canals.

More controversially, enemy aliens resident in Britain, who numbered between 70,000 and 75,000, most of them Germans, also came under close

---

[115] The Pankhursts also attacked Robertson, calling him 'the tool and accomplice of the traitors, Grey, Asquith, and Cecil', language which nearly got *Britannia* suppressed (D. Mitchell, *Women on the Warpath* (London, 1966), 62, 77).

[116] S. E. Koss, *Lord Haldane: Scapegoat For Liberalism* (New York and London, 1969), has many examples of wartime xenophobia.

[117] Another intelligency agency, MI9, was employing a staff of 4,861 by the Armistice.

surveillance. The Aliens Restriction Act of 5 August stipulated that those of military age should be interned, and about 32,000 duly were; others faced repatriation.[118] By the end of September 1914 10,500 German civilians were being housed in internment camps—arguably not a sensible use of scarce resources at a time when so many of Kitchener's volunteers were still being accommodated in tents. But this restriction did not satisfy the Pankhursts, who then called for the revocation of the naturalization of *all* Germans. In August 1918 a petition bearing 1,250,000 signatures, calling for stronger action against aliens, was dispatched to the Prime Minister's residence after a huge rally had been held in Hyde Park. The government, bowing before the storm, gave itself powers to revoke German naturalization papers. Meanwhile the process of repatriation continued—by 1919 there were only 22,254 Germans residents in Britain, compared with 53,324 in 1911.[119]

Most German-owned properties in Britain were also confiscated, while the Trading-With-The-Enemy Act of late 1914 attempted to sever commercial ties with the Central Powers. This proved a more difficult enterprise than its authors anticipated, but popular xenophobia pushed the government in January 1916 into further trading restrictions, which might otherwise not have been implemented. The passing of the Paris Resolutions in December 1915 also served as an earnest of the government's intention of extending the boycott of German goods even after the cessation of war—in an attempt to prevent Germany ever recovering her former economic position. Lloyd George's call, during the later stages of the 1918 election campaign, for German indemnities and reparations was thus merely the culmination of a long-sustained vendetta. All of these anti-German initiatives, it should be noted, seem to have commanded overwhelming popular support.

Governmental attempts at appeasing the Germanophobes, however, could never be entirely successful. Bottomley might have made himself useful to the government by getting the Clyde shipwrights to call off their strike in the spring of 1915, and by making successful morale-boosting tours to the Western Front and to the Grand Fleet. But although he thought that, backed by Northcliffe, he was about to be given Cabinet office in early 1918, Lloyd George held back—and wisely so, since Bottomley was later found guilty of fraudulent conversion on twenty-three counts and sentenced to seven years' penal servitude.

While, from the government's point of view, Bottomley had his uses, the same could not be said of that other maverick, Pemberton Billing, who, by

---

[118] J. C. Bird, *Control of Enemy Aliens in Great Britain, 1914–1918* (New York, 1986), 6, 9, 199.
[119] Panayi, 'Anti-German Riots', 65–6.

linking his 'Germany Must be Destroyed' message to a number of genuine material grievances (for example, food hoarding and profiteering), became an increasing nuisance to the authorities after his election as an Independent MP in May 1916. True, Billing lost some of his influence during the following year, once Smuts had recommended the establishment of an independent air service, because Billing had himself been urging an independent air service, a call to which the government had initially seemed unresponsive.[120] But he was still able to make waves, notably through the famous Pemberton Billing Trial in the early summer of 1918.[121]

Billing's acquittal at the hands of the jury at the end of this most farcical of trials led his followers, who called themselves the 'Vigilantes', to behave in ever-more outrageous ways. At the Clapham by-election in May 1918 their candidate, the anti-Semitic H. H. Beamish (later a prominent Fascist), gave the Conservative a run for his money in a straight fight, and the following month, at Finsbury East, Billing's associate Captain H. S. Spencer featured in a contest so rowdy that it attracted the attention of the Intelligence Services—who half-suspected that 'Vigilante' was somehow in German pay. If this sort of behaviour was a manifestation of patriotism, ministers must have wished that it was not in such abundant supply.[122]

Wartime tension and despair thus produced irrational behaviour among Britons of all backgrounds. But among the bulk of working-class men and women it was probably only a minority who responded with approval to the buffoonery of Billing. It may also be significant that raucously pro-war labour organizations, such as Victor Fisher's British Workers' League, made little progress, despite the fact that its paper had a circulation of 30,000—no doubt because class-conscious workers knew how heavily dependent it was for cash and support on the likes of Lord Milner. Stoicism and wry, self-deprecating humour were the postures more commonly found—whether in 'Blighty' or among the private soldiers serving in the front line—the very reaction that was perhaps to be expected from what one historian has called a 'relatively static, tradition-regulated people'.[123]

Patriotism, then, could take many different forms, just as 'dissidence' was never a homogeneous thing. But it remains true that a sense of national unity had survived the tensions of the war years, however precariously at times, and in some respects emerged in strengthened form. 'God Save the King' started to

[120] M. Paris, *Winged Warfare: The Literature and Theory of Aerial Warfare in Britain, 1859–1917* (Manchester, 1992), 79.
[121] See Ch. 18.
[122] G. R. Searle, *Corruption in British Politics, 1895–1930* (Oxford, 1987), 260–8.
[123] D. Winter, *Death's Men*, 234.

be sung regularly at public entertainments and events during the war—as it continued to be for most of the following century. All the same, the structure of British society, basically intact, had been changed during the war in many important respects.

CHAPTER 20

War and the Reshaping of Identities

1. GENDER AND GENERATION

We have seen that during the war the birth-rate declined: from 23.9 per thousand in 1914 to 19.4 in 1918. Partly in response to this decline, but more generally because the saving of infant lives seemed necessary to replace the carnage of the battlefields, great efforts were made by both government and private agencies to provide support for the expectant mother and her children. Indeed, this seemed nothing less than 'a patriotic and humane duty and the best way to share in tomorrow's national defence'.[1]

However, in the short run these initiatives had a limited effect. There was a drop in the standardized death-rate per million women for complications of pregnancy from 181 in 1914 to 125 in 1918,[2] but this decline was partly the result of the falling birth-rate. Nor was war particularly good for babies and small children. In London the infantile death-rate actually rose in 1915, thanks to a measles epidemic, and though it fell in 1916, it rose again in the last two years of the war.[3] Child mortality (affecting those aged 1 to 4) also rose, not only in 1915 but also in 1918, when influenza, measles, and whooping cough took a heavy toll. The main benefits of the public-health reforms were only to be felt in the 1920s, when the mortality-rate for children fell below the level it had been at before 1914.

For slightly older children and for adolescents the war came as a mixed blessing. For many it presented an exciting challenge. The youth movements threw themselves into the fray with enthusiasm. While most scoutmasters and Rovers enlisted, boy scouts too young for military service were encouraged to acts as orderlies, guards, despatch-runners, and to give air-raid warnings. The Sea Scouts, at Kitchener's request, acted as auxiliary coastguards—their

---

[1] C. Rollet, 'The "Other War" I: Protecting Public Health', in J. Winter and J. -L. Robert (eds.), *Capital Cities at War: Paris, London, Berlin 1914–1919* (Cambridge, 1997), 439. See more, below.

[2] J. M. Winter, *The Great War and the British People* (London, 1985), 132–3.

[3] Ibid. 499.

attempts to identify and report to the authorities those engaged in spying and sabotage may not have been quite as useful![4] After Baden-Powell's young wife Olave had ousted his sister Agnes, the Girl Guides dramatically increased their numbers, under the stimulus of voluntary war work: collecting sphagnum moss (for use in first aid, as a dressing), making sandbags, teaching English to Belgian refugees, and so on.[5]

On the other hand, the war seriously disrupted educational provision. In August 1917 the President of the Board of Education, H. A. L. Fisher, told the Commons that 600,000 children had been put 'prematurely' to work,[6] a consequence of school attendance orders being left unenforced so that adolescent labour could be utilized in agriculture and industry: many teenagers were earning up to £2 a week in the munitions factories. Fisher's Education Bill, which received its third reading in July 1918, was supposed to rectify this setback, but its ambitious proposals could only come into effect once the war had ended—assuming that post-war governments had the will to finance educational extension. Meanwhile the number of children attending secondary school fell during the first year of the war, before rising again. (The universities were far more savagely disrupted: Oxford had 3,181 undergraduates in 1914, but only 491 in 1917.[7])

The war also saw the eruption of a minor wave of adolescent crime, which contemporaries blamed upon the weakening of family structures. While working in the munitions factories, some mothers boarded out their children. The absence from home of so many fathers may also have had an unsettling effect on boys, who were thus deprived of a male role model. Whatever the reason, it must be significant that in Bath, for example, there was a 284 per cent rise in juvenile crime at a time when the general crime-rate was falling.[8]

For many young women, horizons opened out after 1914. Well-paid munitionettes were commonly seen smoking cigarettes, spending their money on entertainments, acting boisterously, and using 'risqué' language. Such females ('flappers', as they were already being known) also tended to wear short skirts, to crop their hair, to don lipstick, and to come and go without the protection of chaperones. These developments caused widespread dismay, not least among older women anxious to preserve traditional notions of feminine delicacy and decorum. 'The war', lamented Louise Creighton, 'has produced a new type of

[4] J. Springhall, *Youth, Empire and Society: British Youth Movements, 1883–1940* (London, 1977), 152–3.

[5] R. A. Voeltz, 'The Antidote to "Khaki Fever"? The Expansion of the British Girl Guides during the First World War', *Journal of Contemporary History*, 27 (1992), 628–30.

[6] G. J. DeGroot, *Blighty: British Society in the Era of the Great War* (London, 1996), 220–1.

[7] A. Marwick, *The Deluge: British Society and the First World War* (London, 1965), 245.

[8] DeGroot, *Blighty*, 221.

girl, absolutely independent, very often wild and undisciplined [who]...
laughs and screams in the streets [and] is eager for any fun and nonsense."[9]
The expanding Girl Guide movement, it was hoped, would direct this adolescent energy into more respectable channels.

But it was young men who were the war's main victims: these, after all, were
the most likely to enlist,[10] the least likely to be protected as a result of working
in a 'reserved occuption', and, once in uniform, the most likely to be exposed to
danger. The costly offensives fought by the BEF in 1918 involved large
numbers of soldiers who were little more than boys. Mortality may have
been 6.3 per cent of all males aged 15–49, but this masks a much higher
death-rate among the younger cohorts: some 80 per cent of all casualties
occurred among the under-thirties.[11] Casualty-rates were especially high for
junior officers who had to lead their men over the top, and these tended to be
younger rather than senior military personnel.

Admittedly, even generals, especially in the early stages of the war, ran a
severe risk of being killed: seventy brigadier-generals and above were killed or
died of their wounds.[12] It would also be unfair to imply that older men
invariably escaped war's horrors. Some positively courted danger: for example,
C. E. Montague, who, when war broke out, was 47 years old with a wife and
seven dependent children, rushed to enlist. Married men, on average older
than bachelors, were indeed exempted under the terms of the first of the
National Service Acts. This did not stop them from volunteering in
droves—cynics said, to escape their wives! But, in any case, the second
Military Service Act removed their exemption, and in 1918 the upper age for
compulsory military service was raised to 50 (55 for doctors).

Nevertheless, it remains a startling fact that, of males aged between 19 and
22 when war broke out, over one in three did not live to see the Armistice, and
that war-related mortality was greatest at the age of 20.[13] 'Soon there will only
be the middle-aged left', lamented the composer Vaughan Williams.[14] The war
also created an emotional chasm between those who donned the King's uniform and those too old to do so, leading to resentment on the part of the former
and guilt on the part of the latter.

[9] P. Levine, ' "Walking the Streets in a Way No Decent Woman Should": Women Police in World War I', *Journal of Modern History*, 66 (1994), 51.

[10] Nearly half of all men aged 19–25 had enlisted before the coming of conscription, 83% of them being single (B. Waites, *A Class Society at War: England 1914–1918* (Leamington Spa, 1987), 188).

[11] D. Winter, *Death's Men: Soldiers of the Great War* (London, 1978), 226.

[12] K. Simpson, 'The Officers', in I. F. W. Beckett and K. Simpson (eds.), *A Nation in Arms: A Social Study of the British Army in the First World War* (Manchester, 1985), 86.

[13] J. Keegan, *The First World War* (London, 1998), 453; Winter, *Great War*, 79, 82.

[14] Cited in T. Wilson, *Myriad Faces of War: Britain and the Great War 1914–1918* (Oxford, 1986: Cambridge, 1988 edn.), 346.

Although fourteen MPs were killed or died of their wounds,[15] the politicians who took the decisions that consigned so many of the young to death and injury mainly came from a generation personally spared the ordeal of military service. Agonies of anxiety over the fate of their sons, however, could not be avoided. Ministers so situated reacted in a variety of ways. Lloyd George, while calling on the nation to make the supreme sacrifice, used his influence to keep his two boys in cushy staff posts, as ADCs to generals.[16] But most of his colleagues suffered the agony of bereavement: Asquith, Bonar Law, Lansdowne, and Walter Long all lost at least one of their sons. So did Rudyard Kipling, the author, after 1918, of the following epitaph on a dead soldier:

> If any question why we died,
> Tell them, because our fathers lied.

One can only guess at the agony of self-reproach that underlay these bitter words. Here, too, lay the source of the later myth of a 'Lost Generation', a cohort of supposedly extra-gifted young men who, had they lived, would somehow have averted the errors made by inter-war British governments.[17]

The very elderly, whatever their gender, also suffered disproportionately, in Britain as in all other combatant countries, mainly because they had a low priority in the competition for scarce resources. Hospital beds, for example, were emptied of long-term patients to make way for war casualties. As a result, well before the onset of the influenza pandemic, the elderly were dying earlier, on average, than in pre-war days, reversing the long-term trend towards greater longevity.[18] It seems that inadequate heating and poorly cooked food, brought about by fuel shortages, were partly responsible for this development, while the increased incidence of death from heart disease cannot have been unconnected with physical isolation and the strain of bereavement and of being separated from other family members.

But for men in general the war did at least have the consolation of legitimizing conventional notions of masculinity. The feminist Edith Picton-Turbervill acknowledged this when she said: 'For men duty was clear, not so for women.'[19] Fighting remained an almost entirely male activity. It was with some reluctance that the Service Ministries sanctioned the use of female

---

[15] 9 Unionists, 4 Liberals, and 1 Irish Nationalist: 2.1% of all MPs. Their ages ranged from C. T. Mills (28) to Willie Redmond (56).

[16] They later both served in positions of danger: see J. Grigg, *Lloyd George: From Peace to War 1912–1916* (London, 1985), 171.

[17] J. M. Winter, 'Britain's "Lost Generation" of the First World War', *Population Studies*, 31 (1977), 449–66.

[18] In London there was an excess of deaths of 2,500, peaking in 1915 (C. Rollet, 'The "Other War" II: Setbacks in Public Health', in Winter and Robert (eds.), *Capital Cities*, 462).

[19] Levine, 'Women Police', 73.

personnel, but in early 1917 volunteer bodies, such as the Queen Mary's Auxiliary Army Corps, were consolidated into the Women's Auxiliary Army Corps (WAAC), followed by the Women's Royal Naval Service (WRNS) and the Women's Royal Air Force (WRAF)—in total over 100,000 servicewomen. But, significantly, these bodies dispensed with officers and made do with controllers and administrators, since it was thought that no woman could hold the King's commission.[20] The strait-laced felt anxiety at the very sight of women in uniform ('self-conscious and not very attractive boys'), who seemed to be transgressing gender boundaries.[21]

In the BEF some 17,000 WAACs served as typists, drivers, telephonists, clerks, cooks, and so on, with a view to releasing more men for combatant duty.[22] However, the rear positions could never be completely insulated from danger, and, as the Germans advanced during their 1918 Spring Offensive, some of these women came under enemy shelling. Nine were killed during an air raid at Abbeville. They were the first female military personnel to die on active service, and were buried with full military honours. In all, several military medals were awarded to women for their coolness under fire—behaviour which brought the WAACs belated respect. Physical danger, as well as the daily confrontation of indescribable horrors in the field hospitals, was also the lot of the 23,000 or so female nurses and the 15,000 female orderlies supplied by the Volunteer Aid Detachment (VAD). Another nurse, the 'martyred' Edith Cavell, quickly achieved heroic status after being executed by the Germans for helping British POWs escape from enemy-occupied Belgium. Among female casualties we must also include the 300 or so 'munitionettes', who died from TNT poisoning or explosions.[23]

Despite these fatalities, many public-spirited women were increasingly conscious that wartime sacrifices were not being equitably spread between men and women. Indeed, some, it has been claimed, 'felt humiliated at their exclusion from the war zone'.[24] This could lead to a mixture of envy and guilt, as expressed by Rose Macaulay in her poem 'Many Sisters to Many Brothers':

---

[20] Simpson, 'Officers', 89–90.

[21] A. Woollacott, 'Khaki Fever and Its Control: Gender, Class, Age and Sexual Morality on the British Homefront in the First World War', *Journal of Contemporary History*, 29 (1994), 250–1. See also S. R. Graysel, ' "The Outward and Visible Sign of Her Patriotism": Women, Uniforms, and National Service During the First World War', *Twentieth Century British History*, 2 (1997), 151–2).

[22] J. M. Bourne, *Britain and the Great War 1914–1918* (London, 1989), 196.

[23] About a third of these died from TNT poisoning, though numbers fell as better precautions and protective clothing became more widely adopted.

[24] C. Tylee, *The Great War and Women's Consciousness* (Basingstoke, 1990), 253–4.

Oh, it's you that have the luck, out there in blood and muck:
You were born beneath a kindly star;
All we dreamt, I and you, you can really go and do,
And I can't, the way things are.[25]

The opening months of the war witnessed what contemporaries disapprovingly called 'khaki fever', as young women (and boys) congregated excitedly around the new tent cities being erected to house the Kitchener armies, pestering the volunteers with their attentions: 'quite young girls from thirteen or fourteen to sixteen', complained *Common Cause*, 'are making themselves a positive nuisance to the men, and are a source of danger to themselves.'[26] Military commanders sometimes felt obliged to impose a curfew around their camps, as at Grantham, for example.

Guilt at exclusion from war service caused many women to put pressure on their menfolk to enlist: 'We Don't Want To Lose You, But We Think You Ought To Go'. The most blatant case of sexual bullying, initially instigated by a retired admiral, Penrose Fitzgerald, involved women distributing white feathers to civilians they thought should be in uniform—many of whom were, in fact, doing valuable work in 'reserved occupations', while others were just overgrown schoolboys! Getting 'shirkers' to enlist was also the objective of the Women of England's Active Service League, founded by the novelist Baroness Orczy, whose members (numbering some 20,000) vowed 'never to be seen in public with any man who, being in every way fit and free for service, has refused to respond to his country's call'.

Not all women succumbed to this kind of patriotic fervour. When the NUWSS, along with the WSPU, suspended its campaign for the vote and threw itself into the national cause, half of the executive committee resigned, among them Mrs Swanwick and Catherine Marshall, who declared: 'war is pre-eminently an outrage on motherhood and all that motherhood means; the destruction of life and the breaking-up of homes is the undoing of women's work as life-givers and home-makers.'[27] These dissidents joined that inveterate rebel Sylvia Pankhurst in forming a small protest group, from which were drawn the 300 or so activists who attempted to send a delegation to the Peace Congress at The Hague in April 1915.[28]

---

[25] C. Reilly (ed.), *Scars Upon My Heart: Women's Poetry and Verse of the First World War* (London, 1981), p. xxxv.

[26] Woollacott, 'Khaki Fever', 330.

[27] Cited in DeGroot, *Blighty*, 197. A similar reaction came from Mrs Despard, who was a sister of Lord French! Swanwick accused 'man' of playing 'the silly, bloody game of massacring the sons of women' (K. Robbins, *The Abolition of War: The "Peace Movement" in Britain 1914–1919* (Cardiff, 1976), 46).

[28] Only three made it to The Hague. Afterwards these women formed a section of the Women's International League, which had 3,687 active members.

But the vast majority of women campaigners threw themselves enthusiastic-ally behind the war effort, Emmeline and Christabel Pankhurst, as we have seen, being particularly bloodthirsty. Some justified their stance with the feminist argument that Germany, through its behaviour in Belgium, had shown itself to be 'a male nation'. Many female poets, of a more conventional cast of mind, also took the chivalric line that Tommy, a latter-day Galahad, was risking his life to save women, who embodied 'Mother England', a land of freedom and peace.[29]

The suffrage societies were not content to base their case on the portrayal of women as passive victims, but also pressed their demand that they be allowed to serve their country by undertaking work that would release men for military duty. On 17 July 1915 the WSPU organized an impressive march to assert this 'right', a march which ended outside the Ministry of Munitions, where it was graciously received by Lloyd George (who had already given the WSPU a £2,000 government grant).

Whitehall had been slow to appreciate that, with the economy suffering severe labour shortages caused by military enlistment, women had a vital contribution to make. By June 1915 the names of 78,946 women were entered on the Board of Trade's Special War Register, but only 1,816 had yet been given actual jobs. In the short run the war put women out of work, because of lay-offs in trades such as millinery and confectionary: only in April 1915 did female employment regain its pre-war level. Nor did the exodus of men into the army automatically create vacancies for women: to start off with, it merely provided more employment opportunities for men.[30]

Despite the fact that women had long been engaged in shell-filling (a repetitive operation for which they were thought particularly suitable), few munitions firms showed much initial enthusiasm for taking on women en masse. However, as the labour shortage intensified, employers had little option but to do so. The turning-point came in 1916. At Woolwich Arsenal the number of women rose from 195 in June 1915 to 11,000 in July 1916, but it then rose again to more than a quarter-of-a-million a year later.[31] In Britain as a whole the number of females employed in munitions production rose from a low point of 82,859 in July 1914 to 340,844 in June 1916 and 947,000 by the end of the war.[32]

Equality in the workplace proved very difficult to achieve. Women still earned substantially less than men, but their average weekly wage, up from

[29] Reilly, *Scars*, pp. xviii–xix.
[30] Wilson, *Myriad Faces*, 717.
[31] T. Bonzon, 'The Labour Market and Industrial Mobilization, 1915–1917', in Winter and Robert (eds.), *Capital Cities*, 187–8.
[32] Bourne, *Great War*, 185, 195.

13*s. 6d.* to 35*s.*, was now about two-thirds of the male wage rather than half, as it had been before the war. This led several male-dominated trade unions to complain about 'undercutting' from women who worked only for pocket money to spend on flashy clothes. There would seem to have been an obvious solution to this difficulty—equal pay; but Lloyd George thought that this would entail 'a social revolution which . . . it is undesirable to attempt in war time'. The government eventually decided to place men and women on the same piece rates, but to keep differentials on time rates. In practice, women were often paid 'basis time'—a standard hourly rate, to which bonuses could be added if the job was done more quickly.[33]

Here, in fact, was an issue on which men and women alike faced a dilemma. Equal pay would undoubtedly have stopped 'undercutting'—which is why some class-conscious women argued that those who placidly accepted a woman's wage for a man's job were falling in with the bosses' desire for cheap labour, and thereby doing a long-term disservice to their 'dear ones behind the guns and trenches'. On the other hand, the introduction of equal pay might well have discouraged employers from hiring women at all. Hence the paradox that some women disclaimed equal pay, while certain 'chauvinistic' male trade unionists mischievously advocated it. The TUC dithered: it thought equal pay for equal work a good idea but one difficult to define, and the trade-union activist Margaret Bondfield wanted women to be paid a minimum of £1 a week, but suggested that equal pay be phased in at some more practical time.[34]

Male objection to female 'interlopers' was often inextricably bound up with the skilled man's suspicions about the threat of 'unfair' competition emanating from unskilled, and especially foreign, workers who had a different (and lower) standard of life. In the midst of so dramatic a time, the war also left undisturbed some of the most entrenched gender assumptions. John Wadsworth, the General Secretary of the Yorkshire Miners, once declared: 'We think a woman's place is at home, looking after the home, husband and family; and if she is a young woman, unmarried, she ought to be learning something better than pit bank work.'[35] Many women openly agreed.

Male workers had one obvious way of curbing women's 'unfair competition': encouraging them to join a trade union. A number of unions did, indeed, take in women for the first time, among them the NUR and the Electrical Trade Union (ETU), though some imposed inferior conditions on these new recruits. Meanwhile unions which already catered for women, such as the Workers Union, were well placed to increase their membership. On the other hand, the

---

[33] G. Braybon, *Women Workers in the First World War* (London, 1981), 81, 78.
[34] Ibid. 80, 99, 101.   [35] Ibid. 74.

Amalgamated Society of Carpenters and Joiners continued to ban women, as did the ASE, even though this bastion of craft unionism was now willing to admit men who had not served an apprenticeship.[36] Despite such obstacles, the numbers of female trade unionists expanded from 437,000 in 1914 to 1,342,000 in 1920.[37]

The total number of women doing waged work did not increase as dramatically during the Great War as is often supposed: 7,311,000 females were employed in 1918, compared with 5,966,000 in 1914, a 22.5 per cent increase.[38] The *Labour Gazette* in 1916 estimated that one in three of these women had 'replaced' a male worker, but many would have been employed before 1914 as domestic servants or would have shifted from small dressmaking establishments, where they were, in their turn, replaced by younger girls.[39] Moreover, by 1918 there were more women substituting in banking, finance, and commerce than in all the metal and chemical trades put together.[40] Although contemporaries were struck by the phenomenon of women invading occupations once thought 'sacred to men', one study finds that by the end of the war five-sixths of women were still doing what was considered to be 'women's work'.[41] The most dramatic exception to this rule was provided by transport, where women took on such traditionally male jobs as van driver and bus conductor. The number of females in the transport sector rose more than sixfold, from 18,200 to 117,200, a higher proportionate increase than in any other occupation.[42]

The war's main impact, by far, was to boost the numbers of *married* women entering the labour market. In the four main engineering firms in Leeds, 44 per cent of all female employees were married women, compared with only 15 per cent in 1911.[43] Whether or not their husbands were in uniform, these women enjoyed a greater economic independence than in pre-war days. 'For the first time in many homes, women were the primary wage-earners, entitled to at least an equal share of the family's food supply.'[44] With the supplementation in some cases of money derived from billeting, married women also had more money with which to feed and clothe their children.

---

[36] Ibid. 82.

[37] The percentage rise was about 160% (Wilson, *Myriad Faces*, 727).

[38] DeGroot says 4,934,000 to 6,193,000, a 25.5% increase (*Blighty*, 128). Germany mobilized its female population more thoroughly (N. Ferguson, *The Pity of War* (Harmondsworth, 1998), 268)—precisely the opposite being the case during the Second World War.

[39] Braybon, *Women Workers*, 46, 49.

[40] Winter, *Great War*, 46.

[41] M. Pugh, *Women and the Women's Movement in Britain 1914–1959* (Basingstoke, 1992), 25.

[42] Bourne, *Great War*, 196.

[43] Braybon, *Women Workers*, 49–50.

[44] Winter, *Great War*, 239.

Many married women whose husbands were serving in the armed services[45] also saw their standard of living improve. Separation allowances (15s. a week for a woman with one child, raised to 23s. by the war's end, with increments for additional children) were set at a miserly level and hedged around with irksome restrictions.[46] Moreover, these payments were only paid to women because of the physical absence of the husband, which may have strengthened male authority by emphasizing women's dependent position. On the other hand, the allowance gave many women, in Eleanor Rathbone's words, 'the sense of security of ease' and a new-found 'dignity'. 'It seems too good to be true, a pound a week and my husband away', one woman exclaimed.[47]

For some women the war offered a legitimate excuse for escaping from the confines of domesticity into a world of excitement and palpable public usefulness. Such opportunities were mainly seized upon by upper- and middle-class females. For example, the Hon. Monica Grenfell trained as a nurse and served in France. A few ventured into even more dangerous locations: Dr Elsie Inglis, a leading light in the Scottish NUWSS, defying initial army advice to 'go home and sit still', led her nurses to Serbia and later to Russia.

However, within working-class communities unmarried women before 1914 had invariably gone out to work, and most of the married women absorbed into the job market after 1914 would have been *returning* to waged work, not tasting a completely new experience. Even so, many of the jobs on offer in the factories offered greater freedom (as well as better remuneration) than, say, domestic service had done. Jobs that seemed 'servile' or demeaning found few takers: for example, only 48,000 women responded to the invitation to work on the land, and soldiers and POWs had to be engaged to bring in the harvest in the last two years of war.[48]

All the same, industrial employment could be attended with much discomfort and danger. Stress, poor housing, and the need to travel long distances away from the parental home contributed to a sharp rise in deaths from respiratory diseases among females aged 10 to 29. And within the factory itself women initially worked up to twelve hours a day, including night shifts, in cramped workshops that had been designed for smaller numbers of men.[49] Better amenities had quickly to be put in place: washrooms and separate toilets were an immediate priority, but some factories were soon installing crèches and

---

[45] Joined after November 1914 by common-law wives.

[46] See below. The government became alarmed at the expense: in 1917–18 £113,287,606 was being spent on allowances, compared with £200,167,123 on soldiers' pay (S. Pedersen, 'Gender, Welfare and Citizenship in Britain during the Great War', *American Historical Review*, 95 (1990), 984).

[47] Ibid. 997–9, 1003.

[48] Wilson, *Myriad Faces*, 720.

[49] Braybon, *Women Workers*, 113.

canteens as well. Seebohm Rowntree's Welfare and Health Section of the Ministry of Munitions set out to convince employers that it was 'both good business and good management, as well as a duty, to regard with sympathetic consideration the health and comfort of their employees', male and female alike.[50] However, such efforts may simply have convinced male trade unionists that 'welfare' was something that was needed for women and children, but not for men, who could look after themselves—so reinforcing older stereotypes.

Unhygienic conditions presented one kind of threat to women's welfare, sexual harassment another—whether from lewd supervisors within the work-shops or from the males they might encounter as they passed through the rougher quarters of the industrial towns. Though real, this danger was prob-ably exaggerated by those, mainly middle-class women of mature years, who, disliking the social freedom of the young, convinced themselves that munition-ettes, in the absence of their mothers, needed protecting from themselves.

To fill this supposed gap, various women-only organizations sprang into existence. The government encouraged employers to appoint female welfare supervisors to monitor both the physical well-being and the moral 'tone' of the women and boys on their payroll. Forming part of the management structure, such supervisors often became deeply unpopular as a result of treating their social inferiors with harshness or with deep condescension: the National Federation of Women Workers, at its 1918 conference, actually called for their abolition, on the ground that they undermined industrial bargaining! Nor did the work of the welfare supervisor necessarily stop at the factory gates, since it also covered women's behaviour outside the workplace.[51]

In this mission to uphold decent standards of behaviour, the welfare super-visors were joined by two groups of women police, the Women Patrols of the National Union of Women Workers (a social purity organization, dating back to 1876) and the more militantly feminist Women's Police Service, which had links with the WSPU.[52] The Women Patrols drew heavily upon the well-to-do: of the 1,080 females trained, 411 (40 per cent) had private means, and others were drawn from nursing, teaching, and the business world. Louise Creighton thought that they should ideally be aged between 30 and 40. Soon some 4,000 NUWW patrols, with Home Office support, were operating the length and breadth of the country.[53] The women police could not themselves make arrests (to do so they had to call for assistance from a male policeman), but, patrolling in pairs and wearing armbands, they maintained a watchful presence in the

---

[50] C. Wrigley, 'The Ministry of Munitions: An Innovatory Department', in K. Burk (ed.), *War and the State* (London, 1982), 50.
[51] Levine, 'Women Police', 54. For class divisions among women, see below.
[52] In September 1918 the Met finally gave official approval to the former, not to the latter.
[53] Levine, 'Women Police', 46, 66–7.

streets and in such public areas as parks, cinemas, music halls, and dance halls. They played an undoubtedly useful role in escorting females who were up before the police courts. More controversially, they sometimes entered private homes in their quest to stamp out 'immorality'—that is, amateur prostitution.

Another body of moralistic vigilantes were the female philanthropists of the Soldiers' and Sailors' Families Association, a body that had initially concerned itself with elevating housecraft and motherhood, but which in the early months of the war also took upon itself the surveillance of servicemen's wives—until responsibility for this work was moved, first to a statutory authority (combining military, political, and philanthropic representatives) and then, from 1917 onwards, to the Ministry of Pensions. The separation allowance could be withdrawn from a woman who misbehaved—for example, by squandering money on drink or cohabiting with another man (the idea being that adultery implicitly breached the marriage contract).[54] Some 2 per cent of claimants were disqualified in this way, constituting about 13,000 out of the 40,000 cases investigated. The Labour Movement railed against this 'inquisitorial system', but, like the voluntary societies and the state, its main concern was to secure justice for the soldiers, not to enhance the respect in which women were held.[55] There were also unjustified slurs of promiscuity against the WAACs.[56]

Were such sexual anxieties justified? War did perhaps relax inhibitions and stimulate the libido. Some young women were apparently tempted to have one last fling with their boyfriend before he set off for the Front, perhaps never to return. As Mary Agnes Hamilton put it: 'How and why refuse appeals, backed up by the hot beating of your own heart, or what at the moment you thought to be your heart, which were put with passion and even pathos by a hero here today and gone tomorrow?'[57]

Perhaps as a result, the illegitimacy-rate rose significantly during the war years (from 4.3 per cent in 1913 to 6.3 per cent in 1918).[58] A letter in the *Morning Post* by the Ulster MP Ronald McNeill, in April 1915, triggered a hysterical debate about 'war nyphomania'.[59] Death-rates among illegitimate babies also went up. This, in turn, alarmed those who felt that the carnage on the Western Front meant that 'replacements' must be found, by whatever

---

[54] The Ministry of Pensions could withdraw the allowance from an unfaithful wife, if her husband disapproved of her behaviour (Pedersen, 'Gender, Welfare and Citizenship', 999).

[55] Ibid. 1000.

[56] A Commission of Inquiry vindicated the good name of the WAACs, finding that, of 6,023 serving in France by 12 March 1918, only 12 had caught venereal disease, while of the 21 pregnancy cases two were married and most of the others had become pregnant before arriving in France (A. Marwick, *Women At War 1914–1918* (London, 1977), 126).

[57] DeGroot, *Blighty*, p. 234.

[58] 1914: 4.2%; 1915: 4.5%; 1916: 4.8%; 1917: 5.5%; 1918: 6.3%; 1919: 5.9%; 1920: 1.6%.

[59] J. Weeks, *Sex, Politics and Society: The Regulation of Sexuality Since 1800* (Harlow, 1981), 208.

means: the National Baby Weeks of 1917 and 1918 declared that the objective was to 'save every savable child'.[60] The work of the National Council For the Unmarried Mother even suggests that, at least for the duration of the emergency, some of the old stigmatization of illegitimacy was being suspended.

More worrying was the startling rise in venereal disease among the troops (by 1917 it was affecting thirty-two out of every thousand men). Even before 1914 those active in public hygiene had been urging that syphilis was a social problem which needed to be faced with greater honesty, and in 1913 the government had set up a Royal Commission of Inquiry. In 1916 this body recommended that treatment be provided gratis, a recommendation acted upon in the same year:[61] with increasing use of the Wasserman test, great medical improvements were soon being made.

But none of this was intended as an endorsement of 'free love'. Significantly, the Royal Commission on Venereal Diseases skirted around the contentious issue of prophylaxis, and the BEF went abroad in 1914 'armed only with a warning on continence from Lord Kitchener, an old friend of the White Cross'.[62] Through the wider dissemination of sheaths, more married couples must have become familiar with contraception during and immediately after the Great War. But Marie Stopes's famous book popularizing birth-control techniques displayed in its very title, *Married Love* (1918), that it was devoted to the enrichment of marriage, spiced with eugenic progress, not sexual pleasure for its own sake. Women may have benefited, in that the growing use of contraception within marriage (Stopes's book sold 2,000 copies in the first fortnight) rescued some wives from a non-stop succession of pregnancies. But the war did not otherwise much advance the cause of sexual 'liberation'. On the contrary, these years saw a proliferation of 'purity' organizations, such as the Association for Moral and Social Hygiene (1915) and the People's League of Health (1917), while a vigilante group, the London Public Morality Council, continued to patrol Hampstead Heath more determinedly than ever.[63] Nor did the double standard disappear: indeed, it was positively enshrined in the notorious Regulation 40D of the Defence of the Realm Act (Easter 1918), which criminalized women who infected men, even if the woman in question had herself been initially infected by her husband—a regulation which none of the mainstream women's organizations saw fit to protest against.[64]

---

[60] G. Braybon and P. Summerfield, *Out of the Cage: Women's Experiences in Two World Wars* (London, 1987), 107.

[61] The state made free supplies of salvarsan to doctors, and free local authority clinics, drawing a 75% Exchequer subsidy, were encouraged in general hospitals.

[62] E. J. Bristow, *Vice and Vigilance: Purity Movements in Britain Since 1700* (London, 1977), 148.

[63] Weeks, *Sex, Politics and Society*, 214–15.

[64] Protest was left to the likes of Mrs Bramwell Booth, of the Salvation Army.

Moreover, the war may actually have strengthened the ideology of domesticity in which woman featured as 'the homemaker for the nation'. Motherhood was now presented as a kind of dangerous, but honourable, state service, akin to soldiering. Mary Stocks developed this line of argument in support of family allowances, and both the Women's Labour League and the WEWNC joined in the cry for state subsidies for the child-bearing mother. The Family Endowment Committee also rested its case in part on the argument that such a system would result in the withdrawal from the labour market of mothers with children under 5. Similarly, in a letter to *The Times*, published in August 1918, Eleanor Rathbone presented the majority of women as mere 'birds of passage in their trades', marriage and the rearing of children being their 'permanent occupation', adding that child allowances would 'put an end to the increasing practice among all the more thrifty and farsighted parents of deliberately limiting the number of children, while the slum dwellers and mentally unfit continue to breed like rabbits, so that the national stock is recruited in increasing proportions from its least fit elements'. These musings differed only slightly from the warnings of a male eugenist such as Caleb Saleeby, who condemned the working mother as committing 'a fundamental sin against the laws of life'.[65] Thus, the Great War, by idealizing motherhood and encouraging talk of woman's 'fruitful womb [replenishing] the wasted ranks', may have forced feminists to redefine 'equality' in ways that emphasized women's special sphere.[66]

Millicent Fawcett was therefore deceiving herself when she proclaimed that war had 'revolutionised men's minds and their conception of the sort of work of which the ordinary everyday woman was capable'.[67] On the contrary, older notions of what constituted a woman's sphere proved to be very deep-rooted, and the pressures of war in some ways reinforced them: for example, the valuable service which women rendered as nurses seemingly supplied proof of their innate fitness for 'caring' roles. Conversely, however little evidence they had to support this contention, many men continued to affirm that women could never replicate their own work with anything like the same efficiency, a prejudice that was particularly strong in farming.[68] Finally, the war can be seen as imposing masculine values on the wider society through its valorization of combat.[69]

---

[65] Braybon, *Women Workers*, 102–4, 119. It was often alleged that working mothers were directly responsible for a rise in infant deaths.

[66] The Countess of Warwick's remarks are cited in S. K. Kent, 'The Politics of Sexual Difference: World War I and the Demise of British Feminism', *Journal of British Studies*, 27 (1988), 234.

[67] Braybon, *Women Workers*, 157.

[68] Pugh, *Women's Movement*, 24.

[69] DeGroot, *Blighty*, 304; Levine, 'Women Police', 77.

Yet women did seem to have emerged from the war with at least one major gain—the vote. To be precise, a clause in the 1918 Representation of the People Act enabled women to vote in parliamentary elections once they had reached the age of 30, provided that they were householders or the wives of householders. On 19 June 1917 this once-controversial proposal passed easily through the Commons, with Asquith himself dramatically reversing his position: during the war, he told MPs, women had 'worked out their own salvation', a famous phrase which helped to entrench the myth that women had received the vote as a 'reward' for their war services.

However, if this were indeed the case, why did the Commons withold the vote from young women below the age of 30, thereby annoying the munitionettes, who had put their health and lives at risk during the war?[70] The explanation is that the coming of women's suffrage was an almost accidental byproduct of the call to give the vote to male soldiers. Responding to this pressure in 1916, Asquith had referred the franchise question, in its many aspects, to an all-party Conference chaired by the Speaker. This Conference eventually produced a comprehensive report, containing thirty-seven important recommendations, among them a proposal (agreed to by a majority of its members) that 'any woman who [was] on the Local Government Register or whose husband [was] on it [might] also vote in Parliamentary Elections', provided she had reached the age of 30 or 35. On a free vote the Commons accepted this recommendation (adopting the lower of the two suggested qualifying ages), with the crucial clause passing by 387 votes to 57. On 9 January 1918 the Lords, by 134 votes to 71, followed suit, after the leader of the Antis, Curzon, had recommended abstention to his friends.

In fact, as we have seen, the intellectual case for enfranchising women had long been won. The war simply created circumstances in which Votes for Women could be granted with minimum political disturbance, since the existence of the National Government meant that the suffrage issue was no longer intertwined with party rivalries. It also helped that the Prime Minister at the time when the crucial decision was taken, Lloyd George, happened to be a lifelong supporter, albeit a tepid one, of the *principle* of women's emancipation. For his part, Asquith, along with many other former 'antis' (including many Conservatives), was looking for an escape from the impossible position into which he had boxed himself in the pre-war years, and this the argument about women's wartime service conveniently furnished.

---

[70] A. Woollacott, *On Her Their Lives Depend: Munitions Workers in the Great War* (London, 1994), 190–1. Admittedly, an exception was made for the 3,372 women who were registered in 1918 as 'naval and military voters', many of them presumably below the age of 30. Like the much larger number of males registered under this franchise they qualified for the vote at the age of 19.

In any case, male MPs could gracefully concede the vote to women in 1917 without fear of being reproached for giving way to violence and agitation; for although some members of the NUWSS had cautiously started to revive their campaign in 1917, they did not make many ripples, and neither government nor Parliament felt itself under serious external pressure.[71] Raising the age-bar for women in any case helped remove male fears by ensuring that men would not be 'swamped' by the new female voters—who comprised only 39.6 per cent of the electorate in 1918, just over 42 per cent thereafter. Mrs Fawcett weakly accepted this restriction, saying that she did not wish to 'risk their prospects for partial success by standing out for more'.[72]

The fact that women gained the vote as a gift from men, rather than forcing it from recalcitrant opponents by their own heroic endeavours, had a dampening effect on the feminist cause for at least a generation. Vera Brittain summed up the situation very accurately: 'With an incongruous irony seldom equalled in the history of revolutions, the spectacular pageant of the woman's movement, vital and colourful with adventure, with initiative, with sacrificial emotion, crept to its quiet, unadvertised triumph in the deepest night of wartime depression.'[73] True, the 1918 Act went beyond the demands of the pre-war suffrage societies by allowing women to *sit* in the Commons. But in the event few tried to do so—only seventeen in the 1918 election, thirty-three in 1922. Even fewer were successful: Countess Markievicz of Sinn Fein, who refused to take her seat, was the only victor in 1918. More significant, for the immediate future, was the passing in December 1918 of the Sex Discrimination Act, which opened up jury service, the magistracy, and the legal profession to women.

It is also questionable whether, in the short run, women had many social and economic gains to show for their wartime exertions. Admittedly, the capacity that they had shown in a variety of civilian occupations was perhaps remembered long after the war had ended, and even without economic independence, women might therefore have been more self-assertive vis-à-vis their male relatives and friends.[74] On the other hand, the unspoken contract during the war had been that women would have to vacate their wartime jobs as soon as the soldiers returned from the Front; the ASE, indeed, openly insisted on this condition, pressurizing the government into passing the Restoration of Pre-War Practices Act in 1919. And after the Armistice brutal language was

[71] Some MPs, it is true, did warn that disorder might recur if the issue was not quickly disposed of (Kent, 'Politics of Sexual Difference', 235).

[72] Ibid. 236.

[73] Cited in Wilson, *Myriad Faces*, 725.

[74] Ibid. 728–9; Woollacott, *On Her Their Lives Depend*, 203.

frequently directed against 'girls clinging on to jobs' that rightly belonged to the returning soldiers.[75]

It is thus hardly surprising that about two-thirds of women had withdrawn from their wartime jobs by 1920;[76] indeed, by July 1921 the proportion of women in waged work was actually lower than in 1911, down from 32.3 per cent to 30.8 per cent. Only in the clerical sector and in the higher professions did women make more or less permanent advances—a continuation of a pre-war trend. Even in the office a 'marriage bar' was commonly operated in the 1920s—with the approval of the National Federation of Women Workers, who urged married women to return to their homes.

Finally, for many women the Great War brought heartache and loneliness, rather than a 'Great Release'. Constant anxiety over the fate of their husbands, sons, brothers, and sweethearts culminated, for all too many, in the agonies of bereavement: men certainly did not have a monopoly of suffering. In the longer run, women had to endure another of the war's legacies: a worsening of the gender imbalance. Among those aged 20 to 34 in England and Wales, there had been 110.7 females to every 100 males in 1911: by 1921 the gap had widened to 119. To put it another way, the female surplus in this age-bracket had risen from 463,300 to 773,300. Perhaps surprisingly, the proportion of single to married women dropped during the 1920s, a development caused by the propensity of women to marry at a younger age.[77] But the harsh reality was that, thanks to the war, one woman in six could look forward to a lifelong spinsterhood.

2. CLASS AND THE MILITARY PARTICIPATION RATIO

The Upper Classes

Although all social classes participated in the great recruiting surge in 1914, 'the soldier's war was more central to some groups than to others'.[78] And no social class was more swept by war fever than the upper and upper-middle classes. Imbued with the strong sense of patriotic duty and *noblesse oblige* which so coloured the public schools, they rushed to enlist in the opening months of war: all but eight of the 5,439 boys who left Winchester between 1909 and 1915 volunteered.[79]

---

[75] Kent, 'Politics of Sexual Difference', 238–9.

[76] The munitionettes were most unhappy at the prospect of returning to their pre-war jobs. They eventually acquiesced in demobilization, but protested if asked to give way for someone other than an ex-serviceman (Woollacott, *On Her Their Lives Depend*, 191, 109).

[77] Wilson, *Myriad Faces*, 722.

[78] A. Gregory, 'Lost Generations: The Impact of Military Casualties on Paris, London, and Berlin', in Winter and Robert (eds), *Capital Cities*, 84.

[79] Ferguson, *Pity of War*, 201.

War validated the social purpose of the landed aristocracy: fighting wars was what families from this background tended to specialize in and to have prepared for all their lives. After 1914 even such a ne'er-do-well as the second Duke of Westminster ('Bendor') discovered a useful role for himself, rejoining his regiment at the age of 35 and leading an armoured car squadron, in which role he showed the bravery, dash, and spirit of chivalric self-sacrifice characteristic of a warrior caste. Although many officers were traumatized by their battle experiences, Julian Grenfell, the eldest son of Lord Desborough, was not being unduly eccentric when, shortly after reaching the Front, he exclaimed: 'I *adore* war. It is like a big picnic without the objectlessness of a picnic. I've never been so well or so happy.'[80] (Within seven months of writing this letter he was dead.)

As the army expanded, the social composition of the officer corps, traditionally aristocratic in tone, became somewhat diluted—those not from normal officer backgrounds eventually comprised about three-quarters of those holding temporary commissions.[81] But although not all army officers came from the upper classes, most males of suitable age born into this stratum received commissions. Of 1,000 Balliol men who joined up, only 3 per cent served in the ranks. In fact, between August 1914 and March 1915 no fewer than 20,577 additional junior officers were recruited from the OTCs—that is to say, mainly from the public schools.[82]

It has been argued that war did nothing to narrow the class divide—young subalterns habitually referring to private soldiers older than themselves as 'lads' and treating them accordingly.[83] But the relationship between officers and men, however paternalistic, was generally quite harmonious, given the circumstances. In their letters home subalterns commonly declared their 'love' for the men under their command, while private soldiers, though prepared to voice their contempt for incompetent and bullying officers, seem to have borne no general grudge against the officer class as a whole, reserving their hatred for the Staff and other 'outsider' groups.[84] (But the Staff were also unpopular with many junior officers: this was a functional, not a class, dispute.)[85] In this respect the Great War may, on balance, have stabilized the pre-war class system, since the military hierarchy both echoed and reinforced the peacetime social order.

The traditional 'ruling class' thus succeeded during the war in answering pre-war Radical sneers that they were mere parasites. But it paid a high price

---

[80] N. Mosley, *Julian Grenfell: His Life and the Times of His Death 1888–1915* (London, 1976), 239.

[81] M. Petter, ' "Temporary Gentlemen" in the Aftermath of the Great War: Rank, Status and the Ex-Officer Problem', *Historical Journal*, 37 (1994), 138.

[82] Simpson, 'Officers', 73.

[83] DeGroot, *Blighty*, 165.

[84] Such as the trench-mortar men, who went away before the enemy inevitably retaliated. See T. Ashworth, *Trench Warfare, 1914–1918: The Live and Let Live System* (London, 1980).

[85] Bourne, *Great War*, 221.

for this increase in respect and social prestige. Admittedly, 96 per cent of all infantry casualties were sustained by private soldiers, but proportionately the officers suffered more. In the armed services as a whole, 13.6 per cent of all serving officers were killed, but only 11.7 per cent of other ranks.[86] The carnage was particularly high among landed and aristocratic families, not least because these were the groups which dominated the officer corps in the opening months of war. The higher up the social scale, the greater the casualty rate. An astonishing 20.7 per cent of serving Old Etonians were killed, another 26.2 per cent wounded. Oxford and Cambridge graduates also suffered proportionately more than did graduates from provincial English universities, who were socially more variegated. And, of peers and their sons aged under 50 in 1914, 18.95 per cent of those who served in the war did not survive it—well above the national average, which was 11.76 per cent throughout the entire armed forces, 12.91 per cent in the army.[87]

Added to such suffering were the economic privations which war brought in its wake. Especially hard hit were aristocratic families in which the death of the head of household was followed by the death in battle of his heir—the estate would then be saddled, in quick succession, with two sets of death duties (or vice versa, as when Sir Edmund Antrobus died shortly after the death of his only son in battle, the result being that the whole of his Amesbury Abbey estate was put on the market in 1915).[88] Like all propertied people, landowners also faced greatly increased tax bills.[89] Admittedly, there was a temporary rise in agricultural prices, but landlords were prevented by the Corn Production Act from raising the rent—even to match wartime inflation. The Board of Income Revenue later calculated that income from real property had fallen from 10 per cent to 7 per cent of national income between 1913–14 and 1923–4.[90]

Finding themselves in straitened circumstances, many landowners were tempted to sell off parts of their estate, whether to sitting farmers or to public bodies—hence the vast land sales following the war, in which almost a quarter of England changed hands. The auctioneers Knight, Frank & Rutley sold 454,972 acres during 1918, including nearly a quarter-of-a-million acres in Scotland belonging to the Duke of Sutherland.[91] Likewise, even wealthy aristocrats such as the Salisburys and the Westminsters found after the war that they could not afford the upkeep of their grand London houses—some of

[86] Winter, *Great War*, 90–1. Officers were even more at risk in the RFC/RAF, but less so in the navy.

[87] Winter, *Great War*, 99, 73.

[88] F. M. L. Thompson, *English Landed Society in the Nineteenth Century* (London, 1963; 1971 edn.), 328.

[89] See below.

[90] Waites, *Class Society*, 93–4. These statistics, however, include small house-owners as well as the possessors of agricultural estates.

[91] Thompson, *Landed Society*, 329.

which subsequently became hotels.[92] The war also accelerated the tendency for landowners to sacrifice their traditional way of life for a business career.

When Lord Lansdowne, in late 1917, released his 'Letter', was he calling for a negotiated peace because he recognized that the war was steadily destroying the economic foundations of the social privileges enjoyed by people of his class? If so, he had a shrewd insight into the movement of events. Charles Masterman, a pre-war scourge of the aristocracy, could lament 'The Passing of Feudalism' and write in the early 1920s about the old landed families in a tone more of pity than of fear or resentment.[93] The pro-war Ben Tillett also voiced praise of the landed gentry, 'which had given their sons nobly and freely'—to the detriment of the 'capitalist class', which he depicted as sitting at home in comfort and security, 'behind the bodies of better men than themselves'.[94] Few peerages, however, actually become extinct.

The Middle Classes

The fortunes of the middle classes were more varied. The one generalization which can confidently be hazarded is that young men from such backgrounds were more likely to end up in uniform than those they considered their social inferiors. Roughly twice as many self-employed professionals and white-collar workers as manual workers enlisted in the voluntary phase of the war.[95] This disparity cannot simply be interpreted as evidence of the greater patriotism of the middle classes, since it broadly continued even under a regime of conscription. In London in 1918 only 45 per cent of the former manufacturing workforce were in uniform, compared to 63 per cent in finance and commerce, and almost 80 per cent in banking.[96] It has been truly said that 'the soldiers of the First World War were as likely to have been clerks or shop assistants in civilian life as to have been miners or engineers'.[97]

Why this differential? It partly came about because few white-collar employees worked in 'reserved occupations', other than those in local government and the civil service.[98] In any case, women could more easily be absorbed into offices than into factories: about one-half of all the females who directly

---

[92] During the war itself these premises had nearly all been appropriated as temporary overspill government offices, for example, Grosvenor House, or hospitals, for example, Londonderry House.

[93] C. F. G. Masterman, *England After War: A Study* (London, 1922), ch. 2.

[94] R. Harrison, 'The War Emergency Workers' National Committee', in A. Briggs and J. Saville (eds.), *Essays in Labour History 1886–1923* (London, 1971), 219.

[95] Winter, *Great War*, 33–4. 41.7% of those employed in the professions, and 40.1% finance and commerce—compared with 22.4% from transport, 28.3% from agriculture, and 28.3% from industry and mining. The sector with the highest enlistment rate was entertainments (41.8%).

[96] A. Gregory, 'Lost Generations', 80

[97] P. E. Dewey, 'Military Recruiting and the British Labour Force During the First World War', *Historical Journal*, 27 (1984), 221.

[98] The enlistment rate in local and central government was 29.4% and 26.4%, respectively.

replaced men were in the commercial sector. Secondly, higher social status carried with it increasing risks of becoming a casualty during the Great War, not least because its possessors were less likely than working men to be rejected as unfit by the army medical boards.

Moreover, as was the case with the aristocracy, most middle-class entrants into the army received commissions.[99] Some of the original 'Pals' Battalions' were drawn from educated groups such as solicitors and stockbrokers, whose members were prepared to serve in the ranks; for example, in late August 1914 a battalion of 'mercantile and professional men' was formed as part of the Gloucestershire Regiment.[100] But such men mostly received commissions in due course, with all the risks that that implied. As a result of all these factors, the fatality rate was relatively high for men from middle-class occupations: only 4–5 per cent of London's pre-war manufacturing workforce died, but 16 per cent of employees in banking did so.[101]

Eugenists worried about the consequences of such differential mortality. The voluntary system, they complained, was particularly harmful because it resulted in the premature deaths (before they had had time to raise families) of the very men on whom racial progress depended, while those endowed with little public spirit were surviving in greater proportions. However, it is difficult to see why, on eugenic grounds, conscription was greatly preferable to voluntarism, since, whatever the enlistment method, the physically and mentally 'unfit' were going to be screened out of the army anyway. By wasting good 'germ plasm', it was war itself, some reluctantly concluded, which stood condemned as 'dysgenic'—though that did not stop the Eugenics Society from broadly supporting the British war effort.[102]

What fate awaited middle-class *civilians*? Here a clear distinction existed between 'winners' and 'losers'. Many businessmen did well out of the war: by 1916 average profits in coal, iron, and engineering, and shipbuilding had risen by 32 per cent above pre-war levels—in the case of the shipbuilding firm Cammel Laird, by over 74 per cent.[103] The consequent outcry about 'profiteering' led to the introduction in the September 1915 Budget of an Excess Profits Duty (EPD). First set at 50 per cent of pre-war profit levels, the rate was successively raised, partly as a sop to Labour; in 1916 it stood at 60 per cent and a year later reached 80 per cent. But, given the pre-war trade boom, the base-line

---

[99] However, about 15–20% of temporary officers were from the manual working class, and more than half in borderline non-manual occupations (Petter, 'Temporary Gentlemen', 138).

[100] Winter, *Great War*, 30–2.

[101] Gregory, 'Lost Generations', 80.

[102] The Eugenics Education Society, worried at these developments, participated in the charitable activities of the Professional Classes War Relief Council.

[103] DeGroot, *Blighty*, 71.

against which profits were being assessed, EPD could hardly be called punitive, though it proved a very handy money-raiser (by the end of the war it accounted for 36 per cent of total state revenue). One historian has suggested that EPD simply 'legitimised high profits rather than removed them'.[104] In any case, the tax was applied only to war production and did not cover coal or food, in both of which prices sharply rose—household coal on average by 20 per cent.[105]

Farmers were another group who, in general, did well out of wartime food shortages. Admittedly, pastoral and dairy farmers faced problems through the reduction in imports of cattle cake and through the diversion of animal-feed supply to meet human consumption. On the other hand, the Corn Production Act of 1917, for all the irksome form-filling that it entailed, came as a godsend to arable farmers, because it guaranteed them a minimum price for wheat and oats until 1922 and fixed their rents at a level that fell well below inflation. The country derived considerable benefit from this arrangement, but it meant that farmers' profits rose from a pre-war range of between 0.3 per cent and 6.1 per cent on their capital to a wartime peak in 1917 of between 10.2 per cent and 14.3 per cent.[106] Government restrictions may have kept profits in check at the end of the war, but there was never any serious possibility of them being subjected to any kind of EPD. Thus, as far as farmers were concerned, this was a time when, to quote one contemporary, 'it was impossible to lose money'.[107]

For other traders the war proved less beneficial. Exporters, cut off from many of their former markets, complained of being harried by successive Trading-with-the-Enemy Acts. Retailers, too, experienced great uncertainty: rationing led to discrepancies in profits, depending on which commodity they sold. Finally, businessmen employed in 'non-essential trades' mostly missed out on the bonanza that came the way of those involved in munitions production and in the distribution of basic foodstuffs.

Middle-class citizens living on fixed incomes were among the war's greatest losers because, as a result of inflation, the prices of basic commodities more than doubled between 1914 and 1918. Those on salaries fared only slightly better. No civil servant was eligible for a cost-of-living increase or a war bonus until July 1916, while the professional men who kept up best were groups such as draughtsmen and architects working in close proximity to manual workers.[108]

---

[104] R. C. Whiting, 'Taxation and the Working Class, 1915–24', *Historical Journal*, 33 (1990), 914.
[105] DeGroot, *Blighty*, 73.
[106] P. E. Dewey, 'British Farming Profits and Government Policy During the First World War', *Economic History Review*, 37 (1984), 387.
[107] A. G. Street, cited in Dewey, 'Farming Profits', 387.
[108] J. Lawrence, 'Material Pressures on the Middle Classes', in Winter and Robert (eds.), *Capital Cities at War*, 237.

To deal with the unfamiliar problem of middle-class distress, a new pressure group, the Professional Classes War Relief Council, was founded. Among its clients were people from the leisure industries, such as musicians, artists, and actors, whose incomes had almost entirely collapsed; those employed in journalism also suffered from raw-material shortages. Such hardship was untypical. Some professional groups, such as lawyers, did well. All the same, between 1914 and 1922 the living standards of professional workers may have fallen by nearly 10 per cent, while non-manual earnings in general lagged behind retail prices, resulting in a significant (albeit temporary) squeezing of the differential between working-class and middle-class incomes.[109]

Rentiers also enjoyed mixed fortunes. British companies 'dealing in rubber, iron and steel, engineering, shipping, oil, and nitrates, consistently paid above average dividends on ordinary capital during the war'.[110] But investors with a stake in companies not directly engaged in war production were less fortunate. The value of Consols (government bonds issued to service the National Debt) also fell. Urban landlords formed another group of losers. The initial rise in house rentals forced the government to intervene with the Rent Restriction Act of 1915. This legislation did not apply to expensive properties, but by fixing the rents of working-class housing (by 1918 they had risen 50 per cent above their 1913 level[111]) it had the effect of severely reducing the urban landlord's income.

On top of all these problems came higher taxes. Although 70 per cent of total war expenditure was met from public borrowing, the Treasury also increased the fiscal burden. It mainly did so by increased direct taxation, which by the end of the war accounted for 80 per cent of state revenues. As a result, whereas in 1914 income tax on incomes over £3,000 p.a. stood at 1s. 2d. in the pound (6 per cent), by 1918–19 it was being levied at rates of 6s. in the pound on incomes over £2,500 (30 per cent). The yield on supertax increased tenfold during the same period. Citizens drawing incomes in excess of £150,000 p.a. were now paying nearly 52 per cent of it in direct taxes.[112] To their bewilderment, Conservative ministers found themselves presiding over rates of taxation many times higher than those they had denounced as 'confiscatory' when introduced by the pre-war Liberal government.

The middle class grew in numbers and importance during the war: in London commercial and financial employment expanded by 34 per cent between 1911 and 1921.[113] But individuals did not necessarily benefit from this development. Once again, we must differentiate. For certain well-positioned middle-class groups, the war scarcely ushered in a period of austerity. Despite petrol rationing, many luxuries were still freely available, especially champagne,

[109] Ibid. 243.   [110] Ibid. 252.   [111] Waites, *Class Society*, 173.
[112] Lawrence, 'Material Pressures', 234.   [113] Ibid. 236.

the consumption of which rocketed.[114] But other middle-class families saw the value of their personal savings decline in real terms, and some had to live off their accumulated capital to get through the war. In Jay Winter's view, this development, though painful, was not for most middle-class people a disaster, and there was a satisfaction to be derived from the thought of making material sacrifices for the good of the nation. Largely for that reason, there was little middle-class protest during the war (though the temporary upsurge in the membership of the National Union of Clerks from under 11,000 in 1915 to over 43,000 in 1919 may be significant).[115] But grievances festered under the surface, and after the Armistice organizations such as the Middle-Classes Union came into being to protest over the way in which their members were being penalized in favour of working men and women, whose contribution to the war effort had been less than theirs.[116] What validity, if any, was there in this complaint?

The Working Class(es)

In practice, as we have seen, the truth was more complex, since the middle class contained both 'winners' and 'losers', who were largely divided from one another by *sector*. The same is true of the working class (or classes). By February 1915 15 per cent of the industrial workforce were in uniform, 28.3 per cent by February 1916. But some occupational groups showed greater patriotic zeal than others. Despite their pre-war reputation for industrial militancy, the miners registered some of the highest enlistment rates: 115,000 of them volunteered in the first month of war alone, some 15 per cent of the entire membership of the MFGB. Munitions, metals, and ship-building also lost between 16 per cent and 24 per cent of their workforce by the summer of 1915. Textile workers, on the other hand, were proportionately under-represented in the army, as were employees in the transport sector. The figures for agricultural labourers (15.6 per cent by February 1915, 28.3 per cent a year later) were almost identical to those for industrial workers.[117]

Worried at the depletion of manpower in the crucial war industries, the Ministry of Munitions adopted a system of 'badging' key workers, a procedure which became much easier after the adoption of conscription, when certain groups could be exempted for economic reasons: 1.4 million industrial workers had been badged by October 1916, 2 million by April 1917, and 2.3 million by October of that year—to the irritation of the War Office, which thought that exemptions were being too readily granted.[118] (Thus conscription, far from flushing out the 'shirkers' as Robertson had hoped, produced, if anything, the

---

[114] DeGroot, *Blighty*, 210, following Burk.   [115] Waites, *Class Society*, 260.
[116] Ibid. 263-4.   [117] Winter, *Great War*, 34-5.   [118] De Groot, *Blighty*, 97.

opposite effect.)[119] Skilled engineers, the backbone of the ASE, enjoyed a virtual exemption from conscription, as we will see. At various points in the war there also occurred a process of releasing from the army those who could render better service to their country by returning to their pre-war jobs.

Conscription introduced another source of differentiation in the form of army medical tests. Of those examined in the last year of the war, 36 per cent were placed in Grade I, 10.3 per cent were declared unfit for any kind of military service, and another 31.3 per cent (placed in Grade III) were deemed to be too sickly to be exposed to combat. In London and Leeds, with their large numbers of immigrants and poorly paid semi-skilled and unskilled workers, the rejection rate was particularly high. In this way many of the urban poor were 'saved by their infirmities'.[120] Over 1 million men were deemed unfit for military service of any kind.

This development partly cancelled out the privileges being enjoyed by the better-paid sectors of the working class, whose skill had gained them exemption from military service. Even so, military death-rates varied from one occupational group to another: in London, for example, they were higher among dockers than among engineers and transport workers.[121] To generalize broadly, a working man's chances of surviving the war were least promising if he was unskilled yet possessed goodish health. But *all* working men were better situated in this respect than those from middle-class occupations.

Those who stayed in 'Blighty' faced both hardships and comfort. In the opening months of the war the unemployment rate among insured workers shot up to 4.2 per cent, largely as a consequence of the disruption of peacetime trade and, for some small firms, transport blockages. As we have seen, women working in the luxury trades were the principal victims of the war in its early stages. But the Prince of Wales Relief Fund, established to deal with such distress, was soon wound up. For one outcome of the army's insatiable demand for manpower was the virtual disappearance of unemployment, which plummeted to 1.2 per cent in 1915 and stood during the following three years at 0.6 per cent, 0.7 per cent, and 0.8 per cent—quite unprecedented figures.

This 'abnormal employment', as some economists called it, created an acute labour shortage, especially in the armaments industry, which, according to a Cabinet Committee in December 1914, was short of some 6,000 workers—16 per cent of employees in the small-arms factories and 23 per cent in chemical and explosive works having already rushed to the colours.[122] To plug the gap, employers turned at first to Belgian refugees and then, with some reluctance, to women. But their primary concern was to hold on to their skilled male workers,

[119] Bourne, *Great War*, 185–6,   [120] Winter, *Great War*, 63.
[121] Gregory, 'Lost Generations', 83–4.   [122] Bourne, *Great War*, 183.

while attempting to 'poach' others from rival establishments. To stop the inflationary pressures which this created, the government in July 1915 introduced the 'leaving certificate' system, which soon covered some 2 million workers across Britain, 30 per cent of the workforce—a deeply unpopular move with trade unionists.[123]

As so often happened in the past, labour shortage led to an expansion of trade-union membership. The numbers affiliated to the TUC, which stood at 4,117,000 in 1914, then steadily rose: to 4,335,000 in 1915, 4,611,000 in 1916, 5,452,000 in 1917, 6,461,000 in 1918, and 7,837,000 in 1919—a 90 per cent increase over 1914.[124] The trade-union movement may not have fully exploited the leverage which it now possessed—Beatrice Webb thought that its leaders too readily succumbed to patriotic blackmail[125]—but the economic situation could hardly have failed to benefit the working-class community.

Initially, it is true, the inflation deliberately engineered by the Treasury brought some hardship in its wake: by early 1915 consumer price levels were generally 10–15 per cent higher and food 20 per cent higher than six months earlier.[126] But real wages soon caught up with prices (and perhaps ran slightly ahead of productivity gains): whereas the cost of living stood at 215 in 1919 compared with the 1914 baseline of 100, weekly wage-rates over the same period rose to between 215 and 220. Agricultural labourers benefited directly from the establishment of a minimum wage (of 25s. a week), even if their gains were lost soon after the Armistice.[127] But industrial workers, who did not enjoy any statutory protection, succeeded in raising their standard of living even more.

Wartime labour could be gruelling: it is reckoned that male war-workers put in ten hours of overtime a week on average, females seven-and-a-half hours.[128] But this brought in extra money, allowing some workers to accumulate substantial savings for the first time in their lives. Occupational upgrading also resulted in higher earnings for many employees, and, with the expansion of the female workforce, thousands of households drew a double income.

Some of this hard-won affluence was then creamed off in higher taxation. After 1916 the income-tax threshold was reduced from £160 to £130, and this, with wage inflation, trebled the number of income-tax payers, bringing substantial numbers of manual workers within its scope. By the end of the war there were 6 million more income-tax payers than in 1914. It is true that only 32 per cent of workers in the £130–160 tax-band paid any income tax at all, thanks to a system of abatements designed to provide relief to families with

---

[123] Bonzon, 'Labour Market', 181. On the 'leaving certificate', see below.
[124] Trade-union density also rose: from 24.7% in 1914 to 46% in 1919.
[125] See below.   [126] DeGroot, *Blighty*, 112.   [127] Waites, *Class Society*, 142.
[128] Winter, *Great War*, 238.

dependent children.[129] Even so, the tax threshold would have had to be raised to £288 to keep up with inflation (Labour politicians suggested a figure of £250), and the fact that this had not happened engendered some ill-will, particularly in South Wales, where the miners attempted to stage a tax revolt. Working-class families were also hit by increased duties on tobacco, beer, spirits, sugar, coffee, and so on, though these were less visible than income tax.[130] Finally, the increased numbers of those drawn into Part II of the National Insurance Scheme found, to their disapproval, that they were involved in pecuniary sacrifices in exchange for unemployment benefits that war workers would not have an immediate occasion to draw.[131]

On the other hand, signs of increased prosperity, at the lower end of the social scale, were there for all to see. For example, pauperism steadily diminished.[132] Similarly, the number of children being fed under the 1906 Act peaked in 31 March 1915 at 422,401: it then dropped to 117,901 in 1916, 64,613 in 1917, and 52,490 in 1918.[133] Vagrancy also declined, as did indictments and convictions for theft.[134]

But, as in the case of the middle class, war-driven developments brought 'winners' and 'losers'. For example, the payment of flat-rate, across-the-board bonuses meant a flattening of wage differentials. Thus, in building, engineering, and railways, the skilled man's wages between 1913 and 1920 rose by less than the cost of living, and only slightly above it in coalmining and cotton; the skilled workers in the electrical trades, aided by their union, the ETU, were among the few to make significant advances. But the semi-skilled did better, while the unskilled did best of all, their wages going up 319 per cent in engineering, 325 per cent in coalmining, 328 per cent in building, 330 per cent in railways, and 331 per cent in cotton.[135] The result was that, whereas in August 1914 a labourer's wage was 59 per cent that of a fitter in engineering, it stood at 76 per cent in April 1919. Such changes, taken in conjunction with a restructuring of the industrial workforce leading to an expansion of semi-skilled employment at the expense of the skilled, generated a certain friction within the working-class community.[136]

---

[129] Whiting, 'Taxation', 897–8.   [130] DeGroot, *Blighty*, 107.

[131] N. Whiteside, 'Welfare Legislation and the Unions During the First World War', *Historical Journal*, 23 (1980), 857–71.

[132] For the impact on Leeds, see Winter, *Great War*, 242.

[133] Waites, *Class Society*, 163.

[134] Winter, *Great War*, 245.

[135] Waites, *Class Society*, 132. Winter notes that whereas labourers in war-related industries did particularly well, those in sectors like building and construction saw their real wages fall; however, by the end of the war 80–90% of the labour force was engaged in war-related work (Winter, *Great War*, 235).

[136] Waites, *Class Society*, 141. Whereas the proportion of industrial employees who were unskilled remained constant between 1914 and 1921, the skilled dropped from 60% to 50%, while the semi-skilled (machinists, and so on) increased from 20% to 30% (p. 153).

Outside the workplace other grievances simmered. Many working-class consumers felt particularly bitter over the sharp rise in food prices which took place at the start of the war—up 20 per cent by the beginning of 1915.[137] Worse was to come: sugar rose by 163 per cent in the first two years of war, while potatoes, milk, and butter eventually doubled in price.[138] These developments were widely blamed on 'profiteers'.

After 1916 the U-boat campaign produced shortages of certain basic commodities. In the final years of war the calorific content of the average diet had dropped by 3 per cent and that of protein by 6 per cent, causing privation which, though small compared with what was being experienced by the peoples of the Central Powers, proved irksome to people working long hours, often under emotional stress. Meals also became more monotonous and less appetizing, despite the encouragement offered in publications such as the *Win the War Cookery Book*. The addition of potato flour gave bread an unpleasant, greyish appearance—flour was also made from barley, maize, and rice. Meanwhile margarine consumption quadrupled, at the expense of butter, although official attempts to popularize horse meat and eels were not a success![139]

However, there were compensations even in the matter of diet, at least as far as many working-class families were concerned. With 6 million men being fed by the army, working-class wives (and their children) now took a higher share of the available civilian rations. By 1918 over a million war workers were also enjoying the benefit of cheap hot meals, dispensed from more than 900 government-subsidized munitions canteens.[140] In addition, the introduction during the last year of the war of a points-based food-rationing system, geared to human needs rather than capacity to pay, did much to even out consumption patterns, to the benefit of the poorer members of society: whereas the skilled man's expenditure on food increased during the war by 85 per cent, that of the semi-skilled man rose by 97.5 per cent, the unskilled man's by 107.7 per cent.[141] (Something similar happened when coal was rationed at the end of the war.)

The other principal worry for working-class families was housing. In those centres of munitions-production which sucked in workers from far and wide, house rents initially soared. This formed the background to the dramatic rent strike on Clydeside in November 1915, which involved 20,000 tenants. The government immediately responded by introducing the Rent Restriction Bill, which fixed rents on working-class houses at pre-war levels—an obvious boon to the tenants covered by the legislation.

But this initiative had a downside. Landlords, many of them seriously out of pocket, lost their incentive and even, in some case, the means to finance

[137] Winter, *Great War*, 112.   [138] DeGroot, *Blighty*, 201.   [139] Ibid. 89, 202–3.
[140] Winter, *Great War*, 211.   [141] Waites, *Class Society*, 135.

repairs—and this at a time when, in addition to the normal processes of dilapidation, housing in some areas was being damaged by air raids. All of this coincided with a virtual cessation of private housebuilding, as the workforce was thinned by military enlistment or diverted into other activities such as factory-construction. As a result, many munitions workers found themselves forced to live in hostels, and the already severe problem of overcrowding grew even worse.[142] By 1918 the government was facing a situation in which another 600,000 houses needed urgently to be built. Moreover, poor-quality, damp housing probably provides one explanation for the worrying rise during the war years in pulmonary-respiratory diseases such as tuberculosis, which particularly affected females in the 15–24 age-brackets.[143]

The overall impact of the war on the nation's health, once thought to be almost entirely benign, now appears to be 'full of contradictory features'.[144] At the very least, traditional plagues such as smallpox, diptheria, and so on were kept at bay, both at the Front and in civilian life—no small achievement, given the upheaval of war. The influenza epidemic of 1918–19, which might be said to contradict this claim, in fact hit all countries, including neutrals, and so cannot solely be treated as war-related. Full employment and higher real wages for the poorest working-class strata obviously promoted physical well-being, not least because it meant that they were being better fed—despite wartime shortages. Indeed, those shortages which obliged consumers to eat less meat and butter but more bread and potatoes seem to have been, on balance, nutritionally advantageous, while the reduction in sugar consumption un-doubtedly proved beneficial to children's teeth and to diabetics and those likely to develop this disease.[145]

Government-imposed controls on alcohol, whether taking the form of restricting opening hours in pubs, raising excise duties, or reducing the strength of beer, had an even more direct impact on the people's health, though this was a side-effect of interventions which were mainly motivated by quite other considerations.[146] Falling alcohol consumption—it fell by 16 per cent

[142] In London the numbers of families sharing a dwelling increased from 15.7% to 20% (DeGroot, *Blighty*, 198).

[143] However, this development may also have owed something to the large numbers of girls, with no built-in immunity, entering the cities from rural areas.

[144] J. Winter, 'Surviving the War: Life Expectation, Illness, and Mortality Rates in Paris, London, and Berlin, 1914–1919', in Winter and Robert (eds.), *Capital Cities at War*, 519.

[145] Winter shows that the cost of working-class food expenditure rose by 60% between 1914 and 1918, while the retail food-price index rose by over 100%, from which he concludes that working-class family saved about 40% of their wartime food bills by changing the composition of their diets (*Great War*, 225).

[146] See below.

from 1914 to 1916 alone[147]—caused a striking reduction in the incidence both of cirrhosis of the liver and of infant deaths by 'overlaying'.

But what of the wider picture? Life-expectancy for men in England and Wales (aged 45 and over) rose between 1911 and 1921 from 49 to 56 years and for women from 53 to 60—an increase substantially in excess of that registered either in the first or in the third decade of the century.[148] But this average conceals many significant variations. For example, as we have seen, because of the shortage of beds and medicines long-term civilian patients, particularly the elderly, had to vacate beds for those whose needs seemed more immediate: in other words, soldiers and those of serviceable age were prioritized.[149] Mortality among girls and young women also rose, though it fell among women in their forties and fifties.

Expectant mothers, on the other hand, did well out of the war. The falling birth-rate (caused mainly by the temporary break-up of families) boosted women's health, and—unsurprisingly—led to an overall decline in deaths from complications of childbirth, a development which resonated throughout British society.[150] By July 1915 about a quarter of the medical profession (including some 14,000 GPs) had joined up,[151] leaving about 20 per cent of the civilian population without adequate medical cover, but this seemingly made little difference to anyone, least of all to women in labour. Women may actually have fared better when obliged to rely upon midwives, who, unlike male doctors, did not use forceps when delivering babies. On the other hand, as we have seen, war was not an unmitigated blessing for babies and infants. There is much about wartime health trends that remains a mystery.

What the war did promote was increased state involvement in public-health matters. With a few exceptions, these initiatives came into effect far too late to show up in wartime vital statistics. However, they were very important for the future, and reflected profound shifts in the relationship between the state and its citizens.

3. THE GROWTH OF THE STATE

Despite the compilation of its 'War Book', the government found itself ill-prepared for war in August 1914. Many of its earliest actions had the appear-

---

[147] DeGroot, *Blighty*, 205.   [148] Winter, *Great War*, 105.
[149] Rollet, 'The "Other War" I', 432.
[150] B. Harris, 'The Demographic Impact of the First World War: An Anthropometric Perspective', *Journal of the Society for the Social History of Medicine*, 6 (1993), 349; L. Bryder, 'The First World War: Healthy or Hungry?', *History Workshop*, 24 (1987), 144–5; I. Loudon, 'Deaths in Childbed from the Eighteenth Century to 1935', *Medical History*, 30 (1986), 1–41.
[151] Winter, *Great War*, 157.

ance of scrambled improvisations. The boldest decision, taken in September, was to control capital movements, the export of which now required a licence, which was normally given only when the national interest was served—an initiative called by one historian 'a clearer break with free trade orthodoxy than the largely symbolic McKenna duties of September 1915'.[152] Trading with the enemy also fell under a general legislative prohibition, much to the annoyance of exporters, who, complaining of a 'needless sacrifice', found plentiful ways of evading these restrictions.[153] But the main aim of government at the start of the war was to promote calm in the markets—hence the adoption of the slogan 'Business as Usual', first employed as an advertising slogan by Harrods.

The 'War Book' was at least useful in suggesting ways by which the railways could prioritize the army's needs. The railway companies were, it is true, left in private ownership, but they all now came under national control—a forerunner of the kind of state intervention later called 'war socialism'. The government also entered the market directly to buy up available sugar stocks, and even made surreptitious purchases of wheat until forced to suspend this operation in March 1915 in the face of an infuriated mercantile community. More far-reaching still was the enactment on 8 August of the Defence of the Realm Act (DORA), which gave the government sweeping power to rule by decree.

But in the opening months of war all else paled beside the need to meet the army's insatiable demand for munitions. The War Office originally preferred to concentrate orders in the hands of ordnance factories and long-established contractors. Lloyd George, on the other hand, wanted to spread orders more widely around the engineering industry, a stance which soon set him at logger-heads with Kitchener and the Master of Ordnance, Stanley von Donop.[154]

In March 1915 Asquith deftly resolved the dispute by putting Lloyd George in charge of a Munitions of War Committee, and giving the government greater powers to direct industry through the DORA (Amendment Number 2) Bill. There followed the so-called 'Treasury Agreement' with trade-union officials (the germ of the later Munitions of War Act). This decreed that profits in the munitions industry should be kept at a maximum of 20 per cent above peacetime levels, and imposed draconian regulations on the aptly named 'controlled establishments', private workshops working on government contracts.

In May the Shells Scandal destroyed Asquith's Liberal ministry, and from the resulting reconstruction Lloyd George emerged as the head of a new Ministry of Munitions, with the War Office stripped of all its powers over

---

[152] D. French, *British Strategy and War Aims, 1914–16* (London, 1986), 90.

[153] J. McDermott, ' "A Needless Sacrifice": British Businessmen and Business as Usual in the First World War', *Albion*, 21 (1989), 282.

[154] D. French, 'The Rise and Fall of "Business as Usual" ', in Burk (ed.), *War and the State*, 22–3.

armaments supply. Much had already been done to boost production.[155] Kitchener, for example, was responsible for overseeing a nineteenfold increase of production. The War Secretary (on 16 March 1915) had also recruited the Liverpudlian shipowner George Booth, the 'man of push and go', charged with mobilizing private industry behind the war effort.

Nevertheless, despite Kitchener's best efforts, the situation facing Lloyd George in May 1915 was dire. There were only enough 18-pounder field-guns to equip twenty-eight divisions, with reserves of ammunition that would last for no more than twelve days. Rifles, smaller guns, and howitzers were in similarly short supply. The greatest shortfall of all was in machine-guns: at least 26,000 of these needed to come off the production line yearly, yet orders had been placed for fewer than 5,500.[156] Nor did the placing of orders guarantee supplies: by 29 May 1915, out of 5,797,274 shell bodies already ordered by the War Office only 1,968,252 had actually been delivered.[157]

Starting with two secretaries, two tables, and a chair, Lloyd George quickly built up a formidable ministry which, by the end of the war, employed a headquarters staff of over 25,000 (with perhaps 65,000 people on its payroll), and directed the production of over 3 million workers.[158] Using the powers conferred on him by the Munitions of War Act, passed in July, Lloyd George and his officials contracted out munitions production so that even inexperienced firms could, with appropriate guidance, adapt their plant to one of its specialized processes—cycle firms, for example, were soon manufacturing shell cases. In addition to the 'controlled establishments', which eventually numbered about 20,000, new state-owned enterprises were established, such as the fifteen National Projectile Factories, the fifteen National Filling Factories, and the four National Cartridge Factories.

These achievements transformed Lloyd George's reputation, making possible his later rise to the premiership. But it had a downside which can easily be overlooked. In fact, the guns and ammunition ordered by the new Ministry were not available in quantity until the following spring, and, as the battle of the Somme showed, many of them were of very poor standard, with shells, for example, often failing to explode—as Kitchener had all along warned. The yearly harvest of unexploded munitions in farms along the Somme continued for the rest of the century.

In his desperate haste to boost production, Lloyd George also took some dangerous short-cuts. Unlike Asquith, Lloyd George was happy to bring businessmen into government, the archetype being Eric Geddes, a railway

[155] Wrigley, 'Ministry of Munitions', 34.   [156] Bourne, *Great War*, 188.
[157] Wrigley, 'Ministry of Munitions', 38.
[158] Bourne, *Great War*, 189. By the end of 1918 39% of the Ministry's staff were women (Wrigley, 'Ministry of Munitions', 42).

manager. But because many businessmen gave their services to the government without charge, the Treasury found it difficult to control their (often questionable) activities.[159] Thus, Albert Herbert, head of the Machine Tool Department, advertised his own firm by issuing circulars on Ministry paper over his own name. Such irregularities damaged the civil service's reputation for honesty and impartiality, and complicated an already tense relationship between the government and the Labour Movement. If the Ministry of Munitions, under Lloyd George, seethed with creativity, it was also riven with departmental rivalries. In any case, the Welshman had never been noted for his administrative efficiency. It needed his successors, Montagu, Addison, and Churchill, to impose system and method on the Ministry's chaotic operations.

Under Lloyd George's inspiration, the Ministry of Munitions transformed the manufacturing world in many important ways—95 per cent of the new munitions factories were powered by electricity;[160] so, too, by the end of the war, were most of the 'controlled establishments'. Mass-production techniques (standardization, simplification, the use of machine tools, etc.) became commonplace throughout industry, as did the adoption of more sophisticated cost-accounting methods and time-and-motion studies. The Ministry was also to the fore in devoting scientific expertise and resources to the search for new armaments systems, a development which resulted not only in better fuses and high explosives and the appearance of new weapons such as the Stokes Mortar, but also in a growing appreciation of the wider commercial benefits of Research and Development.[161]

Even without the government's contribution, the war was transforming the relationship between applied science and manufacturing. Motor vehicles, wireless telegraphy, and the aeronautical industries[162] all received an enormous boost, while technological advances created what were, in effect, a range of new industries geared to the production of such commodities as scientific instruments, glassware, ball bearings, tungsten, benzol, toluol, and liquid ammonia. These innovations came not a minute too soon, for when war broke out the country's munitions factories were still heavily dependent on imports (often German imports, at that) for such crucial items as tungsten, chemicals, electrical equipment, and optical glass.[163] Not until the autumn of 1916 were the British able to manufacture their own magnetos. In some instances the

---

[159] Wrigley, 'Ministry of Munitions', 41.   [160] Ibid. 47.   [161] Bourne, Great War, 190–1.

[162] See Wilson, Myriad Faces, 364, for the growth of the aeronautical industry; also J. Bruce, 'The War in the Air: The Men and their Machines', in H. Cecil and P. H. Liddle (eds.), Facing Armageddon: The First World War Experienced (London, 1996), 196. 'The lack of suitable aeroengines remained Britain's Achilles' heel, and the British had to rely on France for some 16,000 additional engines' (J. H. Morrow, Jnr., The Great War in the Air: Military Aviation from 1909 to 1921 (Shrewsbury, 1993), 369).

[163] In mid-1914 60% of all Britain's optical glass came from the Zeiss Works in Jena, 30% from a French company, and only 10% was manufactured in the UK (P. Alter, The Reluctant Patron: Science

government had to intervene directly in the market, for example, by creating the British Dye Company in the spring of 1915 and giving it a starting capital of £2 million. But, more importantly, the government had to forge an entirely different relationship with the scientific community.

Ever since 1909, the Board of Education had been examining ways of improving scientific research at British universities and making its results more widely available to industry.[164] But little had actually been achieved by 1914. The war then provided dramatic vindication of the long-held views of the 'endowment of science' lobby. In February 1916 thirty-six university teachers and scientists signed a public letter, drawing attention to the 'Neglect of Science', and this was followed three months later by the establishment of the Neglect of Science Committee, chaired by Lord Rayleigh. In December the government responded by creating the Department of Scientific and Industrial Research (DSIR). Walter Runciman, at the Board of Trade, was a key player in this important innovation, with Lloyd George, Haldane, and Addison providing invaluable support. By the middle of the war few would have disagreed with *The Times* when it called the northern civic universities 'branches of the country's defensive forces'.[165] The understandable preoccupation with military injuries was meanwhile responsible for an expansion in the prestige of the Medical Research Council, also established in 1916.

Physicists, chemists, and engineers, now recognized as national assets, were recruited in large numbers by the Service Departments and the Ministry of Munitions, where they assumed direct responsibility for the development of the tank, chemical weapons, synthetic fabrics, and underwater apparatus. They also rendered invaluable service by pointing out areas where product substitution was feasible. For example, a chemist at Manchester University, Professor Chaim Weizmann (better known as the inspirer of a Jewish national home), demonstrated that acetone, an ingredient of cordite, could be made from horse chestnuts.

Yet how were such immensely expensive operations to be paid for and their costs controlled? Unfortunately, as the first wartime Chancellor of the Exchequer, Lloyd George showed little of the long-term vision which characterized his dealings with munitions production. Initially, through the issue of Treasury bills, he deliberately set out to fuel inflation, hoping that this would

---

and the State in Britain (Oxford, 1987), 112). In 1914–15 the Institute of Chemistry commissioned the British Science Guild to investigate the supply of optical glass (R. and K. Macleod, 'War and Economic Development: Government and the Optical Industry in Britain, 1914–18', in J. M. Winter (ed.), *War and Economic Development* (Cambridge, 1975), 171).

[164] See article by MacLeod and Andrews.
[165] 9 Feb. 1916, in Alter, *Reluctant Patron*, 193.

give workers an incentive to seek higher earnings in the war industries.[166] The Treasury's controls over expenditure were also inadequate: for example, although Morgans soon became the sole British agency in New York, little was done to curb or co-ordinate Allied munitions-purchasing in the United States.[167] By the end of March 1915 the British government had also loaned nearly £52 million to its Allies and the Dominions, without giving much thought as to how this gigantic outlay was to be covered.[168] Desperate efforts were soon being made to convince the Allies that Britain did not possess bottomless wealth.[169]

Reginald McKenna, who took charge of the Treasury in May 1915, started off by continuing his predecessor's reliance on borrowing. But the loan, issued on 21 June 1915 in small denominations paying 4.5 per cent interest, was unpopular with the banking community and brought in little more than half of the £1,000 million that McKenna had hoped to raise.[170] An attempt on the part of the British and French governments to raise money on the New York market later in the year proved little more successful.

It was only with McKenna's September 1915 Budget that it was first brought home to the tax-paying public what was involved in fighting a major war. This Budget is now best remembered for the 'McKenna Duties' imposed on luxury imports such as motor cars, cinema films, and musical instruments, a device erroneously supposed to represent a fundamental breach with free trade. Many of its other provisions were far more important. The munitions levy already in place was replaced by the EPD on all war-related industries, fixed at 50 per cent over pre-war profit levels, after allowance had been made for capital investments. Income-tax rates were raised, and the payment threshold lowered, while the supertax rates not only went up, but were also graduated for the first time. Even so, McKenna faced a deficit of £1,285 million, to bridge which he had to resort to further loans.[171]

The April 1916 Budget brought more pain. The standard rate of income tax went up again, this time to 5s. in the pound on incomes over £2,500 p.a. Sugar duty was also increased, and new duties slapped onto a range of new products. EPD went up from 50 per cent to 60 per cent. The Treasury estimated that taxation, in total, would bring in £500 million, £180 million more than had been raised in the preceding year. Extraordinary measures were also taken to discourage investment in American securities, in response to the deteriorating exchange situation with the United States, on whom Britain was becoming precariously dependent.[172] Always sceptical of the Continental entanglement,

[166] French, 'Business as Usual', 23.   [167] Ibid. 121.   [168] Ibid. 19.
[169] French, British Strategy, 127.   [170] Ibid. 123.   [171] Lawrence, 'Material Pressures', 234.
[172] French, British Strategy, 187.

McKenna increasingly came to feel that current policy would sooner or later bankrupt the country—as, indeed, it might have done, had President Wilson not abandoned neutrality when he did. Even with American loans, Bonar Law had to screw up taxation even higher in his budgets of 1917 and 1918.[173]

Lloyd George's own instinct was to win the war by hook or by crook, and only when the peace was over to start worrying about who would pick up the tabs. But the very success of his munitions drive ironically had the effect of allowing the military to pursue an attritional policy, to which he had always entertained objections. It also drew Lloyd George into a damaging dispute on two fronts: against the soldiers who, in their desperation for greater manpower, tried constantly to raid the reservoir of skilled men the Ministry of Munitions needed for munitions production (to say nothing of the need to maintain the prosperity of export-earning businesses); and against the trade unions, who disliked and feared the impact the war was having on their traditional privileges.

Only at the end of the war did the British government have anything that could be called a coherent manpower policy. In August 1916 a Man-Power Distribution Board was established, but it lacked executive powers. Nor did the change of prime minister help the cause of manpower planning. Indeed, Lloyd George's entry into 10 Downing Street involved the abandonment of the far-reaching National Service Bill which Montagu had recently persuaded the Cabinet to accept, so anxious was the new Prime Minister to keep the trade-union leadership on board. So although Lloyd George quickly established a Department of National Service, which he upgraded into a full Ministry in May 1917, he left its Director-General, the luckless Neville Chamberlain, dangling in the wind, with little idea of the extent of his remit. In mid-August Chamberlain was brutally dismissed, to be replaced by Auckland Geddes. As we have seen, it needed the acute manpower crisis of late 1917, followed by the possibility of military defeat in the following spring, to resolve the impasse. It was only in mid-1918 that Geddes, belatedly, received powers that enabled his Ministry to *allocate* labour, as well as to *monitor* its distribution.[174]

During the last two years of the war the problem of munitions production had been largely overcome: under Churchill the volume and variety of the weaponry flooding out of British factories gave the Allied armies the wherewithal to defeat the Central Powers. The main administrative challenges now changed. After Berlin's adoption of unrestricted U-boat warfare the country faced the prospect of being starved into submission, and this highlighted the related problems of shipping and food.

---

[173] It has been argued, however, that Britain acquired leverage over the USA precisely because she was so heavily indebted to the Americans (Ferguson, *Pity of War*, 323).

[174] See Ch. 18.

Shipping shortages had long worried the government. After all, the prime purpose of the McKenna Duties in 1915 had been to economize on shipping space. In that same year vessels were forbidden to ply between two foreign ports without a licence from the Ship Licensing Committee. In January 1916 a Shipping Controller was appointed, operating under the guidance of Lord Curzon, Chairman of the Shipping Control Committee, but the government still largely relied upon the impact of higher freightage rates to reduce the balance of imports. The flaw in this free-market approach, which was also inflationary, was that there could be no guarantee that the process would not lead to the exclusion of necessities.

Only under Lloyd George did the government take a firmer grip. In December 1916 he created a new Ministry of Shipping, quite separate from the Board of Trade, under the direction of the Glaswegian shipowner Joseph Maclay. It was one of his very best appointments. Requisitioning was now extended to cover all ocean-going mercantile ships (one-half of the British fleet, operating in distant waters, had previously been left untouched); the owners became virtually agents of the state, working at a limited rate of profit and on fixed freight charges. Maclay also reorganized the ports, easing congestion by ensuring that ships could more quickly be 'turned round'. Finally, Maclay launched a vast shipbuilding programme, which required many shipwrights and other skilled workers to be brought back from the Front and badged. The results were remarkable: after March 1917 the gross tonnage of ships launched each month exactly doubled, and by June 1917 new ships at last overtook the tonnage lost to submarine attack.

The government supplemented these efforts by taking responsibility for the country's entire imports. Shipping was now concentrated on the shortest possible routes—for example, wheat imports from Australia were largely abandoned for those from North America. In 1918 the government actually managed, in stages, to reduce the volume of imports by 5 million tons—thanks, in large part, to the efficient Milner, whose Priority Committee adjudicated between the claims on materials being made by the armed services and by key civilian industries, and graded imported goods according to their national importance.

At the same time, in December 1916, Lloyd George set up a Food Controller (followed two months later by a Coal Controller). This began a process whereby food production became subject to national planning. When Lloyd George became Prime Minister a Food Production Department already existed, but only as part of the Board of Agriculture. It now became an autonomous agency. With Lord Lee of Fareham as its Director, bold use was made of wide-ranging powers: for example, directing landowners to use their land more efficiently (if recalcitrant, they could be dispossessed and their land worked by County War Executive Committees or leased to other tenants).

Under state direction, 3 million acres of pasture were converted to cereal production, along with commons and parklands. Hampstead Heath was dug up and planted with potatoes.[175]

The 1917 Corn Production Act formed the centrepiece of the government's plan to make Britain more self-sufficient in agricultural products. But, once again, the prioritization of an industry created new manpower problems, which resort to American tractors only partially solved. Labourers had to be brought in from far and wide (only in July 1917 were skilled agricultural workers given exemption). By the end of the war some 84,000 soldiers were working the land, alongside 30,000 POWs and the 16,000 members of the Women's Land Army. Fertilizer remained in short supply (its basic ingredients were also needed for the manufacture of high explosives). Even so, the output of home-grown wheat rose by 0.7 per cent between 1914 and 1917, at a time when that of Germany was dropping catastrophically (by 42.8 per cent), and by 1918 the wheat crop was nearly 65 per cent greater than the pre-war average, while allotments became a significant source of fresh vegetables.

Import substitution took place in other economic sectors. With the aim of reducing the waste of scarce shipping space involved in bulk importation of timber from the United States, patriotic gentlemen were encouraged to donate their private woods to the state, while a few thousand lumbermen came over from Canada to fell them. Similarly, the iron and steel industry learned how to process the ores of Cumberland, instead of relying on the richer 'hematite' ores once imported in bulk from Spain and Scandinavia.

Faced by so many shortages, the government found itself compelled to prevent speculation and profiteering by fixing prices. But, once this had been done, some system of allocation and rationing was needed to take the place of market forces. This happened in the distribution, not only of food, but of commodities such as wool, over which the government acquired a virtual monopoly—this gave an impetus to the formation of trade associations, with which the agencies of the state could strike bargains.

Consumers, too, came under increased control. Food hoarding was made a serious offence, carrying heavy penalties, and sumptuary laws (i.e. laws restricting 'wasteful' expenditure) were passed. The first Food Controller, Lord Devonport, set up 'meat-less days', prohibited the making of expensive sweets and pastries, and, through the Public Meals Order of December 1916, imposed restrictions on what dishes could be sold in restaurants, where meals were limited to two courses midday, three in the evenings.[176] In June 1917 he gave

---

[175] Though with disappointing results: see P. E. Dewey, 'Food Production and Policy in the United Kingdom, 1914–1918', *Transactions of the Royal Historical Society*, 5th ser., 30 (1980), 194.

[176] DeGroot, *Blighty*, 210.

way to Lord Rhondda, who started to prepare a compulsory rationing scheme. In the wake of the irrational queuing which characterized the early months of 1918 (a mania which even spread to munitions workers coming off their night-shift),[177] the Ministry (in which Beveridge and U. F. Wintour, formerly the Director of Army Contracts, played important roles) speeded up the process, and on 8 July a comprehensive rationing system, on the points basis, came into operation.[178] Individuals who registered with a particular shop received coupons for particular foodstuffs. Only in April 1918 did rationing cover meat, and another three months elapsed before most basic commodities were brought into the scheme. But by the end of the war 85 per cent of all food consumed by the civilian population was being bought and sold by the state, which fixed prices and profit margins for each stage of the distribution.

The government also took another set of measures, which had a much greater long-term impact. To eke out scarce grain supplies, not only were millers obliged to increase the extraction rate from flour (barley and oats were meanwhile being diverted from the feeding of animals to the making of bread),[179] but the gravity of beer was also reduced to 50 per cent of its pre-war strength and curbs were placed on distilling.[180]

These economy measures soon merged with the government's campaign against drunkenness, which some ministers, Lloyd George included, thought to be a major cause of absenteeism in the munitions factories and, as such, a grave impediment to the war effort. In 1915, under the authority of DORA, the government had already set up the Central Liquor (Control Board), which rapidly took responsibility for the drinking habits in the area around Gretna, where it acquired 119 licensed premises and bought up breweries in Carlisle and the Maryport district: about one-half of these pubs were declared redundant and closed, others were placed under a strict non-profit-making regime. In other areas where munitions were being made, the Board could reduce opening hours from $19\frac{1}{2}$ to $5\frac{1}{2}$ hours a day. Other government orders imposed a total Sunday closure of pubs, spirit-less Saturdays, and the banning of alcohol sales to those under 18 years of age. Moreover, off-licences could no longer sell spirits in less than quarts, 'chasers' were not allowed, and there was a ban on credit and 'treating'.

As a result of all these changes, by 1918 the production of beer had halved (from 33 to 19 million barrels p.a.), and it was a much weaker beverage that was being sold. Consumption of spirits rose briefly between 1914 and 1915, but a succession of increases in the duty (it had reached 30s. a gallon in 1918, 50s. in 1919) led to an even steeper fall in their sales, down from 35 million gallons

[177] Winter, *Great War*, 216.   [178] DeGroot, *Blighty*, 203.   [179] Ibid. 90–2, 195, 203–4.
[180] Winter, *Great War*, 230. Spirits were also diluted to 30% proof.

in 1915 to 15 millions in 1918.[181] The consequences of these measures for industrial productivity are problematic, but their cumulative effect was undoubtedly helpful to both the nation's health and to public order: prosecutions for drunkenness in England and Wales declined from 157,000 to 32,000, and by a similar ratio in Scotland.[182] Britain was a far more sober society in 1918 than it had ever been before.

The work of the Control Board also had a liberating dimension. Many of the licensed premises it controlled now became recreational centres in a more general sense, serving hot meals and providing billiard tables and newspapers. Such innovations were paralleled by the work of the Health of Munitions Workers Committee at the Ministry of Munitions, which Lloyd George placed under the charge of his old political friend Seebohm Rowntree, who was able to demonstrate that the reduction of excessive factory hours actually *increased* output (by up to 25 per cent), mainly through cutting down the incidence of absenteeism and accidents. But the Ministry also pioneered a range of other reforms, aimed at increasing the productivity of human capital. Model housing was provided in areas such as the neighbourhood of Gretna and on the Well Hall Estate at Eltham. Works canteens also proliferated: by the end of the war, at a cost to the government of £3.5 million, they numbered more than 900 and provided hot meals to over 1 million war workers.[183] Munitions factories never had enough crèches to meet demand, but from 1917 onwards the Ministry contributed 75 per cent of their cost.[184]

As grievances accumulated in the latter stages of the war, state-sponsored welfare came to assume ever greater importance. Asquith's Committee on Reconstruction of 1916, with Montagu as its Chairman, had to plan for such future contingencies as demobilization. Lloyd George then responded to the May strikes in 1917 (described below) by turning the Committee into a full Ministry and placing his loyal lieutenant Christopher Addison at its head. Reconstruction sprouted dozens of specialized committees, concerned with almost every conceivable aspect of social and economic policy, from industrial modernization to the overhaul of industrial insurance, Poor Law reform, educational expansion, housing, and public health. Particularly notable was the way in which the government used the Ministry to conscript various independent experts into the service of the state. Beatrice Webb, for example, sat on the Machinery of Government Committee, chaired by her friend Haldane; Rowntree was another key participant. Prominent trade unionists

[181] J. Burnett, *Liquid Pleasures: A Social History of Drinks in Modern Britain* (London, 1999), 173. The April 1915 Budget doubled the duty on spirits and included measures which resulted in the dilution of whisky, brandy, and rum.
[182] Ibid. 173.   [183] Winter, *Great War*, 211.   [184] Ibid. 222.

were also involved in its work—a shrewd moved, aimed at the Labour Movement's incorporation into the state.

Addison meant well, but one historian has said that the government used the Ministry's myriad committees as a drunken man uses lamp-posts, for support rather than for illumination.[185] Reconstruction certainly suffered from being asked to serve so many different purposes. Buying off social unrest was obviously an important part of its mission, boosting civilian morale another, the short-term raising of industrial productivity yet another. But a fourth reason for the Ministry's existence was the fear that Germany might not be decisively defeated, and that economic controls would thus have to be continued after the war to contain the threat of a German economic resurgence and to ration scarce materials—the assumption which had earlier underlain the 1916 Paris Economic Resolutions.[186]

The need to husband human resources in face of the 'wastage' of life on the battlefield had long interested Addison (a medical man). While still Parliamentary Secretary at the Board of Education, he had been instrumental in framing the 1915 Care of Mothers and Young Children Act, which empowered local authorities to set up facilities for expectant and nursing mothers and for young children, with 50 per cent subsidies from the Local Government Board. By 1917 446 centres were being operated by forty-two voluntary societies, twenty-three by local authorities.[187] The number of full-time health visitors rose from 600 in 1914 to 1,355 in 1918.[188] The wartime 'cult of the baby' inspired other pieces of 'pro-natalist' legislation: for example, the Notification of Births (Extension) Act (1915), the Milk and Dairies Consolidation Act (1915), and the Midwives Act (1918). The Maternity and Child Welfare Act of 1918 consolidated many of these various wartime innovations.[189]

In the final year of war it was also agreed to set up a Ministry of Health, of which Addison was to be the first Minister, with Robert Morant as his Permanent Secretary and Sir George Newman as his Chief Medical Officer. Here, surely, was evidence that the Webbs and their fellow pre-war campaigners for Poor Law reform had belatedly triumphed. Alas, as a result of the obstructionist tactics of the Local Government Board, the new Ministry possessed inadequate powers, particularly in its relationship with local authorities, which remained largely unchanged. Nor had the anxiety of GPs over the possible introduction of a permanent, full-time medical service been allayed—rather the opposite, in fact.

---

[185] S. J. Hurwitz, *State Intervention in Great Britain: A Study of Economic Control and Social Response 1914–1919* (London, 1949; 1968 edn.), 290.

[186] P. Cline, 'Winding Down the War Economy: British Plans for Peacetime Recovery, 1916–19', in Burk (ed.), *War and the State*, 157–81.

[187] DeGroot, *Blighty*, 218.　　[188] Winter, *Great War*, 204.　　[189] Ibid. 188.

And herein lay a dilemma: in the final years of the war Lloyd George and Addison invested Reconstruction with an aura of utopian optimism, raising expectations that would prove difficult to meet. Reconstruction, claimed its spokesmen, would not only be the culmination of the earlier quest for National Efficiency; it would also, with cross-party support, usher in a brave new post-war world. In Addison's words, the aim was 'not so much a question of rebuilding society as it was before the war, but of moulding a better world out of the social and economic conditions which have come into being during the war'. But could this be achieved? And would the Labour Movement be content, in the long run, with the sort of social engineering deemed practical and responsible by Addison and Lloyd George?

The impact of wartime innovation on society may have been problematic: its immediate impact on Whitehall was plain for all to see. By the end of the war the established civil service numbered nearly a quarter of a million officials, plus 150,000 'temporaries', a combined total of nearly 400,000, well over double the figure for 1914. Twelve new ministries were created. Seven of these (Blockade, Reconstruction, Information, Munitions, Shipping, Food Control, and National Service) did not survive into the 1920s, nor were they meant to do so. But another five (Labour, Pensions, Air, Health, and Transport) became a settled part of the country's administration.

Such a dramatic expansion of government meant that peacetime rules for safeguarding the cheapness and probity of the civil service temporarily went out of the window. Competitive examinations, for example, were not fully re-established for recruitment to clerical posts until 1927. In some of the new ministries tension understandably developed between the career civil servants and the newcomers.[190] Similarly, Treasury controls were suspended and not restored until 1920, releasing the spending departments from its former iron grip, leading, many thought, to unbridled extravagance. In 1918 total gross expenditure hit £2,696.2 million—as against £184 million in 1913. Against this development an exaggerated reaction was soon to set in.

In the past Lloyd George has been given too much praise for his role in expanding wartime government. True, his attachment of a secretariat to the War Cabinet, under the efficient Hankey, put a stop to some of the ludicrous muddles that had characterized the Asquith regime. However, the War Cabinet did not exercise the control over Whitehall that it should have done, since, far from concentrating authority in its own hands, it tended to devolve

---

[190] Though in the case of the Ministry of Food 'adventurers' and 'mandarins' were to be found in both camps (J. Harris, 'Bureaucrats and Businessmen in British Food Control, 1916–19', in Burk (ed.), *War and the State*, 135–56).

upwards or downwards,[191] mainly downwards: inheriting 102 Cabinet subcommittees from Asquith, Lloyd George added another sixty-three.[192]

Moreover, as we have seen, several of the new state agencies had either been set up under Asquith or else had been prepared for prior to the change of premiership. But, in any case, the multiplication of ministries, many of them primarily designed to buy off opposition, often created more confusion than they resolved: as, for example, in the overlapping responsibilities of the Ministry of Labour and the Department of National Service. Nor was the Prime Minister's own personality an unmixed blessing. Essentially an improviser, Lloyd George brought a new dynamism to the work of government, but, as has truly been said, dynamism is not the same thing as method.[193]

From the start the government had been anxious not to alienate the Labour Movement. That is why Lloyd George, way back in March 1915, had negotiated the Treasury Agreement with the trade-union leaders, only afterwards presenting his proposals to the employers.[194] But this Agreement, the basis of the later Munitions of War Act, contained many provisions which class-conscious working men were bound to dislike. True, it allowed for trade-union representation on the new munitions tribunals and met their demands, to some extent, on the issue of curbing profiteering. But compulsory arbitration and the suspension of restrictive trade-union practices for the duration of the war posed a long-term threat to the very existence of independent trade unionism. Particularly hated was the institution of the 'leaving certificate' (Clause 7 of the Munitions of War Act), which stipulated that a worker in a 'controlled establishment' could only move jobs if he had first received his employer's permission. David Kirkwood, the colourful Glaswegian shop steward, memorably said of this provision that it had 'the taint of slavery about it'.

The miners' executive had pointedly refused to join trade unionists from other industries in the talks which led to the Treasury Agreement. It was thus hardly a surprise when the miners of South Wales, with full union backing, came out on strike later in July. The government quickly capitulated before this challenge to its authority—as it was later to do, in rather similar circumstances, in November.

But in the engineering industry, where union officials were bound by the Munitions of War Act, discontent was also rife, with many workers sharing Beatrice Webb's belief that their 'leaders' had too readily succumbed to

---

[191] J. Turner, 'Cabinets, Committees and Secretariats: The Higher Direction of War', in Burk (ed.), *War and the State*, 57–83.

[192] Bourne, *Great War*, 130.

[193] DeGroot, *Blighty*, 80.

[194] Admittedly, Runciman was meanwhile negotiating a concordat with the engineering employers.

patriotic blackmail.[195] It was this mistrust of remote union bureaucrats, coupled with a fragmented union structure, which gave rise to a powerful rank-and-file protest movement. In the principal munitions areas power largely passed to local committees of shop stewards, who headed the resistance to the infringements of customary trade-union rights inherent in 'dilution'.

In 1915 the main flashpoint was the Clyde, where, as early as February, there had been a strike, organized by the shop stewards of the Clyde Workers Committee (CWC). The unrest spread. On Christmas Day 1915 angry workmen shouted Lloyd George down when he tried to address them in St George's Square, Glasgow. But officials in the Ministry of Munitions (many of whom had formerly been active in welfare initiatives at the Board of Trade[196]) swiftly counter-attacked: between January and March 1916 the leading troublemakers, John Muir, Tom Bell, and John Maclean, were prosecuted and deported to Edinburgh, and dilution was ruthlessly forced through.

By this time militant trade unionists were in the grip of another fear—the fear that, notwithstanding the pledges they had received, conscription would be extended to industrial life or even be used as an instrument of industrial discipline. The fur really flew when skilled engineers who thought that they had been guaranteed exemption from military service found themselves being called up. This culminated in November in a strike called by the ASE's Sheffield District Committee to contest the conscription of an engineer, Leonard Hargreaves—a strike which quickly spread to Barrow, another important munitions centre (Clydeside, by this time, was relatively calm). Again, the government capitulated. Hargreaves was released, and on 18 November the Trade Cards Agreement was passed, allowing the ASE to decide which of its members could be exempted from military service—the highwater mark of the shop-stewards' movement and of the politics of direct action.

Lloyd George regarded this particular concession as one of Asquith's greatest mistakes,[197] and on 3 April 1917 the War Cabinet unilaterally repudiated it. However, in taking this step at a time when the trade unions were already up in arms over the government's attempts to extend dilution to private establishments, the Prime Minister landed himself in the biggest industrial conflict of the entire war, the 'May strikes'. To defuse the anger, the government prudently moved the unpopular Christopher Addison from Munitions to Reconstruction, fixed the price of certain essential foodstuffs, and offered

---

[195] See diary entry, 2 Jan. 1916, in N. and J. MacKenzie (eds.), *The Diary of Beatrice Webb: Volume Three: 1905–24: 'The Power to Alter Things'* (London, 1984), 244.

[196] J. Hinton, *The First Shop Stewards' Movement* (London, 1973), 30–1.

[197] K. Middlemas, *Politics in Industrial Society: The Experience of the British System Since 1911* (London, 1979; 1980 edn.), 101.

skilled men in the industrial workforce a 12.5 per cent war bonus—which was later extended to semi- and unskilled workers. The protests petered out.

Lloyd George could never quite decide how best to cope with the phenomenon of trade unionism. Spasmodically, he tried to institutionalize the relationship. On forming his government he created two new ministries, Labour and Pensions, filling each with a trade-union stalwart (John Hodge and George Barnes, respectively), as well as finding a place in his War Cabinet for Arthur Henderson. But eight months later he almost casually alienated the all-important Henderson, perhaps feeling, in the light of recent industrial disturbances, that he had exaggerated the latter's influence over rank-and-file workers. On the other hand, there were times when Lloyd George flirted with the idea of going behind the backs of union officialdom and cutting a deal directly with the shop stewards, an initiative from which he was pulled back, not only by the TUC, but also by pressure from the employers' organizations.[198]

Lloyd George's relationship with businessmen was ambiguous. For although the new Prime Minister, supposedly a proponent of 'control', is sometimes presented as someone who broke with old-fashioned economic liberalism, in fact he too, though in a less doctrinaire fashion, accepted the need to work *through* the business community, even at the price of offending the trade unions.

The Ministry of Munitions was, in its creator's own words, 'from first to last a businessman's organisation'. It was certainly stuffed with recruits from private industry, among them Eric Geddes, and William Weir of G. & J. Weir of Cathcart, who was made the Director of Munitions for Scotland.[199] Middlemas thinks that, to an extent which has never been fully documented, employers at the local level actually *ran* the munitions effort: for example, the District Armaments Committee in Manchester consisted solely of members of the largest engineering firms, 'with only exiguous representation by the Ministry of Munitions'.[200] Such employers influenced Lloyd George on the need to keep EPD at relatively low levels to preserve incentives, as well as encouraging him to impose industrial 'discipline' on recalcitrant workers.[201] They also set their face like stone against any extension of nationalization: 'state socialism' might mean state control, but it left industry in private ownership, so that, for example, the day-to-day running of the railways was left to the companies' existing management.[202]

---

[198] Ibid. 81.   [199] Hinton, *Shop Stewards*, 31–2.
[200] Middlemas, *Industrial Society*, 113–14.
[201] Lloyd George's tough speeches on industrial relations in June 1915 had also been inspired by the businessmen in his Ministry (Wrigley, 'Ministry of Munitions', 46).
[202] French, 'Business as Usual', 15.

As Prime Minister, Lloyd George placed several businessmen in charge of Whitehall Departments—part of a wider process whereby, as Beatrice Webb noted in February 1917, the Prime Minister handed over ministries to the 'interests' which they were supposed to regulate: 'In that way, our little Welsh attorney thinks, you combine the least political opposition with the maximum technical knowledge.'[203] Thus Rowlaud Prothero, a land agent, was put in charge of Agriculture; H. A. L. Fisher, a don, was made President of the Board of Education; Maclay, a shipowner, was put in charge of Shipping; and Lord Devonport, a wholesale grocer, headed the new Ministry of Food Control. (Similarly, the first two Ministers of Labour were trade unionists: Hodge and George Roberts, as was the permanent head of the Department, David Shackleton.) In some respects such a development was unavoidable, since the government was undertaking tasks in which it lacked prior experience, and so had to co-opt those with the relevant expertise. However, although Maclay proved to be an excellent administator, businessmen in government often turned out to be failures: Lord Cowdray, the oil mogul, for example, made little impact at the Air Board.

Businessmen also irritated the government by being so slow to form their own business groupings, with a voice analogous to that of the TUC.[204] The gap was partially filled by the British Manufacturers' Association, set up in Birmingham by Dudley Docker, the owner of the *Globe*, which reformed in 1916 as the Federation of British Industries (FBI), with William (now Lord) Weir as one of its senior members. The FBI, which represented mainly the larger firms, called for the creation of a Ministry of Industry, responsible to organized business, working with state-backed export combines. Its demands were echoed by the British Engineers' Association. But, in John Turner's words, 'the relationship between business and the state was not one of domination by either side, but of bargaining between two weak entities which often did not know their own minds'.[205] The FBI, for example, was initially riven by dissension between protectionists and free traders, the latter being particularly mistrustful of any extension of the government's role. As a result, businessmen particularly keen on a pro-tariff policy, headed by Vincent Caillard, broke away to form the British Commonwealth Union (BCU), a militantly imperialistic pressure group, which immediately began preparations for entering the elect-

---

[203] 22 Feb. 1917: M. I. Cole (ed.), *Beatrice Webb's Diaries 1912–1924* (London, 1952), 83.

[204] However, there was by this time an Association of Controlled Establishments, under Lionel Hichens of Cammell Laird. The government employed two senior Foreign Office officials to help form a 'peak organisation' (J. Turner, 'The Politics of "Organised Business" in the First World War', in J. Turner (ed.), *Businessmen and Politics: Studies of Business Activity in British Politics, 1900–1945* (London, 1984), 34).

[205] Ibid. 3.

oral fray, drawing up a 'white list' of candidates who had fully supported the Paris Resolutions and a 'black list' of MPs who had voted against the government on the Maurice Division.[206]

Trade unionists were equally suspicious of any attempt, whether from government or from big business, to manoeuvre them into activities designed to engineer an 'industrial consensus'. So-called Whitley Councils were established in the civil service, but nothing along these 'managerial' lines seemed likely to happen in manufacturing industry. The Conservative Chairman, Arthur Steel-Maitland, might talk about 'a visible and automatic community of interest between masters and men, and about making the latter feel that they are a corporate part of a mutually beneficent organisation'.[207] But sectional struggles, class strife, and the play of politics were not to be neutralized so easily. On the contrary, the Great War was a time of great turmoil, in the course of which the political identities of its citizens underwent a profound transformation.

4. POLITICAL IDENTITIES

The political reconfigurations which war produced did not always follow a predictable course. For example, some socialists welcomed the expansion of the state as prefiguring the kind of collectivism that they wanted to promote once war was over; but so, too, did some 'Social Imperialists', including Lord Milner, reforming Liberals such as Addison, and businessmen in politics such as Eric Geddes.[208] Conversely, many labour activists, more particularly those attracted to syndicalism, reacted with hostility to 'war socialism' and sought to banish the state from industrial life—but so, for diametrically opposed reasons, did many businessmen and prominent figures in both the Liberal and the Conservative Parties. Similar cross-class alliances came into existence over the issue of profiteering—an abuse which enraged the organized working class but which also attracted the contempt of Bottomley's *John Bull* as well as of a middle-of-the-road journal such as *Punch*.[209]

---

[206] See Ch. 18 and below.

[207] Middlemas, *Industrial Society*, 118.

[208] Despite Geddes's later reputation as the wielder of the 'axe', which so damaged the post-war reconstruction programme.

[209] J.-L. Robert, 'The Image of the Profiteer', in Winter and Robert (eds.), *Capital Cities at War*, 107. *Punch* (5 Apr. 1916), against a picture of a well-to-do couple watching two people in a chauffeur-driven Rolls-Royce: 'She: "Good gracious! The Brown-Smiths!! I thought they were so poor." He: "Yes, you see, he's been supplying the Government with shells for quite a fortnight!" ' (Lawrence, 'Material Pressures', 248).

Yet, on balance, class antagonisms intensified during the war. Across the social spectrum there was a growing tendency to speak of the 'working class', rather than the 'working classes', and among manual workers a 'them and us' attitude, applied not only to their social superiors but also to the government, grew more and more commonplace. The 1917 Commissioners of Inquiry into the North-West noted that 'working people have a vague and uneasy feeling that the authorities are not really working in their interest, and if they permit various things to be done which are new to them they will after the war find that their conditions have altered for the worse'.[210]

It is therefore significant that, although the number of days lost in strike action never reached anything near the levels of 1912 or even 1913, there were signs in the last two years of the war that the industrial truce might be breaking down.[211] This faced the government with the dilemma of distinguishing between 'justifiable unrest' and 'deliberate agitation': no easy task, since the one could easily become connected with the other. 'Recent experiences of food shortage', declared the Labour Report of 2 January 1918, 'have unfortunately fortified the argument of those whose aim it is to wage class-warfare.'[212]

Such tensions played into the hands of the socialists. For example, the Socialist Party of Great Britain (SPGB) and the Socialist Labour Party (SLP), breakaways from the SDF founded in 1903 and 1904 respectively, flourished during the war; the latter was particularly strong in Scotland, where it included among its members two of the leading Clydeside shop stewards, John Muir and Arthur MacManus.[213] Trade-union activists, more generally, were influenced by the bitter mood: 'How can there be a truce [between capital and labour],' asked Ernest Bevin in May 1917, 'while one side practices an attitude of dominance to enforce servility by the other?'[214]

But wartime industrial unrest did not easily translate into united political action. For a start, much rank-and-file militancy was directed against the trade-union leadership. 'The support given to the Munitions Act by the Officials', fulminated the Clydeside shop stewards, 'was an act of Treachery to the Working Class', who had been '*Sold*'.[215] It escaped nobody's notice that

---

[210] Waites, *Class Society*, 200–1.

[211] 1912: 40,890,000; 1913: 9,804,000; 1914: 9,878,000; 1915: 2,953,000; 1916: 2,446,000; 1917: 5,647,000; 1918: 5,875,000.

[212] Middlemas, *Industrial Society*, 133, 225.

[213] However, Willie Gallacher and, for a while, John Maclean, the revolutionary defeatist, emerged from the BSP.

[214] Waites, *Class Society*, 67.

[215] J. Hinton, 'The Clyde Workers' Committee and the Dilution Struggle', in A. Briggs and J. Saville (eds.), *Essays in Labour History 1886–1923* (London, 1971), 167. Kirkwood was a member of the ILP, whose paper *Forward* followed a more moderate line.

many of the 'traitors' in question were leading Labour MPs or closely aligned with the PLP.

Moreover, industrial unrest often signified a backlash against those war-accelerated industrial changes which threatened the privileged position of the skilled worker. J. T. Brownlie, the General Secretary of the ASE, revealingly complained that labourers were 'acquiring a knowledge of our trade which may be used to the detriment of skilled craftsmen at the end of the war'.[216] The craft exclusiveness of the engineers (displayed most prominently in their attachment to the Trade Card scheme), attracted deserved mockery from other sectors of the industrial working class. It also limited the effectiveness of the Clyde Workers Commitee which, despite its socialist rhetoric, failed to exploit grievances that concerned *all* working-class families in the vicinity—hence, its detachment from the famous Glasgow rent strike. 'Even the revolution-aries', writes one historian, 'could not escape entanglement in the protective reflexes of the craftsmen, and it was a narrow and self-isolating path that they cut through the turmoil on the Clyde.'[217]

In any case, no clear revolutionary strategy, linking civilians and troops, ever took shape. A few soldiers' soviets emerged in 1917 to protest at wounded men being returned to the line without a certification of fitness from a civilian doctor: there was particular anger over the Review of Exceptions Act (1917), which allowed soldiers discharged as unfit for further duty to be re-examined. However, one reason for Tommy's anger was the belief in the existence of a vast 'army' of 'shirkers' on the home front, so it is not surprising that disgruntled workers and restless troops almost entirely went their separate ways.[218]

It was also a paradox of war, that improved conditions for the poorer strata of the working class, by narrowing wage differentials, caused considerable annoy-ance to those just above them in the social scale. The point was well made in the Report on the labour situation for the week ending 10 December 1919:

During the war the normal relations between different grades and classes of workers, as expressed in wages, have been seriously dislocated, and as a result whole classes of workers feel intense dissatisfaction, not only absolutely, i.e. dissatisfaction with regard to the status and remuneration of labour as such, also relatively, i.e. with their own particular level of wages in comparison with some other class or grade whose wages appear to have been raised disproportionately.[219]

---

[216] Waites, *Class Society*, 195.

[217] Hinton, 'Clyde Workers' Committee', 184.

[218] D. Englander and J. Osborne, 'Jack, Tommy and Henry Dubb: The Armed Forces and the Working Class', *Historical Journal*, 21 (1978), 619–20. The Soviet made no reference to events in Russia.

[219] Waites, *Class Society*, 182–3.

In the long run the war, and its inflationary tendencies, may have created a more cohesive working class, but in the short run that class was riddled with tensions. Robert Roberts's father, a Salford engineer, was riled by the spectacle of the wife of a newly affluent labourer entering his family's corner-shop and asking for a jar of pickled gherkins: 'before the war . . . that one was grateful for a bit o' bread and scrape!'[220]

Nor did the emergence of a more assertive working-class consciousness, insofar as such a development happened at all, signify the incontrovertible triumph of socialism. Socialists such as Ramsay MacDonald liked to present Labour as representing a higher ideal of humanity transcending class divisions, but this kind of rhetoric provoked something of a backlash in certain working-class quarters. Havelock Wilson, the jingo seamen's leader, declared in August 1918 that he 'never knew a trade union which was a success where the working man had to depend on the intellectual'.[221] At the 1916 Labour Conference Wilson and others had actually attempted to form a specifically trade-union Labour Party, and the following year the railwaymen forced through a rule-change which meant that the socialist societies could no longer elect their own representatives to the NEC, this function being transferred to the Conference as a whole, where the big trade-union block votes would be decisive. All of these tensions threatened to splinter the Labour Party beyond repair. Ever since May 1915 the pro- and anti-war elements within the PLP had sat on opposite sides of the House, and the decision to join both coalition governments, in particular, was fiercely contested.

So much for the centrifugal forces bearing down on the Labour Movement. On the other hand, holding it together was a set of common grievances (high food prices, profiteering, inadequate pensions, infringements of traditional trade-union rights, and so on). These may have been 'relatively humdrum second-order questions',[222] but they soon dominated the agenda of a new pressure group, the War Emergency Workers' National Committee (WEWNC). This body was important because it embraced almost all shades of Labour opinion, from the anti-war ILPers W. C. Anderson and Fred Jowett on one wing, to Labour jingoes, such as Havelock Wilson and W. J. Davis, on the other. Middle-of-the-road trade unionists, and the Fabian Sidney Webb, also participated in the WEWNC's work: there was even an important role within it for the eccentric Hyndman of the BSP, a Marxist who was also a 'super-patriot'.

[220] R. Roberts, *The Classic Slum: Salford Life in the First Quarter of the Century* (London, 1971; 1973 edn.), 199.

[221] Waites, *Class Society*, 60–1.

[222] R. Harrison, 'The War Emergency Workers' National Committee', in Briggs and Saville (eds.), *Essays in Labour History*, 256.

Glossing over their very real disagreements on the rights and wrongs of the war, the WEWNC developed a very effective strategy for turning patriotism to its own advantage. The tone was set in a pamphlet of late 1915, *Compulsory Military Service and Industrial Conscription: What They Mean To the Workers*, in which it was claimed that 'the objection of the workers [was] not to Compulsory National Service in any real sense' but to the fact that 'a great number of rich people, men as well as women' did no work and rendered 'no National Service whatever'. Why not impose a supertax of 19s. in the pound on incomes in excess of £1,000 p.a., asked its anonymous author.[223]

Hyndman went on to float the concept of a 'Conscription of Riches', a useful device with which to counter the government's call for conscription of human beings. After the passing of the Military Service Acts, this phrase was redefined to evoke equality of sacrifices between the classes and the need for 'fair play', and Sidney Webb took it up in support of his demand that the war be paid for out of the proceeds of progressive taxation. 'Conscription of Riches' may not have been an entirely satisfactory Labour slogan, since the division between those who fought and those who stayed at home was not really a class division.[224] But its effectiveness, apart from the way that it sidestepped more contentious political issues, lay in the way that it enabled the Labour Movement to sound both radical and patriotic—a consideration that mattered in the final eighteen months of war, when the Labour Movement was beginning to switch its attention from past divisions to its future prospects.

Such united action was possible because both the 'revolutionary defeatists' and 'super-patriots' were very tiny groupings. Real differences within the main body of the party did of course exist, but the organization's federal structure usefully accommodated them—the ILP, for example, providing a protective haven for those critical of the war. Moreover, Henderson and MacDonald, though coming from quite different social and ideological backgrounds, knew that they would have to co-operate with one another in the future, as they had done in the past.

In fact, Labour divisions partially healed over after the 'doormat incident'.[225] Although his place in the War Cabinet had been taken by George Barnes, Henderson himself now began to think of reorganizing Labour so that its leaders would never again have to endure the humiliations that had been visited upon his own head. In the Wansbeck by-election on 29 May 1918 a Labour candidate took on a Coalition Liberal and lost by only 548 votes, and soon afterwards the NEC declined to renew the 'party truce'. It can therefore have come as no suprise when on 14 November, after the signing of the Armistice,

[223] Harrison, 'War Emergency', 240.   [224] Whiting, 'Taxation', 915.   [225] See Ch. 18.

another special Conference, against the advice of its ministerial members, voted by 2,117,000 to 810,000 to pull out of the National Government. What *is* surprising is that Lloyd George should so passively have allowed this to happen.

Labour's underlying situation had meanwhile been much strengthened in a variety of ways. Its experiences in office had given it, for the first time, something of the aura of a party of government, while its political leaders, as well as trade-union officials, had successfully established their right to consultation with government.[226] Meanwhile, at local level, working-class representatives had muscled their way into a variety of public bodies, the government positively encouraging such 'co-option' as a relatively painless way of propitiating working-class discontent. Moreover, given the prevalent apathy concerning 'contracting-out', trade-union expansion was inexorably swelling the party's coffers, making possible an extension of its organization in the country, while the prospect of franchise reform gave its leaders a new optimism about the future. In December 1917 Henderson was telling a startled C. P. Scott that Labour planned to run as many as 500 candidates, most of whom would obviously have to face Liberal opposition. Henderson also indicated at this meeting that he intended to 'enlarge the bounds of the Labour Party and bring in the intellectuals as candidates': in the past, he explained, 'the Labour Party had been too short of brains'.[227]

Henderson obviously had in mind the trickle of UDCers such as Morel, who had finally taken the plunge and aligned themselves with Labour by joining the ILP. Many did this with the encouragement of Herbert Bryan, Secretary of the City of London ILP branch, who prudently refrained from imposing upon them any kind of socialist 'test'. Such middle-class 'entryism' did not pass unchallenged. A railwayman delegate reminded his comrades that 'the middle-class peace men' had betrayed the Labour Party during the Boer War: 'the same old psalm-singing hypocrites', he warned, would do so again.[228] At a selection conference in February 1918 another trade-union delegate said that 'it was about time that they were represented in Parliament by a real Labour man . . . one who had gone through the hoop, knew what it was to go short, and to have a bath in a wash-tub'.[229]

Nevertheless, as Henderson acknowledged, the UDC recruits brought to Labour particular kinds of expertise, notably in international relations, of which it now stood in great need. Their presence as candidates also made

---

[226] Middlemas, *Industrial Society*, 89–90.
[227] 11–12 Dec. 1917: T. Wilson (ed.), *The Political Diaries of C. P. Scott* (London, 1970), 316–17.
[228] M. Swartz, *The Union of Democratic Control in British Politics During the First World War* (Oxford, 1971), 149.
[229] Waites, *Class Society*, 61.

Labour look for the first time less like a sectional grouping, and more like a high-minded vehicle for the attainment of 'ordered social change by constitutional means', to use Henderson's own formulation.

Against this background a special Labour Party Conference met at Nottingham on 23 January 1918, with the aim of overhauling the constitutional arrangements reached in 1900. Unfortunately Henderson's carefully considered plan to alter the party's federal structure ran into the opposition of the miners, who suspected that a more centralized organization would merely increase the influence of the socialist intellectuals and those whom Robert Smillie contemptuously called 'the cranks of the U.D.C. and the Council of Civil Liberties'—at the expense of the genuine working man. Although Henderson, in conjunction with Webb and MacDonald, worked tirelessly for a compromise, his draft constitution was narrowly referred back, and the Conference temporarily adjourned. The miners' executive only gave ground when Henderson proposed to raise the number of trade-union representatives on the NEC from eleven to thirteen (out of twenty-three).

On this basis, the reconvened Conference endorsed the new constitution in the following month. Its most important innovation lay in its provision for individual membership of the party through newly created divisional labour parties (DLPs).[230] This development boded ill for the ILP—whose attempts to regain its unfettered right to control its own representation on the NEC had already been brushed aside. The ILP's diminished influence was immediately revealed with the election in 1918 of a new right-wing, union-dominated NEC. Yet, by one of those ingenious balancing acts at which Labour managers were so adept, wounded socialist susceptibilities were partially assuaged by the Conference's adoption of Clause 4:

To secure for the producers by hand or by brain the full fruits of their industry, and the most equitable distribution thereof that may be possible, upon the basis of the common ownership of the means of production and the best obtainable system of popular administration and control of each industry and service.

For the first time, socialism was inscribed in the party's constitution.

There seems, at first sight, something paradoxical about Labour making this commitment just at the moment when so many ex-Liberals were entering its ranks and when it was seeking to broaden its class appeal. In fact, however, Clause 4, had been skilfully drafted by Sidney Webb, its principal author.[231]

---

[230] This had previously taken place in some areas through the local ward associations, but the practice lacked official sanction.

[231] The Conference had initially been presented with a 'mission statement' couched in terms of the 'Conscription of Riches'.

The wording left open the question of how industries would be managed once they had been socialised (so sidestepping the disagreement between national-izers and syndicalists). Moreover, the reference to 'the producers by hand *or by brain*' shrewdly reached out to those white-collar workers and professional men looking for a party uncontaminated by the past. Labour was now offering itself as an instrument of democratic reform, free from Reaction, on the one hand, and 'Bolshevism', on the other.

It has been argued that Clause 4 was little more than 'an acceptable formula in a Party where there was otherwise little doctrinal agreement'.[232] This may be going too far. Recent events had clearly caused some delegates to reorder their priorities. After all, the state had shown itself capable of controlling and directing great industrial and commercial enterprises, a development which the Fabians saw as a vindication of their own brand of managerial collectivism. And even though both the revolutionary socialists and the intelligentsia asso-ciated with 'guild socialism' positively disliked the whole phenomenon of 'war socialism', no one could now dismiss 'socialism' as a paper scheme devised by utopians and dreamers.

Even so, the ease with which the sponsors of Clause 4 got their resolution accepted by Conference invites the suspicion that the issue of nationalization was not taken with quite the seriousness that it deserved, and that the leader-ship of the big trade unions was only prepared to accept the 'triumph of socialism' because it had been accompanied by organizational changes designed to marginalize the socialists.[233]

Electoral considerations also came into play. Before 1914, with the Lib-Lab Pact in place, it was against Labour's interests to emphasize its differences with the 'capitalist' parties. But by 1918 the 'progressive alliance' had been in abeyance for over three years, and Labour, confident that it could go it alone, now had much to gain, and nothing to lose, by disassociating itself from the divided and demoralized Liberal Party.[234] In that sense the adoption of Clause 4 should be seen as a tactical assertion of its new-found independence. More-over, it is surely significant that Henderson's speeches of this time hardly ever invoked socialism, but simply dilated on what a future Labour government would do.[235] Such an approach also dominated *Labour and the New Social Order*, the manifesto, issued in June, on which the party, fielding an unpreced-ented 388 candidates, contested the 1918 General Election. Labour was clearly

[232] R. McKibbin, *The Evolution of the Labour Party 1910–1924* (Oxford, 1974), 97.

[233] J. M. Winter, *Socialism and the Challenge of War: Ideas and Politics in Britain 1912–18* (London, 1974), ch. 8.

[234] In the new circumstances the Labour Party could also be confident of attracting working-class Irish voters in mainland Britain.

[235] McKibbin, *Evolution of Labour Party*, 99.

going to be a major player in post-war politics, but even its own leading members could, as yet, not foresee quite what kind of party, socially or ideologically, it would turn out to be.

Ambition, rather than a clear sense of purpose, drove Labour on in 1918. Two changes in the political environment particularly influenced its behaviour. The first was ushered in by the 1918 Representation of the People Act, on which the post-war general election would be fought. The all-party Speakers Conference, set up by Asquith in 1916, in response to calls to concede the soldier's vote, had produced an almost unanimous set of recommendations, many of them very radical indeed. As well as dealing on broad and sympathetic lines with the women's question,[236] the report laid down what was effectively the basis of all twentieth-century parliamentary elections through the conferral of adult manhood suffrage, a simplification of the registration process, the meeting of candidates' expenses out of local taxation, the holding of general elections on a single day, and the establishment of a controlled system of postal voting. All of these recommendations duly became law.

Admittedly, not all the features of the Act ran in a democratic direction. Although no one could henceforward cast more than one vote on the same qualification, plural voting was retained—indeed, in one respect plural voting was actually extended in a small way when the accompanying Redistribution Act created new university constituencies, boosting the number of MPs they returned from nine to fifteen.[237] But, rightly or wrongly, Labour organizers thought that, by cheapening the cost of politics and extending the franchise to more working-class males, the new electoral dispensation would work in their favour, and this helped give them the confidence to run more candidates.

There was only one major recommendation in the Speakers' Report which, left to a free vote of the House, eventually fell by the wayside, and that concerned the important issue of abandoning the first-past-the-post voting system. The Conference unanimously recommended that in the larger towns multi-member constituencies, returning four or five Members, should be created, using the system of Proportional Representation known as the Single Transferable Vote (STV). By a majority decision, it also advocated that in the rest of the country the Alternative Vote (AV) system be adopted.

Distracted by the war, Lloyd George failed to give Parliament a lead; nor, with both major parties split on the merits of electoral reform, did any of the party leaders provide their followers with firm guidance. As a result, after a series of confused divisions, often poorly attended, the Commons resolved to

---

[236] See above.
[237] Numbers were reduced to 12 by 1922 after the establishment of the Free State in Southern Ireland.

ignore the Conference's advice and to adopt the Alternative Vote in all territorial constituencies. The House of Lords disagreed, plumping instead for a universal system of PR. With the two Houses deadlocked, the government, anxious to dissolve on the new register, decided to leave the existing system untouched (except in the university constituencies, where a form of STV was introduced), pending a fuller review of all the issues. By the time that this review had been completed, Parliament had lost interest in electoral reform. And so the first-past-the-post system survived, almost by default.

When Henderson had irrevocably committed himself to increasing the number of Labour candidates, he still assumed that AV would be in place by the time of the next general election, so obviating the risk that clashes between Liberals and Labour would allow Conservatives to be elected in droves on a minority of votes cast. In the event, such an electoral change never occurred— an important reason why the twentieth century turned out to be a 'Conservative Century'. The principal losers from all this were, of course, the Liberals— which makes it all the more surprising that Asquith, the Party Leader, did not interest himself more in electoral reform in 1917 and 1918 when the situation was still fluid. Yet Liberal weaknesses were obvious enough to the Labour Party in 1918—hence its eagerness to take on all comers. They had also been apparent to other interested observers for quite some time. Why had the Liberal Party fared so badly since the start of the war, compared not only with Labour but also with the Conservatives?

After 1914 the Liberals underwent a crisis of morale as they came to realize the incompatibility between their ideology and what actions they needed to take to secure victory.[238] The original strategy of 'Business as Usual' presupposed a reliance on the navy, largely to the exclusion of the Continental commitment.[239] When this did not happen, economic Liberals such as McKenna and Runciman were placed in a position where they had constantly to choose between betrayal of their principles and damaging the war effort. The McKenna Duties were a case in point. Their author privately confessed that he wanted them to fail, in order to supply 'a good object lesson as to the impossibility of tariffs in this country', a stratagem which the more astute tariff reformers well understood.[240] But all that most Liberals could see was the partial abandonment of free trade.

The Military Service Acts faced Liberals with an even clearer dilemma. Asquith incurred ridicule on the Conservative backbenches by including 'conscientious objection to undertaking combatant service' as a ground for

---

[238] This is the leading theme in T. Wilson, *The Downfall of the Liberal Party, 1914–35* (London, 1966).

[239] French, 'Business as Usual', 9.

[240] Bourne, *Great War*, 126.

military exemption: when he announced this as government policy, he was greeted with groans, catcalls, and laughter.[241] By contrast, senior Liberal ministers stood by this quintessentially Liberal policy, but it earned them little gratitude or respect from Liberal 'purists'.

On both economic and moral grounds, McKenna and Runciman should logically have urged a negotiated peace. Indeed, once on the backbenches the two men pressed such a course of action on the Liberal Leader after Lansdowne had finally 'gone public' in late 1917. But Asquith, without whom they felt powerless, would never associate himself with such a demand, partly because he acknowledged his own responsibility for Britain having entered the war, and partly out of loyalty to Grey, who felt similarly. Bereft of leadership, those Liberals who saw no point in pushing on to outright victory had little alternative but to opt out of mainstream politics, often proceeding, via the UDC, into the ranks of Labour; perhaps some 2,000 activists, in all, followed this route. Thus, while Asquith was 'waiting and seeing' in the last two years of war, neither giving the government his wholehearted support nor acting like the Leader of the Opposition, a reconfiguration of progressive forces was taking place of which he seemed almost entirely oblivious.

Amongst Liberal loyalists in the party's heartlands, in areas such as the West Riding and the West Country, Asquith continued to enjoy a surprising popularity, perhaps because, despite everything, he alarmed them less than their one-time darling Lloyd George, now allied to the old political enemy. On the other hand, once he had made the fateful decision to invite the Conservatives into his government in May 1915, Asquith found himself implicated in the give-and-take of coalition politics, a situation which strengthened his native pragmatism. Thus, whatever private opinions he may earlier have held, Asquith gave no impression of seeing the conscription issue in anything other than tactical terms. As so often, principle was subordinated to the task of keeping the government afloat. Far from being a doctrinaire upholder of 'Freedom', Asquith was Prime Minister at the time when most of the country's traditional 'freedoms' were temporarily suspended—not just through the establishment of the Ministry of Munitions and the adoption of compulsory military service, but also through the introduction of exchange controls and the passing of the Paris Resolutions.[242]

All the same, Lloyd George as Prime Minister differed from his predecessor in two important respects. By temperament an interventionist, he cut himself off from the inhibiting influences of the likes of McKenna and Runciman.

---

[241] K. Robbins, 'The British Experience of Conscientious Objection', in Cecil and Liddle (eds.), *Facing Armageddon*, 693–4. However, some Unionists, notably Milner and Curzon, did display a humane concern for the plight of the COs (J. Rae, *Conscience and Politics* (Oxford, 1970), 217–22).

[242] See Ch. 17.

Though he, too, often took bold action only under the pressure of events, he at least knew that victory could never be secured on limited liability principles. Moreover, no one could conceivably have asked him, as Ellen Terry famously did of Asquith, 'whether he took any interest in the war'!

Secondly, Lloyd George, who had long held ambiguous views about party, realized that the twin pressures of war and of coalition government had made party increasingly redundant—at least for the time being. That had already become apparent during Asquith's final months in 10 Downing Street, when the war was throwing up novel issues (for example, of strategy) around which strange cross-party alliances, sometimes cemented by personal friendships, quickly formed. This destabilization of party loyalties weakened Asquith, just as it created difficulties for his opposite number, Bonar Law. But Lloyd George relished the freedom which this gave him, as can be seen from the way in which, on becoming Prime Minister, he constructed a 'National Government' which transcended party—in contrast to Asquith, who had always tried to balance competing party interests.

For Conservatives, most of whom in any case felt comfortable with the rhetoric of 'national politics', the weakening of party bonds did not pose too much of a threat. Their Leader Bonar Law was, after all, to all intents and purposes Deputy Prime Minister, a dual responsibility which enabled him to ward off any major collision between his party and the government. By contrast, Asquith's decision to retire to the backbenches, along with most of his former senior Liberal colleagues, had always had the potential to split Liberalism, not least because Asquith continued, without challenge, to retain the office of Leader, with full control over the party funds, the Whips, and the local Liberal machines.

Barely a fortnight into the Lloyd George premiership, an altercation broke out amongst Liberals over who should have the nomination to the recently vacated seat at Derby, and Lloyd George's friends began discussing, informally, whether to build up a rudimentary organization of their own to protect their interests against Asquithian attack—though this attack never seriously materialized at constituency level. Moreover, precisely because he initially lacked a party base of his own, Lloyd George was desperately anxious to get the Liberal press on his side—hence the 'squashing and squaring' which led to such controversial episodes as J. Henry Dalziel's purchase of the *Daily Chronicle* in October, followed by the immediate sacking of its respected editor Robert Donald, who had had the temerity to appoint Maurice as his military correspondent. This coup intensified Asquithian bitterness towards Lloyd George.

Lloyd George showed on several occasions that he was anxious to terminate what threatened to become an unpleasant personal vendetta. But after Asquith had rudely rebuffed Lord Reading's attempt at mediation in May 1917,[243] the Prime Minister found himself in a quandary. Theoretically he could have worked for Liberal reunification—not an attractive option, since it would probably have entailed, sooner or later, a breach with the powerful Conservative Party. Alternately, he could seek to engineer the creation, under his own leadership, of a new 'national party', a topic which he frequently broached in private conversation in late 1917 and early 1918. Addison strongly favoured such an initiative, seeing it as providing political underpinning for the work of 'Reconstruction', a programme of social amelioration that would hopefully combine all that was creative and sensible from the traditions of both major parties. There were also those who felt that it might need both a 'National Government' and a 'National Party' to contain the forces of 'Bolshevism' and to avert the risk of Labour making electoral gains as a result of the division between the two major parties.[244] As well as heterodox Liberals, some Unionists, notably Lord Milner and his circle, were attracted by this project, which became entangled in the spring of 1918 with the possibility of resolving the Irish dispute by federalizing the constitution.[245]

However, Bonar Law saw little point in presiding over the disintegration of his own party simply because the Liberal Leaders seemed about to split theirs. Moreover, Lloyd George's Patronage Secretary, Captain Freddie Guest, in the intervals of assiduously trading honours for contributions to his master's newly established war chest, generally took a cautious line—he clearly did not want to go down in history as one of the authors of the Liberal Party's destruction; still less did Montagu, who hankered after reunion. Instead, Guest began making preparations for a general election on the basis of the new electoral register (the Representation of the People Act had reached the statute book on 6 February 1918), an election which he, along with almost everyone else, assumed would take place while the war was still in progress, with the Coalition Liberals, the Conservatives, and perhaps 'patriotic Labour' presenting a united front to the voters. These plans for a wartime election, however, were interrupted by the German Spring Offensive.

The Maurice Division, the parliamentary dispute over whether the BEF had been under strength on the eve of the German Spring Offensive, then added a new dimension to the debate.[246] Significantly, some eighty-three Liberal MPs had contrived to absent themselves from the division, some of them

[243] See Ch. 18.

[244] G. R. Searle, *Country Before Party: Coalition and the Idea of 'National Government' in Modern Britain 1885–1987* (Harlow, 1995), 110–14.

[245] As late as 21–2 August there was a meeting of these social planners at Criccieth: present were Addison, Kerr, Milner, Hankey, Amery, Henry Norman, and Dudley Ward.

[246] See Ch. 18.

undoubtedly shrinking from the unpleasant necessity of choosing between a
Liberal Leader and a Liberal Premier towards whom they professed equal
allegiance (hitherto most backbench Liberals had been in receipt of both the
official and the Coalition Liberal Whip). But the outcome of the vote not only
dramatized the growing cleavage between the two groups, but also gave Lloyd
George's managers a much better idea than before of who was friend and who
was foe. Thus fore-armed, Guest continued his negotiations with Conservative
Central Office, and by the end of October it had been provisionally agreed that
some 150 Liberals would be treated as supporters of the government and thus
shielded from Conservative attack: eventually 159 were so favoured.[247]

Even so, Lloyd George characteristically kept his options open until the very
last moment. In late September he again put out feelers to Asquith, this time
through his old friend Lord Murray (formerly the Master of Elibank, of
Marconi fame). Asquith was offered the Woolsack and the right to nominate
two of the principal Secretaries of State and six Under-Secretaries, as well as
being given certain assurances on policy. It is not clear with what seriousness
this offer was made, but Asquith yielded not an inch; 'Unless I am very much
mistaken,' Murray privately noted, 'I have been present at the obsequies of the
Liberal Party as I knew it.' At least this rejection saved Guest the embarrassment of having to reallocate seats to government-approved candidates in order
to accommodate the official Liberals—a last-minute adjustment to which
Bonar Law and his officers would surely have objected.

From then onwards events gathered momentum, forcing the Premier to
clarify his political strategy. The sudden and unexpected collapse of the
German armies now meant that the long-planned-for general election would
be one to determine who should make the peace, not who was best fitted to run
the war. Labour's determination to leave the government then left Lloyd
George with few working-class members in his team, apart from a handful of
Labour ministers (notably George Barnes and George Roberts) who, by
defying Conference's instruction to resign, were promptly expelled from the
Labour Party. Lloyd George thus found himself impelled, like it or not, to find
some reason for picking a quarrel with the official Liberal Party, with whom the
Coalition candidates would soon be at war; and here the recent Maurice
Division came in very useful.

It is true that the Maurice vote was not the only factor determining which
Liberal candidates received the 'coupon' (as the joint endorsement from Lloyd
George and Bonar Law was soon being called). But this was mainly because,
out of a total of 411 Liberal candidates (of both wings) who stood in the 1918

[247] See B. McGill, 'Lloyd George's Timing of the 1918 Election', *Journal of British Studies*, 14 (1974),
109–24.

election, only 127 had voted over Maurice (indeed, only 27 per cent of Official and 36 per cent of Coalition Liberal candidates had been in the House at the time). Conversely, forty-three Liberal MPs who *had* participated in the fateful division (17 per cent of the total) were not standing as Liberal candidates.[248] However, the importance of Maurice can be seen from the fact that only 15.7 per cent of the Liberal candidates who had earlier sided with Asquith received a coupon, as against 91.2 per cent of those who had backed the government.[249]

The 'Coupon' election, which took place on 14 December, set the pattern for the party rivalries of the next decade: 133 of the Coalition Liberals were elected, along with ten Coalition Labour and 335 Coalition Conservatives.[250] This was, by any standards, a triumph for Bonar Law, who had successfully worked to gain party advantage from Lloyd George's popularity in the country, without in any way forfeiting the Conservative Party's organizational independence. However, much else was going the Conservatives' way in 1918, including favourable changes to constituency boundaries. This led some party members to wonder whether they had needed to be associated with the Premier at all, a viewpoint strengthened once it had become apparent that the Conservatives held an overall majority within the new House.

For the Official Liberals, on the other hand, the election was an unmitigated disaster. They returned from the fray reduced to a mere twenty-eight Members. Despite generally offering their support to the National Government, while deprecating the haste with which the election had been sprung on the people, Asquith and nearly all his closest colleagues lost their seats— indeed, Runciman, McKenna, and Samuel came bottom of the poll. Moreover, many traditional Liberal voters had found that they had no Liberal candidate to support—a highly demoralizing situation in which to be placed.

Also a worrying portent for the Liberals was the trouncing that Dillon's Irish Nationalists received at the hands of Sinn Fein: the former won only seven seats, the latter seventy-three. But because Sinn Fein refused on principle to take their seats, the role of principal Opposition party devolved on to Labour.[251] Largely as a result of the coupon arrangement, Labour still had only sixty-three MPs, not many more than in pre-war days, and also lost many

---

[248] 8 stood as candidates for some other party, mostly Labour.

[249] 75.7% of 'Asquithians' had to face a couponed candidate, while six (including Asquith) contested a constituency in which no coupon at all had been allocated. Inevitably, in the confusion of the hour, some mistakes were made: 14 Liberal candidates disavowed the 'coupon'.

[250] The Independent Conservatives numbered 23, the Irish Unionists 25. Eight uncouponed Conservatives were returned against couponed Liberals, and another 12 won in constituencies where no coupon had been issued, including East Fife, where Asquith was the Liberal candidate (J. Turner, *British Politics and the Great War* (New Haven, 1992), 333).

[251] Labour must also have been helped by the fact that the first election held on the new register took place at a time when the Labour Party exuded optimism, while the Liberals were all at sea.

of its leading figures, including Henderson as well as MacDonald and Snowden, whose opposition to the war had made them unpopular. On the other hand, even though the coupon had done its work in containing Labour's advance, the party had the satisfaction of polling 2,385,472 votes (22.2 per cent of the total vote), a firm base for the further advances it confidently expected to be making.

Chronology

Publication dates are for first publication in book form.

Date	Politics, Legislation, and Government	State and War
1886	Gladstone's third ministry First Home Rule Bill Contagious Diseases Act repealed General Election Salisbury's second ministry	Penjdeh Incident Lord Iddesleigh Foreign Secretary Royal Niger Company Anglo–German agreement on East Africa
1887	Lord Randolph Churchill resigns Round Table Conference Crimes Act (Ireland) Irish Land Act	Lord Salisbury Foreign Secretary Mediterranean Agreements First Colonial Conference
1888	Local Government Act Irish Land Purchase Act	Imperial British East Africa Company
1889	Technical Instruction Act Start of Parnell divorce case	Naval Defence Act First Official Secrets Act British South Africa Company
1890	Housing of the Working Class Act	Hartington Commission Report Mackinnon Agreement Anglo–Portuguese Convention
1891	Newcastle Programme Parnell cited in O'Shea divorce case Irish Land Purchase Act Factory and Workshop Act Elementary education made free	British Central African Protectorate of Nyasaland
1892	Smallholdings Act General Election Gladstone's fourth ministry Second Home Rule Bill	Earl of Rosebery Foreign Secretary

People, Projects, Events	Intellectual and Cultural Life	Date
Charles Booth launches Life and Labour in London Football Association legalizes professionalism National Vigilance Association (NVA) Mothers' Union	New English Art Club R. L. Stevenson, *Dr Jekyll and Mr Hyde* *English Historical Review*	1886
Queen Victoria's Golden Jubilee	J. Stainer's *Crucifixion* Bram Stoker, *Dracula* National Association for Promotion of Technical Education	1887
'Jack the Ripper' murders Bryant & May matchgirls' strike Foundation of Football League	J. Murray, *New English Dictionary* Guild and School of Handicraft N. Shaw, New Scotland Yard building Port Sunlight	1888
London Dock strike Infant death-rate peaks Indecent Advertisements Act Ladies' anti-suffrage manifesto in *Nineteenth Century* Lipton enters tea market *Comic Cuts*	*Fabian Essays* E. Carpenter, *Civilisation: Its Cause and Cure; Towards Democracy* First unexpurgated English production of Ibsen's *A Dolls House* Grants-in-aid to universities F. Galton, *Natural Inheritance* W. S. Gilbert and A. Sullivan, *Utopia Limited*	1889
	W. James, *Principles of Psychology* A. Marshall, *Principles of Economics*	1890
Start of work on Blackpool Tower Tranby Croft Affair	G. Gissing, *New Grub Street* T. Hardy, *Tess of the D'Urbervilles* W. Morris, *News from Nowhere* Start of J. T. Grein's 'Independent Theatre'	1891
	R. Blatchford, *Merrie England* Death of Tennyson: Alfred Austen made Poet Laureate K. Pearson, *The Grammar of Science*	1892

Date	Politics, Legislation, and Government	State and War
1893	Foundation of Independent Labour Party (ILP)	Ndebele War
1894	Rosebery's ministry Harcourt's 'Death Duties' Budget Local Government Act (parish councils)	Earl Kimberley Foreign Secretary Uganda made British Protectorate Lord Spencer's naval expansion

1895	Salisbury's third ministry
	General Election
		Navy League
		Grey Declaration
		Lord Salisbury Foreign Secretary,
		  Joseph Chamberlain Colonial
		  Secretary
		Defence Committee of Cabinet
		  established
		Jameson Raid
		Kruger Telegram

1896	Irish Land Purchase Act Agricultural Rates Act Education Bill Rosebery resigns Liberal Leadership	Armenian Massacres Start of reconquest of Sudan

1897	Workmen's Compensation Act
	Foundation of National Union of
	  Women's Suffrage Societies
	  (NUWSS)
		Second Colonial Conference

1898	Harcourt retires to backbenches
	Irish Local Government Act
	Death of Gladstone
		Anglo–French Agreement on
		  West Africa
		Lord Milner British High
		  Commissioner in South Africa
		Lord Curzon Viceroy of India
		Battle of Omdurman
		Fashoda Crisis

People, Projects, Events	Intellectual and Cultural Life	Date
National coal strike	O. Wilde's *Salomé* published in French	1893
Nadir of agricultural depression Schism within rugby football Royal Society of St George	G. Moore, *Esther Waters* Cambridge Mechanical Sciences Tripos B. Kidd, *Social Evolution* First issue of the *Yellow Book*	1894
Daimler's invention of internal combustion engine Helby–Matthews case: start of hire-purchase system	Oscar Wilde sent to Reading Gaol O. Wilde, *The Importance of Being Earnest* National Trust founded M. Nordau, *Degeneration* T. Hardy, *Jude the Obscure* Henry Irving knighted Bourneville London School of Economics H. G. Wells, *The Time Machine* Lord Acton becomes Regius Professor of History at Cambridge University Start of Promenade Concerts	1895
Sunday opening of national museums and art galleries Foundation of *Daily Mail* Guglielmo Marconi comes to England	Foundation of National Portrait Gallery Central School of Arts and Crafts A. E. Housman, *A Shropshire Lad* E. Williams, *Made in Germany*	1896
Queen Victoria's Diamond Jubilee Lock-out in engineering industry Diesel invents compression-ignition engine	Tate Gallery of Modern Art Discovery of X-rays H. Ellis, *Sexual Inversion*	1897
	Folk Song Society Peasant Arts Society E. Howard, *Tomorrow* (later *Garden Cities of Tomorrow*)	1898

Date	Politics, Legislation, and Government	State and War
1899	Campbell-Bannerman becomes Liberal Leader National Committee of Organized Labour for Promoting Old Age Pensions Metropolitan Borough Councils established	First Hague Peace Conference Bloemfontein Conference Start of Second South African (Boer) War 'Black Week'
1900	Foundation of Labour Representation Committee General Election ('Khaki')	Battle of Paardeburg Relief of Ladysmith and Mafeking Boxer Rising Annexation of Transvaal and Orange Free State Lord Lansdowne Foreign Secretary Colonial Stock Act
1901	Death of Queen Victoria: Edward VII House of Lords upholds Taff Vale Judgement Rosebery's Chesterfield Speech	Hay–Pauncefote Treaty Commonwealth of Australia
1902	Foundation of Liberal League Balfour's ministry Corn Registration Duty Education Act (England and Wales)	National Service League Anglo-Japanese Treaty Peace of Vereeniging Third Colonial Conference Committee of Imperial Defence
1903	Lib–Lab Pact Death of Lord Salisbury Tariff Reform Campaign Wyndham's Irish Land Act Women's Social and Political Union (WSPU)	Elgin Commission Report First Invasion Inquiry
1904	Licensing Act Report of Inter-Departmental Committee on Physical Deterioration	Esher Committee Report Anglo-French Entente Congo Reform Association Fisher First Sea Lord Dogger Bank Incident
1905	Aliens Act Unemployed Workmen's Act Relugas Pact Campbell-Bannerman's ministry	First Moroccan Crisis Sir E. Grey Foreign Secretary

People, Projects, Events	Intellectual and Cultural Life	Date
Lord Meath's Lads' Drill Association	The 'Stage Society' E. Elgar, *Enigma Variations* Publication of the *Fitzwilliam Virginal Book* Rediscovery of Mendel's paper on sweet-peas	1899
'Moss Empires' floated National Anti-Gambling League (NAGL) Marconi Wireless Telegraphy and Signal Company *Daily Express*	E. Elgar, *Dream of Gerontius* A. Quiller-Couch, *Oxford Book of English Verse* The Curies discover radiation National Physical Laboratory Birmingham University	1900
'Martyrdom' of John Kensit	S. B. Rowntree, *Poverty: A Study of Town Life* H. G. Wells, *Anticipations* E. Elgar 'Pomp and Circumstance' Marches	1901
Daily News churchgoing census, November 1902–November 1903	J. A. Hobson, *Imperialism: A Study* Horniman's Museum E. German, *Merrie England* A. Conan Doyle, *The Hound of the Baskervilles* J. Conrad, *Heart of Darkness* C. R. Ashbee settles in Chipping Campden	1902
Workers' Education Association (WEA) Wright brothers' flight Start of Letchworth Garden City	G. E. Moore, *Principia Ethica* H. James, *The Wings of the Dove* S. Butler, *The Way of All Flesh* G. B. Shaw, *Man and Superman*	1903
Appearance of 'motorized cabs' (taxis)	A. J. Penty founds Guild Socialists J. M. Barrie, *Peter Pan*	1904
Alfred Harmsworth becomes Baron Northcliffe	C. Money, *Poverty and Riches* British Science Guild	1905

Date	Politics, Legislation, and Government	State and War
1906	General Election Education (Provisions of School Meals) Act Education Bill Trades Disputes Act Workers' Compensation Act	Anglo-French Military Conversations Algeciras Conference Launching of *Dreadnought* battleship Transvaal granted responsible government
1907	Irish Councils Bill Campbell-Bannerman Resolutions School medical inspection Moderates win control of LCC	Second Hague Conference Anglo-Russian Entente Self-government for Transvaal Fourth Colonial Conference Haldane's army reforms
1908	Asquith's ministry Miners Eight-Hour Day Act Old Age Pensions	Tweedmouth Letter Conclusion of Second Invasion Inquiry
1909	Reports of Royal Commission on Poor Laws 'People's Budget' Labour Exchanges Irish Land Act Trade Boards Act Osborne Judgement	Finalization of Morley–Minto reforms South Africa Act
1910	General Election (January) Conciliation Committee established Death of Edward VII: George V Constitutional Conference Secret Coalition Talks General Election (December)	Anglo-German naval talks Grey attacked over Persian policy
1911	Parliament Act Payment of MPs National Insurance Act Bonar Law becomes Conservative Leader Ulster Unionist Council establishes 'Provisional Government'	Agadir Crisis Second Official Secrets Act First Imperial Conference George V present at Durbar CID meeting on military–naval strategy

People, Projects, Events	Intellectual and Cultural Life	Date
Farm Labourers' Union Street Betting Act	Everyman's Library Ashton Memorial at Lancaster E. Nesbit, *The Railway Children* R. Kipling, *Puck of Pook's Hill*	1906
Launch of Boy Scouts movement Foundation of National Farmers Union	E. Gosse, *Father and Son* A. R. Orage takes over *The New Age* Eugenics Education Society	1907

Olympic Games in London
Northcliffe purchases
    The Times
	A. Bennett, *Old Wives Tale*
	G. Holst, *Savitri*
	Ezra Pound settles in London
	W. H. Davies, *Autobiography*
	    of a Super-Tramp
	K. Grahame, *Wind in the Willows*
	H. G. Wells, *The War in the*
	    Air
	W. McDougall, *Introduction*
	    to Social Psychology
		1908

Opening of Selfridges
Blériot flies the Channel
	C. F. G. Masterman,
	    The Condition of England
	H. G. Wells, *Tono-Bungay;*
	    Ann Veronica
	First complete performance
	    of F. Delius's *The Mass of Life*
	Imperial College, London,
	    opens
		1909

	Camden Town Group
	'Manet and the Post-Impressionists'
	    Exhibition
	E. M. Forster, *Howards End*
	R. Vaughan Williams, *Fantasia on*
	    a Theme of Thomas Tallis
	B. Russell and A. N. Whitehead,
	    Principia Mathematica
		1910

	L. T. Hobhouse, *Liberalism* First visit of Diaghilev Ballet	1911

Date	Politics, Legislation, and Government	State and War
1912	Third Home Rule Bill Miners' Minimum Wage Act Start of Marconi scandal	Haldane Mission Start of First Balkan War Grey–Cambon letters Establishment of Flying Corps
1913	Franchise and Registration Bill withdrawn Mental Deficiency Act Trade Union Act ('political levy') Start of Land Campaign	Treaty of London ends First Balkan War Start of Second Balkan War
1914	Curragh Incident Education (Provisions of School Meals) Act Buckingham Palace Conference First World War begins Home Rule Bill suspended	Royal Naval Air Service Assassination of Archduke Franz Ferdinand Outbreak of First World War Retreat from Mons First battle of Marne Egypt made British Protectorate Battle of Falklands Islands Founding of Union of Democratic Control
1915	Treasury Agreement First Coalition ministry (Asquith) Establishment of Ministry of Munitions McKenna Duties Conscription crisis	Battle of Neuve Chapelle Dardenelles Campaign Sinking of *Lusitania* Battle of Loos Salonika Expedition Haig replaces John French as Commander-in-Chief
1916	National Service Acts establish conscription Easter Rising Death of Kitchener Second Coalition ministry (Lloyd George)	Battle of Jutland Somme Offensive Battle of Cambrai A. J. Balfour Foreign Secretary
1917	Speaker's Conference reports Reorganization of Sinn Fein Leeds Conference Henderson resigns over Stockholm Conference Corn Production Act	Arras Offensive Fall of Tsar Balfour Declaration Third Ypres (Passchendaele) Offensive Bolsheviks seize power Allenby enters Jerusalem

People, Projects, Events	Intellectual and Cultural Life	Date

Miners strike
Blackpool has electrical
  'Illuminations'
	Start of H. Granville Barker–Lillah
	  McCarthy Shakespeare
	  productions at Savoy
	Second Post-Impressionist
	  Exhibition
		1912

Criminal Law Amendment
  (White Slavery) Act
	'George Bourne', *Change in*
	  the Village
	Georgian Poetry, 1911–1912	

Dublin lock-out	D. H. Lawrence, *Sons and Lovers*
	Robert Bridges becomes Poet
	  Laureate
	London Society of Psychoanalysts
	G. M. Trevelyan, *Clio: A Muse*
	British Society for the Study
	  of Sexual Psychology
		1913

George V attends Cup Final
Prince of Wales Relief Fund
	R. Vaughan Williams, *London*
	  Symphony
	J. Joyce, *Dubliners* published;
	  Portrait of the Artist as a
	  Young Man
	Vorticists launch *Blast*
		1914

Women demand 'right to serve'
War Emergency Workers
  National Committee
Rent strike on Clyde
Central Liquor Control Board
	R. Brooke, *Collected Poems*
	D. H. Lawrence prosecuted
	  for *The Rainbow*
	V. Woolf, *The Voyage Out*
	A. L. Bowley, *Livelihood*
	  and Poverty
	P. Geddes, *Cities in Evolution*
		1915

Federation of British
  Industry (FBI)
	Department of Scientific and
	  Industrial Research
	Medical Research Council
		1916

May Days	T. S. Eliot, *Prufrock and other* *Observations*	1917

Date	Politics, Legislation, and Government	State and War
1918	Representation of the People Act Maurice Debate Pemberton Billing trial Labour Party adopts 'Clause 4'	Demotion of William Robertson German Spring Offensive Battle of Amiens Armistice

People, Projects, Events	Intellectual and Cultural Life	Date
Food rationing on 'points' system Marie Stopes, *Married Love*	L. Strachey, *Eminent Victorians* Death of Wilfred Owen	1918

List of Cabinets

GLADSTONE'S THIRD CABINET

formed February 1886

Prime Minister and First Lord of the Treasury: W. E. Gladstone
Lord Privy Seal: W. E. Gladstone
Lord Chancellor: Lord Herschell
Lord President: Earl Spencer
Chancellor of the Exchequer: Sir W. V. Harcourt
Home Secretary: H. C. E. Childers
Foreign Secretary: Earl of Rosebery
Secretary for War: H. Campbell-Bannerman
Colonial Secretary: Earl Granville
First Lord of the Admiralty: Marquess of Ripon
President of the Board of Trade: A. J. Mundella
Secretary for India: Earl of Kimberley
Secretary for Scotland: G. O. Trevelyan
Chief Secretary for Ireland: John Morley
President of the Local Government Board: Joseph Chamberlain

Changes

April 1886: Chamberlain resigned and was succeeded by James Stansfeld: Trevelyan resigned (his successor was not in the Cabinet).

SALISBURY'S SECOND CABINET

formed August 1886

Prime Minister and First Lord of Treasury: Marquess of Salisbury
Lord Chancellor: Lord Halsbury
Lord Chancellor of Ireland: Lord Ashbourne
Lord President of the Council: Viscount Cranbrook
Chancellor of the Exchequer: Lord Randolph Churchill
Home Secretary: H. Matthews
Foreign Secretary: Earl of Iddesleigh
Secretary for War: W. H. Smith
Colonial Secretary: Hon. Edward Stanhope
First Lord of the Admiralty: Lord George Hamilton
President of the Board of Trade: Lord Stanley
Secretary for India: Viscount Cross
Chief Secretary for Ireland: Sir M. Hicks Beach
Chancellor of the Duchy of Lancaster: Lord John Manners

Changes

November 1886: A. J. Balfour entered Cabinet as Secretary for Scotland. *January 1887*: Lord Randolph Churchill resigned as Chancellor of the Exchequer, to be replaced by G. J. Goschen. Lord Iddesleigh was dismissed as Foreign Secretary, being replaced by Salisbury, whose post as Lord President of the Council passed to W. H. Smith. The latter vacated his post as Secretary for War and was replaced by E. Stanhope, who in turn was succeeded as Colonial Secretary by Lord Knutsford. *March 1887*: A. J. Balfour was replaced as Secretary for Scotland by the Marquess of Lothian and became Chief Secretary for Ireland in place of Sir M. Hicks Beach, who nevertheless retained his place in the Cabinet. *May 1887*: Earl Cadogan entered the Cabinet as Lord Privy Seal and C. T. Ritchie as President of the Local Government Board. *February 1888*: Sir M. Hicks Beach was made President of the Board of Trade, replacing Lord Stanley. *October 1891*: W. H. Smith died, being succeeded as First Lord of the Treasury by A. J. Balfour, who was replaced as Chief Secretary for Ireland by W. L. Jackson.

GLADSTONE'S FOURTH CABINET

formed August 1892

Prime Minister and First Lord of the Treasury: W. E. Gladstone
Lord Privy Seal: W. E. Gladstone
Lord Chancellor: Lord Herschell
Lord President of the Council: Earl of Kimberley
Chancellor of the Exchequer: Sir W. V. Harcourt
Home Secretary: H. H. Asquith
Foreign Secretary: Earl of Rosebery
Secretary for War: H. Campbell-Bannerman
Colonial Secretary: Marquess of Ripon
First Lord of the Admiralty: Earl Spencer
President of the Board of Trade: A. J. Mundella
Secretary for India: Earl of Kimberley
Chief Secretary for Ireland: John Morley
President of the Local Government Board: H. H. Fowler
Chancellor of the Duchy of Lancaster: J. Bryce
Secretary for Scotland: G. O. Trevelyan
Vice-President of the Council (Education): A. H. D. Acland
First Commissioner of Works: G. J. Shaw-Lefevre
Postmaster-General: Arnold Morley

ROSEBERY'S CABINET

formed March 1894

Prime Minister and First Lord of the Treasury: Earl of Rosebery
Lord Chancellor: Lord Herschell
Lord President of the Council: Earl of Rosebery

Lord Privy Seal: Lord Tweedmouth
Chancellor of the Exchequer: Sir W. V. Harcourt
Home Secretary: H. H. Asquith
Foreign Secretary: Earl of Kimberley
Secretary for War: H. Campbell-Bannerman
Colonial Secretary: Marquess of Ripon
First Lord of the Admiralty: Earl Spencer
President of Board of Trade: J. Bryce
Secretary for India: H. H. Fowler
Chief Secretary for Ireland: John Morley
President of Local Government Board: G. J. Shaw-Lefevre
Chancellor of the Duchy of Lancaster: Lord Tweedmouth
Secretary for Scotland: Sir G. O. Trevelyan
Vice-President of the Council (Education): A. H. D. Acland
Postmaster-General: Arnold Morley

SALISBURY'S THIRD MINISTRY

formed June 1895

Prime Minister: Marquess of Salisbury
First Lord of the Treasury: A. J. Balfour
Lord Chancellor: Lord Halsbury
Lord Chancellor of Ireland: Lord Ashbourne
Lord President of the Council: Duke of Devonshire
Lord Privy Seal: Viscount Cross
Chancellor of the Exchequer: Sir M. Hicks Beach
Home Secretary: Sir Matthew White Ridley
Foreign Secretary: Marquess of Salisbury
Secretary for War: Marquess of Lansdowne
Colonial Secretary: Joseph Chamberlain
First Lord of Admiralty: G. J. Goschen
President of the Board of Trade: C. T. Ritchie
Secretary for India: Lord George Hamilton
Lord-Lieutenant of Ireland: Earl Cadogan
President of the Local Government Board: H. Chaplin
Chancellor of the Duchy of Lancaster: Lord James of Hereford
Secretary for Scotland: Lord Balfour of Burleigh
President of the Board of Agriculture: W. Long
First Commissioner of Works: A. Akers-Douglas

Changes

April 1900: the Duke of Devonshire became Lord President of the Board of Education, a new post. *October 1900*: Salisbury became Lord Privy Seal, replacing Viscount Cross, who retired, while vacating the Foreign Office, which was taken over by the Marquess of Lansdowne, who was succeeded as Secretary for War by St John Brodrick. Sir Matthew White Ridley retired as Home Secretary and G. J. Goschen as First Lord of the Admiralty, to be succeeded by C. T. Ritchie and the Earl of Selborne, respectively. Ritchie was replaced as President of the Board of Trade by Gerald Balfour and H. Chaplin as President of the Local Government Board by Walter Long. The latter's position as President of the Board of Agriculture passed to R. W. Hanbury. The Marquess of Londonderry entered the Cabinet as Postmaster-General.

BALFOUR'S CABINET

formed July 1902

Prime Minister: A. J. Balfour
Lord Chancellor: Lord Halsbury
Lord Chancellor of Ireland: Lord Ashbourne
Lord President of Council: Duke of Devonshire
Lord Privy Seal: A. J. Balfour
Chancellor of the Exchequer: C. T. Ritchie
Home Secretary: A. Akers-Douglas
Foreign Secretary: Marquess of Lansdowne
Secretary for War: Hon. St John Brodrick
Colonial Secretary: Joseph Chamberlain
First Lord of the Admiralty: Earl of Selborne
President of Board of Trade: Gerald Balfour
Secretary for India: Lord George Hamilton
Chief Secretary for Ireland: G. Wyndham
President of the Local Government Board: W. Long
Secretary for Scotland: Lord Balfour of Burleigh
President of the Board of Agriculture: R. W. Hanbury
President of the Board of Education: Marquess of Londonderry
Postmaster-General: Austen Chamberlain

Changes

May 1903: R. W. Hanbury was replaced as President of the Board of Agriculture by the Earl of Onslow. *September 1903*: Joseph Chamberlain retired to promote tariff reform, being replaced as Colonial Secretary by the Hon. A. Lyttelton. C. T. Ritchie resigned as Chancellor of the Exchequer, his post being filled by Austen Chamberlain, who was succeeded as Postmaster-General by Lord Stanley. Lord Balfour of Burleigh resigned as Secretary for Scotland and was replaced by G. Murray (Lord Dunedin). Lord George Hamilton resigned as Secretary for India, his post going to St John Brodrick, who was succeeded as Secretary for War by H. O. Arnold-Forster. The Duke of Devonshire resigned as Lord President of the Council and was replaced by the Marquess of Londonderry. The 4th Marquess of Salisbury succeeded A. J. Balfour as Lord Privy Seal. *March 1905*: Selborne left for the post of High Commissioner of South Africa, being replaced at the Admiralty by Earl Cawdor. G. Wyndham resigned as Chief Secretary for Ireland and was succeeded by W. Long, whose post as President of the Local Government Board went to Gerald Balfour. The latter was succeeded as President of the Board of Trade by the 4th Marquess of Salisbury. The Board of Agriculture passed from the Earl of Onslow to the Hon. Ailwyn Fellowes.

CAMPBELL-BANNERMAN'S CABINET

formed December 1905

Prime Minister and First Lord of Treasury: H. Campbell-Bannerman
Lord Chancellor: Lord Loreburn
Lord President of the Council: Earl of Crewe
Lord Privy Seal: Marquess of Ripon
Chancellor of the Exchequer: H. H. Asquith
Home Secretary: Herbert Gladstone
Foreign Secretary: Sir E. Grey
Secretary for War: R. B. Haldane
Colonial Secretary: Earl of Elgin
First Lord of the Admiralty: Lord Tweedmouth
President of the Board of Trade: D. Lloyd George
Secretary for India: John Morley
Chief Secretary for Ireland: J. Bryce
President of the Local Government Board: J. Burns
Chancellor of Duchy of Lancaster: H. H. Fowler
Secretary for Scotland: J. Sinclair
President of Board of Agriculture: Earl Carrington
President of the Board of Education: A. Birrell
Postmaster-General: S. Buxton

Changes

January 1907: J. Bryce left the post of Chief Secretary for Ireland to become British Ambassador at Washington. He was replaced by A. Birrell, who was succeeded at the Board of Education by R. McKenna. *March 1907*: L. Harcourt entered the Cabinet as First Commissioner of Works.

ASQUITH'S LIBERAL CABINET

formed April 1908

Prime Minister and First Lord of Treasury: H. H. Asquith
Lord Chancellor: Lord Loreburn
Lord President of the Council: Lord Tweedmouth
Lord Privy Seal: Marquess of Ripon
Chancellor of the Exchequer: D. Lloyd George
Home Secretary: Herbert Gladstone

Foreign Secretary: Sir E. Grey
Secretary for War: R. B. Haldane (cr. Viscount Haldane, 1911)
Colonial Secretary: Earl of Crewe
First Lord of the Admiralty: R. McKenna
President of the Board of Trade: W. S. Churchill
Secretary for India: Viscount Morley
Chief Secretary for Ireland: A. Birrell
President of the Local Government Board: J. Burns
Chancellor of the Duchy of Lancaster: Sir H. H. Fowler
Secretary for Scotland: J. Sinclair (cr. Lord Pentland, 1909)
President of the Board of Agriculture: Earl Carrington
President of the Board of Education: W. Runciman
First Commissioner of Works: L. Harcourt
Postmaster-General: S. Buxton

Changes

September 1908: Lord Tweedmouth was removed as Lord President of the Council and replaced by Sir H. H. Fowler, created Viscount Wolverhampton, whose position as Chancellor of the Duchy of Lancaster was filled by Lord Edmond Fitzmaurice. *October 1908*: Lord Ripon resigned as Lord Privy Seal, being replaced by the Earl of Crewe, who continued as Colonial Secretary. *June 1909*: H. Samuel replaced Lord Edmond Fitzmaurice as Chancellor of the Duchy of Lancaster. *February 1910*: H. Gladstone was appointed Governor-General of South Africa, being succeeded as Home Secretary by W. S. Churchill, who was replaced as President of the Board of Trade by S. Buxton. The latter was moved from the post of Postmaster-General, being succeeded by H. Samuel, who was succeeded as Chancellor of the Duchy of Lancaster by J. A. Pease. *June 1910*: Viscount Wolverhampton resigned as Lord President of the Council, being succeeded by Earl Beauchamp. *November 1910*: Earl Beauchamp was replaced as Lord President of the Council by Viscount Morley, who was replaced as Indian Secretary by the Earl of Crewe, who was succeeded as Colonial Secretary by L. Harcourt, whom Beauchamp replaced as First Commissioner of Works. *March 1911*: Viscount Morley replaced the Earl of Crewe as Secretary for India until May 1911. *October 1911*: R. McKenna, the First Lord of Admiralty, and W. S. Churchill, Home Secretary, swapped posts. Earl Carrington replaced Crewe as Lord Privy Seal until February 1912. J. A. Pease became President of the Board of Education, replacing W. Runciman, who was appointed President of the Board of Agriculture. C. E. Hobhouse replaced Pease as Chancellor of the Duchy of Lancaster. *February 1912*: Lord Pentland retired as Secretary for Scotland, being replaced by T. McKinnon Wood. *June 1912*: Lord Loreburn retired as Lord Chancellor, being replaced by Viscount Haldane, who was succeeded as Secretary for War by J. E. B. Seely. Sir R. Isaacs, the Attorney-General, entered the Cabinet. *October 1913*: Sir R. Isaacs was appointed Lord Chief Justice, his post as Attorney-General being filled by Sir J. Simon. *February 1914*: J. Burns, President of the Local Government Board, was replaced by H. Samuel, who moved from being Postmaster-General. The latter post was filled by C. E. Hobhouse, who was succeeded as Chancellor of the Duchy of Lancaster by C. F. G. Masterman. J. Burns moved to the Board of Trade to replace S. Buxton, who had been appointed Governor-General of South Africa. *March 1914*: J. E. B. Seely resigned as Secretary for War, the post being filled by H. H. Asquith, the Prime Minister. *August 1914*: J. Burns and Viscount Morley resigned, as President of the Board of Trade and Lord President of the Council, respectively; their places were taken by W. Runciman and Earl Beauchamp. W. Runciman's position as President of the Board of Agriculture was filled by Lord Lucas, Beauchamp's as First Commissioner of Works by Lord Emmott. H. H. Asquith was replaced as Secretary for War by Earl Kitchener. *February 1915*: C. F. G. Masterman resigned as Chancellor of the Duchy of Lancaster, being succeeded by E. Montagu.

ASQUITH'S COALITION CABINET

formed May 1915

Prime Minister: H. H. Asquith (Lib.)
Lord Chancellor: Lord Buckmaster (Lib.)
Lord President of the Council: Marquess of Crewe (Lib.)
Lord Privy Seal: Lord Curzon (Con.)
Chancellor of the Exchequer: R. McKenna (Lib.)
Home Secretary: Sir J. Simon (Lib.)
Foreign Secretary: Sir E. Grey (Lib.)
Secretary for War: Earl Kitchener (Ind.)
Colonial Secretary: A. Bonar Law (Con.)
First Lord of the Admiralty: A. J. Balfour (Con.)
President of the Board of Trade: W. Runciman (Lib.)
Secretary for India: Austen Chamberlain (Con.)
Chief Secretary for Ireland: A. Birrell (Lib.)
President of the Local Government Board: W. Long (Con.)
Chancellor of the Duchy of Lancaster: W. S. Churchill (Lib.)
Secretary for Scotland: T. McKinnon Wood (Lib.)
President of the Board of Agriculture: Earl of Selborne (Con.)
President of the Board of Education: A. Henderson (Lab.)
First Commissioner of Works: L. Harcourt (Lib.)
Attorney-General: Sir E. Carson (Con.)
Minister of Munitions: D. Lloyd George (Lib.)
Minister Without Portfolio: Marquess of Lansdowne (Con.)

Changes

November 1915: E. Carson resigned as Attorney-General and was replaced by F. E. Smith (Con.). W. S. Churchill resigned as Chancellor of the Duchy of Lancaster and was succeeded by Sir H. Samuel (Lib.). *January 1916*: Sir J. Simon resigned as Home Secretary, being replaced by Sir H. Samuel, whose position as Chancellor of the Duchy of Lancaster was taken by E. Montagu (Lib.), who also served as the Financial

Secretary to the Treasury. Lord Robert Cecil (Con.) entered the Cabinet as Minister of Blockade. *July 1916*: the Secretary for War, Earl Kitchener, drowned at sea, was replaced by D. Lloyd George, who was followed as Minister of Munitions by E. Montagu. The latter was replaced as Financial Secretary to the Treasury by T. McKinnon Wood, the former Secretary for Scotland, who was replaced by H. Tennant (Lib.). A. Birrell resigned as Chief Secretary for Ireland and was succeeded by H. Duke (Con.). The Earl of Selborne resigned as President of the Board of Agriculture and was replaced by the Earl of Crawford (Con.). *August 1916*: the Marquess of Crewe, the President of the Council, also became President of the Board of Education, in place of A. Henderson, who was made Paymaster-General.

LLOYD GEORGE'S WAR CABINET

formed December 1916

Prime Minister: David Lloyd George (Lib.)
Andrew Bonar Law (Con.)
Earl Curzon (Con.)
Arthur Henderson (Lab.) Dec. 1916–Aug. 1917
Viscount Milner (Con.) Dec. 1916–Apr. 1918

Changes

June 1917: Jan Smuts (Ind.) joined the War Cabinet. *July 1917*: E. Carson (Con.) joined the War Cabinet. *August 1917*: A. Henderson resigned, to be replaced by G. Barnes (Lab.). *January 1918*: E. Carson resigned. *April 1918*: Viscount Milner left the War Cabinet and was replaced by Austen Chamberlain (Con.).

MINISTERIAL OFFICES OF CABINET RANK

Lord Chancellor: Lord Finlay (Con.)
Lord President of the Council: Lord Curzon (Con.)
Lord Privy Seal: Earl of Crawford (Con.)
Chancellor of the Exchequer: A. Bonar Law (Con.)
Home Secretary: Sir G. Cave (Con.)
Foreign Secretary: A. J. Balfour (Con.)
Secretary for War: Earl of Derby (Con.)
Colonial Secretary: W. Long (Con.)
First Lord of the Admiralty: E. Carson (Con.)
President of the Board of Trade: A. Stanley (Lib.)
Secretary for India: Austen Chamberlain (Con.)
Chief Secretary for Ireland: H. Duke (Con.)
President of the Local Government Board: Lord Rhondda (Lib.)
Chancellor of the Duchy of Lancaster: Sir F. Cawley (Lib.)
Secretary for Scotland: R. Munro (Lib.)
President of the Board of Agriculture: R. Prothero (Con.)

President of the Board of Education: H. A. L. Fisher (Lib.)
Minister of Munitions: C. Addison (Lib.)
Minister of Labour: J. Hodge (Lab.)

Changes

June 1917: Lord Rhondda retired as President of the Local Government Board and was replaced by W. Hayes Fisher (Con.). *July 1917*: E. Carson left the Admiralty for the War Cabinet and was replaced by E. Geddes (Con.). Austen Chamberlain resigned as Secretary for India and was replaced by E. Montagu (Lib.). C. Addison was moved from the Ministry of Munitions to the Ministry of Reconstruction and replaced by W. S. Churchill (Lib.). *August 1917*: J. Hodge moved from the Ministry of Labour to the Ministry of Pensions and was replaced by G. Roberts (Lab.). *February 1918*: Sir F. Cawley was replaced as Chancellor of the Duchy of Lancaster by Lord Beaverbrook (Con.), who combined this office with that of Minister of Information. *April 1918*: the Earl of Derby was replaced as Secretary for War by Viscount Milner (Con.). *May 1918*: H. Duke was made Lord Justice of Appeal and succeeded as Chief Secretary for Ireland by E. Shortt (Lib.). *October 1918*: Viscount French (Ind.) was appointed Lord-Lieutenant of Ireland. *November 1918*: W. Hayes Fisher was replaced as President of the Local Government Board by A. Geddes (Con.) and, as Lord Downham, made Chancellor of the Duchy of Lancaster, in place of Lord Beaverbrook.

GENERAL ELECTIONS

1885–1910

Of the 670 seats:

England	465
Wales	30
Scotland	72
Ireland	103

If Monmouthshire is included in Wales, the figures are:

England	461
Wales	34
Scotland	72
Ireland	103

There were 9 MPs representing the university constituencies, of which 5 were returned in England, 2 in Scotland, 2 in Wales.

If they are excluded, the above figures are, in total, 661, of which:

England	460
Wales	30
Scotland	70
Ireland	101
	or
England	456
Wales	34
Scotland	70
Ireland	101

1886–1918

1886	Con.	Lib. Unionists	Lib.	Irish Nationalist
England	283	56	125	1
Scotland	12	17	43	—
Wales	4	3	23	—
Ireland	17	2	—	84
TOTAL	316	78	191	85

1892	Con.	Lib. Unionist	Lib.	Irish Nationalist
England	236	32	196	1
Scotland	11	11	50	—
Wales	2	—	28	—
Ireland	19	4	—	80*
TOTAL	268	47	274	81

Note: *Including 9 Parnellites.

1895	Con.	Lib. Unionist	Lib.	Irish Nationalist
England	298	51	115	1
Scotland	19	14	39	—
Wales	7	1	22	—
Ireland	17	4	1	81*
TOTAL	341	70	177	82

Note: *Including 12 Parnellites.

1900	Unionist	Lib.	LRC*	Irish Nationalist
England	339	125		1
Scotland	38	34	—	—
Wales	4	26		
Ireland	21	1	—	81
TOTAL	402	186		82

Note: *Labour Representation Committee.

1906	Unionist	Lib.	LRC	Irish Nationalist
England	127	289	48	1
Scotland	12	58	2	
Wales	—	26	4	—
Ireland	18	3	—	82
TOTAL	157	376	54	83

Jan. 1910	Unionist	Lib.	Lab.	Irish Nationalist
England	239	191	34	1
Scotland	11	59	2	—
Wales	2	24	4	—
Ireland	21	1	—	81
TOTAL	273	275	40	82

Dec. 1910	Unionist	Lib.	Lab.	Irish Nationalist
England	241	188	35	1
Scotland	11	58	3	—
Wales	3	23	4	—
Ireland	19	1	—	83
TOTAL	274	270	42	84

1918	Coalition			Unionist	Lib.	Lab.	Irish	Sinn	Others
	Unionist	Lib.	Lab.				Nationalist	Fein	
England	299	91	11	23	19	42	1	—	6
Scotland	30	26	1	2	8	7	—	—	—
Wales*	1	19	1	3	2	10	—	—	—
Ireland	4	—	—	22	—	—	6	73	—
TOTAL	334	136	13	50	29	59	7	73	6

Note: *Including Monmouthshire.

Bibliography

I GENERAL

An invaluable compendium of statistical information is provided in A. H. Halsey, *British Social Trends since 1900* (London, 1988). B. R. Mitchell, *British Historical Statistics* (Cambridge, 1988), is equally useful on economic and demographic data. Politics, including lists of ministers and election results, is comprehensively covered in C. Cook, *British Historical Facts 1830–1900* (London, 1975) and D. Butler and G. Butler, *British Political Facts 1900–1994* (London, 1994).

II NATIONAL IDENTITIES

A good introduction to the complexity of patriotism is J. H. Grainger, *Patriotisms: Britain: 1900–1939* (London, 1986). The relationship between the 'nations' within Great Britain is explored in K. Robbins, *History, Religion and Identity in Modern Britain* (London, 1993), L. Colley, 'Britons and Otherness: An Argument', *Journal of British Studies*, 31 (1992), 309–29, and A. Grant and K. J. Stringer (eds.), *Uniting the Kingdom?* (London, 1995). P. Thane, 'The British Imperial State and the Construction of National Identities', in B. Melman (ed.), *Borderlines: Gender and Identities in War and Peace, 1870–1930* (New York and London, 1998), 29–45, examines ways in which state action helped shape national identities.

On **English identity**, the problem of disentangling the English from their 'Celtic neighbours', is well handled through a study of school primers, S. Heathorn, ' "Let us remember that we, too, are English": Constructions of Citizenship and National Identity in English Elementary School Reading Books, 1880–1914', *Victorian Studies*, 38 (1994–5), 395–427. V. E. Chancellor, *History For Their Masters: Opinion in the English History Textbook, 1800–1914* (Bath, 1970), throws useful light on the inculcation of patriotism. R. T. Shannon, 'John Robert Seeley and the Idea of a National Church', in R. Robson (ed.), *Ideas and Institutions of Victorian Britain* (London, 1967), ch. 9, links 'nationality' with the public role of the Church of England. R. Colls and P. Dodd (eds.), *Englishness: Politics and Culture 1880–1920* (Beckenham, 1986), is a useful collection of essays devoted to the 'construction' of Englishness. R. Colls, *Identity of England* (Oxford, 2002), is a more recent wide-ranging treatment of the same theme.

The best introduction to **immigration** and the reactions it provoked within the host society is to be found in C. Holmes, *John Bull's Other Island: Immigration and British Society 1871–1971* (Basingstoke, 1988). Various ethnic groups feature in C. Holmes (ed.), *Immigrants and Minorities in British Society* (London, 1978), and K. Lunn (ed.), *Hosts, Immigrants and Minorities: Historical Responses to Newcomers in British Society 1870–1914* (New York, 1980).

The issue of **Irish immigration** has attracted a number of studies, among the most useful of which are M. A. G. O Tuathaigh, 'The Irish in Nineteenth-Century Britain: Problems of Integration', *Transactions of the Royal Historical Society*, 5th ser., 31 (1981), 149–73, R. Swift and S. Gilley (eds.), *The Irish in the Victorian City* (London, 1985), R. Swift and S. Gilley (eds.), *The Irish in Britain 1815–1939* (London, 1989), and S. Fielding, *Class and Ethnicity: Irish Catholics in England, 1880–1939* (Buckingham, 1993).

On **Italian** and **German** immigrants, see, respectively, L. Sponza, *Italian Immigrants in Nineteenth-Century Britain: Realities and Images* (Leicester, 1988), and R. Ashton, *Little Germany: Exile and Asylum in Victorian England* (Oxford, 1986). P. Panayi, 'German Business Interests in Britain During the First World War', *Business History*, 32 (1990), 244–58, is not confined entirely to the war years.

The **Jewish** community has been well served by D. Feldman, *Englishmen and Jews: Social Relations and Political Culture 1840–1914* (New Haven and London, 1994), and W. D. Rubinstein, *A History of the Jews in the English-Speaking World: Great Britain* (Basingstoke, 1996). Two specialized studies dealing with aspects of this subject are D. Englander, 'Booth's Jews: The Presentation of Jews and Judaism in "Life and Labour of the People of London" ', *Victorian Studies*, 32 (1989), 551–70, and R. A. Voeltz, ' "A Good Jew and a Good Englishman". The Jewish Lads' Brigade, 1894–1922', *Journal of Contemporary History*, 23 (1988), 119–27.

A lively account of **Indians** in Great Britain is provided in R. Visram, *Ayahs, Lascars and Princes: Indians in Britain 1700–1947* (London, 1986). G. K. Behlmer, 'The Gypsy Problem in Victorian England', *Victorian Studies*, 28 (1985), 231–53, focuses on this much-misunderstood ethnic grouping. **West Indians**, along with other ethnic minorities in London, receive sympathetic treatment in J. Schneer, *London 1900: The Imperial Metropolis* (New Haven and London, 1999).

The complex ways in which national identity were promoted by attitudes to 'abroad' inform three widely different studies: J. Pemble, *The Mediterranean Passion: Victorians and Edwardians in the South* (Oxford, 1987), M. Nelson, *Queen Victoria and the Discovery of the Riviera* (London, 2001), and M. Morgan, *National Identities and Travel in Victorian Britain* (London, 2001).

A good introduction to the understanding of the phenomenon of **imperial emigration** is provided in several essays in A. Porter (ed.), *The Oxford History of the British Empire: Volume 3: The Nineteenth Century* (Oxford, 1999). P. A. Dunae, *Gentlemen Emigrants From the British Public Schools to the Canadian Frontier* (Vancouver, 1981), supplies a detailed case study.

A readable account of **imperialist propaganda**, in the wider sense, is to be found in W. J. Reader, *At Duty's Call: A Study in Obsolete Patriotism* (Manchester, 1988). The shifting meanings of imperialist language are explored in R. Koebner and H. D. Schmidt, *Imperialism: The Story and Significance of a Political Word 1840–1960* (Cambridge, 1965). An examination of the way in which 'imperialism' interpenetrated many aspects of social life is to be found in J. M. MacKenzie, *Propaganda and Empire: The Manipulation of British Public Opinion 1880–1960* (Manchester, 1984), and in J. M. Mackenzie (ed.), *Imperialism and Popular Culture* (Manchester, 1986). There is a stimulating study on how Empire sold commodities and commodities sold the Empire: T. Richards, *The Commodity Culture of Victorian England: Advertising and Spectacle 1851–1914* (Stanford, 1990). The role of 'Empire' in juvenile fiction has attracted a rich literature: see J. Bristow, *Empire Boys: Adventures in a Man's World* (London, 1991), J. McBratney, 'Imperial Subjects, Imperial Space in Kipling's "Jungle Book" ', *Victorian Studies*, 35 (1992), 277–93, and K. Boyd, 'Exemplars and Ingrates: Imperialism and the Boys' Story Paper', *Historical Research*, 67 (1994), 143–55.

Contemporary attempts to construct an intellectual model of **race** form the subject-matter of D. Lorimer, 'Theoretical Racism in Late-Victorian Anthropology, 1870–1900', *Victorian Studies*, 31 (1988), 405–30, and C. Bolt, *Victorian Attitudes to Race* (London, 1971). For the dissemination of **racial imagery**, see J. A. Mangan (ed.), *The Imperial Curriculum: Racial Images and Education in the British Colonial Experience* (London, 1993). D. Cannadine, *Ornamentalism: How the British Saw Their Empire* (Harmondsworth, 2001), is an extended essay showing how race was often undercut by hierarchy, ritual, and display. R. Hyam, *Empire and Sexuality* (London, 1991), provocatively argues that sexual encounters with 'native' peoples helped to broaden cultural horizons.

The relationship between manliness, patriotism, and **chivalry** forms the subject-matter of M. Girouard, *The Return to Camelot: Chivalry and the English Gentleman* (New Haven and London, 1981). On the cult of **St George** throughout the ages, see S. Riches, *St George: Hero, Martyr and Myth* (Stroud, 2000).

III GENDER AND GENERATION

For an advanced investigation of the complexities of **demography**, see R. Woods, *The Demography of Victorian England and Wales* (Cambridge, 2000).

Two useful introductions to the study of **childhood** are J. Walvin, *A Child's World: A Social History of English Childhood 1800–1914* (Harmondsworth, 1982), and H. Hendrick, *Children, Childhood and English Society, 1880–1990* (Cambridge, 1997), the latter of which contains an excellent bibliography. G. Behlmer's monograph, *Child Abuse and Moral Reform in England, 1870–1908* (Stanford, 1982), can be supplemented by the essays in R. Cooter (ed.), *In the Name of the Child: Health and Welfare 1880–1940* (London, 1992).

Two diametrically opposed interpretations of the experience of **schooling** are J. Rose, 'Willingly to School: The Working-Class Response to Elementary Edcuation in Britain, 1875–1918', *Journal of British Studies*, 32 (1993), 114–38, which takes an optimistic line, and L. Rose, *The Erosion of Childhood: Child Oppression in Britain 1860–1918* (London, 1991), which takes a pessimistic one. The growing acceptance of schooling is chronicled in D. Rubinstein, *School Attendance in London, 1870–1914: A Social History* (Hull, 1969).

Contemporary anxieties about '**youth**' have attracted much attention. See S. Humphries, *Hooligans or Rebels? An Oral History of Working-Class Childhood and Youth, 1889–1939* (Oxford, 1981), G. Pearson, *Hooligan: A History of Respectable Fears* (Houndmills, 1983), J. Gillis, *Youth and History* (New York, 1975), and H. Hendrick,

Images of Youth: Age, Class and the Male Youth Problem, 1880–1920 (Oxford, 1990). J. Springhall, *Coming of Age: Adolescence in Britain, 1860–1960* (Dublin [*c*.1986]) registers the new awareness of the period of transition between childhood and adulthood. J. Springhall, *Youth, Empire and Society: British Youth Movements, 1883–1940* (London, 1977), is still the best general guide to the subject. (For the Boy Scouts, see Section XIII below.) The place of youth in the labour market is described in M. J. Childs, 'Boy Labour in Late Victorian and Edwardian England and the Remaking of the Working Class', *Journal of Social History*, 23 (1987), 783–802, and M. Childs, *Labour's Apprentices: Working-Class Lads in Late Victorian and Edwardian England* (London, 1992).

On **old age**, P. Thane, *Old Age in English History: Past Experiences, Present Issues* (Oxford, 2000), is indispensable. P. Johnson, 'The Employment and Retirement of Older Men in England and Wales, 1881–1981', *Economic History Review*, 47 (1994), 106–28, deals authoritatively with its specialized dimension.

Two wide-ranging analyses of **masculinity** are the collection of essays in J. A. Mangan and J. Walvin (eds.), *Manliness and Morality: Middle-Class Masculinity in Britain and America, 1800–1940* (Manchester, [*c*.1987]), and J. Tosh, *A Man's Place: Masculinity and the Middle-Class Home in Victorian England* (New Haven and London, 1999). The construction of masculinity in fiction can be explored through R. H. MacDonald, ' "Reproducing the Middle-Class Boy": From Purity to Patriotism in the Boys' Magazines, 1892–1914', *Journal of Contemporary History*, 24 (1989), 519–39.

For studies of **girls**, see C. Dyhouse, *Girls Growing Up in Late Victorian and Edwardian England* (London, 1981), and S. Mitchell, *The New Girl: Girls' Culture in England, 1880–1915* (New York, 1995). An ambitious attempt to 'organize' girls is chronicled in B. Harrison, 'For Church, Queen and Family: The Girls' Friendly Society, 1874–1920', *Past & Present*, 61 (1973), 107–38. M. Cale, 'Girls and the Perception of Sexual Danger in the Victorian Reformatory System', *History*, 78 (1993), 201–17, is interesting on contemporary perceptions of girls' sexuality.

The literature on **women** is voluminous, and only a brief selection can be given. On **higher education**, see C. Dyhouse, *No Distinction of Sex? Women in British Universities 1870–1939* (London, 1995). On **women and work**, J. Lewis, *Women in England, 1870–1950: Sexual Divisions and Social Change* (New York and London, 1984), is indispensable reading, but P. Thane, 'Late Victorian Women', in T. R. Gourvish and A. O'Day (eds.), *Later Victorian Britain 1867–1900* (Basingstoke, 1988), 175–208, is also highly informative. Opposite ends of the social spectrum are explored in P. Horne, *Ladies of the Manor: Wives and Daughters in Country-House Society 1830–1918* (Stroud, 1991), and E. Ross, *Love and Toil: Motherhood in Outcast London, 1870–1918* (Oxford, 1993). E. Higgs, 'Women, Occupation and Work in the Nineteenth Century Censuses', *History Workshop Journal*, 23 (1987), 59–80, explains the problems of interpreting census data. D. M. Copelman, *London's Women Teachers: Gender, Class and Feminism, 1870–1930* (London, 1996), describes an important and expanding women's profession.

On **social reform and philanthropy**, F. Prochaska, *Women and Philanthropy in 19th Century England* (Oxford, 1980), is important. The movement by working women to control their own environment is described in R. Feurer, 'The Meaning of

"Sisterhood": The British Women's Movement and Protective Labor Legislation, 1870–1900', *Victorian Studies*, 31 (1988), 233–60.

Women and domesticity provides the subject-matter of two important articles, J. Bourke, 'Housewifery in Working-Class England, 1860–1914', *Past & Present*, 143 (1994), 167–97, and P. Levine, ' "So Few Prizes and So Many Blanks": Marriage and Feminism in Late 19th Century England', *Journal of British Studies*, 28 (1989), 150–74. Contemporary views of marriage are illuminated by J. M. Robson, *Marriage or Celibacy? The Daily Telegraph on a Victorian Dilemma* (Toronto, 1995).

Women as **readers** feature in K. Flint, *The Woman Reader, 1837–1914* (Oxford, 1993) and in relation to the **advertising industry** in L. A. Loeb, *Consuming Angels: Advertising and Victorian Women* (Oxford and New York, 1994).

The **public role of women** has attracted a rich literature. D. Rubinstein, *Before the Suffragettes: Women's Emancipation in the 1890s* (Brighton, 1986), corrects misconceptions about the 1890s, while P. Hollis, *Ladies Elect: Women in English Local Government 1865–1914* (Oxford, 1987), demonstrates how effectively women were already using the vote—in local politics. The participation of women in the socialist movement is described in J. Hannam, 'Women and the ILP, 1890–1914', in D. James, T. Jowitt, and K. Laybourn (eds.), *The Centennial History of the Independent Labour Party* (Halifax, 1992), and their contribution to Empire in J. Bush, *Edwardian Ladies and Imperial Power* (Leicester, 2000).

J. Lewis (ed.), *Before the Vote Was Won: Arguments For and Against Women's Suffrage* (New York and London, 1987), examines the controversy about whether women should be enfranchised, and aspects of this debate are also explored by B. Harrison in *Separate Spheres: The Opposition to Women's Suffrage in Britain* (London, 1978) and in 'Women's Health and the Women's Movement in Britain: 1840–1940', in C. Webster (ed.), *Biology, Medicine and Society 1840–1948* (Cambridge, 1971), 15–71. A. Clark, 'Gender, Class and the Nation: Franchise Reform in England, 1832–1928', in J. Vernon (ed.), *Re-Reading the Constitution: New Narratives in the Political History of England's Long Nineteenth Century* (Cambridge, 1996), 230–53, contains some important insights.

On **sexuality**, J. Weeks, *Sex, Politics and Society: The Regulation of Sexuality Since 1800* (Harlow: 2nd edn., 1989), provides the best single introduction to all aspects of sexual behaviour. S. Hynes, *The Edwardian Turn of Mind* (London, 1968), ch. 5, focuses on the 'new' writing about sex. L. A. Hall, ' "Disinterested Enthusiasm for Sexual Misconduct": The British Society for the Study of Sex Psychology, 1913–47', *Journal of Contemporary History*, 30 (1995), 665–86, is an exemplary case study. M. Mason, *The Making of Victorian Sexuality* (Oxford, 1994), is also important.

E. J. Bristow, *Vice and Vigilance: Purity Movements in Britain Since 1700* (London, 1977), is still indispensable on attempts to 'police' sexuality, but it should be supplemented by L. Bland, *Banishing the Beast: English Feminism and Sexual Morality 1885–1914* (Harmondsworth, 1995), which explores the complexities of the contemporary 'feminist' response. The 'cultural studies' approach is adopted in E. Showalter, *Sexual Anarchy: Gender and Culture at the Fin-de-Siecle* (London, 1990), D. E. Nord, *Walking the Victorian Streets: Women, Representation, and the City* (Ithaca and London, 1995), and J. Walkowitz, *City of Dreadful Delight: Narratives of Sexual Danger in Late-Victorian London* (London, 1992). On prostitution, see J. Walkowitz, *Prostitution and Victorian Society* (Cambridge, 1980), and on incest A. S. Wohl, 'Sex and the Single Room: Incest Among the Victorian Working Class', in A. S. Wohl, *The Victorian Family: Structure and Stresses* (London, 1978), 197–216. A. McLaren's ground-breaking *Birth-Control in Nineteenth-Century England* (London, 1978) should now be supplemented by the same author's *Twentieth-Century Sexuality: A History* (Oxford, 1999).

Theatrical and fictional 'transgressions' of conventional sexual boundaries have recently attracted attention: see M. Vicinus, 'Fin-de-Siecle Theatrics: Male Impersonation and Lesbian Desire', in B. Melman (ed.), *Borderlines: Gender and Identities in War and Peace, 1870–1930* (New York and London, 1998), 163–92, D. Trotter, 'Lesbians Before Lesbianism? Sexual Identity in Early Twentieth-Century British Fiction', in ibid. 193–211, and J. S. Bratton, 'Beating the Bounds: Gender Play and Role Reversal in the Edwardian Music Hall', in M. R. Booth and J. L. Kaplan (eds.), *The Edwardian Theatre* (Cambridge, 1996), 86–110.

IV SOCIAL IDENTITIES

J. Harris, *Private Lives, Public Spirit: A Social History of Britain 1870–1914* (Oxford, 1993), has brilliant insights into all the issues discussed under this heading. F. M. L. Thompson, *The Rise of Respectable Society: A Social History of Victorian Britain, 1830–1900* (1988), and J. Bourke, *Working-Class Cultures in Britain 1890–1960: Gender, Class, and Ethnicity* (1994), both provide authoritative introductions, as do the specialized articles in F. M. L. Thompson (ed.), *The Cambridge Social History of Britain 1750–1950*, 3 vols. (Cambridge, 1990), M. D. Daunton (ed.), *The Cambridge Urban History of Britain, vol. 3: 1840–1950* (Cambridge, 2000), and C. Matthew (ed.), *The Nineteenth Century: The British Isles: 1815–1901* (Oxford, 2000).

On locality, P. J. Waller, *Town, City and Nation: England 1850–1914* (Oxford, 1983), is an excellent guide to urban locations, A. Howkins, *Reshaping Rural England: A Social History 1850–1925* (London, 1991), to the structure and problems of the agricultural districts. London is usefully analysed in A. Sutcliffe (ed.), *Metropolis, 1890–1940* (1984), while G. Stedman Jones, in *Outcast London* (Oxford, 1971), subjects the East End to a rigorous Marxist critique. J. K. Walton, *Lancashire: A Social History 1558–1939* (Manchester, 1987), well describes this important and populous region. The often neglected environment of smaller market towns is tackled in J. Brown, *The English Market Town: A Social and Economic History, 1750–1914* (Ramsbury, 1986).

The ideological complexities of the **class system** are brought out in P. Thompson, *The Edwardians: The Remaking of British Society* (London, 1975), which draws heavily on oral testimony. R. McKibbin, *The Ideologies of Class: Social Relations in Britain 1880–1950* (Oxford, 1990), brings together an important collection of the author's articles. G. Routh, *Occupation and Pay in Great Britain 1906–79* (London and Basingstoke, 1980), approaches the subject through an examination of economic data.

D. Cannadine, *Class in Britain* (New Haven and London, 1998), argues for the dominance of the multilayered approach.

On the working class, see M. Savage and A. Miles, *The Remaking of the British Working Class 1840–1940* (London, 1994), and J. Benson (ed.), *The Working Class in England 1875–1914* (Beckenham, 1985). G. S. Jones (see above) explores the issue of working-class stratification, while P. Johnson, 'Conspicuous Consumption and Working-Class Culture in Late Victorian and Edwardian Britain', *Transactions of the Royal Historical Society*, 5th ser., 38 (1988), 27–42, approaches the same subject through consumption patterns. R. Williams, 'The Ragged-Arsed Philanthropists', in D. Alfred (ed.), *The Robert Tressell Lectures, 1981–88* (Rochester, 1988), 19–33, has interesting observations on the 'Lumpenproletariat'.

On 'intermediate' groupings, the foreman class features in J. Melling, ' "Non-Commissioned Officers": British Employers and their Supervisory Workers, 1880–1920', *Social History*, 5 (1980), 183–221, the lower middle class in an important collection of essays edited by G. Crossick, *The Lower Middle Class in Britain, 1870–1914* (London, 1977). G. Crossick and H.-G. Haupt (eds.), *Shopkeepers and Master Artisans in Nineteenth Century Europe* (London, 1984), offers a comparative international perspective.

The middle class is too amorphous to be easily treated as an entity, but the problem of middle-class identity is usefully tackled in a collection of essays, A. Kidd and D. Nicholls (eds), *The Making of the British Middle Class?* (Stroud, 1998). S. Gunn, *The Public Culture of the Victorian Middle Class: Ritual and Authority in the English Industrial City 1840–1914* (Manchester, 2000), elegantly charts the rise and fall of middle-class culture in Birmingham, Leeds, and Manchester. H. Long, *The Edwardian House: The Middle-Class Home in Britain 1880–1914* (Manchester, 1993), illuminates the inhabitants as well as the physical domestic environment.

A good overview of the professions is to be found in T. R. Gourvish, 'The Rise of the Professions', in T. R. Gourvish and A. O'Day (eds.), *Later Victorian Britain 1867–1900* (Basingstoke, 1988), 13–35. D. A. MacKenzie, in *Statistics in Britain 1865–1930* (Edinburgh, 1981), argues, controversially, for the emergence of the professional middle class as a distinctive class in its own right. The medical profession is the subject of two excellent studies by A. Digby, *Making a Medical Living: Doctors and Patients in the English Market for Medicine, 1720–1911* (Cambridge, 1994), and *The Evolution of British General Practice, 1850–1948* (Oxford, 1999). Accounts of particular business groupings are too numerous to itemize, but C. Erickson's ground-breaking study, *British Industrialists: Steel and Hosiery 1850–1950* (Cambridge, 1959), still repays attention. See also Y. Cassis, 'Bankers in English Society in the Late Nineteenth Century', *Economic History Review*, 28 (1985), 210–29. The issue of whether business talent was adversely affected by the process of 'gentrification' is critically assessed in F. M. L. Thompson, *Gentrification and the Enterprise Culture: Britain 1780–1980* (Oxford, 2001).

The landed aristocracy is well served in two major studies: F. M. L. Thompson, *English Landed Society in the Nineteenth Century* (London, 1963), and D. Cannadine, *The Decline and Fall of the British Aristocracy* (New Haven and London, 1990). Using probate records, W. D. Rubinstein anatomizes the distribution of wealth in *Men of*

Property: The Very Wealthy in Britain Since the Industrial Revolution (London, 1981). See also W. Rubinstein, 'Education and the Social Origins of British Elites', *Past & Present*, 112 (1986), 163–207, and 'Wealth, Elites and the Class Structure of Modern Britain', *Past & Present*, 76 (1977), 99–126

Good studies of **industrial restructuring** include P. L. Cottrell, *Industrial Finance 1830–1914* (London, 1979), P. L. Payne, 'The Emergence of the Large-scale Company in Great Britain, 1870–1914', *Economic History Review*, 20 (1967), 519–42, and W. Knox, 'Apprenticeship and De-Skilling in Britain, 1850–1914', *International Review of Social History*, 31 (1986), 166–84.

There is a rich literature on **religion and voluntary associations**. H. McLeod, *Class and Religion in the Late Victorian City* (London, 1974), focuses on London, while the same author's shorter study, *Religion and Society in England, 1850–1914* (Basingstoke, 1996), is written from a national perspective. J. Cox, *The English Churches in a Secular Society: Lambeth, 1870–1930* (Oxford, 1982), further explores the social composition of the church and chapel-goers, as do J. Munson, *The Nonconformists: In Search of a Lost Culture* (London, 1991), and C. G. Brown, *The Death of Christian Britain: Understanding Secularisation 1800–2000* (London and New York, 2001). H. E. Meller's exemplary case study of Bristol, *Leisure and the Changing City, 1870–1914* (London, 1976), examines the impact on social relationships of the movement to provide its citizens with improved leisure facilities.

Two good introductions to **consumption and the mass market** are W. H. Fraser, *The Coming of the Mass Market 1850–1914* (London, 1981), and J. Benson, *The Rise of Consumer Society in Britain, 1880–1980* (Harlow, 1994). Other studies include T. R. Nevett, *Advertising in Britain: A History* (London, 1982), P. Mathias, *Retailing Revolution* (London, 1967), J. B. Jefferys, *Retail Trading in Britain, 1850–1950* (Cambridge, 1954), G. Shaw, 'The Evolution and Impact of Large-Scale Retailing in Britain', in J. Benson and G. Shaw (eds.), *The Evolution of Retail Systems, c.1800–1914* (Leicester, 1992), 135–65. On the Co-operative Movement, see P. Gurney, *Co-operative Culture and the Politics of Consumption in England, 1870–1930* (Manchester, 1996). The implications of retailing for gender relationships are explored in C. Breward, *The Hidden Consumer: Masculinities, Fashion and City Life 1860–1914* (Manchester, 1999), and E. D. Rappaport, *Shopping for Pleasure: Women in the Making of London's West End* (New Jersey, 2000). The preconditions for the development of the popular press are established in D. Vincent, *Literacy and Popular Culture: England 1750–1914* (Cambridge, 1989). A. J. Lee, *The Origins of the Popular Press in England 1855–1914* (London, 1976) is still useful.

On **public schools**, see T. W. Bamford, *The Rise of the Public Schools* (London, 1967), and J. R. de S. Honey, *Tom Brown's Universe: The Development of the Victorian Public School* (London, 1977).

V POLITICAL IDENTITIES

There is no satisfactory single book on the working of the British Constitution in this period, but the following institutional studies all repay careful consideration:

G. W. Cox, *The Efficient Secret: The Cabinet and the Development of Political Parties in Victorian England* (Cambridge, 1987), A. Adonis, *Making Aristocracy Work: The Peerage and the Political System in Britain 1884–1918* (Oxford, 1993), D. Cannadine, 'The Context, Performance and Meaning of Ritual: The British Monarchy and the "Invention of Tradition", *c*.1820–1977', in E. Hobsbawm and T. Ranger (eds.), *The Invention of Tradition* (1983; 1984 edn.), 101–64. Further light on the rehabilitation of monarchy is thrown by T. Richards, 'The Image of Victoria in the Year of Jubilee', *Victorian Studies*, 31 (1987), 7–32. See also R. Quinault, 'Westminster and the Victorian Constitution', *Transactions of the Royal Historical Society*, 2 (1992), 79–104.

On local government, see Section VII, below.

On the electoral system, H. Pelling, *The Social Geography of British Elections, 1885–1910* (London, 1967), describes each constituency in Great Britain, grouping them by region. M. E. J. Chadwick explains 'The Role of Redistribution in the Making of the Third Reform Act', *Historical Journal*, 19 (1976), 665–83, while its consequences are analysed in J. P. D. Dunbabin, 'Some Implications of the 1885 British Shift Towards Single-Member Constituencies: A Note', *English Historical Review*, 109 (1994), 89–100. See also J. P. D. Dunbabin, 'British Elections in the Nineteenth and Twentieth Centuries: A Regional Approach', *English Historical Review*, 95 (1980), 241–67.

The franchise qualifications established by the 1884 Reform Act are clearly laid out in N. Blewett, 'The Franchise in the United Kingdom, 1885–1918', *Past & Present*, 323 (1965), 27–56, but a more up-to-date survey of a complex subject is to be found in D. Tanner, *Political Change and the Labour Party 1900–1918* (Cambridge, 1990), ch. 4. Much additional light on the late-Victorian and Edwardian electoral system has been cast by the debate about whether the 1884 Act can be held accountable for the tardy emergence of the Labour Party. The case for this was first made in H. C. G. Matthew, R. I. McKibbin, and J. A. Kay, 'The Franchise Factor in the Rise of the Labour Party', *English Historical Review*, 91 (1976), 723–52, which provoked lively refutations in P. Clarke, 'Liberals, Labour and the Franchise', *English Historical Review*, 92 (1977), 582–90, and D. Tanner, 'The Parliamentary Electoral System, the "Fourth" Reform Act and the Rise of Labour in England and Wales', *Bulletin of the Institute of Historical Research*, 56 (1983), 205–19. M. Childs, 'Labour Grows Up: The Electoral System, Political Generation and British Politics, 1890–1929', *Twentieth–Century British History*, 6 (1995), 123–44, emphasizes, as does Tanner, the way in which the electoral system discriminated by age.

The issue of party funding is tackled in M. Pinto-Duschinsky, *British Political Finance 1830–1981* (Washington, DC and London, 1981), and T. A. Jenkins, 'The Funding of the Liberal Unionist Party and the Honours System', *English Historical Review* (1990), 921–6. C. O'Leary, *The Elimination of Corrupt Practices in British Elections, 1858–1911* (Oxford, 1962), mainly looks at financial irregularities at constituency level.

On the forging of party identities, original and important insights are contained in J. Lawrence, 'Class and Gender in the Making of Urban Toryism, 1880–1914', *English Historical Review*, 108 (1993), 629–52, and *Speaking for the People: Party, Language and*

Popular Politics in England, 1867–1914 (Cambridge, 1998). P. J. Waller, *Democracy and Sectarianism: A Political and Social History of Liverpool, 1868–1939* (Liverpool, 1981), provides a rich chronicle of sectarian feuding and hatred in Liverpool. **Hostility to party**, in its various manifestations, is discussed in G. R. Searle, *Country Before Party: Coalition and the Idea of 'National Government' in Modern Britain, 1885–1987* (Harlow, 1995), while J. D. Fair, *British Interparty Conferences: A Study of the Procedure of Conciliation in British Politics 1867–1921* (Oxford, 1980), focuses on efforts to break party deadlocks by consensual methods.

The **social base** of parliamentary Conservatism is examined in J. P. Cornford, 'The Parliamentary Foundations of the Hotel Cecil', in R. Robson (ed.), *Ideas and Institutions of Victorian Britain* (London, 1967), 268–311. The changing role of a local 'notable' in one parliamentary constituency is dramatized in the case study by P. F. Clarke, 'British Politics and Blackburn Politics, 1900–1910', *Historical Journal*, 12 (1969), 302–27.

For the **civil service and government departments**, see G. K. Fry, *Statesmen in Disguise: The Changing Role of the Administrative Class of the British Home Civil Service 1853–1966* (London, 1969), H. Roseveare, *The Treasury: The Evolution of a British Institution* (London, 1969), and J. Pellew, *The Home Office 1848–1914: From Clerks to Bureaucrats* (London, 1982).

VI THE POLITICS OF HOME RULE

Liberals: Gladstone is the subject of three outstanding biographies: R. Jenkins, *Gladstone* (London and Basingstoke, 1995), compresses his account into a single volume, but for more detailed insights into the complexities of Irish Home Rule, see H. C. G. Matthew, *Gladstone, Vol. 2: 1875–98* (Oxford, 1995), and R. Shannon, *Gladstone: Heroic Minister 1865–1898* (Harmondsworth, 1999). J. Loughlin, *Gladstone, Home Rule and the Ulster Question 1882–93* (Dublin [c.1986]) argues that Gladstone was fundamentally ignorant of the contemporary Irish scene, D. A. Hamer, *Liberal Politics in the Age of Gladstone and Rosebery: A Study in Leadership and Policy* (Oxford, 1972), shows how he used Ireland tactically to impose order on his party, while M. Barker, *Gladstone and Radicalism: The Reconstruction of Liberal Policy in Britain 1885–1894* (Hassocks, 1975), contends that he was not as obsessed by Ireland as is commonly supposed.

A detailed study of the way the Home Rule crisis split the Liberals at parliamentary level is provided by W. C. Lubenow, *Parliamentary Politics and the Home Rule Crisis: The British House of Commons in 1886* (Oxford, 1988). Chamberlain's motives for breaking with official Liberalism can be explored through R. Jay, *Joseph Chamberlain: A Political Study* (Oxford, 1981). P. Stansky, *Ambitions and Strategies: The Struggle for the Leadership of the Liberal Party in the 1890s* (Oxford, 1964) is still useful on the factionalism that beset the party in the 1890s. On Rosebery, see R. R. James, *Rosebery* (1963), and D. Brooks (ed.), *The Destruction of Lord Rosebery: From the Diary of Sir Edward Hamilton, 1894–1895* (London, 1986).

Unionists: A. Roberts, *Salisbury: Victorian Titan* (London, 1999), is the best introduction to the subject, but should be complemented by D. Steele, *Lord Salisbury:*

A Political Biography (London, 1999), which brings out his progressive impulses. Lord Blake and H. Cecil (eds.), *Salisbury: The Man and His Policies* (Houndmills, 1987), is an important collection of specialized essays. M. Bentley, *Lord Salisbury's World: Conservative Environments in Late Victorian Britain* (Cambridge, 2001) uses Salisbury as a starting point for a study of the late-Victorian thought world. T. A. Jenkins, 'Hartington, Chamberlain and the Unionist Alliance, 1886–1895', *Parliamentary History*, 11 (1992), 108–38, chronicles the shifting personal relationships within the Unionist Alliance. On Lord Randolph Churchill, see R. R. James, *Lord Randolph Churchill* (London, 1969), and R. E. Foster, *Lord Randolph Churchill: A Political Life* (Oxford, 1981). L. P. Curtis, jnr., *Coercion and Conciliation in Ireland 1880–1892: A Study in Conservative Unionism* (Princeton and Oxford, 1963), focuses on the implementation of government policy. C. Campbell, *Fenian Fire: The British Government Plot to Assassinate Queen Victoria* (London, 2002), suggests the lengths to which elements in the British state were prepared to go to discredit Fenianism.

VII THE SOCIAL QUESTION AND SOCIAL POLICY, 1886–1899

A useful short guide to the agricultural depression is R. Perren, *Agriculture in Depression, 1870–1940* (Cambridge, 1995), but for a fuller survey see the authoritative collection of essays, E. J. T. Collins (ed.), *The Agrarian History of England and Wales: Volume Seven: 1850–1914* (Cambridge, 2001). A pessimistic view of the state of British agriculture is offered in A. Offer, *The First World War: An Agrarian Interpretation* (Oxford, 1989). A. O. Armstrong, *Farmworkers: A Social and Economic History, 1770–1980* (London, 1988), examines the impact of change on the farm labourer, as does A. Howkins, *Poor Labouring Men* (London, 1985), which focuses on Radical protest in Norfolk.

On **landed society**, the starting point is still F. M. L. Thompson (see Section IV, above). S. Wade Martins, *A Great Estate at Work: The Holkham Estate and its Inhabitants in the Nineteenth Century* (Cambridge, 1980), offers a case study in economic adaptation. M. E. Montgomery, *Gilded Prostitution: Status, Money and Transatlantic Marriages 1870–1914* (London, 1989), exposes many myths about American heiresses, while P. Mandler, *The Fall and Rise of the Stately Home* (New Haven, 1997), charts changing perceptions of the country house. On the 'Souls', see N. Ellenberg, 'The Souls and London Society at the End of the Nineteenth Century', *Victorian Studies*, 25 (1982), 133–60, and A. Lambert, *Unquiet Souls: The Indian Summer of the British Aristocracy* (London, 1984).

Valuable studies of **the problems of the poor** include A. Digby, *Pauper Palaces* (London, 1978), on the implementation of the Poor Law, and F. B. Smith, *The People's Health 1830–1910* (London, 1979) on public health and the incidence of disease. See also D. J. Oddy, 'Food, Drink and Nutrition', in F. M. L. Thompson (ed.), *The Cambridge Social History of Britain 1750–1950, Vol. 2* (Cambridge, 1990), 251–78, and A. E. Dingle, 'Drink and Working-Class Living Standards in Britain', *Economic History Review*, 25 (1972), 608–22.

Housing receives attention in A. S. Wohl, *The Eternal Slum: Housing and Social Policy in Victorian London* (London, 1977) and M. J. Daunton, *House and the Home in the Victorian City: Working-Class Housing 1850–1914* (London, 1983). Debates on the **standard of living** have spawned a complex literature: an invaluable guide is provided by C. Feinstein in two articles, 'What Really Happened to Real Wages?: Trends in Wages, Prices, and Productivity in the United Kingdom 1880–1913', *Economic History Review*, 43 (1990), 329–55, and 'New Estimates of Average Earnings in the United Kingdom 1880–1913', *Economic History Review*, 43 (1990), 595–632.

Among the many studies of crime and policing, the following are particularly valuable: M. J. Wiener, *Reconstructing the Criminal: Culture, Law, and Policy in England, 1830–1914* (Cambridge, 1990), V. A. C. Gatrell, 'The Decline of Theft and Violence in Victorian and Edwardian England', in V. A. C. Gatrell, B. Lenman, and G. Parker (eds.), *Crimes and the Law: The Social History of Crime in Western Europe Since 1500* (London, 1980), 249–76, D. Woods, 'Community Violence', in J. Benson (ed.), *The Working Class in England, 1875–1914* (Beckenham, 1985), 165–205, D. Jones, *Crime, Protest, Community and Police in Nineteenth-Century Britain* (London, 1982), and C. Emsley, *The English Police: A Political and Social History* (London, 1996).

The **temperance movement** can be explored through A. E. Dingle, *The Campaign for Prohibition in Victorian England: The United Kingdom Alliance, 1872–95* (London, 1980), and L. L. Shiman, *Crusade Against Drink in Victorian England* (Basingstoke, 1988). Opposition to its campaigns by the 'drink interest' forms the theme of D. W. Gutzke, *Protecting the Pub: Brewers and Publicans Against Temperance* (Woodbridge, 1989). The wider economic context is well delineated in T. R. Gourvish and R. G. Wilson, *The British Brewing Industry 1830–1980* (Cambridge, 1994).

Thrift organizations feature in P. H. J. H. Gosden, *Self-Help: Voluntary Associations in Nineteenth-Century Britain* (London, 1973), and P. Johnson, *Saving and Spending: The Working-Class Economy in Britain 1870–1939* (Oxford, 1985). See also S. Cherry, 'Hospital Saturday, Workplace Collections and Issues in Late Nineteenth-Century Hospital Funding', *Medical History*, 44 (2000), 461–88.

The **settlements movement** and the **Charity Organisation Society** are analysed, respectively, in S. Meacham, *Toynbee Hall and Social Reform, 1880–1914* (New Haven, 1987), and R. Humphreys, *Sin, Organised Charity and the Poor Law in Victorian England* (London, 1995). On Charles Booth, E. P. Hennock, 'Poverty and Social Theory in England: The Experience of the 1880s', *Social History*, 1 (1976), 67–91, is still essential reading. More generally, the social survey is explored in the essays in M. Bulmer, K. Bales, and K. K. Sklar (eds.), *The Social Survey in Historical Perspective 1880–1940* (Cambridge, 1991).

Social policy and Unionism provides one of the threads in P. Marsh, *The Discipline of Popular Government: Lord Salisbury's Domestic Statecraft, 1881–1902* (Hassocks, 1978). The subject is treated at greater length, and over a wider timespan, in M. Fforde, *Conservatism and Collectivism, 1886–1914* (Edinburgh, 1990), and E. H. H. Green, *The Crisis of Conservatism: The Politics, Economics and Ideology of the British Conservative Party, 1880–1914* (London, 1995). The **Liberals'** intermittent involvement in social policy is discussed in the books by Hamer and Barker (itemized in

Section VI, above). M. Daunton, *Trusting Leviathan: The Politics of Taxation in Britain 1799–1914* (Cambridge, 2001) deals brilliantly with the fiscal policies pursued by governments of both political complexions.

There is no entirely satisfactory survey of **local government**. However, the causes and consequences of the Local Government Act of 1888 are well analysed in two articles by J. P. D. Dunbabin: 'The Politics of the Establishment of County Councils', *Historical Journal*, 6 (1963), 238–50, and 'Expectations of the New County Councils and Their Realisation', *Historical Journal*, 8 (1965), 353–79. An engaging account of the operation of local government in the rural counties is included in G. D. Phillips, *The Diehards: Aristocratic Society and Politics in Edwardian England* (Cambridge, Mass., 1979). J. M. Lee, *Social Leaders and Public Persons: A Study of County Government in Cheshire* (Oxford, 1963), chronicles change in an urbanized county. The politics of the London County Council are ably handled in K. Young, *Local Politics and the Rise of Party: The London Municipal Society and the Conservative Intervention in Local Elections, 1894–1963* (Leicester, 1975), J. Davis, *Reforming London: The London Government Problem, 1855–1900* (Oxford, 1988), S. D. Pennybacker, *A Vision for London, 1889– 1914: Labour, Everyday Life, and the LCC Experiment* (New York, 1995), and P. Thompson, *Socialists, Liberals and Labour: The Struggle for London 1885–1914* (London, 1967). The work of a reformer who made an impact on local government in Bradford and London is presented in C. Steedman, *Childhood, Culture and Class in Britain: Margaret McMillan, 1860–1931* (London, 1990). More generally, see the excellent study by P. Hollis, *Ladies Elect: Women in English Local Government 1865– 1914* (Oxford, 1987).

On the rise of **Labour**: H. Pelling, *The Origins of the Labour Party 1880–1900* (Oxford, 1965), though old, still serves as a useful starting point. On the trade union, see H. A. Clegg, A. Fox, and A. F. Thompson, *A History of British Trade Unions Since 1889; Volume 1: 1889–1910* (Oxford, 1964). The early utopian phase of socialism is presented in S. Yeo, 'A New Life: The Religion of Socialism in Britain, 1883–1896', *History Workshop*, 4 (1977), 5–56, and also in the somewhat misleadingly entitled volume, S. Pierson, *Marxism and the Origins of British Socialism: The Struggle for a New Consciousness* (Ithaca and London, 1973). Indispensable reading on the ILP is D. Howell, *British Workers and the Independent Labour Party 1888–1906* (Manchester, 1983), while the early history of Fabianism, and much else besides, is covered in R. J. Harrison, *The Life and Times of Sidney and Beatrice Webb 1858–1905: The Formative Years* (Basingstoke, 2000). Among the most useful of many local studies are M. Savage, *The Dynamics of Working-Class Politics: The Labour Movement in Preston, 1890–1940* (Cambridge, 1987), B. Lancaster, *Radicalism, Co-operation and Socialism: Leicester Working-Class Politics, 1860–1906* (Leicester, 1987), and K. Laybourn and J. Reynolds, *Liberalism and the Rise of Labour 1890–1918* (Beckenham, 1984), which focuses on the West Riding of Yorkshire. The anthology by E. F. Biagini and A. J. Reid (eds.), *Currents of Radicalism: Popular Radicalism, Organised Labour and Party Politics in Britain 1850–1914* (Cambridge, 1991), contains two articles of outstanding interest: P. Thane, 'Labour and Local Politics: Radicalism, Democracy and Social Reform, 1880–1914', 244–70, and J. Shepherd, 'Labour and Parliament: The Lib.-Labs. as the First Working-Class

MPs, 1885–1906', 187–213. L. Barrow and I. Bullock, *Democratic Ideas and the British Labour Movement, 1880–1914* (Cambridge, 1996), explains the importance of 'democracy' to an understanding of the early struggles within the Labour movement.

VIII BRITAIN AND THE WIDER WORLD

On the **economics of Empire**, L. E. Davis and R. A. Huttenback, *Mammon and the Pursuit of Empire: The Political Economy of British Imperialism, 1860–1912* (Cambridge, 1986), argues that the Empire was not, on balance, a money-making enterprise, while P. G. Cain and A. G. Hopkins, *British Imperialism: Innovation and Expansion 1688–1914* (London, 1993), emphasizes the importance of 'informal Empire'. W. G. Hynes, *The Economics of Empire: Britain, Africa, and the New Imperialism* (London, 1979), explores the relationship between trade and diplomacy in Africa. See, too, T. A. B. Corley, 'Britain's Overseas Investments in 1914 Revisited', *Business History*, 36 (1994), 71–88.

On **imperialism** generally, the essays in A. Porter (ed.), *The Oxford History of the British Empire: The Nineteenth Century* (Oxford, 1999), and in J. M. Brown and W. R. Louis (eds.), *The Oxford History of the British Empire: Vol. IV: The Twentieth Century* (Oxford, 1999), provide an impressive and up-to-date survey of the field. **Chamberlain**'s work at the Colonial Office is assessed in R. V. Kubicek, *The Administration of Imperialism: Joseph Chamberlain at the Colonial Office* (Durham, NC, 1969), and A. M. Kesner, *Economic Control and Colonial Development: Crown Colony, Financial Management in the Age of Joseph Chamberlain* (Westport, 1981). Among the most useful biographies are Jay, *Chamberlain* (see above) and P. T. Marsh, *Joseph Chamberlain: Entrepreneur in Politics* (New Haven and London, 1994). J. E. Kendle looks at the ambitions of the imperial federalists in *Federal Britain: A History* (London, 1997). M. Perham, *Lugard*, 2 vols. (London, 1956–60), surveys the career of a powerful imperial administrator. The contribution made by the Primrose League to the growth of imperial sentiment is described in M. Pugh, *The Tories and the People 1880–1935* (Oxford, 1985). See also J. Darwin, 'Imperialism and the Victorians: The Dynamics of Territorial Expansion', *English Historical Review*, 112 (1997), 614–42.

Defence organization and strategy are well covered. On the army, see E. M. Spiers, *The Late Victorian Army, 1868–1902* (Manchester, 1992), G. Harries-Jenkins, *The Army in Victorian Society* (London, 1977), and J. Gooch, *The Plans of War: The General Staff and British Military Strategy, c.1900–1916* (London, 1974). H. Kochanski, *Sir Garnet Wolseley: Victorian Hero* (London, 1999), portrays the career of a key military personality. On the navy, A. J. Marder's monumental *The Anatomy of British Sea Power* (Hamden, Conn., 1964), is still indispensable, but the financial constraints within which governments operated are more explicitly dealt with in J. T. Sumida, *In Defence of Naval Supremacy: Finance, Technology, and British Naval Policy 1889–1914* (London, 1993), and P. Smith, 'Ruling the Waves: Government, the Service and the Cost of Naval Supremacy, 1885–99', in P. Smith (ed.), *Government and the Armed Forces in Britain, 1856–1990* (London and Rio Grande, 1996), 21–52. The international background to naval rivalries is covered in P. M. Kennedy, *The Rise and Fall of British Naval Mastery* (London, 1976).

Among important studies of defence strategy, the following should be consulted: D. French, *The British Way in Warfare, 1688–2000* (London, 1990), J. Gooch, 'The Weary Titan: Strategy and Policy in Great Britain, 1890–1914', in W. Murray, M. Knox, and A. Bernstein (eds.), *The Making of Strategy: Rulers, States, and War* (Cambridge, 1994), 278–306, and J. M. Hobson, 'The Military Extraction Gap and the Weary Titan. The Fiscal Sociology of British Defence Policy 1870–1913', *Journal of European Economic History*, 22 (1993), 461–506.

Good overviews of **Salisbury's foreign policy** can be found in J. A. S. Grenville, *Lord Salisbury and Foreign Policy: The Close of the Nineteenth Century* (London, 1964), J. Charmley, *Splendid Isolation? Britain and the Balance of Power 1874–1914* (London, 1999), and T. G. Otte, ' "Floating Downstream"?: Lord Salisbury and British Foreign Policy, 1878–1902', in T. G. Otte (ed.), *The Makers of British Foreign Policy: From Pitt to Thatcher* (Basingstoke, 2002), 98–127, as well as in the biographies of Salisbury listed above. See also D. R. Gillard, 'Salisbury's African Policy and Heligoland Offer of 1890', *English Historical Review*, 75 (1960), 631–53, and A. N. Porter, 'Lord Salisbury, Foreign Policy and Domestic Finance, 1860–1900', in Lord Blake and H. Cecil (eds.), *Salisbury: The Man and His Policies* (Houndsmills, 1987), 148–84.

The **background to the South African War** is expertly delineated in A. N. Porter, *The Origins of the South African War: Joseph Chamberlain and the Diplomacy of Imperialism, 1895–99* (Manchester, 1980), and I. R. Smith, *The Origins of the South African War 1899–1902* (Harlow, 1992).

IX THE SOUTH AFRICAN WAR

On the **military campaign**, L. S. Amery (ed.), *The Times History of the War in South Africa*, 7 vols. (London, 1900–1909), is a very full account by a youthful politician keen to contrast Redvers Buller unfavourably with his hero, Lord Roberts. T. Pakenham, *The Boer War* (London, 1979), goes to the opposite extreme in his assessment of the two generals. A chapter in E. M. Spiers, *The Late Victorian Army, 1868–1902* (Manchester, 1992), seeks to do justice to both men. Pakenham's invaluable volume can now be supplemented with D. Judd and K. Surridge, *The Boer War* (London, 2002), which surveys all aspects of the war. K. T. Surridge, *Managing the South African War, 1899–1902: Politicians v. Generals* (London, 1998), is an accomplished monograph which brings out the underlying tensions between military and civilians, especially the clash between Kitchener and Milner. As well as containing fascinating depictions of the battlefield, E. Lee, *To The Bitter End: A Photographic History of the Boer War, 1899–1902* (London, 1985), has revealing insights into Boer tactics and mentality. Two excellent recent collections of essays, surveying many facets of the war, are D. Lowry (ed.), *The South African War Reappraised* (Manchester, 2000), and D. Omissi and A. Thompson (eds.), *The Impact of the South African War* (Basingstoke, 2002). See also K. Wilson (ed.), *The International Impact of the Boer War* (Chesham, 2001). T. Jeal, *Baden–Powell* (London, 1989), though not uncritical of the hero of Mafeking, does greater justice to him than does the debunking B. Gardner, *Mafeking: A Victorian Legend* (1966).

The **domestic reaction** to the war has attracted controversy. R. Price, *An Imperial War and the British Working Class: Working-Class Attitudes To and Reaction To the Boer War, 1899–1902* (London, 1972), discounts the war's popularity with working men. This account should be balanced by M. D. Blanch, 'British Society and the War', in P. Warwick (ed.), *The South African War: The Anglo-Boer War, 1899–1902* (Harlow, 1980), 210–38, which chronicles war fever. P. Panayi (ed.), *Racial Violence in Britain in the Nineteenth and Twentieth Centuries* (Leicester, 1996 edn.) shows how the German immigrant community became targets for enraged British patriots.

Studies of the out-and-out **opponents of war** include B. Porter, 'The Pro-Boers in Britain', in Warwick (ed.), *South African War*, 239–57, and A. Davey, *The British Pro-Boers, 1871–1902* (Tafelberg, 1978). The war's impact on the Society of Friends is examined in T. C. Kennedy, 'The Quaker Renaissance and the Origins of the Modern British Peace Movement, 1895–1920', *Albion*, 16 (1984), 243–72. K. Surridge, ' "All you soldiers are what we call pro-Boer": The Military Critique of the South African War, 1899–1902', *History*, 82 (1997), 582–600, demonstrates how disillusionment with the war eventually spread among the fighting men. The vast quantity of poetry generated by the war among combatants and civilians alike is ably analysed by W. V. W. Smith, *Drummer Hodge* (London, 1978). J. Schneer, *London 1900: The Imperial Metropolis* (New Haven and London, 1999), vividly portrays the repercussions of the war on London's diverse population.

The war also set off controversies within parties and created alignments which crossed party boundaries. On tensions inside the Unionist Party, much can be gleaned from R. Shannon, *The Age of Salisbury, 1881–1902: Unionism and Empire* (Harlow, 1996), while there is an excellent dissection of Liberal divisions in H. C. G. Matthew, *The Liberal Imperialists: The Ideas and Politics of a Post-Gladstonian Elite* (Oxford, 1973). The standard work on **National Efficiency** is G. R. Searle, *The Quest for National Efficiency: A Study in Politics and Political Thought, 1899–1914* (Oxford, 1971: London and Atlantic Highlands, NJ, 1990 edn.). This theme can be further pursued in E. J. T. Brennan (ed.), *Education for National Efficiency: The Contribution of Sidney and Beatrice Webb* (London, 1975), and G. R. Searle, *Country Before Party: Coalition and the Idea of 'National Government' in Modern Britain 1885–1987* (Harlow, 1995). R. Soloway, 'Counting the Degenerates', *Journal of Contemporary History*, 17 (1982), 137–64, deals with the panic about 'national deterioration'.

The **long-term legacy of the war** is explored in A. L. Friedberg, *The Weary Titan: Britain and the Experience of Relative Decline, 1895–1905* (Princeton, 1988). Its consequences for military reform are laid out in R. Williams, *Defending the Empire: The Conservative Party and British Defence Policy 1899–1915* (New Haven and London, 1991), W. S. Hamer, *The British Army: Civil–Military Relations 1885–1905* (Oxford, 1970), and M. Hendley, ' "Help us to secure a strong, healthy, prosperous and peaceful Britain": The Social Arguments of the Campaign for Compulsory Military Service in Britain, 1899–1914', *Canadian Journal of History*, 31 (1995), 467–88. On imperialist rhetoric, see A. S. Thompson, 'The Language of Imperialism and the Meanings of Empire: Imperial Discourse in British Politics, 1895–1914', *Journal of British Studies*, 36 (1997), 147–77.

X THE BALFOUR GOVERNMENT

On **defence policy**: A. J. Marder's seminal study, *From the Dreadnought to Scapa Flow: Volume 1: The Road to War 1904–1914* (Oxford, 1961), must now be supplemented by N. A. Lambert, *Sir John Fisher's Naval Revolution* (London, 1999). See also R. F. Mackay, *Fisher of Kilverstone* (Oxford, 1973). On military reform, valuable material is contained in B. Bond, *The Victorian Army and the Staff College 1854–1918* (London, 1972), A. Tucker, 'The Issue of Army Reform in the Unionist Government, 1903–5', *Historical Journal*, 9 (1966), 90–100, and in Williams, *Defending the Empire* (see above).

On **foreign policy**: we lack a good, modern account of Lord Lansdowne's important tenure of the Foreign Office, but G. W. Monger, *The End of Isolation: British Foreign Policy 1900–1907* (London, 1963), is still essential reading. Z. S. Steiner, *The Foreign Office and Foreign Policy, 1898–1914* (Cambridge, 1969) supplies the institutional background.

J. Ramsden, *The Age of Balfour and Baldwin, 1902–1940* (London, 1978), provides a good introduction, though its assessment of Balfour's premiership is on the harsh side. Indeed, Balfour still lacks an entirely satisfactory biographical study, though S. H. Zebel, *Balfour: A Political Biography* (Cambridge, 1973), and M. Egremont, *Balfour* (London, 1980), are both useful. The formulation and the consequences of the 1902 **Education Act** are thoroughly discussed in the biographies of the main actors, Balfour, Chamberlain, and Devonshire. R. Betts, *Dr Macnamara 1861–1931* (Liverpool, 1999), in a study of the prominent Liberal educationalist, sheds much light on the role of the National Union of Teachers and of the politics of the London School Board.

Tariff reform: J. Amery, *Joseph Chamberlain and the Tariff Reform Campaign: The Life of Joseph Chamberlain Volumes 5–6* (London, 1969), is rich in documentation. A. Sykes, *Tariff Reform in British Politics 1903–1913* (Oxford, 1979), and E. H. H. Green, *The Crisis of Conservatism: The Politics, Economics and Ideology of the British Conservative Party 1880–1914* (London and New York, 1995) both present tariff reform as a project for the modernization of the Conservative Party. R. A. Rempel, *Unionists Divided: Arthur Balfour, Joseph Chamberlain and the Unionist Free Traders* (Newton Abbot, 1972), shows how Chamberlain's Unionist free-trade opponents quickly became marginalized. A. Howe, *Free Trade and Liberal England, 1846–1946* (Oxford, 1997), explains the vitality and resilience of the wider free-trade movement. K. D. Brown, 'The Trade Union Tariff Reform Association, 1904–1913', *Journal of British Studies*, 9 (1970), 141–53, makes clear why tariff reform failed to attract significant trade-union support. A. Marrison, *British Business and Protection, 1903–1932* (Oxford, 1996), warns against a simplistic conflation of economic interest and political preference. Myths about the vast wealth at the disposal of the Tariff Reform League are exposed in F. Coetzee, 'Pressure Groups, Tory Businessmen and the Aura of Political Corruption Before the First World War', *Historical Journal*, 29 (1986), 833–52. See also two important articles by F. Trentmann, 'The Transformation of Fiscal Reform: Reciprocity, Modernization and the Fiscal Debate Within the Business Community in

Early Twentieth-Century Britain', *Historical Journal*, 39 (1996), 1005–48, and 'The Strange Death of Free Trade: The Erosion of the "Liberal Consensus" in Britain, *c*.1903–32', in E. Biagini (ed.), *Citizenship and Community* (Cambridge, 1996), 219–50.

On the early years of the Labour Party, N. McCord, 'Taff Vale Revisited', *History*, 78 (1993), 243–60, is invaluable. The story of the LRC is meticulously covered in F. Bealey and H. Pelling, *Labour and Politics, 1900–1906* (London, 1958). The 1906 General Election is the subject of a slim but useful work, A. K. Russell, *Liberal Landslide: The General Election of 1906* (Newton Abbot, 1973).

XI LIBERAL WELFARE REFORMS

General: P. Thane, *The Foundations of the Welfare State* (Harlow, 1982), and J. R. Hay, *The Origins of the Liberal Welfare Reforms 1906–1914* (London and Basingstoke, 1975), offer a useful introduction. P. Thane (ed.), *The Origins of British Social Policy* (London, 1978) is a collection of original essays. E. P. Hennock, *British Social Reform and German Precedents: The Case of Social Insurance 1880–1914* (Oxford, 1987), subtly explores the complex relationship between British practice and the German 'model', with particular reference to workmen's compensation and National Insurance. See also J. Lewis, 'The Boundary Between Voluntary and Statutory Social Service in the Late Nineteenth and Early Twentieth Centuries', *Historical Journal*, 39 (1996), 155–77.

On eugenics, G. R. Searle, *Eugenics and Politics in Britain 1900–1914* (Leyden, 1976), emphasizes the way in which eugenics functioned as a critique of state welfare, while G. Jones, *Social Hygiene in Twentieth Century Britain* (Beckenham, 1986) explores the relationship between them. M. Thomson, *The Problem of Mental Deficiency: Eugenics, Democracy, and Social Policy in Britain c.1870–1959* (Oxford, 1998), warns against exaggerating its role in shaping policy towards the mentally deficient. Other useful articles with a bearing on social policy include I. G. Brown, 'Who Were the Eugenicists? A Study of the Formation of an Early Twentieth-Century Pressure Group', *History of Education*, 17 (1988), 295–307, and G. Jones, 'Women and Eugenics in Britain: The Case of Mary Scharlieb, Elisabeth Sloan Chesser, and Stella Browne', *Annals of Science*, 52 (1995), 481–502.

Feminist perspectives on maternalism owe a heavy debt to J. Lewis, *The Politics of Motherhood: Child and Maternal Welfare in England, 1900–1939* (London [*c*.1980]); see, too, her later article, 'Gender, the Family and Women's Agency in the Building of "Welfare States": The British Case', *Social History*, 19 (1994), 37–55. C. Dyhouse, 'Working-Class Mothers and Infant Mortality in England, 1895–1914', in C. Webster (ed.), *Biology, Medicine and Society, 1840–1940* (Cambridge, 1981), 73–98, exposes the ignorance of the lives of working-class women shown by leading medical officers of health, but D. Dwork, *War is Good For Babies and Other Young Children: A History of the Infant and Child Welfare Movement in England 1898–1918* (London and New York, 1987), presents their work in a more sympathetic light. C. Briar, *Working for Women? Gendered Work and Welfare Policies in Twentieth-Century Britain* (London, 1997), usefully covers the years of Liberal reforms as well as the Great War.

Among the many works of **medical history** with insights on the Liberals' welfare agenda, see A. Wear (ed.), *Medicine and Society: Historical Essays* (Cambridge, 1992), J. Lewis, *What Price Community Medicine?* (Brighton, 1986), M. Saks (ed.), *Alternative Medicine in Britain* (Oxford, 1992), and S. Cherry, *Medical Services and Hospitals in Britain, 1860–1939* (Cambridge, 1996).

Welfare legislation: H. N. Bunbury (ed.), *Lloyd George's Ambulance Wagon: Being the Memoirs of William J. Braithwaite 1911–1912* (1957), gives a gripping account of the genesis of the health insurance scheme through the memoirs of the civil servant centrally involved in its early planning. Of the secondary literature, B. B. Gilbert, *The Evolution of National Insurance in Great Britain: The Origins of the Welfare State* (London, 1966), which also deals with old-age pensions and Labour Exchanges, is still the most important single monograph, though some of its conclusions have been modified by later research. Excellent studies of particular legislative initiatives abound, among them: J. Harris, *Unemployment and Politics: A Study in English Social Policy 1886–1914* (Oxford, 1972), J. Macnicol, *The Politics of Retirement in Britain, 1878–1948* (Cambridge, 1998), J. D. Hirst, 'The Growth of Treatment Through the School Medical Service, 1908–18', *Medical History*, 33 (1989), 318–42, N. D. Daglish, 'Robert Morant's Hidden Agenda? The Origins of the Medical Treatment of Schoolchildren', *History of Education*, 19 (1990), 139–48, B. Harris, *The Health of the School Child: A History of the School Medical Service in England and Wales* (Buckingham, 1995), J. Welshman, 'School Meals and Milk in England and Wales, 1906–45', *Medical History*, 41 (1997), 6–29, and S. Blackburn, 'Ideology and Social Policy. The Origins of the Trade Boards Act', *Historical Journal*, 34 (1991), 43–64.

Social conditions during the Edwardian period have attracted an extensive literature, among the most useful of which are P. Horn, *The Victorian and Edwardian Schoolchild* (Avon, 1989), J. S. Hurt, *Elementary Schooling and the Working Classes, 1860–1918* (London, 1979), and A. S. Wohl, *Endangered Lives: Public Health in Victorian Britain* (London, 1983).

Recent work has emphasized the way in which **the state** often took the initiative in the formulation of social policy rather than merely responding to external pressures. Two wide-ranging articles which develop this theme are R. Davidson and R. Lowe, 'Bureaucracy and Innovation in British Welfare Policy 1870–1945', in W. J. Mommsen (ed.), *The Emergence of the Welfare State in Britain and German 1850–1950* (Beckenham, 1981), 263–95, and J. E. Cronin, 'The British State and the Structure of Political Opportunity', *Journal of British Studies*, 27 (1988), 199–231. J. Harris, 'The Transition to High Politics in English Social Policy, 1880–1914', in M. Bentley and J. Stevenson (eds.), in *High and Low Politics in Modern Britain* (Oxford, 1983), 58–79, explains how the state became drawn into the arena of social policy because of a crisis in local government finance. The literature on the key Edwardian civil servants is patchy. No satisfactory biography of Robert Morant exists, but there is an exemplary study by J. Harris, *William Beveridge: A Biography* (Oxford, 1977), which is particularly illuminating on the origins of Labour Exchanges and unemployment insurance.

The contribution of the **Labour Movement** to social welfare is contested territory, but a balanced assessment is provided in P. Thane, 'The Working Class and State

"Welfare" in Britain, 1880–1914', *Historical Journal*, 27 (1984), 877–900. H. A. Clegg, A. Fox, and A. F. Thompson, *A History of British Trade Unions Since 1889, Vol. 1* (Oxford, 1964), supplies the institutional context. J. Stewart, 'Ramsay MacDonald, the Labour Party, and Child Welfare, 1900–1914', *Twentieth-Century British History*, 4 (1993), 105–25, suggests that the early Labour Party was less negative in its attitude to social policy than is often claimed.

The now-classic account of the role of social welfare in **redefining Liberalism** is P. F. Clarke, *Lancashire and the New Liberalism* (Cambridge, 1971), which adopts a regional approach. The same theme is broached, more cautiously, but on a national scale, by H. V. Emy in *Liberals, Radicals and Social Politics 1892–1914* (Cambridge, 1973), and in an important article, 'The Impact of Financial Policy on English Party Politics Before 1914', *Historical Journal*, 25 (1972), 103–31, which should now be read alongside I. Packer, 'The Liberal Cave and the 1914 Budget', *English Historical Review*, 111 (1996), 620–34. B. Murray, *The People's Budget 1909/10: Lloyd George and Liberal Politics* (Oxford, 1980), also explains the ideological turmoil into which the 'new departure' plunged the Liberal ministry. But G. R. Searle, 'The Edwardian Liberal Party and Business', *English Historical Review*, 98 (1983), 26–60, casts doubt on whether Edwardian Liberalism had succeeded in transforming itself into a kind of social democratic party. R. Hay, 'Employers and Social Policy in Britain: The Evolution of Welfare Legislation 1905–14', *Social History*, 2 (1977), 435–55 argues, controversially, that many employers welcomed welfare legislation for their own self-interested reasons.

There are two distinguished surveys of the **New Liberalism**: P. Clarke, *Liberals and Social Democrats* (Cambridge, 1978), which examines the personalities involved, and M. Freeden, *The New Liberalism: An Ideology of Social Reform* (Oxford, 1978), which analyses it as a body of political and social thought.

XII THE LIBERAL GOVERNMENT: YEARS OF CRISIS

A detailed chronology of the years of Liberal rule is provided by P. Rowland, *The Last Liberal Governments: The Promised Land 1905–1910* (London, 1968), and *The Last Liberal Governments: Unfinished Business 1911–14* (London, 1971). The best biography of Asquith remains R. Jenkins, *Asquith* (London, 1964). The fullest biographies of Lloyd George are those by J. Grigg, *Lloyd George The People's Champion: 1902–1911* (London, 1978) and *Lloyd George: From Peace to War 1912–1916* (London, 1985), and by B. B. Gilbert, *David Lloyd George: The Architect of Change 1863–1912* (London, 1987) and *David Lloyd George: Organizer of Victory 1912–16* (London, 1992). See also R. Jenkins, *Churchill: A Biography* (London, 2001).

On the **assault on feudalism**, see J. M. Lee, 'Parliament and the Appointment of Magistrates, The Origin of Advisory Committees', *Parliamentary Affairs*, 7 (1959), 85–94, C. H. E. Zangerl, 'The Social Composition of the County Magistracy in England and Wales, 1831–1887', *Journal of British Studies*, 11 (1971), 113–25, H. V. Emy, 'The Land Campaign: Lloyd George as a Social Reformer', in A. J. P. Taylor (ed.), *Lloyd George: Twelve Essays* (London, 1971), 35–68.

On the **Constitutional Crisis**, R. Jenkins, *Mr Balfour's Poodle* (1954), provides a racy account, but has now largely been superseded. B. K. Murray, *The People's Budget 1909/10* (Oxford, 1980), gives detailed coverage of the 'People's Budget'. The proceedings of the Constitutional Conference have been ably dissected in C. C. Weston, 'The Liberal Leadership and the Lords' Veto, 1907–10', *Historical Journal*, 11 (1968), 508–37, and in J. D. Fair, *British Interparty Conferences: A Study of the Procedure of Conciliation in British Politics 1867–1921* (Oxford, 1980), ch. 4. On the activities of the Opposition peers, see J. Ridley, 'The Unionist Opposition and the House of Lords, 1906–1910', *Parliamentary History*, 11 (1992), 235–52, D. Southern, 'Lord Newton, the Conservative Peers and the Parliament Act of 1911', *English Historical Review*, 96 (1981), 834–40, and G. D. Phillips, 'The "Diehards" and the Myth of the "Backwoodsmen" ', *Journal of British Studies*, 16 (1977), 105–20. N. Blewett, *The Peers, the Parties and the People: The British General Elections of 1910* (London, 1972), is not confined to a study of the two elections but places the whole Constitutional Crisis into its proper context. The Secret Coalition talks are tackled in Searle, *National Efficiency* (see above) and feature prominently in A. M. Gollin, *The Observer and J. L. Garvin 1908–1914* (London, 1960). Much can still be gleaned about the role of the monarchy in the events surrounding the Parliament Act in H. Nicolson, *King George V: His Life and Times* (London, 1952).

On the government's dilemma over **Irish Home Rule**, see P. Jalland, *The Liberals and Ireland: The Ulster Question in British Politics to 1914* (Brighton, 1980), and 'A Liberal Chief Secretary and the Irish Question: Augustine Birrell, 1907–1914', *Historical Journal*, 19 (1976), 421–51. The Conservative response can be followed in R. Blake, *The Unknown Prime Minister: Life and Times of Andrew Bonar Law* (London, 1955), chs. 7, 9–13, and R. J. Q. Adams, *Bonar Law* (London, 1999), chs. 6–8, as well as in several important articles, among them: D. G. Boyce, 'British Conservative Opinion, the Ulster Question and the Partition of Ireland, 1912–21', *Irish Historical Studies*, 17 (1970–1), 89–112, J. Smith, ' "Paralysing the Arms": The Unionists and the Army Annual Act, 1911–1914', *Parliamentary History*, 15 (1996), 191–207, J. Smith, ' "Bluff, Bluster and Brinkmanship": Andrew Bonar Law and the Third Home Rule Bill', *Historical Journal*, 36 (1993), 161–78, and S. Evans, 'The Conservatives and the Redefinition of Unionism, 1912–21', *Twentieth Century History*, 9 (1998), 1–27. F. S. L. Lyons, *John Dillon* (London, 1968), chs. 10–12, is illuminating about the Irish Nationalist leadership. On the Irish Unionists, the work of P. Buckland is indispensable: *Irish Unionism, II, Ulster Unionism and the Origins of Northern Ireland 1886–1922* (Dublin, 1973), should be read alongside 'The Southern Unionists, the Irish Question and British Politics, 1906–14', *Irish Historical Studies*, 15 (1966–7), 228–55. P. Murphy, 'Faction and the Home Rule Crisis, 1912–14', *History*, 71 (1986), 222–34, provides a sure guide through the complex parliamentary manoeuvrings.

The attractions and flaws of 'Home-Rule-All-Round' are debated in P. Jalland, 'United Kingdom Devolution 1910–1914: Political Panacea or Tactical Diversion?', *English Historical Review*, 94 (1979), 757–84, and in J. Kendle, *Ireland and the Federal Solution, 1870–1921* (Kingston, Ont., 1989). Further investigations of developments in Ulster can be pursued through A. T. Q. Stewart, *The Ulster Crisis* (London, 1967), a general survey, and through a specialized study, I. F. W. Beckett (ed.), *The Army and the Curragh Incident 1914* (London, 1986).

All aspects of **corruption** under Liberal rule are covered in G. R. Searle, *Corruption in British Politics, 1895–1930* (Oxford, 1987); the Marconi Scandal is also well handled in B. B. Gilbert, 'David Lloyd George and the Great Marconi Scandal', *Historical Research*, 62 (1989), 295–317. J. Camplin, *The Rise of the Plutocrats: Wealth and Power in Edwardian England* (London, 1978), is a colourful, anecdotal survey of the Edwardian plutocrats.

The literature on the **Great Labour Unrest** is voluminous. H. A. Clegg, *A History of British Trade Unions Since 1889: Volume II: 1911–1933* (Oxford, 1985), is a good place at which to start. Despite their age, B. C. Roberts, *The Trade Union Congress, 1868–1921* (London, 1958), and E. H. Phelps Brown, *The Growth of British Industrial Relations: A Study From the Standpoint of 1906–14* (London, 1959), are also useful. V. Gore, 'Rank-and-File Dissent', in C. Wrigley (ed.), *A History of British Industrial Relations 1875–1914* (Brighton, 1982), 47–73, examines the challenge to the official trade-union leaderships, while B. Holton, *British Syndicalism 1900–1914* (London, 1976), argues, controversially, that British syndicalism was more coherent and influential than it is presented as being in, notably, the essay in H. Pelling, *Popular Politics and Society in Late Victorian Britain* (London, 1968). J. Schneer paints a persuasive portrait of two of the most prominent Labour activists in *Ben Tillett: Portrait of a Labour Leader* (London, 1982) and *George Lansbury* (Manchester, 1990). A. Howkins, *Poor Labouring Men: Rural Radicalism in Norfolk 1870–1923* (London, 1985), shows how unrest affected the agricultural, as well as the industrial, districts. G. A. Phillips, 'The Triple Alliance in 1914', *Economic History Review*, 24 (1971), 55–67, examines how close the country came to a 'general strike' on the eve of the Great War. A sceptical assessment of miners' militancy is presented in R. Church, 'Edwardian Labour Unrest and Coalfield Militancy, 1890–1914', *Historical Journal*, 30 (1987), 841–57.

The state's response to the industrial turbulence is discussed in J. Morgan, *Conflict and Order: The Police and Labour Disputes in England and Wales 1900–1939* (Oxford, 1987), R. Davidson, 'Government Administration', in C. J. Wrigley (ed.), *A History of British Industrial Relations 1875–1914* (Brighton, 1982), 159–83, and B. Porter, *Plots and Paranoia: A History of Political Espionage in Britain, 1790–1988* (London, 1989). C. J. Wrigley, *David Lloyd George and the British Labour Movement* (Hassocks, 1976), deals broadly with the Liberal ministry's dilemma, while A. M. O'Brien, 'Churchill and the Tonypandy Riots', *Welsh Historical Review*, 17 (1994), 67–99, unravels the complexities of this most controversial of episodes.

The challenge posed by the unrest to the parliamentary moderates is excitedly discussed in R. Miliband, *Parliamentary Socialism: A Study in the Politics of Labour* (London, 1961), and, more soberly, in D. Marquand, *Ramsay MacDonald* (London, 1977). K. Laybourn, 'The Failure of Socialist Unity in Britain, c.1893–1914', *Transactions of Royal Historical Society*, 40 (1994), 153–75, is informative about Victor Grayson and the formation of the British Socialist Party.

The role of the Osborne Judgement in creating a new base for the Labour Party is discussed by M. Klarman in two articles, 'Osborne: A Judgement Gone Too Far?',

English Historical Review, 103 (1985), 21–39, and 'Parliamentary Reversal of the Osborne Judgement', *Historical Journal*, 32 (1989), 893–924. R. McKibbin, *The Evolution of the Labour Party 1910–1924* (Oxford, 1974), chronicles Labour's organizational changes on the eve of the Great War, but his claims for a Labour breakthrough in these years is authoritatively challenged, in an important study, by D. Tanner, *Political Change and the Labour Party 1900–1918* (Cambridge, 1990). M. G. Sheppard and J. Halstead, 'Labour's Municipal Election Performance in Provincial England and Wales, 1901–13', *Bulletin of the Society for the Study of Labour History*, 39 (1979), 39–62, traces the upsurge in Labour representation at municipal level, but a cautionary note is sounded by D. Tanner, 'Elections, Statistics, and the Rise of the Labour Party, 1906–1931', *Historical Journal*, 34 (1991), 893–908.

On **women's suffrage**: M. Pugh, *Electoral Reform in War and Peace 1906–18* (London, 1978), places the women's movement in the wider context of suffrage reform. C. Rover, *Women's Suffrage and Party Politics in Britain, 1866–1914* (London and Toronto, 1967), still stands up well as a general introduction. D. Morgan, *Suffragists and Liberals: The Politics of Woman Suffrage in Britain* (Oxford, 1975), concentrates on the Liberal government's attempts to hold itself together in the face of the suffragist challenge. B. Harrison, 'Women's Suffrage at Westminster, 1866–1928', in M. Bentley and J. Stevenson (eds.), *High and Low Politics in Modern Britain* (Oxford, 1983), 80–122, deftly analyses the division lists. S. Holton, *Feminism and Democracy: Women's Suffrage and Reform Politics in Britain 1900–1918* (Cambridge, 1986), examines the tension between 'equal rights' and 'democracy'. A. Rosen, *Rise Up Women! The Militant Campaign of the Women's Social and Political Union 1903–1914* (London, 1974), chronicles the campaign of the WSPU, while L. P. Hume, *The National Union of Women's Suffrage Societies, 1897–1914* (Brighton, 1982) does justice to the too-often neglected activities of constitutional suffragism. M. Pugh, *The March of the Women: A Revisionist Analysis of the Campaign for Women's Suffrage, 1866–1914* (Oxford, 2000), is an excellent up-to-date collection of essays, critical of the WSPU and particularly useful on the Women's Freedom League. J. Liddington and J. Norris, *One Hand Tied Behind Us: The Rise of the Women's Suffrage Movement* (London, 1978), covers the working-class and socialist wing of suffragism. M. Pugh, 'Labour and Women's Suffrage', in K. D. Brown (ed.), *The First Labour Party 1906–1914* (London, 1985), 233–53, traces the complex relationship between Labour and the suffrage movement. The most recent biographical studies are M. Pugh, *The Pankhursts* (Harmondsworth, 2001), and J. Purvis, *Emmeline Pankhurst: A Biography* (London, 2002).

Among many useful articles, the following are worth consulting: J. Park, 'The British Suffrage Activists of 1913: An Analysis', *Past & Present*, 120 (1988), 147–62, R. Billington, 'Women, Politics and Local Liberalism: From Female Suffrage to "Votes for Women" ', *Journal of Regional and Local Studies*, 5 (1985), 1–14, C. Hirschfield, 'Fractured Faith: Liberal Party Women and the Suffrage Issue in Britain, 1892–1914', *Gender and History*, 2 (1990), 173–97, M. Pugh, 'The Limits of Liberalism: Liberals and Women's Suffrage, 1867–1914', in E. F. Biagini (ed.), *Citizenship and Community: Liberals, Radicals and Collective Identities in the British Isles, 1865–1931* (Cambridge, 1996), 45–65, L. Walker, 'Party Political Women: A Comparative Study of Liberal

Women and the Primose League, 1890–1914', in J. Rendall (ed.), *Equal or Different: Women's Politics 1800–1914* (Oxford, 1987), 165–91, and L. E. N. Mayhall, 'Defining Militancy: Radical Protest, the Constitutional Idiom, and Women's Suffrage in Britain, 1908–1909', *Journal of British Studies*, 39 (2000), 340–71.

On the **radical right**, see A. Sykes, 'The Radical Right and the Crisis of Conservatism Before the First World War', *Historical Journal*, 26 (1983), 661–76, and G. Searle, 'The "Revolt from the Right" in Edwardian Britain', in P. Kennedy and A. Nicholls (eds.), *Nationalist and Racialist Movements in Britain and Germany Before 1914* (London, 1981), 21–39. G. Dangerfield, *The Strange Death of Liberal England* (London, 1935), though now largely discredited, still exerts a fascination.

XIII THE ROAD TO WAR

A good overall survey of the **Empire** is provided in R. Hyam, 'The British Empire in the Edwardian Era', in J. M. Brown and W. R. Louis (eds.), *The Oxford History of the British Empire: The Twentieth Century* (Oxford, 1999), 47–63, a valuable collection of essays extending chronologically far beyond the scope of this volume. Further studies worth consulting include: B. Porter, *The Lion's Share: A Short History of British Imperialism 1850–1983* (Harlow, 1975), R. Hyam, *Elgin and Churchill at the Colonial Office 1905–1908: The Watershed of the Empire-Commonwealth* (London and New York, 1968), S. E. Koss, *John Morley at the India Office, 1905–1910* (New Haven, 1969), B. Porter, *Critics of Empire: British Radical Attitudes to Colonialism in Africa 1895–1914* (London and New York, 1968), and J. E. Kendle, *The Colonial and Imperial Conferences 1887–1911* (London, 1967). A. M. Gollin, *Proconsul in Politics: A Study of Lord Milner in Opposition and in Power* (London, 1964), deals authoritatively with this central figure in British imperialism.

Foreign policy in the period leading up to the Great War can best be approached through Z. S. Steiner, *Britain and the Origins of the First World War* (London and Basingstoke, 1977). No single study yet rivals in its range P. M. Kennedy's magisterial *The Rise of the Anglo-German Antagonism 1860–1914* (London, 1980). See also the thought-provoking collections of essays by K. M. Wilson, *Empire and Continent: Studies in British Foreign Policy from the 1880s to the First World War* (London, 1987) and *The Politics of the Entente: Essays on the Determinants of British Foreign Policy, 1904–1914* (Cambridge, 1985), though their heavy emphasis on the Foreign Office's obsession with the Russian threat should be viewed with caution. On the **Russian Entente**, K. Neilson, *Britain and the Last Tsar: British Policy and Russia 1894–1917* (Oxford, 1995), is superb. On the **French Entente and Anglo-French relations**, S. R. Williamson, *The Politics of Grand Strategy: Britain and France Prepare for War, 1904–1914* (Cambridge, Mass., 1969), is still essential reading. G. W. Monger, *The End of Isolation: British Foreign Policy 1900–1907* (London, 1963), examines the start of the Anglo–French military conversations, highlighting the breach between Lansdowne's foreign policy and Grey's.

Grey's tenure of office is sharply criticized in J. Charmley's important revisionist study, *Splendid Isolation? Britain and the Balance of Power 1874–1914* (London, 1999),

Part 3. By contrast, K. Neilson, ' "Control the Whirlwind": Sir Edward Grey as Foreign Secretary, 1906–16', in T. G. Otte (ed.), *The Makers of British Foreign Policy: From Pitt to Thatcher* (Basingstoke, 2002), 128–49, looks sympathetically at Grey's dilemmas, as does Z. S. Steiner, *The Foreign Office and Foreign Policy 1898–1914* (Cambridge, 1969), chs. 3–5, which exonerates the Foreign Secretary from the charge of having been 'captured' by his officials.

The activities of **Grey's Radical critics** are described and analysed in A. J. A. Morris, *Radicalism Against War 1906–1914: The Advocacy of Peace and Retrenchment* (London, 1972), and in the same author's edited collection of essays, *Edwardian Radicalism 1900–1914* (London, 1974). On the **Peace Movement**, M. Ceadel, *Semi-Detached Idealists: The British Peace Movement and International Relations, 1854–1945* (Oxford, 2002), and P. Laity, *The British Peace Movement, 1870–1914* (Oxford, 2002) are both important. S. Koss, *Sir John Brunner: Radical Plutocrat 1842–1919* (Cambridge, 1970), gives an account of one of Grey's most persistent Liberal critics. The parallel campaign being mounted by the Labour/Socialist movement is expertly covered in D. J. Newton, *British Labour, European Socialism and the Struggle for Peace, 1899–1914* (Oxford, 1985).

On **armed services and strategic planning**, see two collections of essays, M. Howard, *The Continental Commitment: The Dilemma of British Defence Policy in the Era of Two World Wars* (Oxford, 1971), and J. Gooch, *The Prospect of War: Studies in Defence Policy 1847–1942* (London, 1981), as well as J. Gooch, 'Adversarial Attitudes: Servicemen, Politicians and Strategic Policy in Edwardian England, 1899–1914', in P. Smith (ed.), *Government and the Armed Forces in Britain 1856–1990* (London and Rio Grande, 1996), 53–74. E. M. Spiers, *Haldane: An Army Reformer* (Edinburgh, 1980), deals with the military reforms. For the continuation of the Fisher era, see the references under Section X, to which should be added the important article, P. O'Brien, 'The Titan Refreshed: Imperial Overstretch and the British Navy Before the First World War', *Past & Present*, 172 (2001), 146–69. N. D'Ombrain, *War Machinery and High Policy: Defence Administration in Peacetime Britain 1902–1914* (Oxford, 1973), is caustic about the failure of the CID to become a centre of strategic planning. The opening chapter of W. J. Philpott, *Anglo-French Relations and Strategy on the Western Front, 1914–1918* (Basingstoke, 1996) explains the origins of the split within the 'Continentalist' camp between the Francophiles and the advocates of the so-called 'Belgian option', a leading proponent of which, Sir John French, is the subject of two useful studies, R. Holmes, *The Little Field Marshal: Sir John French* (London, 1981), and G. H. Cassar, *The Tragedy of Sir John French* (Newark, 1985). The campaign for conscription is covered in the opening chapters of R. J. Q. Adams and P. P. Poirier, *The Conscription Controversy in Great Britain 1900–18* (Basingstoke, 1987).

Spies, spy-mania, and counter-espionage feature in C. Andrew, *Secret Service: The Making of the British Intelligence Community* (London, 1985), B. Porter, *Plots and Paranoia: A History of Political Espionage in Britain, 1790–1988* (London, 1989), D. French, 'Spy Fever in Britain, 1900–1915', *Historical Journal*, 21 (1978), 355–70, and N. Hiley, 'Counter Espionage and Security in Great Britain during the First World War', *English Historical Review*, 101 (1986), 635–61, which also describes their pre-war origins. 'Invasion scare' literature forms the entertaining subject-matter of I. F. Clarke's classic study, *Voices Prophesying War 1763–1984* (Oxford, 1966).

On the early years of **air power**, see A. M. Gollin, *The Impact of Air Power on the British People and Their Government, 1909–14* (Basingstoke, 1989), H. Driver, *The Birth of Military Aviation: Britain, 1903–1914* (London, 1997), and M. Paris, *Winged Warfare: The Literature and Theory of Aerial Warfare in Britain, 1859–1917* (Manchester, 1992).

F. Coetzee, *For Party or Country: Nationaism and the Dilemmas of Popular Conservatism in Edwardian England* (New York, 1990), offers an excellent guide to the **patriotic leagues**, which are also put into international perspective in F. and M. Coetzee, 'Rethinking the Radical Right in Germany and Britain Before 1914', *Journal of Contemporary History*, 21 (1986), 515–37. On **patriotic youth movements**, see Section III, above, plus, on the Boy Scouts, M. Rosenthal, *The Character Factory: Baden-Powell and the Origins of the Boy Scout Movement* (London, 1986), which emphasizes the movement's early social and political conservatism, and A. Warren, 'Sir Robert Baden-Powell, the Scout Movement and Citizen Training in Great Britain, 1900–1920', *English Historical Review*, 101 (1986), 376–98, which qualifies such an interpretation. On patriotic literature, see C. D. Eby, *The Road to Armageddon: The Martial Spirit in English Popular Literature, 1870–1914* (Durham, NC, 1987). As a corrective to such interpretation, N. Ferguson, *The Pity of War* (Harmondsworth, 1998), ch. 1, seeks to expose what he calls 'The Myths of Militarism'.

A succinct survey of how and why the British government opted for war in August 1914 is provided in K. Wilson, 'Britain', in K. Wilson (ed.), *Decisions for War, 1914* (London, 1995), 175–208. The same issues are explored, in greater detail, in H. Strachan, *The First World War: Volume One: To Arms* (Oxford, 2001). D. French, *British Economic and Strategic Planning 1905–1915* (London, 1982), explains why the government was so slow to mobilize the economy for war.

XIV THE PURSUIT OF PLEASURE

On leisure generally, see H. Cunningham, 'Leisure and Culture', in F. M. L. Thompson (ed.), *The Cambridge Social History of Britain 1750–1950: Vol. 2: People and Their Environment* (Cambridge, 1990), 279–339, and J. Walvin, *Leisure and Society 1830–1950* (London and New York, 1978).

J. Wigley traces *The Rise and Fall of the Victorian Sunday* (Manchester, 1980). S. J. D. Green, 'The Religion of the Child in Edwardian Methodism', *Journal of British Studies*, 30 (1991), 377–98, has interesting things to say about the Sunday school. The standard works on **Christian worship** are H. Mcleod, *Class and Religion in the Late Victorian City* (London, 1974), which focuses on London, and his more general study, *Religion and Society in England, 1850–1914* (Basingstoke, 1996). However, these should now be read in conjunction with C. G. Brown, *The Death of Christian Britain* (London, 2001), which challenges the inferences commonly drawn from statistics of church attendance and casts doubt on the secularization thesis. Two valuable accounts of the **secularist movement** are E. Royle, *Radicals, Secularists and Republicans: Popular*

Freethought in Britain, 1866–1915 (Manchester, 1980), and D. Nash, *Secularism, Art and Freedom* (Leicester, 1992).

On '**rational recreation**', the best starting point is provided by two older accounts, D. Reid, 'The Decline of Saint Monday, 1766–1876', *Past & Present*, 71 (1976), 76–101, and P. Bailey, *Leisure and Class in Victorian England* (London, 1978). In an exemplary study of Bristol, H. E. Meller, *Leisure and the Changing City, 1870–1914* (London, 1976), analyses the attempts of community and civic leaders to elevate the urban environment by catering for its inhabitants' spiritual and cultural needs. J. F. C. Harrison, *Learning and Living 1790–1960: A Study in the History of the English Adult Education Movement* (London, 1961), is still useful on the WEA. Other valuable works in this area include D. Vincent, *Literacy and Popular Culture: England 1750–1914* (Cambridge, 1989), J. M. Goldby and A. W. Purdue, *The Civilisation of the Crowd: Popular Culture in England, 1750–1900* (London, 1984), and P. Gurney, *Co-operative Culture and the Politics of Consumption in England 1870–1930* (Manchester, 1996). Particularly important is J. Rose, *The Intellectual Life of the British Working Classes* (New Haven and London, 2001), which, through an examination of what 'serious' working-class readers read, recovers and celebrates the 'lost' world of the **working-class autodidact**. The persistence of an older recreational culture, in the face of new challenges, is stressed in J. K. Walton and R. Poole, 'The Lancashire Wakes in the Nineteenth Century', in R. D. Storch (ed.), *Popular Culture and Custom in Nineteenth-Century England* (London, 1982), 100–24.

A good introduction to the **music hall** is P. Bailey, *Music Hall: The Business of Pleasure* (Milton Keynes, 1986), which can be supplemented by his later *Popular Culture and Performance in the Victorian City* (Cambridge, 1998). The 'cartelization' of the music hall is one of many economic aspects of late-Victorian and Edwardian theatre described in T. C. Davis, *The Economics of the British Stage 1800–1914* (Cambridge, 2000). See, too, her ' "Naughty but nice": Musical Comedy and the Rhetoric of the Girl, 1892–1914', in M. R. Booth and J. L. Kaplan (eds.), *The Edwardian Theatre* (Cambridge, 1996), 36–60. B. M. Walker, *Frank Matcham: Theatre Architect* (Belfast, 1980), is illuminating on the content, as well as on the physical setting, of turn-of-the-century music hall. On the problems of 'cleaning-up' the music hall, see T. C. Davis, 'Indecency and Vigilance in the Music Halls', in R. Foulkes (ed.), *British Theatre in the 1890s* (Cambridge, 1992), 111–31, and P. Bailey, 'Conspiracies of Meaning: Music-Hall and the Knowingness of Popular Culture', *Past & Present*, 146 (1994), 138–70.

The **history of sport** has recently been a growth area. On sport in general, the best single account is R. Holt, *Sport and the British: A Modern History* (Oxford, 1989), but N. Tranter's slim volume, *Sport, Economy and Society in Britain, 1750–1914* (Cambridge, 1998), also offers an expert introduction. The development of professionalism is well covered in W. Vamplew, *Pay Up and Play the Game: Professional Sport in Britain, 1875–1914* (Cambridge, 1988). On the amateur dimension, see J. Lowerson, *Sport and the English Middle Classes, 1870–1914* (Manchester, 1993), which is particularly strong on the spread of golf. On female sport, see C. Parratt, *More Than Mere Amusement: Working-Class Women's Leisure in England 1750–1914* (2001), and

K. E. McCrone, 'Play up! Play up! And Play the Game! Sport at the Late Victorian Girls' Public Schools', in J. A. Mangan and R. J. Park (eds), *From 'Fair Sex' to Feminism: Sport and the Socialization of Women in the Industrial and Post-Industrial Eras* (London [*c*.1987]), 97–129.

Football has been well served in T. Mason, *Association Football and English Society 1863–1915* (Brighton, 1980), and D. Russell, *Football and the English: A Social History of Association Football in England, 1863–1995* (Preston, 1997). C. Korr, 'West Ham United and the Beginning of Professional Football in East London, 1895–1914', *Journal of Contemporary History*, 13 (1978), 211–32, is an interesting case study. W. F. Mandle, 'W. G. Grace as a Victorian Hero', *Historical Studies*, 19 (1980), 353–68, explores the contemporary fascination with cricket. W. Vamplew, *The Turf: A Social and Economic History of Horse Racing* (London, 1976), should be supplemented with M. Huggins, *Flat Racing and British Society 1790–1914* (London, 2000), which stresses the respectability of the turf and the interest taken in it by people from *all* social backgrounds. On cycling as an amateur pastime, see D. Rubinstein, 'Cycling in the 1890s', *Victorian Studies*, 21 (1977), 47–71.

Most seaside resorts have attracted their own histories, but the **seaside holiday** can best be studied through the various writings of J. K. Walton, in particular: *The Blackpool Landlady: A Social History* (Manchester, 1978), *The English Seaside Resort: A Social History, 1750–1914* (Leicester, 1983), and *Blackpool* (Edinburgh, 1998).

On **drinking, smoking, and drugs**, see B. Harrison, 'Pubs', in H. J. Dyos and M. Wolff (eds.), *The Victorian City: Images and Realities, Vol. 1* (London, 1973; 1976 edn.), 161–90, P. Jennings, *The Public House in Bradford, 1770–1970* (Keele, 1995) (an impressive local study), M. Hilton, *Smoking in British Popular Culture 1800–2000* (Manchester, 2000), V. Berridge: *Opium and the People: Opiate Use and Drug Control Policy in Nineteenth and Early Twentieth Century England* (London, 1981: 1999 revised edn., London and New York), and R. Davenport-Hines, *The Pursuit of Oblivion: A History of Narcotics* (London, 2001).

Much can obviously be gleaned about **gambling** from the literature on horse-racing, but the theme can also be followed in C. Chinn, *Better Betting with a Decent Feller: Popular Gambling and the British Working Class* (London, 1991), M. Clapson, *A Bit of a Flutter: Popular Gambling and English Society, c.1823–1961* (Manchester, 1992), R. Munting, *An Economic and Social History of Gambling in Britain and the USA* (1996), and the stimulating article by R. McKibbin, 'Working Class Gambling in Britain, 1880–1939', *Past & Present*, 82 (1979), 147–78. D. Dixon, *From Prohibition to Regulation: Bookmaking, Anti-Gambling, and the Law* (Oxford, 1991), chronicles the activities of the National Anti-Gambling League. Police problems in enforcing the 1906 Street Betting Act are described in A. Davies, *Leisure, Gender and Poverty: Working-Class Culture in Salford and Manchester, 1900–1939* (Buckingham, 1992), ch. 6, and this is also one of the themes of S. Petrow, *Policing Morals: The Metropolitan Police and the Home Office, 1870–1914* (Oxford, 1994).

Many works on sexual 'vice' appear in Section III, above. In addition, see P. Bartley, *Prostitution: Prevention and Reform in England, 1860–1914* (London, 2000), and F. Finnegan, *Poverty and Prostitution: A Study of Victorian Prostitution in York*

(Cambridge, 1979), an exemplary local study. Holywell Street, the headquarters of the pornographic industry, features in L. Nead, *Victorian Babylon: People, Streets and Images in Nineteenth-Century London* (New Haven and London, 2000), though this account focuses on the pre-1886 period. The attempt by vigilantes, as well as the authorities, to suppress and control prostitution and pornography are vividly outlined in E. J. Bristow, *Vice and Vigilance: Purity Movements in Britain Since 1700* (London, 1977). Some of the assumptions underlying these restrictionist campaigns are explored in L. Bland's important *Banishing the Beast: English Feminism and Sexual Morality 1885–1914* (Harmondsworth, 1995).

R. McKibbin, 'Work and Hobbies in Britain, 1880–1950', in J. Winter (ed.), *The Working Class in Modern British History* (Cambridge, 1983), 127–46, is an invaluable guide to a diffuse topic. C. Ehrlich, *The Piano: A History* (Oxford, 1990), deals with domestic music-making. On choirs and brass bands, see the next section.

XV ART AND CULTURE

Here is a small selection of the secondary works which have proved useful in the preparation of this book. Two lively collections of essays exploring aspects of British culture in this period are S. Hynes, *The Edwardian Turn of Mind* (London, 1968), and J. Rose, *The Edwardian Temperament, 1895–1919* (Athens, Ohio, 1981). J. Gross, *The Rise and Fall of the Man of Letters: Aspects of English Literary Life Since 1800* (London, 1969), has interesting observations to make about the world where journalism meets 'serious' literature. S. Nowell-Smith (ed.), *Edwardian England, 1901–1914* (Oxford, 1964), contains several articles surveying branches of the arts, as well as science, scholarship, and technology. B. Ford (ed.), *The Cambridge Guide to the Arts in Britain: Vol. 8: The Edwardian Age and the Inter-War Years* (Cambridge, 1989), is another valuable anthology.

The pioneering work on the **reading public** is R. D. Altick, *The English Common Reader: A Social History of the Mass Reading Public, 1800–1900* (Chicago, 1957), which should be read alongside the more recent studies by Vincent and J. Rose (see Section XIV, above). A spirited indictment of the intelligentsia for its contemptuous response to the broadening of the reading public is mounted by J. Carey, *The Intellectuals and the Masses: Pride and Prejudice Among the Literary Intelligentsia, 1880–1939* (1992). D. Thomas describes the struggle of writers to assert their right of self-expression against the forces of moral repressionism in *A Long Time Burning: The History of Literary Censorship in England* (London, 1969). C. Baldick, *Criticism and Literary Theory 1890 to the Present* (London, 1996), illuminates the emergence of literary criticism as a specialism in its own right.

On **music**, C. Ehrlich, *The Music Profession in Britain Since the Eighteenth Century: A Social History* (Oxford, 1985), provides an admirable introduction. D. Russell, *Popular Music in England, 1840–1914* (Manchester, 1987), is especially good on the activities of brass bands and choirs. On Cecil Sharp, see G. Boyes, *The Imagined Village: Culture, Ideology and the English Folk Revival* (Manchester, 1993), which covers folk dancing as well as music. D. Cannadine, 'Gilbert and Sullivan: The Making and Un-Making of a British "Tradition" ', in R. Porter (ed.), *Myths of the English*

(Cambridge, 1992), 12–32, traces the process whereby operetta transmuted into the musical.

Different aspects of the **theatre** are explored in J. Woodfield, *English Theatre in Transition, 1881–1914* (London [*c*.1984]), M. Sanderson, *From Irving to Olivier: A Social History of the Acting Profession in England, 1888–1983* (London, 1984), D. Kennedy, *Granville Barker and the Dream of Theatre* (Cambridge, 1988), M. R. Booth, *Victorian Spectacular Theatre, 1850–1910* (Boston, Mass., 1981), and T. C. Davis, *The Economics of the British Stage, 1800–1914* (Cambridge, 2000).

D. Farr, *English Art, 1870–1940* (Oxford, 1984), offers a broad survey to the **painting and sculpture** of the period. The centenary of the death of Aubrey Beardsley was the occasion of three valuable studies: P. Raby, *Aubrey Beardsley and the Nineties* (London, 1998), S. Calloway, *Aubrey Beardsley* (London, 1998), and J. H. Desmarais, *The Beardsley Industry: The Critical Reception in England and France, 1893–1914* (Aldershot, 1998).

On **architecture**, see M. Girouard, *The Victorian Country House* (New Haven and London, 1979), and *Sweetness and Light: The 'Queen Anne' Movement, 1860–1900* (Oxford, 1977), A. Service, *Edwardian Architecture* (London, 1977), R. Fellows, *Edwardian Architecture: Style and Technology* (London, 1995), and C. Cunningham, *Victorian and Edwardian Town Halls* (London, 1981).

On the **Arts and Crafts Movement**, see G. Naylor, *The Arts and Crafts Movement: A Study of its Sources, Ideals and Influence on Design Theory* (London, 1971), and M. Greensted, *The Arts and Crafts Movement in the Cotswolds* (Stroud, 1996). S. K. Tillyard, *The Impact of Modernism 1900–1920: Early Modernism and the Arts and Crafts Movement in Edwardian England* (London, 1988), traces its contribution to modernism in the visual arts.

On the **quest for 'Englishness'**: R. Colls and P. Dodd (eds.), *Englishness: Politics and Culture 1880–1920* (Beckenham, 1986), is a useful and wide-ranging anthology. M. J. Wiener, *English Culture and the Decline of the Industrial Spirit 1850–1980* (Cambridge, 1981), is more convincing in its depiction of English culture than in explaining Britain's post-war economic performance. On the role of myth-making in fashioning a sense of 'Englishness', see S. L. Barczewski's important monograph, *Myth and National Identity in Nineteenth Century Britain: The Legends of King Arthur and Robin Hood* (Oxford, 2000).

D. Pick, *Faces of Degeneration: A European Disorder c.1848–c.1918* (Cambridge, 1989), analyses the contemporary obsession with **decadence**. On the artistic **avant-garde**, I. Dunlop, *The Shock of the New: Seven Historical Exhibitions of Modern Art* (London, 1972) deals, *inter alia*, with the 'Manet and the Post-Impressionists' exhibition. W. Martin, *The New Age Under Orage: Chapters in English Cultural History* (Manchester, 1967), conveys the excitement that accompanied the emergence of 'modernism' in its different manifestations. M. Bradbury and J. McFarlane (eds.), *Modernism: A Guide to European Literature 1890–1930* (Harmondsworth, 1976), places the topic in a wider, international perspective.

On **town planning**, see H. Meller, *Towns, Plans and Society in Modern Britain* (Cambridge, 1997). **Letchworth and the garden city movement** are covered in

R. Beevers, *The Garden City Utopia* (London, 1988), M. Miller, *Letchworth: The First Garden City* (Sussex, 1989), and S. Meacham, *Regaining Paradise: Englishness and the Early Garden City Movement* (New Haven and London, 1999).

On **pastoralism and the 'simple life'**, J. Marsh, *Back to the Land: The Pastoral Impulse in England, from 1880 to 1914* (London, 1982), provides a wide-ranging and lively account; also useful are the articles in G. E. Mingay (ed.), *The Rural Idyll* (London, 1989). The contribution of the leading apostle of the 'simple life' receives due acknowledgment in C. Tsuzuki, *Edward Carpenter 1844–1929: Prophet of Human Fellowship* (Cambridge, 1980). M. A. Crowther, 'The Tramp', in R. Porter (ed.), *Myths of the English* (London, 1992), 81–113, examines the romance of the 'open road'. D. Hardy and C. Wood, *Arcadia for All: The Legacy of a Makeshift Landscape* (London and New York, 1984), describes how the not-so-affluent pursued their own rural idyll.

XVI SCIENCE AND LEARNING

On **technology**, A. Briggs, *Victorian Things* (London, 1988), provides a fascinating exploration of the material culture of the nineteenth century and of the social impact made by technical inventions. R. Wohl's lavishly illustrated *A Passion for Wings: Aviation and the Western Imagination, 1908–1918* (New Haven and London, 1994), examines the artistic response to manned flight. See also R. F. Pocock, *The Early British Radio Industry* (Manchester, 1988).

The vast topic of **change in higher education** is opened up in M. Sanderson, *Education and Economic Decline in Britain, 1870 to the 1990s* (Cambridge, 1999), D. Edgerton, *Science, Technology and the British Economic Decline 1870–1970* (Cambridge, 1996), M. Sanderson, 'The English Civic Universities and the "Industrial Spirit", 1870–1914', *Historical Research*, 61 (1988), 90–104, and R. Lowe, 'The Expansion of Higher Education in England', in K. H. Jaraush (ed.), *The Transformation of Higher Learning 1860–1930* (Chicago, 1983).

An overview of **science** can be obtained from A. R. Ubbelohde, 'Science', in S. Nowell-Smith (ed.), *Edwardian England, 1901–1914* (Oxford, 1964), 213–50. R. Macleod, 'Resources of Science in Victorian England', in P. Mathias (ed.), *Science and Society*, (London, 1974), 111–66, is indispensable on the 'endowment of science' movement, a subject also treated at greater length and over a wider period in P. Alter, *The Reluctant Patron: Science and the State in Britain* (Oxford, 1987). F. M. Turner, *Contesting Cultural Authority: Essays in Victorian Intellectual Life* (Cambridge, 1993), is a stimulating collection of essays, Part 2 of which covers 'Science and the Wider Culture'. The antipathy to science is powerfully brought out in D. Porter and R. Porter, 'The Politics of Prevention: Anti-Vaccinationism and Public Health in Nineteenth-Century England', *Medical History*, 32 (1988), 231–52. The ambivalent relationship between science and spirituality is the theme of F. M. Turner, *Between Science and Religion* (New Haven, 1974), and the story of a scientist who straddled these two worlds is told in W. P. Jolly, *Oliver Lodge* (London, 1974).

On **universities**, C. Brooke, *A History of the University of Cambridge: Vol. 4, 1870–1990* (Cambridge, 1993), offers a good overview, and almost all aspects of life at Oxford

University are encompassed in the essays which make up the magisterial official history, the two volumes devoted to the period of this book being M. G. Brock and M. C. Curthoys (eds.), *The History of the University of Oxford: Volume VII: Nineteenth-Century Oxford, Part 2* (Oxford, 2000), and B. Harrison (ed.), *The History of the University of Oxford, Vol. VIII: The Twentieth Century* (Oxford, 1994). M. Sanderson's *The Universities and British Industry 1850–1970* (London, 1972), tells a story of educational adaptation, but a case study of an institution that proved less than successful in this respect is J. Howarth, 'Science Education in Late-Victorian Oxford: A Curious Case of Failure', *English Historical Review*, 102 (1987), 334–67.

The decline of generalist culture and the **rise of academic specialisms** is tackled head-on in T. W. Heyck, *The Transformation of Intellectual Life in Victorian England* (London, 1982). H. Perkin traces the development of organization and professional awareness among university lecturers in *Key Profession: The History of the Association of University Teachers* (London, 1969), and the consequences of this for ministers of religion is the theme of A. J. Engel, *From Clergyman to Don: The Rise of the Academic Profession in Nineteenth-Century Oxford* (Oxford, 1983). R. Simpson tells the complicated story of *How The PhD Came to Britain* (London, 1983). A group which believed in the 'democratic intellect' and did what it could to resist academic specialization is given due acknowledgment in L. Barrow, *Independent Spirits: Spiritualism and English Plebeians 1850–1910* (London, 1986). However, a valuable corrective to all such interpretations is S. Collini, *Public Moralists: Political Thought and Intellectual Life in Britain* (Oxford, 1991), which demonstrates the continuing vitality of an older intellectual tradition.

There follows a short list of studies of particular academic disciplines. **Medicine**: S. Sturdy and R. Cooter, 'Science, Scientific Management, and the Transformation of Medicine in Britain *c.*1870–1950', *History of Science*, 36 (1998), 421–66, and R. Cooter, *Surgery and Society in Peace and War: Orthopaedics and the Origins of Modern Medicine, 1880–1948* (Basingstoke, 1993). **Psychology**: G. Sutherland, *Ability, Merit and Measurement: Mental Testing and English Education, 1880–1940* (Oxford, 1984), and L. S. Hearnshaw, *A Short History of Psychology, 1840–1940* (London, 1964).

English literature: S. Potter, *The Muse in Chains: A Study in Education* (London, 1937), and F. E. Court, *Institutionalizing English Literature: The Culture and Politics of Literary Study, 1750–1900* (Stanford, 1992). **History**: P. R. H. Slee, *Learning and a Liberal Culture: The Study of Modern History in the University of Oxford, 1800–1914* (Manchester [*c.*1986]), R. Soffer, 'Nation, Duty, Character and Confidence: History at Oxford, 1880–1914', *Historical Journal*, 30 (1987), 77–104, D. Cannadine, *G. M. Trevelyan: A Life in History* (London, 1992), and V. Feske, *From Belloc to Churchill: Private Scholars, Public Culture, and the Crisis of British Liberalism 1900–1939* (Chapel Hill and London, 1996).

Anthropology: J. W. Burrow, *Evolution and Society: A Study in Victorian Social Theory* (Cambridge, 1966). **Economics**: J. Maloney, 'Marshall, Cunningham, and the Emerging Economics Profession', *Economic History Review*, 29 (1976), 440–51. **Politics**: S. Collini, D. Winch, and J. Burrow, *That Noble Science of Politics: A Study in Nineteenth-Century Intellectual History* (Cambridge, 1983). **Sociology**: S. Collini,

Liberalism and Sociology: L. T. Hobhouse and Political Argument in England 1880–1914 (Cambridge, 1979), H. Meller, *Patrick Geddes: Social Evolutionist and City Planner* (London, 1990), R. Soffer, *Ethics and Society in England: The Revolution in the Social Sciences, 1870–1914* (Berkeley, 1978), D. P Crook, *Benjamin Kidd: Portrait of a Social Darwinist* (Cambridge, 1984), P. Abrams, *The Origins of British Sociology, 1834–1914* (Chicago, 1968), and R. N. Soffer, 'The Revolution in English Social Thought, 1880–1914', *American Historical Review* (1970), 1938–64. **Philosophy**: A. Quinton, 'Thought', in Nowell-Smith (ed.), *Edwardian England, 1901–1914* (Oxford, 1964), 251–302, and S. M. D. Otter, *British Idealism and Social Explanation: A Study in Late Victorian Thought* (Oxford, 1996).

XVII THE GREAT WAR

General: T. Wilson, *The Myriad Faces of War: Britain and the Great War 1914–1918* (Oxford, 1986), provides an excellent all-round history of Britain's involvement in the war, blending military narrative with political and social analysis, as does J. M. Bourne in *Britain and the Great War 1914–1918* (London, 1989). I. F. W. Beckett, *The Great War 1914–1918* (Harlow, 2001), puts various aspects of the war into a comparative international context. J. Keegan, *The First World War* (London, 1998), is a lively military history, heavily weighted towards the opening campaigns. H. Strachan, *The First World War: Volume One: To Arms* (Oxford, 2001), the first of a monumental three-volume study, is likely to become the definitive account.

The war's impact on the home front is examined in A. Marwick's pioneering *The Deluge: British Society and the First World War* (London, 1965). An excellent survey of the same field is G. J. DeGroot's more recent *Blighty: British Society in the Era of the Great War* (London, 1996). N. Ferguson, *The Pity of War* (Harmondsworth, 1998), a brilliant collection of essays, challenges many received opinions.

Among the many **multi-authored histories** of the war, the following anthologies are useful: P. Liddle (ed.), *Home Fires and Foreign Fields* (London, 1985), S. Constantine, M. W. Kirby, and M. B. Rose (eds), *The First World War in British History* (London, 1995), H. Strachan (ed.), *The Oxford Illustrated History of the First World War* (Oxford, 1998), and J. Bourne, P. Liddle, and I. Whitehead (eds.), *The Great World War, 1914–45*, 2 vols. (London, 2001). H. Cecil and P. H. Liddle (eds.), *Facing Armageddon: The First World War Experienced* (London, 1996), a particularly important volume, examines the experience of war from a wide variety of angles. H. Cecil and P. Liddle (eds.), *At The Eleventh Hour: Reflections, Hopes and Anxieties at the Closing of the Great War, 1918* (Barnsley, 1998), focuses on the Armistice.

Strategy is ably analysed by D. French in two authoritative volumes: *British Strategy and War Aims, 1914–16* (London, 1986), and *The Strategy of the Lloyd George Coalition, 1916–1918* (Oxford, 1995). Much, too, can be gleaned from S. Roskill, *Hankey: Man of Secrets, Vol. 1: 1877–1918* (London, 1970), which contains copious extracts from the diaries of the man at the centre of political and strategic planning. W. J. Phillpott, *Anglo-French Relations and Strategy on the Western Front, 1914–18*

(Basingstoke, 1996), has original things to say about divisions within the 'Westerner' camp. D. Stevenson, *The First World War and International Politics* (London, 1987), covers diplomatic activities during the war. See, too, J. Turner, 'Lloyd George, the War Cabinet, and High Politics', and J. Bourne, 'The World War Context', in P. H. Liddle (ed.), *Passchendaele in Perspective: The Third Battle of Ypres* (London, 1997), 14–29, 3–13.

A range of views on **Haig**'s military command can be encountered in J. Terraine, *Douglas Haig: The Educated Soldier* (London, 1963), G. De Groot, *Douglas Haig, 1861– 1928* (London, 1986), and B. Bond and N. Cave (eds.), *Haig: A Reappraisal 70 Years On* (London, 1999). The effectiveness of the military high command is vigorously defended in G. Sheffield, *Forgotten Victory: The First World War: Myths and Realities* (London, 2001). Issues of **tactics** are explored in the following studies: T. Ashworth, *Trench Warfare, 1914–1918: The Live and Let Live System* (London, 1980), P. Kennedy, 'Britain in the First World War', in A. R. Millett and W. Murray (eds.), *Military Effectiveness: Volume I: The First World War* (Boston, Mass., 1988; 1989 edn.), 31–79, T. Travers, *How the War Was Won: Command and Technology in the British Army on the Western Front, 1917–1918* (London, 1992), P. Griffith (ed.), *British Fighting Methods in the Great War* (London, 1996), and B. Bond (ed.), *Look to Your Front: Studies in the First World War* (Staplehurst, 1999). For recent surveys of the central campaigns of 1916 and 1917, see C. McCarthy, *The Somme* (London, 1995), and P. H. Liddle (ed.), *Passchendaele in Perspective: The Third Battle of Ypres* (London, 1997).

The **soldier's experience of war** is examined generally in D. Winter, *Death's Men: Soldiers of the Great War* (London, 1978), I. F. W. Beckett and K. Simpson (eds.), *A Nation in Arms: A Social Study of the British Army in the First World War* (Manchester, 1985), and P. Simkins, *Kitchener's Army: The Raising of the New Armies, 1914–16* (Manchester, 1988). Issues of recruitment are discussed in P. E. Dewey, 'Military Recruiting and the British Labour Force During the First World War', *Historical Journal*, 27 (1984), 199–223, and J. M. Osborne, 'Defining Their Own Patriotism: British Volunteer Training Corps in the First World War', *Journal of Contemporary History*, 23 (1988), 59–75. J. Bourke, *Dismembering the Male: Men's Bodies, Britain and the Great War* (London, 1996), explores the impact of the war on the male body. D. Hibberd and J. Onions (eds.), *The Poetry of the Great War: An Anthology* (Basingstoke, 1986), covers the writings of both combatants and non-combatants. Articles engaging with matters of army life include D. Englander and J. Osborne, 'Jack, Tommy and Henry Dubb: The Armed Forces and the Working Class', *Historical Journal*, 21 (1978), 593–621, M. Petter, ' "Temporary Gentlemen" in the Aftermath of the Great War: Rank, Status and the Ex-Officer Problem', *Historical Journal*, 37 (1994), 127–52, D. Gill and G. Dallas, 'Mutiny at Etaples Base in 1917', *Past & Present*, 69 (1975), 88–112, and M. Tozer, 'A Sacred Trinity—Cricket, School, Empire: E. W. Hornung and his Young Guard', in J. A. Mangan (ed.), *The Cultural Bond: Sport, Empire, Society* (London, 1992), 11–26. See, too, C. Veitch, 'Play up! Play up! and Win the War!: Football, the Nation and the First World War 1914–15', *Journal of Contemporary History*, 20 (1985), 363–78.

The **war at sea** is addressed in A. J. Marder's *From The Dreadnought to Scapa Flow: Vol. II: The War Years To the Eve of Jutland* (Oxford, 1965) and *From the Dreadnought to Scapa Flow: Vol. III: Jutland and After* (London, 1966). These two classic accounts should now be supplemented with P. Halpern, *A Naval History of World War 1* (Annapolis, Md., 1994).

On the **war in the air**, see J. H. Morrow, Jr., *The Great War in the Air: Military Aviation from 1904 to 1921* (Shrewsbury, 1993), and M. Paris, *Winged Warfare: The Literature and Theory of Aerial Warfare in Britain, 1859–1917* (Manchester, 1992).

On the **politics of war**, the most recent full-length study is J. Turner, *British Politics and the Great War: Coalition and Conflict 1915–1918* (New Haven and London, 1992). The opening months of hostilities are covered in C. Hazlehurst, *Politicians at War July 1914 to May 1915: A Prologue to the Triumph of Lloyd George* (London, 1974). The highly influential account by T. Wilson of *The Downfall of the Liberal Party, 1914–35* (London, 1966), depicts the challenge of war as central to Liberal disintegration. D. Woodward, *Lloyd George and the Generals* (London, 1983), and G. H. Cassar, *Kitchener: Architect of Victory* (London, 1977), explore the troubled relationship between the military and the civilian politicians. See, too, the relevant chapters in S. Koss, *The Rise and Fall of the Political Press in Britain, Vol. 2: The Twentieth-Century Test* (London, 1984), and N. Maurice, *The Maurice Case* (London, 1972).

Many of the detailed episodes are surveyed in specialist articles. Here are some of the most important: M. Pugh, 'Asquith, Bonar Law and the First Coalition', *Historical Journal*, 17 (1974), 813–36, J. G. Little, 'H. H. Asquith and Britain's Manpower Problem, 1914–1915', *Historical Journal*, 82 (1997), J. M. McEwen, 'Lloyd George's Liberal Supporters in December 1916: A Note', *Bulletin of the Institute of Historical Research*, 53 (1980), 265–72, R. J. Q. Adams, 'Andrew Bonar Law and the Fall of the Asquith Government: The December 1916 Cabinet Crisis', *Canadian Journal of History*, 32 (1997), 185–200, M. Fry, 'Political Change in Britain, August 1914 to December 1916: Lloyd George Replaces Asquith: The Issues Underlying the Drama', *Historical Journal*, 31 (1988), 609–27, J. M. McEwen, 'The Press and the Fall of Asquith', *Historical Journal*, 21 (1978), 863–83, J. M. McEwen, 'The Struggle for Mastery in Britain: Lloyd George Versus Asquith, December 1916', *Journal of British Studies*, 18 (1978), 131–56, D. R. Woodward, 'Did Lloyd George Starve the British Army of Men Prior to the German Offensive of 21 March 1918?', *Historical Journal*, 27 (1984), 241–52, and J. O. Stubbs, 'The Unionists and Ireland 1914–1918', *Historical Journal*, 33 (1990), 867–93.

Among the most important **biographies** are those by Jenkins on Asquith and on Churchill (see above). See also J. Grigg, *Lloyd George: From Peace to War 1912–1916* (London, 1985), and *Lloyd George: War Leader* (London, 2002), R. J. Q. Adams, *Bonar Law* (London, 1999), and C. Wrigley, *Arthur Henderson* (Cardiff, 1990).

On '**dissent**', J. Hinton, *The First Shop Stewards' Movement* (London, 1973), deals with unrest on the factory floor, while M. Swartz, *The Union of Democratic Control in British Politics During the First World War* (Oxford, 1971), focuses on the most influential of the government's critics. On the **peace movement**, see K. Robbins,

The Abolition of War: The 'Peace Movement' in Britain 1914–1919 (Cardiff, 1976), and M. Ceadel, *Pacifism in Britain, 1914–1945* (Oxford, 1980), and *Semi-Detached Idealists: The British Peace Movement and International Relations, 1854–1945* (Oxford, 2002). J. Rae, *Conscience and Politics* (Oxford, 1970), is a study of the conscientious objectors.

On **propaganda and censorship**, see C. Lovelace, 'British Press Censorship during the First World War', in G. Boyce et al., *Newspaper History* (London, 1978), 307–19, T. Rose, *Aspects of Political Censorship, 1915–1918* (Hull, 1995), G. S. Messinger, *British Propaganda and the State in the First World War* (Manchester, 1992). B. Millman, *Managing Domestic Dissent in First World War Britain* (London, 2000), emphasizes the repressive aspects of state policy. However, the most effective propaganda in support of the war often came from unofficial quarters: see A. Marrin, *The Last Crusade: The Church of England in the First World War* (Durham, NC, 1974), and S. Wallace, *War and the Image of Germany: British Academics, 1914–1918* (Edinburgh, 1988).

On the issue of enemy **aliens**, see C. Holmes, *Anti-Semitism in British Society 1876–1939* (London, 1979), J. C. Bird, *Control of Enemy Aliens in Great Britain, 1914–1918* (New York, 1986), N. Hiley, 'Counter Espionage and Security in Great Britain During the First World War', *English Historical Review*, 101 (1986), 635–61, and P. Panayi, 'German Business Interests in Britain During the First World War', *Business History*, 32 (1990), 244–58, and 'Anti-German Riots in Britain During the First World War', in P. Panayi (ed.), *Racial Violence in Britain in the Nineteenth and Twentieth Centuries* (Leicester, 1996 edn.), 65–91.

The issue of **national identities** has attracted much attention. A good overview is provided in J. M. Winter, 'British National Identity in the First World War', in S. J. D. Green and R. C. Whiting, *The Boundaries of the State in Modern Britain* (Cambridge, 1996), 261–77. On relationships within the United Kingdom, see D. Fitzpatrick, 'The Logic of Collective Sacrifice: Ireland and the Army, 1914–1918', *Historical Journal*, 38 (1995), 1017–30, E. A. Cameron and I. J. M. Robertson, 'Fighting and Bleeding For the Land: The Scottish Highlands and the Great War', in C. M. M. Macdonald and E. W. McFarland (eds.), *Scotland and the Great War* (East Linton, 1999), 81–102, and C. Hughes, *Mametz: Lloyd George's 'Welsh Army' at the Battle of the Somme* (Gerrards Cross, 1979 and 1982). Imperial relationships are dissected in R. Holland, 'The British Empire and the Great War, 1914–1918', in J. M. Brown and W. R. Louis (eds.), *The Oxford History of the British Empire: Volume IV: The Twentieth Century* (Oxford, 1999), 114–37.

The impact of war on **women** has been much debated. A. Marwick, *Women at War 1914–1918* (London, 1977), and D. Condell and J. Liddiard, *Working for Victory? Images of Women in the First World War* (London, 1987), are both lavishly illustrated. G. Braybon, *Women Workers in the First World War* (London, 1989), serves as a good introduction to the issue of women's work. The 'munitionettes' also figure largely in D. Thom, *Nice Girls and Rude Girls: Women Workers in World War One* (London, 1997), C. Wightman, *More Than Munitions: Women Workers and the Engineering Industries 1900–1950* (London, 1999), A. Woollacott, *On Her Their Lives Depend: Munition Workers in the Great War* (London, 1994), and C. Briar, *Working For Women? Gendered Work and Welfare Policies in Twentieth-Century Britain* (London, 1997). C. Tylee, *The*

Great War and Women's Consciousness (Basingstoke, 1990), and C. Reilly (ed.), *Scars Upon My Heart: Women's Poetry and Verse of the First World War* (London, 1981), explore women's attitudes towards the war.

Accounts of women's political activities can be found in M. Pugh, *Women and the Women's Movement in Britain 1914–1959* (Basingstoke, 1992), A. Wiltsher, *Most Dangerous Women: Feminist Peace Campaigners of the Great War* (London, 1985), M. Pugh, *The Pankhursts* (Houndmills, 2001), and S. K. Kent, 'The Politics of Sexual Difference: World War I and the Demise of British Feminism', *Journal of British Studies*, 27 (1988), 232–53.

Valuable articles include S. Pedersen, 'Gender, Welfare and Citizenship in Britain during the Great War', *American Historical Review*, 95 (1990), 983–1006, P. Levine, ' "Walking the Streets in a Way No Decent Woman Should": Women Police in World War I', *Journal of Modern History*, 66 (1994), 34–78, A. Woollacott, ' "Khaki Fever" and its Control: Gender, Class, Age and Sexual Morality on the British Homefront in the First World War', *Journal of Contemporary History*, 29 (1994), 325–47, S. R. Graysel, ' "The Outward and Visible Sign of Her Patriotism": Women, Uniforms, and National Service During the First World War', *Twentieth Century British History*, 8 (1997), 145–64, R. A. Voeltz, 'The Antidote to "Khaki Fever"? The Expansion of the British Girl Guides During the First World War', *Journal of Contemporary History*, 27 (1992), 627–38.

On the war's impact on the health of the civilian population, J. M. Winter, *The Great War and the British People* (London, 1985), is indispensable reading, though some of its optimistic conclusions must be modified in the light of subsequent research, not least in the ambitious comparative study, J. Winter and J.-L. Robert (eds.), *Capital Cities at War: Paris, London, Berlin 1914–1919* (Cambridge, 1997). See, too, B. Harris, 'The Demographic Impact of the First World War: An Anthropometric Perspective', *Journal of the Society for the History of Medicine*, 343–66, I. Loudon, 'Deaths in Childbed from the Eighteenth Century to 1935', *Medical History*, 30 (1986), 1–41, and L. Bryder, 'The First World War: Healthy or Hungry?', *History Workshop*, 24 (1987), 141–57.

A useful collection of essays dealing with different aspects of **state policy** is K. Burk (ed.), *War and the State: The Transformation of British Government, 1914–1919* (London, 1982). J. E. Cronin, *The Politics of State Expansion: War, State and Society in Twentieth-Century Britain* (London, 1991), takes a global view of the same issues. S. J. Hurwitz, *State Intervention in Great Britain: A Study of Economic Control and Social Response 1914–1919* (1949), is still useful. Arms production is covered in R. J. Q. Adams, *Arms and the Wizard: Lloyd George and the Ministry of Munitions* (London, 1978), manpower planning in K. Grieves, *The Politics of Manpower, 1914–1916* (London, 1988), and R. J. Q. Adams and P. Poirier, *The Conscription Controversy in Great Britain 1900–18* (Houndsmill, 1987). State regulation of alcohol consumption is described in J. Turner, 'State Purchase of the Liquor Trade in the First World War', *Historical Journal*, 23 (1980), 589–615; the background to this issue is laid out in J. Burnett, *Liquid Pleasures: A Social History of Drinks in Modern Britain* (London, 1999). Studies of other areas of state policy include P. E. Dewey, 'Food

Production and Policy in the United Kingdom, 1914–1918', *Transactions of the Royal Historical Society*, 5th ser., 30 (1980), 71–89, P. E. Dewey, 'British Farming Profits and Government Policy During the First World War', *Economic History Review*, 37 (1984), 373–90, N. Whiteside, 'Industrial Welfare and Labour Regulation in Britain at the Time of the First World War', *Industrial Review of Social History*, 25 (1980), 163–207, N. Whiteside, 'Welfare Legislation and the Unions During the First World War', *Historical Journal*, 23 (1980), 857–71, R. C. Whiting, 'Taxation and the Working Class, 1915–24', *Historical Journal*, 33 (1990), 895–916, and M. Daunton, *Just Taxes: The Politics of Taxation in Britain, 1914–1979* (Cambridge, 2002). See also J. M. Winter (ed.), *War and Economic Development* (Cambridge, 1975), 165–203, and R. Cooter, M. Harrison, and S. Sturdy, *War, Medicine and Modernity* (Stroud, 1999).

On **industrial relations**, K. Middlemas, *Politics in Industrial Society: The Experience of the British System Since 1911* (London, 1979), chronicles the halting attempts by government to establish a formal relationship with trade unions and business organizations. An excellent survey of class stratification and class discontents during the war is provided in B. Waites, *A Class Society at War: England 1914–1918* (Leamington Spa, 1987). The turmoil into which the war plunged the Labour Movement is variously explored in R. Wall and J. Winter (eds.), *The Upheaval of War* (Cambridge, 1988), J. Winter, *Socialism and the Challenge of War: Ideas and Politics in Britain* (London, 1974), and A. Briggs and J. Saville (eds.), *Essays in Labour History 1886–1923* (London, 1971). See also C. J. Wrigley, *David Lloyd George and the British Labour Movement* (Hassocks, 1976).

The complex and often fraught relationship between the state and **business** is tackled in a valuable anthology, J. Turner (ed.), *Businessmen and Politics: Studies of Business Activity in British Politics, 1900–1945* (London, 1984). The problems surrounding trade links with enemy countries are scrutinized by J. McDermott in two articles, ' "A Needless Sacrifice": British Businessmen and Business as Usual in the First World War', *Albion*, 21 (1989), 263–82, and 'Trading with the Enemy: British Business and the Law During the First World War', *Canadian Journal of History*, 32 (1997), 201–19. R. P. T. Davenport-Hines, *Dudley Docker: The Life and Times of a Trade Warrior* (Cambridge, 1984), is the biography of the founder of the Federation of British Industries.

On the **realignment on the left** at the end of the war, see R. McKibbin, *The Evolution of the Labour Party 1910–1924* (Oxford, 1974), and J. M. Winter, *Socialism and the Challenge of War: Ideas and Politics in Britain 1912–18* (London, 1974), which examine the transformation of the Labour Party. On Liberal divisions, see above, and also G. L. Bernstein, 'Yorkshire Liberalism During the First World War', *Historical Journal*, 32 (1989), 107–29, E. David, 'The Liberal Party Divided, 1916–1918', *Historical Journal*, 13 (1970), 509–32, and R. E. Dowse, 'The Entry of the Liberals into the Labour Party, 1910–1920', *Yorkshire Bulletin of Economic and Social Research*, 13 (1961), 77–87. The events surrounding the distribution of the 'Coupon' are debated in R. Douglas, 'The Background to the "Coupon" Election Agreements', *English Historical Review*, 86 (1971), 318–36, M. Hart, 'The Liberals, the War and the Franchise', *English Historical Review*, 97 (1982), 820–32, T. Wilson, 'The Coupon and the British General Election of 1918', *Journal of Modern History*, 36 (1964), 28–42, and B. McGill, 'Lloyd George's Timing of the 1918 Election', *Journal of British Studies*, 14 (1974), 109–24. The best account of the election itself is to be found in the closing chapters of J. Turner, *British Politics and the Great War* (see above).

Popular **culture** is surveyed in J. Winter, 'Popular Culture in Wartime Britain', in A. Roshwald and R. Stites (eds.), *European Culture in the Great War: The Arts, Entertainment, and Propaganda, 1914–1918* (Cambridge, 1999), 330–45. J. K. Walton, 'Leisure Towns in Lancashire: The Impact of the First World War in Blackpool and San Sebastian', *Journal of Contemporary History*, 31 (1996), 603–18, looks at seaside resorts. The transformation of the cinema industry forms the theme of a collection of essays, M. Paris (ed.), *The First World War and Popular Cinema, 1914 to the Present* (Edinburgh, 1999). P. Fussell asserts the connection between the war and artistic 'modernism' in *The Great War and Modern Memory* (Oxford, 1975), a once-influential thesis that has been considerably undermined since the publication of J. M. Winter's important *Sites of Memory, Sites of Mourning: The Great War in European Cultural History* (Cambridge, 1995).

Index